THE REALITIES OF LITERATURE

University of South Florida Richard F. Dietrich

The Realities of Literature

The rhetorician would deceive his neighbors,
The sentimentalist himself; while art
Is but a vision of reality.

W. B. Yeats
From "Ego Dominus Tuus"

XEROX COLLEGE PUBLISHING

Waltham, Massachusetts ▪ Toronto

For Linnea, My Wife

The W. B. Yeats extract used as epigraph to this volume has been reprinted from *The Collected Poems of W. B. Yeats* by permission of M. B. Yeats, The Macmillan Company, The Macmillan Company of Canada, and A. P. Watt & Son. Copyright 1918 by The Macmillan Company, renewed 1946 by Bertha Georgie Yeats.

To the Instructor

Anyone who writes an introductory anthology these days must ask himself if this book is really necessary. One must wonder, with the field so crowded, if there is anything left to justify and inspire another text. Obviously I believe there is.

Despite the many fine anthologies already available, with which I have gotten along for better or for worse, I have felt all along that something was lacking in these texts—namely, a clearly expressed and convincingly demonstrated idea that would not only unify the study of literature but would also make that study crucial to the lives of my students. It occurred to me that what my students needed was proof of literature's grasp of reality. In our time, more so than ever before, young people think less in terms of good and evil than in terms of truth and falsehood. The new morality supposes two kinds of people—those who are "real" and those who are "phony." This is the age of "the credibility gap" between those who make official pronouncements and those who disbelieve those pronouncements.

Because of our position in the establishment and our presumed dedication to the teaching of truth, we teachers are caught in our own credibility gap. Our most difficult task is to convince our students that we are not just brainwashing them with the party line but are genuinely interested in developing their self-reliance and independence of mind. We must prove to our students that our efforts are directed ultimately toward opening up the possibilities of life so that they may better choose the life that is legitimate to them. As an English teacher, I can think of no better way of doing this than by explaining and demonstrating how good literature strikes at the very core of reality, exposing it in both its unity and infinite variety. We need further to make students see that good literature is not only the result of vision, but that it can also engender vision in them. Once persuaded of this and armed with a method for the interpretation of literature, they will, I trust, respond more readily to the call of literature. Principally for this reason, I have written this text. The approach that I have hinted at above I have developed in full in the introduction "To the Student."

A few words about the selections. One thing a teacher must have is variety of example. For that reason, this text strives to be as various as possible in its selection from British, American, and continental authors, both modern and traditional, famous and not-so-famous. In the primary table of contents the authors are arranged chronologically and by genre for the most part, the few exceptions occurring for pedagogical reasons; the chronological arrangement is purely for convenience and is not meant to restrict or hinder other approaches. I have, for instance, provided a secondary table of contents at the back of the book that arranges the works according to theme and topic, and there is no reason why other approaches should not be used as well.

Perhaps I should say something about Shakespeare, the most notable omission from the drama section. I deliberately left out a Shakespearean play because I believe everyone will want to select his own. With the many fine editions available in inexpensive paperbacks (Ginn offers the Kittredge-Ribner editions, for instance), you should have no difficulty in supplementing this text. If you are looking for suggestions, I recommend *Antony and Cleopatra* as an excellent contrast for Shaw's *Caesar and Cleopatra*.

I wish to thank Holt, Rinehart & Winston for permission to quote from other texts that I have co-authored, *The Art of Fiction* and *The Art of Drama*. My thanks, too, to those friends and colleagues who offered criticism and encouragement, among them Roger and Julie Sundell, Carmen Avila Broer, Lawrence Broer, and Willie Reader. And my special thanks to my wife, Linnea, without whom this book would have been finished much sooner, but would not have been half as enjoyable.

English as a Foreign Language

Have you ever had the feeling when taking a literature course that you were studying a foreign language? That is, have you found yourself lectured to in literature classes as though the material needed translating? Were you surprised to discover, for instance, that *Huckleberry Finn* is not just a boy's simple adventure tale, as you had thought, but a document of cosmic significance that examines the profoundest of human questions? And after *Huckleberry Finn* had been "translated" into cosmic terms for you, did you lose the joy you perhaps felt at your first reading? If so, you are one of millions, and your complaint joins a swelling chorus of complaints.

The complaints do not come only from students. Many come from poets, dramatists, novelists, and other artists. And many more come from those professors who "translate" for you and spoil all your fun. In short, nearly everybody who has anything to do with literature these days worries about the effect and role of criticism. Is literature being ruined by interpretation? Is the emphasis upon analysis and understanding misplaced? Is there not something radically wrong with education when a student must read a work by Hemingway or Lawrence, O'Neill or Shaw, Yeats or Frost as though it were written in Sanskrit? These are the questions, and the answers are not easily come by.

The Garden of Eden

There is a belief, popular in some quarters, that literature has not always needed translating. According to this view, there was a time in the distant past when man immediately apprehended the meaning of verbal art, without the mid-wifery of translation, in the same way that today a teenager understands "rock" music, or in the way that a child understands a horror movie. In prehistoric times, it is argued, before literature became literature and was spoken and sung rather than written, primitive man was so in tune with nature that symbols drawn from nature by the bards were immediately understood. Everyone knew, for instance, what a crocodile or a dark woods meant, without benefit of explanation. There were no schools of criticism because symbols were all conventional and natural, buried in the psyche of everyone and needing only art to evoke them. Proponents of this view believe that something similar occurred more recently during the Dark Ages and early Middle Ages when the symbols of the faith were immediately understood by even the most illiterate peasants. Further, they believe that this condition still exists, as it always has, in the more backward and out-of-the-way places, as witnessed by the persistence of folk art.

One suspects that this "Garden of Eden" view of the past is a romantic one, colored by our yearning for a simpler day, but for our present purposes it is not necessary to decide that matter, even if we could. What matters is that people are convinced that literature has been over-intellectualized, and a fair reading of history suggests that there were indeed certain times when literature was read with more ease and natural understanding. If this was so, why was it so? What talent of the past have we lost?

The Snake in the Grass

Every melodrama must have its villain, and the villain in the favorite melodrama of literary people is science.[1] In this view, it is sinister science that has tempted the poor innocents into abandoning their former Eden of natural understanding for a more sophisticated and more difficult way of life.

However, if we can forgo the notion of intentional wickedness on the part of scientists, we can better understand the very important role science has had in determining the path of literature since the Renaissance. Almost everything in Western literature from the 17th Century on can be seen as a movement toward or a reaction against the new science. The term "realism" did not come into critical vogue until the 19th Century, but long before then literature was judged by its "realism" or its "truth to nature." The debate over what was real or true between the proponents of literary truth and the proponents of scientific truth waxed hotly for over two centuries until in the early part of the 20th Century the almost complete victory of the scientific view was tacitly evident, though the debate went on. Almost everybody wrote "realistically," in one way or another.

Everywhere we find even those artists who are most antagonistic to science's domination of the arts explaining or justifying their art in scientific terms. Take, for example, one of our foremost painters, Pablo Picasso. Apropos of such paintings as the one below, Picasso had said that "We all know that art is not truth. Art is a lie. . . ."

---

[1] Some would identify the villain as the unimaginative technocrat, who is so easily exploited by others for purely financial or political gain, but behind every technocrat is a scientist providing him with the tools for the mechanization of life.

Picasso's *Guernica*, depicting the bombing of the Spanish town of Guernica by the Nazis during the Spanish Civil War, April 26, 1937.[2]

Picasso went on to say that "Art is a lie that makes us realize truth," but the important thing is that he felt it necessary to say first that art is a lie. Such a statement by an artist of the stature of Picasso would be impossible in a society that was not controlled by science and its peculiar view of reality. For what Picasso means, in part, when he says that art is a lie is that "real" horses do not look like Picasso's horses nor do "real" people look like Picasso's people, "real" in this case meaning photographically real or scientifically verifiable. So complete is the dominance of science that one of our foremost artists cannot hope to be understood if he says flatly, as artists before him have said, that true art never lies; rather he must bow to the trend of the day and imply the unreality of his vision when it is not unreal at all.

It is difficult to convey the absurdity of this, for it is taken as a matter of course that art should justify itself in the familiar terms of science. Perhaps I can best illustrate the absurdity by turning the tables in a *reductio ad absurdum*. Would anyone in his right mind condemn the Second Law of Thermodynamics for its lack of characterization? Of course not. And yet many are willing to condemn a work of art for its lack of "realism," meaning its divergence from the scientific view of reality. Thus literature often is absurdly judged by its adherence to the criteria of science, although no one would dream of judging science by its adherence to the criteria of literature.

---

[2] PICASSO, Pablo. *Guernica* (1937, May-early June). Oil on canvas,   11' 5 1/2" X 25' 5 3/4". On extended loan to The Museum of Modern Art, New York, from the artist.

The Language of Vision

The problem arises from a misunderstanding about the nature and uses of language. The language of literature, as of all art, is different in kind and method and purpose. Unlike the scientific language of observation and report, the language of literature is a total language. It employs such devices as rhythm, metaphor, image, symbol, plot, character, setting, tone, and point of view (among others) to convey feelings and express ideas that will appeal to the whole man—to his senses, emotions, imagination, and intellect. The language of science, *in its pure state*, is directed exclusively to the reasoning intellect, and is thus often supplemented with literary language. Scientists such as Einstein often find themselves employing metaphor, simile, overstatement, parallelism, and other literary and rhetorical devices precisely because purely scientific language is too limited. They must be arguers and communicators as well as scientists. Furthermore, intuition and imagination are as essential to a scientist's career as to an artist's. One cannot go around proclaiming the reality of the invisible atom without being a visionary. And insofar as scientists gain esthetic pleasure from the contemplation of formulae, they share an emotion essential to the artistic. Yet when the scientist functions purely as a scientist (10% of his total life activity?), he wants to use, for the sake of objectivity, language that is as neutral and as unambiguous as possible—thus he prefers mathematical symbols. Now the language of science is a highly useful and necessary language, and no poet could do without its fruits for long (see Thoreau), but because it is limited to discursive terms, it cannot convey the entire range of human experience.

Whereas the language of science seeks to describe the evidences of human experience and generalize them into universal laws, literature attempts to represent or recreate concrete human experience in such a way, and with such an impact, as to bring out meanings invisible to the strictly scientific observer. The author of literature seeks to convey to his readers not only matters capable of verification but also the whole unseen but imaginatively perceived world of human motives, responses, desires, and energies. Although such data can be measured by scientific instruments (as, for instance, a lie detector can signal emotional disturbance), its truth can be apprehended more fully by imagination and intuition, and so its communication to others depends upon a skillful and imaginative use of language.

The distinction I am making is between the language of Vision and the language of vision, the language of the poet's eye versus the language of the ordinary eye. For the sake of the distinction I capitalize poetic Vision here. In science nothing is proven true until it is verified, and verification depends upon the ordinary five senses of the verifier.[3] In literature many things are proven true without the verification of the five senses. All that is required is the "verification" of Vision.

For a lighthearted example, suppose that I have foolishly agreed to fight the heavyweight champion of boxing. About the third round I finally run out of breath from running around the ring, thus allowing the champ to land a punch. After the fight, I am awakened by a man with an offer to write an account of the fight for an important national magazine. What am I to write? Should I write a scientific account or a literary account?[4] First I try a scientific account, in which I list the champ's impressive vital statistics—height: six feet two inches; weight: 210 pounds; arm reach: 35 inches; chest: 48 inches; biceps, etc.—the list could go on from such simple measurements to some highly sophisticated calculations, all of which would be quite useful in assessing the champ's physical stature. But this seems too dull for the general audience, and besides it doesn't really convey the terrible power of the man. So I write a literary account. I write, among other things, that the champ is ten feet tall, has ten arms, hammers growing from each of his ten wrists, and one big bloodshot eye in the middle of his forehead. The question is, when I describe the champ in literary terms, am I telling the truth, am I describing reality as it actually is? The answer of course depends upon your point of view. From the scientific point of view, I am lying. From the literary point of view, I am telling the truth. It depends upon your understanding of the language being used. If you understand that I am employing the language of Vision, you will not make the mistake of scorning the truth and reality of my description.

Look at it this way. What, in the case of my fight with the champ, is essentially true and real? First of all, why is the champ the champ? He is the champ because he has proven to have superior power and skill and ferocity and whatever else it takes to make a champ. Are not the power and the skill and the ferocity objectively inherent in the champ? You will admit that they are. Well, then, which does a better job of conveying the facts of the case, the scientific account or the literary account? There are hundreds, even thousands, of men in the world, including myself, who have measurements more or less like the champ's, and there are many who

---

[3] It is true of course that the scientist relies heavily upon currently unverifiable hypotheses (as, for instance, the mass of Venus can be calculated theoretically, but it has not been verified empirically), but insofar as he proceeds by such guesswork, he is more artist than scientist.

[4] Of course most journalism is neither strictly scientific nor strictly literary, but a combination of the two. I use the extremes here purely for the sake of the argument.

have measurements even more impressive.[5] Scientifically speaking, there is very little in the measurements to account for the champ's overwhelming superiority. Therefore, does not the literary account do a much better job of conveying the essential reality of the champ? And do you see that when I describe the champ as having one big bloodshot eye in the middle of his forehead, this description is not just the product of an overwrought imagination but an accurate account of an essential reality? If the ordinary eye looks at the champ in action and sees only the two usual eyes in the two usual places, the ordinary eye is missing the reality of the champ—his fierce, terrifying concentration, which the literary account does convey. Am I saying that the champ really does have one big bloodshot eye in the middle of his forehead? Yes, I am. Am I saying that everyone will see it that way? No, only those who exercise their Vision empathetically will see it that way. Is it possible to see the champ in some other way? Yes, many different views are possible, and they will all be more or less true. You must judge for yourself the degree of truth in each Vision and how true each Vision is for you.

For another example, suppose that we are able to send witnesses back into the past to view one of the most important events in the evolution of life on earth—the moment when a truly human consciousness first emerged. Our witnesses will consist of two groups—a group of ten scientists and a group of ten poets. For the scientists we will send a team of anthropologists broadly trained in all the sciences. For the poets we will send any ten at random, the only criterion being the excellence of their poetry. What will be the result? How will they report the act of becoming human?

We can safely predict that the anthropologists, insofar as they behave strictly as scientists, will all return with more or less the same report. At least it will be recognizable that they all witnessed the same event. They will return with, among other data, descriptions of the ape-men involved, their environment, and their reaction to the discovery of their own humanity. The scientists will also doubtless return with movies and tape recordings and whatever other measurements and data the machines of science make possible. But whatever variations there may be in the details of their reports, and however widely they disagree on the conclusions to be drawn, it is very likely that the purely scientific part of their reports will be much alike, and it will all point to a hopeful development in the evolution of the species. The information they will bring back will be very useful, and we will be very glad to have it.

But what about our ten poets? What will they bring back? Probably

---

[5]This happens all the time in sports, incidentally. Two opponents are evenly matched, at least on paper, but the one somehow clobbers the other. That's why football coaches talk a lot about "intangibles," and that's why good football coaches are men of Vision.

nothing, except possibly an ecstatic look on their faces and a notepad or something similar bearing weird, indecipherable pen scratchings, which later will be converted into epics, lyric poems, dramas, and the like. Naturally, if you have ten poets witnessing the same event, chances are they will come up with ten radically different accounts, to the extent that one wonders if they all saw the same thing. But suppose that one of them wrote an account remarkably similar to the story of Adam and Eve, except that this version is written in modern free verse and modern diction. What would a literal-minded and somewhat humorless anthropologist say about the tempting of Eve by the serpent and Adam by Eve?

He would probably say, "How wild can you get! Nothing of the sort took place. Imagine, a talking serpent and a God who enjoys walking in the cool of the day! What crude anthropomorphism in these old myths! Furthermore, our tape recorders reveal that the ape-man who made the first discovery of human consciousness was called, if anything, 'Uk' or 'Guk,' not 'Adam.' And there was certainly nothing 'perfect' about this hairy brute before he made the discovery. As a matter of fact, he had just committed rape. And, furthermore, the whole notion of a 'fall' is absolutely wrong, the opposite being closer to the truth. One minute this brute was pure ape and the next minute he was a man. Obviously we have here not a fall but a rise, the rise of man from the animal in the evolution of the species."[6]

"Ah, yes, all very scientific," says our poet, "but hardly all true. You saw everything except the most important fact of all, that the rise of man in the evolution of the species was actually a fall from grace. My story speaks for itself, but if I must explain I must. You scientists seem to understand only your own language, so I'll speak in your tongue, uncomfortable though I find it and limited though it is.

"The truth of the matter is that before man developed a truly human consciousness he was, in a sense, 'perfect.' He was perfect in innocence, as all animals presumably still are. However many times he had committed rape before (or stolen, or murdered, etc.), he had never given a thought to the morality of it—that is, until the day he suddenly evolved a human consciousness. From that day on he was a different ape. From then on he would be troubled by the morality of his acts. He would find himself weighing and considering and judging. He would, in short, discover the awful burden of his unique humanity. Everything else in nature was free to do as it pleased, as its nature dictated. But not man. Man was cursed with the knowledge of good and evil, and must worry himself to death with this knowledge that he had stolen from God. Surely such knowledge

[6]My melodrama requires a dunce to express a popular attitude, but of course most anthropologists are not as literal-minded as this one. For an anthropologist who not only understands literature but is something of a poet himself, read Loren Eiseley.

should be reserved for a superior being. How nice it would be to get back to the good old days when man was an ape and could leave such complicated matters as the knowledge of good and evil to God. What a terrible calamity it was the day that moral consciousness was evolved on this earth! What an awful price to pay! The alienation of human nature from nature resulted in the ultimate alienation of man from God. Thus man's rise from ape to man was also a fall from innocence to experience, from a higher form of life to a lower form. My story of Adam and Eve in the Garden of Eden serves as an excellent and truthful Vision of the fact of perfect bliss that preceded moral consciousness in the development of man. In brief, ignorance is bliss. The remarkable thing to me is that the original teller of this tale, that ancient Semite, had such marvelous Vision that he could see this without witnessing the actual event or knowing anything about Darwin. Very unscientific."

"Well, why didn't you say so?" says the anthropologist. "Now you're making sense. It seems we actually agree. We both agree that man evolved from a lower form of life, scientifically speaking, but you choose to view this evolution as a disaster due to the loss of animal innocence, and this I can quite understand. At least there is no contradiction: If innocence is better than experience, then the innocent would be viewed as a higher form of life, and our evolution would then be a devolution, or fall. Indeed, I can even remember times when I quite sympathized with this morbid view—when I was studying for my Ph.D. exams, for instance. But what I don't understand is why you poets can't come right out and say things in plain English instead of beating around the bush with your stories and riddles and parables and so forth. You really make good sense when you want to."

The poet groaned and spake thusly: "It should come as no surprise to me that you scientists prefer explanations of things to the things themselves, but I never quite adjust to this. To me my story is a beautiful thing, complete unto itself, meaning incarnate, and it does not occur to me either that it needs to be explained or, supreme sacrilege, that anyone would prefer the explanation to the story itself. You mono-linguals are the despair of my life! But I take heart in knowing that your obsession with the language of science leaves you only one life to live, whilst I have two lives to live." Saying this, the poet went his way.

The Best of Both Worlds

My sympathies are with the poet, despite his arrogance, for his is a harder lot, but as a teacher I must insist that both the anthropologist and the poet have a good case. Unless one wishes to be a Neo-Platonist and deny the reality of the material world, something that is very difficult to do these days, there is no choice for a sane person but to live in both worlds, the physical world of the five senses and the spiritual world of the sixth sense (or the seventh sense, or the eighth sense, etc.). This is what the poet means by having two lives to live. A study of history suggests that to exclude either world is to invite insanity, or at least harmful delusions. We laugh at the credulity of the Middle Ages, but is our own age any less credulous? The only difference is that whereas many people in the Middle Ages pretended that only the spiritual world was real, many moderns pretend that only the material world is real, with the result that we are about to blow ourselves up because we have worshipped so exclusively at the shrine of the Almighty Atom. Perhaps it would be better if we were amphibians capable of living naturally in either world, never confusing the two. If we were to do that, why should we have anything less than the best of both worlds? Why should we deny ourselves the benefits of either the Salk vaccine or the plays of George Bernard Shaw? They are both great healers.

The point is this—the language of science is an extremely valuable language to know, and the fruits of learning it have been enormous, but to know that language and only that language is to live but half a life and to be but half a person. To live a fuller life, one must be bi-lingual. One must speak and understand the language of Vision as well as the language of science. And of course one must understand what is really a third language—that combination of both that is the everyday language of most of us.

Most scientists understand perfectly well what I have been saying, and are aware of the degree to which they rely upon Vision to supplement the purely scientific part of their activities. Most scientists are not as naive as my straw-man anthropologist, who represents a popular misconception more than a professional attitude. Yet the fact remains that many students are puzzled by the relevance of literature to their lives, and this puzzlement is largely caused by the remarkable, pervasive influence of certain old-fashioned notions about science and literature in modern schools: the notion, for instance, that "fact" and "reality" are the realm of science whereas the realm of literature is "fancy" and "make-believe," the place where people go to escape reality.[7] Fortunately, up-to-date minds in the academic community are striving to erase such outmoded distinctions and to replace them with the understanding that literature is an important and perhaps indispensable medium for the conveyance of fact and the perception of reality.

So, back to the original question of why English is taught as a foreign language. Perhaps there was a time when people more naturally understood the language of Vision and thus no critics or teachers of it were

---

[7]Note how the word "fiction" is used in popular parlance. More often than not "fiction" is an antonym for "fact," as in the frequently heard question—"Is it fact, or fiction?"

necessary. True or not, it is for certain that people of our century are so conditioned by their science-oriented culture that the language of Vision is not one that most people can understand without a translator. Thus we have all those college courses dedicated to explaining art, translating it into rational, discursive, non-metaphorical language. If the teachers of these courses sometimes feel rather uncomfortable in their work, it is because they understand how artists feel about criticism ("My story speaks for itself"), and they understand the curse of education, that it can interfere with our responses to life. We wish that we could respond to literature as a child responds to a horror movie or as most people respond to music, but unfortunately we must translate first, then respond, hoping that the response will not be killed by the effort of translation, and that translation will actually enhance the response. Understanding the difficulties, teachers sometimes despair, but they are inspired to carry on by the hope that if they translate literature for students in an interesting way, students will eventually learn the language of Vision for themselves, so expertly one hopes that literature will stimulate Vision without needing to be laboriously translated.

The Varieties of Visionary Experience

When you have finally learned to read the language of Vision, you will have learned how various a language it is. For the sake of the argument between science and literature, I have been emphasizing literature's ability to convey reality and fact. But that of course is only one of its functions. For literature can not only convey things as they are, it can also show us life as it seems to be, or life as it ought to be, or life as it should not be, or life as it might be, to name a few of the possibilities. And of course any of these can be portrayed comically or tragically or something in between, in an almost infinite number of forms. There have been many theories of literature, some maintaining that literature should make no direct moral comment but just show us life as it is, or seems to be, or might be, and others maintaining that literature should make a direct moral comment by showing us how life should be or should not be. But as for the writers themselves, whatever their methods or intentions, their one allegiance should be to the truth of their Vision. If they are faithful to that and are good artists, they will seldom go wrong, all theories of literature notwithstanding.

It is much easier for the student of literature to go wrong. The endeavors of interpretation and evaluation are fraught with dangers. Your instructor may have much to say on these subjects. For the present, I would like to point out a couple of problems that are most in need of comment.

The first is that dread disease known as symbolitis. Of all the plagues visited upon English teachers and their students, this is surely one of the most destructive. When it strikes, hardly a sane person is to be found anywhere. So that you will be on guard against it, let me describe its symptoms. Symbolitis occurs when you feel embarrassed because you enjoyed the purely literal level of a story and couldn't find any symbols. Or, to put it the opposite way, symbolitis occurs when you feel triumphant because you found more symbols than anybody else and believe the symbolic level of meaning to be more important than the literal. The most extreme case of symbolitis occurs when you treat the literal story as though it had no value in itself but existed only for the sake of the symbolic meanings.[8] In the worst cases, the symbolic interpretation and the literal reading either contradict one another or have very little necessary connection.

To cure symbolitis is to realize that the great body of literature uses what might be called "natural symbolism," which can be apprehended on the level of feeling without translation, but which if translated takes little more than common sense to figure out. If a story has a man stumbling in a drunken stupor onto a railroad track in the face of an onrushing train, you may safely assume that the train symbolizes impending death. If the story is about the crushing effects of materialism on a man who is unable to cope with modern civilization, you may even assume that the train symbolizes the crushing effects of materialism. But if you go so far as to read into this scene a confrontation between man and the Devil, then you are asking for trouble, even if the author describes the train as "devilish" or "hell-bent on destruction." There is, after all, a difference between a "devilish" train and the Devil, just as there is a distinction between a "devilish" materialism and the Devil.

Of course I do not mean to imply that all symbolism is natural or that authors do not at times intend to evoke the most tenuous of associations. Some authors employ a symbolism that is so private, or so nationalistic, or so arcanely societal that only initiates can detect it without years of intensive study. James Joyce and William Butler Yeats are fine examples of authors who make it difficult for their readers by employing symbols whose meanings are not widely known. Joyce sometimes evokes meanings that only a Catholic Dubliner who was also an intimate friend of his would know, and Yeats sometimes relies on the esoteric symbolism of Theosophy, Buddhism, and other spiritual societies. Fortunately, their work is so rich in meaning on all levels that it is possible to read them with profit and enjoyment without fully understanding the more esoteric points. It would make an interesting study to account for this esoteric trend in modern literature. Consider for yourself what role science has played in driving the

---

[8] In allegory the literal story *does* exist primarily for the sake of a meaning other than the literal, but allegories are very rare, especially in modern literature.

modern writer into artistic isolation and alienation. Is there some connection between our loss of the ability to understand the language of Vision and the modern writer's extremely esoteric use of that language?

The second problem is that of evaluation. A certain kind of skepticism is as valuable in evaluating literature as it is in testing scientific hypotheses, for not all literature is great and true. I have included works in this anthology that are not works of great Vision precisely so that you may exercise your judgment upon them. You must judge each work on the basis of its truth and art. Many people have great Vision, but few have the art to express Vision truthfully. Conversely, many people are extremely skilled in the craft and technique of literary expression, but their art may lack Vision. You should especially be on your guard against works that tend to be mere literary exercises. Such works may employ symbolism, for instance, in so mechanical a fashion that they seem to have been inspired more by a desire to copy other people's Visions than to recreate their own.

The problem of evaluation is perhaps the most difficult one you will face, for the simple reason that you probably have not been trained properly to evaluate literature. The problem is caused, once again, partly by our science-oriented culture with its roots in Aristotelian logic, but also by our two-valued religious sensibility. We are conditioned by science and conventional religion to think in terms of absolutes. We feel so much more secure in a world in which two plus two always equals four, as it does in conventional math, or in a world divided neatly among the saved and the damned, as it is in conventional theology, that we are inclined to view the entire world in such absolute terms. But literature does not deal in absolutes. As I have said, ten different poets might express their Vision of evolution in ten radically different ways, yet all might be equally true to their Vision and equally great in their art, or they might not. So too ten other painters might paint the experience of *Guernica* in ways radically different from Picasso's, yet Picasso's would still be as true and as realistic as any of them. You must judge for yourself, and there are no tables of multiplication or ten commandments to help you. There are no right answers and no wrong answers. All that you can rely on is your experience in life, your knowledge of art, and the sensitivity of your Vision. If you develop Vision in your own life, you will be a better judge of the Visions of others, and their Visions will mean more to you.

Contents

PART 2 / FICTION

PART 3 / DRAMA

THE REALITIES OF LITERATURE

Part 1

POETRY

On a Horse Who Bit a Clergyman

The steed bit his master;
   How came this to pass?
He heard the good pastor
   Say, "All flesh is grass."

Eighteenth Century

Ogden Nash (b. 1902)

Very Like a Whale

One thing that literature would be greatly the better for
Would be a more restricted employment by authors of simile and
   metaphor.
Authors of all races, be they Greeks, Roman, Teutons or Celts,
Can't seem just to say that anything is the thing it is but have to go out
   of their way to say that it is like something else.
What does it mean when we are told   5
That the Assyrian came down like a wolf on the fold?
In the first place, George Gordon Byron had had enough experience
To know that it probably wasn't just one Assyrian, it was a lot of
   Assyrians.
However, as too many arguments are apt to induce apoplexy and thus
   hinder longevity,
We'll let it pass as one Assyrian for the sake of brevity.   10
Now then, this particular Assyrian, the one whose cohorts were gleam-
   ing in purple and gold,
Just what does the poet mean when he says he came down like a wolf
   on the fold?
In heaven and earth more than is dreamed of in our philosophy there
   are a great many things,

SOURCE: Reprinted from *Verses From 1929 On* by Ogden Nash with the permission of
Little, Brown and Company. Copyright 1934 by The Curtis Publishing Co.

3

But I don't imagine that among them there is a wolf with purple and
gold cohorts or purple and gold anythings.
No, no, Lord Byron, before I'll believe that this Assyrian was actually 15
like a wolf I must have some kind of proof;
Did he run on all fours and did he have a hairy tail and a big red mouth
and big white teeth and did he say Woof woof woof?
Frankly I think it very unlikely, and all you were entitled to say, at the
very most,
Was that the Assyrian cohorts came down like a lot of Assyrian cohorts
about to destroy the Hebrew host.
But that wasn't fancy enough for Lord Byron, oh dear me no, he had
to invent a lot of figures of speech and then interpolate them,
With the result that whenever you mention Old Testament soldiers to 20
people they say Oh yes, they're the ones that a lot of wolves dressed
up in gold and purple ate them.
That's the kind of thing that's being done all the time by poets, from
Homer to Tennyson;
They're always comparing ladies to lilies and veal to venison.
How about the man who wrote,
Her little feet stole in and out like mice beneath her petticoat?
Wouldn't anybody but a poet think twice   25
Before stating that his girl's feet were mice?
Then they always say things like that after a winter storm
The snow is a white blanket. Oh it is, is it, all right then, you sleep under
a six-inch blanket of snow and I'll sleep under a half-inch blanket
of unpoetical blanket material and we'll see which one keeps warm,
And after that maybe you'll begin to comprehend dimly
What I mean by too much metaphor and simile.   30

The Bible, King James Version

Psalm 23

The Lord is my shepherd;
I shall not want.
He maketh me to lie down in green pastures;
He leadeth me beside the still waters;
He restoreth my soul.   5
He leadeth me in the paths of righteousness for his name's sake.
Yea, though I walk through the valley of the shadow of death,
I will fear no evil, for thou art with me.
Thy rod and thy staff they comfort me.
Thou preparest a table before me in the presence of mine enemies;   10

Thou anointest my head with oil;
My cup runneth over.
Surely goodness and mercy shall follow me all the days of my life,
And I will dwell in the house of the Lord for ever.

The Bay–Psalm Book

A Psalm of David

The Lord to me a shepherd is; want therefore shall not I.
He in the folds of tender grass doth cause me down to lie.
To waters calm me gently leads, restore my soul doth he;
He doth in paths of righteousness for his name's sake lead me.
Yea, though in valley of death's shade I walk, none ill I'll fear   5
Because thou art with me; thy rod and staff my comfort are.
For me a table thou hast spread in presence of my foes;
Thou dost anoint my head with oil; my cup it overflows.
Goodness and mercy surely shall all my days follow me,
And in the Lord's house I shall dwell so long as days shall be.   10

Anonymous

Sir Patrick Spence

The king sits in Dumferling toune,
  Drinking the blude-reid wine:
"O whar will I get guid sailor
  To sail this schip of mine?"

Up and spak an eldern knicht,   5
  Sat at the kings richt kne:
"Sir Patrick Spence is the best sailor
  That sails upon the se."

The king has written a braid° letter,   *broad*
  And signed it wi' his hand,   10
And sent it to Sir Patrick Spence,
  Was walking on the sand.

The first line that Sir Patrick red,
  A loud lauch lauchèd he;
The next line that Sir Patrick red,
  The teir blinded his ee.   15

"O wha° is this has don this deid,   *who*
  This ill deid don to me,
To send me out this time o' the yeir,
  To sail upon the se!   20

"Mak haste, mak haste, my mirry men all,
  Our guid schip sails the morne."
"O say na sae°, my master deir,   *so*
  For I feir a deadlie storme.

"Late late yestreen I saw the new moone,   25
  Wi' the auld moone in hir arme,
And I feir, I feir, my deir master,
  That we will cum to harme."

O our Scots nobles wer richt laith°   *loath*
  To weet° their cork-heild schoone°;   *wet; shoes*
Bot lang owre° a' the play wer playd,   *ere*
  Their hats they swam aboone°.   *above (their heads)*

O lang, lang may their ladies sit,
  Wi' their fans into their hand,
Or ere° they se Sir Patrick Spence   *long before*
  Cum sailing to the land.

O lang, lang may the ladies stand,
  Wi' their gold kems° in their hair,   *combs*
Waiting for their ain° deir lords,   *own*
  For they'll se thame na mair.   40

Haf owre°, haf owre to Aberdour,   *halfway over*
  It's fiftie fadom deip,
And thair lies guid Sir Patrick Spence,
  Wi' the Scots lords at his feit.

Scottish Popular Ballad

Anonymous

Get Up and Bar the Door

It fell about the Martinmas time,
    And a gay time it was then,
When our goodwife got puddings to make,
    And she's boiled them in the pan.

The wind sae cauld blew south and north,   5
    And blew into the floor;
Quoth our goodman to our goodwife,
    "Gae out and bar the door."

"My hand is in my hussyfskap,°   *housework*
    Goodman, as ye may see;   10
An it shoud nae be barred this hundred year,
    It's no be barred for me."

They made a paction 'tween them twa,
    They made it firm and sure,
That the first word whaeer shoud speak,   15
    Shoud rise and bar the door.

Then by there came two gentlemen,
    At twelve o'clock at night,
And they could neither see house nor hall,
    Nor coal nor candle-light.   20

"Now whether is this a rich man's house,
    Or whether is it a poor?"
But neer a word wad ane o' them speak,
    For barring of the door.

And first they ate the white puddings,   25
    And then they ate the black;
Tho' muckle° thought the goodwife to hersel,   *much*
    Yet neer a word she spake.

Then said the one unto the other,
    "Here, man, tak ye my knife;
Do ye tak aff the auld man's beard,   30
    And I'll kiss the goodwife."

"But there's nae water in the house,
   And what shall we do than?"
"What ails ye at the pudding-broo,   35
   That boils into the pan?"

O up then started our goodman,
   An angry man was he:
"Will ye kiss my wife before my een,°   *eyes*
   And scad° me wi' pudding-bree?"   *scald*

Then up and started our goodwife,
   Gied three skips on the floor:
"Goodman, you've spoken the foremost word,
   Get up and bar the door."

Scottish Popular Ballad

Anonymous

Western Wind

Western wind, when wilt thou blow,
The° small rain down can rain?   *(so that) the*
Christ, if my love were in my arms,
And I in my bed again!

English; Sixteenth Century

Paul Simon (b. 1942)

The Dangling Conversation[1]

It's a still-life water color
   of a now-late afternoon,
As the sun shines through the curtain lace
   and shadows wash the room,
And we sit and drink our coffee
   couched in our indifference
   like shells upon the shore
   you can hear the ocean roar.

In the dangling conversation
and the superficial sighs
and the borders of our lives.

And you read your Emily Dickinson
and I my Robert Frost,
And we note our place with book-markers
and measure what we've lost,
Like a poem poorly written
we are verses out of rhythm
couplets out of rhyme
in syncopated time.

And the dangling conversation
and the superficial sighs
are the borders of our lives.

Yes we speak of things that matter
with words that must be said,
Can analysis be worthwhile?
is the theater really dead?
And how the room is softly faded
and I kiss your shadow
I cannot feel your hand
you're a stranger now unto me.

Lost in the dangling conversation
and the superficial sighs
and the borders of our lives.

5

10

Flowers Never Bend with the Rainfall

Through the hard doors of sleep
Pass shadows dark and deep,
My mind dances and weeps in confusion.

I don't know what is real,
I can't touch what I feel,
And I hide behind the shield of my illusion.

So I'll continue to continue to pretend my life will never end,
And flowers never bend with the rainfall.

5

The mirror on my wall
Casts an image dark and small,   10
But I'm not sure at all it's my reflection.

I'm blinded by the light
Of God and truth and right,
And I wander in the night without direction.

   So I'll continue to continue to pretend my life will never end,   15
And flowers never bend with the rainfall.

No matter if you're born
To play the king or pawn,
For the line is thinly drawn 'tween joy and sorrow.

So my fantasy becomes reality,   20
And I must be what I must be
And face tomorrow.

   So I'll continue to continue to pretend my life will never end,
And flowers never bend with the rainfall.

Edmund Spenser (1552?–1599)

Like as a ship, that through the ocean wide

Like as a ship, that through the ocean wide
By conduct of some star, doth make her way,
When as a storm hath dimmed her trusty guide,
Out of her course doth wander far astray;
So I, whose star, that wont with her bright ray   5
Me to direct, with clouds is overcast,
Do wander now in darkness and dismay,
Through hidden perils round about me placed.
Yet hope I well that, when this storm is passed,
My Helice,[1] the lodestar of my life,   10
Will shine again and look on me at last
With lovely light to clear my cloudy grief.
   Till then I wander carefull, comfortless,
   In secret sorrow, and sad pensiveness.

                      Sonnet 34

[1]Ursa Major.

Sir Philip Sidney (1554–1586)

Loving in truth, and fain in verse my love to show

Loving in truth, and fain in verse my love to show,
That she, dear she, might take some pleasure of my pain,
Pleasure might cause her read, reading might make her know,
Knowledge might pity win, and pity grace obtain,
I sought fit words to paint the blackest face of woe;   5
Studying inventions fine, her wits to entertain,
Oft turning others' leaves to see if thence would flow
Some fresh and fruitful showers upon my sunburned brain.
But words came halting forth, wanting invention's stay;
Invention, nature's child, fled stepdame Study's blows,   10
And others' feet still seemed but strangers in my way.
Thus, great with child to speak, and helpless in my throes,
Biting my truant pen, beating myself for spite,
"Fool," said my muse to me, "look in thy heart and write."

Sonnet 1

Christopher Marlowe (1564–1593)

Like untuned golden strings all women are

Like untuned golden strings all women are,
Which Long time lie untouched, will harshly jar.
Vessels of brass, oft handled, brightly shine;
What difference betwixt the richest mine
And basest mold, but use? for both, not used,   5
Are of like worth. Then treasure is abused,
When misers keep it; being put to loan,
In time it will return us two for one.
Rich robes themselves and others do adorn;
Neither themselves nor others, if not worn.   10
Who builds a palace, and rams up the gate,
Shall see it ruinous and desolate.

from Hero and Leander

William Shakespeare (1564–1616)

Shall I compare thee to a summer's day?

Shall I compare thee to a summer's day?
Thou art more lovely and more temperate.
Rough winds do shake the darling buds of May,
And summer's lease hath all too short a date.
Sometime too hot the eye of heaven shines,   5
And often is his gold complexion dimmed;
And every fair from fair sometime declines,
By chance, or nature's changing course, untrimmed.
But thy eternal summer shall not fade,
Nor lose possession of that fair thou ow'st°;   *ownest, has*
Nor shall death brag thou wand'rest in his shade,
When in eternal lines to time thou grow'st.
    So long as men can breathe or eyes can see,
    So long lives this, and this gives life to thee.

Sonnet 18

When to the sessions of sweet silent thought

When to the sessions of sweet silent thought
I summon up remembrance of things past,
I sigh the lack of many a thing I sought,
And with old woes new wail my dear time's waste.
Then can I drown an eye, unused to flow,   5
For precious friends hid in death's dateless night,
And weep afresh love's long-since cancelled woe,
And moan the expense of many a vanished sight.
Then can I grieve at grievances foregone,
And heavily from woe to woe tell o'er   10
The sad account of fore-bemoaned moan,
Which I new pay as if not paid before.
    But if the while I think on thee, dear friend,
    All losses are restored, and sorrows end.

Sonnet 30

That time of year thou mayst in me behold

That time of year thou mayst in me behold
When yellow leaves, or none, or few, do hang
Upon those boughs which shake against the cold,
Bare ruined choirs where late the sweet birds sang.
In me thou see'st the twilight of such day   5
As after sunset fadeth in the west,
Which by-and-by black night doth take away,
Death's second self that seals up all in rest.
In me thou see'st the glowing of such fire
That on the ashes of his youth doth lie,   10
As the deathbed whereon it must expire,
Consumed with that which it was nourished by.
    This thou perceiv'st, which makes thy love more strong,
    To love that well which thou must leave ere long.

Sonnet 73

Let me not to the marriage of true minds

Let me not to the marriage of true minds
Admit impediments. Love is not love
Which alters when it alteration finds,
Or bends with the remover° to remove.   *the inconstant lover*
O, no! it is an ever-fixèd mark   5
That looks on tempests and is never shaken;
It is the star to every wand'ring bark,
Whose worth's unknown, although his height be taken.
Love's not Time's fool, though rosy lips and cheeks
Within his bending sickle's compass come;   10
Love alters not with his brief hours and weeks,
But bears it out even to the edge of doom.
    If this be error and upon me proved,
    I never writ, nor no man ever loved.

Sonnet 116

The expense of spirit in a waste of shame

The expense of spirit in a waste of shame
Is lust in action; and, till action, lust
Is perjured, murderous, bloody, full of blame,
Savage, extreme, rude, cruel, not to trust;   *to be trusted*
Enjoyed no sooner but despisèd straight;   5
Past reason hunted, and no sooner had,
Past reason hated, as a swallowed bait
On purpose laid to make the taker mad;
Mad in pursuit, and in possession so;
Had, having, and in quest to have, extreme;   10
A bliss in proof—and proved, a very woe;
Before, a joy proposed; behind, a dream.
　　All this the world well knows; yet none knows well
　　To shun the heaven that leads men to this hell.

Sonnet 129

My mistress' eyes are nothing like the sun

My mistress' eyes are nothing like the sun;
Coral is far more red than her lips' red;
If snow be white, why then her breasts are dun;
If hairs be wires, black wires grow on her head.
I have seen roses damasked red and white,   5
But no such roses see I in her cheeks;
And in some perfumes is there more delight
Than in the breath that from my mistress reeks.
I love to hear her speak, yet well I know
That music hath a far more pleasing sound;   10
I grant I never saw a goddess go:
My mistress, when she walks, treads on the ground.
　　And yet, by heaven, I think my love as rare
　　As any she, belied with false compare.

Sonnet 130

All the world's a stage

All the world's a stage,
And all the men and women merely players.
They have their exits and their entrances,
And one man in his time plays many parts,
His acts being seven ages. At first, the infant,   5
Mewling and puking in the nurse's arms.
Then the whining schoolboy, with his satchel
And shining morning face, creeping like snail
Unwillingly to school. And then the lover,
Sighing like furnace, with a woeful ballad   10
Made to his mistress' eyebrow. Then a soldier,
Full of strange oaths and bearded like the pard,
Jealous in honor, sudden and quick in quarrel,
Seeking the bubble reputation
Even in the cannon's mouth. And then the justice,   15
In fair round belly with good capon lined,
With eyes severe and beard of formal cut,
Full of wise saws and modern instances;
And so he plays his part. The sixth age shifts
Into the lean and slippered pantaloon,   20
With spectacles on nose and pouch on side;
His youthful hose, well saved, a world too wide
For his shrunk shank, and his big manly voice,
Turning again toward childish trebel, pipes
And whistles in his sound. Last scene of all,   25
That ends this strange eventful history,
Is second childishness and mere oblivion,
Sans teeth, sans eyes, sans taste, sans everything.

from *As You Like It*

Sweet are the uses of adversity

Sweet are the uses of adversity,
Which, like the toad, ugly and venomous,
Wears yet a precious jewel in his head;
And this our life, exempt from public haunt,
Find tongues in trees, books in the running brooks,   5
Sermons in stones, and good in everything.

from *As You Like It*

William Cowper (1731–1800)

The man to solitude accustom'd long

The man to solitude accustom'd long
Perceives in ev'ry thing that lives a tongue;
Not animals alone, but shrubs and trees,
Have speech for him, and understood with ease.

from "The Needless Alarm"

Samuel Daniel (1562–1619)

Fair is my love, and cruel as she's fair

Fair is my love, and cruel as she's fair:
    Her brow shades frowns, although her eyes are sunny;
    Her smiles are lightning, though her pride despair;
    And her disdains are gall, her favors honey.
A modest maid, decked with a blush of honor,   5
    Whose feet do tread green paths of youth and love;
    The wonder of all eyes that look upon her,
    Sacred on earth, designed a saint above.
Chastity and beauty, which were deadly foes,
    Live reconcilèd friends within her brow;   10
    And had she pity to conjoin with those,
    Then who had heard the plaints I utter now?
For had she not been fair and thus unkind,
My muse had slept, and none had known my mind.

Sonnet 6, from *Delia*

Love Is a Sickness

Love is a sickness full of woes,
    All remedies refusing;
A plant that with most cutting grows,
    Most barren with best using.
        Why so?   5
    More we enjoy it, more it dies;
If not enjoyed it sighing cries,
        Hey ho.

Love is a torment of the mind,
  A tempest everlasting;
And Jove hath made it of a kind
  Not well, nor full, nor fasting.
    Why so?
  More we enjoy it, more it dies;
If not enjoyed it sighing cries,
  Hey ho.

10

15

from *Hymen's Triumph*

Michael Drayton (1563–1631)

To the Senses

When conquering love did first my heart assail,
Unto mine aid I summoned every sense,
Doubting, if that proud tyrant should prevail,
My heart should suffer for mine eyes' offence;
But he with beauty first corrupted sight,
My hearing bribed with her tongue's harmony,
My taste, by her sweet lips drawn with delight,
My smelling won with her breath's spicery;
But when my touching came to play his part
(The king of senses, greater than the rest),
He yields love up the keys unto my heart,
And tells the other how they should be blest;
  And thus by those of whom I hoped for aid,
  To cruel love my soul was first betrayed.

5

10

Thomas Campion (1567–1620)

There is a garden in her face

  There is a garden in her face
Where roses and white lilies grow;
  A heav'nly paradise is that place
Wherein all pleasant fruits do flow.
    There cherries grow which none may buy
    Till "Cherry-ripe"[1] themselves do cry.

5

---

[1]Cry of fruit-peddlers in London streets.

Those cherries fairly do enclose
Of orient pearl a double row,
 Which when her lovely laughter shows,
They look like rose-buds filled with snow;   10
 Yet them nor° peer nor prince can buy,   *neither*
 Till "Cherry-ripe" themselves do cry.

 Her eyes like angels watch them still;
Her brows like bended bows do stand,
 Threat'ning with piercing frowns to kill   15
All that attempt, with eye or hand
 Those sacred cherries to come nigh
 Till "Cherry-ripe" themselves do cry.

from *The Third and Fourth Book of Airs*

Barnaby Barnes (1569?–1609)

Burn On, Sweet Fire

Burn on, sweet fire, for I live by that fuel
 Whose smoke is as an incense to my soul.
Each sigh prolongs my smart. Be fierce and cruel,
 My fair Parthenophe.[1] Frown and control,
Vex, torture, scald, disgrace me. Do thy will!   5
 Stop up thine ears; with flint immure thine heart,
And kill me with thy looks, if they would kill.
 Thine eyes, those crystal phials which impart
The perfect balm to my dead-wounded breast;
 Thine eyes, the quivers whence those darts were drawn   10
Which me to thy love's bondage have addressed;
 Thy smile and frown, night-star and daylight's dawn,
Burn on, frown on, vex, stop thine ears, torment me!
 More, for thy beauty borne, would not repent me.

[1]The girl's name.

Ben Jonson (1572–1637)

Song: *To Celia*

Drink to me only with thine eyes,
    And I will pledge with mine;
Or leave a kiss but in the cup,
    And I'll not ask for wine.
The thirst that from the soul doth rise   5
    Doth ask a drink divine;
But might I of Jove's nectar sup,
    I would not change for thine.

I sent thee late a rosy wreath,
    Not so much honoring thee   10
As giving it a hope that there
    It could not withered be.
But thou thereon didst only breathe,
    And sent'st it back to me;
Since when it grows, and smells, I swear,   15
    Not of itself but thee.

Doing a Filthy Pleasure Is

Doing a filthy pleasure is, and short;
And done, we straight repent us of the sport.
Let us not, then, rush blindly on unto it
Like lustful beasts, that only know to do it,
For lust will languish, and that heat decay.   5
But thus, thus, keeping endless holiday,
Let us together closely lie, and kiss;
There is no labor, nor no shame in this.
This hath pleased, doth please, and long will please; never
Can this decay, but is beginning ever.   10

The Hourglass

Do but consider this small dust,
Here running in the glass,
    By atoms moved;
Could you believe that this
The body was   5
    Of one that loved?
And in his Mistress' flame, playing like a fly,
    Turned to cinders by her eye?
        Yes; and in death, as life, unblest,
            To have't expressed,   10
Even ashes of lovers find no rest.

Though I am young, and cannot tell[1]

Though I am young, and cannot tell
    Either what Death or Love is well,
Yet I have heard they both bear darts,
    And both do aim at human hearts.
And then again, I have been told   5
    Love wounds with heat, as Death with cold;
So that I fear they do but bring
    Extremes to touch, and mean one thing.

As in a ruin[2] we it call
    One thing to be blown up, or fall;
Or to our end like way may have   10
    By a flash of lightning, or a wave;
So Love's inflaméd shaft or brand
    May kill as soon as Death's cold hand;
Except Love's fires the virtue have   15
    To fright the frost out of the grave.

---

[1]This song is sung in *The Sad Shepherd* by Caroline.
[2]Demolition, explosion.

John Fletcher (1579–1625)

Take, oh take those lips away

Take, oh take those lips away,
    That so sweetly were forsworn,
And those eyes like break of day,
    Lights that do mislead the morn;
But my kisses bring again,   5
    Seals of love, though sealed in vain.

Hide, oh hide those hills of snow,
    Which thy frozen bosom bears,
On whose tops the pinks that grow
    Are of those that April wears;   10
But first set my poor heart free,
    Bound in those icy chains by thee.

Song from *The Bloody Brother*

Robert Herrick (1591–1674)

Corinna's Going A-Maying

Get up! get up for shame! the blooming morn
Upon her wings presents the god unshorn.[1]
    See how Aurora[2] throws her fair
    Fresh-quilted colors through the air:
    Get up, sweet slug-a-bed, and see   5
    The dew bespangling herb and tree.
Each flower has wept and bowed toward the east
Above an hour since, yet you not dressed;
    Nay, not so much as out of bed?
    When all the birds have matins[3] said,   10
    And sung their thankful hymns, 'tis sin,
    Nay, profanation to keep in,
When as a thousand virgins on this day
Spring, sooner than the lark, to fetch in May.

[1]Apollo, the sun god, often depicted with long, flowing hair.
[2]Goddess of the dawn.
[3]Morning prayers.

Rise and put on your foliage, and be seen   15
To come forth, like the springtime, fresh and green,
    And sweet as Flora.[4] Take no care
    For jewels for your gown or hair;
    Fear not, the leaves will strew
    Gems in abundance upon you;   20
Besides, the childhood of the day has kept,
Against you come, some orient pearls unwept;
    Come and receive them while the light
    Hangs on the dew-locks of the night,
    And Titan[5] on the eastern hill   25
    Retires himself, or else stands still
Till you come forth. Wash, dress, be brief in praying:
Few beads[6] are best when once we go a-Maying.

Come, my Corinna, come; and, coming, mark
How each field turns a street, each street a park   30
    Made green and trimmed with trees; see how
    Devotion gives each house a bough
    Or branch: each porch, each door ere this,
    An ark, a tabernacle is,
Made up of white-thorn neatly interwove,   35
As if here were those cooler shades of love.
    Can such delights be in the street
    And open fields, and we not see't?
    Come, we'll abroad; and let's obey
    The proclamation made for May,   40
And sin no more, as we have done, by staying;
But, my Corinna, come, let's go a-Maying.

---

[4]Flower goddess.

[5]The sun god Helios representing the physical sun, as Apollo represents its spiritual manifestation.

[6]Prayer beads, rosary.

There's not a budding boy or girl this day
But is got up and gone to bring in May;
   A deal of youth, ere this, is come   45
   Back, and with white-thorn laden home.
   Some have dispatched their cakes and cream
   Before that we have left to dream;
And some have wept, and wooed, and plighted troth,
And chose their priests, ere we can cast off sloth.   50
   Many a green gown has been given,
   Many a kiss, both odd and even;
   Many a glance, too, has been sent
   From out the eye, love's firmament;
Many a jest told of the keys betraying   55
This night, and locks picked; yet we're not a-Maying.

Come, let us go while we are in our prime,
And take the harmless folly of the time.
   We shall grow old apace, and die
   Before we know our liberty.
   Our life is short, and our days run   60
   As fast away as does the sun;
And, as a vapor or a drop of rain
Once lost, can ne'er be found again;
   So when or you or I are made   65
   A fable, song, or fleeting shade,
   All love, all liking, all delight
   Lies drowned with us in endless night.
Then while time serves, and we are but decaying,
Come, my Corinna, come, let's go a-Maying.   70

To the Virgins, to Make Much of Time

Gather ye rose-buds while ye may,
   Old Time is still a-flying;
And this same flower that smiles today,
   Tomorrow will be dying.

The glorious lamp of heaven, the sun,   5
   The higher he's a-getting,
The sooner will his race be run,
   And nearer he's to setting.

That age is best which is the first,
   When youth and blood are warmer;   10
But being spent, the worse, and worst
   Times still succeed the former.

Then be not coy, but use your time,
   And while ye say, go marry;
For having lost but once your prime,   15
   You may for ever tarry.

Delight in Disorder

A sweet disorder in the dress
Kindles in clothes a wantonness:
A lawn about the shoulders thrown
Into a fine distraction,
An erring lace, which here and there   5
Enthralls the crimson stomacher,
A cuff neglectful, and thereby
Ribands to flow confusedly,
A winning wave (deserving note)
In the tempestuous petticoat,   10
A careless shoe-string, in whose tie
I see a wild civility,
Do more bewitch me than when art
Is too precise in every part.

Upon Julia's Voice

So smooth, so sweet, so silv'ry is thy voice,
As, could they hear, the damned would make no noise,
But listen to thee (walking in thy chamber)
Melting melodious words, to lutes of amber.

Upon Julia's Clothes

Whenas in silks my Julia goes,
Then, then, methinks, how sweetly flows
That liquefaction of her clothes.

Next, when I cast mine eyes and see
That brave vibration each way free,   5
O how that glittering taketh me!

Anonymous

Herrick's Julia Improved

When all in silk my Julia's dressed,
She flows along, be it confessed,
As if her clothes had deliquesced.

Next, if and when I her behold,
Her oscillations are so bold,   5
She glistens like a lump of gold.

Edmund Waller (1606–1687)

Song: *Go, Lovely Rose*

 Go, lovely rose,
Tell her that wastes her time and me
 That now she knows,
When I resemble her to thee,
How sweet and fair she seems to be.   5

 Tell her that's young
And shuns to have her graces spied
 That hadst thou sprung
In deserts where no men abide,
Thou must have uncommended died.   10

Small is the worth
Of beauty from the light retired;
  Bid her come forth,
Suffer herself to be desired,
And not blush so to be admired.   15

  Then die, that she
The common fate of all things rare
  May read in thee:
How small a part of time they share
That are so wondrous sweet and fair!   20

Sir John Suckling (1609–1642)

Why so pale and wan, fond lover?

Why so pale and wan, fond lover?
  Prithee, why so pale?
Will, when looking well can't move her,
  Looking ill prevail?
  Prithee, why so pale?   5

Why so dull and mute, young sinner?
  Prithee, why so mute?
Will, when speaking well can't win her,
  Saying nothing do't?
  Prithee, why so mute?   10

Quit, quit, for shame; this will not move,
  This cannot take her.
If of herself she will not love.
  Nothing can make her:
  The devil take her!   15

Song from *Aglaura*

Richard Lovelace (1618–1658)

To Lucasta, on Going to the Wars

Tell me not, Sweet, I am unkind
    That from the nunnery
Of thy chaste breast and quiet mind,
    To war and arms I fly.

True, a new mistress now I chase,
    The first foe in the field;   5
And with a stronger faith embrace
    A sword, a horse, a shield.

Yet this inconstancy is such
    As you too shall adore;   10
I could not love thee, Dear, so much,
    Loved I not Honor more.

Andrew Marvell (1621–1678)

To His Coy Mistress

Had we but world enough, and time,
This coyness°, lady, were no crime.   *modesty, reluctance*
We would sit down and think which way
To walk, and pass our long love's day.
Thou by the Indian Ganges' side   5
Should'st rubies find; I by the tide
Of Humber[1] would complain. I would
Love you ten years before the Flood,
And you should, if you please, refuse
Till the conversion of the Jews.   10
My vegetable love should grow
Vaster than empires, and more slow.
An hundred years should go to praise
Thine eyes, and on thy forehead gaze,
Two hundred to adore each breast,   15
But thirty thousand to the rest.

---

[1]River that flows by Marvell's town of Hull.

An age at least to every part,
And the last age should show your heart.
For, lady, you deserve this state,
Nor would I love at lower rate.   20
    But at my back I always hear
Time's winged chariot hurrying near;
And yonder all before us lie
Deserts of vast eternity.
Thy beauty shall no more be found,   25
Nor in thy marble vault shall sound
My echoing song; then worms shall try
That long preserved virginity,
And your quaint honor turn to dust,
And into ashes all my lust.   30
The grave's a fine and private place,
But none, I think, do there embrace.
    Now therefore, while the youthful hue
Sits on thy skin like morning dew,
And while thy willing soul transpires   35
At every pore with instant° fires,   *eager*
Now let us sport us while we may;
And now, like am'rous birds of prey,
Rather at once our time devour,
Than languish in his slow-chapped° power,[2]   *slow-jawed*
Let us roll all our strength, and all
Our sweetness, up into one ball;
And tear our pleasures with rough strife
Thorough° the iron gates of life.   *through*
Thus, though we cannot make our sun   45
Stand still[3] yet we will make him run.

---

[2]Perhaps alludes to the Greek god Chronos (Father Time), who devoured his children to
  forestall their rebellion.

[3]Zeus bade the sun stand still so that he might enjoy a longer night with Alcmene.

John Donne (1572–1631)

Song: Go and catch a falling star

Go and catch a falling star,
　　Get with child a mandrake root,[1]
Tell me where all past years are,
　　Or who cleft the Devil's foot,
Teach me to hear mermaids singing,　　　　　　　　5
　　Or to keep off envy's stinging,
　　　　And find
　　　　What wind
Serves to advance an honest mind.

If thou be'st borne to strange sights,　　　　　　　10
　　Things invisible to see,
Ride ten thousand days and nights,
　　Till age snow white hairs on thee,
Thou, when thou return'st, wilt tell me
　　All strange wonders that befell thee,　　　　　15
　　　　And swear
　　　　Nowhere
Lives a woman true, and fair.

If thou findst one, let me know,
　　Such a pilgrimage were sweet—　　　　　　　20
Yet do not, I would not go,
　　Though at next door we might meet;
Though she were true, when you met her,
　　And last, till you write your letter,
　　　　Yet she　　　　　　　　　　　　25
　　　　Will be
False, ere I come, to two, or three.

---

[1]Supposedly an aphrodisiac and known for being fork-shaped like a human being.

The Flea

Mark but this flea, and mark in this
How little that which thou deniest me is;
It sucked me first, and now sucks thee,
And in this flea our two bloods mingled be.
Thou knowest that this cannot be said   5
A sin, nor shame, nor loss of maidenhead;
   Yet this enjoys before it woo,
   And pampered swells with one blood made of two,
   And this, alas, is more than we would do.

O stay! Three lives in one flea spare,   10
Where we almost, yea, more than married are;
This flea is you and I, and this
Our marriage bed and marriage temple is.
Though parents grudge, and you, we're met
And cloistered in these living walls of jet.   15
   Though use make you apt to kill me,
   Let not to that, self-murder added be,
   And sacrilege, three sins in killing three.

Cruel and sudden! Hast thou since
Purpled thy nail in blood of innocence?   20
Wherein could this flea guilty be,
Except in that drop which it sucked from thee?
Yet thou triumph'st and saist that thou
Find'st not thyself, nor me, the weaker now.
   'Tis true. Then learn how false, fears be;   25
   Just so much honor, when thou yield'st to me,
   Will waste, as this flea's death took life from thee.

A Valediction: Forbidding Mourning

As virtuous men pass mildly away,
   And whisper to their souls to go,
Whilst some of their sad friends do say
   The breath goes now, and some say no:

So let us melt, and make no noise,   5
   No tear-floods, nor sigh-tempests move;
'Twere profanation of our joys
   To tell the laity our love.

Moving of th' earth° brings harms and fears;   *earthquake*
   Men reckon what it did and meant;   10
But trepidation of the spheres,[1]
   Though greater far, is innocent°.   *harmless, unnoticeable*

Dull súblunary° lovers' love   *earthly*
   (Whose soul is sense) cannot admit
Absence, because it doth remove   15
   Those things which elemented° it.   *constituted*

But we, by a love so much refined
   That ourselves know not what it is,
Inter-assurèd of the mind,
   Care less, eyes, lips, and hands to miss.   20

Our two souls, therefore, which are one,
   Though I must go, endure not yet
A breach, but an expansiòn,
   Like gold to airy thinness beat.

If they be two, they are two so   25
   As stiff twin compasses are two:
Thy soul, the fixed foot, makes no show
   To move, but doth, if th' other do.

And though it in the center sit,
   Yet when the other far doth roam,
It leans and harkens after it,   30
   And grows erect as that comes home.

Such wilt thou be to me, who must,
   Like th' other foot, obliquely run;
Thy firmness makes my circle just°,   *perfect*
   And makes me end where I begun.

---

[1]In Ptolemaic astronomy, the concentric spheres surrounding the earth.

The Ecstasy

Where, like a pillow on a bed,
    A pregnant bank swelled up to rest
The violet's reclining head,
    Sat we two, one another's best.

Our hands were firmly cemented   5
    With a fast balm, which thence did spring;
Our eye-beams[1] twisted, and did thread
    Our eyes upon one double string;

So to entergraft° our hands, as yet   *graft together*
    Was all the means to make us one;   10
And pictures in our eyes to get°   *beget*
    Was all our propagation.

As 'twixt two equal armies Fate
    Suspends uncertain victory,
Our souls, which to advance their state   15
    Were gone out, hung 'twixt her and me.

And whilst our souls negotiate there,
    We like sepulchral statues lay;
All day, the same our postures were
    And we said nothing, all the day.   20

If any, so by love refined
    That he soul's language understood,
And by good love were grown all mind,
    Within convenient distance stood,

He, though he knew not which soul spake   25
    Because both meant, both spake the same,
Might thence a new concoction take,
    And part far purer than he came.

This ecstasy doth unperplex,
    We said, and tell us what we love.   30
We see by this it was not sex;
    We see we saw not what did move.

---

[1] It was thought that actual streams of images came from the eyes to an object.

But as all several° souls contain   *individual, separate*
    Mixtures of things, they know not what,
Love these mixed souls doth mix again   35
    And makes both one, each this and that.

A single violet transplant,
    The strength, the color, and the size,
All which before was poor and scant,
    Redoubles still, and multiplies.   40

When love with one another so
    Interinanimates two souls,
That abler soul, which thence doth flow,
    Defects of loneliness controls.

We, then, who are this new soul, know   45
    Of what we are composed and made,
For the atomies of which we grow
    Are souls, whom no change can invade.

But oh, alas, so long, so far,
    Our bodies why do we forbear?   50
They are ours, though they are not we; we are
    The intelligences[2] they the sphere.

We owe them thanks, because they thus
    Did us to us at first convey,
Yielded their forces, sense, to us,   55
    Nor are dross to us, but allay°.   *alloy*

On man heaven's influence works not so
    But that it first imprints the air;[3]
So soul into the soul may flow,
    Though it to body first repair.   60

As our blood labors to beget
    Spirits[4] as like souls as it can,
Because such fingers need to knit
    That subtle knot which makes us man,

---

[2]In Ptolemaic astronomy, the powers that move the heavenly spheres.
[3]The medium through which heavenly bodies affect man.
[4]Subtle vapors manufactured by the blood that link body and soul together.

So must pure lovers' souls descend   65
   To affections and to faculties
Which sense may reach and apprehend:
   Else a great prince in prison lies.

To our bodies turn we then, that so
   Weak men on love revealed may look;   70
Love's mysteries in souls do grow,
   But yet the body is his book.

And if some lover, such as we,
   Have heard this dialogue of one,
Let him still mark us; he shall see   75
   Small change when we're to bodies gone.

Batter my heart, three-personed God

Batter my heart, three-personed God, for you
As yet but knock, breathe, shine, and seek to mend;
That I may rise and stand, o'erthrow me, and bend
Your force to break, blow, burn, and make me new.
I, like an usurped town to another due,   5
Labor to admit to you, but oh, to no end;
Reason, your viceroy in me, me should defend,
But is captived, and proves weak or untrue.
Yet dearly I love you, and would be lovèd fain
But am betrothed unto your enemy;   10
Divorce me, untie or break that knot again;
Take me to you, imprison me, for I,
Except you enthrall me, never shall be free,
Nor ever chaste, except you ravish me.

Holy Sonnet 14

Death, be not proud

Death, be not proud, though some have called thee
Mighty and dreadful, for thou art not so,
For those whom thou think'st thou dost overthrow
Die not, poor Death, nor yet canst thou kill me.
From rest and sleep, which but thy picture be,   5
Much pleasure, then from thee much more must flow;
And soonest our best men with thee do go—
Rest of their bones and souls' delivery!
Thou'rt slave to fate, chance, kings and desperate men,
And dost with poison, war, and sickness dwell,   10
And poppy or charms can make us sleep as well,
And better than thy stroke; why swell'st thou then?
One short sleep past, we wake eternally,
And death shall be no more: Death, thou shalt die!

Holy Sonnet 10

Antiquary

If in his study he hath so much care
To hang all old strange things, let his wife beware.

A Lame Beggar

"I am unable," yonder beggar cries,
"To stand or move!" If he say true, he lies.

Sir John Harrington (1561–1612)

Of Treason

Treason doth never prosper; what's the reason?
For if it prosper, none dare call it treason.

George Herbert (1593–1633)

Easter Wings

Lord, who createdst man in wealth and store,
Though foolishly he lost the same,
Decaying more and more
Till he became
Most poor;   5
With thee
Oh, let me rise
As larks, harmoniously,
And sing this day thy victories;
Then shall the fall further the flight in me.   10

My tender age in sorrow did begin;
And still with sicknesses and shame
Thou didst so punish sin,
That I became
Most thin.   15
With thee
Let me combine,
And feel this day thy victory;
For if I imp° my wing on thine,   *graft*
Affliction shall advance the flight in me.   20

The Pulley

When God at first made man,
Having a glass of blessings standing by—
Let us (said he) pour on him all we can;
Let the world's riches, which dispersèd lie,
Contract into a span.   5

So strength first made a way,
Then beauty flowed, then wisdom, honor, pleasure:
When almost all was out, God made a stay,
Perceiving that, alone of all His treasure,
Rest in the bottom lay.   10

For if I should (said he)
Bestow this jewel also on My creature,
He would adore My gifts instead of Me,
And rest in Nature, not the God of Nature:
    So both should losers be.   15

    Yet let him keep the rest,
But keep them with repining restlessness;
Let him be rich and weary, that at least,
If goodness lead him not, yet weariness
    May toss him to My breast.   20

Redemption

Having been a tenant long to a rich Lord,
    Not thriving, I resolvèd to be bold,
    And make a suit unto him to afford
A new small-rented lease and cancel th' old.
In heaven at his manor I him sought.   5
    They told me there that he was lately gone
    About some land which he had dearly bought
Long since on earth, to take possessiòn.
I straight returned, and knowing his great birth,
    Sought him accordingly in great resorts,   10
    In cities, theaters, gardens, parks, and courts.
At length I heard a ragged noise and mirth
    Of thieves and murderers; there I him espied,
Who straight "Your suit is granted," said, and died.

The Windows

Lord, how can man preach thy eternal word?
    He is a brittle, crazy glass;
Yet in thy temple thou dost him afford
    This glorious and transcendent place,
    To be a window through thy grace.   5

But when thou dost anneal in glass thy story,
  Making thy life to shine within
The holy preacher's, then the light and glory
  More reverend grows, and more doth win,
  Which else shows waterish, bleak, and thin.   10

Doctrine and life, colors and light in one,
  When they combine and mingle, bring
A strong regard and awe; but speech alone
  Doth vanish like a flaring thing,
  And in the ear, not conscience, ring.   15

Virtue

Sweet day, so cool, so calm, so bright,
The bridal of the earth and sky:
The dew shall weep thy fall tonight,
  For thou must die.

Sweet rose, whose hue, angry and brave,   5
Bids the rash gazer wipe his eye:
Thy root is ever in its grave,
  And thou must die.

Sweet spring, full of sweet days and roses,
A box where sweets compacted lie;   10
My music shows ye have your closes°,   *cadences*
  And all must die.

Only a sweet and virtuous soul,
Like seasoned timber, never gives;
But though the whole world turn to coal,   15
  Then chiefly lives.

Anonymous

Thus Passeth

Oh Nature! World! Oh Life! Oh Time!
Why aren't you always in your prime?
Why doesn't summer always stay?
Why aren't the flowers always gay?
Why is love's song so short a tune?   5
Why isn't January June?
I sigh to see all young girls grow
Older and older, their hair like snow.
All things on earth thus pass away:
Nothing save virtue lasts for aye.   10

Twentieth Century

John Milton (1608–1674)

When I consider how my light is spent

(On His Blindness)

When I consider how my light is spent,
    Ere half my days in this dark world and wide,
    And that one talent[1] which is death to hide
    Lodged with me useless, though my soul more bent
To serve therewith my Maker, and present   5
    My true account, lest He returning chide;
    "Doth God exact day-labor, light denied?"
    I fondly° ask. But Patience, to prevent   *foolishly*
That murmur, soon replies, "God doth not need
    Either man's work or His own gifts. Who best   10
    Bear His mild yoke, they serve Him best. His state
Is kingly: thousands at His bidding speed,
    And post o'er land and ocean without rest;
    They also serve who only stand and wait."

---

[1]For Christ's parable of the talents (measures of money), see Matthew 25:14-30.

Lycidas [1]

In this monody the author bewails a learned friend, unfortunately drowned in his passage from Chester on the Irish Seas, 1637. And by occasion foretells the ruin of our corrupted clergy then in their height.

Yet once more, O ye laurels,[2] and once more,
Ye myrtles brown°, with ivy never sere,   *dark*
I come to pluck your berries harsh and crude°,   *immature*
And with forced fingers rude
Shatter your leaves before the mellowing year.   5
Bitter constraint and sad occasion dear
Compels me to disturb your season due;
For Lycidas is dead, dead ere his prime,
Young Lycidas, and hath not left his peer.
Who would not sing for Lycidas? he knew   10
Himself to sing, and build the lofty rhyme.
He must not float upon his wat'ry bier
Unwept, and welter° to the parching wind,   *toss about*
Without the meed° of some melodious tear.   *tribute*
    Begin, then, Sisters of the Sacred Well   15
That from beneath the seat of Jove doth spring,
Begin, and somewhat loudly sweep the string.
Hence with denial vain and coy excuse:
So may some gentle Muse°   *poet*
With lucky words favor my destined urn,   20
And, as he passes, turn,
And bid fair peace be to my sable shroud!
For we were nursed upon the self-same hill,
Fed the same flocks, by fountain, shade, and rill;
    Together both, ere the high lawns appeared   25
Under the opening eyelids of the Morn,
We drove a-field, and both together heard
What time the gray-fly winds° her sultry horn,   *sounds*
Batt'ning° our flocks with the fresh dews of night,   *feeding*
Oft till the star that rose at evening bright   30
Toward Heav'n's descent had sloped his westering wheel.
Meanwhile the rural ditties were not mute,

---

[1]Lycidas was a conventional name for a young shepherd in pastoral poetry. The "learned friend" refers to Edward King, a fellow poet and student at Cambridge, who had planned a career in the ministry.

[2]Laurels and myrtles are evergreens in the crowns traditionally awarded to poets.

Tempered to the oaten° flute,   *made of an oat stalk*
Rough satyrs danced, and fauns with cloven heel
From the glad sound would not be absent long;   35
And old Damaetas³ loved to hear our song.
　But, O the heavy change, now thou art gone,
Now thou art gone, and never must return!
Thee, Shepherd, thee the woods and desert caves,
With wild thyme and the gadding° vine o'ergrown,   *wandering*
And all their echoes mourn.
The willows, and the hazel copses green,
Shall now no more be seen
Fanning their joyous leaves to thy soft lays.
As killing as the canker to the rose,   45
Or taint-worm to the weanling herds that graze,
Or frost to flowers, that their gay wardrobe wear
When first the white thorn blows°;   *blossoms*
Such, Lycidas, thy loss to shepherd's ear.
　Where were ye, Nymphs, when the remorseless deep   50
Closed o'er the head of your loved Lycidas?
For neither were ye playing on the steep
Where your old bards, the famous Druids, lie,
Nor yet on the shaggy top of Mona⁴ high,
Nor yet where Deva⁵ spreads her wizard stream.   55
Ay me! I fondly° dream!   *foolishly*
"Had ye been there"—for what could that have done?
What could the Muse herself that Orpheus bore,
The Muse herself, for her enchanting son,
Whom universal Nature did lament,   60
When, by the rout° that made the hideous roar,   *mob*
His gory visage down the stream was sent,
Down the swift Hebrus to the Lesbian shore?
　Alas! what boots it° with uncessant care   *what good does it do*
To tend the homely, slighted, shepherd's trade,   65
And strictly meditate the thankless Muse?
Were it not better done as others use°,   *do*
To sport with Amaryllis⁶ in the shade,
Or with the tangles of Neaera's⁶ hair?
Fame is the spur that the clear spirit doth raise   70

---

³Some Cambridge tutor perhaps.
⁴Roman name for the Isle of Man, near which King was drowned.
⁵The river Dee between England and Wales, whose shifts in course were thought to augur
　good luck for one country or the other.
⁶Conventional names for shepherdesses.

(That last infirmity of noble mind)
To scorn delights and live laborious days;
But the fair guerdon when we hope to find,
And think to burst out into sudden blaze,
Comes the blind Fury with th' abhorrèd shears,   75
And slits the thin-spun life. "But not the praise,"
Phoebus replied, and touched my trembling ears:[7]
"Fame is no plant that grows on mortal soil,
Nor in the glistering° foil[8]   *glittering*
Set off to the world, nor in broad rumor° lies,   *reputation*
But lives and spreads aloft by those pure eyes
And perfect witness of all-judging Jove;
As he pronounces lastly on each deed,
Of so much fame in Heav'n expect thy meed."
    O fountain Arethuse,[9] and thou honored flood,   85
Smooth-sliding Mincius,[9] crowned with vocal reeds,
That strain I heard was of a higher mood:
But now my oat proceeds,
And listens to the Herald of the Sea,
That came in Neptune's plea.[10]   90
He asked the waves, and asked the felon winds,
What hard mishap hath doomed this gentle swain?
And questioned every gust of rugged wings
That blows from off each beakèd promontory:
They knew not of his story;   95
And sage Hippotades their answer brings,
That not a blast was from his dungeon strayed:
The air was calm, and on the level brine
Sleek Panope[11] with all her sisters played.
It was that fatal and perfidious bark,   100
Built in th' eclipse°, and rigged with curses dark,   *bad omen*
That sunk so low that sacred head of thine.
    Next, Camus,[12] reverend sire, went footing slow,
His mantle hairy, and his bonnet sedge,
Inwrought with figures dim, and on the edge   105
Like to that sanguine flower inscribed with woe.

---

[7]Gesture signifying "Remember!"

[8]A setting of gold or silver leaf that would make a gem more brilliant.

[9]A fountain and river near the birthplaces of Theocritus and Virgil, respectively the most
  celebrated writer of Greek pastorals and of Latin pastorals.

[10]The sea-god's plea of "not guilty."

[11]A sea nymph whose name means "one who sees all."

[12]Spirit of the river Cam and personification of Cambridge University.

"Ah! who hath reft," quoth he, "my dearest pledge?"
Last came, and last did go,
The pilot° of the Galilean lake;   *St. Peter*
Two massy keys he bore of metals twain   110
(The golden opes, the iron shuts amain°).   *with force*
He shook his mitered locks, and stern bespake:—
"How well could I have spared for thee, young swain,
Enow° of such, as for their bellies' sake,   *enough*
Creep, and intrude, and climb into the fold!   115
Of other care they little reck'ning make
Than how to scramble at the shearers' feast,
And shove away the worthy bidden guest.
Blind mouths! that scarce themselves know how to hold
A sheep-hook, or have learned aught else the least   120
That to the faithful herdsman's art belongs!
What recks it them? What need they? they are sped°;   *prosperous*
And, when they list°, their lean and flashy songs   *so incline*
Grate on their scrannel° pipes of wretched straw;   *feeble, harsh*
The hungry sheep look up, and are not fed,   125
But, swoll'n with wind and the rank mist they draw,
Rot inwardly, and foul contagion spread;
Besides what the grim wolf[13] with privy° paw   *stealthy*
Daily devours apace, and nothing said;
But that two-handed engine[14] at the door   130
Stands ready to smite once, and smite no more."
        Return, Alpheus; the dread voice is past
That shrunk thy streams; return, Sicilian Muse,[15]
And call the vales, and bid them hither cast
Their bells and flow'rets of a thousand hues.   135
Ye valleys low, where the mild whispers use°   *resort*
Of shades, and wanton winds, and gushing brooks,
On whose fresh lap the swart star[16] sparely looks,
Throw hither all your quaint enameled eyes,
That on the green turf suck the honied showers,   140
And purple all the ground with vernal flowers.
Bring the rathe° primrose that forsaken dies,   *early*
The tufted crow-toe, and pale jessamine,
The white pink, and the pansy freaked° with jet,   *streaked*

---

[13]The Church of Rome, whose priests were winning converts.

[14]Alludes perhaps to the punishing sword of God visualized as a lightning bolt (Revelation 19:15).

[15]Inspired Theocritus, a native of Sicily.

[16]Sirius, at its zenith in summer, supposedly turned vegetation black.

The glowing violet,   145
The musk-rose, and the well-attired woodbine,
With cowslips wan that hang the pensive head,
And every flower that sad embroidery wears;
Bid amaranthus all his beauty shed,
And daffadillies fill their cups with tears,   150
To strew the laureate hearse where Lycid lies.
For so, to interpose a little ease,
Let our frail thoughts dally with false surmise,
Ay me! whilst thee the shores and sounding seas
Wash far away, where'er thy bones are hurled;   155
Whether beyond the stormy Hebrides,
Where thou, perhaps, under the whelming tide
Visit'st the bottom of the monstrous° world;   *full of sea-monsters*
Or whether thou, to our moist vows° denied,   *prayers*
Sleep'st by the fable of Bellerus[17] old,   160
Where the great Vision of the guarded mount[18]
Looks toward Namancos and Bayona's[19] hold°:   *stronghold*
Look homeward, angel, now, and melt with ruth°;   *pity*
And, O ye dolphins,[20] waft the hapless youth.

    Weep no more, woeful shepherds, weep no more,   165
For Lycidas, your sorrow, is not dead,
Sunk though he be beneath the wat'ry floor:
So sinks the day-star in the ocean bed
And yet anon repairs his drooping head,
And tricks° his beams, and with new-spangled ore°   *arrays; gold*
Flames in the forehead of the morning sky:
So Lycidas sunk low, but mounted high,
Through the dear might of Him that walked the waves,
Where, other groves and other streams along,
With nectar pure his oozy locks he laves,   175
And hears the unexpressive nuptial song,[21]
In the blest kingdoms meek of Joy and Love.
There entertain him all the Saints above,
In solemn troops, and sweet societies,
That sing, and singing in their glory move,   180
And wipe the tears forever from his eyes.
Now, Lycidas, the shepherds weep no more;

---

[17]Legendary giant of Land's End, the far tip of Cornwall.
[18]St. Michael's Mount, off Land's End, presumed to be under the protection of St. Michael.
[19]On the coast of Spain.
[20]In Greek legend, the kindly fish who carried the drowning or the drowned to shore.
[21]Inexpressibly beautiful song for the marriage feast of the Lamb (Revelation 19:9).

Henceforth thou art the Genius° of the shore,   *guardian spirit*
In thy large recompense, and shalt be good
To all that wander in that perilous flood.   185

                                                                                              rustic (or
    Thus sang the uncouth° swain to th' oaks and rills,   *little-known)*
While the still Morn went out with sandals gray;
He touched the tender stops of various quills°,   *reeds of a shepherd's pipe*
With eager thought warbling his Doric lay:²²
And now the sun had stretched out all the hills,   190
And now was dropped into the western bay.
At last he rose, and twitched° his mantle blue: *donned*
Tomorrow to fresh woods and pastures new.

Henry Vaughan (1622–1695)

The Retreat

Happy those early days when I
Shined in my angel-infancy!
Before I understood this place
Appointed for my second race,
Or taught my soul to fancy aught   5
But a white celestial thought;
When yet I had not walked above
A mile or two from my first love,
And looking back at that short space,
Could see a glimpse of his bright face;   10
When on some gilded cloud or flower
My gazing soul would dwell an hour,
And in those weaker glories spy
Some shadows of eternity;
Before I taught my tongue to wound   15
My conscience with a sinful sound,
Or had the black art to dispense
A sev'ral sin to ev'ry sense;
But felt through all this fleshly dress
Bright shoots of everlastingness.   20
    Oh, how I long to travel back
And tread again that ancient track!—

---

²²Pastoral poem. Doric is the dialect of Greek employed by Theocritus.

That I might once more reach that plain
Where first I left my glorious train,
From whence th' enlightened spirit sees   25
That shady city of palm trees.
But, ah, my soul with too much stay
Is drunk, and staggers in the way.
Some men a forward motion love,
But I by backward steps would move,   30
And when this dust falls to the urn,
In that state I came, return.

John Dryden (1631–1700)

A Song for St. Cecilia's Day[1]

1

From harmony, from heavenly harmony
    This universal frame began:
        When Nature underneath a heap
            Of jarring atoms lay,
            And could not heave her head,   5
The tuneful voice was heard from high:
    "Arise, ye more than dead."
Then cold, and hot, and moist, and dry,
In order to their stations leap,
        And Music's power obey.
From harmony, from heavenly harmony   10
    This universal frame began:
        From harmony to harmony
Through all the compass of the notes it ran,
The diapason[2] closing full in man.   15

---

[1] St. Cecilia, a Roman and early Christian martyr, long regarded as the patroness of music and the supposed inventor of the organ. Her Festival day (November 22) was observed in England by religious services and public concerts, which included an ode set to music for the occasion.

[2] The entire compass of tones in the scale, implicitly compared to the Great Chain of Being.

2

What passion cannot Music raise and quell!
    When Jubal[3] struck the corded shell,
    His listening brethren stood around,
    And, wondering, on their faces fell
    To worship that celestial sound.   20
Less than a god they thought there could not dwell
    Within the hollow of that shell
    That spoke so sweetly and so well.
What passion cannot Music raise and quell!

3

    The trumpet's loud clangor   25
      Excites us to arms,
    With shrill notes of anger,
      And mortal alarms.
    The double double double beat
      Of the thundering drum   30
Cries: "Hark! the foes come;
Charge, charge, 'tis too late to retreat."

4

The soft complaining flute
In dying notes discovers
The woes of hopeless lovers,   35
Whose dirge is whispered by the warbling lute.

5

    Sharp violins proclaim
Their jealous pangs, and desperation,
Fury, frantic indignation,
Depth of pains, and height of passion,   40
    For the fair, disdainful dame.

---

[3]The inventor of the harp and organ, according to Genesis 4:21. Jubal's harp is imagined
to have been made of a tortoise shell.

6

But O! what art can teach,
    What human voice can reach,
The sacred organ's praise?
    Notes inspiring holy love,   45
Notes that wing their heavenly ways
    To mend the choirs above.

7

Orpheus° could lead the savage race;   *son of a muse*
And trees unrooted left their place,
    Sequacious° of the lyre;   *following*
But bright Cecilia raised the wonder higher:
When to her organ vocal breath was given,
An angel heard, and straight appeared,
    Mistaking earth for heaven.

GRAND CHORUS

As from the power of sacred lays   55
    The spheres began to move,
And sung the great Creator's praise
    To all the blest above;
So, when the last and dreadful hour
This crumbling pageant shall devour,   60
The trumpet shall be heard on high,
The dead shall live, the living die,
And Music shall untune the sky.

Why should a foolish marriage vow

1

Why should a foolish marriage vow,
    Which long ago was made,
Oblige us to each other now,
    When passion is decayed?
We loved, and we loved, as long as we could,   5
    Till our love was loved out in us both;
But our marriage is dead when the pleasure is fled:
    'Twas pleasure first made it an oath.

2

If I have pleasures for a friend,
  And farther love in store,
What wrong has he whose joys did end,   10
  And who could give no more?
'Tis a madness that he should be jealous of me,
  Or that I should bar him of another:
For all we can gain is to give ourselves pain,   15
  When neither can hinder the other.

Song from *Marriage à la Mode*

Jonathan Swift (1667–1745)

A Description of the Morning

Now hardly here and there an Hackney-Coach
Appearing, show'd the Ruddy Morns Approach.
Now Betty from her Masters Bed had flown,
And softly stole to discompose her own.
The Slipshod Prentice from his Masters Door,   5
Had par'd the Dirt, and Sprinkled round the Floor.
Now Moll had whirl'd her Mop with dex'trous Airs,
Prepar'd to Scrub the Entry and the Stairs.
The Youth with Broomy Stumps began to trace
The Kennel-Edge, where Wheels had worn the Place.   10
The Smallcoal-Man was heard with Cadence deep,
'Till drown'd in Shriller Notes of Chimney-Sweep,
Duns at his Lordships Gate began to meet,
And Brickdust Moll had Scream'd through half the street.
The Turnkey now his Flock returning sees,   15
Duly let out a Nights to Steal for Fees.
The watchful Bailiffs take their silent Stands,
And School-Boys lag with Satchels in their Hands.

Verses on the Death of Dr. Swift, D.S.P.D.

Occasioned by reading a maxim in Rochefoucault
"Dans l'adversitè de nos meilleurs amis nous trouvons
quelquechose, qui ne nous deplaist pas."

As Rochefoucault his maxims drew
From nature, I believe 'em true;
They argue no corrupted mind
In him; the fault is in mankind.

This maxim more than all the rest   5
Is thought too base for human breast;
"In all distresses of our friends
We first consult our private ends,
While nature kindly bent to ease us,
Points out some circumstance to please us."   10

If this perhaps your patience move
Let reason and experience prove.

We all behold with envious eyes,
Our equal raised above our size;
Who would not at a crowded show,   15
Stand high himself, keep others low?
I love my friend as well as you,
But would not have him stop my view;
Then let him have the higher post;
I ask but for an inch at most.   20

If in a battle you should find,
One, whom you love of all mankind,
Had some heroic action done,
A champion killed, or trophy won;
Rather than thus be over-topt,   25
Would you not wish his laurels cropt?

Dear honest Ned is in the gout,
Lies rackt with pain, and you without:
How patiently you hear him groan!
How glad the case is not your own!   30

What poet would not grieve to see,
His brethren write as well as he?
But rather than they should excel,
He'd wish his rivals all in Hell.

Her end when emulation misses,   35
She turns to envy, stings and hisses:
The strongest friendship yields to pride,
Unless the odds be on our side.

Vain human kind! Fantastic race!
Thy various follies, who can trace?
Self-love, ambition, envy, pride,   40
Their empire in our hearts divide:
Give others riches, power, and station,
'Tis all on me an usurpation.
I have no title to aspire;   45
Yet, when you sink, I seem the higher.
In Pope, I cannot read a line,
But with a sigh, I wish it mine:
When he can in one couplet fix
More sense than I can do in six: 50
It gives me such a jealous fit,
I cry, pox take him, and his wit.

Why must I be outdone by Gay,
In my own hum'rous biting way?

Arbuthnot is no more my friend,   55
Who dares to irony pretend;
Which I was born to introduce,
Refin'd it first, and shew'd its use.

St. John, as well as Pultney knows,
That I had some repute for prose;   60
And till they drove me out of date,
Could maul a Minister of State:
If they have mortified my pride,
And made me throw my pen aside;
If with such talents Heav'n hath blest 'em   65
Have I not reason to detest 'em?

To all my foes, dear Fortune, send
Thy gifts, but never to my friend:
I tamely can endure the first,
But, this with envy makes me burst.   70

Thus much may serve by way of proem,
Proceed we therefore to our poem.

The time is not remote, when I
Must by the course of nature die:
When I foresee my special friends,   75
Will try to find their private ends:
Tho' it is hardly understood,
Which way my death can do them good:
Yet, thus methinks, I hear 'em speak:
See, how the Dean begins to break: 80
Poor gentleman, he droops apace,
You plainly find it in his face:
That old vertigo in his head,
Will never leave him, till he's dead:
Besides, his memory decays,   85
He recollects not what he says;
He cannot call his friends to mind;
Forgets the place where last he din'd:
Plies you with stories o'er and o'er,
He told them fifty times before.   90
How does he fancy we can sit,
To hear his out-of-fashion'd wit?
But he takes up with younger folks,
Who for his wine will bear his jokes:
Faith, he must make his stories shorter,   95
Or change his comrades once a quarter:
In half the time, he talks them round;
There must another set be found.

For poetry, he's past his prime,
He takes an hour to find a rhyme: 100
His fire is out, his wit decay'd,
His fancy sunk, his muse a jade.
I'd have him throw away his pen;
But there's no talking to some men.

And, then their tenderness appears,   105
By adding largely to my years:
"He's older than he would be reckon'd,
And well remembers Charles the Second.

"He hardly drinks a pint of wine;
And that, I doubt, is no good sign.
His stomach too begins to fail: 110
Last year we thought him strong and hale;
But now, he's quite another thing;
I wish he may hold out till Spring."

Then hug themselves, and reason thus;   115
"It is not yet so bad with us."

In such a case they talk in tropes,
And, by their fears express their hopes:
Some great misfortune to portend,
No enemy can match a friend;   120
With all the kindness they profess,
The merit of a lucky guess,
(When daily howd'y's come of course,
And servants answer; *Worse and worse*)
Would please 'em better than to tell,   125
That, God be prais'd, the Dean is well.
Then he who prophecy'd the best,
Approves his foresight to the rest:
"You know, I always fear'd the worst,
And often told you so at first:"   130
He'd rather choose that I should die,
Than his prediction prove a lie.
Not one foretells I shall recover;
But, all agree, to give me over.

Yet should some neighbour feel a pain,   135
Just in the parts, where I complain;
How many a message would he send?
What hearty prayers that I should mend?
Enquire what regimen I kept;
What gave me ease, and how I slept?   140
And more lament, when I was dead,
Than all the sniv'llers round my bed.

My good companions, never fear,
For though you may mistake a year;
Though your prognostics run too fast,   145
They must be verified at last.

Behold the fatal day arrive!
"How is the Dean? He's just alive.
Now the departing prayer is read:
He hardly breathes. The Dean is dead."   150
Before the passing-bell begun,
The news thro' half the town has run.
"O, may we all for death prepare!
What has he left? And who's his heir?
I know no more than what the news is,   155
'Tis all bequeath'd to public uses.
To public use! A perfect whim!
What had the public done for him!
Mere envy, avarice, and pride!
He gave it all:—But first he died.   160
And had the Dean, in all the nation,
No worthy friend, no poor relation?
So ready to do strangers good,
Forgetting his own flesh and blood?"

Now Grub-Street wits are all employ'd;   165
With elegies, the town is cloy'd:
Some paragraph in ev'ry paper,
To curse the Dean, or bless the Drapier.

The doctors tender of their fame,
Wisely on me lay all the blame: 170
"We must confess his case was nice;
But he would never take advice:
Had he been rul'd, for aught appears,
He might have liv'd these twenty years:
For when we open'd him we found,   175
That all his vital parts were sound."

From Dublin soon to London spread,
'Tis told at Court, the Dean is dead.

Kind Lady Suffolk in the spleen,
Runs laughing up to tell the Queen.   180
The Queen, so gracious, mild, and good,
Cries, "Is he gone? 'Tis time he should.

He's dead you say; why let him rot;
I'm glad the medals were forgot.
I promised them, I own; but when?   185
I only was the Princess then;
But now as Consort of the King,
You know 'tis quite a different thing."

   Now, Chartres at Sir Robert's levee
Tells, with a sneer, the tidings heavy:
"Why, is he dead without his shoes?"   190
(Cries Bob) "I'm sorry for the news;
Oh, were the wretch but living still,
And in his place my good friend Will;
Or, had a mitre on his head   195
Provided Bolingbroke were dead."

   Now Curl his shop from rubbish drains,
Three genuine tomes of Swift's Remains.
And then to make them pass the glibber,
Revised by Tibbalds, Moore, and Cibber.
He'll treat me as he does my betters.   200
Publish my will, my life, my letters.
Revive the libels born to die;
Which Pope must bear, as well as I.

   Here shift the scene, to represent   205
How those I love, my death lament.
Poor Pope will grieve a month; and Gay
A week; and Arbuthnot a day.

   St. John himself will scarce forbear,
To bite his pen, and drop a tear.   210
The rest will give a shrug and cry,
I'm sorry; but we all must die.
Indifference clad in wisdom's guise,
All fortitude of mind supplies:
For how can stony bowels melt,   215
In those who never pity felt;
When *we* are lash'd, *they* kiss the rod;
Resigning to the will of God.

The fools, my juniors by a year,
Are tortur'd with suspense and fear.   220
Who wisely thought my age a screen,
When death approach'd, to stand between:
The screen remov'd, their hearts are trembling,
They mourn for me without dissembling.

My female friends, whose tender hearts   225
Have better learn'd to act their parts.
Receive the News in doleful dumps,
"The Dean is dead, (and what is trumps?)
Then Lord have mercy on his soul.
(Ladies I'll venture for the vole.)   230
Six Deans they say must bear the pall.
(I wish I knew what king to call.)
Madam, your husband will attend
The funeral of so good a friend.
No Madam, 'tis a shocking sight,   235
And he's engag'd to-morrow night!
My Lady Club would take it ill,
If he should fail her at Quadrille.
He lov'd the Dean. (I lead a heart.)
But dearest friends, they say, must part.   240
His time was come, he ran his race;
We hope he's in a better place."

Why do we grieve that friends should die?
No loss more easy to supply.
One year is past; a different scene;   245
No further mention of the Dean;
Who now, alas, no more is mist,
Than if he never did exist.

Where's now this fav'rite of Apollo?
Departed; and his works must follow:
Must undergo the common fate;   250
His kind of wit is out of date.
Some country squire to Lintot goes,
Enquires for Swift in verse and prose:
Says Lintot, "I have heard the name:
He died a year ago." The same.   255
He searcheth all his shop in vain;
"Sir you may find them in Duck-lane:
I sent them with a load of books,
Last Monday to the pastry-cooks.
To fancy they cou'd live a year!   260
I find you're but a stranger here.
The Dean was famous in his time;
And had a kind of knack at rhyme:
His way of writing now is past;
The town hath got a better taste: 265
I keep no antiquated stuff;
But, spick and span I have enough.
Pray, do but give me leave to shew 'em;
Here's Colley Cibber's Birth-day Poem.
This Ode you never yet have seen,   270
By Stephen Duck, upon the Queen.
Then, here's a Letter finely penn'd
Against the Craftsman and his friend;
It clearly shows that all reflection
On ministers, is disaffection.   275
Next, here's Sir Robert's Vindication,
And Mr. Henly's last Oration:
The hawkers have not got 'em yet,
You Honour please to buy a set?
                                                      280

"Here's Wolston's Tracts, the twelfth edition:
'Tis read by ev'ry politician:
The Country Members, when in town,
To all their Boroughs send them down:
You never met a thing so smart;   285
The courtiers have them all by heart;
Those Maids of Honour (who can read)
Are taught to use them for their Creed.
The Rev'rend author's good intention,
Hath been rewarded with a pension: 290
He doth an honour to his gown,
By bravely running priest-craft down:
He shews, as sure as God's in *Glo'ster*,
That Jesus was a grand imposter:
That all his miracles were cheats,   295
Perform'd as jugglers do their feats:
The Church had never such a writer:
A shame, he hath not got a mitre!"

Suppose me dead; and then suppose
A club assembled at the Rose;   300
Where from discourse of this and that,
I grow the subject of their chat:
    And, while they toss my name about,
With favour some, and some without;
One quite indiff'rent in the cause,   305
My character impartial draws:

"The Dean, if we believe report,
Was never ill received at Court:
As for his works in verse and prose,
I own my self no judge of those: 310
Nor, can I tell what critics thought 'em:
But, this I know, all people bought 'em;
As with a moral view design'd
To cure the vices of mankind:
His vein, ironically grave,   315
Expos'd the fool, and lash'd the knave:
To steal a hint was never known,
But what he writ was all his own.

"He never thought an honour done him,
Because a Duke was proud to own him;   320
Would rather slip aside, and choose
To talk with wits in dirty shoes:
Despis'd the fools with stars and garters,
So often seen caressing Chartres:
He never courted men in station,   325
Nor persons had in admiration:
Of no man's greatness was afraid,
Because he sought for no man's aid.

"Though trusted long in great affairs,
He gave himself no haughty airs: 330
Without regarding private ends,
Spent all his credit for his friends:
And only chose the wise and good;
No flatt'rers; no allies in blood;
But succour'd virtue in distress,   335
And seldom fail'd of good success;
As numbers in their hearts must own,
Who, but for him, had been unknown.

"With Princes kept a due decorum,
But never stood in awe before 'em: 340
He follow'd David's lesson just,
In Princes never put thy trust.
And, would you make him truly sour;
Provoke him with a slave in power:
The Irish Senate, if you named,   345
With what impatience he declaimed!
Fair LIBERTY was all his cry;
For her he stood prepar'd to die;
For her he boldly stood alone;
For her he oft expos'd his own.   350
Two Kingdoms, just as faction led,
Had set a price upon his head;
But, not a traitor could be found,
To sell him for six hundred pound.

"Had he but spar'd his tongue and pen,   355
He might have rose like other men:
But, power was never in his thought;
And, wealth he valu'd not a groat:
Ingratitude he often found,
And pitied those who meant the wound: 360
But, kept the tenor of his mind,
To merit well of human kind:
Nor made a sacrifice of those
Who still were true, to please his foes.
He labour'd many a fruitless hour   365
To reconcile his friends in power;
Saw mischief by a faction brewing,
While they pursu'd each others' ruin.
But, finding vain was all his care,
He left the Court in mere despair.   370

"And, oh! how short are human schemes!
Here ended all our golden dreams.
What St. John's skill in State affairs,
What Ormond's valour, Oxford's cares,
To save their sinking country lent,   375
Was all destroy'd by one event.
Too soon that precious life was ended,
On which alone, our weal depended.
When up a dangerous faction starts,
With wrath and vengeance in their hearts: 380
By solemn League and Cov'nant bound,
To ruin, slaughter, and confound;
To turn religion to a fable,
And make the government a Babel:

"Pervert the law, disgrace the gown,   385
Corrupt the senate, rob the crown;
To sacrifice old England's glory,
And make her infamous in story.
When such a tempest shook the land,
How could unguarded virtue stand?   390

"With horror, grief, despair the Dean
Beheld the dire destructive scene:

His friends in exile, or the Tower,
Himself within the frown of Power;
Pursued by base envenom'd pens,   395
Far to the land of slaves and fens;
A servile race in folly nurs'd,
Who truckle most, when treated worst.

"By innocence and resolution,
He bore continual persecution;   400
While numbers to preferment rose;
Whose merits were, to be his foes.
When, ev'n his own familiar friends
Intent upon their private ends;
Like renegadoes now he feels,   405
Against him lifting up their heels.

"The Dean did by his pen defeat
An infamous destructive cheat.
Taught fools their int'rest how to know;
And gave them arms to ward the blow.   410
Envy hath own'd it was his doing,
To save that helpless land from ruin,
While they who at the steerage stood,
And reapt the profit, sought his blood.

"To save them from their evil fate,   415
In him was held a crime of state.
A wicked monster on the bench,
Whose fury blood could never quench;
As vile and profligate a villain,
As modern Scroggs, or old Tressilian;   420
Who long all justice had discarded,
Nor fear'd he GOD, nor man regarded;
Vow'd on the Dean his rage to vent,
And make him of his zeal repent;
But Heav'n his innocence defends,   425
The grateful people stand his friends;
Not strains of law, nor Judges' frown,
Nor topics brought to please the Crown,
Nor witness hir'd, nor jury pick'd,
Prevail to bring him in convict.   430

"In exile with a steady heart,
He spent his Life's declining part;
Where, folly, pride, and faction sway,
Remote from St. John, Pope, and Gay.

"His friendship there to few confin'd,   435
Were always of the middling kind:
No fools of rank, a mungril breed,
Who fain would pass for lords indeed:
Where titles give no right or power,
And peerage is a wither'd flower,   440
He would have held it a disgrace,
If such a wretch had known his face.
On rural squires, that kingdom's bane,
He vented oft his wrath in vain:
Biennial squires, to market brought;   445
Who sell their souls and votes for naught;
The nation stript go joyful back,
To rob the Church, their tenants rack,
Go snacks with thieves and rapparees,
And, keep the peace, to pick up fees: 450
In every job to have a share,
A jail or barrack to repair;
And turn the tax for public roads
Commodious to their own abodes.

"Perhaps I may allow, the Dean   455
Had too much satire in his vein:
And seem'd determin'd not to starve it,

Because no age could more deserve it.
Yet, malice never was his aim;
He lash'd the vice but spar'd the name.   460
No individual could resent,
Where thousands equally were meant.
His satire points at no defect,
But what all mortals may correct;
For he abhorr'd that senseless tribe,   465
Who call it humour when they jibe:
He spar'd a hump or crooked nose,
Whose owners set not up for beaux.
True genuine dulness moved his pity,
Unless it offer'd to be witty.   470
Those, who their ignorance confess'd,
He ne'er offended with a jest;
But laugh'd to hear an idiot quote,
A verse from Horace, learn'd by rote.

"He knew an hundred pleasant stories,   475
With all the turns of Whigs and Tories:
Was cheerful to his dying day,
And friends would let him have his way.

"He gave the little wealth he had,
To build a house for fools and mad: 480
And shew'd by one satyric touch,
No nation wanted it so much:
That Kingdom he hath left his debtor,
I wish it soon may have a better."

Alexander Pope (1688–1744)

The sound must seem an echo to the sense

True ease in writing comes from Art, not Chance,
As those move easiest who have learn'd to dance.
'Tis not enough no harshness gives offence;
The sound must seem an echo to the sense.
Soft is the strain when zephyr gently blows,   5
And the smooth stream in smoother numbers flows;
But when loud surges lash the sounding shore,
The hoarse rough verse should like the torrent roar.
When Ajax strives some rock's vast weight to throw,
The line, too, labours, and the words move slow: 10
Not so when swift Camilla[1] scours the plain,
Flies o'er th' unbending corn, and skims along the main.

from *An Essay on Criticism*

You Beat Your Pate

You beat your Pate, and fancy Wit will come:
Knock as you please, there's no body at home.

Epitaph Intended for Sir Isaac Newton

Nature, and Nature's Laws lay hid in Night.
God said, Let Newton be! and All was Light.

---

[1] A swift-footed maiden in the *Aeneid*.

The proper study of mankind is man

Hope humbly then; with trembling pinions soar;
Wait the great teacher, Death, and God adore.
What future bliss, he gives not thee to know,
But gives that hope to be thy blessing now;
Hope springs eternal in the human breast—   5
Man never is, but always to be blessed.
The soul, uneasy and confined from home,
Rests and expatiates in a life to come.
Lo, the poor Indian! whose untutored mind
Sees God in clouds, or hears him in the wind;   10
His soul proud science never taught to stray
Far as the solar walk, or milky way,
Yet simple nature to his hope has given,
Behind the cloud-topped hill, an humbler heaven.

Know then thyself, presume not God to scan,   15
The proper study of mankind is man.
Placed on this isthmus of a middle state,
A being darkly wise, and rudely great:
With too much knowledge for the sceptic side,
With too much weakness for the stoic's pride,   20
He hangs between; in doubt to act, or rest;
In doubt to deem himself a god, or beast;
In doubt his mind or body to prefer;
Born but to die, and reasoning but to err;
Alike in ignorance, his reason such,   25
Whether he thinks too little or too much:
Chaos of thought and passion, all confused;
Still by himself abused or disabused;
Created half to rise and half to fall;
Great lord of all things, yet a prey to all;   30
Sole judge of truth, in endless error hurled:
The glory, jest, and riddle of the world!
Whate'er the passion—knowledge, fame, or pelf,
Not one will change his neighbor with himself.
The learned is happy nature to explore,   35
The fool is happy that he knows no more;
The rich is happy in the plenty given,
The poor contents him with the care of Heaven.
See the blind beggar dance, the cripple sing,
The sot a hero, lunatic a king;   40

The starving chemist in his golden views
Supremely blest, the poet in his muse.
See some strange comfort every state attend,
And pride bestowed on all, a common friend;
See some fit passion every age supply,   45
Hope travels through nor quits us when we die.
    Behold the child, by nature's kindly law,
Pleased with a rattle, tickled with a straw:
Some livelier plaything gives his youth delight,
A little louder, but as empty quite: 50
Scarfs, garters, gold, amuse his riper stage,
And beads and prayer-books are the toys of age:
Pleased with this bauble still, as that before;
Till tired he sleeps, and life's poor play is o'er.

from *An Essay on Man*

Robert Burns (1759–1796)

A Red, Red Rose

O, my luve is like a red, red rose,
    That's newly sprung in June;
O, my luve is like the melody
    That's sweetly played in tune.

As fair art thou, my bonny lass,   5
    So deep in luve am I,
And I will luve thee still, my dear,
    Till a'° the seas gang° dry.   *all; go*

Till a' the seas gang dry, my dear,
    And the rocks melt wi' the sun;
And I will luve thee still, my dear,   10
    While the sands o' life shall run.

And fare thee weel, my only luve,
    And fare thee weel a while;
And I will come again, my luve,   15
    Though it were ten thousand mile!

Green Grow the Rashes, O

CHORUS

GREEN grow the rashes,° O;   *rushes*
   Green grow the rashes, O;
The sweetest hours that e'er I spend,
   Are spent amang the lasses, O!

There's nought but care on ev'ry han',   5
   In ev'ry hour that passes, O;
What signifies the life o' man,
   An' twere na for the lasses, O.

The warly° race may riches chase,   *worldly*
   An' riches still may fly them, O;   10
An' tho' at last they catch them fast,
   Their hearts can ne'er enjoy them, O.

But gie me a canny° hour at e'en,   *happy*
   My arms about my dearie, O;
An' warly cares, an' warly men,   15
May a' gae tapsalteerie,° O!   *topsey-turvey*

For you sae douce,° ye sneer at this,   *sedate, sober*
   Ye're nought but senseless asses, O:
The wisest man the warl' saw,
   He dearly lov'd the lasses, O.   20

Auld nature swears, the lovely dears
   Her noblest work she classes, O;
Her prentice han' she try'd on man,
   An' then she made the lasses, O.

To a Mouse

On Turning Her Up in Her Nest with the Plough, November 1785

Wee, sleekit,° cow'rin', tim'rous beastie,   *sleek*
O what a panic's in thy breastie!
Thou need na start awa sae hasty,
      Wi' bickering brattle!°   *scampering haste*
I wad be laith to rin an' chase thee   5
      Wi' murd'ring pattle!°   *plough-staff*

I'm truly sorry man's dominion
Has broken Nature's social union,
An' justifies that ill opinion
      Which makes thee startle   10
At me, thy poor earth-born companion,
      An' fellow-mortal!

I doubt na, whiles,° but thou may thieve;   *at times*
What then? poor beastie, thou maun live!
A daimen-icker in a thrave[1]   15
      'S a sma' request:
I'll get a blessin' wi' the lave,°   *nest*
      And never miss 't!

Thy wee bit housie, too, in ruin!
Its silly wa's the win's are strewin'!   20
An' naething, now, to big° a new ane,   *build*
      O' foggage° green!   *coarse grass*
An' bleak December's winds ensuin',
      Baith snell° an' keen!   *biting*

Thou saw the fields laid bare and waste,   25
An' weary winter comin' fast,
An' cozie here, beneath the blast,
      Thou thought to dwell,
Till crash! the cruel coulter past
      Out-thro' thy cell.   30

---

[1]An occasional ear in a shock of grain.

That wee bit heap o' leaves an' stibble
Has cost thee mony a weary nibble!
Now thou's turn'd out, for a' thy trouble,
  But house or hald,°   *without house or home*
To thole° the winter's sleety dribble,   *endure*
  An' cranreuch° cauld!   *hoarfrost*

But, Mousie, thou art no thy lane,°   *not alone*
In proving foresight may be vain:
The best laid schemes o' mice an' men
  Gang aft a-gley,°   *awry*
An' lea'e us nought but grief an' pain
  For promis'd joy.

Still thou art blest compar'd wi' me!
The present only toucheth thee:
But och! I backward cast my e'e
  On prospects drear!   45
An' forward tho' I canna see,
  I guess an' fear!

William Blake (1757–1827)

The Lamb

Little lamb, who made thee?
Dost thou know who made thee?
Gave thee life, and bid thee feed
By the stream and o'er the mead;
Gave thee clothing of delight,   5
Softest clothing, woolly, bright;
Gave thee such a tender voice,
Making all the vales rejoice?
 Little lamb, who made thee?
 Dost thou know who made thee?   10

Little lamb, I'll tell thee,
Little lamb, I'll tell thee:
He is callèd by thy name,
For he calls himself a Lamb.
He is meek, and he is mild;   15
He became a little child.
I a child, and thou a lamb,
We are callèd by his name.
    Little lamb, God bless thee!
    Little lamb, God bless thee!   20

from *Songs of Innocence*

The Tyger

Tyger! Tyger! burning bright
In the forests of the night,
What immortal hand or eye
Could frame thy fearful symmetry?

In what distant deeps or skies   5
Burnt the fire of thine eyes?
On what wings dare he aspire?
What the hand dare seize the fire?

And what shoulder, and what art,
Could twist the sinews of thy heart?   10
And when thy heart began to beat,
What dread hand? and what dread feet?

What the hammer? what the chain?
In what furnace was thy brain?
What the anvil? what dread grasp   15
Dare its deadly terrors clasp?

When the stars threw down their spears,
And watered heaven with their tears,
Did he smile his work to see?
Did he who made the Lamb make thee?   20

Tyger! Tyger! burning bright
In the forests of the night,
What immortal hand or eye
Dare frame thy fearful symmetry?

from *Songs of Experience*

The Clod and the Pebble

"Love seeketh not itself to please,
    Nor for itself hath any care,
But for another gives its ease,
    And builds a Heaven in Hell's despair."

So sung a little Clod of Clay   5
    Trodden with the cattle's feet,
But a Pebble of the brook
    Warbled out these metres meet:

"Love seeketh only self to please,
    To bind another to its delight,   10
Joys in another's loss of ease,
    And builds a Hell in Heaven's despite."

A Divine Image

Cruelty has a human heart,
And Jealousy a human face;
Terror the human form divine,
And Secrecy the human dress.

The human dress is forgèd iron,   5
The human form a fiery forge,
The human face a furnace sealed,
The human heart is hungry gorge.

London

I wander through each chartered street,
Near where the chartered Thames does flow,
And mark in every face I meet
Marks of weakness, marks of woe.

In every cry of every man,   5
In every infant's cry of fear,
In every voice, in every ban,
The mind-forged manacles I hear.

How the chimney-sweeper's cry
Every black'ning church appalls;   10
And the hapless soldier's sigh
Runs in blood down palace walls.

But most through midnight streets I hear
How the youthful harlot's curse
Blasts the new-born infant's tear,   15
And blights with plagues the marriage hearse.

The Garden of Love

I went to the Garden of Love,
And saw what I never had seen:
A Chapel was built in the midst,
Where I used to play on the green.

And the gates of this Chapel were shut,   5
And "Thou shalt not" writ over the door:
So I turned to the Garden of Love
That so many sweet flowers bore;

And I saw it was filled with graves,
And tomb-stones where flowers should be;   10
And Priests in black gowns were walking their rounds,
And binding with briars my joys and desires.

Eternity

He who binds to himself a joy
Does the wingèd life destroy;
But he who kisses the joy as it flies
Lives in eternity's sun rise.

Abstinence Sows Sand All Over

Abstinence sows sand all over
The ruddy limbs and flaming hair,
But Desire Gratified
Plants fruits of life and beauty there.

The Angel that presided o'er my birth

The Angel that presided o'er my birth
Said, "Little creature, formed of Joy and Mirth,
Go love without the help of any thing on earth."

The Sick Rose

O Rose, thou art sick!
The invisible worm
That flies in the night,
In the howling storm,

Has found out thy bed
Of crimson joy,
And his dark secret love
Does thy life destroy.

5

A Poison Tree

I was angry with my friend:
I told my wrath, my wrath did end.
I was angry with my foe:
I told it not, my wrath did grow.

And I water'd it in fears,   5
Night and morning with my tears;
And I sunned it with smiles,
And with soft deceitful wiles.

And it grew both day and night,
Till it bore an apple bright;   10
And my foe beheld it shine,
And he knew that it was mine,

And into my garden stole
When the night had veil'd the pole:
In the morning glad I see   15
My foe outstretch'd beneath the tree.

To see a world in a grain of sand

To see a world in a grain of sand
And a heaven in a wild flower,
Hold infinity in the palm of your hand
And eternity in an hour.

from "Auguries of Innocence"

Mock on, Mock on Voltaire, Rousseau

Mock on, Mock on Voltaire, Rousseau:
Mock on, Mock on; 'tis all in vain!
You throw the sand against the wind,
And the wind blows it back again.

And every sand becomes a Gem   5
Reflected in the beams divine;
Blown back they blind the mocking eye,
But still in Israel's paths they shine.

The Atoms of Democritus
And Newton's Particles of light   10
Are sands upon the Red sea shore,
Where Israel's tents do shine so bright.

William Wordsworth (1770–1850)

Composed upon Westminster Bridge

Earth has not anything to show more fair:
Dull would he be of soul who could pass by
A sight so touching in its majesty.
This city now doth, like a garment, wear
The beauty of the morning; silent, bare,   5
Ships, towers, domes, theaters, and temples lie
Open unto the fields, and to the sky—
All bright and glittering in the smokeless air.
Never did sun more beautifully steep
In his first splendor valley, rock, or hill;   10
Ne'er saw I, never felt, a calm so deep!
The river glideth at his own sweet will.
Dear God! the very houses seem asleep,
And all that mighty heart is lying still!

London, 1802

Milton! thou shouldst be living at this hour:
England hath need of thee: she is a fen
Of stagnant waters: altar, sword, and pen,
Fireside, the heroic wealth of hall and bower,
Have forfeited their ancient English dower   5
Of inward happiness. We are selfish men;
Oh! raise us up, return to us again;
And give us manners, virtue, freedom, power.
Thy soul was like a Star, and dwelt apart;
Thou hadst a voice whose sound was like the sea: 10
Pure as the naked heavens, majestic, free,
So didst thou travel on life's common way,
In cheerful godliness; and yet thy heart
The lowliest duties on herself did lay.

The World Is Too Much with Us

The world is too much with us; late and soon,
Getting and spending, we lay waste our powers:
Little we see in Nature that is ours;
We have given our hearts away, a sordid boon!
This Sea that bares her bosom to the moon;   5
The winds that will be howling at all hours,
And are up-gathered now like sleeping flowers;
For this, for everything, we are out of tune;
It moves us not. — Great God! I'd rather be
A Pagan suckled in a creed outworn;   10
So might I, standing on this pleasant lea,
Have glimpses that would make me less forlorn;
Have sight of Proteus rising from the sea;
Or hear old Triton blow his wreathèd horn.

Lines Written in Early Spring

I heard a thousand blended notes,
While in a grove I sat reclined,
In that sweet mood when pleasant thoughts
Bring sad thoughts to the mind.

To her fair works did Nature link   5
The human soul that through me ran;
And much it grieved my heart to think
What man has made of man.

Through primrose tufts, in that green bower,
The periwinkle trailed its wreaths;
And 'tis my faith that every flower   10
Enjoys the air it breathes.

The birds around me hopped and played,
Their thoughts I cannot measure—
But the least motion which they made,
It seemed a thrill of pleasure.   15

The budding twigs spread out their fan,
To catch the breezy air;
And I must think, do all I can,
That there was pleasure there.   20

If this belief from heaven be sent,
If such be Nature's holy plan,
Have I not reason to lament
What man has made of man?

My heart leaps up

My heart leaps up when I behold
  A rainbow in the sky;
So was it when my life began;
So is it now I am a man;
So be it when I shall grow old.   5
  Or let me die!
The Child is father of the Man;
And I could wish my days to be
Bound each to each by natural piety.

The Tables Turned

An Evening Scene on the Same Subject

Up! up! my friend, and quit your books,
Or surely you'll grow double;
Up! up! my friend, and clear your looks;
Why all this toil and trouble?

The sun, above the mountain's head,   5
A freshening luster mellow
Through all the long green fields has spread,
His first sweet evening yellow.

Books! 'tis a dull and endless strife;
Come, hear the woodland linnet,   10
How sweet his music! on my life,
There's more of wisdom in it.

And hark! how blithe the throstle sings!
He, too, is no mean preacher;
Come forth into the light of things,   15
Let Nature be your teacher.

She has a world of ready wealth,
Our minds and hearts to bless—
Spontaneous wisdom breathed by health,
Truth breathed by cheerfulness.   20

One impulse from a vernal wood
May teach you more of man,
Of moral evil and of good,
Than all the sages can.

Sweet is the lore which Nature brings;   25
Our meddling intellect
Misshapes the beauteous forms of things—
We murder to dissect.

Enough of Science and of Art;
Close up those barren leaves;   30
Come forth, and bring with you a heart
That watches and receives.

Samuel Taylor Coleridge (1772–1834)

Kubla Khan

Or, a Vision in a Dream. A Fragment.

In Xanadu did Kubla Khan
A stately pleasure-dome decree:
Where Alph, the sacred river, ran
Through caverns measureless to man
    Down to a sunless sea.   5
So twice five miles of fertile ground
With walls and towers were girdled round;
And there were gardens bright with sinuous rills,
Where blossomed many an incense-bearing tree;
And here were forests ancient as the hills,   10
Enfolding sunny spots of greenery.

But oh! that deep romantic chasm which slanted
Down the green hill athwart a cedarn cover!
A savage place! as holy and enchanted
As e'er beneath a waning moon was haunted   15
By woman wailing for her demon-lover!
And from this chasm, with ceaseless turmoil seething,
As if this earth in fast thick pants were breathing,
A mighty fountain momently was forced:
Amid whose swift half-intermitted burst   20
Huge fragments vaulted like rebounding hail,
Or chaffy grain beneath the thresher's flail:
And 'mid these dancing rocks at once and ever
It flung up momently the sacred river.
Five miles meandering with a mazy motion   25
Through wood and dale the sacred river ran,
Then reached the caverns measureless to man,
And sank in tumult to a lifeless ocean:
And 'mid this tumult Kubla heard from far
Ancestral voices prophesying war!   30
    The shadow of the dome of pleasure
    Floated midway on the waves;
    Where was heard the mingled measure
    From the fountain and the caves.
It was a miracle of rare device,   35
A sunny pleasure-dome with caves of ice!

    A damsel with a dulcimer
    In a vision once I saw:
    It was an Abyssinian maid,
    And on her dulcimer she played,   40
    Singing of Mount Abora.
    Could I revive within me
    Her symphony and song,
    To such a deep delight 'twould win me,
That with music loud and long,   45
I would build that dome in air,
That sunny dome! those caves of ice!
And all who heard should see them there,
And all should cry, Beware! Beware!
His flashing eyes, his floating hair!   50
Weave a circle round him thrice,
And close your eyes with holy dread,
For he on honey-dew hath fed,
And drunk the milk of Paradise.

Metrical Feet

Trochee trips from long to short;
From long to long in solemn sort
Slow Spondee stalks: strong foot! yet ill able
Ever to come up with Dactyl trisyllable;
Iambics march from short to long;
With a leap and a bound the swift Anapests throng;
One syllable long, with one short at each side.
Amphibrachys hastes with a stately stride;
First and last being long, middle short, Amphimacer
Strikes his thundering hoofs like a proud high-bred racer.

On a Volunteer Singer

Swans sing before they die—'twere no bad thing
Should certain persons die before they sing.

On Donne's Poetry

With Donne, whose muse on dromedary trots,
Wreathe iron pokers into true-love knots;
Rhyme's sturdy cripple, fancy's maze and clue,
Wit's forge and fire-blast, meaning's press and screw.

The Hour-Glass

O think, fair maid! these sands that pass
In slender threads adown this glass,
Were once the body of some swain,
Who lov'd too well and lov'd in vain,
And let one soft sigh heave thy breast,
That not in life alone unblest
E'en lovers' ashes find no rest.

George Gordon, Lord Byron (1788–1824)

She Walks in Beauty

She walks in beauty, like the night
Of cloudless climes and starry skies,
And all that's best of dark and bright
Meet in her aspect and her eyes;
Thus mellowed to that tender light   5
Which heaven to gaudy day denies.

One shade the more, one ray the less,
Had half impaired the nameless grace
Which waves in every raven tress
Or softly lightens o'er her face,   10
Where thoughts serenely sweet express
How pure, how dear their dwelling-place.

And on that cheek and o'er that brow
So soft, so calm, yet eloquent,
The smiles that win, the tints that glow   15
But tell of days in goodness spent,
A mind at peace with all below,
A heart whose love is innocent.

John Keats (1795–1821)

On First Looking into Chapman's Homer

Much have I traveled in the realms of gold,
And many goodly states and kingdoms seen;
Round many western islands have I been
Which bards in fealty to Apollo hold.
Oft of one wide expanse had I been told   5
That deep-browed Homer ruled as his demesne;
Yet did I never breathe its pure serene
Till I heard Chapman speak out loud and bold:
Then felt I like some watcher of the skies
When a new planet swims into his ken;   10
Or like stout Cortez when with eagle eyes
He stared at the Pacific—and all his men
Looked at each other with a wild surmise—
Silent, upon a peak in Darien.[1]

---

[1] Now Panama.

Ode to a Nightingale

My heart aches, and a drowsy numbness pains
　　My sense, as though of hemlock I had drunk,
Or emptied some dull opiate to the drains
　　One minute past, and Lethe-wards[1]　had sunk:
'Tis not through envy of thy happy lot, 5
　　But being too happy in thy happiness—
　　　　That thou, light-wingèd Dryad° of the trees, *nymph or spirit*
　　　　　　In some melodious plot
　　　　Of beechen green, and shadows numberless,
　　　　　　Singest of summer in full-throated ease. 10

O for a draught of vintage! that hath been
　　Cooled a long age in the deep-delvèd earth,
Tasting of Flora and the country green,
　　Dance, and Provençal song, and sunburnt mirth!
O for a beaker full of the warm South, 15
　　Full of the true, the blushful Hippocrene[2],
　　　　With beaded bubbles winking at the brim,
　　　　　　And purple-stainèd mouth;
　　　　That I might drink, and leave the world unseen,
　　　　　　And with thee fade away into the forest dim: 20

Fade far away, dissolve, and quite forget
　　What thou among the leaves has never known,
The weariness, the fever, and the fret
　　Here, where men sit and hear each other groan;
Where palsy shakes a few, sad, last grey hairs, 25
　　Where youth grows pale, and specter-thin, and dies;
　　　　Where but to think is to be full of sorrow
　　　　　　And leaden-eyed despairs,
　　　　Where Beauty cannot keep her lustrous eyes,
　　　　　　Or new Love pine at them beyond to-morrow. 30

---

[1]River in Hades, a taste of whose waters caused forgetfulness.
[2]Fountain sacred to the Muses, on Mt. Helicon, whose waters gave poetic inspiration.

Away! away! for I will fly to thee,
  Not charioted by Bacchus[3] and his pards,
But on the viewless wings of Poesy,
  Though the dull brain perplexes and retards:
Already with thee! tender is the night,   35
  And haply the Queen-Moon is on her throne,
    Clustered around by all her starry Fays°;   *Fairies*
      But here there is no light,
Save what from heaven is with the breezes blown
    Through verdurous glooms and winding mossy ways.   40

I cannot see what flowers are at my feet,
  Nor what soft incense hangs upon the boughs,
But, in embalmèd darkness, guess each sweet
  Wherewith the seasonable month endows
The grass, the thicket, and the fruit tree wild;   45
  White hawthorn, and the pastoral eglantine;
    Fast fading violets covered up in leaves;
      And mid-May's eldest child,
The coming musk rose, full of dewy wine,
    The murmurous haunt of flies on summer eves.   50

Darkling° I listen; and, for many a time   *in darkness*
  I have been half in love with easeful Death,
Called him soft names in many a musèd rhyme,
  To take into the air my quiet breath;
Now more than ever seems it rich to die,   55
  To cease upon the midnight with no pain,
    While thou art pouring forth thy soul abroad
      In such an ecstasy!
Still wouldst thou sing, and I have ears in vain—
  To thy high requiem become a sod.   60

Thou wast not born for death, immortal Bird!
  No hungry generations tread thee down;
The voice I hear this passing night was heard
  In ancient days by emperor and clown:
Perhaps the self-same song that found a path   65
  Through the sad heart of Ruth, when, sick for home,
    She stood in tears amid the alien corn;
      The same that oft-times hath
Charmed magic casements, opening on the foam
  Of perilous seas, in faery lands forlorn.   70

---

[3]The god of wine was sometimes depicted riding in a leopard-drawn chariot.

Forlorn! the very word is like a bell
 To toll me back from thee to my sole self!
Adieu! the fancy cannot cheat so well
 As she is famed to do, deceiving elf.
Adieu! adieu! thy plaintive anthem fades   75
  Past the near meadows, over the still stream,
   Up the hillside; and now 'tis buried deep
    In the next valley glades:
 Was it a vision, or a waking dream?
  Fled is that music:—Do I wake or sleep?   80

Ode on a Grecian Urn

Thou still unravished bride of quietness,
 Thou foster-child of silence and slow time,
Sylvan historian, who canst thus express
 A flowery tale more sweetly than our rhyme:
What leaf-fringed legend haunts about thy shape   5
 Of deities or mortals, or of both,
  In Tempe[1] or the dales of Arcady[1]?
 What men or gods are these? What maidens loth?
What mad pursuit? What struggle to escape?
  What pipes and timbrels? What wild ecstasy?   10

Heard melodies are sweet, but those unheard
 Are sweeter; therefore, ye soft pipes, play on;
Not to the sensual° ear, but, more endeared,   *physical*
 Pipe to the spirit ditties of no tone:
Fair youth, beneath the trees, thou canst not leave   15
 Thy song, nor ever can those trees be bare;
  Bold Lover, never, never canst thou kiss,
Though winning near the goal—yet, do not grieve;
  She cannot fade, though thou hast not thy bliss,
 For ever wilt thou love, and she be fair!   20

---

[1]Valleys in Greece.

Ah, happy, happy boughs! that cannot shed
   Your leaves, nor ever bid the Spring adieu;
And, happy melodist, unwearièd,
   For ever piping songs for ever new;
More happy love! more happy, happy love!   25
   For ever warm and still to be enjoyed,
      For ever panting, and for ever young;
All breathing human passion far above,
   That leaves a heart high-sorrowful and cloyed,
      A burning forehead, and a parching tongue.   30

Who are these coming to the sacrifice?
   To what green altar, O mysterious priest,
Lead'st thou that heifer lowing at the skies,
   And all her silken flanks with garlands drest?
What little town by river or sea shore,   35
   Or mountain-built with peaceful citadel,
      Is emptied of this folk, this pious morn?
And, little town, thy streets for evermore
   Will silent be; and not a soul to tell
      Why thou art desolate, can e'er return.   40

O Attic² shape! Fair attitude! with brede°   *design*
   Of marble men and maidens overwrought,
With forest branches and the trodden weed;
   Thou, silent form, dost tease us out of thought
As doth Eternity: Cold Pastoral!   45
   When old age shall this generation waste,
      Thou shalt remain, in midst of other woe
Than ours, a friend to man, to whom thou say'st,
Beauty is truth, truth beauty,—that is all
   Ye know on earth, and all ye need to know.   50

Percy Bysshe Shelley (1792–1822)

Ode to the West Wind

I

O wild West Wind, thou breath of Autumn's being,
Thou, from whose unseen presence the leaves dead
Are driven, like ghosts from an enchanter fleeing,

---

²Athenian, possessing a classical simplicity and grace.

Yellow, and black, and pale, and hectic red,
Pestilence-stricken multitudes: O thou,   5
Who chariotest to their dark wintry bed

The wingèd seeds, where they lie cold and low,
Each like a corpse within its grave, until
Thine azure sister of the spring shall blow

Her clarion o'er the dreaming earth, and fill   10
(Driving sweet buds like flocks to feed in air)
With living hues and odors plain and hill:

Wild Spirit, which art moving everywhere;
Destroyer and preserver; hear, O, hear!

II

Thou on whose stream, 'mid the steep sky's commotion,   15
Loose clouds like earth's decaying leaves are shed,
Shook from the tangled boughs of Heaven and Ocean,
Angels of rain and lightning: there are spread
On the blue surface of thine airy surge,
Like the bright hair uplifted from the head   20

Of some fierce Maenad[1], even from the dim verge
Of the horizon to the zenith's height,
The locks of the approaching storm. Thou dirge

Of the dying year, to which this closing night
Will be the dome of a vast sepulcher,   25
Vaulted with all thy congregated might
Of vapors, from whose solid atmosphere
Black rain, and fire, and hail will burst: O, hear!

III

Thou who didst waken from his summer dreams
The blue Mediterranean, where he lay,   30
Lulled by the coil of his crystalline streams,

Beside a pumice isle in Baiae's bay,
And saw in sleep old palaces and towers
Quivering within the wave's intenser day,

---

[1]In ancient Greece, a woman of the cult of the god Dionysus, who would show her
devotion by dancing herself into a frenzy.

All overgrown with azure moss, and flowers   35
So sweet, the sense faints picturing them! Thou
For whose path the Atlantic's level powers

Cleave themselves into chasms, while far below
The sea-blooms and the oozy woods which wear
The sapless foliage of the ocean, know   40

Thy voice, and suddenly grow gray with fear,
And tremble and despoil themselves: O, hear!

IV

If I were a dead leaf thou mightest bear;
If I were a swift cloud to fly with thee;
A wave to pant beneath thy power, and share   45

The impulse of thy strength, only less free
Than thou, O uncontrollable! If even
I were as in my boyhood, and could be

The comrade of thy wanderings over heaven,
As then, when to outstrip thy skiey speed   50
Scarce seemed a vision; I would ne'er have striven

As thus with thee in prayer in my sore need.
Oh! lift me as a wave, a leaf, a cloud!
I fall upon the thorns of life! I bleed!

A heavy weight of hours has chained and bowed   55
One too like thee: tameless, and swift, and proud.

V

Make me thy lyre, even as the forest is:
What if my leaves are falling like its own!
The tumult of thy mighty harmonies

Will take from both a deep, autumnal tone,   60
Sweet though in sadness. Be thou, spirit fierce,
My spirit! Be thou me, impetuous one!

Drive my dead thoughts over the universe
Like withered leaves, to quicken a new birth!
And, by the incantation of this verse,   65

Scatter, as from an unextinguished hearth
Ashes and sparks, my words among mankind!
Be through my lips to unawakened earth

The trumpet of a prophecy! O wind,
If Winter comes, can Spring be far behind?   70

One Word Is Too Often Profaned

One word is too often profaned
    For me to profane it,
One feeling too falsely disdain'd
    For thee to disdain it;
One hope is too like despair   5
    For prudence to smother,
And Pity from thee more dear
    Than that from another.

I can give not what men call love;
    But wilt thou accept not   10
The worship the heart lifts above
    And the Heavens reject not,—
The desire of the moth for the star,
    Of the night for the morrow,
The devotion to something afar   15
    From the sphere of our sorrow?

The One remains, the many change and pass

The One remains, the many change and pass;
Heaven's light forever shines, Earth's shadows fly;
Life, like a dome of many-coloured glass,
Stains the white radiance of Eternity,
Until Death tramples it to fragments.—Die,   5
If thou wouldst be with that which thou dost seek!
Follow where all is fled!—Rome's azure sky,
Flowers, ruins, statues, music, words, are weak
The glory they transfuse with fitting truth to speak.

from "Adonais"

Mutability

We are as clouds that veil the midnight moon;
    How restlessly they speed, and gleam, and quiver,
Streaking the darkness radiantly!—yet soon
    Night closes round, and they are lost forever:

Or like forgotten lyres, whose dissonant strings   5
    Give various response to each varying blast,
To whose frail frame no second motion brings
    One mood or modulation like the last.

We rest.—A dream has power to poison sleep;
    We rise.—One wandering thought pollutes the day;   10
We feel, conceive or reason, laugh or weep;
    Embrace fond woe, or cast our cares away:

It is the same!—For, be it joy or sorrow,
    The path of its departure still is free:
Man's yesterday may ne'er be like his morrow;   15
    Nought may endure but Mutability.

Ozymandias

I met a traveler from an antique land
Who said: Two vast and trunkless legs of stone
Stand in the desert. Near them, on the sand,
Half sunk, a shattered visage lies, whose frown,
And wrinkled lip, and sneer of cold command,   5
Tell that its sculptor well those passions read
Which yet survive, stamped on these lifeless things,
The hand that mocked° them and the heart that fed;   *imitated*
And on the pedestal these words appear:
"My name is Ozymandias, king of kings: 10
Look on my works, ye Mighty, and despair!"
Nothing beside remains. Round the decay
Of that colossal wreck, boundless and bare
The lone and level sands stretch far away.

Arthur Guiterman (1871–1943)

On the Vanity of Earthly Greatness [1]

The tusks that clashed in mighty brawls
Of mastodons, are billiard balls.

The sword of Charlemagne the Just
Is ferric oxide, known as rust.

The grizzly bear whose potent hug   5
Was feared by all, is now a rug.

Great Caesar's bust is on the shelf,
And I don't feel so well myself.

Alfred, Lord Tennyson (1809–1892)

Ulysses

It little profits that an idle king,
By this still hearth, among these barren crags,
Matched with an agèd wife, I mete and dole
Unequal laws unto a savage race
That hoard, and sleep, and feed, and know not me.   5
I cannot rest from travel; I will drink
Life to the lees. All times I have enjoyed
Greatly, have suffered greatly, both with those
That loved me, and alone; on shore, and when
Through scudding drifts the rainy Hyades[1]   10
Vexed the dim sea. I am become a name;
For always roaming with a hungry heart
Much have I seen and known—cities of men
And manners, climates, councils, governments,
Myself not least, but honored of them all—   15
And drunk delight of battle with my peers,
Far on the ringing plains of windy Troy.
I am a part of all that I have met;

SOURCE: [1] Copyright by Mrs. Arthur Guiterman. Reprinted with permission.

[1] Daughters of Atlas, who were transformed into a group of stars. Their rising with the sun was thought to be a sign of rain.

Yet all experience is an arch wherethrough
Gleams that untraveled world whose margin fades   20
Forever and forever when I move.
How dull it is to pause, to make an end,
To rust unburnished, not to shine in use!
As though to breathe were life! Life piled on life
Were all too little, and of one to me   25
Little remains; but every hour is saved
From that eternal silence, something more,
A bringer of new things; and vile it were
For some three suns to store and hoard myself,
And this grey spirit yearning in desire   30
To follow knowledge like a sinking star,
Beyond the utmost bound of human thought.
      This is my son, mine own Telemachus,
To whom I leave the scepter and the isle—
Well-loved of me, discerning to fulfill   35
This labor, by slow prudence to make mild
A rugged people, and through soft degrees
Subdue them to the useful and the good.
Most blameless is he, centered in the sphere
Of common duties, decent not to fail   40
In offices of tenderness, and pay
Meet adoration to my household gods,
When I am gone. He works his work, I mine.
      There lies the port; the vessel puffs her sail;
There gloom the dark, broad seas. My mariners,   45
Souls that have toiled, and wrought, and thought with me—
That ever with a frolic welcome took
The thunder and the sunshine, and opposed
Free hearts, free foreheads—you and I are old;
Old age hath yet his honor and his toil.   50
Death closes all; but something ere the end,
Some work of noble note, may yet be done,
Not unbecoming men that strove with Gods.
The lights begin to twinkle from the rocks;
The long day wanes; the slow moon climbs; the deep   55
Moans round with many voices. Come, my friends,
'Tis not too late to seek a newer world.
Push off, and sitting well in order smite
The sounding furrows; for my purpose holds
To sail beyond the sunset, and the baths   60
Of all the western stars, until I die.
It may be that the gulfs will wash us down;

It may be we shall touch the Happy Isles[2],
And see the great Achilles, whom we knew.
Though much is taken, much abides; and though   65
We are not now that strength which in old days
Moved earth and heaven, that which we are, we are—
One equal temper of heroic hearts,
Made weak by time and fate, but strong in will
To strive, to seek, to find, and not to yield.   70

Tears, Idle Tears

Tears, idle tears, I know not what they mean,
Tears from the depth of some divine despair
Rise in the heart, and gather to the eyes,
In looking on the happy autumn-fields,
And thinking of the days that are no more.   5

Fresh as the first beam glittering on a sail,
That brings our friends up from the under-world,
Sad as the last which reddens over one
That sinks with all we love below the verge;
So sad, so fresh, the days that are no more.   10

Ah, sad and strange as in dark summer dawns
The earliest pipe of half-awakened birds
To dying ears, when unto dying eyes
The casement slowly grows a glimmering square;
So sad, so strange, the days that are no more.   15

Dear as remembered kisses after death,
And sweet as those by hopeless fancy feigned
On lips that are for others; deep as love,
Deep as first love, and wild with all regret;
O Death in Life, the days that are no more.   20

---

[2]Elysium, a paradise believed to be attainable by sailing west.

Locksley Hall

Comrades, leave me here a little, while as yet 'tis early morn;
Leave me here, and when you want me, sound upon the bugle horn.

'Tis the place, and all around it, as of old, the curlews call,
Dreary gleams[1] about the moorland flying over Locksley Hall;

Locksley Hall, that in the distance overlooks the sandy tracts,   5
And the hollow ocean-ridges roaring into cataracts.

Many a night from yonder ivied casement, ere I went to rest,
Did I look on great Orion sloping slowly to the west.

Many a night I saw the Pleiads[2], rising through the mellow shade,
Glitter like a swarm of fireflies tangled in a silver braid.   10

Here about the beach I wandered, nourishing a youth sublime
With the fairy tales of science, and the long result of time;

When the centuries behind me like a fruitful land reposed;
When I clung to all the present for the promise that it closed;°   *enclosed*

When I dipped into the future far as human eye could see,   15
Saw the vision of the world and all the wonder that would be.—

In the spring a fuller crimson comes upon the robin's breast;
In the spring the wanton lapwing gets himself another crest;

In the spring a livelier iris changes on the burnished dove;
In the spring a young man's fancy lightly turns to thoughts of love.   20

Then her cheek was pale and thinner than should be for one so young,
And her eyes on all my motions with a mute observance hung.

And I said, "My cousin Amy, speak, and speak the truth to me,
Trust me, cousin, all the current of my being sets to thee."

On her pallid cheek and forehead came a color and a light,   25
As I have seen the rosy red flushing in the northern night.

---

[1]Tennyson stated that "gleams" does not refer to "curlews" flying but to streaks of light.
[2]The Pleiades, a seven-starred constellation.

And she turned—her bosom shaken with a sudden storm of sighs—
All the spirit deeply dawning in the dark of hazel eyes—

Saying, "I have hid my feelings, fearing they should do me wrong";
Saying, "Dust thou love me, cousin?" weeping, "I have loved thee
    long."   30

Love took up the glass of Time, and turned it in his glowing hands;
Every moment, lightly shaken, ran itself in golden sands.

Love took up the harp of Life, and smote on all the chords with might;
Smote the chord of Self, that, trembling, passed in music out of sight.

Many a morning on the moorland did we hear the copses ring,   35
And her whisper thronged my pulses with the fullness of the spring.

Many an evening by the waters did we watch the stately ships,
And our spirits rushed together at the touching of the lips.

O my cousin, shallow-hearted! O my Amy, mine no more!
O the dreary, dreary moorland! O the barren, barren shore!   40

Falser than all fancy fathoms, falser than all songs have sung,
Puppet to a father's threat, and servile to a shrewish tongue!

Is it well to wish thee happy?—having known me—to decline
On a range of lower feelings and a narrower heart than mine!

Yet it shall be; thou shalt lower to his level day by day,   45
What is fine within thee growing coarse to sympathize with clay.

As the husband is, the wife is; thou art mated with a clown,
And the grossness of his nature will have weight to drag thee down.

He will hold thee, when his passion shall have spent its novel force,
Something better than his dog, a little dearer than his horse.   50

What is this? his eyes are heavy; think not they are glazed with wine.
Go to him, it is thy duty; kiss him, take his hand in thine.

It may be my lord is weary, that his brain is overwrought;
Soothe him with thy finer fancies, touch him with thy lighter thought.

He will answer to the purpose, easy things to understand—   55
Better thou wert dead before me, though I slew thee with my hand!

Better thou and I were lying, hidden from the heart's disgrace,
Rolled in one another's arms, and silent in a last embrace.

Cursed be the social wants that sin against the strength of youth!
Cursed be the social lies that warp us from the living truth!   60

Cursed be the sickly forms that err from honest Nature's rule!
Cursed be the gold that gilds the straitened° forehead of the   *narrowed*
    fool!

Well—'tis well that I should bluster!—Hadst thou less unworthy
    proved—
Would to God—for I had loved thee more than ever wife was loved.

Am I mad, that I should cherish that which bears but bitter fruit?   65
I will pluck it from my bosom, though my heart be at the root.

Never, though my mortal summers to such length of years should come
As the many-wintered crow[3] that leads the clanging rookery home.

Where is comfort? in division of the records of the mind?
Can I part her from herself, and love her, as I knew her, kind?   70

I remember one that perished: sweetly did she speak and move;
Such a one do I remember, whom to look at was to love.

Can I think of her as dead, and love her for the love she bore?
No—she never loved me truly; love is love for evermore.

Comfort? comfort scorned of devils! this is truth the poet[4] sings,   75
That a sorrow's crown of sorrow is remembering happier things.

Drug thy memories, lest thou learn it, lest thy heart be put to proof,
In the dead unhappy night, and when the rain is on the roof.

Like a dog, he hunts in dreams, and thou art staring at the wall,
Where the dying night-lamp flickers, and the shadows rise and fall.   80

---

[3]A rook, a long-lived bird.
[4]Dante (*Inferno* V.121-123).

Then a hand shall pass before thee, pointing to his drunken sleep,
To thy widowed marriage-pillows, to the tears that thou wilt weep.

Thou shalt hear the "Never, never," whispered by the phantom years.
And a song from out the distance in the ringing of thine ears;

And an eye shall vex thee, looking ancient kindness on thy pain.   85
Turn thee, turn thee on thy pillow; get thee to thy rest again.

Nay, but Nature brings thee solace; for a tender voice will cry.
'Tis a purer life than thine, a lip to drain thy trouble dry.

Baby lips will laugh me down; my latest rival brings thee rest.
Baby fingers, waxen touches, press me from the mother's breast.   90

O, the child too clothes the father with a dearness not his due.
Half is thine and half is his; it will be worthy of the two.

O, I see thee old and formal, fitted to thy petty part,
With a little hoard of maxims preaching down a daughter's heart.

"They were dangerous guides the feelings—she herself was not
    exempt—   95
Truly, she herself had suffered"—Perish in thy self-contempt!

Overlive it—lower yet—be happy! wherefore should I care?
I myself must mix with action, lest I wither by despair.

What is that which I should turn to, lighting upon days like these?
Every door is barred with gold, and opens but to golden keys.   100

Every gate is thronged with suitors, all the markets overflow.
I have but an angry fancy; what is that which I should do?

I had been content to perish, falling on the foeman's ground,
When the ranks are rolled in vapor, and the winds are laid with
    sound.[5]

But the jingling of the guinea helps the hurt that Honor feels,   105
And the nations do but murmur, snarling at each other's heels.

---

[5]It was once believed that the firing of artillery stilled the winds.

Can I but relive in sadness? I will turn that earlier page.
Hide me from my deep emotion, O thou wondrous Mother-Age!

Make me feel the wild pulsation that I felt before the strife,
When I heard my days before me, and the tumult of my life;   110

Yearning for the large excitement that the coming years would yield,
Eager-hearted as a boy when first he leaves his father's field,

And at night along the dusky highway near and nearer drawn,
Sees in heaven the light of London flaring like a dreary dawn;

And his spirit leaps within him to be gone before him then,   115
Underneath the light he looks at, in among the throngs of men;

Men, my brothers, men the workers, ever reaping something new;
That which they have done but earnest° of the things that they   *a pledge*
   shall do.

For I dipped into the future, far as human eye could see,
Saw the Vision of the world, and all the wonder that would be;   120

Saw the heavens fill with commerce, argosies of magic sails,
Pilots of the purple twilight, dropping down with costly bales;

Heard the heavens fill with shouting, and there rained a ghastly dew
From the nations' airy navies grappling in the central blue;

Far along the world-wide whisper of the south wind rushing warm,   125
With the standards of the peoples plunging through the thunderstorm;

Till the war drum throbbed no longer, and the battle flags were furled
In the Parliament of man, the Federation of the world.

There the common sense of most shall hold a fretful realm in awe,
And the kindly earth shall slumber, lapped in universal law.   130

So I triumphed ere my passion sweeping through me left me dry,
Left me with the palsied heart, and left me with the jaundiced eye;

Eye, to which all order festers, all things here are out of joint.
Science moves, but slowly, slowly, creeping on from point to point;

Slowly comes a hungry people, as a lion, creeping nigher,   135
Glares at one that nods and winks behind a slowly-dying fire.

Yet I doubt not through the ages one increasing purpose runs,
And the thoughts of men are widened with the process of the suns.

What is that to him that reaps not harvest of his youthful joys,
Though the deep heart of existence beat forever like a boy's?   140

Knowledge comes, but wisdom lingers, and I linger on the shore,
And the individual withers, and the world is more and more.

Knowledge comes, but wisdom lingers, and he bears a laden breast,
Full of sad experience, moving toward the stillness of his rest.

Hark, my merry comrades call me, sounding on the bugle horn,   145
They to whom my foolish passion were a target for their scorn.

Shall it not be scorn to me to harp on such a moldered string?
I am shamed through all my nature to have loved so slight a thing.

Weakness to be wroth with weakness! woman's pleasure, woman's
    pain—
Nature made them blinder motions bounded in a shallower brain.   150

Woman is the lesser man, and all thy passions, matched with mine,
Are as moonlight unto sunlight, and as water unto wine—

Here at least, where nature sickens, nothing. Ah, for some retreat
Deep in yonder shining Orient, where my life began to beat,

Where in wild Mahratta-battle[6] fell my father evil-starred—   155
I was left a trampled orphan, and a selfish uncle's ward.

Or to burst all links of habit—there to wander far away,
On from island unto island at the gateways of the day.

Larger constellations burning, mellow moons and happy skies,
Breadths of tropic shade and palms in cluster, knots of Paradise.   160

---

[6]A reference to wars waged by a Hindu people against the British forces in India (1803
and 1817).

Never comes the trader, never floats an European flag,
Slides the bird o'er lustrous woodland, swings the trailer° from the   *vine*
  crag,
Droops the heavy-blossomed bower, hangs the heavy-fruited tree—
Summer isles of Eden lying in dark purple spheres of sea.

There methinks would be enjoyment more than in this march of mind, 165
In the steamship, in the railway, in the thoughts that shake mankind.

There the passions cramped no longer shall have scope and breathing
  space;
I will take some savage woman, she shall rear my dusky race.

Iron-jointed, supple-sinewed, they shall dive, and they shall run,
Catch the wild goat by the hair, and hurl their lances in the sun;   170

Whistle back the parrot's call, and leap the rainbows of the brooks.
Not with blinded eyesight poring over miserable books—

Fool, again the dream, the fancy! but I *know* my words are wild,
But I count the gray barbarian lower than the Christian child.

I, to herd with narrow foreheads, vacant of our glorious gains.   175
Like a beast with lower pleasures, like a beast with lower pains!

Mated with a squalid savage—what to me were sun or clime?
I the heir of all the ages, in the foremost files of time—

I that rather held it better men should perish one by one,
Than that earth should stand at gaze like Joshua's moon in Ajalon!   180

Not in vain the distance beacons. Forward, forward let us range,
Let the great world spin forever down the ringing grooves of change.

Through the shadow of the globe we sweep into the younger day;
Better fifty years of Europe than a cycle of Cathay.[7]

Mother-Age—for mine I knew not—help me as when life begun;   185
Rift the hills, and roll the waters, flash the lightnings, weigh the sun.

---

[7]China, regarded in the 19th century as a static, unprogressive country.

O, I see the crescent promise of my spirit hath not set.
Ancient founts of inspiration well through all my fancy yet.

Howsoever these things be, a long farewell to Locksley Hall!
Now for me the woods may wither, now for me the roof-tree fall.   190

Comes a vapor from the margin, blackening over heath and holt,
Cramming all the blast before it, in its breast a thunderbolt.

Let it fall on Locksley Hall, with rain or hail, or fire or snow;
For the mighty wind arises, roaring seaward, and I go.

Robert Browning (1812–1889)

My Last Duchess

Ferrara[1]

That's my last Duchess painted on the wall,
Looking as if she were alive. I call
That piece a wonder, now; Frà Pandolf's[2] hands
Worked busily a day, and there she stands.
Will 't please you sit and look at her? I said   5
"Frà Pandolf" by design, for never read
Strangers like you that pictured countenance,
The depth and passion of its earnest glance,
But to myself they turned (since none puts by
The curtain I have drawn for you, but I)   10
And seemed as they would ask me, if they durst,
How such a glance came there; so, not the first
Are you to turn and ask thus. Sir, 'twas not
Her husband's presence only, called that spot
Of joy into the Duchess' cheek; perhaps   15
Frà Pandolf chanced to say, "Her mantle laps
Over my lady's wrist too much," or "Paint
Must never hope to reproduce the faint
Half-flush that dies along her throat." Such stuff
Was courtesy, she thought, and cause enough   20
For calling up that spot of joy. She had

[1]A city in northern Italy. Browning may have modeled his speaker after Alonzo, Duke of Ferrara (1533–1598).
[2]Fictitious names of artists.

A heart—how shall I say?—too soon made glad,
Too easily impressed; she liked whate'er
She looked on, and her looks went everywhere.
Sir, 'twas all one! My favor at her breast,   25
The dropping of the daylight in the West,
The bough of cherries some officious fool
Broke in the orchard for her, the white mule
She rode with round the terrace—all and each
Would draw from her alike the approving speech,   30
Or blush, at least. She thanked men,—good! But thanked
Somehow—I know not how—as if she ranked
My gift of a nine-hundred-years' old name
With anybody's gift. Who'd stoop to blame
This sort of trifling? Even had you skill   35
In speech—which I have not—to make your will
Quite clear to such an one, and say, "Just this
Or that in you disgusts me; here you miss,
Or there exceed the mark"—and if she let
Herself be lessoned so, nor plainly set   40
Her wits to yours, forsooth, and made excuse—
E'en then would be some stooping; and I choose
Never to stoop. Oh, sir, she smiled, no doubt,
Whene'er I passed her; but who passed without
Much the same smile? This grew; I gave commands;   45
Then all smiles stopped together. There she stands
As if alive. Will 't please you rise? We'll meet
The company below, then. I repeat,
The Count your master's known munificence
Is ample warrant that no just pretense   50
Of mine for dowry will be disallowed;
Though his fair daughter's self, as I avowed
At starting, is my object. Nay, we'll go
Together down, sir. Notice Neptune, though,
Taming a sea-horse, thought a rarity,   55
Which Claus of Innsbruck² cast in bronze for me!

Matthew Arnold (1822–1888)

Dover Beach

The sea is calm tonight.
The tide is full, the moon lies fair
Upon the straits;—on the French coast the light
Gleams and is gone; the cliffs of England stand,
Glimmering and vast, out in the tranquil bay.   5
Come to the window, sweet is the night-air!
Only, from the long line of spray
Where the sea meets the moon-blanched land,
Listen! you hear the grating roar
Of pebbles which the waves draw back, and fling,   10
At their return, up the high strand,
Begin, and cease, and then again begin,
With tremulous cadence slow, and bring
The eternal note of sadness in.

Sophocles long ago   15
Heard it on the Aegean, and it brought
Into his mind the turbid ebb and flow
Of human misery; we
Find also in the sound a thought,
Hearing it by this distant northern sea.   20

The Sea of Faith
Was once, too, at the full, and round earth's shore
Lay like the folds of a bright girdle furled.
But now I only hear
Its melancholy, long, withdrawing roar,   25
Retreating, to the breath
Of the night-wind, down the vast edges drear
And naked shingles of the world.

Ah, love, let us be true
To one another! for the world, which seems   30
To lie before us like a land of dreams,
So various, so beautiful, so new,
Hath really neither joy, nor love, nor light,
Nor certitude, nor peace, nor help for pain;
And we are here as on a darkling plain   35
Swept with confused alarms of struggle and flight,
Where ignorant armies clash by night.

Arthur Hugh Clough (1819–1861)

The Latest Decalogue

Thou shalt have one God only; who
Would be at the expense of two?
No graven images may be
Worshipped, except the currency:
Swear not at all; for for thy curse   5
Thine enemy is none the worse;
At church on Sunday to attend
Will serve to keep the world thy friend:
Honour thy parents; that is, all
From whom advancement may befall: 10
Thou shalt not kill; but needst not strive
Officiously to keep alive:
Do not adultery commit;
Advantage rarely comes of it:
Thou shalt not steal; an empty feat,   15
When it's so lucrative to cheat:
Bear not false witness; let the lie
Have time on its own wings to fly:
Thou shalt not covet; but tradition
Approves all forms of competition.   20
The sum of all is, thou shalt love,
If any body, God above:
At any rate shall never labour
More than thyself to love thy neighbour.

Lewis Carroll (1832–1898)

Jabberwocky

'Twas brillig, and the slithy toves
   Did gyre and gimble in the wabe:
All mimsy were the borogoves,
   And the mome raths outgrabe.

"Beware the Jabberwock, my son!   5
   The jaws that bite, the claws that catch!
Beware the Jubjub bird, and shun
   The frumious Bandersnatch!"

He took his vorpal sword in hand;
  Long time the manxome foe he sought—   10
So rested he by the Tumtum tree,
  And stood awhile in thought.

And, as in uffish thought he stood,
  The Jabberwock, with eyes of flame,
Came whiffling through the tulgey wood,   15
  And burbled as it came!

One, two! One, two! And through and through
  The vorpal blade went snicker-snack!
He left it dead, and with its head
  He went galumphing back.   20

"And hast thou slain the Jabberwock?
  Come to my arms, my beamish boy!
O frabjous day! Callooh, Callay!"
  He chortled in his joy.

'Twas brillig, and the slithy toves   25
  Did gyre and gimble in the wabe:
All mimsy were the borogoves,
  And the mome raths outgrabe.

William Ernest Henley (1849–1903)

Madam Life's a piece in bloom

Madam Life's a piece in bloom
  Death goes dogging everywhere:
She's the tenant of the room,
  He's the ruffian on the stair.

You shall see her as a friend,   5
  You shall bilk him once or twice;
But he'll trap you in the end,
  And he'll stick you for her price.

With his kneebones at your chest,
   And his knuckles in your throat,
You would reason—plead—protest!   10
   Clutching at her petticoat;

But she's heard it all before,
   Well she knows you've had your fun,
Gingerly she gains the door,
   And your little job is done.   15

Thomas Hardy (1840–1928)

Hap

If but some vengeful god would call to me
From up the sky, and laugh: "Thou suffering thing,
Know that thy sorrow is my ecstasy,
That thy love's loss is my hate's profiting!"

Then would I bear it, clench myself, and die,   5
Steeled by the sense of ire unmerited;
Half-eased in that a Powerfuller than I
Had willed and meted me the tears I shed.

But not so. How arrives it joy lies slain,
And why unblooms the best hope ever sown?   10
—Crass Casualty obstructs the sun and rain,
And dicing Time for gladness casts a moan. . . .
These purblind Doomsters had as readily strown
Blisses about my pilgrimage as pain.

The Man He Killed

"Had he and I but met
   By some old ancient inn,
We should have sat us down to wet
   Right many a nipperkin!

SOURCE: Reprinted from *Collected Poems* by Thomas Hardy with the permission of his Estate; The Macmillan Company, New York; Macmillan & Co., Ltd., London; and The Macmillan Company of Canada, Ltd., Toronto. Copyright 1925 by The Macmillan Company.

"But ranged as infantry,   5
    And staring face to face,
I shot at him as he at me,
    And killed him in his place.

"I shot him dead because—
    Because he was my foe,   10
Just so: my foe of course he was;
    That's clear enough; although

"He thought he'd 'list, perhaps,
    Off-hand like—just as I—
Was out of work—had sold his traps—   15
    No other reason why.

"Yes; quaint and curious war is!
    You shoot a fellow down
You'd treat if met where any bar is,
    Or help to half-a-crown."   20

A. E. Housman (1859–1936)

To an Athlete Dying Young

The time you won your town the race
We chaired you through the market-place;
Man and boy stood cheering by,
And home we brought you shoulder-high.

Today, the road all runners come,   5
Shoulder-high we bring you home,
And set you at your threshold down,
Townsman of a stiller town.

Smart lad, to slip betimes away
From fields where glory does not stay,   10
And early though the laurel grows
It withers quicker than the rose.

SOURCE: Reprinted from "A Shropshire Lad," Authorized Edition, from *The Collected Poems of A. E. Housman,* with the permission of The Society of Authors as the literary representative of the Estate of A. E. Housman and the publishers, Jonathan Cape, Ltd. and Holt, Rinehart and Winston, Inc. Copyright 1939, 1940, © 1959 by Holt, Rinehart and Winston, Inc. Copyright © 1967, 1968 by Robert E. Symons.

Eyes the shady night has shut
Cannot see the record cut,
And silence sounds no worse than cheers
After earth has stopped the ears.

Now you will not swell the rout
Of lads that wore their honors out,
Runners whom renown outran
And the name died before the man.

So set, before its echoes fade,
The fleet foot on the sill of shade,
And hold to the low lintel up
The still-defended challenge-cup.

And round that early-laureled head
Will flock to gaze the strengthless dead,
And find unwithered on its curls
The garland briefer than a girl's.

15

20

25

"Is my team ploughing?"

"Is my team ploughing,
　That I was used to drive
And hear the harness jingle
　When I was man alive?"

Ay, the horses trample,
　The harness jingles now;
No change though you lie under
　The land you used to plough.

"Is football playing
　Along the river shore,
With lads to chase the leather,
　Now I stand up no more?"

5

10

SOURCE: Reprinted from "A Shropshire Lad," Authorized Edition, from *The Collected Poems of A. E. Housman,* with the permission of The Society of Authors as the literary representative of the Estate of A. E. Housman and the publishers, Jonathan Cape, Ltd. and Holt, Rinehart and Winston, Inc. Copyright 1939, 1940, © 1959 by Holt, Rinehart and Winston, Inc. Copyright © 1967, 1968 by Robert E. Symons.

Ay, the ball is flying,
   The lads play heart and soul;
The goal stands up, the keeper   15
   Stands up to keep the goal.

"Is my girl happy,
   That I thought hard to leave,
And has she tired of weeping
   As she lies down at eve?"   20

Ay, she lies down lightly,
   She lies not down to weep:
Your girl is well contented.
   Be still, my lad, and sleep.

"Is my friend hearty,   25
   Now I am thin and pine,
And has he found to sleep in
   A better bed than mine?"

Yes, lad, I lie easy,
   I lie as lads would choose;
I cheer a dead man's sweetheart,   30
   Never ask me whose.

When I Was One-and-Twenty

When I was one-and-twenty
   I heard a wise man say,
"Give crowns and pounds and guineas
   But not your heart away;
Give pearls away and rubies   5
   But keep your fancy free."
But I was one-and-twenty,
   No use to talk to me.

SOURCE: Reprinted from "A Shropshire Lad," Authorized Edition, from *The Collected Poems of A. E. Housman*, with the permission of The Society of Authors as the literary representative of the Estate of A. E. Housman and the publishers, Jonathan Cape, Ltd. and Holt, Rinehart and Winston, Inc. Copyright 1939, 1940, © 1959 by Holt, Rinehart and Winston, Inc. Copyright © 1967, 1968 by Robert E. Symons.

When I was one-and-twenty
  I heard him say again,
"The heart out of the bosom
  Was never given in vain;
'Tis paid with sighs a-plenty
  And sold for endless rue."
And I am two-and-twenty,
  And oh, 'tis true, 'tis true.

10

15

"*Terence, this is stupid stuff*"

"Terence[1], this is stupid stuff:
You eat your victuals fast enough;
There can't be much amiss, 'tis clear,
To see the rate you drink your beer.
But oh, good Lord, the verse you make,
It gives a chap the belly-ache.
The cow, the old cow, she is dead;
It sleeps well, the horned head:
We poor lads, 'tis our turn now
To hear such tunes as killed the cow.
Pretty friendship 'tis to rhyme
Your friends to death before their time
Moping melancholy mad:
Come, pipe a tune to dance to, lad."

    Why, if 'tis dancing you would be,
There's brisker pipes than poetry.
Say, for what were hop-yards meant,
Or why was Burton built on Trent?
Oh many a peer of England brews
Livelier liquor than the Muse,
And malt does more than Milton can
To justify God's ways to man.

5

10

15

20

SOURCE: Reprinted from "A Shropshire Lad," Authorized Edition, from *The Collected Poems of A. E. Housman* with the permission of The Society of Authors as the literary representative of the Estate of A. E. Housman and the publishers, Jonathan Cape, Ltd. and Holt, Rinehart and Winston, Inc. Copyright 1939, 1940, © 1959 by Holt, Rinehart and Winston, Inc. Copyright © 1967, 1968 by Robert E. Symons.

[1] As a name for himself, the narrator takes that of a Roman poet, author of satiric comedies.

Ale, man, ale's the stuff to drink
For fellows whom it hurts to think:
Look into the pewter pot   25
To see the world as the world's not.
And faith, 'tis pleasant till 'tis past:
The mischief is that 'twill not last.
Oh I have been to Ludlow fair
And left my necktie God knows where,   30
And carried half-way home, or near,
Pints and quarts of Ludlow beer:
Then the world seemed none so bad,
And I myself a sterling lad;
And down in lovely muck I've lain,   35
Happy till I woke again.
Then I saw the morning sky:
Heigho, the tale was all a lie;
The world, it was the old world yet,
I was I, my things were wet,   40
And nothing now remained to do
But begin the game anew.

    Therefore, since the world has still
Much good, but much less good than ill,
And while the sun and moon endure   45
Luck's a chance, but trouble's sure,
I'd face it as a wise man would,
And train for ill and not for good.
'Tis true, the stuff I bring for sale
Is not so brisk a brew as ale: 50
Out of a stem that scored the hand
I wrung it in a weary land.
But take it: if the smack is sour,
The better for the embittered hour;
It should do good to heart and head   55
When your soul is in my soul's stead;
And I will friend you, if I may,
In the dark and cloudy day.

    There was a king reigned in the East:
There, when kings will sit to feast,   60
They get their fill before they think
With poisoned meat and poisoned drink.
He gathered all that springs to birth
From the many-venomed earth;

First a little, thence to more,   65
He sampled all her killing store;
And easy, smiling, seasoned sound,
Sate the king when healths went round.
They put arsenic in his meat
And stared aghast to watch him eat;   70
They poured strychnine in his cup
And shook to see him drink it up:
They shook, they stared as white's their shirt:
Them it was their poison hurt.
—I tell the tale that I heard told.   75
Mithridates, he died old.

G. K. Chesterton (1874–1936)

The Donkey

When fishes flew and forests walked
   And figs grew upon thorn,
Some moment when the moon was blood
   Then surely I was born;

With monstrous head and sickening cry   5
   And ears like errant wings,
The devil's walking parody
   On all four-footed things.

The tattered outlaw of the earth,
   Of ancient crooked will;   10
Starve, scourge, deride me: I am dumb,
   I keep my secret still.

Fools! For I also had my hour;
   One far fierce hour and sweet:
There was a shout about my ears,   15
   And palms before my feet.

Edgar Allan Poe (1809–1849)

Sonnet—To Science

Science! true daughter of Old Time thou art!
    Who alterest all things with thy peering eyes.
Why preyest thou thus upon the poet's heart,
    Vulture, whose wings are dull realities?
How should he love thee? or how deem thee wise,   5
    Who wouldst not leave him in his wandering
To seek for treasure in the jewelled skies,
    Albeit he soared with an undaunted wing?
Hast thou not dragged Diana from her car?
    And driven the Hamadryad from the wood   10
To seek a shelter in some happier star?
    Hast thou not torn the Naiad from her flood,
The Elfin from the green grass, and from me
    The summer dream beneath the tamarind tree?

Walt Whitman (1819–1892)

Beginning My Studies

Beginning my studies the first step pleas'd me so much,
The mere fact consciousness, these forms, the power of motion,
The least insect or animal, the senses, eyesight, love,
The first step I say awed me and pleas'd me so much,
I have hardly gone and hardly wish'd to go any farther,   5
But stop and loiter all the time to sing it in ecstatic songs.

When I Heard the Learn'd Astronomer

When I heard the learn'd astronomer,
When the proofs, the figures, were ranged in columns before me,
When I was shown the charts and diagrams, to add, divide, and
measure them,
When I sitting heard the astronomer where he lectured with
much applause in the lecture-room,
How soon unaccountable I became tired and sick,
Till rising and gliding out I wandered off by myself,
In the mystical moist night-air, and from time to time
Looked up in perfect silence at the stars.

5

A Noiseless Patient Spider

A noiseless patient spider,
I mark'd where on a little promontory it stood isolated,
Mark'd how to explore the vacant vast surrounding,
It launch'd forth filament, filament, filament, out of itself,
Ever unreeling them, ever tirelessly speeding them.

5

And you O my soul where you stand,
Surrounded, detached, in measureless oceans of space,
Ceaselessly musing, venturing, throwing, seeking the spheres to
connect them,
Till the bridge you will need be form'd, till the ductile anchor hold,
Till the gossamer thread you fling catch somewhere, O my soul.

10

Emily Dickinson (1830–1886)

There is no Frigate like a Book

There is no Frigate like a Book
   To take us Lands away,
Nor any Coursers like a Page
   Of prancing Poetry.

This Traverse may the poorest take   5
   Without oppress of Toll;
How frugal is the chariot
   That bears a human soul!

I taste a liquor never brewed

I taste a liquor never brewed—
From Tankards scooped in Pearl—
Not all the Vats upon the Rhine[1]
Yield such an Alcohol!

Inebriate of Air—am I—   5
And Debauchee of Dew—
Reeling—thro endless summer days—
From inns of Molten Blue—

When "Landlords" turn the drunken Bee
Out of the Foxglove's door—   10
When Butterflies—renounce their "drams"—
I shall but drink the more!

SOURCE: Reprinted from *The Poems of Emily Dickinson,* edited by Thomas H. Johnson, with the permission of the Trustees of Amherst College, The Belknap Press of Harvard University Press, and Little, Brown and Co. Copyright 1951, 1955 by the President and Fellows of Harvard College.

[1]Another version of this line is: "Not all the Frankfort Berries."

Till Seraphs swing their snowy Hats—
And Saints—to windows run—
To see the little Tippler
Leaning against the—Sun.[2]

15

It dropped so low — in my Regard[1]

It dropped so low—in my Regard—
I heard it hit the Ground—
And go to pieces on the Stones
At bottom of my Mind—

Yet blamed the Fate that fractured—*less*   5
Than I denounced Myself,
For entertaining Plated Wares
Upon my Silver Shelf—

Edwin Arlington Robinson (1869–1935)

Richard Cory[2]

Whenever Richard Cory went down town,
We people on the pavement looked at him:
He was a gentleman from sole to crown,
Clean favored, and imperially slim.

And he was always quietly arrayed,   5
And he was always human when he talked;
But still he fluttered pulses when he said,
"Good-morning," and he glittered when he walked.

SOURCE: [1]Reprinted from *The Poems of Emily Dickinson,* edited by Thomas H. Johnson, with the permission of the Trustees of Amherst College, The Belknap Press of Harvard University Press, and Little, Brown and Co. Copyright 1951, 1955 by the President and Fellows of Harvard College.

SOURCE: [2]Reprinted from *The Children of the Night* by Edwin Arlington Robinson with the permission of Charles Scribner's Sons.

[2]There are two other versions of this line: "Come staggering toward the sun" and "From Manzanilla come," Manzanilla being a seaport in Cuba famous for its rum trade.

And he was rich—yes, richer than a king—
And admirably schooled in every grace: 10
In fine°, we thought that he was everything   *in short*
To make us wish that we were in his place.

So on we worked, and waited for the light,
And went without the meat, and cursed the bread;
And Richard Cory, one calm summer night,   15
Went home and put a bullet through his head.

Miniver Cheevy

Miniver Cheevy, child of scorn,
    Grew lean while he assailed the seasons;
He wept that he was ever born,
    And he had reasons.

Miniver loved the days of old   5
    When swords were bright and steeds were prancing;
The vision of a warrior bold
    Would set him dancing.

Miniver sighed for what was not,
    And dreamed, and rested from his labors;   10
He dreamed of Thebes and Camelot,
    And Priam's neighbors.

Miniver mourned the ripe renown
    That made so many a name so fragrant;
He mourned Romance, now on the town,   15
    And Art, a vagrant.

Miniver loved the Medici,
    Albeit he had never seen one;
He would have sinned incessantly
    Could he have been one.   20

SOURCE: Reprinted from *The Town Down the River* by Edwin Arlington Robinson with the permission of Charles Scribner's Sons. Copyright 1907 by Charles Scribner's Sons. Copyright 1938 by Ruth Nivison.

Miniver cursed the commonplace
  And eyed a khaki suit with loathing;
He missed the mediæval grace
  Of iron clothing.

Miniver scorned the gold he sought,   25
  But sore annoyed was he without it;
Miniver thought, and thought, and thought,
  And thought about it.

Miniver Cheevy, born too late,
  Scratched his head and kept on thinking;   30
Miniver coughed, and called it fate,
  And kept on drinking.

Stephen Crane (1871–1900)

A Man Said to the Universe

A man said to the universe:
"Sir, I exist!"
"However," replied the universe,
"The fact has not created in me
A sense of obligation."   5

The Heart

In the desert
I saw a creature, naked, bestial,
Who, squatting upon the ground,
Held his heart in his hands,
And ate of it.   5

I said, "Is it good, friend?"
"It is bitter—bitter," he answered;
"But I like it
Because it is bitter,
And because it is my heart."   10

The Wayfarer

The wayfarer,
Perceiving the pathway to truth,
Was struck with astonishment.
It was thickly grown with weeds.
"Ha," he said,   5
"I see that none has passed here
In a long time."
Later he saw that each weed
Was a singular knife.
"Well," he mumbled at last,   10
"Doubtless there are other roads."

When the Prophet, a Complacent Fat Man

When the prophet, a complacent fat man,
Arrived at the mountain-top,
He cried: "Woe to my knowledge!
I intended to see good white lands
And bad black lands,   5
But the scene is grey."

Robert Frost (1874–1963)

Departmental

An ant on the tablecloth
Ran into a dormant moth
Of many times his size.
He showed not the least surprise.
His business wasn't with such.   5
He gave it scarcely a touch,

SOURCE: Reprinted from *Complete Poems of Robert Frost* with the permission of Holt, Rinehart and Winston, Inc. Copyright 1916, 1923, 1928 by Holt, Rinehart and Winston, Inc. Copyright 1936, 1944, 1951, © 1956 by Robert Frost. Copyright © 1964 by Lesley Frost Ballantine.

And was off on his duty run.
Yet if he encountered one
Of the hive's enquiry squad
Whose work is to find out God   10
And the nature of time and space,
He would put him onto the case.
Ants are a curious race;
One crossing with hurried tread
The body of one of their dead   15
Isn't given a moment's arrest—
Seems not even impressed.
But he no doubt reports to any
With whom he crosses antennae,
And they no doubt report   20
To the higher up at court.
Then word goes forth in Formic:
"Death's come to Jerry McCormic,
Our selfless forager Jerry.
Will the special Janizary°   *soldier*
Whose office it is to bury
The dead of the commissary
Go bring him home to his people.
Lay him in state on a sepal.
Wrap him for shroud in a petal.   30
Embalm him with ichor of nettle.
This is the word of your Queen."
And presently on the scene
Appears a solemn mortician;
And taking formal position   35
With feelers calmly atwiddle,
Seizes the dead by the middle,
And heaving him high in air,
Carries him out of there.
No one stands round to stare.   40
It is nobody else's affair.
It couldn't be called ungentle.
But how thoroughly departmental.

The Road Not Taken

Two roads diverged in a yellow wood,
And sorry I could not travel both
And be one traveler, long I stood
And looked down one as far as I could
To where it bent in the undergrowth;   5

Then took the other, as just as fair,
And having perhaps the better claim,
Because it was grassy and wanted wear;
Though as for that the passing there
Had worn them really about the same,   10

And both that morning equally lay
In leaves no step had trodden black.
Oh, I kept the first for another day!
Yet knowing how way leads on to way,
I doubted if I should ever come back.   15

I shall be telling this with a sigh
Somewhere ages and ages hence:
Two roads diverged in a wood, and I—
I took the one less traveled by,
And that has made all the difference.   20

Neither Out Far Nor In Deep

The people along the sand
All turn and look one way.
They turn their back on the land.
They look at the sea all day.

SOURCE: Reprinted from *Complete Poems of Robert Frost* with the permission of Holt, Rinehart and Winston, Inc. Copyright 1916, 1923, 1928 by Holt, Rinehart and Winston, Inc. Copyright 1936, 1944, 1951, © 1956 by Robert Frost. Copyright © 1964 by Lesley Frost Ballantine.

As long as it takes to pass   5
A ship keeps raising its hull;
The wetter ground like glass
Reflects a standing gull.

The land may vary more;
But wherever the truth may be—
The water comes ashore,   10
And the people look at the sea.

They cannot look out far.
They cannot look in deep.
But when was that ever a bar   15
To any watch they keep?

There Are Roughly Zones

We sit indoors and talk of the cold outside.
And every gust that gathers strength and heaves
Is a threat to the house. But the house has long been tried.
We think of the tree. If it never again has leaves,
We'll know, we say, that this was the night it died.   5
It is very far north, we admit, to have brought the peach.
What comes over a man, is it soul or mind—
That to no limits and bounds he can stay confined?
You would say his ambition was to extend the reach
Clear to the Arctic of every living kind.   10
Why is his nature forever so hard to teach
That though there is no fixed line between wrong and right,
There are roughly zones whose laws must be obeyed.
There is nothing much we can do for the tree tonight,
But we can't help feeling more than a little betrayed   15
That the northwest wind should rise to such a height
Just when the cold went down so many below.
The tree has no leaves and may never have them again.
We must wait till some months hence in the spring to know.
But if it is destined never again to grow,   20
It can blame this limitless trait in the hearts of men.

SOURCE: Reprinted From *Complete Poems of Robert Frost* with the permission of Holt, Rine-
hart and Winston, Inc. Copyright 1916, 1923, 1928 by Holt, Rinehart and Winston, Inc.
Copyright 1936, 1944, 1951, © 1956 by Robert Frost. Copyright © 1964 by Lesley Frost
Ballantine.

West-Running Brook

"Fred, where is north?"

                    "North? North is there, my love.
The brook runs west."

                    "West-running Brook then call it."
(West-running Brook men call it to this day.)   5
"What does it think it's doing running west
When all the other country brooks flow east
To reach the ocean? It must be the brook
Can trust itself to go by contraries
The way I can with you—and you with me—   10
Because we're—we're—I don't know what we are.
What are we?"

           "Young or new?"

                  "We must be something.

We've said we two. Let's change that to we three.   15
As you and I are married to each other,
We'll both be married to the brook. We'll build
Our bridge across it, and the bridge shall be
Our arm thrown over it asleep beside it.

Look, look, it's waving to us with a wave   20
To let us know it hears me."
                                        "Why, my dear,
That wave's been standing off this jut of shore—"
(The black stream, catching on a sunken rock,
Flung backward on itself in one white wave,   25
And the white water rode the black forever,
Not gaining but not losing, like a bird
White feathers from the struggle of whose breast
Flecked the dark stream and flecked the darker pool
Below the point, and were at last driven wrinkled   30
In a white scarf against the far shore alders.)
"That wave's been standing off this jut of shore
Ever since rivers, I was going to say,
Were made in heaven. It wasn't waved to us."

"It wasn't, yet it was. If not to you   35
It was to me—in an annunciation."

"Oh, if you take it off to lady-land,
As't were the country of the Amazons
We men must see you to the confines of
And leave you there, ourselves forbid to enter,—   40
It is your brook! I have no more to say."

"Yes, you have, too. Go on. You thought of something."

"Speaking of contraries, see how the brook
In that white wave runs counter to itself.
It is from that in water we were from   45
Long, long before we were from any creature.
Here we, in our impatience of the steps,
Get back to the beginning of beginnings,
The stream of everything that runs away.
Some say existence like a Pirouot   50
And Pirouette, forever in one place,
Stands still and dances, but it runs away,
It seriously, sadly, runs away
To fill the abyss' void with emptiness.
It flows beside us in this water brook,   55
But it flows over us. It flows between us
To separate us for a panic moment.
It flows between us, over us, and *with* us.
And it is time, strength, tone, light, life and love—
And even substance lapsing unsubstantial;   60
The universal cataract of death
That spends to nothingness—and unresisted,
Save by some strange resistance in itself,
Not just a swerving, but a throwing back,
As if regret were in it and were sacred.   65
It has this throwing backward on itself
So that the fall of most of it is always
Raising a little, sending up a little.
Our life runs down in sending up the clock.
The brook runs down in sending up our life.   70
The sun runs down in sending up the brook.
And there is something sending up the sun.
It is this backward motion toward the source,
Against the stream, that most we see ourselves in,
The tribute of the current to the source.   75
It is from this in nature we are from.
It is most us."

                    "Today will be the day
You said so."

                    "No, today will be the day   80
You said the brook was called West-running Brook."

"Today will be the day of what we both said."

Fire and Ice[1]

Some say the world will end in fire,
Some say in ice.
From what I've tasted of desire
I hold with those who favor fire.
But if it had to perish twice,   5
I think I know enough of hate
To say that for destruction ice
Is also great
And would suffice.

Charles Baudelaire (1821–1867)

The Metamorphoses of a Vampire[2]
                                          Translated by
                                          Donald Justice

The woman, meanwhile, from strawberry lips,
Twisting and turning like a snake on coals,
And kneading her breasts against her corset stays,
Lets flow these words, which seem infused with musk
"My lips are moist, I know the science well   5
Of losing the old conscience deep in bed.
I dry all tears on my triumphant breasts
And set old men to laughing like young boys.
For those who see me naked and unveiled
I take the place of sun, and moon, and stars!   10
Dear scholar, I am so learned in this art
That when I smother a man in my smooth arms,
Or when I abandon to their teeth my bosom,
The timid man, the rake, the weak, the strong
Shiver these cushions so before they swoon   15
The impotent angels would damn themselves for me."

When she had sucked the marrow from my bones,
And, languishing, I turned towards her to give
Her one more kiss of love, I only saw
Her sticky loins—a winesack filled with pus!   20
I shut my eyes in a cold fright, and when
I opened them again to the live light,
Beside me lay no mannequin whose power
Seemed to have come from drinking human blood:
There trembled a confusion of old bones   25
Which squeaked in turning like a weathervane,
Or like a signboard on an iron pole
Swung by the wind through the long winter nights.

Gerard Manley Hopkins (1844–1889)

God's Grandeur

The world is charged with the grandeur of God.
   It will flame out, like shining from shook foil;
   It gathers to a greatness, like the ooze of oil
Crushed. Why do men then now not reck his rod?
Generations have trod, have trod, have trod;   5
   And all is seared with trade; bleared, smeared with toil;
   And wears man's smudge and shares man's smell: the soil
Is bare now, nor can foot feel, being shod.

And for all this, nature is never spent;
   There lives the dearest freshness deep down things;   10
And though the last lights off the black West went
   Oh, morning, at the brown brink eastward, springs—
Because the Holy Ghost over the bent
   World broods with warm breast and with ah! bright wings.

The Windhover ¹   *To Christ our Lord*

  I caught this morning morning's minion, kingdom of daylight's
    dauphin, dapple-dawn-drawn Falcon, in his riding
  Of the rolling level underneath him steady air, and striding
High there, how he rung upon the rein of a wimpling wing²
In his ecstasy! then off, off forth on swing,
    As a skate's heel sweeps smooth on a bow-bend: the hurl and
      gliding   5
  Rebuffed the big wind. My heart in hiding
Stirred for a bird,—the achieve of, the mastery of the thing!

Brute beauty and valor and act, oh, air, pride, plume, here
    Buckle! AND the fire that breaks from thee then, a billion
Times told lovelier, more dangerous, O my chevalier!   10

    No wonder of it: shéer plód makes plow down sillion°   *furrow*
Shine, and blue-bleak embers, ah my dear,
    Fall, gall themselves, and gash gold-vermilion.

SOURCE: The Hopkins poems are reprinted from *The Poems of Gerard Manley Hopkins*, edited by W. H. Gardner. Reprinted with the permission of Oxford University Press.

Thou Art Indeed Just, Lord

*Justus quidem tu es, Domine, si disputem tecum: verumtamen justa loquar ad te:
Quare via impiorum prosperatur? etc.*[1]

Thou art indeed just, Lord, if I contend
With thee; but, sir, so what I plead is just.
Why do sinners' ways prosper? and why must
Disappointment all I endeavour end?
   Wert thou my enemy, O thou my friend,   5
How wouldst thou worse, I wonder, than thou dost
Defeat, thwart me? Oh, the sots and thralls of lust
Do in spare hours more thrive than I that spend,
Sir, life upon thy cause. See, banks and brakes
Now, leavèd how thick! lacèd they are again   10
With fretty chervil, look, and fresh wind shakes
Them; birds build—but not I build; no, but strain,
Time's eunuch, and not breed one work that wakes.
Mine, O thou lord of life, send my roots rain.

Carrion Comfort

Not, I'll not, carrion comfort, Despair, not feast on thee;
Not untwist—slack they may be—these last strands of man
In me ór, most weary, cry *I can no more.* I can;
Can something, hope, wish day come, not choose not to be.
But ah, but O thou terrible, why wouldst thou rude on me   5
Thy wring-world right foot rock? lay a lionlimb against me? scan
With darksome devouring eyes my bruisèd bones? and fan,
O in turns of tempest, me heaped there; me frantic to avoid thee
   and flee?

---

[1]The Latin is from Jeremiah 12:1 and is translated by the first three lines of the poem.

Why? That my chaff might fly; my grain lie, sheer and clear.
Nay in all that toil, that coil, since (seems) I kissed the rod,   10
Hand rather, my heart lo! lapped strength, stole joy, would laugh,
   chéer.
Cheer whom though? the hero whose heaven-handling flung me,
   fóot tród
Me? or me that fought him? O which one? is it each one?
   That night, that year
Of now done darkness I wretch lay wrestling with (my God!) my
   God.   15

William Butler Yeats (1865–1939)

The Lake Isle of Innisfree

I will arise and go now, and go to Innisfree,
And a small cabin build there, of clay and wattles made:
Nine bean rows will I have there, a hive for the honey bee,
   And live alone in the bee-loud glade.

And I shall have some peace there, for peace comes dropping slow,   5
Dropping from the veils of the morning to where the cricket sings;
There midnight's all a glimmer, and noon a purple glow,
   And evening full of the linnet's wings.

I will arise and go now, for always night and day
I hear lake water lapping with low sounds by the shore;   10
While I stand on the roadway, or on the pavements gray,
   I hear it in the deep heart's core.

SOURCE: Reprinted from *Collected Poems* by William Butler Yeats with the permission of
M. B. Yeats, The Macmillan Company of Canada, and The Macmillan Company, New York.
Copyright 1906 by The Macmillan Company. Copyright 1934 by William Butler Yeats.

A Prayer for Old Age[1]

God guard me from those thoughts men think
In the mind alone;
He that sings a lasting song
Thinks in a marrow-bone;

From all that makes a wise old man
That can be praised of all;
O what am I that I should not seem
For the song's sake a fool?

I pray—for fashion's word is out
And prayer comes round again—
That I may seem, though I die old,
A foolish, passionate man.

Leda and the Swan[2]

A sudden blow: the great wings beating still
Above the staggering girl, her thighs caressed
By the dark webs, her nape caught in his bill,
He holds her helpless breast upon his breast.

How can those terrified vague fingers push
The feathered glory from her loosening thighs?
And how can body, laid in that white rush,
But feel the strange heart beating where it lies?

A shudder in the loins engenders there
The broken wall, the burning roof and tower
And Agamemnon dead.

Being so caught up,
So mastered by the brute blood of the air,
Did she put on his knowledge with his power
Before the indifferent beak could let her drop?

15

The Magi [1]

Now as at all times I can see in the mind's eye,
In their stiff, painted clothes, the pale unsatisfied ones
Appear and disappear in the blue depth of the sky
With all their ancient faces like rain-beaten stones,
And all their helms of silver hovering side by side,
And all their eyes still fixed, hoping to find once more,
Being by Calvary's turbulence unsatisfied,
The uncontrollable mystery on the bestial floor.

5

The Second Coming [2]

Turning and turning in the widening gyre
The falcon cannot hear the falconer;
Things fall apart; the centre cannot hold;
Mere anarchy is loosed upon the world,
The blood-dimmed tide is loosed, and everywhere
The ceremony of innocence is drowned;
The best lack all conviction, while the worst
Are full of passionate intensity.

5

SOURCE: [1] Reprinted from *Collected Poems* by William Butler Yeats by permission of M. B. Yeats, The Macmillan Company of Canada, and The Macmillan Company, New York. Copyright 1916 by The Macmillan Company. Copyright 1944 by Bertha Georgie Yeats.

SOURCE: [2] Reprinted from *Collected Poems* by William Butler Yeats by permission of M. B. Yeats, The Macmillan Company of Canada, and The Macmillan Company, New York. Copyright 1924 by The Macmillan Company. Copyright 1952 by Bertha Georgie Yeats.

Surely some revelation is at hand;
Surely the Second Coming is at hand.   10
The Second Coming! Hardly are those words out
When a vast image out of *Spiritus Mundi*
Troubles my sight: somewhere in sands of the desert
A shape with lion body and the head of a man,
A gaze blank and pitiless as the sun,   15
Is moving its slow thighs, while all about it
Reel shadows of the indignant desert birds.
The darkness drops again; but now I know
That twenty centuries of stony sleep
Were vexed to nightmare by a rocking cradle,   20
And what rough beast, its hour come round at last,
Slouches towards Bethlehem to be born?

Sailing to Byzantium

That is no country for old men. The young
In one another's arms, birds in the trees
—Those dying generations—at their song,
The salmon-falls, the mackerel-crowded seas,
Fish, flesh, or fowl, commend all summer long   5
Whatever is begotten, born, and dies.
Caught in that sensual music all neglect
Monuments of unaging intellect.

An aged man is but a paltry thing,
A tattered coat upon a stick, unless   10
Soul clap its hands and sing, and louder sing
For every tatter in its mortal dress,
Nor is there singing school but studying
Monuments of its own magnificence;
And therefore I have sailed the seas and come   15
To the holy city of Byzantium.

SOURCE: Reprinted from *Collected Poems* by William Butler Yeats with the permission of M. B. Yeats, The Macmillan Company of Canada, and The Macmillan Company, New York. Copyright 1928 by The Macmillan Company. Copyright 1956 by Georgie Yeats.

O sages standing in God's holy fire
As in the gold mosaic of a wall,
Come from the holy fire, perne in a gyre°,   *spin down in a spiral*
And be the singing-masters of my soul.   20
Consume my heart away; sick with desire
And fastened to a dying animal
It knows not what it is; and gather me
Into the artifice of eternity.

Once out of nature I shall never take   25
My bodily form from any natural thing,
But such a form as Grecian goldsmiths make
Of hammered gold and gold enameling
To keep a drowsy Emperor awake;
Or set upon a golden bough to sing   30
To lords and ladies of Byzantium
Of what is past, or passing, or to come.

Byzantium

The unpurged images of day recede;
The Emperor's drunken soldiery are abed;
Night resonance recedes, night-walkers' song
After great cathedral gong;
A starlit or a moonlit dome disdains   5
All that man is,
All mere complexities,
The fury and the mire of human veins.

Before me floats an image, man or shade,
Shade more than man, more image than a shade;   10
For Hades' bobbin bound in mummy-cloth
May unwind the winding path;
A mouth that has no moisture and no breath
Breathless mouths may summon;
I hail the superhuman;   15
I call it death-in-life and life-in-death.

SOURCE: Reprinted from *Collected Poems* by William Butler Yeats with the permission of M. B. Yeats, The Macmillan Company of Canada, and The Macmillan Company, New York. Copyright 1933 by The Macmillan Company. Copyright 1961 by Bertha Georgie Yeats.

Miracle, bird or golden handiwork,
More miracle than bird or handiwork,
Planted on the star-lit golden bough,
Can like the cocks of Hades crow,   20
Or, by the moon embittered, scorn aloud
In glory of changeless metal
Common bird or petal
And all complexities of mire or blood.

At midnight on the Emperor's pavement flit   25
Flames that no faggot feeds, nor steel has lit,
Nor storm disturbs, flames begotten of flame,
Where blood-begotten spirits come
And all complexities of fury leave,
Dying into a dance,   30
An agony of trance,
An agony of flame that cannot singe a sleeve.

Astraddle on the dolphin's mire and blood,
Spirit after spirit! The smithies break the flood,
The golden smithies of the Emperor!   35
Marbles of the dancing floor
Break bitter furies of complexity,
Those images that yet
Fresh images beget,
That dolphin-torn, that gong-tormented sea.   40

Wallace Stevens (1879–1955)

Peter Quince at the Clavier [1]

I

Just as my fingers on these keys
Make music, so the selfsame sounds
On my spirit make a music, too.

SOURCE: Reprinted from *The Collected Poems of Wallace Stevens* with the permission of Alfred A. Knopf, Inc. Copyright 1923, 1951 by Wallace Stevens.

[1] In Shakespeare's *Midsummer Night's Dream*, Peter Quince is a clownish carpenter who stages a mock-tragic play. In *The History of Susanna* in the Apocrypha, two lustful elders who covet Susanna, a virtuous married woman, hide in her garden, spy on her as she bathes, then threaten to make false accusations against her unless she submits to them. When she refuses, they cry out, and her servants come running. All ends well when the prophet Daniel cross-examines the elders and proves them liars.

Music is feeling, then, not sound;
And thus it is that what I feel,
Here in this room, desiring you,

Thinking of your blue-shadowed silk,
Is music. It is like the strain
Waked in the elders by Susanna.

Of a green evening, clear and warm,
She bathed in her still garden, while
The red-eyed elders watching, felt

The basses of their beings throb
In witching chords, and their thin blood
Pulse pizzicati of Hosanna.

II

In the green water, clear and warm,
Susanna lay.
She searched
The touch of springs,
And found
Concealed imaginings.
She sighed,
For so much melody.

Upon the bank, she stood
In the cool
Of spent emotions.
She felt, among the leaves,
The dew
Of old devotions.

She walked upon the grass,
Still quavering.
The winds were like her maids,
On timid feet,
Fetching her woven scarves,
Yet wavering.

A breath upon her hand
Muted the night
She turned—
A cymbal crashed,
And roaring horns.   40

III

Soon, with a noise like tambourines,
Came her attendant Byzantines.

They wondered why Susanna cried
Against the elders by her side;

And as they whispered, the refrain   45
Was like a willow swept by rain.

Anon, their lamps' uplifted flame
Revealed Susanna and her shame.

And then, the simpering Byzantines
Fled, with a noise like tambourines.   50

IV

Beauty is momentary in the mind—
The fitful tracing of a portal;
But in the flesh it is immortal.

The body dies; the body's beauty lives.
So evenings die, in their green going,   55
A wave, interminably flowing.
So gardens die, their meek breath scenting
The cowl of winter, done repenting.
So maidens die, to the auroral
Celebration of a maiden's choral.   60

Susanna's music touched the bawdy strings
Of those white elders; but, escaping,
Left only Death's ironic scraping.
Now, in its immortality, it plays
On the clear viol of her memory,   65
And makes a constant sacrament of praise.

How to Live. What to Do

Last evening the moon rose above this rock
Impure upon a world unpurged.
The man and his companion stopped
To rest before the heroic height.

Coldly the wind fell upon them   5
In many majesties of sound:
They that had left the flame-freaked sun
To seek a sun of fuller fire.

Instead there was this tufted rock
Massively rising high and bare   10
Beyond all trees, the ridges thrown
Like giant arms among the clouds.

There was neither voice nor crested image,
No chorister, nor priest. There was
Only the great height of the rock   15
And the two of them standing still to rest.

There was the cold wind and the sound
It made, away from the muck of the land
That they had left, heroic sound
Joyous and jubilant and sure.   20

SOURCE: Reprinted from *The Collected Poems of Wallace Stevens* with the permission of Alfred A. Knopf, Inc. Copyright 1936, 1964 by Holly Stevens Stephenson.

A High-Toned Old Christian Woman [1]

Poetry is the supreme fiction, madame.
Take the moral law and make a nave of it
And from the nave build haunted heaven. Thus,
The conscience is converted into palms,
Like windy citherns[1] hankering for hymns.   5
We agree in principle. That's clear. But take
The opposing law and make a peristyle,[2]
And from the peristyle project a masque[3]
Beyond the planets. Thus, our bawdiness,
Unpurged by epitaph, indulged at last,   10
Is equally converted into palms,
Squiggling like saxophones. And palm for palm,
Madame, we are where we began. Allow,
Therefore, that in the planetary scene
Your disaffected flagellants, well-stuffed,   15
Smacking their muzzy bellies in parade,
Proud of such novelties of the sublime,
Such tink and tank and tunk-a-tunk-tunk,
May, merely may, madame, whip from themselves
A jovial hullabaloo among the spheres.   20
This will make widows wince. But fictive things
Wink as they will. Wink most when widows wince.

The House Was Quiet and the World Was Calm [2]

The house was quiet and the world was calm.
The reader became the book; and summer night

Was like the conscious being of the book.
The house was quiet and the world was calm.

SOURCE: 1 Reprinted from *The Collected Poems of Wallace Stevens* with the permission of Alfred A. Knopf, Inc. Copyright 1923, 1951 by Wallace Stevens.

SOURCE: 2 Reprinted from *The Collected Poems of Wallace Stevens* with the permission of Alfred A. Knopf, Inc. Copyright 1942, 1947 by Wallace Stevens.

[1]medieval lutelike instruments.

[2]a system of roof-supporting columns.

[3]a head or face, often grotesque, used as an adornment.

The words were spoken as if there was no book,   5
Except that the reader leaned above the page,

Wanted to lean, wanted much most to be
The scholar to whom his book is true, to whom

The summer night is like a perfection of thought.
The house was quiet because it had to be.   10

The quiet was part of the meaning, part of the mind:
The access of perfection to the page.

And the world was calm. The truth in a calm world,
In which there is no other meaning, itself

Is calm, itself is summer and night, itself   15
Is the reader leaning late and reading there.

Study of Images I

It does no good to speak of the big, blue bush
Of day. If the study of his images
Is the study of man, this image of Saturday,

This Italian symbol, this Southern landscape, is like
A waking, as in images we awake,   5
Within the very object that we seek,

Participants of its being. It is, we are.
He is, we are. Ah, bella! He is, we are,
Within the big, blue bush and its vast shade

At evening and at night. It does no good.   10
Stop at the terraces of mandolins,
False, faded and yet inextricably there,

The pulse of the object, the heat of the body grown cold
Or cooling in late leaves, not false except
When the image itself is false, a mere desire,   15

Not faded, if images are all we have.
They can be no more faded than ourselves.
The blood refreshes with its stale demands.

Men Made Out of Words [1]

What should we be without the sexual myth,
The human revery or poem of death?

Castratos of moon-mash—Life consists
Of propositions about life. The human

Revery is a solitude in which   5
We compose these propositions, torn by dreams,

By the terrible incantations of defeats
And by the fear that defeats and dreams are one.

The whole race is a poet that writes down
The eccentric propositions of its fate.   10

William Carlos Williams (1883–1963)

The Jungle [2]

It is not the still weight
of the tree, the
breathless interior of the wood,
tangled with wrist-thick

vines, the flies, reptiles,   5
the forever fearful monkeys
screaming and running
in the branches—

SOURCE: [1] Reprinted from *The Collected Poems of Wallace Stevens* with the permission of Alfred A. Knopf, Inc. Copyright 1947 by Wallace Stevens.

SOURCE: [2] Reprinted from *Collected Earlier Poems* by William Carlos Williams with the permission of New Directions Publishing Corporation. Copyright 1938 by William Carlos Williams.

but
a girl waiting,
shy, brown, soft-eyed—   10
to guide you
                    Upstairs, sir.

The Dance [1]

In Breughel's great picture, The Kermess,
the dancers go round, they go round and
around, the squeal and the blare and the
tweedle of bagpipes, a bugle and fiddles
tipping their bellies (round as the thick-   5
sided glasses whose wash they impound)
their hips and their bellies off balance
to turn them. Kicking and rolling about
the Fair Grounds, swinging their butts, those
shanks must be sound to bear up under such   10
rollicking measures, prance as they dance
in Breughel's great picture, The Kermess.

John Hall Wheelock (b. 1886)

Hippopotamothalamion [2,1]

A hippopotamus had a bride
  Of rather singular beauty,
When he lay down at her side
  'Twas out of love, not duty—
  Hers was an exceptional beauty   5
Take, oh take those lips away, etc.

SOURCE: [1] Reprinted from *Collected Later Poems* by William Carlos Williams with the permission of New Directions Publishing Corporation. Copyright 1944 by William Carlos Williams.

SOURCE: [2] Reprinted from *New Poems by American Poets, No. 2*, edited by Rolphe Humphries with the permission of Ballantine Books, Inc. Copyright © 1957 by Ballantine Books, Inc.

[1] "A Nuptial Song for Hippopotamuses."

He met her in Central Nigeria,
  While she was resident there,
Where life is distinctly superior
  And a hippo can take down her hair—   10
  And, God, but she was fair!
Take, oh take those lips away, etc.

She was coming up from her morning swim
  When first they chanced to meet:
He looked at her, she looked at him,   15
  And stood with reluctant feet
  Where mud and river meet.
Take, oh take those lips away, etc.

Their eye-beams, twisted on one thread,
  Instantaneously did twine,   20
And he made up poetry out of his head,
  Such as: "Dear heart, be mine"—
  And he quoted, line for line,
"Hail to thee, blithe spirit," etc.

Now, hippopotamoid courtesy   25
  Is strangely meticulous—
A beautiful thing, you will agree,
  In a hippopotamus—
  And she answered, briefly, thus:
"Hail to thee, blithe spirit," etc.   30

Perhaps she was practicing the arts
  That grace old Hippo's daughter,
The coquetries that win all hearts,
  For even as he besought her
  She slid into the water.   35
Out, out, brief candle, etc.

Now on the borders of the wood,
  Whence love had drawn him hither,
He paces in an anguished mood,
  Darting hither and thither   40
  In a terrific dither.
Out, out, brief candle, etc.

The course of true love never yet
   Ran smooth, so we are told,
With thorns its pathway is beset
   And perils manifold,
   And has been from of old.
Out, out, brief candle, etc.

Yet soon a happier morning smiles,
   The marriage feast is spread—
The flower girls were crocodiles
   When hippopotamus led
   Hippopotamus, with firm tread
   A bride to the bridal bed.
Milton, thou should'st be living at this hour.

45

50

55

T. S. Eliot (1888–1965)

The Love Song of J. Alfred Prufrock

S'io credessi che mia risposta fosse a persona che mai tornasse al mondo, questa fiamma staria senza più scosse. Ma per ciò che giammai di questo fondo non tornò vivo alcun, s'i'odo il vero, senza tema d'infamia ti rispondo.[1]

Let us go then, you and I,
When the evening is spread out against the sky
Like a patient etherized upon a table;
Let us go, through certain half-deserted streets,
The muttering retreats
Of restless nights in one-night cheap hotels
And sawdust restaurants with oyster-shells:
Streets that follow like a tedious argument
Of insidious intent
To lead you to an overwhelming question . . .
Oh, do not ask, "What is it?"
Let us go and make our visit.

5

10

SOURCE: Reprinted from *Collected Poems 1909–1962* by T. S. Eliot with the permission of Faber and Faber, Ltd., London and Harcourt Brace Jovanovich, Inc., New York. Copyright 1936 by Harcourt Brace Jovanovich, Inc. Copyright © 1963, 1964 by T. S. Eliot.

[1]The epigraph, from Dante's *Inferno,* is the speech of one dead and damned, who thinks that his hearer also is going to remain in Hell. Count Guido da Montefeltro, whose sin has been to give false counsel after a corrupt prelate had offered him prior absolution and whose punishment is to be wrapped in a constantly burning flame, offers to tell Dante his story: "If I thought my reply were to someone who could ever return to the world, this flame would waver no more. But since, I'm told, nobody ever escapes from this pit, I'll tell you without fear of ill fame."

In the room the women come and go
Talking of Michelangelo.

The yellow fog that rubs its back upon the window-panes,   15
The yellow smoke that rubs its muzzle on the window-panes,
Licked its tongue into the corners of the evening,
Lingered upon the pools that stand in drains,
Let fall upon its back the soot that falls from chimneys,
Slipped by the terrace, made a sudden leap,   20
And seeing that it was a soft October night,
Curled once about the house, and fell asleep.

And indeed there will be time
For the yellow smoke that slides along the street
Rubbing its back upon the window-panes;   25
There will be time, there will be time
To prepare a face to meet the faces that you meet;
There will be time to murder and create,
And time for all the works and days of hands
That lift and drop a question on your plate;   30
Time for you and time for me,
And time yet for a hundred indecisions,
And for a hundred visions and revisions,
Before the taking of a toast and tea.

In the room the women come and go   35
Talking of Michelangelo.

And indeed there will be time
To wonder, "Do I dare?" and, "Do I dare?"
Time to turn back and descend the stair,
With a bald spot in the middle of my hair—   40
(They will say: "How his hair is growing thin!")
My morning coat, my collar mounting firmly to the chin,
My necktie rich and modest, but asserted by a simple pin—

(They will say: "But how his arms and legs are thin!")
Do I dare   45

Disturb the universe?
In a minute there is time
For decisions and revisions which a minute will reverse.
For I have known them all already, known them all—
Have known the evenings, mornings, afternoons,   50
I have measured out my life with coffee spoons;
I know the voices dying with a dying fall
Beneath the music from a farther room.
   So how should I presume?

And I have known the eyes already, known them all—   55
The eyes that fix you in a formulated phrase,
And when I am formulated, sprawling on a pin,
When I am pinned and wriggling on the wall,
Then how should I begin
To spit out all the butt-ends of my days and ways?   60
   And how should I presume?

And I have known the arms already, known them all—
Arms that are braceleted and white and bare
(But in the lamplight, downed with light brown hair!)
Is it perfume from a dress
That makes me so digress?   65
Arms that lie along a table, or wrap about a shawl.
   And should I then presume?
   And how should I begin?

     .   .   .   .   .

Shall I say, I have gone at dusk through narrow streets   70
And watched the smoke that rises from the pipes
Of lonely men in shirt-sleeves, leaning out of windows? . . .

I should have been a pair of ragged claws
Scuttling across the floors of silent seas.

     .   .   .   .   .

And the afternoon, the evening, sleeps so peacefully!   75
Smoothed by long fingers,
Asleep . . . tired . . . or it malingers,
Stretched on the floor, here beside you and me.
Should I, after tea and cakes and ices,
Have the strength to force the moment to its crisis?   80
But though I have wept and fasted, wept and prayed,
Though I have seen my head (grown slightly bald) brought in upon a
     platter,
I am no prophet—and here's no great matter;
I have seen the moment of my greatness flicker,
And I have seen the eternal Footman hold my coat, and snicker,   85
And in short, I was afraid.

And would it have been worth it, after all,
After the cups, the marmalade, the tea,
Among the porcelain, among some talk of you and me,
Would it have been worth while,   90
To have bitten off the matter with a smile,
To have squeezed the universe into a ball
To roll it toward some overwhelming question,
To say: "I am Lazarus, come from the dead,
Come back to tell you all, I shall tell you all"—   95
If one, settling a pillow by her head,
     Should say: "That is not what I meant at all.
     That is not it, at all."

And would it have been worth it, after all,
Would it have been worth while,   100
After the sunsets and the dooryards and the sprinkled streets,
After the novels, after the teacups, after the skirts that trail along the
     floor—
And this, and so much more?—
It is impossible to say just what I mean!

But as if a magic lantern threw the nerves in patterns on a screen: 105
Would it have been worth while
If one, settling a pillow or throwing off a shawl,
And turning toward the window, should say:
   "That is not it at all,
    That is not what I meant, at all." 110

    .   .   .   .   .

No! I am not Prince Hamlet, nor was meant to be;
Am an attendant lord, one that will do
To swell a progress, start a scene or two,
Advise the prince; no doubt, an easy tool,
Deferential, glad to be of use, 115
Politic, cautious, and meticulous;
Full of high sentence, but a bit obtuse;
At times, indeed, almost ridiculous—
Almost, at times, the Fool.

I grow old . . . I grow old . . . 120
I shall wear the bottoms of my trousers rolled.

Shall I part my hair behind? Do I dare to eat a peach?
I shall wear white flannel trousers, and walk upon the beach.
I have heard the mermaids singing, each to each.

I do not think that they will sing to me. 125

I have seen them riding seaward on the waves
Combing the white hair of the waves blown back
When the wind blows the water white and black.

We have lingered in the chambers of the sea
By sea-girls wreathed with seaweed red and brown 130
Till human voices wake us, and we drown.

The Hollow Men

A penny for the Old Guy.[1]

[I]

We are the hollow men
We are the stuffed men
Leaning together
Headpiece filled with straw. Alas!
Our dried voices, when   5
We whisper together
Are quiet and meaningless
As wind in dry grass
Or rats' feet over broken glass
In our dry cellar   10
Shape without form, shade without color,
Paralyzed force, gesture without motion;

Those who have crossed
With direct eyes, to death's other Kingdom
Remember us—if at all—not as lost   15
Violent souls, but only
As the hollow men
The stuffed men.

[2]

Eyes I dare not meet in dreams
In death's dream kingdom   20
These do not appear:
There, the eyes are
Sunlight on a broken column
There, is a tree swinging
And voices are   25
In the wind's singing
More distant and more solemn
Than a fading star.

SOURCE: Reprinted from *Collected Poems 1909–1962* by T. S. Eliot with the permission of Faber and Faber, Ltd., London and Harcourt Brace Jovanovich, Inc., New York. Copyright 1936 by Harcourt Brace Jovanovich, Inc. Copyright © 1963, 1964 by T. S. Eliot.

[1]Phrase used by English children begging money to buy fireworks for Guy Fawkes Day.

Let me be no nearer
In death's dream kingdom
Let me also wear   30
Such deliberate disguises
Rat's coat, crowskin, crossed staves
In a field
Behaving as the wind behaves   35
No nearer—

Not that final meeting
In the twilight kingdom

[3]

This is the dead land
This is cactus land
Here the stone images   40
Are raised, here they receive
The supplication of a dead man's hand
Under the twinkle of a fading star.

Is it like this
In death's other kingdom   45
Waking alone
At the hour when we are
Trembling with tenderness
Lips that would kiss   50
Form prayers to broken stone.

[4]

The eyes are not here
There are no eyes here
In this valley of dying stars
In this hollow valley
This broken jaw of our lost kingdoms   55

In this last of meeting places
We grope together
And avoid speech
Gathered on this beach of the tumid river   60

Sightless, unless
The eyes reappear
As the perpetual star
Multifoliate rose
Of death's twilight kingdom   65
The hope only
Of empty men.

[5]

Here we go round the prickly pear
Prickly pear prickly pear
Here we go round the prickly pear   70
At five o'clock in the morning.

Between the idea
And the reality
Between the motion
And the act   75
Falls the Shadow

                                    For Thine is the Kingdom

Between the conception
And the creation
Between the emotion   80
And the response
Falls the Shadow

                                         Life is very long

Between the desire
And the spasm   85
Between the potency
And the existence
Between the essence
And the descent
Falls the Shadow   90

                                    For Thine is the Kingdom

For Thine is
Life is
For Thine is the

This is the way the world ends
This is the way the world ends
This is the way the world ends
Not with a bang but a whimper.

John Crowe Ransom (b. 1888)

Two Sonnets: I. Yea, II. Nay

I. Yea

It was beside the fire that I had lit,
Out of the rain that drummed upon my roof,
She leant against my bosom, fluttering it,
And stared beyond my world, far, far aloof.

And neither spoke, and thus we might have sat
Till angry Gabriel trumpeted for change,
But she said, "Heart of stone, look not like that!
O unconcessive husband, you are strange."

For joy I could not answer, being taxed
By such a star, so distant in the sky,
With being cold. But think how the poor heart waxed,
The chidden wonder of women, the huge I!

And I played the god; disdaining her no more
I smiled, and drew her closer than before.

II. Nay

With such strong arms I shut my love about,
She rested there, which was to me a token
This was a house she never could walk without,
Securely bricked, and never to be broken.

But no, the tight imprisonment was vain,
Too physical and wide to catch a heart;
When we had come most near, and scarce were twain,
Some soul was still unmet, and much apart.

SOURCE: Reprinted from *Chills and Fever* by John Crowe Ransom with the permission of Alfred A. Knopf, Inc. Copyright 1924 by Alfred A. Knopf, Inc. Copyright 1952 by John Crowe Ransom.

Therefore I knew the most unperjured lips
That ever sweetly bargained love's exchange   10
Must lie; love must be blacked with this eclipse,
That she and I could live, and still be strange!

Archibald MacLeish (b. 1892)

Ars Poetica

A poem should be palpable and mute
As a globed fruit,

Dumb
As old medallions to the thumb,

Silent as the sleeve-worn stone   5
Of casement ledges where the moss has grown—

A poem should be wordless
As the flight of birds.

A poem should be motionless in time
As the moon climbs,   10

Leaving, as the moon releases
Twig by twig the night-entangled trees,

Leaving, as the moon behind the winter leaves,
Memory by memory the mind—

A poem should be motionless in time   15
As the moon climbs.

A poem should be equal to:
Not true.

For all the history of grief
An empty doorway and a maple leaf.   20

SOURCE: Reprinted from *Collected Poems 1917–1952* by Archibald MacLeish with the permission of Houghton Mifflin Company. Copyright 1952 by Archibald MacLeish.

For love
The leaning grasses and two lights above the sea—

A poem should not mean
But be.

You, Andrew Marvell

And here face down beneath the sun,
And here upon earth's noonward height
To feel the always coming on,
The always rising of the night.

To feel creep up the curving east   5
The earthly chill of dusk and slow
Upon those under lands the vast
And ever-climbing shadow grow,

And strange at Ecbatan the trees
Take leaf by leaf the evening, strange,   10
The flooding dark about their knees,
The mountains over Persia change,

And now at Kermanshah the gate,
Dark, empty, and the withered grass,
And through the twilight now the late   15
Few travelers in the westward pass.

And Baghdad darken and the bridge
Across the silent river gone,
And through Arabia the edge
Of evening widen and steal on,   20

SOURCE: Reprinted from *Collected Poems 1917–1952* by Archibald MacLeish with the permission of Houghton Mifflin Company. Copyright 1952 by Archibald MacLeish.

And deepen on Palmyra's street
The wheel rut in the ruined stone,
And Lebanon fade out and Crete
High through the clouds and overblown,

And over Sicily the air   25
Still flashing with the landward gulls,
And loom and slowly disappear
The sails above the shadowy hulls,

And Spain go under and the shore
Of Africa, the gilded sand,   30
And evening vanish and no more
The low pale light across that land,

Nor now the long light on the sea—
And here face downward in the sun
To feel how swift, how secretly,   35
The shadow of the night comes on. . . .

Wilfred Owen (1893–1918)

Greater Love

Red lips are not so red
   As the stained stones kissed by the English dead.
Kindness of wooed and wooer
Seems shame to their love pure.
O Love, your eyes lose lure   5
   When I behold eyes blinded in my stead!

Your slender attitude
   Trembles not exquisite like limbs knife-skewed,
Rolling and rolling there
Where God seems not to care;   10
Till the fierce love they bear
   Cramps them in death's extreme decrepitude.

SOURCE: Reprinted from *The Collected Poems of Wilfred Owen* with the permission of Chatto and Windus, Ltd., London; New Directions Publishing Corporation, New York; and Harold Owen. Copyright Chatto & Windus, Ltd. 1946, © 1963.

Your voice sings not so soft,—
   Though even as wind murmuring through raftered loft,—
Your dear voice is not dear,   15
Gentle, and evening clear,
As theirs whom none now hear,
   Now earth has stopped their piteous mouths that
      coughed.
Heart, you were never hot,
   Nor large, nor full like hearts made great with shot;   20
And though your hand be pale,
Paler are all which trail
Your cross through flame and hail:
   Weep, you may weep, for you may touch them not.

The Parable of the Old Men and the Young

So Abram rose, and clave the wood, and went,
And took the fire with him, and a knife.
And as they sojourned both of them together,
Isaac the first-born spake and said, "My Father,
Behold the preparations, fire and iron,   5
But where the lamb for this burnt-offering?"
Then Abram bound the youth with belts and straps,
And builded parapets and trenches there,
And stretched forth the knife to slay his son.
When lo! an angel called him out of heaven,   10
Saying, "Lay not thy hand upon the lad,
Neither do anything to him. Behold,
A ram, caught in a thicket by its horns;
Offer the Ram of Pride instead of him."
But the old man would not so, but slew his son,—   15
And half the seed of Europe, one by one.

SOURCE: Reprinted from *The Collected Poems of Wilfred Owen* with the permission of Chatto and Windus, Ltd., London; New Directions Publishing Corporation, New York; and Harold Owen. Copyright Chatto & Windus, Ltd. 1946, © 1963.

Arms and the Boy [1]

Let the boy try along this bayonet-blade
How cold steel is, and keen with hunger of blood;
But with all malice, like a madman's flash;
And thinly drawn with famishing for flesh.

Lend him to stroke these blind, blunt bullet-heads   5
Which long to nuzzle in the hearts of lads,
Or give him cartridges of fine zinc teeth,
Sharp with the sharpness of grief and death.

For his teeth seem for laughing round an apple.
There lurk no claws behind his fingers supple;   10
And God will grow no talons at his heels,
Nor antlers through the thickness of his curls.

E. E. Cummings (1894–1962)

in Just- [2]

in Just-
spring   when the world is mud-
luscious the little
lame balloonman

whistles   far   and wee

and eddieandbill come
running from marbles and
piracies and it's
spring

SOURCE: [1] Reprinted from *The Collected Poems of Wilfred Owen* with the permission of Chatto and Windus, Ltd., London; New Directions Publishing Corporation, New York; and Harold Owen. Copyright Chatto & Windus, Ltd. 1946, © 1963.

SOURCE: [2] Reprinted from *Poems 1923–1954* by E. E. Cummings with the permission of Harcourt Brace Jovanovich, Inc. Copyright 1923, 1951 by E. E. Cummings.

when the world is puddle-wonderful   10

the queer
old balloonman whistles
far   and   wee

and bettyandisbel come dancing

from hop-scotch and jump-rope and   15

it's
spring
and
    the

        goat-footed   20

balloonMan   whistles
far
and
wee

---

nobody loses all the time

   i had an uncle named
   Sol who was a born failure and
   nearly everybody said he should have gone
   into vaudeville perhaps because my Uncle Sol could
   sing McCann He Was A Diver on Xmas Eve like Hell Itself which   5
   may or may not account for the fact that my Uncle

   Sol indulged in that possibly most inexcusable
   of all to use a highfalootin phrase
   luxuries that is or to
   wit farming and be   10
   it needlessly
   added

SOURCE: Reprinted from *Poems 1923–1954* by E. E. Cummings with the permission of Harcourt Brace Jovanovich, Inc. Copyright 1926 by Horace Liveright. Copyright 1954 by E. E. Cummings.

my Uncle Sol's farm
failed because the chickens
ate the vegetables so   15
my Uncle Sol had a
chicken farm till the
skunks ate the chickens when

my Uncle Sol
had a skunk farm but   20
the skunks caught cold and
died and so
my Uncle Sol imitated the
skunks in a subtle manner

or by drowning himself in the watertank   25
but somebody who'd given my Uncle Sol a Victor
Victrola and records while he lived presented to
him upon the auspicious occasion of his decease a
scrumptious not to mention splendiferous funeral with
tall boys in black gloves and flowers and everything and   30

i remember we all cried like the Missouri
when my Uncle Sol's coffin lurched because
somebody pressed a button
(and down went
my Uncle   35
Sol

and started a worm farm)

_____

since feeling is first

since feeling is first
who pays any attention
to the syntax of things
will never wholly kiss you;

_____

wholly to be a fool
while Spring is in the world   5

my blood approves,
and kisses are a better fate
than wisdom
lady i swear by all flowers. Don't cry   10
—the best gesture of my brain is less than
your eyelids' flutter which says

we are for each other: then
laugh, leaning back in my arms
for life's not a paragraph   15

And death i think is no parenthesis

O sweet spontaneous

O sweet spontaneous
earth how often have
the
doting

       fingers of   5
prurient philosophers pinched
and
poked

thee
, has the naughty thumb
of science prodded   10
thy

     beauty   how
often have religions taken
thee upon their scraggy knees
squeezing and   15

SOURCE: Reprinted from *Poems 1923–1954* by E. E. Cummings with the permission of Harcourt Brace Jovanovich, Inc. Copyright 1923, 1951 by E. E. Cummings.

buffeting thee that thou mightest conceive
gods
      (but
true   20

to the incomparable
couch of death thy
rhythmic
lover

      thou answerest   25

them only with

          spring)

Space being(don't forget to remember)Curved

Space being(don't forget to remember)Curved
(and that reminds me who said o yes Frost
Something there is which isn't fond of walls)

an electromagnetic(now I've lost
the)Einstein expanded Newton's law preserved   5
conTinuum(but we read that beFore)

of Course life being just a Reflex you
know since Everything is Relative or

to sum it All Up god being Dead(not to

mention inTerred)   10
             LONG LIVE that Upwardlooking

SOURCE: Reprinted from *Poems 1923–1954* by E. E. Cummings with the permission of Harcourt Brace Jovanovich, Inc. Copyright 1931, 1959 by E. E. Cummings.

Serene Illustrious and Beatific
Lord of Creation, MAN:
                                    at a least crooking
of Whose compassionate digit,earth's most terrific   15

quadruped swoons into billiardBalls!

---

when serpents bargain for the right to squirm

when serpents bargain for the right to squirm
and the sun strikes to gain a living wage—
when thorns regard their roses with alarm
and rainbows are insured against old age

when every thrush may sing no new moon in   5
if all screech-owls have not okayed his voice
—and any wave signs on the dotted line
or else an ocean is compelled to close

when the oak begs permission of the birch
to make an acorn—valleys accuse their   10
mountains of having altitude—and march
denounces april as a saboteur

then we'll believe in that incredible
unanimal mankind(and not until)

SOURCE: Reprinted from *Poems 1923–1954* by E. E. Cummings with the permission of Harcourt Brace Jovanovich, Inc. Copyright 1950 by E. E. Cummings.

"next to of course god america i"

"next to of course god america i
love you land of the pilgrims' and so forth oh
say can you see by the dawn's early my
country 'tis of centuries come and go
and are no more what of it we should worry   5
in every language even deafanddumb
thy sons acclaim your glorious name by gorry
by jingo by gee by gosh by gum
why talk of beauty what could be more beautiful than these heroic happy dead   10
who rushed like lions to the roaring slaughter
they did not stop to think they died instead
then shall the voice of liberty be mute?"

He spoke.   And drank rapidly a glass of water

SOURCE: Reprinted from *Poems 1923–1954* by E. E. Cummings with the permission of Harcourt Brace Jovanovich, Inc. Copyright 1926 by Horace Liveright. Copyright 1954 by E. E. Cummings.

Poem, Or Beauty Hurts Mr. Vinal

take it from me kiddo
believe me
my country, 'tis of

you, land of the Cluett
Shirt Boston Garter and Spearmint   5
Girl With The Wrigley Eyes(of you
land of the Arrow Ide
and Earl &
Wilson
Collars) of you i   10
sing: land of Abraham Lincoln and Lydia E. Pinkham,
land above all of Just Add Hot Water and Serve—
from every B. V. D.

let freedom ring

amen. i do however protest, anent the un   15
-spontaneous and otherwise scented merde which
greets one (Everywhere Why) as divine poesy per
that and this radically defunct periodical. i would

suggest that certain ideas gestures
rhymes, like Gillette Razor Blades   20
having been used and reused
to the mystical moment of dullness emphatically are
Not To be Resharpened. (Case in point

if we are to believe these gently O sweetly
melancholy trillers amid the thrillers   25
these crepuscular violinists among my and your
skyscrapers—Helen & Cleopatra were Just Too Lovely,
The Snail's On The Thorn enter Morn and God's
In His andsoforth

SOURCE: Reprinted from *Poems 1923–1954* by E. E. Cummings with the permission of
Harcourt Brace Jovanovich, Inc. Copyright 1926 by Horace Liveright. Copyright 1954 by
E. E. Cummings.

do you get me?)according   30
to such supposedly indigenous
throstles Art is O World O Life
a formula:example, Turn Your Shirttails Into
Drawers and If It Isn't An Eastman It Isn't A
Kodak therefore my friends let   35
us now sing each and all fortissimo A-
mer
i

ca, I
love,   40
You. And there're a
hun-dred-mil-lion-oth-ers, like
all of you successfully if
delicately gelded(or spaded)
gentlemen(and ladies)—pretty   45

littleliverpill-
hearted-Nujolneeding-There's-A-Reason
americans(who tensetendoned and with
upward vacant eyes, painfully
perpetually crouched, quivering, upon the   50
sternly allotted sandpile
—how silently
emit a tiny violetflavoured nuisance:Odor?

ono.
comes out like a ribbon lies flat on the brush   55

---

pity this busy monster,manunkind

pity this busy monster,manunkind,

not. Progress is a comfortable disease:
your victim(death and life safely beyond)

plays with the bigness of his littleness
—electrons deify one razorblade   5
into a mountainrange;lenses extend

SOURCE: Reprinted from *Poems 1923–1954* by E. E. Cummings with the permission of Harcourt Brace Jovanovich, Inc. Copyright 1944 by E. E. Cummings.

unwish through curving wherewhen till unwish
returns on its unself.
                              A world of made
is not a world of born—pity poor flesh   10

and trees,poor stars and stones,but never this
fine specimen of hypermagical

ultraomnipotence.   We doctors know

a hopeless case if—listen:there's a hell
of a good universe next door;let's go   15

---

anyone lived in a pretty how town

anyone lived in a pretty how town
(with up so floating many bells down)
spring summer autumn winter
he sang his didn't he danced his did.

Women and men(both little and small)   5
cared for anyone not at all
they sowed their isn't they reaped their same
sun moon stars rain

children guessed(but only a few
and down they forgot as up they grew
autumn winter spring summer)   10
that noone loved him more by more

when by now and tree by leaf
she laughed his joy she cried his grief
bird by snow and stir by still
anyone's any was all to her   15

someones married their everyones
laughed their cryings and did their dance
(sleep wake hope and then)they
said their nevers they slept their dream   20

stars rain sun moon
(and only the snow can begin to explain
how children are apt to forget to remember
with up so floating many bells down)

one day anyone died i guess   25
(and noone stooped to kiss his face)
busy folk buried them side by side
little by little and was by was

all by all and deep by deep
and more by more they dream their sleep   30
noone and anyone earth by april
wish by spirit and if by yes.

Women and men(both dong and ding)
summer and autumn winter spring
reaped their sowing and went their came   35
sun moon stars rain

---

you shall above all things be glad and young

you shall above all things be glad and young.
For if you're young,whatever life you wear

it will become you;and if you are glad
whatever's living will yourself become.
Girlboys may nothing more than boygirls need: 5
i can entirely her only love

whose any mystery makes every man's
flesh put space on;and his mind take off time

that you should ever think, may god forbid
and(in his mercy)your true lover spare: 10
for that way knowledge lies,the foetal grave
called progress,and negation's dead undoom.

I'd rather learn from one bird how to sing
than teach ten thousand stars how not to dance

SOURCE: Reprinted from *Poems 1923–1954* by E. E. Cummings with the permission of Harcourt Brace Jovanovich, Inc. Copyright 1938 by E. E. Cummings. Copyright 1966 by Marion Morehouse Cummings.

Kenneth Fearing (b. 1902)

Portrait (2)

The clear brown eyes, kindly and alert, with 12-20 vision, give confident
   regard to the passing world through R. K. Lampert & Company lenses
   framed in gold;
His soul, however, is all his own;

Arndt Brothers necktie and hat (with feather) supply a touch of youth.
With his soul his own, he drives, drives, chats and drives,
The first and second bicuspids, lower right, replaced by bridgework,
   while two incisors have porcelain crowns;   5

(Render unto Federal, state and city Caesar, but not unto time;
Render nothing unto time until Amalgamated Death serves final notice,
   in proper form;

   The vault is ready;
   The will has been drawn by Clagget, Clagget, Clagget & Brown;
   The policies are adequate, Confidential's best, reimbursing for disa-
      bility, partial or complete, with double indemnity should the end
   be a pure and simple accident)   10

Nothing unto time,
Nothing unto change, nothing unto fate,
Nothing unto you, and nothing unto me, or to any other known or
   unknown party or parties, living or deceased;

But Mercury shoes, with special arch supports, take much of the wear
   and tear:
On the course, a custombuilt driver corrects a tendency to slice;   15
Love's ravages have been repaired (it was a textbook case) by Drs.
   Schultz, Lightner, Mannheim, and Goode,
While all of it is enclosed in excellent tweed, with Mr. Baumer's per-
   sonal attention to the shoulders and the waist;

And all of it now roving, chatting amiably through space in a Plymouth
   6.
With his soul (his own) at peace, soothed by Walter Lippmann, and
   sustained by Haig & Haig.

SOURCE: Reprinted from *Afternoon of a Pawnbroker and Other Poems* by Kenneth Fearing
with the permission of Indiana University Press, Bloomington, Indiana. Copyright 1943 by
Kenneth Fearing.

Travelogue in a Shooting-Gallery

There is a jungle, there is a jungle, there is a vast, vivid, wild, wild,
    marvelous, marvelous, marvelous jungle,
Open to the public during business hours,
A jungle not very far from an Automat, between a hat store there, and
    a radio shop.

There, there, whether it rains, or it snows, or it shines,
Under the hot, blazing, cloudless, tropical neon skies that the manage-
    ment always arranges there,   5
Rows and rows of marching ducks, dozens and dozens and dozens of
    ducks, move steadily along on smoothly-oiled ballbearing feet,
Ducks as big as telephone books, slow and fearless and out of this
    world,
While lines and lines of lions, lions, rabbits, panthers, elephants, croco-
    diles, zebras, apes,
Filled with jungle hunger and jungle rage and jungle love,
Stalk their prey on endless, endless rotary belts through never-ending
    forests, and burning deserts, and limitless veldts,   10
To the sound of tom-toms, equipped with silencers, beaten by thou-
    sands of savages hidden there.

And there it is that all the big game hunters go, there the traders and
    the explorers come,
Leanfaced men with windswept eyes who arrive by streetcar, auto or
    subway, taxi or on foot, streetcar or bus,
And they nod, and they say, and they need no more:
"There . . . there . . .   15
There they come and there they go."

And weighing machines, in this civilized jungle, will read your soul like
    an open book, for a penny at a time, and tell you all,
There, there, where smoking is permitted,
In a jungle that lies, like a rainbow's end, at the very end of every trail,
There, in the only jungle in the whole wide world where ducks are
    waiting for streetcars,   20
And hunters can be psychoanalyzed, while they smoke and wait for
    ducks.

SOURCE: Reprinted from *Afternoon of a Pawnbroker and Other Poems* by Kenneth Fearing
with the permission of Harcourt Brace Jovanovich, Inc., New York, and Indiana University
Press, Bloomington, Indiana. Copyright 1943 by Kenneth Fearing.

Langston Hughes (1902–1967)

Deferred

This year, maybe, do you think I can graduate?
I'm already two years late.
Dropped out six months when I was seven,
a year when I was eleven,
then got put back when we came North.   5
To get through high at twenty's kind of late—
But maybe this year I can graduate.

Maybe now I can have that white enamel stove
I dreamed about when we first fell in love
eighteen years ago.   10
But you know,
rooming and everything
then kids,
cold-water flat and all that.
But now my daughter's married   15
And my boy's most grown—
quit school to work—
and where we're moving
there ain't no stove—
Maybe I can buy that white enamel stove!   20

Me, I always did want to study French.
It don't make sense—
I'll never go to France,
but night schools teach French.
Now at last I've got a job   25
where I get off at five,
in time to wash and dress,
so, si'l-vous plait, I'll study French!

Someday,
I'm gonna buy two new suits   30
at once!

All I want is
one more bottle of gin.

SOURCE: Reprinted from *Montage of a Dream Deferred* by Langston Hughes with the permission of Harold Ober Associates, Inc. Copyright 1951 by Langston Hughes.

All I want is to see
my furniture paid for.   35

All I want is a wife who will
work with me and not against me. Say,
baby, could you see your way clear?

Heaven, heaven, is my home!
This world I'll leave behind   40
When I set my feet in glory
I'll have a throne for mine!

I want to pass the civil service.

I want a television set.

You know, as old as I am,   45
I ain't never
owned a decent radio yet?

I'd like to take up Bach.

Montage
of a dream   50
deferred.

Buddy, have you heard?

Richard Eberhart (b.1904)

On a Squirrel Crossing the Road in Autumn, in New England

It is what he does not know,
Crossing the road under the elm trees,
About the mechanism of my car,
About the Commonwealth of Massachusetts,
About Mozart, India, Arcturus,   5

SOURCE: Reprinted from *Collected Poems 1930–1960* by Richard Eberhart with the permission of Chatto & Windus, Ltd., London and Oxford University Press, Inc., New York. Copyright ©1960 by Richard Eberhart.

That wins my praise. I engage
At once in whirling squirrel-praise.

He obeys the orders of nature
Without knowing them.
It is what he does not know   10
That makes him beautiful.
Such a knot of little purposeful nature!
I who can see him as he cannot see himself
Repose in the ignorance that is his blessing.

It is what man does not know of God   15
Composes the visible poem of the world.

                    . . . Just missed him!

The Horse Chestnut Tree

Boys in sporadic but tenacious droves
Come with sticks, as certainly as Autumn,
To assault the great horse chestnut tree.

There is a law governs their lawlessness.
Desire is in them for a shining amulet   5
And the best are those that are highest up.

They will not pick them easily from the ground.
With shrill arms they fling to the higher branches,
To hurry the work of nature for their pleasure.

I have seen them trooping down the street   10
Their pockets stuffed with chestnuts shucked, unshucked.
It is only evening keeps them from their wish.

Sometimes I run out in a kind of rage
To chase the boys away: I catch an arm,
Maybe, and laugh to think of being the lawgiver.   15

SOURCE: Reprinted from *Collected Poems 1930–1960* by Richard Eberhart with the permission of Chatto & Windus, Ltd., London and Oxford University Press, Inc., New York. Copyright ©1960 by Richard Eberhart.

I was once such a young sprout myself
And fingered in my pocket the prize and trophy.
But still I moralize upon the day

And see that we, outlaws on God's property,
Fling out imagination beyond the skies,   20
Wishing a tangible good from the unknown.

And likewise death will drive us from the scene
With the great flowering world unbroken yet,
Which we held in idea, a little handful.

On Shooting Particles beyond the World

*"White Sands, N. M. Dec. 18 (UP). 'We first throw a little something into the skies,'
Zwicky said. 'Then a little more, then a shipload of instruments—then ourselves.' "*

On this day man's disgust is known
Incipient before but now full blown
With minor wars of major consequence,
Duly building empirical delusions.

Now this little creature in a rage   5
Like new-born infant screaming compleat angler
Objects to the whole globe itself
And with a vicious lunge he throws

Metal particles beyond the orbit of mankind.
Beethoven shaking his first at death,   10
A giant dignity in human terms,
Is nothing to this imbecile fury.

The world is too much for him. The green
Of earth is not enough, love's deities,
Peaceful intercourse, happiness of nations,   15
The wild animal dazzled on the desert.

SOURCE: Reprinted from *Collected Poems 1930–1960* by Richard Eberhart, with the permission of Chatto & Windus, Ltd., London and Oxford University Press, Inc., New York. Copyright ©1960 by Richard Eberhart.

If the maniac would only realize
The comforts of his padded cell
He would have penetrated the
Impenetrability of the spiritual.   20

It is not intelligent to go too far.
How he frets that he can't go too!
But his particles would maim a star,
His free-floating bombards rock the moon.

Good Boy! We pat the baby to eructate,   25
We pat him then for eructation.
Good Boy Man! Your innards are put out,
From now all space will be your vomitorium.

The atom bomb accepted this world,
Its hatred of man blew death in his face.   30
But not content, he'll send slugs beyond,
His particles of intellect will spit on the sun.

Not God he'll catch, in the mystery of space.
He flaunts his own out-cast state
As he throws his imperfections outward bound,   35
And his shout that gives a hissing sound.

Villanelle

Christ is walking in your blood today,
His gentle tread you cannot hear nor see.
He tramples down your militant wish to slay.

The whelped deaths you dealt in your war's day
Arise howling, they will never make you free.   5
Christ is walking in your blood today.

You did it easily in the heat of the fray.
You did not know what you could do, could be.
He tramples down the massive wish to slay.

You are the front and fore of passion's play,   10
Of deepest knowledge you have lost the key.
Christ is walking in your blood today.

To kill is one, is not the essential way
Of action, which you then could not foresee.
He will wash the welling blood. Not slay.   15

A child becomes a man who learns to pray,
A child-like silence on a moveless sea.
Redeemed you may be of the will to slay.
Christ fermentative be all your blood today.

The Fury of Aerial Bombardment

You would think the fury of aerial bombardment
Would rouse God to relent; the infinite spaces
Are still silent. He looks on shock-pried faces.
History, even, does not know what is meant.

You would feel that after so many centuries   5
God would give man to repent; yet he can kill
As Cain could, but with multitudinous will,
No farther advanced than in his ancient furies.

Was man made stupid to see his own stupidity?
Is God by definition indifferent, beyond us all?   10
Is the eternal truth man's fighting soul
Wherein the Beast ravens in its own avidity?

Of Van Wettering I speak, and Averill,
Names on a list, whose faces I do not recall
But they are gone to early death, who late in school   15
Distinguished the belt feed lever from the belt holding pawl.

SOURCE: Reprinted from *Collected Poems 1930–1960*, by Richard Eberhart, with the permission of Chatto & Windus, Ltd., London and Oxford University Press, Inc., New York. Copyright © 1960 by Richard Eberhart.

Phyllis McGinley (b.1905)

The Angry Man [1]

The other day I chanced to meet
An angry man upon the street—
A man of wrath, a man of war,
A man who truculently bore
Over his shoulder, like a lance,
A banner labeled "Tolerance."   5

And when I asked him why he strode
Thus scowling down the human road,
Scowling, he answered, "I am he
Who champions total liberty—
Intolerance being, ma'am, a state   10
No tolerant man can tolerate."

"When I meet rogues," he cried, "who choose
To cherish oppositional views,
Lady, like this, and in this manner,
I lay about me with my banner   15
Till they cry mercy, ma'am." His blows
Rained proudly on prospective foes.
Fearful, I turned and left him there
Still muttering, as he thrashed the air,
"Let the Intolerant beware!"   20

A. D. Hope (b. 1907)

Imperial Adam [2]

Imperial Adam, naked in the dew,
Felt his brown flanks and found the rib was gone.
Puzzled he turned and saw where, two and two,
The mighty spoor of Jahweh marked the lawn.

SOURCE: [1] Reprinted from *Times Three* by Phyllis McGinley with the permission of The Viking Press, Inc. Copyright 1954 by Phyllis McGinley.

SOURCE: [2] Reprinted from *Collected Poems 1930–1965* by A. D. Hope with the permission of The Viking Press, Inc. Copyright 1963, 1966 in all countries of the International Copyright Union by A. D. Hope. All rights reserved.

Then he remembered through mysterious sleep   5
The surgeon fingers probing at the bone,
The voice so far away, so rich and deep:
"It is not good for him to live alone."

Turning once more he found Man's counterpart
In tender parody breathing at his side.   10
He knew her at first sight, he knew by heart
Her allegory of sense unsatisfied.

The pawpaw drooped its golden breasts above
Less generous than the honey of her flesh;
The innocent sunlight showed the place of love;   15
The dew on its dark hairs winked crisp and fresh.

This plump gourd severed from his virile root,
She promised on the turf of Paradise
Delicious pulp of the forbidden fruit;
Sly as the snake she loosed her sinuous thighs,   20

And waking, smiled up at him from the grass;
Her breasts rose softly and he heard her sigh—
From all the beasts whose pleasant task it was
In Eden to increase and multiply

Adam had learned the jolly deed of kind: 25
He took her in his arms and there and then,
Like the clean beasts, embracing from behind,
Began in joy to found the breed of men.

Then from the spurt of seed within her broke
Her terrible and triumphant female cry,   30
Split upward by the sexual lightning stroke.
It was the beasts now who stood watching by:

The gravid elephant, the calving hind,
The breeding bitch, the she-ape big with young
Were the first gentle midwives of mankind;   35
The teeming lioness rasped her with her tongue;

The proud vicuña nuzzled her as she slept
Lax on the grass; and Adam watching too
Saw how her dumb breasts at their ripening wept,
The great pod of her belly swelled and grew,   40

And saw its water break, and saw, in fear,
Its quaking muscles in the act of birth,
Between her legs a pigmy face appear,
And the first murderer lay upon the earth.

W. H. Auden (b. 1907)

"O Where Are You Going?"

"O where are you going?" said reader to rider,
"That valley is fatal when furnaces burn,
Yonder's the midden whose odours will madden,
That gap is the grave where the tall return."

"O do you imagine," said fearer to farer,   5
"That dusk will delay on your path to the pass,
Your diligent looking discover the lacking
Your footsteps feel from granite to grass?"

"O what was that bird," said horror to hearer,
"Did you see that shape in the twisted trees?   10
Behind you swiftly the figure comes softly,
The spot on your skin is a shocking disease?"

"Out of this house"—said rider to reader,
"Yours never will"—said farer to fearer,
"They're looking for you"—said hearer to horror,   15
As he left them there, as he left them there.

SOURCE: Reprinted from *Collected Shorter Poems 1927–1957* by W. H. Auden with the permission of Faber and Faber, Ltd., London and Random House, Inc., New York. Copyright 1934, 1962 by W. H. Auden.

The Unknown Citizen

(To JS/07/M/378   *This Marble Monument Is Erected by the State)*

He was found by the Bureau of Statistics to be
One against whom there was no official complaint,
And all the reports on his conduct agree
That, in the modern sense of an old-fashioned word, he was a saint,
For in everything he did he served the Greater Community.   5
Except for the War till the day he retired
He worked in a factory and never got fired,
But satisfied his employers, Fudge Motors Inc.
Yet he wasn't a scab or odd in his views,
For his Union reports that he paid his dues,   10
(Our report on his Union shows it was sound)
And our Social Psychology workers found
That he was popular with his mates and liked a drink.
The Press are convinced that he bought a paper every day
And that his reactions to advertisements were normal in every way.   15
Policies taken out in his name prove that he was fully insured,
And his Health-card shows he was once in hospital but left it cured.
Both Producers Research and High-Grade Living declare
He was fully sensible to the advantages of the Installment Plan
And had everything necessary to the Modern Man,   20
A phonograph, a radio, a car and a frigidaire.
Our researchers into Public Opinion are content
That he held the proper opinions for the time of year;
When there was peace, he was for peace; when there was war, he went.
He was married and added five children to the population,   25
Which our Eugenist says was the right number for a parent of his
     generation,
And our teachers report that he never interfered with their education.
Was he free? Was he happy? The question is absurd:
Had anything been wrong, we should certainly have heard.

SOURCE: Reprinted from *Collected Shorter Poems 1927–1957* by W. H. Auden with the permission of Faber and Faber, Ltd., London and Random House, Inc., New York. Copyright 1940, 1968 by W. H. Auden.

In Memory of W. B. Yeats *(d. Jan. 1939)*

I

He disappeared in the dead of winter:
The brooks were frozen, the airports almost deserted,
And snow disfigured the public statues;
The mercury sank in the mouth of the dying day.
What instruments we have agree   5
The day of his death was a dark cold day.

Far from his illness
The wolves ran on through the evergreen forests,
The peasant river was untempted by the fashionable quays;
By mourning tongues
The death of the poet was kept from his poems.   10

But for him it was his last afternoon as himself,
An afternoon of nurses and rumours;
The provinces of his body revolted,
The squares of his mind were empty,
Silence invaded the suburbs,   15
The current of his feeling failed; he became his admirers.

Now he is scattered among a hundred cities
And wholly given over to unfamiliar affections,
To find his happiness in another kind of wood   20
And be punished under a foreign code of conscience.
The words of a dead man
Are modified in the guts of the living.

But in the importance and noise of to-morrow
When the brokers are roaring like beasts on the floor of the Bourse, 25
And the poor have the sufferings to which they are fairly accustomed,
And each in the cell of himself is almost convinced of his freedom,
A few thousand will think of this day
As one thinks of a day when one did something slightly unusual.
What instruments we have agree   30
The day of his death was a dark cold day.

SOURCE: Reprinted from *Collected Shorter Poems 1927-1957* by W. H. Auden with the permission of Faber and Faber, Ltd., London and Random House, Inc., New York. Copyright 1940, 1968 by W. H. Auden.

II

You were silly like us; your gift survived it all:
The parish of rich women, physical decay,
Yourself. Mad Ireland hurt you into poetry.
Now Ireland has her madness and her weather still,   35
For poetry makes nothing happen: it survives
In the valley of its making where executives
Would never want to tamper, flows on south
From ranches of isolation and the busy griefs,
Raw towns that we believe and die in; it survives,   40
A way of happening, a mouth.

III

Earth, receive an honoured guest:
William Yeats is laid to rest.
Let the Irish vessel lie
Emptied of its poetry.   45

In the nightmare of the dark
All the dogs of Europe bark,
And the living nations wait,
Each sequestered in its hate;

Intellectual disgrace   50
Stares from every human face,
And the seas of pity lie
Locked and frozen in each eye.

Follow, poet, follow right
To the bottom of the night,   55
With your unconstraining voice
Still persuade us to rejoice;

With the farming of a verse
Make a vineyard of the curse,
Sing of human unsuccess   60
In a rapture of distress;

In the deserts of the heart
Let the healing fountain start,
In the prison of his days
Teach the free man how to praise.   65

Theodore Roethke (1908–1963)

Dolor

I have known the inexorable sadness of pencils,
Neat in their boxes, dolor of pad and paper-weight,
All the misery of manilla folders and mucilage,
Desolation in immaculate public places,
Lonely reception room, lavatory, switchboard,   5
The unalterable pathos of basin and pitcher,
Ritual of multigraph, paper-clip, comma,
Endless duplication of lives and objects.
And I have seen dust from the walls of institutions,
Finer than flour, alive, more dangerous than silica,   10
Sift, almost invisible, through long afternoons of tedium,
Dropping a fine film on nails and delicate eyebrows,
Glazing the pale hair, the duplicate gray standard faces.

SOURCE: Reprinted from *The Collected Poems of Theodore Roethke* with the permission of Doubleday & Company, Inc. Copyright 1943 by Modern Poetry Association, Inc.

Elder Olson (b. 1909)

Plot Improbable, Character Unsympathetic

I was born in a bad slum
Where no one had to die
To show his skeleton.
The wind came through the walls,
A three-legged rat and I   5
Fought all day for swill.
My father was crazed, my mother cruel
My brothers chopped the stairs for fuel,
I tumbled my sisters in a broken bed
And jiggled them till all were dead.   10
Then I ran away and lived with my lice
On my wits, a knife, and a pair of dice,
Slept like a rat in the river reeds,
Got converted fifty times
To fifty different creeds   15
For bowls of mission broth,
Till I killed the grocer and his wife
With a stove-poker and a butcher-knife.
The mayor said, Hang him high,
The merchants said, He won't buy or sell,   20
The bishop said, He won't pay to pray.
They flung me into a jail,
But I, I broke out,
Beat my bars to a bell,
Ran all around the town   25
Dingling my sweet bell,
And the mayor wanted it for his hall,
The merchants wanted to buy it,
The bishop wanted it for his church,
But I broke my bell in two,   30
Of one half a huge bullet made,
Of the other an enormous gun,
Took all the people of all the world
And rolled them into one,
And when the World went by   35
With a monocle in his eye,
With a silk hat on his head,
Took aim and shot him dead.

SOURCE: Reprinted from *The Scarecrow Christ* by Elder Olson with the permission of Farrar, Straus & Giroux. Copyright 1954 by Elder Olson.

Stephen Spender (b. 1909)

An Elementary School Classroom in a Slum

Far far from gusty waves, these children's faces.
Like rootless weeds the torn hair round their paleness.
The tall girl with her weighed-down head. The paper-
seeming boy with rat's eyes. The stunted unlucky heir
Of twisted bones, reciting a father's gnarled disease,   5
His lesson from his desk. At back of the dim class,
One unnoted, sweet and young: his eyes live in a dream
Of squirrels' game, in tree room, other than this.

On sour cream walls, donations. Shakespeare's head
Cloudless at dawn, civilized dome riding all cities.   10
Belled, flowery, Tyrolese valley. Open-handed map
Awarding the world its world. And yet, for these
Children, these windows, not this world, are world,
Where all their future's painted with a fog,
A narrow street sealed in with a lead sky,   15
Far far from rivers, capes, and stars of words.

Surely Shakespeare is wicked, the map a bad example
With ships and sun and love tempting them to steal—
For lives that slyly turn in their cramped holes
From fog to endless night? On their slag heap, these children   20
Wear skins peeped through by bones and spectacles of steel
With mended glass, like bottle bits on stones.
All of their time and space are foggy slum
So blot their maps with slums as big as doom.

Unless, governor, teacher, inspector, visitor,   25
This map becomes their window and these windows
That open on their lives like crouching tombs
Break, O break open, till they break the town
And show the children to the fields and all their world
Azure on their sands, to let their tongues   30
Run naked into books, the white and green leaves open
The history theirs whose language is the sun.

SOURCE: Reprinted from *Collected Poems 1928–1953* by Stephen Spender with the permission of Faber and Faber, Ltd., London and Random House, Inc., New York. Copyright 1942 by Stephen Spender.

Josephine Miles (b. 1911)

Government Injunction Restraining Harlem Cosmetic Co.

They say La Jac Brite Pink Skin Bleach avails not,
They say its Orange Beauty Glow does not glow,
Nor the face grow five shades lighter nor the heart
Five shades lighter. They say no.

They deny good luck, love, power, romance, and inspiration   5
From La Jac Brite ointment and incense of all kinds,
And condemn in writing skin brightening and whitening
And whitening of minds.

There is upon the federal trade commission a burden of glory
So to defend the fact, so to impel   10
The plucking of hope from the hand, honor from the complexion,
Sprite from the spell.

SOURCE: Reprinted from *Poems 1930–1960* by Josephine Miles with the permission of Indiana University Press.

Kenneth Patchen (b. 1911)

In Order To[1]

Apply for the position (I've forgotten now for what) I
had to marry the Second Mayor's daughter by twelve noon.
The order arrived three minutes of.

I already had a wife; the Second Mayor was childless:
but I did it.

Next they told me to shave off my father's beard. All
right. No matter that he'd been a eunuch, and had succumbed
in early childhood: I did it, I shaved him.

Then they told me to burn a village; next, a fair-sized town;
then, a city; a bigger city; a small, down-at-heels country;
then one of 'the great powers'; then another (another, another)— In fact, they went right on until they'd told me
to burn up every man-made thing on the face of the earth!
And I did it, I burned away every last trace, I left nothing,
nothing of any kind whatever.

Then they told me to blow it all to hell and gone! And I
blew it all to hell and gone (oh, didn't I!) . . .

Now, they said, put it back together again; put it all back
the way it was when you started.

Well . . . it was my turn then to tell *them* something!
Shucks, I didn't want any job that bad.

Anonymous

My Mother's Hands

Such beautiful, beautiful hands!
   They're neither white nor small;
And you, I know, would scarcely think
   That they were fair at all.
I've looked on hands whose form and hue   5
   A sculptor's dream might be;
Yet are those wrinkled, aged hands
   Most beautiful to me.

SOURCE: [1]Reprinted from *Collected Poems* by Kenneth Patchen with the permission of New
Directions Publishing Corporation. Copyright 1954 by New Directions Publishing Corporation.

Such beautiful, beautiful hands!
  Though heart were weary and sad,   10
These patient hands kept toiling on,
  That the children might be glad;
I always weep, as looking back
  To childhood's distant day,
I think how those hands rested not,   15
  When mine were at their play.

Such beautiful, beautiful hands!
  They're growing feeble now,
For time and pain have left their mark
  On hands, and heart, and brow.   20
Alas! alas! the nearing time,
  And the sad, sad day to me,
When 'neath the daisies, out of sight,
  These hands will folded be.

But oh, beyond this shadow land,   25
  Where all is bright and fair,
I know full well these dear old hands
  Will palms of victory bear;
Where crystal streams through endless years
  Flow over golden sands,   30
And where the old grow young again,
  I'll clasp my mother's hands.

                                        Nineteenth Century

George Barker (b. 1913)

To My Mother [1]

Most near, most dear, most loved and most far,
Under the window where I often found her
Sitting as huge as Asia, seismic with laughter,
Gin and chicken helpless in her Irish hand,
Irresistible as Rabelais, but most tender for   5
The lame dogs and hurt birds that surround her,—
She is a procession no one can follow after
But be like a little dog following a brass band.
She will not glance up at the bomber, or condescend
To drop her gin and scuttle to a cellar,   10
But lean on the mahogany table like a mountain
Whom only faith can move, and so I send
O all my faith, and all my love to tell her
That she will move from mourning into morning.

Delmore Schwartz (1913–1966)

The Heavy Bear Who Goes with Me [2]   *"the withness of the body"*
                                                          —Whitehead

The heavy bear who goes with me,
A manifold honey to smear his face,
Clumsy and lumbering here and there,
The central ton of every place,
The hungry beating brutish one   5
In love with candy, anger, and sleep,
Crazy factotum, dishevelling all,
Climbs the building, kicks the football,
Boxes his brother in the hate-ridden city.

SOURCE: [1] Reprinted from *Collected Poems 1930–1955* by George Barker with the permission of Faber and Faber, Ltd., London and October House, Inc., New York. Copyright © 1957, 1962, 1965 by George Granville Barker.

SOURCE: [2] Reprinted from *Selected Poems: Summer Knowledge* by Delmore Schwartz with the permission of New Directions Publishing Corporation. Copyright 1938 by New Directions Publishing Corporation.

Breathing at my side, that heavy animal,   10
That heavy bear who sleeps with me,
Howls in his sleep for a world of sugar,
A sweetness intimate as the water's clasp,
Howls in his sleep because the tight-rope
Trembles and shows the darkness beneath.   15
—The strutting show-off is terrified,
Dressed in his dress-suit, bulging his pants,
Trembles to think that his quivering meat
Must finally wince to nothing at all.

That inescapable animal walks with me,   20
Has followed me since the black womb held,
Moves where I move, distorting my gesture,
A caricature, a swollen shadow,
A stupid clown of the spirit's motive,
Perplexes and affronts with his own darkness,   25
The secret life of belly and bone,
Opaque, too near, my private, yet unknown,
Stretches to embrace the very dear
With whom I would walk without him near,
Touches her grossly, although a word   30
Would bare my heart and make me clear,
Stumbles, flounders, and strives to be fed,
Dragging me with him in his mouthing care,
Amid the hundred million of his kind,
The scrimmage of appetite everywhere.   35

Karl Shapiro (b. 1913)

The Dirty Word

The dirty word hops in the cage of the mind like the Pondi-
cherry vulture, stomping with its heavy left claw on the sweet
meat of the brain and tearing it with its vicious beak, ripping
and chopping the flesh. Terrified, the small boy bears the big bird
of the dirty word into the house, and grunting, puffing,   5
carries it up the stairs to his own room in the skull. Bits of
black feather cling to his clothes and his hair as he locks the
staring creature in the dark closet.

SOURCE: Reprinted from *Poems 1940–1953* by Karl Shapiro with the permission of Random House, Inc. Copyright 1947 by Karl Shapiro.

All day the small boy returns to the closet to examine and feed the bird, to caress and kick the bird, that now snaps and 10 flaps its wings savagely whenever the door is opened. How the boy trembles and delights at the sight of the white excrement of the bird! How the bird leaps and rushes against the walls of the skull, trying to escape from the zoo of the vocabulary! How wildly snaps the sweet meat of the brain in its rage.   15

And the bird outlives the man, being freed at the man's death-funeral by a word from the rabbi.

(But I one morning went upstairs and opened the door and entered the closet and found in the cage of my mind the great bird dead. Softly I wept it and softly removed it and softly 20 buried the body of the bird in the hollyhock garden of the house I lived in twenty years before. And out of the worn black feathers of the wing have I made these pens to write these elegies, for I have outlived the bird, and I have murdered it in my early manhood.)   25

Auto Wreck

Its quick soft silver bell beating, beating,
And down the dark one ruby flare
Pulsing out red light like an artery,
The ambulance at top speed floating down
Past beacons and illuminated clocks   5
Wings in a heavy curve, dips down,
And brakes speed, entering the crowd.
The doors leap open, emptying light;
Stretchers are laid out, the mangled lifted
And stowed into the little hospital.   10
Then the bell, breaking the hush, tolls once,
And the ambulance with its terrible cargo
Rocking, slightly rocking, moves away,
As the doors, an afterthought, are closed.

SOURCE: Reprinted from *Poems 1940-1953* by Karl Shapiro with the permission of Random House, Inc. Copyright 1941 by Karl Shapiro.

We are deranged, walking among the cops   15
Who sweep glass and are large and composed.
One is still making notes under the light.
One with a bucket douches ponds of blood
Into the street and gutter.
One hangs lanterns on the wrecks that cling,   20
Empty husks of locusts, to iron poles.

Our throats were tight as tourniquets,
Our feet were bound with splints, but now,
Like convalescents intimate and gauche,
We speak through sickly smiles and warn   25
With the stubborn saw of common sense,
The grim joke and the banal resolution.
The traffic moves around with care,
But we remain, touching a wound
That opens to our richest horror.   30
Already old, the question Who shall die?
Becomes unspoken Who is innocent?
For death in war is done by hands;
Suicide has cause and stillbirth, logic;
And cancer, simple as a flower, blooms.   35
But this invites the occult mind,
Cancels our physics with a sneer,
And spatters all we knew of denouement
Across the expedient and wicked stones.

Dylan Thomas (1914–1953)

Fern Hill

Now as I was young and easy under the apple boughs
About the lilting house and happy as the grass was green,
        The night above the dingle° starry,   *wooded valley*
        Time let me hail and climb
        Golden in the heydays of his eyes,   5

SOURCE: Reprinted from *Collected Poems of Dylan Thomas* with the permission of J. M. Dent & Sons, Ltd., London and New Directions Publishing Corporation, New York. Copyright 1939, 1943, 1946 by New Directions Publishing Corporation. Copyright 1952 by Dylan Thomas.

And honored among wagons I was prince of the apple towns
And once below a time I lordly had the trees and leaves
    Trail with daisies and barley
    Down the rivers of the windfall light.

And as I was green and carefree, famous among the barns   10
About the happy yard and singing as the farm was home,
    In the sun that is young once only,
      Time let me play and be
    Golden in the mercy of his means,
And green and golden I was huntsman and herdsman, the calves   15
Sang to my horn, the foxes on the hills barked clear and cold,
    And the sabbath rang slowly
    In the pebbles of the holy streams.

All the sun long it was running, it was lovely, the hay
Fields high as the house, the tunes from the chimneys, it was air   20
    And playing, lovely and watery
      And fire green as grass.
    And nightly under the simple stars
As I rode to sleep the owls were bearing the farm away,
All the moon long I heard, blessed among stables, the nightjars   25
    Flying with the ricks, and the horses
      Flashing into the dark.

And then to awake, and the farm, like a wanderer white
With the dew, come back, the cock on his shoulder: it was all
    Shining, it was Adam and maiden,   30
      The sky gathered again
    And the sun grew round that very day.
So it must have been after the birth of the simple light
In the first, spinning place, the spellbound horses walking warm
    Out of the whinnying green stable   35
      On to the fields of praise.

And honored among foxes and pheasants by the gay house
Under the new made clouds and happy as the heart was long,
    In the sun born over and over,
      I ran my heedless ways,   40
    My wishes raced through the house high hay
And nothing I cared, at my sky blue trades, that time allows
In all his tuneful turning so few and such morning songs
    Before the children green and golden
      Follow him out of grace,   45

Nothing I cared, in the lamb white days, that time would take me
Up to the swallow thronged loft by the shadow of my hand,
    In the moon that is always rising,
      Nor that riding to sleep
    I should hear him fly with the high fields   50
And wake to the farm forever fled from the childless land.
Oh as I was young and easy in the mercy of his means,
      Time held me green and dying
    Though I sang in my chains like the sea.

The Force That Through the Green Fuse Drives the Flower

The force that through the green fuse drives the flower
Drives my green age; that blasts the roots of trees
Is my destroyer.
And I am dumb to tell the crooked rose
My youth is bent by the same wintry fever.   5

The force that drives the water through the rocks
Drives my red blood; that dries the mouthing streams
Turns mine to wax.
And I am dumb to mouth unto my veins
How at the mountain spring the same mouth sucks.   10

The hand that whirls the water in the pool
Stirs the quicksand; that ropes the blowing wind
Hauls my shroud sail.
And I am dumb to tell the hanging man
How of my clay is made the hangman's lime.   15

The lips of time leech to the fountain head;
Love drips and gathers, but the fallen blood
Shall calm her sores.
And I am dumb to tell a weather's wind
How time has ticked a heaven round the stars.   20

And I am dumb to tell the lover's tomb
How at my sheet goes the same crooked worm.

SOURCE: Reprinted from *Collected Poems of Dylan Thomas* with the permission of J. M. Dent
& Sons, Ltd., London and New Directions Publishing Corporation, New York. Copyright
1939, 1943, 1946 by New Directions Publishing Corporation. Copyright 1952 by Dylan
Thomas.

And Death Shall Have No Dominion

And death shall have no dominion.
Dead men naked they shall be one
With the man in the wind and the west moon;
When their bones are picked clean and the clean bones gone,
They shall have stars at elbow and foot;   5
Though they go mad they shall be sane,
Though they sink through the sea they shall rise again;
Though lovers be lost love shall not;
And death shall have no dominion.

And death shall have no dominion.   10
Under the windings of the sea
They lying long shall not die windily;
Twisting on racks when sinews give way,
Strapped to a wheel, yet they shall not break;
Faith in their hands shall snap in two,   15
And the unicorn evils run them through;
Split all ends up they shan't crack;
And death shall have no dominion.

And death shall have no dominion.
No more may gulls cry at their ears   20
Or waves break loud on the seashores;
Where blew a flower may a flower no more
Lift its head to the blows of the rain;
Though they be mad and dead as nails,
Heads of the characters hammer through daisies;   25
Break in the sun till the sun breaks down,
And death shall have no dominion.

SOURCE: Reprinted from *Collected Poems of Dylan Thomas* with the permission of J. M. Dent
& Sons, Ltd., London and New Directions Publishing Corporation, New York. Copyright
1939, 1943, 1946 by New Directions Publishing Corporation. Copyright 1952 by Dylan
Thomas.

Do Not Go Gentle into That Good Night

Do not go gentle into that good night,
Old age should burn and rave at close of day;
Rage, rage against the dying of the light.

Though wise men at their end know dark is right,
Because their words had forked no lightning they   5
Do not go gentle into that good night.

Good men, the last wave by, crying how bright
Their frail deeds might have danced in a green bay,
Rage, rage against the dying of the light.

Wild men who caught and sang the sun in flight,   10
And learn, too late, they grieved it on its way,
Do not go gentle into that good night.

Grave men, near death, who see with blinding sight
Blind eyes could blaze like meteors and be gay,
Rage, rage against the dying of the light.   15

And you, my father, there on the sad height,
Curse, bless, me now with your fierce tears, I pray.
Do not go gentle into that good night.
Rage, rage against the dying of the light.

SOURCE: Reprinted from *Collected Poems of Dylan Thomas* with the permission of J. M. Dent & Sons, Ltd., London and New Directions Publishing Corporation, New York. Copyright 1939, 1943, 1946 by New Directions Publishing Corporation. Copyright 1952 by Dylan Thomas.

In My Craft or Sullen Art

In my craft or sullen art
Exercised in the still night
When only the moon rages
And the lovers lie abed
With all their griefs in their arms,   5
I labour by singing light
Not for ambition or bread
Or the strut and trade of charms
On the ivory stages
But for the common wages   10
Of their most secret heart.

Not for the proud man apart
From the raging moon I write
On these spindrift pages
Nor for the towering dead   15
With their nightingales and psalms
But for the lovers, their arms
Round the griefs of the ages,
Who pay no praise or wages
Nor heed my craft or art.   20

If I Were Tickled by the Rub of Love

If I were tickled by the rub of love,
A rooking girl who stole me for her side,
Broke through her straws, breaking my bandaged string.
If the red tickle as the cattle calve
Still set to scratch a laughter from my lung,   5
I would not fear the apple nor the flood
Nor the bad blood of spring.

Shall it be male or female? say the cells,
And drop the plum like fire from the flesh.
If I were tickled by the hatching hair,   10
The winging bone that sprouted in the heels,
The itch of man upon the baby's thigh,
I would not fear the gallows nor the axe
Nor the crossed sticks of war.

Shall it be male or female? say the fingers   15
That chalk the walls with green girls and their men.
I would not fear the muscling-in of love
If I were tickled by the urchin hungers
Rehearsing heat upon a raw-edged nerve.
I would not fear the devil in the loin   20
Nor the outspoken grave.

If I were tickled by the lovers' rub
That wipes away not crow's-foot nor the lock
Of sick old manhood on the fallen jaws,
Time and the crabs and the sweethearting crib   25
Would leave me cold as butter for the flies,
The sea of scums could drown me as it broke
Dead on the sweethearts' toes.

This world is half the devil's and my own,
Daft with the drug that's smoking in a girl   30
And curling round the bud that forks her eye.
An old man's shank one-marrowed with my bone,
And all the herrings smelling in the sea,
I sit and watch the worm beneath my nail
Wearing the quick away.   35

And that's the rub, the only rub that tickles.
The knobbly ape that swings along his sex
From damp love-darkness and the nurse's twist
Can never raise the midnight of a chuckle,
Nor when he finds a beauty in the breast   40
Of lover, mother, lovers, or his six
Feet in the rubbing dust.

And what's the rub? Death's feather on the nerve?
Your mouth, my love, the thistle in the kiss?
My Jack of Christ born thorny on the tree?   45
The words of death are dryer than his stiff,
My wordy wounds are printed with your hair.
I would be tickled by the rub that is:
Man be my metaphor.

Henry Reed (b. 1914)

Naming of Parts

Today we have naming of parts. Yesterday,
We had daily cleaning. And tomorrow morning,
We shall have what to do after firing. But today,
Today we have naming of parts. Japonica
Glistens like coral in all of the neighboring gardens,   5
    And today we have naming of parts.

This is the lower sling swivel. And this
Is the upper sling swivel, whose use you will see,
When you are given your slings. And this is the piling swivel,
Which in your case you have not got. The branches   10
Hold in the gardens their silent, eloquent gestures,
    Which in our case we have not got.

This is the safety-catch, which is always released
With an easy flick of the thumb. And please do not let me
See anyone using his finger. You can do it quite easy   15
If you have any strength in your thumb. The blossoms
Are fragile and motionless, never letting anyone see
    Any of them using their finger.

And this you can see is the bolt. The purpose of this
Is to open the breech, as you see. We can slide it   20
Rapidly backwards and forwards: we call this
Easing the spring. And rapidly backwards and forwards
The early bees are assaulting and fumbling the flowers:
    They call it easing the Spring.

SOURCE: Reprinted from *A Map of Verona and Other Poems* by Henry Reed with the permission of Harcourt Brace Jovanovich, Inc., New York and Jonathan Cape, Ltd., London. Copyright 1947 by Henry Reed.

They call it easing the Spring: it is perfectly easy   25
If you have any strength in your thumb: like the bolt,
And the breech, and the cocking-piece, and the point of balance,
Which in our case we have not got; and the almond-blossom
Silent in all of the gardens and the bees going backwards and forwards,
  For today we have naming of parts.   30

Randall Jarrell (1914–1965)

New Georgia

Sometimes as I woke, the branches beside the stars
Were to me, as I drowsed, the bars of my cell;
The creepers lumped through my blanket, hard as a bed
In the old ward, in the time before the war—

In the days when, supperless, I moaned in sleep   5
With the stripes of beating, the old, hard, hampering dream
That lay like the chains on my limbs; till I woke
To a world and a year that used me, when I had learned to obey.

By the piece with the notch on the stock, by the knife from the States,
The tags' chain stirs with the wind; and I sleep   10
Paid, dead, and a soldier. Who fights for his own life
Loses, loses: I have killed for my world, and am free.

The Death of the Ball Turret Gunner [1]

From my mother's sleep I fell into the State
And I hunched in its belly till my wet fur froze.
Six miles from earth, loosed from its dream of life,
I woke to black flak and the nightmare fighters.
When I died they washed me out of the turret with a hose.   5

SOURCE: Reprinted from *The Complete Poems of Randall Jarrell* with the permission of Farrar,
Straus & Giroux, Inc. Copyright © 1945, 1969 by Mrs. Randall Jarrell.

[1]Of this poem Mr. Jarrell has written: "A ball turret was a plexiglass sphere set into the
belly of a B-17 or B-24, and inhabited by two .50 caliber machine-guns and one man,
a short small man. When this gunner tracked with his machine-guns a fighter attacking
his bomber from below, he revolved with the turret; hunched upside-down in his little
sphere, he looked like the fetus in the womb. The fighters which attacked him were
armed with cannon firing explosive shells. The hose was a steam hose."

Robert Lowell (b. 1917)

Skunk Hour

(For Elizabeth Bishop)

Nautilus Island's hermit
heiress still lives through winter in her Spartan cottage;
her sheep still graze above the sea.
Her son's a bishop. Her farmer
is first selectman in our village;   5
she's in her dotage.

Thirsting for
the hierarchic privacy
of Queen Victoria's century
she buys up all   10
the eyesores facing her shore,
and lets them fall.

The season's ill—
we've lost our summer millionaire,
who seemed to leap from an L. L. Bean   15
catalogue. His nine-knot yawl
was auctioned off to lobstermen.
A red fox stain covers Blue Hill.

And now our fairy
decorator brightens his shop for fall;   20
his fishnet's filled with orange cork,
orange, his cobbler's bench and awl;
there is no money in his work,
he'd rather marry.

One dark night,   25
my Tudor Ford climbed the hill's skull;
I watched for love-cars. Lights turned down,
they lay together, hull to hull,
where the graveyard shelves on the town. . . .
My mind's not right.   30

A car radio bleats,
"Love, O careless Love. . . ." I hear
my ill-spirit sob in each blood cell,
as if my hand were at its throat. . . .
I myself am hell;   35
nobody's here—

only skunks, that search
in the moonlight for a bite to eat.
They march on their soles up Main Street:
white stripes, moonstruck eyes' red fire   40
under the chalk-dry and spar spire
of the Trinitarian Church.

I stand on top
of our back steps and breathe the rich air—
a mother skunk with her column of kittens swills the garbage pail.   45
She jabs her wedge-head in a cup
of sour cream, drops her ostrich tail,
and will not scare.

Richard Wilbur (b. 1921)

Love Calls Us to the Things of This World

The eyes open to a cry of pulleys,
And spirited from sleep, the astounded soul
Hangs for a moment bodiless and simple
As false dawn.
       Outside the open window   5
The morning air is all awash with angels.

Some are in bed-sheets, some are in blouses,
Some are in smocks: but truly there they are.
Now they are rising together in calm swells
Of halcyon feeling, filling whatever they wear   10
With the deep joy of their impersonal breathing;

SOURCE: Reprinted from *Things of This World* by Richard Wilbur with the permission of
Harcourt Brace Jovanovich, Inc. Copyright ©1956 by Richard Wilbur.

Now they are flying in place, conveying
The terrible speed of their omnipresence, moving
And staying like white water; and now of a sudden
They swoon down into so rapt a quiet
That nobody seems to be there.   15
                    The soul shrinks

From all that it is about to remember,
From the punctual rape of every blessèd day,
And cries,   20
        "Oh, let there be nothing on earth but laundry,
Nothing but rosy hands in the rising steam
And clear dances done in the sight of heaven."

Yet, as the sun acknowledges
With a warm look the world's hunks and colors,   25
The soul descends once more in bitter love
To accept the waking body, saying now
In a changed voice as the man yawns and rises,

"Bring them down from their ruddy gallows;
Let there be clean linen for the backs of thieves;   30
Let lovers go fresh and sweet to be undone,
And the heaviest nuns walk in a pure floating
Of dark habits,
             keeping their difficult balance."

Still, Citizen Sparrow

Still, citizen sparrow, this vulture which you call
Unnatural, let him but lumber again to air
Over the rotten office, let him bear
The carrion ballast up, and at the tall

Tip of the sky lie cruising. Then you'll see   5
That no more beautiful bird is in heaven's height,
No wider more placid wings, no watchfuller flight;
He shoulders nature there, the frightfully free,

SOURCE: Reprinted from *Ceremony and Other Poems* by Richard Wilbur with the permission of Harcourt Brace Jovanovich, Inc. Copyright 1948, 1949, 1950 by Richard Wilbur.

The naked-headed one. Pardon him, you
Who dart in the orchard aisles, for it is he   10
Devours death, mocks mutability,
Has heart to make an end, keeps nature new.

Thinking of Noah, childheart, try to forget
How for so many bedlam hours his saw
Soured the song of birds with its wheezy gnaw,   15
And the slam of his hammer all the day beset

The people's ears. Forget that he could bear
To see the towns like coral under the keel,
And the fields so dismal deep. Try rather to feel
How high and weary it was, on the waters where   20

He rocked his only world, and everyone's.
Forgive the hero, you who would have died
Gladly with all you knew; he rode that tide
To Ararat; all men are Noah's sons.

Kingsley Amis (b.1922)

A Dream of Fair Women

The door still swinging to, and girls revive,
Aeronauts in the utmost altitudes
    Of boredom fainting, dive
Into the bright oxygen of my nod;
Angels as well, a squadron of draped nudes,   5
    They roar towards their god.

Militant all, they fight to take my hat,
No more as yet; the other men retire
    Insulted, gestured at;
Each girl presses on me her share of what   10
Makes up the barn-door target of desire:
    And I am a crack shot.

SOURCE: Reprinted from *A Case of Samples* by Kingsley Amis, with the permission of Curtis Brown, Ltd., London and Victor Gollancz, Ltd., London.

Speech fails them, amorous, but each one's look,
Endorsed in other ways, begs me to sign
   Her body's autograph-book;
"Me first, Kingsley; I'm cleverest" each declares,
But no gourmet races downstairs to dine,
   Nor will I race upstairs.

Feigning aplomb, perhaps for half an hour,
I hover, and am shown by each princess
   The entrance to her tower;
Open, in that its tenant throws the key
At once to anyone, but not unless
   The anyone is me.

Now from the corridor their fathers cheer,
Their brothers, their young men; the cheers increase
   As soon as I appear;
From each I win a handshake and sincere
Congratulations; from the chief of police
   A nod, a wink, a leer.

This over, all delay is over too;
The first eight girls (the roster now agreed)
   Leap on me, and undo . . .
But honesty impels me to confess
That this is 'all a dream', which was, indeed,
   Not difficult to guess.

But wait; not 'just a dream', because, though good
And beautiful, it is also true, and hence
   Is rarely understood;
Who would choose any feasible ideal
In here and now's giant circumference,
   If that small room were real?

Only the best; the others find, have found
Love's ordinary distances too great,
   And eager, stand their ground;
Map-drunk explorers, dry-land sailors, they
See no arrival that can compensate
   For boredom on the way;

15

20

25

30

35

40

45

And, seeming doctrinaire, but really weak,
Limelighted dolls guttering in their brain,   50
   They come with me, to seek
The halls of theoretical delight,
The women of that ever-fresh terrain,
   The night after to-night.

Masters

That horse whose rider fears to jump will fall,
Riflemen miss if orders sound unsure;
They only are secure who seem secure;
   Who lose their voice, lose all.

Those whom heredity or guns have made   5
Masters, must show it by a common speech;
Expected words in the same tone from each
   Will always be obeyed.

Likewise with stance, with gestures, and with face;
No more than mouth need move when words are said,   10
No more than hand to strike, or point ahead;
   Like slaves, limbs learn their place.

In triumph as in mutiny unmoved,
These make their public act their private good,
Their words in lounge or courtroom understood,   15
   But themselves never loved.

The eyes that will not look, the twitching cheek,
The hands that sketch what mouth would fear to own,
These only make us known, and we are known
   Only as we are weak: 20

By yielding mastery the will is freed,
For it is by surrender that we live,
And we are taken if we wish to give,
   Are needed if we need.

SOURCE: Reprinted from *A Case of Samples* by Kingsley Amis with the permission of Curtis Brown, Ltd., London and Victor Gollancz, Ltd., London.

Anthony Hecht (b.1923)

The Dover Bitch   **for Andrews Wanning**

A Criticism of Life

So there stood Matthew Arnold and this girl
With the cliffs of England crumbling away behind them,
And he said to her, "Try to be true to me,
And I'll do the same for you, for things are bad
All over, etc., etc."   5
Well now, I knew this girl. It's true she had read
Sophocles in a fairly good translation
And caught that bitter allusion to the sea,
But all the time he was talking she had in mind
The notion of what his whiskers would feel like   10
On the back of her neck. She told me later on
That after a while she got to looking out
At the lights across the channel, and really felt sad,
Thinking of all the wine and enormous beds
And blandishments in French and the perfumes.   15
And then she got really angry. To have been brought
All the way down from London, and then be addressed
As sort of a mournful cosmic last resort
Is really tough on a girl, and she was pretty.
Anyway, she watched him pace the room   20
And finger his watch-chain and seem to sweat a bit,
And then she said one or two unprintable things.
But you mustn't judge her by that. What I mean to say is,
She's really all right. I still see her once in a while
And she always treats me right. We have a drink   25
And I give her a good time, and perhaps it's a year
Before I see her again, but there she is,
Running to fat, but dependable as they come,
And sometimes I bring her a bottle of *Nuit d'Amour*.

SOURCE: Reprinted from *The Hard Hours* by Anthony Hecht with the permission of Atheneum. Copyright 1954, © 1960 by Anthony E. Hecht. Appeared originally in *The Transatlantic Review*.

La Condition Botanique

Romans, rheumatic, gouty, came
To bathe in Ischian springs where water steamed,
Puffed and enlarged their bold imperial thoughts, and which
Later Madame Curie declared to be so rich
In radioactive content as she deemed   5
Should win them everlasting fame.

Scattered throughout their ice and snow
The Finns have built airtight cabins of log
Where they may lie, limp and entranced by the sedative purr
Of steam pipes, or torment themselves with flails of fir   10
To stimulate the blood, and swill down grog,
Setting the particles aglow.

Similarly the Turks, but know
Nothing of the more delicate thin sweat
Of plants, breathing their scented oxygen upon   15
Brooklyn's botanical gardens, roofed with glass and run
So to the pleasure of each leafy pet,
Manured, addressed in Latin, so

To its thermostatic happiness—
Spreading its green and innocence to the ground   20
Where pipes, like Satan masquerading as the snake,
Coil and uncoil their frightful liquid length, and make
Gurglings of love mixed with a rumbling sound
Of sharp intestinal distress—

So to its pleasure, as I said,   25
That each particular vegetable may thrive,
Early and late, as in the lot first given Man,
Sans interruption, as when Universal Pan
Led on the Eternal Spring. The spears of chive,
The sensitive plant, showing its dread,   30

SOURCE: Reprinted from *The Hard Hours* by Anthony Hecht with the permission of Atheneum. Copyright 1954, ©1960 by Anthony E. Hecht. Appeared originally in *The Summoning of Stones* by Anthony Hecht.

The Mexican flytrap, that can knit
Its quilled jaws pitilessly, and would hurt
A fly with pleasure, leading Riley's life in bed
Of peat moss and of chemicals, and is thoughtfully fed
Flies for the entrée, flies for the dessert,   35
    Fruit flies for fruit, and all of it

Administered as by a wife—
Lilith our lady, patroness of plants,
Who sings, *Lullay myn lykyng, myn owyn dere derlyng,*
Madrigals nightly to the spiny stalk in sterling   40
Whole notes of admiration and romance—
    This, then, is what is called The Life.

And we, like disinherited heirs,
Old Adams, can inspect the void estate
At visiting hours: the unconditional garden spot,   45
The effortless innocence preserved, for God knows what,
And think, as we depart by the toll gate:
    No one has lived here these five thousand years.

Our world is turned on points, is whirled
On wheels, Tibetan prayer wheels, French verb wheels,   50
The toothy wheels of progress, the terrible torque
Insisting, and in the sky, even above New York
Rotate the marvelous four-fangled seals
    Ezekiel saw. The mother-of-pearled

Home of the bachelor oyster lies   55
Fondled in fluent shifts of bile and lime
As sunlight strikes the water, and it is of our world,
And will appear to us sometime where the finger is curled
Between the frets upon a mandolin,
    Fancy cigar boxes, and eyes   60

Of ceremonial masks; and all
The places where Kilroy inscribed his name,
For instance, the ladies' rest room in the Gare du Nord,
The iron rump of Buddha, whose hallowed, hollowed core
Admitted tourists once but all the same   65
    Housed a machine gun, and let fall

A killing fire from its eyes
During the war; and Polyphemus hurled
Tremendous rocks that stand today off Sicily's coast
Signed with the famous scrawl of our most traveled ghost;   70
    And all these various things are of our world
      But what's become of Paradise?

    Ah, it is lodged in glass, survives
    In Brooklyn, like a throwback, out of style,
Like an incomprehensible veteran of the Grand   75
Army of the Republic in the reviewing stand
    Who sees young men in a mud-colored file
      March to the summit of their lives,

    For glory, for their country, with the flag
Joining divergent stars of North and South   80
In one blue field of heaven, till they fall in blood
And are returned at last unto their native mud—
    The eyes weighed down with stones, the sometimes mouth
      Helpless to masticate or gag

    Its old inheritance of earth.   85
    In the sweat of thy face shalt thou manage, said the Lord.
And we, old Adams, stare through the glass panes and wince,
Fearing to see the ancestral apple, pear, or quince,
    The delicacy of knowledge, the fleshed Word,
      The globe of wisdom that was worth   90

    Our lives, or so our parents thought,
    And turn away to strengthen our poor breath
And body, keep the flesh rosy with hopeful dreams,
Peach-colored, practical, to decorate the bones, with schemes
    Of life insurance, Ice-Cream-After-Death,   95
      Hormone injections, against the *mort'*

    Saison, largely to babble praise
    Of Simeon Pyrites, patron saint
Of our Fools' Paradise, whose glittering effigy
Shines in God's normal sunlight till the blind men see   10(
    Visions as permanent as artists paint:
      The body's firm, nothing decays

Upon the heirloom set of bones
In their gavotte. Yet we look through the glass
Where green lies ageless under snow-stacked roofs in steam-   105
Fitted apartments, and reflect how bud and stem
Are wholly flesh, and the immaculate grass
Does without buttressing of bones.

In open field or public bed
With ultraviolet help, man hopes to learn   110
The leafy secret, pay his most outstanding debt
To God in the salt and honesty of his sweat,
And in his streaming face manly to earn
His daily and all-nourishing bread.

Robert Huff (b.1924)

Getting Drunk with Daughter

Caught without wife and mother, child,
We squat close, scratching gibberish in the sand,
Inspect your castle, peek into the pail
Where shells await your signal to attack
The stick gate, strike down squads of stones,   5
And storm the tower of the Feather Queen,
When, perchspine arrow in his head,
Lord Cork falls dead, his bride carted away.
And my pailful of ice is melting down
Around what will be two dead soldiers soon.   10

Odors remind me your cheeks reeked with kisses:
Whiskey, tobacco, dentures—sourdough—
When Father found you on the trail he misses.
Too bad the old man had to see you grow
Into my blonde wag with your woman's wishes,   15
Playing pretend wife, Daughter . . . even though
He threw himself to rags and knows his bliss is
Walking the sweaty mares he can't let go.

SOURCE: Reprinted from *The Course* by Robert Huff, with the permission of Robert Huff and the publisher, Wayne State University Press. Copyright 1966 by Robert Huff.

Precocious runt. Noting our shapely neighbor
Is amber from toenails to Brillo hair,   20
Has rolled, and drops her top and props her cleavage,
You grin above your army. Dear, her spine's
Not likely to compete with you or Bourbon
Since your're your mother's small ape from behind.
Oh, I know you know I know love likes beaches—   25
For blood outruns the heart, no doubt,
But mine runs to your lordship's mortal splinter.
I've one cork left. So let the spearmen start.

Tomorrow's going to come. We'll be together.
The sun will bake us, and we'll let our bones   30
Fly with the wastrel gulls, who love this weather,
Enlisting stronger sticks, more stalwart stones.
Your mother's got a feather where she itches.
Your daddy's got a fishbone in his brain.
The world lies down and waits in all its ditches.   35
But you and I aren't going to let it rain.

How Not to Make a Model in a Bottle in a Bar in Ithaca

When I am stiff enough to swing
I'll crack that flask. I'll sow
The amber cornered in my hand
Until the pieces grow

Into its golden likeness and   5
The measure starts to flow.
When light's contrived on everything
In miniature, we'll row

Easily as the oarlocks sing
(We and our wake aglow!)   10
Into the shining neck of it
To wander, for it's so

SOURCE: Reprinted from *The Course* by Robert Huff, with the permission of Robert Huff and the publisher, Wayne State University Press. Copyright 1966 by Robert Huff.

That Beauty may in bottles fit,
But making her is, oh,
Like something else. Once in the drift,   15
Where would you want to go?

David Ferry (b.1924)

Adam's Dream

The sycamores and sidewalks of
His neighborhood were private park
And dark retreat, where he could walk
In congress sweet

With his kind neighbors, sleep and love,   5
And where their gossip, or nice talk,
Discriminated beast from bird
By proper word:

      Adam yawned, and there were cats;
      Blinked, and there were antelopes;   10
      Stretched, and everywhere he reached
      A mile of meadow bloomed.

      He cocked his eye, and fishes leaped
      In every brook to praise him;
      He rose to walk, and rabbits ran   15
      As couriers to every green
      Community to tell of him.

      He only glanced at any tree,
      Its birds at once began to sing;
      He nodded, and the region budded;   20
      He put the bloom on everything.

      He was the lord of all the park,
      And he was lonely in the dark,
      Till Eve came smiling out of his side
      To be his bride.   25

SOURCE: Reprinted from *On the Way to the Island* by David Ferry with the permission of
Wesleyan University Press. Copyright © 1953 by David Ferry. Several stanzas of this poem
were first published in *The New Yorker*.

"Sweet rib," he said, astonished at her,
"This is *my* green environ!"
Eve answered no word, but for reply
The wilderness was in her eye.

Adam awoke, the snow had come,   30
And drifts of daylight covered the park;
And his sweet friends, and their sweet talk,
Were dumb.

W. D. Snodgrass (b.1926)

The Examination

Under the thick beams of that swirly smoking light,
   The black robes are clustering, huddled in together.
Hunching their shoulders, they spread short, broad sleeves like night-
   Black grackles' wings and reach out bone-yellow leather-

Y fingers, each to each. And are prepared. Each turns   5
   His single eye—or since one can't discern their eyes,
That reflective, single, moon-pale disc which burns
   Over each brow—to watch this uncouth shape that lies

Strapped to their table. One probes with his ragged nails
   The slate-sharp calf, explores the thigh and the lean thews   10
Of the groin. Others raise, red as piratic sails,
   His wing, stretching, trying the pectoral sinews.

One runs his finger down the whet of that cruel
   Golden beak, lifts back the horny lids from the eyes,
Peers down in one bright eye, malign as a jewel   15
   And steps back suddenly. "He is anaesthetized?"

"He is. He is. Yes. Yes." The tallest of them, bent
   Down by the head, rises. "This drug possesses powers
Sufficient to still all gods in this firmament.
   This is Garuda who was fierce. He's yours for hours.   20

SOURCE:　Reprinted from *After Experience* by W. D. Snodgrass with the permission of Harper & Row, Publishers, Inc. Copyright ©1961 by W. D. Snodgrass.

"We shall continue, please." Now, once again, he bends
    To the skull, and its clamped tissues. Into the cra-
Nial cavity, he plunges both of his hands
    Like obstetric forceps and lifts out the great brain.

Holds it aloft, then gives it to the next who stands   25
    Beside him. Each, in turn, accepts it, although loath,
Turns it this way, that way, feels it between his hands
    Like a wasp's nest or some sickening outsized growth.

They must decide what thoughts each part of it must think;
    They tap it, then listen beside, each suspect lobe,   30
Next, with a crow's quill dipped into India ink,
    Mark on its surface, as if on a map or globe,

Those dangerous areas which need to be excised.
    They rinse it, then apply antiseptics to it;
Now, silver saws appear which, inch by inch, slice   35
    Through its ancient folds and ridges, like thick suet.

It's rinsed, dried, and daubed with thick salves. The smoky saws
    Are scrubbed, resterilized, and polished till they gleam.
The brain is repacked in its case. Pinched in their claws,
    Glimmering needles stitch it up, that leave no seam.   40

Meantime, one of them has set blinders to the eyes,
    Inserted light packing beneath each of the ears
And caulked the nostrils in. One, with thin twine, ties
    The genitals off. With long wooden-handled shears,

Another chops pinions out of the scarlet wings.   45
    It's hoped that with disuse he will forget the sky
Or, at least, in time, learn, among other things,
    To fly no higher than his superiors fly.

Well; that's a beginning. The next time, they can split
    His tongue and teach him to talk correctly, can give   50
Him memory of fine books and choose clothing fit
    For the integrated area where he'll live.

Their candidate may live to give them thanks one day.
    He will recover and may hope for such success
He might return to join their ranks. Bowing away,   55
    They nod, whispering, "One of ours; one of ours. Yes. Yes."

Allen Ginsberg (b.1926)

A Supermarket in California

What thoughts I have of you tonight, Walt Whitman, for I walked down the sidestreets under the trees with a headache self-conscious looking at the full moon.

In my hungry fatigue, and shopping for images, I went into the neon fruit supermarket, dreaming of your enumerations!

What peaches and what penumbras! Whole families shopping at night! Aisles full of husbands! Wives in the avocados, babies in the tomatoes— and you Garcia Lorca, what were you doing down by the watermelons?

I saw you, Walt Whitman, childless, lonely old grubber, poking among the meats in the refrigerator and eyeing the grocery boys.

I heard you asking questions of each: Who killed the pork chops? What price bananas? Are you my Angel?   5

I wandered in and out of the brilliant stacks of cans following you, and followed in my imagination by the store detective.

We strode down the open corridors together in our solitary fancy tasting artichokes, possessing every frozen delicacy, and never passing the cashier.

Where are we going, Walt Whitman? The doors close in an hour. Which way does your beard point tonight?

(I touch your book and dream of our odyssey in the supermarket and feel absurd.)

Will we walk all night through solitary streets? The trees add shade to shade, lights out in the houses, we'll both be lonely.   10

Will we stroll dreaming of the lost America of love past blue automobiles in driveways, home to our silent cottage?

Ah, dear father, graybeard, lonely old courage-teacher, what America did you have when Charon quit poling his ferry and you got out on a smoking bank and stood watching the boat disappear on the black waters of Lethe?

SOURCE: Reprinted from *Howl* by Allen Ginsberg with the permission of City Lights Books. Copyright © 1956,1959 by Allen Ginsberg.

Donald Hall (b. 1928)

My Son, My Executioner [1]

My son, my executioner,
  I take you in my arms,
Quiet and small and just astir,
  And whom my body warms.

Sweet death, small son, our instrument   5
  Of immortality,
Your cries and hungers document
  Our bodily decay.

We twenty-five and twenty-two,
  Who seemed to live forever,   10
Observe enduring life in you
  And start to die together.

Thom Gunn (b. 1929)

Black Jackets [2]

In the silence that prolongs the span
Rawly of music when the record ends,
  The red-haired boy who drove a van
In weekday overalls but, like his friends,

  Wore cycle boots and jacket here   5
To suit the Sunday hangout he was in,
  Heard, as he stretched back from his beer,
Leather creak softly round his neck and chin.

SOURCE: [1] Reprinted from *Exiles and Marriages* by Donald Hall (New York: Viking Press) with the permission of Curtis Brown, Ltd; Copyright © 1955 by Donald Hall.

SOURCE: [2] Reprinted from *My Sad Captain* by Thom Gunn with the permission of University of Chicago Press, Faber and Faber, Ltd., London, and the poet. Copyright 1961 by Thom Gunn.

Before him, on a coal-black sleeve
Remote exertion had lined, scratched, and burned .   10
  Insignia that could not revive
The heroic fall or climb where they were earned.

On the other drinkers bent together,
Concocting selves for their impervious kit,
  He saw it as no more than leather   15
Which, taut across the shoulders grown to it,

Sent through the dimness of a bar
As sudden and anonymous hints of light
  As those that shipping give, that are
Now flickers in the Bay, now lost in night.   20

He stretched out like a cat, and rolled
The bitterish taste of beer upon his tongue,
  And listened to a joke being told:
The present was the things he stayed among.

If it was only loss he wore,   25
He wore it to assert, with fierce devotion,
  Complicity and nothing more.
He recollected his initiation,

And one especially of the rites.
For on his shoulders they had put tattoos: 30
  The group's name on the left, The Knights,
And on the right the slogan Born To Lose.

X. J. Kennedy (b. 1929)

*In a Prominent Bar
in Secaucus One Day*

**To the tune of "The Old Orange Flute"
or the tune of "Sweet Betsy from Pike"**

In a prominent bar in Secaucus one day
Rose a lady in skunk with a topheavy sway,
Raised a knobby red finger—all turned from their beer—
While with eyes bright as snowcrust she sang high and clear:

SOURCE: Reprinted from *Nude Descending a Staircase* by X. J. Kennedy with the permission
of Doubleday & Company, Inc.

"Now who of you'd think from an eyeload of me   5
That I once was a lady as proud as could be?
Oh I'd never sit down by a tumbledown drunk
If it wasn't, my dears, for the high cost of junk.

"All the gents used to swear that the white of my calf
Beat the down of the swan by a length and a half.   10
In the kerchief of linen I caught to my nose
Ah, there never fell snot, but a little gold rose.

"I had seven gold teeth and a toothpick of gold,
My Virginia cheroot was a leaf of it rolled
And I'd light it each time with a thousand in cash—   15
Why the bums used to fight if I flicked them an ash.

"Once the toast of the Biltmore, the belle of the Taft,
I would drink bottle beer at the Drake, never draft,
And dine at the Astor on Salisbury steak
With a clean tablecloth for each bite I did take.   20

"In a car like the Roxy I'd roll to the track,
A steel-guitar trio, a bar in the back,
And the wheels made no noise, they turned over so fast,
Still it took you ten minutes to see me go past.

"When the horses bowed down to me that I might choose,   25
I bet on them all, for I hated to lose.
Now I'm saddled each night for my butter and eggs
And the broken threads race down the backs of my legs.

"Let you hold in mind, girls, that your beauty must pass
Like a lovely white clover that rusts with its grass.   30
Keep your bottoms off barstools and marry you young
Or be left—an old barrel with many a bung.

"For when time takes you out for a spin in his car
You'll be hard-pressed to stop him from going too far
And be left by the roadside, for all your good deeds,   35
Two toadstools for tits and a face full of weeds."

All the house raised a cheer, but the man at the bar
Made a phonecall and up pulled a red patrol car
And she blew us a kiss as they copped her away
From the prominent bar in Secaucus, N.J.   40

Gary Snyder (b. 1930)

Piute Creek, August 1955

Milton by Firelight

"O hell, what do mine eyes
    with grief behold?"
Working with an old
Singlejack miner, who can sense
The vein and cleavage
In the very guts of rock, can   5
Blast granite, build
Switchbacks that last for years
Under the beat of snow, thaw, mule-hooves.
What use, Milton, a silly story
Of our lost general parents,
    eaters of fruit?   10

The Indian, the chainsaw boy,
And a string of six mules
Came riding down to camp
Hungry for tomatoes and green apples.
Sleeping in saddle-blankets   15
Under a bright night-sky
Han River slantwise by morning.
Jays squall
Coffee boils

In ten thousand years the Sierras   20
Will be dry and dead, home of the scorpion.
Ice-scratched slabs and bent trees.
No paradise, no fall,
Only the weathering land
The wheeling sky,   25
Man, with his Satan
Scouring the chaos of the mind.
Oh Hell!

SOURCE: Reprinted from *A Range of Poems* with the permission of Gary Snyder and Fulcrum Press, London. Copyright © Gary Snyder.

Fire down
Too dark to read, miles from a road
The bell-mare clangs in the meadow
That packed dirt for a fill-in
Scrambling through loose rocks
On an old trail
All of a summer's day.

30

35

Gregory Corso (b. 1930)

Marriage

Should I get married? Should I be good?
Astound the girl next door with my velvet suit and faustus hood?
Don't take her to movies but to cemeteries
tell all about werewolf bathtubs and forked clarinets
then desire her and kiss her and all the preliminaries
and she going just so far and I understanding why
not getting angry saying You must feel! It's beautiful to feel!
Instead take her in my arms lean against an old crooked tombstone
and woo her the entire night the constellations in the sky—

5

When she introduces me to her parents
back straightened, hair finally combed, strangled by a tie,
should I sit knees together on their 3rd degree sofa
and not ask Where's the bathroom?
How else to feel other than I am,
often thinking Flash Gordon soap—
O how terrible it must be for a young man
seated before a family and the family thinking
We never saw him before! He wants our Mary Lou!
After tea and homemade cookies they ask What do you do for a living?

10

15

Should I tell them? Would they like me then?
Say All right get married, we're losing a daughter
but we're gaining a son—
And should I then ask Where's the bathroom?

20

SOURCE: Reprinted from *The Happy Birthday of Death* by Gregory Corso with the permission of New Directions Publishing Corporation. Copyright © 1960 by New Directions Publishing Corporation.

O God, and the wedding! All her family and her friends
and only a handful of mine all scroungy and bearded   25
just wait to get at the drinks and food—
And the priest! he looking at me as if I masturbated
asking me Do you take this woman for your lawful wedded wife?
And I trembling what to say say Pie Glue!
I kiss the bride all those corny men slapping me on the back   30
She's all yours, boy! Ha-ha-ha!
And in their eyes you could see some obscene honeymoon going on—
Then all that absurd rice and clanky cans and shoes
Niagara Falls! Hordes of us! Husbands! Wives! Flowers! Chocolates!
All streaming into cozy hotels   35
All going to do the same thing tonight
The indifferent clerk he knowing what was going to happen
The lobby zombies they knowing what
The whistling elevator man he knowing
The winking bellboy knowing   40
Everybody knowing! I'd be almost inclined not to do anything!
Stay up all night! Stare that hotel clerk in the eye!
Screaming: I deny honeymoon! I deny honeymoon!
running rampant into those almost climactic suites
yelling Radio belly! Cat shovel!   45
O I'd live in Niagara forever! in a dark cave beneath the Falls
I'd sit there the Mad Honeymooner
devising ways to break marriages, a scourge of bigamy
a saint of divorce—

But I should get married I should be good   50
How nice it'd be to come home to her
and sit by the fireplace and she in the kitchen
aproned young and lovely wanting my baby
and so happy about me she burns the roast beef

and comes crying to me and I get up from my big papa chair 55
saying Christmas teeth! Radiant brains! Apple deaf!
God what a husband I'd make! Yes, I should get married!
So much to do! like sneaking into Mr Jones' house late at night
and cover his golf clubs with 1920 Norwegian books
Like hanging a picture of Rimbaud on the lawnmower 60
like pasting Tannu Tuva postage stamps all over the picket fence
like when Mrs Kindhead comes to collect for the Community Chest
grab her and tell her There are unfavorable omens in the sky!
And when the mayor comes to get my vote tell him
When are you going to stop people killing whales! 65
And when the milkman comes leave him a note in the bottle
Penguin dust, bring me penguin dust, I want penguin dust—

Yet if I should get married and it's Connecticut and snow
and she gives birth to a child and I am sleepless, worn,
up for nights, head bowed against a quiet window, the past behind me, 70

finding myself in the most common of situations a trembling man
knowledged with responsibility not twig-smear nor Roman coin
    soup—
O what would that be like!
Surely I'd give it for a nipple a rubber Tacitus
For a rattle a bag of broken Bach records
Tack Della Francesca all over its crib 75
Sew the Greek alphabet on its bib
And build for its playpen a roofless Parthenon
No, I doubt I'd be that kind of father
not rural not snow no quiet window
but hot smelly tight New York City 80
seven flights up, roaches and rats in the walls

a fat Reichian wife screeching over potatoes Get a job!
And five nose running brats in love with Batman
and the neighbors all toothless and dry haired   85
like those hag masses of the 18th century
all wanting to come in and watch TV
The landlord wants his rent
Grocery store Blue Cross Gas & Electric Knights of Columbus
Impossible to lie back and dream Telephone snow, ghost parking—   90
No! I should not get married I should never get married!
But—imagine If I were married to a beautiful sophisticated woman
tall and pale wearing an elegant black dress and long black gloves
holding a cigarette holder in one hand and a highball in the other
and we lived high up in a penthouse with a huge window   95
from which we could see all of New York and ever farther on clearer
    days

No, can't imagine myself married to that pleasant prison dream—

O but what about love! I forget love
not that I am incapable of love
it's just that I see love as odd as wearing shoes—   100
I never wanted to marry a girl who was like my mother
And Ingrid Bergman was always impossible
And there's maybe a girl now but she's already married
And I don't like men and—
But there's got to be somebody!   105
Because what if I'm 60 years old and not married,
all alone in a furnished room with pee stains on my underwear
and everybody else is married! All the universe married but me!

Ah, yet well I know that were a woman possible as I am possible
then marriage would be possible—   110
Like SHE in her lonely alien gaud waiting her Egyptian lover
so I wait—bereft of 2,000 years and the bath of life.

Willie Reader (b.1931)

Six Haiku: American Style

1

High on the blue rim
  of the far hill a goat crops
    at the early stars.

SOURCE: Reprinted with the permission of Willie Reader. First printed in *American Haiku*, Vol. IV, No. 2 (1966).

2

That perfect dipper
  holding no water and cupping
    nothing but stars.

First printed in *South Florida Review*, No. 2, Spring 1968.

3

I had not thought
  the winter wind had such nails
    on its soft white hands.

First printed in *South Florida Review*, No. 2, Spring 1968.

4

Tolerance is not
  to begrudge a prairie rattler
    his place in the sun.

First printed in *Florida Poetry And*, No. 2, Spring 1968.

5

On Saturday night
  the old unmelodious zinc tub
    has a new ring.

First printed in *South Florida Review*, No. 1, Spring 1967.

6

Wheeling on the edge
  of an echo, the grey bat
    veers into black . . .

Sylvia Plath (1932–1963)

The Bee Meeting

Who are these people at the bridge to meet me? They are the
 villagers—
The rector, the midwife, the sexton, the agent for bees.
In my sleeveless summery dress I have no protection,
And they are all gloved and covered, why did nobody tell me?
They are smiling and taking out veils tacked to ancient hats.   5

I am nude as a chicken neck, does nobody love me?
Yes, here is the secretary of bees with her white shop smock,
Buttoning the cuffs at my wrists and the slit from my neck to my knees.
Now I am milkweed silk, the bees will not notice.
They will not smell my fear, my fear, my fear.   10

Which is the rector now, is it that man in black?
Which is the midwife, is that her blue coat?
Everybody is nodding a square black head, they are knights in visors,
Breastplates of cheesecloth knotted under the armpits.
Their smiles and their voices are changing. I am led through a beanfield.   15

Strips of tinfoil winking like people,
Feather dusters fanning their hands in a sea of bean flowers,
Creamy bean flowers with black eyes and leaves like bored hearts.
Is it blood clots the tendrils are dragging up that string?
No, no, it is scarlet flowers that will one day be edible.   20

Now they are giving me a fashionable white straw Italian hat
And a black veil that moulds to my face, they are making me one of
 them.
They are leading me to the shorn grove, the circle of hives.
Is it the hawthorn that smells so sick?
The barren body of hawthorn, etherizing its children.   25

SOURCE: Reprinted from *Ariel* by Sylvia Plath with the permission of Harper & Row,
Publishers, Inc., New York and Olwyn Hughes, London. Copyright © 1963 by Ted Hughes.

Is it some operation that is taking place?
It is the surgeon my neighbours are waiting for,
This apparition in a green helmet,
Shining gloves and white suit.
Is it the butcher, the grocer, the postman, someone I know? 30

I cannot run, I am rooted, and the gorse hurts me
With its yellow purses, its spiky armoury.
I could not run without having to run forever.
The white hive is snug as a virgin,
Sealing off her brood cells, her honey, and quietly humming. 35

Smoke rolls and scarves in the grove.
The mind of the hive thinks this is the end of everything.
Here they come, the outriders, on their hysterical elastics.
If I stand very still, they will think I am cow parsley,
A gullible head untouched by their animosity, 40

Not even nodding, a personage in a hedgerow.
The villagers open the chambers, they are hunting the queen.
Is she hiding, is she eating honey? She is very clever.
She is old, old, old, she must live another year, and she knows it.
While in their fingerjoint cells the new virgins 45

Dream of a duel they will win inevitably,
A curtain of wax dividing them from the bride flight,
The upflight of the murderess into a heaven that loves her.
The villagers are moving the virgins, there will be no killing.
The old queen does not show herself, is she so ungrateful? 50

I am exhausted, I am exhausted——
Pillar of white in a blackout of knives.
I am the magician's girl who does not flinch.
The villagers are untying their disguises, they are shaking hands.
Whose is that long white box in the grove, what have they
 accomplished, why am I cold? 55

The Arrival of the Bee Box

I ordered this, this clean wood box.
Square as a chair and almost too heavy to lift.
I would say it was the coffin of a midget
Or a square baby
Were there not such a din in it.   5

The box is locked, it is dangerous.
I have to live with it overnight.
And I can't keep away from it.
There are no windows, so I can't see what is in there.
There is only a little grid, no exit.   10

I put my eye to the grid.
It is dark, dark,
With the swarmy feeling of African hands
Minute and shrunk for export,
Black on black, angrily clambering.   15

How can I let them out?
It is the noise that appals me most of all,
The unintelligible syllables.
It is like a Roman mob,
Small, taken one by one, but my god, together!   20

I lay my ear to furious Latin.
I am not a Caesar.
I have simply ordered a box of maniacs.
They can be sent back.
They can die, I need feed them nothing, I am the owner.   25

I wonder how hungry they are.
I wonder if they would forget me
If I just undid the locks and stood back and turned into a tree.
There is the laburnum, its blond colonnades,
And the petticoats of the cherry.   30

SOURCE: Reprinted from *Ariel* by Sylvia Plath with the permission of Harper & Row, Publishers, Inc., New York and Olwyn Hughes, London. Copyright ©1963 by Ted Hughes.

They might ignore me immediately
In my moon suit and funeral veil.
I am no source of honey
So why should they turn on me?
Tomorrow I will be sweet God, I will set them free.   35

The box is only temporary.

Geoffrey Hill (b. 1932)

Genesis

I

Against the burly air I strode,
Where the tight ocean heaves its load,
Crying the miracles of God.

And first I brought the sea to bear
Upon the dead weight of the land;
And the waves flourished at my prayer,   5
The rivers spawned their sand.

And where the streams were salt and full
The tough pig-headed salmon strove,
Curbing the ebb and the tide's pull,
To reach the steady hills above.   10

II

The second day I stood and saw
The osprey plunge with triggered claw,
Feathering blood along the shore,
To lay the living sinew bare.   15

And the third day I cried: "Beware
The soft-voiced owl, the ferret's smile,
The hawk's deliberate stoop in air,
Cold eyes, and bodies hooped in steel,
Forever bent upon the kill."   20

SOURCE: Reprinted with the permission of Dufour Editions Inc., Chester Springs, Pennsyl-
vania.

III

And I renounced, on the fourth day,
This fierce and unregenerate clay,

Building as a huge myth for man
The watery Leviathan,
And made the glove-winged albatross   25
Scour the ashes of the sea
Where Capricorn and Zero cross,
A brooding immortality—
Such as the charmed phoenix has
In the unwithering tree.   30

IV

The phoenix burns as cold as frost;
And, like a legendary ghost,
The phantom-bird goes wild and lost,
Upon a pointless ocean tossed.

So, the fifth day, I turned again   35
To flesh and blood and the blood's pain.

V

On the sixth day, as I rode
In haste about the works of God,
With spurs I plucked the horse's blood.

By blood we live, the hot, the cold,   40
To ravage and redeem the world:
There is no bloodless myth will hold.

And by Christ's blood are men made free
Though in close shrouds their bodies lie
Under the rough pelt of the sea;   45

Though Earth has rolled beneath her weight
The bones that cannot bear the light.

Part 2

FICTION

Nathaniel Hawthorne (1804–1864)

EARTH'S HOLOCAUST

Once upon a time—but whether in the time past or time to come, is a matter of little or no moment—this wide world had become so overburthened with an accumulation of worn-out trumpery, that the inhabitants determined to rid themselves of it by a general bonfire. The site fixed upon, at the representation of the insurance companies, and as being as central a spot as any other on the globe, was one of the broadest prairies of the West, where no human habitation would be endangered by the flames, and where a vast assemblage of spectators might commodiously admire the show. Having a taste for sights of this kind, and imagining, likewise, that the illumination of the bonfire might reveal some profundity or moral truth, heretofore hidden in mist or darkness, I made it convenient to journey thither and be present. At my arrival, although the heap of condemned rubbish was as yet comparatively small, the torch had already been applied. Amid that boundless plain, in the dusk of the evening, like a far-off star alone in the firmament, there was merely visible one tremulous gleam, whence none could have anticipated so fierce a blaze as was destined to ensue. With every moment, however, there came foot-travellers, women holding up their aprons, men on horseback, wheelbarrows, lumbering baggage wagons, and other vehicles, great and small, and from far and near, laden with articles that were judged fit for nothing but to be burnt.

"What materials have been used to kindle the flame?" inquired I of a bystander, for I was desirous of knowing the whole process of the affair from beginning to end.

The person whom I addressed was a grave man, fifty years old, or thereabout, who had evidently come thither as a looker-on; he struck me immediately as having weighed for himself the true value of life and its circumstances, and therefore as feeling little personal interest in whatever judgment the world might form of them. Before answering my question, he looked me in the face, by the kindling light of the fire.

"Oh, some very dry combustibles," replied he, "and extremely suitable to the purpose—no other, in fact, than yesterday's newspapers, last month's magazines, and last year's withered leaves. Here, now, comes some antiquated trash, that will take fire like a handful of shavings."

As he spoke, some rough-looking men advanced to the verge of the bonfire, and threw in, as it appeared, all the rubbish of the Herald's office; the blazonry of coat-armor, the crests and devices of illustrious families; pedigrees that extended back, like lines of light, into the midst of the dark ages, together with stars, garters, and embroidered collars, each of which, as paltry a bubble as it might appear to the uninstructed eye, had once possessed vast significance, as was still, in truth, reckoned among the most precious of moral or material facts, by the worshippers of the gorgeous past. Mingled with this confused heap, which was tossed into the flames by armfuls at once, were innumerable badges of knighthood, comprising those of all the European sovereignties, and Napoleon's decoration of the Legion of Honor, the ribands of which were entangled with those of the ancient order of St. Louis. There, too, were the medals of our own society of Cincinnati, by means of which, as history tells us, an order of hereditary knights came near being constituted out of the king-quellers of the Revolution. And besides, there were the patents of nobility of German counts and barons, Spanish grandees, and English peers, from the worm-eaten instruments signed by William the Conqueror, down to the brand-new parchment of the latest lord who has received his honors from the fair hand of Victoria.

At sight of these dense volumes of smoke, mingled with vivid jets of flame that gushed and eddied forth from this immense pile of earthly distinctions, the multitude of plebeian spectators set up a joyous shout, and clapt their hands with an emphasis that made the welkin echo. That was their moment of triumph, achieved, after long ages, over creatures of the same clay and the same spiritual infirmities, who had dared to assume the privileges due only to Heaven's better workmanship. But now there rushed towards the blazing heap a grey-haired man, of stately presence, wearing a coat from the breast of which a star, or other badge of rank, seemed to have been forcibly wrenched away. He had not the tokens of intellectual power in his face; but still there was the demeanor—the habitual, and almost native dignity—of one who had been born to the idea of his own social superiority, and had never felt it questioned till that moment.

"People," cried he, gazing at the ruin of what was dearest to his eyes with grief and wonder, but nevertheless, with a degree of stateliness; "people, what have you done! This fire is consuming all that marked your advance from barbarism, or that could have prevented your relapse thither. We—the men of the privileged orders—were those who kept alive, from age to age, the old chivalrous spirit; the gentle and generous thought; the higher, the purer, the more refined and delicate life! With the nobles, too, you cast off the poet, the painter, the sculptor—all the beautiful arts; for we were their patrons, and created the atmosphere in which they flourish. In abolishing the majestic distinctions of rank, society loses not only its grace, but its steadfastness—"

More he would doubtless have spoken, but here there arose an outcry, sportive, contemptuous, and indignant, that altogether drowned the appeal of the fallen nobleman, insomuch that, casting one look of despair at his own half-burnt pedigree, he shrunk back into the crowd, glad to shelter himself under his new-found insignificance.

"Let him thank his stars that we have not flung him into the same fire!" shouted a rude figure, spurning the embers with his foot. "And, henceforth, let no man dare to show a piece of musty parchment as his warrant for lording it over his fellows! If he have strength of arm, well and good; it is one species of superiority. If he have wit, wisdom, courage, force of character, let these attributes do for him what they may. But, from this day forward, no mortal must hope for place and consideration by reckoning up the mouldy bones of his ancestors! That nonsense is done away."

"And in good time," remarked the grave observer by my side, in a low voice, however—"if no worse nonsense comes in its place. But, at all events, this species of nonsense has fairly lived out its life."

There was little space to muse or moralize over the embers of this time-honored rubbish; for, before it was half burnt out, there came another multitude from beyond the sea, bearing the purple robes of royalty, and the crowns, globes, and sceptres of emperors and kings. All these had been condemned as useless baubles, playthings, at best, fit only for the infancy of the world, or rods to govern and chastise it in its nonage; but with which universal manhood, at its full-grown stature, could no longer brook to be insulted. Into such contempt had these regal insignia now fallen, that the gilded crown and tinseled robes of the player-king, from Drury-Lane Theatre, had been thrown in among the rest, doubtless as a mockery of his brother-monarchs on the great stage of the world. It was a strange sight to discern the crown-jewels of England, glowing and flashing in the midst of the fire. Some of them had been delivered down from the time of the Saxon princes; others were purchased with vast revenues, or, perchance, ravished from the dead brows of the native potentates of Hindostan; and the whole now blazed with a dazzling lustre, as if a star had fallen in that spot, and been shattered into fragments. The splendor of the ruined monarchy had no reflection, save in those inestimable precious stones. But enough on this subject. It were but tedious to describe how the Emperor of Austria's mantle was converted to tinder, and how the posts and pillars of the French throne became a heap of coals, which it was impossible to distinguish from those of any other wood. Let me add, however, that I noticed one of the exiled Poles stirring up the bonfire with the Czar of Russia's sceptre, which he afterwards flung into the flames.

"The smell of singed garments is quite intolerable here," observed my new acquaintance, as the breeze enveloped us in the smoke of a royal wardrobe. "Let us get to windward, and see what they are doing on the other side of the bonfire."

We accordingly passed around, and were just in time to witness the arrival of a vast procession of Washingtonians—as the votaries of temperance call themselves now-a-days—accompanied by thousands of the Irish disciples of Father Mathew, with that great apostle at their head. They brought a rich contribution to the bonfire; being nothing less than all the hogsheads and barrels of liquor in the world, which they rolled before them across the prairie.

"Now, my children," cried Father Mathew, when they reached the verge of the fire—"one shove more, and the work is done! And now let us stand off and see Satan deal with his own liquor!"

Accordingly, having placed their wooden vessels within reach of the flames, the procession stood off at a safe distance, and soon beheld them burst into a blaze that reached the clouds, and threatened to set the sky itself on fire. And well it might. For here was the whole world's stock of spirituous liquors, which, instead of kindling a frenzied light in the eyes of individual topers, as of yore, soared upwards with a bewildering gleam that startled all mankind. It was the aggregate of that fierce fire which would otherwise have scorched the hearts of millions. Meantime, numberless bottles of precious wine were flung into the blaze, which lapped up the contents as if it loved them, and grew, like other drunkards, the merrier and fiercer for what it quaffed. Never again will the insatiable thirst of the fire-fiend be so pampered! Here were the treasures of famous bon-vivants—liquors that had been tossed on ocean, and mellowed in the sun, and hoarded long in the recesses of the earth—the pale, the gold, the ruddy juice of whatever vineyards were most delicate—the entire vintage of Tokay—all mingling in one stream with the vile fluids of the common pot-house, and contributing to heighten the self-same blaze. And while it rose in a gigantic spire, that seemed to wave against the arch of the firmament, and combine itself with the light of stars, the multitude gave a shout, as if the broad earth were exulting in its deliverance from the curse of ages.

But the joy was not universal. Many deemed that human life would be gloomier than ever, when that brief illumination should sink down. While the reformers were at work, I overheard muttered expostulations from several respectable gentlemen with red noses, and wearing gouty shoes; and a ragged worthy, whose face looked like a hearth where the fire is burnt out, now expressed his discontent more openly and boldly.

"What is this world good for," said the last toper, "now that we can never be jolly anymore? What is to comfort the poor man in sorrow and perplexity?—how is he to keep his heart warm against the cold winds of this cheerless earth?—and what do you propose to give him in exchange for the solace that you take away? How are old friends to sit together by the fireside, without a cheerful glass between them? A plague upon your reformation! It is a sad world, a cold world, a selfish world, a low world, not worth an honest fellow's living in, now that good fellowship is gone forever!"

This harangue excited great mirth among the bystanders. But, preposterous as was the sentiment, I could not help commiserating the forlorn condition of the last toper, whose boon-companions had dwindled away from his side, leaving the poor fellow without a soul to countenance him in sipping his liquor, nor indeed any liquor to sip. Not that this was quite the true state of the case; for I had observed him, at a critical moment, filch a bottle of fourth-proof brandy that fell beside the bonfire, and hide it in his pocket.

The spirituous and fermented liquors being thus disposed of, the zeal of the reformers next induced them to replenish the fire with all the boxes of tea and bags of coffee in the world. And now came the planters of Virginia, bringing their crops of tobacco. These, being cast upon the heap of inutility, aggregated it to the size of a mountain, and incensed the atmosphere with such potent fragrance that methought we should never draw pure breath again. The present sacrifice seemed to startle the lovers of the weed more than any that they had hitherto witnessed.

"Well, they've put my pipe out," said an old gentleman, flinging it into the flames in a pet. "What is this world coming to? Everything rich and racy,—all the spice of life—is to be condemned as useless. Now that they have kindled the bonfire, if these nonsensical reformers would fling themselves into it, all would be well enough!"

"Be patient," responded a staunch conservative; "it will come to that in the end. They will first fling us in, and finally themselves."

From the general and systematic measures of reform, I now turned to consider the individual contributions to this memorable bonfire. In many instances these were of a very amusing character. One poor fellow threw in his empty purse, and another a bundle of counterfeit or insolvable bank notes. Fashionable ladies threw in their last season's bonnets, together with heaps of ribbons, yellow lace, and much other half-worn milliner's ware; all of which proved even more evanescent in the fire than it had been in the fashion. A multitude of lovers of both sexes—discarded maids or bachelors, and couples mutually weary of one another—tossed in bundles of perfumed letters and enamored sonnets. A hack politician, being deprived of bread by the loss of office, threw in his teeth, which happened to be false ones. The Rev. Sidney Smith,—having voyaged across the Atlantic for that sole purpose—came up to the bonfire with a bitter grin, and threw in certain repudiated bonds, fortified though they were with the broad seal of a sovereign state. A little boy of five years old, in the premature manliness of the present epoch, threw in his playthings; a college graduate, his diploma; an apothecary, ruined by the spread of homoeopathy, his whole stock of drugs and medicines; a physician, his library; a parson, his old sermons; and a fine gentleman of the old school, his code of manners, which he had formerly written down for the benefit of the next generation. A widow, resolving on a second marriage, slily threw in her dead husband's miniature. A young man, jilted by his mistress, would willingly have flung his own desperate heart into the flames, but could find no means to wrench it out of his bosom. An American author, whose works were neglected by the public, threw his pen and paper into the bonfire, and betook himself to some less discouraging occupation. It somewhat startled me to overhear a number of ladies, highly respectable in appearance, proposing to fling their gowns and petticoats into the flames, and assume the garb, together with the manners, duties, offices, and responsibilities, of the opposite sex.

What favor was accorded to this scheme, I am unable to say; my attention being suddenly drawn to a poor, deceived, and half-delirious girl, who, exclaiming that she was the most worthless thing alive or dead, attempted to cast herself into the fire, amid all that wrecked and broken trumpery of the world. A good man, however, ran to her rescue.

"Patience, my poor girl!" said he, as he drew her back from the fierce embrace of the destroying angel. "Be patient, and abide Heaven's will. So long as you possess a living soul, all may be restored to its first freshness. These things of matter, and creations of human fantasy, are fit for nothing but to be burnt, when once they have had their day. But your day is eternity!"

"Yes," said the wretched girl, whose frenzy seemed now to have sunk down into deep despondency; "yes, and the sunshine is blotted out of it!"

It was now rumored among the spectators that all the weapons and munitions of war were to be thrown into the bonfire, with the exception of the world's stock of gunpowder, which, as the safest mode of disposing of it, had already been drowned in the sea. This intelligence seemed to awaken great diversity of opinion. The hopeful philanthropist esteemed it a token that the millenium was already come; while persons of another stamp, in whose view mankind was a breed of bull-dogs, prophesied that all the old stoutness, fervor, nobleness, generosity, and magnanimity of the race would disappear; these qualities, as they affirmed, requiring blood for their nourishment. They comforted themselves, however, in the belief that the proposed abolition of war was impracticable, for any length of time together.

Be that as it might, numberless great guns, whose thunder had long been the voice of battle—the artillery of the Armada, the battering-trains of Marlborough, and the adverse cannon of Napoleon and Wellington—were

trundled into the midst of the fire. By the continual addition of dry combustibles, it had now waxed so intense that neither brass nor iron could
withstand it. It was wonderful to behold how these terrible instruments
of slaughter melted away like playthings of wax. Then the armies of the
earth wheeled around the mighty furnace, with their military music playing triumphant marches, and flung in their muskets and swords. The
standard-bearers, likewise, cast one look upward at their banners, all tattered with shot-holes, and inscribed with the names of victorious fields,
and, giving them a last flourish on the breeze, they lowered them into the
flame, which snatched them upward in its rush toward the clouds. This
ceremony being over, the world was left without a single weapon in its
hands, except, possibly, a few old king's arms and rusty swords, and other
trophies of the Revolution, in some of our state armories. And now the
drums were beaten and the trumpets brayed all together, as a prelude to
the proclamation of universal and eternal peace, and the announcement
that glory was no longer to be won by blood; but that it would henceforth
be the contention of the human race to work out the greatest mutual good,
and that beneficence, in the future annals of the earth, would claim the
praise of valor. The blessed tidings were accordingly promulgated, and
caused infinite rejoicings among those who had stood aghast at the horror
and absurdity of war.

But I saw a grim smile pass over the seared visage of a stately old
commander—by his war-worn figure and rich military dress, he might
have been one of Napoleon's famous marshals—who, with the rest of the
world's soldiery, had just flung away the sword that had been familiar to
his right hand for half a century.

"Aye, aye!" grumbled he. "Let them proclaim what they please; but, in
the end, we shall find that all this foolery has only made more work for
the armorers and cannon-founders."

"Why, sir," exclaimed I, in astonishment, "do you imagine that the
human race will ever so far return on the steps of its past madness as to
weld another sword, or cast another cannon?"

"There will be no need," observed, with a sneer, one who neither felt
benevolence, nor had faith in it. "When Cain wished to slay his brother,
he was at no loss for a weapon."

"We shall see," replied the veteran commander. "If I am mistaken, so
much the better; but in my opinion—without pretending to philosophize
about the matter—the necessity of war lies far deeper than these honest
gentlemen suppose. What! Is there a field for all the petty disputes of
individuals, and shall there be no great law court for the settlement of
national difficulties? The battle-field is the only court where such suits can
be tried!"

"You forget, general," rejoined I, "that, in this advanced stage of civilization, Reason and Philanthropy combined will constitute just such a tribunal as is requisite."

"Ah, I had forgotten that, indeed!" said the old warrior, as he limped away.

The fire was now to be replenished with materials that had hitherto been considered of even greater importance to the well-being of society, than the warlike munitions which we had already seen consumed. A body of reformers had travelled all over the earth, in quest of the machinery by which the different nations were accustomed to inflict the punishment of death. A shudder passed through the multitude, as these ghastly emblems were dragged forward. Even the flames seemed at first to shrink away, displaying the shape and murderous contrivance of each in a full blaze of light, which, of itself, was sufficient to convince mankind of the long and deadly error of human law. Those old implements of cruelty—those horrible monsters of mechanism—those inventions which it seemed to demand something worse than man's natural heart to contrive, and which had lurked in the dusky nooks of ancient prisons, the subject of terror-stricken legend—were now brought forth to view. Headsmen's axes, with the rust of noble and royal blood upon them, and a vast collection of halters that had choked the breath of plebeian victims, were thrown in together. A shout greeted the arrival of the guillotine, which was thrust forward on the same wheels that had borne it from one to another of the blood-stained streets of Paris. But the loudest roar of applause went up, telling the distant sky of the triumph of the earth's redemption, when the gallows made its appearance. An ill-looking fellow, however, rushed forward, and, putting himself in the path of the reformers, bellowed hoarsely, and fought with brute fury to stay their progress.

It was little matter of surprise, perhaps, that the executioner should thus do his best to vindicate and uphold the machinery by which he himself had his livelihood, and worthier individuals their death. But it deserved special note, that men of a far different sphere,—even of that class in whose guardianship the world is apt to trust its benevolence—were found to take the hangman's view of the question.

"Stay, my brethren!" cried one of them. "You are misled by a false philanthropy!—you know not what you do. The gallows is a Heaven-ordained instrument! Bear it back, then, reverently, and set it up in its old place; else the world will fall to speedy ruin and desolation!"

"Onward, onward!" shouted a leader in the reform. "Into the flames with the accursed instrument of man's bloody policy. How can human law inculcate benevolence and love, while it persists in setting up the gallows as its chief symbol? One heave more, good friends, and the world will be redeemed from its greatest error!"

A thousand hands, that, nevertheless, loathed the touch, now lent their assistance, and thrust the ominous burthen far, far, into the centre of the raging furnace. There its fatal and abhorred image was beheld, first black, then a red coal, then ashes.

"That was well done!" exclaimed I.

"Yes, it was well done," replied—but with less enthusiasm than I expected—the thoughtful observer who was still at my side; "well done, if the world be good enough for the measure. Death, however, is an idea that cannot easily be dispensed with, in any condition between the primal innocence and that other purity and perfection, which, perchance, we are destined to attain after travelling round the full circle. But, at all events, it is well that the experiment should now be tried."

"Too cold! too cold!" impatiently exclaimed the young and ardent leader in this triumph. "Let the heart have its voice here, as well as the intellect. And as for ripeness—and as for progress—let mankind always do the highest, kindest, noblest thing that, at any given period, it has attained the perception of; and surely that thing cannot be wrong, nor wrongly timed."

I know not whether it were the excitement of the scene, or whether the good people around the bonfire were really growing more enlightened every instant; but they now proceeded to measures, in the full length of which I was hardly prepared to keep them company. For instance, some threw their marriage certificates into the flames, and declared themselves candidates for a higher, holier, and more comprehensive union than that which had subsisted from the birth of time, under the form of the connubial tie. Others hastened to the vaults of banks, and to the coffers of the rich—all of which were open to the first comer, on this fated occasion—and brought entire bales of paper-money to enliven the blaze, and tons of coin to be melted down by its intensity. Henceforth, they said, universal benevolence, uncoined and exhaustless, was to be the golden currency of the world. At this intelligence, the bankers, and speculators in the stocks, grew pale; and a pickpocket, who had reaped a rich harvest among the crowd, fell down in a deadly fainting-fit. A few men of business burnt their day-books and ledgers, the notes and obligations of their creditors, and all other evidences of debts due to themselves; while perhaps a somewhat larger number satisfied their zeal for reform with the sacrifice of any uncomfortable recollection of their own indebtment. There was then a cry, that the period was arrived when the title-deeds of landed property should be given to the flames, and the whole soil of the earth revert to the public, from whom it had been wrongfully abstracted, and most unequally distributed among individuals. Another party demanded that all written constitutions, set forms of government, legislative acts, statute-books, and everything else on which human invention had endeavored to stamp its arbitrary laws, should at once be destroyed, leaving the consummated world as free as the man first created.

Whether any ultimate action was taken with regard to these proposi- tions, is beyond my knowledge; for, just then, some matters were in progress that concerned my sympathies more nearly.

"See!—see!—what heaps of books and pamphlets!" cried a fellow, who did not seem to be a lover of literature. "Now we shall have a glorious blaze!"

"That's just the thing," said a modern philosopher. "Now we shall get rid of the weight of dead men's thought, which has hitherto pressed so heavily on the living intellect that it has been incompetent to any effectual self-exertion. Well done, my lads! Into the fire with them! Now you are enlightening the world, indeed!"

"But what is to become of the Trade?" cried a frantic bookseller.

"Oh, by all means, let them accompany their merchandise," coolly observed an author. "It will be a noble funeral pile!"

The truth was, that the human race had now reached a stage of progress so far beyond what the wisest and wittiest men of former ages had ever dreamed of, that it would have been a manifest absurdity to allow the earth to be any longer encumbered with their poor achievements in the literary line. Accordingly, a thorough and searching investigation had swept the booksellers' shops, hawkers' stands, public and private libraries, and even the little book-shelf by the country fireside, and had brought the world's entire mass of printed paper, bound or in sheets, to swell the already mountain-bulk of our illustrious bonfire. Thick, heavy folios, containing the labors of lexicographers, commentators, and encyclopedists, were flung in, and, falling among the embers with a leaden thump, smouldered away to ashes, like rotten wood. The small, richly gilt French tomes of the last age, with the hundred volumes of Voltaire among them, went off in a brilliant shower of sparkles, and little jets of flame; while the current literature of the same nation burnt red and blue, and threw an infernal light over the visages of the spectators, converting them all to the aspect of parti-colored fiends. A collection of German stories emitted a scent of brimstone. The English standard authors made excellent fuel, generally exhibiting the properties of sound oak logs. Milton's works, in particular, sent up a powerful blaze, gradually reddening into a coal, which promised to endure longer than almost any other material of the pile. From Shake- speare there gushed a flame of such marvellous splendor that men shaded their eyes as against the sun's meridian glory; nor even when the works of his own elucidators were flung upon him did he cease to flash forth a dazzling radiance from beneath the ponderous heap. It is my belief that he is still blazing as fervidly as ever.

"Could a poet but light a lamp at that glorious flame," remarked I, "he might then consume the midnight oil to some good purpose."

"That is the very thing which modern poets have been too apt to do, or at least to attempt," answered a critic. "The chief benefit to be expected from this conflagration of past literature undoubtedly is, that writers will henceforth be compelled to light their lamps at the sun or stars."

"If they can reach so high," said I. "But that task requires a giant, who may afterward distribute the light among inferior men. It is not every one that can steal the fire from heaven, like Prometheus; but when once he had done the deed, a thousand hearths were kindled by it."

It amazed me much to observe how indefinite was the proportion between the physical mass of any given author, and the property of brilliant and long-continued combustion. For instance, there was not a quarto volume of the last century—nor, indeed, of the present—that could compete, in that particular, with a child's little gilt-covered book, containing Mother Goose's Melodies. The Life and Death of Tom Thumb outlasted the biography of Marlborough. An epic—indeed, a dozen of them—was converted to white ashes, before the single sheet of an old ballad was half consumed. In more than one case, too, when volumes of applauded verse proved incapable of anything better than a stifling smoke, an unregarded ditty of some nameless bard—perchance in the corner of a newspaper— soared up among the stars, with a flame as brilliant as their own. Speaking of the properties of flame, methought Shelley's poetry emitted a purer light than almost any other productions of his day; contrasting beautifully with the fitful and lurid gleams, and gushes of black vapor, that flashed and eddied from the volumes of Lord Byron. As for Tom Moore, some of his songs diffused an odor like a burning pastille.

I felt particular interest in watching the combustion of American authors, and scrupulously noted, by my watch, the precise number of moments that changed most of them from shabbily printed books to indistinguishable ashes. It would be invidious, however, if not perilous, to betray these awful secrets; so that I shall content myself with observing, that it was not invariably the writer most frequent in the public mouth that made the most splendid appearance in the bonfire. I especially remember, that a great deal of excellent inflammability was exhibited in a thin volume of poems by Ellery Channing; although, to speak the truth, there were certain portions that hissed and spluttered in a very disagreeable fashion. A curious phenomenon occurred in reference to several writers, native as well as foreign. Their books, though of highly respectable figure, instead of bursting into a blaze, or even smoldering out their substance in smoke, suddenly melted away, in a manner that proved them to be ice.

If it be no lack of modesty to mention my own works, it must here be confessed, that I looked for them with fatherly interest, but in vain. Too probably, they were changed to vapor by the first action of the heat; at best, I can only hope that, in their quiet way, they contributed a glimmering spark or two to the splendor of the evening.

"Alas! and woe is me!" thus bemoaned himself a heavy-looking gentleman in green spectacles. "The world is utterly ruined, and there is nothing to live for any longer! The business of my life is snatched from me. Not a volume to be had for love or money!"

"This," remarked the sedate observer beside me, "is a book-worm—one of those men who are born to gnaw dead thoughts. His clothes, you see, are covered with the dust of libraries. He has no inward fountain of ideas; and, in good earnest, now that the old stock is abolished, I do not see what is to become of the poor fellow. Have you no word of comfort for him?"

"My dear sir," said I, to the desperate book-worm, "is not Nature better than a book?—is not the human heart deeper than any system of philosophy?—is not life replete with more instruction than past observers have found it possible to write down in maxims? Be of good cheer! The great book of Time is still spread wide open before us; and, if we read it aright, it will be to us a volume of eternal Truth."

"Oh, my books, my books, my precious, printed books!" reiterated the forlorn book-worm. "My only reality was a bound volume; and now they will not leave me even a shadowy pamphlet!"

In fact, the last remnant of the literature of all the ages was now descending upon the blazing heap, in the shape of a cloud of pamphlets from the press of the New World. These, likewise, were consumed in the twinkling of an eye, leaving the earth, for the first time since the days of Cadmus, free from the plague of letters—an enviable field for the authors of the next generation!

"Well!—and does anything remain to be done?" inquired I, somewhat anxiously. "Unless we set fire to the earth itself, and then leap boldly off into infinite space, I know not that we can carry reform to any further point."

"You are vastly mistaken, my good friend," said the observer. "Believe me, the fire will not be allowed to settle down without the addition of fuel that will startle many persons, who have lent a willing hand thus far."

Nevertheless, there appeared to be a relaxation of effort, for a little time, during which, probably, the leaders of the movement were considering what should be done next. In the interval, a philosopher threw his theory into the flames; a sacrifice which, by those who knew how to estimate it, was pronounced the most remarkable that had yet been made. The combustion, however, was by no means brilliant. Some indefatigable people, scorning to take a moment's ease, now employed themselves in collecting all the withered leaves and fallen boughs of the forest, and thereby recruited the bonfire to a greater height than ever. But this was mere by-play.

"Here comes the fresh fuel that I spoke of," said my companion.

To my astonishment, the persons who now advanced into the vacant space around the mountain fire, bore surplices and other priestly garments, mitres, crosiers, and a confusion of Popish and Protestant emblems, with which it seemed their purpose to consummate the great Act of Faith. Crosses, from the spires of old cathedrals, were cast upon the heap with as little remorse as if the reverence of centuries, passing in long array beneath the lofty towers, had not looked up to them as the holiest of symbols. The font, in which infants were consecrated to God; the sacramental vessels, whence Piety received the hallowed draught; were given to the same destruction. Perhaps it most nearly touched my heart to see, among these devoted relics, fragments of the humble communion tables and undecorated pulpits, which I recognized as having been torn from the meeting-houses of New England. Those simple edifices might have been permitted to retain all of sacred embellishments that their Puritan founders had bestowed, even though the mighty structure of St. Peter's had sent its spoils to the fire of this terrible sacrifice. Yet I felt that these were but the externals of religion, and might most safely be relinquished by spirits that best knew their deep significance.

"All is well," said I cheerfully. "The wood-paths shall be the aisles of our cathedral—the firmament itself shall be its ceiling! What needs an earthly roof between the Deity and his worshippers? Our faith can well afford to lose all the drapery that even the holiest men have thrown around it, and be only the more sublime in its simplicity."

"True," said my companion. "But will they pause here?"

The doubt implied in his question was well founded. In the general destruction of books already described, a holy volume—that stood apart from the catalogue of human literature, and yet, in one sense, was at its head—had been spared. But the Titan of innovation—angel or fiend, double in his nature, and capable of deeds befitting both characters—at first shaking down only the old and rotten shapes of things, had now, as it appeared, laid his terrible hand upon the main pillars which supported the whole edifice of our moral and spiritual state. The inhabitants of the earth had grown too enlightened to define their faith within a form of words, or to limit the spiritual by any analogy to our material existence. Truths, which the heavens trembled at, were now but a fable of the world's infancy. Therefore, as the final sacrifice of human error, what else remained to be thrown upon the embers of that awful pile, except the Book, which, though a celestial revelation to past ages, was but a voice from a lower sphere, as regarded the present race of man? It was done! Upon the blazing heap of falsehood and worn out truth—things that the earth had never needed, or had ceased to need, or had grown childishly weary of— fell the ponderous church Bible, the great old volume, that had lain so long on the cushion of the pulpit, and whence the pastor's solemn voice had given holy utterance on so many a Sabbath day. There, likewise, fell the family Bible, which the long-buried patriarch had read to his children— in prosperity or sorrow, by the fireside and in the summer shade of trees —and had bequeathed downward, as the heirloom of generations. There fell the bosom Bible, the little volume that had been the soul's friend of some sorely tried child of dust, who thence took courage, whether his trial were for life or death, steadfastly confronting both in the strong assurance of immortality.

All these were flung into the fierce and riotous blaze; and then a mighty wind came roaring across the plain, with a desolate howl, as if it were the angry lamentations of the Earth for the loss of Heaven's sunshine, and it shook the gigantic pyramid of flame, and scattered the cinders of half-consumed abominations around upon the spectators.

"This is terrible!" said I, feeling that my cheek grew pale, and seeing a like change in the visages about me.

"Be of good courage yet," answered the man with whom I had so often spoken. He continued to gaze steadily at the spectacle, with a singular calmness, as if it concerned him merely as an observer. "Be of good courage —nor yet exult too much; for there is far less both of good and evil, in the effect of this bonfire, than the world might be willing to believe."

"How can that be?" exclaimed I, impatiently. "Has it not consumed everything? Has it not swallowed up, or melted down, every human or divine appendage of our mortal state that had substance enough to be acted on by fire? Will there be anything left us tomorrow morning, better or worse than a heap of embers and ashes?"

"Assuredly there will," said my grave friend. "Come hither tomorrow morning—or whenever the combustible portion of the pile shall be quite burnt out—and you will find among the ashes everything really valuable that you have seen cast into the flames. Trust me, the world of tomorrow will again enrich itself with the gold and diamonds which have been cast off by the world of today. Not a truth is destroyed—nor buried so deep among the ashes, but it will be raked up at last."

This was a strange assurance. Yet I felt inclined to credit it; the more especially as I beheld among the wallowing flames a copy of the Holy Scriptures, the pages of which, instead of being blackened into tinder, only assumed a more dazzling whiteness as the finger-marks of human imperfection were purified away. Certain marginal notes and commentaries, it is true, yielded to the intensity of the fiery test, but without detriment to the smallest syllable that had flamed from the pen of inspiration.

"Yes—there is the proof of what you say," answered I, turning to the observer. "But if only what is evil can feel the action of the fire, then, surely, the conflagration has been of inestimable utility. Yet if I understand aright, you intimate a doubt whether the world's expectation of benefit would be realized by it."

"Listen to the talk of these worthies," said he, pointing to a group in front of the blazing pile. "Possibly they may teach you something useful, without intending it."

The persons whom he indicated consisted of that brutal and most earthy figure who had stood forth so furiously in defence of the gallows—the hangman, in short—together with the last thief and the last murderer; all three of whom were clustered about the last toper. The latter was liberally passing the brandy bottle, which he had rescued from the general destruction of wines and spirits. This little convivial party seemed at the lowest pitch of despondency; as considering that the purified world must needs be utterly unlike the sphere that they had hitherto known, and therefore but a strange and desolate abode for gentlemen of their kidney.

"The best counsel for all of us is," remarked the hangman, "that—as soon as we have finished the last drop of liquor—I help you, my three friends, to a comfortable end upon the nearest tree, and then hang myself on the same bough. This is no world for us any longer."

"Poh, poh, my good fellows!" said a dark-complexioned personage, who now joined the group—his complexion was indeed fearfully dark, and his eyes glowed with a redder light than that of the bonfire—"Be not so cast down, my dear friends; you shall see good days yet. There is one thing that these wiseacres have forgotten to throw into the fire, and without which all the rest of the conflagration is just nothing at all; yes—though they had burnt the earth itself to a cinder!"

"And what may that be?" eagerly demanded the last murderer.

"What but the human heart itself!" said the dark visaged stranger, with a portentous grin. "And unless they hit upon some method of purifying that foul cavern, forth from it will re-issue all the shapes of wrong and misery—the same old shapes, or worse ones—which they have taken such a vast deal of trouble to consume to ashes. I have stood by, this live-long night, and laughed in my sleeve at the whole business. Oh, take my word for it, it will be the old world yet!"

This brief conversation supplied me with a theme for lengthened thought. How sad a truth—if true it were—that Man's age-long endeavor for perfection had served only to render him the mockery of the Evil Principle, from the fatal circumstance of an error at the very root of the matter! The heart—the heart—there was the little yet boundless sphere, wherein existed the original wrong, of which the crime and misery of this outward world were merely types. Purify that inward sphere; and the many shapes of evil that haunt the outward, and which now seem almost our only realities, will turn to shadowy phantoms, and vanish of their own accord. But if we go no deeper than the Intellect, and strive, with merely that feeble instrument, to discern and rectify what is wrong, our whole accomplishment will be a dream; so unsubstantial, that it matters little whether the bonfire, which I have so faithfully described, were what we choose to call a real event, and a flame that would scorch the finger—or only a phosphoric radiance, and a parable of my own brain!

THE DREAM OF A RIDICULOUS MAN

A Fantastic Story

I

I am a ridiculous man. They call me a madman now. That would be a distinct rise in my social position were it not that they still regard me as being as ridiculous as ever. But that does not make me angry any more. They are all dear to me now even while they laugh at me—yes, even then they are for some reason particularly dear to me. I shouldn't have minded laughing with them—not at myself, of course, but because I love them— had I not felt so sad as I looked at them. I feel sad because they do not know the truth, whereas I know it. Oh, how hard it is to be the only man to know the truth! But they won't understand that. No, they will not understand.

And yet in the past I used to be terribly distressed at appearing to be ridiculous. No, not appearing to be, but being. I've always cut a ridiculous figure. I suppose I must have known it from the day I was born. At any rate, I've known for certain that I was ridiculous ever since I was seven years old. Afterwards I went to school, then to the university, and—well —the more I learned, the more conscious did I become of the fact that I was ridiculous. So that for me my years of hard work at the university seem in the end to have existed for the sole purpose of demonstrating and proving to me, the more deeply engrossed I became in my studies, that I was an utterly absurd person. And as during my studies, so all my life. Every year the same consciousness that I was ridiculous in every way strengthened and intensified in my mind. They always laughed at me. But not one of them knew or suspected that if there were one man on earth who knew better than anyone else that he was ridiculous, that man was I. And this—I mean, the fact that they did not know it—was the bitterest pill for me to swallow. But there I was myself at fault. I was always so proud that I never wanted to confess it to anyone. No, I wouldn't do that for anything in the world. As the years passed, this pride increased in me

Source: Reprinted from *The Best Short Stories of Fyodor Dostoevsky,* translated by David Magarshack. Reprinted with the permission of Random House, Inc. All rights reserved.

so that I do believe that if ever I had by chance confessed it to any one I should have blown my brains out the same evening. Oh, how I suffered in the days of my youth from the thought that I might not myself resist the impulse to confess it to my schoolfellows. But ever since I became a man I grew for some unknown reason a little more composed in my mind, though I was more and more conscious of that awful characteristic of mine. Yes, most decidedly for some unknown reason, for to this day I have not been able to find out why that was so. Perhaps it was because I was becoming terribly disheartened owing to one circumstance which was beyond my power to control, namely, the conviction which was gaining upon me that nothing in the whole world *made any difference.* I had long felt it dawning upon me, but I was fully convinced of it only last year, and that, too, all of a sudden, as it were. I suddenly felt that it made *no* difference to me whether the world existed or whether nothing existed anywhere at all. I began to be acutely conscious that *nothing existed in my own lifetime.* At first I couldn't help feeling that at any rate in the past many things had existed; but later on I came to the conclusion that there had not been anything even in the past, but that for some reason it had merely seemed to have been. Little by little I became convinced that there would be nothing in the future, either. It was then that I suddenly ceased to be angry with people and almost stopped noticing them. This indeed disclosed itself in the smallest trifles. For instance, I would knock against people while walking in the street. And not because I was lost in thought —I had nothing to think about—I had stopped thinking about anything at that time: it made no difference to me. Not that I had found an answer to all the questions. Oh, I had not settled a single question, and there were thousands of them! But *it made no difference to me,* and all the questions disappeared.

And, well, it was only after that that I learnt the truth. I learnt the truth last November, on the third of November, to be precise, and every moment since then has been imprinted indelibly on my mind. It happened on a dismal evening, as dismal an evening as could be imagined. I was returning home at about eleven o'clock and I remember thinking all the time that there could not be a more dismal evening. Even the weather was foul. It had been pouring all day, and the rain too was the coldest and most dismal rain that ever was, a sort of menacing rain—I remember that—a rain with a distinct animosity towards people. But about eleven o'clock it had stopped suddenly, and a horrible dampness descended upon everything, and it became much damper and colder than when it had been raining. And a sort of steam was rising from everything, from every cobble in the street, and from every side-street if you peered closely into it from the street as far as the eye could reach. I could not help feeling that if the gaslight had been extinguished everywhere, everything would have seemed much more cheerful, and that the gaslight oppressed the heart so much just because it shed a light upon it all. I had had scarcely any dinner that day. I had been spending the whole evening with an engineer who had two more friends visiting him. I never opened my mouth, and I expect I must have got on their nerves. They were discussing some highly controversial subject, and suddenly got very excited over it. But it really did not make any difference to them. I could see that. I knew that their excitement was not genuine. So I suddenly blurted it out. "My dear fellows," I said, "you don't really care a damn about it, do you?" They were not in the least offended, but they all burst out laughing at me. That was because I had said it without meaning to rebuke them, but simply because it made no difference to me. Well, they realized that it made no difference to me, and they felt happy.

When I was thinking about the gaslight in the streets, I looked up at the sky. The sky was awfully dark, but I could clearly distinguish the torn wisps of cloud and between them fathomless dark patches. All of a sudden I became aware of a little star in one of those patches and I began looking at it intently. That was because the little star gave me an idea: I made up my mind to kill myself that night. I had made up my mind to kill myself already two months before and, poor as I am, I bought myself an excellent revolver and loaded it the same day. But two months had elapsed and it was still lying in the drawer. I was so utterly indifferent to everything that I was anxious to wait for the moment when I would not be so indifferent and then kill myself. Why—I don't know. And so every night during these two months I thought of shooting myself as I was going home. I was only waiting for the right moment. And now the little star gave me an idea, and I made up my mind then and there that it should *most certainly* be that night. But why the little star gave me the idea—I don't know.

And just as I was looking at the sky, this little girl suddenly grasped me by the elbow. The street was already deserted and there was scarcely a soul to be seen. In the distance a cabman was fast asleep on his box. The girl was about eight years old. She had a kerchief on her head, and she wore only an old, shabby little dress. She was soaked to the skin, but what stuck in my memory was her little torn wet boots. I still remember them. They caught my eye especially. She suddenly began tugging at my elbow and calling me. She was not crying, but saying something in a loud, jerky sort of voice, something that did not make sense, for she was trembling all over and her teeth were chattering from cold. She seemed to be terrified of something and she was crying desperately, "Mummy! Mummy!" I turned round to look at her, but did not utter a word and went on walking. But she ran after me and kept tugging at my clothes, and there was a sound in her voice which in very frightened children signifies despair. I know that sound. Though her words sounded as if they were choking her, I realized that her mother must be dying somewhere very near, or that something similar was happening to her, and that she had run out to call someone, to find someone who would help her mother. But I did not go with her; on the contrary, something made me drive her away. At first I told her to go and find a policeman. But she suddenly clasped her hands and, whimpering and gasping for breath, kept running at my side and would not leave me. It was then that I stamped my foot and shouted at her. She just cried, "Sir! Sir! . . ." and then she left me suddenly and rushed headlong across the road: another man appeared there and she evidently rushed from me to him.

I climbed to the fifth floor. I live apart from my landlord. We all have separate rooms as in a hotel. My room is very small and poor. My window is a semicircular skylight. I have a sofa covered with American cloth, a table with books on it, two chairs and a comfortable armchair, a very old armchair indeed, but low-seated and with a high back serving as a headrest. I sat down in the armchair, lighted the candle, and began thinking. Next door in the other room behind the partition, the usual bedlam was going on. It had been going on since the day before yesterday. A retired army captain lived there, and he had visitors—six merry gentlemen who drank vodka and played faro with an old pack of cards. Last night they had a fight and I know that two of them were for a long time pulling each other about by the hair. The landlady wanted to complain, but she is dreadfully afraid of the captain. We had only one more lodger in our rooms, a thin little lady, the wife of an army officer, on a visit to Petersburg with her three little children who had all been taken ill since their arrival at our house. She and her children were simply terrified of the captain and they lay shivering and crossing themselves all night long, and the youngest child had a sort of nervous attack from fright. This captain (I know that for a fact) sometimes stops people on Nevsky Avenue and asks them for a few coppers, telling them he is very poor. He can't get a job in the Civil Service, but the strange thing is (and that's why I am telling you this) that the captain had never once during the month he had been living with us made me feel in the least irritated. From the very first, of course, I would not have anything to do with him, and he himself was bored with me the very first time we met. But however big a noise they raised behind their partition and however many of them there were in the captain's room, it makes no difference to me. I sit up all night and, I assure you, I don't hear them at all—so completely do I forget about them. You see, I stay awake all night till daybreak, and that has been going on for a whole year now. I sit up all night in the armchair at the table—doing nothing. I read books only in the daytime. At night I sit like that without even thinking about anything in particular: some thoughts wander in and out of my mind, and I let them come and go as they please. In the night the candle burns out completely.

I sat down at the table, took the gun out of the drawer, and put it down in front of me. I remember asking myself as I put it down, "Is it to be then?" and I replied with complete certainty, "It is!" That is to say, I was going to shoot myself. I knew I should shoot myself that night for certain. What I did not know was how much longer I should go on sitting at the table till I shot myself. And I should of course have shot myself, had it not been for the little girl.

II

You see, though nothing made any difference to me, I could feel pain, for instance, couldn't I? If anyone had struck me, I should have felt pain. The same was true so far as my moral perceptions were concerned. If anything happened to arouse my pity, I should have felt pity, just as I used to do at the time when things did make a difference to me. So I had felt pity that night: I should most decidedly have helped a child. Why then did I not help the little girl? Because of a thought that had occurred to me at the time: when she was pulling at me and calling me, a question suddenly arose in my mind and I could not settle it. It was an idle question, but it made me angry. What made me angry was the conclusion I drew from the reflection that if I had really decided to do away with myself that night, everything in the world should have been more indifferent to me than ever. Why then should I have suddenly felt that I was not indifferent and be sorry for the little girl? I remember that I was very sorry for her, so much so that I felt a strange pang which was quite incomprehensible in my position. I'm afraid I am unable better to convey that fleeting sensation of mine, but it persisted with me at home when I was sitting at the table, and I was very much irritated. I had not been so irritated for a long time past. One train of thought followed another. It was clear to me that so long as I was still a human being and not a meaningless cipher, and till I became a cipher, I was alive, and consequently able to suffer, be angry, and feel shame at my actions. Very well. But if, on the other hand, I were going to kill myself in, say, two hours, what did that little girl matter to me and what did I care for shame or anything else in the world? I was going to turn into a cipher, into an absolute cipher. And surely the realization that I should soon cease to exist *altogether*, and hence everything would cease to exist, ought to have had some slight effect on my feeling of pity for the little girl or on my feeling of shame after so mean an action. Why after all did I stamp and shout so fiercely at the little girl? I did it because I thought that not only did I feel no pity, but that it wouldn't matter now if I were guilty of the most inhuman baseness, since in another two hours everything would become extinct. Do you believe me when I tell you that that was the only reason why I shouted like that? I am almost convinced of it now. It seemed clear to me that life and the world in some way or other depended on me now. It might almost be said that the world seemed to be created for me alone. If I were to shoot myself, the world would cease to exist—for me at any rate. To say nothing of the possibility that nothing would in fact exist for anyone after me and the whole world would dissolve as soon as my consciousness became extinct, would disappear in a twinkling like a phantom, like some integral part of my consciousness, and vanish without leaving a trace behind, for all this world and all these people exist perhaps only in my consciousness.

I remember that as I sat and meditated, I began to examine all these questions which thronged in my mind one after another from quite a different angle, and thought of something quite new. For instance, the strange notion occurred to me that if I had lived before on the moon or on Mars and had committed there the most shameful and dishonorable action that can be imagined, and had been so disgraced and dishonored there as can be imagined and experienced only occasionally in a dream, a nightmare, and if, finding myself afterwards on earth, I had retained the memory of what I had done on the other planet, and moreover knew that I should never in any circumstances go back there—if that were to have happened, should I or should I not have felt, as I looked from the earth upon the moon, that *it made no difference* to me? Should I or should I not have felt ashamed of that action? The questions were idle and useless, for the gun was already lying before me and there was not a shadow of doubt in my mind that *it* was going to take place for certain, but they excited and maddened me. It seemed to me that I could not die now without having settled something first. The little girl, in fact, had saved me, for by these questions I put off my own execution.

Meanwhile things had grown more quiet in the captain's room: they had finished their card game and were getting ready to turn in for the night, and now were only grumbling and swearing at each other in a halfhearted sort of way. It was at that moment that I suddenly fell asleep in my armchair at the table, a thing that had never happened to me before.

I fell asleep without being aware of it at all. Dreams, as we all know, are very curious things: certain incidents in them are presented with quite uncanny vividness, each detail executed with the finishing touch of a jeweler, while others you leap across as though entirely unaware of, for instance, space and time. Dreams seem to be induced not by reason but by desire, not by the head but by the heart, and yet what clever tricks my reason has sometimes played on me in dreams! And furthermore what incomprehensible things happen to it in a dream. My brother, for instance, died five years ago. I sometimes dream about him: he takes a keen interest in my affairs, we are both very interested, and yet I know very well all through my dream that my brother is dead and buried. How is it that I am not surprised that, though dead, he is here beside me, doing his best to help me? Why does my reason accept all this without the slightest hesitation? But enough. Let me tell you about my dream. Yes, I dreamed that dream that night. My dream of the third of November. They are making fun of me now by saying that it was only a dream. But what does it matter whether it was a dream or not, so long as that dream revealed the Truth to me? For once you have recognized the truth and seen it, you know it is the one and only truth and that there can be no other, whether you are asleep or awake. But never mind. Let it be a dream, but remember that I had intended to cut short by suicide that life that means so much to us, and that my dream—my dream—oh, it revealed to me a new, grand, regenerated, strong life!

Listen.

III

I have said that I fell asleep imperceptibly and even while I seemed to be revolving the same thoughts again in my mind. Suddenly I dreamed that I picked up the gun and, sitting in my armchair, pointed it straight at my heart—at my heart, and not at my head. For I had firmly resolved to shoot myself through the head, through the right temple, to be precise. Having aimed the gun at my breast, I paused for a second or two, and suddenly my candle, the table and the wall began moving and swaying before me. I fired quickly.

In a dream you sometimes fall from a great height, or you are being murdered or beaten, but you never feel any pain unless you really manage somehow or other to hurt yourself in bed, when you feel pain and almost always wake up from it. So it was in my dream: I did not feel any pain, but it seemed as though with my shot everything within me was shaken and everything was suddenly extinguished, and a terrible darkness descended all around me. I seemed to have become blind and dumb. I was lying on something hard, stretched out full length on my back. I saw nothing and could not make the slightest movement. All round me people were walking and shouting. The captain was yelling in his deep bass voice, the landlady was screaming and—suddenly another hiatus, and I was being carried in a closed coffin. I could feel the coffin swaying and I was thinking about it, and for the first time the idea flashed through my mind that I was dead, dead as a doornail, that I knew it, that there was not the least doubt about it, that I could neither see nor move, and yet I could feel and reason. But I was soon reconciled to that and, as usually happens in dreams, I accepted the facts without questioning them.

And now I was buried in the earth. They all went away, and I was left alone, entirely alone. I did not move. Whenever before I imagined how I should be buried in a grave, there was only one sensation I actually associated with the grave, namely, that of damp and cold. And so it was now. I felt that I was very cold, especially in the tips of my toes, but I felt nothing else.

I lay in my grave and, strange to say, I did not expect anything, accepting the idea that a dead man had nothing to expect as an incontestable fact. But it was damp. I don't know how long a time passed, whether an hour, or several days, or many days. But suddenly a drop of water, which had seeped through the lid of the coffin, fell on my closed left eye. It was followed by another drop a minute later, then after another minute by another drop, and so on. One drop every minute. All at once deep indignation blazed up in my heart, and I suddenly felt a twinge of physical pain in it. "That's my wound," I thought. "It's the shot I fired. There's a bullet there. . . ." And drop after drop still kept falling every minute on my closed eyelid. And suddenly I called (not with my voice, for I was motionless, but with the whole of my being) upon Him who was responsible for all that was happening to me:

"Whoever Thou art, and if anything more rational exists than what is happening here, let it, I pray Thee, come to pass here too. But if Thou are revenging Thyself for my senseless act of self-destruction by the infamy and absurdity of life after death, then know that no torture that may be inflicted upon me can ever equal the contempt which I shall go on feeling in silence, though my martyrdom last for aeons upon aeons!"

I made this appeal and was silent. The dead silence went on for almost a minute, and one more drop fell on my closed eyelid, but I knew, I knew and believed infinitely and unshakably that everything would without a doubt change immediately. And then my grave was opened. I don't know, that is, whether it was opened or dug open, but I was seized by some dark and unknown being and we found ourselves in space. I suddenly regained my sight. It was a pitch-black night. Never, never had there been such darkness! We were flying through space at a terrific speed and we had already left the earth behind us. I did not question the being who was carrying me. I was proud and waited. I was telling myself that I was not afraid, and I was filled with admiration at the thought that I was not afraid. I cannot remember how long we were flying, nor can I give you an idea of the time; it all happened as it always does happen in dreams when you leap over space and time and the laws of nature and reason, and only pause at the points which are especially dear to your heart. All I remember is that I suddenly beheld a little star in the darkness.

"Is that Sirius?" I asked, feeling suddenly unable to restrain myself, for I had made up my mind not to ask any questions.

"No," answered the being who was carrying me, "that is the same star you saw between the clouds when you were coming home."

I knew that its face bore some resemblance to a human face. It is a strange fact but I did not like that being, and I even felt an intense aversion for it. I had expected complete non-existence and that was why I had shot myself through the heart. And yet there I was in the hands of a being, not human of course, but which *was*, which existed. "So there is life beyond the grave!" I thought with the curious irrelevance of a dream, but at heart I remained essentially unchanged. "If I must *be* again," I thought, "and live again at someone's unalterable behest, I won't be defeated and humiliated!"

"You know I'm afraid of you and that's why you despise me," I said suddenly to my companion, unable to refrain from the humiliating remark with its implied admission, and feeling my own humiliation in my heart like the sharp prick of a needle.

He did not answer me, but I suddenly felt that I was not despised, that no one was laughing at me, that no one was even pitying me, and that our journey had a purpose, an unknown and mysterious purpose that concerned only me. Fear was steadily growing in my heart. Something was communicated to me from my silent companion—mutely but agonizingly —and it seemed to permeate my whole being. We were speeding through dark and unknown regions of space. I had long since lost sight of the constellations familiar to me. I knew that there were stars in the heavenly spaces whose light took thousands and millions of years to reach the earth. Possibly we were already flying through those spaces. I expected something in the terrible anguish that wrung my heart. And suddenly a strangely familiar and incredibly nostalgic feeling shook me to the very core: I suddenly caught sight of our sun! I knew that it could not possibly be *our* sun that gave birth to our earth, and that we were millions of miles away from our sun, but for some unknown reason I recognized with every fiber of my being that it was precisely the same sun as ours, its exact copy and twin. A sweet, nostalgic feeling filled my heart with rapture: the old familiar power of the same light which had given me life stirred an echo in my heart and revived it, and I felt the same life stirring within me for the first time since I had been in the grave.

"But if it is the sun, if it's exactly the same sun as ours," I cried, "then where is the earth?"

And my companion pointed to a little star twinkling in the darkness with an emerald light. We were making straight for it.

"But are such repetitions possible in the universe? Can that be nature's law? And if that is an earth there, is it the same earth as ours? Just the same poor, unhappy, but dear, dear earth, and beloved for ever and ever? Arousing like our earth the same poignant love for herself even in the most ungrateful of her children?" I kept crying, deeply moved by an uncontrollable, rapturous love for the dear old earth I had left behind.

The face of the poor little girl I had treated so badly flashed through my mind.

"You shall see it all," answered my companion, and a strange sadness sounded in his voice.

But we were rapidly approaching the planet. It was growing before my eyes. I could already distinguish the ocean, the outlines of Europe, and suddenly a strange feeling of some great and sacred jealousy blazed up in my heart.

"How is such a repetition possible and why? I love, I can only love the earth I've left behind, stained with my blood when, ungrateful wretch that I am, I extinguished my life by shooting myself through the heart. But never, never have I ceased to love that earth, and even on the night I parted from it I loved it perhaps more poignantly than ever. Is there suffering on this new earth? On our earth we can truly love only with suffering and through suffering! We know not how to love otherwise. We know no other love. I want suffering in order to love. I want and thirst this very minute to kiss, with tears streaming down my cheeks, the one and only earth I have left behind. I don't want, I won't accept life on any other! . . ."

But my companion had already left me. Suddenly, and without as it were being aware of it myself, I stood on this other earth in the bright light of a sunny day, fair and beautiful as paradise. I believe I was standing on one of the islands which on our earth form the Greek archipelago, or somewhere on the coast of the mainland close to this archipelago. Oh, everything was just as it is with us, except that everything seemed to be bathed in the radiance of some public festival and of some great and holy triumph attained at last. The gentle emerald sea softly lapped the shore and kissed it with manifest, visible, almost conscious love. Tall, beautiful trees stood in all the glory of their green luxuriant foliage, and their innumerable leaves (I am sure of that) welcomed me with their soft, tender rustle, and seemed to utter sweet words of love. The lush grass blazed with bright and fragrant flowers. Birds were flying in flocks through the air and, without being afraid of me, alighted on my shoulders and hands and joyfully beat against me with their sweet fluttering wings. And at last I saw and came to know the people of this blessed earth. They came to me themselves. They surrounded me. They kissed me. Children of the sun, children of their sun—oh, how beautiful they were! Never on our earth had I beheld such beauty in man. Only perhaps in our children during the very first years of their life could one have found a remote, though faint, reflection of this beauty. The eyes of these happy people shone with a bright luster. Their faces were radiant with understanding and a serenity of mind that had reached its greatest fulfilment. Those faces were joyous; in the words and voices of these people there was a child-like gladness. Oh, at the first glance at their faces I at once understood all, all! It was an earth unstained by the Fall, inhabited by people who had not sinned and who lived in the same paradise as that in which, according to the legends of mankind, our first parents lived before they sinned, with the only difference that all the earth here was everywhere the same paradise. These people, laughing happily, thronged round me and overwhelmed me with their caresses; they took me home with them, and each of them was anxious to set my mind at peace. Oh, they asked me no questions, but seemed to know everything already (that was the impression I got), and they longed to remove every trace of suffering from my face as soon as possible.

IV

Well, you see, again let me repeat: All right, let us assume it was only a dream! But the sensation of the love of those innocent and beautiful people has remained with me for ever, and I can feel that their love is even now flowing out to me from over there. I have seen them myself. I have known them thoroughly and been convinced. I loved them and I suffered for them afterwards. Oh, I knew at once even all the time that there were many things about them I should never be able to understand. To me, a modern Russian progressive and a despicable citizen of Petersburg, it seemed inexplicable that, knowing so much, they knew nothing of our science, for instance. But I soon realized that their knowledge was derived from, and fostered by emotions other than those to which we were accustomed on earth, and that their aspirations, too, were quite different. They desired nothing. They were at peace with themselves. They did not strive to gain knowledge of life as we strive to understand it because their lives were full. But their knowledge was higher and deeper than the knowledge we derive from our science; for our science seeks to explain what life is and strives to understand it in order to teach others how to live, while they knew how to live without science. I understood that, but I couldn't understand their knowledge. They pointed out their trees to me and I could not understand the intense love with which they looked on them; it was as though they were talking with beings like themselves. And, you know, I don't think I am exaggerating in saying that they talked with them! Yes, they had discovered their language, and I am sure the trees understood them. They looked upon all nature like that—the animals which lived peaceably with them and did not attack them, but loved them, conquered by their love for them. They pointed out the stars to me and talked to me about them in a way that I could not understand, but I am certain that in some curious way they communed with the stars in the heavens, not only in thought, but in some actual, living way. Oh, these people were not concerned whether I understood them or not; they loved me without it. But I too knew that they would never be able to understand me, and for that reason I hardly ever spoke to them about our earth. I merely kissed the earth on which they lived in their presence, and worshipped them without any words. And they saw that and let me worship them without being ashamed that I was worshipping them, for they themselves loved much. They did not suffer for me when, weeping, I sometimes kissed their feet, for in their hearts they were joyfully aware of the strong affection with which they would return my love. At times I asked myself in amazement how they had managed never to offend a person like me and not once arouse in a person like me a feeling of jealousy and envy. Many times I asked myself how I—a braggart and a liar—could refrain from telling them all I knew of science and philosophy, of which of course they had no idea? How it had never occurred to me to impress them with my store of learning, or impart my learning to them out of the love I bore them?

They were playful and high-spirited like children. They wandered about their beautiful woods and groves, they sang their beautiful songs, they lived on simple food—the fruits of their trees, the honey from their woods, and the milk of the animals that loved them. To obtain their food and clothes, they did not work very hard or long. They knew love and they begot children, but I never noticed in them those outbursts of *cruel* sensuality which overtake almost everybody on our earth, whether man or woman, and are the only source of almost every sin of our human race. They rejoiced in their new-born children as new sharers in their bliss. There were no quarrels or jealousy among them, and they did not even know what the words meant. Their children were the children of them all, for they were all one family. There was scarcely any illness among them, though there was death; but their old people died peacefully, as though falling asleep, surrounded by the people who took leave of them, blessing them and smiling at them, and themselves receiving with bright smiles the farewell wishes of their friends. I never saw grief or tears on those occasions. What I did see was love that seemed to reach the point of rapture, but it was a gentle, self-sufficient, and contemplative rapture. There was reason to believe that they communicated with the departed after death, and that their earthly union was not cut short by death. They found it almost impossible to understand me when I questioned them about life eternal, but apparently they were so convinced of it in their minds that for them it was no question at all. They had no places of worship, but they had a certain awareness of a constant, uninterrupted, and living union with the Universe at large. They had no specific religions, but instead they had a certain knowledge that when their earthly joy had reached the limits imposed upon it by nature, they—both the living and the dead—would reach a state of still closer communion with the Universe at large. They looked forward to that moment with joy, but without haste and without pining for it, as though already possessing it in the vague stirrings of their hearts, which they communicated to each other.

In the evening, before going to sleep, they were fond of gathering together and singing in melodious and harmonious choirs. In their songs they expressed all the sensations the parting day had given them. They praised it and bade it farewell. They praised nature, the earth, the sea, and the woods. They were also fond of composing songs about one another, and they praised each other like children. Their songs were very simple, but they sprang straight from the heart and they touched the heart. And not only in their songs alone, but they seemed to spend all their lives in perpetual praise of one another. It seemed to be a universal and all-embracing love for each other. Some of their songs were solemn and ecstatic, and I was scarcely able to understand them at all. While understanding the words, I could never entirely fathom their meaning. It remained somehow beyond the grasp of my reason, and yet it sank unconsciously deeper and deeper into my heart. I often told them that I had had a presentiment of it years ago and that all that joy and glory had been perceived by me while I was still on our earth as a nostalgic yearning, bordering at times on unendurably poignant sorrow; that I had had a presentiment of them all and of their glory in the dreams of my heart and in the reveries of my soul; that often on our earth I could not look at the setting sun without tears. . . . That there always was a sharp pang of anguish in my hatred of the men of our earth; why could I not hate them without loving them too? why could I not forgive them? And in my love for them, too, there was a sharp pang of anguish: why could I not love them without hating them? They listened to me, and I could tell that they did not know what I was talking about. But I was not sorry to have spoken to them of it, for I knew that they appreciated how much and how anxiously I yearned for those I had forsaken. Oh yes, when they looked at me with their dear eyes full of love, when I realized that in their presence my heart, too, became as innocent and truthful as theirs, I did not regret my inability to understand them, either. The sensation of the fullness of life left me breathless, and I worshipped them in silence.

Oh, everyone laughs in my face now and everyone assures me that I could not possibly have seen and felt anything so definite, but was merely conscious of a sensation that arose in my own feverish heart, and that I invented all those details myself when I woke up. And when I told them that they were probably right, good Lord, what mirth that admission of mine caused and how they laughed at me! Why, of course, I was overpowered by the mere sensation of that dream and it alone survived in my sorely wounded heart. But none the less the real shapes and forms of my dream, that is, those I actually saw at the very time of my dream, were filled with such harmony and were so enchanting and beautiful, and so intensely true, that on awakening I was indeed unable to clothe them in our feeble words so that they were bound as it were to become blurred in my mind; so is it any wonder that perhaps unconsciously I was myself afterwards driven to make up the details which I could not help distorting, particularly in view of my passionate desire to convey some of them at least as quickly as I could. But that does not mean that I have no right to believe that it all did happen. As a matter of fact, it was quite possibly a thousand times better, brighter, and more joyful than I describe it. What if it was only a dream? All that couldn't possibly not have been. And do you know, I think I'll tell you a secret: perhaps it was no dream at all! For what happened afterwards was so awful, so horribly true, that it couldn't possibly have been a mere coinage of my brain seen in a dream. Granted that my heart was responsible for my dream, but could my heart alone have been responsible for the awful truth of what happened to me afterwards? Surely my paltry heart and my vacillating and trivial mind could not have risen to such a revelation of truth! Oh, judge for yourselves: I have been concealing it all the time, but now I will tell you the whole truth. The fact is, I— corrupted them all!

V

Yes, yes, it ended in my corrupting them all! How it could have happened I do not know, but I remember it clearly. The dream encompassed thousands of years and left in me only a vague sensation of the whole. I only know that the cause of the Fall was I. Like a horrible trichina, like the germ of the plague infecting whole kingdoms, so did I infect with myself all that happy earth that knew no sin before me. They learnt to lie, and they grew to appreciate the beauty of a lie. Oh, perhaps, it all began *innocently,* with a jest, with a desire to show off, with amorous play, and perhaps indeed only with a germ, but this germ made its way into their hearts and they liked it. The voluptuousness was soon born, voluptuousness begot jealousy, and jealousy—cruelty. . . . Oh, I don't know, I can't remember, but soon, very soon the first blood was shed; they were shocked and horrified, and they began to separate and to shun one another. They formed alliances, but it was one against another. Recriminations began, reproaches. They came to know shame, and they made shame into a virtue. The conception of honor was born, and every alliance raised its own standard. They began torturing animals, and the animals ran away from them into the forests and became their enemies. A struggle began for separation, for isolation, for personality, for mine and thine. They began talking in different languages. They came to know sorrow, and they loved sorrow. They thirsted for suffering, and they said that Truth could only be attained through suffering. It was then that science made its appearance among them. When they became wicked, they began talking of brotherhood and humanity and understood the meaning of those ideas. When they became guilty of crimes, they invented justice, and drew up whole codes of law, and to ensure the carrying out of their laws they erected a guillotine. They only vaguely remembered what they had lost, and they would not believe that they ever were happy and innocent. They even laughed at the possibility of their former happiness and called it a dream. They could not even imagine it in any definite shape or form, but the strange and wonderful thing was that though they had lost faith in their former state of happiness and called it a fairy-tale, they longed so much to be happy and innocent once more that, like children, they succumbed to the desire of their hearts, glorified this desire, built temples, and began offering up prayers to their own idea, their own "desire," and at the same time firmly believed that it could not be realized and brought about, though they still worshipped it and adored it with tears. And yet if they could have in one way or another returned to the state of happy innocence they had lost, and if someone had shown it to them again and had asked them whether they desired to go back to it, they would certainly have refused. The answer they gave me was, "What if we are dishonest, cruel, and unjust? We *know* it and we are sorry for it, and we torment ourselves for it, and inflict pain upon ourselves, and punish ourselves more perhaps than the merciful Judge who will judge us and whose name we do not know. But we have science and with its aid we shall again discover truth, though we shall accept it only when we perceive it with our reason. Knowledge is higher than feeling, and the consciousness of life is higher than life. Science will give us wisdom. Wisdom will reveal to us the laws. And the knowledge of the laws of happiness is higher than happiness." That is what they said to me, and having uttered those words, each of them began to love himself better than anyone else, and indeed they could not do otherwise. Every one of them became so jealous of his own personality that he strove with might and main to belittle and humble it in others; and therein he saw the whole purpose of his life. Slavery made its appearance, even voluntary slavery: the weak eagerly submitted themselves to the will of the strong on condition that the strong helped them to oppress those who were weaker than themselves. Saints made their appearance, saints who came to these people with tears and told them of their pride, of their loss of proportion and harmony, of their loss of shame. They were laughed to scorn and stoned to death. Their sacred blood was spilt on the threshold of the temples. But then men arose who began to wonder how they could all be united again, so that everybody should, without ceasing to love himself best of all, not interfere with everybody else and so that all of them should live together in a society which would at least seem to be founded on mutual understanding. Whole wars were fought over this idea. All the combatants at one and the same time firmly believed that science, wisdom, and the instinct of self-preservation would in the end force mankind to unite into a harmonious and intelligent society, and therefore, to hasten matters, the "very wise" did their best to exterminate as rapidly as possible the "not so wise" who did not understand their idea, so as to prevent them from interfering with its triumph. But the instinct of self-preservation began to weaken rapidly. Proud and voluptuous men appeared who frankly demanded all or nothing. In order to obtain everything they did not hesitate to resort to violence, and if it failed—to suicide. Religions were founded to propagate the cult of non-existence and self-destruction for the sake of the everlasting peace in nothingness. At last these people grew weary of their senseless labors and suffering appeared on their faces, and these people proclaimed that suffering was beauty, for in suffering alone was there thought. They glorified suffering in their songs. I walked among them, wringing my hands and weeping over them, but I loved them perhaps more than before when there was no sign of suffering in their faces and when they were innocent and—oh, so beautiful! I loved the earth they had polluted even more than when it had been a paradise, and only because sorrow had made its appearance on it. Alas, I always loved sorrow and affliction, but only for myself, only for myself; for them I wept now, for I pitied them. I stretched out my hands to them, accusing, cursing, and despising myself. I told them that I alone was responsible for it all—I alone; that it was I who had brought them corruption, contamination, and lies! I implored them to crucify me, and I taught them how to make the cross. I could not kill myself; I had not the courage to do it; but I longed to receive martyrdom at their hands. I thirsted for martyrdom, I yearned for my blood to be shed to the last drop in torment and suffering. But they only laughed at me, and in the end they began looking upon me as a madman. They justified me. They said that they had got what they themselves wanted and that what was now could not have been otherwise. At last they told me that I was becoming dangerous to them and that they would lock me up in a lunatic asylum if I did not hold my peace. Then sorrow entered my soul with such force that my heart was wrung and I felt as though I were dying, and then—well, then I awoke.

It was morning, that is, the sun had not risen yet, but it was about six o'clock. When I came to, I found myself in the same armchair, my candle had burnt out, in the captain's room they were asleep, and silence, so rare in our house, reigned around. The first thing I did was to jump up in great amazement. Nothing like this had ever happened to me before, not even so far as the most trivial details were concerned. Never, for instance, had I fallen asleep like this in my armchair. Then, suddenly, as I was standing and coming to myself, I caught sight of my gun lying there ready and loaded. But I pushed it away from me at once! Oh, how I longed for life, life! I lifted up my hands and called upon eternal Truth—no, not called upon it, but wept. Rapture, infinite and boundless rapture intoxicated me. Yes, life and—preaching! I made up my mind to preach from that very moment and, of course, to go on preaching all my life. I am going to preach, I want to preach. What? Why, truth. For I have beheld truth, I have beheld it with mine own eyes, I have beheld it in all its glory!

And since then I have been preaching. Moreover, I love all who laugh at me more than all the rest. Why that is so, I don't know and I cannot explain, but let it be so. They say that even now I often get muddled and confused and that if I am getting muddled and confused now, what will be later on? It is perfectly true. I do get muddled and confused and it is quite possible that I shall be getting worse later. And, of course, I shall get muddled several times before I find out how to preach, that is, what words to use and what deeds to perform, for that is all very difficult! All this is even now as clear to me as daylight, but, pray, tell me who does not get muddled and confused? And yet all follow the same path, at least all strive to achieve the same thing, from the philosopher to the lowest criminal, only by different roads. It is an old truth, but this is what is new: I cannot even get very much muddled and confused. For I have beheld the Truth. I have beheld it and I know that people can be happy and beautiful without losing their ability to live on earth. I will not and I cannot believe that evil is the normal condition among men. And yet they all laugh at this faith of mine. But how can I help believing it? I have beheld it—the Truth—it is not as though I had invented it with my mind: I have beheld it, I have beheld it, and the *living image* of it has filled my soul for ever. I have beheld it in all its glory and I cannot believe that it cannot exist among men. So how can I grow muddled and confused? I shall of course lose my way and I'm afraid that now and again I may speak with words that are not my own, but not for long: the living image of what I beheld will always be with me and it will always correct me and lead me back on to the right path. Oh, I'm in fine fettle, and I am of good cheer. I will go on and on for a thousand years, if need be. Do you know, at first I did not mean to tell you that I corrupted them, but that was a mistake—there you have my first mistake! But Truth whispered to me that I was *lying,* and so preserved me and set me on the right path. But I'm afraid I do not know how to establish a heaven on earth, for I do not know how to put it into words. After my dream I lost the knack of putting things into words. At least, into the most necessary and most important words. But never mind, I shall go on and I shall keep on talking, for I have indeed beheld it with my own eyes, though I cannot describe what I saw. It is this the scoffers do not understand. "He had a dream," they say, "a vision, a hallucination!" Oh dear, is this all they have to say? Do they really think that is very clever? And how proud they are! A dream! What is a dream? And what about our life? Is that not a dream too? I will say more: even—yes, even if this never comes to pass, even if there never is a heaven on earth (that, at any rate, I can see very well!), even then I shall go on preaching. And really how simple it all is: in one day, *in one hour,* everything could be arranged at once! The main thing is to love your neighbor as yourself—that is the main thing, and that is everything, for nothing else matters. Once you do that, you will discover at once how everything can be arranged. And yet it is an old truth, a truth that has been told over and over again, but in spite of that it finds no place among men! "The consciousness of life is higher than life, the knowledge of happiness is higher than happiness"—that is what we have to fight against! And I shall, I shall fight against it! If only we all wanted it, everything could be arranged immediately.

And—I did find that little girl. . . . And I shall go on! I shall go on!

THE REAL THING

I

When the porter's wife,who used to answer the house-bell,announced "A gentleman and a lady, sir," I had, as I often had in those days—the wish being father to the thought—an immediate vision of sitters. Sitters my visitors in this case proved to be; but not in the sense I should have preferred. There was nothing at first however to indicate that they mightn't have come for a portrait. The gentleman, a man of fifty, very high and very straight, with a moustache slightly grizzled and a dark grey walking-coat admirably fitted, both of which I noted professionally—I don't mean as a barber or yet as a tailor—would have struck me as a celebrity if celebrities often were striking. It was a truth of which I had for some time been conscious that a figure with a good deal of frontage was, as one might say, almost never a public institution. A glance at the lady helped to remind me of this paradoxical law: she also looked too distinguished to be a "personality." Moreover one would scarcely come across two variations together.

Neither of the pair immediately spoke—they only prolonged the preliminary gaze suggesting that each wished to give the other a chance. They were visibly shy; they stood there letting me take them in—which, as I afterwards perceived, was the most practical thing they could have done. In this way their embarrassment served their cause. I had seen people painfully reluctant to mention that they desired anything so gross as to be represented on canvas; but the scruples of my new friends appeared almost insurmountable. Yet the gentleman might have said "I should like a portrait of my wife," and the lady might have said "I should like a portrait of my husband." Perhaps they weren't husband and wife—this naturally would make the matter more delicate. Perhaps they wished to be done together—in which case they ought to have brought a third person to break the news.

"We come from Mr. Rivet," the lady finally said with a dim smile that had the effect of a moist sponge passed over a "sunk" piece of painting, as well as of a vague allusion to vanished beauty. She was as tall and straight, in her degree, as her companion, and with ten years less to carry.

She looked as sad as a woman could look whose face was not charged with expression; that is her tinted oval mask showed waste as an exposed surface shows friction. The hand of time had played over her freely, but to an effect of elimination. She was slim and stiff, and so well-dressed, in dark blue cloth, with lappets and pockets and buttons, that it was clear she employed the same tailor as her husband. The couple had an indefinable air of prosperous thrift—they evidently got a good deal of luxury for their money. If I was to be one of their luxuries, it would behoove me to consider my terms.

"Ah, Claude Rivet recommended me?" I echoed; and I added that it was very kind of him, though I could reflect that, as he only painted landscape, this wasn't a sacrifice.

The lady looked very hard at the gentleman, and the gentleman looked round the room. Then, staring at the door a moment and stroking his moustache, he rested his pleasant eyes on me with the remark: "He said you were the right one."

"I try to be, when people want to sit."

"Yes, we should like to," said the lady anxiously.

"Do you mean together?"

My visitors exchanged a glance. "If you could do anything with *me* I suppose it would be double," the gentleman stammered.

"Oh, yes, there's naturally a higher charge for two figures than for one."

"We should like to make it pay," the husband confessed.

"That's very good of you," I returned, appreciating so unwonted a sympathy—for I supposed he meant pay the artist.

A sense of strangeness seemed to dawn on the lady. "We mean for the illustrations—Mr. Rivet said you might put one in."

"Put in—an illustration?" I was equally confused.

"Sketch her off, you know," said the gentleman, colouring.

It was only then that I understood the service Claude Rivet had rendered me; he had told them how I worked in black and white, for magazines, for storybooks, for sketches of contemporary life, and consequently had copious employment for models. These things were true, but it was not less true—I may confess it now; whether because the aspiration was to lead to everything or to nothing I leave the reader to guess—that I couldn't get the honours, to say nothing of the emoluments, of a great painter of portraits out of my head. My "illustrations" were my pot-boilers; I looked to a different branch of art—far and away the most interesting it had always seemed to me—to perpetuate my fame. There was no shame in looking to it also to make my fortune; but that fortune was by so much further from being made from the moment my visitors wished to be "done" for something. I was disappointed; for in the pictorial sense I had immediately seen them. I had seized their type—I had already settled what I would do with it. Something that wouldn't absolutely have pleased them, I afterwards reflected.

"Ah, you're—you're—a—?" I began as soon as I had mastered my surprise. I couldn't bring out the dingy word "models": it seemed so little to fit the case.

"We haven't had much practice," said the lady.

"We've got to *do* something, and we've thought that an artist in your line might perhaps make something of us," her husband threw off. He further mentioned that they didn't know many artists and that they had gone first, on the off chance—he painted views of course, but sometimes put in figures; perhaps I remembered—to Mr. Rivet, whom they had met a few years before at a place in Norfolk where he was sketching.

"We used to sketch a little ourselves," the lady hinted.

"It's very awkward, but we absolutely *must* do something," her husband went on.

"Of course we're not so *very* young," she admitted with a wan smile.

With the remark that I might as well know something more about them the husband had handed me a card extracted from a neat new pocketbook —their appurtenances were all of the freshest—and inscribed with the words "Major Monarch." Impressive as these words were they didn't carry my knowledge much further; but my visitor presently added: "I've left the army and we've had the misfortune to lose our money. In fact our means are dreadfully small."

"It's awfully trying—a regular strain," said Mrs Monarch.

They evidently wished to be discreet—to take care not to swagger because they were gentlefolk. I felt them willing to recognize this as something of a drawback, at the same time that I guessed at an underlying sense—their consolation in adversity—that they *had* their points. They certainly had; but these advantages struck me as preponderantly social; such, for instance, as would help to make a drawing-room look well. However, a drawing-room was always, or ought to be, a picture.

In consequence of his wife's allusion to their age Major Monarch observed: "Naturally it's more for the figure that we thought of going in. We can still hold ourselves up." On the instant I saw that the figure was indeed their strong point. His "naturally" didn't sound vain, but it lighted up the question. *"She* has the best one," he continued, nodding at his wife with a pleasant after-dinner absence of circumlocution. I could only reply, as if we were in fact sitting over our wine, that this didn't prevent his own from being very good; which led him in turn to make answer: "We thought that if you ever have to do people like us we might be something like it. *She* particularly—for a lady in a book, you know."

I was so amused by them that, to get more of it, I did my best to take their point of view; and though it was an embarrassment to find myself appraising physically, as if they were animals on hire or useful blacks, a pair whom I should have expected to meet only in one of the relations in which criticism is tacit, I looked at Mrs. Monarch judicially enough to be able to exclaim after a moment with conviction: "Oh, yes, a lady in a book!" She was singularly like a bad illustration.

"We'll stand up, if you like," said the Major; and he raised himself before me with a really grand air.

I could take his measure at a glance—he was six feet two and a perfect gentleman. It would have paid any club in process of formation and in want of a stamp to engage him at a salary to stand in the principal window. What struck me at once was that in coming to me they had rather missed their vocation; they could surely have been turned to better account for advertising purposes. I couldn't of course see the thing in detail, but I could see them make somebody's fortune—I don't mean their own. There was something in them for a waistcoat-maker, an hotel-keeper or a soap-vendor. I could imagine "We always use it" pinned on their bosoms with the greatest effect; I had a vision of the brilliancy with which they would launch a table d'hôte.

Mrs. Monarch sat still, not from pride but from shyness, and presently her husband said to her: "Get up, my dear, and show how smart you are." She obeyed, but she had no need to get up to show it. She walked to the end of the studio and then came back blushing, her fluttered eyes on the partner of her appeal. I was reminded of an incident I had accidentally had a glimpse of in Paris—being with a friend there, a dramatist about to produce a play, when an actress came to him to ask to be entrusted with a part. She went through her paces before him, walked up and down as Mrs. Monarch was doing. Mrs Monarch did it quite as well, but I abstained from applauding. It was very odd to see such people apply for such poor pay. She looked as if she had ten thousand a year. Her husband had used the word that described her: she was in the London current jargon essentially and typically "smart." Her figure was, in the same order of ideas, conspicuously and irreproachably "good." For a woman of her age her waist was surprisingly small; her elbow moreover had the orthodox crook. She held her head at the conventional angle, but why did she come to *me?* She ought to have tried on jackets at a big shop. I feared my visitors were not only destitute but "artistic"—which would be a great complication. When she sat down again I thanked her, observing that what a draughts-man most valued in his model was the faculty of keeping quiet.

"Oh, *she* can keep quiet," said Major Monarch. Then he added jocosely: "I've always kept her quiet."

"I'm not a nasty fidget, am I?" It was going to wring tears from me, I felt, the way she hid her head, ostrich-like, in the other broad bosom.

The owner of this expanse addressed his answer to me. "Perhaps it isn't out of place to mention—because we ought to be quite businesslike, oughtn't we?—that when I married her she was known as the Beautiful Statue."

"Oh dear!" said Mrs. Monarch ruefully.

"Of course I should want a certain amount of expression," I rejoined.

"Of *course!*"—and I had never heard such unanimity.

"And then I suppose you know that you'll get awfully tired."

"Oh, we *never* get tired!" they eagerly cried.

"Have you had any kind of practice?"

They hesitated—they looked at each other. "We've been photographed —*immensely,* " said Mrs. Monarch.

"She means the fellows have asked us themselves," added the Major.

"I see—because you're so good-looking."

"I don't know what they thought, but they were always after us."

"We always got our photographs for nothing," smiled Mrs. Monarch.

"We might have brought some, my dear," her husband remarked.

"I'm not sure we have any left. We've given quantities away," she explained to me.

"With our autographs and that sort of thing," said the Major.

"Are they to be got in the shops?" I inquired as a harmless pleasantry.

"Oh, yes, *hers*—they used to be."

"Not now," said Mrs. Monarch with her eyes on the floor.

II

I could fancy the "sort of thing" they put on the presentation copies of their photographs, and I was sure they wrote a beautiful hand. It was odd how quickly I was sure of everything that concerned them. If they were now so poor as to have to earn shillings and pence they could never have had much of a margin. Their good looks had been their capital, and they had good-naturedly made the most of the career that this resource marked out for them. It was in their faces, the blankness, the deep intellectual repose of the twenty years of country-house visiting that had given them pleasant intonations. I could see the sunny drawing-rooms, sprinkled with periodicals she didn't read, in which Mrs. Monarch had continuously sat; I could see the wet shrubberies in which she had walked, equipped to admiration for either exercise. I could see the rich covers the Major had helped to shoot and the wonderful garments in which, late at night, he repaired to the smoking-room to talk about them. I could imagine their leggings and waterproofs, their knowing tweeds and rugs, their rolls of sticks and cases of tackle and neat umbrellas; and I could evoke the exact appearance of their servants and the compact variety of their luggage on platforms of country stations.

They gave small tips, but they were liked; they didn't do anything themselves, but they were welcome. They looked so well everywhere; they gratified the general relish for stature, complexion and "form." They knew it without fatuity or vulgarity, and they respected themselves in consequence. They weren't superficial; they were thorough and kept themselves up—it had been their line. People with such a taste for activity had to have some line. I could feel how even in a dull house they could have been counted on for the joy of life. At present something had happened—it didn't matter what, their little income had grown less, it had grown least —and they had to do something for pocket-money. Their friends could like them, I made out, without liking to support them. There was something about them that represented credit—their clothes, their manners, their type; but if credit is a large empty pocket in which an occasional chink reverberates, the chink at least must be audible. What they wanted of me was help to make it so. Fortunately they had no children—I soon divined that. They would also perhaps wish our relations to be kept secret: this was why it was "for the figure"—the reproduction of the face would betray them.

I liked them—I felt, quite as their friends must have done—they were so simple; and I had no objection to them if they would suit. But somehow with all their perfections I didn't easily believe in them. After all they were amateurs, and the ruling passion of my life was the detestation of the amateur. Combined with this was another perversity—an innate preference for the represented subject over the real one: the defect of the real one was so apt to be a lack of representation. I liked things that appeared; then one was sure. Whether they *were* or not was a subordinate and almost always a profitless question. There were other considerations, the first of which was that I already had two or three recruits in use, notably a young person with big feet, in alpaca, from Kilburn, who for a couple of years had come to me regularly for my illustrations and with whom I was still —perhaps ignobly—satisfied. I frankly explained to my visitors how the case stood, but they had taken more precautions than I supposed. They had reasoned out their opportunity, for Claude Rivet had told them of the projected *édition de luxe* of one of the writers of our day—the rarest of the novelists—who, long neglected by the multitudinous vulgar and dearly prized by the attentive (need I mention Philip Vincent?), had had the happy fortune of seeing, late in life, the dawn and then the full light of a higher criticism; an estimate in which on the part of the public there was something really of expiation. The edition preparing, planned by a publisher of taste, was practically an act of high reparation; the woodcuts with which it was to be enriched were the homage of English art to one of the most independent representatives of English letters. Major and Mrs. Monarch confessed to me they had hoped I might be able to work *them* into my branch of the enterprise. They knew I was to do the first of the books, "Rutland Ramsay," but I had to make clear to them that my participation in the rest of the affair—this first book was to be a test—must depend on the satisfaction I should give. If this should be limited my employers would drop me with scarce common forms. It was therefore a crisis for me, and naturally I was making special preparations, looking about for new people, should they be necessary, and securing the best types. I admitted however that I should like to settle down to two or three good models who would do for everything.

"Should we have often to—a—put on special clothes?" Mrs. Monarch timidly demanded.

"Dear, yes—that's half the business."

"And should we be expected to supply our own costumes?"

"Oh, no; I've got a lot of things. A painter's models put on—or put off—anything he likes."

"And you mean—a—the same?"

"The same?"

Mrs. Monarch looked at her husband again.

"Oh, she was just wondering," he explained, "if the costumes are in *general* use." I had to confess that they were, and I mentioned further that some them—I had a lot of genuine greasy last-century things—had served their time, a hundred years ago, on living world-stained men and women; on figures not perhaps so far removed, in that vanished world, from *their* type, the Monarchs', *quoi!* of a breeched and bewigged age. "We'll put on anything that *fits,*" said the Major.

"Oh, I arrange that—they fit in the pictures."

"I'm afraid I should do better for the modern books. I'd come as you like," said Mrs. Monarch.

"She has got a lot of clothes at home: they might do for contemporary life," her husband continued.

"Oh, I can fancy scenes in which you'd be quite natural." And indeed I could see the slipshod rearrangements of stale properties—the stories I tried to produce pictures for without the exasperation of reading them—whose sandy tracts the good lady might help to people. But I had to return to the fact that for this sort of work—the daily mechanical grind—I was already equipped: the people I was working with were fully adequate.

"We only thought we might be more like *some* characters," said Mrs. Monarch mildly, getting up.

Her husband also rose; he stood looking at me with a dim wistfulness that was touching in so fine a man. "Wouldn't it be rather a pull sometimes to have—a—to have—?" He hung fire; he wanted me to help him by phrasing what he meant. But I couldn't—I didn't know. So he brought it out awkwardly: "The *real* thing; a gentleman, you know, or a lady." I was quite ready to give a general assent—I admitted that there was a great deal in that. This encouraged Major Monarch to say, following up his appeal with an unacted gulp: "It's awfully hard—we've tried everything." The gulp was communicative; it proved too much for his wife. Before I knew it Mrs. Monarch had dropped again upon a divan and burst into tears. Her husband sat down beside her, holding one of her hands; whereupon she quickly dried her eyes with the other, while I felt embarrassed as she looked up at me. "There isn't a confounded job I haven't applied for— waited for—prayed for. You can fancy we'd be pretty bad first. Secretary-ships and that sort of thing? You might as well ask for a peerage. I'd be *anything*—I'm strong; a messenger or a coal-heaver. I'd put on a gold-laced cap and open carriage-doors in front of the haberdasher's; I'd hang about a station to carry portmanteaus; I'd be a postman. But they won't *look* at you; there are thousands as good as yourself already on the ground. *Gentlemen,* poor beggars, who've drunk their wine, who've kept their hunt-ers!"

I was as reassuring as I knew how to be, and my visitors were presently on their feet again while, for the experiment, we agreed on an hour. We were discussing it when the door opened and Miss Churm came in with a wet umbrella. Miss Churm had to take the omnibus to Maida Vale and then walk half a mile. She looked a trifle blowsy and slightly splashed. I scarcely ever saw her come in without thinking afresh how odd it was that, being so little in herself, she should yet be so much in others. She was a meagre little Miss Churm, but was such an ample heroine of romance. She was only a freckled cockney, but she could represent everything, from a fine lady to a shepherdess; she had the faculty as she might have had a fine voice or long hair. She couldn't spell and she loved beer, but she had two or three "points," and practice, and a knack, and mother-wit, and a whimsical sensibility, and a love of the theatre, and seven sisters, and not an ounce of respect, especially for the *h*. The first thing my visitors saw was that her umbrella was wet, and in their spotless perfection they visibly winced at it. The rain had come on since their arrival.

"I'm all in a soak; there *was* a mess of people in the 'bus. I wish you lived near a stytion," said Miss Churm. I requested her to get ready as quickly as possible, and she passed into the room in which she always changed her dress. But before going out she asked me what she was to get into this time.

"It's the Russian princess, don't you know?" I answered; "the one with the 'golden eyes,' in black velvet, for the long thing in the *Cheapside.*"

"Golden eyes? I *say!*" cried Miss Churm, while my companions watched her with intensity as she withdrew. She always arranged herself, when she was late, before I could turn round; and I kept my visitors a little on purpose, so that they might get an idea, from seeing her, what would be expected of themselves. I mentioned that she was quite my notion of an excellent model—she was really very clever.

"Do you think she looks like a Russian princess?" Major Monarch asked with lurking alarm.

"When I make her, yes."

"Oh, if you have to *make* her—!" he reasoned, not without point.

"That's the most you can ask. There are so many who are not make-able."

"Well, now, *here's* a lady"—and with a persuasive smile he passed his arm into his wife's—"who's already made!"

"Oh, I'm not a Russian princess," Mrs. Monarch protested a little coldly. I could see she had known some and didn't like them. There at once was a complication of a kind I never had to fear with Miss Churm.

This young lady came back in black velvet—the gown was rather rusty and very low on her lean shoulders—and with a Japanese fan in her red hands. I reminded her that in the scene I was doing she had to look over someone's head. "I forget whose it is; but it doesn't matter. Just look over a head."

"I'd rather look over a stove," said Miss Churm; and she took her station near the fire. She fell into position, settled herself into a tall attitude, gave a certain backward inclination to her head and a certain forward droop to her fan, and looked, at least to my prejudiced sense, distinguished and charming, foreign and dangerous. We left her looking so while I went downstairs with Major and Mrs. Monarch.

"I believe I could come about as near it as that," said Mrs. Monarch.

"Oh, you think she's shabby, but you must allow for the alchemy of art."

However, they went off with an evident increase of comfort founded on their demonstrable advantage in being the real thing. I could fancy them shuddering over Miss Churm. She was very droll about them when I went back, for I told her what they wanted.

"Well, if *she* can sit I'll tyke to bookkeeping," said my model.

"She's very ladylike," I replied as an innocent form of aggravation.

"So much the worse for *you.* That means she can't turn round."

"She'll do for the fashionable novels."

"Oh, yes, she'll *do* for them!" my model humorously declared. "Ain't they bad enough without her?" I had often sociably denounced them to Miss Churm.

III

It was for the elucidation of a mystery in one of these works that I first tried Mrs. Monarch. Her husband came with her, to be useful if necessary —it was sufficiently clear that as a general thing he would prefer to come with her. At first I wondered if this were for "propriety's" sake—if he were going to be jealous and meddling. The idea was too tiresome, and if it had been confirmed it would speedily have brought our acquaintance to a close. But I soon saw there was nothing in it and that if he accompanied Mrs. Monarch it was—in addition to the chance of being wanted—simply because he had nothing else to do. When they were separate his occupation was gone, and they never *had* been separate. I judged rightly that in their awkward situation their close union was their main comfort and that this union had no weak spot. It was a real marriage, an encouragement to the hesitating, a nut for pessimists to crack. Their address was humble—I remember afterwards thinking it had been the only thing about them that was really professional—and I could fancy the lamentable lodgings in which the Major would have been left alone. He could sit there more or less grimly with his wife—he couldn't sit there anyhow without her.

He had too much tact to try and make himself agreeable when he couldn't be useful; so when I was too absorbed in my work to talk he simply sat and waited. But I liked to hear him talk—it made my work, when not interrupting it, less mechanical, less special. To listen to him was to combine the excitement of going out with the economy of staying at home. There was only one hindrance—that I seemed not to know any of the people this brilliant couple had known. I think he wondered extremely, during the term of our intercourse, whom the deuce I *did* know. He hadn't a stray sixpence of an idea to fumble for, so we didn't spin it very fine; we confined ourselves to questions of leather and even of liquor—saddlers and breeches-makers and how to get excellent claret cheap—and matters like "good trains" and the habits of small game. His lore on these last subjects was astonishing—he managed to interweave the station-master with the ornithologist. When he couldn't talk about greater things he could talk cheerfully about small, and since I couldn't accompany him into reminiscences of the fashionable world he could lower the conversation without a visible effort to my level.

So earnest a desire to please was touching in a man who could so easily have knocked one down. He looked after the fire and had an opinion on the draught of the stove without my asking him, and I could see that he thought many of my arrangements not half knowing. I remember telling him that if I were only rich I'd offer him a salary to come and teach me how to live. Sometimes he gave a random sigh of which the essence might have been: "Give me even such a bare old barrack as *this,* and I'd do something with it!" When I wanted to use him he came alone; which was an illustration of the superior courage of women. His wife could bear her solitary second floor, and she was in general more discreet; showing by various small reserves that she was alive to the propriety of keeping our relations markedly professional—not letting them slide into sociability. She wished it to remain clear that she and the Major were employed, not cultivated, and if she approved of me as a superior, who could be kept in his place, she never thought me quite good enough for an equal.

She sat with great intensity, giving the whole of her mind to it, and was capable of remaining for an hour almost as motionless as before a photographer's lens. I could see she had been photographed often, but somehow the very habit that made her good for that purpose unfitted her for mine. At first I was extremely pleased with her ladylike air, and it was a satisfaction, on coming to follow her lines, to see how good they were and how far they could lead the pencil. But after a little skirmishing I began to find her too insurmountably stiff; do what I would with it my drawing looked like a photograph or a copy of a photograph. Her figure had no variety of expression—she herself had no sense of variety. You may say that this was my business and was only a question of placing her. Yet I placed her in every conceivable position and she managed to obliterate their differences. She was always a lady certainly, and into the bargain was always the same lady. She was the real thing, but always the same thing. There were moments when I rather writhed under the serenity of her confidence that she *was* the real thing. All her dealings with me and all her husband's were an implication that this was lucky for *me*. Meanwhile I found myself trying to invent types that approached her own, instead of making her own transform itself—in the clever way that was not impossible for instance to poor Miss Churm. Arrange as I would and take the precautions I would, she always came out, in my pictures, too tall—landing me in the dilemma of having represented a fascinating woman as seven feet high, which (out of respect perhaps to my own very much scantier inches) was far from my idea of such a personage.

The case was worse with the Major—nothing I could do would keep *him* down, so that he became useful only for representation of brawny giants. I adored variety and range, I cherished human accidents, the illustrative note; I wanted to characterize closely, and the thing in the world I most hated was the danger of being ridden by a type. I had quarrelled with some of my friends about it; I had parted company with them for maintaining that one *had* to be, and that if the type was beautiful—witness Raphael and Leonardo—the servitude was only a gain. I was neither Leonardo nor Raphael—I might only be a presumptuous young modern searcher; but I held that everything was to be sacrificed sooner than character. When they claimed that the obsessional form could easily *be* character I retorted, perhaps superficially, "Whose?" It couldn't be everybody's—it might end in being nobody's.

After I had drawn Mrs. Monarch a dozen times I felt surer even than before that the value of such a model as Miss Churm resided precisely in the fact that she had no positive stamp, combined of course with the other fact that what she did have was a curious and inexplicable talent for imitation. Her usual appearance was like a curtain which she could draw up at request for a capital performance. This performance was simply suggestive; but it was a word to the wise—it was vivid and pretty. Sometimes even I thought it, though she was plain herself, too insipidly pretty; I made it a reproach to her that the figures drawn from her were monotonously *(bêtement,* as we used to say) graceful. Nothing made her more angry: it was so much her pride to feel she could sit for characters that had nothing in common with each other. She would accuse me at such moments of taking away her "reputytion."

It suffered a certain shrinkage, this queer quantity, from the repeated visits of my new friends. Miss Churm was greatly in demand, never in want of employment, so I had no scruple in putting her off occasionally, to try them more at my ease. It was certainly amusing at first to do the real thing—it was amusing to do Major Monarch's trousers. They *were* the real thing, even if he did come out colossal. It was amusing to do his wife's back hair—it was so mathematically neat—and the particular "smart" tension of her tight stays. She lent herself especially to positions in which the face was somewhat averted or blurred; she abounded in ladylike back views and *profils perdus.* When she stood erect she took naturally one of the attitudes in which court painters represent queens and princesses; so that I found myself wondering whether, to draw out this accomplishment, I couldn't get the editor of the *Cheapside* to publish a really royal romance, "A Tale of Buckingham Palace." Sometimes, however, the real thing and the make-believe came into contact; by which I mean that Miss Churm, keeping an appointment or coming to make one on days when I had much work in hand, encountered her invidious rivals. The encounter was not on their part, for they noticed her no more than if she had been the housemaid; not from intentional loftiness, but simply because as yet, professionally, they didn't know how to fraternize, as I could imagine they would have liked—or at least that the Major would. They couldn't talk about the omnibus—they always walked; and they didn't know what else to try— she wasn't interested in good trains or cheap claret. Besides, they must have felt—in the air—that she was amused at them, secretly derisive of their ever knowing how. She wasn't a person to conceal the limits of her faith if she had had a chance to show them. On the other hand Mrs. Monarch didn't think her tidy; for why else did she take pains to say to me—it was going out of the way, for Mrs. Monarch—that she didn't like dirty women?

One day when my young lady happened to be present with my other sitters—she even dropped in, when it was convenient, for a chat—I asked her to be so good as to lend a hand in getting tea, a service with which she was familiar and which was one of a class that, living as I did in a small way, with slender domestic resources, I often appealed to my models to render. They liked to lay hands on my property, to break the sitting, and sometimes the china—it made them feel Bohemian. The next time I saw

Miss Churm after this incident she surprised me greatly by making a scene about it—she accused me of having wished to humiliate her. She hadn't resented the outrage at the time, but had seemed obliging and amused, enjoying the comedy of asking Mrs. Monarch, who sat vague and silent, whether she would have cream and sugar, and putting an exaggerated simper into the question. She had tried intonations—as if she too wished to pass for the real thing—till I was afraid my other visitors would take offence.

Oh, they were determined not to do this, and their touching patience was the measure of their great need. They would sit by the hour, uncomplaining, till I was ready to use them; they would come back on the chance of being wanted and would walk away cheerfully if it failed. I used to go to the door with them to see in what magnificent order they retreated. I tried to find other employment for them—I introduced them to several artists. But they didn't "take," for reasons I could appreciate, and I became rather anxiously aware that after such disappointments they fell back upon me with a heavier weight. They did me the honour to think me most *their* form. They weren't romantic enough for the painters, and in those days there were few serious workers in black-and-white. Besides, they had an eye to the great job I had mentioned to them—they had secretly set their hearts on supplying the right essence for my pictorial vindication of our fine novelist. They knew that for this undertaking I should want no costume effects, none of the frippery of past ages—that it was a case in which everything would be contemporary and satirical and presumably genteel. If I could work them into it their future would be assured, for the labour would of course be long and the occupation steady.

One day Mrs. Monarch came without her husband—she explained his absence by his having had to go to the City. While she sat there in her usual relaxed majesty there came at the door a knock which I immediately recognized as the subdued appeal of a model out of work. It was followed by the entrance of a young man whom I at once saw to be a foreigner and who proved in fact an Italian acquainted with no English word but my name, which he uttered in a way that made it seem to include all others. I hadn't then visited his country, nor was I proficient in his tongue; but as he was not so meanly constituted—what Italian is?—as to depend only on that member for expression he conveyed to me, in familiar but graceful mimicry, that he was in search of exactly the employment in which the lady before me was engaged. I was not struck with him at first, and while I continued to draw I dropped few signs of interest or encouragement. He stood his ground, however—not importunately, but with a dumb dog-like fidelity in his eyes that amounted to innocent impudence, the manner of a devoted servant—he might have been in the house for years—unjustly suspected. Suddenly it struck me that this very attitude and expression made a picture; whereupon I told him to sit down and wait till I should be free. There was another picture in the way he obeyed me, and I observed as I worked that there were others still in the way he looked wonderingly, with his head thrown back, about the high studio. He might have been crossing himself in Saint Peter's. Before I finished I said to myself, "The fellow's a bankrupt orange-monger, but a treasure."

When Mrs. Monarch withdrew he passed across the room like a flash to open the door for her, standing there with the rapt, pure gaze of the young Dante spellbound by the young Beatrice. As I never insisted, in such situations, on the blankness of the British domestic, I reflected that he had the making of a servant—and I needed one, but couldn't pay him to be only that—as well as of a model; in short I resolved to adopt my bright adventurer if he would agree to officiate in the double capacity. He jumped at my offer, and in the event my rashness—for I had really known nothing about him—wasn't brought home to me. He proved a sympathetic though a desultory ministrant, and had in a wonderful degree the *sentiment de la pose*. It was uncultivated, instinctive, a part of the happy instinct that had guided him to my door and helped him to spell out my name on the card nailed to it. He had had no other introduction to me than a guess, from the shape of my high north window, seen outside, that my place was a studio and that as a studio it would contain an artist. He had wandered to England in search of fortune, like other itinerants, and had embarked, with a partner and a small green handcart, on the sale of penny ices. The ices had melted away and the partner had dissolved in their train. My young man wore tight yellow trousers with reddish stripes and his name was Oronte. He was sallow but fair, and when I put him into some old clothes of my own he looked like an Englishman. He was as good as Miss Churm, who could look, when requested, like an Italian.

IV

I thought Mrs. Monarch's face slightly convulsed when, on her coming back with her husband, she found Oronte installed. It was strange to have to recognize in a scrap of a lazzarone a competitor to her magnificent Major. It was she who scented danger first, for the Major was anecdotally unconscious. But Oronte gave us tea, with a hundred eager confusions— he had never been concerned in so queer a process—and I think she thought better of me for having at last an "establishment." They saw a couple of drawings that I had made of the establishment, and Mrs. Monarch hinted that it never would have struck her he had sat for them. "Now the drawings you make from *us,* they look exactly like us," she reminded me, smiling in triumph; and I recognized that this was indeed just their defect. When I drew the Monarchs I couldn't anyhow get away from them —get into the character I wanted to represent; and I hadn't the least desire my model should be discoverable in my picture. Miss Churm never was, and Mrs. Monarch thought I hid her, very properly, because she was vulgar; whereas if she was lost it was only as the dead who go to heaven are lost—in the gain of an angel the more.

By this time I had got a certain start with "Rutland Ramsay," the first novel in the great projected series; that is, I had produced a dozen drawings, several with the help of the Major and his wife, and I had sent them in for approval. My understanding with the publishers, as I have already hinted, had been that I was to be left to do my work, in this particular case, as I liked, with the whole book committed to me; but my connexion with the rest of the series was only contingent. There were moments when, frankly, it *was* a comfort to have the real thing under one's hand; for there were characters in "Rutland Ramsay" that were very much like it. There were people presumably as erect as the Major and women of as good a fashion as Mrs. Monarch. There was a great deal of country-house life— treated, it is true, in a fine fanciful ironical generalised way—and there was a considerable implication of knickerbockers and kilts. There were certain things I had to settle at the outset; such things for instance as the exact appearance of the hero and the particular bloom and figure of the heroine. The author of course gave me a lead, but there was a margin for interpretation. I took the Monarchs into my confidence, I told them frankly what I was about, I mentioned my embarrassments and alternatives. "Oh, take *him!*" Mrs. Monarch murmured sweetly, looking at her husband; and "What could you want better than my wife?" the Major inquired with the comfortable candour that now prevailed between us.

I wasn't obliged to answer these remarks—I was only obliged to place my sitters. I wasn't easy in mind, and I postponed a little timidly perhaps the solving of my question. The book was a large canvas, the other figures were numerous, and I worked off at first some of the episodes in which the hero and the heroine were not concerned. When once I had set *them* up I should have to stick to them—I couldn't make my young man seven feet high in one place and five feet nine in another. I inclined on the whole to the latter measurement, though the Major more than once reminded me that *he* looked about as young as any one. It was indeed quite possible to arrange him, for the figure, so that it would have been difficult to detect his age. After the spontaneous Oronte had been with me a month, and after I had given him to understand several times over that his native exuberance would presently constitute an insurmountable barrier to our further intercourse, I waked to a sense of his heroic capacity. He was only five feet seven, but the remaining inches were latent. I tried him almost secretly at first, for I was really rather afraid of the judgement my other models would pass on such a choice. If they regarded Miss Churm as little better than a snare what would they think of the representation of a person so little the real thing as an Italian street-vendor of a protagonist formed by a public school?

If I went a little in fear of them it wasn't because they bullied me, because they had got an oppressive foothold, but because in their really pathetic decorum and mysteriously permanent newness they counted on me so intensely. I was therefore very glad when Jack Hawley came home: he was always of such good counsel. He painted badly himself, but there was no one like him for putting his finger on the place. He had been absent from England for a year; he had been somewhere—I don't remember where —to get a fresh eye. I was in a good deal of dread of any such organ, but we were old friends; he had been away for months and a sense of emptiness was creeping into my life. I hadn't dodged a missile for a year.

He came back with a fresh eye, but with the same old black velvet blouse, and the first evening he spent in my studio we smoked cigarettes till the small hours. He had done no work himself, he had only got the eye; so the field was clear for the production of my little things. He wanted to see what I had produced for the *Cheapside,* but he was disappointed in the exhibition. That at least seemed the meaning of two or three comprehensive groans which, as he lounged on my big divan, his leg folded under him, looking at my latest drawings, issued from his lips with the smoke of the cigarette.

"What's the matter with you?" I asked.

"What's the matter with *you?"*

"Nothing save that I'm mystified."

"You are indeed. You're quite off the hinge. What's the meaning of this new fad?" And he tossed me, with visible irreverence, a drawing in which I happened to have depicted both my elegant models. I asked if he didn't think it good, and he replied that it struck him as execrable, given the sort of thing I had always represented myself to him as wishing to arrive at; but I let that pass—I was so anxious to see exactly what he meant. The two figures in the picture looked colossal, but I supposed this was *not* what he meant, inasmuch as, for aught he knew to the contrary, I might have been trying for some such effect. I maintained that I was working exactly in the same way as when he last had done me the honour to tell me I might do something some day. "Well, there's a screw loose somewhere," he answered; "wait a bit and I'll discover it." I depended upon him to do so: where else was the fresh eye? But he produced at last nothing more luminous than "I don't know—I don't like your types." This was lame for a critic who had never consented to discuss with me anything but the question of execution, the direction of strokes and the mystery of values.

"In the drawings you've been looking at I think my types are very handsome."

"Oh, they won't do!"

"I've been working with new models."

"I see you have. *They* won't do."

"Are you very sure of that?"

"Absolutely—they're stupid."

"You mean *I* am—for I ought to get round that."

"You *can't*—with such people. Who are they?"

I told him, so far as was necessary, and he concluded heartlessly: *"Ce sont des gens qu'il faut mettre à la porte."*

"You've never seen them; they're awfully good"—I flew to their defense.

"Not seen them? Why all this recent work of yours drops to pieces with them. It's all I want to see of them."

"No one else has said anything against it—the *Cheapside* people are pleased."

"Every one else is an ass, and the *Cheapside* people the biggest asses of all. Come, don't pretend at this time of day to have pretty illusions about the public, especially about publishers and editors. It's not for *such* animals you work—it's for those who know, *coloro che sanno;* so keep straight for *me* if you can't keep straight for yourself. There was a certain sort of thing you used to try for—and a very good thing it was. But this twaddle isn't *in* it." When I talked with Hawley later about "Rutland Ramsay" and its possible successors he declared that I must get back into my boat again or I should go to the bottom. His voice in short was the voice of warning.

I noted the warning, but I didn't turn my friends out of doors. They bored me a good deal; but the very fact that they bored me admonished me not to sacrifice them—if there was anything to be done with them—simply to irritation. As I look back at this phase they seem to me to have pervaded my life not a little. I have a vision of them as most of the time in my studio, seated against the wall on an old velvet bench to be out of the way, and resembling the while a pair of patient courtiers in a royal ante-chamber. I'm convinced that during the coldest weeks of the winter they held their ground because it saved them fire. Their newness was losing its gloss, and it was impossible not to feel them objects of charity. Whenever Miss Churm arrived they went away, and after I was fairly launched in "Rutland Ramsay" Miss Churm arrived pretty often. They managed to express to me tacitly that they supposed I wanted her for the low life of the book, and I let them suppose it, since they had attempted to study the work—it was lying about the studio—without discovering that it dealt only with the highest circles. They had dipped into the most brilliant of our novelists without deciphering many passages. I still took an hour from them, now and again, in spite of Jack Hawley's warning: it would be time enough to dismiss them, if dismissal should be necessary, when the rigour of the season was over. Hawley had made their acquaintance—he had met them at my fireside—and thought them a ridiculous pair. Learning that he was a painter they tried to approach him, to show him too that they were the real thing; but he looked at them, across the big room, as if they were miles away: they were a compendium of everything he most objected to in the social system of his country. Such people as that, all convention and patent-leather, with ejaculations that stopped conversation, had no business in a studio. A studio was a place to learn to see, and how could you see through a pair of feather-beds?

The main inconvenience I suffered at their hands was that at first I was shy of letting it break upon them that my artful little servant had begun to sit to me for "Rutland Ramsay." They knew I had been odd enough— they were prepared by this time to allow oddity to artists—to pick a foreign vagabond out of the streets when I might have had a person with whiskers and credentials; but it was some time before they learned how high I rated his accomplishments. They found him in an attitude more than once, but they never doubted I was doing him as an organ-grinder. There were several things they never guessed, and one of them was that for a striking scene in the novel, in which a footman briefly figured, it occurred to me to make use of Major Monarch as the menial. I kept putting this off, I didn't like to ask him to don the livery—besides the difficulty of finding a livery to fit him. At last, one day late in the winter, when I was at work on the despised Oronte, who caught one's idea on the wing, and was in the glow of feeling myself go very straight, they came in, the Major and his wife, with their society laugh about nothing (there was less and less to laugh at); came in like country-callers—they always reminded me of that—who have walked across the park after church and are presently persuaded to stay to luncheon. Luncheon was over, but they could stay to tea—I knew they wanted it. The fit was on me, however, and I couldn't let my ardour cool and my work wait, with the fading daylight, while my model prepared it. So I asked Mrs. Monarch if she would mind laying it out—a request which for an instant brought all the blood to her face. Her eyes were on her husband's for a second, and some mute telegraphy passed between them. Their folly was over the next instant; his cheerful shrewdness put an end to it. So far from pitying their wounded pride, I must add, I was moved to give it as complete a lesson as I could. They bustled about together and got out the cups and saucers and made the kettle boil. I know they felt as if they were waiting on my servant, and when the tea was prepared I said: "He'll have a cup, please—he's tired." Mrs. Monarch brought him one where he stood, and he took it from her as if he had been a gentleman at a party squeezing a crush-hat with an elbow.

Then it came over me that she had made a great effort for me—made it with a kind of nobleness—and that I owed her a compensation. Each time I saw her after this I wondered what the compensation could be. I couldn't go on doing the wrong thing to oblige them. Oh, it *was* the wrong thing, the stamp of the work for which they sat—Hawley was not the only person to say it now. I sent in a large number of the drawings I had made for "Rutland Ramsay," and I received a warning that was more to the point than Hawley's. The artistic adviser of the house for which I was working was of opinion that many of my illustrations were not what had been looked for. Most of these illustrations were the subjects in which the Monarchs had figured. Without going into the question of what *had* been looked for, I had to face the fact that at this rate I shouldn't get the other books to do. I hurled myself in despair on Miss Churm—I put her through all her paces. I not only adopted Oronte publicly as my hero, but one morning when the Major looked in to see if I didn't require him to finish a *Cheapside* figure for which he had begun to sit the week before, I told him I had changed my mind—I'd do the drawing from my man. At this my visitor turned pale and stood looking at me. "Is *he* your idea of an English gentleman?" he asked.

I was disappointed, I was nervous, I wanted to get on with my work; so I replied with irritation: "Oh my dear Major—I can't be ruined for *you!*"

It was a horrid speech, but he stood another moment—after which, without a word, he quitted the studio. I drew a long breath, for I said to myself that I shouldn't see him again. I hadn't told him definitely that I was in danger of having my work rejected, but I was vexed at his not having felt the catastrophe in the air, read with me the moral of our fruitless collaboration, the lesson that in the deceptive atmosphere of art even the highest respectability may fail of being plastic.

I didn't owe my friends money, but I did see them again. They reappeared together three days later, and, given all the other facts, there was something tragic in that one. It was a clear proof they could find nothing else in life to do. They had threshed the matter out in a dismal conference —they had digested the bad news that they were not in for the series. If they weren't useful to me even for the *Cheapside,* their function seemed difficult to determine, and I could only judge at first that they had come, forgivingly, decorously, to take a last leave. This made me rejoice in secret that I had little leisure for a scene; I had placed both my other models in position together and I was pegging away at a drawing from which I hoped to derive glory. It had been suggested by the passage in which Rutland Ramsay, drawing up a chair to Artemisia's piano-stool, says extraordinary things to her while she ostensibly fingers out a difficult piece of music. I had done Miss Churm at the piano before—it was an attitude in which she knew how to take on an absolutely poetic grace. I wished the two figures to "compose" together with intensity, and my little Italian had entered perfectly into my conception. The pair were vividly before me, the piano had been pulled out; it was a charming show of blended youth and murmured love, which I had only to catch and keep. My visitors stood and looked at it, and I was friendly to them over my shoulder.

They made no response, but I was used to silent company and went on with my work, only a little disconcerted—even though exhilarated by the sense that *this* was at least the ideal thing—at not having got rid of them after all. Presently I heard Mrs. Monarch's sweet voice beside or rather above me: "I wish her hair were a little better done." I looked up and she was staring with a strange fixedness at Miss Churm, whose back was turned to her. "Do you mind my just touching it?" she went on—a question which made me spring up for an instant as with the instinctive fear that she might do the young lady a harm. But she quieted me with a glance I shall never forget—I confess I should like to have been able to paint *that* —and went for a moment to my model. She spoke to her softly, laying a hand on her shoulder and bending over her; and as the girl, understanding, gratefully assented, she disposed her rough curls, with a few quick passes, in such a way as to make Miss Churm's head twice as charming. It was one of the most heroic personal services I've ever seen rendered. Then Mrs. Monarch turned away with a low sigh and, looking about her as if for something to do, stooped to the floor with a noble humility and picked up a dirty rag that had dropped out of my paint-box.

The Major meanwhile had also been looking for something to do, and, wandering to the other end of the studio, saw before him my breakfast-things neglected, unremoved. "I say, can't I be useful *here?*" he called out to me with an irrepressible quaver. I assented with a laugh that I fear was awkward, and for the next ten minutes, while I worked, I heard the light clatter of china and the tinkle of spoons and glass. Mrs. Monarch assisted her husband—they washed up my crockery, they put it away. They wandered off into my little scullery, and I afterwards found that they had cleaned my knives and that my slender stock of plate had an unprecedented surface. When it came over me, the latent eloquence of what they were doing, I confess that my drawing was blurred for a moment—the picture swam. They had accepted their failure, but they couldn't accept their fate. They had bowed their heads in bewilderment to the perverse and cruel law in virtue of which the real thing could be so much less precious than the unreal; but they didn't want to starve. If my servants were my models, then my models might be my servants. They would reverse the parts—the others would sit for the ladies and gentlemen and *they* would do the work. They would still be in the studio—it was an intense dumb appeal to me not to turn them out. "Take us on," they wanted to say—"we'll do *anything.*"

My pencil dropped from my hand; my sitting was spoiled and I got rid of my sitters, who were also evidently rather mystified and awestruck. Then, alone with the Major and his wife I had a most uncomfortable moment. He put their prayer into a single sentence: "I say, you know— just let *us* do for you, can't you?" I couldn't—it was dreadful to see them emptying my slops; but I pretended I could, to oblige them, for about a week. Then I gave them a sum of money to go away, and I never saw them again. I obtained the remaining books, but my friend Hawley repeats that Major and Mrs. Monarch did me a permanent harm, got me into false ways. If it be true I'm content to have paid the price—for the memory.

THE LAGOON

The white man, leaning with both arms over the roof of the little house in the stern of the boat, said to the steersman—

"We will pass the night in Arsat's clearing. It is late."

The Malay only grunted, and went on looking fixedly at the river. The white man rested his chin on his crossed arms and gazed at the wake of the boat. At the end of the straight avenue of forests cut by the intense glitter of the river, the sun appeared unclouded and dazzling, poised low over the water that shone smoothly like a band of metal. The forests, sombre and dull, stood motionless and silent on each side of the broad stream. At the foot of big, towering trees, trunkless nipa palms rose from the mud of the bank, in bunches of leaves enormous and heavy, that hung unstirring over the brown swirl of eddies. In the stillness of the air every tree, every leaf, every bough, every tendril of creeper and every petal of minute blossoms seemed to have been bewitched into an immobility perfect and final. Nothing moved on the river but the eight paddles that rose flashing regularly, dipped together with a single splash; while the steersman swept right and left with a periodic and sudden flourish of his blade describing a glinting semicircle above his head. The churned-up water frothed alongside with a confused murmur. And the white man's canoe, advancing upstream in the short-lived disturbance of its own making, seemed to enter the portals of a land from which the very memory of motion had forever departed.

The white man, turning his back upon the setting sun, looked along the empty and broad expanse of the sea-reach. For the last three miles of its course the wandering, hesitating river, as if enticed irresistibly by the freedom of an open horizon, flows straight into the sea, flows straight to the east—to the east that harbours both light and darkness. Astern of the boat the repeated call of some bird, a cry discordant and feeble, skipped

Source: Reprinted from *Tales of Unrest* by Joseph Conrad, with the permission of the Trustees of the Joseph Conrad Estate and J. M. Dent & Sons Ltd., London.

along over the smooth water and lost itself, before it could reach the other shore, in the breathless silence of the world.

The steersman dug his paddle into the stream, and held hard with stiffened arms, his body thrown forward. The water gurgled aloud; and suddenly the long straight reach seemed to pivot on its centre, the forests swung in a semicircle, and the slanting beams of sunset touched the broadside of the canoe with a fiery glow, throwing the slender and distorted shadows of its crew upon the streaked glitter of the river. The white man turned to look ahead. The course of the boat had been altered at right-angles to the stream, and the carved dragon-head of its prow was pointing now at a gap in the fringing bushes of the bank. It glided through, brushing the overhanging twigs, and disappeared from the river like some slim and amphibious creature leaving the water for its lair in the forests.

The narrow creek was like a ditch: tortuous, fabulously deep; filled with gloom under the thin strip of pure and shining blue of the heaven. Immense trees soared up, invisible behind the festooned draperies of creepers. Here and there, near the glistening blackness of the water, a twisted root of some tall tree showed amongst the tracery of small ferns, black and dull, writhing and motionless, like an arrested snake. The short words of the paddlers reverberated loudly between the thick and sombre walls of vegetation. Darkness oozed out from between the trees, through the angled maze of the creepers, from behind the great fantastic and unstirring leaves; the darkness, mysterious and invincible; the darkness scented and poisonous of impenetrable forests.

The men poled in the shoaling water. The creek broadened, opening out into a wide sweep of a stagnant lagoon. The forests receded from the marshy bank, leaving a level strip of bright green, reedy grass to frame the reflected blueness of the sky. A fleecy pink cloud drifted high above, trailing the delicate colouring of its image under the floating leaves and the silvery blossoms of the lotus. A little house, perched on high piles, appeared black in the distance. Near it, two tall nibong palms, that seemed to have come out of the forests in the background, leaned slightly over the ragged roof, with a suggestion of sad tenderness and care in the droop of their leafy and soaring heads.

The steersman, pointing with his paddle, said, "Arsat is there. I see his canoe fast between the piles."

The polers ran along the sides of the boat glancing over their shoulders at the end of the day's journey. They would have preferred to spend the night somewhere else than on this lagoon of weird aspect and ghostly reputation. Moreover, they disliked Arsat, first as a stranger, and also because he who repairs a ruined house, and dwells in it, proclaims that he is not afraid to live amongst the spirits that haunt the places abandoned by mankind. Such a man can disturb the course of fate by glances or words;

while his familiar ghosts are not easy to propitiate by casual wayfarers upon whom they long to wreak the malice of their human master. White men care not for such things, being unbelievers and in league with the Father of Evil, who leads them unharmed through the invisible dangers of this world. To the warnings of the righteous they oppose an offensive pretence of disbelief. What is there to be done?

So they thought, throwing their weight on the end of their long poles. The big canoe glided on swiftly, noiselessly, and smoothly, towards Arsat's clearing, till, in a great rattling of poles thrown down, and the loud murmurs of "Allah be praised!" it came with a gentle knock against the crooked piles below the house.

The boatmen with uplifted faces shouted discordantly, "Arsat! O Arsat!" Nobody came. The white man began to climb the rude ladder giving access to the bamboo platform before the house. The juragan of the boat said sulkily, "We will cook in the sampan, and sleep on the water."

"Pass my blankets and the basket," said the white man, curtly.

He knelt on the edge of the platform to receive the bundle. Then the boat shoved off, and the white man, standing up, confronted Arsat, who had come out through the low door of his hut. He was a man young, powerful, with broad chest and muscular arms. He had nothing on but his sarong. His head was bare. His big, soft eyes stared eagerly at the white man, but his voice and demeanour were composed as he asked, without any words of greeting—

"Have you medicine, Tuan?"

"No," said the visitor in a startled tone. "No. Why? Is there sickness in the house?"

"Enter and see," replied Arsat, in the same calm manner, and turning short round, passed again through the small doorway. The white man, dropping his bundles, followed.

In the dim light of the dwelling he made out on a couch of bamboos a woman stretched on her back under a broad sheet of red cotton cloth. She lay still, as if dead; but her big eyes, wide open, glittered in the gloom, staring upwards at the slender rafters, motionless and unseeing. She was in a high fever, and evidently unconscious. Her cheeks were sunk slightly, her lips were partly open, and on the young face there was the ominous and fixed expression—the absorbed, contemplating expression of the unconscious who are going to die. The two men stood looking down at her in silence.

"Has she been long ill?" asked the traveller.

"I have not slept for five nights," answered the Malay, in a deliberate tone. "At first she heard voices calling her from the water and struggled against me who held her. But since the sun of to-day rose she hears nothing—she hears not me. She sees nothing. She sees not me—me!"

He remained silently for a minute, then asked softly—

"Tuan, will she die?"

"I fear so," said the white man, sorrowfully. He had known Arsat years ago, in a far country in times of trouble and danger, when no friendship is to be despised. And since his Malay friend had come unexpectedly to dwell in the hut on the lagoon with a strange woman, he had slept many times there, in his journeys up and down the river. He liked the man who knew how to keep faith in council and how to fight without fear by the side of his white friend. He liked him—not so much perhaps as a man likes his favourite dog—but still he liked him well enough to help and ask no questions, to think sometimes vaguely and hazily in the midst of his own pursuits, about the lonely man and the long-haired woman with audacious face and triumphant eyes, who lived together hidden by the forests—alone and feared.

The white man came out of the hut in time to see the enormous conflagration of sunset put out by the swift and stealthy shadows that, rising like a black and impalpable vapour above the tree-tops, spread over the heaven, extinguishing the crimson glow of floating clouds and the red brilliance of departing daylight. In a few moments all the stars came out above the intense blackness of the earth and the great lagoon gleaming suddenly with reflected lights resembled an oval patch of night sky flung down into the hopeless and abysmal night of the wilderness. The white man had some supper out of the basket, then collecting a few sticks that lay about the platform, made up a small fire, not for warmth, but for the sake of the smoke, which would keep off the mosquitos. He wrapped himself in the blankets and sat with his back against the reed wall of the house, smoking thoughtfully.

Arsat came through the doorway with noiseless steps and squatted down by the fire. The white man moved his outstretched legs a little.

"She breathes," said Arsat in a low voice, anticipating the expected question. "She breathes and burns as if with a great fire. She speaks not; she hears not—and burns!"

He paused for a moment, then asked in a quiet, incurious tone—

"Tuan . . . will she die?"

The white man moved his shoulders uneasily and muttered in a hesitating manner—

"If such is her fate."

"No, Tuan," said Arsat, calmly. "If such is my fate. I hear, I see, I wait. I remember . . . Tuan, do you remember the old days? Do you remember my brother?"

"Yes," said the white man. The Malay rose suddenly and went in. The other, sitting still outside, could hear the voice in the hut. Arsat said: "Hear me! Speak!" His words were succeeded by a complete silence. "O Diamelen!" he cried, suddenly. After that cry there was a deep sigh. Arsat came out and sank down again in his old place.

They sat in silence before the fire. There was no sound within the house, there was no sound near them; but far away on the lagoon they could hear the voices of the boatmen ringing fitful and distinct on the calm water. The fire in the bows of the sampan shone faintly in the distance with a hazy red glow. Then it died out. The voices ceased. The land and the water slept invisible, unstirring and mute. It was as though there had been nothing left in the world but the glitter of stars streaming, ceaseless and vain, through the black stillness of the night.

The white man gazed straight before him into the darkness with wide-open eyes. The fear and fascination, the inspiration and the wonder of death—of death, near, unavoidable, and unseen, soothed the unrest of his race and stirred the most indistinct, the most intimate of his thoughts. The ever-ready suspicion of evil, the gnawing suspicion that lurks in our hearts, flowed out into the stillness round him—into the stillness profound and dumb, and made it appear untrustworthy and infamous, like the placid and impenetrable mask of an unjustifiable violence. In that fleeting and powerful disturbance of his being the earth enfolded in the starlight peace became a shadowy country of inhuman strife, a battle-field of phantoms terrible and charming, august or ignoble, struggling ardently for the possession of our helpless hearts. An unquiet and mysterious country of inextinguishable desires and fears.

A plaintive murmur rose in the night; a murmur saddening and startling, as if the great solitudes of surrounding woods had tried to whisper into his ear the wisdom of their immense and lofty indifference. Sounds hesitating and vague floated in the air round him, shaped themselves slowly into words; and at last flowed on gently in a murmuring stream of soft and monotonous sentences. He stirred like a man waking up and changed his position slightly. Arsat, motionless and shadowy, sitting with bowed head under the stars, was speaking in a low and dreamy tone—

" . . . for where can we lay down the heaviness of our trouble but in a friend's heart? A man must speak of war and of love. You, Tuan, know what war is, and you have seen me in time of danger seek death as other men seek life! A writing may be lost; a lie may be written; but what the eye has seen is truth and remains in the mind!"

"I remember," said the white man, quietly. Arsat went on with mournful composure—

"Therefore I shall speak to you of love. Speak in the night. Speak before both night and love are gone—and the eye of day looks upon my sorrow and my shame; upon my blackened face; upon my burnt-up heart."

A sigh, short and faint, marked an almost imperceptible pause, and then his words flowed on, without a stir, without a gesture.

"After the time of trouble and war was over and you went away from my country in the pursuit of your desires, which we, men of the islands, cannot understand, I and my brother became again, as we had been before, the sword-bearers of the Ruler. You know we were men of family, belonging to a ruling race, and more fit than any to carry on our right shoulder the emblem of power. And in the time of prosperity Si Dendring showed us favour, as we, in time of sorrow, had showed to him the faithfulness of our courage. It was a time of peace. A time of deer-hunts and cock-fights; of idle talks and foolish squabbles between men whose bellies are full and weapons are rusty. But the sower watched the young rice-shoots grow up without fear, and the traders came and went, departed lean and returned fat into the river of peace. They brought news, too. Brought lies and truth mixed together, so that no man knew when to rejoice and when to be sorry. We heard from them about you also. They had seen you here and had seen you there. And I was glad to hear, for I remembered the stirring times, and I always remembered you, Tuan, till the time came when my eyes could see nothing in the past, because they had looked upon the one who is dying there—in the house."

He stopped to exclaim in an intense whisper, "O Mara bahia! O Calamity!" then went on speaking a little louder:

"There's no worse enemy and no better friend than a brother, Tuan, for one brother knows another, and in perfect knowledge is strength for good or evil. I loved my brother. I went to him and told him that I could see nothing but one face, hear nothing but one voice. He told me: 'Open your heart so that she can see what is in it—and wait. Patience is wisdom. Inchi Midah may die or our Ruler may throw off his fear of a woman!' . . . I waited! . . . You remember the lady with the veiled face, Tuan, and the fear of our Ruler before her cunning and temper. And if she wanted her servant, what could I do? But I fed the hunger of my heart on short glances and stealthy words. I loitered on the path to the bath-houses in the daytime, and when the sun had fallen behind the forest I crept along the jasmine hedges of the woman's courtyard. Unseeing, we spoke to one another through the scent of flowers, through the veil of leaves, through the blades of long grass that stood still before our lips; so great was our prudence, so faint was the murmur of our great longing. The time passed swiftly . . . and there were whispers amongst women—and our enemies watched—my brother was gloomy, and I began to think of killing and of a fierce death. . . . We are of a people who take what they want—like you whites. There is a time when a man should forget loyalty and respect. Might and authority are given to rulers, but to all men is given love and strength and courage. My brother said, 'You shall take her from their midst. We are two who are like one.' And I answered, 'Let it be soon, for I find no warmth in sunlight that does not shine upon her.' Our time came when the Ruler and all the great people went to the mouth of the river to fish by torchlight. There were hundreds of boats, and on the white sand, between the water and the forests, dwellings of leaves were built for the households of the Rajah. The smoke of cooking-fires was like a blue mist of the evening, and many voices rang in it joyfully. While they were making the boats ready to beat up the fish, my brother came to me and said, 'To-night!' I looked to my weapons, and when the time came our canoe took its place in the circle of boats carrying the torches. The lights blazed on the water, but behind the boats there was darkness. When the shouting began and the excitement made them like mad we dropped out. The water shallowed our fire, and we floated back to the shore that was dark with only here and there the glimmer of embers. We could hear the talk of slave-girls amongst the sheds. Then we found a place deserted and silent. We waited there. She came. She came running along the shore, rapid and leaving no trace, like a leaf driven by the wind into the sea. My brother said gloomily, 'Go and take her; carry her into our boat.' I lifted her in my arms. She panted. Her heart was beating against my breast. I said, 'I take you from those people. You came to the cry of my heart, but my arms take you into my boat against the will of the great!' 'It is right,' said my brother. 'We are men who take what we want and can hold it against many. We should have taken her in daylight.' I said, 'Let us be off'; for since she was in my boat I began to think of our Ruler's many men. 'Yes. Let us be off,' said my brother. 'We are cast out and this boat is our country now—and the sea is our refuge.' He lingered with his foot on the shore, and I entreated him to hasten, for I remembered the strokes of her heart against my breast and thought that two men cannot withstand a hundred. We left, paddling downstream close to the bank; and as we passed by the creek where they were fishing, the great shouting had ceased, but the murmur of voices was loud like the humming of insects flying at noonday. The boats floated, clustered together, in the red light of torches, under a black roof of smoke; and men talked of their sport. Men that boasted, and praised, and jeered—men that would have been our friends in the morning, but on that night were already our enemies. We paddled swiftly past. We had no more friends in the country of our birth. She sat in the middle of the canoe with covered face; silent as she is now; unseeing as she is now—and I had no regret at what I was leaving because I could hear her breathing close to me—as I can hear her now."

He paused, listened with his ear turned to the doorway, then shook his head and went on:

"My brother wanted to shout the cry of challenge—one cry only—to let the people know we were freeborn robbers who trusted our arms and the great sea. And again I begged him in the name of our love to be silent. Could I not hear her breathing close to me? I knew the pursuit would come quick enough. My brother loved me. He dipped his paddle without a splash. He only said, 'There is half a man in you now—the other half is in that woman. I can wait. When you are a whole man again, you will come back with me here to shout defiance. We are sons of the same mother.' I made no answer. All my strength and all my spirit were in my hands that held the paddle—for I longed to be with her in a safe place beyond the reach of men's anger and of women's spite. My love was so great, that I thought it could guide me to a country where death was unknown, if I could only escape from Inchi Midah's fury and from our Ruler's sword. We paddled with haste, breathing through our teeth. The blades bit deep into the smooth water. We passed out of the river; we flew in clear channels amongst the shallows. We skirted the black coast; we skirted the sand beaches where the sea speaks in whispers to the land; and the gleam of white sand flashed back past our boat, so swiftly she ran upon the water. We spoke not. Only once I said, 'Sleep, Diamelen, for soon you may want all your strength.' I heard the sweetness of her voice, but I never turned my head. The sun rose and still we went on. Water fell from my face like rain from a cloud. We flew in the light and heat. I never looked back, but I knew that my brother's eyes, behind me, were looking steadily ahead, for the boat went as straight as a bushman's dart, when it leaves the end of the sumpitan. There was no better paddler, no better steersman than my brother. Many times, together, we had won races in that canoe. But we never had put out our strength as we did then—then, when for the last time we paddled together! There was no braver or stronger man in our country than my brother. I could not spare the strength to turn my head and look at him, but every moment I heard the hiss of his breath getting louder behind me. Still he did not speak. The sun was high. The heat clung to my back like a flame of fire. My ribs were ready to burst, but I could no longer get enough air into my chest. And then I felt I must cry out with my last breath, 'Let us rest!' . . . 'Good!' he answered; and his voice was firm. He was strong. He was brave. He knew not fear and no fatigue . . . My brother!"

A murmur powerful and gentle, a murmur vast and faint; the murmur of trembling leaves, of stirring boughs, ran through the tangled depths of the forests, ran over the starry smoothness of the lagoon, and the water between the piles lapped the slimy timber once with a sudden splash. A breath of warm air touched the two men's faces and passed on with a mournful sound—a breath loud and short like an uneasy sigh of the dreaming earth.

Arsat went on in an even, low voice.

"We ran our canoe on the white beach of a little bay close to a long tongue of land that seemed to bar our road; a long wooded cape going far into the sea. My brother knew that place. Beyond the cape a river has its entrance, and through the jungle of that land there is a narrow path. We made a fire and cooked rice. Then we lay down to sleep on the soft sand in the shade of our canoe, while she watched. No sooner had I closed my eyes than I heard her cry of alarm. We leaped up. The sun was halfway down the sky already, and coming in sight in the opening of the bay we saw a prau manned by many paddlers. We knew it at once; it was one of our Rajah's praus. They were watching the shore, and saw us. They beat the gong, and turned the head of the prau into the bay. I felt my heart become weak within my breast. Diamelen sat on the sand and covered her face. There was no escape by sea. My brother laughed. He had the gun you had given him, Tuan, before you went away, but there was only a handful of powder. He spoke to me quickly: 'Run with her along the path. I shall keep them back, for they have no firearms, and landing in the face of a man with a gun is certain death for some. Run with her. On the other side of that wood there is a fisherman's house—and a canoe. When I have fired all the shots I will follow. I am a great runner, and before they can come up we shall be gone. I will hold out as long as I can, for she is but a woman —that can neither run nor fight, but she has your heart in her weak hands.' He dropped behind the canoe. The prau was coming. She and I ran, and as we rushed along the path I heard shots. My brother fired—once—twice —and the booming of the gong ceased. There was silence behind us. That neck of land is narrow. Before I heard my brother fire the third shot I saw the shelving shore, and I saw the water again; the mouth of a broad river We crossed a grassy glade. We ran down to the water. I saw a low hut above the black mud, and a small canoe hauled up. I heard another shot behind me. I thought, 'That is his last charge. We rushed down to the canoe; a man came running from the hut, but I leaped on him, and we rolled together in the mud. Then I got up, and he lay still at my feet. I don't know whether I had killed him or not. I and Diamelen pushed the canoe afloat. I heard yells behind me, and I saw my brother run across the glade. Many men were bounding after him, I took her in my arms and threw her into the boat, then leaped in myself. When I looked back I saw that my brother had fallen. He fell and was up again, but the men were closing round him. He shouted, 'I am coming!' The men were close to him. I looked. Many men. Then I looked at her. Tuan, I pushed the canoe! I pushed it into deep water. She was kneeling forward looking at me, and I said, 'Take your paddle,' while I struck the water with mine. Tuan, I heard him cry. I heard him cry my name twice; and I heard voices shouting, 'Kill! Strike!' I never turned back. I heard him calling my name again with a great shriek, as when life is going out together with the voice—and I never turned my head. My own name! . . . My brother! Three times he called— but I was not afraid of life. Was she not there in that canoe? And could I not with her find a country where death is forgotten—where death is unknown!"

The white man sat up. Arsat rose and stood, an indistinct and silent figure above the dying embers of the fire. Over the lagoon a mist drifting and low had crept, erasing slowly the glittering images of the stars. And now a great expanse of white vapour covered the land: it flowed cold and gray in the darkness, eddied in noiseless whirls round the tree-trunks and about the platform of the house, which seemed to float upon a restless and impalpable illusion of a sea. Only far away the tops of the trees stood outlined on the twinkle of heaven, like a sombre and forbidding shore—a coast deceptive, pitiless and black.

Arsat's voice vibrated loudly in the profound peace.

"I had her there! I had her! To get her I would have faced all mankind. But I had her—and—"

His words went out ringing into the empty distances. He paused, and seemed to listen to them dying away very far—beyond help and beyond recall. Then he said quietly—

"Tuan, I loved my brother."

A breath of wind made him shiver. High above his head, high above the silent sea of mist the drooping leaves of the palms rattled together with a mournful and expiring sound. The white man stretched his legs. His chin rested on his chest, and he murmured sadly without lifting his head—

"We all love our brothers."

Arsat burst out with an intense whispering violence—

"What did I care who died? I wanted peace in my own heart."

He seemed to hear a stir in the house—listened—then stepped in noiselessly. The white man stood up. A breeze was coming in fitful puffs. The stars shone paler as if they had retreated into the frozen depths of immense space. After a chill gust of wind there were a few seconds of perfect calm and absolute silence. Then from behind the black and wavy line of the forests a column of golden light shot up into the heavens and spread over the semicircle of the eastern horizon. The sun had risen. The mist lifted, broke into drifting patches, vanished into thin flying wreaths; and the unveiled lagoon lay, polished and black, in the heavy shadows at the foot of the wall of trees. A white eagle rose over it with a slanting and ponderous flight, reached the clear sunshine and appeared dazzlingly brilliant for a moment, then soaring higher, became a dark and motionless speck before it vanished into the blue as if it had left the earth forever. The white man, standing gazing upwards before the doorway, heard in the hut a confused and broken murmur of distracted words ending with a loud groan. Suddenly Arsat stumbled out with outstretched hands, shivered and stood still for some time with fixed eyes. Then, he said—

"She burns no more."

Before his face the sun showed its edge above the treetops rising steadily. The breeze freshened; a great brilliance burst upon the lagoon, sparkled on the rippling water. The forests came out of the clear shadows of the morning, became distinct, as if they had rushed nearer—to stop short in a great stir of leaves, of nodding boughs, of swaying branches. In the merciless sunshine the whisper of unconscious life grew louder, speaking in an incomprehensible voice round the dumb darkness of that human sorrow. Arsat's eyes wandered slowly, then stared at the rising sun.

"I can see nothing," he said half aloud to himself.

"There is nothing," said the white man, moving to the edge of the platform and waving his hand to his boat. A shout came faintly over the lagoon and the sampan began to glide towards the abode of the friend of ghosts.

"If you want to come with me, I will wait all the morning," said the white man, looking away upon the water.

"No, Tuan," said Arsat, softly. "I shall not eat or sleep in this house, but I must first see my road. Now I can see nothing—see nothing! There is no light and no peace in the world; but there is death—death for many. We are sons of the same mother—and I left him in the midst of enemies; but I am going back now."

He drew a long breath and went on in a dreamy tone:

"In a little while I shall see clear enough to strike—to strike. But she has died, and . . . now . . . darkness."

He flung his arms wide open, let them fall along his body, then stood still with unmoved face and stony eyes, staring at the sun. The white man got down into his canoe. The polers ran smartly along the sides of the boat, looking over their shoulders at the beginning of a weary journey. High in the stern, his head muffled up in white rags, the juragan sat moody, letting his paddle trail in the water. The white man, leaning with both arms over the grass roof of the little cabin, looked back at the shining ripple of the boat's wake. Before the sampan passed out of the lagoon into the creek he lifted his eyes. Arsat had not moved. He stood lonely in the searching sunshine; and he looked beyond the great light of a cloudless day into the darkness of a world of illusions.

MARIO AND THE MAGICIAN

The atmosphere of Torre di Venere remains unpleasant in the memory. From the first moment the air of the place made us uneasy, we felt irritable, on edge; then at the end came the shocking business of Cipolla, that dreadful being who seemed to incorporate, in so fateful and so humanly impressive a way, all the peculiar evilness of the situation as a whole. Looking back, we had the feeling that the horrible end of the affair had been preordained and lay in the nature of things; that the children had to be present at it was an added impropriety, due to the false colors in which the weird creature presented himself. Luckily for them they did not know where the comedy left off and the tragedy began; and we let them remain in their happy belief that the whole thing had been a play up till the end.

Torre di Venere lies some fifteen kilometers from Portoclemente, one of the most popular summer resorts on the Tyrrhenian Sea. Portoclemente is urban and elegant and full to overflowing for months on end. Its gay and busy main street of shops and hotels runs down to a wide sandy beach covered with tents and pennanted sand-castles and sunburnt humanity, where at all times a lively social bustle reigns, and much noise. But this same spacious and inviting fine-sanded beach, this same border of pine grove and near, presiding mountains, continues all the way along the coast. No wonder then that some competition of a quiet kind should have sprung up further on. Torre di Venere—the tower that gave the town its name is gone long since, one looks for it in vain—is an offshoot of the larger resort, and for some years remained an idyll for the few, a refuge for more unworldly spirits. But the usual history of such places repeated itself: peace has had to retire further along the coast, to Marina Petriera and dear knows where else. We all know how the world at once seeks peace and puts her to flight—rushing upon her in the fond idea that they two will wed, and where she is, there it can be at home. It will even set up its Vanity Fair in a spot and be capable of thinking that peace is still by its side. Thus Torre—though its atmosphere so far is more modest and contemplative than that of Portoclemente—has been quite taken up, by both Italians and foreigners. It is no longer the thing to go to Portoclemente—though still so much the thing that it is as noisy and crowded as ever. One goes next door, so to speak: to Torre. So much more refined, even, and cheaper to boot. And the attractiveness of these qualities persists, though the qualities themselves long ago ceased to be evident. Torre has got a Grand Hotel. Numerous pensions have sprung up, some modest, some pretentious. The people who own or rent the villas and pinetas overlooking the sea no longer have it all their own way on the beach. In July and August it looks just like the beach at Portoclemente: it swarms with a screaming, squabbling, merrymaking crowd, and the sun, blazing down like mad, peels the skin off their necks. Garish little flat-bottomed boats rock on the glittering blue, manned by children, whose mothers hover afar and fill the air with anxious cries of Nino! and Sandro! and Bice! and Maria! Peddlers step across the legs of recumbent sun-bathers, selling flowers and corals, oysters, lemonade, and *cornetti al burro,* and crying their wares in the breathy, full-throated southern voice.

Such was the scene that greeted our arrival in Torre: pleasant enough, but after all, we thought, we had come too soon. It was the middle of August, the Italian season was still at its height, scarcely the moment for strangers to learn to love the special charms of the place. What an afternoon crowd in the cafés on the front! For instance, in the Esquisito, where we sometimes sat and were served by Mario, that very Mario of whom I shall have presently to tell. It is well-nigh impossible to find a table; and the various orchestras contend together in the midst of one's conversation with bewildering effect. Of course, it is in the afternoon that people come over from Portoclemente. The excursion is a favorite one for the restless denizens of that pleasure resort, and a Fiat motor-bus plies to and fro, coating inch-thick with dust the oleander and laurel hedges along the highroad—a notable if repulsive sight.

Yes, decidedly one should go to Torre in September, when the great public has left. Or else in May, before the water is warm enough to tempt the Southerner to bathe. Even in the before and after seasons Torre is not empty, but life is less national and more subdued. English, French, and German prevail under the tent-awnings and in the pension dining-rooms; whereas in August—in the Grand Hotel, at least, where, in default of private addresses, we had engaged rooms—the stranger finds the field so occupied by Florentine and Roman society that he feels quite isolated and even temporarily *déclassé.*

We had, rather to our annoyance, this experience on the evening we arrived, when we went in to dinner and were shown to our table by the waiter in charge. As a table, it had nothing against it, save that we had already fixed our eyes upon those on the veranda beyond, built out over the water, where little red-shaded lamps glowed—and there were still some tables empty, though it was as full as the dining-room within. The children went into raptures at the festive sight, and without more ado we announced our intention to take our meals by preference in the veranda. Our words, it appeared, were prompted by ignorance; for we were informed, with somewhat embarrassed politeness, that the cozy nook outside was reserved for the clients of the hotel: *ai nostri clienti.* Their clients? But we were their clients. We were not tourists or tippers, but boarders for a stay of some three or four weeks. However, we forbore to press for an explanation of the difference between the likes of us and that clientèle to whom it was vouchsafed to eat out there in the glow of the red lamps, and took our dinner by the prosaic common light of the dining-room chandelier—a thoroughly ordinary and monotonous hotel bill of fare, be it said. In Pensione Eleonora, a few steps landward, the table, as we were to discover, was much better.

And thither it was that we moved, three or four days later, before we had had time to settle in properly at the Grand Hotel. Not on account of the veranda and the lamps. The children, straightway on the best of terms with waiters and pages, absorbed in the joys of life on the beach, promptly forgot those colorful seductions. But now there arose, between ourselves and the veranda clientèle—or perhaps more correctly with the compliant management—one of those little unpleasantnesses which can quite spoil the pleasure of a holiday. Among the guests were some high Roman aristocracy, a Principe X and his family. These grand folk occupied rooms close to our own, and Principessa, a great and a passionately maternal lady, was thrown into a panic by the vestiges of a whooping-cough which our little ones had lately got over, but which now and then still faintly troubled the unshatterable slumbers of our youngest-born. The nature of this illness is not clear, leaving some play for the imagination. So we took no offense at our elegant neighbor for clinging to the widely held view that whooping-cough is acoustically contagious and quite simply fearing lest her children yield to the bad example set by ours. In the fullness of her feminine self-confidence she protested to the management, which then, in the person of the proverbial frock-coated manager, hastened to represent to us, with many expressions of regret, that under the circumstances they were obliged to transfer us to the annexe. We did our best to assure him that the disease was in its very last stages, that it was actually over, and presented no danger of infection to anybody. All that we gained was permission to bring the case before the hotel physician—not one chosen by us—by whose verdict we must then abide. We agreed, convinced that thus we should at once pacify the Princess and escape the trouble of moving. The doctor appeared, and behaved like a faithful and honest servant of science. He examined the child and gave his opinion: the disease was quite over, no danger of contagion was present. We drew a long breath and considered the incident closed—until the manager announced that despite the doctor's verdict it would still be necessary for us to give up our rooms and retire to the *dépendance.* Byzantinism like this outraged us. It is not likely that the Principessa was responsible for the willful breach of faith. Very likely the fawning management had not even dared to tell her what the physician said. Anyhow, we made it clear to his understanding that we preferred to leave the hotel altogether and at once—and packed our trunks. We could do so with a light heart, having already set up casual friendly relations with Casa Eleonora. We had noticed its pleasant exterior and formed the acquaintance of its proprietor, Signora Angiolieri, and her husband: she slender and black-haired, Tuscan in type, probably at the beginning of the thirties, with the dead ivory complexion of the southern woman, he quiet and bald and carefully dressed. They owned a larger establishment in Florence and presided only in summer and early autumn over the branch in Torre di Venere. But earlier, before her marriage, our new landlady had been companion, fellow-traveler, wardrobe mistress, yes, friend, of Eleonora Duse and manifestly regarded that period as the crown of her career. Even at our first visit she spoke of it with animation. Numerous photographs of the great actress, with affectionate inscriptions, were displayed about the drawing-room, and other souvenirs of their life together adorned the little tables and étagères. This cult of a so interesting past was calculated, of course, to heighten the advantages of the signora's present business. Nevertheless our pleasure and interest were quite genuine as we were conducted through the house by its owner and listened to her sonorous and staccato Tuscan voice relating anecdotes of that immortal mistress, depicting her suffering saintliness, her genius, her profound delicacy of feeling.

Thither, then, we moved our effects, to the dismay of the staff of the Grand Hotel, who, like all Italians, were very good to children. Our new quarters were retired and pleasant, we were within easy reach of the sea through the avenue of young plane trees that ran down to the esplanade. In the clean, cool dining-room Signora Angiolieri daily served the soup with her own hands, the service was attentive and good, the table capital. We even discovered some Viennese acquaintances, and enjoyed chatting with them after luncheon, in front of the house. They, in their turn, were the means of our finding others—in short, all seemed for the best, and we were heartily glad of the change we had made. Nothing was now wanting to a holiday of the most gratifying kind.

And yet no proper gratification ensued. Perhaps the stupid occasion of our change of quarters pursued us to the new ones we had found. Personally, I admit that I do not easily forget these collisions with ordinary humanity, the naïve misuse of power, the injustice, the sycophantic corruption. I dwelt upon the incident too much, it irritated me in retrospect —quite futilely, of course, since such phenomena are only all too natural and all too much the rule. And we had not broken off relations with the

Grand Hotel. The children were as friendly as ever there, the porter mended their toys, and we sometimes took tea in the garden. We even saw the Principessa. She would come out, with her firm and delicate tread, her lips emphatically corallined, to look after her children, playing under the supervision of their English governess. She did not dream that we were anywhere near, for so soon as she appeared in the offing we sternly forbade our little one even to clear his throat.

The heat—if I may bring it in evidence—was extreme. It was African. The power of the sun, directly one left the border of the indigo-blue wave, was so frightful, so relentless, that the mere thought of the few steps between the beach and luncheon was a burden, clad though one might be only in pajamas. Do you care for that sort of thing? Weeks on end? Yes, of course, it is proper to the south, it is classic weather, the sun of Homer, the climate wherein human culture came to flower—and all the rest of it. But after a while it is too much for me, I reach a point where I begin to find it dull. The burning void of the sky, day after day, weighs one down; the high coloration, the enormous naïveté of the unrefracted light—they do, I dare say, induce light heartedness, a carefree mood born of immunity from downpours and other meteorological caprices. But slowly, slowly, there makes itself felt a lack: the deeper, more complex needs of the northern soul remain unsatisfied. You are left barren—even, it may be, in time, a little contemptuous. True, without that stupid business of the whooping-cough I might not have been feeling these things. I was annoyed, very likely I wanted to feel them and so half-unconsciously seized upon an idea lying ready to hand to induce, or if not to induce, at least to justify and strengthen, my attitude. Up to this point, then, if you like, let us grant some ill will on our part. But the sea; and the mornings spent extended upon the fine sand in face of its eternal splendors—no, the sea could not conceivably induce such feelings. Yet it was none the less true that, despite all previous experience, we were not at home on the beach, we were not happy.

It was too soon, too soon. The beach, as I have said, was still in the hands of the middle-class native. It is a pleasing breed to look at, and among the young we saw much shapeliness and charm. Still, we were necessarily surrounded by a great deal of very average humanity—a middle-class mob, which, you will admit, is not more charming under this sun than under one's own native sky. The voices these women have! It was sometimes hard to believe that we were in the land which is the western cradle of the art of song. *"Fuggièro!"* I can still hear that cry, as for twenty mornings long I heard it close behind me, breathy, full-throated, hideously stressed, with a harsh open *e*, uttered in accents of mechanical despair. *"Fuggièro! Rispondi almeno!"* Answer when I call you! The *sp* in *rispondi* was pronounced like *shp*, as Germans pronounce it; and this, on top of what I felt already, vexed my sensitive soul. The cry was addressed to a repulsive youngster whose

sunburn had made disgusting raw sores on his shoulders. He outdid anything I have ever seen for ill-breeding, refractoriness, and temper and was
a great coward to boot, putting the whole beach in an uproar, one day,
because of his outrageous sensitiveness to the slightest pain. A sand-crab
had pinched his toe in the water, and the minute injury made him set up
a cry of heroic proportions—the shout of an antique hero in his agony—
that pierced one to the marrow and called up visions of some frightful
tragedy. Evidently he considered himself not only wounded, but poisoned
as well; he crawled out on the sand and lay in apparently intolerable
anguish, groaning *"Ohi!"* and *"Ohimè!"* and threshing about with arms
and legs to ward off his mother's tragic appeals and the questions of the
bystanders. An audience gathered round. A doctor was fetched—the same
who had pronounced objective judgment on our whooping-cough—and
here again acquitted himself like a man of science. Good-naturedly he
reassured the boy, telling him that he was not hurt at all, he should simply
go into the water again to relieve the smart. Instead of which, Fuggièro was
borne off the beach, followed by a concourse of people. But he did not fail
to appear next morning, nor did he leave off spoiling our children's sand-
castles. Of course, always by accident. In short, a perfect terror.

And this twelve-year-old lad was prominent among the influences that,
imperceptibly at first, combined to spoil our holiday and render it un-
wholesome. Somehow or other, there was a stiffness, a lack of innocent
enjoyment. These people stood on their dignity—just why, and in what
spirit, it was not easy at first to tell. They displayed much self-respecting-
ness; towards each other and towards the foreigner their bearing was that
of a person newly conscious of a sense of honor. And wherefore? Gradually we realized the political implications and understood that we were in
the presence of a national ideal. The beach, in fact, was alive with patriotic
children—a phenomenon as unnatural as it was depressing. Children are
a human species and a society apart, a nation of their own, so to speak.
On the basis of their common form of life, they find each other out with
the greatest ease, no matter how different their small vocabularies. Ours
soon played with natives and foreigners alike. Yet they were plainly both
puzzled and disappointed at times. There were wounded sensibilities, displays of assertiveness—or rather hardly assertiveness, for it was too self-
conscious and too didactic to deserve the name: There were quarrels over
flags, disputes about authority and precedence. Grown-ups joined in, not
so much to pacify as to render judgment and enunciate principles. Phrases
were dropped about the greatness and dignity of Italy, solemn phrases that
spoilt the fun. We saw our two little ones retreat, puzzled and hurt, and
were put to it to explain the situation. These people, we told them, were
just passing through a certain stage, something rather like an illness, perhaps; not very pleasant, but probably unavoidable.

We had only our own carelessness to thank that we came to blows in the end with this "stage"—which, after all, we had seen and sized up long before now. Yes, it came to another "cross-purposes," so evidently the earlier ones had not been sheer accident. In a word, we became an offense to the public morals. Our small daughter—eight years old, but in physical development a good year younger and thin as a chicken—had had a good long bathe and gone playing in the warm sun in her wet costume. We told her that she might take off her bathing-suit, which was stiff with sand, rinse it in the sea, and put it on again, after which she must take care to keep it cleaner. Off goes the costume and she runs down naked to the sea, rinses her little jersey, and comes back. Ought we to have foreseen the outburst of anger and resentment which her conduct, and thus our conduct, called forth? Without delivering a homily on the subject, I may say that in the last decade our attitude towards the nude body and our feelings regarding it have undergone, all over the world, a fundamental change. There are things we "never think about" any more, and among them is the freedom we had permitted to this by no means provocative little childish body. But in these parts it was taken as a challenge. The patriotic children hooted. Fuggièro whistled on his fingers. The sudden buzz of conversation among the grown people in our neighborhood boded no good. A gentleman in city togs, with a not very apropos bowler hat on the back of his head, was assuring his outraged womenfolk that he proposed to take punitive measures; he stepped up to us, and a philippic descended on our unworthy heads, in which all the emotionalism of the sense-loving south spoke in the service of morality and discipline. The offense against decency of which we had been guilty was, he said, the more to be condemned because it was also a gross ingratitude and an insulting breach of his country's hospitality. We had criminally injured not only the letter and spirit of the public bathing regulations, but also the honor of Italy; he, the gentleman in the city togs, knew how to defend that honor and proposed to see to it that our offense against the national disunity should not go unpunished.

We did our best, bowing respectfully, to give ear to this eloquence. To contradict the man, overheated as he was, would probably be to fall from one error into another. On the tips of our tongues we had various answers: as, that the word "hospitality," in its strictest sense, was not quite the right one, taking all the circumstances into consideration. We were not literally the guests of Italy, but of Signora Angiolieri, who had assumed the role of dispenser of hospitality some years ago on laying down that of familiar friend to Eleonora Duse. We longed to say that surely this beautiful country had not sunk so low as to be reduced to a state of hypersensitive prudishness. But we confined ourselves to assuring the gentleman that any lack of respect, any provocation on our parts, had been the furthest from our thoughts. And as a mitigating circumstance we pointed out the tender age and physical slightness of the little culprit. In vain. Our protests were waved away, he did not believe in them; our defense would not hold water. We must be made an example of. The authorities were notified, by telephone, I believe, and their representative appeared on the beach. He said the case was *"molto grave."* We had to go with him to the Municipio up in the Piazza, where a higher official confirmed the previous verdict of *"molto grave,"* launched into a stream of the usual didactic phrases—the selfsame tune and words as the man in the bowler hat—and levied a fine and ransom of fifty lire. We felt that the adventure must willy-nilly be worth to us this much of a contribution to the economy of the Italian government; paid, and left. Ought we not at this point to have left Torre as well?

If we only had! We should thus have escaped that fatal Cipolla. But circumstances combined to prevent us from making up our minds to a change. A certain poet says that it is indolence that makes us endure uncomfortable situations. The *aperçu* may serve as an explanation for our inaction. Anyhow, one dislikes voiding the field immediately upon such an event. Especially if sympathy from other quarters encourages one to defy it. And in the Villa Eleonora they pronounced as with one voice upon the injustice of our punishment. Some Italian after-dinner acquaintances found that the episode put their country in a very bad light, and proposed taking the man in the bowler hat to task, as one fellow-citizen to another. But the next day he and his party had vanished from the beach. Not on our account, of course. Though it might be that the consciousness of his impending departure had added energy to his rebuke; in any case his going was a relief. And, furthermore, we stayed because our stay had by now become remarkable in our own eyes, which is worth something in itself, quite apart from the comfort or discomfort involved. Shall we strike sail, avoid a certain experience so soon as it seems not expressly calculated to increase our enjoyment or our self-esteem? Shall we go away whenever life looks like turning in the slightest uncanny, or not quite normal, or even rather painful and mortifying? No, surely not. Rather stay and look matters in the face, brave them out; perhaps precisely in so doing lies a lesson for us to learn. We stayed on and reaped as the awful reward of our constancy the unholy and staggering experience with Cipolla.

I have not mentioned that the after season had begun, almost on the very day we were disciplined by the city authorities. The worshipful gentleman in the bowler hat, our denouncer, was not the only person to leave the resort. There was a regular exodus, on every hand you saw luggage-carts on their way to the station. The beach denationalized itself. Life in Torre, in the cafés and the pinetas, became more homelike and more European. Very likely we might even have eaten at a table in the glass veranda, but we refrained, being content at Signora Angiolieri's—as content, that is, as our evil star would let us be. But at the same time with this turn for the better came a change in the weather: almost to an hour it showed itself in harmony with the holiday calendar of the general public. The sky was overcast; not that it grew any cooler, but the unclouded heat of the entire eighteen days since our arrival, and probably long before that, gave place to a stifling sirocco air, while from time to time a little ineffectual rain sprinkled the velvety surface of the beach. Add to which, that two-thirds of our intended stay at Torre had passed. The colorless, lazy sea, with sluggish jellyfish floating in its shallows, was at least a change. And it would have been silly to feel retrospective longings after a sun that had caused us so many sighs when it burned down in all its arrogant power.

At this juncture, then, it was that Cipolla announced himself. Cavaliere Cipolla he was called on the posters that appeared one day stuck up everywhere, even in the dining-room of Pensione Eleonora. A traveling virtuso, an entertainer, *"forzatore, illusionista, prestidigitatore,"* as he called himself, who proposed to wait upon the highly respectable population of Torre di Venere with a display of extraordinary phenomena of a mysterious and staggering kind. A conjuror! The bare announcement was enough to turn our children's heads. They had never seen anything of the sort, and now our present holiday was to afford them this new excitement. From that moment on they besieged us with prayers to take tickets for the performance. We had doubts, from the first, on the score of the lateness of the hour, nine o'clock; but gave way, in the idea that we might see a little of what Cipolla had to offer, probably no great matter, and then go home. Besides, of course, the children could sleep late next day. We bought four tickets of Signora Angiolieri herself, she having taken a number of the stalls on commission to sell them to her guests. She could not vouch for the man's performance, and we had no great expectations. But we were conscious of a need for diversion, and the children's violent curiosity proved catching.

The Cavaliere's performance was to take place in a hall where during the season there had been a cinema with a weekly program. We had never been there. You reached it by following the main street under the wall of the *"palazzo,"* a ruin with a "For sale" sign, that suggested a castle and had obviously been built in lordlier days. In the same street were the chemist, the hairdresser, and all the better shops; it led, so to speak, from the feudal past the bourgeois into the proletarian, for it ended off between two rows of poor fishing-huts, where old women sat mending nets before the doors. And here, among the proletariat, was the hall, not much more, actually, than a wooden shed, though a large one, with a turreted entrance, plastered on either side with layers of gay placards. Some while after dinner, then, on the appointed evening, we wended our way thither in the dark, the children dressed in their best and blissful with the sense of so much irregularity. It was sultry, as it had been for days; there was heat lightning now and then, and a little rain; we proceeded under umbrellas. It took us a quarter of an hour.

Our tickets were collected at the entrance, our places we had to find ourselves. They were in the third row left, and as we sat down we saw that, late though the hour was for the performance, it was to be interpreted with even more laxity. Only very slowly did an audience—who seemed to be relied upon to come late—begin to fill the stalls. These comprised the whole auditorium; there were no boxes. This tardiness gave us some concern. The children's cheeks were already flushed as much with fatigue as with excitement. But even when we entered, the standing-room at the back and in the side aisles was already well occupied. There stood the manhood of Torre di Venere, all and sundry, fisherfolk, rough-and-ready youths with bare forearms crossed over their striped jerseys. We were all pleased with the presence of this native assemblage, which always adds color and animation to occasions like the present; and the children were frankly delighted. For they had friends among these people—acquaintances picked up on afternoon strolls to the further ends of the beach. We would be turning homeward, at the hour when the sun dropped into the sea, spent with the huge effort it had made and gilding with reddish gold the oncoming surf; and we would come upon bare-legged fisherfolk standing in rows, bracing and hauling with long-drawn cries as they drew in the nets and harvested in dripping baskets their catch, often so scanty, of *frutta di mare*. The children looked on, helped to pull, brought out their little stock of Italian words, made friends. So now they exchanged nods with the "standing-room" clientèle; there was Guiscardo, there Antonió, they knew them by name and waved and called across in half-whispers, getting answering nods and smiles that displayed rows of healthy white teeth. Look, there is even Mario, Mario from the Exquisito, who brings us the chocolate. He wants to see the conjuror, too, and he must have come early, for he is almost in front; but he does not see us, he is not paying attention; that is a way he has, even though he is a waiter. So we wave instead to the man who lets out the little boats on the beach; he is there too, standing at the back.

It had got to a quarter past nine, it got to almost half past. It was natural that we should be nervous. When would the children get to bed? It had been a mistake to bring them, for now it would be very hard to suggest breaking off their enjoyment before it had got well under way. The stalls had filled in time; all Torre, apparently, was there: the guests of the Grand Hotel, the guests of Villa Eleonora, familiar faces from the beach. We heard English and German and the sort of French that Rumanians speak with Italians. Madame Angiolieri herself sat two rows behind us, with her quiet, bald-headed spouse, who kept stroking his mustache with the two middle fingers of his right hand. Everybody had come late, but nobody too late. Cipolla made us wait for him.

He made us wait. That is probably the way to put it. He heightened the suspense by his delay in appearing. And we could see the point of this, too —only not when it was carried to extremes. Towards half past nine the audience began to clap—an amiable way of expressing justifiable impatience, evincing as it does an eagerness to applaud. For the little ones, this was a joy in itself—all children love to clap. From the popular sphere came loud cries of *"Pronti!" "Cominciamo!"* And lo, it seemed now as easy to begin as before it had been hard. A gong sounded, greeted by the standing rows with a many-voiced "Ah-h!" and the curtains parted. They revealed a platform furnished more like a schoolroom than like the theater of a conjuring performance—largely because of the blackboard in the left foreground. There was a common yellow hat-stand, a few ordinary straw-bottomed chairs, and further back a little round table holding a water carafe and glass, also a tray with a liqueur glass and a flask of pale yellow liquid. We had still a few seconds of time to let these things sink in. Then, with no darkening of the house, Cavaliere Cipolla made his entry.

He came forward with a rapid step that expressed his eagerness to appear before his public and gave rise to the illusion that he had already come a long way to put himself at their service—whereas, of course, he had only been standing in the wings. His costume supported the fiction. A man of an age hard to determine, but by no means young; with a sharp, ravaged face, piercing eyes, compressed lips, small black waxed mustache, and a so-called imperial in the curve between mouth and chin. He was dressed for the street with a sort of complicated evening elegance, in a wide black pelerine with velvet collar and satin lining; which, in the hampered state of his arms, he held together in front with his white-gloved hands. He had a white scarf round his neck; a top hat with a curving brim sat far back on his head. Perhaps more than anywhere else the eighteenth century is still alive in Italy, and with it the charlatan and mountebank type so characteristic of the period. Only there, at any rate, does one still encounter really well-preserved specimens. Cipolla had in his whole appearance much of the historic type; his very clothes helped to conjure up the traditional figure with its blatantly, fantastically foppish air. His pretentious costume sat upon him, or rather hung upon him, most curiously, being in one place drawn too tight, in another a mass of awkward folds. There was something not quite in order about this figure, both front and back—that was plain later on. But I must emphasize the fact that there was not a trace of personal jocularity or clownishness in his pose, manner, or behavior. On the contrary, there was complete seriousness, an absence of any humorous appeal; occasionally even a cross-grained pride, along with that curious, self-satisfied air so characteristic of the deformed. None of all this, however, prevented his appearance from being greeted with laughter from more than one quarter of the hall.

All the eagerness had left his manner. The swift entry had been merely an expression of energy, not of zeal. Standing at the footlights he negligently drew off his gloves, to display long yellow hands, one of them adorned with a seal ring with a lapis-lazuli in a high setting. As he stood there, his small hard eyes, with flabby pouches beneath them, roved appraisingly about the hall, not quickly, rather in a considered examination, pausing here and there upon a face with his lips clipped together, not speaking a word. Then with a display of skill as surprising as it was casual, he rolled his gloves into a ball and tossed them across a considerable distance into the glass on the table. Next from an inner pocket he drew forth a packet of cigarettes; you could see by the wrapper that they were the cheapest sort the government sells. With his fingertips he pulled out a cigarette and lighted it, without looking, from a quick-firing benzine lighter. He drew the smoke deep into his lungs and let it out again, tapping his foot, with both lips drawn in an arrogant grimace and the gray smoke streaming out between broken and saw-edged teeth.

With a keenness equal to his own his audience eyed him. The youths at the rear scowled as they peered at this cocksure creature to search out his secret weaknesses. He betrayed none. In fetching out and putting back the cigarettes his clothes got in his way. He had to turn back his pelerine, and in so doing revealed a riding-whip with a silver claw-handle that hung by a leather thong from his left forearm and looked decidedly out of place. You could see that he had on not evening clothes but a frock-coat, and under this, as he lifted it to get at his pocket, could be seen a striped sash worn about the body. Somebody behind me whispered that this sash went with this title of Cavaliere. I give the information for what it may be worth —personally, I never heard that the title carried such insignia with it. Perhaps the sash was sheer pose, like the way he stood there, without a word, casually and arrogantly puffing smoke into his audience's face.

People laughed, as I said. The merriment had become almost general when somebody in the "standing seats," in a loud, dry voice, remarked: *"Buona sera."*

Cipolla cocked his head. "Who was that?" asked he, as though he had been dared. "Who was that just spoke? Well? First so bold and now so modest? *Paura,* eh?" He spoke with a rather high, asthmatic voice, which yet had a metallic quality. He waited.

"That was me," a youth at the rear broke into the stillness, seeing himself thus challenged. He was not far from us, a handsome fellow in a woolen shirt, with his coat hanging over one shoulder. He wore his curly, wiry hair in a high, disheveled mop, the style affected by the youth of the awakened Fatherland; it gave him an African appearance that rather spoiled his looks. *"Bè!* That was me. It was your business to say it first, but I was trying to be friendly."

More laughter. The chap had a tongue in his head. *"Ha sciolto lo scilin-guágnolo,"* I heard near me. After all, the retort was deserved.

"Ah, bravo!" answered Cipolla. "I like you, *giovanotto.* Trust me, I've had my eye on you for some time. People like you are just in my line. I can use them. And you are the pick of the lot, that's plain to see. You do what you like. Or is it possible you have ever not done what you liked—or even, maybe, what you didn't like? What somebody else liked, in short? Hark ye, my friend, that might be a pleasant change for you, to divide up the willing and the doing and stop tackling both jobs at once. Division of labor, *sistema americano, sa'!* For instance, suppose you were to show your tongue to this elect and honorable audience here—your whole tongue, right down to the roots?"

"No, I won't," said the youth, hostilely. "Sticking out your tongue shows a bad bringing-up."

"Nothing of the sort," retorted Cipolla. "You would only be *doing* it. With all due respect to your bringing-up, I suggest that before I count ten, you will perform a right turn and stick out your tongue at the company here further than you knew yourself that you could stick it out."

He gazed at the youth, and his piercing eyes seemed to sink deeper into their sockets. *"Uno!"* said he. He had let his riding-whip slide down his arm and made it whistle once through the air. The boy faced about and put out his tongue, so long, so extendedly, that you could see it was the very uttermost in tongue which he had to offer. Then turned back, stony-faced, to his former position.

"That was me," mocked Cipolla, with a jerk of his head towards the youth. *"Bè!* That was me." Leaving the audience to enjoy its sensations, he turned towards the little round table, lifted the bottle, poured out a small glass of what was obviously cognac, and tipped it up with a practiced hand.

The children laughed with all their hearts. They had understood practically nothing of what had been said, but it pleased them hugely that something so funny should happen, straightaway, between that queer man up there and somebody out of the audience. They had no preconception of what an "evening" would be like and were quite ready to find this a priceless beginning. As for us, we exchanged a glance and I remember that involuntarily I made with my lips the sound that Cipolla's whip had made when it cut the air. For the rest, it was plain that people did not know what to make of a preposterous beginning like this to a sleight-of-hand performance. They could not see why the *giovanotto,* who after all in a way had been their spokesman, should suddenly have turned on them to vent his incivility. They felt that he had behaved like a silly ass and withdrew

their countenances from him in favor of the artist, who now came back
from his refreshment table and addressed them as follows:

"Ladies and gentlemen," said he, in his wheezing, metallic voice, "you
saw just now that I was rather sensitive on the score of the rebuke this
hopeful young linguist saw fit to give me"—*"questo linguista di belle spe-
ranze"* was what he said, and we all laughed at the pun. "I am a man who
sets some store by himself, you may take it from me. And I see no point
in being wished a good-evening unless it is done courteously and in all
seriousness. For anything else there is no occasion. When a man wishes me
a good-evening he wishes himself one, for the audience will have one only
if I do. So this lady-killer of Torre di Venere" (another thrust) "did well
to testify that I have one tonight and that I can dispense with any wishes
of his in the matter: I can boast of having good evenings almost without
exception. One not so good does come my way now and again, but very
seldom. My calling is hard and my health not of the best. I have a little
physical defect which prevented me from doing my bit in the war for the
greater glory of the Fatherland. It is perforce with my mental and spiritual
parts that I conquer life—which after all only means conquering oneself.
And I flatter myself that my achievements have aroused interest and respect among the educated public. The leading newspapers have lauded me,
the *Corriere della Sera* did me the courtesy of calling me a phenomenon, and
in Rome the brother of the *Duce* honored me by his presence at one of my
evenings. I should not have thought that in a relatively less important
place" (laughter here, at the expense of poor little Torre) "I should have
to give up the small personal habits which brilliant and elevated audiences
had been ready to overlook. Nor did I think I had to stand being heckled
by a person who seems to have been rather spoilt by the favors of the fair
sex." All this of course at the expense of the youth whom Cipolla never
tired of presenting in the guise of *donnaiuolo* and rustic Don Juan. His
persistent thin-skinnedness and animosity were in striking contrast to the
self-confidence and the worldly success he boasted of. One might have
assumed that the *giovanotto* was merely the chosen butt of Cipolla's cus-
tomary professional sallies, had not the very pointed witticisms betrayed
a genuine antagonism. No one looking at the physical parts of the two men
need have been at a loss for the explanation, even if the deformed man had
not constantly played on the other's supposed success with the fair sex.
"Well," Cipolla went on, "before beginning our entertainment this evening, perhaps you will permit me to make myself comfortable."

And he went towards the hat-stand to take off his things.

"Parla benissimo," asserted somebody in our neighborhood. So far, the
man had done nothing; but what he had said was accepted as an achievement, by means of that he had made an impression. Among southern
peoples speech is a constituent part of the pleasure of living, it enjoys far

livelier social esteem than in the north. That national cement, the mother tongue, is paid symbolic honors down here, and there is something blithely symbolical in the pleasure people take in their respect for its forms and phonetics. They enjoy speaking, they enjoy listening; and they listen with discrimination. For the way a man speaks serves as a measure of his personal rank; carelessness and clumsiness are greeted with scorn, elegance and mastery are rewarded with social éclat. Wherefore the small man too, where it is a question of getting his effect, chooses his phrase nicely and turns it with care. On this count, then, at least, Cipolla had won his audience; though he by no means belonged to the class of men which the Italian, in a singular mixture of moral and esthetic judgments, labels "*simpatico.*"

After removing his hat, scarf, and mantle he came to the front of the stage, settling his coat, pulling down his cuffs with their large cuff-buttons, adjusting his absurd sash. He had very ugly hair; the top of his head, that is, was almost bald, while a narrow, black-varnished frizz of curls ran from front to back as though stuck on; the side hair, likewise blackened, was brushed forward to the corners of the eyes—it was, in short, the hairdressing of an old-fashioned circus-director, fantastic, but entirely suited to his outmoded personal type and worn with so much assurance as to take the edge off the public's sense of humor. The little physical defect of which he had warned us was now all too visible, though the nature of it was even now not very clear: the chest was too high, as is usual in such cases; but the corresponding malformation of the back did not sit between the shoulders, it took the form of a sort of hips or buttocks hump, which did not indeed hinder his movements but gave him a grotesque and dipping stride at every step he took. However, by mentioning his deformity beforehand he had broken the shock of it, and a delicate propriety of feeling appeared to reign throughout the hall.

"At your service," said Cipolla. "With your kind permission, we will begin the evening with some arithmetical tests."

Arithmetic? That did not sound much like sleight-of-hand. We began to have our suspicions that the man was sailing under a false flag, only we did not yet know which was the right one. I felt sorry on the children's account; but for the moment they were content simply to be there.

The numerical test which Cipolla now introduced was as simple as it was baffling. He began by fastening a piece of paper to the upper right-hand corner of the blackboard; then lifting it up, he wrote something underneath. He talked all the while, relieving the dryness of his offering by a constant flow of words, and showed himself a practiced speaker, never at a loss for conversational turns of phrase. It was in keeping with the nature of his performance, and at the same time vastly entertained the children, that he went on to eliminate the gap between stage and audience, which had already been bridged over by the curious skirmish with the fisher lad: he had representatives from the audience mount the stage, and himself descended the wooden steps to seek personal contact with his public. And again, with individuals, he fell into his former taunting tone. I do not know how far that was a deliberate feature of his system; he preserved a serious, even a peevish air, but his audience, at least the more popular section, seemed convinced that that was all part of the game. So then, after he had written something and covered the writing by the paper, he desired that two persons should come up on the platform and help to perform the calculations. They would not be difficult, even for people not clever at figures. As usual, nobody volunteered, and Cipolla took care not to molest the more select portion of his audience. He kept to the populace. Turning to two sturdy young louts standing behind us, he beckoned them to the front, encouraging and scolding by turns. They should not stand there gaping, he said, unwilling to oblige the company. Actually, he got them in motion; with clumsy tread they came down the middle aisle, climbed the steps, and stood in front of the blackboard, grinning sheepishly at their comrades' shouts and applause. Cipolla joked with them for a few minutes, praised their heroic firmness of limb and the size of their hands, so well calculated to do this service for the public. Then he handed one of them the chalk and told him to write down the numbers as they were called out. But now the creature declared that he could not write! *"Non so scrivere,"* said he in his gruff voice, and his companion added that neither did he.

God knows whether they told the truth or whether they wanted to make game of Cipolla. Anyhow, the latter was far from sharing the general merriment which their confession aroused. He was insulted and disgusted. He sat there on a straw-bottomed chair in the center of the stage with his legs crossed, smoking a fresh cigarette out of his cheap packet; obviously it tasted the better for the cognac he had indulged in while the yokels were stumping up the steps. Again he inhaled the smoke and let it stream out between curling lips. Swinging his leg, with his gaze sternly averted from the two shamelessly chuckling creatures and from the audience as well, he stared into space as one who withdraws himself and his dignity from the contemplation of an utterly despicable phenomenon.

"Scandalous," said he, in a sort of icy snarl. "Go back to your places! In Italy everybody can write—in all her greatness there is no room for ignorance and unenlightenment. To accuse her of them, in the hearing of this international company, is a cheap joke, in which you yourselves cut a very poor figure and humiliate the government and the whole country as well. If it is true that Torre di Venere is indeed the last refuge of such ignorance, then I must blush to have visited the place—being, as I already was, aware of its inferiority to Rome in more than one respect—"

Here Cipolla was interrupted by the youth with the Nubian coiffure and his jacket across his shoulder. His fighting spirit, as we now saw, had only abdicated temporarily, and he now flung himself into the breach in defense of his native heath.

"That will do," said he loudly. "That's enough jokes about Torre. We all come from the place and we won't stand strangers making fun of it. These two chaps are our friends. Maybe they are no scholars, but even so they may be straighter than some folks in the room who are so free with their boasts about Rome, though they did not build it either."

That was capital. The young man had certainly cut his eyeteeth. And this sort of spectacle was good fun, even though it still further delayed the regular performance. It is always fascinating to listen to an altercation. Some people it simply amuses, they take a sort of kill-joy pleasure in not being principals. Others feel upset and uneasy, and my sympathies are with these latter, although on the present occasion I was under the impression that all this was part of the show—the analphabetic yokels no less than the *giovanotto* with the jacket. The children listened well pleased. They understood not at all, but the sound of the voices made them hold their breath. So this was a "magic evening"—at least it was the kind they have in Italy. They expressly found it "lovely."

Cipolla had stood up and with two of his scooping strides was at the footlights.

"Well, well, see who's here!" said he with grim cordiality. "An old acquaintance! A young man with his heart at the end of his tongue" (he used the word *linguaccia,* which means a coated tongue, and gave rise to much hilarity). "That will do, my friends," he turned to the yokels. "I do not need you now, I have business with this deserving young man here, *con questo torregiano di Venere,* this tower of Venus, who no doubt expects the gratitude of the fair as a reward for his prowess—"

"Ah, non scherziamo! We're talking earnest," cried out the youth. His eyes flashed, and he actually made as though to pull off his jacket and proceed to direct methods of settlement.

Cipolla did not take him too seriously. We had exchanged apprehensive glances; but he was dealing with a fellow-countryman and had his native soil beneath his feet. He kept quite cool and showed complete mastery of the situation. He looked at his audience, smiled, and made a sideways motion of the head towards the young cockerel as though calling the public to witness how the man's bumptiousness only served to betray the simplicity of his mind. And then, for the second time, something strange happened, which set Cipolla's calm superiority in an uncanny light, and in some mysterious and irritating way turned all the explosiveness latent in the air into matter for laughter.

Cipolla drew still nearer to the fellow, looking him in the eye with a peculiar gaze. He even came half-way down the steps that led into the auditorium on our left, so that he stood directly in front of the troublemaker, on slightly higher ground. The riding-whip hung from his arm.

"My son, you do not feel much like joking," he said. "It is only too natural, for anyone can see that you are not feeling too well. Even your tongue, which leaves something to be desired on the score of cleanliness, indicates acute disorder of the gastric system. An evening entertainment is no place for people in your state; you yourself, I can tell, were of several minds whether you would not do better to put on a flannel bandage and go to bed. It was not good judgment to drink so much of that very sour white wine this afternoon. Now you have such a colic you would like to double up with the pain. Go ahead, don't be embarrassed. There is a distinct relief that comes from bending over, in cases of intestinal cramp."

He spoke thus, word for word, with quiet impressiveness and a kind of stern sympathy, and his eyes, plunged the while deep in the young man's, seemed to grow very tired and at the same time burning above their enlarged tear-ducts—they were the strangest eyes, you could tell that not manly pride alone was preventing the young adversary from withdrawing his gaze. And presently, indeed, all trace of its former arrogance was gone from the bronzed young face. He looked openmouthed at the Cavaliere and the open mouth was drawn in a rueful smile.

"Double over," repeated Cipolla. "What else can you do? With a colic like that you *must* bend. Surely you will not struggle against the performance of a perfectly natural action just because somebody suggests it to you?"

Slowly the youth lifted his forearms, folded and squeezed them across his body; it turned a little sideways, then bent, lower and lower, the feet shifted, the knees turned inward, until he had become a picture of writhing pain, until he all but groveled upon the ground. Cipolla let him stand for some seconds thus, then made a short cut through the air with his whip and went with his scooping stride back to the little table, where he poured himself out a cognac.

"Il boit beaucoup," asserted a lady behind us. Was that the only thing that struck her? We could not tell how far the audience grasped the situation. The fellow was standing upright again, with a sheepish grin—he looked as though he scarcely knew how it had all happened. The scene had been followed with tense interest and applauded at the end; there were shouts of *"Bravo, Cipolla!"* and *"Bravo, giovanotto!"* Apparently the issue of the duel was not looked upon as a personal defeat for the young man. Rather the audience encouraged him as one does an actor who succeeds in an unsympathetic role. Certainly his way of screwing himself up with cramp had been highly picturesque, its appeal was directly calculated to impress the gallery—in short, a fine dramatic performance. But I am not sure how

far the audience were moved by that natural tactfulness in which the south excels, or how far it penetrated into the nature of what was going on.

The Cavaliere, refreshed, had lighted another cigarette. The numerical tests might now proceed. A young man was easily found in the back row who was willing to write down on the blackboard the numbers as they were dictated to him. Him too we knew; the whole entertainment had taken on an intimate character through our acquaintance with so many of the actors. This was the man who worked at the greengrocer's in the main street; he had served us several times, with neatness and dispatch. He wielded the chalk with clerkly confidence, while Cipolla descended to our level and walked with his deformed gait through the audience, collecting numbers as they were given, in two, three, and four places, and calling them out to the grocer's assistant, who wrote them down in a column. In all this, everything on both sides was calculated to amuse, with its jokes and its oratorical asides. The artist could not fail to hit on foreigners, who were not ready with their figures, and with them he was elaborately patient and chivalrous, to the great amusement of the natives, whom he reduced to confusion in their turn, by making them translate numbers that were given in English or French. Some people gave dates concerned with great events in Italian history. Cipolla took them up at once and made patriotic comments. Somebody shouted "Number one!" The Cavaliere, incensed at this as at every attempt to make game of him, retorted over his shoulder that he could not take less than two-place figures. Whereupon another joker cried out "Number two!" and was greeted with the applause and laughter which every reference to natural functions is sure to win among southerners.

When fifteen numbers stood in a long straggling row on the board, Cipolla called for a general adding-match. Ready reckoners might add in their heads, but pencil and paper were not forbidden. Cipolla, while the work went on, sat on his chair near the blackboard, smoked and grimaced, with the complacent, pompous air cripples so often have. The five-place addition was soon done. Somebody announced the answer, somebody else confirmed it, a third had arrived at a slightly different result, but the fourth agreed with the first and second. Cipolla got up, tapped some ash from his coat, and lifted the paper at the upper right-hand corner of the board to display the writing. The correct answer, a sum close on a million, stood there; he had written it down beforehand.

Astonishment, and loud applause. The children were overwhelmed. How had he done that, they wanted to know. We told them it was a trick, not easily explainable offhand. In short, the man was a conjuror. This was what a sleight-of-hand evening was like, so now they knew. First the fisherman had cramp, and then the right answer was written down beforehand—it was all simply glorious, and we saw with dismay that despite the hot eyes and the hand of the clock at almost half past ten, it would be very hard to get them away. There would be tears. And yet it was plain that this magician did not "magick"—at least not in the accepted sense, of manual dexterity—and that the entertainment was not at all suitable for children. Again, I do not know, either, what the audience really thought. Obviously there was grave doubt whether its answers had been given of "free choice"; here and there an individual might have answered of his own motion, but on the whole Cipolla certainly selected his people and thus kept the whole procedure in his own hands and directed it towards the given result. Even so, one had to admire the quickness of his calculations, however much one felt disinclined to admire anything else about the performance. Then his patriotism, his irritable sense of dignity—the Cavaliere's own countrymen might feel in their element with all that and continue in a laughing mood; but the combination certainly gave us outsiders food for thought.

Cipolla himself saw to it—though without giving them a name—that the nature of his powers should be clear beyond a doubt to even the least-instructed person. He alluded to them, of course, in his talk—and he talked without stopping—but only in vague, boastful, self-advertising phrases. He went on a while with experiments on the same lines as the first, merely making them more complicated by introducing operations in multiplying, subtracting, and dividing; then he simplified them to the last degree in order to bring out the method. He simply had numbers "guessed" which were previously written under the paper; and the guess was nearly always right. One guesser admitted that he had had in mind to give a certain number when Cipolla's whip went whistling through the air, and a quite different one slipped out, which proved to be the "right" one. Cipolla's shoulders shook. He pretended admiration for the powers of the people he questioned. But in all his compliments there was something fleering and derogatory; the victims could scarcely have relished them much, although they smiled, and although they might easily have set down some part of the applause to their own credit. Moreover, I had not the impression that the artist was popular with his public. A certain ill will and reluctance were in the air, but courtesy kept such feelings in check, as did Cipolla's competency and his stern self-confidence. Even the riding-whip, I think, did much to keep rebellion from becoming overt.

From tricks with numbers he passed to tricks with cards. There were two packs, which he drew out of his pockets, and so much I still remember, that the basis of the tricks he played with them was as follows: from the first pack he drew three cards and thrust them without looking at them inside his coat. Another person then drew three out of the second pack, and these turned out to be the same as the first three—not invariably all the three, for it did happen that only two were the same. But in the majority of cases Cipolla triumphed, showing his three cards with a little bow in acknowledgment of the applause with which his audience conceded his possession of strange powers—strange whether for good or evil. A young man in the front row, to our right, an Italian, with proud, finely chiseled features, rose up and said that he intended to assert his own will in his choice and consciously to resist any influence, of whatever sort. Under these circumstances, what did Cipolla think would be the result? "You will," answered the Cavaliere, "make my task somewhat more difficult thereby. As for the result, your resistance will not alter it in the least. Freedom exists, and also the will exists; but freedom of the will does not exist, for a will that aims at its own freedom aims at the unknown. You are free to draw or not to draw. But if you draw, you will draw the right cards—the more certainly, the more willfully obstinate your behavior."

One must admit that he could not have chosen his words better, to trouble the waters and confuse the mind. The refractory youth hesitated before drawing. Then he pulled out a card and at once demanded to see if it was among the chosen three. "But why?" queried Cipolla. "Why do things by halves?" Then, as the other defiantly insisted, *'E servito,'* said the juggler, with a gesture of exaggerated servility; and held out the three cards fanwise, without looking at them himself. The left-hand card was the one drawn.

Amid general applause, the apostle of freedom sat down. How far Cipolla employed small tricks and manual dexterity to help out his natural talents, the deuce only knew. But even without them the result would have been the same: the curiosity of the entire audience was unbounded and universal, everybody both enjoyed the amazing character of the entertainment and unanimously conceded the professional skill of the performer. *'Lavora bene,'* we heard, here and there in our neighborhood; it signified the triumph of objective judgment over antipathy and repressed resentment.

After his last, incomplete, yet so much the more telling success, Cipolla had at once fortified himself with another cognac. Truly he did "drink a lot" and the fact made a bad impression. But obviously he needed the liquor and the cigarettes for the replenishment of his energy, upon which, as he himself said, heavy demands were made in all directions. Certainly in the intervals he looked very ill, exhausted and hollow-eyed. Then the little glassful would redress the balance, and the flow of lively, self-confident chatter run on, while the smoke he inhaled gushed out gray from his lungs. I clearly recall that he passed from the card-tricks to parlor games —the kind based on certain powers which in human nature are higher or else lower than human reason: on intuition and "magnetic" transmission; in short, upon a low type of manifestation. What I do not remember is the precise order things came in. And I will not bore you with a description of these experiments; everybody knows them, everybody has at one time or another taken part in this finding of hidden articles, this blind carrying out of a series of acts, directed by a force that proceeds from organism to organism by unexplored paths. Everybody has had his little glimpse into the equivocal, impure, inexplicable nature of the occult, has been conscious of both curiosity and contempt, has shaken his head over the human tendency of those who deal in it to help themselves out with humbuggery, though, after all, the humbuggery is no disproof whatever of the genuineness of the other elements in the dubious amalgam. I can only say here that each single circumstance gains in weight and the whole greatly in impressiveness when it is a man like Cipolla who is the chief actor and guiding spirit in the sinister business. He sat smoking at the rear of the stage, his back to the audience while they conferred. The object passed from hand to hand which it was his task to find, with which he was to perform some action agreed upon beforehand. Then he would start to move zigzag through the hall, with his head thrown back and one hand outstretched, the other clasped in that of guide who was in the secret but enjoined to keep himself perfectly passive, with his thoughts directed upon the agreed goal. Cipolla moved with the bearing typical in these experiments: now groping upon a false start, now with a quick forward thrust, now pausing as though to listen and by sudden inspiration correcting his course. The roles seemed reversed, the stream of influence was moving in the contrary direction, as the artist himself pointed out, in his ceaseless flow of discourse. The suffering, receptive, performing part was now his, the will he had before imposed on others was shut out, he acted in obedience to a voiceless common will which was in the air. But he made it perfectly clear that it all came to the same thing. The capacity for self-surrender, he said, for becoming a tool, for the most unconditional and utter self-abnegation, was but the reverse side of that other power to will and to command. Commanding and obeying formed together one single principle, one indissoluble unity; he who knew how to obey knew also how to command, and conversely; the one idea was comprehended in the other, as people and leader were comprehended in one another. But that which was *done,* the highly exacting and exhausting performance, was in every case his, the leader's and mover's, in whom the will became obedience, the obedience will, whose person was the cradle and womb of both, and who thus suffered enormous hardship. Repeatedly he emphasized the fact that his lot was a hard one—presumably to account for his need of stimulant and his frequent recourse to the little glass.

Thus he groped his way forward, like a blind seer, led and sustained by the mysterious common will. He drew a pin set with a stone out of its hiding-place in an Englishwoman's shoe, carried it, halting and pressing on by turns, to another lady—Signora Angiolieri—and handed it to her on bended knee, with the words it had been agreed he was to utter. "I present you with this in token of my respect," was the sentence. Their sense was obvious, but the words themselves not easy to hit upon, for the reason that they had been agreed on in French; the language complication seemed to us a little malicious, implying as it did a conflict between the audience's natural interest in the success of the miracle, and their desire to witness the humiliation of this presumptuous man. It was a strange sight: Cipolla on his knees before the signora, wrestling, amid efforts at speech, after knowledge of the preordained words. "I must say something," he said, "and I feel clearly what it is I must say. But I also feel that if it passed my lips it would be wrong. Be careful not to help me unintentionally!" he cried out, though very likely that was precisely what he was hoping for. *"Pensez très fort,"* he cried all at once, in bad French, and then burst out with the required words—in Italian, indeed, but with the final substantive pronounced in the sister tongue, in which he was probably far from fluent: he said *vénération* instead of *venerazione,* with an impossible nasal. And this partial success, after the complete success before it, the finding of the pin, the presentation of it on his knees to the right person—was almost more impressive than if he had got the sentence exactly right, and evoked bursts of admiring applause.

Cipolla got up from his knees and wiped the perspiration from his brow. You understand that this experiment with the pin was a single case, which I describe because it sticks in my memory. But he changed his method several times and improvised a number of variations suggested by his contact with his audience; a good deal of time thus went by. He seemed to get particular inspiration from the person of our landlady; she drew him on to the most extraordinary displays of clairvoyance. "It does not escape me, madame," he said to her, "that there is something unusual about you, some special and honorable distinction. He who has eyes to see descries about your lovely brow an aureola—if I mistake not, it once was stronger than now—a slowly paling radiance . . . hush, not a word! Don't help me. Beside you sits your husband—yes?" He turned towards the silent Signor Angiolieri. "You are the husband of this lady, and your happiness is complete. But in the midst of this happiness memories rise . . . the past, signora, so it seems to me, plays an important part in your present. You knew a king . . . has not a king crossed your path in bygone days?"

"No," breathed the dispenser of our midday soup, her golden-brown eyes gleaming in the noble pallor of her face.

"No? No, not a king; I meant that generally, I did not mean literally a king. Not a king, not a prince, and a prince after all, a king of loftier realm; it was a great artist, at whose side you once—you would contradict me, and yet I am not wholly wrong. Well, then! It was a woman, a great, a world-renowned woman artist, whose friendship you enjoyed in your tender years, whose sacred memory overshadows and transfigures your whole existence. Her name? Need I utter it, whose fame has long been bound up with the Fatherland's, immortal as its own? Eleonora Duse," he finished, softly and with much solemnity.

The little woman bowed her head, overcome. The applause was like a patriotic demonstration. Nearly everyone there knew about Signora Angiolieri's wonderful past; they were all able to confirm the Cavaliere's intuition—not least the present guests of Casa Eleonora. But we wondered how much of the truth he had learned as the result of professional inquiries made on his arrival. Yet I see no reason at all to cast doubt, on rational grounds, upon powers which, before our very eyes, became fatal to their possessor.

At this point there was an intermission. Our lord and master withdrew. Now I confess that almost ever since the beginning of my tale I have looked forward with dread to this moment in it. The thoughts of men are mostly not hard to read; in this case they are very easy. You are sure to ask why we did not choose this moment to go away—and I must continue to owe you an answer. I do not know why. I cannot defend myself. By this time it was certainly eleven, probably later. The children were asleep. The last series of tests had been too long, nature had had her way. They were sleeping in our laps, the little one on mine, the boy on his mother's. That was, in a way, a consolation; but at the same time it was also ground for compassion and a clear leading to take them home to bed. And I give you my word that we wanted to obey this touching admonition, we seriously wanted to. We roused the poor things and told them it was now high time to go. But they were no sooner conscious than they began to resist and implore—you know how horrified children are at the thought of leaving before the end of a thing. No cajoling has any effect, you have to use force. It was so lovely, they wailed. How did we know what was coming next? Surely we could not leave until after the intermission; they liked a little nap now and again—only not go home, only not go to bed, while the beautiful evening was still going on!

We yielded, but only for the moment, of course—so far as we knew— only for a little while, just a few minutes longer. I cannot excuse our staying, scarcely can I even understand it. Did we think, having once said A, we had to say B—having once brought the children hither we had to let them stay? No, it is not good enough. Were we ourselves so highly entertained? Yes, and no. Our feelings for Cavaliere Cipolla were of a very mixed kind, but so were the feelings of the whole audience, if I mistake not, and nobody left. Were we under the sway of a fascination which emanated from this man who took so strange a way to earn his bread; a fascination which he gave out independently of the program and even between the tricks and which paralyzed our resolve? Again, sheer curiosity may account for something. One was curious to know how such an evening turned out; Cipolla in his remarks having all along hinted that he had tricks in his bag stranger than any he had yet produced.

But all that is not it—or at least it is not all of it. More correct it would be to answer the first question with another. Why had we not left Torre di Venere itself before now? To me the two questions are one and the same, and in order to get out of the impasse I might simply say that I had answered it already. For, as things had been in Torre in general: queer, uncomfortable, troublesome, tense, oppressive, so precisely they were here in this hall tonight. Yes, more than precisely. For it seemed to be the fountainhead of all the uncanniness and all the strained feelings which had oppressed the atmosphere of our holiday. This man whose return to the stage we were awaiting was the personification of all that; and, as we had not gone away in general, so to speak, it would have been inconsistent to do it in the particular case. You may call this an explanation, you may call it inertia, as you see fit. Any argument more to the purpose I simply do not know how to adduce.

Well, there was an interval of ten minutes, which grew into nearly twenty. The children remained awake. They were enchanted by our compliance, and filled the break to their own satisfaction by renewing relations with the popular sphere, with Antonio, Guiscardo, and the canoe man. They put their hands to their mouths and called messages across, appealing to us for the Italian words. "Hope you have a good catch tomorrow, a whole netful!" They called to Mario, Esquisito Mario: *"Mario, una cioccolata e biscotti!"* And this time he heeded and answered with a smile: *"Subito, signorini!"* Later we had reason to recall this kindly, if rather absent and pensive smile.

Thus the interval passed, the gong sounded. The audience, which had scattered in conversation, took their places again, the children sat up straight in their chairs with their hands in their laps. The curtain had not been dropped. Cipolla came forward again, with his dipping stride, and began to introduce the second half of the program with a lecture.

Let me state once for all that this self-confident cripple was the most powerful hypnotist I have ever seen in my life. It was pretty plain now that he threw dust in the public eye and advertised himself as a prestidigitator on account of police regulations which would have prevented him from making his living by the exercise of his powers. Perhaps this eye-wash is the usual thing in Italy; it may be permitted or even connived at by the authorities. Certainly the man had from the beginning made little concealment of the actual nature of his operations; and this second half of the program was quite frankly and exclusively devoted to one sort of experiment. While he still practiced some rhetorical circumlocutions, the tests themselves were one long series of attacks upon the will-power, the loss or compulsion of volition. Comic, exciting, amazing by turns, by midnight they were still in full swing; we ran the gamut of all the phenomena this natural-unnatural field has to show, from the unimpressive at one end of the scale to the monstrous at the other. The audience laughed and applauded as they followed the grotesque details; shook their heads, clapped their knees, fell very frankly under the spell of this stern, self-assured personality. At the same time I saw signs that they were not quite complacent, not quite unconscious of the peculiar ignominy which lay, for the individual and for the general, in Cipolla's triumphs.

Two main features were constant in all the experiments: the liquor glass and the claw-handled riding-whip. The first was always invoked to add fuel to his demoniac fires; without it, apparently, they might have burned out. On this score we might even have felt pity for the man; but the whistle of his scourge, the insulting symbol of his domination, before which we all cowered, drowned out every sensation save a dazed and out-braved submission to his power. Did he then lay claim to our sympathy to boot? I was struck by a remark he made—it suggested no less. At the climax of his experiments, by stroking and breathing upon a certain young man who had offered himself as a subject and already proved himself a particularly susceptible one, he had not only put him into the condition known as deep trance and extended his insensible body by neck and feet across the backs of two chairs, but had actually sat down on the rigid form as on a bench, without making it yield. The sight of this unholy figure in a frock-coat squatted on the stiff body was horrible and incredible; the audience, convinced that the victim of this scientific diversion must be suffering, expressed its sympathy: *"Ah, poveretto!"* Poor soul, poor soul! *"Poor soul!"* Cipolla mocked them, with some bitterness. "Ladies and gentlemen, you are barking up the wrong tree. *Sono io il poveretto.* I am the person who is suffering, I am the one to be pitied." We pocketed the information. Very good. Maybe the experiment was at his expense, maybe it was he who had suffered the cramp when the *giovanotto* over there had made the faces. But appearances were all against it; and one does not feel like saying *poveretto* to a man who is suffering to bring about the humiliation of others.

I have got ahead of my story and lost sight of the sequence of events. To this day my mind is full of the Cavaliere's feats of endurance; only I do not recall them in their order—which does not matter. So much I do know: that the longer and more circumstantial tests, which got the most applause, impressed me less than some of the small ones which passed quickly over. I remember the young man whose body Cipolla converted into a board, only because of the accompanying remarks which I have quoted. An elderly lady in a cane-seated chair was lulled by Cipolla in the delusion that she was on a voyage to India and gave a voluble account of her adventures by land and sea. But I found this phenomenon less impressive than one which followed immediately after the intermission. A tall, well-built, soldierly man was unable to lift his arm, after the hunchback had told him that he could not and given a cut through the air with his whip. I can still see the face of that stately, mustachioed colonel smiling and clenching his teeth as he struggled to regain his lost freedom of action. A staggering performance! He seemed to be exerting his will, and in vain; the trouble, however, was probably simply that he could not will. There was involved here that recoil of the will upon itself which paralyzes choice —as our tyrant had previously explained to the Roman gentleman.

Still less can I forget the touching scene, at once comic and horrible, with Signora Angiolieri. The Cavaliere, probably in his first bold survey of the room, had spied out her ethereal lack of resistance to his power. For actually he bewitched her, literally drew her out of her seat, out of her row, and away with him whither he willed. And in order to enhance his effect, he bade Signor Angiolieri call upon his wife by her name to throw, as it were, all the weight of his existence and his rights in her into the scale, to rouse by the voice of her husband everything in his spouse's soul which could shield her virtue against the evil assaults of magic. And how vain it all was! Cipolla was standing at some distance from the couple, when he made a single cut with his whip through the air. It caused our landlady to shudder violently and turn her face towards him. "Sofronia!" cried Signor Angiolieri—we had not known that Signora Angiolieri's name was Sofronia. And he did well to call, everybody saw that there was no time to lose. His wife kept her face turned in the direction of the diabolical Cavaliere, who with his ten long yellow fingers was making passes at his victim, moving backwards as he did so, step by step. Then Signora Angiolieri, her pale face gleaming, rose up from her seat, turned right round, and began to glide after him. Fatal and forbidding sight! Her face as though moonstruck, stiff-armed, her lovely hands lifted a little at the wrists, the feet as it were together, she seemed to float slowly out of her row and after the tempter. "Call her, sir, keep on calling," prompted the redoubtable man. And Signor Angiolieri, in a weak voice, called: "Sofronia!" Ah, again and again he called; as his wife went further off he even curved one hand round his lips and beckoned with the other as he called. But the poor voice of love and duty echoed unheard, in vain, behind the lost one's back; the signora swayed along, moonstruck, deaf, enslaved; she glided into the middle aisle and down it towards the fingering hunchback, towards the door. We were convinced, we were driven to the conviction, that she would have followed her master, had he so willed it, to the ends of the earth.

"Accidente!" cried out Signor Angiolieri, in genuine affright, springing up as the exit was reached. But at the same moment the Cavaliere put aside, as it were, the triumphal crown and broke off. "Enough, signora, I thank you," he said, and offered his arm to lead her back to her husband. "Signor," he greeted the latter, "here is your wife. Unharmed, with my

compliments, I give her into your hands. Cherish with all the strength of your manhood a treasure which is so wholly yours, and let your zeal be quickened by knowing that there are powers stronger than reason or virtue, and not always so magnanimously ready to relinquish their prey!"

Poor Signor Angiolieri, so quiet, so bald! He did not look as though he would know how to defend his happiness, even against powers much less demoniac than these which were now adding mockery to frightfulness. Solemnly and pompously the Cavaliere retired to the stage, amid applause to which his eloquence gave double strength. It was this particular episode, I feel sure, that set the seal upon his ascendancy. For now he made them dance, yes, literally; and the dancing lent a dissolute, abandoned, topsy-turvy air to the scene, a drunken abdication of the critical spirit which had so long resisted the spell of this man. Yes, he had had to fight to get the upper hand—for instance against the animosity of the young Roman gentleman, whose rebellious spirit threatened to serve others as a rallying-point. But it was precisely upon the importance of example that the Cavaliere was so strong. He had the wit to make his attack at the weakest point and to choose as his first victim that feeble, ecstatic youth whom he had previously made into a board. The master had but to look at him, when this young man would fling himself back as though struck by lightning, place his hands rigidly at his sides, and fall into a state of military somnambulism, in which it was plain to any eye that he was open to the most absurd suggestion that might be made to him. He seemed quite content in his abject state, quite pleased to be relieved of the burden of voluntary choice. Again and again he offered himself as a subject and gloried in the model facility he had in losing consciousness. So now he mounted the platform, and a single cut of the whip was enough to make him dance to the Cavaliere's orders, in a kind of complacent ecstasy, eyes closed, head nodding, lank limbs flying in all directions.

It looked unmistakably like enjoyment, and other recruits were not long in coming forward: two other young men, one humbly and one well dressed, were soon jigging alongside the first. But now the gentleman from Rome bobbed up again, asking defiantly if the Cavaliere would engage to make him dance too, even against his will.

"Even against your will," answered Cipolla, in unforgettable accents. That frightful *"anche se non vuole"* still rings in my ears. The struggle began. After Cipolla had taken another little glass and lighted a fresh cigarette he stationed the Roman at a point in the middle aisle and himself took up a position some distance behind him, making his whip whistle through the air as he gave the order: *"Balla!"* His opponent did not stir. *"Balla!"* repeated the Cavaliere incisively, and snapped his whip. You saw the young man move his neck round in his collar; at the same time one hand lifted slightly at the wrist, one ankle turned outward. But that was all, for the time at least; merely a tendency to twitch, now sternly repressed, now seeming about to get the upper hand. It escaped nobody that here a heroic obstinacy, a fixed resolve to resist, must needs be conquered; we were beholding a gallant effort to strike out and save the honor of the human race. He twitched but danced not; and the struggle was so prolonged that the Cavaliere had to divide his attention between it and the stage, turning now and then to make his riding-whip whistle in the direction of the dancers, as it were to keep them in leash. At the same time he advised the audience that no fatigue was involved in such activities, however long they went on, since it was not the automatons up there who danced, but himself. Then once more his eye would bore itself in the back of the Roman's neck and lay siege to the strength of purpose which defied him.

One saw it waver, that strength of purpose, beneath the repeated summons and whip-crackings. Saw with an objective interest which yet was not quite free from traces of sympathetic emotion—from pity, even from a cruel kind of pleasure. If I understand what was going on, it was negative character of the young man's fighting position which was his undoing. It is likely that *not* willing is not a practicable state of mind; *not* to want to do something may be in the long run a mental content impossible to subsist on. Between not willing a certain thing and not willing at all—in other words, yielding to another person's will—there may lie too small a space for the idea of freedom to squeeze into. Again, there were the Cavaliere's persuasive words, woven in among the whip-crackings and commands, as he mingled effects that were his own secret with others of a bewilderingly psychological kind. *"Balla!"* said he. "Who wants to torture himself like that? Is forcing yourself your idea of freedom? *Una ballatina!* Why, your arms and legs are aching for it. What a relief to give way to them—there, you are dancing already! That is no struggle any more, it is a pleasure!" And so it was. The jerking and twitching of the refractory youth's limbs had at last got the upper hand; he lifted his arms, then his knees, his joints quite suddenly relaxed, he flung his legs and danced, and amid bursts of applause the Cavaliere led him to join the row of puppets on the stage. Up there we could see his face as he "enjoyed" himself; it was clothed in a broad grin and the eyes were half-shut. In a way, it was consoling to see that he was having a better time than he had had in the hour of his pride.

His "fall" was, I may say, an epoch. The ice was completely broken, Cipolla's triumph had reached its height. The Circe's wand, that whistling leather whip with the claw handle, held absolute sway. At one time—it must have been well after midnight—not only were there eight or ten persons dancing on the little stage, but in the hall below a varied animation reigned, and a long-toothed Anglo-Saxoness in a pince-nez left her seat of her own motion to perform a tarantella in the center aisle. Cipolla was lounging in a cane-seated chair at the left of the stage, gulping down the smoke of a cigarette and breathing it impudently out through his bad teeth. He tapped his foot and shrugged his shoulders, looking down upon the abandoned scene in the hall; now and then he snapped his whip backwards at a laggard upon the stage. The children were awake at the moment. With shame I speak of them. For it was not good to be here, least of all for them; that we had not taken them away can only be explained by saying that we had caught the general devil-may-careness of the hour. By that time it was all one. Anyhow, thank goodness, they lacked understanding for the disreputable side of the entertainment, and in their innocence were perpetually charmed by the unheard-of indulgence which permitted them to be present at such a thing as a magician's "evening." Whole quarter-hours at a time they drowsed on our laps, waking refreshed and rosy-cheeked, with sleep-drunken eyes, to laugh to bursting at the leaps and jumps the magician made those people up there make. They had not thought it would be so jolly; they joined with their clumsy little hands in every round of applause. And jumped for joy upon their chairs, as was their wont, when Cipolla beckoned to their friend Mario from the Esquisito, beckoned to him just like a picture in a book, holding his hand in front of his nose and bending and straightening the fore-finger by turns.

Mario obeyed. I can see him now going up the stairs to Cipolla, who continued to beckon him, in that droll, picture-book sort of way. He hesitated for a moment at first; that, too, I recall quite clearly. During the whole evening he had lounged against a wooden pillar at the side entrance, with his arms folded, or else with his hands thrust into his jacket pockets. He was on our left, near the youth with the militant hair, and had followed the performance attentively, so far as we had seen, if with no particular animation and God knows how much comprehension. He could not much relish being summoned thus, at the end of the evening. But it was only too easy to see why he obeyed. After all, obedience was his calling in life; and then, how should a simple lad like him find it within his human capacity to refuse compliance to a man so throned and crowned as Cipolla at that hour? Willy-nilly he left his column and with a word of thanks to those making way for him he mounted the steps with a doubtful smile on his full lips.

Picture a thickset youth of twenty years, with clipt hair, a low forehead, and heavy-lidded eyes of an indefinite gray, shot with green and yellow. These things I knew from having spoken with him, as we often had. There was a saddle of freckles on the flat nose, the whole upper half of the face retreated behind the lower, and that again was dominated by thick lips that parted to show the salivated teeth. These thick lips and the veiled look of the eyes lent the whole face a primitive melancholy—it was that which had drawn us to him from the first. In it was not the faintest trace of brutality —indeed, his hands would have given the lie to such an idea, being unusually slender and delicate even for a southerner. They were hands by which one liked being served.

We knew him humanly without knowing him personally, if I may make that distinction. We saw him nearly every day, and felt a certain kindness for his dreamy ways, which might at times be actual inattentiveness, suddenly transformed into a redeeming zeal to serve. His mien was serious, only the children could bring a smile to his face. It was not sulky, but uningratiating, without intentional effort to please—or, rather, it seemed to give up being pleasant in the conviction that it could not succeed. We should have remembered Mario in any case, as one of those homely recollections of travel which often stick in the mind better than more important ones. But of his circumstances we knew no more than that his father was a petty clerk in the Municipio and his mother took in washing.

His white waiter's-coat became him better than the faded striped suit he wore, with a gay colored scarf instead of a collar, the ends tucked into his jacket. He neared Cipolla, who however did not leave off that motion of his finger before his nose, so that Mario had to come still closer, right up to the chair-seat and the master's legs. Whereupon the latter spread out his elbows and seized the lad, turning him so that we had a view of his face. Then gazed him briskly up and down, with a careless, commanding eye.

"Well, *ragazzo mio,* how comes it we make acquaintance so late in the day? But believe me, I made yours long ago. Yes, yes, I've had you in my eye this long while and known what good stuff you were made of. How could I go and forget you again? Well, I've had a good deal to think about. . . . Now tell me, what is your name? The first name, that's all I want."

"My name is Mario," the young man answered, in a low voice.

"Ah, Mario. Very good. Yes, yes, there is such a name, quite a common name, a classic name too, one of those which preserve the heroic traditions of the Fatherland. *Bravo! Salve!*" And he flung up his arm slantingly above his crooked shoulder, palm outward, in the Roman salute. He may have been slightly tipsy by now, and no wonder; but he spoke as before, clearly, fluently, and with emphasis. Though about this time there had crept into his voice a gross, autocratic note, and a kind of arrogance was in his sprawl.

"Well, now, Mario *mio,*" he went on, "it's a good thing you came this evening, and that's a pretty scarf you've got on; it is becoming to your style of beauty. It must stand you in good stead with the girls, the pretty pretty girls of Torre—"

From the row of youths, close by the place where Mario had been standing, sounded a laugh. It came from the youth with the militant hair. He stood there, his jacket over his shoulder, and laughed outright, rudely and scornfully.

Mario gave a start. I think it was a shrug, but he may have started and then hastened to cover the movement by shrugging his shoulders, as much as to say that the neckerchief and the fair sex were matters of equal indifference to him.

The Cavaliere gave a downward glance.

"We needn't trouble about him," he said. "He is jealous, because your scarf is so popular with the girls, maybe partly because you and I are so friendly up here. Perhaps he'd like me to put him in mind of his colic—I could do it free of charge. Tell me, Mario. You've come here this evening for a bit of fun—and in the daytime you work in an ironmonger's shop?"

"In a café," corrected the youth.

"Oh, in a café. That's where Cipolla nearly came a cropper! What you are is a cup-bearer, a Ganymede—I like that, it is another classical allusion —*Salvietta!*" Again the Cavaliere saluted, to the huge gratification of his audience.

Mario smiled too. "But before that," he interpolated, in the interest of accuracy, "I worked for a while in a shop in Portoclemente." He seemed visited by a natural desire to assist the prophecy by dredging out its essential features.

"There, didn't I say so? In an ironmonger's shop?"

"They kept combs and brushes," Mario got round it.

"Didn't I say that you were not always a Ganymede? Not always at the sign of the serviette? Even when Cipolla makes a mistake, it is a kind that makes you believe in him. Now tell me: Do you believe in me?"

An indefinite gesture.

"A half-way answer," commented the Cavaliere. "Probably it is not easy to win your confidence. Even for me, I can see, it is not so easy. I see in your features a reserve, a sadness, *un tratto di malinconia* . . . tell me" (he seized Mario's hand persuasively) "have you troubles?"

"Nossignore," answered Mario, promptly and decidedly.

"You *have* troubles," insisted the Cavaliere, bearing down the denial by the weight of his authority. "Can't I see? Trying to pull the wool over Cipolla's eyes, are you? Of course, about the girls—it is a girl, isn't it? You have love troubles?"

Mario gave a vigorous head-shake. And again the *giovanotto's* brutal laugh rang out. The Cavaliere gave heed. His eyes were roving about somewhere in the air; but he cocked an ear to the sound, then swung his whip backwards, as he had once or twice before in his conversation with Mario, that none of his puppets might flag in their zeal. The gesture had nearly cost him his new prey: Mario gave a sudden start in the direction of the steps. But Cipolla had him in his clutch.

"Not so fast," said he. "That would be fine, wouldn't it? So you want to skip, do you, Ganymede, right in the middle of the fun, or, rather, when it is just beginning? Stay with me, I'll show you something nice. I'll convince you. You have no reason to worry, I promise you. This girl—you know her and others know her too—what's her name? Wait! I read the name in your eyes, it is on the tip of my tongue and yours too—"

"Silvestra!" shouted the *giovanotto* from below.

The Cavaliere's face did not change.

"Aren't there the forward people?" he asked, not looking down, more as in undisturbed converse with Mario. "Aren't there the young fighting-cocks that crow in season and out? Takes the word out of your mouth, the conceited fool, and seems to think he has some special right to it. Let him be. But Silvestra, your Silvestra—ah, what a girl that is! What a prize! Brings your heart into your mouth to see her walk or laugh or breathe, she is so lovely. And her round arms when she washes, and tosses her head back to get the hair out of her eyes! An angel from paradise!"

Mario stared at him, his head thrust forward. He seemed to have forgotten the audience, forgotten where he was. The red rings round his eyes had got larger, they looked as though they were painted on. His thick lips parted.

"And she makes you suffer, this angel," went on Cipolla, "or, rather, you make yourself suffer for her—there is a difference, my lad, a most important difference, let me tell you. There are misunderstandings in love, maybe nowhere else in the world are there so many. I know what you are thinking: what does this Cipolla, with his little physical defect, know about love? Wrong, all wrong, he knows a lot. He has a wide and powerful understanding of its workings, and it pays to listen to his advice. But let's leave Cipolla out, cut him out altogether and think only of Silvestra, your peerless Silvestra! What! Is she to give any young gamecock the preference, so that he can laugh while you cry? To prefer him to a chap like you, so full of feeling and so sympathetic? Not very likely, is it? It is impossible —we know better, Cipolla and she. If I were to put myself in her place and choose between the two of you, a tarry lout like that—a codfish, a sea-urchin—and a Mario, a knight of the serviette, who moves among gentlefolk and hands round refreshments with an air—my word, but my heart would speak in no uncertain tones—it knows to whom I gave it long ago. It is time that he should see and understand, my chosen one! It is time that you see me and recognize me, Mario, my beloved! Tell me, who am I?"

It was grisly, the way the betrayer made himself irresistible, wreathed and coquetted with his crooked shoulder, languished with the puffy eyes, and showed his splintered teeth in a sickly smile. And alas, at his beguiling words, what was come of our Mario? It is hard for me to tell, hard as it was for me to see; for here was nothing less than an utter abandonment of the inmost soul, a public exposure of timid and deluded passion and rapture. He put his hands across his mouth, his shoulders rose and fell with his pantings. He could not, it was plain, trust his eyes and ears for joy, and the one thing he forgot was precisely that he could not trust them. "Silvestra!" he breathed, from the very depths of his vanquished heart.

"Kiss me!" said the hunchback. "Trust me, I love thee. Kiss me here." And with the tip of his index finger, hand, arm, and little finger outspread, he pointed to his cheek, near the mouth. And Mario bent and kissed him.

It had grown very still in the room. That was a monstrous moment, grotesque and thrilling, the moment of Mario's bliss. In that evil span of time, crowded with a sense of the illusiveness of all joy, one sound became audible, and that not quite at once, but on the instant of the melancholy and ribald meeting between Mario's lips and the repulsive flesh which thrust itself forward for his caress. It was the sound of a laugh, from the *giovanotto* on our left. It broke into the dramatic suspense of the moment, coarse, mocking, and yet—or I must have been grossly mistaken—with an undertone of compassion for the poor bewildered, victimized creature. It had a faint ring of that *"Poveretto"* which Cipolla had declared was wasted on the wrong person, when he claimed the pity for his own.

The laugh still rang in the air when the recipient of the caress gave his whip a little swish, low down, close to his chair-leg, and Mario started up and flung himself back. He stood in that posture staring, his hands one over the other on those desecrated lips. Then he beat his temples with his clenched fists, over and over; turned and staggered down the steps, while the audience applauded, and Cipolla sat there with his hands in his lap, his shoulders shaking. Once below, and even while in full retreat, Mario hurled himself round with legs flung wide apart; one arm flew up, and two flat shattering detonations crashed through applause and laughter.

There was instant silence. Even the dancers came to a full stop and stared about, struck dumb. Cipolla bounded from his seat. He stood with his arms spread out, slanting as though to ward everybody off, as though next moment he would cry out: "Stop! Keep back! Silence! What was that?" Then, in that instant, he sank back in his seat, his head rolling on his chest; in the next he had fallen sideways to the floor, where he lay motionless, a huddled heap of clothing, with limbs awry.

The commotion was indescribable. Ladies hid their faces, shuddering, on the breasts of their escorts. There were shouts for a doctor, for the police. People flung themselves on Mario in a mob, to disarm him, to take away the weapon that hung from his fingers—that small, dull-metal, scarcely pistol-shaped tool with hardly any barrel—in how strange and unexpected a direction had fate leveled it!

An now—now finally, at last—we took the children and led them towards the exit, past the pair of *carabinieri* just entering. Was that the end, they wanted to know, that they might go in peace? Yes, we assured them, that was the end. An end of horror, a fatal end. And yet a liberation—for I could not, and I cannot, but find it so!

E. M. Forster (1879–1969)

THE CELESTIAL OMNIBUS

The boy who resided at Agathox Lodge, 28, Buckingham Park Road, Surbiton, had often been puzzled by the old sign-post that stood almost opposite. He asked his mother about it, and she replied that it was a joke, and not a very nice one, which had been made many years back by some naughty young men, and that the police ought to remove it. For there were two strange things about this sign-post: firstly, it pointed up a blank alley, and, secondly, it had painted on it, in faded characters, the words, "To Heaven."

"What kind of young men were they?" he asked.

"I think your father told me that one of them wrote verses, and was expelled from the University and came to grief in other ways. Still, it was a long time ago. You must ask your father about it. He will say the same as I do, that it was put up as a joke."

"So it doesn't mean anything at all?"

She sent him up-stairs to put on his best things, for the Bonses were coming to tea, and he was to hand the cake-stand.

It struck him, as he wrenched on his tightening trousers, that he might do worse than ask Mr. Bons about the sign-post. His father, though very kind, always laughed at him—shrieked with laughter whenever he or any other child asked a question or spoke. But Mr. Bons was serious as well as kind. He had a beautiful house and lent one books, he was a church-warden, and a candidate for the County Council; he had donated to the Free Library enormously, he presided over the Literary Society, and had Members of Parliament to stop with him—in short, he was probably the wisest person alive.

Yet even Mr. Bons could only say that the sign-post was a joke—the joke of a person named Shelley.

"Of course!" cried the mother; "I told you so, dear. That was the name."

"Had you never heard of Shelley?" asked Mr. Bons.

"No," said the boy, and hung his head.

"But is there no Shelley in this house?"

"Why yes!" exclaimed the lady, in much agitation. "Dear Mr. Bons, we aren't such Philistines as that. Two at the least. One a wedding present, and the other, smaller print, in one of the spare rooms."

"I believe we have seven Shelleys," said Mr. Bons, with a slow smile. Then he brushed the cake crumbs off his stomach, and, together with his daughter, rose to go.

The boy, obeying a wink from his mother, saw them all the way to the garden gate, and when they had gone he did not at once return to the house, but gazed for a little up and down Buckingham Park Road.

His parents lived at the right end of it. After No. 39 the quality of the houses dropped very suddenly, and 64 had not even a separate servants' entrance. But at the present moment the whole road looked rather pretty, for the sun had just set in splendour, and the inequalities of rent were drowned in a saffron afterglow. Small birds twittered, and the breadwinners' train shrieked musically down through the cutting—that wonderful cutting which has drawn to itself the whole beauty out of Surbiton, and clad itself, like any Alpine valley, with the glory of the fir and the silver birch and the primrose. It was this cutting that had first stirred desires within the boy—desires for something just a little different, he knew not what, desires that would return whenever things were sunlit, as they were this evening, running up and down inside him, up and down, up and down, till he would feel quite unusual all over, and as likely as not would want to cry. This evening he was even sillier, for he slipped across the road towards the sign-post and began to run up the blank alley.

The alley runs between high walls—the walls of the gardens of "Ivanhoe" and "Belle Vista" respectively. It smells a little all the way, and is scarcely twenty yards long, including the turn at the end. So not unnaturally the boy soon came to a standstill. "I'd like to kick that Shelley," he exclaimed, and glanced idly at a piece of paper which was pasted on the wall. Rather an odd piece of paper, and he read it carefully before he turned back. This is what he read:

S. and C. R. C. C.

Alteration in Service.

Owing to lack of patronage the Company are regretfully compelled to suspend the hourly service, and to retain only the

Sunrise and Sunset Omnibuses,

which will run as usual. It is to be hoped that the public will patronize an

arrangement which is intended for their convenience. As an extra induce-
ment, the Company will, for the first time, now issue

Return Tickets!

(available one day only), which may be obtained of the driver. Passengers
are again reminded that *no tickets are issued at the other end,* and that no
complaints in this connection will receive consideration from the Company.
Nor will the company be responsible for any negligence or stupidity on the
part of Passengers, nor for Hailstorms, Lightning, Loss of Tickets, nor for any
Act of God.

For the Direction.

Now he had never seen this notice before, nor could he imagine where
the omnibus went to. S. of course was for Surbiton, and R.C.C. meant Road
Car Company. But what was the meaning of the other C.? Coombe and
Malden, perhaps, or possibly "City." Yet it could not hope to compete with
the South-Western. The whole thing, the boy reflected, was run on hopelessly unbusiness-like lines. Why no tickets from the other end? And what
an hour to start! Then he realized that unless the notice was a hoax, an
omnibus must have been starting just as he was wishing the Bonses good-
bye. He peered at the ground through the gathering dusk, and there he saw
what might or might not be the marks of wheels. Yet nothing had come
out of the alley. And he had never seen an omnibus at any time in the
Buckingham Park Road. No: it must be a hoax, like the sign-posts, like the
fairy tales, like the dreams upon which he would wake suddenly in the
night. And with a sigh he stepped from the alley—right into the arms of
his father.

Oh, how his father laughed! "Poor, poor Popsey!" he cried. "Diddums!
Diddums! Diddums think he'd walky-palky up to Evvink!" And his
mother, also convulsed with laughter, appeared on the steps of Agathox
Lodge. "Don't, Bob!" She gasped. "Don't be so naughty! Oh, You'll kill
me! Oh, leave the boy alone!"

But all that evening the joke was kept up. The father implored to be
taken too. Was it a very tiring walk? Need one wipe one's shoes on the
doormat? And the boy went to bed feeling faint and sore, and thankful for
only one thing—that he had not said a word about the omnibus. It was
a hoax, yet though his dreams it grew more and more real, and the streets
of Surbiton, through which he saw it driving, seemed instead to become
hoaxes and shadows. And very early in the morning he woke with a cry,
for he had had a glimpse of its destination.

He struck a match, and its light fell not only on his watch but also on
his calendar, so that he knew it to be half-an-hour to sunrise. It was pitch
dark, for the fog had come down from London in the night, and all Surbiton was wrapped in its embraces. Yet he sprang out and dressed himself,

for he was determined to settle once for all which was real: the omnibus or the streets. "I shall be a fool one way or the other," he thought, "until I know." Soon he was shivering in the road under the gas lamp that guarded the entrance to the alley.

To enter the alley itself required some courage. Not only was it horribly dark, but he now realized that it was an impossible terminus for an omnibus. If it had not been for a policeman, whom he heard approaching through the fog, he would never have made the attempt. The next moment he had made the attempt and failed. Nothing. Nothing but a blank alley and a very silly boy gaping at its dirty floor. It *was* a hoax. "I'll tell papa and mamma," he decided. "I deserve it. I deserve that they should know. I am too silly to be alive." And he went back to the gate of Agathox Lodge.

There he remembered that his watch was fast. The sun was not risen; it would not rise for two minutes. "Give the bus every chance," he thought cynically, and returned into the alley.

But the omnibus was there.

It had two horses, whose sides were still smoking from their journey, and its two great lamps shone through the fog against the alley's walls, changing their cobwebs and moss into tissues of fairyland. The driver was huddled up in a cape. He faced the blank wall, and how he managed to drive in so neatly and so silently was one of the many things that the boy never discovered. Nor could he imagine how ever he would drive out.

"Please," his voiced quavered through the foul brown air. "Please, is that an omnibus?"

"Omnibus est," said the driver, without turning round. There was a moment's silence. The policeman passed, coughing, by the entrance of the alley. The boy crouched in the shadow, for he did not want to be found out. He was pretty sure, too, that it was a Pirate; nothing else, he reasoned, would go from such odd places and at such odd hours.

"About when do you start?" He tried to sound nonchalant.

"At sunrise."

"How far do you go?"

"The whole way."

"And can I have a return ticket which will bring me all the way back?"

"You can."

"Do you know, I half think I'll come." The driver made no answer. The sun must have risen, for he unhitched the brake. And scarcely had the boy jumped in before the omnibus was off.

How? Did it turn? There was no room. Did it go forward? There was a blank wall. Yet it was moving—moving at a stately pace through the fog, which had turned from brown to yellow. The thought of warm bed and warmer breakfast made the boy feel faint. He wished he had not come. His parents would not have approved. He would have gone back to them if the weather had not made it impossible. The solitude was terrible; he was the only passenger. And the omnibus, though well-built, was cold and somewhat musty. He drew his coat round him, and in so doing chanced to feel his pocket. It was empty. He had forgotten his purse.

"Stop!" he shouted. "Stop!" And then, being of a polite disposition, he glanced up at the painted notice-board so that he might call the driver by name. "Mr. Browne! stop; Oh, do please stop!"

Mr. Browne did not stop, but he opened a little window and looked in at the boy. His face was a surprise, so kind it was and modest.

"Mr. Browne, I've left my purse behind. I've not got a penny. I can't pay for the ticket. Will you take my watch, please? I am in the most awful hole."

"Tickets on this line," said the driver, "whether single or return, can be purchased by coinage from no terrene mint. And a chronometer, though it had solaced the vigils of Charlemagne, or measured the slumbers of Laura, can acquire by no mutation the double-cake that charms the fang-less Cerberus of Heaven!" So saying, he handed in the necessary ticket, and, while the boy said "Thank you," continued: "Titular pretensions, I know it well, are vanity. Yet they merit no censure when uttered on a laughing lip, and in an homonymous world are in some sort useful, since they do serve to distinguish one Jack from his fellow. Remember me, therefore, as Sir Thomas Browne."

"Are you a Sir? Oh, sorry!" He had heard of these gentlemen drivers. "It *is* good of you about the ticket. But if you go on at this rate, however does your bus pay?"

"It does not pay. It was not intended to pay. Many are the faults of my equipage; it is compounded too curiously of foreign woods; its cushions tickle erudition rather than promote repose; and my horses are nourished not on the evergreen pastures of the moment, but on the dried bents and clovers of Latinity. But that it pays!—that error at all events was never intended and never attained."

"Sorry again," said the boy rather hopelessly. Sir Thomas looked sad, fearing that, even for a moment, he had been the cause of sadness. He invited the boy to come up and sit beside him on the box, and together they journeyed on through the fog, which was now changing from yellow to white. There were no houses by the road; so it must be either Putney Heath or Wimbledon Common.

"Have you been a driver always?"

"I was a physician once."

"But why did you stop? Weren't you good?"

"As a healer of bodies I had scant success, and several score of my patients preceded me. But as a healer of the spirit I have succeeded beyond my hopes and my deserts. For though my draughts were not better nor subtler than those of other men, yet by reason of the cunning goblets wherein I offered them, the queasy soul was ofttimes tempted to sip and be refreshed."

"The queasy soul," he murmured; "if the sun sets with trees in front of it, and you suddenly come strange all over, is that a queasy soul?"

"Have you felt that?"

"Why yes."

After a pause he told the boy a little, a very little, about the journey's end. But they did not chatter much, for the boy, when he liked a person, would as soon sit silent in his company as speak, and this, he discovered, was also the mind of Sir Thomas Browne and of many others with whom he was to be acquainted. He heard, however, about the young man Shelley, who was now quite a famous person, with a carriage of his own, and about some of the other drivers who are in the service of the Company. Meanwhile the light grew stronger, though the fog did not disperse. It was now more like mist than fog, and at times would travel quickly across them, as if it was part of a cloud. They had been ascending, too, in a most puzzling way; for over two hours the horses had been pulling against the collar, and even if it were Richmond Hill they ought to have been at the top long ago. Perhaps it was Epsom, or even the North Downs; yet the air seemed keener than that which blows on either. And as to the name of their destination, Sir Thomas Browne was silent.

Crash!

"Thunder, by Jove!" said the boy, "and not so far off either. Listen to the echoes! It's more like mountains."

He thought, not very vividly, of his father and mother. He saw them sitting down to sausages and listening to the storm. He saw his own empty place. Then there would be questions, alarms, theories, jokes, consolations. They would expect him back at lunch. To lunch he would not come, nor to tea, but he would be in for dinner, and so his day's truancy would be over. If he had had his purse he would have bought them presents—not that he should have known what to get them.

Crash!

The peal and the lightening came together. The cloud quivered as if it were alive, and torn streamers of mist rushed past. "Are you afraid?" asked Sir Thomas Browne.

"What is there to be afraid of? Is it much farther?"

The horses of the omnibus stopped just as a ball of fire burst up and exploded with a ringing noise that was deafening but clear, like the noise of a blacksmith's forge. All the cloud was shattered.

"Oh, listen, Sir Thomas Browne! No, I mean look; we shall get a view at last. No, I mean listen; that sounds like a rainbow!"

The noise had died into the faintest murmur, beneath which another murmur grew, spreading stealthily, steadily, in a curve that widened but did not vary. And in widening curves a rainbow was spreading from the horses' feet into the dissolving mists.

"But how beautiful! What colours! Where will it stop? It is more like the rainbows you can tread on. More like dreams."

The colour and the sound grew together. The rainbow spanned an enormous gulf. Clouds rushed under it and were pierced by it, and still it grew, reaching forward, conquering the darkness, until it touched something that seemed more solid than a cloud.

The boy stood up. "What is that out there?" he called. "What does it rest on, out at that other end?"

In the morning sunshine a precipice shone forth beyond the gulf. A precipice—or was it a castle? The horses moved. They set their feet upon the rainbow.

"Oh, look!" the boy shouted. "Oh, listen! Those caves—or are they gateways? Oh, look between those cliffs at those ledges. I see people! I see trees!"

"Look also below," whispered Sir Thomas. "Neglect not the diviner Acheron."

The boy looked below, past the flames of the rainbow that licked against their wheels. The gulf also had cleared, and in its depths there flowed an everlasting river. One sunbeam entered and struck a green pool, and as they passed over he saw three maidens rise to the surface of the pool, singing, and playing with something that glistened like a ring.

"You down in the water—" he called.

They answered, "You up on the bridge—" There was a burst of music. "You up on the bridge, good luck to you. Truth in the depth, truth on the height."

"You down in the water, what are you doing?"

Sir Thomas Browne replied: "They sport in the mancipiary possession of their gold"; and the omnibus arrived.

The boy was in disgrace. He sat locked up in the nursery of Agathox Lodge, learning poetry for a punishment. His father had said, "My boy! I can pardon anything but untruthfulness," and had caned him, saying at each stroke, "There is *no* omnibus, *no* driver, *no* bridge, *no* mountain; you are a *truant*, a *gutter snipe*, a *liar*." His father could be very stern at times. His mother had begged him to say he was sorry. But he could not say that. It was the greatest day of his life, in spite of the caning and the poetry at the end of it.

He had returned punctually at sunset—driven not by Sir Thomas Browne, but by a maiden lady who was full of quiet fun. They had talked of omnibuses and also of barouche landaus. How far away her gentle voice seemed now! Yet is was scarcely three hours since he had left her up the alley.

His mother called through the door. "Dear, you are to come down and to bring your poetry with you."

He came down and found that Mr. Bons was in the smoking-room with his father. It had been a dinner party.

"Here is the great traveller!" said his father grimly. "Here is the young gentleman who drives in an omnibus over rainbows, while young ladies sing to him." Pleased with his wit, he laughed.

"After all," said Mr. Bons, smiling, "there is something a little like it in Wagner. It is odd how, in quite illiterate minds, you will find glimmers of Artistic Truth. The case interests me. Let me plead for the culprit. We have all romanced in our time, haven't we?"

"Hear how kind Mr. Bons is," said his mother, while his father said, "Very well. Let him say his Poem, and that will do. He is going away to my sister on Tuesday, and *she* will cure him of his alley-sloping." (Laughter.) "Say your Poem."

The boy began. "'Standing aloof in giant ignorance.'"

His father laughed again—roared. "One for you, my son! 'Standing aloof in giant ignorance!' I never knew these poets talked sense. Just describes you. Here, Bons, you go in for poetry. Put him through it, will you, while I fetch up the whisky?"

"Yes, give me the Keats," said Mr. Bons. "Let him say his Keats to me."

So for a few moments the wise man and the ignorant boy were left alone in the smoking-room.

"'Standing aloof in giant ignorance, of thee I dream and of the Cyclades, as one who sits ashore and longs perchance to visit—'"

"Quite right. To visit what?"

"'To visit dolphin coral in deep seas, '" said the boy, and burst into tears.

"Come, come! why do you cry?"

"Because—because all these words that only rhymed before, now that I've come back they're me."

Mr. Bons laid the Keats down. The case was more interesting than he had expected. *"You?"* he exclaimed. "This sonnet, *you?"*

"Yes—and look further on: 'Aye, on the shores of darkness there is light, and precipices show untrodden green.' It *is* so, sir. All these things are true."

"I never doubted it," said Mr. Bons, with closed eyes.

"You—then you believe me? You believe in the omnibus and the driver and the storm and that return ticket I got for nothing and—"

"Tut, tut! No more of your yarns, my boy. I meant that I never doubted the essential truth of Poetry. Some day, when you have read more, you will understand what I mean."

"But Mr. Bons, it *is* so. There *is* light upon the shores of darkness. I have seen it coming. Light and a wind."

"Nonsense," said Mr. Bons.

"If I had stopped! They tempted me. They told me to give up my ticket —for you cannot come back if you lose your ticket. They called from the river for it, and indeed I was tempted, for I have never been so happy as among those precipices. But I thought of my mother and father, and that I must fetch them. Yet they will not come, though the road starts opposite our house. It has all happened as the people up there warned me, and Mr. Bons has disbelieved me like every one else. I have been caned. I shall never see that mountain again."

"What's that about me?" said Mr. Bons, sitting up in his chair very suddenly.

"I told them about you, and how clever you were, and how many books you had, and they said, 'Mr. Bons will certainly disbelieve you.'"

"Stuff and nonsense, my young friend. You grow impertinent. I—well —I will settle the matter. Not a word to your father. I will cure you. Tomorrow evening I will myself call here to take you for a walk, and at sunset we will go up this alley opposite and hunt for your omnibus, you silly little boy."

His face grew serious, for the boy was not disconcerted, but leapt about the room singing, "Joy! joy! I told them you would believe me. We will drive together over the rainbow. I told them that you would come." After all, could there be anything in the story? Wagner? Keats? Shelley? Sir Thomas Browne? Certainly the case was interesting.

And on the morrow evening, though it was pouring with rain, Mr. Bons did not omit to call at Agathox Lodge.

The boy was ready, bubbling with excitement, and skipping about in a way that rather vexed the President of the Literary Society. They took a turn down Buckingham Park Road, and then—having seen that no one was watching them—slipped up the alley. Naturally enough (for the sun was setting) they ran straight against the omnibus.

"Good heavens!" exclaimed Mr. Bons. "Good gracious heavens!"

It was not the omnibus in which the boy had driven first, nor yet that in which he had returned. There were three horses—black, gray, and white, the gray being the finest. The driver, who turned round at the mention of goodness and of heaven, was a sallow man with terrifying jaws and sunken eyes. Mr. Bons, on seeing him, gave a cry as if of recognition, and began to tremble violently.

The boy jumped in.

"Is it possible?" cried Mr. Bons. "Is the impossible possible?"

"Sir; come in, sir. It is such a fine omnibus. Oh, here is his name—Dan some one."

Mr. Bons sprang in too. A blast of wind immediately slammed the omnibus door, and the shock jerked down all the omnibus blinds, which were very weak on their springs.

"Dan . . . Show me. Good gracious heavens! we're moving."

"Hooray!" said the boy.

Mr. Bons became flustered. He had not intended to be kidnapped. He could not find the door-handle, nor push up the blinds. The omnibus was quite dark, and by the time he had struck a match, night had come on outside also. They were moving rapidly.

"A strange, a memorable adventure," he said, surveying the interior of the omnibus, which was large, roomy, and constructed with extreme regularity, every part exactly answering to every other part. Over the door (the handle of which was outside) was written, "Lasciate ogni baldanza voi che entrate"—at least, that was what was written, but Mr. Bons said that it was Lashy arty something, and that baldanza was a mistake for speranza. His voice sounded as if he was in church. Meanwhile, the boy called to the cadaverous driver for two return tickets. They were handed in without a word. Mr. Bons covered his face with his hand and again trembled. "Do you know who that is!" he whispered, when the little window had shut upon them. "It is the impossible."

"Well, I don't like him as much as Sir Thomas Browne, though I shouldn't be surprised if he had even more in him."

"More in him?" He stamped irritably. "By accident you have made the greatest discovery of the century, and all you can say is that there is more in this man. Do you remember those vellum books in my library, stamped with red lilies? This—sit still, I bring you stupendous news!—*this is the man who wrote them.*"

The boy sat quite still. "I wonder if we shall see Mrs. Gamp?" he asked, after a civil pause.

"Mrs.—?"

"Mrs. Gamp and Mrs. Harris. I like Mrs. Harris. I came upon them quite suddenly. Mrs. Gamp's bandboxes have moved over the rainbow so badly. All the bottoms have fallen out, and two of the pippins off her bedstead tumbled into the stream."

"Out there sits the man who wrote my vellum books!" thundered Mr. Bons, "and you talk to me of Dickens and of Mrs. Gamp?"

"I know Mrs. Gamp so well," he apologized. "I could not help being glad to see her. I recognized her voice. She was telling Mrs. Harris about Mrs. Prig."

"Did you spend the whole day in her elevating company?"

"Oh, no. I raced. I met a man who took me out beyond to a race-course. You run, and there are dolphins out at sea."

"Indeed. Do you remember the man's name?"

"Achilles. No; he was later. Tom Jones."

Mr. Bons sighed heavily. "Well, my lad, you have made a miserable mess of it. Think of a cultured person with your opportunities! A cultured person would have known all these characters and known what to have said to each. He would not have wasted his time with a Mrs. Gamp or a Tom Jones. The creations of Homer, of Shakespeare, and of Him who drives us now, would alone have contented him. He would not have raced. He would have asked intelligent questions."

"But Mr. Bons," said the boy humbly, "you will be a cultured person. I told them so."

"True, true, and I beg of you not to disgrace me when we arrive. No gossiping. No running. Keep close to my side, and never speak to these Immortals unless they speak to you. Yes, and give me the return tickets. You will be losing them."

The boy surrendered the tickets, but felt a little sore. After all, he had found the way to this place. It was hard first to be disbelieved and then to be lectured. Meanwhile, the rain had stopped, and moonlight crept into the omnibus through the cracks in the blinds.

"But how is there to be a rainbow?" cried the boy.

"You distract me," snapped Mr. Bons. "I wish to meditate on beauty. I wish to goodness I was with a reverent and sympathetic person."

The lad bit his lip. He made a hundred good resolutions. He would imitate Mr. Bons all the visit. He would not laugh, or run, or sing, or do any of the vulgar things that must have disgusted his new friends last time. He would be very careful to pronounce their names properly, and to remember who knew whom. Achilles did not know Tom Jones—at least, so Mr. Bons said. The Duchess of Malfi was older than Mrs. Gamp—at least, so Mr. Bons said. He would be self-conscious, reticent, and prim. He would never say he liked any one. Yet, when the blind flew up at a chance touch of his head, all these good resolutions went to the winds, for the omnibus had reached the summit of a moonlit hill, and there was the chasm, and there, across it, stood the old precipices, dreaming, with their feet in the everlasting river. He exclaimed, "The mountain! Listen to the new tune in the water! Look at the camp fires in the ravines," and Mr. Bons, after a hasty glance, retorted, "Water? Camp fires? Ridiculous rubbish. Hold your tongue. There is nothing at all."

Yet, under his eyes, a rainbow formed, compounded not of sunlight and storm, but of moonlight and the spray of the river. The three horses put their feet upon it. He thought it the finest rainbow he had seen, but he did not dare to say so, since Mr. Bons said that nothing was there. He leant out—the window had opened—and sang the tune that rose from the sleeping waters.

"The prelude to Rhinegold?" said Mr. Bons suddenly. "Who taught you these *leit motifs?*" He, too, looked out of the window. Then he behaved very oddly. He gave a choking cry, and fell back on to the omnibus floor. He writhed and kicked. His face was green.

"Does the bridge make you dizzy?" the boy asked.

"Dizzy!" gasped Mr. Bons. "I want to go back. Tell the driver."

But the driver shook his head.

"We are nearly there," said the boy. "They are asleep. Shall I call? They will be so pleased to see you, for I have prepared them."

Mr. Bons moaned. They moved over the lunar rainbow, which ever and ever broke away behind their wheels. How still the night was! Who would be sentry at the Gate?

"I am coming," he shouted, again forgetting the hundred resolutions. "I am returning—I, the boy."

"The boy is returning," cried a voice to other voices, who repeated, "The boy is returning."

"I am bringing Mr. Bons with me."

Silence.

"I should have said Mr. Bons is bringing me with him."

Profound silence.

"Who stands sentry?"

"Achilles."

And on the rocky causeway, close to the springing of the rainbow bridge, he saw a young man who carried a wonderful shield.

"Mr. Bons, it is Achilles, armed."

"I want to go back," said Mr. Bons.

The last fragment of the rainbow melted, the wheels sang upon the living rock, the door of the omnibus burst open. Out leapt the boy—he could not resist—and sprang to meet the warrior, who, stooping suddenly, caught him on his shield.

"Achilles!" he cried, "let me get down, for I am ignorant and vulgar, and I must wait for that Mr. Bons of whom I told you yesterday."

But Achilles raised him aloft. He crouched on the wonderful shield, on heroes and burning cities, on vineyards graven in gold, on every dear passion, every joy, on the entire image of the Mountain that he had discovered, encircled, like it, with an everlasting stream. "No, no," he protested, "I am not worthy. It is Mr. Bons who must be up here."

But Mr. Bons was whimpering, and Achilles trumpeted and cried, "Stand upright upon my shield!"

"Sir, I did not mean to stand! something made me stand. Sir, why do you delay? Here is only the great Achilles, whom you knew."

Mr. Bons screamed, "I see no one. I see nothing. I want to go back." Then he cried to the driver, "Save me! Let me stop in your chariot. I have honoured you. I have quoted you. I have bound you in vellum. Take me back to my world."

The driver replied, "I am the means and not the end. I am the food and not the life. Stand by yourself, as that boy has stood. I cannot save you. For poetry is a spirit; and they that would worship it must worship in spirit and in truth."

Mr. Bons—he could not resist—crawled out of the beautiful omnibus. His face appeared, gaping horribly. His hands followed, one gripping the step, the other beating the air. Now his shoulders emerged, his chest, his stomach. With a shriek of "I see London," he fell—fell against the hard, moonlit rock, fell into it as if it were water, fell through it, vanished, and was seen by the boy no more.

"Where have you fallen to, Mr. Bons? Here is a procession arriving to honour you with music and torches. Here come the men and women whose names you know. The mountain is awake, the river is awake, over the race-course the sea is awaking those dolphins, and it is all for you. They want you——"

There was the touch of fresh leaves on his forehead. Some one had crowned him.

ΤΕΛΟΣ

From the *Kingston Gazette, Surbiton Times, and
Raynes Park Observer.*

The body of Mr. Septimus Bons has been found in a shockingly mutilated condition in the vicinity of the Bermondsey gas-works. The deceased's pockets contained a sovereign-purse, a silver cigar-case, a bijou pronouncing dictionary, and a couple of omnibus tickets. The unfortunate gentleman had apparently been hurled from a considerable height. Foul play is suspected, and a thorough investigation is pending by the authorities.

ARABY

North Richmond Street, being blind, was a quiet street except at the hour when the Christian Brothers' School set the boys free. An uninhabited house of two storeys stood at the blind end, detached from its neighbours in a square ground. The other houses of the street, conscious of decent lives within them, gazed at one another with brown imperturbable faces.

The former tenant of our house, a priest, had died in the back drawing-room. Air, musty from having been long enclosed, hung in all the rooms, and the waste room behind the kitchen was littered with old useless papers. Among these I found a few paper-covered books, the pages of which were curled and damp: *The Abbot,* by Walter Scott, *The Devout Communicant* and *The Memoirs of Vidocq.* I liked the last best because its leaves were yellow. The wild garden behind the house contained a central apple-tree and a few straggling bushes under one of which I found the late tenant's rusty bicycle-pump. He had been a very charitable priest; in his will he had left all his money to institutions and the furniture of his house to his sister.

When the short days of winter came dusk fell before we had well eaten our dinners. When we met in the street the houses had grown sombre. The space of sky above us was the colour of everchanging violet and towards it the lamps of the street lifted their feeble lanterns. The cold air stung us and we played till our bodies glowed. Our shouts echoed in the silent street. The career of our play brought us through the dark muddy lanes behind the houses where we ran the gauntlet of the rough tribes from the cottages, to the back doors of the dark dripping gardens where odours arose from the ashpits, to the dark odorous stables where a coachman smoothed and combed the horse or shook music from the buckled harness. When we returned to the street light from the kitchen windows had filled the areas. If my uncle was seen turning the corner we hid in the shadow until we had seen him safely housed. Or if Mangan's sister came out on the doorstep to call her brother in to his tea we watched her from our shadow peer up and down the street. We waited to see whether she would remain or go in and, if she remained, we left our shadow and walked up to Mangan's steps resignedly. She was waiting for us, her figure defined by the light from the half-opened door. Her brother always teased her before he obeyed and I stood by the railings looking at her. Her dress swung as she moved her body and the soft rope of her hair tossed from side to side.

Every morning I lay on the floor in the front parlour watching her door. The blind was pulled down to within an inch of the sash so that I could not be seen. When she came out on the doorstep my heart leaped. I ran to the hall, seized my books and followed her. I kept her brown figure always in my eye and, when we came near the point at which our ways diverged, I quickened my pace and passed her. This happened morning after morning. I had never spoken to her, except for a few casual words, and yet her name was like a summons to all my foolish blood.

Her image accompanied me even in places the most hostile to romance. On Saturday evenings when my aunt went marketing I had to go to carry some of the parcels. We walked through the flaring streets, jostled by drunken men and bargaining women, amid the curses of labourers, the shrill litanies of shop-boys who stood on guard by the barrels of pigs' cheeks, the nasal chanting of street-singers, who sang a *come-all-you* about O'Donovan Rossa, or a ballad about the troubles in our native land. These noises converged in a single sensation of life for me: I imagined that I bore my chalice safely through a throng of foes. Her name sprang to my lips at moments in strange prayers and praises which I myself did not understand. My eyes were often full of tears (I could not tell why) and at times a flood from my heart seemed to pour itself out into my bosom. I thought little of the future. I did not know whether I would ever speak to her or not or, if I spoke to her, how I could tell her of my confused adoration. But my body was like a harp and her words and gestures were like fingers running upon the wires.

One evening I went into the back drawing-room in which the priest had died. It was a dark rainy evening and there was no sound in the house. Through one of the broken panes I heard the rain impinge upon the earth, the fine incessant needles of water playing in the sodden beds. Some distant lamp or lighted window gleamed below me. I was thankful that I could see so little. All my senses seemed to desire to veil themselves and, feeling that I was about to slip from them, I pressed the palms of my hands together until they trembled, murmuring: *"O love! O love!"* many times.

At last she spoke to me. When she addressed the first words to me I was so confused that I did not know what to answer. She asked me was I going to *Araby*. I forgot whether I answered yes or no. It would be a splendid bazaar, she said she would love to go.

"And why can't you?" I asked.

While she spoke she turned a silver bracelet round and round her wrist. She could not go, she said, because there would be a retreat that week in her convent. Her brother and two other boys were fighting for their caps and I was alone at the railings. She held one of the spikes, bowing her head towards me. The light from the lamp opposite our door caught the white curve of her neck, lit up her hair that rested there and, falling, lit up the hand upon the railing. It fell over one side of her dress and caught the white border of a petticoat, just visible as she stood at ease.

"It's well for you," she said.

"If I go," I said, "I will bring you something."

What innumerable follies laid waste my waking and sleeping thoughts after that evening! I wished to annihilate the tedious intervening days. I chafed against the work of school. At night in my bedroom and by day in the classroom her image came between me and the page I strove to read. The syllables of the word *Araby* were called to me through the silence in which my soul luxuriated and cast an Eastern enchantment over me. I asked for leave to go to the bazaar on Saturday night. My aunt was surprised and hoped it was not some Freemason affair. I answered few questions in class. I watched my master's face pass from amiability to sternness; he hoped I was not beginning to idle. I could not call my wandering thoughts together. I had hardly any patience with the serious work of life which, now that it stood between me and my desire, seemed to me child's play, ugly monotonous child's play.

On Saturday morning I reminded my uncle that I wished to go to the bazaar in the evening. He was fussing at the hallstand, looking for the hat-brush, and answered me curtly:

"Yes, boy, I know."

As he was in the hall I could not go into the front parlour and lie at the window. I left the house in bad humour and walked slowly towards the school. The air was pitilessly raw and already my heart misgave me.

When I came home to dinner my uncle had not yet been home. Still it was early. I sat staring at the clock for some time and, when its ticking began to irritate me, I left the room. I mounted the staircase and gained the upper part of the house. The high cold empty gloomy rooms liberated me and I went from room to room singing. From the front window I saw my companions playing below in the street. Their cries reached me weakened and indistinct and, leaning my forehead against the cool glass, I looked over at the dark house where she lived. I may have stood there for an hour, seeing nothing but the brown-clad figure cast by my imagination, touched discreetly by the lamplight at the curved neck, at the hand upon the railings and at the border below the dress.

When I came downstairs again I found Mrs. Mercer sitting at the fire. She was an old garrulous woman, a pawnbroker's widow, who collected used stamps for some pious purpose. I had to endure the gossip of the tea-table. The meal was prolonged beyond an hour and still my uncle did not come. Mrs. Mercer stood up to go: she was sorry she couldn't wait any longer, but it was after eight o'clock and she did not like to be out late, as the night air was bad for her. When she had gone I began to walk up and down the room, clenching my fists. My aunt said:

"I'm afraid you may put off your bazaar for this night of Our Lord."

At nine o'clock I heard my uncle's latchkey in the halldoor. I heard him talking to himself and heard the hallstand rocking when it had received the weight of the overcoat. I could interpret these signs. When he was midway through his dinner I asked him to give me the money to go to the bazaar. He had forgotten.

"The people are in bed and after their first sleep now," he said.

I did not smile. My aunt said to him energetically:

"Can't you give him the money and let him go? You've kept him late enough as it is."

My uncle said he was very sorry he had forgotten. He said he believed in the old saying: "All work and no play makes Jack a dull boy." He asked me where I was going and, when I had told him a second time he asked me did I know *The Arab's Farewell to his Steed.* When I left the kitchen he was about to recite the opening lines of the piece to my aunt.

I held a florin tightly in my hand as I strode down Buckingham Street towards the station. The sight of the streets thronged with buyers and glaring with gas recalled to me the purpose of my journey. I took my seat in a third-class carriage of a deserted train. After an intolerable delay the train moved out of the station slowly. It crept onward among ruinous houses and over the twinkling river. At Westland Row Station a crowd of people pressed to the carriage doors; but the porters moved them back, saying that it was a special train for the bazaar. I remained alone in the bare carriage. In a few minutes the train drew up beside an improvised wooden platform. I passed out on to the road and saw by the lighted dial of a clock that it was ten minutes to ten. In front of me was a large building which displayed the magical name.

I could not find any sixpenny entrance and, fearing that the bazaar would be closed, I passed in quickly through a turnstile, handing a shilling to a weary-looking man. I found myself in a big hall girdled at half its height by a gallery. Nearly all the stalls were closed and the greater part of the hall was in darkness. I recognized a silence like that which pervades a church after a service. I walked into the centre of the bazaar timidly. A few people were gathered about the stalls which were still open. Before a curtain, over which the words *Café Chantant* were written in coloured lamps, two men were counting money on a salver. I listened to the fall of the coins.

Remembering with difficulty why I had come I went over to one of the stalls and examined porcelain vases and flowered tea-sets. At the door of the stall a young lady was talking and laughing with two young gentlemen. I remarked their English accents and listened vaguely to their conversation.

"O, I never said such a thing!"

"O, but you did!"

"O, but I didn't!"

"Didn't she say that?"

"Yes. I heard her."

"O, there's a . . . fib!"

Observing me the young lady came over and asked me did I wish to buy anything. The tone of her voice was not encouraging; she seemed to have spoken to me out of a sense of duty. I looked humbly at the great jars that stood like eastern guards at either side of the dark entrance to the stall and murmured:

"No, thank you."

The young lady changed the position of one of the vases and went back to the two young men. They began to talk of the same subject. Once or twice the young lady glanced at me over her shoulder.

I lingered before her stall, though I knew my stay was useless, to make my interest in her wares seem the more real. Then I turned away slowly and walked down the middle of the bazaar. I allowed the two pennies to fall against the sixpence in my pocket. I heard a voice call from one end of the gallery that the light was out. The upper part of the hall was now completely dark.

Gazing up into the darkness I saw myself as a creature driven and derided by vanity; and my eyes burned with anguish and anger.

William Carlos Williams (1883–1963)

THE USE OF FORCE

They were new patients to me, all I had was the name, Olson. Please come down as soon as you can, my daughter is very sick.

When I arrived I was met by the mother, a big startled looking woman, very clean and apologetic who merely said, Is this the doctor? and let me in. In the back, she added. You must excuse us, doctor, we have her in the kitchen where it is warm. It is very damp here sometimes.

The child was fully dressed and sitting on her father's lap near the kitchen table. He tried to get up, but I motioned for him not to bother, took off my overcoat and started to look things over. I could see that they were all very nervous, eyeing me up and down distrustfully. As often, in such cases, they weren't telling me more than they had to, it was up to me to tell them; that's why they were spending three dollars on me.

The child was fairly eating me up with her cold, steady eyes, and no expression to her face whatever. She did not move and seemed, inwardly, quiet; an unusually attractive little thing, and as strong as a heifer in appearance. But her face was flushed, she was breathing rapidly, and I realized that she had a high fever. She had magnificent blonde hair, in profusion. One of those picture children often reproduced in advertising leaflets and the photogravure sections of the Sunday papers.

She's had a fever for three days, began the father, and we don't know what it comes from. My wife has given her things, you know, like people do, but it don't do no good. And there's been a lot of sickness around. So we tho't you'd better look her over and tell us what is the matter.

As doctors often do I took a trial shot at it as a point of departure. Has she had a sore throat?

Both parents answered me together, No . . . No, she says her throat don't hurt her.

Does your throat hurt you? added the mother to the child. But the little girl's expression didn't change, nor did she move her eyes from my face.

Have you looked?

I tried to, said the mother, but I couldn't see.

As it happens, we had been having a number of cases of diphtheria in the school to which this child went during that month and we were all, quite apparently, thinking of that, though no one had as yet spoken of the thing.

Well, I said, suppose we take a look at the throat first. I smiled in my best professional manner and asking for the child's first name I said, come on, Mathilda, open your mouth and let's take a look at your throat.

Nothing doing.

Aw, come on, I coaxed, just open your mouth wide and let me take a look. Look, I said opening both hands wide, I haven't anything in my hands. Just open up and let me see.

Such a nice man, put in the mother. Look how kind he is to you. Come on, do what he tells you to. He won't hurt you.

At that I ground my teeth in disgust. If only they wouldn't use the word "hurt" I might be able to get somewhere. But I did not allow myself to be hurried or disturbed, but speaking quietly and slowly I approached the child again.

As I moved my chair a little nearer, suddenly with one catlike movement both her hands clawed instinctively for my eyes and she almost reached them too. In fact she knocked my glasses flying and they fell, though unbroken, several feet away from me on the kitchen floor.

Both the mother and father almost turned themselves inside out in embarrassment and apology. You bad girl, said the mother, taking her and shaking her by one arm. Look what you've done. The nice man. . . .

For heaven's sake, I broke in. Don't call me a nice man to her. I'm here to look at her throat on the chance that she might have diphtheria and possibly die of it. But that's nothing to her. Look here, I said to the child, we're going to look at your throat. You're old enough to understand what I'm saying. Will you open it now by yourself or shall we have to open it for you?

Not a move. Even her expression hadn't changed. Her breaths however were coming faster and faster. Then the battle began. I had to do it. I had to have a throat culture for her own protection. But first I told the parents that it was entirely up to them. I explained the danger but said that I would not insist on a throat examination so long as they would take the responsibility.

If you don't do what the doctor says you'll have to go to the hospital, the mother admonished her severely.

Oh yeah? I had to smile to myself. After all, I had already fallen in love with the savage brat, the parents were contemptible to me. In the ensuing struggle they grew more and more abject, crushed, exhausted while she surely rose to magnificent heights of insane fury of effort bred of her terror of me.

The father tried his best, and he was a big man but the fact that she was his daughter, his shame at her behavior and his dread of hurting her made him release her just at the critical moment several times when I had almost achieved success, till I wanted to kill him. But his dread also that she might have diphtheria made him tell me to go on, go on though he himself was almost fainting, while the mother moved back and forth behind us raising and lowering her hands in an agony of apprehension.

Put her in front of you on your lap, I ordered, and hold both her wrists.

But as soon as he did the child let out a scream. Don't, you're hurting me. Let go of my hands. Let them go I tell you. Then she shrieked terrifyingly, hysterically. Stop it! Stop it! You're killing me!

Do you think she can stand it, doctor! said the mother.

You get out, said the husband to his wife. Do you want her to die of diphtheria?

Come on now, hold her, I said.

Then I grasped the child's head with my left hand and tried to get the wooden tongue depressor between her teeth. She fought, with clenched teeth, desperately! But now I also had grown furious—at a child. I tried to hold myself down but I couldn't. I know how to expose a throat for inspection. And I did my best. When finally I got the wooden spatula behind the last teeth and just the point of it into the mouth cavity, she opened up for an instant but before I could see anything she came down again and gripping the wooden blade between her molars she reduced it to splinters before I could get it out again.

Aren't you ashamed, the mother yelled at her. Aren't you ashamed to act like that in front of the doctor?

Get me a smooth-handled spoon of some sort, I told the mother. We're going through with this. The child's mouth was already bleeding. Her tongue was cut and she was screaming in wild hysterical shrieks. Perhaps I should have desisted and come back in an hour or more. No doubt it would have been better. But I have seen at least two children lying dead in bed of neglect in such cases, and feeling that I must get a diagnosis now or never I went at it again. But the worst of it was that I too had got beyond reason. I could have torn the child apart in my own fury and enjoyed it. It was a pleasure to attack her. My face was burning with it.

The damned little brat must be protected against her own idiocy, one says to one's self at such times. Others must be protected against her. It is social necessity. And all these things are true. But a blind fury, a feeling of adult shame, bred of a longing for muscular release are the operatives. One goes on to the end.

In a final unreasoning assault I overpowered the child's neck and jaws.

I forced the heavy silver spoon back of her teeth and down her throat till she gagged. And there it was—both tonsils covered with membrane. She had fought valiantly to keep me from knowing her secret. She had been hiding that sore throat for three days at least and lying to her parents in order to escape just such an outcome as this.

Now truly she *was* furious. She had been on the defensive before but now she attacked. Tried to get off her father's lap and fly at me while tears of defeat blinded her eyes.

A HUNGER ARTIST

During these last decades the interest in professional fasting has markedly diminished. It used to pay very well to stage such great performances under one's own management, but today that is quite impossible. We live in a different world now. At one time the whole town took a lively interest in the hunger artist; from day to day of his fast the excitement mounted; everybody wanted to see him at least once a day; there were people who bought season tickets for the last few days and sat from morning till night in front of his small barred cage; even in the nighttime there were visiting hours, when the whole effect was heightened by torch flares; on fine days the cage was set out in the open air, and then it was the children's special treat to see the hunger artist; for their elders he was often just a joke that happened to be in fashion, but the children stood open-mouthed, holding each other's hands for greater security, marveling at him as he sat there pallid in black tights, with his ribs sticking out so prominently, not even on a seat but down among straw on the ground, sometimes giving a courteous nod, answering questions with a constrained smile, or perhaps stretching an arm through the bars so that one might feel how thin it was, and then again withdrawing deep into himself, paying no attention to anyone or anything, not even to the all-important striking of the clock that was the only piece of furniture in his cage, but merely staring into vacancy with half-shut eyes, now and then taking a sip from a tiny glass of water to moisten his lips.

Besides casual onlookers there were also relays of permanent watchers selected by the public, usually butchers, strangely enough, and it was their task to watch the hunger artist day and night, three of them at a time, in case he should have some secret recourse to nourishment. This was nothing but a formality, instituted to reassure the masses, for the initiates knew well enough that during his fast the artist would never in any circumstances, not even under forcible compulsion, swallow the smallest morsel of food; the honor of his profession forbade it. Not every watcher, of course, was capable of understanding this, there were often groups of night watchers who were very lax in carrying out their duties and deliberately huddled together in a retired corner to play cards with great absorption, obviously intending to give the hunger artist the chance of a little refreshment, which they supposed he could draw from some private hoard. Nothing annoyed the artist more than such watchers; they made him miserable; they made his fast seem unendurable; sometimes he mastered his feebleness sufficiently to sing during their watch for as long as he could keep going, to show them how unjust their suspicions were. But that was of little use; they only wondered at his cleverness in being able to fill his mouth even while singing. Much more to his taste were the watchers who sat close up to the bars, who were not content with the dim night lighting of the hall but focused him in the full glare of the electric pocket torch given them by the impresario. The harsh light did not trouble him at all. In any case he could never sleep properly, and he could always drowse a little, whatever the light, at any hour, even when the hall was thronged with noisy onlookers. He was quite happy at the prospect of spending a sleepless night with such watchers; he was ready to exchange jokes with them, to tell them stories out of his nomadic life, anything at all to keep them awake and demonstrate to them again that he had no eatables in his cage and that he was fasting as not one of them could fast. But his happiest moment was when the morning came and an enormous breakfast was brought them, at his expense, on which they flung themselves with the keen appetite of healthy men after a weary night of wakefulness. Of course there were people who argued that this breakfast was an unfair attempt to bribe the watchers, but that was going rather too far, and when they were invited to take on a night's vigil without a breakfast, merely for the sake of the cause, they made themselves scarce, although they stuck stubbornly to their suspicions.

Such suspicions, anyhow, were a necessary accompaniment to the profession of fasting. No one could possibly watch the hunger artist continuously, day and night, and so no one could produce first-hand evidence that the fast had really been rigorous and continous; only the artist himself could know that; he was therefore bound to be the sole completely satisfied spectator of his own fast. Yet for other reasons he was never satisfied; it was not perhaps mere fasting that had brought him to such skeleton thinness that many people had regretfully to keep away from his exhibitions, because the sight of him was too much for them, perhaps it was dissatisfaction with himself that had worn him down. For he alone knew, what no other initiate knew, how easy it was to fast. It was the easiest thing in the world. He made no secret of this, yet people did not believe him; at the best they set him down as modest, most of them, however, thought he was out for publicity or else was some kind of cheat who found it easy to fast because he had discovered a way of making it easy, and then had the impudence to admit the fact, more or less. He had to put up with all that, and in the course of time had got used to it, but his inner dissatisfaction always rankled, and never yet, after any term of fasting—this must be granted to his credit—had he left the cage of his own free will. The longest period of fasting was fixed by his impresario at forty days, beyond that term he was not allowed to go, not even in great cities, and there was good reason for it, too. Experience had proved that for about forty days the interest of the public could be stimulated by a steadily increasing pressure of advertisement, but after that the town began to lose interest, sympathetic support began notably to fall off; there were of course local variations as between one town and another or one country and another, but as a general rule forty days marked the limit. So on the fortieth day the flower-bedecked cage was opened, enthusiastic spectators filled the hall, a military band played, two doctors entered the cage to measure the results of the fast, which were announced through a megaphone, and finally two young ladies appeared, blissful at having been selected for the honor, to help the hunger artist down the few steps leading to a small table on which was spread a carefully chosen invalid repast. And at this very moment the artist always turned stubborn. True, he would entrust his bony arms to the outstretched helping hands of the ladies bending over him, but stand up he would not. Why stop fasting at this particular moment, after forty days of it? He had held out for a long time, an illimitably long time; why stop now, when he was in his best fasting form, or rather, not yet quite in his best fasting form? Why should he be cheated of the fame he would get for fasting longer, for being not only the record hunger artist of all time, which presumably he was already, but for beating his own record by a performance beyond human imagination, since he felt that there were no limits to his capacity for fasting? His public pretended to admire him so much, why should it have so little patience with him; if he could endure fasting longer, why shouldn't the public endure it? Besides, he was tired, he was comfortable sitting in the straw, and now he was supposed to lift himself to his full height and go down to a meal the very thought of which gave him a nausea that only the presence of the ladies kept him from betraying, and even that with an effort. And he looked up into the eyes of the ladies who were apparently so friendly and in reality so cruel, and shook his head, which felt too heavy on its strengthless neck. But then there happened yet again what always happened. The impresario came forward, without a word—for the band made speech impossible—lifted his arms in the air above the artist, as if inviting Heaven to look down upon its creature here in the straw, this suffering martyr, which indeed he was, although in quite another sense; grasped him round the emaciated waist, with exaggerated caution, so that the frail condition he was in might be appreciated; and committed him to the care of the blenching ladies, not without secretly giving him a shaking so that his legs and body tottered and swayed. The artist now submitted completely; his head lolled on his breast as if it had landed there by chance; his body was hollowed out; his legs in a spasm of self-preservation clung close to each other at the knees, yet scraped on the ground as if it were not really solid ground, as if they were only trying to find solid ground; and the whole weight of his body, a featherweight after all, relapsed onto one of the ladies, who, looking round for help and panting a little—this post of honor was not at all what she had expected it to be—first stretched her neck as far as she could to keep her face at least free from contact with the artist, then finding this impossible, and her more fortunate companion not coming to her aid but merely holding extended on her own trembling hand the little bunch of knucklebones that was the artist's, to the great delight of the spectators burst into tears and had to be replaced by an attendant who had long been stationed in readiness. Then came the food, a little of which the impresario managed to get between the artist's lips, while he sat in a kind of half-fainting trance, to the accompaniment of cheerful patter designed to distract the public's attention from the artist's condition; after that, a toast was drunk to the public, supposedly prompted by a whisper from the artist in the impresario's ear; the band confirmed it with a mighty flourish, the spectators melted away, and no one had any cause to be dissatisfied with the proceedings, no one except the hunger artist himself, he only, as always.

So he lived for many years, with small regular intervals of recuperation, in visible glory, honored by the world, yet in spite of that troubled in spirit, and all the more troubled because no one would take his trouble seriously. What comfort could he possibly need? What more could he possibly wish for? And if some good-natured person, feeling sorry for him, tried to console him by pointing out that his melancholy was probably caused by fasting, it could happen, especially when he had been fasting for some time, that he reacted with an outburst of fury and to the general alarm began to shake the bars of his cage like a wild animal. Yet the impresario had a way of punishing these outbreaks which he rather enjoyed putting into operation. He would apologize publicly for the artist's behavior, which was only to be excused, he admitted, because of the irritability caused by fasting; a condition hardly to be understood by well-fed people; then by natural transition he went on to mention the artist's equally incomprehensible boast that he could fast for much longer than he was doing; he praised the high ambition, the good will, the great self-denial undoubtedly implicit in such a statement; and then quite simply countered it by bringing out photographs, which were also on sale to the public, showing the artist on the fortieth day of a fast lying in bed almost dead from exhaustion. This perversion of the truth, familiar to the artist though it was, always unnerved him afresh and proved too much for him. What was a consequence of the premature ending of his fast was here presented as the cause of it! To fight against this lack of understanding, against a whole world of nonunderstanding, was impossible. Time and again in good faith he stood by the bars listening to the impresario, but as soon as the photographs appeared he always let go and sank with a groan back on to his straw, and the reassured public could once more come close and gaze at him.

A few years later when the witnesses of such scenes called them to mind, they often failed to understand themselves at all. For meanwhile the aforementioned change in public interest had set in; it seemed to happen almost overnight; there may have been profound causes for it, but who was going to bother about that; at any rate the pampered hunger artist suddenly found himself deserted one fine day by the amusement seekers, who went streaming past him to other more favored attractions. For the last time the impresario hurried him over half Europe to discover whether the old interest might still survive here and there; all in vain; everywhere, as if by secret agreement, a positive revulsion from professional fasting was in evidence. Of course it could not really have sprung up so suddenly as all that, and many premonitory symptoms which had not been sufficiently remarked or suppressed during the rush and glitter of success now came retrospectively to mind, but it was now too late to take any countermeasures. Fasting would surely come into fashion again at some future date, yet that was no comfort for those living in the present. What, then, was the hunger artist to do? He had been applauded by thousands in his time and could hardly come down to showing himself in a street booth at village fairs, and as for adopting another profession, he was not only too old for that but too fanatically devoted to fasting. So he took leave of the impresario, his partner in an unparalleled career, and hired himself to a large circus; in order to spare his own feelings he avoided reading the conditions of his contract.

A large circus with its enormous traffic in replacing and recruiting men, animals and apparatus can always find a use for people at any time, even for a hunger artist, provided of course that he does not ask too much, and in this particular case anyhow it was not only the artist who was taken on but his famous and long-known name as well; indeed considering the peculiar nature of his performance, which was not impaired by advancing age, it could not be objected that here was an artist past his prime, no longer at the height of his professional skill, seeking a refuge in some quiet corner of a circus; on the contrary, the hunger artist averred that he could fast as well as ever, which was entirely credible; he even alleged that if he were allowed to fast as he liked, and this was at once promised him without more ado, he could astound that world by establishing a record never yet achieved, a statement which certainly provoked a smile among the other professionals, since it left out of account the change in public opinion, which the hunger artist in his zeal conveniently forgot.

He had not, however, actually lost his sense of the real situation and took it as a matter of course that he and his cage should be stationed, not in the middle of the ring as a main attraction, but outside, near the animal cages, on a site that was after all easily accessible. Large and gaily painted placards made a frame for the cage and announced what was to be seen inside it. When the public came thronging out in the intervals to see the animals, they could hardly avoid passing the hunger artist's cage and stopping there for a moment, perhaps they might even have stayed longer had not those pressed behind them in the narrow gangway, who did not understand why they should be held up on their way towards the excitements of the menagerie, made it impossible for anyone to stand gazing quietly for any length of time. And that was the reason why the hunger artist, who had of course been looking forward to these visiting hours as the main achievement of his life, began instead to shrink from them. At first he could hardly wait for the intervals; it was exhilarating to watch the crowds come streaming his way, until only too soon—not even the most obstinate self-deception, clung to almost consciously, could hold out against the fact—the conviction was borne in upon him that these people, most of them, to judge from their actions, again and again, without exception, were all on their way to the menagerie. And the first sight of them from the distance remained the best. For when they reached his cage he was at once deafened by the storm of shouting and abuse that arose from the two contending factions, which renewed themselves continuously, of those who wanted to stop and stare at him—he soon began to dislike them more than the others—not out of real interest but only out of obstinate self-assertiveness, and those who wanted to go straight on to the animals. When the first great rush was past, the stragglers came along, and these, whom nothing could have prevented from stopping to look at him as long as they had breath, raced past with long strides, hardly even glancing at him, in their haste to get to the menagerie in time. And all too rarely did it happen that he had a stroke of luck, when some father of a family fetched up before him with his children, pointed a finger at the hunger artist and explained at length what the phenomenon meant, telling stories of earlier years when he himself had watched similar but much more thrilling performances, and the children, still rather uncomprehending, since neither inside nor outside school had they been sufficiently prepared for this lesson—what did they care about fasting?—yet showed by the brightness of their intent eyes that new and better times might be coming. Perhaps, said the hunger artist to himself many a time, things would be a little better if his cage were set not quite so near the menagerie. That made it too easy for people to make their choice, to say nothing of what he suffered from the stench of the menagerie, the animal's restlessness by night, the carrying past of raw lumps of flesh for the beasts of prey, the roaring at feeding times, which depressed him continually. But he did not dare to lodge a complaint with the management; after all, he had the animals to thank for the troops of people who passed his cage, among whom there might always be one here and there to take an interest in him, and who could tell where they might seclude him if he called attention to his existence and thereby to the fact that, strictly speaking, he was only an impediment on the way to the menagerie.

A small impediment, to be sure, one that grew steadily less. People grew familiar with the strange idea that they could be expected, in times like these, to take an interest in a hunger artist, and with this familiarity the verdict went out against him. He might fast as much as he could, and he did so; but nothing could save him now, people passed him by. Just try to explain to anyone the art of fasting! Anyone who has no feeling for it cannot be made to understand it. The fine placards grew dirty and illegible, they were torn down; the little notice board telling the number of fast days achieved, which at first was changed carefully every day, had long stayed at the same figure, for after the first few weeks even this small task seemed pointless to the staff; and so the artist simply fasted on and on, as he had once dreamed of doing, and it was no trouble to him, just as he had always foretold, but no one counted the days, no one, not even the artist himself, knew what records he was already breaking, and his heart grew heavy. And when once in a time some leisurely passer-by stopped, made merry over the old figure on the board and spoke of swindling, that was in its way the stupidest lie ever invented by indifference and inborn malice, since it was not the hunger artist who was cheating; he was working honestly, but the world was cheating him of his record.

Many more days went by, however, and that too came to an end. An overseer's eye fell on the cage one day and he asked the attendants why this perfectly good stage should be left standing there unused with dirty straw inside it; nobody knew, until one man, helped out by the notice board, remembered about the hunger artist. They poked into the straw with sticks and found him in it. "Are you still fasting?" asked the overseer. "When on earth do you mean to stop?" "Forgive me, everybody," whispered the hunger artist; only the overseer, who had his ear to the bars, understood him. "Of course," said the overseer, and tapped his forehead with a finger to let the attendants know what state the man was in, "we forgive you." "I always wanted you to admire my fasting," said the hunger artist. "We do admire it," said the overseer, affably. "But you shouldn't admire it," said the hunger artist. "Well, then we don't admire it," said the overseer, "but why shouldn't we admire it?" "Because I have to fast, I can't help it," said the hunger artist. "What a fellow you are," said the overseer, "and why can't you help it?" "Because," said the hunger artist, lifting his head a little and speaking with his lips pursed, as if for a kiss, right into the overseer's ear, so that no syllable might be lost, "because I couldn't find the food I liked. If I had found it, believe me, I should have made no fuss and stuffed myself like you or anyone else." These were his last words, but in his dimming eyes remained the firm though no longer proud persuasion that he was still continuing to fast.

"Well, clear this out now!" said the overseer, and they buried the hunger artist, straw and all. Into the cage they put a young panther. Even the most insensitive felt it refreshing to see this wild creature leaping around the cage that had so long been dreary. The panther was all right. The food he liked was brought him without hesitation by the attendants; he seemed not even to miss his freedom; his noble body, furnished almost to the bursting point with all that it needed, seemed to carry freedom around with it too; somewhere in his jaws it seemed to lurk; and the joy of life streamed with such ardent passion from his throat that for the onlookers it was not easy to stand the shock of it. But they braced themselves, crowded round the cage, and did not want ever to move away.

D. H. Lawrence (1885–1930)

THE ROCKING-HORSE WINNER

There was a woman who was beautiful, who started with all the advantages, yet she had no luck. She married for love, and the love turned to dust. She had bonny children, yet she felt they had been thrust upon her, and she could not love them. They looked at her coldly, as if they were finding fault with her. And hurriedly she felt she must cover up some fault in herself. Yet what it was that she must cover up she never knew. Nevertheless, when her children were present, she always felt the centre of her heart go hard. This troubled her, and in her manner she was all the more gentle and anxious for her children, as if she loved them very much. Only she herself knew that at the centre of her heart was a hard little place that could not feel love, no, not for anybody. Everybody else said of her: "She is such a good mother. She adores her children." Only she herself, and her children themselves, knew it was not so. They read it in each other's eyes.

There were a boy and two little girls. They lived in a pleasant house, with a garden, and they had discreet servants, and felt themselves superior to anyone in the neighbourhood.

Although they lived in style, they felt always an anxiety in the house. There was never enough money. The mother had a small income, and the father had a small income, but not nearly enough for the social position which they had to keep up. The father went into town to some office. But though he had good prospects, these prospects never materialized. There was always the grinding sense of the shortage of money, though the style was always kept up.

At last the mother said: "I will see if I can't make something." But she did not know where to begin. She racked her brains, and tried this thing and the other, but could not find anything successful. The failure made deep lines come into her face. Her children were growing up, they would have to go to school. There must be more money, there must be more money. The father, who was always very handsome and expensive in his

361

tastes, seemed as if he never would be able to do anything worth doing. And the mother, who had a great belief in herself, did not succeed any better, and her tastes were just as expensive.

And so the house came to be haunted by the unspoken phrase: There must be more money! There must be more money! The children could hear it all the time, though nobody said it aloud. They heard it at Christmas, when the expensive and splendid toys filled the nursery. Behind the shining modern rocking horse, behind the smart doll's-house, a voice would start whispering: "There must be more money! There must be more money!" And the children would stop playing, to listen for a moment. They would look into each other's eyes, to see if they had all heard. And each one saw in the eyes of the other two that they too had heard. "There must be more money! There must be more money!"

It came whispering from the springs of the still-swaying rocking horse, and even the horse, bending his wooden, champing head, heard it. The big doll, sitting so pink and smirking in her new pram, could hear it quite plainly, and seemed to be smirking all the more self-consciously because of it. The foolish puppy, too, that took the place of the Teddy bear, he was looking so extraordinarily foolish for no other reason but that he heard the secret whisper all over the house: "There must be more money!"

Yet nobody ever said it aloud. The whisper was everywhere, and therefore no one spoke it. Just as no one ever says: "We are breathing!" in spite of the fact that breath is coming and going all the time.

"Mother," said the boy Paul one day, "why don't we keep a car of our own? Why do we always use uncle's, or else a taxi?"

"Because we're the poor members of the family," said the mother.

"But why are we, mother?"

"Well—I suppose," she said slowly and bitterly, "it's because your father has no luck."

The boy was silent for some time.

"Is luck money, mother?" he asked, rather timidly.

"No, Paul. Not quite. It's what causes you to have money."

"Oh!" said Paul vaguely. "I thought when Uncle Oscar said filthy lucker, it meant money."

"Filthy lucre does mean money," said the mother. "But it's lucre, not luck."

"Oh!" said the boy. "Then what is luck, mother?"

"It's what causes you to have money. If you're lucky you have money. That's why it's better to be born lucky than rich. If you're rich, you may lose your money. But if you're lucky, you will always get more money."

"Oh! Will you? And is father not lucky?"

"Very unlucky, I should say," she said bitterly.

The boy watched her with unsure eyes.

"Why?" he asked.

"I don't know. Nobody ever knows why one person is lucky and another unlucky."

"Don't they? Nobody at all? Does nobody know?"

"Perhaps God. But He never tells."

"He ought to, then. And aren't you lucky either, mother?"

"I can't be, if I married an unlucky husband."

"But by yourself, aren't you?"

"I used to think I was, before I married. Now I think I am very unlucky indeed."

"Why?"

"Well—never mind! Perhaps I'm not really," she said.

The child looked at her, to see if she meant it. But he saw, by the lines of her mouth, that she was only trying to hide something from him.

"Well, anyhow," he said stoutly, "I'm a lucky person."

"Why?" said his mother, with a sudden laugh.

He stared at her. He didn't even know why he had said it.

"God told me," he asserted, brazening it out.

"I hope He did, dear!" she said, again with a laugh, but rather bitter.

"He did, mother!"

"Excellent!" said the mother, using one of her husband's exclamations.

The boy saw she did not believe him; or, rather, that she paid no attention to his assertion. This angered him somewhat, and made him want to compel her attention.

He went off by himself, vaguely, in a childish way, seeking for the clue to "luck." Absorbed, taking no heed of other people, he went about with a sort of stealth, seeking inwardly for luck. He wanted luck, he wanted it, he wanted it. When the two girls were playing dolls in the nursery, he would sit on his big rocking horse, charging madly into space, with a frenzy that made the little girls peer at him uneasily. Wildly the horse careered, the waving dark hair of the boy tossed, his eyes had a strange glare in them. The little girls dared not speak to him.

When he had ridden to the end of his mad little journey, he climbed down and stood in front of his rocking horse, staring fixedly into its lowered face. Its red mouth was slightly open, its big eye was wide and glassy-bright.

"Now!" he would silently command the snorting steed. "Now, take me to where there is luck! Now take me!"

And he would slash the horse on the neck with the little whip he had asked Uncle Oscar for. He knew the horse could take him to where there was luck, if only he forced it. So he would mount again, and start on his furious ride, hoping at last to get there. He knew he could get there.

"You'll break your horse, Paul!" said the nurse.

"He's always riding like that! I wish he'd leave off!" said his elder sister Joan.

But he only glared down on them in silence. Nurse gave him up. She could make nothing of him. Anyhow he was growing beyond her.

One day his mother and his Uncle Oscar came in when he was on one of his furious rides. He did not speak to them.

"Hallo, you young jockey! Riding a winner?" said his uncle.

"Aren't you growing too big for a rocking horse? You're not a very little boy any longer, you know," said the mother.

But Paul only gave a blue glare from his big, rather close-set eyes. He would speak to nobody when he was in full tilt. His mother watched him with an anxious expression on her face.

At last he suddenly stopped forcing his horse into the mechanical gallop, and slid down.

"Well, I got there!" he announced fiercely, his blue eyes still flaring, and his sturdy long legs straddling apart.

"Where did you get to?" asked his mother.

"Where I wanted to go," he flared back at her.

"That's right, son!" said Uncle Oscar. "Don't you stop till you get there. What's the horse's name?"

"He doesn't have a name," said the boy.

"Gets on without all right?" asked the uncle.

"Well, he has different names. He was called Sansovino last week."

"Sansovino, eh? Won the Ascot. How did you know his name?"

"He always talks about horse races with Bassett," said Joan.

The uncle was delighted to find that his small nephew was posted with all the racing news. Bassett, the young gardener, who had been wounded in the left foot in the war and had got his present job through Oscar Cresswell, whose batman he had been, was a perfect blade of the "turf." He lived in the racing events, and the small boy lived with him.

Oscar Cresswell got it all from Bassett.

"Master Paul comes and asks me, so I can't do more than tell him, sir," said Bassett, his face terribly serious, as if he were speaking of religious matters.

"And does he ever put anything on a horse he fancies?"

"Well—I don't want to give him away—he's a young sport, a fine sport, sir. Would you mind asking him yourself? He sort of takes a pleasure in it, and perhaps he'd feel I was giving him away, sir, if you don't mind."

Bassett was serious as a church.

The uncle went back to his nephew, and took him off for a ride in the car.

"Say, Paul, old man, do you ever put anything on a horse?" the uncle asked.

The boy watched the handsome man closely.

"Why, do you think I oughtn't to?" he parried.

"Not a bit of it! I thought perhaps you might give me a tip for the Lincoln."

The car sped on into the country, going down to Uncle Oscar's place in Hampshire.

"Honour bright?" said the nephew.

"Honour bright, son!" said the uncle.

"Well, then, Daffodil."

"Daffodil! I doubt it, sonny. What about Mirza?"

"I only know the winner," said the boy. "That's Daffodil."

"Daffodil, eh?"

There was a pause. Daffodil was an obscure horse comparatively.

"Uncle!"

"Yes, son?"

"You won't let it go any further, will you? I promised Bassett."

"Bassett be damned, old man! What's he got to do with it?"

"We're partners. We've been partners from the first. Uncle, he lent me my first five shillings, which I lost. I promised him, honour bright, it was only between me and him; only you gave me that ten-shilling note I started winning with, so I thought you were lucky. You won't let it go any further, will you?"

The boy gazed at his uncle from those big, hot, blue eyes, set rather close together. The uncle stirred and laughed uneasily.

"Right you are, son! I'll keep your tip private. Daffodil, eh? How much are you putting on him?"

"All except twenty pounds," said the boy. "I keep that in reserve."

The uncle thought it a good joke.

"You keep twenty pounds in reserve, do you, you young romancer? What are you betting, then?"

"I'm betting three hundred," said the boy gravely. "But it's between you and me, Uncle Oscar! Honour bright?"

The uncle burst into a roar of laughter.

"It's between you and me all right, you young Nat Gould," he said, laughing. "But where's your three hundred?"

"Bassett keeps it for me. We're partners."

"You are, are you! And what is Bassett putting on Daffodil?"

"He won't go quite as high as I do, I expect. Perhaps he'll go a hundred and fifty."

"What, pennies?" laughed the uncle.

"Pounds," said the child, with a surprised look at his uncle. "Bassett keeps a bigger reserve than I do."

Between wonder and amusement Uncle Oscar was silent. He pursued the matter no further, but he determined to take his nephew with him to the Lincoln races.

"Now, son," he said, "I'm putting twenty on Mirza, and I'll put five for you on any horse you fancy. What's your pick?"

"Daffodil, uncle."

"No, not the fiver on Daffodil!"

"I should if it was my own fiver," said the child.

"Good! Good! Right you are! A fiver for me and a fiver for you on Daffodil."

The child had never been to a race meeting before, and his eyes were blue fire. He pursed his mouth tight, and watched. A Frenchman just in front had put his money on Lancelot. Wild with excitement, he flayed his arms up and down, yelling "Lancelot! Lancelot!" in his French accent.

Daffodil came in first, Lancelot second, Mirza third. The child, flushed and with eyes blazing, was curiously serene. His uncle brought him four five-pound notes, four to one.

"What am I to do with these?" he cried, waving them before the boy's eyes.

"I suppose we'll talk to Bassett," said the boy. "I expect I have fifteen hundred now; and twenty in reserve; and this twenty."

His uncle studied him for some moments.

"Look here, son!" he said. "You're not serious about Bassett and that fifteen hundred, are you?"

"Yes, I am. But it's between you and me, uncle. Honour bright!"

"Honour bright all right, son! But I must talk to Bassett."

"If you'd like to be a partner, uncle, with Bassett and me, we could all be partners. Only, you'd have to promise, honour bright, uncle, not to let it go beyond us three. Bassett and I are lucky, and you must be lucky, because it was your ten shillings I started winning with. . . ."

Uncle Oscar took both Bassett and Paul into Richmond Park for an afternoon, and there they talked.

"It's like this, you see, sir," Bassett said. "Master Paul would get me talking about racing events, spinning yarns, you know, sir. And he was always keen on knowing if I'd made or if I'd lost. It's about a year since, now, that I put five shillings on Blush of Dawn for him—and we lost. Then the luck turned, with that ten shillings he had from you, that we put on Singhalese. And since that time, it's been pretty steady, all things considering. What do you say, Master Paul?"

"We're all right when we're sure," said Paul. "It's when we're not quite sure that we go down."

"Oh, but we're careful then," said Bassett.

"But when are you sure?" smiled Uncle Oscar.

"It's Master Paul, sir," said Bassett, in a secret, religious voice. "It's as if he had it from heaven. Like Daffodil, now, for the Lincoln. That was as sure as eggs."

"Did you put anything on Daffodil?" asked Oscar Cresswell.

"Yes, sir, I made my bit."

"And my nephew?"

Bassett was obstinately silent, looking at Paul.

"I made twelve hundred, didn't I, Bassett? I told uncle I was putting three hundred on Daffodil."

"That's right," said Bassett, nodding.

"But where's the money?" asked the uncle.

"I keep it safe locked up, sir. Master Paul he can have it any minute he likes to ask for it."

"What, fifteen hundred pounds?"

"And twenty! and forty, that is, with the twenty he made on the course."

"It's amazing!" said the uncle.

"If Master Paul offers you to be partners, sir, I would, if I were you; if you'll excuse me," said Bassett.

Oscar Cresswell thought about it.

"I'll see the money," he said.

They drove home again, and sure enough, Bassett came round to the garden-house with fifteen hundred pounds in notes. The twenty pounds reserve was left with Joe Glee, in the Turf Commission deposit.

"You see, it's all right, uncle, when I'm sure! Then we go strong, for all we're worth. Don't we, Bassett?"

"We do that, Master Paul."

"And when are you sure?" said the uncle, laughing.

"Oh, well, sometimes I'm absolutely sure, like about Daffodil," said the boy; "and sometimes I have an idea; and sometimes I haven't even an idea, have I, Bassett? Then we're careful, because we mostly go down."

"You do, do you? And when you're sure, like about Daffodil, what makes you sure, sonny?"

"Oh, well, I don't know," said the boy uneasily. "I'm sure, you know, uncle; that's all."

"It's as if he had it from heaven, sir," Bassett reiterated.

"I should say so!" said the uncle.

But he became a partner. And when the Leger was coming on, Paul was "sure" about Lively Spark, which was a quite inconsiderable horse. The boy insisted on putting a thousand on the horse, Bassett went for five hundred, and Oscar Cresswell two hundred. Lively Spark came in first, and the betting had been ten to one against him. Paul had made ten thousand.

"You see," he said, "I was absolutely sure of him."

Even Oscar Cresswell had cleared two thousand.

"Look here, son," he said, "this sort of thing makes me nervous."

"It needn't, uncle! Perhaps I shan't be sure again for a long time."

"But what are you going to do with your money?" asked the uncle.

"Of course," said the boy, "I started it for mother. She said she had no luck, because father is unlucky, so I thought if I was lucky, it might stop whispering."

"What might stop whispering?"

"Our house. I hate our house for whispering."

"What does it whisper?"

"Why—why"—the boy fidgeted—"why, I don't know. But it's always short of money, you know, uncle."

"I know it, son, I know it."

"You know people send mother writs, don't you, uncle?"

"I'm afraid I do," said the uncle.

"And then the house whispers, like people laughing at you behind your back. It's awful, that is! I thought if I was lucky. . . ."

"You might stop it," added the uncle.

The boy watched him with big blue eyes that had an uncanny cold fire in them, and he said never a word.

"Well, then!" said the uncle. "What are we doing?"

"I shouldn't like mother to know I was lucky," said the boy.

"Why not, son?"

"She'd stop me."

"I don't think she would."

"Oh!"—and the boy writhed in an odd way—"I don't want her to know, uncle."

"All right, son! We'll manage it without her knowing."

They managed it very easily. Paul, at the other's suggestion, handed over five thousand pounds to his uncle, who deposited it with the family lawyer, who was then to inform Paul's mother that a relative had put five thousand pounds into his hands, which sum was to be paid out a thousand pounds at a time, on the mother's birthday, for the next five years.

"So she'll have a birthday present of a thousand pounds for five successive years," said Uncle Oscar. "I hope it won't make it all the harder for her later."

Paul's mother had her birthday in November. The house had been "whispering" worse than ever lately, and, even in spite of his luck, Paul could not bear up against it. He was very anxious to see the effect of the birthday letter, telling his mother about the thousand pounds.

When there were no visitors, Paul now took his meals with his parents, as he was beyond the nursery control. His mother went into town nearly every day. She had discovered that she had an odd knack of sketching furs and dress materials, so she worked secretly in the studio of a friend who was the chief "artist" for the leading drapers. She drew the figures of ladies in furs and ladies in silk and sequins for the newspaper advertisements. This young woman artist earned several thousand pounds a year, but Paul's mother only made several hundreds, and she was again dissatisfied.

She so wanted to be first in something, and she did not succeed, even in making sketches for drapery advertisements.

She was down to breakfast on the morning of her birthday. Paul watched her face as she read her letters. He knew the lawyer's letter. As his mother read it, her face hardened and became more expressionless. Then a cold, determined look came on her mouth. She hid the letter under the pile of others, and said not a word about it.

"Didn't you have anything nice in the post for your birthday, mother?" said Paul.

"Quite moderately nice," she said, her voice cold and absent.

She went away to town without saying more.

But in the afternoon Uncle Oscar appeared. He said Paul's mother had had a long interview with the lawyer, asking if the whole five thousand could be advanced at once, as she was in debt.

"What do you think, uncle?" said the boy.

"I leave it to you, son."

"Oh, let her have it, then! We can get some more with the other," said the boy.

"A bird in the hand is worth two in the bush, laddie!" said Uncle Oscar.

"But I'm sure to know for the Grand National; or the Lincolnshire; or else the Derby. I'm sure to know for one of them," said Paul.

So Uncle Oscar signed the agreement, and Paul's mother touched the whole five thousand. Then something very curious happened. The voices in the house suddenly went mad, like a chorus of frogs on a spring evening. There were certain new furnishings, and Paul had a tutor. He was really going to Eton, his father's school, in the following autumn. There were flowers in the winter, and a blossoming of the luxury Paul's mother had been used to. And yet the voices in the house, behind the sprays of mimosa and almond blossom, and from under the piles of iridescent cushions, simply trilled and screamed in a sort of ecstasy: "There must be more money! Oh-h-, there must be more money. Oh now, now-w! Now-w-w —there must be more money!—more than ever! More than ever!"

It frightened Paul terribly. He studied away at his Latin and Greek with his tutors. But his intense hours were spent with Bassett. The Grand National had gone by: he had not "known," and had lost a hundred pounds. Summer was at hand. He was in agony for the Lincoln. But even for the Lincoln he didn't "know" and he lost fifty pounds. He became wild-eyed and strange, as if something were going to explode in him.

"Let it alone, son! Don't you bother about it!" urged Uncle Oscar. But it was as if the boy couldn't really hear what his uncle was saying.

"I've got to know for the Derby! I've got to know for the Derby!" the child reiterated, his big blue eyes blazing with a sort of madness.

His mother noticed how overwrought he was.

"You'd better go to the seaside. Wouldn't you like to go now to the seaside, instead of waiting? I think you'd better," she said, looking down at him anxiously, her heart curiously heavy because of him.

But the child lifted his uncanny blue eyes.

"I couldn't possibly go before the Derby, mother!" he said. "I couldn't possibly!"

"Why not?" she said, her voice becoming heavy when she was opposed. "Why not? You can still go from the seaside to see the Derby with your Uncle Oscar, if that's what you wish. No need for you to wait here. Besides, I think you care too much about these races. It's a bad sign. My family has been a gambling family, and you won't know till you grow up how much damage it has done. But it has done damage. I shall have to send Bassett away, and ask Uncle Oscar not to talk racing to you, unless you promise to be reasonable about it; go away to the seaside and forget it. You're all nerves!"

"I'll do what you like, mother, so long as you don't send me away till after the Derby," the boy said.

"Send you away from where? Just from this house?"

"Yes," he said, gazing at her.

"Why, you curious child, what makes you care about this house so much, suddenly? I never knew you loved it."

He gazed at her without speaking. He had a secret within a secret, something he had not divulged, even to Bassett or to his Uncle Oscar.

But his mother, after standing undecided and a little bit sullen for some moments, said:

"Very well, then! Don't go to the seaside till after the Derby, if you don't wish it. But promise me you won't let your nerves go to pieces. Promise you won't think so much about horse racing and events, as you call them!"

"Oh, no," said the boy casually. "I won't think much about them, mother. You needn't worry. I wouldn't worry, mother, if I were you."

"If you were me and I were you," said his mother, "I wonder what we should do!"

"But you know you needn't worry, mother, don't you?" the boy repeated.

"I should be awfully glad to know it," she said wearily.

"Oh, well, you can, you know. I mean, you ought to know you needn't worry," he insisted.

"Ought I? Then I'll see about it," she said.

Paul's secret of secrets was his wooden horse, that which had no name. Since he was emancipated from a nurse and a nursery-governess, he had had his rocking horse removed to his own bedroom at the top of the house.

"Surely, you're too big for a rocking horse!" his mother had remonstrated.

"Well, you see, mother, till I can have a real horse, I like to have some sort of animal about," had been his quaint answer.

"Do you feel he keeps you company?" she laughed.

"Oh, yes! He's very good, he always keeps me company, when I'm there," said Paul.

So the horse, rather shabby, stood in an arrested prance in the boy's bedroom.

The Derby was drawing near, and the boy grew more and more tense. He hardly heard what was spoken to him, he was very frail, and his eyes were really uncanny. His mother had sudden seizures of uneasiness about him. Sometimes, for half-an-hour, she would feel a sudden anxiety about him that was almost anguish. She wanted to rush to him at once, and know he was safe.

Two nights before the Derby, she was at a big party in town, when one of her rushes of anxiety about her boy, her first-born, gripped her heart till she could hardly speak. She fought with the feeling, might and main, for she believed in common sense. But it was too strong. She had to leave the dance and go downstairs to telephone to the country. The children's nursery-governess was terribly surprised and startled at being rung up in the night.

"Are the children all right, Miss Wilmot?"

"Oh, yes, they are quite all right."

"Master Paul? Is he all right?"

"He went to bed as right as a trivet. Shall I run up and look at him?"

"No," said Paul's mother reluctantly. "No! Don't trouble. It's all right. Don't sit up. We shall be home fairly soon." She did not want her son's privacy intruded upon.

"Very good," said the governess.

It was about one o'clock when Paul's mother and father drove up to their house. All was still. Paul's mother went to her room and slipped off her white fur coat. She had told her maid not to wait up for her. She heard her husband downstairs, mixing a whisky-and-soda.

And then, because of the strange anxiety at her heart, she stole upstairs to her son's room. Noiselessly she went along the upper corridor. Was there a faint noise? What was it?

She stood, with arrested muscles, outside his door, listening. There was a strange, heavy, and yet not loud noise. Her heart stood still. It was a soundless noise, yet rushing and powerful. Something huge, in violent, hushed motion. What was it? What in God's name was it? She ought to know. She felt that she knew the noise. She knew what it was.

Yet she could not place it. She couldn't say what it was. And on and on it went, like a madness.

Softly, frozen with anxiety and fear, she turned the door handle.

The room was dark. Yet in the space near the window, she heard and saw something plunging to and fro. She gazed in fear and amazement.

Then suddenly she switched on the light, and saw her son, in his green pyjamas, madly surging on the rocking horse. The blaze of light suddenly lit him up, as he urged the wooden horse, and lit her up, as she stood, blonde, in her dress of pale green and crystal, in the doorway.

"Paul!" she cried. "Whatever are you doing?"

"It's Malabar!" he screamed, in a powerful, strange voice. "It's Malabar."

His eyes blazed at her for one strange and senseless second, as he ceased urging his wooden horse. Then he fell with a crash to the ground, and she, all her tormented motherhood flooding upon her, rushed to gather him up.

But he was unconscious, and unconscious he remained, with some brain-fever. He talked and tossed, and his mother sat stonily by his side.

"Malabar! It's Malabar! Bassett, Bassett, I know! It's Malabar!"

So the child cried, trying to get up and urge the rocking horse that gave him his inspiration.

"What does he mean by Malabar?" asked the heart-frozen mother.

"I don't know," said the father stonily.

"What does he mean by Malabar?" she asked her brother Oscar.

"It's one of the horses running for the Derby," was the answer.

And, in spite of himself, Oscar Cresswell spoke to Bassett, and himself put a thousand on Malabar: at fourteen to one.

The third day of the illness was critical: they were waiting for a change. The boy, with his rather long, curly hair, was tossing ceaselessly on the pillow. He neither slept nor regained consciousness, and his eyes were like blue stones. His mother sat, feeling her heart had gone, turned actually into a stone.

In the evening, Oscar Cresswell did not come, but Bassett sent a message, saying could he come up for one moment, just one moment? Paul's mother was very angry at the intrusion, but on second thought she agreed. The boy was the same. Perhaps Bassett might bring him to consciousness.

The gardener, a shortish fellow with a little brown moustache, and sharp little brown eyes, tiptoed into the room, touched his imaginary cap to Paul's mother, and stole to the bedside, staring with glittering, smallish eyes, at the tossing, dying child.

"Master Paul!" he whispered. "Master Paul! Malabar came in first all right, a clean win. I did as you told me. You've made over seventy thousand pounds, you have; you've got over eighty thousand. Malabar came in all right, Master Paul."

"Malabar! Malabar! Did I say Malabar, mother? Did I say Malabar? Do you think I'm lucky, mother? I knew Malabar, didn't I? Over eighty thousand pounds! I call that lucky, don't you, mother? Over eighty thousand pounds! I knew, didn't I know I knew? Malabar came in all right. If

I ride my horse till I'm sure, then I tell you, Bassett, you can go as high as you like. Did you go for all you were worth, Bassett?"

"I went a thousand on it, Master Paul."

"I never told you, mother, that if I can ride my horse, and get there, then I'm absolutely sure—oh, absolutely! Mother, did I ever tell you? I am lucky."

"No, you never did," said the mother.

But the boy died in the night.

And even as he lay dead, his mother heard her brother's voice saying to her: "My God, Hester, you're eighty-odd thousand to the good and a poor devil of a son to the bad. But, poor devil, poor devil, he's best gone out of a life where he rides his rocking horse to find a winner."

William Faulkner (1897–1962)

BARN BURNING

The store in which the Justice of the Peace's court was sitting smelled of cheese. The boy, crouched on his nail keg at the back of the crowded room, knew he smelled cheese, and more: from where he sat he could see the ranked shelves close-packed with the solid, squat, dynamic shapes of tin cans whose labels his stomach read, not from the lettering which meant nothing to his mind but from the scarlet devils and the silver curve of fish —this, the cheese which he knew he smelled and the hermetic meat which his intestines believed he smelled coming in intermittent gusts momentary and brief between the other constant one, the smell and sense just a little of fear because mostly of despair and grief, the old fierce pull of blood. He could not see the table where the Justice sat and before which his father and his father's enemy (*our enemy* he thought in that despair; *ourn! mine and hisn both! He's my father!*) stood, but he could hear them, the two of them that is, because his father had said no word yet:

"But what proof have you, Mr. Harris?"

"I told you. The hog got into my corn. I caught it up and sent it back to him. He had no fence that would hold it. I told him so, warned him. The next time I put the hog in my pen. When he came to get it I gave him enough wire to patch up his pen. The next time I put the hog up and kept it. I rode down to his house and saw the wire I gave him still rolled on to the spool in his yard. I told him he could have the hog when he paid me a dollar pound fee. That evening a nigger came with the dollar and got the hog. He was a strange nigger. He said, 'He say to tell you wood and hay kin burn.' I said, 'What?' 'That whut he say to tell you,' the nigger said. 'Wood and hay kin burn.' That night my barn burned. I got the stock out but I lost the barn."

"Where is the nigger? Have you got him?"

"He was a strange nigger, I tell you. I don't know what became of him."

"But that's not proof. Don't you see that's not proof?"

"Get that boy up here. He knows." For a moment the boy thought too that the man meant his older brother until Harris said, "Not him. The little one. The boy," and, crouching, small for his age, small and wiry like his father, in patched and faded jeans even too small for him, with straight, uncombed, brown hair and eyes gray and wild as storm scud, he saw the men between himself and the table part and become a lane of grim faces, at the end of which he saw the Justice, a shabby, collarless, graying man in spectacles, beckoning him. He felt no floor under his bare feet; he seemed to walk beneath the palpable weight of the grim turning faces. His father, stiff in his black Sunday coat donned not for the trial but for the moving, did not even look at him. *He aims for me to lie,* he thought, again with that frantic grief and despair. *And I will have to do hit.*

"What's your name, boy?" the Justice said.

"Colonel Sartoris Snopes," the boy whispered.

"Hey?" the Justice said. "Talk louder. Colonel Sartoris? I reckon anybody named for Colonel Sartoris in this country can't help but tell the truth, can they?" The boy said nothing. *Enemy! Enemy!* he thought; for a moment he could not even see, could not see that the Justice's face was kindly nor discern that his voice was troubled when he spoke to the man named Harris: "Do you want me to question this boy?" But he could hear, and during those subsequent long seconds while there was absolutely no sound in the crowded little room save that of quiet and intent breathing it was as if he had swung outward at the end of a grape vine, over a ravine, and at the top of the swing had been caught in a prolonged instant of mesmerized gravity, weightless in time.

"No!" Harris said violently, explosively. "Damnation! Send him out of here!" Now time, the fluid world, rushed beneath him again, the voices coming to him again through the smell of cheese and sealed meat, the fear and despair and the old grief of blood:

"This case is closed. I can't find against you, Snopes, but I can give you advice. Leave this country and don't come back to it."

His father spoke for the first time, his voice cold and harsh, level, without emphasis: "I aim to. I don't figure to stay in a country among people who . . . " he said something unprintable and vile, addressed to no one.

"That'll do," the Justice said. "Take your wagon and get out of this country before dark. Case dismissed."

His father turned, and he followed the stiff black coat, the wiry figure walking a little stiffly from where a Confederate provost's man's musket ball had taken him in the heel on a stolen horse thirty years ago, followed the two backs now, since his older brother had appeared from somewhere in the crowd, no taller than the father but thicker, chewing tobacco steadily, between the two lines of grim-faced men and out of the store and across the worn gallery and down the sagging steps and among the dogs and half-grown boys in the mild May dust, where as he passed a voice hissed:

"Barn burner!"

Again he could not see, whirling; there was a face in a red haze, moon-like, bigger than the full moon, the owner of it half again his size, he leaping in the red haze toward the face, feeling no blow, feeling no shock when his head struck the earth, scrabbling up and leaping again, feeling no blow this time either and tasting no blood, scrabbling up to see the other boy in full flight and himself already leaping into pursuit as his father's hand jerked him back, the harsh, cold voice speaking above him: "Go get in the wagon."

It stood in a grove of locusts and mulberries across the road. His two hulking sisters in their Sunday dresses and his mother and her sister in calico and sunbonnets were already in it, sitting on and among the sorry residue of the dozen and more movings which even the boy could remember—the battered stove, the broken beds and chairs, the clock inlaid with mother-of-pearl, which would not run, stopped at some fourteen minutes past two o'clock of a dead and forgotten day and time, which had been his mother's dowry. She was crying, though when she saw him she drew her sleeve across her face and began to descend from the wagon. "Get back," the father said.

"He's hurt. I got to get some water and wash his . . . "

"Get back in the wagon," his father said. He got in too, over the tailgate. His father mounted to the seat where the older brother already sat and struck the gaunt mules two savage blows with the peeled willow, but without heat. It was not even sadistic; it was exactly that same quality which in later years would cause his decendants to over-run the engine before putting a motor car into motion, striking and reining back in the same movement. The wagon went on, the store with its quiet crowd of grimly watching men dropped behind; a curve in the road hid it. *Forever,* he thought. *Maybe he's done satisfied now, now that he has . . .* stopping himself, not to say it aloud even to himself. His mother's hand touched his shoulder.

"Does hit hurt?" she said.

"Naw," he said. "Hit don't hurt Lemme be."

"Can't you wipe some of the blood off before hit dries?"

"I'll wash to-night," he said. "Lemme be, I tell you."

The wagon went on. He did not know where they were going. None of them ever did or ever asked, because it was always somewhere, always a house of sorts waiting for them a day or two days or even three days away. Likely his father had already arranged to make a crop on another farm before he . . . Again he had to stop himself. He (the father) always did.

There was something about his wolflike independence and even courage when the advantage was at least neutral which impressed strangers, as if they got from his latent ravening ferocity not so much a sense of dependability as a feeling that his ferocious conviction in the rightness of his own actions would be of advantage to all whose interest lay with his.

That night they camped, in a grove of oaks and beeches where a spring ran. The nights were still cool and they had a fire against it, of a rail lifted from a nearby fence and cut into lengths—a small fire, neat, niggard almost, a shrewd fire; such fires were his father's habit and custom always, even in freezing weather. Older, the boy might have remarked this and wondered why not a big one; why should now a man who had not only seen the waste and extravagance of war, but who had in his blood an inherent voracious prodigality with material not his own, have burned everything in sight? Then he might have gone a step farther and thought that that was the reason: that niggard blaze was the living fruit of nights passed during those four years in the woods hiding from all men, blue or gray, with his strings of horses (captured horses, he called them). And older still, he might have divined the true reason: that the element of fire spoke to some deep mainspring of his father's being, as the element of steel or of powder spoke to other men, as the one weapon for the preservation of integrity, else breath were not worth the breathing, and hence to be regarded with respect and used with discretion.

But he did not think this now and he had seen those same niggard blazes all his life. He merely ate his supper beside it and was already half asleep over his iron plate when his father called him, and once more he followed the stiff back, the stiff and ruthless limp, up the slope and on to the starlit road where, turning, he could see his father against the stars but without face or depth—a shape black, flat, and bloodless as though cut from tin in the iron folds of the frockcoat which had not been made for him, the voice harsh like tin and without heat like tin:

"You were fixing to tell them. You would have told him." He didn't answer. His father struck him with the flat of his hand on the side of the head, hard but without heat, exactly as he had struck the two mules at the store, exactly as he would strike either of them with any stick in order to kill a horsefly, his voice still without heat or anger: "You're getting to be a man. You got to learn. You got to learn to stick to your own blood or you ain't going to have any blood to stick to you. Do you think either of them, any man there this morning, would? Don't you know all they wanted was a chance to get at me because they knew I had them beat? Eh?" Later, twenty years later, he was to tell himself, "If I had said they wanted only truth, justice, he would have hit me again." But now he said nothing. He was not crying. He just stood there. "Answer me," his father said.

"Yes," he whispered. His father turned.

"Get on to bed. We'll be there to-morrow."

To-morrow they were there. In the early afternoon the wagon stopped before a paintless two-room house identical almost with the dozen others it had stopped before even in the boy's ten years, and again, as on the other dozen occasions, his mother and aunt got down and began to unload the wagon, although his two sisters and his father and brother had not moved.

"Likely hit ain't fitten for hawgs," one of the sisters said.

"Nevertheless, fit it will and you'll hog it and like it," his father said. "Get out of them chairs and help your Ma unload."

The two sisters got down, big, bovine, in a flutter of cheap ribbons; one of them drew from the jumbled wagon bed a battered lantern, the other a worn broom. His father handed the reins to the older son and began to climb stiffly over the wheel. "When they get unloaded, take the team to the barn and feed them." Then he said, and at first the boy thought he was still speaking to his brother: "Come with me."

"Me?" he said.

"Yes," his father said. "You."

"Abner," his mother said. His father paused and looked back—the harsh level stare beneath the shaggy, graying, irascible brows.

"I reckon I'll have a word with the man that aims to begin to-morrow owning me body and soul for the next eight months."

They went back up the road. A week ago—or before last night, that is —he would have asked where they were going, but not now. His father had struck him before last night but never before had he paused afterward to explain why; it was as if the blow and the following calm, outrageous voice still rang, repercussed, divulging nothing to him save the terrible handicap of being young, the light weight of his few years, just heavy enough to prevent his soaring free of the world as it seemed to be ordered but not heavy enough to keep him footed solid in it, to resist it and try to change the course of its events.

Presently he could see the grove of oaks and cedars and the other flowering trees and shrubs where the house would be, though not the house yet. They walked beside a fence massed with honeysuckle and Cherokee roses and came to a gate swinging open between two brick pillars, and now, beyond a sweep of drive, he saw the house for the first time and at that instant he forgot his father and the terror and despair both, and even when he remembered his father again (who had not stopped) the terror and despair did not return. Because, for all the twelve movings, they had sojourned until now in a poor country, a land of small farms and fields and houses, and he had never seen a house like this before. *Hit's big as a courthouse,* he thought quietly, with a surge of peace and joy whose reason he could not have thought into words, being too young for that: *They are safe from him. People whose lives are a part of this peace and dignity are beyond his touch, he no more to them than a buzzing wasp: capable of stinging for a little moment but that's all; the spell of this peace and dignity rendering even the barns and stable and cribs which belong to it impervious to the puny flames he might contrive* . . . this, the peace and joy, ebbing for an instant as he looked again at the stiff black back, the stiff and implacable limp of the figure which was not dwarfed by the house, for the reason that it had never looked big anywhere and which now, against the serene columned backdrop, had more than ever that impervious quality of something cut ruthlessly from tin, depthless, as though, sidewise to the sun, it would cast no shadow. Watching him, the boy remarked the absolutely undeviating course which his father held and saw the stiff foot come squarely down in a pile of fresh droppings where a horse had stood in the drive and which his father could have avoided by a simple change of stride. But it ebbed only for a moment, though he could not have thought this into words either, walking on in the spell of the house, which he could even want but without envy, without sorrow, certainly never with that ravening and jealous rage which unknown to him walked in the ironlike black coat before him: *Maybe he will feel it too. Maybe it will even change him now from what maybe he couldn't help but be.*

They crossed the portico. Now he could hear his father's stiff foot as it came down on the boards with clocklike finality, a sound out of all proportion to the displacement of the body it bore and which was not dwarfed either by the white door before it, as though it had attained to a sort of vicious and ravening minimum not to be dwarfed by anything—the flat, wide, black hat, the formal coat of broadcloth which had once been black but which had now that friction-glazed greenish cast of the bodies of old house flies, the lifted sleeve which was too large, the lifted hand like a curled claw. The door opened so promptly that the boy knew the Negro must have been watching them all the time, an old man with neat grizzled hair, in a linen jacket, who stood barring the door with his body, saying, "Wipe yo foots, white man, fo you come in here. Major ain't home no-how."

"Get out of my way, nigger," his father said, without heat too, flinging the door back and the Negro also and entering, his hat still on his head. And now the boy saw the prints of the stiff foot on the doorjamb and saw them appear on the pale rug behind the machinelike deliberation of the foot which seemed to bear (or transmit) twice the weight which the body compassed. The Negro was shouting "Miss Lula! Miss Lula!" somewhere behind them, then the boy, deluged as though by a warm wave by a suave turn of carpeted stair and a pendant glitter of chandeliers and a mute gleam of gold frames, heard the swift feet and saw her too, a lady—perhaps he had never seen her like before either—in a gray, smooth gown with lace at the throat and an apron tied at the waist and the sleeves turned back, wiping cake or biscuit dough from her hands with a towel as she came up the hall, looking not at his father at all but at the track on the blond rug with an expression of incredulous amazement.

"I tried," the Negro cried. "I tole him to . . . "

"Will you please go away?" she said in a shaking voice. "Major de Spain is not at home. Will you please go away?"

His father had not spoken again. He did not speak again. He did not even look at her. He just stood stiff in the center of the rug, in his hat, the shaggy iron-gray brows twitching slightly above the pebble-colored eyes as he appeared to examine the house with brief deliberation. Then with the same deliberation he turned; the boy watched him pivot on the good leg and saw the stiff foot drag round the arc of the turning, leaving a final long and fading smear. His father never looked at it, he never once looked down at the rug. The Negro held the door. It closed behind them, upon the hysteric and indistinguishable woman-wail. His father stopped at the top of the steps and scraped his boot clean on the edge of it. At the gate he stopped again. He stood for a moment, planted stiffly on the stiff foot, looking back at the house. "Pretty and white, ain't it?" he said. "That's sweat. Nigger sweat. Maybe it ain't white enough yet to suit him. Maybe he wants to mix some white sweat with it."

Two hours later the boy was chopping wood behind the house within which his mother and aunt and the two sisters (the mother and aunt, not the two girls, he knew that; even at this distance and muffled by walls the flat loud voices of the two girls emanated an incorrigible idle inertia) were setting up the stove to prepare a meal, when he heard the hooves and saw the linen-clad man on a fine sorrel mare, whom he recognized even before he saw the rolled rug in front of the Negro youth following on a fat bay carriage horse—a suffused, angry face vanishing, still at full gallop, beyond the corner of the house where his father and brother were sitting in the two tilted chairs; and a moment later, almost before he could have put the axe down, he heard the hooves again and watched the sorrel mare go back out of the yard, already galloping again. Then his father began to shout one of the sister's names, who presently emerged backward from the kitchen door dragging the rolled rug along the ground by one end while the other sister walked behind it.

"If you ain't going to tote, go on and set up the wash-pot," the first said.

"You, Sarty!" the second shouted. "Set up the wash-pot!" His father appeared at the door, framed against that shabbiness, as he had been against that other bland perfection, impervious to either, the mother's anxious face at his shoulder.

"Go on," the father said. "Pick it up." The two sisters stooped, broad, lethargic; stooping, they presented an incredible expanse of pale cloth and a flutter of tawdry ribbons.

"If I thought enough of a rug to have to git hit all the way from France I wouldn't keep hit where folks coming in would have to tromp on hit," the first said. They raised the rug.

"Abner," the mother said. "Let me do it."

"You go back and git dinner," his father said. "I'll tend to this."

From the woodpile through the rest of the afternoon the boy watched them, the rug spread flat in the dust beside the bubbling wash-pot, the two sisters stooping over it with that profound and lethargic reluctance, while the father stood over them in turn, implacable and grim, driving them though never raising his voice again. He could smell the harsh homemade lye they were using; he saw his mother come to the door once and look toward them with an expression not anxious now but very like despair; he saw his father turn, and he fell to with the axe and saw from the corner of his eye his father raise from the ground a flattish fragment of field stone and examine it and return to the pot, and this time his mother actually spoke: "Abner. Abner. Please don't. Please, Abner."

Then he was done too. It was dusk; the whippoorwills had already begun. He could smell coffee from the room where they would presently eat the cold food remaining from the mid-afternoon meal, though when he entered the house he realized they were having coffee again probably because there was a fire on the hearth, before which the rug now lay spread over the backs of the two chairs. The tracks of his father's foot were gone. Where they had been were now long, water-cloudy scorifications resembling the sporadic course of a lilliputian mowing machine.

It still hung there while they ate the cold food and then went to bed, scattered without order or claim up and down the two rooms, his mother in one bed, where his father would later lie, the older brother in the other, himself, the aunt, and the two sisters on pallets on the floor. But his father was not in bed yet. The last thing the boy remembered was the depthless, harsh silhouette of the hat and coat bending over the rug and it seemed to him that he had not even closed his eyes when the silhouette was standing over him, the fire almost dead behind it, the stiff foot prodding him awake. "Catch up the mule," his father said.

When he returned with the mule his father was standing in the black door, the rolled rug over his shoulder. "Ain't you going to ride?" he said.

"No. Give me your foot."

He bent his knee into his father's hand, the wiry, surprising power flowed smoothly, rising, he rising with it, on the mule's bare back (they had owned a saddle once; the boy could remember it though not when or where) and with the same effortlessness his father swung the rug up in front of him. Now in the starlight they retraced the afternoon's path, up the dusty road rife with honeysuckle, through the gate and up the black tunnel of the drive to the lightless house, where he sat on the mule and felt the rough warp of the rug drag across his thighs and vanish.

"Don't you want me to help?" he whispered. His father did not answer and now he heard again that stiff foot striking the hollow portico with that wooden and clocklike deliberation, that outrageous overstatement of the weight it carried. The rug, hunched, not flung (the boy could tell that even in the darkness) from his father's shoulder struck the angle of wall and floor with a sound unbelievably loud, thunderous, then the foot again, unhurried and enormous; a light came on in the house and the boy sat, tense, breathing steadily and quietly and just a little fast, though the foot itself did not increase its beat at all, descending the steps now; now the boy could see him.

"Don't you want to ride now?" he whispered. "We kin both ride now," the light within the house altering now, flaring up and sinking. *He's coming down the stairs now,* he thought. He had already ridden the mule up beside the horse block; presently his father was up behind him and he doubled the reins over and slashed the mule across the neck, but before the animal could begin to trot the hard, thin arm came round him, the hard, knotted hand jerking the mule back to a walk.

In the first red rays of the sun they were in the lot, putting plow gear on the mules. This time the sorrel mare was in the lot before he heard it at all, the rider collarless and even bareheaded, trembling, speaking in a shaking voice as the woman in the house had done, his father merely looking up once before stooping again to the hame he was buckling, so that the man on the mare spoke to his stooping back:

"You must realize you have ruined that rug. Wasn't there anybody here, any of your women . . . " he ceased, shaking, the boy watching him, the older brother leaning now in the stable door, chewing, blinking slowly and steadily at nothing apparently. "It cost a hundred dollars. But you never had a hundred dollars. You never will. So I'm going to charge you twenty bushels of corn against your crop. I'll add it in your contract and when you come to the commissary you can sign it. That won't keep Mrs. de Spain quiet but maybe it will teach you to wipe your feet off before you enter her house again."

Then he was gone. The boy looked at his father, who still had not spoken or even looked up again, who was now adjusting the logger-head in the hame.

"Pap," he said. His father looked at him—the inscrutable face, the shaggy brows beneath which the gray eyes glinted coldly. Suddenly the boy went toward him, fast, stopping as suddenly. "You done the best you could!" he cried. "If he wanted hit done different why didn't he wait and tell you how? He won't git no twenty bushels! He won't git none! We'll gether hit and hide hit! I kin watch . . . "

"Did you put the cutter back in that straight stock like I told you?"

"No, sir," he said.

"Then go do it."

That was Wednesday. During the rest of that week he worked steadily, at what was within his scope and some which was beyond it, with an industry that did not need to be driven nor even commanded twice; he had this from his mother, with the difference that some at least of what he did he liked to do, such as splitting wood with the half-size axe which his mother and aunt had earned, or saved money somehow, to present him with at Christmas. In company with the two older women (and on one afternoon, even one of the sisters), he built pens for the shoat and the cow which were a part of his father's contract with the landlord, and one afternoon, his father being absent, gone somewhere on one of the mules, he went to the field.

They were running a middle buster now, his brother holding the plow straight while he handled the reins, and walking beside the straining mule, the rich black soil shearing cool and damp against his bare ankles, he thought *Maybe this is the end of it. Maybe even that twenty bushels that seems hard to have to pay for just a rug will be a cheap price for him to stop forever and always from being what he used to be;* thinking, dreaming now, so that his brother had to speak sharply to him to mind the mule: *Maybe he even won't collect the twenty bushels. Maybe it will all add up and balance and vanish— corn, rug, fire; the terror and grief, the being pulled two ways like between two teams of horses—gone, done with forever and ever.*

Then it was Saturday; he looked up from beneath the mule he was harnessing and saw his father in the black coat and hat. "Not that," his father said. "The wagon gear." And then, two hours later, sitting in the wagon bed behind his father and brother on the seat, the wagon accomplished a final curve, and he saw the weathered paintless store with its tattered tobacco and patent-medicine posters and the tethered wagons and saddle animals below the gallery. He mounted the gnawed steps behind his father and brother, and there again was the lane of quiet, watching faces for the three of them to walk through. He saw the man in spectacles sitting at the plank table and he did not need to be told this was a Justice of the Peace; he sent one glare of fierce, exultant, partisan defiance at the man in collar and cravat now, whom he had seen but twice before in his life, and that on a galloping horse, who now wore on his face an expression not of rage but of amazed unbelief which the boy could not have known was at the incredible circumstance of being sued by one of his own tenants, and came and stood against his father and cried at the Justice: "He ain't done it! He ain't burnt . . . "

"Go back to the wagon," his father said.

"Burnt?" the Justice said. "Do I understand this rug was burned too?"

"Does anybody here claim it was?" his father said. "Go back to the wagon." But he did not, he merely retreated to the rear of the room, crowded as that other had been, but not to sit down this time, instead, to stand pressing among the motionless bodies, listening to the voices:

"And you claim twenty bushels of corn is too high for the damage you did to the rug?"

"He brought the rug to me and said he wanted the tracks washed out of it. I washed the tracks out and took the rug back to him."

"But you didn't carry the rug back to him in the same condition it was in before you made the tracks on it."

His father did not answer, and now for perhaps half a minute there was no sound at all save that of breathing, the faint, steady suspiration of complete and intent listening.

"You decline to answer that, Mr. Snopes?" Again his father did not answer. "I'm going to find against you, Mr. Snopes. I'm going to find that you were responsible for the injury to Major de Spain's rug and hold you liable for it. But twenty bushels of corn seems a little high for a man in your circumstances to have to pay. Major de Spain claims it cost a hundred dollars. October corn will be worth about fifty cents. I figure that if Major de Spain can stand a ninety-five dollar loss on something he paid cash for, you can stand a five-dollar loss you haven't earned yet. I hold you in damages to Major de Spain to the amount of ten bushels of corn over and above your contract with him, to be paid to him out of your crop at gathering time. Court adjourned."

It had taken no time hardly, the morning was but half begun. He thought they would return home and perhaps back to the field, since they were late, far behind all other farmers. But instead his father passed on behind the wagon, merely indicating with his hand for the older brother to follow with it, and crossed the road toward the blacksmith shop opposite, pressing on after his father, overtaking him, speaking, whispering up at the harsh, calm face beneath the weathered hat: "He won't git no ten bushels neither. He won't git one. We'll . . . " until his father glanced for an instant down at him, the face absolutely calm, the grizzled eyebrows tangled above the cold eyes, the voice almost pleasant, almost gentle:

"You think so? Well, we'll wait till October anyway."

The matter of the wagon—the setting of a spoke or two and the tightening of the tires—did not take long either, the business of the tires accomplished by driving the wagon into the spring branch behind the shop and letting it stand there, the mules nuzzling into the water from time to time, and the boy on the seat with the idle reins, looking up the slope and through the sooty tunnel of the shed where the slow hammer rang and where his father sat on an upended cypress bolt, easily, either talking or listening, still sitting there when the boy brought the dripping wagon up out of the branch and halted it before the door.

"Take them on to the shade and hitch," his father said. He did so and returned. His father and the smith and a third man squatting on his heels inside the door were talking, about crops and animals; the boy, squatting too in the ammoniac dust and hoof-parings and scales of rust, heard his father tell a long and unhurried story out of the time before the birth of the older brother even when he had been a professional horse-trader. And then his father came up beside him where he stood before a tattered last year's circus poster on the other side of the store, gazing rapt and quiet at the scarlet horses, the incredible poisings and convolutions of tulle and tights and the painted leers of comedians, and said, "It's time to eat."

But not at home. Squatting beside his brother against the front wall, he watched his father emerge from the store and produce from a paper sack a segment of cheese and divide it carefully and deliberately into three with his pocket knife and produce crackers from the same sack. They all three squatted on the gallery and ate, slowly, without talking; then in the store again, they drank from a tin dipper tepid water smelling of the cedar bucket and of living beech trees. And still they did not go home. It was a horse lot this time, a tall rail fence upon and along which men stood and sat and out of which one by one horses were led, to be walked and trotted and then cantered back and forth along the road while the slow swapping and buying went on and the sun began to slant westward, they—the three of them—watching and listening, the older brother with his muddy eyes and his steady, inevitable tobacco, the father commenting now and then on certain of the animals, to no one in particular.

It was after sundown when they reached home. They ate supper by lamplight, then, sitting on the doorstep, the boy watched the night fully accomplish, listening to the whippoorwills and the frogs, when he heard his mother's voice: "Abner! No! No! Oh, God. Oh, God. Abner!" and he rose, whirled, and saw the altered light through the door where a candle stub now burned in a bottleneck on the table and his father, still in the hat and coat, at once formal and burlesque as though dressed carefully for some shabby and ceremonial violence, emptying the reservoir of the lamp back into the five-gallon kerosene can from which it had been filled, while the mother tugged at his arm until he shifted the lamp to the other hand and flung her back, not savagely or viciously, just hard, into the wall, her hands flung out against the wall for balance, her mouth open and in her face the same quality of hopeless despair as had been in her voice. Then his father saw him standing in the door.

"Go to the barn and get that can of oil we were oiling the wagon with," he said. The boy did not move. Then he could speak.

"What . . ." he cried. "What are you . . ."

"Go get that oil," his father said. "Go."

Then he was moving, running, outside the house, toward the stable: this the old habit, the old blood which he had not been permitted to choose for himself, which had been bequeathed him willy nilly and which had run for so long (and who knew where, battening on what of outrage and savagery and lust) before it came to him. *I could keep on,* he thought. *I could run on and on and never look back, never need to see his face again. Only I can't. I can't,* the rusted can in his hand now, the liquid sploshing in it as he ran back to the house and into it, into the sound of his mother's weeping in the next room, and handed the can to his father.

"Ain't you going to even send a nigger?" he cried. "At least you sent a nigger before!"

This time his father didn't strike him. The hand came even faster than the blow had, the same hand which had set the can on the table with almost excruciating care flashing from the can toward him too quick for him to follow it, gripping him by the back of his shirt and on to tiptoe before he had seen it quit the can, the face stooping at him in breathless and frozen ferocity, the cold, dead voice speaking over him to the older brother who leaned against the table, chewing with that steady, curious, sidewise motion of cows.

"Empty the can into the big one and go on. I'll catch up with you."

"Better tie him up to the bedpost," the brother said.

"Do like I told you," the father said. Then the boy was moving, his bunched shirt and the hard, bony hand between his shoulder-blades, his toes just touching the floor, across the room and into the other one, past the sisters sitting with spread heavy thighs in the two chairs over the cold hearth, and to where his mother and aunt sat side by side on the bed, the aunt's arm about his mother's shoulders.

"Hold him," the father said. The aunt made a startled movement. "Not you," the father said. "Lennie. Take hold of him. I want to see you do it." His mother took him by the wrist. "You'll hold him better than that. If he gets loose don't you know what he is going to do? He will go up yonder." He jerked his head toward the road. "Maybe I'd better tie him."

"I'll hold him," his mother whispered.

"See you do then." Then his father was gone, the stiff foot heavy and measured upon the boards, ceasing at last.

Then he began to struggle. His mother caught him in both arms, he jerking and wrenching at them. He would be stronger in the end, he knew that. But he had no time to wait for it. "Lemme go!" he cried. "I don't want to have to hit you!"

"Let him go!" the aunt said. "If he don't go, before God, I am going up there myself!"

"Don't you see I can't?" his mother cried. "Sarty! Sarty! No! No! Help me, Lizzie!"

Then he was free. His aunt grasped at him but it was too late. He whirled, running, his mother stumbled forward onto her knees behind him, crying to the nearer sister: "Catch him, Net! Catch him!" But that was too late too, the sister (the sisters were twins, born at the same time, yet either of them now gave the impression of being, encompassing as much living meat and volume and weight as any other two of the family) not yet having begun to rise from the chair, her head, face, alone merely turned, presenting to him in the flying instant an astonishing expanse of young female features untroubled by any surprise even, wearing only an expression of bovine interest. Then he was out of the room, out of the house, in the mild dust of the starlit road and the heavy rifeness of honey-suckle, the pale ribbon unspooling with terrific slowness under his running feet, reaching the gate at last and turning in, running, his heart and lungs drumming, on up the drive toward the lighted house, the lighted door. He did not knock, he burst in, sobbing for breath, incapable for the moment of speech; he saw the astonished face of the Negro in the linen jacket without knowing when the Negro had appeared.

"De Spain!" he cried, panted. "Where's . . . " then he saw the white man too emerging from a white door down the hall. "Barn!" he cried. "Barn!"

"What?" the white man said. "Barn?"

"Yes!" the boy cried. "Barn!"

"Catch him!" the white man shouted.

But it was too late this time too. The Negro grasped his shirt, but the entire sleeve, rotten with washing, carried away, and he was out that door too and in the drive again, and had actually never ceased to run even while he was screaming into the white man's face.

Behind him the white man was shouting, "My horse! Fetch my horse!" and he thought for an instant of cutting across the park and climbing the fence into the road, but he did not know the park nor how high the vine-massed fence might be and he dared not risk it. So he ran on down the drive, blood and breath roaring; presently he was in the road again though he could not see it. He could not hear either: the galloping mare was almost upon him before he heard her, and even then he held his course, as if the very urgency of his wild grief and need must in a moment more find him wings, waiting until the ultimate instant to hurl himself aside and into the weed-choked roadside ditch as the horse thundered past and on, for an instant in furious silhouette against the stars, the tranquil early summer night sky which, even before the shape of the horse and rider vanished, stained abruptly and violently upward: a long, swirling roar incredible and soundless, blotting the stars, and he springing up and into the road again, running again, knowing it was too late yet still running even after he heard the shot and, an instant later, two shots, pausing now without knowing he had ceased to run, crying "Pap! Pap!", running again before he knew he had begun to run, stumbling, tripping over something and scrabbling up again without ceasing to run, looking backward over his shoulder at the glare as he got up, running on among the invisible trees, panting, sobbing, "Father! Father!"

At midnight he was sitting on the crest of a hill. He did not know it was midnight and he did not know how far he had come. But there was no glare behind him now and he sat now, his back toward what he had called home for four days anyhow, his face toward the dark woods which he would enter when breath was strong again, small, shaking steadily in the chill darkness, hugging himself into the remainder of his thin, rotten shirt, the grief and despair now no longer terror and fear but just grief and despair. *Father. My father,* he thought. "He was brave!" he cried suddenly, aloud but not loud, no more than a whisper: "He was! He was in the war! He was in Colonel Sartoris' cav'ry!" not knowing that his father had gone to that war a private in the fine old European sense, wearing no uniform, admitting the authority of and giving fidelity to no man or army or flag, going to war as Malbrouck himself did: for booty—it meant nothing and less than nothing to him if it were enemy booty or his own.

The slow constellations wheeled on. It would be dawn and then sun-up after a while and he would be hungry. But that would be to-morrow and now he was only cold, and walking would cure that. His breathing was easier now and he decided to get up and go on, and then he found that he had been asleep because he knew it was almost dawn, the night almost over. He could tell that from the whippoorwills. They were everywhere now among the dark trees below him, constant and inflectioned and ceaseless, so that, as the instant for giving over to the day birds drew nearer and nearer, there was no interval at all between them. He got up. He was a little stiff, but walking would cure that too as it would the cold, and soon there would be the sun. He went on down the hill, toward the dark woods within which the liquid silver voices of the birds called unceasing—the rapid and urgent beating of the urgent and quiring heart of the late spring night. He did not look back.

Ernest Hemingway (1899–1961)

A CLEAN, WELL-LIGHTED PLACE

It was late and every one had left the café except an old man who sat in the shadow the leaves of the tree made against the electric light. In the daytime the street was dusty, but at night the dew settled the dust and the old man liked to sit late because he was deaf and now at night it was quiet and he felt the difference. The two waiters inside the café knew that the old man was a little drunk, and while he was a good client they knew that if he became too drunk he would leave without paying, so they kept watch on him.

"Last week he tried to commit suicide," one waiter said.

"Why?"

"He was in despair."

"What about?"

"Nothing."

"How do you know it was nothing?"

"He has plenty of money."

They sat together at a table that was close against the wall near the door of the café and looked at the terrace where the tables were all empty except where the old man sat in the shadow of the leaves of the tree that moved slightly in the wind. A girl and a soldier went by in the street. The street light shone on the brass number on his collar. The girl wore no head covering and hurried beside him.

"The guard will pick him up," one waiter said.

"What does it matter if he gets what he's after?"

"He had better get off the street now. The guard will get him. They went by five minutes ago."

The old man sitting in the shadow rapped on his saucer with his glass. The younger waiter went over to him.

"What do you want?"

The old man looked at him. "Another brandy," he said.

"You'll be drunk," the waiter said. The old man looked at him. The waiter went away.

"He'll stay all night," he said to his colleague. "I'm sleepy now. I never get into bed before three o'clock. He should have killed himself last week."

The waiter took the brandy bottle and another saucer from the counter inside the café and marched out to the old man's table. He put down the saucer and poured the glass full of brandy.

"You should have killed yourself last week," he said to the deaf man. The old man motioned with his finger. "A little more," he said. The waiter poured on into the glass so that the brandy slopped over and ran down the stem into the top saucer of the pile. "Thank you," the old man said. The waiter took the bottle back inside the café. He sat down at the table with his colleague again.

"He's drunk now," he said.

"He's drunk every night."

"What did he want to kill himself for?"

"How should I know?"

"How did he do it?"

"He hung himself with a rope."

"Who cut him down?"

"His niece."

"Why did they do it?"

"Fear for his soul."

"How much money has he got?"

"He's got plenty."

"He must be eighty years old."

"Anyway I should say he was eighty."

"I wish he would go home. I never get to bed before three o'clock. What kind of hour is that to go to bed?"

"He stays up because he likes it."

"He's lonely. I'm not lonely. I have a wife waiting in bed for me."

"He had a wife once too."

"A wife would be no good to him now."

"You can't tell. He might be better with a wife."

"His niece looks after him. You said she cut him down."

"I know."

"I wouldn't want to be that old. An old man is a nasty thing."

"Not always. This old man is clean. He drinks without spilling. Even now, drunk. Look at him."

"I don't want to look at him. I wish he would go home. He has no regard for those who must work."

The old man looked from his glass across the square, then over at the waiters.

"Another brandy," he said, pointing to his glass. The waiter who was in a hurry came over.

"Finished," he said, speaking with that omission of syntax stupid people employ when talking to drunken people or foreigners. "No more tonight. Close now."

"Another," said the old man.

"No. Finished." The waiter wiped the edge of the table with a towel and shook his head.

The old man stood up, slowly counted the saucers, took a leather coin purse from his pocket and paid for the drinks, leaving half a peseta tip.

The waiter watched him go down the street, a very old man walking unsteadily but with dignity.

"Why didn't you let him stay and drink?" the unhurried waiter asked. They were putting up the shutters. "It is not half-past two."

"I want to go home to bed."

"What is an hour?"

"More to me than to him."

"An hour is the same."

"You talk like an old man yourself. He can buy a bottle and drink at home."

"It's not the same."

"No, it is not," agreed the waiter with a wife. He did not wish to be unjust. He was only in a hurry.

"And you? You have no fear of going home before your usual hour?"

"Are you trying to insult me?"

"No, hombre, only to make a joke."

"No," the waiter who was in a hurry said, rising from pulling down the metal shutters. "I have confidence. I am all confidence."

"You have youth, confidence, and a job," the older waiter said. "You have everything."

"And what do you lack?"

"Everything but work."

"You have everything I have."

"No. I have never had confidence and I am not young."

"Come on. Stop talking nonsense and lock up."

"I am of those who like to stay late at the café," the older waiter said. "With all those who do not want to go to bed. With all those who need a light for the night."

"I want to go home and into bed."

"We are of two different kinds," the older waiter said. He was now dressed to go home. "It is not only a question of youth and confidence although those things are very beautiful. Each night I am reluctant to close up because there may be some one who needs the café."

"Hombre, there are bodegas open all night long."

"You do not understand. This is a clean and pleasant café. It is well lighted. The light is very good and also, now, there are shadows of the leaves."

"Good night," said the younger waiter.

"Good night," the other said. Turning off the electric light he continued the conversation with himself. It is the light of course but it is necessary that the place be clean and pleasant. You do not want music. Certainly you do not want music. Nor can you stand before a bar with dignity although that is all that is provided for these hours. What did he fear? It was not fear or dread. It was a nothing that he knew too well. It was all a nothing and a man was nothing too. It was only that and light was all it needed and a certain cleanness and order. Some lived in it and never felt it but he knew it all was nada y pues nada y nada y pues nada. Our nada who art in nada, nada be thy name thy kingdom nada thy will be nada in nada as it is in nada. Give us this nada our daily nada and nada us our nada as we nada our nadas and nada us not into nada but deliver us from nada; pues nada. Hail nothing full of nothing, nothing is with thee. He smiled and stood before a bar with a shining steam pressure coffee machine.

"What's yours?" asked the barman.

"Nada."

"Otro loco màs," said the barman and turned away.

"A little cup," said the waiter.

The barman poured it for him.

"The light is very bright and pleasant but the bar is unpolished," the waiter said.

The barman looked at him but did not answer. It was too late at night for conversation.

"You want another copita?" the barman asked.

"No, thank you," said the waiter and went out. He disliked bars and bodegas. A clean, well-lighted café was a very different thing. Now, without thinking further, he would go home to his room. He would lie in the bed and finally, with daylight, he would go to sleep. After all, he said to himself, it is probably only insomnia. Many must have it.

John Steinbeck (1902–1968)

FLIGHT

About fifteen miles below Monterey, on the wild coast, the Torres family had their farm, a few sloping acres above a cliff that dropped to the brown reefs and to the hissing white waters of the ocean. Behind the farm the stone mountains stood up against the sky. The farm buildings huddled like little clinging aphids on the mountain skirts, crouched low to the ground as though the wind might blow them into the sea. The little shack, the rattling, rotting barn were grey-bitten with sea salt, beaten by the damp wind until they had taken on the color of the granite hills. Two horses, a red cow and a red calf, half a dozen pigs and a flock of lean, multicolored chickens stocked the place. A little corn was raised on the sterile slope, and it grew short and thick under the wind, and all the cobs formed on the landward sides of the stalks.

Mama Torres, a lean, dry woman with ancient eyes, had ruled the farm for ten years, ever since her husband tripped over a stone in the field one day and fell full length on a rattlesnake. When one is bitten on the chest there is not much that can be done.

Mama Torres had three children, two undersized black ones of twelve and fourteen, Emilio and Rosy, whom Mama kept fishing on the rocks below the farm when the sea was kind and when the truant officer was in some distant part of Monterey County. And there was Pepé, the tall smiling son of nineteen, a gentle, affectionate boy, but very lazy. Pepé had a tall head, pointed at the top, and from its peak, coarse black hair grew down like a thatch all around. Over his smiling little eyes Mama cut a straight bang so he could see. Pepé had sharp Indian cheek bones and an eagle nose, but his mouth was as sweet and shapely as a girl's mouth, and his chin was fragile and chiseled. He was loose and gangling, all legs and feet and wrists, and he was very lazy. Mama thought him fine and brave, but she never told him so. She said, "Some lazy cow must have got into thy father's family, else how could I have a son like thee." And she said,

"When I carried thee, a sneaking lazy coyote came out of the brush and looked at me one day. That must have made thee so."

Pepé smiled sheepishly and stabbed at the ground with his knife to keep the blade sharp and free from rust. It was his inheritance, that knife, his father's knife. The long heavy blade folded back into the black handle. There was a button on the handle. When Pepé pressed the button, the blade leaped out ready for use. The knife was with Pepé always, for it had been his father's knife.

One sunny morning when the sea below the cliff was glinting and blue and the white surf creamed on the reef, when even the stone mountains looked kindly, Mama Torres called out the door of the shack, "Pepé, I have a labor for thee."

There was no answer. Mama listened. From behind the barn she heard a burst of laughter. She lifted her full long skirt and walked in the direction of the noise.

Pepé was sitting on the ground with his back against a box. His white teeth glistened. On either side of him stood the two black ones, tense and expectant. Fifteen feet away a redwood post was set in the ground. Pepé's right hand lay limply in his lap, and in the palm the big black knife rested. The blade was closed back into the handle. Pepé looked smiling at the sky.

Suddenly Emilio cried, "Ya!"

Pepé's wrist flicked like the head of a snake. The blade seemed to fly open in mid-air, and with a thump the point dug into the redwood post, and the black handle quivered. The three burst into excited laughter. Rosy ran to the post and pulled out the knife and brought it back to Pepé. He closed the blade and settled the knife carefully in his listless palm again. He grinned self-consciously at the sky.

"Ya!"

The heavy knife lanced out and sunk into the post again. Mama moved forward like a ship and scattered the play.

"All day you do foolish things with the knife, like a toy-baby," she stormed. "Get up on thy huge feet that eat up shoes. Get up!" She took him by one loose shoulder and hoisted at him. Pepé grinned sheepishly and came half-heartedly to his feet. "Look!" Mama cried. "Big lazy, you must catch the horse and put on him thy father's saddle. You must ride to Monterey. The medicine bottle is empty. There is no salt. Go thou now, Peanut! Catch the horse."

A revolution took place in the relaxed figure of Pepé. "To Monterey, me? Alone? Sí, Mama."

She scowled at him. "Do you think, big sheep, that you will buy candy. No, I will give you only enough for the medicine and the salt."

Pepé smiled. "Mama, you will put the hatband on the hat?"

She relented then. "Yes, Pepé. You may wear the hatband."

His voice grew insinuating, "And the green handkerchief, Mama?"

"Yes, if you go quickly and return with no trouble, the silk green handkerchief will go. If you make sure to take off the handkerchief when you eat so no spot may fall on it. . . ."

"Sí, Mama. I will be careful. I am a man."

"Thou? A man? Thou art a peanut."

He went into the rickety barn and brought out a rope, and he walked agilely enough up the hill to catch the horse.

When he was ready and mounted before the door, mounted on his father's saddle that was so old that the oaken frame showed through torn leather in many places, then Mama brought out the round black hat with the tooled leather band, and she reached up and knotted the green silk handkerchief about his neck. Pepé's blue denim coat was much darker than his jeans, for it had been washed much less often.

Mama handed up the big medicine bottle and the silver coins. "That for the medicine," she said, "and that for the salt. That for a candle to burn for the papa. That for *dulces* for the little ones. Our friend Mrs. Rodriguez will give you dinner and maybe a bed for the night. When you go to the church say only ten Paternosters and only twenty-five Ave Marias. Oh! I know, big coyote. You would sit there flapping your mouth over Aves all day while you looked at the candles and the holy pictures. That is not good devotion to stare at the pretty things."

The black hat, covering the high pointed head and black thatched hair of Pepé, gave him dignity and age. He sat the rangy horse well. Mama thought how handsome he was, dark and lean and tall. "I would not send thee now alone, thou little one, except for the medicine," she said softly. "It is not good to have no medicine, for who knows when the toothache will come, or the sadness of the stomach. These things are."

"Adios, Mama," Pepé cried. "I will come back soon. You may send me often alone. I am a man."

"Thou art a foolish chicken."

He straightened his shoulders, flipped the reins against the horse's shoulder and rode away. He turned once and saw that they still watched him, Emilio and Rosy and Mama. Pepé grinned with pride and gladness and lifted the tough buckskin horse to a trot.

When he had dropped out of sight over a little dip in the road, Mama turned to the black ones, but she spoke to herself. "He is nearly a man now," she said. "It will be a nice thing to have a man in the house again." Her eyes sharpened on the children. "Go to the rocks now. The tide is going out. There will be abalones to be found." She put the iron hooks into their hands and saw them down the steep trail to the reefs. She brought the smooth stone *metate* to the doorway and sat grinding her corn to flour and looking occasionally at the road over which Pepé had gone. The

noonday came and then the afternoon, when the little ones beat the abalones on a rock to make them tender and Mama patted the tortillas to make
them thin. They ate their dinner as the red sun was plunging down toward
the ocean. They sat on the doorsteps and watched the big white moon
come over the mountain tops.

Mama said, "He is now at the house of our friend Mrs. Rodriguez. She
will give him nice things to eat and maybe a present."

Emilio said, "Some day I too will ride to Monterey for medicine. Did
Pepé come to be a man today?"

Mama said wisely, "A boy gets to be a man when a man is needed.
Remember this thing. I have known boys forty years old because there was
no need for a man."

Soon afterwards they retired, Mama in her big oak bed on one side of
the room, Emilio and Rosy in their boxes full of straw and sheepskins on
the other side of the room.

The moon went over the sky and the surf roared on the rocks. The
roosters crowed the first call. The surf subsided to a whispering surge
against the reef. The moon dropped toward the sea. The roosters crowed
again.

The moon was near down to the water when Pepé rode on a winded horse
to his home flat. His dog bounced out and circled the horse yelping with
pleasure. Pepé slid off the saddle to the ground. The weathered little shack
was silver in the moonlight and the square shadow of it was black to the
north and east. Against the east the piling mountains were misty with
light; their tops melted into the sky.

Pepé walked wearily up the three steps and into the house. It was dark
inside. There was a rustle in the corner.

Mama cried out from her bed, "Who comes? Pepé, is it thou?"

"Sí, Mama."

"Did you get the medicine?"

"Sí, Mama."

"Well, go to sleep, then. I thought you would be sleeping at the house
of Mrs. Rodriguez." Pepé stood silently in the dark room. "Why do you
stand there, Pepé? Did you drink wine?"

"Sí, Mama."

"Well, go to bed then and sleep out the wine."

His voice was tired and patient, but very firm. "Light the candle, Mama.
I must go away into the mountains."

"What is this, Pepé? You are crazy." Mama struck a sulphur match and
held the little blue burr until the flame spread up the stick. She set light
to the candle on the floor beside her bed. "Now, Pepé, what is this you
say?" She looked anxiously into his face.

He was changed. The fragile quality seemed to have gone from his chin. His mouth was less full than it had been, the lines of the lips were straighter, but in his eyes the greatest change had taken place. There was no laughter in them any more, nor any bashfulness. They were sharp and bright and purposeful.

He told her in a tired monotone, told her everything just as it happened. A few people came into the kitchen of Mrs. Rodriguez. There was wine to drink. Pepé drank wine. The little quarrel—the man started toward Pepé and then the knife—it went almost by itself. It flew, it darted before Pepé knew it. As he talked, Mama's face grew stern, and it seemed to grow more lean. Pepé finished. "I am a man now, Mama. The man said names to me I could not allow."

Mama nodded. "Yes, thou art a man, my poor little Pepé. Thou art a man. I have seen it coming on thee. I have watched you throwing the knife into the post, and I have been afraid." For a moment her face had softened, but now it grew stern again. "Come! We must get you ready. Go. Awaken Emilio and Rosy. Go quickly."

Pepé stepped over to the corner where his brother and sister slept among the sheepskins. He leaned down and shook them gently. "Come, Rosy! Come, Emilio! The mama says you must arise."

The little black ones sat up and rubbed their eyes in the candlelight. Mama was out of bed now, her long black skirt over her nightgown. "Emilio," she cried. "Go up and catch the other horse for Pepé. Quickly, now! Quickly." Emilio put his legs in his overalls and stumbled sleepily out the door.

"You heard no one behind you on the road?" Mama demanded.

"No, Mama. I listened carefully. No one was on the road."

Mama darted like a bird about the room. From a nail on the wall she took a canvas water bag and threw it on the floor. She stripped a blanket from her bed and rolled it into a tight tube and tied the ends with string. From a box beside the stove she lifted a flour sack half full of black stringy jerky. "Your father's black coat, Pepé. Here, put it on."

Pepé stood in the middle of the floor watching her activity. She reached behind the door and brought out the rifle, a long 38-56, worn shiny the whole length of the barrel. Pepé took it from her and held it in the crook of his elbow. Mama brought a little leather bag and counted the cartridges into his hand. "Only ten left," she warned. "You must not waste them."

Emilio put his head in the door. " *'Qui 'st 'l caballo,* Mama."

"Put on the saddle from the other horse. Tie on the blanket. Here, tie the jerky to the saddle horn."

Still Pepé stood silently watching his mother's frantic activity. His chin looked hard, and his sweet mouth was drawn and thin. His little eyes followed Mama about the room almost suspiciously.

Rosy asked softly, "Where goes Pepé?"

Mama's eyes were fierce. "Pepé goes on a journey. Pepé is a man now. He has a man's thing to do."

Pepé straightened his shoulders. His mouth changed until he looked very much like Mama.

At last the preparation was finished. The loaded horse stood outside the door. The water bag dripped a line of moisture down the bay shoulder.

The moonlight was being thinned by the dawn and the big white moon was near down to the sea. The family stood by the shack. Mama confronted Pepé. "Look my son! Do not stop until it is dark again. Do not sleep even though you are tired. Take care of the horse in order that he may not stop of weariness. Remember to be careful with the bullets—there are only ten. Do not fill thy stomach with jerky or it will make thee sick. Eat a little jerky and fill thy stomach with grass. When thou comest to the high mountains, if thou seest any of the dark watching men, go not near to them nor try to speak to them. And forget not thy prayers." She put her lean hands on Pepé's shoulders, stood on her toes and kissed him formally on both cheeks, and Pepé kissed her on both cheeks. Then he went to Emilio and Rosy and kissed both of their cheeks.

Pepé turned back to Mama. He seemed to look for a little softness, a little weakness in her. His eyes were searching, but Mama's face remained fierce. "Go now," she said. "Do not wait to be caught like a chicken."

Pepé pulled himself into the saddle. "I am a man," he said.

It was the first dawn when he rode up the hill toward the little canyon which let a trail into the mountains. Moonlight and daylight fought with each other, and the two warring qualities made it difficult to see. Before Pepé had gone a hundred yards, the outlines of his figure were misty; and long before he entered the canyon, he had become a grey, indefinite shadow.

Mama stood stiffly in front of her doorstep, and on either side of her stood Emilio and Rosy. They cast furtive glances at Mama now and then.

When the grey shape of Pepé melted into the hillside and disappeared, Mama relaxed. She began the high, whining keen of the death wail. "Our beautiful—our brave," she cried. "Our protector, our son is gone." Emilio and Rosy moaned beside her. "Our beautiful—our brave, he is gone." It was the formal wail. It rose to a high piercing whine and subsided to a moan. Mama raised it three times and then she turned and went into the house and shut the door.

Emilio and Rosy stood wondering in the dawn. They heard Mama whimpering in the house. They went out to sit on the cliff above the ocean. They touched shoulders. "When did Pepé come to be a man?" Emilio asked.

"Last night," said Rosy. "Last night in Monterey." The ocean clouds turned red with the sun that was behind the mountains.

"We will have no breakfast," said Emilio. "Mama will not want to cook." Rosy did not answer him. "Where is Pepé gone?" he asked.

Rosy looked around at him. She drew her knowledge from the quiet air. "He has gone on a journey. He will never come back."

"Is he dead? Do you think he is dead?"

Rosy looked back at the ocean again. A little steamer, drawing a line of smoke sat on the edge of the horizon. "He is not dead," Rosy explained. "Not yet."

Pepé rested the big rifle across the saddle in front of him. He let the horse walk up the hill and he didn't look back. The stony slope took on a coat of short brush so that Pepé found the entrance to a trail and entered it.

When he came to the canyon opening, he swung once in his saddle and looked back, but the houses were swallowed in the misty light. Pepé jerked forward again. The high shoulder of the canyon closed in on him. His horse stretched out its neck and sighed and settled to the trail.

It was a well-worn path, dark soft leaf-mould earth strewn with broken pieces of sandstone. The trail rounded the shoulder of the canyon and dropped steeply into the bed of the stream. In the shallows the water ran smoothly, glinting in the first morning sun. Small round stones on the bottom were as brown as rust with sun moss. In the sand along the edges of the stream the tall, rich wild mint grew, while in the water itself the cress, old and tough, had gone to heavy seed.

The path went into the stream and emerged on the other side. The horse sloshed into the water and stopped. Pepé dropped his bridle and let the beast drink of the running water.

Soon the canyon sides became steep and the first giant sentinel redwoods guarded the trail, great round red trunks bearing foliage as green and lacy as ferns. Once Pepé was among the trees, the sun was lost. A perfumed and purple light lay in the pale green of the underbrush. Gooseberry bushes and blackberries and tall ferns lined the stream, and overhead the branches of the redwoods met and cut off the sky.

Pepé drank from the water bag, and he reached into the flour sack and brought out a black string of jerky. His white teeth gnawed at the string until the tough meat parted. He chewed slowly and drank occasionally from the water bag. His little eyes were slumberous and tired, but the muscles of his face were hard set. The earth of the trail was black now. It gave up a hollow sound under the walking hoofbeats.

The stream fell more sharply. Little waterfalls splashed on the stones. Five-fingered ferns hung over the water and dripped spray from their fingertips. Pepé rode half over in his saddle, dangling one leg loosely. He picked a bay leaf from a tree beside the way and put it into his mouth for a moment to flavor the dry jerky. He held the gun loosely across the pommel.

Suddenly he squared in his saddle, swung the horse from the trail and kicked it hurriedly up behind a big redwood tree. He pulled up the reins tight against the bit to keep the horse from whinnying. His face was intent and his nostrils quivered a little.

A hollow pounding came down the trail, and a horseman rode by, a fat man with red cheeks and a white stubble beard. His horse put down its head and blubbered at the trail when it came to the place where Pepé had turned off. "Hold up!" said the man and he pulled up his horse's head.

When the last sound of the hoofs died away, Pepé came back into the trail again. He did not relax in the saddle any more. He lifted the big rifle and swung the lever to throw a shell into the chamber, and then he let down the hammer to half cock.

The trail grew very steep. Now the redwood trees were smaller and their tops were dead, bitten dead where the wind reached them. The horse plodded on; the sun went slowly overhead and started down toward the afternoon.

Where the stream came out of a side canyon, the trail left it. Pepé dismounted and watered his horse and filled up his water bag. As soon as the trail had parted from the stream, the trees were gone and only the thick brittle sage and manzanita and chaparral edged the trail. And the soft black earth was gone, too, leaving only the light tan broken rock for the trail bed. Lizards scampered away into the brush as the horse rattled over the little stones.

Pepé turned in his saddle and looked back. He was in the open now: he could be seen from a distance. As he ascended the trail the country grew more rough and terrible and dry. The way wound about the bases of great square rocks. Little grey rabbits skittered in the brush. A bird made a monotonous high creaking. Eastward the bare rock mountaintops were pale and powder-dry under the dropping sun. The horse plodded up and up the trail toward a little V in the ridge which was the pass.

Pepé looked suspiciously back every minute or so, and his eyes sought the tops of the ridges ahead. Once, on a white barren spur, he saw a black figure for a moment, but he looked quickly away, for it was one of the dark watchers. No one knew who the watchers were, nor where they lived, but it was better to ignore them and never to show interest in them. They did not bother one who stayed on the trail and minded his own business.

The air was parched and full of light dust blown by the breeze from the eroding mountains. Pepé drank sparingly from his bag and corked it tightly and hung it on the horn again. The trail moved up the dry shale hillside, avoiding rocks, dropping under clefts, climbing in and out of old water scars. When he arrived at the little pass he stopped and looked back for a long time. No dark watchers were to be seen now. The trail behind was empty. Only the high tops of the redwoods indicated where the stream flowed.

Pepé rode on through the pass. His little eyes were nearly closed with weariness, but his face was stern, relentless and manly. The high mountain wind coasted sighing through the pass and whistled on the edges of the big blocks of broken granite. In the air, a red-tailed hawk sailed over close to the ridge and screamed angrily. Pepé went slowly through the broken jagged pass and looked down on the other side.

The trail dropped quickly, staggering among broken rock. At the bottom of the slope there was a dark crease, thick with brush, and on the other side of the crease a little flat, in which a grove of oak trees grew. A scar of green grass cut across the flat. And behind the flat another mountain rose, desolate with dead rocks and starving little black bushes. Pepé drank from the bag again for the air was so dry that it encrusted his nostrils and burned his lips. He put the horse down the trail. The hooves slipped and struggled on the steep way, starting little stones that rolled off into the brush. The sun was gone behind the westward mountain now, but still it glowed brilliantly on the oaks and on the grassy flat. The rocks and the hillsides still sent up waves of the heat they had gathered from the day's sun.

Pepé looked up to the top of the next dry withered ridge. He saw a dark form against the sky, a man's figure standing on top of a rock, and he glanced away quickly not to appear curious. When a moment later he looked up again, the figure was gone.

Downward the trail was quickly covered. Sometimes the horse floundered for footing, sometimes set his feet and slid a little way. They came at last to the bottom where the dark chaparral was higher than Pepé's head. He held up his rifle on one side and his arm on the other to shield his face from the sharp brittle fingers of the brush.

Up and out of the crease he rode, and up a little cliff. The grassy flat was before him, and the round comfortable oaks. For a moment he studied the trail down which he had come, but there was no movement and no sound from it. Finally he rode out over the flat, to the green streak, and at the upper end of the damp he found a little spring welling out of the earth and dropping into a dug basin before it seeped out over the flat.

Pepé filled his bag first, and then he let the thirsty horse drink out of the pool. He led the horse to the clump of oaks, and in the middle of the grove, fairly protected from sight on all sides, he took off the saddle and the bridle and laid them on the ground. The horse stretched his jaws sideways and yawned. Pepé knotted the lead rope about the horse's neck and tied him to a sapling among the oaks, where he could graze in a fairly large circle.

When the horse was gnawing hungrily at the dry grass, Pepé went to the saddle and took a black string of jerky from the sack and strolled to an oak tree on the edge of the grove, from under which he could watch the trail. He sat down in the crisp dry oak leaves and automatically felt for his big black knife to cut the jerky, but he had no knife. He leaned back on his elbow and gnawed at the tough strong meat. His face was blank, but it was a man's face.

The bright evening light washed the eastern ridge, but the valley was darkening. Doves flew down from the hills to the spring, and the quail came running out of the brush and joined them, calling clearly to one another.

Out of the corner of his eye Pepé saw a shadow grow out of the bushy crease. He turned his head slowly. A big spotted wildcat was creeping toward the spring, belly to the ground, moving like thought.

Pepé cocked his rifle and edged the muzzle slowly around. Then he looked apprehensively up the trail and dropped the hammer again. From the ground beside him he picked an oak twig and threw it toward the spring. The quail flew up with a roar and the doves whistled away. The big cat stood up: for a long moment he looked at Pepé with cold yellow eyes, and then fearlessly walked back into the gulch.

The dusk gathered quickly in the deep valley. Pepé muttered his prayers, put his head down on his arm and went instantly to sleep.

The moon came up and filled the valley with cold blue light, and the wind swept rustling down from the peaks. The owls worked up and down the slopes looking for rabbits. Down in the brush of the gulch a coyote gabbled. The oak trees whispered softly in the night breeze.

Pepé started up, listening. His horse had whinnied. The moon was just slipping behind the western ridge, leaving the valley in darkness behind it. Pepé sat tensely gripping his rifle. From far up the trail he heard an answering whinny and the crash of shod hooves on the broken rock. He jumped to his feet, ran to his horse and led it under the trees. He threw on the saddle and cinched it tight for the steep trail, caught the unwilling head and forced the bit into the mouth. He felt the saddle to make sure the water bag and the sack of jerky were there. Then he mounted and turned up the hill.

It was velvet dark. The horse found the entrance to the trail where it left the flat, and started up, stumbling and slipping on the rocks. Pepé's hand rose up to his head. His hat was gone. He had left it under the oak tree.

The horse had struggled far up the trail when the first change of dawn came into the air, a steel greyness as light mixed thoroughly with dark. Gradually the sharp snaggled edge of the ridge stood out above them, rotten granite tortured and eaten by the winds of time. Pepé had dropped his reins on the horn, leaving direction to the horse. The brush grabbed at his legs in the dark until one knee of his jeans was ripped.

Gradually the light flowed down over the ridge. The starved brush and rocks stood out in the half light, strange and lonely in high perspective.

Then there came warmth into the light. Pepé drew up and looked back, but he could see nothing in the darker valley below. The sky turned blue over the coming sun. In the waste of the mountainside, the poor dry brush grew only three feet high. Here and there, big outcroppings of unrotted granite stood up like mouldering houses. Pepé relaxed a little. He drank from his water bag and bit off a piece of jerky. A single eagle flew over, high in the light.

Without warning Pepé's horse screamed and fell on its side. He was almost down before the rifle crash echoed up from the valley. From a hole behind the struggling shoulder, a stream of bright crimson blood pumped and stopped and pumped and stopped. The hooves threshed on the ground. Pepé lay half stunned beside the horse. He looked slowly down the hill. A piece of sage clipped off beside his head and another crash echoed up from side to side of the canyon. Pepé flung himself frantically behind a bush.

He crawled up the hill on his knees and one hand. His right hand held the rifle up off the ground and pushed it ahead of him. He moved with the instinctive care of an animal. Rapidly he wormed his way toward one of the big outcroppings of granite on the hill above him. Where the brush was high he doubled up and ran, but where the cover was slight he wriggled forward on his stomach, pushing the rifle ahead of him. In the last little distance there was no cover at all. Pepé poised and then he darted across the space and flashed around the corner of the rock.

He leaned panting against the stone. When his breath came easier he moved along behind the big rock until he came to a narrow split that offered a thin section of vision down the hill. Pepé lay on his stomach and pushed the rifle barrel through the slit and waited.

The sun reddened the western ridges now. Already the buzzards were settling down toward the place where the horse lay. A small brown bird scratched in the dead sage leaves directly in front of the rifle muzzle. The coasting eagle flew back toward the rising sun.

Pepé saw a little movement in the brush far below. His grip tightened on the gun. A little brown doe stepped daintily out on the trail and crossed it and disappeared into the brush again. For a long time Pepé waited. Far below he could see the little flat and the oak trees and the slash of green. Suddenly his eyes flashed back at the trail again. A quarter of a mile down there had been a quick movement in the chaparral. The rifle swung over. The front sight nestled in the v of the rear sight. Pepé studied for a moment and then raised the rear sight a notch. The little movement in the brush came again. The sight settled on it. Pepé squeezed the trigger. The explosion crashed down the mountain and up the other side, and came rattling back. The whole side of the slope grew still. No more movement. And then a white streak cut into the granite of the slit and a bullet whined away and a crash sounded up from below. Pepé felt a sharp pain in his right hand.

A sliver of granite was sticking out from between his first and second knuckles and the point protruded from his palm. Carefully he pulled out the sliver of stone. The wound bled evenly and gently. No vein nor artery was cut.

Pepé looked into a little dusty cave in the rock and gathered a handful of spider web, and he pressed the mass into the cut, plastering the soft web into the blood. The flow stopped almost at once.

The rifle was on the ground. Pepé picked it up, levered a new shell into the chamber. And then he slid into the brush on his stomach. Far to the right he crawled, and then up the hill, moving slowly and carefully, crawling to cover and resting and then crawling again.

In the mountains the sun is high in its arc before it penetrates the gorges. The hot face looked over the hill and brought instant heat with it. The white light beat on the rocks and reflected from them and rose up quivering from the earth again, and the rocks and bushes seemed to quiver behind the air.

Pepé crawled in the general direction of the ridge peak, zig-zagging for cover. The deep cut between his knuckles began to throb. He crawled close to a rattlesnake before he saw it, and when it raised its dry head and made a soft beginning whirr, he backed up and took another way. The quick grey lizards flashed in front of him, raising a tiny line of dust. He found another mass of spider web and pressed it against his throbbing hand.

Pepé was pushing the rifle with his left hand now. Little drops of sweat ran to the ends of his coarse black hair and rolled down his cheeks. His lips and tongue were growing thick and heavy. His lips writhed to draw saliva into his mouth. His little dark eyes were uneasy and suspicious. Once when a grey lizard paused in front of him on the parched ground and turned its head sideways he crushed it flat with a stone.

When the sun slid past noon he had not gone a mile. He crawled exhaustedly a last hundred yards to a patch of high sharp manzanita, crawled desperately, and when the patch was reached he wriggled in among the tough gnarly trunks and dropped his head on his left arm. There was little shade in the meager brush, but there was cover and safety. Pepé went to sleep as he lay and the sun beat on his back. A few little birds hopped close to him and peered and hopped away. Pepé squirmed in his sleep and he raised and dropped his wounded hand again and again.

The sun went down behind the peaks and the cool evening came, and then the dark. A coyote yelled from the hillside, Pepé started awake and looked about with misty eyes. His hand was swollen and heavy; a little thread of pain ran up the inside of his arm and settled in a pocket in his armpit. He peered about and then stood up, for the mountains were black and the moon had not yet risen. Pepé stood up in the dark. The coat of his father pressed on his arm. His tongue was swollen until it nearly filled his mouth. He wriggled out of the coat and dropped it in the brush, and then he struggled up the hill, falling over rocks and tearing his way through the brush. The rifle knocked against stones as he went. Little dry avalanches of gravel and shattered stone went whispering down the hill behind him.

After a while the old moon came up and showed the jagged ridge top ahead of him. By moonlight Pepé traveled more easily. He bent forward so that his throbbing arm hung away from his body. The journey uphill was made in dashes and rests, a frantic rush up a few yards and then a rest. The wind coasted down the slope rattling the dry stems of the bushes.

The moon was at meridian when Pepé came at last to the sharp back-bone of the ridge top. On the last hundred yards of the rise no soil had clung under the wearing winds. The way was on solid rock. He clambered to the top and looked down on the other side. There was a draw like the last below him, misty with moonlight, brushed with dry struggling sage and chaparral. On the other side the hill rose up sharply and at the top the jagged rotten teeth of the mountain showed against the sky. At the bottom of the cut the brush was thick and dark.

Pepé stumbled down the hill. His throat was almost closed with thirst. At first he tried to run, but immediately he fell and rolled. After that he went more carefully. The moon was just disappearing behind the mountains when he came to the bottom. He crawled into the heavy brush feeling with his fingers for water. There was no water in the bed of the stream, only damp earth. Pepé laid his gun down and scooped up a handful of mud and put it in his mouth, and then he spluttered and scraped the earth from his tongue with his finger, for the mud drew at his mouth like a poultice. He dug a hole in the stream bed with his fingers, dug a little basin to catch water; but before it was very deep his head fell forward on the damp ground and he slept.

The dawn came and the heat of the day fell on the earth, and still Pepé slept. Late in the afternoon his head jerked up. He looked slowly around. His eyes were slits of wariness. Twenty feet away in the heavy brush a big tawny mountain lion stood looking at him. Its long thick tail waved grace-fully, its ears were erect with interest, not laid back dangerously. The lion squatted down on its stomach and watched him.

Pepé looked at the hole he had dug in the earth. A half inch of muddy water had collected in the bottom. He tore the sleeve from his hurt arm, with his teeth ripped out a little square, soaked it in the water and put it in his mouth. Over and over he filled the cloth and sucked it.

Still the lion sat and watched him. The evening came down but there was no movement on the hills. No birds visited the dry bottom of the cut. Pepé looked occasionally at the lion. The eyes of the yellow beast drooped as though he were about to sleep. He yawned and his long thin red tongue curled out. Suddenly his head jerked around and his nostrils quivered. His big tail lashed. He stood up and slunk like a tawny shadow into the thick brush.

A moment later Pepé heard the sound, the faint far crash of horses' hooves on gravel. And he heard something else, a high whining yelp of a dog.

Pepé took his rifle in his left hand and he glided into the brush almost as quietly as the lion had. In the darkening evening he crouched up the hill toward the next ridge. Only when the dark came did he stand up. His energy was short. Once it was dark he fell over the rocks and slipped to his knees on the steep slope, but he moved on and on up the hill, climbing and scrabbling over the broken hillside.

When he was far up toward the top, he lay down and slept for a little while. The withered moon, shining on his face, awakened him. He stood up and moved up the hill. Fifty yards away he stopped and turned back, for he had forgotten his rifle. He walked heavily down and poked about in the brush, but he could not find his gun. At last he lay down to rest. The pocket of pain in his armpit had grown more sharp. His arm seemed to swell out and fall with every heartbeat. There was no position lying down where the heavy arm did not press against his armpit.

With the effort of a hurt beast, Pepé got up and moved again toward the top of the ridge. He held his swollen arm away from his body with his left hand. Up the steep hill he dragged himself, a few steps and a rest, and a few more steps. At last he was nearing the top. The moon showed the uneven sharp back of it against the sky.

Pepé's brain spun in a big spiral up and away from him. He slumped to the ground and lay still. The rock ridge top was only a hundred feet above him.

The moon moved over the sky. Pepé half turned on his back. His tongue tried to make words, but only a thick hissing came from between his lips.

When the dawn came, Pepé pulled himself up. His eyes were sane again. He drew his great puffed arm in front of him and looked at the angry wound. The black line ran up from his wrist to his armpit. Automatically he reached in his pocket for the big black knife, but it was not there. His eyes searched the ground. He picked up a sharp blade of stone and scraped at the wound, sawed at the proud flesh and then squeezed the green juice out in big drops. Instantly he threw back his head and whined like a dog. His whole right side shuddered at the pain, but the pain cleared his head.

In the grey light he struggled up the last slope to the ridge and crawled over and lay down behind a line of rocks. Below him lay a deep canyon exactly like the last, waterless and desolate. There was no flat, no oak trees, not even heavy brush in the bottom of it. And on the other side a sharp ridge stood up, thinly brushed with starving sage, littered with broken granite. Strewn over the hill there were giant outcroppings, and on the top the granite teeth stood out against the sky.

The new day was light now. The flame of the sun came over the ridge and fell on Pepé where he lay on the ground. His coarse black hair was littered with twigs and bits of spider web. His eyes had retreated back into his head. Between his lips the tip of his black tongue showed.

He sat up and dragged his great arm into his lap and nursed it, rocking his body and moaning in his throat. He threw back his head and looked up into the pale sky. A big black bird circled nearly out of sight, and far to the left another was sailing near.

He lifted his head to listen, for a familiar sound had come to him from the valley he had climbed out of; it was the crying yelp of hounds, excited and feverish, on a trail.

Pepé bowed his head quickly. He tried to speak rapid words but only a thick hiss came from his lips. He drew a shaky cross on his breast with his left hand. It was a long struggle to get to his feet. He crawled slowly and mechanically to the top of a big rock on the ridge peak. Once there, he arose slowly, swaying to his feet, and stood erect. Far below he could see the dark brush where he had slept. He braced his feet and stood there, black against the morning sky.

There came a ripping sound at his feet. A piece of stone flew up and a bullet droned off into the next gorge. The hollow crash echoed up from below. Pepé looked down for a moment and then pulled himself straight again.

His body jarred back. His left hand fluttered helplessly toward his breast. The second crash sounded from below. Pepé swung forward and toppled from the rock. His body struck and rolled over and over, starting a little avalanche. And when at last he stopped against a bush, the avalanche slid slowly down and covered up his head.

Frank O'Connor (1903–1966)

MY OEDIPUS COMPLEX

Father was in the army all through the war—the first war, I mean—so, up to the age of five, I never saw much of him, and what I saw did not worry me. Sometimes I woke and there was a big figure in khaki peering down at me in the candlelight. Sometimes in the early morning I heard the slamming of the front door and the clatter of nailed boots down the cobbles of the lane. These were Father's entrances and exits. Like Santa Claus he came and went mysteriously.

In fact, I rather liked his visits, though it was an uncomfortable squeeze between Mother and him when I got into the big bed in the early morning. He smoked, which gave him a pleasant musty smell, and shaved, an operation of astounding interest. Each time he left a trail of souvenirs—model tanks and Gurkha knives with handles made of bullet cases, and German helmets and cap badges and button-sticks, and all sorts of military equipment—carefully stowed away in a long box on top of the wardrobe, in case they ever came in handy. There was a bit of the magpie about Father; he expected everything to come in handy. When his back was turned, Mother let me get a chair and rummage through his treasures. She didn't seem to think so highly of them as he did.

The war was the most peaceful period of my life. The window of my attic faced southeast. My mother had curtained it, but that had small effect. I always woke with the first light and, with all the responsibilities of the previous day melted, feeling myself rather like the sun, ready to illumine and rejoice. Life never seemed so simple and clear and full of possibilities as then. I put my feet out from under the clothes—I called them Mrs. Left and Mrs. Right—and invented dramatic situations for them in which they discussed the problems of the day. At least Mrs. Right did; she was very demonstrative, but I hadn't the same control of Mrs. Left, so she mostly contented herself with nodding agreement.

They discussed what Mother and I should do during the day, what

Source: Reprinted from *The Stories of Frank O'Connor* with the permission of Alfred A. Knopf, Inc., New York, and A. D. Peters & Company, London.

Santa Claus should give a fellow for Christmas, and what steps should be taken to brighten the home. There was that little matter of the baby, for instance. Mother and I could never agree about that. Ours was the only house in the terrace without a new baby, and Mother said we couldn't afford one till Father came back from the war because they cost seventeen and six. That showed how simple she was. The Geneys up the road had a baby, and everyone knew they couldn't afford seventeen and six. It was probably a cheap baby, and Mother wanted something really good, but I felt she was too exclusive. The Geney's baby would have done us fine.

Having settled my plans for the day, I got up, put a chair under the attic window, and lifted the frame high enough to stick out my head. The window overlooked the front gardens of the terrace behind ours, and beyond these it looked over a deep valley to the tall, red-brick houses terraced up the opposite hillside, which were all still in shadow, while those at our side of the valley were all lit up, though with long strange shadows that made them seem unfamiliar; rigid and painted.

After that I went into Mother's room and climbed into the big bed. She woke and I began to tell her of my schemes. By this time, though I never seem to have noticed it, I was petrified in my nightshirt, and I thawed as I talked until, the last frost melted, I fell asleep beside her and woke again only when I heard her below in the kitchen, making the breakfast.

After breakfast we went into town; heard Mass at St. Augustine's and said a prayer for Father, and did the shopping. If the afternoon was fine we either went for a walk in the country or a visit to Mother's great friend in the convent, Mother St. Dominic. Mother had them all praying for Father, and every night, going to bed, I asked God to send him back safe from the war to us. Little, indeed, did I know what I was praying for!

One morning, I got into the big bed, and there, sure enough, was Father in his usual Santa Claus manner, but later, instead of uniform, he put on his best blue suit, and Mother was as pleased as anything. I saw nothing to be pleased about, because, out of uniform, Father was altogether less interesting, but she only beamed, and explained that our prayers had been answered, and off we went to Mass to thank God for having brought Father safely home.

The irony of it! That very day when he came in to dinner he took off his boots and put on his slippers, donned the dirty old cap he wore about the house to save him from colds, crossed his legs, and began to talk gravely to Mother, who looked anxious. Naturally, I disliked her looking anxious, because it destroyed her good looks, so I interrupted him.

"Just a moment, Larry!" she said gently.

This was only what she said when we had boring visitors, so I attached no importance to it and went on talking.

"Do be quiet, Larry!" she said impatiently. "Don't you hear me talking to Daddy?"

This was the first time I had heard those ominous words, "talking to Daddy," and I couldn't help feeling that if this was how God answered prayers, he couldn't listen to them very attentively.

"Why are you talking to Daddy?" I asked with as great a show of indifference as I could muster.

"Because Daddy and I have business to discuss. Now, don't interrupt again!"

In the afternoon, at Mother's request, Father took me for a walk. This time we went into town instead of out the country, and I thought at first, in my usual optimistic way, that it might be an improvement. It was nothing of the sort. Father and I had quite different notions of a walk in town. He had no proper interest in trams, ships, and horses, and the only thing that seemed to divert him was talking to fellows as old as himself. When I wanted to stop he simply went on, dragging me behind him by the hand; when he wanted to stop I had no alternative but to do the same. I noticed that it seemed to be a sign that he wanted to stop for a long time whenever he leaned against a wall. The second time I saw him do it I got wild. He seemed to be settling himself forever. I pulled him by the coat and trousers, but, unlike Mother who, if you were too persistent, got into a wax and said: "Larry, if you don't behave yourself, I'll give you a good slap," Father had an extraordinary capacity for amiable inattention. I sized him up and wondered would I cry, but he seemed to be too remote to be annoyed even by that. Really, it was like going for a walk with a mountain! He either ignored the wrenching and pummeling entirely, or else glanced down with a grin of amusement from his peak. I had never met anyone so absorbed in himself as he seemed.

At teatime, "talking to Daddy" began again, complicated this time by the fact that he had an evening paper, and every few minutes he put it down and told Mother something new out of it. I felt this was foul play. Man for man, I was prepared to compete with him any time for Mother's attention, but when he had it all made up for him by other people it left me no chance. Several times I tried to change the subject without success.

"You must be quiet while Daddy is reading, Larry," Mother said impatiently.

It was clear that she either genuinely liked talking to Father better than talking to me, or else that he had some terrible hold on her which made her afraid to admit the truth.

"Mummy," I said that night when she was tucking me up, "do you think if I prayed hard God would send Daddy back to the war?"

She seemed to think about that for a moment.

"No dear," she said with a smile. "I don't think he would."

"Why wouldn't he, Mummy?"

"Because there isn't a war any longer, dear."

"But, Mummy, couldn't God make another war, if He liked?"

"He wouldn't like to, dear. It's not God who makes wars, but bad people."

"Oh!" I said.

I was disappointed about that. I began to think that God wasn't quite what he was cracked up to be.

Next morning I woke at my usual hour, feeling like a bottle of champagne. I put out my feet and invented a long conversation in which Mrs. Right talked of the trouble she had with her own father till she put him in the Home. I didn't quite know what the Home was but it sounded the right place for Father. Then I got my chair and stuck my head out of the attic window. Dawn was just breaking, with a guilty air that made me feel I had caught it in the act. My head bursting with stories and schemes, I stumbled in next door, and in the half-darkness scrambled into the big bed. There was no room at Mother's side so I had to get between her and Father. For the time being I had forgotten about him, and for several minutes I sat bolt upright, racking my brains to know what I could do with him. He was taking up more than his fair share of the bed, and I couldn't get comfortable, so I gave him several kicks that made him grunt and stretch. He made room all right, though. Mother waked and felt for me. I settled back comfortably in the warmth of the bed with my thumb in my mouth.

"Mummy!" I hummed, loudly and contentedly.

"Sssh! dear," she whispered. "Don't wake Daddy!"

This was a new development, which threatened to be even more serious than "talking to Daddy." Life without my early-morning conferences was unthinkable.

"Why?" I asked severely.

"Because poor Daddy is tired."

This seemed to me a quite inadequate reason, and I was sickened by the sentimentality of her "poor Daddy." I never liked that sort of gush; it always struck me as insincere.

"Oh!" I said lightly. Then in my most winning tone: "Do you know where I want to go with you today, Mummy?"

"No, dear," she sighed.

"I want to go down the Glen and fish for thornybacks with my new net, and then I want to go out to the Fox and Hounds, and—"

"Don't-wake-Daddy!" she hissed angrily, clapping her hand across my mouth.

But it was too late. He was awake, or nearly so. He grunted and reached for the matches. Then he stared incredulously at his watch.

"Like a cup of tea, dear?" asked Mother in a meek, hushed voice I had never heard her use before. It sounded almost as though she were afraid.

"Tea?" he exclaimed indignantly. "Do you know what the time is?"

"And after that I want to go up the Rathcooney Road," I said loudly, afraid I'd forget something in all those interruptions.

"Go to sleep at once, Larry!" she said sharply.

I began to snivel. I couldn't concentrate, the way that pair went on, and smothering my early-morning schemes was like burying a family from the cradle.

Father said nothing, but lit his pipe and sucked it, looking out into the shadows without minding Mother or me. I knew he was mad. Every time I made a remark Mother hushed me irritably. I was mortified. I felt it wasn't fair; there was even something sinister in it. Every time I had pointed out to her the waste of making two beds when we could both sleep in one, she had told me it was healthier like that, and now here was this man, this stranger, sleeping with her without the least regard for her health!

He got up early and made tea, but though he brought Mother a cup he brought none for me.

"Mummy," I shouted, "I want a cup of tea, too."

"Yes, dear," she said patiently. "You can drink from Mummy's saucer."

That settled it. Either Father or I would have to leave the house. I didn't want to drink from Mother's saucer; I wanted to be treated as an equal in my own home, so, just to spite her, I drank it all and left none for her. She took that quietly, too.

But that night when she was putting me to bed she said gently:

"Larry, I want you to promise me something."

"What is it?" I asked.

"Not to come in and disturb poor Daddy in the morning. Promise?"

"Poor Daddy" again! I was becoming suspicious of everything involving that quite impossible man.

"Why?" I asked.

"Because poor Daddy is worried and tired and he doesn't sleep well."

"Why doesn't he, Mummy?"

"Well, you know, don't you, that while he was at the war Mummy got the pennies from the Post Office?"

"From Miss MacCarthy?"

"That's right. But now, you see, Miss MacCarthy hasn't any more pennies, so Daddy must go out and find us some. You know what would happen if he couldn't?"

"No," I said, "tell us."

"Well, I think we might have to go out and beg for them like the poor old woman on Fridays. We wouldn't like that, would we?"

"No," I agreed. "We wouldn't."

"So you'll promise not to come in and wake him?"

"Promise."

Mind you, I meant that. I knew pennies were a serious matter, and I was all against having to go out and beg like the old woman on Fridays. Mother laid out all my toys in a complete ring round the bed so that, whatever way I got out, I was bound to fall over one of them.

When I woke I remembered my promise all right. I got up and sat on the floor and played—for hours, it seemed to me. Then I got my chair and looked out the attic window for more hours. I wished it was time for Father to wake; I wished someone would make me a cup of tea. I didn't feel in the least like the sun; instead, I was bored and so very, very cold! I simply longed for the warmth and depth of the big featherbed.

At last I could stand it no longer. I went into the next room. As there was still no room at Mother's side I climbed over her and she woke with a start.

"Larry," she whispered, gripping my arm very tightly, "what did you promise?"

"But I did, Mummy," I wailed, caught in the very act. "I was quiet for ever so long."

"Oh, dear, and you're perished!" she said sadly, feeling me all over. "Now, if I let you stay will you promise not to talk?"

"But I want to talk, Mummy," I wailed.

"That has nothing to do with it," she said with a firmness that was new to me. "Daddy wants to sleep. Now, do you understand that?"

I understood it only too well. I wanted to talk, he wanted to sleep— whose house was it, anyway?

"Mummy," I said with equal firmness, "I think it would be healthier for Daddy to sleep in his own bed."

That seemed to stagger her, because she said nothing for a while.

"Now, once for all," she went on, "you're to be perfectly quiet or go back to your own bed. Which is it to be?"

The injustice of it got me down. I had convicted her out of her own mouth of inconsistency and unreasonableness, and she hadn't even attempted to reply. Full of spite, I gave Father a kick, which she didn't notice but which made him grunt and open his eyes in alarm.

"What time is it?" he asked in a panic-stricken voice, not looking at Mother but at the door, as if he saw someone there.

"It's early yet," she replied soothingly. "It's only the child. Go to sleep again. . . . Now, Larry," she added, getting out of bed, "you've wakened Daddy and you must go back."

This time, for all her quiet air, I knew she meant it, and knew that my principal rights and privileges were as good as lost unless I asserted them at once. As she lifted me, I gave a screech, enough to wake the dead, not to mind Father. He groaned.

"That damn child! Doesn't he ever sleep?"

"It's only a habit, dear," she said quietly, though I could see she was vexed.

"Well, it's time he got out of it," shouted Father, beginning to heave in the bed. He suddenly gathered all the bedclothes about him, turned to the wall, and then looked back over his shoulder with nothing showing only two small, spiteful, dark eyes. The man looked very wicked.

To open the bedroom door, Mother had to let me down, and I broke free and dashed for the farthest corner, screeching. Father sat bolt upright in bed.

"Shut up, you little puppy!" he said in a choking voice.

I was so astonished that I stopped screeching. Never, never had anyone spoken to me in that tone before. I looked at him incredulously and saw his face convulsed with rage. It was only then that I fully realized how God had coddled me, listening to my prayers for the safe return of this monster.

"Shut up, you!" I bawled, beside myself.

"What's that you said?" shouted Father, making a wild leap out of the bed.

"Mick, Mick!" cried Mother. "Don't you see the child isn't used to you?"

"I see he's better fed than taught," snarled Father, waving his arms wildly. "He wants his bottom smacked."

All his previous shouting was as nothing to these obscene words referring to my person. They really made my blood boil.

"Smack your own!" I screamed hysterically. "Smack your own! Shut up! Shut up!"

At this he lost his patience and let fly at me. He did it with the lack of conviction you'd expect of a man under Mother's horrified eyes, and it ended up as a mere tap, but the sheer indignity of being struck at all by a stranger, a total stranger who had cajoled his way back from the war into our big bed as a result of my innocent intercession, made me completely dotty. I shrieked and shrieked, and danced in my bare feet, and Father, looking awkward and hairy in nothing but a short grey army shirt, glared down at me like a mountain out for murder. I think it must have been then that I realized he was jealous too. And there stood Mother in her nightdress, looking as if her heart was broken between us. I hoped she felt as she looked. It seemed to me that she deserved it all.

From that morning out my life was a hell. Father and I were enemies, open and avowed. We conducted a series of skirmishes against one another, he trying to steal my time with Mother and I his. When she was sitting on my bed, telling me a story, he took to looking for some pair of old boots which he alleged he had left behind him at the beginning of the war. While he talked to Mother I played loudly with my toys to show my total lack of concern. He created a terrible scene one evening when he came in from work and found me at his box, playing with his regimental badges,

Gurkha knives and botton-sticks. Mother got up and took the box from me.

"You mustn't play with Daddy's toys unless he lets you, Larry," she said severely. "Daddy doesn't play with yours."

For some reason Father looked at her as if she had struck him and then turned away with a scowl.

"Those are not toys," he growled, taking down the box again to see had I lifted anything. "Some of those curios are very rare and valuable."

But as time went on I saw more and more how he managed to alienate Mother and me. What made it worse was that I couldn't grasp his method or see what attraction he had for Mother. In every possible way he was less winning than I. He had a common accent and made noises at his tea. I thought for a while that it might be the newspapers she was interested in, so I made up bits of news of my own to read to her. Then I thought it might be the smoking, which I personally thought attractive, and took his pipes and went round the house dribbling into them till he caught me. I even made noises at my tea, but Mother only told me I was disgusting. It all seemed to hinge round that unhealthy habit of sleeping together, so I made a point of dropping into their bedroom and nosing round, talking to myself, so that they wouldn't know I was watching them, but they were never up to anything that I could see. In the end it beat me. It seemed to depend on being grown-up and giving people rings, and I realized I'd have to wait.

But at the same time I wanted him to see that I was only waiting, not giving up the fight. One evening when he was being particularly obnoxious, chattering away well above my head, I let him have it.

"Mummy," I said, "do you know what I'm going to do when I grow up?"

"No, dear," she replied. "What?"

"I'm going to marry you," I said quietly.

Father gave a great guffaw out of him, but he didn't take me in. I knew it must only be pretence. And Mother, in spite of everything, was pleased. I felt she was probably relieved to know that one day Father's hold on her would be broken.

"Won't that be nice?" she said with a smile.

"It'll be very nice," I said confidently. "Because we're going to have lots and lots of babies."

"That's right, dear," she said placidly. "I think we'll have one soon, and then you'll have plenty of company."

I was no end pleased about that because it showed that in spite of the way she gave in to Father she still considered my wishes. Besides, it would put the Geneys in their place.

It didn't turn out like that, though. To begin with, she was very preoccupied—I supposed about where she would get the seventeen and six—

and though Father took to staying out late in the evenings it did me no particular good. She stopped taking me for walks, became as touchy as blazes, and smacked me for nothing at all. Sometimes I wished I'd never mentioned the confounded baby—I seemed to have a genius for bringing calamity on myself.

And calamity it was! Sonny arrived in the most appalling hullabaloo— even that much he couldn't do without a fuss—and from the first moment I disliked him. He was a difficult child—so far as I was concerned he was always difficult—and demanded far too much attention. Mother was simply silly about him, and couldn't see when he was only showing off. As company he was worse than useless. He slept all day, and I had to go round the house on tiptoe to avoid waking him. It wasn't any longer a question of not waking Father. The slogan now was "Don't-wake-Sonny!" I couldn't understand why the child wouldn't sleep at the proper time, so whenever Mother's back was turned I woke him. Sometimes to keep him awake I pinched him as well. Mother caught me at it one day and gave me a most unmerciful flaking.

One evening, when Father was coming in from work, I was playing trains in the front garden. I let on not to notice him; instead, I pretended to be talking to myself, and said in a loud voice: "If another bloody baby comes into this house, I'm going out."

Father stopped dead and looked at me over his shoulder.

"What's that you said?" he asked sternly.

"I was only talking to myself," I replied, trying to conceal my panic. "It's private."

He turned and went in without a word. Mind you, I intended it as a solemn warning, but its effect was quite different. Father started being quite nice to me. I could understand that, of course. Mother was quite sickening about Sonny. Even at mealtimes she'd get up and gawk at him in the cradle with an idiotic smile, and tell Father to do the same. He was always polite about it, but he looked so puzzled you could see he didn't know what she was talking about. He complained of the way Sonny cried at night, but she only got cross and said that Sonny never cried except when there was something up with him—which was a flaming lie, because Sonny never had anything up with him, and only cried for attention. It was really painful to see how simple-minded she was. Father wasn't attractive, but he had a fine intelligence. He saw through Sonny, and now he knew that I saw through him as well.

One night I woke with a start. There was someone beside me in the bed. For one wild moment I felt sure it must be Mother, having come to her senses and left Father for good, but then I heard Sonny in convulsions in the next room, and Mother saying: "There! There! There!" and I knew it wasn't she. It was Father. He was lying beside me, wide awake, breathing hard and apparently as mad as hell.

After a while it came to me what he was mad about. It was his turn now. After turning me out of the big bed, he had been turned out himself. Mother had no consideration now for anyone but that poisonous pup, Sonny. I couldn't help feeling sorry for Father. I had been through it all myself, and even at that age I was magnanimous. I began to stroke him down and say: "There! There!" He wasn't exactly responsive.

"Aren't you asleep either?" he snarled.

"Ah, come on and put your arm around us, can't you?" I said, and he did, in a sort of way. Gingerly, I suppose, is how you'd describe it. He was very bony but better than nothing.

At Christmas he went out of his way to buy me a really nice model railway.

Lionel Trilling (b. 1905)

OF THIS TIME, OF THAT PLACE

I

It was a fine September day. By noon it would be summer again, but now it was true autumn with a touch of chill in the air. As Joseph Howe stood on the porch of the house in which he lodged, ready to leave for his first class of the year, he thought with pleasure of the long indoor days that were coming. It was a moment when he could feel glad of his profession.

On the lawn the peach tree was still in fruit and young Hilda Aiken was taking a picture of it. She held the camera tight against her chest. She wanted the sun behind her, but she did not want her own long morning shadow in the foreground. She raised the camera, but that did not help, and she lowered it, but that made things worse. She twisted her body to the left, then to the right. In the end she had to step out of the direct line of the sun. At last she snapped the shutter and wound the film with intense care.

Howe, watching her from the porch, waited for her to finish and called good morning. She turned, startled, and almost sullenly lowered her glance. In the year Howe had lived at the Aikens', Hilda had accepted him as one of her family, but since his absence of the summer she had grown shy. Then suddenly she lifted her head and smiled at him, and the humorous smile confirmed his pleasure in the day. She picked up her book-bag and set off for school.

The handsome houses on the streets to the college were not yet fully awake, but they looked very friendly. Howe went by the Bradby house where he would be a guest this evening at the first dinner party of the year. When he had gone the length of the picket fence, the whitest in town, he turned back. Along the path there was a fine row of asters and he went through the gate and picked one for his buttonhole. The Bradbys would be pleased if they happened to see him invading their lawn and the knowledge of this made him even more comfortable.

He reached the campus as the hour was striking. The students were hurrying to their classes. He himself was in no hurry. He stopped at his

Source: Copyright ©1943 by Lionel Trilling. Reprinted with the permission of The Viking Press, Inc.

dim cubicle of an office and lit a cigarette. The prospect of facing his class had suddenly presented itself to him and his hands were cold; the lawful seizure of power he was about to make seemed momentous. Waiting did not help. He put out his cigarette, picked up a pad of theme paper, and went to his classroom.

As he entered, the rattle of voices ceased, and the twenty-odd freshmen settled themselves and looked at him appraisingly. Their faces seemed gross, his heart sank at their massed impassivity, but he spoke briskly.

"My name is Howe," he said, and turned and wrote it on the blackboard. The carelessness of the scrawl confirmed his authority. He went on, "My office is 412 Slemp Hall, and my office-hours are Monday, Wednesday and Friday from eleven-thirty to twelve-thirty."

He wrote, "M., W., F., 11:30-12:30." He said, "I'll be glad to see any of you at that time. Or if you can't come then, you can arrange with me for some other time."

He turned again to the blackboard and spoke over his shoulder. "The text for the course is Jarman's *Modern Plays,* revised edition. The Co-op has it in stock." He wrote the name, underlined "revised edition" and waited for it to be taken down in the new notebooks.

When the bent heads were raised again he began his speech of prospectus. "It is hard to explain—" he said, and paused as they composed themselves. "It is hard to explain what a course like this is intended to do. We are going to try to learn something about modern literature and something about prose composition."

As he spoke, his hands warmed and he was able to look directly at the class. Last year on the first day the faces seemed just as cloddish, but as the term wore on they became gradually alive and quite likable. It did not seem possible that the same thing could happen again.

"I shall not lecture in this course," he continued. "Our work will be carried on by discussion and we will try to learn by an exchange of opinion. But you will soon recognize that my opinion is worth more than anyone else's here."

He remained grave as he said it, but two boys understood and laughed. The rest took permission from them and laughed too. All Howe's private ironies protested the vulgarity of the joke, but the laughter made him feel benign and powerful.

When the little speech was finished, Howe picked up the pad of paper he had brought. He announced that they would write an extemporaneous theme. Its subject was traditional, "Who I am and why I came to Dwight College." By now the class was more at ease and it gave a ritualistic groan of protest. Then there was a stir as fountain pens were brought out and the writing-arms of the chairs were cleared, and the paper was passed about. At last, all the heads bent to work, and the room became still.

Howe sat idly at his desk. The sun shone through the tall clumsy windows. The cool of the morning was already passing. There was a scent of autumn and of varnish and the stillness of the room was deep and oddly touching. Now and then a student's head was raised and scratched in the old, elaborate students' pantomine that calls the teacher to witness honest intellectual effort.

Suddenly a tall boy stood within the frame of the open door. "Is this," he said, and thrust a large nose into a college catalogue, "is this the meeting place of English 1A? The section instructed by Dr. Joseph Howe?"

He stood on the very sill of the door, as if refusing to enter until he was perfectly sure of all his rights. The class looked up from work, found him absurd and gave a low mocking cheer.

The teacher and the new student, with equal pointedness, ignored the disturbance. Howe nodded to the boy, who pushed his head forward and then jerked it back in a wide elaborate arc to clear his brow of a heavy lock of hair. He advanced into the room and halted before Howe, almost at attention. In a loud, clear voice he announced, "I am Tertan, Ferdinand R., reporting at the direction of Head of Department Vincent."

The heraldic formality of this statement brought forth another cheer. Howe looked at the class with a sternness he could not really feel, for there was indeed something ridiculous about this boy. Under his displeased regard the rows of heads dropped to work again. Then he touched Tertan's elbow, led him up to the desk and stood so as to shield their conversation from the class.

"We are writing an extemporaneous theme," he said. "The subject is, 'Who I am and why I came to Dwight College.'"

He stripped a few sheets from the pad and offered them to the boy. Tertan hesitated and then took the paper, but he held it only tentatively. As if with the effort of making something clear, he gulped, and a slow smile fixed itself on his face. It was at once knowing and shy.

"Professor," he said, "to be perfectly fair to my classmates"—he made a large gesture over the room—"and to you"—he inclined his head to Howe—"this would not be for me an extemporaneous subject."

Howe tried to understand. "You mean you've already thought about it —you've heard we always give the same subject? That doesn't matter."

Again the boy ducked his head and gulped. It was the gesture of one who wishes to make a difficult explanation with perfect candor. "Sir," he said, and made the distinction with great care, "the topic I did not expect, but I have given much ratiocination to the subject."

Howe smiled and said, "I don't think that's an unfair advantage. Just go ahead and write."

Tertan narrowed his eyes and glanced sidewise at Howe. His strange mouth smiled. Then in quizzical acceptance, he ducked his head, threw back the heavy, dank lock, dropped into a seat with a great loose noise and began to write rapidly.

The room fell silent again and Howe resumed his idleness. When the bell rang, the students who had groaned when the task had been set now groaned again because they had not finished. Howe took up the papers and held the class while he made the first assignment. When he dismissed it, Tertan bore down on him, his slack mouth held ready for speech.

"Some professors," he said, "are pedants. They are Dryasdusts. However, some professors are free souls and creative spirits. Kant, Hegel and Nietzsche were all professors." With this pronouncement he paused. "It is my opinion," he continued, "that you occupy the second category."

Howe looked at the boy in surprise and said with good-natured irony, "With Kant, Hegel and Nietzsche?"

Not only Tertan's hand and head but his whole awkward body waved away the stupidity. "It is the kind and not the quantity of the kind," he said sternly.

Rebuked, Howe said as simply and seriously as he could, "It would be nice to think so." He added, "Of course I am not a professor."

This was clearly a disappointment but Tertan met it. "In the French sense," he said with composure. "Generically, a teacher."

Suddenly he bowed. It was such a bow, Howe fancied, as a stage-director might teach an actor playing a medieval student who takes leave of Abelard—stiff, solemn, with elbows close to the body and feet together. Then, quite as suddenly, he turned and left.

A queer fish, and as soon as Howe reached his office, he sifted through the batch of themes and drew out Tertan's. The boy had filled many sheets with his unformed headlong scrawl. "Who am I?" he had begun. "Here, in a mundane, not to say commercialized academe, is asked the question which from time long immemorially out of mind has accreted doubts and thoughts in the psyche of man to pester him as a nuisance. Whether in St. Augustine (or Austin as sometimes called) or Miss Bashkirtsieff or Frederic Amiel or Empedocles, or in less lights of the intellect than these, this posed question has been ineluctable."

Howe took out his pencil. He circled "academe" and wrote "vocab." in the margin. He underlined "time long immemorially out of mind" and wrote "Diction!" But this seemed inadequate for what was wrong. He put down his pencil and read ahead to discover the principle of error in the theme. "Today as ever, in spite of gloomy prophets of the dismal science (economics) the question is uninvalidated. Out of the starry depths of heaven hurtles this spear of query demanding to be caught on the shield of the mind ere it pierces the skull and the limbs be unstrung."

Baffled but quite caught, Howe read on. "Materialism, by which is meant the philosophic concept and not the moral idea, provides no aegis against the question which lies beyond the tangible (metaphysics). Existence without alloy is the question presented. Environment and heredity relegated aside, the rags and old clothes of practical life discarded, the name and the instrumentality of livelihood do not, as the prophets of the dismal science insist on in this connection, give solution to the interrogation which not from the professor merely but veritably from the cosmos is given. I think, therefore I am (cogito etc.) but who am I? Tertan I am, but what is Tertan? Of this time, of that place, of some parentage, what does it matter?"

Existence without alloy: the phrase established itself. Howe put aside Tertan's paper and at random picked up another. "I am Arthur J. Casebeer, Jr.," he read. "My father is Arthur J. Casebeer and my grandfather was Arthur J. Casebeer before him. My mother is Nina Wimble Casebeer. Both of them are college graduates and my father is in insurance. I was born in St. Louis eighteen years ago and we still make our residence there."

Arthur J. Casebeer, who knew who he was, was less interesting than Tertan, but more coherent. Howe picked up Tertan's paper again. It was clear that none of the routine marginal comments, no "sent. str." or "punct." or "vocab." could cope with this torrential rhetoric. He read ahead, contenting himself with underscoring the errors against the time when he should have the necessary "conference" with Tertan.

It was a busy and official day of cards and sheets, arrangements and small decisions, and it gave Howe pleasure. Even when it was time to attend the first of the weekly Convocations he felt the charm of the beginning of things when intention is still innocent and uncorrupted by effort. He sat among the young instructors on the platform, and joined in their humorous complaints at having to assist at the ceremony, but actually he got a clear satisfaction from the ritual of prayer and prosy speech, and even from wearing his academic gown. And when the Convocation was over the pleasure continued as he crossed the campus, exchanging greetings with men he had not seen since the spring. They were people who did not yet, and perhaps never would, mean much to him, but in a year they had grown amiably to be part of his life. They were his fellow-townsmen.

The day had cooled again at sunset, and there was a bright chill in the September twilight. Howe carried his voluminous gown over his arm, he swung his doctoral hood by its purple neckpiece, and on his head he wore his mortarboard with its heavy gold tassel bobbing just over his eye. These were the weighty and absurd symbols of his new profession and they pleased him. At twenty-six Joseph Howe had discovered that he was neither so well off nor so bohemian as he had once thought. A small income, adequate when supplemented by a sizable cash legacy, was genteel poverty when the cash was all spent. And the literary life—the room at the Lafayette, or the small apartment without a lease, the long summers on the Cape, the long afternoons and the social evenings—began to weary him. His writing filled his mornings and should perhaps have filled his life, yet it did not. To the amusement of his friends, and with a certain sense that he was betraying his own freedom, he had used the last of his legacy for a year at Harvard. The small but respectable reputation of his two volumes of verse had proved useful—he continued at Harvard on a fellowship and when he emerged as Doctor Howe he received an excellent appointment, with prospects, at Dwight.

He had his moments of fear when all that had ever been said of the dangers of the academic life had occurred to him. But after a year in which he had tested every possibility of corruption and seduction he was ready to rest easy. His third volume of verse, most of it written in his first years of teaching, was not only ampler but, he thought, better than its predecessors.

There was a clear hour before the Bradby dinner party and Howe looked forward to it. But he was not to enjoy it, for lying with his mail on the hall table was a copy of this quarter's issue of *Life and Letters,* to which his landlord subscribed. Its severe cover announced that its editor, Frederic Woolley, had this month contributed an essay called "Two Poets," and Howe, picking it up, curious to see who the two poets might be, felt his own name start out at him with cabalistic power—Joseph Howe. As he continued to turn the pages his hand trembled.

Standing in the dark hall, holding the neat little magazine, Howe knew that his literary contempt for Frederic Woolley meant nothing, for he suddenly understood how he respected Woolley in the way of the world. He knew this by the trembling of his hand. And of the little world as well as the great, for although the literary groups of New York might dismiss Woolley, his name carried high authority in the academic world. At Dwight it was even a revered name, for it had been here at the college that Frederic Woolley had made the distinguished scholarly career from which he had gone on to literary journalism. In middle life he had been induced to take the editorship of *Life and Letters,* a literary monthly not widely read but heavily endowed, and in its pages he had carried on the defense of what he sometimes called the older values. He was not without wit, he had great knowledge and considerable taste, and even in the full movement of the "new" literature he had won a certain respect for his refusal to accept it. In France, even in England, he would have been connected with a more robust tradition of conservatism, but America gave him an audience not much better than genteel. It was known in the college that to the subsidy of *Life and Letters* the Bradbys contributed a great part.

As Howe read, he saw that he was involved in nothing less than an event. When the Fifth Series of *Studies in Order and Value* came to be collected, this latest of Frederic Woolley's essays would not be merely another step in the old direction. Clearly and unmistakably, it was a turning point. All his literary life Woolley had been concerned with the relation of literature to morality, religion, and the private and delicate pieties, and he had been unalterably opposed to all that he had called "inhuman humanitarianism." But here, suddenly, dramatically late, he had made an about-face, turning to the public life and to the humanitarian politics he had so long despised. This was the kind of incident the histories of literature make much of. Frederic Woolley was opening for himself a new career and winning a kind of new youth. He contrasted the two poets, Thomas Wormser, who was admirable, Joseph Howe, who was almost dangerous. He spoke of the "precious subjectivism" of Howe's verse. "In times like ours," he wrote, "with millions facing penury and want, one feels that the qualities of the *tour d'ivoire* are well-nigh inhuman, nearly insulting. The *tour d'ivoire* becomes the *tour d'ivresse*, and it is not self-intoxicated poets that our people need." The essay said more: "The problem is one of meaning. I am not ignorant that the creed of the esoteric poets declares that a poem does not and should not *mean* anything, that it *is* something. But poetry is what the poet makes it, and if he is a true poet he makes what his society needs. And what is needed now is the tradition in which Mr. Wormser writes, the true tradition of poetry. The Howes do no harm, but they do no good when positive good is demanded of all responsible men. Or do the Howes indeed do no harm? Perhaps Plato would have said they do, that in some ways theirs is the Phrygian music that turns men's minds from the struggle. Certainly it is true that Thomas Wormser writes in the lucid Dorian mode which sends men into battle with evil."

It was easy to understand why Woolley had chosen to praise Thomas Wormser. The long, lilting lines of *Corn Under Willows* hymned, as Woolley put it, the struggle for wheat in the Iowa fields, and expressed the real lives of real people. But why out of the dozen more notable examples he had chosen Howe's little volume as the example of "precious subjectivism" was hard to guess. In a way it was funny, this multiplication of himself into "the Howes." And yet this becoming the multiform political symbol by whose creation Frederic Woolley gave the sign of a sudden new life, this use of him as a sacrifice whose blood was necessary for the rites of rejuvenation, made him feel oddly unclean.

Nor could Howe get rid of a certain practical resentment. As a poet he had a special and respectable place in the college life. But it might be another thing to be marked as the poet of a wilful and selfish obscurity.

As he walked to the Bradbys', Howe was a little tense and defensive. It seemed to him that all the world knew of the "attack" and agreed with it. And, indeed, the Bradbys had read the essay but Professor Bradby, a kind and pretentious man, said, "I see my old friend knocked you about a bit, my boy," and his wife Eugenia looked at Howe with her childlike blue eyes and said, "I shall *scold* Frederic for the untrue things he wrote about you. You aren't the least obscure." They beamed at him. In their genial snobbery they seemed to feel that he had distinguished himself. He was the leader of Howeism. He enjoyed the dinner party as much as he had thought he would.

And in the following days, as he was more preoccupied with his duties the incident was forgotten. His classes had ceased to be mere groups. Student after student detached himself from the mass and required or claimed a place in Howe's awareness. Of them all it was Tertan who first and most violently signaled his separate existence. A week after classes had begun Howe saw his silhouette on the frosted glass of his office door. It was motionless for a long time, perhaps stopped by the problem of whether or not to knock before entering. Howe called, "Come in!" and Tertan entered with his shambling stride.

He stood beside the desk, silent and at attention. When Howe asked him to sit down, he responded with a gesture of head and hand, as if to say that amenities were beside the point. Nevertheless, he did take the chair. He put his ragged, crammed briefcase between his legs. His face, which Howe now observed fully for the first time, was confusing, for it was made up of florid curves, the nose arched in the bone and voluted in the nostril, the mouth loose and soft and rather moist. Yet the face was so thin and narrow as to seem the very type of asceticism. Lashes of unusual length veiled the eyes and, indeed, it seemed as if there was a veil over the countenance. Before the words actually came, the face screwed itself into an attitude of preparation for them.

"You can confer with me now?" Tertan said.

"Yes, I'd be glad to. There are several things in your two themes I want to talk to you about." Howe reached for the packet of themes on his desk and sought for Tertan's. But the boy was waving them away.

"These are done perforce," he said. "Under the pressure of your requirement. They are not significant; mere duties." Again his great hand flapped vaguely to dismiss his themes. He leaned forward and gazed at his teacher.

"You are," he said, "a man of letters? You are a poet?" It was more declaration than question.

"I should like to think so," Howe said.

At first Tertan accepted the answer with a show of appreciation, as though the understatement made a secret between himself and Howe. Then he chose to misunderstand. With his shrewd and disconcerting control of expression, he presented to Howe a puzzled grimace. "What does that mean?" he said.

Howe retracted the irony. "Yes, I am a poet." It sounded strange to say.

"That," Tertan said, "is a wonder." He corrected himself with his ducking head. "I mean that is wonderful."

Suddenly, he dived at the miserable briefcase between his legs, put it on his knees, and began to fumble with the catch, all intent on the difficulty it presented. Howe noted that his suit was worn thin, his shirt almost unclean. He became aware, even, of a vague and musty odor of garments worn too long in unaired rooms. Tertan conquered the lock and began to concentrate upon a search into the interior. At last he held in his hand what he was after, a torn and crumpled copy of *Life and Letters.*

"I learned it from here," he said, holding it out.

Howe looked at him sharply, his hackles a little up. But the boy's face was not only perfectly innocent, it even shone with a conscious admiration. Apparently nothing of the import of the essay had touched him except the wonderful fact that his teacher was a "man of letters." Yet this seemed too stupid, and Howe, to test it, said, "The man who wrote that doesn't think it's wonderful."

Tertan made a moist hissing sound as he cleared his mouth of saliva. His head, oddly loose on his neck, wove a pattern of contempt in the air. "A critic," he said, "who admits *prima facie* that he does not understand." Then he said grandly, "It is the inevitable fate."

It was absurd, yet Howe was not only aware of the absurdity but of a tension suddenly and wonderfully relaxed. Now that the "attack" was on the table between himself and this strange boy, and subject to the boy's funny and absolutely certain contempt, the hidden force of his feeling was revealed to him in the very moment that it vanished. All unsuspected, there had been a film over the world, a transparent but discoloring haze of danger. But he had no time to stop over the brightened aspect of things. Tertan was going on. "I also am a man of letters. Putative."

"You have written a good deal?" Howe meant to be no more than polite, and he was surprised at the tenderness he heard in his words.

Solemnly the boy nodded, threw back the dank lock, and sucked in a deep, anticipatory breath. "First, a work of homiletics, which is a defense of the principles of religious optimism against the pessimism of Schopenhauer and the humanism of Nietzsche."

"Humanism? Why do you call it humanism?"

"It is my nomenclature for making a deity of man," Tertan replied negligently. "Then three fictional works, novels. And numerous essays in science, combating materialism. Is it your duty to read these if I bring them to you?"

Howe answered simply, "No, it isn't exactly my duty, but I shall be happy to read them."

Tertan stood up and remained silent. He rested his bag on the chair. With a certain compunction—for it did not seem entirely proper that, of two men of letters, one should have the right to blue-pencil the other, to grade him or to question the quality of his "sentence structure"—Howe reached for Tertan's papers. But before he could take them up, the boy suddenly made his bow-to-Abelard, the stiff inclination of the body with the hands seeming to emerge from the scholar's gown. Then he was gone.

But after his departure something was still left of him. The timbre of his curious sentences, the downright finality of so quaint a phrase as "It is the inevitable fate" still rang in the air. Howe gave the warmth of his feeling to the new visitor who stood at the door announcing himself with a genteel clearing of the throat.

"Doctor Howe, I believe?" the student said. A large hand advanced into the room and grasped Howe's hand. "Blackburn, sir, Theodore Blackburn, vice-president of the Student Council. A great pleasure, sir."

Out of a pair of ruddy cheeks a pair of small eyes twinkled good-naturedly. The large face, the large body were not so much fat as beefy and suggested something "typical"—monk, politician, or innkeeper.

Blackburn took the seat beside Howe's desk. "I may have seemed to introduce myself in my public capacity, sir," he said. "But it is really as an individual that I came to see you. That is to say, as one of your students to be."

He spoke with an English intonation and he went on, "I was once an English major, sir."

For a moment Howe was startled, for the roast-beef look of the boy and the manner of his speech gave a second's credibility to one sense of his statement. Then the collegiate meaning of the phrase asserted itself, but some perversity made Howe say what was not really in good taste even with so forward a student, "Indeed? What regiment?"

Blackburn stared and then gave a little pouf-pouf of laughter. He waved the misapprehension away. "Very good, sir. It certainly is an ambiguous term." He chuckled in appreciation of Howe's joke, then cleared his throat to put it aside. "I look forward to taking your course in the romantic poets, sir," he said earnestly. "To me the romantic poets are the very crown of English literature."

Howe made a dry sound, and the boy, catching some meaning in it, said, "Little as I know them, of course. But even Shakespeare who is so dear to us of the Anglo-Saxon tradition is in a sense but the preparation for Shelley, Keats and Byron. And Wadsworth."

Almost sorry for him, Howe dropped his eyes. With some embarrassment, for the boy was not actually his student, he said softly, "Wordsworth."

"Sir?"

"Wordsworth, not Wadsworth. You said Wadsworth."

"Did I, sir?" Gravely he shook his head to rebuke himself for the error. "Wordsworth, of course—slip of the tongue." Then, quite in command again, he went on. "I have a favor to ask of you, Doctor Howe. You see, I began my college course as an English major,"—he smiled—"as I said."

"Yes?"

"But after my first year I shifted. I shifted to the social sciences. Sociology and government—I find them stimulating and very *real*." He paused, out of respect for reality. "But now I find that perhaps I have neglected the other side."

"The other side?" Howe said.

"Imagination, fancy, culture. A well-rounded man." He trailed off as if there were perfect understanding between them. "And so, sir, I have decided to end my senior year with your course in the romantic poets."

His voice was filled with an indulgence which Howe ignored as he said flatly and gravely, "But that course isn't given until the spring term."

"Yes, sir, and that is where the favor comes in. Would you let me take your romantic prose course? I can't take it for credit, sir, my program is full, but just for background it seems to me that I ought to take it. I do hope," he concluded in a manly way, "that you will consent."

"Well, it's no great favor, Mr. Blackburn. You can come if you wish, though there's not much point in it if you don't do the reading."

The bell rang for the hour and Howe got up.

"May I begin with this class, sir?" Blackburn's smile was candid and boyish.

Howe nodded carelessly and together, silently, they walked to the classroom down the hall. When they reached the door Howe stood back to let his student enter, but Blackburn moved adroitly behind him and grasped him by the arm to urge him over the threshold. They entered together with Blackburn's hand firmly on Howe's biceps, the student inducting the teacher into his own room. Howe felt a surge of temper rise in him and almost violently he disengaged his arm and walked to the desk, while Blackburn found a seat in the front row and smiled at him.

II

The question was, At whose door must the tragedy be laid?

All night the snow had fallen heavily and only now was abating in sparse little flurries. The windows were valanced high with white. It was very quiet; something of the quiet of the world had reached the class, and Howe found that everyone was glad to talk or listen. In the room there was a comfortable sense of pleasure in being human.

Casebeer believed that the blame for the tragedy rested with heredity. Picking up the book he read, "The sins of the fathers are visited on their children." This opinion was received with general favor. Nevertheless, Johnson ventured to say that the fault was all Pastor Manders' because the Pastor had made Mrs. Alving go back to her husband and was always hiding the truth. To this Hibbard objected with logic enough, "Well then, it was really all her husband's fault. He *did* all the bad things." De Witt, his face bright with an impatient idea, said that the fault was all society's. "By society I don't mean upper-crust society," he said. He looked around a little defiantly, taking in any members of the class who might be members of upper-crust society. "Not in that sense. I mean the social unit."

Howe nodded and said, "Yes, of course."

"If the society of the time had progressed far enough in science," De Witt went on, "then there would be no problem for Mr. Ibsen to write about. Captain Alving plays around a little, gives way to perfectly natural biological urges, and he gets a social disease, a venereal disease. If the disease is cured, no problem. Invent salvarsan and the disease is cured. The problem of heredity disappears and li'l Oswald just doesn't get paresis. No paresis, no problem—no problem, no play."

"Or take birth-control, for instance," De Witt went on. "If Mrs. Alving had some knowledge of contraception, she wouldn't have had to have li'l Oswald at all. No li'l Oswald, no play."

The class was suddenly quieter. In the back row Stettenhover swung his great football shoulders in a righteous sulking gesture, first to the right, then to the left. He puckered his mouth ostentatiously. Intellect was always ending up by talking dirty.

Tertan's hand went up, and Howe said, "Mr. Tertan." The boy shambled to his feet and began his long characteristic gulp. Howe made a motion with his fingers, as small as possible, and Tertan ducked his head and smiled an apology. He sat down. The class laughed. With more than half the term gone, Tertan had not been able to remember that one did not rise to speak. He seemed unable to carry on the life of the intellect without this mark of respect for it. To Howe the boy's habit of rising seemed to accord with the formal shabbiness of his dress. He never wore the casual sweaters and jackets of his classmates. Into the free and comfortable air of the college classroom he brought the stuffy sordid strictness of some crowded, metropolitan high school.

"Speaking from one sense," Tertan began slowly, "there is no blame ascribable. From the sense of determinism, who can say where the blame lies? The preordained is the preordained and it cannot be said without rebellion against the universe, a palpable absurdity."

In the back row Stettenhover slumped suddenly in his seat, his heels held out before him, making a loud, dry, disgusted sound. His body sank until his neck rested on the back of his chair. He folded his hands across his belly and looked significantly out of the window, exasperated not only with Tertan, but with Howe, with the class, with the whole system designed to encourage this kind of thing. There was a certain insolence in the movement and Howe flushed. As Tertan continued to speak, Howe stalked casually toward the window and placed himself in the line of Stettenhover's vision. He stared at the great fellow, who pretended not to see him. There was so much power in the big body, so much contempt in the Greek-athlete face under the crisp Greek-athlete curls, that Howe felt almost physical fear. But at last Stettenhover admitted him to focus and under his disapproving gaze sat up with slow indifference. His eyebrows raised high in resignation, he began to examine his hands. Howe relaxed and turned his attention back to Tertan.

"Flux of existence," Tertan was saying, "produces all things so that judgment wavers. Beyond the phenomena, what? But phenomena are adumbrated and to them we are limited."

Howe saw it for a moment as perhaps it existed in the boy's mind—the world of shadows which are cast by a great light upon a hidden reality as in the old myth of the Cave. But the little brush with Stettenhover had tired him, and he said irritably, "But come to the point, Mr. Tertan."

He said it so sharply that some of the class looked at him curiously. For three months he had gently carried Tertan through his verbosities, to the vaguely respectful surprise of the other students, who seemed to conceive that there existed between this strange classmate and their teacher some special understanding from which they were content to be excluded. Tertan looked at him mildly, and at once came brilliantly to the point. "This is the summation of the play," he said and took up his book and read, "'Your poor father never found any outlet for the overmastering joy of life that was in him. And I brought no holiday into his home, either. Everything seemed to turn upon duty and I am afraid I made your father's home unbearable to him, Oswald.' Spoken by Mrs. Alving."

Yes that was surely the "summation of the play" and Tertan had hit it, as he hit, deviously and eventually, the literary point of almost everything. But now, as always, he was wrapping it away from sight. "For most mortals," he said, "there are only joys of biological urgings, gross and crass, such as the sensuous Captain Alving. For certain few there are the transmutations beyond these to a contemplation of the utter whole."

Oh, the boy was mad. And suddenly the word, used in hyperbole, intended almost for the expression of exasperated admiration, became literal. Now that the word was used, it became simply apparent to Howe that Tertan was mad.

It was a monstrous word and stood like a bestial thing in the room. Yet it so completely comprehended everything that had puzzled Howe, it so arranged and explained what for three months had been perplexing him that almost at once its horror became domesticated. With this word Howe was able to communicate to Tertan the value of a single criticism or correction of his wild, verbose themes. Their conferences had been frequent and long but had done nothing to reduce to order the splendid confusion of the boy's ideas. Yet, impossible though its expression was, Tertan's incandescent mind could always strike for a moment into some dark corner of thought.

And now it was suddenly apparent that it was not a faulty rhetoric that Howe had to contend with. With his new knowledge he looked at Tertan's face and wondered how he could have so long deceived himself. Tertan was still talking, and the class had lapsed into a kind of patient unconsciousness, a coma of respect for words which, for all that most of them knew, might be profound. Almost with a suffusion of shame, Howe believed that in some dim way the class had long ago had some intimation of Tertan's madness. He reached out as decisively as he could to seize the thread of Tertan's discourse before it should be entangled further.

"Mr. Tertan says that the blame must be put upon whoever kills the joy of living in another. We have been assuming that Captain Alving was a wholly bad man, but what if we assume that he became bad only because Mrs. Alving, when they were first married, acted toward him in the prudish way she says she did?"

It was a ticklish idea to advance to freshmen and perhaps not profitable. Not all of them were following.

"That would put the blame on Mrs. Alving herself, whom most of you admire. And she herself seems to think so." He glanced at his watch. The hour was nearly over. "What do you think, Mr. De Witt?"

De Witt rose to the idea; he wanted to know if society couldn't be blamed for educating Mrs. Alving's temperament in the wrong way. Casebeer was puzzled, Stettenhover continued to look at his hands until the bell rang.

Tertan, his brows louring in thought, was making as always for a private word. Howe gathered his books and papers to leave quickly. At this moment of his discovery and with the knowledge still raw, he could not engage himself with Tertan. Tertan sucked in his breath to prepare for speech and Howe made ready for the pain and confusion. But at that moment Casebeer detached himself from the group with which he had been conferring and which he seemed to represent. His constituency remained at a tactful distance. The mission involved the time of an assigned essay. Casebeer's presentation of the plea—it was based on the freshmen's heavy duties at the fraternities during Carnival Week—cut across Tertan's preparations for speech. "And so some of us fellows thought," Casebeer concluded with heavy solemnity, "that we could do a better job, give our minds to it more, if we had more time."

Tertan regarded Casebeer with mingled curiosity and revulsion. Howe not only said that he would postpone the assignment but went on to talk about the Carnival, and even drew the waiting constituency into the conversation. He was conscious of Tertan's stern and astonished stare, then of his sudden departure.

Now that the fact was clear, Howe knew that he must act on it. His course was simple enough. He must lay the case before the Dean. Yet he hesitated. His feeling for Tertan must now, certainly, be in some way invalidated. Yet could he, because of a word, hurry to assign to official and reasonable solicitude what had been, until this moment, so various and warm? He could at least delay and, by moving slowly, lend a poor grace to the necessary, ugly act of making his report.

It was with some notion of keeping the matter in his own hands that he went to the Dean's office to look up Tertan's records. In the outer office the Dean's secretary greeted him brightly, and at his request brought him the manila folder with the small identifying photograph pasted in the corner. She laughed. "He was looking for the birdie in the wrong place," she said.

Howe leaned over her shoulder to look at the picture. It was as bad as all the Dean's-office photographs were, but it differed from all that Howe had ever seen. Tertan, instead of looking into the camera, as no doubt he had been bidden, had, at the moment of exposure, turned his eyes upward. His mouth, as though conscious of the trick played on the photographer, had the sly superior look that Howe knew.

The secretary was fascinated by the picture. "What a funny boy," she said. "He looks like Tartuffe!"

And so he did, with the absurd piety of the eyes and the conscious slyness of the mouth and the white face bloated by the bad lens.

"Is he *like* that?" the secretary said.

"Like Tartuffe? No."

From the photograph there was little enough comfort to be had. The records themselves gave no clue to madness, though they suggested sadness enough. Howe read of a father, Stanislaus Tertan, born in Budapest and trained in engineering in Berlin, once employed by the Hercules Chemical Corporation—this was one of the factories that dominated the sound end of the town—but now without employment. He read of a mother Erminie (Youngfellow) Tertan, born in Manchester, educated at a Normal School at Leeds, now housewife by profession. The family lived on Greenbriar Street which Howe knew as a row of once elegant homes near what was now the factory district. The old mansion had long ago been divided into small and primitive apartments. Of Ferdinand himself there was little to learn. He lived with his parents, had attended Detroit high school and had transferred to the local school in his last year. His rating for intelligence, as expressed in numbers, was high, his scholastic record was remarkable, he held a college scholarship for his tuition.

Howe laid the folder on the secretary's desk. "Did you find what you wanted to know?" she asked.

The phrases from Tertan's momentous first theme came back to him. "Tertan I am, but what is Tertan? Of this time, of that place, of some parentage, what does it matter?"

"No, I didn't find it," he said.

Now that he had consulted the sad, half-meaningless record he knew all the more firmly that he must not give the matter out of his own hands. He must not release Tertan to authority. Not that he anticipated from the Dean anything but the greatest kindness for Tertan. The Dean would have the experience and skill which he himself could not have. One way or another the Dean could answer the question, "What is Tertan?" Yet this was precisely what he feared. He alone could keep alive—not forever but for a somehow important time—the question. "What is Tertan?" He alone could keep it still a question. Some sure instinct told him that he must not surrender the question to a clean official desk in a clear official light to be dealt with, settled and closed.

He heard himself saying, "Is the Dean busy at the moment? I'd like to see him."

His request came thus unbidden, even forbidden, and it was one of the surprising and startling incidents of his life. Later when he reviewed the events, so disconnected in themselves, or so merely odd, of the story that unfolded for him that year, it was over this moment, on its face the least notable, that he paused longest. It was frequently to be with fear and never without a certainty of its meaning in his own knowledge of himself that he would recall this simple, routine request, and the feeling of shame and freedom it gave him as he sent everything down the official chute. In the end, of course, no matter what he did to "protect" Tertan, he would have had to make the same request and lay the matter on the Dean's clean desk. But it would always be a landmark of his life that, at the very moment when he was rejecting the official way, he had been, without will or intention, so gladly drawn to it.

After the storm's last delicate flurry, the sun had come out. Reflected by the new snow, it filled the office with a golden light which was almost musical in the way it made all the commonplace objects of efficiency shine with a sudden sad and noble significance. And the light, now that he noticed it made the utterance of his perverse and unwanted request even more momentous.

The secretary consulted the engagement pad. "He'll be free any minute. Don't you want to wait in the parlor?"

She threw open the door of the large and pleasant room in which the Dean held his Committee meetings, and in which his visitors waited. It was designed with a homely elegance on the masculine side of the eighteenth-century manner. There was a small coal fire in the grate and the handsome mahogany table was strewn with books and magazines. The large windows gave on the snowy lawn, and there was such a fine width of window that the white casements and walls seemed at this moment but a continuation of the snow, the snow but an extension of casement and walls. The out-doors seemed taken in and made safe, the indoors seemed luxuriously freshened and expanded.

Howe sat down by the fire and lighted a cigarette. The room had its intended effect upon him. He felt comfortable and relaxed, yet nicely organized, some young diplomatic agent of the eighteenth century, the newly fledged Swift carrying out Sir William Temple's business. The rawness of Tertan's case quite vanished. He crossed his legs and reached for a magazine.

It was that famous issue of *Life and Letters* that his idle hand had found and his blood raced as he sifted through it, and the shape of his own name, Joseph Howe, sprang out at him, still cabalistic in its power. He tossed the magazine back on the table as the door of the Dean's office opened and the Dean ushered out Theodore Blackburn.

"Ah, Joseph!" the Dean said.

Blackburn said, "Good morning, Doctor." Howe winced at the title and caught the flicker of amusement over the Dean's face. The Dean stood with his hand high on the door-jamb and Blackburn, still in the doorway, remained standing almost under the long arm.

Howe nodded briefly to Blackburn, snubbing his eager deference. "Can you give me a few minutes?" he said to the Dean.

"All the time you want. Come in." Before the two men could enter the office, Blackburn claimed their attention with a long full "er." As they turned to him, Blackburn said, "Can *you* give *me* a few minutes, Doctor Howe?" His eyes sparkled at the little audacity he had committed, the slightly impudent play with hierarchy. Of the three of them Blackburn kept himself the lowest, but he reminded Howe of his subaltern relation to the Dean.

"I mean, of course," Blackburn went on easily, "when you've finished with the Dean."

"I'll be in my office shortly," Howe said, turned his back on the ready "Thank you, sir," and followed the Dean into the inner room.

"Energetic boy," said the Dean. "A bit beyond himself but very energetic. Sit down."

The Dean lighted a cigarette, leaned back in his chair, sat easy and silent for a moment, giving Howe no signal to go ahead with business. He was a young Dean, not much beyond forty, a tall handsome man with sad, ambitious eyes. He had been a Rhodes scholar. His friends looked for great things from him, and it was generally said that he had notions of education which he was not yet ready to try to put into practice.

His relaxed silence was meant as a compliment to Howe. He smiled and said, "What's the business, Joseph?"

"Do you know Tertan—Ferdinand Tertan, a freshman?"

The Dean's cigarette was in his mouth and his hands were clasped behind his head. He did not seem to search his memory for the name. He said, "What about him?"

Clearly the Dean knew something, and he was waiting for Howe to tell him more. Howe moved only tentatively. Now that he was doing what he had resolved not to do, he felt more guilty at having been so long deceived by Tertan and more need to be loyal to his error.

"He's a strange fellow," he ventured. He said stubbornly, "In a strange way he's very brilliant." He concluded, "But very strange."

The springs of the Dean's swivel chair creaked as he came out of his sprawl and leaned forward to Howe. "Do you mean he's so strange that it's something you could give a name to?"

Howe looked at him stupidly. "What do you mean?" he said.

"What's his trouble?" the Dean said more neutrally.

"He's very brilliant, in a way. I looked him up and he has a top intelligence rating. But somehow, and it's hard to explain just how, what he says is always on the edge of sense and doesn't quite make it."

The Dean looked at him and Howe flushed up. The Dean had surely read Woolley on the subject of "the Howes" and the *tour d'ivresse*. Was that quick glance ironical?

The Dean picked up some papers from his desk, and Howe could see that they were in Tertan's impatient scrawl. Perhaps the little gleam in the Dean's glance had come only from putting facts together.

"He sent me this yesterday," the Dean said. "After an interview I had with him. I haven't been able to do more than glance at it. When you said what you did, I realized there was something wrong."

Twisting his mouth, the Dean looked over the letter. "You seem to be involved," he said without looking up. "By the way, what did you give him at mid-term?"

Flushing, setting his shoulders, Howe said firmly, "I gave him A-minus."

The Dean chuckled. "Might be a good idea if some of our nicer boys went crazy—just a little." He said, "Well," to conclude the matter and handed the papers to Howe. "See if this is the same thing you've been finding. Then we can go into the matter again."

Before the fire in the parlor, in the chair that Howe had been occupying, sat Blackburn. He sprang to his feet as Howe entered.

"I said my office, Mr. Blackburn." Howe's voice was sharp. Then he was almost sorry for the rebuke, so clearly and naively did Blackburn seem to relish his stay in the parlor, close to authority.

"I'm in a bit of a hurry, sir," he said, "and I did want to be sure to speak to you, sir."

He was really absurd, yet fifteen years from now he would have grown up to himself, to the assurance and mature beefiness. In banks, in consular offices, in brokerage firms, on the bench, more seriously affable, a little sterner, he would make use of his ability to be administered by his job. It was almost reassuring. Now he was exercising his too-great skill on Howe. "I owe you an apology, sir," he said.

Howe knew that he did, but he showed surprise.

"I mean, Doctor, after your having been so kind about letting me attend your class, I stopped coming." He smiled in deprecation. "Extracurricular activities take up so much of my time. I'm afraid I undertook more than I could perform."

Howe had noticed the absence and had been a little irritated by it after Blackburn's elaborate plea. It was an absence that might be interpreted as a comment on the teacher. But there was only one way for him to answer. "You've no need to apologize," he said. "It's wholly your affair."

Blackburn beamed. "I'm so glad you feel that way about it, sir. I was worried you might think I had stayed away because I was influenced by —" he stopped and lowered his eyes.

Astonished, Howe said, "Influenced by what?"

"Well, by—" Blackburn hesitated and for answer pointed to the table on which lay the copy of *Life and Letters*. Without looking at it, he knew where to direct his hand. "By the unfavorable publicity, sir." He hurried on. "And that brings me to another point, sir. I am secretary of Quill and Scroll, sir, the student literary society, and I wonder if you would address us. You could read your own poetry, sir, and defend your own point of view. It would be very interesting."

It was truly amazing. Howe looked long and cruelly into Blackburn's face, trying to catch the secret of the mind that could have conceived this way of manipulating him, this way so daring and inept—but not entirely inept—with its malice so without malignity. The face did not yield its secret. Howe smiled broadly and said, "Of course I don't think you were influenced by the unfavorable publicity."

"I'm still going to take—regularly, for credit—your romantic poets course next term," Blackburn said.

"Don't worry, my dear fellow, don't worry about it."

Howe started to leave and Blackburn stopped him with, "But about Quill, sir?"

"Suppose we wait until next term? I'll be less busy then."

And Blackburn said, "Very good, sir, and thank you."

In his office the little encounter seemed less funny to Howe, was even in some indeterminate way disturbing. He made an effort to put it from his mind by turning to what was sure to disturb him more, the Tertan letter read in the new interpretation. He found what he had always found, the same florid leaps beyond fact and meaning, the same headlong certainty. But as his eye passed over the familiar scrawl it caught his own name, and for the second time that hour he felt the race of his blood.

"The Paraclete," Tertan had written to the Dean, "from a Greek word meaning to stand in place of, but going beyond the primitive idea to mean traditionally the helper, the one who comforts and assists, cannot without fundamental loss be jettisoned. Even if taken no longer in the supernatural sense, the concept remains deeply in the human consciousness inevitably. Humanitarianism is no reply, for not every man stands in the place of every other man for this other comrade's comfort. But certain are chosen out of the human race to be the consoler of some other. Of these, for example, is Joseph Barker Howe, Ph.D. Of intellects not the first yet of true intellect and lambent instructions, given to that which is intuitive and irrational, not to what is logical in the strict word, what is judged by him is of the heart and not the head. Here is one chosen, in that he chooses himself to stand in the place of another for comfort and consolation. To him more than another I give my gratitude, with all respect to our Dean who reads this, a noble man, but merely dedicated, not consecrated. But not in the aspect of the Paraclete only is Dr. Joseph Barker Howe established, for he must be the Paraclete to another aspect of himself, that which is driven and persecuted by the lack of understanding in the world at large, so that he in himself embodies the full history of man's tribulations and, overflowing upon others, notably the present writer, is the ultimate end."

This was love. There was no escape from it. Try as Howe might to remember that Tertan was mad and all his emotions invalidated, he could not destroy the effect upon him of his student's stern, affectionate regard. He had betrayed not only a power of mind but a power of love. And, however firmly he held before his attention the fact of Tertan's madness, he could do nothing to banish the physical sensation of gratitude he felt. He had never thought of himself as "driven and persecuted" and he did not now. But still he could not make meaningless his sensation of gratitude. The pitiable Tertan sternly pitied him, and comfort came from Tertan's never-to-be-comforted mind.

III

In an academic community, even an efficient one, official matters move slowly. The term drew to a close with no action in the case of Tertan, and Joseph Howe had to confront a curious problem. How should he grade his strange student, Tertan?

Tertan's final examination had been no different from all his other writing, and what did one "give" such a student? De Witt must have his A, that was clear. Johnson would get a B. With Casebeer it was a question of a B-minus or a C-plus, and Stettenhover, who had been crammed, by the team tutor to fill half a blue-book with his thin feminine scrawl, would have his C-minus which he would accept with mingled indifference and resentment. But with Tertan it was not so easy.

The boy was still in the college process and his name could not be omitted from the grade sheet. Yet what should a mind under suspicion of madness be graded? Until the medical verdict was given, it was for Howe to continue as Tertan's teacher and to keep his judgment pedagogical. Impossible to give him an F: he had not failed. B was for Johnson's stolid mediocrity. He could not be put on the edge of passing with Stettenhover, for he exactly did not pass. In energy and richness of intellect he was perhaps even De Witt's superior, and Howe toyed grimly with the notion of giving him an A, but that would lower the value of the A De Witt had won with his beautiful and clear, if still arrogant, mind. There was a notation which the Registrar recognized—Inc., for Incomplete, and in the horrible comedy of the situation, Howe considered that. But really only a mark of M for Mad would serve.

In his perplexity, Howe sought the Dean, but the Dean was out of town. In the end, he decided to maintain the A-minus he had given Tertan at mid-term. After all, there had been no falling away from that quality. He entered it on the grade sheet with something like bravado.

Academic time moves quickly. A college year is not really a year, lacking as it does three months. And it is endlessly divided into units which, at their beginning, appear larger than they are—terms, half-terms, months, weeks. And the ultimate unit, the hour, is not really an hour, lacking as it does ten minutes. And so the new term advanced rapidly, and one day the fields about the town were all brown, cleared of even the few thin patches of snow which had lingered so long.

Howe, as he lectured on the romantic poets, became conscious of Blackburn emanating wrath. Blackburn did it well, did it with enormous dignity. He did not stir in his seat, he kept his eyes fixed on Howe in perfect attention, but he abstained from using his notebook, there was no mistaking what he proposed to himself as an attitude. His elbow on the writing-wing of the chair, his chin on the curled fingers of his hand, he was the embodiment of intellectual indignation. He was thinking his own thoughts, would give no public offense, yet would claim his due, was not to be intimidated. Howe knew that he would present himself at the end of the hour.

Blackburn entered the office without invitation. He did not smile; there was no cajolery about him. Without invitation he sat down beside Howe's desk. He did not speak until he had taken the blue-book from his pocket. He said, "What does this mean, sir?"

It was a sound and conservative student tactic. Said in the usual way it meant, "How could you have so misunderstood me?" or "What does this mean for my future in the course?" But there were none of the humbler tones in Blackburn's way of saying it.

Howe made the established reply, "I think that's for you to tell me."
Blackburn continued icy. "I'm sure I can't, sir."

There was a silence between them. Both dropped their eyes to the blue-book on the desk. On its cover Howe had penciled: "F. This is very poor work."

Howe picked up the blue-book. There was always the possibility of injustice. The teacher may be bored by the mass of papers and not wholly attentive. A phrase, even the student's handwriting, may irritate him un-reasonably. "Well," said Howe, "Let's go through it."

He opened the first page. "Now here: you write, 'In *The Ancient Mariner,* Coleridge lives in and transports us to a honey-sweet world where all is rich and strange, a world of charm to which we can escape from the humdrum existence of our daily lives, the world of romance. Here, in this warm and honey-sweet land of charming dreams we can relax and enjoy ourselves.'"

Howe lowered the paper and waited with a neutral look for Blackburn to speak. Blackburn returned the look boldly, did not speak, sat stolid and lofty. At last Howe said, speaking gently, "Did you mean that, or were you just at a loss for something to say?"

"You imply that I was just 'Bluffing'?" The quotation marks hung palpable in the air about the word.

"I'd like to know. I'd prefer believing that you were bluffing to believing that you really thought this."

Blackburn's eyebrows went up. From the height of a great and firm-based idea he looked at his teacher. He clasped the crags for a moment and then pounced, craftily, suavely. "Do you mean, Doctor Howe, that there aren't two opinions possible?"

It was superbly done in its air of putting all of Howe's intellectual life into the balance. Howe remained patient and simple. "Yes, many opinions are possible, but not this one. Whatever anyone believes of *The Ancient Mariner,* no one can in reason believe that it represents a—a honey-sweet world in which we can relax."

"But that is what I *feel,* sir."

This was well-done, too. Howe said, "Look, Mr. Blackburn. Do you really relax with hunger and thirst, the heat and the sea-serpents, the dead men with staring eyes, Life in Death and the skeletons? Come now, Mr. Blackburn."

Blackburn made no answer, and Howe pressed forward. "Now, you say of Wordsworth, 'Of peasant stock himself, he turned from the effete life of the salons and found in the peasant the hope of flaming revolution which would sweep away all the old ideas. This is the subject of his best poems.'"

Beaming at his teacher with youthful eagerness, Blackburn said, "Yes, sir, a rebel, a bringer of light to suffering mankind. I see him as a kind of Prothemeus."

"A kind of what?"

"Prothemeus, sir."

"Think, Mr. Blackburn. We were talking about him only today and I mentioned his name a dozen times. You don't mean Prothemeus. You mean—" Howe waited, but there was no response.

"You mean Prometheus."

Blackburn gave no assent, and Howe took the reins. "You've done a bad job here, Mr. Blackburn, about as bad as could be done." He saw Blackburn stiffen and his genial face harden again. "It shows either a lack of preparation or a complete lack of understanding." He saw Blackburn's face begin to go to pieces and he stopped.

"Oh, sir," Blackburn burst out, "I've never had a mark like this before, never anything below a B, never. A thing like this has never happened to me before."

It must be true, it was a statement too easily verified. Could it be that other instructors accepted such flaunting nonsense? Howe wanted to end the interview. "I'll set it down to lack of preparation," he said. "I know you're busy. That's not an excuse, but it's an explanation. Now, suppose you really prepare, and then take another quiz in two weeks. We'll forget this one and count the other."

Blackburn squirmed with pleasure and gratitude. "Thank you, sir. You're really very kind, very kind."

Howe rose to conclude the visit. "All right, then—in two weeks."

It was that day that the Dean imparted to Howe the conclusion of the case of Tertan. It was simple and a little anti-climatic. A physician had been called in, and had said the word, given the name.

"A classic case, he called it," the Dean said. "Not a doubt in the world," he said. His eyes were full of miserable pity, and he clutched at a word. "A classic case, a classic case." To his aid and to Howe's there came the Parthenon and the form of the Greek drama, the Aristotelian logic, Racine and the Well-Tempered Clavichord, the blueness of the Aegean and its clear sky, Classic—that is to say, without a doubt, perfect in its way, a veritable model, and, as the Dean had been told, sure to take a perfectly predictible and inevitable course to a foreknown conclusion.

It was only pity that stood in the Dean's eyes. For a moment there was fear too. "Terrible," he said, "it is simply terrible."

Then he went on briskly. "Naturally, we've told the boy nothing. And naturally, we won't. His tuition's paid by his scholarship, and we'll continue him on the rolls until the end of the year. That will be the kindest. After that the matter will be out of control. We'll see, of course, that he gets into the proper hands. I'm told there will be no change, he'll go on like this, be as good as this, for four to six months. And so we'll just go along as usual."

So Tertan continued to sit in Section 5 of English 1A, to his classmates still a figure of curiously dignified fun, symbol to most of them of the respectable but absurd intellectual life. But to his teacher he was now very different. He had not changed—he was still the greyhound casting for the scent of ideas, and Howe could see that he was still the same Tertan, but he could not feel it. What he felt as he looked at the boy sitting in his accustomed place was the hard blank of a fact. The fact itself was formidable and depressing. But what Howe was chiefly aware of was that he had permitted the metamorphosis of Tertan from person to fact.

As much as possible he avoided seeing Tertan's upraised hand and eager eye. But the fact did not know of its mere factuality, it continued its existence as if it were Tertan, hand up and eye questioning, and one day it appeared in Howe's office with a document.

"Even the spirit who lives egregiously, above the herd, must have its relations with the fellowman," Tertan declared. He laid the document on Howe's desk. It was headed "Quill and Scroll Society of Dwight College. Application for Membership."

"In most ways these are crass minds," Tertan said, touching the paper. "Yet as a whole, bound together in their common love of letters, they transcend their intellectual lacks since it is not a paradox that the whole is greater than the sum of its parts."

"When are the elections?" Howe asked.

"They take place tomorrow."

"I certainly hope you will be successful."

"Thank you. Would you wish to implement that hope?" A rather dirty finger pointed to the bottom of the sheet. "A faculty recommender is necessary," Tertan said stiffly, and waited.

"And you wish me to recommend you?"

"It would be an honor."

"You may use my name."

Tertan's finger pointed again. "It must be a written sponsorship, signed by the sponsor." There was a large blank space on the form under the heading, "Opinion of Faculty Sponsor."

This was almost another thing and Howe hesitated. Yet there was nothing else to do and he took out his fountain pen. He wrote, "Mr. Ferdinand Tertan is marked by his intense devotion to letters and by his exceptional love of all things of the mind." To this he signed his name, which looked bold and assertive on the white page. It disturbed him, the strange affirming power of a name. With a businesslike air, Tertan whipped up the paper, folding it with decision, and put it into his pocket. He bowed and took his departure, leaving Howe with the sense of having done something oddly momentous.

And so much now seemed odd and momentous to Howe that should not have seemed so. It was odd and momentous, he felt, when he sat with Blackburn's second quiz before him, and wrote in an excessively firm hand the grade of C-minus. The paper was a clear, an indisputable failure. He was carefully and consciously committing a cowardice. Blackburn had told the truth when he had pleaded his past record. Howe had consulted it in the Dean's office. It showed no grade lower than a B-minus. A canvass of some of Blackburn's previous instructors had brought vague attestations to the adequate powers of a student imperfectly remembered, and sometimes surprise that his abilities could be questioned at all.

As he wrote the grade, Howe told himself that his cowardice sprang from an unwillingness to have more dealings with a student he disliked. He knew it was simpler than that. He knew he feared Blackburn: that was the absurd truth. And cowardice did not solve the matter after all. Blackburn, flushed with a first success, attacked at once. The minimal passing grade had not assuaged his feelings and he sat at Howe's desk and again the blue-book lay between them. Blackburn said nothing. With an enormous impudence, he was waiting for Howe to speak and explain himself.

At last Howe said sharply and rudely, "Well?" His throat was tense and the blood was hammering in his head. His mouth was tight with anger at himself for his disturbance.

Blackburn's glance was almost baleful. "This is impossible, sir."

"But there it is," Howe answered.

"Sir?" Blackburn had not caught the meaning but his tone was still haughty.

Impatiently Howe said, "There it is, plain as day. Are you here to complain again?"

"Indeed I am, sir." There was surprise in Blackburn's voice that Howe should ask the question.

"I shouldn't complain if I were you. You did a thoroughly bad job on your first quiz. This one is a little, only a very little better." This was not true. If anything, it was worse.

"That might be a matter of opinion, sir."

"It is a matter of opinion. Of my opinion."

"Another opinion might be different, sir."

"You really believe that?" Howe said.

"Yes." The omission of the "sir" was monumental.

"Whose, for example?"

"The Dean's, for example." Then the fleshy jaw came forward a little. "Or a certain literary critic's, for example."

It was colossal and almost too much for Blackburn himself to handle. The solidity of his face almost crumpled under it. But he withstood his own audacity and went on. "And the Dean's opinion might be guided by the knowledge that the person who gave me this mark is the man whom a famous critic, the most eminent judge of literature in this country, called a drunken man. The Dean might think twice about whether such a man is fit to teach Dwight students."

Howe said in quiet admonition, "Blackburn, you're mad," meaning no more than to check the boy's extravagance.

But Blackburn paid no heed. He had another shot in the locker. "And the Dean might be guided by the information, of which I have evidence, documentary evidence,"—he slapped his breast pocket twice—"that this same person personally recommended to the college literary society, the oldest in the country, that he personally recommended a student who is crazy, who threw the meeting into an uproar—a psychiatric case. The Dean might take that into account."

Howe was never to learn the details of that "uproar." He had always to content himself with the dim but passionate picture which at that moment sprang into his mind, of Tertan standing on some abstract height and madly denouncing the multitude of Quill and Scroll who howled him down.

He sat quiet a moment and looked at Blackburn. The ferocity had entirely gone from the student's face. He sat regarding his teacher almost benevolently. He had played a good card and now, scarcely at all unfriendly, he was waiting to see the effect. Howe took up the blue-book and negligently sifted through it. He read a page, closed the book, struck out the C-minus and wrote an F.

"Now you may take the paper to the Dean," he said. "You may tell him that after reconsidering it, I lowered the grade."

The gasp was audible. "Oh, sir!" Blackburn cried. "Please!" His face was agonized. "It means my graduation, my livelihood, my future. Don't do this to me."

"It's done already."

Blackburn stood up. "I spoke rashly, sir, hastily. I had no intention, no real intention, of seeing the Dean. It rests with you—entirely, entirely. I *hope* you will restore the first mark."

"Take the matter to the Dean or not, just as you choose. The grade is what you deserve and it stands."

Blackburn's head dropped. "And will I be failed at mid-term, sir?"

"Of course."

From deep out of Blackburn's great chest rose a cry of anguish. "Oh, sir, if you want me to go down on my knees to you, I will, I will."

Howe looked at him in amazement.

"I will, I will. On my knees, sir. This mustn't, mustn't happen."

He spoke so literally, meaning so very truly that his knees and exactly his knees were involved and seeming to think that he was offering something of tangible value to his teacher, that Howe, whose head had become icy clear in the nonsensical drama, thought, "The boy is mad," and began to speculate fantastically whether something in himself attracted or developed aberration. He could see himself standing absurdly before the Dean and saying, "I've found another. This time it's the vice-president of the Council, the manager of the debating team and secretary of Quill and Scroll."

One more such discovery, he thought, and he himself would be discovered! And there, suddenly, Blackburn was on his knees with a thump, his huge thighs straining his trousers, his hand outstretched in a great gesture of supplication.

With a cry, Howe shoved back his swivel chair and it rolled away on its casters half across the little room. Blackburn knelt for a moment to nothing at all, then got to his feet.

Howe rose abruptly. He said, "Blackburn, you will stop acting like an idiot. Dust your knees off, take your paper and get out. You've behaved like a fool and a malicious person. You have half a term to do a decent job. Keep your silly mouth shut and try to do it. Now get out."

Blackburn's head was low. He raised it and there was a pious light in his eyes. "Will you shake hands, sir?" he said. He thrust out his hand.

"I will not," Howe said.

Head and hand sank together. Blackburn picked up his blue-book and walked to the door. He turned and said, "Thank you, sir." His back, as he departed, was heavy with tragedy and stateliness.

IV

After years of bad luck with weather, the College had a perfect day for Commencement. It was wonderfully bright, the air so transparent, the wind so brisk that no one could resist talking about it.

As Howe set out for the campus he heard Hilda calling from the back yard. She called, "Professor, professor," and came running to him.

Howe said, "What's this 'professor' business?"

"Mother told me," Hilda said. "You've been promoted. And I want to take your picture."

"Next year," said Howe. "I won't be a professor until next year. And you know better than to call anybody 'professor.'"

"It was just in fun," Hilda said. She seemed disappointed.

"But you can take my picture if you want. I won't look much different next year." Still, it was frightening. It might mean that he was to stay in this town all his life.

Hilda brightened. "Can I take it in this?" she said, and touched the gown he carried over his arm.

Howe laughed. "Yes, you can take it in this."

"I'll get my things and meet you in front of Otis," Hilda said. "I have the background all picked out."

On the campus the Commencement crowd was already large. It stood about in eager, nervous little family groups. As he crossed, Howe was greeted by a student, capped and gowned, glad of the chance to make an event for his parents by introducing one of his teachers. It was while Howe stood there chatting that he saw Tertan.

He had never seen anyone quite so alone, as though a circle had been woven about him to separate him from the gay crowd on the campus. Not that Tertan was not gay, he was the gayest of all. Three weeks had passed since Howe had last seen him, the weeks of examination, the lazy week before Commencement, and this was now a different Tertan. On his head he wore a panama hat, broad-brimmed and fine, of the shape associated with South American planters. He wore a suit of raw silk, luxurious, but yellowed with age and much too tight, and he sported a whangee cane. He walked sedately, the hat tilted at a devastating angle, the stick coming up and down in time to his measured tread. He had, Howe guessed, outfitted himself to greet the day in the clothes of that ruined father whose existence was on record in the Dean's office. Gravely and arrogantly he surveyed the scene—in it, his whole bearing seemed to say, but not of it. With his haughty step, with his flashing eye, Tertan was coming nearer. Howe did not wish to be seen. He shifted his position slightly. When he looked again, Tertan was not in sight.

The chapel clock struck the quarter hour. Howe detached himself from his chat and hurried to Otis Hall at the far end of the campus. Hilda had not yet come. He went up into the high portico and, using the glass of the door for a mirror, put on his gown, adjusted the hood on his shoulders and set the mortar-board on his head. When he came down the steps, Hilda had arrived.

Nothing could have told him more forcibly that a year had passed than the development of Hilda's photographic possessions from the box camera of the previous fall. By a strap about her neck was hung a leather case, so thick and strong, so carefully stitched and so molded to its contents that it could only hold a costly camera. The appearance was deceptive, Howe knew, for he had been present at the Aikens' pre-Christmas conference about its purchase. It was only a fairly good domestic camera. Still, it looked very impressive. Hilda carried another leather case from which she drew a collapsible tripod. Decisively she extended each of its gleaming legs and set it up on the path. She removed the camera from its case and fixed it to the tripod. In its compact efficiency the camera almost had a life of its own, but Hilda treated it with easy familiarity, looked into its eye, glanced casually at its gauges. Then from a pocket she took still another leather case and drew from it a small instrument through which she looked first at Howe, who began to feel inanimate and lost, and then at the sky. She made some adjustment on the instrument, then some adjustment on the camera. She swept the scene with her eye, found a spot on it and beckoned to Howe. With each new leather case, with each new instrument, and with each new adjustment she had grown in ease and now she said, "Joe, will you stand here?"

Obediently Howe stood where he was bidden. She had yet another instrument. She took out a tape-measure on a mechanical spool. Kneeling down before Howe, she put the little metal ring of the tape under the tip of his shoe. At her request, Howe pressed it with his toe. When she had measured her distance, she nodded to Howe who released the tape. At a touch, it sprang back into the spool. "You have to be careful if you're going to get what you want," Hilda said. "I don't believe in all this snap-snap-snapping," she remarked loftily. Howe nodded in agreement, although he was beginning to think Hilda's care excessive.

Now at last the moment had come. Hilda squinted into the camera, moved the tripod slightly. She stood to the side, holding the plunger of the shutter-cable. "Ready," she said. "Will you relax, Joseph, please?" Howe realized that he was standing frozen. Hilda stood poised and precise as a setter, one hand holding the little cable, the other extended with curled dainty fingers like a dancer's, as if expressing to her subject the precarious delicacy of the moment. She pressed the plunger and there was a click. At once she stirred to action, got behind the camera, turned a new exposure. "Thank you," she said. "Would you stand under that tree and let me do a character study with light and shade?"

The childish absurdity of the remark restored Howe's ease. He went to the little tree. The patterns the leaves made on his gown was what Hilda was after. He had just taken a satisfactory position when he heard in the unmistakable voice, "Ah, Doctor! Having your picture taken?"

Howe gave up the pose and turned to Blackburn who stood on the walk, his hands behind his back, a little too large for his bachelor's gown. Annoyed that Blackburn should see him posing for a character study in light and shade, Howe said irritably, "Yes, having my picture taken."

Blackburn beamed at Hilda. "And the little photographer?" he said. Hilda fixed her eyes on the ground and stood closer to her brilliant and aggressive camera. Blackburn, teetering on his heels, his hands behind his back, wholly prelatical and benignly patient, was not abashed at the silence. At last Howe said, "If you'll excuse us, Mr. Blackburn, we'll go on with the picture."

"Go right ahead, sir. I'm running along." But he only came closer. "Doctor Howe," he said fervently, "I want to tell you how glad I am that I was able to satisfy your standards at last."

Howe was surprised at the hard, insulting brightness of his own voice, and even Hilda looked up curiously as he said, "Nothing you have ever done has satisfied me, and nothing you could ever do would satisfy me, Blackburn."

With a glance at Hilda, Blackburn made a gesture as if to hush Howe —as though all his former bold malice had taken for granted a kind of understanding between himself and his teacher, a secret which must not be betrayed to a third person. "I only meant, sir," he said, "that I was able to pass your course after all."

Howe said, "You didn't pass my course. I passed you out of my course. I passed you without even reading your paper. I wanted to be sure the college would be rid of you. And when all the grades were in and I did read your paper, I saw I was right not to have read it first."

Blackburn presented a stricken face. "It was very bad, sir?"

But Howe had turned away. The paper had been fantastic. The paper had been, if he wished to see it so, mad. It was at this moment the Dean came up behind Howe and caught his arm. "Hello, Joseph," he said. "We'd better be getting along, it's almost late."

He was not a familiar man, but when he saw Blackburn, who approached to greet him, he took Blackburn's arm, too. "Hello, Theodore," he said. Leaning forward on Howe's arm and on Blackburn's, he said, "Hello, Hilda dear." Hilda replied quietly, "Hello, Uncle George."

Still clinging to their arms, still linking Howe and Blackburn, the Dean said, "Another year gone, Joe, and we've turned out another crop. After you've been here a few years, you'll find it reasonably upsetting—you wonder how there can be so many graduating classes while you stay the same. But of course you don't stay the same." Then he said, "Well," sharply, to dismiss the thought. He pulled Blackburn's arm and swung him around to Howe. "Have you heard about Teddy Blackburn?" he asked. "He has a job already, before graduation—the first man of his class to be placed." Expectant of congratulations, Blackburn beamed at Howe. Howe remained silent.

"Isn't that good?" the Dean said. Still Howe did not answer and the Dean, puzzled and put out, turned to Hilda. "That's a very fine-looking camera, Hilda." She touched it with affectionate pride.

"Instruments of precision," said a voice. "Instruments of precision." Of the three with joined arms, Howe was the nearest to Tertan, whose gaze took in all the scene except the smile and the nod which Howe gave him. The boy leaned on his cane. The broad-brimmed hat, canting jauntily over his eye, confused the image of his face that Howe had established, suppressed the rigid lines of the ascetic and brought out the baroque curves. It made an effect of perverse majesty.

"Instruments of precision," said Tertan for the last time, addressing no one, making a casual comment to the universe. And it occurred to Howe that Tertan might not be referring to Hilda's equipment. The sense of the thrice-woven circle of the boy's loneliness smote him fiercely. Tertan stood in majestic jauntiness, superior to all the scene, but his isolation made Howe ache with a pity of which Tertan was more the cause than the object, so general and indiscriminate was it.

Whether in his sorrow he made some unintended movement toward Tertan which the Dean checked, or whether the suddenly tightened grip on his arm was the Dean's own sorrow and fear, he did not know. Tertan watched them in the incurious way people watch a photograph being taken, and suddenly the thought that, to the boy, it must seem that the three were posing for a picture together made Howe detach himself almost rudely from the Dean's grasp.

"I promised Hilda another picture," he announced—needlessly, for Tertan was no longer there, he had vanished in the last sudden flux of visitors who, now that the band had struck up, were rushing nervously to find seats.

"You'd better hurry," the Dean said. "I'll go along, it's getting late for me." He departed and Blackburn walked stately by his side.

Howe again took his position under the little tree which cast its shadow over his face and gown. "Just hurry, Hilda, won't you?" he said. Hilda held the cable at arm's length, her other arm crooked and her fingers crisped. She rose on her toes and said "Ready," and pressed the release. "Thank you," she said gravely and began to dismantle her camera as he hurried off to join the procession.

THE GUEST

The schoolmaster was watching the two men climb toward him. One was on horseback, the other on foot. They had not yet tackled the abrupt rise leading to the schoolhouse built on the hillside. They were toiling onward, making slow progress in the snow, among the stones, on the vast expanse of the high, deserted plateau. From time to time the horse stumbled. Without hearing anything yet, he could see the breath issuing from the horse's nostrils. One of the men, at least, knew the region. They were following the trail although it had disappeared days ago under a layer of dirty white snow. The schoolmaster calculated that it would take them half an hour to get onto the hill. It was cold; he went back into the school to get a sweater.

He crossed the empty, frigid classroom. On the blackboard the four rivers of France, drawn with four different colored chalks, had been flowing toward their estuaries for the past three days. Snow had suddenly fallen in mid-October after eight months of drought without the transition of rain, and the twenty pupils, more or less, who lived in the villages scattered over the plateau had stopped coming. With fair weather they would return. Daru now heated only the single room that was his lodging, adjoining the classroom and giving also onto the plateau to the east. Like the class windows, his window looked to the south too. On that side the school was a few kilometers from the point where the plateau began to slope toward the south. In clear weather could be seen the purple mass of the mountain range where the gap opened onto the desert.

Somewhat warmed, Daru returned to the window from which he had first seen the two men. They were no longer visible. Hence they must have tackled the rise. The sky was not so dark, for the snow had stopped falling during the night. The morning had opened with a dirty light which had scarcely become brighter as the ceiling of clouds lifted. At two in the afternoon it seemed as if the day were merely beginning. But still this was better than those three days when the thick snow was falling amidst unbroken darkness with little gusts of wind that rattled the double door of the classroom. Then Daru had spent long hours in his room, leaving it only to go to the shed and feed the chickens or get some coal. Fortunately the delivery truck from Tadjid, the nearest village to the north, had brought his supplies two days before the blizzard. It would return in forty-eight hours.

Besides, he had enough to resist a siege, for the little room was cluttered with bags of wheat that the administration left as a stock to distribute to those of his pupils whose families had suffered from the drought. Actually they had all been victims because they were all poor. Every day Daru would distribute a ration to the children. They had missed it, he knew, during these bad days. Possibly one of the fathers or big brothers would come this afternoon and he could supply them with grain. It was just a matter of carrying them over to the next harvest. Now shiploads of wheat were arriving from France and the worst was over. But it would be hard to forget that poverty, that army of ragged ghosts wandering in the sunlight, the plateaus burned to a cinder month after month, the earth shriveled up little by little, literally scorched, every stone bursting into dust under one's foot. The sheep had died then by thousands and even a few men, here and there, sometimes without anyone's knowing.

In contrast with such poverty, he who lived almost like a monk in his remote schoolhouse, nonetheless satisfied with the little he had and with the rough life, had felt like a lord with his whitewashed walls, his narrow couch, his unpainted shelves, his well, and his weekly provision of water and food. And suddenly this snow, without warning, without the foretaste of rain. This is the way the region was, cruel to live in, even without men —who didn't help matters either. But Daru had been born here. Everywhere else, he felt exiled.

He stepped out onto the terrace in front of the schoolhouse. The two men were now halfway up the slope. He recognized the horseman as Balducci, the old gendarme he had known for a long time. Balducci was holding on the end of a rope an Arab who was walking behind him with hands bound and head lowered. The gendarme waved a greeting to which Daru did not reply, lost as he was in contemplation of the Arab dressed in a faded blue jellaba, his feet in sandals but covered with socks of heavy raw wool, his head surmounted by a narrow, short *chèche*.[1] They were approaching. Balducci was holding back his horse in order not to hurt the Arab, and the group was advancing slowly.

Within earshot, Balducci shouted: "One hour to do the three kilometers from El Ameur!" Daru did not answer. Short and square in his thick sweater, he watched them climb. Not once had the Arab raised his head.

----

[1] *chèche:* a cloth cap.

"Hello," said Daru when they got up onto the terrace. "Come in and warm up." Balducci painfully got down from his horse without letting go the rope. From under his bristling mustache he smiled at the schoolmaster. His little dark eyes, deep-set under a tanned forehead, and his mouth surrounded with wrinkles made him look attentive and studious. Daru took the bridle, led the horse to the shed, and came back to the two men, who were now waiting for him in the school. He led them into his room. "I am going to heat up the classroom," he said. "We'll be more comfortable there." When he entered the room again, Balducci was on the couch. He had undone the rope tying him to the Arab, who had squatted near the stove. His hands still bound, the *chèche* pushed back on his head, he was looking toward the window. At first Daru noticed only his huge lips, fat, smooth, almost Negroid; yet his nose was straight, his eyes were dark and full of fever. The *chèche* revealed an obstinate forehead and, under the weathered skin now rather discolored by the cold, the whole face had a restless and rebellious look that struck Daru when the Arab, turning his face toward him, looked him straight in the eyes. "Go into the other room," said the schoolmaster, "and I'll make you some mint tea." "Thanks," Balducci said. "What a chore! How I long for retirement." And addressing his prisoner in Arabic: "Come on, you." The Arab got up and, slowly, holding his bound wrists in front of him, went into the classroom.

With the tea, Daru brought a chair. But Balducci was already enthroned on the nearest pupil's desk and the Arab had squatted against the teacher's platform facing the stove, which stood between the desk and the window. When he held out the glass of tea to the prisoner, Daru hesitated at the sight of his bound hands. "He might perhaps be untied." "Sure," said Balducci. "That was for the trip." He started to get to his feet. But Daru, setting the glass on the floor, had knelt beside the Arab. Without saying anything, the Arab watched him with his feverish eyes. Once his hands were free, he rubbed his swollen wrists against each other, took the glass of tea, and sucked up the burning liquid in swift little sips.

"Good," said Daru. "And where are you headed?"

Balducci withdrew his mustache from the tea. "Here, son."

"Odd pupils! And you're spending the night?"

"No. I'm going back to El Ameur. And you will deliver this fellow to Tinguit. He is expected at police headquarters."

Balducci was looking at Daru with a friendly little smile.

"What's this story?" asked the schoolmaster. "Are you pulling my leg?"

"No, son. Those are the orders."

"The orders? I'm not . . ." Daru hesitated, not wanting to hurt the old Corsican. "I mean, that's not my job."

"What! What's the meaning of that? In wartime people do all kinds of jobs."

"Then I'll wait for the declaration of war!"

Balducci nodded.

"O.K. But the orders exist and they concern you too. Things are brewing, it appears. There is talk of a forthcoming revolt. We are mobilized, in a way."

Daru still had his obstinate look.

"Listen, son," Balducci said. "I like you and you must understand. There's only a dozen of us at El Ameur to patrol throughout the whole territory of a small department and I must get back in a hurry. I was told to hand this guy over to you and return without delay. He couldn't be kept there. His village was beginning to stir; they wanted to take him back. You must take him to Tinguit tomorrow before the day is over. Twenty kilometers shouldn't faze a husky fellow like you. After that, all will be over. You'll come back to your pupils and your comfortable life."

Behind the wall the horse could be heard snorting and pawing the earth. Daru was looking out the window. Decidedly, the weather was clearing and the light was increasing over the snowy plateau. When all the snow was melted, the sun would take over again and once more would burn the fields of stone. For days, still, the unchanging sky would shed its dry light on the solitary expanse where nothing had any connection with man.

"After all," he said, turning around toward Balducci, "what did he do?" And, before the gendarme had opened his mouth, he asked: "Does he speak French?"

"No, not a word. We had been looking for him for a month, but they were hiding him. He killed his cousin."

"Is he against us?"

"I don't think so. But you can never be sure."

"Why did he kill?"

"A family squabble, I think. One owed the other grain, it seems. It's not at all clear. In short, he killed his cousin with a billhook. You know, like a sheep, *kreezk!*"

Balducci made the gesture of drawing a blade across his throat and the Arab, his attention attracted, watched him with a sort of anxiety. Daru felt a sudden wrath against the man, against all men with their rotten spite, their tireless hates, their blood lust.

But the kettle was singing on the stove. He served Balducci more tea, hesitated, then served the Arab again, who, a second time, drank avidly. His raised arms made the jellaba fall open and the schoolmaster saw his thin, muscular chest.

"Thanks, kid," Balducci said. "And now, I'm off."

He got up and went toward the Arab, taking a small rope from his pocket.

"What are you doing?" Daru asked dryly.

Balducci, disconcerted, showed him the rope.

"Don't bother."

The old gendarme hesitated. "It's up to you. Of course, you are armed?"

"I have my shotgun."

"Where?"

"In the trunk."

"You ought to have it near your bed."

"Why? I have nothing to fear."

"You're crazy, son. If there's an uprising, no one is safe, we're all in the same boat."

"I'll defend myself. I'll have time to see them coming."

Balducci began to laugh, then suddenly the mustache covered the white teeth.

"You'll have time? O.K. That's just what I was saying. You have always been a little cracked. That's why I like you, my son was like that."

At the same time he took out his revolver and put it on the desk.

"Keep it; I don't need two weapons from here to El Ameur."

The revolver shone against the black paint of the table. When the gendarme turned toward him, the schoolmaster caught the smell of leather and horseflesh.

"Listen, Balducci," Daru said suddenly, "every bit of this disgusts me, and first of all your fellow here. But I won't hand him over. Fight, yes, if I have to. But not that."

The old gendarme stood in front of him and looked at him severely.

"You're being a fool," he said slowly. "I don't like it either. You don't get used to putting a rope on a man even after years of it, and you're even ashamed—yes, ashamed. But you can't let them have their way."

"I won't hand him over," Daru said again.

"It's an order, son, and I repeat it."

"That's right. Repeat to them what I've said to you: I won't hand him over."

Balducci made a visible effort to reflect. He looked at the Arab and at Daru. At last he decided.

"No, I won't tell them anything. If you want to drop us, go ahead; I'll not denounce you. I have an order to deliver the prisoner and I'm doing so. And now you'll just sign this paper for me."

"There's no need. I'll not deny that you left him with me."

"Don't be mean with me. I know you'll tell the truth. You're from hereabouts and you are a man. But you must sign, that's the rule."

Daru opened his drawer, took out a little square bottle of purple ink, the red wooden penholder with the "sergeant-major" pen he used for making models of penmanship, and signed. The gendarme carefully folded the paper and put it into his wallet. Then he moved toward the door.

"I'll see you off," Daru said.

"No," said Balducci. "There's no use being polite. You insulted me."

He looked at the Arab, motionless in the same spot, sniffed peevishly, and turned away toward the door. "Good-by son," he said. The door shut behind him. Balducci appeared suddenly outside the window and then disappeared. His footsteps were muffled by the snow. The horse stirred on the other side of the wall and several chickens fluttered in fright. A moment later Balducci reappeared outside the window leading the horse by the bridle. He walked toward the little rise without turning around and disappeared from sight with the horse following him. A big stone could be heard bouncing down. Daru walked back toward the prisoner, who, without stirring, never took his eyes off him. "Wait," the schoolmaster said in Arabic and went toward the bedroom. As he was going through the door, he had a second thought, went to the desk, took the revolver, and stuck it in his pocket. Then, without looking back, he went into his room.

For some time he lay on his couch watching the sky gradually close over, listening to the silence. It was this silence that had seemed painful to him during the first days here, after the war. He had requested a post in the little town at the base of the foothills separating the upper plateaus from the desert. There, rocky walls, green and black to the north, pink and lavender to the south, marked the frontier of eternal summer. He had been named to a post farther north, on the plateau itself. In the beginning, the solitude and the silence had been hard for him on these wastelands peopled only by stones. Occasionally, furrows suggested cultivation, but they had been dug to uncover a certain kind of stone good for building. The only plowing here was to harvest rocks. Elsewhere a thin layer of soil accumulated in the hollows would be scraped out to enrich paltry village gardens. This is the way it was: bare rock covered three quarters of the region. Towns sprang up, flourished, then disappeared; men came by, loved one another or fought bitterly, then died. No one in this desert, neither he nor his guest, mattered. And yet, outside this desert neither of them, Daru knew, could have really lived.

When he got up, no noise came from the classroom. He was amazed at the unmixed joy he derived from the mere thought that the Arab might have fled and that he would be alone with no decision to make. But the prisoner was there. He had merely stretched out between the stove and the desk. With eyes open, he was staring at the ceiling. In that position, his thick lips were particularly noticeable, giving him a pouting look. "Come," said Daru. The Arab got up and followed him. In the bedroom, the schoolmaster pointed to a chair near the table under the window. The Arab sat down without taking his eyes off Daru.

"Are you hungry?"

"Yes," the prisoner said.

Daru set the table for two. He took flour and oil, shaped a cake in a frying-pan, and lighted the little stove that functioned on bottled gas.

While the cake was cooking, he went out to the shed to get cheese, eggs, dates, and condensed milk. When the cake was done he set it on the window sill to cool, heated some condensed milk diluted with water, and beat up the eggs into an omelette. In one of his motions he knocked against the revolver stuck in his right pocket. He set the bowl down, went into the classroom, and put the revolver in his desk drawer. When he came back to the room, night was falling. He put on the light and served the Arab. "Eat," he said. The Arab took a piece of the cake, lifted it eagerly to his mouth, and stopped short.

"And you?" he asked.

"After you. I'll eat too."

The thick lips opened slightly. The Arab hesitated, then bit into the cake determinedly.

The meal over, the Arab looked at the schoolmaster. "Are you the judge?"

"No, I'm simply keeping you until tomorrow."

"Why do you eat with me?"

"I'm hungry."

The Arab fell silent. Daru got up and went out. He brought back a folding bed from the shed, set it up between the table and the stove, perpendicular to his own bed. From a large suitcase which, upright in a corner, served as a shelf for papers, he took two blankets and arranged them on the camp bed. Then he stopped, felt useless, and sat down on his bed. There was nothing more to do or to get ready. He had to look at this man. He looked at him, therefore, trying to imagine his face bursting with rage. He couldn't do so. He could see nothing but the dark yet shining eyes and the animal mouth.

"Why did you kill him?" he asked in a voice whose hostile tone surprised him.

The Arab looked away.

"He ran away. I ran after him."

He raised his eyes to Daru again and they were full of a sort of woeful interrogation. "Now what will they do to me?"

"Are you afraid?"

He stiffened, turning his eyes away.

"Are you sorry?"

The Arab stared at him openmouthed. Obviously he did not understand. Daru's annoyance was growing. At the same time he felt awkward and self-conscious with his big body wedged between the two beds.

"Lie down there," he said impatiently. "That's your bed."

The Arab didn't move. He called to Daru:

"Tell me!"

The schoolmaster looked at him.

"Is the gendarme coming back tomorrow?"

"I don't know."

"Are you coming with us?"

"I don't know. Why?"

The prisoner got up and stretched out on top of the blankets, his feet toward the window. The light from the electric bulb shone straight into his eyes and he closed them at once.

"Why?" Daru repeated, standing beside the bed.

The Arab opened his eyes under the blinding light and looked at him, trying not to blink.

"Come with us," he said.

In the middle of the night, Daru was still not asleep. He had gone to bed after undressing completely; he generally slept naked. But when he suddenly realized that he had nothing on, he hesitated. He felt vulnerable and the temptation came to him to put his clothes back on. Then he shrugged his shoulders; after all, he wasn't a child and, if need be, he could break his adversary in two. From his bed he could observe him, lying on his back, still motionless with his eyes closed under the harsh light. When Daru turned out the light, the darkness seemed to coagulate all of a sudden. Little by little, the night came back to life in the window where the starless sky was stirring gently. The schoolmaster soon made out the body lying at his feet. The Arab still did not move, but his eyes seemed open. A faint wind was prowling around the schoolhouse. Perhaps it would drive away the clouds and the sun would reappear.

During the night the wind increased. The hens fluttered a little and then were silent. The Arab turned over on his side with his back to Daru, who thought he heard him moan. Then he listened for his guest's breathing, become heavier and more regular. He listened to that breath so close to him and mused without being able to go to sleep. In this room where he had been sleeping alone for a year, this presence bothered him. But it bothered him also by imposing on him a sort of brotherhood he knew well but refused to accept in the present circumstances. Men who share the same rooms, soldiers or prisoners, develop a strange alliance as if, having cast off their armor with their clothing, they fraternized every evening, over and above their differences, in the ancient community of dream and fatigue. But Daru shook himself; he didn't like such musings, and it was essential to sleep.

A little later, however, when the Arab stirred slightly, the schoolmaster was still not asleep. When the prisoner made a second move, he stiffened, on the alert. The Arab was lifting himself slowly on his arms with almost the motion of a sleepwalker. Seated upright in bed, he waited motionless without turning his head toward Daru, as if he were listening attentively. Daru did not stir; it had just occurred to him that the revolver was still in the drawer of his desk. It was better to act at once. Yet he continued to observe the prisoner, who, with the same slithery motion, put his feet on the ground, waited again, then began to stand up slowly. Daru was about to call out to him when the Arab began to walk, in a quite natural but extraordinarily silent way. He was heading toward the door at the end of the room that opened into the shed. He lifted the latch with precaution and went out, pushing the door behind him but without shutting it. Daru had not stirred. "He is running away," he merely thought. "Good riddance!" Yet he listened attentively. The hens were not fluttering; the guest must be on the plateau. A faint sound of water reached him, and he didn't know what it was until the Arab again stood framed in the doorway, closed the door carefully, and came back to bed without a sound. Then Daru turned his back on him and fell asleep. Still later he seemed, from the depths of his sleep, to hear furtive steps around the schoolhouse. "I'm dreaming! I'm dreaming!" he repeated to himself. And he went on sleeping.

When he awoke, the sky was clear; the loose window let in a cold, pure air. The Arab was asleep, hunched up under the blankets now, his mouth open, utterly relaxed. But when Daru shook him, he started dreadfully, staring at Daru with wild eyes as if he had never seen him and such a frightened expression that the schoolmaster stepped back. "Don't be afraid. It's me. You must eat." The Arab nodded his head and said yes. Calm had returned to his face, but his expression was vacant and listless.

The coffee was ready. They drank it seated together on the folding bed as they munched their pieces of the cake. Then Daru led the Arab under the shed and showed him the faucet where he washed. He went back into the room, folded the blankets and the bed, made his own bed and put the room in order. Then he went through the classroom and out onto the terrace. The sun was already rising in the blue sky; a soft, bright light was bathing the deserted plateau. On the ridge the snow was melting in spots. The stones were about to reappear. Crouched on the edge of the plateau, the schoolmaster looked at the deserted expanse. He thought of Balducci. He had hurt him, for he had sent him off in a way as if he didn't want to be associated with him. He could still hear the gendarme's farewell and, without knowing why, he felt strangely empty and vulnerable. At that moment, from the other side of the schoolhouse, the prisoner coughed. Daru listened to him almost despite himself and then, furious, threw a pebble that whistled through the air before sinking into the snow. That man's stupid crime revolted him, but to hand him over was contrary to honor. Merely thinking of it made him smart with humiliation. And he cursed at one and the same time his own people who had sent him this Arab and the Arab too who had dared to kill and not managed to get away. Daru got up, walked in a circle on the terrace, waited motionless, and then went back into the schoolhouse.

The Arab, leaning over the cement floor of the shed, was washing his teeth with two fingers. Daru looked at him and said: "Come." He went back into the room ahead of the prisoner. He slipped a hunting-jacket on over his sweater and put on walking-shoes. Standing, he waited until the Arab had put on his *chèche* and sandals. They went into the classroom and the schoolmaster pointed to the exit, saying: "Go ahead." The fellow didn't budge. "I'm coming," said Daru. The Arab went out. Daru went back into the room and made a package of pieces of rusk, dates, and sugar. In the classroom, before going out, he hesitated a second in front of his desk, then crossed the threshold and locked the door. "That's the way," he said. He started toward the east, followed by the prisoner. But, a short distance from the schoolhouse, he thought he heard a slight sound behind them. He retraced his steps and examined the surroundings of the house; there was no one there. The Arab watched him without seeming to understand. "Come on," said Daru.

They walked for an hour and rested beside a sharp peak of limestone. The snow was melting faster and faster and the sun was drinking up the puddles at once, rapidly cleaning the plateau, which gradually dried and vibrated like the air itself. When they resumed walking, the ground rang under their feet. From time to time a bird rent the space in front of them with a joyful cry. Daru breathed in deeply the fresh morning light. He felt a sort of rapture before the vast familiar expanse, now almost entirely yellow under its dome of blue sky. They walked an hour more, descending toward the south. They reached a level height made up of crumbly rocks. From there on, the plateau sloped down, eastward, toward a low plain where there were a few spindly trees and, to the south, toward outcroppings of rock that gave the landscape a chaotic look.

Daru surveyed the two directions. There was nothing but the sky on the horizon. Not a man could be seen. He turned toward the Arab, who was looking at him blankly. Daru held out the package to him. "Take it," he said. "There are dates, bread, and sugar. You can hold out for two days. Here are a thousand francs too." The Arab took the package and the money but kept his full hands at chest level as if he didn't know what to do with what was being given him. "Now look," the schoolmaster said as he pointed in the direction of the east, "there's the way to Tinguit. You have a two-hour walk. At Tinguit you'll find the administration and the police. They are expecting you." The Arab looked toward the east, still holding the package and the money against his chest. Daru took his elbow and turned him rather roughly toward the south. At the foot of the height on which they stood could be seen a faint path. "That's the trail across the plateau. In a day's walk from here you'll find pasturelands and the first nomads. They'll take you in and shelter you according to their law." The Arab had now turned toward Daru and a sort of panic was visible in his expression. "Listen," he said. Daru shook his head: "No, be quiet. Now I'm leaving you." He turned his back on him, took two long steps in the direction of the school, looked hesitantly at the motionless Arab, and started off again. For a few minutes he heard nothing but his own step resounding on the cold ground and did not turn his head. A moment later, however, he turned around. The Arab was still there on the edge of the hill, his arms hanging now, and he was looking at the schoolmaster. Daru felt something rise in his throat. But he swore with impatience, waved vaguely, and started off again. He had already gone some distance when he again stopped and looked. There was no longer anyone on the hill.

Daru hesitated. The sun was now rather high in the sky and was beginning to beat down on his head. The schoolmaster retraced his steps, at first somewhat uncertainly, then with decision. When he reached the little hill, he was bathed in sweat. He climbed it as fast as he could and stopped, out of breath, at the top. The rock-fields to the south stood out sharply against the blue sky, but on the plain to the east a steamy heat was already rising. And in that slight haze, Daru, with heavy heart, made out the Arab walking slowly on the road to prison.

A little later, standing before the window of the classroom, the schoolmaster was watching the clear light bathing the whole surface of the plateau, but he hardly saw it. Behind him on the blackboard, among the winding French rivers, sprawled the clumsily chalked-up words he had just read: "You handed over our brother. You will pay for this." Daru looked at the sky, the plateau, and, beyond, the invisible lands stretching all the way to the sea. In this vast landscape he had loved so much, he was alone.

KING OF THE BINGO GAME

The woman in front of him was eating roasted peanuts that smelled so good that he could barely contain his hunger. He could not even sleep and wished they'd hurry and begin the bingo game. There, on his right, two fellows were drinking wine out of a bottle wrapped in a paper bag, and he could hear soft gurgling in the dark. His stomach gave a low, gnawing growl. "If this was down South," he thought, "all I'd have to do is lean over and say, 'Lady, gimme a few of those peanuts, please ma'm,' and she'd pass me the bag and never think nothing of it." Or he could ask the fellows for a drink in the same way. Folks down South stuck together that way; they didn't even have to know you. But up here it was different. Ask somebody for something, and they'd think you were crazy. Well, I ain't crazy. I'm just broke, 'cause I got no birth certificate to get a job, and Laura 'bout to die 'cause we got no money for a doctor. But I ain't crazy. And yet a pinpoint of doubt was focused in his mind as he glanced toward the screen and saw the hero stealthily entering a dark room and sending the beam of a flashlight along a wall of bookcases. This is where he finds the trapdoor, he remembered. The man would pass abruptly through the wall and find the girl tied to a bed, her legs and arms spread wide, and her clothing torn to rags. He laughed softly to himself. He had seen the picture three times, and this was one of the best scenes.

On his right the fellow whispered wide-eyed to his companion, "Man, look a-yonder!"

"Damn!"

"Wouldn't I like to have her tied up like that . . . "

"Hey! That fool's letting her loose!"

"Aw, man, he loves her."

"Love or no love!"

The man moved impatiently beside him, and he tried to involve himself in the scene. But Laura was on his mind. Tiring quickly of watching the picture he looked back to where the white beam filtered from the projection room above the balcony. It started small and grew large, specks of dust dancing in its whiteness as it reached the screen. It was strange how the beam always landed right on the screen and didn't mess up and fall somewhere else. But they had it all fixed. Everything was fixed. Now suppose when they showed that girl with her dress torn the girl started taking off the rest of her clothes, and when the guy came in he didn't untie her but kept her there and went to taking off his own clothes? *That* would be something to see. If a picture got out of hand like that those guys up there would go nuts. Yeah, and there'd be so many folks in here you couldn't find a seat for nine months! A strange sensation played over his skin. He shuddered. Yesterday he'd seen a bedbug on a woman's neck as they walked out into the bright street. But exploring his thigh through a hole in his pocket he found only goose pimples and old scars.

The bottle gurgled again. He closed his eyes. Now a dreamy music was accompanying the film and train whistles were sounding in the distance, and he was a boy again walking along a railroad trestle down South, and seeing the train coming, and running back as fast as he could go, and hearing the whistle blowing, and getting off the trestle to solid ground just in time, with the earth trembling beneath his feet, and feeling relieved as he ran down the cinder-strewn embankment onto the highway, and looking back and seeing with terror that the train had left the track and was following him right down the middle of the street, and all the white people laughing as he ran screaming . . .

"Wake up there, buddy! What the hell do you mean hollering like that? Can't you see we trying to enjoy this here picture?"

He stared at the man with gratitude.

"I'm sorry, old man," he said. "I musta been dreaming."

"Well, here, have a drink. And don't be making no noise like that, damn!"

His hands trembled as he tilted his head. It was not wine, but whiskey. Cold rye whiskey. He took a deep swoller, decided it was better not to take another, and handed the bottle back to its owner.

"Thanks, old man," he said.

Now he felt the cold whiskey breaking a warm path straight through the middle of him, growing hotter and sharper as it moved. He had not eaten all day, and it made him light-headed. The smell of the peanuts stabbed him like a knife, and he got up and found a seat in the middle aisle. But no sooner did he sit than he saw a row of intense-faced young girls, and got up again, thinking, "You chicks musta been Lindy-hopping somewhere." He found a seat several rows ahead as the lights came on, and he saw the screen disappear behind a heavy red and gold curtain; then the curtain rising, and the man with the microphone and a uniformed attendant coming on the stage.

He felt for his bingo cards, smiling. The guy at the door wouldn't like it if he knew about his having *five* cards. Well, not everyone played the bingo game; and even with five cards he didn't have much of a chance. For Laura, though, he had to have faith. He studied the cards, each with its different numerals, punching the free center hole in each and spreading them neatly across his lap; and when the lights faded he sat slouched in his seat so that he could look from his cards to the bingo wheel with but a quick shifting of his eyes.

Ahead, at the end of the darkness, the man with the microphone was pressing a button attached to a long cord and spinning the bingo wheel and calling out the number each time the wheel came to rest. And each time the voice rang out his finger raced over the cards for the number. With five cards he had to move fast. He became nervous; there were too many cards, and the man went too fast with his grating voice. Perhaps he should just select one and throw the others away. But he was afraid. He became warm. Wonder how much Laura's doctor would cost? Damn that, watch the cards! And with despair he heard the man call three in a row which he missed on all five cards. This way he'd never win . . .

When he saw the row of holes punched across the third card, he sat paralyzed and heard the man call three more numbers before he stumbled forward, screaming,

"Bingo! Bingo!"

"Let that fool up there," someone called.

"Get up there, man!"

He stumbled down the aisle and up the steps to the stage into a light so sharp and bright that for a moment it blinded him, and he felt that he had moved into the spell of some strange, mysterious power. Yet it was as familiar as the sun, and he knew it was the perfectly familiar bingo.

The man with the microphone was saying something to the audience as he held out his card. A cold light flashed from the man's finger as the card left his hand. His knees trembled. The man stepped closer, checking the card against the numbers chalked on the board. Suppose he had made a mistake? The pomade on the man's hair made him feel faint, and he backed away. But the man was checking the card over the microphone now, and he had to stay. He stood tense, listening.

"Under the O, forty-four," the man chanted. "Under the I, seven. Under the G, three. Under the B, ninety-six. Under the N, thirteen!"

His breath came easier as the man smiled at the audience.

"Yessir, ladies and gentlemen, he's one of the chosen people!"

The audience rippled with laughter and applause.

"Step right up to the front of the stage."

He moved slowly forward, wishing that the light was not so bright.

"To win tonight's jackpot of $36.90 the wheel must stop between the double-zero, understand?"

He nodded, knowing the ritual from the many days and nights he had watched the winners march across the stage to press the button that controlled the spinning wheel and receive the prizes. And now he followed the instructions as though he'd crossed the slippery stage a million prize-winning times.

The man was making some kind of a joke, and he nodded vacantly. So tense had he become that he felt a sudden desire to cry and shook it away. He felt vaguely that his whole life was determined by the bingo wheel; not only that which would happen now that he was at last before it, but all that had gone before, since his birth, and his mother's birth and the birth of his father. It had always been there, even though he had not been aware of it, handing out the unlucky cards and numbers of his days. The feeling persisted, and he started quickly away. I better get down from here before I make a fool of myself, he thought.

"Here, boy," the man called. "You haven't started yet."

Someone laughed as he went hesitantly back.

"Are you all reet?"

He grinned at the man's jive talk, but no words would come, and he knew it was not a convincing grin. For suddenly he knew that he stood on the slippery brink of some terrible embarrassment.

"Where are you from, boy?" the man asked.

"Down South."

"He's from down South, ladies and gentlemen," the man said. "Where from? Speak right into the mike."

"Rocky Mont," he said. "Rock' Mont, North Car'lina."

"So you decided to come down off that mountain to the U.S.," the man laughed. He felt that the man was making a fool of him, but then something cold was placed in his hand, and the lights were no longer behind him.

Standing before the wheel he felt alone, but that was somehow right, and he remembered his plan. H would give the wheel a short quick twirl. Just a touch of the button. He had watched it many times, and always it came close to double zero when it was short and quick. He steeled himself; the fear had left, and he felt a profound sense of promise, as though he were about to be repaid for all the things he'd suffered all his life. Trembling, he pressed the button. There was a whirl of lights, and in a second he realized with finality that though he wanted to, he could not stop. It was as though he held a high-powered line in his naked hand. His nerves tightened. As the wheel increased its speed it seemed to draw him more and more into its power, as though it held his fate; and with it came a deep need to submit, to whirl, to lose himself in its swirl of color. He could not stop it now, he knew. So let it be.

The button rested snuggly in his palm where the man had placed it. And now he became aware of the man beside him, advising him through the microphone, while behind the shadowy audience hummed with noisy voices. He shifted his feet. There was still that feeling of helplessness within him, making part of him desire to turn back, even now that the jackpot was right in his hand. He squeezed the button until his fist ached. Then, like the sudden shriek of a subway whistle, a doubt tore through his head. Suppose he did not spin the wheel long enough? What could he do, and how could he tell? And then he knew, even as he wondered, that as long as he pressed the button, he could control the jackpot. He and only he could determine whether or not it was to be his. Not even the man with the microphone could do anything about it now. He felt drunk. Then, as though he had come down from a high hill into a valley of people, he heard the audience yelling.

"Come down from there, you jerk!"

"Let somebody else have a chance . . . "

"Ole Jack thinks he done found the end of the rainbow . . . "

The last voice was not unfriendly, and he turned and smiled dreamily into the yelling mouths. Then he turned his back squarely on them.

"Don't take too long, boy," a voice said.

He nodded. They were yelling behind him. Those folks did not understand what had happened to him. They had been playing the bingo game day in and night out for years, trying to win rent money or hamburger change. But not one of those wise guys had discovered this wonderful thing. He watched the wheel whirling past the numbers and experienced a burst of exaltation: This is God! This is the really truly God! He said it aloud, "This is God!"

He said it with such absolute conviction that he feared he would fall fainting into the footlights. But the crowd yelled so loud that they could not hear. Those fools, he thought. I'm here trying to tell them the most wonderful secret in the world, and they're yelling like they gone crazy. A hand fell upon his shoulder.

"You'll have to make a choice now, boy. You've taken too long."

He brushed the hand violently away.

"Leave me alone, man. I know what I'm doing!"

The man looked surprised and held on to the microphone for support. And because he did not wish to hurt the man's feelings he smiled, realizing with a sudden pang that there was no way of explaining to the man just why he had to stand there pressing the button forever.

"Come here," he called tiredly.

The man approached, rolling the heavy microphone across the stage.

"Anybody can play this bingo game, right?" he said.

"Sure, but . . . "

He smiled, feeling inclined to be patient with this slick looking white man with his blue sport shirt and his sharp gabardine suit.

"That's what I thought," he said. "Anybody can win the jackpot as long as they get the lucky number, right?"

"That's the rule, but after all . . . "

"That's what I thought," he said. "And the big prize goes to the man who knows how to win it?"

The man nodded speechlessly.

"Well then, go on over there and watch me win like I want to. I ain't going to hurt nobody," he said "and I'll show you how to win. I mean to show the whole world how it's got to be done."

And because he understood, he smiled again to let the man know that he held nothing against him for being white and impatient. Then he refused to see the man any longer and stood pressing the button, the voices of the crowd reaching him like sounds in distant streets. Let them yell. All the Negroes down there were just ashamed because he was black like them. He smiled inwardly, knowing how it was. Most of the time he was ashamed of what Negroes did himself. Well, let them be ashamed for something this time. Like him. He was like a long thin black wire that was being stretched and wound upon the bingo wheel; wound until he wanted to scream; wound, but this time himself controlling the winding and the sadness and the shame, and because he did, Laura would be all right. Suddenly the lights flickered. He staggered backwards. Had something gone wrong? All this noise. Didn't they know that although he controlled the wheel, it also controlled him, and unless he pressed the button forever and forever and ever it would stop, leaving him high and dry, dry and high on this hard high slippery hill and Laura dead? There was only one chance; he had to do whatever the wheel demanded. And gripping the button in despair, he discovered with surprise that it imparted a nervous energy. His spine tingled. He felt a certain power.

Now he faced the raging crowd with defiance, its screams penetrating his eardrums like trumpets shrieking from a jukebox. The vague faces glowing in the bingo lights gave him a sense of himself that he had never known before. He was running the show, by God! They had to react to him, for he was their luck. This is *me*, he thought. Let the bastards yell. Then someone was laughing inside him, and he realized that somehow he had forgotten his own name. It was a sad, lost feeling to lose your name, and a crazy thing to do. That name had been given him by the white man who had owned his grandfather a long lost time ago down South. But maybe those wise guys knew his name.

"Who am I?" he screamed.

"Hurry up and bingo, you jerk!"

They didn't know either, he thought sadly. They didn't even know their own names, they were all poor nameless bastards. Well, he didn't need that old name; he was reborn. For as long as he pressed the button he was The-man-who-pressed-the-button -who-held-the-prize -who-was-the-King-of-Bingo. That was the way it was, and he'd have to press the button even if nobody understood, even though Laura did not understand.

"Live!" he shouted.

The audience quieted like the dying of a huge fan.

"Live, Laura, baby. I got holt of it now, sugar. Live!"

He screamed it, tears streaming down his face. "I got nobody but YOU!"

The screams tore from his very guts. He felt as though the rush of blood to his head would burst out in baseball seams of small red droplets, like a head beaten by police clubs. Bending over he saw a trickle of blood splashing the toe of his shoe. With his free hand he searched his head. It was his nose. God, suppose something has gone wrong? He felt that the whole audience had somehow entered him and was stamping its feet in his stomach, and he was unable to throw them out. They wanted the prize, that was it. They wanted the secret for themselves. But they'd never get it; he would keep the bingo wheel whirling forever, and Laura would be safe in the wheel. But would she? It had to be, because if she were not safe the wheel would cease to turn; it could not go on. He had to get away, *vomit* all, and his mind formed an image of himself running with Laura in his arms down the tracks of the subway just ahead of an A train, running desperately *vomit* with people screaming for him to come out but knowing no way of leaving the tracks because to stop would bring the train crushing down upon him and to attempt to leave across the other tracks would mean to run into a hot third rail as high as his waist which threw blue sparks that blinded his eyes until he could hardly see.

He heard singing and the audience was clapping its hands.

> *Shoot the liquor to him, Jim, boy!*
> *Clap-clap-clap*
> *Well a-calla the cop*
> *He's blowing his top!*
> *Shoot the liquor to him, Jim, boy!*

Bitter anger grew within him at the singing. They think I'm crazy. Well let 'em laugh. I'll do what I got to do.

He was standing in an attitude of intense listening when he saw that they were watching something on the stage behind him. He felt weak. But when he turned he saw no one. If only his thumb did not ache so. Now they were applauding. And for a moment he thought that the wheel had stopped. But that was impossible, his thumb still pressed the button. Then he saw them. Two men in uniform beckoned from the end of the stage. They were coming toward him, walking in step, slowly, like a tap-dance team returning for a third encore. But their shoulders shot forward, and he backed away, looking wildly about. There was nothing to fight them with. He had only the long black cord which led to a plug somewhere back stage, and he couldn't use that because it operated the bingo wheel. He backed slowly, fixing the men with his eyes as his lips stretched over his teeth in a tight, fixed grin; moved toward the end of the stage and realizing that he couldn't go much further, for suddenly the cord became taut and he couldn't afford to break the cord. But he had to do something. The audience was howling. Suddenly he stopped dead, seeing the men halt, their legs lifted as in an interrupted step of a slow-motion dance. There was nothing to do but run in the other direction and he dashed forward, slipping and sliding. The men fell back, surprised. He struck out violently going past.

"Grab him!"

He ran, but all too quickly the cord tightened, resistingly, and he turned and ran back again. This time he slipped them, and discovered by running in a circle before the wheel he could keep the cord from tightening. But this way he had to flail his arms to keep the men away. Why couldn't they leave a man alone? He ran, circling.

"Ring down the curtain," someone yelled. But they couldn't do that. If they did the wheel flashing from the projection room would be cut off. But they had him before he could tell them so, trying to pry open his fist, and he was wrestling and trying to bring his knees into the fight and holding on to the button, for it was his life. And now he was down, seeing a foot coming down, crushing his wrist cruelly, down, as he saw the wheel whirling serenely above.

"I can't give it up," he screamed. Then quietly, in a confidential tone, "Boys, I really can't give it up."

It landed hard against his head. And in the blank moment they had it away from him, completely now. He fought them trying to pull him up from the stage as he watched the wheel spin slowly to a stop. Without surprise he saw it rest at double-zero.

"You see," he pointed bitterly.

"Sure, boy, sure, it's O. K.," one of the men said smiling.

And seeing the man bow his head to someone he could not see, he felt very, very happy; he would receive what all the winners received.

But as he warmed in the justice of the man's tight smile he did not see the man's slow wink, nor see the bow-legged man behind him step clear of the swiftly descending curtain and set himself for a blow. He only felt the dull pain exploding in his skull, and he knew even as it slipped out of him that his luck had run out on the stage.

BLACK IS MY FAVORITE COLOR

Charity Sweetness sits in the toilet eating her two hardboiled eggs while I'm having my ham sandwich and coffee in the kitchen. That's how it goes only don't get the idea of ghettoes. If there's a ghetto I'm the one that's in it. She's my cleaning woman from Father Divine and comes in once a week to my small three-room apartment on my day off from the liquor store. "Peace," she says to me, "Father reached on down and took me right up in Heaven." She's a small person with a flat body, frizzy hair, and a quiet face that the light shines out of, and Mama had such eyes before she died. The first time Charity Sweetness came in to clean, a little more than a year and a half, I made the mistake to ask her to sit down at the kitchen table with me and eat her lunch. I was still feeling not so hot after Ornita left but I'm the kind of a man—Nat Lime, forty-four, a bachelor with a daily growing bald spot on the back of my head, and I could lose frankly fifteen pounds—who enjoys company so long as he has it. So she cooked up her two hardboiled eggs and sat down and took a small bite out of one of them. But after a minute she stopped chewing and she got up and carried the eggs in a cup in the bathroom, and since then she eats there. I said to her more than once, "Okay, Charity Sweetness, so have it your way, eat the eggs in the kitchen by yourself and I'll eat when you're done," but she smiles absentminded, and eats in the toilet. It's my fate with colored people.

Although black is still my favorite color you wouldn't know it from my luck except in short quantities even though I do all right in the liquor store business in Harlem, on Eighth Avenue between 110th and 111th. I speak with respect. A large part of my life I've had dealings with Negro people, most on a business basis but sometimes for friendly reasons with genuine feeling on both sides. I'm drawn to them. At this time of my life I should have one or two good colored friends but the fault isn't necessarily mine. If they knew what was in my heart towards them, but how can you tell that to anybody nowadays? I've tried more than once but the language of the heart either is a dead language or else nobody understands it the way you speak it. Very few. What I'm saying is, personally for me there's only one human color and that's the color of blood. I like a black person if not because he's black, then because I'm white. It comes to the same thing. If I wasn't white my first choice would be black. I'm satisfied to be white because I have no other choice. Anyway, I got an eye for color. I appreciate. Who wants everybody to be the same? Maybe it's like some kind of a talent. Nat Lime might be a liquor dealer in Harlem, but once in the jungle in New Guinea in the Second War, I got the idea when I shot at a running Jap and missed him, that I had some kind of a talent, though maybe it's the kind where you have a marvelous idea now and then but in the end what do they come to? After all, it's a strange world.

Where Charity Sweetness eats her eggs makes me think about Buster Wilson when we were both boys in the Williamsburg section of Brooklyn. There was this long block of run-down dirty frame houses in the middle of a not-so-hot white neighborhood full of pushcarts. The Negro houses looked to me like they had been born and died there, dead not long after the beginning of the world. I lived on the next street. My father was a cutter with arthritis in both hands, big red knuckles and swollen fingers so he didn't cut, and my mother was the one who went to work. She sold paper bags from a second-hand pushcart in Ellery Street. We didn't starve but nobody ate chicken unless we were sick or the chicken was. This was my first acquaintance with a lot of black people and I used to poke around on their poor block. I think I thought, brother, if there can be like this, what can't there be? I mean I caught an early idea what life was about. Anyway I met Buster Wilson there. He used to play marbles by himself. I sat on the curb across the street, watching him shoot one marble lefty and the other one righty. The hand that won picked up the marbles. It wasn't so much of a game but he didn't ask me to come over. My idea was to be friendly, only he never encouraged, he discouraged. Why did I pick him out for a friend? Maybe because I had no others then, we were new in the neighborhood, from Manhattan. Also I liked his type. Buster did everything alone. He was a skinny kid and his brothers' clothes hung on him like worn-out potato sacks. He was a beanpole boy, about twelve, and I was then ten. His arms and legs were burnt out matchsticks. He always wore a brown wool sweater, one arm half unraveled, the other went down to the wrist. His long and narrow head had a white part cut straight in the short woolly hair, maybe with a ruler there, by his father, a barber but too drunk to stay a barber. In those days though I had little myself I was old enough to know who was better off, and the whole block of colored houses made me feel bad in the daylight. But I went there as much as I could because the street was full of life. In the night it looked different, it's hard to tell a cripple in the dark. Sometimes I was afraid to walk by the houses when they were dark and quiet. I was afraid there were people looking at me that I couldn't see. I liked it better when they had parties at night and everybody had a good time. The musicians played their banjos and saxophones and the houses shook with the music and laughing. The young girls, with their pretty dresses and ribbons in their hair, caught me in my throat when I saw them through the windows.

But with the parties came drinking and fights. Sundays were bad days after the Saturday night parties. I remember once that Buster's father, also long and loose, always wearing a dirty gray Homburg hat, chased another black man in the street with a half-inch chisel. The other one, maybe five feet high, lost his shoe and when they wrestled on the ground he was already bleeding through his suit, a thick red blood smearing the sidewalk. I was frightened by the blood and wanted to pour it back in the man who was bleeding from the chisel. On another time Buster's father was playing in a crap game with two big bouncy red dice, in the back of an alley between two middle houses. Then about six men started fist-fighting there, and they ran out of the alley and hit each other in the street. The neighbors, including children, came out and watched, everybody afraid but nobody moving to do anything. I saw the same thing near my store in Harlem, years later, a big crowd watching two men in the street, their breaths hanging in the air on a winter night, murdering each other with switch knives, but nobody moved to call a cop. I didn't either. Anyway, I was just a young kid but I still remember how the cops drove up in a police paddy wagon and broke up the fight by hitting everybody they could hit with big nightsticks. This was in the days before LaGuardia. Most of the fighters were knocked out cold, only one or two got away. Buster's father started to run back in his house but a cop ran after him and cracked him on his Homburg hat with a club, right on the front porch. Then the Negro men were lifted up by the cops, one at the arms and the other at the feet, and they heaved them in the paddy wagon. Buster's father hit the back of the wagon and fell, with his nose spouting very red blood, on top of three other men. I personally couldn't stand it, I was scared of the human race so I ran home, but I remember Buster watching without any expression in his eyes. I stole an extra fifteen cents from my mother's pocketbook and I ran back and asked Buster if he wanted to go to the movies. I would pay. He said yes. This was the first time he talked to me.

So we went more than once to the movies. But we never got to be friends. Maybe because it was a one-way proposition—from me to him. Which includes my invitations to go with me, my (poor mother's) movie money, Hershey chocolate bars, watermelon slices, even my best Nick Carter and Merriwell books that I spent hours picking up in the junk shops, and that he never gave me back. Once he let me go in his house to get a match so we could smoke some butts we found, but it smelled so heavy, so impossible, I died till I got out of there. What I saw in the way of furniture I won't mention—the best was falling apart in pieces. Maybe we went to the movies all together five or six matinees that spring and in the summertime, but when the shows were over he usually walked home by himself.

"Why don't you wait for me, Buster?" I said. "We're both going in the same direction."

But he was walking ahead and didn't hear me. Anyway he didn't answer.

One day when I wasn't expecting it he hit me in the teeth. I felt like crying but not because of the pain. I spit blood and said, "What did you hit me for? What did I do to you?"

"Because you a Jew bastard. Take your Jew movies and your Jew candy and shove them up your Jew ass."

And he ran away.

I thought to myself how was I to know he didn't like the movies. When I was a man I thought, you can't force it.

Years later, in the prime of my life, I met Mrs. Ornita Harris. She was standing by herself under an open umbrella at the bus stop, crosstown 110th, and I picked up her green glove that she had dropped on the wet sidewalk. It was in the end of November. Before I could ask her was it hers, she grabbed the glove out of my hand, closed her umbrella, and stepped in the bus. I got on right after her.

I was annoyed so I said, "If you'll pardon me, Miss, there's no law that you have to say thanks, but at least don't make a criminal out of me."

"Well, I'm sorry," she said, "but I don't like white men trying to do me favors."

I tipped my hat and that was that. In ten minutes I got off the bus but she was already gone.

Who expected to see her again but I did. She came into my store about a week later for a bottle of scotch.

"I would offer you a discount," I told her, "but I know you don't like a certain kind of a favor and I'm not looking for a slap in the face."

Then she recognized me and got a little embarrassed.

"I'm sorry I misunderstood you that day."

"So mistakes happen."

The result was she took the discount. I gave her a dollar off.

She used to come in about every two weeks for a fifth of Haig and Haig. Sometimes I waited on her, sometimes my helpers, Jimmy or Mason, also colored, but I said to give the discount. They both looked at me but I had nothing to be ashamed. In the spring when she came in we used to talk once in a while. She was a slim woman, dark but not the most dark, about thirty years I would say, also well built, with a combination nice legs and a good-size bosom that I like. Her face was pretty, with big eyes and high cheek bones, but lips a little thick and nose a little broad. Sometimes she didn't feel like talking, she paid for the bottle, less discount, and walked out. Her eyes were tired and she didn't look to me like a happy woman.

I found out her husband was once a window cleaner on the big buildings, but one day his safety belt broke and he fell fifteen stories. After the funeral she got a job as a manicurist in a Times Square barber shop. I told her I was a bachelor and lived with my mother in a small three-room apartment on West Eighty-third near Broadway. My mother had cancer, and Ornita said she was very sorry.

One night in July we went out together. How that happened I'm still not so sure. I guess I asked her and she didn't say no. Where do you go out with a Negro woman? We went to the Village. We had a good dinner and walked in Washington Square Park. It was a hot night. Nobody was surprised when they saw us, nobody looked at us like we were against the law. If they looked maybe they saw my new lightweight suit that I bought yesterday and my shiny bald spot when we walked under a lamp, also how pretty she was for a man of my type. We went in a movie on West Eighth Street. I didn't want to go in but she said she had heard about the picture. We went in like strangers and we came out like strangers. I wondered what was in her mind and I thought to myself, whatever is in there it's not a certain white man that I know. All night long we went together like we were chained. After the movie she wouldn't let me take her back to Harlem. When I put her in a taxi she asked me, "Why did we bother?"

For the steak, I wanted to say. Instead I said, "You're worth the bother."

"Thanks anyway."

Kiddo, I thought to myself after the taxi left, you just found out what's what, now the best thing is forget her.

It's easy to say. In August we went out the second time. That was the night she wore a purple dress and I thought to myself, my God, what colors. Who paints that picture paints a masterpiece. Everybody looked at us but I had pleasure. That night when she took off her dress it was in a furnished room I had the sense to rent a few days before. With my sick mother, I couldn't ask her to come to my apartment, and she didn't want me to go home with her where she lived with her brother's family on West 115th near Lenox Avenue. Under her purple dress she wore a black slip, and when she took that off she had white underwear. When she took off the white underwear she was black again. But I know where the next white was, if you want to call it white. And that was the night I think I fell in love with her, the first time in my life though I have liked one or two nice girls I used to go with when I was a boy. It was a serious proposition. I'm the kind of a man when I think of love I'm thinking of marriage. I guess that's why I am a bachelor.

That same week I had a holdup in my place, two big men—both black —with revolvers. One got excited when I rang open the cash register so he could take the money and he hit me over the ear with his gun. I stayed in the hospital a couple of weeks. Otherwise I was insured. Ornita came to see me. She sat on a chair without talking much. Finally I saw she was uncomfortable so I suggested she ought to go home.

"I'm sorry it happened," she said.

"Don't talk like it's your fault."

When I got out of the hospital my mother was dead. She was a wonderful person. My father died when I was thirteen and all by herself she kept the family alive and together. I sat shive for a week and remembered how she sold paper bags on her pushcart. I remembered her life and what she tried to teach me. Nathan, she said, if you ever forget you are a Jew a goy will remind you. Mama, I said, rest in peace on this subject. But if I do something you don't like, remember, on earth it's harder than where you are. Then when my week of mourning was finished, one night I said, "Ornita, let's get married. We're both honest people and if you love me like I love you it won't be such a bad time. If you don't like New York I'll sell out here and we'll move someplace else. Maybe to San Francisco where nobody knows us. I was there for a week in the Second War and I saw white and colored living together."

"Nat," she answered me, "I like you but I'd be afraid. My husband woulda killed me."

"Your husband is dead."

"Not in my memory."

"In that case I'll wait."

"Do you know what it'd be like—I mean the life we could expect?"

"Ornita," I said, "I'm the kind of a man, if he picks his own way of life he's satisfied."

"What about children? Were you looking forward to half-Jewish polka dots?"

"I was looking forward to children."

"I can't," she said.

Can't is can't. I saw she was afraid and the best thing was not to push. Sometimes when we met she was so nervous that whatever we did she couldn't enjoy it. At the same time I still thought I had a chance. We were together more and more. I got rid of my furnished room and she came to my apartment—I gave away Mama's bed and bought a new one. She stayed with me all day on Sundays. When she wasn't so nervous she was affectionate, and if I know what love is, I had it. We went out a couple of times a week, the same way—usually I met her in Times Square and sent her home in a taxi, but I talked more about marriage and she talked less against it. One night she told me she was still trying to convince herself but she was almost convinced. I took an inventory of my liquor stock so I could put the store up for sale.

Ornita knew what I was doing. One day she quit her job, the next day she took it back. She also went away a week to visit her sister in Philadelphia for a little rest. She came back tired but said maybe. Maybe is maybe so I'll wait. The way she said it it was closer to yes. That was the winter two years ago. When she was in Philadelphia I called up a friend of mine from the Army, now CPA, and told him I would appreciate an invitation for an evening. He knew why. His wife said yes right away. When Ornita came back we went there. The wife made a fine dinner. It wasn't a bad time and they told us to come again. Ornita had a few drinks. She looked relaxed, wonderful. Later, because of a twenty-four hour taxi strike I had to take her home on the subway. When we got to the 116th Street station she told me to stay on the train, and she would walk the couple of blocks to her house. I didn't like a woman walking alone on the streets at that time of the night. She said she never had any trouble but I insisted nothing doing. I said I would walk to her stoop with her and when she went upstairs I would go back to the subway.

On the way there, on 115th in the middle of the block before Lenox, we were stopped by three men—maybe they were boys. One had a black hat with a half-inch brim, one a green cloth hat, and the third wore a black leather cap. The green hat was wearing a short coat and the other two had long ones. It was under a street light but the leather cap snapped a six-inch switchblade open in the light.

"What you doin' with this white son of a bitch?" he said to Ornita.

"I'm minding my own business," she answered him, "and I wish you would too."

"Boys," I said, "we're all brothers. I'm a reliable merchant in the neighborhood. This young lady is my dear friend. We don't want any trouble. Please let us pass."

"You talk like a Jew landlord," said the green hat. "Fifty a week for a single room."

"No charge fo' the rats," said the half-inch brim.

"Believe me, I'm no landlord. My store is 'Nathan's Liquors' between Hundred Tenth and Eleventh. I also have two colored clerks, Mason and Jimmy, and they will tell you I pay good wages as well as I give discounts to certain customers."

"Shut your mouth, Jewboy," said the leather cap, and he moved the knife back and forth in front of my coat button. "No more black pussy for you."

"Speak with respect about this lady, please."

I got slapped on my mouth.

"That ain't no lady," said the long face in the half-inch brim, "that's black pussy. She deserve to have evvy bit of her hair shave off. How you like to have evvy bit of your hair shave off, black pussy?"

"Please leave me and this gentleman alone or I'm gonna scream long and loud. That's my house three doors down."

They slapped her. I never heard such a scream. Like her husband was falling fifteen stories.

I hit the one that slapped her and the next I knew I was lying in the gutter with a pain in my head. I thought, goodbye, Nat, they'll stab me for sure, but all they did was take my wallet and run in three different directions.

Ornita walked back with me to the subway and she wouldn't let me go home with her again.

"Just get home safely."

She looked terrible. Her face was gray and I still remembered her scream. It was a terrible winter night, very cold February, and it took me an hour and ten minutes to get home. I felt bad for leaving her but what could I do?

We had a date downtown the next night but she didn't show up, the first time.

In the morning I called her in her place of business.

"For God's sake, Ornita, if we got married and moved away we wouldn't have that kind of trouble that we had. We wouldn't come in that neighborhood any more."

"Yes, we would. I have family there and don't want to move anyplace else. The truth of it is I can't marry you, Nat. I got troubles enough of my own."

"I coulda sworn you love me."

"Maybe I do but I can't marry you."

"For God's sake, why?"

"I got enough trouble of my own."

I went that night in a cab to her brother's house to see her. He was a quiet man with a thin mustache. "She gone," he said, "left for a long visit to some close relatives in the South. She said to tell you she appreciate your intentions but didn't think it will work out."

"Thank you kindly," I said.

Don't ask me how I got home.

Once on Eighth Avenue, a couple of blocks from my store, I saw a blind man with a white cane tapping on the sidewalk. I figured we were going in the same direction so I took his arm.

"I can tell you're white," he said.

A heavy colored woman with a full shopping bag rushed after us.

"Never mind," she said, "I know where he live."

She pushed me with her shoulder and I hurt my leg on the fire hydrant.

That's how it is. I give my heart and they kick me in my teeth.

"Charity Sweetness—you hear me?—come out of that goddamn toilet!"

A FATHER-TO-BE

The strangest notions had a way of forcing themselves into Rogin's mind. Just thirty-one and passable-looking, with short black hair, small eyes, but a high, open forehead, he was a research chemist, and his mind was generally serious and dependable. But on a snowy Sunday evening while this stocky man, buttoned to the chin in a Burberry coat and walking in his preposterous gait—feet turned outward—was going toward the subway, he fell into a peculiar state.

He was on his way to have supper with his fiancée. She had phoned him a short while ago and said, "You'd better pick up a few things on the way."

"What do we need?"

"Some roast beef, for one thing. I bought a quarter of a pound coming home from my aunt's."

"Why a quarter of a pound, Joan?" said Rogin, deeply annoyed. "That's just about enough for one good sandwich."

"So you have to stop at a delicatessen. I had no more money."

He was about to ask, "What happened to the thirty dollars I gave you on Wednesday?," but he knew that would not be right.

"I had to give Phyllis money for the cleaning woman," said Joan.

Phyllis, Joan's cousin, was a young divorcée, extremely wealthy. The two women shared an apartment.

"Roast beef," he said, "and what else?"

"Some shampoo, sweetheart. We've used up all the shampoo. And hurry, darling, I've missed you all day."

"And I've missed you," said Rogin, but to tell the truth he had been worrying most of the time. He had a younger brother whom he was putting through college. And his mother, whose annuity wasn't quite enough in these days of inflation and high taxes, needed money, too. Joan had debts he was helping her to pay, for she wasn't working. She was looking for something suitable to do. Beautiful, well-educated, aristocratic in her atti-

Source: Copyright ©1955 by Saul Bellow. Reprinted from *Mosby's Memoirs And Other Stories* by Saul Bellow, with the permission of The Viking Press, Inc. Originally published in *The New Yorker*.

tude, she couldn't clerk in a dime store; she couldn't model clothes (Rogin thought this made girls vain and stiff, and he didn't want her to); she couldn't be a waitress or a cashier. What could she be? Well, something would turn up, and meantime Rogin hesitated to complain. He paid her bills—the dentist, the department store, the osteopath, the doctor, the psychiatrist. At Christmas, Rogin almost went mad. Joan bought him a velvet smoking jacket with frog fasteners, a beautiful pipe, and a pouch. She bought Phyllis a garnet brooch, an Italian silk umbrella, and a gold cigarette holder. For other friends, she bought Dutch pewter and Swedish glassware. Before she was through, she had spent five hundred dollars of Rogin's money. He loved her too much to show his suffering. He believed she had a far better nature than his. She didn't worry about money. She had a marvellous character, always cheerful, and she really didn't need a psychiatrist at all. She went to one because Phyllis did and it made her curious. She tried too much to keep up with her cousin, whose father had made millions in the rug business.

While the woman in the drugstore was wrapping the shampoo bottle, a clear idea suddenly arose in Rogin's thoughts: Money surrounds you in life as the earth does in death. Superimposition is the universal law. Who is free? No one is free. Who has no burdens? Everyone is under pressure. The very rocks, the waters of the earth, beasts, men, children—everyone has some weight to carry. This idea was extremely clear to him at first. Soon it became rather vague, but it had a great effect nevertheless, as if someone had given him a valuable gift. (Not like the velvet smoking jacket he couldn't bring himself to wear, or the pipe it choked him to smoke.) The notion that all were under pressure and affliction, instead of saddening him, had the opposite influence. It put him in a wonderful mood. It was extraordinary how happy he became and, in addition, clear-sighted. His eyes all at once were opened to what was around him. He saw with delight how the druggist and the woman who wrapped the shampoo bottle were smiling and flirting, how the lines of worry in her face went over into lines of cheer and the druggist's receding gums did not hinder his kidding and friendliness. And in the delicatessen, also, it was amazing how much Rogin noted and what happiness it gave him simply to be there.

Delicatessens on Sunday night, when all other stores are shut, will overcharge you ferociously, and Rogin would normally have been on guard, but he was not tonight, or scarcely so. Smells of pickle, sausage, mustard, and smoked fish overjoyed him. He pitied the people who would buy the chicken salad and chopped herring; they could do it only because their sight was too dim to see what they were getting—the fat flakes of pepper on the chicken, the soppy herring, mostly vinegar-soaked stale bread. Who would buy them? Late risers, people living alone, waking up in the darkness of the afternoon, finding their refrigerators empty, or people whose gaze was turned inward. The roast beef looked not bad, and Rogin ordered a pound.

While the storekeeper was slicing the meat, he yelled at a Puerto Rican kid who was reaching for a bag of chocolate cookies, "Hey, you want to pull me down the whole display on yourself? You, *chico,* wait a half a. minute." This storekeeper, though he looked like one of Pancho Villa's bandits, the kind that smeared their enemies with syrup and staked them down on anthills, a man with toadlike eyes and stout hands made to clasp pistols hung around his belly, was not so bad. He was a New York man, thought Rogin—who was from Albany himself—a New York man toughened by every abuse of the city, trained to suspect everyone. But in his own realm, on the board behind the counter, there was justice. Even clemency.

The Puerto Rican kid wore a complete cowboy outfit—a green hat with white braid, guns, chaps, spurs, boots, and gauntlets—but he couldn't speak any English. Rogin unhooked the cellophane bag of hard circular cookies and gave it to him. The boy tore the cellophane with his teeth and began to chew one of those dry chocolate discs. Rogin recognized his state —the energetic dream of childhood. Once, he, too, had found these dry biscuits delicious. It would have bored him now to eat one. What else would Joan like? Rogin thought fondly. Some strawberries? "Give me some frozen strawberries. No, raspberries, she likes those better. And heavy cream. And some rolls, cream cheese, and some of those rubber-looking gherkins."

"What rubber?"

"Those, deep green, with eyes. Some ice cream might be in order, too."

He tried to think of a compliment, a good comparison, an endearment, for Joan when she'd open the door. What about her complexion? There was really nothing to compare her sweet, small, daring, shapely, timid, defiant, loving face to. How difficult she was, and how beautiful!

As Rogin went down into the stony, odorous, metallic, captive air of the subway, he was diverted by an unusual confession made by a man to his friend. These were two very tall men, shapeless in their winter clothes, as if their coats concealed suits of chain mail.

"So, how long have you known me?" said one.

"Twelve years."

"Well, I have an admission to make," he said. "I've decided that I might as well. For years I've been a heavy drinker. You didn't know. Practically an alcoholic."

But his friend was not surprised, and he answered immediately, "Yes, I did know."

"You knew? Impossible! How could you?"

Why, thought Rogin, as if it could be a secret! Look at that long, austere, alcohol-washed face, that drink-ruined nose, the skin by his ears like turkey wattles, and those whiskey—saddened eyes.

"Well, I did know, though."

"You couldn't have. I can't believe it." He was upset, and his friend didn't seem to want to soothe him. "But it's all right now," he said. "I've been going to a doctor and taking pills, a new revolutionary Danish discovery. It's a miracle. I'm beginning to believe they can cure you of anything and everything. You can't beat the Danes in science. They do everything. They turned a man into a woman."

"That isn't how they stop you from drinking, is it?"

"No. I hope not. This is only like aspirin. It's super-aspirin. They call it the aspirin of the future. But if you use it, you have to stop drinking."

Rogin's illuminated mind asked of itself while the human tides of the subway swayed back and forth, and cars linked and transparent like fish bladders raced under the streets: How come he thought nobody would know what everybody couldn't help knowing? And, as a chemist, he asked himself what kind of compound this new Danish drug might be, and started thinking about various inventions of his own, synthetic albumen, a cigarette that lit itself, a cheaper motor fuel. Ye gods, but he needed money! As never before. What was to be done? His mother was growing more and more difficult. On Friday night, she had neglected to cut up his meat for him, and he was hurt. She had sat at the table motionless, with her long-suffering face, severe, and let him cut his own meat, a thing she almost never did. She had always spoiled him and made his brother envy him. But what she expected now! Oh, Lord, how he had to pay, and it had never even occurred to him formerly that these things might have a price.

Seated, one of the passengers, Rogin recovered his calm, happy, even clairvoyant state of mind. To think of money was to think as the world wanted you to think; then you'd never be your own master. When people said they couldn't do something for love or money, they meant that love and money were opposite passions and one the enemy of the other. He went on to reflect how little people knew about this, how they slept through life, how small a light the light of consciousness was. Rogin's clean, snub-nosed face shone while his heart was torn with joy at these deeper thoughts of our ignorance. You might take this drunkard as an example, who for long years thought his closest friends never suspected he drank. Rogin looked up and down the aisle for this remarkable knightly symbol, but he was gone.

However, there was no lack of things to see. There was a small girl with a new white muff; into the muff a doll's head was sewn, and the child was happy and affectionately vain of it, while her old man, stout and grim, with a huge scowling nose, kept picking her up and resetting her in the seat, as if he were trying to change her into something else. Then another child, led by her mother, boarded the car, and this other child carried the very same doll-faced muff, and this greatly annoyed both parents. The woman, who looked like a difficult, contentious woman, took her daughter away. It seemed to Rogin that each child was in love with its own muff and didn't even see the other, but it was one of his foibles to think he understood the hearts of little children.

A foreign family next engaged his attention. They looked like Central Americans to him. On one side the mother, quite old, dark-faced, white-haired, and worn out; on the other a son with the whitened, porous hands of a dishwasher. But what was the dwarf who sat between them—a son or a daughter? The hair was long and wavy and the cheeks smooth, but the shirt and tie were masculine. The overcoat was feminine, but the shoes —the shoes were a puzzle. A pair of brown oxfords with an outer seam like a man's, but Baby Louis heels like a woman's—a plain toe like a man's, but a strap across the instep like a woman's. No stockings. That didn't help much. The dwarf's fingers were beringed, but without a wedding band. There were small grim dents in the cheeks. The eyes were puffy and concealed, but Rogin did not doubt that they could reveal strange things if they chose and that this was a creature of remarkable understanding. He had for many years owned De la Mare's "Memoirs of a Midget." Now he took a resolve; he would read it. As soon as he had decided, he was free from his consuming curiosity as to the dwarf's sex and was able to look at the person who sat beside him.

Thoughts very often grow fertile in the subway, because of the motion, the great company, the subtlety of the rider's state as he rattles under streets and rivers, under the foundations of great buildings, and Rogin's mind had already been strangely stimulated. Clasping the bag of groceries from which there rose odors of bread and pickle spice, he was following a train of reflections, first about the chemistry of sex determination, the X and Y chromosomes, hereditary linkages, the uterus, afterward about his brother as a tax exemption. He recalled two dreams of the night before. In one, an undertaker had offered to cut his hair, and he had refused. In another, he had been carrying a woman on his head. Sad dreams, both! Very sad! Which was the woman—Joan or Mother? And the undertaker —his lawyer? He gave a deep sigh, and by force of habit began to put together his synthetic albumen that was to revolutionize the entire egg industry.

Meanwhile, he had not interrupted his examination of the passengers and had fallen into a study of the man next to him. This was a man whom he had never in his life seen before but with whom he now suddenly felt linked through all existence. He was middle-aged, sturdy, with clear skin and blue eyes. His hands were clean, well-formed, but Rogin did not approve of them. The coat he wore was a fairly expensive blue check such as Rogin would never have chosen for himself. He would not have worn blue suède shoes, either, or such a faultless hat, a cumbersome felt animal of a hat encircled by a high, fat ribbon. There are all kinds of dandies, not all of them are of the flaunting kind; some are dandies of respectability, and Rogin's fellow-passenger was one of these. His straight-nosed profile was handsome, yet he had betrayed his gift, for he was flat-looking. But in his flat way he seemed to warn people that he wanted no difficulties with them, he wanted nothing to do with them. Wearing such blue suède shoes, he could not afford to have people treading on his feet, and he seemed to draw about himself a circle of privilege, notifying all others to mind their own business and let him read his paper. He was holding a *Tribune,* and perhaps it would be overstatement to say that he was reading. He was holding it.

His clear skin and blue eyes, his straight and purely Roman nose—even the way he sat—all strongly suggested one person to Rogin: Joan. He tried to escape the comparison, but it couldn't be helped. This man not only looked like Joan's father, whom Rogin detested; he looked like Joan herself. Forty years hence, a son of hers, provided she had one, might be like this. A son of hers? Of such a son, he himself, Rogin, would be the father. Lacking in dominant traits as compared with Joan, his heritage would not appear. Probably the children would resemble her. Yes, think forty years ahead, and a man like this, who sat by him knee to knee in the hurtling car among their fellow-creatures, unconscious participants in a sort of great carnival of transit—such a man would carry forward what had been Rogin.

This was why he felt bound to him through all existence. What were forty years reckoned against eternity! Forty years were gone, and he was gazing at his own son. Here he was. Rogin was frightened and moved. "My son! My son!" he said to himself, and the pity of it almost made him burst into tears. The holy and frightful work of the masters of life and death brought this about. We were their instruments. We worked toward ends we thought were our own. But no! The whole thing was so unjust. To suffer, to labor, to toil and force your way through the spikes of life, to crawl through its darkest caverns, to push through the worst, to struggle under the weight of economy, to make money—only to become the father of a fourth-rate man of the world like this, so flat-looking, with his ordinary, clean, rosy, uninteresting, self-satisfied, fundamentally bourgeois face. What a curse to have a dull son! A son like this, who could never understand his father. They had absolutely nothing, but nothing, in common, he and this neat, chubby, blue-eyed man. He was so pleased, thought Rogin, with all he owned and all he did and all he was that he could hardly unfasten his lip. Look at that lip, sticking up at the tip like a little thorn or egg tooth. He wouldn't give anyone the time of day. Would this perhaps be general forty years from now? Would personalities be chillier as the world aged and grew colder? The inhumanity of the next generation incensed Rogin. Father and son had no sign to make to each other. Terrible! Inhuman! What a vision of existence it gave him. Man's personal aims were nothing, illusion. The life force occupied each of us in turn in its progress toward its own fulfillment, trampling on our individual humanity, using us for its own ends like mere dinosaurs or bees, exploiting love heartlessly, making us engage in the social process, labor, struggle for money, and submit to the law of pressure, the universal law of layers, superimposition!

What the blazes am I getting into? Rogin thought. To be the father of a throwback to *her* father. The image of this white-haired, gross, peevish old man with his ugly selfish blue eyes revolted Rogin. This was how his grandson would look. Joan, with whom Rogin was now more and more displeased, could not help that. For her, it was inevitable. But did it have to be inevitable for him? Well, then, Rogin, you fool, don't be a damned instrument. Get out of the way!

But it was too late for this, because he had already experienced the sensation of sitting next to his own son, his son and Joan's. He kept staring at him, waiting for him to say something, but the presumptive son remained coldly silent though he must have been aware of Rogin's scrutiny. They even got out at the same stop—Sheridan Square. When they stepped to the platform, the man, without even looking at Rogin, went away in a different direction in his detestable blue-checked coat, with his rosy, nasty face.

The whole thing upset Rogin very badly. When he approached Joan's door and heard Phyllis's little dog Henri barking even before he could knock, his face was very tense. "I won't be used," he declared to himself. "I have my own right to exist." Joan had better watch out. She had a light way of bypassing grave questions he had given earnest thought to. She always assumed no really disturbing thing would happen. He could not afford the luxury of such a carefree, debonair attitude himself, because he had to work hard and earn money so that disturbing things would *not* happen. Well, at the moment this situation could not be helped, and he really did not mind the money if he could feel that she was not necessarily the mother of such a son as his subway son or entirely the daughter of that awful, obscene father of hers. After all, Rogin was not himself so much like either of his parents, and quite different from his brother.

Joan came to the door, wearing one of Phyllis's expensive housecoats. It suited her very well. At first sight of her happy face, Rogin was brushed by the shadow of resemblance; the touch of it was extremely light, almost figmentary, but it made his flesh tremble.

She began to kiss him, saying, "Oh, my baby. You're covered with snow. Why didn't you wear your hat? It's all over its little head"—her favorite third-person endearment.

"Well, let me put down this bag of stuff. Let me take off my coat," grumbled Rogin, and escaped from her embrace. Why couldn't she wait making up to him? "It's so hot in here. My face is burning. Why do you keep the place at this temperature? And that damned dog keeps barking. If you didn't keep it cooped up, it wouldn't be so spoiled and noisy. Why doesn't anybody ever walk him?"

"Oh, it's not really so hot here! You've just come in from the cold. Don't you think this housecoat fits me better than Phyllis? Especially across the hips. She thinks so, too. She may sell it to me."

"I hope not," Rogin almost exclaimed.

She brought a towel to dry the melting snow from his short, black hair. The flurry of rubbing excited Henri intolerably, and Joan locked him up in the bedroom, where he jumped persistently against the door with a rhythmic sound of claws on the wood.

Joan said, "Did you bring the shampoo?"

"Here it is."

"Then I'll wash your hair before dinner. Come."

"I don't want it washed."

"Oh, come on," she said, laughing.

Her lack of consciousness of guilt amazed him. He did not see how it could be. And the carpeted, furnished, lamplit, curtained room seemed to stand against his vision. So that he felt accusing and angry, his spirit sore and bitter, but it did not seem fitting to say why. Indeed, he began to worry lest the reason for it all slip away from him.

They took off his coat and his shirt in the bathroom, and she filled the sink. Rogin was full of his troubled emotions; now that his chest was bare he could feel them even more distinctly inside, and he said to himself, "I'll have a thing or two to tell her pretty soon. I'm not letting them get away with it. 'Do you think,' he was going to tell her, 'that I alone was made to carry the burden of the whole world on me? Do you think I was born just to be taken advantage of and sacrificed? Do you think I'm just a natural resource, like a coal mine, or oil well, or fishery, or the like? Remember, that I'm a man is no reason why I should be loaded down. I have a soul in me no bigger or stronger than yours. Take away the externals, like the muscles, deeper voice, and so forth, and what remains? A pair of spirits, practically alike. So why shouldn't there also be equality? I can't always be the strong one.'"

"Sit here," said Joan, bringing up a kitchen stool to the sink. "Your hair's gotten all matted."

He sat with his breast against the cool enamel, his chin on the edge of the basin, the green, hot, radiant water reflecting the glass and the tile, and the sweet, cool, fragrant juice of the shampoo poured on his head. She began to wash him.

"You have the healthiest-looking scalp," she said. "It's all pink."

He answered, "Well, it should be white. There must be something wrong with me."

"But there's absolutely nothing wrong with you," she said, and pressed against him from behind, surrounding him, pouring the water gently over him until it seemed to him that the water came from within him, it was the warm fluid of his own secret loving spirit overflowing into the sink, green and foaming, and the words he had rehearsed he forgot, and his anger at his son-to-be disappeared altogether, and he sighed, and said to her from the water-filled hollow of the sink, "You always have such wonderful ideas, Joan. You know? You have a kind of instinct, a regular gift."

Carson McCullers (1917–1967)

A TREE, A ROCK, A CLOUD

It was raining that morning, and still very dark. When the boy reached the streetcar café he had almost finished his route and he went in for a cup of coffee. The place was an all-night café owned by a bitter and stingy man called Leo. After the raw, empty street, the café seemed friendly and bright: along the counter there were a couple of soldiers, three spinners from the cotton mill, and in a corner a man who sat hunched over with his nose and half his face down in a beer mug. The boy wore a helmet such as aviators wear. When he went into the café he unbuckled the chin strap and raised the right flap up over his pink little ear; often as he drank his coffee someone would speak to him in a friendly way. But this morning Leo did not look into his face and none of the men were talking. He paid and was leaving the café when a voice called out to him:

"Son! Hey Son!"

He turned back and the man in the corner was crooking his finger and nodding to him. He had brought his face out of the beer mug and he seemed suddenly very happy. The man was long and pale, with a big nose and faded orange hair.

"Hey Son!"

The boy went toward him. He was an undersized boy of about twelve, with one shoulder drawn higher than the other because of the weight of the paper sack. His face was shallow, freckled, and his eyes were round child eyes.

"Yeah Mister?"

The man laid one hand on the paper boy's shoulders, then grasped the boy's chin and turned his face slowly from one side to the other. The boy shrank back uneasily.

"Say! What's the big idea?"

The boy's voice was shrill; inside the café it was suddenly very quiet. The man said slowly, "I love you."

All along the counter the men laughed. The boy, who had scowled and

Source: Copyright © 1951 by Carson McCullers. Reprinted from *The Ballad of the Sad Cafe* by Carson McCullers, with the permission of Houghton Mifflin Company.

sidled away, did not know what to do. He looked over the counter at Leo, and Leo watched him with a weary, brittle jeer. The boy tried to laugh also. But the man was serious and sad.

"I did not mean to tease you, Son," he said. "Sit down and have a beer with me. There is something I have to explain."

Cautiously, out of the corner of his eye, the paper boy questioned the men along the counter to see what he should do. But they had gone back to their beer or their breakfast and did not notice him. Leo put a cup of coffee on the counter and a little jug of cream.

"He is a minor," Leo said.

The paper boy slid himself up onto the stool. His ear beneath the upturned flap of the helmet was very small and red. The man was nodding at him soberly. "It is important," he said. Then he reached in his hip pocket and brought out something which he held up in the palm of his hand for the boy to see.

"Look very carefully," he said.

The boy stared, but there was nothing to look at very carefully. The man held in his big, grimy palm a photograph. It was the face of a woman, but blurred, so that only the hat and the dress she was wearing stood out clearly.

"See?" the man asked.

The boy nodded and the man placed another picture in his palm. The woman was standing on a beach in a bathing suit. The suit made her stomach very big, and that was the main thing you noticed.

"Got a good look?" He leaned over closer and finally asked: "You ever seen her before?"

The boy sat motionless, staring slantwise at the man. "Not so I know of."

"Very well." The man blew on the photographs and put them back into his pocket. "That was my wife."

"Dead?" the boy asked.

Slowly the man shook his head. He pursed his lips as though about to whistle and answered in a long-drawn way: "Nuuu—" he said. "I will explain."

The beer on the counter before the man was in a large brown mug. He did not pick it up to drink. Instead he bent down and, putting his face over the rim, he rested there for a moment. Then with both hands he tilted the mug and sipped.

"Some night you'll go to sleep with your big nose in a mug and drown," said Leo. "Prominent transient drowns in beer. That would be a cute death."

The paper boy tried to signal to Leo. While the man was not looking he screwed up his face and worked his mouth to question soundlessly: "Drunk?" But Leo only raised his eyebrows and turned away to put some pink strips of bacon on the grill. The man pushed the mug away from him, straightened himself, and folded his loose crooked hands on the counter. His face was sad as he looked at the paper boy. He did not blink, but from time to time the lids closed down with delicate gravity over his pale green eyes. It was nearing dawn and the boy shifted the weight of the paper sack.

"I am talking about love," the man said. "With me it is a science."

The boy half slid down from the stool. But the man raised his forefinger, and there was something about him that held the boy and would not let him go away.

"Twelve years ago I married the woman in the photograph. She was my wife for one year, nine months, three days, and two nights. I loved her. Yes. . . ." He tightened his blurred, rambling voice and said again: "I loved her. I thought also that she loved me. I was a railroad engineer. She had all home comforts and luxuries. It never crept into my brain that she was not satisfied. But do you know what happened?"

"Mgneeow!" said Leo.

The man did not take his eyes from the boy's face. "She left me. I came in one night and the house was empty and she was gone. She left me."

"With a fellow?" the boy asked.

Gently the man placed his palm down on the counter. "Why naturally, Son. A woman does not run off like that alone."

The café was quiet, the soft rain black and endless in the street outside. Leo pressed down the frying bacon with the prongs of his long fork. "So you have been chasing the floozie for eleven years. You frazzled old rascal!"

For the first time the man glanced at Leo. "Please don't be vulgar. Besides, I was not speaking to you." He turned back to the boy and said in a trusting and secretive undertone. "Let's not pay any attention to him. O.K.?"

The paper boy nodded doubtfully.

"It was like this," the man continued. "I am a person who feels many things. All my life one thing after another has impressed me. Moonlight. The leg of a pretty girl. One thing after another. But the point is that when I had enjoyed anything there was a peculiar sensation as though it was laying around loose in me. Nothing seemed to finish itself up or fit in with the other things. Women? I had my portion of them. The same. Afterwards laying around loose in me. I was a man who had never loved."

Very slowly he closed his eyelids, and the gesture was like a curtain drawn at the end of a scene in a play. When he spoke again his voice was excited and the words came fast—the lobes of his large, loose ears seemed to tremble.

"Then I met this woman. I was fifty-one years old and she always said she was thirty. I met her at a filling station and we were married within three days. And do you know what it was like? I just can't tell you. All

I had ever felt was gathered together around this woman. Nothing lay around loose in me any more but was finished up by her."

The man stopped suddenly and stroked his long nose. His voice sank down to a steady and reproachful undertone: "I'm not explaining this right. What happened was this. There were these beautiful feelings and loose little pleasures inside me. And this woman was something like an assembly line for my soul. I run these little pieces of myself through her and I come out complete. Now do you follow me?"

"What was her name?" the boy asked.

"Oh," he said. "I called her Dodo. But that is immaterial."

"Did you try to make her come back?"

The man did not seem to hear. "Under the circumstances you can imagine how I felt when she left me."

Leo took the bacon from the grill and folded two strips of it between a bun. He had a gray face, with slitted eyes, and a pinched nose saddled by faint blue shadows. One of the mill workers signaled for more coffee and Leo poured it. He did not give refills on coffee free. The spinner ate breakfast there every morning, but the better Leo knew his customers the stingier he treated them. He nibbled his own bun as though he grudged it to himself.

"And you never got hold of her again?"

The boy did not know what to think of the man, and his child's face was uncertain with mingled curiosity and doubt. He was new on the paper route; it was still strange to him to be out in the town in the black, queer early morning.

"Yes," the man said. "I took a number of steps to get her back. I went around trying to locate her. I went to Tulsa where she had folks. And to Mobile. I went to every town she had ever mentioned to me, and I hunted down every man she had formerly been connected with. Tulsa, Atlanta, Chicago, Cheehaw, Memphis. . . . For the better part of two years I chased around the country trying to lay hold of her."

"But the pair of them had vanished from the face of the earth!" said Leo.

"Don't listen to him," the man said confidentially. "And also just forget those two years. They are not important. What matters is that around the third year a curious thing begun to happen to me."

"What?" the boy asked.

The man leaned down and tilted his mug to take a sip of beer. But as he hovered over the mug his nostrils fluttered slightly; he sniffed the staleness of the beer and did not drink. "Love is a curious thing to begin with. At first I thought only of getting her back. It was a kind of mania. But then as time went on I tried to remember her. But do you know what happened?"

"No," the boy said.

"When I laid myself down on a bed and tried to think about her my mind became a blank. I couldn't see her. I would take out her pictures and look. No good. Nothing doing. A blank. Can you imagine it?"

"Say Mac!" Leo called down the counter. "Can you imagine this bozo's mind a blank!"

Slowly, as though fanning away flies, the man waved his hand. His green eyes were concentrated and fixed on the shallow little face of the paper boy.

"But a sudden piece of glass on a sidewalk. Or a nickle tune in a music box. A shadow on a wall at night. And I would remember. It might happen in a street and I would cry or bang my head against a lamppost. You follow me?"

"A piece of glass . . ." the boy said.

"Anything. I would walk around and I had no power of how and when to remember her. You think you can put up a kind of shield. But remembering don't come to a man face forward—it corners around sideways. I was at the mercy of everything I saw and heard. Suddenly instead of me combing the countryside to find her she begun to chase me around in my very soul. *She* chasing *me*, mind you! and in my soul."

The boy asked finally: "What part of the country were you in then?"

"Ooh," the man groaned. "I was a sick mortal. It was like smallpox. I confess, Son, that I boozed. I fornicated. I committed any sin that suddenly appealed to me. I am loath to confess it but I will do so. When I recall that period it is all curdled in my mind, it was so terrible."

The man leaned his head down and tapped his forehead on the counter. For a few seconds he stayed bowed over in this position, the back of his stringy neck covered with orange furze, his hands with their long warped fingers held palm to palm in an attitude of prayer. Then the man straightened himself; he was smiling and suddenly his face was bright and tremulous and old.

"It was in the fifth year that it happened," he said. "And with it I started my science."

Leo's mouth jerked with a pale, quick grin. "Well none of we boys are getting any younger," he said. Then with sudden anger he balled up a dishcloth he was holding and threw it down hard on the floor. "You draggletailed old Romeo!"

"What happened?" the boy asked.

The old man's voice was high and clear: "Peace," he answered.

"Huh?"

"It is hard to explain scientifically, Son," he said. "I guess the logical explanation is that she and I had fleed around from each other for so long that finally we just got tangled up together and lay down and quit. Peace. A queer and beautiful blankness. It was spring in Portland and the rain came every afternoon. All evening I just stayed there on my bed in the dark. And that is how the science come to me."

The windows in the streetcar were pale blue with light. The two soldiers paid for their beers and opened the door—one of the soldiers combed his hair and wiped off his muddy puttees before they went outside. The three mill workers bent silently over their breakfasts. Leo's clock was ticking on the wall.

"It is this. And listen carefully. I meditated on love and reasoned it out. I realized what is wrong with us. Men fall in love for the first time. And what do they fall in love with?"

The boy's soft mouth was partly open and he did not answer.

"A woman," the old man said. "Without science, with nothing to go by, they undertake the most dangerous and sacred experience in God's earth. They fall in love with a woman. Is that correct, Son?"

"Yeah," the boy said faintly.

"They start at the wrong end of love. They begin at the climax. Can you wonder it is so miserable? Do you know how men should love?"

The old man reached over and grasped the boy by the collar of his leather jacket. He gave him a gentle little shake and his green eyes gazed down unblinking and grave.

"Son, do you know how love should be begun?"

The boy sat small and listening and still. Slowly he shook his head. The old man leaned closer and whispered:

"A tree. A rock. A cloud."

It was still raining outside in the street: a mild, gray, endless rain. The mill whistle blew for the six o'clock shift and the three spinners paid and went away. There was no one in the café but Leo, the old man, and the little paper boy.

"The weather was like this in Portland," he said. "At the time my science was begun. I meditated and I started very cautious. I would pick up something from the street and take it home with me. I bought a goldfish and I concentrated on the goldfish and I loved it. I graduated from one thing to another. Day by day I was getting this technique. On the road from Portland to San Diego——"

"Aw shut up!" screamed Leo suddenly. "Shut up! Shut up!"

The old man still held the collar of the boy's jacket; he was trembling and his face was earnest and bright and wild. "For six years now I have gone around by myself and build up my science. And now I am a master. Son, I can love anything. No longer do I have to think about it even. I see a street full of people and a beautiful light comes in me. I watch a bird in the sky. Or I meet a traveler on the road. Everything, Son. And anybody. All stranger and all loved! Do you realize what a science like mine can mean?"

The boy held himself stiffly, his hands curled tight around the counter edge. Finally he asked: "Did you ever really find that lady?"

"What? What say, Son?"

"I mean," the boy asked timidly. "Have you fallen in love with a woman again?"

The old man loosened his grasp on the boy's collar. He turned away and for the first time his green eyes had a vague and scattered look. He lifted his mug from the counter, drank down the yellow beer. His head was shaking slowly from side to side. Then finally he answered: "No, Son. You see that is the last step in my science. I go cautious. And I am not quite ready yet."

"Well!" said Leo. "Well well well!"

The old man stood in the open doorway. "Remember," he said. Framed there in the gray damp light of the early morning he looked shrunken and seedy and frail. But his smile was bright. "Remember I love you," he said with a last nod. And the door closed quietly behind him.

The boy did not speak for a long time. He pulled down the bangs on his forehead and slid his grimy little forefinger around the rim of his empty cup. Then without looking at Leo he finally asked:

"Was he drunk?"

"No," said Leo shortly.

The boy raised his clear voice higher. "Then was he a dope fiend?"

"No."

The boy looked up at Leo, and his flat little face was desperate, his voice urgent and shrill. "Was he crazy? Do you think he was a lunatic?" The paper boy's voice dropped suddenly with doubt. "Leo? Or not?"

But Leo would not answer him. Leo had run a night café for fourteen years, and he held himself to be a critic of craziness. There were the town characters and also the transients who roamed in from the night. He knew the manias of all of them. But he did not want to satisfy the questions of the waiting child. He tightened his pale face and was silent.

So the boy pulled down the right flap of his helmet and as he turned to leave he made the only comment that seemed safe to him, the only remark that could not be laughed down and despised:

"He sure has done a lot of traveling."

THIS MORNING, THIS EVENING, SO SOON

"You are full of nightmares," Harriet tells me. She is in her dressing gown and has cream all over her face. She and my older sister, Louisa, are going out to be girls together. I suppose they have many things to talk about—they have *me* to talk about, certainly—and they do not want my presence. I have been given a bachelor's evening. The director of the film which has brought us such incredible and troubling riches will be along later to take me out to dinner.

I watch her face. I know that it is quite impossible for her to be as untroubled as she seems. Her self-control is mainly for my benefit—my benefit, and Paul's. Harriet comes from orderly and progressive Sweden and has reacted against all the advanced doctrines to which she has been exposed by becoming steadily and beautifully old-fashioned. We never fought in front of Paul, not even when he was a baby. Harriet does not so much believe in protecting children as she does in helping them to build a foundation on which they can build and build again, each time life's high-flying steel ball knocks down everything they have built.

Whenever I become upset, Harriet becomes very cheerful and composed. I think she began to learn how to do this over eight years ago, when I returned from my only visit to America. Now, perhaps, it has become something she could not control if she wished to. This morning, at breakfast, when I yelled at Paul, she averted Paul's tears and my own guilt by looking up and saying, "My God, your father is cranky this morning, isn't he?"

Paul's attention was immediately distracted from his wounds, and the unjust inflictor of those wounds, to his mother's laughter. He watched her.

"It is because he is afraid they will not like his songs in New York. Your father is an *artiste, mon chou,* and they are very mysterious people, *les artistes.* Millions of people are waiting for him in New York, they are begging him to come, and they will give him a *lot* of money, but he is afraid they will not like him. Tell him he is wrong."

She succeeded in rekindling Paul's excitement about places he has never seen. I was also, at once, reinvested with all my glamour. I think it is sometimes extremely difficult for Paul to realize that the face he sees on record sleeves and in the newspapers and on the screen is nothing more or less than the face of his father—who sometimes yells at him. Of course, since he is only seven—going on eight, he will be eight years old this winter—he cannot know that I am baffled, too.

"Of course, you are wrong, you are silly," he said with passion—and caused me to smile. His English is strongly accented and is not, in fact, as good as his French, for he speaks French all day at school. French is really his first language, the first he ever heard. "You are the greatest singer in France"—sounding exactly as he must sound when he makes this pronouncement to his schoolmates—"the greatest *American* singer"—this concession was so gracefully made that it was not a concession at all, it added inches to my stature, America being only a glamorous word for Paul. It is the place from which his father came, and to which he now is going, a place which very few people have ever seen. But his aunt is one of them and he looked over at her. "Mme. Dumont says so, and she says he is a *great actor, too.*" Louisa nodded, smiling. "And she has seen *Les Fauves Nous Attendent*—five times!" This clinched it, of course. Mme. Dumont is our concierge and she has known Paul all his life. I suppose he will not begin to doubt anything she says until he begins to doubt everything.

He looked over at me again. "So you are wrong to be afraid."

"I was wrong to yell at you, too. I won't yell at you any more today."

"All right." He was very grave.

Louisa poured more coffee. "He's going to knock them dead in New York. You'll see."

"Mais bien sur," said Paul, doubtfully. He does not quite know what "knock them dead" means, though he was sure, from her tone, that she must have been agreeing with him. He does not quite understand this aunt, whom he met for the first time two months ago, when she arrived to spend the summer with us. Her accent is entirely different from anything he has ever heard. He does not really understand why, since she is my sister and his aunt, she should be unable to speak French.

Harriet, Louisa, and I looked at each other and smiled. "Knock them dead," said Harriet, "means *d'avoir un succès fou.* But you will soon pick up all the American expressions." She looked at me and laughed. "So will I."

"That's what he's afraid of." Louisa grinned. "We have *got* some expressions, believe me. Don't let anybody ever tell you America hasn't got a culture. Our culture is as thick as clabber milk."

"Ah," Harriet answered, "I know. I know."

"I'm going to be practicing later," I told Paul.

His face lit up. *"Bon."* This meant that, later, he would come into my study and lie on the floor with his papers and crayons while I worked out with the piano and the tape recorder. He knew that I was offering this as an olive branch. All things considered, we get on pretty well, my son and I.

He looked over at Louisa again. She held a coffee cup in one hand and a cigarette in the other; and something about her baffled him. It was early, so she had not yet put on her face. Her short, thick, graying hair was rougher than usual, almost as rough as my own—later, she would be going to the hairdresser's; she is fairer than I, and better-looking; Louisa, in fact, caught all the looks in the family. Paul knows that she is my older sister and that she helped to raise me, though he does not, of course, know what this means. He knows that she is a schoolteacher in the *American* South, which is not, for some reason, the same place as South America. I could see him trying to fit all these exotic details together into a pattern which would explain her strangeness—strangeness of accent, strangeness of manner. In comparison with the people he has always known, Louisa must seem, for all her generosity and laughter and affection, peculiarly uncertain of herself, peculiarly hostile and embattled.

I wondered what he would think of his Uncle Norman, older and much blacker than I, who lives near the Alabama town in which we were born. Norman will meet us at the boat.

Now Harriet repeats, "Nightmares, nightmares. Nothing ever turns out as badly as you think it will—in fact," she adds laughing, "I am happy to say that that would scarcely be possible."

Her eyes seek mine in the mirror—dark-blue eyes, pale skin, black hair. I had always thought of Sweden as being populated entirely by blondes, and I thought that Harriet was abnormally dark for a Swedish girl. But when we visited Sweden, I found out differently. "It is all a great racial salad, Europe, that is why I am sure that I will never understand your country," Harriet said. That was in the days when we never imagined that we would be going to it.

I wonder what she is really thinking. Still, she is right, in two days we will be on a boat, and there is simply no point in carrying around my load of apprehension. I sit down on the bed, watching her fix her face. I realize that I am going to miss this old-fashioned bedroom. For years, we've talked about throwing out the old junk which came with the apartment and replacing it with less massive, modern furniture. But we never have.

"Oh, everything will probably work out," I say. "I've been in a bad mood all day long. I just can't sing any more." We both laugh. She reaches for a wad of tissues and begins wiping off the cream. "I wonder how Paul will like it, if he'll make friends—that's all."

"Paul will like any place where you are, where we are. Don't you worry about Paul."

Paul has never been called any names, so far. Only, once he asked us what the word *métis* meant and Harriet explained to him that it meant mixed blood, adding that the blood of just about everybody in the world was mixed by now. Mme. Dumont contributed bawdy and detailed corroboration from her own family tree, the roots of which were somewhere in Corsica; the moral of the story, as she told it, was that women were weak, men incorrigible, and *le bon Dieu* appallingly clever. Mme. Dumont's version is the version I prefer, but it may not be, for Paul, the most utilitarian.

Harriet rises from the dressing table and comes over to sit in my lap. I fall back with her on the bed, and she smiles down into my face.

"Now, don't worry," she tells me, "please try not to worry. Whatever is coming, we will manage it all very well, you will see. We have each other and we have our son and we know what we want. So, we are luckier than most people."

I kiss her on the chin. "I'm luckier than most men."

"I'm a very lucky woman, too."

And for a moment we are silent, alone in our room, which we have shared so long. The slight rise and fall of Harriet's breathing creates an intermittent pressure against my chest, and I think how, if I had never left America, I would never have met her and would never have established a life of my own, would never have entered my own life. For everyone's life begins on a level where races, armies, and churches stop. And yet everyone's life is always shaped by races, churches, and armies; races, churches, armies menace, and have taken, many lives. If Harriet had been born in America, it would have taken her a long time, perhaps forever, to look on me as a man like other men; if I had met her in America, I would never have been able to look on her as a woman like all other women. The habits of public rage and power would also have been our private compulsions, and would have blinded our eyes. We would never have been able to love each other. And Paul would never have been born.

Perhaps, if I had stayed in America, I would have found another woman and had another son. But that other woman, that other son are in the limbo of vanished possibilities. I might also have become something else, instead of an actor-singer, perhaps a lawyer, like my brother, or a teacher, like my sister. But no, I am what I have become and this woman beside me is my wife, and I love her. All the sons I might have had mean nothing, since I *have* a son, I named him, Paul, for my father, and I love him.

I think of all the things I have seen destroyed in America, all the things that I have lost there, all the threats it holds for me and mine.

I grin up at Harriet. "Do you love me?"

"Of course not. I simply have been madly plotting to get to America all these years."

"What a patient wench you are."

"The Swedes are very patient."

She kisses me again and stands up. Louisa comes in, also in a dressing gown.

"I hope you two aren't sitting in here yakking about the *subject.*" She looks at me. "My, you are the sorriest-looking celebrity I've ever seen. I've always wondered why people like you hired press agents. Now I know." She goes to Harriet's dressing table. "Honey, do you mind if I borrow some of that *mad* nail polish?"

Harriet goes over to the dressing table. "I'm not sure I know *which* mad nail polish you mean."

Harriet and Louisa, somewhat to my surprise, get on very well. Each seems to find the other full of the weirdest and most delightful surprises. Harriet has been teaching Louisa French and Swedish expressions, and Louisa has been teaching Harriet some of the saltier expressions of the black South. Whenever one of them is not playing straight man to the other's accent, they become involved in long speculations as to how a language reveals the history and the attitudes of a people. They discovered that all the European languages contain a phrase equivalent to "to work like a nigger." ("Of course," says Louisa, "they've had black men working for them for a long time.") "Language is experience and language is power," says Louisa, after regretting that she does not know any of the African dialects. "That's what I keep trying to tell those dirty bastards down South. They get their own experience into the language, we'll have a great language. But, no, they all want to talk like white folks." Then she leans forward, grasping Harriet by the knee. "I tell them, honey, white folks ain't saying *nothing.* Not a thing are they saying—and *some* of them know it, they *need* what you got, the whole world needs it." Then she leans back, in disgust. "You think they listen to me? Indeed they do not. They just go right on, trying to talk like white folks." She leans forward again, in tremendous indignation. "You know some folks are *ashamed* of Mahalia Jackson? *Ashamed* of her, one of the greatest singers alive! They think she's common." Then she looks about the room as though she held a bottle in her hand and were looking for a skull to crack.

I think it is because Louisa has never been able to talk like this to any white person before. All the white people she has ever met needed, in one way or another, to be reassured, consoled, to have their consciences pricked but not blasted; could not, could not afford to hear a truth which would shatter, irrevocably, their image of themselves. It is astonishing the lengths to which a person, or a people, will go in order to avoid a truthful mirror. But Harriet's necessity is precisely the opposite: it is of the utmost importance that she learn everything that Louisa can tell her, and then learn more, much more. Harriet is really trying to learn from Louisa how best to protect her husband and her son. This is why they are going out alone tonight. They will have, tonight, as it were, a final council of war. I may be moody, but they, thank God, are practical.

Now Louisa turns to me while Harriet rummages about on the dressing table. "What time is Vidal coming for you?"

"Oh, around seven-thirty, eight o'clock. He says he's reserved tables for us in some very chic place, but he won't say where." Louisa wriggles her shoulders, raises her eyebrows, and does a tiny bump and grind. I laugh. "That's right. And then I guess we'll go out and get drunk."

"I hope to God you do. You've been about as cheerful as a cemetery these last few days. And, that way, your hangover will keep you from bugging us tomorrow."

"What about *your* hangovers? I know the way you girls drink."

"Well, we'll be paying for our own drinks," says Harriet, "so I don't think we'll have that problem. But *you're* going to be feted, like an international movie star."

"You sure you don't want to change your mind and come out with Vidal and me?"

"We're sure," Louisa says. She looks down at me and gives a small, amused grunt. "An international movie star. And I used to change your diapers. I'll be damned." She is grave for a moment. "Mama'd be proud of you, you know that?" We look at each other and the air between us is charged with secrets which not even Harriet will ever know. "Now, get the hell out of here, so we can get dressed."

"I'll take Paul on down to Mme. Dumont's."

Paul is to have supper with her children and spend the night there.

"For the last time," says Mme. Dumont and she rubs her hand over Paul's violently curly black hair. *"Tu vas nous manquer, tu sais?"* Then she looks up at me and laughs. "He doesn't care. He is only interested in seeing the big ship and all the wonders of New York. Children are never sad to make journeys."

"I would be very sad to go," says Paul, "but my father must go to New York to work and he wants me to come with him."

Over his head, Mme. Dumont and I smile at each other. *"Il est malin, ton gosse!"* She looks down at him again. "And do you think, my little diplomat, that you will like New York?"

"We aren't only going to New York," Paul answers, "we are going to California, too."

"Well, do you think you will like California?"

Paul looks at me. "I don't know. If we don't like it, we'll come back."

"So simple. Just like that," says Mme. Dumont. She looks at me. "It is the best way to look at life. Do come back. You know, we feel that you belong to us, too, here in France."

"I hope you do," I say. "I hope you do. I have always felt—always felt at home here." I bend down and Paul and I kiss each other on the cheek. We have always done so—but will we be able to do so in America? American fathers never kiss American sons. I straighten, my hand on Paul's shoulder. "You be good. I'll pick you up for breakfast, or, if you get up first you come and pick me up and we can hang out together tomorrow, while you *Maman* and your Aunt Louisa finish packing. They won't want two men hanging around the house."

"D'accord. Where shall we hang out?" On the last two words he stumbles a little and imitates me.

"Maybe we can go to the zoo, I don't know. And I'll take you to lunch at the Eiffel Tower, would you like that?"

"Oh, yes," he says, "I'd love that." When he is pleased, he seems to glow. All the energy of his small, tough, concentrated being charges an unseen battery and adds an incredible luster to his eyes, which are large and dark brown—like mine—and to his skin, which always reminds me of the colors of honey and the fires of the sun.

"OK, then." I shake hands with Mme. Dumont. *"Bonsoir, Madame,"* I ring for the elevator, staring at Paul. *"Ciao, Pauli."*

"Bonsoir, Papa."

And Mme. Dumont takes him inside.

Upstairs, Harriet and Louisa are finally powdered, perfumed, and jeweled, and ready to go: dry martinis at the Ritz, supper, "in some *very* expensive little place," says Harriet, and perhaps the Folies Bergère afterwards. "A real cornball, tourist evening," says Louisa. "I'm working on the theory that if I can get Harriet to act like an American now, she won't have so much trouble later."

"I very much doubt," Harriet says, "that I will be able to endure the Folies Bergère for three solid hours."

"Oh, then we'll duck across town to Harry's New York bar and drink mint juleps," says Louisa.

I realize that, quite apart from everything else, Louisa is having as much fun as she has ever had in her life. Perhaps she, too, will be sad to leave Paris, even though she has only known it for such a short time.

"Do people drink those in New York?" Harriet asks. I think she is making a list of the things people do or do not do in New York.

"Some people do." Louisa winks at me. "Do you realize that this Swedish chick's picked up an Alabama drawl?"

We laugh together. The elevator chugs to a landing.

"We'll stop and say goodnight to Paul," Harriet says. She kisses me. "Give our best to Vidal."

"Right. Have a good time. Don't let any Frenchmen run off with Louisa."

"I did not come to Paris to be protected, and if I had, this wild chick *you* married couldn't do it. I just *might* upset everybody and come home with a French count." She presses the elevator button and the cage goes down.

I walk back into our dismantled apartment. It stinks of departure. There are bags and crates in the hall which will be taken away tomorrow, there are no books in the bookcases, the kitchen looks as though we never cooked a meal there, never dawdled there, in the early morning or late at night, over coffee. Presently, I must shower and shave but now I pour myself a drink and light a cigarette and step out on our balcony. It is dusk, the brilliant light of Paris is beginning to fade, and the green of the trees is darkening.

I have lived in this city for twelve years. This apartment is on the top floor of a corner building. We look out over the trees and the roof tops to the Champ de Mars, where the Eiffel Tower stands. Beyond this field is the river, which I have crossed so often, in so many states of mind. I have crossed every bridge in Paris, I have walked along every *quai*. I know the river as one finally knows a friend, know it when it is black, guarding all the lights of Paris in its depths, and seeming, in its vast silence, to be communing with the dead who lie beneath it; when it is yellow, evil, and roaring, giving a rough time to tugboats and barges, and causing people to remember that it has been known to rise, it has been known to kill; when it is peaceful, a slick dark, dirty green, playing host to rowboats and *les bateaux mouches* and throwing up from time to time an extremely unhealthy fish. The men who stand along the *quais* all summer with their fishing lines gratefully accept the slimy object and throw it in a rusty can. I have always wondered who eats those fish.

And I walk up and down, up and down, glad to be alone.

It is August, the month when all Parisians desert Paris and one has to walk miles to find a barbershop or a laundry open in some tree-shadowed, silent side street. There is a single person on the avenue, a paratrooper walking toward École Militaire. He is also walking, almost certainly, and rather sooner than later, toward Algeria. I have a friend, a good-natured boy who was always hanging around the clubs in which I worked in the old days, who has just returned from Algeria, with a recurring, debilitating fever, and minus one eye. The government has set his pension at the sum, arbitrary if not occult, of fifty-three thousand francs every three months. Of course, it is quite impossible to live on this amount of money without working—but who will hire a half-blind invalid? This boy has been spoiled forever, long before his thirtieth birthday, and there are thousands like him all over France.

And there are fewer Algerians to be found on the street of Paris now.

The rug sellers, the peanut vendors, the postcard peddlers and money changers have vanished. The boys I used to know during my first years in Paris are scattered—or corralled—the Lord knows where.

Most of them had no money. They lived three and four together in rooms with a single skylight, a single hard cot, or in buildings that seemed abandoned, with cardboard in the windows, with erratic plumbing in a wet, cobblestoned yard, in dark, dead-end alleys, or on the outer, chilling heights of Paris.

The Arab cafés are closed—those dark, acrid cafés in which I used to meet with them to drink tea, to get high on hashish, to listen to the obsessive, stringed music which has no relation to any beat, any time, that I have ever known. I once thought of the North Africans as my brothers and that is why I went to their cafés. They were very friendly to me, perhaps one or two of them remained really fond of me even after I could no longer afford to smoke Lucky Strikes and after my collection of American sport shirts had vanished—mostly into their wardrobes. They seemed to feel that they had every right to them, since I could only have wrested these things from the world by cunning—it meant nothing to say that I had had no choice in the matter; perhaps I had wrested these things from the world by treason, by refusing to be identified with the misery of my people. Perhaps, indeed, I identified myself with those who were responsible for this misery.

And this was true. Their rage, the only note in all their music which I could not fail to recognize, to which I responded, yet had the effect of setting us more than ever at a division. They were perfectly prepared to drive all Frenchmen into the sea, and to level the city of Paris. But I could not hate the French, because they left me alone. And I love Paris, I will always love it, it is the city which saved my life. It saved my life by allowing me to find out who I am.

It was on a bridge, one tremendous, April morning, that I knew I had fallen in love. Harriet and I were walking hand in hand. The bridge was the Pont Royal, just before us was the great *horloge,* high and lifted up, saying ten to ten; beyond this, the golden statue of Joan of Arc, with her sword uplifted. Harriet and I were silent, for we had been quarreling about something. Now, when I look back, I think we had reached that state when an affair must either end or become something more than an affair.

I looked sideways at Harriet's face, which was still. Her dark-blue eyes were narrowed against the sun, and her full, pink lips were still slightly sulky, like a child's. In those days, she hardly ever wore make-up. I was in my shirt sleeves. Her face made me want to laugh and run my hand over her short dark hair. I wanted to pull her to me and say, *Baby, don't be mad at me,* and at that moment something tugged at my heart and made me catch my breath. There were millions of people all around us, but I was alone with Harriet. She was alone with me. Never, in all my life, until that moment, had I been alone with anyone. The world had always been with us, between us, defeating the quarrel we could not achieve, and making love impossible. During all the years of my life, until that moment, I had carried the menacing, the hostile, killing world with me everywhere. No matter what I was doing or saying or feeling, one eye had always been on the world—that world which I had learned to distrust almost as soon as I learned my name, that world on which I knew one could never turn one's back, the white man's world. And for the first time in my life I was free of it; it had not existed for me; I had been quarreling with my girl. It was our quarrel, it was entirely between us, it had nothing to do with anyone else in the world. For the first time in my life I had not been afraid of the patriotism of the mindless, in uniform or out, who would beat me up and treat the woman who was with me as though she were the lowest of untouchables. For the first time in my life I felt that no force jeopardized my right, felt that the woman was not, in her own eyes or in the eyes of the world, degraded by my presence.

The sun fell over everything, like a blessing, people were moving all about us, I will never forget the feeling of Harriet's small hand in mine, dry and trusting, and I turned to her, slowing our pace. She looked up at me with her enormous, blue eyes, and she seemed to wait. I said, *"Harriet. Harriet. Tu sais, il y a quelque chose de très grave qui m'est arrivé. Je t'aime. Je t'aime. Tu me comprends,* or shall I say it in English?"

This was eight years ago, shortly before my first and only visit home.

That was when my mother died. I stayed in America for three months. When I came back, Harriet thought that the change in me was due to my grief—I was very silent, very thin. But it had not been my mother's death which accounted for the change. I had known that my mother was going to die. I had not known what America would be like for me after nearly four years away.

I remember standing at the rail and watching the distance between myself and Le Havre increase. Hands fell, ceasing to wave, handkerchiefs ceased to flutter, people turned away, they mounted their bicycles or got into their cars and rode off. Soon, Le Havre was nothing but a blur. I thought of Harriet, already miles from me in Paris, and I pressed my lips tightly together in order not to cry.

Then, as Europe dropped below the water, as the days passed and passed, as we left behind us the skies of Europe and the eyes of everyone on the ship began, so to speak, to refocus, waiting for the first glimpse of America, my apprehension began to give way to a secret joy, a checked anticipation. I thought of such details as showers, which are rare in Paris, and I thought of such things as rich, cold, American milk and heavy, chocolate cake. I wondered about my friends, wondered if I had any left, and wondered if they would be glad to see me.

The Americans on the boat did not seem to be so bad, but I was fascinated, after such a long absence from it, by the nature of their friendliness. It was a friendliness which did not suggest, and was not intended to suggest, any possibility of friendship. Unlike Europeans, they dropped titles and used first names almost at once, leaving themselves, unlike the Europeans, with nowhere thereafter to go. Once one had become "Pete" or "Jane" or "Bill" all that could decently be known was known and any suggestion that there might be further depths, a person, so to speak, behind the name, was taken as a violation of that privacy which did not, paradoxically, since they trusted it so little, seem to exist among Americans. They apparently equated privacy with the unspeakable things they did in the bathroom or bedroom, which they related only to the analyst, and then read about in the pages of best sellers. There was an eerie and unnerving irreality about everything they said and did, as though they were all members of the same team and were acting on orders from some invincibly cheerful and tirelessly inventive coach. I was fascinated by it. I found it oddly moving, but I cannot say that I was displeased. It had not occurred to me before that Americans, who had never treated me with any respect, had no respect for each other.

On the last night but one, there was a gala in the big ballroom and I sang. It had been a long time since I had sung before so many Americans. My audience had mainly been penniless French students, in the weird, Left Bank bistros I worked in those days. Still, I was a great hit with them and by this time I had become enough of a drawing card, in the Latin quarter and in St. Germain des Prés, to have attracted a couple of critics, to have had my picture in *France-soir,* and to have acquired a legal work permit which allowed me to make a little more money. Just the same, no matter how industrious and brilliant some of the musicians had been, or how devoted my audience, they did not know, they could not know, what my songs came out of. They did not know what was funny about it. It was impossible to translate: it damn well better be funny, or Laughing to keep from crying, or What did *I* do to be so black and blue?

The moment I stepped out on the floor, they began to smile, something opened in them, they were ready to be pleased. I found in their faces, as they watched me, smiling, waiting, an artless relief, a profound reassurance. Nothing was more familiar to them than the sight of a dark boy, singing, and there were few things on earth more necessary. It was under cover of darkness, my own darkness, that I could sing for them of the joys, passions, and terrors they smuggled about with them like steadily depreciating contraband. Under cover of the midnight fiction that I was unlike them because I was black, they could stealthily gaze at those treasures which they had been mysteriously forbidden to possess and were never permitted to declare.

I sang *I'm Coming, Virginia,* and *Take This Hammer,* and *Precious Lord.* They wouldn't let me go and I came back and sang a couple of the oldest blues I knew. Then someone asked me to sing *Swanee River,* and I did, astonished that I could, astonished that this song, which I had put down long ago, should have the power to move me. Then, if only, perhaps, to make the record complete, I wanted to sing *Strange Fruit,* but, on this number, no one can surpass the great, tormented Billie Holiday. So I finished with *Great Getting-Up Morning* and I guess I can say that if I didn't stop the show I certainly ended it. I got a big hand and I drank at a few tables and I danced with a few girls.

After one more day and one more night, the boat landed in New York. I woke up, I was bright awake at once, and I thought, *We're here.* I turned on all the lights in my small cabin and I stared into the mirror as though I were committing my face to memory. I took a shower and I took a long time shaving and I dressed myself very carefully. I walked the long ship corridors to the dining room, looking at the luggage piled high before the elevators and beside the steps. The dining room was nearly half empty and full of a quick and joyous excitement which depressed me even more. People ate quickly, chattering to each other, anxious to get upstairs and go on deck. Was it my imagination or was it true that they seemed to avoid my eyes? A few people waved and smiled, but let me pass; perhaps it would have made them uncomfortable, this morning, to try to share their excitement with me; perhaps they did not want to know whether or not it was possible for me to share it. I walked to my table and sat down. I munched toast as dry as paper and drank a pot of coffee. Then I tipped my waiter, who bowed and smiled and called me "sir" and said that he hoped to see me on the boat again. "I hope so, too," I said.

And was it true, or was it my imagination, that a flash of wondering comprehension, a flicker of wry sympathy, then appeared in the waiter's eyes? I walked upstairs to the deck.

There was a breeze from the water but the sun was hot and made me remember how ugly New York summers could be. All of the deck chairs had been taken away and people milled about in the space where the deck chairs had been, moved from one side of the ship to the other, clambered up and down the steps, crowded the rails, and they were busy taking photographs—of the harbor, of each other, of the sea, of the gulls. I walked slowly along the deck, and an impulse stronger than myself drove me to the rail. There it was, the great, unfinished city, with all its towers blazing in the sun. It came toward us slowly and patiently, like some enormous, cunning, and murderous beast, ready to devour, impossible to escape. I watched it come closer and I listened to the people around me, to their excitement and their pleasure. There was no doubt that it was real. I watched their shining faces and wondered if I were mad. For a moment I longed, with all my heart, to be able to feel whatever they were feeling, if only to know what such a feeling was like. As the boat moved slowly into the harbor, they were being moved into safety. It was only I who was being floated into danger. I turned my head, looking for Europe, but all that stretched behind me was the sky, thick with gulls. I moved away from the rail. A big, sandy-haired man held his daughter on his shoulders, showing her the Statue of Liberty. I would never know what this statue meant to others, she had always been an ugly joke for me. And the American flag was flying from the top of the ship, above my head. I had seen the French flag drive the French into the most unspeakable frenzies, I had seen the flag which was nominally mine used to dignify the vilest purposes: now I would never, as long as I lived, know what others saw when they saw a flag. "There's no place like home," said a voice close by, and I thought *There damn sure isn't.* I decided to go back to my cabin and have a drink.

There was a cablegram from Harriet in my cabin. It said: Be good. Be quick. I'm waiting. I folded it carefully and put it in my breast pocket. Then I wondered if I would ever get back to her. How long would it take me to earn the money to get out of this land? Sweat broke out on my forehead and I poured myself some whiskey from my nearly empty bottle. I paced the tiny cabin. It was silent. There was no one down in the cabins now.

I was not sober when I faced the uniforms in the first-class lounge. There were two of them; they were not unfriendly. They looked at my passport, they looked at me. "You've been away a long time," said one of them.

"Yes," I said, "it's been a while."

"What did you do over there all that time?"—with a grin meant to hide more than it revealed, which hideously revealed more than it could hide.

I said, "I'm a singer," and the room seemed to rock around me. I held on to what I hoped was a calm, open smile. I had not had to deal with these faces in so long that I had forgotten how to do it. I had once known how to pitch my voice precisely between curtness and servility, and known what razor's edge of a pickaninny's smile would turn away wrath. But I had forgotten all the tricks on which my life had once depended. Once I had been an expert at baffling these people, at setting their teeth on edge, and dancing just outside the trap laid for me. But I was not an expert now. These faces were no longer merely the faces of two white men, who were my enemies. They were the faces of two white people whom I did not understand, and I could no longer plan my moves in accordance with what I knew of their cowardice and their needs and their strategy. That moment on the bridge had undone me forever.

"That's right," said one of them, "that's what it says, right here on the passport. Never heard of you, though." They looked up at me. "Did you do a lot of singing over there?"

"Some."

"What kind—concerts?"

"No." I wondered what I looked like, sounded like. I could tell nothing from their eyes. "I worked a few nightclubs."

"Nightclubs, eh? I guess they liked you over there."

"Yes," I said, "they seemed to like me all right."

"Well"—and my passport was stamped and handed back to me—"let's hope they like you over here."

"Thanks." They laughed—was it at me, or was it my imagination? and I picked up the one bag I was carrying and threw my trench coat over one shoulder and walked out of the first-class lounge. I stood in the slow-moving, murmuring line which led to the gangplank. I looked straight ahead and watched heads, smiling faces, step up to the shadow of the gangplank awning and then swiftly descend out of sight. I put my passport back in my breast pocket—*Be quick. I'm waiting*—and I held my landing card in my hand. Then, suddenly, there I was, standing on the edge of the boat, staring down the long ramp to the ground. At the end of the plank, on the ground, stood a heavy man in a uniform. His cap was pushed back from his gray hair and his face was red and wet. He looked up at me. This was the face I remembered, the face of my nightmares; perhaps hatred had caused me to know this face better than I would ever know the face of any lover. "Come on, boy," he cried, "come on, come on!"

And I almost smiled. I was home. I touched my breast pocket. I thought of a song I sometimes sang, *When will I ever get to be a man?* I came down the gangplank, stumbling a little, and gave the man my landing card.

Much later in the day, a customs inspector checked my baggage and waved me away. I picked up my bags and started walking down the long stretch which led to the gate, to the city.

And I heard someone call my name.

I looked up and saw Louisa running toward me. I dropped my bags and grabbed her in my arms and tears came to my eyes and rolled down my face. I did not know whether the tears were for joy at seeing her, or from rage, or both.

"How are you? How are you? You look wonderful, but, oh, haven't you lost weight? It's wonderful to see you again."

I wiped my eyes. "It's wonderful to see you, too, I bet you thought I was never coming back."

Louisa laughed. "I wouldn't have blamed you if you hadn't. These people are just as corny as ever, I swear I don't believe there's any hope for them. How's you French? Lord, when I think that it was I who studied French and now I can't speak a word. And you never went near it and you probably speak it like a native."

I grinned. *'Pas mal. Te me défends pas mal.'* We started down the wide steps into the street. "My God," I said. "New York." I was not aware of its towers now. We were in the shadow of the elevated highway but the thing which most struck me was neither light nor shade, but noise. It came from a million things at once, from trucks and tires and clutches and brakes and doors; from machines shuttling and stamping and rolling and cutting and pressing; from the building of tunnels, the checking of gas mains, the laying of wires, the digging of foundations; from the chattering of rivets, the scream of the pile driver, the clanging of great shovels; from the battering down and the raising up of walls; from millions of radios and television sets and juke boxes. The human voices distinguished themselves from the roar only by their note of strain and hostility. Another fleshy man, uniformed and red faced, hailed a cab for us and touched his cap politely but could only manage a peremptory growl: "Right this way, miss. Step up, sir." He slammed the cab door behind us. Louisa directed the driver to the New Yorker Hotel.

"Do they take us there?"

She looked at me. "They got laws in New York, honey, it'd be the easiest thing in the world to spend all your time in court. But over at the New Yorker, I believe they've already got the message." She took my arm. "You see? In spite of all this chopping and booming, this place hasn't really changed very much. You still can't hear yourself talk."

And I thought to myself, Maybe that's the point.

Early the next morning we checked out of the hotel and took the plane for Alabama.

I am just stepping out of the shower when I hear the bell ring. I dry myself hurriedly and put on a bathrobe. It is Vidal, of course, and very elegant he is, too, with his bushy gray hair quite lustrous, his swarthy, cynical, gypsylike face shaved and lotioned. Usually he looks just any old way. But tonight his brief bulk is contained in a dark-blue suit and he has an ironical pearl stickpin in his blue tie.

"Come in, make yourself a drink. I'll be with you in a second."

"I am, *hélas!*, on time. I trust you will forgive me for my thoughtlessness."

But I am already back in the bathroom. Vidal puts on a record: Mahalia Jackson, singing *I'm Going to Live the Life I Sing About in My Song.*

When I am dressed, I find him sitting in a chair before the open window. The daylight is gone, but it is not exactly dark. The trees are black now against the darkening sky. The lights in windows and the lights of motorcars are yellow and ringed. The street lights have not yet been turned on. It is as though, out of deference to the departed day, Paris waited a decent interval before assigning her role to a more theatrical but inferior performer.

Vidal is drinking a whiskey and soda. I pour myself a drink. He watches me.

"Well. How are you, my friend? You are nearly gone. Are you happy to be leaving us?"

"No." I say this with more force than I had intended. Vidal raises his eyebrows, looking amused and distant. "I never really intended to go back there. I certainly never intended to raise my kid there—"

"Mais, mon cher," Vidal says, calmly, "you are an intelligent man, you must have known that you would probably be returning one day." He pauses. "And, as for Pauli—did it never occur to you that he might wish one day to see the country in which his father and his father's fathers were born?"

"To do that, really, he'd have to go to Africa."

"America will always mean more to him than Africa, you know that."

"I don't know." I throw my drink down and pour myself another. "Why should he want to cross all that water just to be called a nigger? America never gave him anything."

"It gave him his father."

I look at him, "You mean, his father escaped."

Vidal throws back his head and laughs. If Vidal likes you, he is certain to laugh at you and his laughter can be very unnerving, too. And, now, in the silence, he asks me, "Do you really think that you have escaped anything? Come. I know you for a better man than that." He walks to the table which holds the liquor. "In that movie of ours which has made you so famous, and, as I now see, so troubled, what are you playing, after all? What is the tragedy of this half-breed troubadour if not, precisely, that he has taken all the possible roads to escape and that all these roads have failed him?" He pauses, with the bottle in one hand, and looks at me. "Do you remember the trouble I had to get a performance out of you? How you hated me, you sometimes looked as though you wanted to shoot me! And do you remember when the role of Chico began to come alive?" He pours his drink. "Think back, remember. I am a very great director, *mais pardon!* I could not have got such a performance out of anyone but you. And what were you thinking of, what was in your mind, what nightmare were you living with when you began, at last, to play the role—truthfully?" He walks back to his seat.

Chico, in the film, is the son of a Martinique woman and a French *colon* who hates both his mother and his father. He flees from the island to the capital, carrying his hatred with him. This hatred has now grown, naturally, to include all dark women and all white men, in a word, everyone. He descends into the underworld of Paris, where he dies. *Les fauves*—the wild beasts—refers to the life he has fled and to the life which engulfs him. When I agreed to do the role, I felt that I could probably achieve it by bearing in mind the North Africans I had watched in Paris for so long. But this did not please Vidal. The blowup came while we were rehearsing a fairly simple, straightforward scene. Chico goes into a sleazy Pigalle dance hall to beg the French owner for a particularly humiliating job. And this Frenchman reminds him of his father.

"You are playing this boy as though you thought of him as the noble savage," Vidal said, icily. *"Ça vient d'où*—all these ghastly mannerisms you are using all the time?"

Everyone fell silent, for Vidal rarely spoke this way. This silence told me that everyone, the actor with whom I was playing the scene and all the people in the "dance hall," shared Vidal's opinion of my performance and were relieved that he was going to do something about it. I was humiliated and too angry to speak; but perhaps I also felt, at the very bottom of my heart, a certain relief, an unwilling respect.

"You are doing it all wrong," he said, more gently. Then, "Come, let us have a drink together."

We walked into his office. He took a bottle and two glasses out of his desk. "Forgive me, but you put me in mind of some of those English *lady* actresses who love to play *putain* as long as it is always clear to the audience that they are really ladies. So perhaps they read a book, not usually, *hélas!, Fanny Hill,* and they have their chauffeurs drive them through Soho once or twice—and they come to the stage with a performance so absolutely loaded with detail, every bit of it meaningless, that there can be no doubt that they are acting. It is what the British call a triumph." He poured two cognacs. "That is what you are doing. Why? Who do you think this boy is, what do you think he is feeling, when he asks for this job?" He watched me carefully and I bitterly resented his look. "You come from America. The situation is not so pretty there for boys like you. I know you may not have been as poor as—as some—but is it really impossible for you to understand what a boy like Chico feels? Have you never, yourself, been in a similar position?"

I hated him for asking the question because I knew he knew the answer to it. "I would have had to be a very lucky black man not to have been in such a position."

"You would have had to be a very lucky *man.*"

"Oh, God," I said, "please don't give me any of this equality-in-anguish business."

"It is perfectly possible," he said, sharply, "that there is not another kind."

Then he was silent. He sat down behind his desk. He cut a cigar and lit it, puffing up clouds of smoke, as though to prevent us from seeing each other too clearly. "Consider this," he said. "I am a French director who has never seen your country. I have never done you any harm, except, perhaps, historically—I mean, because I am white—but I cannot be blamed for that—"

"But *I* can be," I said, "and I am! I've never understood why, if *I* have to pay for the history written in the color of my skin, *you* should get off scot-free!" But I was surprised at my vehemence, I had not known I was going to say these things, and by the fact that I was trembling and from the way he looked at me I knew that, from a professional point of view anyway, I was playing into his hands.

"What makes you think I *do?*" His face looked weary and stern. "I am a Frenchman. Look at France. You think that I—we—are not paying for our history?" He walked to the window, staring out at the rather grim little town in which the studio was located. "If it is revenge that you want, well, then, let me tell you, you will have it. You will probably have it, whether you want it or not, our stupidity will make it inevitable." He turned back into the room."But I beg you not to confuse me with the happy people of your country, who scarcely know that there is such a thing as history and so, naturally, imagine that they can escape, as you put it, scot-free. That is what you are doing, that is what I was about to say. I was about to say that I am a French director and I have never been in your country and I have never done you any harm—but you are not talking to that man, in this room, now. You are not talking to Jean Luc Vidal, but to some other white man, whom you remember, who has nothing to do with me." He paused and went back to his desk. "Oh, most of the time you are not like this, I know. But it is there all the time, it must be, because when you are upset, this is what comes out. So you are not playing Chico truthfully, you are lying about him, and I will not let you do it. When you go back, now, and play this scene again, I want you to remember what has just happened in this room. You brought your past into this room. That is what Chico does when he walks into the dance hall. The Frenchman whom he begs for a job is not merely a Frenchman—he is the father who disowned and betrayed him and all the Frenchmen whom he hates." He smiled and poured me another cognac. "Ah! If it were not for *my* history, I would not have so much trouble to get the truth out of you." He looked into my face, half smiling. "And you, you are angry—are you not?—that I *ask* you for the truth. You think I have no right to ask." Then he said something which he knew would enrage me. "Who are you then, and what good has it done you to come to France, and how will you raise your son? Will you teach him never to tell the truth to anyone?" And he moved behind his desk and looked at me, as though from behind a barricade.

"You have no right to talk to me this way."

"Oh, yes, I do," he said. "I have a film to make and a reputation to maintain and I am going to get a performance out of you." He looked at his watch. "Let us go back to work."

I watch him now, sitting quietly in my living room, tough, cynical, crafty old Frenchman, and I wonder if he knows that the nightmare at the bottom of my mind, as I played the role of Chico, was all the possible fates of Paul.

This is but another way of saying that I relived the disasters which had nearly undone me; but, because I was thinking of Paul, I discovered that I did not want my son ever to feel toward me as I had felt toward my own father. He had died when I was eleven, but I had watched the humiliations he had to bear, and I had pitied him. But was there not, in that pity, however painfully and unwillingly, also some contempt? For how could I *know* what he had borne? I knew only that I was his son. However he had loved me, whatever he had borne, I, his son, was despised. Even had he lived, he could have done nothing to prevent it, nothing to protect me. The best that he could hope to do was to prepare me for it; and even at that he had failed. How can one be prepared for the spittle in the face, all the tireless ingenuity which goes into the spite and fear of small, unutterably miserable people, whose greatest terror is the singular identity, whose joy, whose safety, is entirely dependent on the humiliation and anguish of others?

But for Paul, I swore it, such a day would never come. I would throw my life and my work between Paul and the nightmare of the world. I would make it impossible for the world to treat Paul as it had treated my father and me.

Mahalia's record ends. Vidal rises to turn it over. "Well?" He looks at me very affectionately. "Your nightmares, please!"

"Oh, I was thinking of that summer I spent in Alabama, when my mother died." I stop. "You know, but when we finally filmed that bar scene, I was thinking of New York. I was scared in Alabama, but I almost went crazy in New York. I was sure I'd never make it back here—back here to Harriet. And I knew if I didn't, it was going to be the end of me." Now Mahalia is singing *When the Saints Go Marching In.* "I got a job in the town as an elevator boy, in the town's big department store. It was a special favor, one of my father's white friends got it for me. For a long time, in the South, we all—depended—on the—*kindness*—of white friends." I take out a handkerchief and wipe my face. "But this man didn't like me. I guess I didn't seem grateful enough, wasn't enough like my father, what he thought my father was. And I couldn't get used to the town again, I'd been away too long, I hated it. It's a terrible town, anyway, the whole thing looks as though it's been built around a jailhouse. There's a room in the courthouse, a room where they beat you up. Maybe you're walking along the street one night, it's usually at night, but it happens in the daytime, too. And the police car comes up behind you and the cop says, 'Hey, boy. Come on over here.' So you go on over. He says, 'Boy, I believe you're drunk.' And, you see, if you say, 'No, no sir,' he'll beat you because you're calling him a liar. And if you say anything else, unless it's something to make him laugh, he'll take you in and beat you, just for fun. The trick is to think of some way for them to have their fun without beating you up."

The street lights of Paris click on and turn all the green leaves silver. "Or

to go along with the ways *they* dream up. And they'll do anything, anything at all, to prove that you're no better than a dog and to make you feel
like one. And they hated me because I'd been North and I'd been to Europe.
People kept saying, I hope you didn't bring no foreign notions back here
with you boy. And I'd say, 'No sir,' or 'No ma'am,' but I never said it right.
And there was a time, all of them remembered it, when I *had* said it right.
But now they could tell that I despised them—I guess, no matter what, I
wanted them to know that I despised them. But I didn't despise them any
more than everyone else did, only the others never let it show. They knew
how to keep the white folks happy, and it was easy—you just had to keep
them feeling like they were God's favor to the universe. They'd walk
around with great, big, foolish grins on their faces and the colored folks
loved to see this, because they hated them so much. "Just look at So-and-
So," somebody'd say. "His white is *on* him today." And when we didn't
hate them, we pitied them. In America, that's usually what it means to
have a white friend. You pity the poor bastard because he was born
believing the world's a great place to be, and you know it's not, and you
can see that he's going to have a terrible time getting used to this idea, if
he ever gets used to it."

Then I think of Paul again, those eyes which still imagine that I can do
anything, that skin, the color of honey and fire, his jet-black, curly hair.
I look out at Paris again, and I listen to Mahalia. "Maybe it's better to have
the terrible times first. I don't know. Maybe, then, you can have, *if* you
live, a better life, a real life, because you had to fight so hard to get it away
—you know?—from the mad dog who held it in his teeth. But then your
life has all those tooth marks, too, all those tatters, and all that blood." I
walk to the bottle and raise it. "One for the road?"

"Thank you," says Vidal.

I pour us a drink, and he watches me. I have never talked so much before,
not about those things anyway. I know that Vidal has nightmares, because
he knows so much about them, but he has never told me what his are. I
think that he probably does not talk about his nightmares any more. I
know that the war cost him his wife and his son, and that he was in prison
in Germany. He very rarely refers to it. He has a married daughter who
lives in England, and he rarely speaks of her. He is like a man who has
learned to live on what is left of an enormous fortune.

We are silent for a moment.

"Please go on," he says, with a smile. "I am curious about the reality
behind the reality of your performance."

"My sister, Louisa, never married," I say, abruptly, "because, once,
years ago, she and the boy she was going with and two friends of theirs
were out driving in a car and the police stopped them. The girl who was
with them was very fair and the police pretended not to believe her when

she said she was colored. They made her get out and stand in front of the headlights of the car and pull down her pants and raise her dress—they said that was the only way they could be sure. And you can imagine what they said, and what they did—and they were lucky, at that, that it didn't go any further. But none of the men could do anything about it. Louisa couldn't face the boy again, and I guess he couldn't face her." Now it is really growing dark in the room and I cross to the light switch. "You know, I know what that boy felt, I've felt it. They want you to feel that you're not a man, maybe that's the only way they can feel like men, I don't know. I walked around New York with Harriet's cablegram in my pocket as though it were some atomic secret, in *code*, and they'd kill me if they ever found out what it meant. You know, there's something wrong with people like that. And thank God Harriet was here, she *proved* that the world was bigger than the world they wanted me to live in, I *had* to get back here, get to a place where people were too busy with their own lives, *their private lives,* to make fantasies about mine, to set up walls around mine." I look at him. The light in the room has made the night outside blue-black and golden and the great searchlight of the Eiffel Tower is turning in the sky. "That's what it's like in America, for me, anyway. I always feel that I don't exist there, except in someone else's—usually dirty—mind. I don't know if you know what that means, but I do, and I don't want to put Harriet through that and I don't want to raise Paul there."

"Well," he says at last, "you are not required to remain in America forever, are you? You will sing in that elegant club which apparently feels that it cannot, much longer, so much as open its doors without you, and you will probably accept the movie offer, you would be very foolish not to. You will make a lot of money. Then, one day, you will remember that airlines and steamship companies are still in business and that France still exists. *That* will certainly be cause for astonishment."

Vidal was a Gaullist before de Gaulle came to power. But he regrets the manner of de Gaulle's rise and he is worried about de Gaulle's regime. "It is not the fault of *mon général,*" he sometimes says, sadly. "Perhaps it is history's fault. I *suppose* it must be history which always arranges to bill a civilization at the very instant it is least prepared to pay."

Now he rises and walks out on the balcony, as though to reassure himself of the reality of Paris. Mahalia is singing *Didn't It Rain?* I walk out and stand beside him.

"You are a good boy—Chico," he says. I laugh. "You believe in love. You do not know all the things love cannot do, but"—he smiles—"love will teach you that."

We go, after dinner, to a Left Bank discothèque which can charge outrageous prices because Marlon Brando wandered in there one night. By accident, according to Vidal. "Do you know how many people in Paris are becoming rich—to say nothing of those, *hélas!,* who are going broke—on the off chance that Marlon Brando will lose his way again?"

He has not, presumably, lost his way tonight, but the discothèque is crowded with those strangely faceless people who are a part of the night life of all great cities, and who always arrive, moments, hours, or decades late, on the spot made notorious by an event or a movement or a handful of personalities. So here are American boys, anything but beardless, scratching around for Hemingway; American girls, titillating themselves with Frenchmen and existentialism, while waiting for the American boys to shave off their beards; French painters, busily pursuing the revolution which ended thirty years ago; and the young, bored, perverted, American *arrivistes* who are buying their way into the art world via flattery and liquor, and the production of canvases as arid as their greedy little faces. Here are boys, of all nations, one step above the pimp, who are occasionally walked across a stage or trotted before a camera. And the girls, their enemies, whose faces are sometimes seen in ads, one of whom will surely have a tantrum before the evening is out.

In a corner, as usual, surrounded, as usual, by smiling young men, sits the drunken blonde woman who was once the mistress of a famous, dead painter. She is a figure of some importance in the art world, and so rarely has to pay for either her drinks or her lovers. An older Frenchman, who was once a famous director, is playing *quatre cent vingt-et-un* with the woman behind the cash register. He nods pleasantly to Vidal and me as we enter, but makes no move to join us, and I respect him for this. Vidal and I are obviously cast tonight in the role vacated by Brando: our entrance justifies the prices and sends a kind of shiver through the room. It is marvelous to watch the face of the waiter as he approaches, all smiles and deference and grace, not so much honored by our presence as achieving his reality from it; excellence, he seems to be saying, gravitates naturally toward excellence. We order two whiskey and sodas. I know why Vidal sometimes comes here. He is lonely. I do not think that he expects ever to love one woman again, and so he distracts himself with many.

Since this is a discothèque, jazz is blaring from the walls and record sleeves are scattered about with a devastating carelessness. Two of them are mine and no doubt, presently, someone will play the recording of the songs I sang in the film.

"I thought," says Vidal, with a malicious little smile, "that your farewell to Paris would not be complete without a brief exposure to the perils of fame. Perhaps it will help prepare you for America, where, I am told, the populace is yet more carnivorous than it is here."

I can see that one of the vacant models is preparing herself to come to our table and ask for an autograph, hoping, since she is pretty—she has, that is, the usual female equipment, dramatized in the usual, modern way —to be invited for a drink. Should the maneuver succeed, one of her boy friends or girl friends will contrive to come by the table, asking for a light or a pencil or a lipstick, and it will be extremely difficult not to invite this person to join us, too. Before the evening ends, we will be surrounded. I don't, now, know what I expected of fame, but I suppose it never occurred to me that the light could be just as dangerous, just as killing, as the dark.

"Well, let's make it brief," I tell him. "Sometimes I wish that you weren't quite so fond of me."

He laughs. "There are some very interesting people here tonight. Look."

Across the room from us, and now staring at our table, are a group of American Negro students, who are probably visiting Paris for the first time. There are four of them, two boys and two girls, and I suppose that they must be in their late teens or early twenties. One of the boys, a gleaming, curly-haired, golden-brown type—the color of his mother's fried chicken—is carrying a guitar. When they realize we have noticed them, they smile and wave—wave as though I were one of their possessions, as, indeed, I am. Golden-brown is a mime. He raises his guitar, drops his shoulders, and his face falls into the lugubrious lines of Chico's face as he approaches death. He strums a little of the film's theme music, and I laugh and the table laughs. It is as though we were all back home and had met for a moment, on a Sunday morning, say, before a church or a poolroom or a barbershop.

And they have created a sensation in the discothèque, naturally, having managed, with no effort whatever, to outwit all the gleaming boys and girls. Their table, which had been of no interest only a moment before, has now become the focus of a rather pathetic attention; their smiles have made it possible for the others to smile, and to nod in our direction.

"Oh," says Vidal, "he does that far better than you ever did, perhaps I will make him a star."

"Feel free, *m'sieu, le bon Dieu,* I got mine." But I can see that his attention has really been caught by one of the girls, slim, tense, and dark, who seems, though it is hard to know how one senses such things, to be treated by the others with a special respect. And, in fact, the table now seems to be having a council of war, to be demanding her opinion or her cooperation. She listens, frowning, laughing; the quality, the force of her intelligence causes her face to keep changing all the time, as though a light played on it. And, presently, with a gesture she might once have used to scatter feed to chickens, she scoops up from the floor one of those dangling rag bags women love to carry. She holds it loosely by the drawstrings, so that it is banging somewhere around her ankle, and walks over to our table. She has an honest, forthright walk, entirely unlike the calculated, pelvic workout by means of which most women get about. She is small, but sturdily, economically, put together.

As she reaches our table, Vidal and I rise, and this throws her for a second. (It has been a long time since I have seen such an attractive girl.)

Also, everyone, of course, is watching us. It is really a quite curious moment. They have put on a record of Chico singing a sad, angry Martinique ballad; my own voice is coming at us from the walls as the girl looks from Vidal to me, and smiles.

"I guess you know," she says, "we weren't *about* to let you get out of here without bugging you just a little bit. We've only been in Paris just a couple of days and we thought for sure that we wouldn't have a chance of running into you anywhere, because it's in all the papers that you're coming home."

"Yes," I say, "yes. I'm leaving the day after tomorrow."

"Oh!" She grins. "Then we really *are* lucky." I find that I have almost forgotten the urchin-like grin of a colored girl. "I guess, before I keep babbling on, I'd better introduce myself. My name is Ada Holmes."

We shake hands. "This is Monsieur Vidal, the director of the film."

"I'm very honored to meet you, sir."

"Will you join us for a moment? Won't you sit down?" And Vidal pulls a chair out for her.

But she frowns contritely. "I really ought to get back to my friends." She looks at me. "I really just came over to say, for myself and all the kids, that we've got your records and we've seen your movie, and it means so much to us"—and she laughs, breathlessly, nervously, it is somehow more moving than tears—"more than I can say. Much more. And we wanted to know if you and your friend"—she looks at Vidal—"your *director*, Monsieur Vidal, would allow us to buy you a drink? We'd be honored if you would."

"It is we who are honored," says Vidal, promptly, "*and* grateful. We were getting terribly bored with one another, thank God you came along."

The three of us laugh, and we cross the room.

The three at the table rise, and Ada makes the introductions. The other girl, taller, and paler than Ada, is named Ruth. One of the boys is named Talley —"short for Talliafero"—and Golden-brown's name is Pete. "Man," he tells me, "I dig you the most. You tore me up, baby, tore me *up*."

"You tore up a lot of people," Talley says, cryptically, and he and Ruth laugh. Vidal does not know, but I do, that Talley is probably referring to white people.

They are from New Orleans and Tallahassee and North Carolina; are college students, and met on the boat. They have been in Europe all summer, in Italy and Spain, but are only just getting to Paris.

"We meant to come sooner," says Ada, "but we could never make up our minds to leave a place. I thought we'd never pry Ruth loose from Venice."

"I resigned myself," says Pete, "and just say in the Piazza San Marco, drinking gin fizz and being photographed with the pigeons, while Ruth had herself driven *all* up and down the Grand Canal." He looks at Ruth. "Finally, thank heaven, it rained."

"She was working off her hostilities," says Ada, with a grin. "We thought we might as well let her do it in Venice, the opportunities in North Carolina are really terribly limited."

"There are some very upset people walking around down there," Ruth says, "and a couple of tours around the Grand Canal might do them a world of good."

Pete laughs. "Can't you just see Ruth escorting them to the edge of the water?"

"I haven't lifted my hand in anger yet," Ruth says, "but, oh Lord," and she laughs, clenching and unclenching her fists.

"You haven't been back for a long time, have you?" Talley asks me.

"Eight years. I haven't really lived there for twelve years."

Pete whistles. "I fear you are in for some surprises, my friend. There have been some changes made." Then, "Are you afraid?"

"A little."

"We all are," says Ada, "that's why I was so glad to get away for a little while."

"Then you haven't been back since Black Monday," Talley says. He laughs. "That's how it's gone down in Confederate history." He turns to Vidal. "What do people think about it here?"

Vidal smiles, delighted. "It seems extraordinarily infantile behavior, even for Americans, from whom, I must say, I have never expected very much in the way of maturity." Everyone at the table laughs. Vidal goes on. "But I cannot really talk about it, I do not understand it. I have never really understood Americans; I am an old man now, and I suppose I never will. There is something very nice about them, something very winning, but they seem so ignorant—so ignorant of life. Perhaps it is strange, but the only people from your country with whom I have ever made contact are black people—like my good friend, my discovery, here," and he slaps me on the shoulder. "Perhaps it is because we, in Europe, whatever else we do not know, or have forgotten, know about suffering. We have suffered here. You have suffered, too. But most Americans do not yet know what anguish is. It is too bad, because the life of the West is in their hands." He turns to Ada. "I cannot help saying that I think it is a scandal —and we may all pay very dearly for it—that a civilized nation should elect to represent it a man who is so simple that he thinks the world is simple." And silence falls at the table and the four young faces stare at him.

"Well," says Pete, at last, turning to me, "you won't be bored, man, when you get back there."

"It's much too nice a night," I say, "to stay cooped up in this place, where all I can hear is my own records." We laugh. "Why don't we get out of here and find a sidewalk café?" I tap Pete's guitar. "Maybe we can find out if you've got any talent."

"Oh, talent I've got," says Pete, "but character, man, I'm lacking."

So, after some confusion about the bill, for which Vidal has already made himself responsible, we walk out into the Paris night. It is very strange to feel that, very soon now, these boulevards will not exist for me. People will be walking up and down, as they are tonight, and lovers will be murmuring in the black shadows of the plane trees, and there will be these same still figures on the benches or in the parks—but they will not exist for me, I will not be here. For a long while Paris will no longer exist for me, except in my mind; and only in the minds of some people will I exist any longer for Paris. After departure, only invisible things are left, perhaps the life of the world is held together by invisible chains of memory and loss and love. So many things, so many people, depart! And we can only repossess them in our minds. Perhaps this is what the old folks meant, what my mother and my father meant, when they counseled us to keep the faith.

We have taken a table at the Deux Magots and Pete strums on his guitar and begins to play this song:

> *Preach the word, preach the word, preach the word!*
> *If I never, never see you any more.*
> *Preach the word, preach the word.*
> *And I'll meet you on Canaan's shore.*

He has a strong, clear, boyish voice, like a young preacher's, and he is smiling as he sings his song. Ada and I look at each other and grin, and Vidal is smiling. The waiter looks a little worried, for we are already beginning to attract a crowd, but it is a summer night, the gendarmes on the corner do not seem to mind, and there will be time, anyway, to stop us.

Pete was not there, none of us were, the first time this song was needed; and no one now alive can imagine what the time was like. But the song has come down the bloodstained ages. I suppose this to mean that the song is still needed, still has its work to do.

The others are all, visibly, very proud of Pete; and we all join him, and people stop to listen:

> *Testify! Testify!*
> *If I never, never see you any more!*
> *Testify! Testify!*
> *I'll meet you on Canaan's shore!*

In the crowd that has gathered to listen to us, I see a face I know, the face of a North African prize fighter, who is no longer in the ring. I used to know him well in the old days, but have not seen him for a long time. He looks quite well, his face is shining, he is quite decently dressed. And something about the way he holds himself, not quite looking at our table, tells me that he has seen me, but does not want to risk a rebuff. So I call him. "Boona!"

And he turns, smiling, and comes loping over to our table, his hands in his pockets. Pete is still singing and Ada and Vidal have taken off on a conversation of their own. Ruth and Talley look curiously, expectantly, at Boona. Now that I have called him over, I feel somewhat uneasy. I realize that I do not know what he is doing now, or how he will get along with any of these people, and I can see in his eyes that he is delighted to be in the presence of two young girls. There are virtually no North African women in Paris, and not even the dirty, rat-faced girls who live, apparently, in cafés are willing to go with an Arab. So Boona is always looking for a girl, and because he is so deprived and because he is not Western, his techniques can be very unsettling. I know he is relieved that the girls are not French and not white. He looks briefly at Vidal and Ada. Vidal, also, though for different reasons, is always looking for a girl.

But Boona has always been very nice to me. Perhaps I am sorry that I called him over, but I did not want to snub him.

He claps one hand to the side of my head, as is his habit. *"Comment vas-tu, mon frère?* I have not seen you, oh, for long time." And he asks me, as in the old days, "You all right? Nobody bother you?" And he laughs. "Ah! *Tu as fait le chemin, toi!* Now you are *vedette,* big star—wonderful!" He looks around the table, made a little uncomfortable by the silence that has fallen, now that Pete has stopped singing. "I have seen you in the movies—you know?—and I tell everybody, I know *him!"* He points to me, and laughs, and Ruth and Talley laugh with him. "That's right, man, you make me real proud, you make me cry!"

"Boona, I want you to meet some friends of mine." And I go round the table: "Ruth, Talley, Ada, Pete"—and he bows and shakes hands, his dark eyes gleaming with pleasure—*"et Monsieur Vidal, le metteur en scène du film qui t'a arraché des larmes."*

"Enchanté." But his attitude toward Vidal is colder, more distrustful. "Of course I have heard of Monsieur Vidal. He is the director of many films, many of them made me cry." This last statement is utterly, even insolently, insincere.

But Vidal, I think, is relieved that I will now be forced to speak to Boona and will leave him alone with Ada.

"Sit down," I say, "have a drink with us, let me have your news. What's been happening with you, what are you doing with yourself these days?"

"Ah," he sits down, "nothing very brilliant, my brother." He looks at me quickly, with a little smile. "You know, we have been having hard times here."

"Where are you from?" Ada asks him.

His brilliant eyes take her in entirely, but she does not flinch. "I am from Tunis." He says it proudly, with a little smile.

"From Tunis. I have never been to Africa, I would love to go one day."

He laughs. "Africa is a big place. Very big. There are many countries in Africa, many"—he looks briefly at Vidal—"different kinds of people, many colonies."

"But Tunis," she continues, in her innocence, "is free? Freedom is happening all over Africa. That's why I would like to go there."

"I have not been back for a long time," says Boona, "but all the news I get from Tunis, from my people, is not good."

"Wouldn't you like to go back?" Ruth asks.

Again he looks at Vidal. "That is not so easy."

Vidal smiles. "You know what I would like to do? There's a wonderful Spanish place not far from here, where we can listen to live music and dance a little." He turns to Ada. "Would you like that?"

He is leaving it up to me to get rid of Boona, and it is, of course, precisely for this reason that I cannot do it. Besides, it is no longer so simple.

"Oh, I'd love that," says Ada, and she turns to Boona. "Won't you come, too?"

"Thank you, mam'selle," he says, softly, and his tongue flicks briefly over his lower lip, and he smiles. He is very moved, people are not often nice to him.

In the Spanish place there are indeed a couple of Spanish guitars, drums, castanets, and a piano, but the uses to which these are being put carry one back, as Pete puts it, to the levee. "These are the wailingest Spanish cats I ever heard," says Ruth. "They didn't learn how to do this in Spain, no, they didn't, they been rambling. You ever hear anything like this going on in Spain?" Talley takes her out on the dance floor, which is already crowded. A very handsome Frenchwoman is dancing with an enormous, handsome black man, who seems to be her lover, who seems to have taught her how to dance. Apparently, they are known to the musicians, who egg them on with small cries of *"Olé!"* It is a very good-natured crowd, mostly foreigners, Spaniards, Swedes, Greeks. Boona takes Ada out on the dance floor while Vidal is answering some questions put to him by Pete on the entertainment situation in France. Vidal looks a little put out, and I am amused.

We are there for perhaps an hour, dancing, talking, and I am, at last, a little drunk. In spite of Boona, who is a very good and tireless dancer, Vidal continues his pursuit of Ada, and I begin to wonder if he will make it and I begin to wonder if I want him to.

I am still puzzling out my reaction when Pete, who has disappeared, comes in through the front door, catches my eye, and signals to me. I leave the table and follow him into the streets.

He looks very upset. "I don't want to bug you, man," he says, "but I fear your boy has goofed."

I know he is not joking. I think he is probably angry at Vidal because of Ada, and I wonder what I can do about it and why he should be telling me.

I stare at him, gravely, and he says, "It looks like he stole some money."

"Stole *money?* Who, Vidal?"

And then, of course, I get it, in the split second before he says, impatiently, "No, are you kidding? Your friend, the Tunisian."

I do not know what to say or what to do, and so I temporize with questions. All the time I am wondering if this can be true and what I can do about it if it is. The trouble is, I know that Boona steals, he would probably not be alive if he didn't, but I cannot say so to these children, who probably still imagine that everyone who steals is a thief. But he has never, to my knowledge, stolen from a friend. It seems unlike him. I have always thought of him as being better than that, and smarter than that. And so I cannot believe it, but neither can I doubt it. I do not know anything about Boona's life, these days. This causes me to realize that I do not really know much about Boona.

"Who did he steal it from?"

"From Ada. Out of her bag."

"How much?"

"Ten dollars. It's not an awful lot of money, but"—he grimaces—"none of us *have* an awful lot of money."

"I know." The dark side street on which we stand is nearly empty. The only sound on the street is the muffled music of the Spanish club. "How do you know it was Boona?"

He anticipates my own unspoken rejoinder. "Who else could it be? Besides—somebody *saw* him do it."

"Somebody saw him?"

"Yes."

I do not ask him who this person is, for fear that he will say it is Vidal.

"Well," I say, "I'll try to get it back." I think that I will take Boona aside and then replace the money myself. "Was it in dollars or in francs?"

"In francs."

I have no dollars and this makes it easier. I do not know how I can possibly face Boona and accuse him of stealing money from my friends. I would rather give him the benefit of even the faintest doubt. But, "Who saw him?" I ask.

"Talley. But we didn't want to make a thing about it—"

"Does Ada know it's gone?"

"Yes." He looks at me helplessly. "I know this makes you feel pretty bad, but we thought we'd better tell you, rather than"—lamely—"anybody else."

Now, Ada comes out of the club, carrying her ridiculous handbag, and with her face all knotted and sad. "Oh," she says, "I hate to cause all this trouble, it's not worth it, not for ten lousy dollars." I am astonished to see that she has been weeping, and tears come to her eyes now.

I put my arm around her shoulder. "Come on, now. You're not causing anybody any trouble and, anyway, it's nothing to cry about."

"It isn't your fault, Ada," Pete says, miserably.

"Oh, I ought to get a sensible handbag," she says, "like you're always telling me to do," and she laughs a little, then looks at me. "Please don't try to do anything about it. Let's just forget it."

"What's happening inside?" I ask her.

"Nothing. They're just talking. I think Mr. Vidal is dancing with Ruth. He's a great dancer, that little Frenchman."

"He's a great talker, too," Pete says.

"Oh, he doesn't mean anything," says Ada, "he's just having fun. He probably doesn't get a chance to talk to many American girls."

"He certainly made up for lost time tonight."

"Look," I say, "if Talley and Boona are alone, maybe you better go back in. We'll be in in a minute. Let's try to keep this as quiet as we can."

"Yeah," he says, "okay. We're going soon anyway, okay?"

"Yes," she tells him, "right away."

But as he turns away, Boona and Talley step out into the street, and it is clear that Talley feels that he has Boona under arrest. I almost laugh, the whole thing is beginning to resemble one of those mad French farces with people flying in and out of doors; but Boona comes straight to me.

"They say I stole money, my friend. You know me, you are the only one here who knows me, you know I would not do such a thing."

I look at him and I do not know what to say. Ada looks at him with her eyes full of tears and looks away. I take Boona's arm.

"We'll be back in a minute," I say. We walk a few paces up the dark, silent street.

"She say I take her money," he says. He, too, looks as though he is about to weep—but I do not know for which reason. "You know me, you know me almost twelve years, you think I do such a thing?"

Talley saw you, I want to say, but I cannot say it. Perhaps Talley only thought he saw him. Perhaps it is easy to see a boy who looks like Boona with his hand in an American girl's purse.

"If you do not believe me," he says, "search me. Search me!" and he opens his arms wide, theatrically, and now there are tears standing in his eyes.

I do not know what his tears mean, but I certainly cannot search him.

I want to say, I know you steal, I know you have to steal. Perhaps you took the money out of this girl's purse in order to eat tomorrow, in order not be thrown into the streets tonight, in order to stay out of jail. This girl means nothing to you, after all, she is only an American, an American like me. Perhaps, I suddenly think, no girl means anything to you, or ever will again, they have beaten you too hard and kept you out in the gutter too long. And I also think, if you would steal from her, then of course you would lie to me, neither of us means anything to you; perhaps, in your eyes, we are simply luckier gangsters in a world which is run by gangsters. But I cannot say any of these things to Boona. I cannot say, Tell me the truth, nobody cares about the money any more.

So I say, "Of course I will not search you." And I realize that he knew I would not.

"I think it is that Frenchman who say I am a thief. They think we all are thieves." His eyes are bright and bitter. He looks over my shoulder. "They have all come out of the club now."

I look around and they are all there, in a little dark knot on the sidewalk.

"Don't worry," I say. "It doesn't matter."

"You believe me? My brother?" And his eyes look into mine with a terrible intensity.

"Yes," I force myself to say, "yes, of course, I believe you. Someone made a mistake, that's all."

"You know, the way American girls run around, they have their sack open all the time, she could have lost the money anywhere. Why she blame me? Because I come from Africa?" Tears are glittering on his face. "Here she come now."

And Ada comes up the street with her straight, determined walk. She walks straight to Boona and takes his hand. "I am sorry," she says, "for everything that happened. Please believe me. It isn't worth all this fuss. I'm sure you're a very nice person, and"—she falters—"I must have lost the money, I'm sure I lost it." She looks at him. "It isn't worth hurting your feelings, and I'm terribly sorry about it."

"I no take your money," he says. "Really, truly, I no take it. Ask him" —pointing to me, grabbing me by the arm, shaking me—"he know me for years, he will tell you that I never, never steal!"

"I'm sure," she says. "I'm sure."

I take Boona by the arm again. "Let's forget it. Let's forget it all. We're all going home now, and one of these days we'll have a drink again and we'll forget all about it, all right?"

"Yes," says Ada, "let us forget it." And she holds out her hand.

Boona takes it, wonderingly. His eyes take her in again. "You are a very nice girl. Really. A very nice girl."

"I'm sure you're a nice person, too." She pauses. "Goodnight."

"Goodnight," he says, after a long silence.

Then he kisses me on both cheeks. *"Au revoir, mon frère."*

"Au revoir, Boona."

After a moment we turn and walk away, leaving him standing there. "Did he take it?" asks Vidal.

"I tell you, I *saw* him," says Talley.

"Well," I say, "it doesn't matter now." I look back and see Boona's stocky figure disappearing down the street.

"No," says Ada, "it doesn't matter." She looks up. "It's almost morning."

"I would gladly," says Vidal, stammering, "gladly—"

But she is herself again. "I wouldn't think of it. We had a wonderful time tonight, a wonderful time, and I wouldn't think of it." She turns to me with the urchin-like grin. "It was wonderful meeting you. I hope you won't have too much trouble getting used to the States again."

"Oh, I don't think I will," I say. And then, "I hope you won't."

"No," she says, "I don't think anything they can do will surprise me any more."

"Which way are we all going?" asks Vidal. "I hope someone will share my taxi with me."

But he lives in the sixteenth arrondissement, which is not in anyone's direction. We walk him to the line of cabs standing under the clock at Odéon.

And we look each other in the face, in the growing morning light. His face looks weary and lined and lonely. He puts both hands on my shoulders and then puts one hand on the nape of my neck. "Do not forget me, Chico," he says. "You must come back and see us, one of these days. Many of us depend on you for many things."

"I'll be back," I say. "I'll never forget you."

He raises his eyebrows and smiles. *"Alors, Adieu."*

"Adieu, Vidal."

"I was happy to meet all of you," he says. He looks at Ada. "Perhaps we will meet again before you leave."

"Perhaps," she says. "Goodby, Monsieur Vidal."

"Goodby."

Vidal's cab drives away. "I also leave you now," I say. "I must go home and wake up my son and prepare for our journey."

I leave them standing on the corner, under the clock, which points to six. They look very strange and lost and determined, the four of them. Just before my cab turns off the boulevard, I wave to them and they wave back.

Mme. Dumont is in the hall, mopping the floor.

"Did all my family get home?" I ask. I feel very cheerful, I do not know why.

"Yes," she says, "they are all here. Paul is still sleeping."

"May I go in and get him?"

She looks at me in surprise. "Of course."

So I walk into her apartment and walk into the room where Paul lies sleeping. I stand over his bed for a long time.

Perhaps my thoughts traveled—travel through to him. He opens his eyes and smiles up at me. He puts a fist to his eyes and raises his arms. *"Bonjour, Papa."*

I lift him up. *"Bonjour.* How do you feel today?"

"Oh, I don't know yet," he says.

I laugh. I put him on my shoulder and walk out into the hall. Mme. Dumont looks up at him with her radiant, aging face.

"Ah," she says, "you are going on a journey! How does it feel?"

"He doesn't know yet," I tell her. I walk to the elevator door and open it, dropping Paul down to the crook of my arm.

She laughs again. "He will know later. What a journey! *Jusqu'au nouveau monde!"*

I open the cage and we step inside. "Yes," I say, "all the way to the new world." I press the button and the cage, holding my son and me, goes up.

Flannery O'Connor (1925–1964)

EVERYTHING THAT RISES MUST CONVERGE

Her doctor had told Julian's mother that she must lose twenty pounds on account of her blood pressure, so on Wednesday nights Julian had to take her downtown on the bus for a reducing class at the Y. The reducing class was designed for working girls over fifty, who weighed from 165 to 200 pounds. His mother was one of the slimmer ones, but she said ladies did not tell their age or weight. She would not ride the buses by herself at night since they had been integrated, and because the reducing class was one of her few pleasures, necessary for her health, and *free,* she said Julian could at least put himself out to take her, considering all she did for him. Julian did not like to consider all she did for him, but every Wednesday night he braced himself and took her.

She was almost ready to go, standing before the hall mirror, putting on her hat, while he, his hands behind him, appeared pinned to the door frame, waiting like Saint Sebastian for the arrows to begin piercing him. The hat was new and had cost her seven dollars and a half. She kept saying, "Maybe I shouldn't have paid that for it. No, I shouldn't have. I'll take it off and return it tomorrow. I shouldn't have bought it."

Julian raised his eyes to heaven. "Yes, you should have bought it," he said. "Put it on and let's go." It was a hideous hat. A purple velvet flap came down on one side of it and stood up on the other; the rest of it was green and looked like a cushion with the stuffing out. He decided it was less comical than jaunty and pathetic. Everything that gave her pleasure was small and depressed him.

She lifted the hat one more time and set it down slowly on top of her head. Two wings of gray hair protruded on either side of her florid face, but her eyes, sky-blue, were as innocent and untouched by experience as they must have been when she was ten. Were it not that she was a widow who had struggled fiercely to feed and clothe and put him through school

525

and who was supporting him still, "until he got on his feet," she might have been a little girl that he had to take to town.

"It's all right, it's all right," he said. "Let's go." He opened the door himself and started down the walk to get her going. The sky was a dying violet and the houses stood out darkly against it, bulbous liver-colored monstrosities of a uniform ugliness though no two were alike. Since this had been a fashionable neighborhood forty years ago, his mother persisted in thinking they did well to have an apartment in it. Each house had a narrow collar of dirt around it in which sat, usually, a grubby child. Julian walked with his hands in his pockets, his head down and thrust forward and his eyes glazed with the determination to make himself completely numb during the time he would be sacrificed to her pleasure.

The door closed and he turned to find the dumpy figure, surmounted by the atrocious hat, coming toward him. "Well," she said, "you only live once and paying a little more for it, I at least won't meet myself coming and going."

"Some day I'll start making money," Julian said gloomily—he knew he never would—"and you can have one of those jokes whenever you take the fit." But first they would move. He visualized a place where the nearest neighbors would be three miles away on either side.

"I think you're doing fine," she said, drawing on her gloves. "You've only been out of school a year. Rome wasn't built in a day."

She was one of the few members of the Y reducing class who arrived in hat and gloves and who had a son who had been to college. "It takes time," she said, "and the world is in such a mess. This hat looked better on me than any of the others, though when she brought it out I said, 'Take that thing back. I wouldn't have it on my head,' and she said, 'Now wait till you see it on,' and when she put it on me, I said, 'We-ull,' and she said, 'If you ask me, that hat does something for you and you do something for the hat, and besides,' she said, 'with that hat, you won't meet yourself coming and going.' "

Julian thought he could have stood his lot better if she had been selfish, if she had been an old hag who drank and screamed at him. He walked along, saturated in depression, as if in the midst of his martyrdom he had lost his faith. Catching sight of his long, hopeless, irritated face, she stopped suddenly with a grief-stricken look, and pulled back on his arm. "Wait on me," she said. "I'm going back to the house and take this thing off and tomorrow I'm going to return it. I was out of my head. I can pay the gas bill with that seven-fifty."

He caught her arm in a vicious grip. "You are not going to take it back," he said. "I like it."

"Well," she said, "I don't think I ought . . ."

"Shut up and enjoy it," he muttered, more depressed than ever.

"With the world in the mess it's in," she said, "it's a wonder we can enjoy anything. I tell you, the bottom rail is on the top."

Julian sighed.

"Of course," she said, "if you know who you are, you can go anywhere." She said this every time he took her to the reducing class. "Most of them in it are not our kind of people," she said, "but I can be gracious to anybody. I know who I am."

"They don't give a damn for your graciousness," Julian said savagely. "Knowing who you are is good for one generation only. You haven't the foggiest idea where you stand now or who you are."

She stopped and allowed her eyes to flash at him. "I most certainly do know who I am," she said, "and if you don't know who you are, I'm ashamed of you."

"Oh hell," Julian said.

"Your great-grandfather was a former governor of this state," she said. "Your grandfather was a prosperous landowner. Your grandmother was a Godhigh."

"Will you look around you," he said tensely, "and see where you are now?" and he swept his arm jerkily out to indicate the neighborhood, which the growing darkness at least made less dingy.

"You remain what you are," she said. "Your great-grandfather had a plantation and two hundred slaves."

"There are no more slaves," he said irritably.

"They were better off when they were," she said. He groaned to see that she was off on that topic. She rolled onto it every few days like a train on an open track. He knew every stop, every junction, every swamp along the way, and knew the exact point at which her conclusion would roll majestically into the station: "It's ridiculous. It's simply not realistic. They should rise, yes, but on their own side of the fence."

"Let's skip it," Julian said.

"The ones I feel sorry for," she said, "are the ones that are half white. They're tragic."

"Will you skip it?"

"Suppose we were half white. We would certainly have mixed feelings."

"I have mixed feelings now," he groaned.

"Well let's talk about something pleasant," she said. "I remember going to Grandpa's when I was a little girl. Then the house had double stairways that went up to what was really the second floor—all the cooking was done on the first. I used to like to stay down in the kitchen on account of the way the walls smelled. I would sit with my nose pressed against the plaster and take deep breaths. Actually the place belonged to the Godhighs but your grandfather Chestny paid the mortgage and saved it for them. They were in reduced circumstances," she said, "but reduced or not, they never forgot who they were."

"Doubtless that decayed mansion reminded them," Julian muttered. He never spoke of it without contempt or thought of it without longing. He had seen it once when he was a child before it had been sold. The double stairways had rotted and been torn down. Negroes were living in it. But it remained in his mind as his mother had known it. It appeared in his dreams regularly. He would stand on the wide porch, listening to the rustle of oak leaves, then wander through the high-ceilinged hall into the parlor that opened onto it and gaze at the worn rugs and faded draperies. It occurred to him that it was he, not she, who could have appreciated it. He preferred its threadbare elegance to anything he could name and it was because of it that all the neighborhoods they had lived in had been a torment to him—whereas she had hardly known the difference. She called her insensitivity "being adjustable."

"And I remember the old darky who was my nurse, Caroline. There was no better person in the world. I've always had a great respect for my colored friends," she said. "I'd do anything in the world for them and they'd . . ."

"Will you for God's sake get off that subject?" Julian said. When he got on a bus by himself, he made it a point to sit down beside a Negro, in reparation as it were for his mother's sins.

"You're mighty touchy tonight," she said. "Do you feel all right?"

"Yes I feel all right," he said. "Now lay off."

She pursed her lips. "Well, you certainly are in a vile humor," she observed. "I just won't speak to you at all."

They had reached the bus stop. There was no bus in sight and Julian, his hands still jammed in his pockets and his head thrust forward, scowled down the empty street. The frustration of having to wait on the bus as well as ride on it began to creep up his neck like a hot hand. The presence of his mother was borne in upon him as she gave a pained sigh. He looked at her bleakly. She was holding herself very erect under the preposterous hat, wearing it like a banner of her imaginary dignity. There was in him an evil urge to break her spirit. He suddenly unloosened his tie and pulled it off and put it in his pocket.

She stiffened. "Why must you look like *that* when you take me to town?" she said. "Why must you deliberately embarrass me?"

"If you'll never learn where you are," he said, "you can at least learn where I am."

"You look like a—thug," she said.

"Then I must be one," he murmured.

"I'll just go home," she said. "I will not bother you. If you can't do a little thing like that for me . . ."

Rolling his eyes upward, he put his tie back on. "Restored to my class," he muttered. He thrust his face toward her and hissed, "True culture is in the mind, the *mind,*" he said, and tapped his head, "the mind."

"It's in the heart," she said, "and in how you do things and how you do things is because of who you *are.*"

"Nobody in the damn bus cares who you are."

"I care who I am," she said icily.

The lighted bus appeared on top of the next hill and as it approached, they moved out into the street to meet it. He put his hand under her elbow and hoisted her up on the creaking step. She entered with a little smile, as if she were going into a drawing room where everyone had been waiting for her. While he put in the tokens, she sat down on one of the broad front seats for three which faced the aisle. A thin woman with protruding teeth and long yellow hair was sitting on the end of it. His mother moved up beside her and left room for Julian beside herself. He sat down and looked at the floor across the aisle where a pair of thin feet in red and white canvas sandals were planted.

His mother immediately began a general conversation meant to attract anyone who felt like talking. "Can it get any hotter?" she said and removed from her purse a folding fan, black with a Japanese scene on it, which she began to flutter before her.

"I reckon it might could," the woman with the protruding teeth said, "but I know for a fact my apartment couldn't get no hotter."

"It must get the afternoon sun," his mother said. She sat forward and looked up and down the bus. It was half filled. Everybody was white. "I see we have the bus to ourselves," she said. Julian cringed.

"For a change," said the woman across the aisle, the owner of the red and white canvas sandals. "I come on one the other day and they were thick as fleas—up front and all through."

"The world is in a mess everywhere," his mother said. "I don't know how we've let it get in this fix."

"What gets my goat is all those boys from good families stealing automobile tires," the woman with the protruding teeth said. "I told my boy, I said you may not be rich but you been raised right and if I ever catch you in any such mess, they can send you on to the reformatory. Be exactly where you belong."

"Training tells," his mother said. "Is your boy in high school?"

"Ninth grade," the woman said.

"My son just finished college last year. He wants to write but he's selling typewriters until he gets started," his mother said.

The woman leaned forward and peered at Julian. He threw her such a malevolent look that she subsided against the seat. On the floor across the aisle there was an abandoned newspaper. He got up and got it and opened it out in front of him. His mother discreetly continued the conversation in a lower tone but the woman across the aisle said in a loud voice, "Well that's nice. Selling typewriters is close to writing. He can go right from one to the other."

"I tell him," his mother said, "that Rome wasn't built in a day."

Behind the newspaper Julian was withdrawing into the inner compartment of his mind where he spent most of his time. This was a kind of mental bubble in which he established himself when he could not bear to be a part of what was going on around him. From it he could see out and judge but in it he was safe from any kind of penetration from without. It was the only place where he felt free of the general idiocy of his fellows. His mother had never entered it but from it he could see her with absolute clarity.

The old lady was clever enough and he thought that if she had started from any of the right premises, more might have been expected of her. She lived according to the laws of her own fantasy world, outside of which he had never seen her set foot. The law of it was to sacrifice herself for him after she had first created the necessity to do so by making a mess of things. If he had permitted her sacrifices, it was only because her lack of foresight had made them necessary. All of her life had been a struggle to act like a Chestny without the Chestny goods, and to give him everything she thought a Chestny ought to have; but since, said she, it was fun to struggle, why complain? And when you had won, as she had won, what fun to look back on the hard times! He could not forgive her that she had enjoyed the struggle and that she thought *she* had won.

What she meant when she said she had won was that she had brought him up successfully and had sent him to college and that he had turned out so well—good looking (her teeth had gone unfilled so that his could be straightened), intelligent (he realized he was too intelligent to be a success), and with a future ahead of him (there was of course no future ahead of him). She excused his gloominess on the grounds that he was still growing up and his radical ideas on his lack of practical experience. She said he didn't yet know a thing about "life," that he hadn't even entered the real world—when already he was as disenchanted with it as a man of fifty.

The further irony of all this was that in spite of her, he had turned out so well. In spite of going to only a third-rate college, he had, on his own initiative, come out with a first-rate education; in spite of growing up dominated by a small mind, he had ended up with a large one; in spite of all her foolish views, he was free of prejudice and unafraid to face facts. Most miraculous of all, instead of being blinded by love for her as she was for him, he had cut himself emotionally free of her and could see her with complete objectivity. He was not dominated by his mother.

The bus stopped with a sudden jerk and shook him from his meditation. A woman from the back lurched forward with little steps and barely escaped falling in his newspaper as she righted herself. She got off and a large Negro got on. Julian kept his paper lowered to watch. It gave him a certain satisfaction to see injustice in daily operation. It confirmed his view that with a few exceptions there was no one worth knowing within a radius of three hundred miles. The Negro was well dressed and carried a briefcase. He looked around and then sat down on the other end of the seat where the woman with the red and white canvas sandals was sitting. He immediately unfolded a newspaper and obscured himself behind it. Julian's mother's elbow at once prodded insistently into his ribs. "Now you see why I won't ride on these buses by myself," she whispered.

The woman with the red and white canvas sandals had risen at the same time the Negro sat down and had gone further back in the bus and taken the seat of the woman who had got off. His mother leaned forward and cast her an approving look.

Julian rose, crossed the aisle, and sat down in the place of the woman with the canvas sandals. From this position, he looked serenely across at his mother. Her face had turned an angry red. He stared at her, making his eyes the eyes of a stranger. He felt his tension suddenly lift as if he had openly declared war on her.

He would have liked to get in conversation with the Negro and to talk with him about art or politics or any subject that would be above the comprehension of those around them, but the man remained entrenched behind his paper. He was either ignoring the change of seating or had never noticed it. There was no way for Julian to convey his sympathy.

His mother kept her eyes fixed reproachfully on his face. The woman with the protruding teeth was looking at him avidly as if he were a type of monster new to her.

"Do you have a light?" he asked the Negro.

Without looking away from his paper, the man reached in his pocket and handed him a packet of matches.

"Thanks," Julian said. For a moment he held the matches foolishly. A NO SMOKING sign looked down upon him from over the door. This alone would not have deterred him; he had no cigarettes. He had quit smoking some months before because he could not afford it. "Sorry," he muttered and handed back the matches. The Negro lowered the paper and gave him an annoyed look. He took the matches and raised the paper again.

His mother continued to gaze at him but she did not take advantage of his momentary discomfort. Her eyes retained their battered look. Her face seemed to be unnaturally red, as if her blood pressure had risen. Julian allowed no glimmer of sympathy to show on his face. Having got the advantage, he wanted desperately to keep it and carry it through. He would have liked to teach her a lesson that would last her a while, but there seemed no way to continue the point. The Negro refused to come out from behind his paper.

Julian folded his arms and looked stolidly before him, facing her but as if he did not see her, as if he had ceased to recognize her existence. He visualized a scene in which, the bus having reached their stop, he would remain in his seat and when she said, "Aren't you going to get off?" he would look at her as at a stranger who had rashly addressed him. The corner they got off on was usually deserted, but it was well lighted and it would not hurt her to walk by herself the four blocks to the Y. He decided to wait until the time came and then decide whether or not he would let her get off by herself. He would have to be at the Y at ten to bring her back, but he could leave her wondering if he was going to show up. There was no reason for her to think she could always depend on him.

He retired again into the high-ceilinged room sparsely settled with large pieces of antique furniture. His soul expanded momentarily but then he became aware of his mother across from him and the vision shriveled. He studied her coldly. Her feet in little pumps dangled like a child's and did not quite reach the floor. She was training on him an exaggerated look of reproach. He felt completely detached from her. At that moment he could with pleasure have slapped her as he would have slapped a particularly obnoxious child in his charge.

He began to imagine various unlikely ways by which he could teach her a lesson. He might make friends with some distinguished Negro professor or lawyer and bring him home to spend the evening. He would be entirely justified but her blood pressure would rise to 300. He could not push her to the extent of making her have a stroke, and moreover, he had never been successful at making any Negro friends. He had tried to strike up an acquaintance on the bus with some of the better types, with ones that looked like professors or ministers or lawyers. One morning he had sat down next to a distinguished-looking dark brown man who had answered his questions with a sonorous solemnity but who had turned out to be an undertaker. Another day he had sat down beside a cigar-smoking Negro with a diamond ring on his finger, but after a few stilted pleasantries, the Negro had rung the buzzer and risen, slipping two lottery tickets into Julian's hand as he climbed over him to leave.

He imagined his mother lying desperately ill and his being able to secure only a Negro doctor for her. He toyed with that idea for a few minutes and then dropped it for a momentary vision of himself participating as a sympathizer in a sit-in demonstration. This was possible but he did not linger with it. Instead, he approached the ultimate horror. He brought home a beautiful suspiciously Negroid woman. Prepare yourself, he said. There is nothing you can do about it. This is the woman I've chosen. She's intelligent, dignified, even good, and she's suffered and she hasn't thought it *fun.* Now persecute us, go ahead and persecute us. Drive her out of here, but remember, you're driving me too. His eyes were narrowed and through the indignation he had generated, he saw his mother across the aisle, purple-faced, shrunken to the dwarf-like proportions of her moral nature, sitting like a mummy beneath the ridiculous banner of her hat.

He was tilted out of his fantasy again as the bus stopped. The door opened with a sucking hiss and out of the dark a large, gaily dressed, sullen-looking colored woman got on with a little boy. The child, who might have been four, had on a short plaid suit and a Tyrolean hat with a blue feather in it. Julian hoped that he would sit down beside him and that the woman would push in beside his mother. He could think of no better arrangement.

As she waited for her tokens, the woman was surveying the seating possibilities—he hoped with the idea of sitting where she was least wanted. There was something familiar-looking about her but Julian could not place what it was. She was a giant of a woman. Her face was set not only to meet opposition but to seek it out. The downward tilt of her large lower lip was like a warning sign: DON'T TAMPER WITH ME. Her bulging figure was encased in a green crepe dress and her feet overflowed in red shoes. She had on a hideous hat. A purple velvet flap came down on one side of it and stood up on the other; the rest of it was green and looked like a cushion with the stuffing out. She carried a mammoth red pocketbook that bulged throughout as if it were stuffed with rocks.

To Julian's disappointment, the little boy climbed up on the empty seat beside his mother. His mother lumped all children, black and white, into the common category, "cute," and she thought little Negroes were on the whole cuter than little white children. She smiled at the little boy as he climbed on the seat.

Meanwhile the woman was bearing down upon the empty seat beside Julian. To his annoyance, she squeezed herself into it. He saw his mother's face change as the woman settled herself next to him and he realized with satisfaction that this was more objectionable to her than it was to him. Her face seemed almost gray and there was a look of dull recognition in her eyes, as if suddenly she had sickened at some awful confrontation. Julian saw that it was because she and the woman had, in a sense, swapped sons. Though his mother would not realize the symbolic significance of this, she would feel it. His amusement showed plainly on his face.

The woman next to him muttered something unintelligible to herself. He was conscious of a kind of bristling next to him, a muted growling like that of an angry cat. He could not see anything but the red pocketbook upright on the bulging green thighs. He visualized the woman as she had stood waiting for her tokens—the ponderous figure, rising from the red shoes upward over the solid hips, the mammoth bosom, the haughty face, to the green and purple hat.

His eyes widened.

The vision of the two hats, identical, broke upon him with the radiance of a brilliant sunrise. His face was suddenly lit with joy. He could not believe that Fate had thrust upon his mother such a lesson. He gave a loud chuckle so that she would look at him and see that he saw. She turned her eyes on him slowly. The blue in them seemed to have turned a bruised purple. For a moment he had an uncomfortable sense of her innocence, but it lasted only a second before principle rescued him. Justice entitled him to laugh. His grin hardened until it said to her as plainly as if he were saying aloud: Your punishment exactly fits your pettiness. This should teach you a permanent lesson.

Her eyes shifted to the woman. She seemed unable to bear looking at him and to find the woman preferable. He became conscious again of the bristling presence at his side. The woman was rumbling like a volcano about to become active. His mother's mouth began to twitch slightly at one corner. With a sinking heart, he saw incipient signs of recovery on her face and realized that this was going to strike her suddenly as funny and was going to be no lesson at all. She kept her eyes on the woman and an amused smile came over her face as if the woman were a monkey that had stolen her hat. The little Negro was looking up at her with large fascinated eyes. He had been trying to attract her attention for some time.

"Carver!" the woman said suddenly. "Come heah!"

When he saw that the spotlight was on him at last, Carver drew his feet up and turned himself toward Julian's mother and giggled.

"Carver!" the woman said. "You heah me? Come heah!"

Carver slid down from the seat but remained squatting with his back against the base of it, his head turned slyly around toward Julian's mother, who was smiling at him. The woman reached a hand across the aisle and snatched him to her. He righted himself and hung backwards on her knees, grinning at Julian's mother. "Isn't he cute?" Julian's mother said to the woman with the protruding teeth.

"I reckon he is," the woman said without conviction.

The Negress yanked him upright but he eased out of her grip and shot across the aisle and scrambled, giggling wildly, onto the seat beside his love.

"I think he likes me," Julian's mother said, and smiled at the woman. It was the smile she used when she was being particularly gracious to an inferior. Julian saw everything lost. The lesson had rolled off her like rain on a roof.

The woman stood up and yanked the little boy off the seat as if she were snatching him from contagion. Julian could feel the rage in her at having no weapon like his mother's smile. She gave the child a sharp slap across his leg. He howled once and then thrust his head into her stomach and kicked his feet against her shins. "Be-have," she said vehemently.

The bus stopped and the Negro who had been reading the newspaper got off. The woman moved over and set the little boy down with a thump between herself and Julian. She held him firmly by the knee. In a moment he put his hands in front of his face and peeped at Julian's mother through his fingers.

"I see yoooooooo!" she said and put her hand in front of her face and peeped at him.

The woman slapped his hand down. "Quit yo' foolishness," she said, "before I knock the living Jesus out of you!"

Julian was thankful that the next stop was theirs. He reached up and pulled the cord. The woman reached up and pulled it at the same time. Oh my God, he thought. He had the terrible intuition that when they got off the bus together, his mother would open her purse and give the little boy a nickel. The gesture would be as natural to her as breathing. The bus stopped and the woman got up and lunged to the front, dragging the child, who wished to stay on, after her. Julian and his mother got up and followed. As they neared the door, Julian tried to relieve her of her pocketbook.

"No," she murmured, "I want to give the little boy a nickel."

"No!" Julian hissed. "No!"

She smiled down at the child and opened her bag. The bus door opened and the woman picked him up by the arm and descended with him, hanging at her hip. Once in the street she set him down and shook him.

Julian's mother had to close her purse while she got down the bus step but as soon as her feet were on the ground, she opened it again and began to rummage inside. "I can't find but a penny," she whispered, "but it looks like a new one."

"Don't do it!" Julian said fiercely between his teeth. There was a streetlight on the corner and she hurried to get under it so that she could better see into her pocketbook. The woman was heading off rapidly down the street with the child still hanging backward on her hand.

"Oh little boy!" Julian's mother called and took a few quick steps and caught up with them just beyond the lamppost. "Here's a bright new penny for you," and she held out the coin, which shone bronze in the dim light.

The huge woman turned and for a moment stood, her shoulders lifted and her face frozen with frustrated rage, and stared at Julian's mother. Then all at once she seemed to explode like a piece of machinery that had been given one ounce of pressure too much. Julian saw the black fist swing out with the red pocketbook. He shut his eyes and cringed as he heard the woman shout, "He don't take nobody's pennies!" When he opened his eyes, the woman was disappearing down the street with the little boy staring wide-eyed over her shoulder. Julian's mother was sitting on the sidewalk.

"I told you not to do that," Julian said angrily. "I told you not to do that!"

He stood over her for a minute, gritting his teeth. Her legs were stretched out in front of her and her hat was on her lap. He squatted down and looked her in the face. It was totally expressionless. "You got exactly what you deserved," he said. "Now get up."

He picked up her pocketbook and put what had fallen out back in it. He picked the hat up off her lap. The penny caught his eye on the sidewalk and he picked that up and let it drop before her eyes into the purse. Then he stood up and leaned over and held his hands out to pull her up. She remained immobile. He sighed. Rising above them on either side were black apartment buildings, marked with irregular rectangles of light. At the end of the block a man came out of a door and walked off in the opposite direction. "All right," he said, "suppose somebody happens by and wants to know why you're sitting on the sidewalk?"

She took the hand and, breathing hard, pulled heavily up on it and then stood for a moment, swaying slightly as if the spots of light in the darkness were circling around her. Her eyes, shadowed and confused, finally settled on his face. He did not try to conceal his irritation. "I hope this teaches you a lesson," he said. She leaned forward and her eyes raked his face. She seemed trying to determine his identity. Then, as if she found nothing familiar about him, she started off with a headlong movement in the wrong direction.

"Aren't you going on to the Y?" he asked.

"Home," she muttered.

"Well, are we walking?"

For answer she kept going. Julian followed along, his hands behind him. He saw no reason to let the lesson she had had go without backing it up with an explanation of its meaning. She might as well be made to understand what had happened to her. "Don't think that was just an uppity Negro woman," he said. "That was the whole colored race which will no longer take your condescending pennies. That was your black double. She can wear the same hat as you, and to be sure," he added gratuitously (because he thought it was funny), "it looked better on her than it did on you. What all this means," he said, "is that the old world is gone. The old manners are obsolete and your graciousness is not worth a damn." He thought bitterly of the house that had been lost for him. "You aren't who you think you are," he said.

She continued to plow ahead, paying no attention to him. Her hair had come undone on one side. She dropped her pocketbook and took no notice. He stooped and picked it up and handed it to her but she did not take it.

"You needn't act as if the world had come to an end," he said, "because it hasn't. From now on you've got to live in a new world and face a few realities for a change. Buck up," he said, "it won't kill you."

She was breathing fast.

"Let's wait on the bus," he said.

"Home," she said thickly.

"I hate to see you behave like this," he said. "Just like a child. I should be able to expect more of you." He decided to stop where he was and make her stop and wait for a bus. "I'm not going any farther," he said, stopping. "We're going on the bus."

She continued to go on as if she had not heard him. He took a few steps and caught her arm and stopped her. He looked into her face and caught his breath. He was looking into a face he had never seen before. "Tell Grandpa to come get me," she said.

He stared, stricken.

"Tell Caroline to come get me," she said.

Stunned, he let her go and she lurched forward again, walking as if one leg were shorter than the other. A tide of darkness seemed to be sweeping her from him. "Mother!" he cried. "Darling, sweetheart, wait!" Crumpling, she fell to the pavement. He dashed forward and fell at her side, crying, "Mamma, Mamma!" He turned her over. Her face was fiercely distorted. One eye, large and staring, moved slightly to the left as if it had become unmoored. The other remained fixed on him, raked his face again, found nothing and closed.

"Wait here, wait here!" he cried and jumped up and began to run for help toward a cluster of lights he saw in the distance ahead of him. "Help, help!" he shouted, but his voice was thin, scarcely a thread of sound. The lights drifted farther away the faster he ran and his feet moved numbly as if they carried him nowhere. The tide of darkness seemed to sweep him back to her, postponing from moment to moment his entry into the world of guilt and sorrow.

NIGHT–SEA JOURNEY

One way or another, no matter which theory of our journey is correct, it's myself I address; to whom I rehearse as to a stranger our history and condition, and will disclose my secret hope though I sink for it.

"Is the journey my invention? Do the night, the sea, exist at all, I ask myself, apart from my experience of them? Do I myself exist, or is this a dream? Sometimes I wonder. And if I am, who am I? The Heritage I supposedly transport? But how can I be both vessel and contents? Such are the questions that beset my intervals of rest.

"My trouble is, I lack conviction. Many accounts of our situation seem plausible to me—where and what we are, why we swim and whither. But implausible ones as well, perhaps especially those, I must admit as possibly correct. Even likely. If at times, in certain humors—stroking in unison, say, with my neighbors and chanting with them 'Onwards! Upwards!'—I have supposed that we have after all a common Maker, Whose nature and motives we may not know, but Who engendered us in some mysterious wise and launched us forth toward some end known but to Him—if (for a moodslength only) I have been able to entertain such notions, very popular in certain quarters, it is because our night-sea journey partakes of their absurdity. One might even say: I can believe them *because* they are absurd.

"Has that been said before?

"Another paradox: it appears to be these recesses from swimming that sustain me in the swim. Two measures onward and upward, flailing with the rest, then I float exhausted and dispirited, brood upon the night, the sea, the journey, while the flood bears me a measure back and down: slow progress, but I live, I live, and make my way, aye, past many a drowned comrade in the end, stronger, worthier than I, victims of their unremitting *joie de nager.* I have seen the best swimmers of my generation go under. Numberless the number of the dead! Thousands drown as I think this thought, millions as I rest before returning to the swim. And scores, hundreds of millions have expired since we surged forth, brave in our innocence, upon our dreadful way. 'Love! Love!' we sang then, a quarter-billion strong, and churned the warm sea white with joy of swimming! Now all are gone down—the buoyant, the sodden, leaders and followers, all gone under, while wretched I swim on. Yet these same reflective intervals that keep me afloat have led me into wonder, doubt, despair—strange emotions for a swimmer!—have led me, even, to suspect . . . that our night-sea journey is without meaning.

"Indeed, if I have yet to join the hosts of the suicides, it is because (fatigue apart) I find it no meaningfuller to drown myself than to go on swimming.

"I know that there are those who seem actually to enjoy the night-sea; who claim to love swimming for its own sake, or sincerely believe that 'reaching the Shore,' 'transmitting the Heritage' (*Whose* Heritage, I'd like to know? And to whom?) is worth the staggering cost. I do not. Swimming itself I find at best not actively unpleasant, more often tiresome, not infrequently a torment. Arguments from function and design don't impress me: granted that we can and do swim, that in a manner of speaking our long tails and streamlined heads are 'meant for' swimming; it by no means follows—for me, at least—that we *should* swim, or otherwise endeavor to 'fulfill our destiny.' Which is to say, Someone Else's destiny, since ours, so far as I can see, is merely to perish, one way or another, soon or late. The heartless zeal of our (departed) leaders, like the blind ambition and good cheer of my own youth, appalls me now; for the death of my comrades I am inconsolable. If the night-sea journey has any justification, it is not for us swimmers ever to discover it.

"Oh, to be sure, 'Love!' one heard on every side: 'Love it is that drives and sustains us!' I translate: We don't know *what* drives and sustains us, only that we are most miserably driven and, imperfectly, sustained. *Love* is how we call our ignorance of what whips us. 'To reach the Shore,' then: but what if the Shore exists only in the fancies of us swimmers, who dream it to account for the dreadful fact that we swim, have always and only swum, and continue swimming without respite (myself excepted) until we die? Supposing even that there *were* a Shore—that, as a cynical companion of mine once imagined, we rise from the drowned to discover that all those vulgar superstitions and exalted metaphors are literal truths: the giant Maker of us all, the Shores of Light beyond our night-sea journey!— whatever would a swimmer do there? The fact is, when we imagine the Shore, what comes to mind is just the opposite of our present condition: no more night, no more sea, no more journeying. In short, the blissful estate of the drowned.

"'Ours not to stop and think; ours but to swim and sink. . . .' Because a moment's thought reveals the pointlessness of swimming. 'No matter,' I've heard some say, even as they gulped their last: 'The night-sea journey may be absurd, but here we swim, will-we nill-we, against the flood, onward and upward, toward a Shore that may not exist and couldn't be reached even if it did.' The thoughtful swimmer's choices, then, they say, are two: give over thrashing and go under for good, or embrace the absurdity: affirm in and for itself the night-sea journey; swim on with neither motive nor destination, for the sake of swimming, and compassionate moreover with your fellow swimmer, we being all at sea and equally in the dark. I find neither course acceptable. If not even the hypothetical Shore can justify a sea full of drowned comrades, to speak of the swim-in-itself as somehow doing so strikes me as obscene. I continue to swim—but only because blind habit, blind instinct, and blind fear of drowning are still more strong than the horror of our journey. And if on occasion I have assisted a fellow thrasher, joined in the cheers and songs, even passed along to others strokes of genius from the drownèd great, it's that I shrink by temperament from making myself conspicuous. To paddle off in one's own direction, assert one's independent right-of-way, overrun one's fellows without compunction in pursuit of selfish ends, or dedicate oneself entirely to pleasures and diversions without regard for conscience—I can't finally condemn those who journey in this wise; in half my moods I envy them and despise the weak vitality that keeps me from following their example. But in reasonabler moments I remind myself that it's their very freedom and self-responsibility I reject, as more dramatically absurd, in our senseless circumstances, than tailing along in conventional fashion. Suicides, rebels, affirmers of the paradox—nay-sayers and yea-sayers alike to our fatal journey—I finally shake my head at them. And I splash sighing past their corpses, one by one, as past a hundred sorts of others: friends, enemies, brothers, fools, sages, brutes—and nobodies, million upon million. I envy them all.

"A poor irony: that I, who find abhorrent and tautological the doctrine of survival of the fittest (*fitness* meaning, in my experience, nothing more than survival ability, a talent whose only demonstration is the fact of survival, but whose chief ingredients seem to be strength, guile, and callousness), may be the sole remaining swimmer! But the doctrine is false as well as repellent: Chance drowns the worthy with the unworthy, bears up the unfit with the fit by whatever definition, and makes the night-sea journey essentially *haphazard* as well as murderous and unjustified.

"'You only swim once.' Why bother, then?

"'Except ye drown, ye shall not reach the Shore of Life.' Poppycock.

"One of my late companions—that same cynic with the curious fancy, among the first to drown—entertained us with odd conjectures while we waited to begin our journey. A favorite theory of his was that the Father does exist, and did indeed make us and the sea we swim—but not a-purpose or even consciously; He made us as it were despite Himself, as we make waves with every tail thrash, and may be unaware of our existence. Another was that He knows we're here but doesn't care what happens to us, inasmuch as He creates (voluntarily or not) other seas and swimmers at more or less regular intervals. In bitterer moments, such as just before he drowned, my friend even supposed that our Maker wished us unmade; there was indeed a Shore, he'd argue, which could save at least some of us from drowning and toward which it was our function to struggle—but for reasons unknowable to us He wanted desperately to prevent our reaching that happy place and fulfilling our destiny. Our 'Father,' in short, was our adversary and would-be killer! No less outrageous, and offensive to traditional opinion, were the fellow's speculations on the nature of our Maker: That He might well be no swimmer Himself at all, but some sort of monstrosity, perhaps even tailless; that He might be stupid, malicious, insensible, perverse, or asleep and dreaming; that the end for which He created and launched us forth, and which we flagellate ourselves to fathom, was perhaps immoral, even obscene. *Et cetera, et cetera:* there was no end to the chap's conjectures, or the impoliteness of his fancy; I have reason to suspect that his early demise, whether planned by 'our Maker' or not, was expedited by certain fellow swimmers indignant at his blasphemies.

"In other moods, however (he was as given to moods as I), his theorizing would become half-serious, so it seemed to me, especially upon the subjects of Fate and Immortality, to which our youthful conversations often turned. Then his harangues, if no less fantastical, grew solemn and obscure, and if he was still baiting us, his passion undid the joke. His objection to popular opinions of the hereafter, he would declare, was their claim to general validity. Why need believers hold that *all* the drownèd rise to be judged at journey's end, and nonbelievers that drowning is final without exception? In *his* opinion (so he'd vow at least), nearly everyone's fate was permanent death; indeed he took a sour pleasure in supposing that every 'Maker' made thousands of separate seas in His creative lifetime, each populated like ours with millions of swimmers, and that in almost every instance both sea and swimmers were utterly annihilated, whether accidentally or by malevolent design. (Nothing if not pluralistical, he imagined there might be millions and billions of 'Fathers,' perhaps in some 'night-sea' of their own!) However—and here he turned infidels against him with the faithful—he professed to believe that in possibly a single night-sea per thousand, say, one of its quarter-billion swimmers (that is, one swimmer in two-hundred-fifty billions) achieved a qualified immortality. In some cases the rate might be slightly higher; in others it was vastly lower, for just as there are swimmers of every degree of proficiency, including some who drown before the journey starts, unable to swim at all, and others created drownèd, as it were, so he imagined what can only be termed impotent Creators, Makers unable to Make, as well as uncommonly fertile ones and all grades between. And it pleased him to deny any necessary relation between a Maker's productivity and His other virtues—including, even, the quality of His creatures.

"I could go on (*he* surely did) with his elaboration of these mad notions —such as that swimmers in other night-seas needn't be of our kind; that Makers themselves might belong to different *species,* so to speak; that our particular Maker mightn't Himself be immortal, or that we might be not only His emissaries but His 'immortality,' continuing His life and our own, transmogrified, beyond our individual deaths. Even this modified immortality (meaningless to me) he conceived as relative and contingent, subject to accidental or deliberate termination: his pet hypothesis was that Makers and swimmers *each generate the other*—against all odds, their number being so great—and that any given 'immortality chain' could terminate after any number of cycles, so that what was 'immortal' (still speaking relatively) was only the cyclic process of incarnation, which itself might have a beginning and an end. Alternatively he liked to imagine cycles within cycles, either finite or infinite: for example, the 'night-sea,' as it were, in which Makers 'swam' and created night-seas and swimmers like ourselves, might be the creation of a larger Maker, Himself one of many, Who in turn, etc. Time itself he regarded as relative to our experience, like magnitude: who knew but what, with each thrash of our tails, minuscule seas and swimmers, whole eternities, came to pass—as ours, perhaps, and our Maker's Maker's, was elapsing between the strokes of some super-tail, in a slower order of time?

"Naturally I hooted with the others at this nonsense. We were young then, and had only the dimmest notion of what lay ahead; in our ignorance we imagined night-sea journeying to be a positively heroic enterprise. Its meaning and value we never questioned; to be sure, some must go down by the way, a pity no doubt, but to win a race requires that others lose, and like all my fellows I took for granted that I would be the winner. We milled and swarmed, impatient to be off, never mind where or why, only to try our youth against the realities of night and sea; if we indulged the skeptic at all it was as a droll, half-contemptible mascot. When he died in the initial slaughter, no one cared.

"And even now I don't subscribe to all his views—but I no longer scoff. The horror of our history has purged me of opinions, as of vanity, confidence, spirit, charity, hope, vitality, everything—except dull dread and a kind of melancholy, stunned persistence. What leads me to recall his fancies is my growing suspicion that I, of all swimmers, may be the sole survivor of this fell journey, tale bearer of a generation. This suspicion, together with the recent sea change, suggests to me now that nothing is impossible, not even my late companion's wildest visions, and brings me to a certain desperate resolve, the point of my chronicling.

"Very likely I have lost my senses. The carnage at our setting out; our decimation by whirlpool, poisoned cataract, and sea convulsion; the panic stampedes, mutinies, slaughters, mass suicides; the mounting evidence that none will survive the journey—add to these anguish and fatigue; it were a miracle if sanity stayed afloat. Thus I admit, with the other possibilities, that the present sweetening and calming of the sea, and what seems to be a kind of vasty presence, song, or summons from the near upstream, may be hallucinations of disordered sensibility. . . .

"Perhaps, even, I am drowned already. Surely I was never meant for the rough-and-tumble of the swim; not impossibly I perished at the outset and have only imagined the night-sea journey from some final deep. In any case I'm no longer young. For it is we spent old swimmers, disabused of every illusion, who are most vulnerable to dreams.

"Sometimes I think I am my drownèd friend.

"Out with it: I've begun to believe, not only that *She* exists, but that She lies not far ahead, and stills the sea, and draws me Herward! Aghast, I recollect his maddest notion: that our destination (which existed, mind, in but one night-sea out of hundreds and thousands) was no Shore, as commonly conceived, but a mysterious being, indescribable except by paradox and vaguest figure: wholly different from us swimmers, yet our complement; the death of us, yet our salvation and resurrection; simultaneously our journey's end, midpoint, and commencement; not membered and thrashing like us, but a motionless or hugely gliding sphere of unimaginable dimension; self-contained, yet dependent absolutely, in some wise, upon the chance (always monstrously improbable) that one of us will survive the night-sea journey and reach . . . Her! *Her,* he called it, or *She,* which is to say, Other-than-a-he. I shake my head; the thing is too preposterous; it is myself I talk to, to keep my reason in this awful darkness. There is no She! There is no You! I rave to myself; it's Death alone that hears and summons. To the drowned, all seas are calm. . . .

"Listen: my friend maintained that in every order of creation there are two sorts of creators, contrary yet complementary, one of which gives rise to seas and swimmers, the other to the Night-which-contains-the-sea and to What-waits-at-the-journey's-end: the former, in short, to destiny, the latter to destination (and both profligately, involuntarily, perhaps indifferently or unwittingly). The 'purpose' of the night-sea journey—but not necessarily of the journeyer or of either Maker!—my friend could describe only in abstractions: *consummation, transfiguration, union of contraries, transcension of categories.* When we laughed he would shrug and admit that he understood the business no better than we, and thought it ridiculous, dreary, possibly obscene. 'But one of you,' he'd add with his wry smile, 'may be the Hero destined to complete the night-sea journey and be one with Her. Chances are, of course, you won't make it.' He himself, he declared, was not even going to try; the whole idea repelled him; if we chose to dismiss it as an ugly fiction, so much the better for us; thrash, splash, and be merry, we were soon enough drowned. But there it was, he could not say how he knew or why he bothered to tell us, any more than he could say what would happen after She and the Hero, Shore and Swimmer, 'merged identities' to become something both and neither. He quite agreed with me that if the issue of that magical union had no memory of the night-sea journey, for example, it enjoyed a poor sort of immortality; even poorer if, as he rather imagined, a swimmer-hero plus a She equalled or became merely another Maker of future night-seas and the rest, at such incredible expense of life. This being the case—he was persuaded it was—the merciful thing to do was refuse to participate; the genuine heroes, in his opinion, were the suicides, and the hero of heroes would be the swimmer who, in the very presence of the Other, refused Her proffered 'immortality' and thus put an end to at least one cycle of catastrophes.

"How we mocked him! Our moment came, we hurtled forth, pretending to glory in the adventure, thrashing, singing, cursing, strangling, rationalizing, rescuing, killing, inventing rules and stories and relationships, giving up, struggling on, but dying all, and still in darkness, until only a battered remnant was left to croak 'Onward, upward,' like a bitter echo. Then they too fell silent—victims, I can only presume, of the last frightful wave—and the moment came when I also, utterly desolate and spent, thrashed my last and gave myself over to the current, to sink or float as might be, but swim no more. Whereupon, marvelous to tell, in an instant the sea grew still! Then warmly, gently, the great tide turned, began to bear me, as it does now, onwards and upwards will-I nill-I, like a flood of joy—and I recalled with dismay my dead friend's teaching.

"I am not deceived. This new emotion is Her doing; the desire that possesses me is Her bewitchment. Lucidity passes from me; in a moment I'll cry 'Love!', bury myself in Her side, and be 'transfigured.' Which is to say, I die already; this fellow transported by passion is not I; *I am he who abjures and rejects the night-sea journey! I. . . .*

"I am all love. 'Come!' She whispers, and I have no will.

"You and I may be about to become, whatever You are: with the last twitch of my real self I beg You to listen. It is *not* love that sustains me! No; though Her magic makes me burn to sing the contrary, and though I drown even now for the blasphemy, I will say the truth. What has fetched me across this dreadful sea is a single hope, gift of my poor dead comrade: that You may be stronger-willed than I, and that by sheer force of concentration I may transmit to You, along with Your official Heritage, a private legacy of awful recollection and negative resolve. Mad as it may be, my dream is that some unimaginable embodiment of myself (or myself plus Her if that's how it must be) will come to find itself expressing, in however garbled or radical a translation, some reflection of these reflections. If against all odds this comes to pass, may You to whom, through whom I speak, do what I cannot: terminate this aimless, brutal business! Stop Your hearing against Her song! Hate love!

"Still alive, afloat, afire. Farewell then my penultimate hope: that one may be sunk for direst blasphemy on the very shore of the Shore. Can it be (my old friend would smile) that only utterest nay-sayers survive the night? But even that were Sense, and there is no sense, only senseless love, senseless death. Whoever echoes these reflections: be more courageous than their author! An end to night-sea journeys! Make no more! And forswear me when I shall forswear myself, deny myself, plunge into Her who summons, singing . . .

"'Love! Love! Love!'"

A & P

In walks these three girls in nothing but bathing suits. I'm in the third checkout slot, with my back to the door, so I don't see them until they're over by the bread. The one that caught my eye first was the one in the plaid green two-piece. She was a chunky kid, with a good tan and a sweet broad soft-looking can with those two crescents of white just under it, where the sun never seems to hit, at the top of the backs of her legs. I stood there with my hand on a box of HiHo crackers trying to remember if I rang it up or not. I ring it up again and the customer starts giving me hell. She's one of these cash-register-watchers, a witch about fifty with rouge on her cheekbones and no eyebrows, and I know it made her day to trip me up. She'd been watching cash registers for fifty years and probably never seen a mistake before.

By the time I got her feathers smoothed and her goodies into a bag— she gives me a little snort in passing, if she'd been born at the right time they would have burned her over in Salem—by the time I get her on her way the girls had circled around the bread and were coming back, without a pushcart, back my way along the counters, in the aisle between the checkouts and the Special bins. They didn't even have shoes on. There was this chunky one, with the two-piece—it was bright green and the seams on the bra were still sharp and her belly was still pretty pale so I guessed she just got it (the suit)—there was this one, with one of those chubby berry-faces, the lips all bunched together under her nose, this one, and a tall one, with black hair that hadn't quite frizzed right, and one of those sunburns right across under the eyes, and a chin that was too long—you know, the kind of girl other girls think is very "striking" and "attractive" but never quite makes it, as they very well know, which is why they like her so much—and then the third one, that wasn't quite so tall. She was the queen. She kind of led them, the other two peeking around and making their shoulders round. She didn't look around, not this queen, she just walked straight on slowly, on these long white prima-donna legs. She came down a little hard on her heels, as if she didn't walk in her bare feet that much, putting down her heels and then letting the weight move along to her toes as if she was testing the floor with every step, putting a little deliberate extra action into it. You never know for sure how girls' minds work (do you really think it's a mind in there or just a little buzz like a bee in a glass jar?) but you got the idea she had talked the other two into coming in here with her, and now she was showing them how to do it, walk slow and hold yourself straight.

She had on a kind of dirty-pink—beige maybe, I don't know—bathing suit with a little nubble all over it and, what got me, the straps were down. They were off her shoulders looped loose around the cool tops of her arms, and I guess as a result the suit had slipped a little on her, so all around the top of the cloth there was this shining rim. If it hadn't been there you wouldn't have known there could have been anything whiter than those shoulders. With the straps pushed off, there was nothing between the top of the suit and the top of her head except just *her,* this clean bare plane of the top of her chest down from the shoulder bones like a dented sheet of metal tilted in the light. I mean, it was more than pretty.

She had sort of oaky hair that the sun and salt had bleached, done up in a bun that was unravelling, and a kind of prim face. Walking into the A & P with your straps down, I suppose it's the only kind of face you *can* have. She held her head so high her neck, coming up out of those white shoulders, looked kind of stretched, but I didn't mind. The longer her neck was, the more of her there was.

She must have felt in the corner of her eye me and over my shoulder Stokesie in the second slot watching, but she didn't tip. Not this queen. She kept her eyes moving across the racks, and stopped, and turned so slow it made my stomach rub the inside of my apron, and buzzed to the other two, who kind of huddled against her for relief, and then they all three of them went up the cat - and - dog - food - breakfast - cereal - macaroni - rice - raisins - seasonings - spreads - spaghetti - soft - drinks - crackers - and - cookies aisle. From the third slot I look straight up this aisle to the meat counter, and I watched them all the way. The fat one with the tan sort of fumbled with the cookies, but on second thought she put the package back. The sheep pushing their carts down the aisle—the girls were walking against the usual traffic (not that we have one-way signs or any-thing)—were pretty hilarious. You could see them, when Queenie's white shoulders dawned on them, kind of jerk, or hop, or hiccup, but their eyes snapped back to their own baskets and on they pushed. I bet you could set off dynamite in an A & P and the people would by and large keep reaching and checking oatmeal off their lists and muttering "Let me see, there was a third thing, began with A, asparagus, no, ah, yes, applesauce!"

or whatever it is they do mutter. But there was no doubt, this jiggled them. A few houseslaves in pin curlers even looked around after pushing their carts past to make sure what they had seen was correct.

You know, it's one thing to have a girl in a bathing suit down on the beach, where what with the glare nobody can look at each other much anyway, and another thing in the cool of the A & P, under the fluorescent lights, against all those stacked packages, with her feet paddling along naked over our checkerboard green-and-cream rubber-tile floor.

"Oh Daddy," Stokesie said beside me. "I feel so faint."

"Darling," I said. "Hold me tight." Stokesie's married, with two babies chalked up on his fuselage already, but as far as I can tell that's the only difference. He's twenty-two, and I was nineteen this April.

"Is it done?" he asks, the responsible married man finding his voice. I forgot to say he thinks he's going to be manager some sunny day, maybe in 1990 when it's called the Great Alexandrov and Petrooshki Tea Company or something.

What he meant was, our town is five miles from a beach, with a big summer colony out on the Point, but we're right in the middle of town, and the women generally put on a shirt or shorts or something before they get out of the car into the street. And anyway these are usually women with six children and varicose veins mapping their legs and nobody, including them, could care less. As I say, we're right in the middle of town, and if you stand at our front doors you can see two banks and the Congregational church and the newspaper store and three real-estate offices and about twenty-seven old freeloaders tearing up Central Street because the sewer broke again. It's not as if we're on the Cape; we're north of Boston and there's people in this town haven't seen the ocean for twenty years.

The girls had reached the meat counter and were asking McMahon something. He pointed, they pointed, and they shuffled out of sight behind a pyramid of Diet Delight peaches. All that was left for us to see was old McMahon patting his mouth and looking after them sizing up their joints. Poor kids, I began to feel sorry for them, they couldn't help it.

Now here comes the sad part of the story, at least my family says it's sad, but I don't think it's so sad myself. The store's pretty empty, it being Thursday afternoon, so there was nothing much to do except lean on the register and wait for the girls to show up again. The whole store was like a pinball machine and I didn't know which tunnel they'd come out of. After a while they come around out of the far aisle, around the light bulbs, records at discount of the Caribbean Six or Tony Martin Sings or some such gunk you wonder they waste the wax on, sixpacks of candy bars, and plastic toys done up in cellophane that fall apart when a kid looks at them anyway. Around they come, Queenie still leading the way, and holding a little gray jar in her hand. Slots Three through Seven are unmanned and

I could see her wondering between Stokes and me, but Stokesie with his usual luck draws an old party in baggy gray pants who stumbles up with four giant cans of pineapple juice (what do these bums *do* with all that pineapple juice? I've often asked myself) so the girls come to me. Queenie puts down the jar and I take it into my fingers icy cold. Kingfish Fancy Herring Snacks in Pure Sour Cream: 49 cents. Now her hands are empty, not a ring or a bracelet, bare as God made them, and I wonder where the money's coming from. Still with that prim look she lifts a folded dollar bill out of the hollow at the center of her nubbled pink top. The jar went heavy in my hand. Really, I thought that was so cute.

Then everybody's luck begins to run out. Lengel comes in from haggling with a truck full of cabbages on the lot and is about to scuttle into that door marked MANAGER behind which he hides all day when the girls touch his eye. Lengel's pretty dreary, teaches Sunday school and the rest, but he doesn't miss that much. He comes over and says, "Girls, this isn't the beach."

Queenie blushes, though maybe it's just a brush of sunburn I was noticing for the first time, now that she was so close. "My mother asked me to pick up a jar of herring snacks." Her voice kind of startled me, the way voices do when you see the people first, coming out so flat and dumb yet kind of tony, too, the way it ticked over "pick up" and "snacks." All of a sudden I slid right down her voice into her living room. Her father and the other men were standing around in ice-cream coats and bow ties and the women were in sandals picking up herring snacks on toothpicks off a big glass plate and they were all holding drinks the color of water with olives and sprigs of mint in them. When my parents have somebody over they get lemonade and if it's a real racy affair Schlitz in tall glasses with "They'll Do It Every Time" cartoons stencilled on.

"That's all right," Lengel said. "But this isn't the beach." His repeating this struck me as funny, as if it had just occurred to him, and he had been thinking all these years the A & P was a great big dune and he was the head lifeguard. He didn't like my smiling—as I say he doesn't miss much —but he concentrates on giving the girls that sad Sunday-school-superintendent stare.

Queenie's blush is no sunburn now, and the plump one in plaid, that I liked better from the back—a really sweet can—pipes up, "We weren't doing any shopping. We just came in for the one thing."

"That makes no difference," Lengel tells her, and I could see from the way his eyes went that he hadn't noticed she was wearing a two-piece before. "We want you decently dressed when you come in here."

"We *are* decent," Queenie says suddenly, her lower lip pushing, getting sore now that she remembers her place, a place from which the crowd that runs the A & P must look pretty crummy. Fancy Herring Snacks flashed in her very blue eyes.

"Girls, I don't want to argue with you. After this come in here with your shoulders covered. It's our policy." He turns his back. That's policy for you. Policy is what the kingpins want. What the others want is juvenile delinquency.

All this while, the customers had been showing up with their carts but, you know, sheep, seeing a scene, they had all bunched up on Stokesie, who shook open a paper bag as gently as peeling a peach, not wanting to miss a word. I could feel in the silence everybody getting nervous, most of all Lengel, who asks me, "Sammy, have you rung up their purchase?"

I thought and said "No" but it wasn't about that I was thinking. I go through the punches, 4, 9, GROC, TOT—it's more complicated than you think, and after you do it often enough, it begins to make a little song, that you hear words to, in my case "Hello *(bing)* there, you *(gung)* hap-py *pee-pul (splat)!'*"—the *splat* being the drawer flying out. I uncrease the bill, tenderly as you may imagine, it just having come from between the two smoothest scoops of vanilla I had ever known were there, and pass a half and a penny into her narrow pink palm, and nestle the herrings in a bag and twist its neck and hand it over, all the time thinking.

The girls, and who'd blame them, are in a hurry to get out, so I say "I quit" to Lengel quick enough for them to hear, hoping they'll stop and watch me, their unsuspected hero. They keep right on going, into the electric eye; the door flies open and they flicker across the lot to their car, Queenie and Plaid and Big Tall Goony-Goony (not that as raw material she was so bad), leaving me with Lengel and a kink in his eyebrow.

"Did you say something, Sammy?"

"I said I quit."

"I thought you did."

"You didn't have to embarrass them."

"It was they who were embarrassing us."

I started to say something that come out "Fiddle-de-doo." It's a saying of my grandmother's, and I know she would have been pleased.

"I don't think you know what you're saying," Lengel said.

"I know you don't" I said. "But I do." I pull the bow at the back of my apron and start shrugging it off my shoulders. A couple customers that had been heading for my slot begin to knock against each other, like scared pigs in a chute.

Lengel sighs and begins to look very patient and old and gray. He's been a friend of my parents for years. "Sammy, you don't want to do this to your Mom and Dad," he tells me. It's true, I don't. But it seems to me that once you begin a gesture it's fatal not to go through with it. I fold the apron, "Sammy" stitched in red on the pocket, and put it on the counter, and drop the bow tie on top of it. The bow tie is theirs, if you've ever wondered. "You'll feel this for the rest of your life," Lengel says, and I know that's true, too, but remembering how he made that pretty girl blush makes me so scrunchy inside I punch the No Sale tab and the machine whirs "pee-pul" and the drawer splats out. One advantage to this scene taking place in summer, I can follow this up with a clean exit, there's no fumbling around getting your coat and galoshes, I just saunter into the electric eye in my white shirt that my mother ironed the night before, and the door heaves itself open, and outside the sunshine is skating around on the asphalt.

I look around for my girls, but they're gone, of course. There wasn't anybody but some young married screaming with her children about some candy they didn't get by the door of a powder-blue Falcon station wagon. Looking back in the big windows, over the bags of peat moss and aluminum lawn furniture stacked on the pavement, I could see Lengel in my place in the slot, checking the sheep through. His face was dark gray and his back stiff, as if he'd just had an injection of iron, and my stomach kind of fell as I felt how hard the world was going to be to me hereafter.

THE CONVERSION OF THE JEWS

"You're a real one for opening your mouth in the first place," Itzie said. "What do you open your mouth all the time for?"

"I didn't bring it up, Itz, I didn't," Ozzie said.

"What do you care about Jesus Christ for anyway?"

"I didn't bring up Jesus Christ. He did. I didn't even know what he was talking about. Jesus is historical, he kept saying. Jesus is historical." Ozzie mimicked the momumental voice of Rabbi Binder.

"Jesus was a person that lived like you and me," Ozzie continued. "That's what Binder said—"

"Yeah? . . . So what! What do I give two cents whether he lived or not. And what do you gotta open your mouth!" Itzie Lieberman favored closed-mouthedness, especially when it came to Ozzie Freedman's questions. Mrs. Freedman had to see Rabbi Binder twice before about Ozzie's questions and this Wednesday at four-thirty would be the third time. Itzie preferred to keep *his* mother in the kitchen; he settled for behind-the-back subtleties such as gestures, faces, snarls and other less delicate barnyard noises.

"He was a real person, Jesus, but he wasn't like God, and we don't believe he is God." Slowly, Ozzie was explaining Rabbi Binder's position to Itzie, who had been absent from Hebrew School the previous afternoon.

"The Catholics," Itzie said helpfully, "they believe in Jesus Christ, that he's God." Itzie Lieberman used "the Catholics" in its broadest sense—to include the Protestants.

Ozzie received Itzie's remark with a tiny head bob, as though it were a footnote, and went on. "His mother was Mary, and his father probably was Joseph," Ozzie said. "But the New Testament says his real father was God."

"His *real* father?"

"Yeah," Ozzie said, "that's the big thing, his father's supposed to be God."

"Bull."

"That's what Rabbi Binder says, that it's impossible—"

"Sure it's impossible. That stuff's all bull. To have a baby you gotta get laid," Itzie theologized. "Mary hadda get laid."

"That's what Binder says: 'The only way a woman can have a baby is to have intercourse with a man.'"

"He said *that,* Ozz?" For a moment it appeared that Itzie had put the theological question aside. "He said that, intercourse?" A little curled smile shaped itself in the lower half of Itzie's face like a pink mustache. "What you guys do, Ozz, you laugh or something?"

"I raised my hand."

"Yeah? Whatja say?"

"That's when I asked the question."

Itzie's face lit up. "Whatja ask about—intercourse?"

"No, I asked the question about God, how if He could create the heaven and earth in six days, and make all the animals and the fish and the light in six days—the light especially, that's what always gets me, that He could make the light. Making fish and animals, that's pretty good—"

"That's damn good." Itzie's appreciation was honest but unimaginative: it was as though God had just pitched a one-hitter.

"But making light . . . I mean when you think about it, it's really something," Ozzie said. "Anyway, I asked Binder if He could make all that in six days, and He could *pick* the six days he wanted right out of nowhere, why couldn't He let a woman have a baby without having intercourse."

"You said intercourse, Ozz, to Binder?"

"Yeah."

"Right in class?"

"Yeah."

Itzie smacked the side of his head.

"I mean, no kidding around," Ozzie said, "that'd really be nothing. After all that other stuff, that'd practically be nothing."

Itzie considered a moment. "What'd Binder say?"

"He started all over again explaining how Jesus was historical and how he lived like you and me but he wasn't God. So I said I understood that. What I wanted to know was different."

What Ozzie wanted to know was always different. The first time he had wanted to know how Rabbi Binder could call the Jews "The Chosen People" if the Declaration of Independence claimed all men to be created equal. Rabbi Binder tried to distinguish for him between political equality and spiritual legitimacy, but what Ozzie wanted to know, he insisted vehemently, was different. That was the first time his mother had to come.

Then there was the plane crash. Fifty-eight people had been killed in a plane crash at La Guardia. In studying a casualty list in the newspaper his mother had discovered among the list of those dead eight Jewish names (his grandmother had nine but she counted Miller as a Jewish name); because of the eight she said the plane crash was "a tragedy." During free-discussion time on Wednesday Ozzie had brought to Rabbi Binder's attention this matter of "some of his relations" always picking out the Jewish names. Rabbi Binder had begun to explain cultural unity and some other things when Ozzie stood up at his seat and said that what he wanted to know was different. Rabbi Binder insisted that he sit down and it was then that Ozzie shouted that he wished all fifty-eight were Jews. That was the second time his mother came.

"And he kept explaining about Jesus being historical, and so I kept asking him. No kidding, Itz, he was trying to make me look stupid."

"So what he finally do?"

"Finally he starts screaming that I was deliberately simple-minded and a wise guy, and that my mother had to come, and this was the last time. And that I'd never get bar-mitzvahed if he could help it. Then, Itz, then he starts talking in that voice like a statue, real slow and deep, and he says that I better think over what I said about the Lord. He told me to go to his office and think it over." Ozzie leaned his body towards Itzie. "Itz, I thought it over for a solid hour, and now I'm convinced God could do it."

Ozzie had planned to confess his latest transgression to his mother as soon as she came home from work. But it was a Friday night in November and already dark, and when Mrs. Freedman came through the door she tossed off her coat, kissed Ozzie quickly on the face, and went to the kitchen table to light the three yellow candles, two for the Sabbath and one for Ozzie's father.

When his mother lit the candles she would move her two arms slowly towards her, dragging them through the air, as though persuading people whose minds were half made up. And her eyes would get glassy with tears. Even when his father was alive Ozzie remembered that her eyes had gotten glassy, so it didn't have anything to do with his dying. It had something to do with lighting the candles.

As she touched the flaming match to the unlit wick of a Sabbath candle, the phone rang, and Ozzie, standing only a foot from it, plucked off the receiver and held it muffled to his chest. When his mother lit candles Ozzie felt there should be no noise; even breathing, if you could manage it, should be softened. Ozzie pressed the phone to his breast and watched his mother dragging whatever she was dragging, and he felt his own eyes get glassy. His mother was a round, tired, gray-haired penguin of a woman whose gray skin had begun to feel the tug of gravity and the weight of her own history. Even when she was dressed up she didn't look like a chosen person. But when she lit candles she looked like something better; like a woman who knew momentarily that God could do anything.

After a few mysterious minutes she was finished. Ozzie hung up the phone and walked to the kitchen table where she was beginning to lay the two places for the four-course Sabbath meal. He told her that she would have to see Rabbi Binder next Wednesday at four-thirty, and then he told her why. For the first time in their life together she hit Ozzie across the face with her hand.

All through the chopped liver and chicken soup part of the dinner Ozzie cried; he didn't have any appetite for the rest.

On Wednesday, in the largest of the three basement classrooms of the synagogue, Rabbi Marvin Binder, a tall, handsome, broad-shouldered man of thirty with thick strong-fibered black hair, removed his watch from his pocket and saw that it was four o'clock. At the rear of the room Yakov Blotnik, the seventy-one-year-old custodian, slowly polished the large window, mumbling to himself, unaware that it was four o'clock or six o'clock, Monday or Wednesday. To most of the students Yakov Blotnik's mumbling, along with his brown curly beard, scythe nose, and two heel-trailing black cats, made of him an object of wonder, a foreigner, a relic, towards whom they were alternately fearful and disrespectful. To Ozzie the mumbling had always seemed a monotonous, curious prayer; what made it curious was that old Blotnik had been mumbling so steadily for so many years, Ozzie suspected he had memorized the prayers and forgotten all about God.

"It is now free-discussion time," Rabbi Binder said. "Feel free to talk about any Jewish matter at all—religion, family, politics, sports—"

There was silence. It was a gusty, clouded November afternoon and it did not seem as though there ever was or could be a thing called baseball. So nobody this week said a word about that hero from the past, Hank Greenberg—which limited free discussion considerably.

And the soul-battering Ozzie Freedman had just received from Rabbi Binder had imposed its limitation. When it was Ozzie's turn to read aloud from the Hebrew book the rabbi had asked him petulantly why he didn't read more rapidly. He was showing no progress. Ozzie said he could read faster but that if he did he was sure not to understand what he was reading. Nevertheless, at the rabbi's repeated suggestion Ozzie tried, and showed a great talent, but in the midst of a long passage he stopped short and said he didn't understand a word he was reading, and started in again at a drag-footed pace. Then came the soul-battering.

Consequently when free-discussion time rolled around none of the students felt too free. The rabbi's invitation was answered only by the mumbling of feeble old Blotnik.

"Isn't there anything at all you would like to discuss?" Rabbi Binder asked again, looking at his watch. "No questions or comments?"

There was a small grumble from the third row. The rabbi requested that Ozzie rise and give the rest of the class the advantage of his thought.

Ozzie rose. "I forget it now," he said, and sat down in his place.

Rabbi Binder advanced a seat towards Ozzie and poised himself on the edge of the desk. It was Itzie's desk and the rabbi's frame only a dagger's-length away from his face snapped him to sitting attention.

"Stand up again, Oscar," Rabbi Binder said calmly, "and try to assemble your thoughts."

Ozzie stood up. All his classmates turned in their seats and watched as he gave an unconvincing scratch to his forehead.

"I can't assemble any," he announced, and plunked himself down.

"Stand up!" Rabbi Binder advanced from Itzie's desk to the one directly in front of Ozzie; when the rabbinical back was turned Itzie gave it five-fingers off the tip of his nose, causing a small titter in the room. Rabbi Binder was too absorbed in squelching Ozzie's nonsense once and for all to bother with titters. "Stand up, Oscar. What's your question about?"

Ozzie pulled a word out of the air. It was the handiest word. "Religion."

"Oh, now you remember?"

"Yes."

"What is it?"

Trapped, Ozzie blurted the first thing that came to him. "Why can't He make anything He wants to make!"

As Rabbi Binder prepared an answer, a final answer, Itzie, ten feet behind him, raised one finger on his left hand, gestured it meaningfully towards the rabbi's back, and brought the house down.

Binder twisted quickly to see what had happened and in the midst of the commotion Ozzie shouted into the rabbi's back what he couldn't have shouted to his face. It was a loud, toneless sound that had the timbre of something stored inside for about six days.

"You don't know! You don't know anything about God!"

The rabbi spun back towards Ozzie. "What?"

"You don't know—you don't—"

"Apologize, Oscar, apologize!" It was a threat.

"You don't—"

Rabbi Binder's hand flicked out at Ozzie's cheek. Perhaps it had only been meant to clamp the boy's mouth shut, but Ozzie ducked and the palm caught him squarely on the nose.

The blood came in a short, red spurt on to Ozzie's shirt front.

The next moment was all confusion. Ozzie screamed, "You bastard, you bastard!" and broke for the classroom door. Rabbi Binder lurched a step backwards, as though his own blood had started flowing violently in the opposite direction, then gave a clumsy lurch forward and bolted out the door after Ozzie. The class followed after the rabbi's huge blue-suited back, and before old Blotnik could turn from his window, the room was empty and everyone was headed full speed up the three flights leading to the roof.

If one should compare the light of day to the life of man: sunrise to birth; sunset—the dropping down over the edge—to death; then as Ozzie Freedman wiggled through the trapdoor of the synagogue roof, his feet kicking backwards bronco-style at Rabbi Binder's outstretched arms—at that moment the day was fifty years old. As a rule, fifty or fifty-five reflects accurately the age of late afternoons in November, for it is in that month, during those hours, that one's awareness of light seems no longer a matter of seeing, but of hearing: light begins clicking away. In fact, as Ozzie locked shut the trapdoor in the rabbi's face, the sharp click of the bolt into the lock might momentarily have been mistaken for the sound of the heavier gray that had just throbbed through the sky.

With all his weight Ozzie kneeled on the locked door; any instant he was certain that Rabbi Binder's shoulder would fling it open, splintering the wood into shrapnel and catapulting his body into the sky. But the door did not move and below him he heard only the rumble of feet, first loud then dim, like thunder rolling away.

A question shot through his brain. "Can this be *me?*" For a thirteen-year-old who had just labeled his religious leader a bastard, twice, it was not an improper question. Louder and louder the question came to him—"Is it me? Is it me?"—until he discovered himself no longer kneeling, but racing crazily toward the edge of the roof, his eyes crying, his throat screaming, and his arms flying everywhichway as though not his own.

"Is it me? Is it me Me ME ME ME! It has to be me—but is it!"

It is the question a thief must ask himself the night he jimmies open his first window, and it is said to be the question with which bridegrooms quiz themselves before the altar.

In the few wild seconds it took Ozzie's body to propel him to the edge of the roof, his self-examination began to grow fuzzy. Gazing down at the street he became confused as to the problem beneath the question: was it, is-it-me-who-called-Binder-a-Bastard? or, is-it-me-prancing-around-on-the-roof? However, the scene below settled all, for there is an instant in any action when whether it is you or somebody else is academic. The thief crams the money in his pockets and scoots out the window. The bridegroom signs the hotel register for two. And the boy on the roof finds a streetful of people gaping at him, necks stretched backwards, faces up, as though he were the ceiling of the Hayden Planetarium. Suddenly you know it's you.

"Oscar! Oscar Freedman!" A voice rose from the center of the crowd, a voice that, could it have been seen, would have looked like the writing on a scroll. "Oscar Freedman, get down from there. Immediately!" Rabbi Binder was pointing one arm stiffly up at him; and at the end of that arm, one finger aimed menacingly. It was the attitude of a dictator, but one— the eyes confessed all—whose personal valet had spit neatly in his face.

Ozzie didn't answer. Only for a blink's length did he look towards Rabbi Binder. Instead his eyes began to fit together the world beneath him, to sort out people from places, friends from enemies, participants from spectators. In little jagged starlike clusters his friends stood around Rabbi Binder, who was still pointing. The topmost point on a star compounded not of angels but of five adolescent boys was Itzie. What a world it was, with those stars below, Rabbi Binder below . . . Ozzie, who a moment earlier hadn't been able to control his own body, started to feel the meaning of the word control: he felt Peace and he felt Power.

"Oscar Freedman, I'll give you three to come down."

Few dictators give their subjects three to do anything; but, as always, Rabbi Binder only looked dictatorial.

"Are you ready, Oscar?"

Ozzie nodded his head yes, although he had no intention in the world —the lower one of the celestial one he'd just entered—of coming down even if Rabbi Binder should give him a million.

"All right then," said Rabbi Binder. He ran a hand through his black Samson hair as though it were the gesture prescribed for uttering the first digit. Then, with his other hand cutting a circle out of the small piece of sky around him, he spoke. "One!"

There was no thunder. On the contrary, at that moment, as though "one" was the cue for which he had been waiting, the world's least thunderous person appeared on the synagogue steps. He did not so much come out the synagogue door as lean out, onto the darkening air. He clutched at the doorknob with one hand and looked up at the roof.

"Oy!"

Yakov Blotnik's old mind hobbled slowly, as if on crutches, and though he couldn't decide precisely what the boy was doing on the roof, he knew it wasn't good—that is, it wasn't-good-for-the-Jews. For Yakov Blotnik life had fractionated itself simply: things were either good-for-the-Jews or no-good-for-the-Jews.

He smacked his free hand to his in-sucked cheek, gently. "Oy, Gut!" And then quickly as he was able, he jacked down his head and surveyed the street. There was Rabbi Binder (like a man at an auction with only three dollars in his pocket, he had just delivered a shaky "Two!"); there were the students, and that was all. So far it-wasn't-so-bad-for-the-Jews. But the boy had to come down immediately, before anybody saw. The problem: how to get the boy off the roof?

Anybody who has ever had a cat on the roof knows how to get him down. You call the fire department. Or first you call the operator and you ask her for the fire department. And the next thing there is great jamming of brakes and clanging of bells and shouting of instructions. And then the cat is off the roof. You do the same thing to get a boy off the roof.

That is, you do the same thing if you are Yakov Blotnik and you once had a cat on the roof.

When the engines, all four of them, arrived, Rabbi Binder had four times given Ozzie the count of three. The big hook-and-ladder swung around the corner and one of the firemen leaped from it, plunging headlong towards the yellow fire hydrant in front of the synagogue. With a huge wrench be began to unscrew the top nozzle. Rabbi Binder raced over to him and pulled at his shoulder.

"There's no fire . . ."

The fireman mumbled back over his shoulder and, heatedly, continued working at the nozzle.

"But there's no fire, there's no fire . . ." Binder shouted. When the fireman mumbled again, the rabbi grasped his face with both hands and pointed it up at the roof.

To Ozzie it looked as though Rabbi Binder was trying to tug the fireman's head out of his body, like a cork from a bottle. He had to giggle at the picture they made: it was a family portrait—rabbi in black skullcap, fireman in red fire hat, and the little yellow hydrant squatting beside like a kid brother, bareheaded. From the edge of the roof Ozzie waved at the portrait, a one-handed, flapping, mocking wave; in doing it his right foot slipped from under him. Rabbi Binder covered his eyes with his hands.

Firemen work fast. Before Ozzie had even regained his balance, a big, round, yellowed net was being held on the synagogue lawn. The firemen who held it looked up at Ozzie with stern, feelingless faces.

One of the firemen turned his head towards Rabbi Binder. "What, is the kid nuts or something?"

Rabbi Binder unpeeled his hands from his eyes, slowly, painfully, as if they were tape. Then he checked: nothing on the sidewalk, no dents in the net.

"Is he gonna jump, or what?" the fireman shouted.

In a voice not at all like a statue, Rabbi Binder finally answered. "Yes, Yes, I think so . . . He's been threatening to . . ."

Threatening to? Why, the reason he was on the roof, Ozzie remembered, was to get away; he hadn't even thought about jumping. He had just run to get away, and the truth was that he hadn't really headed for the roof as much as he'd been chased there.

"What's his name, the kid?"

"Freedman," Rabbi Binder answered. "Oscar Freedman."

The fireman looked up at Ozzie. "What is it with you, Oscar? You gonna jump, or what?"

Ozzie did not answer. Frankly, the question had just arisen.

"Look, Oscar, if you're gonna jump, jump—and if you're not gonna jump, don't jump. But don't waste our time, willya?"

Ozzie looked at the fireman and then at Rabbi Binder. He wanted to see Rabbi Binder cover his eyes one more time.

"I'm going to jump."

And then he scampered around the edge of the roof to the corner, where there was no net below, and he flapped his arms at his sides, swishing the air and smacking his palms to his trousers on the downbeat. He began screaming like some kind of engine, "Wheeeee . . . wheeeee," and leaning way out over the edge with the upper half of his body. The firemen whipped around to cover the ground with the net. Rabbi Binder mumbled a few words to Somebody and covered his eyes. Everything happened quickly, jerkily, as in a silent movie. The crowd, which had arrived with the fire engines, gave out a long, Fourth-of-July fireworks oooh-aahhh. In the excitement no one had paid the crowd much heed, except, of course, Yakov Blotnik, who swung from the doorknob counting heads. "Fier und tsvantsik . . . finf und tsvantsik . . . Oy, Gut!" It wasn't like this with the cat.

Rabbi Binder peeked through his fingers, checked the sidewalk and net. Empty. But there was Ozzie racing to the other corner. The firemen raced with him but were unable to keep up. Whenever Oscar wanted to he might jump and splatter himself upon the sidewalk, and by the time the firemen scooted to the spot all they could do with their net would be to cover the mess.

"Wheeeee . . . wheeeee . . ."

"Hey, Oscar," the winded fireman yelled, "What the hell is this, a game or something?"

"Wheeeee . . . wheeeee . . ."

"Hey, Oscar—"

But he was off now to the other corner, flapping his wings fiercely. Rabbi Binder couldn't take it any longer—the fire engines from nowhere, the screaming suicidal boy, the net. He fell to his knees, exhausted, and with his hands curled together in front of his chest like a little dome, he pleaded, "Oscar, stop it, Oscar. Don't jump, Oscar. Please come down . . . Please don't jump."

And further back in the crowd a single voice, a single young voice, shouted a lone word to the boy on the roof.

"Jump!"

It was Itzie. Ozzie momentarily stopped flapping.

"Go ahead, Ozz—jump!" Itzie broke off his point of the star and courageously, with the inspiration not of a wise-guy but of a disciple, stood alone. "Jump, Ozz, jump!"

Still on his knees, his hands still curled, Rabbi Binder twisted his body back. He looked at Itzie, then, agonizingly, back to Ozzie.

"Oscar, Don't jump! Please, Don't Jump . . . please please . . ."

"Jump!" This time it wasn't Itzie but another point of the star. By the time Mrs. Freedman arrived to keep her four-thirty appointment with Rabbi Binder, the whole little upside down heaven was shouting and pleading for Ozzie to jump, and Rabbi Binder no longer was pleading with him not to jump, but was crying into the dome of his hands.

Understandably Mrs. Freedman couldn't figure out what her son was doing on the roof. So she asked.

"Ozzie, my Ozzie, what are you doing? My Ozzie, what is it?"

Ozzie stopped wheeeeeing and slowed his arms down to a cruising flap, the kind birds use in soft winds, but he did not answer. He stood against the low, clouded, darkening sky—light clicked down swiftly now, as on a small gear—flapping softly and gazing down at the small bundle of a woman who was his mother.

"What are you doing, Ozzie?" She turned towards the kneeling Rabbi Binder and rushed so close that only a paper-thickness of dusk lay between her stomach and his shoulders.

"What is my baby doing?"

Rabbi Binder gaped up at her but he too was mute. All that moved was the dome of his hands; it shook back and forth like a weak pulse.

"Rabbi, get him down! He'll kill himself. Get him down, my only baby . . ."

"I can't," Rabbi Binder said, "I can't . . ." and he turned his handsome head towards the crowd of boys behind him. "It's them. Listen to them."

And for the first time Mrs. Freedman saw the crowd of boys, and she heard what they were yelling.

"He's doing it for them. He won't listen to me. It's them." Rabbi Binder spoke like one in a trance.

"For them?"

"Yes."

"Why for them?"

"They want him to . . ."

Mrs. Freedman raised her two arms upward as though she were conducting the sky. "For them he's doing it!" And then in a gesture older than pyramids, older than prophets and floods, her arms came slapping down to her sides. "A martyr I have. Look!" She tilted her head to the roof. Ozzie was still flapping softly. "My martyr."

"Oscar, come down, *please,*" Rabbi Binder groaned.

In a startlingly even voice Mrs. Freedman called to the boy on the roof. "Ozzie, come down, Ozzie. Don't be a martyr, my baby."

As though it were a litany, Rabbi Binder repeated her words. "Don't bè a martyr, my baby. Don't be a martyr."

"Gawhead, Ozz—*be* a Martin!" It was Itzie. "Be a Martin, be a Martin," and all the voices joined in singing for Martindom, whatever *it* was. "Be a Martin, be a Martin . . ."

Somehow when you're on a roof the darker it gets the less you can hear. All Ozzie knew was that two groups wanted two new things: his friends were spirited and musical about what they wanted; his mother and the rabbi were even-toned, chanting, about what they didn't want. The rabbi's voice was without tears now and so was his mother's.

The big net stared up at Ozzie like a sightless eye. The big, clouded sky pushed down. From beneath it looked like a gray corrugated board. Suddenly, looking up into that unsympathetic sky, Ozzie realized all the strangeness of what these people, his friends, were asking: they wanted him to jump, to kill himself; they were singing about it now—it made them that happy. And there was an even greater strangeness: Rabbi Binder was on his knees, trembling. If there was a question to be asked now it was not "Is it me?" but rather "Is it us? . . . Is it us?"

Being on the roof, it turned out, was a serious thing. If he jumped would the singing become dancing? Would it? What would jumping stop? Yearningly, Ozzie wished he could rip open the sky, plunge his hands through, and pull out the sun; and on the sun, like a coin, would be stamped JUMP or DON'T JUMP.

Ozzie's knees rocked and sagged a little under him as though they were setting him for a dive. His arms tightened, stiffened, froze, from shoulders to fingernails. He felt as if each part of his body were going to vote as to whether he should kill himself or not—and each part as though it were independent of *him.*

The light took an unexpected click down and the new darkness, like a gag, hushed the friends singing for this and the mother and rabbi chanting for that.

Ozzie stopped counting votes, and in a curiously high voice, like one who wasn't prepared for speech, he spoke.

"Mamma?"

"Yes, Oscar."

"Mamma, get down on your knees, like Rabbi Binder."

"Oscar—"

"Get down on your knees," he said, "or I'll jump."

Ozzie heard a whimper, then a quick rustling, and when he looked down where his mother had stood he saw the top of a head and beneath that a circle of dress. She was kneeling beside Rabbi Binder.

He spoke again. "Everybody kneel." There was the sound of everybody kneeling.

Ozzie looked around. With one hand he pointed towards the synagogue entrance. "Make *him* kneel."

There was a noise, not of kneeling, but of body-and-cloth stretching. Ozzie could hear Rabbi Binder saying in a gruff whisper, ". . . or he'll *kill* himself," and when next he looked there was Yakov Blotnik off the door-knob and for the first time in his life upon his knees in the Gentile posture of prayer.

As for the firemen—it is not as difficult as one might imagine to hold a net taut while you are kneeling.

Ozzie looked around again; and then he called to Rabbi Binder.

"Rabbi?"

"Yes, Oscar."

"Rabbi Binder, do you believe in God."

"Yes."

"Do you believe God can do Anything?" Ozzie leaned his head out into the darkness. "Anything?"

"Oscar, I think—"

"Tell me you believe God can do Anything."

There was a second's hesitation. Then: "God can do Anything."

"Tell me you believe God can make a child without intercourse."

"He can."

"Tell me!"

"God," Rabbi Binder admitted, "can make a child without intercourse."

"Mamma, you tell me."

"God can make a child without intercourse," his mother said.

"Make *him* tell me." There was no doubt who *him* was.

In a few moments Ozzie heard an old comical voice say something to the increasing darkness about God.

Next, Ozzie made everybody say it. And then he made them all say they believed in Jesus Christ—first one at a time, then all together.

When the catechizing was through it was the beginning of evening. From the street it sounded as if the boy on the roof might have sighed.

"Ozzie?" A woman's voice dared to speak. "You'll come down now?"

There was no answer, but the woman waited, and when a voice finally did speak it was thin and crying, and exhausted as that of an old man who has just finished pulling the bells.

"Mamma, don't you see—you shouldn't hit me. He shouldn't hit me. You shouldn't hit me about God, Mamma. You should never hit anybody about God—"

"Ozzie, please come down now."

"Promise me, promise me you'll never hit anybody about God."

He had asked only his mother, but for some reason everyone kneeling in the street promised he would never hit anybody about God.

Once again there was silence.

"I can come down now Mamma," the boy on the roof finally said. He turned his head both ways as though checking the traffic lights. "Now I can come down . . ."

And he did, right into the center of the yellow net that glowed in the evening's edge like an overgrown halo.

Part 3

DRAMA

Sophocles (496–406 B.C.)

OEDIPUS REX

An English Version by Dudley Fitts and Robert Fitzgerald

CHARACTERS

OEDIPUS:	*King of Thebes*
A PRIEST	
CREON:	*brother of Iocastê*
TEIRESIAS:	*a blind seer*
IOCASTÊ:	*the Queen, wife of Oedipus*
MESSENGER	
SHEPHERD OF LAÏOS	
SECOND MESSENGER	
CHORUS OF THEBAN ELDERS	

[THE SCENE: *Before the palace of Oedipus, King of Thebes. A central door and two lateral doors open onto a platform which runs the length of the façade. On the platform, right and left, are altars; and three steps lead down into the "orchestra," or chorus-ground. At the beginning of the action these steps are crowded by suppliants who have brought branches and chaplets of olive leaves and who lie in various attitudes of despair.* OEDIPUS *enters.*]

SOURCE: Reprinted with the permission of Harcourt Brace Jovanovich, Inc. Copyright 1949 by Harcourt Brace & World, Inc.

Prologue [1]

OEDIPUS: My children, generations of the living
   In the line of Kadmos,[2] nursed at his ancient hearth:
   Why have you strewn yourselves before these altars
   In supplication, with your boughs and garlands?
   The breath of incense rises from the city   5
   With a sound of prayer and lamentation.
                             Children,
   I would not have you speak through messengers,
   And therefore I have come myself to hear you—
   I, Oedipus, who bear the famous name.   10
   [*to a* PRIEST]
   You, there, since you are eldest in the company,
   Speak for them all, tell me what preys upon you,
   Whether you come in dread, or crave some blessing:
   Tell me, and never doubt that I will help you
   In every way I can; I should be heartless   15
   Were I not moved to find you suppliant here.
PRIEST: Great Oedipus, O powerful King of Thebes!
   You see how all the ages of our people
   Cling to your altar steps: here are boys
   Who can barely stand alone, and here are priests   20
   By weight of age, as I am a priest of God,
   And young men chosen from those yet unmarried;
   As for the others, all that multitude,
   They wait with olive chaplets in the squares,
   At the two shrines of Pallas, and where Apollo   25
   Speaks in the glowing embers.
                       Your own eyes
   Must tell you: Thebes is in her extremity
   And can not lift her head from the surge of death.
   A rust consumes the buds and fruits of the earth;   30
   The herds are sick; children die unborn,
   And labor is vain. The god of plague and pyre
   Raids like detestable lightning through the city,
   And all the house of Kadmos is laid waste,

---

[1]This play consists of a prologue, a párodos, four scenes—each followed by an ode—and
an éxodos. The **parodos** is the ode sung by the chorus as it enters; the **exodos** is that part
of the play which follows the last ode. The play, then, is composed of a beginning (prologue
and párodos) in which the situation is defined and explored; a middle (the four scenes and
their terminal odes) in which the plot develops, with choral commentary, to the catastrophic
discovery; and an end (the éxodos) in which the consequences of the discovery are explored
and, in part, realized.

[2]Founder of Thebes, great-great-grandfather of Oedipus.

All emptied, and all darkened: Death alone   35
Battens upon the misery of Thebes.

You are not one of the immortal gods, we know;
Yet we have come to you to make our prayer
As to the man of all men best in adversity
And wisest in the ways of God. You saved us   40
From the Sphinx,³ that flinty singer, and the tribute
We paid to her so long; yet you were never
Better informed than we, nor could we teach you:
It was some god breathed in you to set us free.

Therefore, O mighty King, we turn to you: 45
Find us our safety, find us a remedy,
Whether by counsel of the gods or men.
A king of wisdom tested in the past
Can act in a time of troubles, and act well.
Noblest of men, restore   50
Life to your city! Think how all men call you
Liberator for your triumph long ago;
Ah, when your years of kingship are remembered,
Let them not say *We rose, but later fell*—
Keep the State from going down in the storm!   55
Once, years ago, with happy augury,
You brought us fortune; be the same again!
No man questions your power to rule the land:
But rule over men, not over a dead city!
Ships are only hulls, citadels are nothing,   60
When no life moves in the empty passageways.
OEDIPUS: Poor children! You may be sure I know
All that you longed for in your coming here.
I know that you are deathly sick; and yet,
Sick as you are, not one is as sick as I.   65
Each of you suffers in himself alone
His anguish, not another's; but my spirit
Groans for the city, for myself, for you.

I was not sleeping, you are not waking me.
No, I have been in tears for a long while   70
And in my restless thought walked many ways.

---

³Monster that settled near Thebes and slew all passers-by who failed to solve the riddle
she asked of them: "What being has four feet in the morning, two at noon, and three at
night?" Years before the play's opening Oedipus had rescued Thebes by solving the riddle
("Man"), whereupon the Sphinx killed herself, and the Thebans made Oedipus their king.

In all my search, I found one helpful course,
And that I have taken: I have sent Creon,
Son of Menoikeus, brother of the Queen,
To Delphi, Apollo's place of revelation,   75
To learn there, if he can,
What act or pledge of mine may save the city.
I have counted the days, and now, this very day,
I am troubled, for he has overstayed his time.
What is he doing? He has been gone too long.   80
Yet whenever he comes back, I should do ill
To scant whatever hint the god may give.
PRIEST: It is a timely promise. At this instant
They tell me Creon is here.
OEDIPUS: O Lord Apollo!   85
May his news be fair as his face is radiant!
PRIEST: It could not be otherwise: he is crowned with bay,[4]
The chaplet is thick with berries.
OEDIPUS: We shall soon know;
He is near enough to hear us now.   90
                    [*Enter* CREON.]
                                   O Prince:
Brother: son of Menoikeus:
What answer do you bring us from the god?
CREON: It is favorable. I can tell you, great afflictions   95
Will turn out well, if they are taken well.
OEDIPUS: What was the oracle? These vague words
Leave me still hanging between hope and fear.
CREON: Is it your pleasure to hear me with all these
Gathered around us? I am prepared to speak,
But should we not go in?   100
OEDIPUS: Let them all hear it.
It is for them I suffer, more than for myself.
CREON: Then I will tell you what I heard at Delphi.

In plain words
The god commands us to expel from the land of Thebes   105
An old defilement that it seems we shelter.
It is a deathly thing, beyond expiation.
We must not let it feed upon us longer.
OEDIPUS: What defilement? How shall we rid ourselves of it?
CREON: By exile or death, blood for blood. It was   110
Murder that brought the plague-wind on the city.

---

[4]The laurel, sacred to Apollo and, when worn in wreaths or crowns, symbolic of victory.

OEDIPUS: Murder of whom? Surely the god has named him?
CREON: My lord: long ago Laïos was our king,
  Before you came to govern us.
OEDIPUS: I know;   115
  I learned of him from others; I never saw him.
CREON: He was murdered; and Apollo commands us now
  To take revenge upon whoever killed him.
OEDIPUS: Upon whom? Where are they? Where shall we find a clue
  To solve that crime, after so many years?   120
CREON: Here in this land, he said. If we make enquiry,
  We may touch things that otherwise escape us.
OEDIPUS: Tell me: Was Laïos murdered in his house,
  Or in the fields, or in some foreign country?   125
CREON: He said he planned to make a pilgrimage.
  He did not come home again.
OEDIPUS: And was there no one,
  No witness, no companion, to tell what happened?
CREON: They were all killed but one, and he got away   130
  So frightened that he could remember one thing only.
OEDIPUS: What was that one thing? One may be the key
  To everything, if we resolve to use it.
CREON: He said that a band of highwaymen attacked them,
  Outnumbered them, and overwhelmed the King.   135
OEDIPUS: Strange, that a highwayman should be so daring—
  Unless some faction here bribed him to do it.
CREON: We thought of that. But after Laïos' death
  New troubles arose and we had no avenger.
OEDIPUS: What troubles could prevent your hunting down the killers?   140
CREON: The riddling Sphinx's song
  Made us deaf to all mysteries but her own.
OEDIPUS: Then once more I must bring what is dark to light.
  It is most fitting that Apollo shows,
  As you do, this compunction for the dead.   145
  You shall see how I stand by you, as I should,
  To avenge the city and the city's god,
  And not as though it were for some distant friend,
  But for my own sake, to be rid of evil.
  Whoever killed King Laïos might—who knows?—   150
  Decide at any moment to kill me as well.
  By avenging the murdered king I protect myself.

  Come, then, my children: leave the altar steps,
  Lift up your olive boughs!
                One of you go   155

And summon the people of Kadmos to gather here.
I will do all that I can; you may tell them that. [*Exit a* PAGE.]
So, with the help of God,[5]
We shall be saved—or else indeed we are lost.

PRIEST: Let us rise, children. It was for this we came,   160
And now the King has promised it himself.
Phoibos has sent us an oracle; may he descend
Himself to save us and drive out the plague.

[*Exeunt* OEDIPUS *and* CREON *into the palace by the central door. The* PRIEST *and the* SUPPLIANTS *disperse R. and L. After a short pause the* CHORUS *enters the orchestra.*]

Párodos

CHORUS: What is the god singing in his profound   STROPHE 1
Delphi of gold and shadow?   165
What oracle for Thebes, the sunwhipped city?

Fear unjoints me, the roots of my heart tremble.

Now I remember, O Healer, your power, and wonder:
Will you send doom like a sudden cloud, or weave it
Like nightfall of the past?   170

Ah no: be merciful, issue of holy sound:
Dearest to our expectancy: be tender!

Let me pray to Athenê, the immortal daughter of Zeus,   ANTISTROPHE 1
And to Artemis her sister
Who keeps her famous throne in the market ring,   175
And to Apollo, bowman at the far butts of heaven—

O gods, descend! Like three streams leap against
The fires of our grief, the fires of darkness;
Be swift to bring us rest!

As in the old time from the brilliant house   180
Of air you stepped to save us, come again!

Now our afflictions have no end.   STROPHE 2
Now all our stricken host lies down
And no man fights off death with his mind;

---

[5] Apollo, god of music, archery, healing, light (**Phoibos** , as he is sometimes called, means *light* or *pure*), and truth. Through his oracle he mediates between man and the gods.

The noble plowland bears no grain,   185
And groaning mothers can not bear—

See, how our lives like birds take wing,
Like sparks that fly when a fire soars,
To the shore of the god of evening.

The plague burns on, it is pitiless,   ANTISTROPHE 2
Though pallid children laden with death
Lie unwept in the stony ways,

And old gray women by every path
Flock to the strand about the altars

There to strike their breasts and cry   195
Worship of Zeus in wailing prayers:
Be kind, God's golden child!⁶

There are no swords in this attack by fire,   STROPHE 3
No shields, but we are ringed with cries.

Send the besieger plunging from our homes   200
Into the vast sea-room of the Atlantic
Or into the waves that foam eastward of Thrace—

For the day ravages what the night spares—

Destroy our enemy, lord of the thunder!
Let him be riven by lightning from heaven!   205

Phoibos Apollo, stretch the sun's bowstring,   ANTISTROPHE 3
That golden cord, until it sing for us,
Flashing arrows in heaven!
                        Artemis, Huntress,
Race with flaring lights upon our mountains!   210

O scarlet⁷ god, O golden-banded brow,
O Theban⁸ Bacchos in a storm of Maenads,
                    [*Enter* OEDIPUS, *center.*]
Whirl upon Death, that all the Undying hate!
Come with blinding cressets, come in joy!

---

⁶Athena, daughter of Zeus.
⁷Flushed with wine.
⁸Born in Thebes and descended on his mortal side from Kadmos.

Scene I

OEDIPUS: Is this your prayer? It may be answered. Come,   21
    Listen to me, act as the crisis demands,
    And you shall have relief from all these evils.

    Until now I was a stranger to this tale,
    As I had been a stranger to the crime.
    Could I track down the murderer without a clue?   22
    But now, friends,
    As one who became a citizen after the murder,
    I make this proclamation to all Thebans:
    If any man knows by whose hands Laïos, son of Labdakos,
    Met his death, I direct that man to tell me everything,   22
    No matter what he fears for having so long withheld it.
    Let it stand as promised that no further trouble
    Will come to him, but he may leave the land in safety.

    Moreover: If anyone knows the murderer to be foreign,
    Let him not keep silent: he shall have his reward from me.   23
    However, if he does conceal it; if any man
    Fearing for his friend or for himself disobeys this edict,
    Hear what I propose to do:

    I solemnly forbid the people of this country,
    Where power and throne are mine, ever to receive that man   23
    Or speak to him, no matter who he is, or let him
    Join in sacrifice, lustration, or in prayer.
    I decree that he be driven from every house,
    Being, as he is, corruption itself to us: the Delphic
    Voice of Zeus has pronounced this revelation.   2
    Thus I associate myself with the oracle
    And take the side of the murdered king.

    As for the criminal, I pray to God—
    Whether it be a lurking thief, or one of a number—
    I pray that that man's life be consumed in evil and wretchedness. 2
    And as for me, this curse applies no less
    If it should turn out that the culprit is my guest here,
    Sharing my hearth.
                You have heard the penalty.
    I lay it on you now to attend to this   2
    For my sake, for Apollo's, for the sick
    Sterile city that heaven has abandoned.

Suppose the oracle had given you no command:
Should this defilement go uncleansed for ever?
You should have found the murderer: your king,   255
A noble king, had been destroyed!
                              Now I,
Having the power that he held before me,
Having his bed, begetting children there
Upon his wife, as he would have, had he lived—   260
Their son would have been my children's brother,
If Laïos had had luck in fatherhood!
(But surely ill luck rushed upon his reign)—
I say I take the son's part, just as though
I were his son, to press the fight for him   265
And see it won! I'll find the hand that brought
Death to Labdakos' and Polydoros' child,
Heir of Kadmos' and Agenor's line.[9]
And as for those who fail me,
May the gods deny them the fruit of the earth,   270
Fruit of the womb, and may they rot utterly!
Let them be wretched as we are wretched, and worse!

For you, for loyal Thebans, and for all
Who find my actions right, I pray the favor
Of justice, and of all the immortal gods.   275
CHORAGOS:[10] Since I am under oath, my lord, I swear
    I did not do the murder, I can not name
    The murderer. Might not the oracle
    That has ordained the search tell where to find him?
OEDIPUS: An honest question. But no man in the world   280
    Can make the gods do more than the gods will.
CHORAGOS: There is one last expedient—
OEDIPUS: Tell me what it is.
    Though it seem slight, you must not hold it back.
CHORAGOS: A lord clairoyant to the lord Apollo,   285
    As we all know, is the skilled Teiresias.
    One might learn much about this from him, Oedipus.
OEDIPUS: I am not wasting time:
    Creon spoke of this, and I have sent for him—
    Twice, in fact; it is strange that he is not here.   290
CHORAGOS: The other matter—that old report—seems useless.

---

[9]The child is Laïos, whose male ancestry Oedipus traces back: Laïos-Labdakos-Polydoros-Kadmos-Agenor.

[10]Leader of the chorus.

OEDIPUS: Tell me. I am interested in all reports.

CHORAGOS: The King was said to have been killed by highwaymen.

OEDIPUS: I know. But we have no witnesses to that.

CHORAGOS: If the killer can feel a particle of dread,   295
  Your curse will bring him out of hiding!

OEDIPUS: No.
  The man who dared that act will fear no curse.

  [*Enter the blind seer* TEIRESIAS, *led by a* PAGE.]

CHORAGOS: But there is one man who may detect the criminal.
  This is Teiresias, this is the holy prophet   300
  In whom, alone of all men, truth was born.

OEDIPUS: Teiresias: seer: student of mysteries,
  Of all that's taught and all that no man tells,
  Secrets of Heaven and secrets of the earth:
  Blind though you are, you know the city lies   305
  Sick with plague; and from this plague, my lord,
  We find that you alone can guard or save us.

  Possibly you did not hear the messengers?
  Apollo, when we sent to him,
  Sent us back word that this great pestilence   310
  Would lift, but only if we established clearly
  The identity of those who murdered Laïos.
  They must be killed or exiled.

                        Can you use
  Birdflight or any art of divination   315
  To purify yourself, and Thebes, and me
  From this contagion? We are in your hands.
  There is no fairer duty
  Than that of helping others in distress.

TEIRESIAS: How dreadful knowledge of the truth can be   320
  When there's no help in truth! I knew this well,
  But did not act on it: else I should not have come.

OEDIPUS: What is troubling you? Why are your eyes so cold?

TEIRESIAS: Let me go home. Bear your own fate, and I'll
  Bear mine. It is better so: trust what I say.   325

OEDIPUS: What you say is ungracious and unhelpful
  To your native country. Do not refuse to speak.

TEIRESIAS: When it comes to speech, your own is neither temperate
  Nor opportune. I wish to be more prudent.

OEDIPUS: In God's name, we all beg you—   330

TEIRESIAS: You are all ignorant.
  No; I will never tell you what I know.
  Now it is my misery; then, it would be yours.

OEDIPUS: What! You do know something, and will not tell us?
You would betray us all and wreck the State? 335
TEIRESIAS: I do not intend to torture myself, or you.
Why persist in asking? You will not persuade me.
OEDIPUS: What a wicked old man you are! You'd try a stone's
Patience! Out with it! Have you no feeling at all?
TEIRESIAS: You call me unfeeling. If you could only see 340
The nature of your own feelings . . .
OEDIPUS: Why,
Who would not feel as I do? Who could endure
Your arrogance toward the city?
TEIRESIAS: What does it matter! 345
Whether I speak or not, it is bound to come.
OEDIPUS: Then, if "it" is bound to come, you are bound to tell me.
TEIRESIAS: No, I will not go on. Rage as you please.
OEDIPUS: Rage? Why not!
                                       And I'll tell you what I think: 350
You planned it, you had it done, you all but
Killed him with your own hands: if you had eyes,
I'd say the crime was yours, and yours alone.
TEIRESIAS: So? I charge you, then,
Abide by the proclamation you have made: 355
From this day forth
Never speak again to these men or to me;
You yourself are the pollution of this country.
OEDIPUS: You dare say that! Can you possibly think you have
Some way of going free, after such insolence? 360
TEIRESIAS: I have gone free. It is the truth sustains me.
OEDIPUS: Who taught you shamelessness? It was not your craft.
TEIRESIAS: You did. You made me speak. I did not want to.
OEDIPUS: Speak what? Let me hear it again more clearly.
TEIRESIAS: Was it not clear before? Are you tempting me? 365
OEDIPUS: I did not understand it. Say it again.
TEIRESIAS: I say that you are the murderer whom you seek.
OEDIPUS: Now twice you have spat out infamy. You'll pay for it!
TEIRESIAS: Would you care for more? Do you wish to be really angry?
OEDIPUS: Say what you will. Whatever you say is worthless. 370
TEIRESIAS: I say that you live in hideous love with her
Who is nearest you in blood. You are blind to the evil.
OEDIPUS: It seems you can go on mouthing like this for ever.
TEIRESIAS: I can, if there is power in truth.
OEDIPUS: There is: 375
But not for you, not for you,
You sightless, witless, senseless, mad old man!

TEIRESIAS: You are the madman. There is no one here
　　Who will not curse you soon, as you curse me.
OEDIPUS: You child of endless night! You can not hurt me　　　　380
　　Or any other man who sees the sun.
TEIRESIAS: True: it is not from me your fate will come.
　　That lies within Apollo's competence,
　　As it is his concern.
OEDIPUS: 　　　　　　　Tell me:　　　　　　　　　　　　　385
　　Are you speaking for Creon, or for yourself?
TEIRESIAS: Creon is no threat. You weave your own doom.
OEDIPUS: Wealth, power, craft of statesmanship!
　　Kingly position, everywhere admired!
　　What savage envy is stored up against these,　　　　　390
　　If Creon, whom I trusted, Creon my friend,
　　For this great office which the city once
　　Put in my hands unsought—if for this power
　　Creon desires in secret to destroy me!

　　He has bought this decrepit fortune-teller, this　　　　395
　　Collector of dirty pennies, this prophet fraud—
　　Why, he is no more clairvoyant than I am!
　　　　　　　　　　　　　　　　　Tell us:
　　Has your mystic mummery ever approached the truth?
　　When that hellcat the Sphinx was performing here,　　　400
　　What help were you to these people?
　　Her magic was not for the first man who came along:
　　It demanded a real exorcist. Your birds—
　　What good were they? or the gods, for the matter of that?
　　But I came by,　　　　　　　　　　　　　　　　　405
　　Oedipus, the simple man, who knows nothing—
　　I thought it out for myself, no birds helped me!
　　And this is the man you think you can destroy,
　　That you may be close to Creon when he's king!
　　Well, you and your friend Creon, it seems to me,　　　410
　　Will suffer most. If you were not an old man,
　　You would have paid already for your plot.
CHORAGOS: We can not see that his words or yours
　　Have been spoken except in anger, Oedipus,
　　And of anger we have no need. How can God's will　　　415
　　Be accomplished best? That is what most concerns us.
TEIRESIAS: You are a king. But where argument's concerned
　　I am your man, as much a king as you.
　　I am not your servant, but Apollo's.
　　I have no need of Creon to speak for me.　　　　　　420

Listen to me. You mock my blindness, do you?
But I say that you, with both your eyes, are blind:
You can not see the wretchedness of your life,
Nor in whose house you live, no, nor with whom.
Who are your father and mother? Can you tell me?   425
You do not even know the blind wrongs
That you have done them, on earth and in the world below.
But the double lash of your parents' curse will whip you
Out of this land some day, with only night
Upon your precious eyes.   430
Your cries then—where will they not be heard?
What fastness of Kithairon[11] will not echo them?
And that bridal-descant of yours—you'll know it then,
The song they sang when you came here to Thebes
And found your misguided berthing.   435
All this, and more, that you can not guess at now,
Will bring you to yourself among your children.

Be angry, then. Curse Creon. Curse my words.
I tell you, no man that walks upon the earth
Shall be rooted out more horribly than you.   440
OEDIPUS: Am I to bear this from him?—Damnation
  Take you! Out of this place! Out of my sight!
TEIRESIAS: I would not have come at all if you had not asked me.
OEDIPUS: Could I have told that you'd talk nonsense, that
  You'd come here to make a fool of yourself, and of me?   445
TEIRESIAS: A fool? Your parents thought me sane enough.
OEDIPUS: My parents again!—Wait: who were my parents?
TEIRESIAS: This day will give you a father, and break your heart.
OEDIPUS: Your infantile riddles! Your damned abracadabra!
TEIRESIAS: You were a great man once at solving riddles.   450
OEDIPUS: Mock me with that if you like; you will find it true.
TEIRESIAS: It was true enough. It brought about your ruin.
OEDIPUS: But if it saved this town?
TEIRESIAS [*to the* PAGE]: Boy, give me your hand.
OEDIPUS: Yes, boy; lead him away.   455
                    —While you are here
  We can do nothing. Go; leave us in peace.
TEIRESIAS: I will go when I have said what I have to say.
  How can you hurt me? And I tell you again:
  The man you have been looking for all this time,   460
  The damned man, the murderer of Laïos,
  That man is in Thebes. To your mind he is foreign-born,

---

[11]Mountain near Thebes where the infant Oedipus was left to die.

But it will soon be shown that he is a Theban,
A revelation that will fail to please.

                       A blind man,   465
Who has his eyes now; a penniless man, who is rich now;
And he will go tapping the strange earth with his staff.
To the children with whom he lives now he will be
Brother and father—the very same; to her
Who bore him, son and husband—the very same   470
Who came to his father's bed, wet with his father's blood.

Enough. Go think that over.
If later you find error in what I have said,
You may say that I have no skill in prophecy.

    [*Exit* TEIRESIAS, *led by his* PAGE. OEDIPUS *goes into the palace.*]

Ode I

CHORUS: The Delphic stone of prophecies[12]   STROPHE 1
  Remembers ancient regicide
  And a still bloody hand.
  That killer's hour of flight has come.
  He must be stronger than riderless
  Coursers of untiring wind,   48
  For the son of Zeus[13] armed with his father's thunder
  Leaps in lightning after him;
  And the Furies follow him, the sad Furies.

  Holy Parnassos'[14] peak of snow   ANTISTROPHE 1
  Flashes and blinds that secret man,   48
  That all shall hunt him down:
  Though he may roam the forest shade
  Like a bull gone wild from pasture
  To rage through glooms of stone.
  Doom comes down on him; flight will not avail him;   49
  For the world's heart calls him desolate,
  And the immortal Furies follow, for ever follow.

  But now a wilder thing is heard   STROPHE 2
  From the old man skilled at hearing Fate in the wingbeat of a bird.

---

[12]Platform of rock on which stood the temple of the Delphic oracle.
[13]Apollo.
[14]Mountain, sacred to Apollo, on the side of which Delphi and its oracle stood.

Bewildered as a blown bird, my soul hovers and can not find   495
Foothold in this debate, or any reason or rest of mind.
But no man ever brought—none can bring
Proof of strife between Thebes' royal house,
Labdakos' line, and the son of Polybos;
And never until now has any man brought word   500
Of Laïos' dark death staining Oedipus the King.

Divine Zeus and Apollo hold   ANTISTROPHE 2
Perfect intelligence alone of all tales ever told;
And well though this diviner works, he works in his own night;
No man can judge that rough unknown or trust in second sight,   505
For wisdom changes hands among the wise.
Shall I believe my great lord criminal
At a raging word that a blind old man let fall?
I saw him, when the carrion woman faced him of old,
Prove his heroic mind! These evil words are lies.   510

Scene II

CREON: Men of Thebes:
    I am told that heavy accusations
    Have been brought against me by King Oedipus.

I am not the kind of man to bear this tamely.

If in these present difficulties   515
He holds me accountable for any harm to him
Through anything I have said or done—why, then,
I do not value life in this dishonor.
It is not as though this rumor touched upon
Some private indiscretion. The matter is grave.   520
The fact is that I am being called disloyal
To the State, to my fellow citizens, to my friends.
CHORAGOS: He may have spoken in anger, not from his mind.
CREON: But did you not hear him say I was the one
    Who seduced the old prophet into lying?   525
CHORAGOS: The thing was said; I do not know how seriously.
CREON: But you were watching him! Were his eyes steady?
    Did he look like a man in his right mind?
CHORAGOS: I do not know.
    I can not judge the behavior of great men.   530
    But here is the King himself.

[*Enter* OEDIPUS.]

OEDIPUS: So you dared come back.
Why? How brazen of you to come to my house,
You murderer!
                    Do you think I do not know   535
That you plotted to kill me, plotted to steal my throne?
Tell me, in God's name: am I coward, a fool,
That you should dream you could accomplish this?
A fool who could not see your slippery game?
A coward, not to fight back when I saw it?   540
You are the fool, Creon, are you not? hoping
Without support or friends to get a throne?
Thrones may be won or bought: you could do neither.

CREON: Now listen to me. You have talked; let me talk, too.
You can not judge unless you know the facts.   545

OEDIPUS: You speak well: there is one fact; but I find it hard
To learn from the deadliest enemy I have.

CREON: That above all I must dispute with you.

OEDIPUS: That above all I will not hear you deny.

CREON: If you think there is anything good in being stubborn   550
Against all reason, then I say you are wrong.

OEDIPUS: If you think a man can sin against his own kind
And not be punished for it, I say you are mad.

CREON: I agree. But tell me: what have I done to you?

OEDIPUS: You advised me to send for that wizard, did you not?   555

CREON: I did. I should do it again.

OEDIPUS: Very well. Now tell me:
How long has it been since Laïos—

CREON: What of Laïos?

OEDIPUS: Since he vanished in that onset by the road?   560

CREON: It was long ago, a long time.

OEDIPUS: And this prophet,
Was he practicing here then?

CREON: He was; and with honor, as now.

OEDIPUS: Did he speak of me at that time?   565

CREON: He never did;
At least, not when I was present.

OEDIPUS: But . . . the enquiry?
I suppose you held one?

CREON: We did, but we learned nothing. 570

OEDIPUS: Why did the prophet not speak against me then?

CREON: I do not know; and I am the kind of man
Who holds his tongue when he has no facts to go on.

OEDIPUS: There's one fact that you know, and you could tell it.
CREON: What fact is that? If I know it, you shall have it. 575
OEDIPUS: If he were not involved with you, he could not say
 That it was I who murdered Laïos.
CREON: If he says that, you are the one that knows it?—
 But now it is my turn to question you.
OEDIPUS: Put your questions. I am no murderer. 580
CREON: First, then: You married my sister?
OEDIPUS: I married your sister.
CREON: And you rule the kingdom equally with her?
OEDIPUS: Everything that she wants she has from me.
CREON: And I am the third, equal to both of you? 585
OEDIPUS: That is why I call you a bad friend.
CREON: No. Reason it out, as I have done.
 Think of this first: Would any sane man prefer
 Power, with all a king's anxieties,
 To that same power and the grace of sleep? 590
 Certainly not I.
 I have never longed for the king's power—only his rights.
 Would any wise man differ from me in this?
 As matters stand, I have my way in everything
 With your consent, and no responsibilities. 595
 If I were king, I should be a slave to policy.

 How could I desire a scepter more
 Than what is now mine—untroubled influence?
 No, I have not gone mad; I need no honors,
 Except those with the perquisites I have now. 600
 I am welcome everywhere; every man salutes me,
 And those who want your favor seek my ear,
 Since I know how to manage what they ask.
 Should I exchange this ease for that anxiety?
 Besides, no sober mind is treasonable. 605
 I hate anarchy
 And never would deal with any man who likes it.

 Test what I have said. Go to the priestess
 At Delphi, ask if I quoted her correctly.
 And as for this other thing: if I am found 610
 Guilty of treason with Teiresias,
 Then sentence me to death! You have my word
 It is a sentence I should cast my vote for—
 But not without evidence!

You do wrong   615

When you take good men for bad, bad men for good.
A true friend thrown aside—why, life itself
Is not more precious!

In time you will know this well:

For time, and time alone, will show the just man,   620
Though scoundrels are discovered in a day.
CHORAGOS: This is well said, and a prudent man would ponder it.
Judgments too quickly formed are dangerous.
OEDIPUS: But is he not quick in his duplicity?
And shall I not be quick to parry him?   625
Would you have me stand still, hold my peace, and let
This man win everything, through my inaction?
CREON: And you want—what is it, then? To banish me?
OEDIPUS: No, not exile. It is your death I want,
So that all the world may see what treason means.   630
CREON: You will persist, then? You will not believe me?
OEDIPUS: How can I believe you?
CREON: Then you are a fool.
OEDIPUS: To save myself?
CREON: In justice, think of me.   635
OEDIPUS: You are evil incarnate.
CREON: But suppose that you are wrong?
OEDIPUS: Still I must rule.
CREON: But not if you rule badly.
OEDIPUS: O city, city!   640
CREON: It is my city, too!
CHORAGOS: Now, my lords, be still. I see the Queen,
Iocastê, coming from her palace chambers;
And it is time she came, for the sake of you both.
This dreadful quarrel can be resolved through her.   645

[Enter IOCASTÊ.]

IOCASTÊ: Poor foolish men, what wicked din is this?
With Thebes sick to death, is it not shameful
That you should rake some private quarrel up?
[to OEDIPUS]
Come into the house.

—And you, Creon, go now: 650

Let us have no more of this tumult over nothing.
CREON: Nothing? No, sister: what your husband plans for me
Is one of two great evils: exile or death.
OEDIPUS: He is right.

Why, woman I have caught him squarely   655

Plotting against my life.
CREON: No! Let me die.

Accurst if ever I have wished you harm!
IOCASTÊ: Ah, believe it, Oedipus!
  In the name of the gods, respect this oath of his   660
  For my sake, for the sake of these people here!

CHORAGOS: Open your mind to her, my lord. Be ruled by her,   STROPHE 1
  I beg you!
OEDIPUS: What would you have me do?
CHORAGOS: Respect Creon's word. He has never spoken like a fool,
  And now he has sworn an oath.   665
OEDIPUS: You know what you ask?
CHORAGOS: I do.
OEDIPUS: Speak on, then.
CHORAGOS: A friend so sworn should not be baited so,
  In blind malice, and without final proof.   670
OEDIPUS: You are aware, I hope, that what you say
  Means death for me, or exile at the least.

CHORAGOS: No, I swear by Helios,[15] first in Heaven!   STROPHE 2
  May I die friendless and accurst,
    The worst of deaths, if ever I meant that!   675
      It is the withering fields
        That hurt my sick heart:
        Must we bear all these ills,
          And now your bad blood as well?
OEDIPUS: Then let him go. And let me die, if I must,   680
  Or be driven by him in shame from the land of Thebes.
  It is your unhappiness, and not his talk,
  That touches me.
        As for him—
  Wherever he is, I will hate him as long as I live.   685
CREON: Ugly in yielding, as you were ugly in rage!
  Natures like yours chiefly torment themselves.
OEDIPUS: Can you not go? Can you not leave me?
CREON: I can.
  You do not know me; but the city knows me,   690
  And in its eyes I am just, if not in yours.

                  [*Exit* CREON.]

CHORAGOS: Lady Iocastê, did you not ask the King to go to   ANTISTROPHE 1
his chambers?
IOCASTÊ: First tell me what has happened.
CHORAGOS: There was suspicion without evidence; yet it rankled
  As even false charges will.   695

———
[15]The sun-god.

IOCASTÊ: On both sides?
CHORAGOS: On both.
IOCASTÊ: But what was said?
CHORAGOS: Oh let it rest, let it be done with!
    Have we not suffered enough?   700
OEDIPUS: You see to what your decency has brought you: .
    You have made difficulties where my heart saw none.

CHORAGOS: Oedipus, it is not once only I have told you—   ANTISTROPHE 2
    You must know I should count myself unwise
    To the point of madness, should I now forsake you—   70
            You, under whose hand,
                In the storm of another time,
                Our dear land sailed out free.
                But now stand fast at the helm!
IOCASTÊ: In God's name, Oedipus, inform your wife as well: 71
    Why are you so set in this hard anger?
OEDIPUS: I will tell you, for none of these men deserves
    My confidence as you do. It is Creon's work,
    His treachery, his plotting against me.
IOCASTÊ: Go on, if you can make this clear to me.   71
OEDIPUS: He charges me with the murder of Laïos.
IOCASTÊ: Has he some knowledge? Or does he speak from hearsay?
OEDIPUS: He would not commit himself to such a charge,
    But he has brought in that damnable soothsayer
    To tell his story.   72
IOCASTÊ: Set your mind at rest.
    If it is a question of soothsayers, I tell you
    That you will find no man whose craft gives knowledge
    Of the unknowable.
                    Here is my proof: 72

An oracle was reported to Laïos once
(I will not say from Phoibos himself, but from
His appointed ministers, at any rate)
That his doom would be death at the hands of his own son—
His son, born of his flesh and of mine!   7.
Now, you remember the story: Laïos was killed
By marauding strangers where three highways meet;
But his child had not been three days in this world
Before the King had pierced the baby's ankles
And had him left to die on a lonely mountain.   7.

Thus, Apollo never caused that child

To kill his father, and it was not Laïos' fate
To die at the hands of his son, as he had feared.
This is what prophets and prophecies are worth!
Have no dread of them.   740
                    It is God himself
Who can show us what he wills, in his own way.
OEDIPUS: How strange a shadowy memory crossed my mind,
   Just now while you were speaking; it chilled my heart.
IOCASTÊ: What do you mean? What memory do you speak of?   745
OEDIPUS: If I understand you, Laïos was killed
   At a place where three roads meet.
IOCASTÊ: So it was said;
   We have no later story.
OEDIPUS: Where did it happen?   750
IOCASTÊ: Phokis, it is called: at a place where the Theban Way
   Divides into the roads toward Delphi and Daulia.
OEDIPUS: When?
IOCASTÊ: We had the news not long before you came
   And proved the right to your succession here.   755
OEDIPUS: Ah, what net has God been weaving for me?
IOCASTÊ: Oedipus! Why does this trouble you?
OEDIPUS: Do not ask me yet.
   First, tell me how Laïos looked, and tell me
   How old he was.   760
IOCASTÊ: He was tall, his hair just touched
   With white; his form was not unlike your own.
OEDIPUS: I think that I myself may be accurst
   By my own ignorant edict.
IOCASTÊ: You speak strangely.   765
   It makes me tremble to look at you, my King.
OEDIPUS: I am not sure that the blind man can not see.
   But I should know better if you were to tell me—
IOCASTÊ: Anything—though I dread to hear you ask it.
OEDIPUS: Was the King lightly escorted, or did he ride   770
   With a large company, as a ruler should?
IOCASTÊ: There were five men with him in all: one was a herald;
   And a single chariot, which he was driving.
OEDIPUS: Alas, that makes it plain enough!
                              But who—   775
   Who told you how it happened?
IOCASTÊ: A household servant,
   The only one to escape.
OEDIPUS: And is he still
   A servant of ours?   780

IOCASTÊ: No; for when he came back at last
  And found you enthroned in the place of the dead king,
  He came to me, touched my hand with his, and begged
  That I would send him away to the frontier district
  Where only the shepherds go—   785
  As far away from the city as I could send him.
  I granted his prayer; for although the man was a slave,
  He had earned more than this favor at my hands.
OEDIPUS: Can he be called back quickly?
IOCASTÊ: Easily.   790
  But why?
OEDIPUS: I have taken too much upon myself
  Without enquiry; therefore I wish to consult him.
IOCASTÊ: Then he shall come.
                    But am I not one also   795
  To whom you might confide these fears of yours?
OEDIPUS: That is your right; it will not be denied you,
  Now least of all; for I have reached a pitch
  Of wild foreboding. Is there anyone
  To whom I should sooner speak?   800

  Polybos of Corinth is my father.
  My mother is a Dorian: Meropê.
  I grew up chief among the men of Corinth
  Until a strange thing happened—
  Not worth my passion, it may be, but strange.   805

  At a feast, a drunken man maundering in his cups
  Cries out that I am not my father's son!

  I contained myself that night, though I felt anger
  And a sinking heart. The next day I visited
  My father and mother, and questioned them. They stormed,   810
  Calling it all the slanderous rant of a fool;
  And this relieved me. Yet the suspicion
  Remained always aching in my mind;
  I knew there was talk; I could not rest;
  And finally, saying nothing to my parents,   815
  I went to the shrine at Delphi.

  The god dismissed my question without reply;
  He spoke of other things.
                    Some were clear,

Full of wretchedness, dreadful, unbearable: 820
As, that I should lie with my own mother, breed
Children from whom all men would turn their eyes;
And that I should be my father's murderer.

I heard all this, and fled. And from that day
Corinth to me was only in the stars   825
Descending in that quarter of the sky,
As I wandered farther and farther on my way
To a land where I should never see the evil
Sung by the oracle. And I came to this country
Where, so you say, King Laïos was killed.   830

I will tell you all that happened there, my lady.

There were three highways
Coming together at a place I passed;
And there a herald came towards me, and a chariot
Drawn by horses, with a man such as you describe   835
Seated in it. The groom leading the horses
Forced me off the road at his lord's command;
But as this charioteer lurched over towards me
I struck him in my rage. The old man saw me
And brought his double goad down upon my head   840
As I came abreast.
                    He was paid back, and more!
Swinging my club in this right hand I knocked him
Out of his car, and he rolled on the ground.
                                        I killed him.   845

I killed them all.
Now if that stranger and Laïos were—kin,
Where is a man more miserable than I?
More hated by the gods? Citizen and alien alike
Must never shelter me or speak to me—   850
I must be shunned by all.
                        And I myself
Pronounced this malediction upon myself!
Think of it: I have touched you with these hands,
These hands that killed your husband. What defilement!   855

Am I all evil, then? It must be so,
Since I must flee from Thebes, yet never again

See my own countrymen, my own country,
For fear of joining my mother in marriage
And killing Polybos, my father.   860
                              Ah,
If I was created so, born to this fate,
Who could deny the savagery of God?

O holy majesty of heavenly powers!
May I never see that day! Never!   865
Rather let me vanish from the race of men
Than know the abomination destined me!

CHORAGOS: We too, my lord, have felt dismay at this.
But there is hope: you have yet to hear the shepherd.

OEDIPUS: Indeed, I fear no other hope is left me.   870

IOCASTÊ: What do you hope from him when he comes?

OEDIPUS: This much:
If his account of the murder tallies with yours,
Then I am cleared.

IOCASTÊ: What was it that I said   875
Of such importance?

OEDIPUS: Why, "marauders," you said,
Killed the King, according to this man's story.
If he maintains that still, if there were several,
Clearly the guilt is not mine: I was alone.   880
But if he says one man, singlehanded, did it,
Then the evidence all points to me.

IOCASTÊ: You may be sure that he said there were several;
And can he call back that story now? He can not.
The whole city heard it as plainly as I.   885
But suppose he alters some detail of it:
He can not ever show that Laïos' death
Fulfilled the oracle: for Apollo said
My child was doomed to kill him; and my child—
Poor baby!—it was my child that died first.   890
No. From now on, where oracles are concerned,
I would not waste a second thought on any.

OEDIPUS: You may be right.
                              But come: let someone go
For the shepherd at once. This matter must be settled.   89(

IOCASTÊ: I will send for him.
I would not wish to cross you in anything,
And surely not in this.—Let us go in.

                              [*Exeunt into the palace.*]

Ode II

CHORUS: Let me be reverent in the ways of right,   STROPHE 1
   Lowly the paths I journey on;   900
   Let all my words and actions keep
   The laws of the pure universe
   From highest Heaven handed down.
   For Heaven is their bright nurse,
   Those generations of the realms of light;   905
   Ah, never of mortal kind were they begot,
   Nor are they slaves of memory, lost in sleep:
   Their Father is greater than Time, and ages not.

   The tyrant is a child of Pride   ANTISTROPHE 1
   Who drinks from his great sickening cup   910
   Recklessness and vanity,
   Until from his high crest headlong
   He plummets to the dust of hope.
   That strong man is not strong.
   But let no fair ambition be denied;   915
   May God protect the wrestler for the State
   In government, in comely policy,
   Who will fear God, and on His ordinance wait.

   Haughtiness and the high hand of disdain   STROPHE 2
   Tempt and outrage God's holy law;   920
   And any mortal who dares hold
   No immortal Power in awe
   Will be caught up in a net of pain:
   The price for which his levity is sold.
   Let each man take due earnings, then,   925
   And keep his hands from holy things,
   And from blasphemy stand apart—
   Else the crackling blast of heaven
   Blows on his head, and on his desperate heart;
   Though fools will honor impious men,   930
   In their cities no tragic poet sings.

   Shall we lose faith in Delphi's obscurities,   ANTISTROPHE 2
   We who have heard the world's core
   Discredited, and the sacred wood
   Of Zeus at Elis praised no more?   935
   The deeds and the strange prophecies

Must make a pattern yet to be understood.
Zeus, if indeed you are lord of all,
Throned in light over night and day,
Mirror this in your endless mind: 940
Our masters call the oracle
Words on the wind, and the Delphic vision blind!
Their hearts no longer know Apollo,
And reverence for the gods has died away.

Scene III

[*Enter* IOCASTÊ.]

IOCASTÊ: Princes of Thebes, it has occurred to me   945
To visit the altars of the gods, bearing
These branches as a suppliant, and this incense.
Our King is not himself: his noble soul
Is overwrought with fantasies of dread,
Else he would consider   950
The new prophecies in the light of the old.
He will listen to any voice that speaks disaster,
And my advice goes for nothing.
[*She approaches the altar, R.*]
                                    To you, then, Apollo,
Lycean lord,[16] since you are nearest, I turn in prayer.   955
Receive these offerings, and grant us deliverance
From defilement. Our hearts are heavy with fear
When we see our leader distracted, as helpless sailors
Are terrified by the confusion of their helmsman.
[*Enter* MESSENGER.]

MESSENGER: Friends, no doubt you can direct me: 960
Where shall I find the house of Oedipus,
Or, better still, where is the King himself?

CHORAGOS: It is this very place, stranger; he is inside.
This is his wife and mother of his children.

MESSENGER: I wish her happiness in a happy house,   965
Blest in all the fulfillment of her marriage.

IOCASTÊ: I wish as much for you: your courtesy
Deserves a like good fortune. But now, tell me:
Why have you come? What have you to say to us?

MESSENGER: Good news, my lady, for your house and your husband.   970

IOCASTÊ: What news? Who sent you here?

MESSENGER: I am from Corinth.

---

[16]Lord of light.

The news I bring ought to mean joy for you,
Though it may be you will find some grief in it.
IOCASTÊ: What is it? How can it touch us in both ways?   975
MESSENGER: The people of Corinth, they say,
Intend to call Oedipus to be their king.
IOCASTÊ: But old Polybos—is he not reigning still?
MESSENGER: No. Death holds him in his sepulchre.
IOCASTÊ: What are you saying? Polybos is dead?   980
MESSENGER: If I am not telling the truth, may I die myself.
IOCASTÊ [*to a* MAID-SERVANT]: Go in, go quickly; tell this to your master.

O riddlers of God's will, where are you now!
This was the man whom Oedipus, long ago,
Feared so, fled so, in dread of destroying him—   985
But it was another fate by which he died.
                    [*Enter* OEDIPUS, *center.*]
OEDIPUS: Dearest Iocastê, why have you sent for me?
IOCASTÊ: Listen to what this man says, and then tell me
What has become of the solemn prophecies.
OEDIPUS: Who is this man? What is his news for me?   990
IOCASTÊ: He has come from Corinth to announce your father's death!
OEDIPUS: Is it true, stranger? Tell me in your own words.
MESSENGER: I can not say it more clearly: the King is dead.
OEDIPUS: Was it by treason? Or by an attack of illness?
MESSENGER: A little thing brings old men to their rest.   995
OEDIPUS: It was sickness, then?
MESSENGER: Yes, and his many years.
OEDIPUS: Ah!
Why should a man respect the Pythian hearth,[17]   or
Give heed to the birds that jangle above his head?   1000
They prophesied that I should kill Polybos,
Kill my own father; but he is dead and buried,
And I am here—I never touched him, never,
Unless he died of grief for my departure,
And thus, in a sense, through me. No. Polybos   1005
Has packed the oracles off with him underground.
They are empty words.
IOCASTÊ: Had I not told you so?
OEDIPUS: You had; it was my faint heart that betrayed me.
IOCASTÊ: From now on never think of those things again.   1010
OEDIPUS: And yet—must I not fear my mother's bed?
IOCASTÊ: Why should anyone in this world be afraid,

---

[17]Delphic oracle, where Apollo slew the serpent *Python.*

Since Fate rules us and nothing can be foreseen?
A man should live only for the present day.

Have no more fear of sleeping with your mother: 1015
How many men, in dreams, have lain with their mothers!
No reasonable man is troubled by such things.
OEDIPUS: That is true; only—
If only my mother were not still alive!
But she is alive. I can not help my dread.   1020
IOCASTÊ: Yet this news of your father's death is wonderful.
OEDIPUS: Wonderful. But I fear the living woman.
MESSENGER: Tell me, who is this woman that you fear?
OEDIPUS: It is Meropê, man; the wife of King Polybos.
MESSENGER: Meropê? Why should you be afraid of her?   1025
OEDIPUS: An oracle of the gods, a dreadful saying.
MESSENGER: Can you tell me about it or are you sworn to silence?
OEDIPUS: I can tell you, and I will.
Apollo said through his prophet that I was the man
Who should marry his own mother, shed his father's blood   1030
With his own hands. And so, for all these years
I have kept clear of Corinth, and no harm has come—
Though it would have been sweet to see my parents again.
MESSENGER: And is this the fear that drove you out of Corinth?
OEDIPUS: Would you have me kill my father?   1035
MESSENGER: As for that
You must be reassured by the news I gave you.
OEDIPUS: If you could reassure me, I would reward you.
MESSENGER: I had that in mind, I will confess: I thought
I could count on you when you returned to Corinth.   1040
OEDIPUS: No: I will never go near my parents again.
MESSENGER: Ah, son, you still do not know what you are doing—
OEDIPUS: What do you mean? In the name of God tell me!
MESSENGER: —If these are your reasons for not going home.
OEDIPUS: I tell you, I fear the oracle may come true.   1045
MESSENGER: And guilt may come upon you through your parents?
OEDIPUS: That is the dread that is always in my heart.
MESSENGER: Can you not see that all your fears are groundless?
OEDIPUS: How can you say that? They are my parents, surely?
MESSENGER: Polybos was not your father.   1050
OEDIPUS: Not my father?
MESSENGER: No more your father than the man speaking to you.
OEDIPUS: But you are nothing to me!
MESSENGER: Neither was he.
OEDIPUS: Then why did he call me son?   1055

MESSENGER: I will tell you:
Long ago he had you from my hands, as a gift.
OEDIPUS: Then how could he love me so, if I was not his?
MESSENGER: He had no children, and his heart turned to you.
OEDIPUS: What of you? Did you buy me? Did you find me by chance? 1060
MESSENGER: I came upon you in the crooked pass of Kithairon.
OEDIPUS: And what were you doing there?
MESSENGER: Tending my flocks.
OEDIPUS: A wandering shepherd?
MESSENGER: But your savior, son, that day. 1065
OEDIPUS: From what did you save me?
MESSENGER: Your ankles should tell you that.
OEDIPUS: Ah, stranger, why do you speak of that childhood pain?
MESSENGER: I cut the bonds that tied your ankles together.
OEDIPUS: I have had the mark as long as I can remember. 1070
MESSENGER: That was why you were given the name you bear.[18]
OEDIPUS: God! Was it my father or my mother who did it?
Tell me!
MESSENGER: I do not know. The man who gave you to me
Can tell you better than I. 1075
OEDIPUS: It was not you that found me, but another?
MESSENGER: It was another shepherd gave you to me.
OEDIPUS: Who was he? Can you tell me who he was?
MESSENGER: I think he was said to be one of Laïos' people.
OEDIPUS: You mean the Laïos who was king here years ago? 1080
MESSENGER: Yes; King Laïos; and the man was one of his herdsmen.
OEDIPUS: Is he still alive? Can I see him?
MESSENGER: These men here
Know best about such things.
OEDIPUS: Does anyone here 1085
Know this shepherd that he is talking about?
Have you seen him in the fields, or in the town?
If you have, tell me. It is time things were made plain.
CHORAGOS: I think the man he means is that same shepherd
You have already asked to see. Iocastê perhaps 1090
Could tell you something.
OEDIPUS: Do you know anything
About him, Lady? Is he the man we have summoned?
Is that the man this shepherd means?
IOCASTÊ: Why think of him? 1095
Forget this herdsman. Forget it all.
This talk is a waste of time.

---

[18] *Oedipus* means *swollen-foot*.

OEDIPUS: How can you say that,
When the clues to my true birth are in my hands?
IOCASTÊ: For God's love, let us have no more questioning!   1100
Is your life nothing to you?
My own is pain enough for me to bear.
OEDIPUS: You need not worry. Suppose my mother a slave,
And born of slaves: no baseness can touch you.
IOCASTÊ: Listen to me, I beg you: do not do this thing!   110
OEDIPUS: I will not listen; the truth must be made known.
IOCASTÊ: Everything that I say is for your own good!
OEDIPUS: My own good
Snaps my patience, then; I want none of it.
IOCASTÊ: You are fatally wrong! May you never learn who you are!   111
OEDIPUS: Go, one of you, and bring the shepherd here.
Let us leave this woman to brag of her royal name.
IOCASTÊ: Ah, miserable!
That is the only word I have for you now.
That is the only word I can ever have.   111

> *[Exit into the palace.]*

CHORAGOS: Why has she left us, Oedipus? Why has she gone
In such a passion of sorrow? I fear this silence:
Something dreadful may come of it.
OEDIPUS: Let it come!
However base my birth, I must know about it.   112
The Queen, like a woman, is perhaps ashamed
To think of my low origin. But I
Am a child of Luck; I cannot be dishonored.
Luck is my mother; the passing months, my brothers,
Have seen me rich and poor.   112
                              If this is so,
How could I wish that I were someone else?
How could I not be glad to know my birth?

Ode III

CHORUS: If ever the coming time were known
To my heart's pondering,   113
Kithairon, now by Heaven I see the torches
At the festival of the next full moon,
And see the dance, and hear the choir sing
A grace to your gentle shade:
Mountain where Oedipus was found,   113
O mountain guard of a noble race!

May the god who heals us lend his aid,
And let that glory come to pass
For our king's cradling-ground.

Of the nymphs that flower beyond the years,   ANTISTROPHE
Who bore you, royal child,   1140
To Pan of the hills or the timberline Apollo,
Cold in delight where the upland clears,
Or Hermês for whom Kyllenê's[19] heights are piled?
Or flushed as evening cloud,   1145
Great Dionysos, roamer of mountains,
He—was it he who found you there,
And caught you up in his own proud
Arms from the sweet god-ravisher[20]
Who laughed by the Muses' fountains?[21]   1150

Scene IV

OEDIPUS: Sirs: though I do not know the man,
  I think I see him coming, this shepherd we want:
  He is old, like our friend here, and the men
  Bringing him seem to be servants of my house.
  But you can tell, if you have ever seen him.   1155
        [*Enter* SHEPHERD *escorted by servants.*]
CHORAGOS: I know him, he was Laïos' man. You can trust him.
OEDIPUS: Tell me first, you from Corinth: is this the shepherd
  We were discussing?
MESSENGER: This is the very man.
OEDIPUS [*to* SHEPHERD]: Come here. No, look at me. You must answer   1160
  Everything I ask.—You belonged to Laïos?
SHEPHERD: Yes: born his slave, brought up in his house.
OEDIPUS: Tell me: what kind of work did you do for him?
SHEPHERD: I was a shepherd of his, most of my life.
OEDIPUS: Where mainly did you go for pasturage?   1165
SHEPHERD: Sometimes Kithairon, sometimes the hills near-by.
OEDIPUS: Do you remember ever seeing this man out there?
SHEPHERD: What would he be doing there? This man?
OEDIPUS: This man standing here. Have you ever seen him before?
SHEPHERD: No. At least, not to my recollection.   1170

---

[19]Highest mountain in the Peloponnesus, sacred to Hermes.
[20]Nymph whom the chorus conjecture to have been Oedipus' mother.
[21]Springs of Helicon, sacred to Apollo and the Muses.

MESSENGER: And that is not strange, my lord. But I'll refresh
   His memory: he must remember when we two
   Spent three whole seasons together, March to September,
   On Kithairon or thereabouts. He had two flocks;
   I had one. Each autumn I'd drive mine home   1175
   And he would go back with his to Laïos' sheepfold.—
   Is this not true, just as I have described it?
SHEPHERD: True, yes; but it was all so long ago.
MESSENGER: Well, then: do you remember, back in those days,
   That you gave me a baby boy to bring up as my own?   1180
SHEPHERD: What if I did? What are you trying to say?
MESSENGER: King Oedipus was once that little child.
SHEPHERD: Damn you, hold your tongue!
OEDIPUS: No more of that!
   It is your tongue needs watching, not this man's.   1185
SHEPHERD: My King, my Master, what is it I have done wrong?
OEDIPUS: You have not answered his question about the boy.
SHEPHERD: He does not know . . . He is only making trouble . . .
OEDIPUS: Come, speak plainly, or it will go hard with you.
SHEPHERD: In God's name, do not torture an old man!   1190
OEDIPUS: Come here, one of you; bind his arms behind him.
SHEPHERD: Unhappy king! What more do you wish to learn?
OEDIPUS: Did you give this man the child he speaks of?
SHEPHERD: I did.
   And I would to God I had died that very day.   1195
OEDIPUS: You will die now unless you speak the truth.
SHEPHERD: Yet if I speak the truth, I am worse than dead.
OEDIPUS: Very well; since you insist upon delaying—
SHEPHERD: No! I have told you already that I gave him the boy.
OEDIPUS: Where did you get him? From your house? From somewhere else? 1200
SHEPHERD: Not from mine, no. A man gave him to me.
OEDIPUS: Is that man here? Do you know whose slave he was?
SHEPHERD: For God's love, my King, do not ask me any more!
OEDIPUS: You are a dead man if I have to ask you again.
SHEPHERD: Then . . . Then the child was from the palace of Laïos.   1205
OEDIPUS: A slave child? or a child of his own line?
SHEPHERD: Ah, I am on the brink of dreadful speech!
OEDIPUS: And I of dreadful hearing. Yet I must hear.
SHEPHERD: If you must be told, then . . .
                          They said it was Laïos' child;   1210
   But it is your wife who can tell you about that.
OEDIPUS: My wife!—Did she give it to you?
SHEPHERD: My lord, she did.
OEDIPUS: Do you know why?

SHEPHERD: I was told to get rid of it.   1215
OEDIPUS: An unspeakable mother!
SHEPHERD: There had been prophecies . . .
OEDIPUS: Tell me.
SHEPHERD: It was said that the boy would kill his own father.
OEDIPUS: Then why did you give him over to this old man?   1220
SHEPHERD: I pitied the baby, my King,
    And I thought that this man would take him far away
    To his own country.
                    He saved him—but for what a fate!
    For if you are what this man says you are,   1225
    No man living is more wretched than Oedipus.
OEDIPUS: Ah God!
    It was true!
            All the prophecies!
                    —Now,   1230
    O Light, may I look on you for the last time!
    I, Oedipus,
    Oedipus, damned in his birth, in his marriage damned,
    Damned in the blood he shed with his own hand!
                                    [*He rushes into the palace.*]

Ode IV

CHORUS: Alas for the seed of men.   STROPHE 1

    What measure shall I give these generations
    That breathe on the void and are void
    And exist and do not exist?

    Who bears more weight of joy
    Than mass of sunlight shifting in images,   1240
    Or who shall make his thought stay on
    That down time drifts away?

    Your splendor is all fallen.

    O naked brow of wrath and tears,
    O change of Oedipus!   1245
    I who saw your days call no man blest—
    Your great days like ghosts gone.

    That mind was a strong bow.   ANTISTROPHE 1
    Deep, how deep you drew it then, hard archer,

At a dim fearful range,   1250
And brought dear glory down!

You overcame the stranger—
The virgin with her hooking lion claws—
And though death sang, stood like a tower
To make pale Thebes take heart.   1255

Fortress against our sorrow!

Divine king, giver of laws,
Majestic Oedipus!
No prince in Thebes had ever such renown,
No prince won such grace of power.   1260

And now of all men ever known   STROPHE 2
Most pitiful is this man's story:
His fortunes are most changed, his state
Fallen to a low slave's
Ground under bitter fate.   1265

O Oedipus, most royal one!
The great door that expelled you to the light
Gave at night—ah, gave night to your glory:
As to the father, to the fathering son.

All understood too late.   1270

How could that queen whom Laïos won,
The garden that he harrowed at his height,
Be silent when that act was done?

But all eyes fail before time's eye,   ANTISTROPHE 2
All actions come to justice there.   1275
Though never willed, though far down the deep past,
Your bed, your dread sirings,
Are brought to book at last.
Child by Laïos doomed to die,
Then doomed to lose that fortunate little death,   1280
Would God you never took breath in this air
That with my wailing lips I take to cry:

For I weep the world's outcast.

Blind I was, and cannot tell why;

Asleep, for you had given ease of breath;   1285
A fool, while the false years went by.

Exodos

[*Enter, from the palace,* SECOND MESSENGER.]
2ND MESSENGER: Elders of Thebes, most honored in this land,
  What horrors are yours to see and hear, what weight
  Of sorrow to be endured, if, true to your birth,
  You venerate the line of Labdakos!   1290
  I think neither Istros nor Phasis,²² those great rivers,
  Could purify this place of the corruption
  It shelters now, or soon must bring to light—
  Evil not done unconsciously, but willed.

  The greatest griefs are those we cause ourselves.   1295
CHORAGOS: Surely, friend, we have grief enough already;
  What new sorrow do you mean?
2ND MESSENGER: The Queen is dead.
CHORAGOS: Iocastê? Dead? But at whose hand?
2ND MESSENGER: Her own.   1300
  The full horror of what happened you cannot know,
  For you did not see it; but I, who did, will tell you
  As clearly as I can how she met her death.

  When she had left us,
  In passionate silence, passing through the court,   1305
  She ran to her apartment in the house,
  Her hair clutched by the fingers of both hands.
  She closed the doors behind her; then, by that bed
  Where long ago the fatal son was conceived—
  That son who should bring about his father's death—   1310
  We heard her call upon Laïos, dead so many years,
  And heard her wail for the double fruit of her marriage,
  A husband by her husband, children by her child.
  Exactly how she died I do not know:
  For Oedipus burst in moaning and would not let us   1315
  Keep vigil to the end: it was by him
  As he stormed about the room that our eyes were caught.
  From one to another of us he went, begging a sword,
  Cursing the wife who was not his wife, the mother
  Whose womb had carried his own children and himself.   1320
  I do not know: it was none of us aided him,

---

²²The Danube and the Rion, conventional types of great rivers.

But surely one of the gods was in control!
For with a dreadful cry
He hurled his weight, as though wrenched out of himself,
At the twin doors: the bolts gave, and he rushed in.   1325
And there we saw her hanging, her body swaying
From the cruel cord she had noosed about her neck.
A great sob broke from him, heartbreaking to hear,
As he loosed the rope and lowered her to the ground.

I would blot out from my mind what happened next!   1330
For the King ripped from her gown the golden brooches
That were her ornament, and raised them, and plunged them down
Straight into his own eyeballs, crying, "No more,
No more shall you look on the misery about me,
The horrors of my own doing! Too long you have known   1335
The faces of those whom I should never have seen,
Too long been blind to those for whom I was searching!
From this hour, go in darkness!" And as he spoke,
He struck at his eyes—not once, but many times;
And the blood spattered his beard,   1340
Bursting from his ruined sockets like red hail.
So from the unhappiness of two this evil has sprung,
A curse on the man and woman alike. The old
Happiness of the house of Labdakos
Was happiness enough: where is it today?   1345
It is all wailing and ruin, disgrace, death—all
The misery of mankind that has a name—
And it is wholly and forever theirs.

CHORAGOS: Is he in agony still? Is there no rest for him?

2ND MESSENGER: He is calling for someone to lead him to the gates   1350
So that all the children of Kadmos may look upon
His father's murderer, his mother's—no,
I can not say it!
         And then he will leave Thebes,
Self-exiled, in order that the curse   1355
Which he himself pronounced may depart from the house.
He is weak, and there is none to lead him,
So terrible is his suffering.
         But you will see:
Look, the doors are opening; in a moment   1360
You will see a thing that would crush a heart of stone.

[*The central door is opened;* OEDIPUS, *blinded, is led in.*]

CHORAGOS: Dreadful indeed for men to see.

Never have my own eyes
Looked on a sight so full of fear.

Oedipus!   1365
What madness came upon you, what daemon
Leaped on your life with heavier
Punishment than a mortal man can bear?
No: I cannot even
Look at you, poor ruined one.   1370
And I would speak, question, ponder,
If I were able. No.
You make me shudder.
OEDIPUS: God.   God.
   Is there a sorrow greater?   1375
   Where shall I find harbor in this world?
   My voice is hurled far on a dark wind.
   What has God done to me?
CHORAGOS: Too terrible to think of, or to see.
OEDIPUS: O cloud of night,   STROPHE 1
   Never to be turned away: night coming on,
   I can not tell how: night like a shroud!

   My fair winds brought me here.
                              O God. Again
   The pain of the spikes where I had sight,   1385
   The flooding pain
   Of memory, never to be gouged out.
CHORAGOS: This is not strange.
   You suffer it all twice over, remorse in pain,
   Pain in remorse.   1390

OEDIPUS: Ah dear friend   ANTISTROPHE 1
   Are you faithful even yet, you alone?
   Are you still standing near me, will you stay here,
   Patient, to care for the blind?
                              The blind man!   1395
   Yet even blind I know who it is attends me,
   By the voice's tone—
   Though my new darkness hide the comforter.
CHORAGOS: Oh fearful act!
   What god was it drove you to rake black   1400
   Night across your eyes?

OEDIPUS: Apollo. Apollo. Dear   STROPHE 2
   Children, the god was Apollo.

He brought my sick, sick fate upon me.
But the blinding hand was my own!   1405
How could I bear to see
When all my sight was horror everywhere?
CHORAGOS: Everywhere; that is true.
OEDIPUS: And now what is left?
Images? Love? A greeting even,   1410
Sweet to the senses? Is there anything?
Ah, no, friends: lead me away.
Lead me away from Thebes.
                              Lead the great wreck
And hell of Oedipus, whom the gods hate.   1415
CHORAGOS: Your fate is clear, you are not blind to that.
Would God you had never found it out!

OEDIPUS: Death take the man who unbound   ANTISTROPHE 2
My feet on that hillside
And delivered me from death to life! What life?   1420
If only I had died,
This weight of monstrous doom
Could not have dragged me and my darlings down.
CHORAGOS: I would have wished the same.
OEDIPUS: Oh never to have come here   1425
With my father's blood upon me! Never
To have been the man they call his mother's husband!
Oh accurst! Oh child of evil,
To have entered that wretched bed—
                              the selfsame one!   1430
More primal than sin itself, this fell to me.
CHORAGOS: I do not know how I can answer you.
You were better dead than alive and blind.
OEDIPUS: Do not counsel me any more. This punishment
That I have laid upon myself is just.   1435
If I had eyes,
I do not know how I could bear the sight
Of my father, when I came to the house of Death,
Or my mother: for I have sinned against them both
So vilely that I could not make my peace   1440
By strangling my own life.
                              Or do you think my children,
Born as they were born, would be sweet to my eyes?
Ah never, never! Nor this town with its high walls,
Nor the holy images of the gods.   1445
                              For I,
Thrice miserable!—Oedipus, noblest of all the line

Of Kadmos, have condemned myself to enjoy
These things no more, by my own malediction
Expelling that man whom the gods declared   1450
To be a defilement in the house of Laïos.
After exposing the rankness of my own guilt,
How could I look men frankly in the eyes?
No, I swear it,
If I could have stifled my hearing at its source,   1455
I would have done it and made all this body
A tight cell of misery, blank to light and sound:
So I should have been safe in a dark agony
Beyond all recollection.
                         Ah Kithairon!   1460
Why did you shelter me? When I was cast upon you,
Why did I not die? Then I should never
Have shown the world my execrable birth.

Ah Polybos! Corinth, city that I believed
The ancient seat of my ancestors: how fair   1465
I seemed, your child! And all the while this evil
Was cancerous within me!
                         For I am sick
In my daily life, sick in my origin.

O three roads, dark ravine, woodland and way   1470
Where three roads met: you, drinking my father's blood,
My own blood, spilled by my own hand: can you remember
The unspeakable things I did there, and the things
I went on from there to do?
                         O marriage, marriage!   1475
The act that engendered me, and again the act
Performed by the son in the same bed—
                         Ah, the net
Of incest, mingling fathers, brothers, sons,
With brides, wives, mothers: the last evil   1480
That can be known by men: no tongue can say
How evil!
         No. For the love of God, conceal me
Somewhere far from Thebes; or kill me; or hurl me
Into the sea, away from men's eyes forever.   1485

Come, lead me. You need not fear to touch me.
Of all men, I alone bear this guilt.
                    [*Enter* CREON.]
CHORAGOS: We are not the ones to decide; but Creon here
    May fitly judge of what you ask. He only

Is left to protect the city in your place.   1490
OEDIPUS: Alas, how can I speak to him? What right have I
　　To beg his courtesy whom I have deeply wronged?
CREON: I have not come to mock you, Oedipus,
　　Or to reproach you, either.
　　　　　　　　[*to* ATTENDANTS]—You, standing there: 1495
　　If you have lost all respect for man's dignity,
　　At least respect the flame of Lord Helios:
　　Do not allow this pollution to show itself
　　Openly here, an affront to the earth
　　And Heaven's rain and the light of day. No, take him   1500
　　Into the house as quickly as you can.
　　For it is proper
　　That only the close kindred see his grief.
OEDIPUS: I pray you in God's name, since your courtesy
　　Ignores my dark expectation, visiting   1505
　　With mercy this man of all men most execrable:
　　Give me what I ask—for your good, not for mine.
CREON: And what is it that you would have me do?
OEDIPUS: Drive me out of this country as quickly as may be
　　To a place where no human voice can ever greet me.   1510
CREON: I should have done that before now—only,
　　God's will had not been wholly revealed to me.
OEDIPUS: But his command is plain: the parricide
　　Must be destroyed. I am that evil man.
CREON: That is the sense of it, yes; but as things are,   1515
　　We had best discover clearly what is to be done.
OEDIPUS: You would learn more about a man like me?
CREON: You are ready now to listen to the god.
OEDIPUS: I will listen. But it is to you
　　That I must turn for help. I beg you, hear me.   1520

The woman in there—
Give her whatever funeral you think proper:
She is your sister.
　　　　　　—But let me go, Creon!
Let me purge my father's Thebes of the pollution   1525
Of my living here, and go out to the wild hills,
To Kithairon, that has won such fame with me,
The tomb my mother and father appointed for me,
And let me die there, as they willed I should.
And yet I know   1530
Death will not ever come to me through sickness
Or in any natural way: I have been preserved
For some unthinkable fate. But let that be.

As for my sons, you need not care for them.
They are men, they will find some way to live.   1535
But my poor daughters, who have shared my table,
Who never before have been parted from their father—
Take care of them, Creon; do this for me.
And will you let me touch them with my hands
A last time, and let us weep together?   1540
Be kind, my lord,
Great prince, be kind!

                  Could I but touch them,
They would be mine again, as when I had my eyes.
            [*Enter* ANTIGONE *and* ISMENE, *attended.*]
Ah, God!   1545
Is it my dearest children I hear weeping?
Has Creon pitied me and sent my daughters?
CREON: Yes, Oedipus: I knew that they were dear to you
In the old days, and know you must love them still.
OEDIPUS: May God bless you for this—and be a friendlier   1550
Guardian to you than he has been to me!

Children, where are you?
Come quickly to my hands: they are your brother's—
Hands that have brought your father's once clear eyes
To this way of seeing—   1555
                 Ah dearest ones,
I had neither sight nor knowledge then, your father
By the woman who was the source of his own life!
And I weep for you—having no strength to see you—,
I weep for you when I think of the bitterness   1560
That men will visit upon you all your lives.
What homes, what festivals can you attend
Without being forced to depart again in tears?
And when you come to marriageable age,
Where is the man, my daughters, who would dare   1565
Risk the bane that lies on all my children?
Is there any evil wanting? Your father killed
His father; sowed the womb of her who bore him;
Engendered you at the fount of his own existence!

That is what they will say of you.   1570

                   Then, whom
Can you ever marry? There are no bridegrooms for you,
And your lives must wither away in sterile dreaming.

O Creon, son of Menoikeus!
You are the only father my daughters have,   1575
Since we, their parents, are both of us gone forever.
They are your own blood: you will not let them
Fall into beggary and loneliness;
You will keep them from the miseries that are mine!
Take pity on them; see, they are only children,   1580
Friendless except for you. Promise me this,
Great Prince, and give me your hand in token of it.
[CREON *clasps his right hand.*]
Children:
I could say much, if you could understand me,
But as it is, I have only this prayer for you: 1585
Live where you can, be as happy as you can—
Happier, please God, than God has made your father!
CREON: Enough. You have wept enough. Now go within.
OEDIPUS: I must; but it is hard.
CREON: Time eases all things.   1590
OEDIPUS: But you must promise—
CREON: Say what you desire.
OEDIPUS: Send me from Thebes!
CREON: God grant that I may!
OEDIPUS: But since God hates me . . .   1595
CREON: No, he will grant your wish.
OEDIPUS: You promise?
CREON: I cannot speak beyond my knowledge.
OEDIPUS: Then lead me in.
CREON: Come now, and leave your children.   1600
OEDIPUS: No! Do not take them from me!
CREON: Think no longer
That you are in command here, but rather think
How, when you were, you served your own destruction.
        [*Exeunt into the house all but the* CHORUS; *the* CHORAGOS
                chants directly to the audience.]
CHORAGOS: Men of Thebes: look upon Oedipus.   1605
This is the king who solved the famous riddle
And towered up, most powerful of men.
No mortal eyes but looked on him with envy,
Yet in the end ruin swept over him.

Let every man in mankind's frailty   1610
Consider his last day; and let none
Presume on his good fortune until he find
Life, at his death, a memory without pain.

Henrik Ibsen (1828–1906)

AN ENEMY OF THE PEOPLE

A Play in Five Acts (1882)

CHARACTERS

DR. THOMAS STOCKMANN:	*physician at the Baths*
MRS. KATHERINE STOCKMANN:	*his wife*
PETRA:	*their daughter, a schoolteacher*
EJLIF MORTEN	*their sons, aged thirteen and ten*
PETER STOCKMANN:	*the doctor's elder brother; Mayor and Chief of Police; Chairman of the Board at the Baths*
MORTEN KIIL:	*owner of a tannery; Mrs. Stockmann's foster-father*
HOVSTAD:	*editor of The People's Messenger*
BILLING:	*his colleague on the paper*
CAPTAIN HORSTER	
ASLAKSEN:	*a printer* *Citizens of various types and standing; some women and a number of schoolboys* *The action takes place in a town on the South Coast of Norway.*

ACT I

[SCENE: DR. STOCKMANN'S *sitting-room. It is evening. The room is plainly but neatly appointed and furnished. In the right-hand wall are two doors; the farther*

SOURCE: Reprinted from *Ghosts; An Enemy of the People; The Warriors at Helgeland* by Henrik Ibsen, translated by R. Farquharson Sharp, with the permission of E. P. Dutton & Co., Inc., New York and J. M. Dent & Sons Ltd., London.

leads out to the hall, the nearer to the doctor's study. In the left-hand wall, opposite the door leading to the hall, is a door leading to the other rooms occupied by the family. In the middle of the same wall stands the stove, and, further forward, a couch with a looking-glass hanging over it and an oval table in front of it. On the table, a lighted lamp, with a lampshade. At the back of the room, an open door leads to the dining-room. BILLING *is seen sitting at the dining table, on which a lamp is burning. He has a napkin tucked under his chin, and* MRS. STOCKMANN *is standing by the table handing him a large plate-full of roast beef. The other places at the table are empty, and the table somewhat in disorder, a meal having evidently recently been finished.*]

MRS. STOCKMANN: You see, if you come an hour late, Mr. Billing, you have to put up with cold meat.

BILLING [*as he eats*]: It is uncommonly good, thank you—remarkably good.

MRS. STOCKMANN: My husband makes such a point of having his meals punctually, you know—

BILLING: That doesn't affect me a bit. Indeed, I almost think I enjoy a meal all the better when I can sit down and eat all by myself and undisturbed.

MRS. STOCKMANN: Oh well, as long as you are enjoying it—. [*Turns to the hall door, listening.*] I expect that is Mr. Hovstad coming too.

BILLING: Very likely.

[PETER STOCKMANN *comes in. He wears an overcoat and his official hat, and carries a stick.*]

PETER STOCKMANN: Good evening, Katherine.

MRS. STOCKMANN [*coming forward into the sitting-room*]: Ah, good evening— is it you? How good of you to come up and see us!

PETER STOCKMANN: I happened to be passing, and so—[*looks into the dining-room*]. But you have company with you, I see.

MRS. STOCKMANN [*a little embarrassed*]: Oh, no—it was quite by chance he came in. [*Hurriedly.*] Won't you come in and have something, too?

PETER STOCKMANN: I! No, thank you. Good gracious—hot meat at night! Not with my digestion.

MRS. STOCKMANN: Oh, but just once in a way—

PETER STOCKMANN: No, no, my dear lady; I stick to my tea and bread and butter. It is much more wholesome in the long run—and a little more economical, too.

MRS. STOCKMANN [*smiling*]: Now you mustn't think that Thomas and I are spendthrifts.

PETER STOCKMANN: Not you, my dear; I would never think that of you. [*Points to the Doctor's study.*] Is he not at home?

MRS. STOCKMANN: No, he went for a little turn after supper—he and the boys.

PETER STOCKMANN: I doubt if that is a wise thing to do. [*Listens.*] I fancy I hear him coming now.

MRS. STOCKMANN: No, I don't think it is he. [*A knock is heard at the door.*] Come in! [HOVSTAD *comes in from the hall.*] Oh, it is you, Mr. Hovstad!

HOVSTAD: Yes, I hope you will forgive me, but I was delayed at the printers. Good evening, Mr. Mayor.

PETER STOCKMANN [*bowing a little distantly*]: Good evening. You have come on business, no doubt.

HOVSTAD: Partly. It's about an article for the paper.

PETER STOCKMANN: So I imagined. I hear my brother has become a prolific contributor to the "People's Messenger."

HOVSTAD: Yes, he is good enough to write in the "People's Messenger" when he has any home truths to tell.

MRS. STOCKMANN [*to* HOVSTAD]: But won't you—? [*Points to the dining-room.*]

PETER STOCKMANN: Quite so, quite so. I don't blame him in the least, as a writer, for addressing himself to the quarters where he will find the readiest sympathy. And, besides that, I personally have no reason to bear any ill will to your paper, Mr. Hovstad.

HOVSTAD: I quite agree with you.

PETER STOCKMANN: Taking one thing with another, there is an excellent spirit of toleration in the town—an admirable municipal spirit. And it all springs from the fact of our having a great common interest to unite us—an interest that is in an equally high degree the concern of every right-minded citizen—

HOVSTAD: The Baths, yes.

PETER STOCKMANN: Exactly—our fine, new, handsome Baths. Mark my words, Mr. Hovstad—the Baths will become the focus of our municipal life! Not a doubt of it!

MRS. STOCKMANN: That is just what Thomas says.

PETER STOCKMANN: Think how extraordinarily the place has developed within the last year or two! Money has been flowing in, and there is some life and some business doing in the town. Houses and landed property are rising in value every day.

HOVSTAD: And unemployment is diminishing.

PETER STOCKMANN: Yes, that is another thing. The burden of the poor rates has been lightened, to the great relief of the propertied classes; and that relief will be even greater if only we get a really good summer this year, and lots of visitors—plenty of invalids, who will make the Baths talked about.

HOVSTAD: And there is a good prospect of that, I hear.

PETER STOCKMANN: It looks very promising. Enquiries about apartments and that sort of thing are reaching us every day.

HOVSTAD: Well, the doctor's article will come in very suitably.

PETER STOCKMANN: Has he been writing something just lately?

HOVSTAD: This is something he wrote in the winter; a recommendation of the Baths—an account of the excellent sanitary conditions here. But I held the article over, temporarily.

PETER STOCKMANN: Ah,—some little difficulty about it, I suppose?

HOVSTAD: No, not at all; I thought it would be better to wait till the spring, because it is just at this time that people begin to think seriously about their summer quarters.

PETER STOCKMANN: Quite right; you were perfectly right, Mr. Hovstad.

HOVSTAD: Yes, Thomas is really indefatigable when it is a question of the Baths.

PETER STOCKMANN: Well—remember, he is the Medical Officer to the Baths.

HOVSTAD: Yes, and what is more, they owe their existence to him.

PETER STOCKMANN: To him? Indeed! It is true I have heard from time to time that some people are of that opinion. At the same time I must say I imagined that I took a modest part in the enterprise.

MRS. STOCKMANN: Yes, that is what Thomas is always saying.

HOVSTAD: But who denies it, Mr. Stockmann? You set the thing going and made a practical concern of it; we all know that. I only meant that the idea of it came first from the doctor.

PETER STOCKMANN: Oh, ideas—yes! My brother has had plenty of them in his time—unfortunately. But when it is a question of putting an idea into practical shape, you have to apply to a man of different mettle, Mr. Hovstad. And I certainly should have thought that in this house at least—

MRS. STOCKMANN: My dear Peter—

HOVSTAD: How can you think that—?

MRS. STOCKMANN: Won't you go in and have something, Mr. Hovstad? My husband is sure to be back directly.

HOVSTAD: Thank you, perhaps just a morsel. [*Goes into the dining-room.*]

PETER STOCKMANN [*lowering his voice a little*]: It is a curious thing that these farmers' sons never seem to lose their want of tact.

MRS. STOCKMANN: Surely it is not worth bothering about! Cannot you and Thomas share the credit as brothers?

PETER STOCKMANN: I should have thought so; but apparently some people are not satisfied with a share.

MRS. STOCKMANN: What nonsense! You and Thomas get on so capitally together. [*Listens.*] There he is at last, I think. [*Goes out and opens the door leading to the hall.*]

DR. STOCKMANN [*laughing and talking outside*]: Look here—here is another guest for you, Katherine. Isn't that jolly! Come in, Captain Horster; hang your coat upon this peg. Ah, you don't wear an overcoat. Just think, Katherine; I met him in the street and could hardly persuade him to come up! [CAPTAIN HORSTER *comes into the room and greets* MRS. STOCK-MANN. *He is followed by* DR. STOCKMANN.] Come along in, boys. They are ravenously hungry again, you know. Come along, Captain Horster; you must have a slice of beef. [*Pushes* HORSTER *into the dining-room.* EJLIF *and* MORTEN *go in after them.*]

MRS. STOCKMANN: But, Thomas, don't you see—?

DR. STOCKMANN [*turning in the doorway*]: Oh, is it you, Peter? [*Shakes hands with him.*] Now that is very delightful.

PETER STOCKMANN: Unfortunately I must go in a moment—

DR. STOCKMANN: Rubbish! There is some toddy just coming in. You haven't forgotten the toddy, Katherine?

MRS. STOCKMANN: Of course not; the water is boiling now. [*Goes into the dining-room.*]

PETER STOCKMANN: Toddy too!

DR. STOCKMANN: Yes, sit down and we will have it comfortably.

PETER STOCKMANN: Thanks, I never care about an evening's drinking.

DR. STOCKMANN: But this isn't an evening's drinking.

PETER STOCKMANN: It seems to me—. [*Looks towards the dining-room.*] It is extraordinary how they can put away all that food.

DR. STOCKMANN [*rubbing his hands*]: Yes, isn't it splendid to see young people eat? They have always got an appetite, you know! That's as it should be. Lots of food—to build up their strength! They are the people who are going to stir up the fermenting forces of the future, Peter.

PETER STOCKMANN: May I ask what they will find here to "stir up," as you put it?

DR. STOCKMANN: Ah, you must ask the young people that—when the time comes. We shan't be able to see it, of course. That stands to reason— two old fogies, like us—

PETER STOCKMANN: Really, really! I must say that is an extremely odd expression to—

DR. STOCKMANN: Oh, you mustn't take me too literally, Peter. I am so heartily happy and contented, you know. I think it is such an extraordinary piece of good fortune to be in the middle of all this growing, germinating life. It is a splendid time to live in! It is as if a whole new world were being created around one.

PETER STOCKMANN: Do you really think so?

DR. STOCKMANN: Ah, naturally you can't appreciate it as keenly as I. You have lived all your life in these surroundings, and your impressions have got blunted. But I, who have been buried all these years in my little corner up north, almost without ever seeing a stranger who might bring new ideas with him—well, in my case it has just the same effect as if I had been transported into the middle of a crowded city.

PETER STOCKMANN: Oh, a city—!

DR. STOCKMANN: I know, I know; it is all cramped enough here, compared with many other places. But there is life here—there is promise—there are innumerable things to work for and fight for; and that is the main thing. [*Calls.*] Katherine, hasn't the postman been here?

MRS. STOCKMANN [*from the dining-room*]: No.

DR. STOCKMANN: And then to be comfortably off, Peter! That is something one learns to value, when one has been on the brink of starvation, as we have.

PETER STOCKMANN: Oh, surely—

DR. STOCKMANN: Indeed I can assure you we have often been very hard put to it, up there. And now to be able to live like a lord! Today, for instance, we had roast beef for dinner—and, what is more, for supper too. Won't you come and have a little bit? Or let me show it you, at any rate? Come here—

PETER STOCKMANN: No, no—not for worlds!

DR. STOCKMANN: Well, but just come here then. Do you see, we have got a table-cover?

PETER STOCKMANN: Yes, I noticed it.

DR. STOCKMANN: And we have got a lamp-shade too. Do you see? All out of Katherine's savings! It makes the room so cosy. Don't you think so? Just stand here for a moment—no, no, not there—just here, that's it! Look now, when you get the light on it altogether—I really think it looks very nice, doesn't it?

PETER STOCKMANN: Oh, if you can afford luxuries of this kind—

DR. STOCKMANN: Yes, I can afford it now. Katherine tells me I earn almost as much as we spend.

PETER STOCKMANN: Almost—yes!

DR. STOCKMANN: But a scientific man must live in a little bit of style. I am quite sure an ordinary civil servant spends more in a year than I do.

PETER STOCKMANN: I daresay. A civil servant—a man in a well-paid position—

DR. STOCKMANN: Well, any ordinary merchant, then! A man in that position spends two or three times as much as—

PETER STOCKMANN: It just depends on circumstances.

DR. STOCKMANN: At all events I assure you I don't waste money unprofitably. But I can't find it in my heart to deny myself the pleasure of entertaining my friends. I need that sort of thing, you know. I have lived for so long shut out of it all, that it is a necessity of life to me to mix with young, eager, ambitious men, men of liberal and active minds; and that describes every one of those fellows who are enjoying their supper in there. I wish you knew more of Hovstad—

PETER STOCKMANN: By the way, Hovstad was telling me he was going to print another article of yours.

DR. STOCKMANN: An article of mine?

PETER STOCKMANN: Yes, about the Baths. An article you wrote in the winter.

DR. STOCKMANN: Oh, that one! No, I don't intend that to appear just for the present.

PETER STOCKMANN: Why not? It seems to me that this would be the most opportune moment.

DR. STOCKMANN: Yes, very likely—under normal conditions. [*Crosses the room.*]

PETER STOCKMANN [*following him with his eyes*]: Is there anything abnormal about the present conditions?

DR. STOCKMANN [*standing still*]: To tell you the truth, Peter, I can't say just at this moment—at all events not tonight. There may be much that is very abnormal about the present conditions—and it is possible there may be nothing abnormal about them at all. It is quite possible it may be merely my imagination.

PETER STOCKMANN: I must say it all sounds most mysterious. Is there something going on that I am to be kept in ignorance of? I should have imagined that I, as Chairman of the governing body of the Baths—

DR. STOCKMANN: And I should have imagined that I—. Oh, come, don't let us fly out at one another, Peter.

PETER STOCKMANN: Heaven forbid! I am not in the habit of flying out at people, as you call it. But I am entitled to request most emphatically that all arrangements shall be made in a business-like manner, through the proper channels, and shall be dealt with by the legally constituted authorities. I can allow no going behind our backs by any roundabout means.

DR. STOCKMANN: Have I ever at any time tried to go behind your backs!

PETER STOCKMANN: You have an ingrained tendency to take your own way, at all events; and that is almost equally inadmissible in a well-ordered community. The individual ought undoubtedly to acquiesce in subordinating himself to the community—or, to speak more accurately, to the authorities who have the care of the community's welfare.

DR. STOCKMANN: Very likely. But what the deuce has all this got to do with me?

PETER STOCKMANN: That is exactly what you never appear to be willing to learn, my dear Thomas. But, mark my words, some day you will have to suffer for it—sooner or later. Now I have told you. Good-bye.

DR. STOCKMANN: Have you taken leave of your senses? You are on the wrong scent altogether.

PETER STOCKMANN: I am not usually that. You must excuse me now if I— [*calls into the dining-room*]. Good night, Katherine. Good night, gentlemen. [*Goes out.*]

MRS. STOCKMANN [*coming from the dining-room*]: Has he gone?

DR. STOCKMANN: Yes, and in such a bad temper.

MRS. STOCKMANN: But, dear Thomas, what have you been doing to him again?

DR. STOCKMANN: Nothing at all. And, anyhow, he can't oblige me to make my report before the proper time.

MRS. STOCKMANN: What have you got to make a report to him about?

DR. STOCKMANN: Hm! Leave that to me, Katherine.—It is an extraordinary thing that the postman doesn't come.

[HOVSTAD, BILLING *and* HORSTER *have got up from the table and come into the sitting-room.* EJLIF *and* MORTEN *come in after them.*]

BILLING [*stretching himself*]: Ah!—one feels a new man after a meal like that.

HOVSTAD: The mayor wasn't in a very sweet temper tonight, then.

DR. STOCKMANN: It is his stomach; he has a wretched digestion.

HOVSTAD: I rather think it was us two of the "People's Messenger" that he couldn't digest.

MRS. STOCKMANN: I thought you came out of it pretty well with him.

HOVSTAD: Oh yes; but it isn't anything more than a sort of truce.

BILLING: That is just what it is! That word sums up the situation.

DR. STOCKMANN: We must remember that Peter is a lonely man, poor chap. He has no home comforts of any kind; nothing but everlasting business. And all that infernal weak tea wash that he pours into himself! Now then, my boys, bring chairs up to the table. Aren't we going to have that toddy, Katherine?

MRS. STOCKMANN [*going into the dining-room*]: I am just getting it.

DR. STOCKMANN: Sit down here on the couch beside me, Captain Horster. We so seldom see you—. Please sit down, my friends. [*They sit down at the table.* MRS. STOCKMANN *brings a tray, with a spirit-lamp, glasses, bottles, etc., upon it.*]

MRS. STOCKMANN: There you are! This is arrack, and this is rum, and this one is the brandy. Now every one must help themselves.

DR. STOCKMANN [*taking a glass*]: We will. [*They all mix themselves some toddy.*] And let us have the cigars. Ejlif, you know where the box is. And you, Morten, can fetch my pipe. [*The two boys go into the room on the right.*] I have a suspicion that Ejlif pockets a cigar now and then!—but I take no notice of it. [*Calls out.*] And my smoking-cap too, Morten. Katherine, you can tell him where I left it. Ah, he has got it. [*The boys bring the various things.*] Now, my friends. I stick to my pipe, you know. This one has seen plenty of bad weather with me up north. [*Touches glasses with them.*] Your good health! Ah, it is good to be sitting snug and warm here.

MRS. STOCKMANN [*who sits knitting*]: Do you sail soon, Captain Horster?

HORSTER: I expect to be ready to sail next week.

MRS. STOCKMANN: I suppose you are going to America?

HORSTER: Yes, that is the plan.

MRS. STOCKMANN: Then you won't be able to take part in the coming election.

HORSTER: Is there going to be an election?

BILLING: Didn't you know?

HORSTER: No, I don't mix myself up with those things.

BILLING: But do you not take an interest in public affairs?

HORSTER: No, I don't know anything about politics.

BILLING: All the same, one ought to vote, at any rate.

HORSTER: Even if one doesn't know anything about what is going on?

BILLING: Doesn't know! What do you mean by that? A community is like a ship; every one ought to be prepared to take the helm.

HORSTER: Maybe that is all very well on shore; but on board ship it wouldn't work.

HOVSTAD: It is astonishing how little most sailors care about what goes on on shore.

BILLING: Very extraordinary.

DR. STOCKMANN: Sailors are like birds of passage; they feel equally at home in any latitude. And that is only an additional reason for our being all the more keen, Hovstad. Is there to be anything of public interest in tomorrow's "Messenger"?

HOVSTAD: Nothing about municipal affairs. But the day after tomorrow I was thinking of printing your article—

DR. STOCKMANN: Ah, devil take it—my article! Look here, that must wait a bit.

HOVSTAD: Really? We had just got convenient space for it, and I thought it was just the opportune moment—

DR. STOCKMANN: Yes, yes, very likely you are right; but it must wait all the same. I will explain to you later. [PETRA *comes in from the hall, in hat and cloak and with a bundle of exercise books under her arm.*]

PETRA: Good evening.

DR. STOCKMANN: Good evening, Petra; come along.

[*Mutual greetings;* PETRA *takes off her things and puts them down on a chair by the door.*]

PETRA: And you have all been sitting here enjoying yourselves, while I have been out slaving!

DR. STOCKMANN: Well, come and enjoy yourself too!

BILLING: May I mix a glass for you?

PETRA [*coming to the table*]: Thanks, I would rather do it; you always mix it too strong. But I forgot, father—I have a letter for you. [*Goes to the chair where she has laid her things.*]

DR. STOCKMANN: A letter? From whom?

PETRA [*looking in her coat pocket*]: The postman gave it to me just as I was going out—

DR. STOCKMANN [*getting up and going to her*]: And you only give to me now!

PETRA: I really had not time to run up again. There it is!

DR. STOCKMANN [*seizing the letter*]: Let's see, let's see, child! [*Looks at the address.*] Yes, that's all right!

MRS. STOCKMANN: Is it the one you have been expecting so anxiously, Thomas?

DR. STOCKMANN: Yes, it is. I must go to my room now and—. Where shall I get a light, Katherine? Is there no lamp in my room again?

MRS. STOCKMANN: Yes, your lamp is already lit on your desk.

DR. STOCKMANN: Good, good. Excuse me for a moment—. [*Goes into his study.*]

PETRA: What do you suppose it is, mother?

MRS. STOCKMANN: I don't know; for the last day or two he has always been asking if the postman has not been.

BILLING: Probably some country patient.

PETRA: Poor old dad!—he will overwork himself soon. [*Mixes a glass for herself.*] There, that will taste good!

HOVSTAD: Have you been teaching in the evening school again today?

PETRA [*sipping from her glass*]: Two hours.

BILLING: And four hours of school in the morning—

PETRA: Five hours.

MRS. STOCKMANN: And you have still got exercises to correct, I see.

PETRA: A whole heap, yes.

HORSTER: You are pretty full up with work too, it seems to me.

PETRA: Yes—but that is good. One is so delightfully tired after it.

BILLING: Do you like that?

PETRA: Yes, because one sleeps so well then.

MORTEN: You must be dreadfully wicked, Petra.

PETRA: Wicked?

MORTEN: Yes, because you work so much. Mr. Rörlund says work is a punishment for our sins.

EJLIF: Pooh, what a duffer you are, to believe a thing like that!

MRS. STOCKMANN: Come, come, Ejlif!

BILLING [*laughing*]: That's capital!

HOVSTAD: Don't you want to work as hard as that, Morten?

MORTEN: No, indeed I don't.

HOVSTAD: What do you want to be, then?

MORTEN: I should like best to be a Viking.

EJLIF: You would have to be a pagan then.

MORTEN: Well, I could become a pagan, couldn't I?

BILLING: I agree with you, Morten! My sentiments, exactly.

MRS. STOCKMANN [*signalling to him*]: I am sure that is not true, Mr. Billing.

BILLING: Yes, I swear it is! I am a pagan, and I am proud of it. Believe me, before long we shall all be pagans.

MORTEN: And then shall be allowed to do anything we like?

BILLING: Well, you see, Morten—.

MRS. STOCKMANN: You must go to your room now, boys; I am sure you have some lessons to learn for tomorrow.

EJLIF: I should like so much to stay a little longer—

MRS. STOCKMANN: No, no; away you go, both of you. [*The boys say good night and go into the room on the left.*]

HOVSTAD: Do you really think it can do the boys any harm to hear such things?

MRS. STOCKMANN: I don't know; but I don't like it.

PETRA: But you know, mother, I think you really are wrong about it.

MRS. STOCKMANN: Maybe, but I don't like it—not in our own home.

PETRA: There is so much falsehood both at home and at school. At home one must not speak, and at school we have to stand and tell lies to the children.

HORSTER: Tell lies?

PETRA: Yes, don't you suppose we have to teach them all sorts of things that we don't believe?

BILLING: That is perfectly true.

PETRA: If only I had the means I would start a school of my own, and it would be conducted on very different lines.

BILLING: Oh, bother the means—!

HORSTER: Well if you are thinking of that, Miss Stockmann, I shall be delighted to provide you with a schoolroom. The great big old house my father left me is standing almost empty; there is an immense dining-room downstairs—

PETRA [*laughing*]: Thank you very much; but I am afraid nothing will come of it.

HOVSTAD: No, Miss Petra is much more likely to take to journalism, I expect. By the way, have you had time to do anything with that English story you promised to translate for us?

PETRA: No, not yet; but you shall have it in good time.

[DR. STOCKMANN *comes in from his room with an open letter in his hand.*]

DR. STOCKMANN [*waving the letter*]: Well, now the town will have something new to talk about, I can tell you!

BILLING: Something new?

MRS. STOCKMANN: What is this?

DR. STOCKMANN: A great discovery, Katherine.

HOVSTAD: Really?

MRS. STOCKMANN: A discovery of yours?

DR. STOCKMANN: A discovery of mine. [*Walks up and down.*] Just let them come saying, as usual, that it is all fancy and a crazy man's imagination! But they will be careful what they say this time, I can tell you!

PETRA: But, father, tell us what it is.

DR. STOCKMANN: Yes, yes—only give me time, and you shall know all about it. If only I had Peter here now! It just shows how we men can go about forming our judgments, when in reality we are as blind as any moles—

HOVSTAD: What are you driving at, Doctor?

DR. STOCKMANN [*standing still by the table*]: Isn't it the universal opinion that our town is a healthy spot?

HOVSTAD: Certainly.

DR. STOCKMANN: Quite an unusually healthy spot, in fact—a place that deserves to be recommended in the warmest possible manner either for invalids or for people who are well—

MRS. STOCKMANN: Yes, but my dear Thomas—

DR. STOCKMANN: And we have been recommending it and praising it—I have written and written, both in the "Messenger" and in pamphlets—

HOVSTAD: Well, what then?

DR. STOCKMANN: And the Baths—we have called them the "main artery of the town's life-blood," the "nerve-centre of our town," and the devil knows what else—

BILLING: "The town's pulsating heart" was the expression I once used on an important occasion—

DR. STOCKMANN: Quite so. Well, do you know what they really are, these great, splendid, much praised Baths, that have cost so much money— do you know what they are?

HOVSTAD: No, what are they?

MRS. STOCKMANN: Yes, what are they?

DR. STOCKMANN: The whole place is a pesthouse!

PETRA: The Baths, father?

MRS. STOCKMANN [*at the same time*]: Our Baths!

HOVSTAD: But, Doctor—

BILLING: Absolutely incredible!

DR. STOCKMANN: The whole Bath establishment is a whited, poisoned sepulchre, I tell you—the gravest possible danger to the public health! All the nastiness up at Mölledal, all that stinking filth, is infecting the water in the conduit-pipes leading to the reservoir; and the same cursed, filthy poison oozes out on the shore too—

HORSTER: Where the bathing-place is?

DR. STOCKMANN: Just there.

HOVSTAD: How do you come to be so certain of all this, Doctor?

DR. STOCKMANN: I have investigated the matter most conscientiously. For a long time past I have suspected something of the kind. Last year we had some very strange cases of illness among the visitors—typhoid cases, and cases of gastric fever—

MRS. STOCKMANN: Yes, that is quite true.

DR. STOCKMANN: At the time, we supposed the visitors had been infected before they came; but later on, in the winter, I began to have a different opinion; and so I set myself to examine the water, as well as I could.

MRS. STOCKMANN: Then that is what you have been so busy with?

DR. STOCKMANN: Indeed I have been busy, Katherine. But here I had none of the necessary scientific apparatus; so I sent samples, both of the drinking-water and of the sea-water, up to the University, to have an accurate analysis made by a chemist.

HOVSTAD: And have you got that?

DR. STOCKMANN [*showing him the letter*]: Here it is! It proves the presence of decomposing organic matter in the water—it is full of infusoria. The water is absolutely dangerous to use, either internally or externally.

MRS. STOCKMANN: What a mercy you discovered it in time.

DR. STOCKMANN: You may well say so.

HOVSTAD: And what do you propose to do now, Doctor?

DR. STOCKMANN: To see the matter put right—naturally.

HOVSTAD: Can that be done?

DR. STOCKMANN: It must be done. Otherwise the Baths will be absolutely useless and wasted. But we need not anticipate that; I have a very clear idea what we shall have to do.

MRS. STOCKMANN: But why have you kept this all so secret, dear?

DR. STOCKMANN: Do you suppose I was going to run about the town gossiping about it, before I had absolute proof? No, thank you. I am not such a fool.

PETRA: Still, you might have told us—

DR. STOCKMANN: Not a living soul. But tomorrow you may run around to the old Badger—

MRS. STOCKMANN: Oh, Thomas! Thomas!

DR. STOCKMANN: Well, to your grandfather, then. The old boy will have something to be astonished at! I know he thinks I am cracked—and there are lots of other people think so too, I have noticed. But now these good folks shall see—they shall just see—! [*Walks about, rubbing his hands.*] There will be a nice upset in the town, Katherine; you can't imagine what it will be. All the conduit-pipes will have to be relaid.

HOVSTAD [*getting up*]: All the conduit-pipes—?

DR. STOCKMANN: Yes, of course. The intake is too low down; it will have to be lifted to a position much higher up.

PETRA: Then you were right after all.

DR. STOCKMANN: Ah, you remember, Petra—I wrote opposing the plans before the work was begun. But at that time no one would listen to me. Well, I am going to let them have it, now! Of course I have prepared a report for the Baths Committee; I have had it ready for a week, and was only waiting for this to come. [*Shows the letter.*] Now it shall go off at once. [*Goes into his room and comes back with some papers.*] Look at that! Four closely written sheets!—and the letter shall go with them. Give me a bit of paper, Katherine—something to wrap them up in. That will do! Now give it to—to—[*stamps his foot*]—what the deuce is her name?— give it to the maid, and tell her to take it at once to the Mayor.

[MRS. STOCKMANN *takes the packet and goes out through the dining-room.*]

PETRA: What do you think uncle Peter will say, father?

DR. STOCKMANN: What is there for him to say? I should think he would be very glad that such an important truth has been brought to light.

HOVSTAD: Will you let me print a short note about your discovery in the "Messenger"?

DR. STOCKMANN: I shall be very much obliged if you will.

HOVSTAD: It is very desirable that the public should be informed of it without delay.

DR. STOCKMANN: Certainly.

MRS. STOCKMANN [*coming back*]: She has just gone with it.

BILLING: Upon my soul, Doctor, you are going to be the foremost man in the town!

DR. STOCKMANN [*walking about happily*]: Nonsense! As a matter of fact I have done nothing more than my duty. I have only made a lucky find —that's all. Still, all the same—

BILLING: Hovstad, don't you think the town ought to give Dr. Stockmann some sort of testimonial?

HOVSTAD: I will suggest it, anyway.

BILLING: And I will speak to Aslaksen about it.

DR. STOCKMANN: No, my good friends, don't let us have any of that non-sense. I won't hear of anything of the kind. And if the Baths Committee should think of voting me an increase of salary, I will not accept it. Do you hear, Katherine?—I won't accept it.

MRS. STOCKMANN: You are quite right, Thomas.

PETRA [*lifting her glass*]: Your health, father!

HOVSTAD and BILLING: Your health, Doctor! Good health!

HORSTER [*touches glasses with* DR. STOCKMANN]: I hope it will bring you noth-ing but good luck.

DR. STOCKMANN: Thank you, thank you, my dear fellows! I feel tremen-dously happy! It is a splendid thing for a man to be able to feel that he has done a service to his native town and to his fellow-citizens. Hurrah, Katherine! (*He puts his arms round her and whirls her round and round, while she protests with laughing cries. They all laugh, clap their hands, and cheer the* DOCTOR. *The boys put their heads in at the door to see what is going on.*)

ACT II

[SCENE: *The same. The door into the dining-room is shut. It is morning.* MRS.

STOCKMANN, *with a sealed letter in her hand, comes in from the dining-room, goes to the door of the* DOCTOR'S *study, and peeps in.*]

MRS. STOCKMANN: Are you in, Thomas?

DR. STOCKMANN [*from within his room*]: Yes, I have just come in. [*Comes into the room.*] What is it?

MRS. STOCKMANN: A letter from your brother.

DR. STOCKMANN: Aha, let us see! [*Opens the letter and reads:*] "I return herewith the manuscript you sent me"—[*reads on in a low murmur*] Hm!—

MRS. STOCKMANN: What does he say?

DR. STOCKMANN [*putting the papers in his pocket*]: Oh, he only writes that he will come up here himself about midday.

MRS. STOCKMANN: Well, try and remember to be at home this time.

DR. STOCKMANN: That will be all right; I have got through all my morning visits.

MRS. STOCKMANN: I am extremely curious to know how he takes it.

DR. STOCKMANN: You will see he won't like its having been I, and not he, that made the discovery.

MRS. STOCKMANN: Aren't you a little nervous about that?

DR. STOCKMANN: Oh, he really will be pleased enough, you know. But, at the same time, Peter is so confoundedly afraid of anyone's doing any service to the town except himself.

MRS. STOCKMANN: I will tell you what, Thomas—you should be good natured, and share the credit of this with him. Couldn't you make out that it was he who set you on the scent of this discovery?

DR. STOCKMANN: I am quite willing. If only I can get the thing set right. I—

[MORTEN KIIL *puts his head in through the door leading from the hall, looks round in an enquiring manner, and chuckles.*]

MORTEN KIIL [*slyly*]: Is it—is it true?

MRS. STOCKMANN [*going to the door*]: Father!—is it you?

DR. STOCKMANN: Ah, Mr. Kiil—good morning, good morning!

MRS. STOCKMANN: But come along in.

MORTEN KIIL: If it is true, I will; if not, I am off.

DR. STOCKMANN: If what is true?

MORTEN KIIL: This tale about the water supply. Is it true?

DR. STOCKMANN: Certainly it is true. But how did you come to hear it?

MORTEN KIIL [*coming in*]: Petra ran in on her way to the school—

DR. STOCKMANN: Did she?

MORTEN KIIL: Yes; and she declares that—. I thought she was only making a fool of me, but it isn't like Petra to do that.

DR. STOCKMANN: Of course not. How could you imagine such a thing!

MORTEN KIIL: Oh well, it is better never to trust anybody; you may find you have been made a fool of before you know where you are. But it is really true, all the same?

DR. STOCKMANN: You can depend upon it that it is true. Won't you sit down? [*Settles him on the couch.*] Isn't it a real bit of luck for the town—

MORTEN KIIL [*suppressing his laughter*]: A bit of luck for the town?

DR. STOCKMANN: Yes, that I made the discovery in good time.

MORTEN KIIL [*as before*]: Yes, yes, yes!—But I should never have thought you the sort of man to pull your own brother's leg like this!

DR. STOCKMANN: Pull his leg!

MRS. STOCKMANN: Really, father dear—

MORTEN KIIL [*resting his hands and his chin on the handle of his stick and winking slyly at the* DOCTOR]: Let me see, what was the story? Some kind of beast that had got into the water-pipes, wasn't it?

DR. STOCKMANN: Infusoria—yes.

MORTEN KIIL: And a lot of these beasts had got in, according to Petra—a tremendous lot.

DR. STOCKMANN: Certainly; hundreds of thousands of them, probably.

MORTEN KIIL: But no one can see them—isn't that so?

DR. STOCKMANN: Yes; you can't see them.

MORTEN KIIL [*with a quiet chuckle*]: Damme—it's the finest story I have ever heard!

DR. STOCKMANN: What do you mean?

MORTEN KIIL: But you will never get the Mayor to believe a thing like that.

DR. STOCKMANN: We shall see.

MORTEN KIIL: Do you think he will be fool enough to—?

DR. STOCKMANN: I hope the whole town will be fools enough.

MORTEN KIIL: The whole town! Well, it wouldn't be a bad thing. It would just serve them right, and teach them a lesson. They think themselves so much cleverer than we old fellows. They hounded me out of the council; they did, I tell you—they hounded me out. Now they shall pay for it. You pull their legs too, Thomas!

DR. STOCKMANN: Really, I—

MORTEN KIIL: You pull their legs! [*Gets up.*] If you can work it so that the Mayor and his friends all swallow the same bait, I will give ten pounds to a charity—like a shot!

DR. STOCKMANN: That is very kind of you.

MORTEN KIIL: Yes, I haven't got much money to throw away, I can tell you; but if you can work this, I will give five pounds to a charity at Christmas.

[HOVSTAD *comes in by the hall door.*]

HOVSTAD: Good morning! [*Stops.*] Oh, I beg your pardon—

DR. STOCKMANN: Not at all; come in.

MORTEN KIIL [*with another chuckle*]: Oho!—is he in this too?

HOVSTAD: What do you mean?

DR. STOCKMANN: Certainly he is.

MORTEN KIIL: I might have known it! It must get into the papers. You know how to do it, Thomas! Set your wits to work. Now I must go.

DR. STOCKMANN: Won't you stay a little while?

MORTEN KIIL: No, I must be off now. You keep up this game for all it is worth; you won't repent it, I'm damned if you will!

[*He goes out;* MRS. STOCKMANN *follows him into the hall.*]

DR. STOCKMANN [*laughing*]: Just imagine—the old chap doesn't believe a word of all this about the water supply.

HOVSTAD: Oh that was it, then?

DR. STOCKMANN: Yes, that was what we were talking about. Perhaps it is the same thing that brings you here?

HOVSTAD: Yes, it is. Can you spare me a few minutes, Doctor?

DR. STOCKMANN: As long as you like, my dear fellow.

HOVSTAD: Have you heard from the Mayor yet?

DR. STOCKMANN: Not yet. He is coming here later.

HOVSTAD: I have given the matter a great deal of thought since last night.

DR. STOCKMANN: Well?

HOVSTAD: From your point of view, as a doctor and a man of science, this affair of the water-supply is an isolated matter. I mean, you do not realise that it involves a great many other things.

DR. STOCKMANN: How, do you mean?—Let us sit down, my dear fellow. No, sit here on the couch. [HOVSTAD *sits down on the couch,* DR. STOCKMANN *on a chair on the other side of the table.*] Now then. You mean that—?

HOVSTAD: You said yesterday that the pollution of the water was due to impurities in the soil.

DR. STOCKMANN: Yes, unquestionably it is due to that poisonous morass up at Mölledal.

HOVSTAD: Begging your pardon, doctor, I fancy it is due to quite another morass altogether.

DR. STOCKMANN: What morass?

HOVSTAD: The morass that the whole life of our town is built on and is rotting in.

DR. STOCKMANN: What the deuce are you driving at, Hovstad?

HOVSTAD: The whole of the town's interests have, little by little, got into the hands of a pack of officials.

DR. STOCKMANN: Oh, come!—they are not all officials.

HOVSTAD: No, but those that are not officials are at any rate the officials' friends and adherents; it is the wealthy folk, the old families in the town, that have got us entirely in their hands.

DR. STOCKMANN: Yes, but after all they are men of ability and knowledge.

HOVSTAD: Did they show any ability or knowledge when they laid the conduit-pipes where they are now?

DR. STOCKMANN: No, of course that was a great piece of stupidity on their part. But that is going to be set right now.

HOVSTAD: Do you think that will be all such plain sailing?

DR. STOCKMANN: Plain sailing or no, it has got to be done, anyway.

HOVSTAD: Yes, provided the press takes up the question.

DR. STOCKMANN: I don't think that will be necessary, my dear fellow, I am certain my brother—

HOVSTAD: Excuse me, doctor; I feel bound to tell you I am inclined to take the matter up.

DR. STOCKMANN: In the paper?

HOVSTAD: Yes. When I took over the "People's Messenger" my idea was to break up this ring of self-opinionated old fossils who had got hold of all the influence.

DR. STOCKMANN: But you know you told me yourself what the result had been; you nearly ruined your paper.

HOVSTAD: Yes, at the time we were obliged to climb down a peg or two, it is quite true; because there was a danger of the whole project of the Baths coming to nothing if they failed us. But now the scheme has been carried through, and we can dispense with these grand gentlemen.

DR. STOCKMANN: Dispense with them, yes; but we owe them a great debt of gratitude.

HOVSTAD: That shall be recognised ungrudgingly. But a journalist of my democratic tendencies cannot let such an opportunity as this slip. The bubble of official infallibility must be pricked. This superstition must be destroyed, like any other.

DR. STOCKMANN: I am whole-heartedly with you in that, Mr. Hovstad; if it is a superstition, away with it!

HOVSTAD: I should be very reluctant to bring the Mayor into it, because he is your brother. But I am sure you will agree with me that truth should be the first consideration.

DR. STOCKMANN: That goes without saying. [*With sudden emphasis.*] Yes, but —but—

HOVSTAD: You must not misjudge me. I am neither more self-interested nor more ambitious than most men.

DR. STOCKMANN: My dear fellow—who suggests anything of that kind?

HOVSTAD: I am of humble origin, as you know; and that has given me opportunities of knowing what is the most crying need in the humbler ranks of life. It is that they should be allowed some part in the direction of public affairs, Doctor. That is what will develop their faculties and intelligence and self respect—

DR. STOCKMANN: I quite appreciate that.

HOVSTAD: Yes—and in my opinion a journalist incurs a heavy responsibility

if he neglects a favourable opportunity of emancipating the masses—
the humble and oppressed. I know well enough that in exalted circles
I shall be called an agitator, and all that sort of thing; but they may call
what they like. If only my conscience doesn't reproach me, then—
DR. STOCKMANN: Quite right! Quite right, Mr. Hovstad. But all the same—
devil take it! [*A knock is heard at the door.*] Come in!

[ASLAKSEN *appears at the door. He is poorly but decently dressed, in black, with
a slightly crumpled white neck-cloth; he wears gloves and has a felt hat in his
hand.*]

ASLAKSEN [*bowing*]: Excuse my taking the liberty, Doctor—
DR. STOCKMANN [*getting up*]: Ah, it is you, Aslaksen!
ASLAKSEN: Yes, Doctor.
HOVSTAD [*standing up*]: Is it me you want, Aslaksen?
ASLAKSEN: No; I didn't know I should find you here. No, it was the Doctor
    I—
DR. STOCKMANN: I am quite at your service. What is it?
ASLAKSEN: Is what I heard from Mr. Billing true, sir—that you mean to
    improve our water-supply?
DR. STOCKMANN: Yes, for the Baths.
ASLAKSEN: Quite so, I understand. Well, I have come to say that I will back
    that up by every means in my power.
HOVSTAD [*to the* DOCTOR]: You see!
DR. STOCKMANN: I shall be very grateful to you, but—
ASLAKSEN: Because it may be no bad thing to have us small tradesmen at
    your back. We form, as it were, a compact majority in the town—if we
    choose. And it is always a good thing to have the majority with you,
    Doctor.
DR. STOCKMANN: This is undeniably true; but I confess I don't see why such
    unusual precautions should be necessary in this case. It seems to me that
    such a plain, straightforward thing—
ASLAKSEN: Oh, it may be very desirable, all the same. I know our local
    authorities so well; officials are not generally very ready to act on
    proposals that come from other people. That is why I think it would not
    be at all amiss if we made a little demonstration.
HOVSTAD: That's right.
DR. STOCKMANN: Demonstration, did you say? What on earth are you going
    to make a demonstration about?
ASLAKSEN: We shall proceed with the greatest moderation, Doctor. Modera-
    tion is always my aim; it is the greatest virtue in a citizen—at least, I
    think so.
DR. STOCKMANN: It is well known to be a characteristic of yours, Mr. As-
    laksen.
ASLAKSEN: Yes, I think I may pride myself on that. And this matter of the

water-supply is of the greatest importance to us small tradesmen. The Baths promise to be a regular gold-mine for the town. We shall all make our living out of them, especially those of us who are householders. That is why we will back up the project as strongly as possible. And as I am at present Chairman of the Householders' Association—

DR. STOCKMANN: Yes—?

ASLAKSEN: And, what is more, local secretary of the Temperance Society— you know, sir, I suppose, that I am a worker in the temperance cause?

DR. STOCKMANN: Of course, of course.

ASLAKSEN: Well, you can understand that I come into contact with a great many people. And as I have the reputation of a temperate and law-abiding citizen—like yourself, Doctor—I have a certain influence in the town, a little bit of power, if I may be allowed to say so.

DR. STOCKMANN: I know that quite well, Mr. Aslaksen.

ASLAKSEN: So you see it would be an easy matter for me to set on foot some testimonial, if necessary.

DR. STOCKMANN: A testimonial?

ASLAKSEN: Yes, some kind of an address of thanks from the townsmen for your share in a matter of such importance to the community. I need scarcely say that it would have to be drawn up with the greatest regard to moderation, so as not to offend the authorities—who, after all, have the reins in their hands. If we pay strict attention to that, no one can take it amiss, I should think!

HOVSTAD: Well, and even supposing they didn't like it—

ASLAKSEN: No, no, no; there must be no discourtesy to the authorities, Mr. Hovstad. It is no use falling foul of those upon whom our welfare so closely depends. I have done that in my time, and no good ever comes of it. But no one can take exception to a reasonable and frank expression of a citizen's views.

DR. STOCKMANN [*shaking him by the hand*]: I can't tell you, dear Mr. Aslaksen, how extremely pleased I am to find such hearty support among my fellow-citizens. I am delighted—delighted! Now, you will take a small glass of sherry, eh?

ASLAKSEN: No, thank you; I never drink alcohol of that kind.

DR. STOCKMANN: Well, what do you say to a glass of beer, then?

ASLAKSEN: Nor that either, thank you, Doctor. I never drink anything as early as this. I am going into town now to talk this over with one or two householders, and prepare the ground.

DR. STOCKMANN: It is tremendously kind of you, Mr. Aslaksen; but I really cannot understand the necessity for all these precautions. It seems to me that the thing should go of itself.

ASLAKSEN: The authorities are somewhat slow to move, Doctor. Far be it from me to seem to blame them—

HOVSTAD: We are going to stir them up in the paper tomorrow, Aslaksen.

ASLAKSEN: But not violently, I trust, Mr. Hovstad. Proceed with moderation, or you will do nothing with them. You may take my advice; I have gathered my experience in the school of life. Well, I must say good-bye, Doctor. You know now that we small tradesmen are at your back at all events, like a solid wall. You have the compact majority on your side, Doctor.

DR. STOCKMANN: I am very much obliged, dear Mr. Aslaksen. [*Shakes hands with him.*] Good-bye, good-bye.

ASLAKSEN: Are you going my way, towards the printing-office, Mr. Hovstad?

HOVSTAD: I will come later; I have something to settle up first.

ASLAKSEN: Very well. [*Bows and goes out;* STOCKMANN *follows him into the hall.*]

HOVSTAD [*as* STOCKMANN *comes in again*]: Well, what do you think of that, Doctor? Don't you think it is high time we stirred a little life into all this slackness and vacillation and cowardice?

DR. STOCKMANN: Are you referring to Aslaksen?

HOVSTAD: Yes, I am. He is one of those who are floundering in a bog—decent enough fellow though he may be, otherwise. And most of the people here are in just the same case—see-sawing and edging first to one side and then to the other, so overcome with caution and scruple that they never dare to take any decided step.

DR. STOCKMANN: Yes, but Aslaksen seemed to me so thoroughly well-intentioned.

HOVSTAD: There is one thing I esteem higher than that; and that is for a man to be self-reliant and sure of himself.

DR. STOCKMANN: I think you are perfectly right there.

HOVSTAD: That is why I want to seize this opportunity, and try if I cannot manage to put a little virility into these well-intentioned people for once. The idol of Authority must be shattered in this town. This gross and inexcusable blunder about the water-supply must be brought home to the mind of every municipal voter.

DR. STOCKMANN: Very well; if you are of opinion that it is for the good of the community, so be it. But not until I have had a talk with my brother.

HOVSTAD: Anyway, I will get a leading article ready; and if the Mayor refuses to take the matter up—

DR. STOCKMANN: How can you suppose such a thing possible?

HOVSTAD: It is conceivable. And in that case—

DR. STOCKMANN: In that case I promise you—. Look here, in that case you may print my report—every word of it.

HOVSTAD: May I? Have I your word for it?

DR. STOCKMANN [*giving him the MS.*]: Here it is; take it with you. It can do no harm for you to read it through, and you can give it back to me later on.

HOVSTAD: Good, good! That is what I will do. And now good-bye, Doctor.

DR. STOCKMANN: Good-bye, good-bye. You will see everything will run quite smoothly, Mr. Hovstad—quite smoothly.

HOVSTAD: Hm!—we shall see. [*Bows and goes out.*]

DR. STOCKMANN [*opens the dining-room door and looks in*]: Katherine! Oh, you are back, Petra?

PETRA [*coming in*]: Yes, I have just come from the school.

MRS. STOCKMANN [*coming in*]: Has he not been here yet?

DR. STOCKMANN: Peter? No. But I have had a long talk with Hovstad. He is quite excited about my discovery. I find it has a much wider bearing than I at first imagined. And he has put his paper at my disposal if necessity should arise.

MRS. STOCKMANN: Do you think it will?

DR. STOCKMANN: Not for a moment. But at all events it makes me feel proud to know that I have the liberal-minded independent press on my side. Yes, and—just imagine—I have had a visit from the Chairman of the Householders' Association!

MRS. STOCKMANN: Oh! What did he want?

DR. STOCKMANN: To offer me his support too. They will support me in a body if it should be necessary. Katherine—do you know what I have got behind me?

MRS. STOCKMANN: Behind you? No, what have you got behind you?

DR. STOCKMANN: The compact majority.

MRS. STOCKMANN: Really? Is that a good thing for you, Thomas?

DR. STOCKMANN: I should think it was a good thing. [*Walks up and down rubbing his hands.*] By Jove, it's a fine thing to feel this bond of brotherhood between oneself and one's fellow citizens!

PETRA: And to be able to do so much that is good and useful, father.

DR. STOCKMANN: And for one's own native town into the bargain, my child!

MRS. STOCKMANN: That was a ring at the bell.

DR. STOCKMANN: It must be he, then. [*A knock is heard at the door.*] Come in!

PETER STOCKMANN [*comes in from the hall*]: Good morning.

DR. STOCKMANN: Glad to see you, Peter!

MRS. STOCKMAN: Good morning, Peter. How are you?

PETER STOCKMANN: So so, thank you. [*To* DR. STOCKMANN.] I received from you yesterday, after office hours, a report dealing with the condition of the water at the Baths.

DR. STOCKMANN: Yes. Have you read it?

PETER STOCKMANN: Yes, I have.

DR. STOCKMANN: And what have you to say to it?

PETER STOCKMANN [*with a sidelong glance*]: Hm!—

MRS. STOCKMANN: Come along, Petra. [*She and* PETRA *go into the room on the left.*]

PETER STOCKMANN [*after a pause*]: Was it necessary to make all these investigations behind my back?

DR. STOCKMANN: Yes, because until I was absolutely certain about it—

PETER STOCKMANN: Then you mean that you are absolutely certain now?

DR. STOCKMANN: Surely you are convinced of that.

PETER STOCKMANN: Is it your intention to bring this document before the Baths Committee as a sort of official communication?

DR. STOCKMANN: Certainly. Something must be done in the matter—and that quickly.

PETER STOCKMANN: As usual, you employ violent expressions in your report. You say, amongst other things, that what we offer visitors in our Baths is a permanent supply of poison.

DR. STOCKMANN: Well, can you describe it any other way, Peter? Just think —water that is poisonous, whether you drink it or bathe in it! And this we offer to the poor sick folk who come to us trustfully and pay us at an exorbitant rate to be made well again!

PETER STOCKMANN: And your reasoning leads you to this conclusion, that we must build a sewer to draw off the alleged impurities from Mölledal and must relay the water conduits.

DR. STOCKMANN: Yes. Do you see any other way out of it? I don't.

PETER STOCKMANN: I made a pretext this morning to go and see the town engineer, and, as if only half seriously, broached the subject of these proposals as a thing we might perhaps have to take under consideration some time later on.

DR. STOCKMANN: Some time later on!

PETER STOCKMANN: He smiled at what he considered to be my extravagance, naturally. Have you taken the trouble to consider what your proposed alterations would cost? According to the information I obtained, the expenses would probably mount up to fifteen or twenty thousand pounds.

DR. STOCKMANN: Would it cost so much?

PETER STOCKMANN: Yes; and the worst part of it would be that the work would take at least two years.

DR. STOCKMANN: Two years? Two whole years?

PETER STOCKMANN: At least. And what are we to do with the Baths in the meantime? Close them? Indeed we should be obliged to. And do you suppose any one would come near the place after it had got about that the water was dangerous?

DR. STOCKMANN: Yes but, Peter, that is what it is.

PETER STOCKMANN: And all this at this juncture—just as the Baths are beginning to be known. There are other towns in the neighbourhood with qualifications to attract visitors for bathing purposes. Don't you suppose they would immediately strain every nerve to divert the entire stream of strangers to themselves? Unquestionably they would; and then where should we be? We should probably have to abandon the whole thing, which has cost us so much money—and then you would have ruined your native town.

DR. STOCKMANN: I—should have ruined—!

PETER STOCKMANN: It is simply and solely through the Baths that the town has before it any future worth mentioning. You know that just as well as I.

DR. STOCKMANN: But what do you think ought to be done, then?

PETER STOCKMANN: Your report has not convinced me that the condition of the water at the Baths is as bad as you represent it to be.

DR. STOCKMANN: I tell you it is even worse!—or at all events it will be in summer, when the warm weather comes.

PETER STOCKMANN: As I said, I believe you exaggerate the matter considerably. A capable physician ought to know what measures to take—he ought to be capable of preventing injurious influences or of remedying them if they become obviously persistent.

DR. STOCKMANN: Well? What more?

PETER STOCKMANN: The water supply for the Baths is now an established fact, and in consequence must be treated as such. But probably the Committee, at its discretion, will not be disinclined to consider the question of how far it might be possible to introduce certain improvements consistently with a reasonable expenditure.

DR. STOCKMANN: And do you suppose that I will have anything to do with such a piece of trickery as that?

PETER STOCKMANN: Trickery! !

DR. STOCKMANN: Yes, it would be a trick—a fraud, a lie, a downright crime towards the public, towards the whole community!

PETER STOCKMANN: I have not, as I remarked before, been able to convince myself that there is actually any imminent danger.

DR. STOCKMANN: You have! It is impossible that you should not be convinced. I know I have represented the facts absolutely truthfully and fairly. And you know it very well, Peter, only you won't acknowledge it. It was owing to your action that both the Baths and the water-conduits were built where they are; and that is what you won't acknowledge—that damnable blunder of yours. Pooh!—do you suppose I don't see through you?

PETER STOCKMANN: And even if that were true? If I perhaps guard my reputation somewhat anxiously, it is in the best interests of the town. Without moral authority I am powerless to direct public affairs as seems, to my judgment, to be best for the common good. And on that account—and for various other reasons too—it appears to me to be a matter of importance that your report should not be delivered to the Committee. In the interests of the public, you must withhold it. Then, later on, I will raise the question and we will do our best, privately; but nothing of this unfortunate affair—not a single word of it—must come to the ears of the public.

DR. STOCKMANN: I am afraid you will not be able to prevent that now, my dear Peter.

PETER STOCKMANN: It must and shall be prevented.

DR. STOCKMANN: It is no use, I tell you. There are too many people that know about it.

PETER STOCKMANN: That know about it? Who? Surely you don't mean those fellows on the "People's Messenger"?

DR. STOCKMANN: Yes, they know. The liberal-minded independent press is going to see that you do your duty.

PETER STOCKMANN [*after a short pause*]: You are an extraordinarily independent man, Thomas. Have you given no thought to the consequences this may have for yourself?

DR. STOCKMANN: Consequences?—for me?

PETER STOCKMANN: For you and yours, yes.

DR. STOCKMANN: What the deuce do you mean?

PETER STOCKMANN: I believe I have always behaved in a brotherly way to you—have always been ready to oblige or to help you?

DR. STOCKMANN: Yes, you have, and I am grateful to you for it.

PETER STOCKMANN: There is no need. Indeed, to some extent I was forced to do so—for my own sake. I always hoped that, if I helped to improve your financial position, I should be able to keep some check on you.

DR. STOCKMANN: What!! Then it was only for your own sake—!

PETER STOCKMANN: Up to a certain point, yes. It is painful for a man in an official position to have his nearest relative compromising himself time after time.

DR. STOCKMANN: And do you consider that I do that?

PETER STOCKMANN: Yes, unfortunately, you do, without even being aware of it. You have a restless, pugnacious, rebellious disposition. And then there is that disastrous propensity of yours to want to write about every sort of possible and impossible thing. The moment an idea comes into your head, you must needs go and write a newspaper article or a whole pamphlet about it.

DR. STOCKMANN: Well, but is it not the duty of a citizen to let the public share in any new ideas he may have?

PETER STOCKMANN: Oh, the public doesn't require any new ideas. The public is best served by the good, old-established ideas it already has.

DR. STOCKMANN: And that is your honest opinion?

PETER STOCKMANN: Yes, and for once I must talk frankly to you. Hitherto I have tried to avoid doing so, because I know how irritable you are; but now I must tell you the truth, Thomas. You have no conception what an amount of harm you do yourself by your impetuosity. You complain of the authorities, you even complain of the government—you are always pulling them to pieces; you insist that you have been neglected and persecuted. But what else can such a cantankerous man as you expect?

DR. STOCKMANN: What next! Cantankerous, am I?

PETER STOCKMANN: Yes, Thomas, you are an extremely cantankerous man to work with—I know that to my cost. You disregard everything that you ought to have consideration for. You seem completely to forget that it is me you have to thank for your appointment here as medical officer to the Baths—

DR. STOCKMANN: I was entitled to it as a matter of course!—I and nobody else! I was the first person to see that the town could be made into a flourishing watering-place, and I was the only one who saw it at that time. I had to fight single-handed in support of the idea for many years; and I wrote and wrote—

PETER STOCKMANN: Undoubtedly. But things were not ripe for the scheme then—though, of course, you could not judge of that in your out-of-the way corner up north. But as soon as the opportune moment came I— and the others—took the matter into our hands—

DR. STOCKMANN: Yes, and made this mess of all my beautiful plan. It is pretty obvious now what clever fellows you were!

PETER STOCKMANN: To my mind the whole thing only seems to mean that you are seeking another outlet for your combativeness. You want to pick a quarrel with your superiors—an old habit of yours. You cannot put up with any authority over you. You look askance at anyone who occupies a superior official position; you regard him as a personal enemy, and then any stick is good enough to beat him with. But now I have called your attention to the fact that the town's interests are at stake—and, incidentally, my own too. And therefore I must tell you, Thomas, that you will find me inexorable with regard to what I am about to require you to do.

DR. STOCKMANN: And what is that?

PETER STOCKMANN: As you have been so indiscreet as to speak of this delicate matter to outsiders, despite the fact that you ought to have treated it as entirely official and confidential, it is obviously impossible to hush it up now. All sorts of rumours will get about directly, and everybody who has a grudge against us will take care to embellish these rumours. So it will be necessary for you to refute them publicly.

DR. STOCKMANN: I! How? I don't understand.

PETER STOCKMANN: What we shall expect is that, after making further investigations, you will come to the conclusion that the matter is not by any means as dangerous or as critical as you imagined in the first instance.

DR. STOCKMANN: Oho!—so that is what you expect!

PETER STOCKMANN: And, what is more, we shall expect you to make public profession of your confidence in the Committee and in their readiness to consider fully and conscientiously what steps may be necessary to remedy any possible defects.

DR. STOCKMANN: But you will never be able to do that by patching and tinkering at it—never! Take my word for it, Peter; I mean what I say, as deliberately and emphatically as possible.

PETER STOCKMANN: As an officer under the Committee, you have no right to any individual opinion.

DR. STOCKMANN [*amazed*]: No right?

PETER STOCKMANN: In your official capacity, no. As a private person, it is quite another matter. But as a subordinate member of the staff of the Baths, you have no right to express any opinion which runs contrary to that of your superiors.

DR. STOCKMANN: This is too much! I, a doctor, a man of science, have no right to—!

PETER STOCKMANN: The matter in hand is not simply a scientific one. It is a complicated matter, and has its economic as well as its technical side.

DR. STOCKMANN: I don't care what it is! I intend to be free to express my opinion on any subject under the sun.

PETER STOCKMANN: As you please—but not on any subject concerning the Baths. That we forbid.

DR. STOCKMANN [*shouting*]: You forbid—! You! A pack of—

PETER STOCKMANN: *I* forbid it—I, your chief; and if I forbid it, you have to obey.

DR. STOCKMANN [*controlling himself*]: Peter—if you were not my brother—

PETRA [*throwing open the door*]: Father, you shan't stand this!

MRS. STOCKMANN [*coming in after her*]: Petra, Petra!

PETER STOCKMANN: Oh, so you have been eavesdropping.

MRS. STOCKMANN: You were talking so loud, we couldn't help—

PETRA: Yes, I was listening.

PETER STOCKMANN: Well, after all, I am very glad—

DR. STOCKMANN [*going up to him*]: You were saying something about forbidding and obeying?

PETER STOCKMANN: You obliged me to take that tone with you.

DR. STOCKMANN: And so I am to give myself the lie, publicly?

PETER STOCKMANN: We consider it absolutely necessary that you should make some such public statement as I have asked for.

DR. STOCKMANN: And if I do not—obey?

PETER STOCKMANN: Then we shall publish a statement ourselves to reassure the public.

DR. STOCKMANN: Very well; but in that case I shall use my pen against you. I stick to what I have said; I will show that I am right and that you are wrong. And what will you do then?

PETER STOCKMANN: Then I shall not be able to prevent your being dismissed.

DR. STOCKMANN: What—?

PETRA: Father—dismissed!

MRS. STOCKMANN: Dismissed!

PETER STOCKMANN: Dismissed from the staff of the Baths. I shall be obliged to propose that you shall immediately be given notice, and shall not be allowed any further participation in the Baths' affairs.

DR. STOCKMANN: You would dare to do that!

PETER STOCKMANN: It is you that are playing the daring game.

PETRA: Uncle, that is a shameful way to treat a man like father!

MRS. STOCKMANN: Do hold your tongue, Petra!

PETER STOCKMANN [*looking at* PETRA]: Oh, so we volunteer our opinions already, do we? Of course. [*To* MRS. STOCKMANN.] Katherine, I imagine you are the most sensible person in this house. Use any influence you may have over your husband, and make him see what this will entail for his family as well as—

DR. STOCKMANN: My family is my own concern and nobody else's!

PETER STOCKMANN: —for his own family, as I was saying, as well as for the town he lives in.

DR. STOCKMANN: It is I who have the real good of the town at heart! I want to lay bare the defects that sooner or later must come to the light of day. I will show whether I love my native town.

PETER STOCKMANN: You, who in your blind obstinacy want to cut off the most important source of the town's welfare?

DR. STOCKMANN: The source is poisoned, man! Are you mad? We are making our living by retailing filth and corruption! The whole of our flourishing municipal life derives its sustenance from a lie!

PETER STOCKMANN: All imagination—or something even worse. The man who can throw out such offensive insinuations about his native town must be an enemy to our community.

DR. STOCKMANN [*going up to him*]: Do you dare to—!

MRS. STOCKMANN [*throwing herself between them*]: Thomas!

PETRA [*catching her father by the arm*]: Don't lose your temper, father!

PETER STOCKMANN: I will not expose myself to violence. Now you have had a warning; so reflect on what you owe to yourself and your family. Good-bye. [*Goes out.*]

DR. STOCKMANN [*walking up and down*]: Am I to put up with such treatment as this? In my own house, Katherine! What do you think of that!

MRS. STOCKMANN: Indeed it is both shameful and absurd, Thomas—

PETRA: If only I could give uncle a piece of my mind—

DR. STOCKMANN: It is my own fault. I ought to have flown out at him long ago!—shown my teeth!—bitten! To hear him call me an enemy to our community! Me! I shall not take that lying down, upon my soul!

MRS. STOCKMANN: But, dear Thomas, your brother has power on his side—

DR. STOCKMANN: Yes, but I have right on mine, I tell you.

MRS. STOCKMANN: Oh yes, right—right. What is the use of having right on your side if you have not got might?

PETRA: Oh, mother!—how can you say such a thing!

DR. STOCKMANN: Do you imagine that in a free country it is no use having right on your side? You are absurd, Katherine. Besides, haven't I got the liberal-minded independent press to lead the way, and the compact majority behind me? That is might enough, I should think!

MRS. STOCKMANN: But, good heavens, Thomas, you don't mean to—?

DR. STOCKMANN: Don't mean to what?

MRS. STOCKMANN: To set yourself up in opposition to your brother.

DR. STOCKMANN: In God's name, what else do you suppose I should do but take my stand on right and truth?

PETRA: Yes, I was just going to say that.

MRS. STOCKMANN: But it won't do you any earthly good. If they won't do it, they won't.

DR. STOCKMANN: Oho, Katherine! Just give me time, and you will see how I will carry the war into their camp.

MRS. STOCKMANN: Yes, you carry the war into their camp, and you get your dismissal—that is what you will do.

DR. STOCKMANN: In any case I shall have done my duty towards the public —towards the community. I, who am called its enemy!

MRS. STOCKMANN: But towards your family, Thomas? Towards your own home! Do you think that is doing your duty towards those you have to provide for?

PETRA: Ah, don't think always first of us, mother.

MRS. STOCKMANN: Oh, it is easy for you to talk; you are able to shift for yourself, if need be. But remember the boys, Thomas; and think a little too of yourself, and of me—

DR. STOCKMANN: I think you are out of your senses, Katherine! If I were to be such a miserable coward as to go on my knees to Peter and his damned crew, do you suppose I should ever know an hour's peace of mind all my life afterwards?

MRS. STOCKMANN: I don't know anything about that; but God preserve us from the peace of mind we shall have, all the same, if you go on defying him! You will find yourself again without the means of subsistence, with no income to count upon. I should think we had had enough of that in the old days. Remember that, Thomas; think what that means.

DR. STOCKMANN [*collecting himself with a struggle and clenching his fists*]: And this is what this slavery can bring upon a free, honourable man! Isn't it horrible, Katherine?

MRS. STOCKMANN: Yes, it is sinful to treat you so, it is perfectly true. But, good heavens, one has to put up with so much injustice in this world. —There are the boys, Thomas! Look at them! What is to become of them? Oh, no, you can never have the heart—. [EJLIF *and* MORTEN *have come in while she was speaking, with their school books in their hands.*]

DR. STOCKMANN: The boys—! [*Recovers himself suddenly.*] No, even if the whole world goes to pieces, I will never bow my neck to this yoke! [*Goes towards his room.*]

MRS. STOCKMANN [*following him*]: Thomas—what are you going to do!

DR. STOCKMANN [*at his door*]: I mean to have the right to look my sons in the face when they are grown men. [*Goes into his room.*]

MRS. STOCKMANN [*bursting into tears*]: God help us all!

PETRA: Father is splendid! He will not give in.

[*The boys look on in amazement;* PETRA *signs to them not to speak.*]

ACT III

[SCENE: *The editorial office of the "People's Messenger." The entrance door is on the left-hand side of the back wall; on the right-hand side is another door with glass panels through which the printing-room can be seen. Another door in the right-hand wall. In the middle of the room is a large table covered with papers, newspapers and books. In the foreground on the left a window, before which stand a desk and a high stool. There are a couple of easy chairs by the table, and other chairs standing along the wall. The room is dingy and uncomfortable; the furniture is old, the chairs stained and torn. In the printing-room the compositors are seen at work, and a printer is working a hand-press.* HOVSTAD *is sitting at the desk, writing.* BILLING *comes in from the right with* DR. STOCKMANN'S *manuscript in his hand.*]

BILLING: Well, I must say!

HOVSTAD [*still writing*]: Have you read it through?

BILLING [*laying the MS. on the desk*]: Yes, indeed I have.

HOVSTAD: Don't you think the Doctor hits them pretty hard?

BILLING: Hard? Bless my soul, he's crushing! Every word falls like—how shall I put it?—like the blow of a sledge-hammer.

HOVSTAD: Yes, but they are not the people to throw up the sponge at the first blow.

BILLING: That is true; and for that reason we must strike blow upon blow until the whole of this aristocracy tumbles to pieces. As I sat there reading this, I almost seemed to see a revolution in being.

HOVSTAD [*turning round*]: Hush!—Speak so that Aslaksen cannot hear you.

BILLING [*lowering his voice*]: Aslaksen is a chicken-hearted chap, a coward; there is nothing of the man in him. But this time you will insist on your own way, won't you? You will put the Doctor's article in?

HOVSTAD: Yes, and if the Mayor doesn't like it—

BILLING: That will be the devil of a nuisance.

HOVSTAD: Well, fortunately we can turn the situation to good account, whatever happens. If the Mayor will not fall in with the Doctor's project, he will have all the small tradesmen down on him—the whole of the Householders' Association and the rest of them. And if he does fall in with it, he will fall out with the whole crowd of large shareholders in the Baths, who up to now have been his most valuable supporters—

BILLING: Yes, because they will certainly have to fork out a pretty penny—

HOVSTAD: Yes, you may be sure they will. And in this way the ring will be broken up, you see, and then in every issue of the paper we will enlighten the public on the Mayor's incapability on one point and another, and make it clear that all the positions of trust in the town, the whole control of municipal affairs, ought to be put in the hands of the Liberals.

BILLING: That is perfectly true! I see it coming—I see it coming; we are on the threshold of a revolution!

[*A knock is heard at the door.*]

HOVSTAD: Hush! [*Calls out.*] Come in! [DR. STOCKMANN *comes in by the street door.* HOVSTAD *goes to meet him.*] Ah, it is you, Doctor! Well?

DR. STOCKMANN: You may set to work and print it, Mr. Hovstad!

HOVSTAD: Has it come to that, then?

BILLING: Hurrah!

DR. STOCKMANN: Yes, print away. Undoubtedly it has come to that. Now they must take what they get. There is going to be a fight in the town, Mr. Billing!

BILLING: War to the knife, I hope! We will get our knives to their throats, Doctor!

DR. STOCKMANN: This article is only a beginning. I have already got four or five more sketched out in my head. Where is Aslaksen?

BILLING [*calls into the printing-room*]: Aslaksen, just come here for a minute!

HOVSTAD: Four or five more articles, did you say? On the same subject?

DR. STOCKMANN: No—far from it, my dear fellow. No, they are about quite another matter. But they all spring from the question of the water-supply and the drainage. One thing leads to another, you know. It is like beginning to pull down an old house, exactly.

BILLING: Upon my soul, it's true; you find you are not done till you have pulled all the old rubbish down.

ASLAKSEN [*coming in*]: Pulled down? You are not thinking of pulling down the Baths surely, Doctor?

HOVSTAD: Far from it, don't be afraid.

DR. STOCKMANN: No, we meant something quite different. Well, what do you think of my article, Mr. Hovstad?

HOVSTAD: I think it is simply a masterpiece—

DR. STOCKMANN: Do you really think so? Well, I am very pleased, very pleased.

HOVSTAD: It is so clear and intelligible. One need have no special knowledge to understand the bearing of it. You will have every enlightened man on your side.

ASLAKSEN: And every prudent man too, I hope?

BILLING: The prudent and the imprudent—almost the whole town.

ASLAKSEN: In that case we may venture to print it.

DR. STOCKMANN: I should think so!

HOVSTAD: We will put it in tomorrow morning.

DR. STOCKMANN: Of course—you must not lose a single day. What I wanted to ask you, Mr. Aslaksen, was if you would supervise the printing of it yourself.

ASLAKSEN: With pleasure.

DR. STOCKMANN: Take care of it as if it were a treasure! No misprints—every word is important. I will look in again a little later; perhaps you will be able to let me see a proof. I can't tell you how eager I am to see it in print, and see it burst upon the public—

BILLING: Burst upon them—yes, like a flash of lightning!

DR. STOCKMANN: —and to have it submitted to the judgment of my intelligent fellow-townsmen. You cannot imagine what I have gone through today. I have been threatened first with one thing and then with another; they have tried to rob me of my most elementary rights as a man—

BILLING: What! Your rights as a man!

DR. STOCKMANN: — they have tried to degrade me, to make a coward of me, to force me to put personal interests before my most sacred convictions—

BILLING: That is too much—I'm damned if it isn't.

HOVSTAD: Oh, you mustn't be surprised at anything from that quarter.

DR. STOCKMANN: Well, they will get the worst of it with me; they may assure themselves of that. I shall consider the "People's Messenger" my sheet-anchor now, and every single day I will bombard them with one article after another, like bomb-shells—

ASLAKSEN: Yes, but—

BILLING: Hurrah!—it is war, it is war!

DR. STOCKMANN: I shall smite them to the ground—I shall crush them—I shall break down all their defences, before the eyes of the honest public! That is what I shall do!

ASLAKSEN: Yes, but in moderation, Doctor—proceed with moderation—

BILLING: Not a bit of it, not a bit of it! Don't spare the dynamite!

DR. STOCKMANN: Because it is not merely a question of water-supply and drains now, you know. No—it is the whole of our social life that we have got to purify and disinfect—

BILLING: Spoken like a deliverer!

DR. STOCKMANN: All the incapables must be turned out, you understand—

and that in every walk of life! Endless vistas have opened themselves to my mind's eye today. I cannot see it all quite clearly yet, but I shall in time. Young and vigorous standard-bearers—those are what we need and must seek, my friends; we must have new men in command at all our outposts.

BILLING: Hear, hear!

DR. STOCKMANN: We only need to stand by one another, and it will all be perfectly easy. The revolution will be launched like a ship that runs smoothly off the stocks. Don't you think so?

HOVSTAD: For my part I think we have now a prospect of getting the municipal authority into the hands where it should lie.

ASLAKSEN: And if only we proceed with moderation, I cannot imagine that there will be any risk.

DR. STOCKMANN: Who the devil cares whether there is any risk or not! What I am doing, I am doing in the name of truth and for the sake of my conscience.

HOVSTAD: You are a man who deserves to be supported, Doctor.

ASLAKSEN: Yes, there is no denying that the Doctor is a true friend to the town—a real friend to the community, that he is.

BILLING: Take my word for it, Aslaksen, Dr. Stockmann is a friend of the people.

ASLAKSEN: I fancy the Householders' Association will make use of that expression before long.

DR. STOCKMANN [*affected, grasps their hands*]: Thank you, thank you, my dear staunch friends. It is very refreshing to me to hear you say that; my brother called me something quite different. By Jove, he shall have it back, with interest! But now I must be off to see a poor devil—. I will come back, as I said. Keep a very careful eye on the manuscript, Aslaksen, and don't for worlds leave out any of my notes of exclamation! Rather put one or two more in! Capital, capital! Well, good-bye for the present—good-bye, good-bye!

[*They show him to the door, and bow him out.*]

HOVSTAD: He may prove an invaluably useful man to us.

ASLAKSEN: Yes, so long as he confines himself to this matter of the Baths. But if he goes farther afield, I don't think it would be advisable to follow him.

HOVSTAD: Hm!—that all depends—

BILLING: You are so infernally timid, Aslaksen!

ASLAKSEN: Timid? Yes, when it is a question of the local authorities, I am timid, Mr. Billing; it is a lesson I have learnt in the school of experience, let me tell you. But try me in higher politics, in matters that concern the government itself, and then see if I am timid.

BILLING: No, you aren't, I admit. But this is simply contradicting yourself.

ASLAKSEN: I am a man with a conscience, and that is the whole matter. If you attack the government, you don't do the community any harm, anyway; those fellows pay no attention to attacks, you see—they go on just as they are, in spite of them. But *local* authorities are different; they *can* be turned out, and then perhaps you may get an ignorant lot into office who may do irreparable harm to the householders and everybody else.

HOVSTAD: But what of the education of citizens by self government—don't you attach any importance to that?

ASLAKSEN: When a man has interests of his own to protect, he cannot think of everything, Mr. Hovstad.

HOVSTAD: Then I hope I shall never have interests of my own to protect!

BILLING: Hear, hear!

ASLAKSEN [*with a smile*]: Hm! [*Points to the desk.*] Mr. Sheriff Stensgaard was your predecessor at that editorial desk.

BILLING [*spitting*]: Bah! That turncoat.

HOVSTAD: I am not a weathercock—and never will be.

ASLAKSEN: A politician should never be too certain of anything, Mr. Hovstad. And as for you, Mr. Billing, I should think it is time for you to be taking in a reef or two in your sails, seeing that you are applying for the post of secretary to the Bench.

BILLING: I—!

HOVSTAD: Are you, Billing?

BILLING: Well, yes—but you must clearly understand I am only doing it to annoy the bigwigs.

ASLAKSEN: Anyhow, it is no business of mine. But if I am to be accused of timidity and of inconsistency in my principles, this is what I want to point out: my political past is an open book. I have never changed, except perhaps to become a little more moderate, you see. My heart is still with the people; but I don't deny that my reason has a certain bias towards the authorities—the local ones, I mean. [*Goes into the printing-room.*]

BILLING: Oughtn't we to try and get rid of him, Hovstad?

HOVSTAD: Do you know anyone else who will advance the money for our paper and printing bill?

BILLING: It is an infernal nuisance that we don't possess some capital to trade on.

HOVSTAD [*sitting down at his desk*]: Yes, if we only had that, then—

BILLING: Suppose you were to apply to Dr. Stockmann?

HOVSTAD [*turning over some papers*]: What is the use? He has got nothing.

BILLING: No, but he has got a warm man in the background, old Morten Kiil—"the Badger," as they call him.

HOVSTAD [*writing*]: Are you so sure *he* has got anything?

BILLING: Good Lord, of course he has! And some of it must come to the Stockmanns. Most probably he will do something for the children, at all events.

HOVSTAD [*turning half round*]: Are you counting on that?

BILLING: Counting on it? Of course I am not counting on anything.

HOVSTAD: That is right. And I should not count on the secretaryship to the Bench either, if I were you; for I can assure you—you won't get it.

BILLING: Do you think I am not quite aware of that? My object is precisely *not* to get it. A slight of that kind stimulates a man's fighting power— it is like getting a supply of fresh bile—and I am sure one needs that badly enough in a hole-and-corner place like this, where it is so seldom anything happens to stir one up.

HOVSTAD [*writing*]: Quite so, quite so.

BILLING: Ah, I shall be heard of yet!—Now I shall go and write the appeal to the Householders' Association. [*Goes into the room on the right.*]

HOVSTAD [*sitting at his desk, biting his penholder, says slowly*]: Hm!—that's it, is it. [*A knock is heard.*] Come in! [PETRA *comes in by the outer door.* HOVSTAD *gets up.*] What, you!—here?

PETRA: Yes, you must forgive me—

HOVSTAD [*pulling a chair forward*]: Won't you sit down?

PETRA: No, thank you; I must go again in a moment.

HOVSTAD: Have you come with a message from your father, by any chance?

PETRA: No, I have come on my own account. [*Takes a book out of her coat pocket.*] Here is the English story.

HOVSTAD: Why have you brought it back?

PETRA: Because I am not going to translate it.

HOVSTAD: But you promised me faithfully—

PETRA: Yes, but then I had not read it. I don't suppose you have read it either?

HOVSTAD: No, you know quite well I don't understand English; but—

PETRA: Quite so. That is why I wanted to tell you that you must find something else. [*Lays the book on the table.*] You can't use this for the "People's Messenger."

HOVSTAD: Why not?

PETRA: Because it conflicts with all your opinions.

HOVSTAD: Oh, for that matter—

PETRA: You don't understand me. The burden of this story is that there is a supernatural power that looks after the so-called good people in this world and makes everything happen for the best in their case—while all the so-called bad people are punished.

HOVSTAD: Well, but that is all right. That is just what our readers want.

PETRA: And are you going to be the one to give it to them? For myself, I do not believe a word of it. You know quite well that things do not happen so in reality.

HOVSTAD: You are perfectly right; but an editor cannot always act as he would prefer. He is often obliged to bow to the wishes of the public in unimportant matters. Politics are the most important thing in life—for a newspaper, anyway; and if I want to carry my public with me on the path that leads to liberty and progress, I must not frighten them away. If they find a moral tale of this sort in the serial at the bottom of the page, they will be all the more ready to read what is printed above it; they feel more secure, as it were.

PETRA: For shame! You would never go and set a snare like that for your readers; you are not a spider!

HOVSTAD [*smiling*]: Thank you for having such a good opinion of me. No; as a matter of fact that is Billing's idea and not mine.

PETRA: Billing's!

HOVSTAD: Yes; anyway he propounded that theory here one day. And it is Billing who is so anxious to have that story in the paper; I don't know anything about the book.

PETRA: But how can Billing, with his emancipated views—

HOVSTAD: Oh, Billing is a many-sided man. He is applying for the post of secretary to the Bench, too, I hear.

PETRA: I don't believe it, Mr. Hovstad. How could he possibly bring himself to do such a thing?

HOVSTAD: Ah, you must ask him that.

PETRA: I should never have thought it of him.

HOVSTAD [*looking more closely at her*]: No? Does it really surprise you so much?

PETRA: Yes. Or perhaps not altogether. Really, I don't quite know—

HOVSTAD: We journalists are not much worth, Miss Stockmann.

PETRA: Do you really mean that?

HOVSTAD: I think so sometimes.

PETRA: Yes, in the ordinary affairs of everyday life, perhaps; I can understand that. But now, when you have taken a weighty matter in hand—

HOVSTAD: This matter of your father's, you mean?

PETRA: Exactly. It seems to me that now you must feel you are a man worth more than most.

HOVSTAD: Yes, today I do feel something of that sort.

PETRA: Of course you do, don't you? It is a splendid vocation you have chosen—to smooth the way for the march of unappreciated truths, and new and courageous lines of thought. If it were nothing more than because you stand fearlessly in the open and take up the cause of an injured man—

HOVSTAD: Especially when that injured man is—ahem!—I don't rightly know how to—

PETRA: When that man is so upright and so honest, you mean?

HOVSTAD [*more gently*]: Especially when he is your father, I meant.

PETRA [*suddenly checked*]: *That?*

HOVSTAD: Yes, Petra—Miss Petra.

PETRA: Is it *that,* that is first and foremost with you? Not the matter itself? Not the truth?—not my father's big generous heart?

HOVSTAD: Certainly—of course—that too.

PETRA: No, thank you; you have betrayed yourself, Mr. Hovstad, and now I shall never trust you again in anything.

HOVSTAD: Can you really take it so amiss in me that it is mostly for your sake—?

PETRA: What I am angry with you for, is for not having been honest with my father. You talked to him as if the truth and the good of the community were what lay nearest to your heart. You have made fools of both my father and me. You are not the man you made yourself out to be. And that I shall never forgive you—never!

HOVSTAD: You ought not to speak so bitterly, Miss Petra—least of all now.

PETRA: Why not now, especially?

HOVSTAD: Because your father cannot do without my help.

PETRA [*looking him up and down*]: Are you that sort of man too? For shame!

HOVSTAD: No, no, I am not. This came upon me so unexpectedly—you must believe that.

PETRA: I know what to believe. Good-bye.

ASLAKSEN [*coming from the printing-room, hurriedly and with an air of mystery*]: Damnation, Hovstad!—[*Sees* PETRA.] Oh, this is awkward—

PETRA: There is the book; you must give it to some one else. [*Goes towards the door.*]

HOVSTAD [*following her*]: But, Miss Stockmann—

PETRA: Good-bye. [*Goes out.*]

ASLAKSEN: I say—Mr. Hovstad—

HOVSTAD: Well, well!—what is it?

ASLAKSEN: The Mayor is outside in the printing-room.

HOVSTAD: The Mayor, did you say?

ASLAKSEN: Yes, he wants to speak to you. He came in by the back door— didn't want to be seen, you understand.

HOVSTAD: What can he want? Wait a bit—I will go myself. [*Goes to the door of the printing-room, opens it, bows and invites* PETER STOCKMANN *in.*] Just see, Aslaksen, that no one—

ASLAKSEN: Quite so. [*Goes into the printing-room.*]

PETER STOCKMANN: You did not expect to see me here, Mr. Hovstad?

HOVSTAD: No, I confess I did not.

PETER STOCKMANN [*looking round*]: You are very snug in here—very nice indeed.

HOVSTAD: Oh—

PETER STOCKMANN: And here I come, without any notice, to take up your time!

HOVSTAD: By all means, Mr. Mayor. I am at your service. But let me relieve you of your— [*takes* STOCKMANN'S *hat and stick and puts them on a chair*]. Won't you sit down?

PETER STOCKMANN [*sitting down by the table*]: Thank you. [HOVSTAD *sits down.*] I have had an extremely annoying experience today, Mr. Hovstad.

HOVSTAD: Really? Ah well, I expect with all the various business you have to attend to—

PETER STOCKMANN: The Medical Officer of the Baths is responsible for what happened today.

HOVSTAD: Indeed? The Doctor?

PETER STOCKMANN: He has addressed a kind of report to the Baths Committee on the subject of certain supposed defects in the Baths.

HOVSTAD: Has he indeed?

PETER STOCKMANN: Yes—has he not told you? I thought he said—

HOVSTAD: Ah, yes—it is true he did mention something about—

ASLAKSEN [*coming from the printing-room*]: I ought to have that copy—

HOVSTAD [*angrily*]: Ahem!—there it is on the desk.

ASLAKSEN [*taking it*]: Right.

PETER STOCKMANN: But look there—that is the thing I was speaking of!

ASLAKSEN: Yes, that is the Doctor's article, Mr. Mayor.

HOVSTAD: Oh, is *that* what you were speaking about?

PETER STOCKMANN: Yes, that is it. What do you think of it?

HOVSTAD: Oh, I am only a layman—and I have only taken a very cursory glance at it.

PETER STOCKMANN: But you are going to print it?

HOVSTAD: I cannot very well refuse a distinguished man—

ASLAKSEN: I have nothing to do with editing the paper, Mr. Mayor—

PETER STOCKMANN: I understand.

ASLAKSEN: I merely print what is put into my hands.

PETER STOCKMANN: Quite so.

ASLAKSEN: And so I must— [*moves off towards the printing-room*].

PETER STOCKMANN: No, wait a moment, Mr. Aslaksen. You will allow me, Mr. Hovstad?

HOVSTAD: If you please, Mr. Mayor.

PETER STOCKMANN: You are a discreet and thoughtful man, Mr. Aslaksen.

ASLAKSEN: I am delighted to hear you think so, sir.

PETER STOCKMANN: And a man of very considerable influence.

ASLAKSEN: Chiefly among the small tradesmen, sir.

PETER STOCKMANN: The small tax-payers are the majority—here as everywhere else.

ASLAKSEN: That is true.

PETER STOCKMANN: And I have no doubt you know the general trend of opinion among them, don't you?

ASLAKSEN: Yes I think I may say I do, Mr. Mayor.

PETER STOCKMANN: Yes. Well, since there is such a praiseworthy spirit of self-sacrifice among the less wealthy citizens of our town—

ASLAKSEN: What?

HOVSTAD: Self-sacrifice?

PETER STOCKMANN: It is pleasing evidence of a public-spirited feeling, extremely pleasing evidence. I might almost say I hardly expected it. But you have a closer knowledge of public opinion than I.

ASLAKSEN: But, Mr. Mayor—

PETER STOCKMANN: And indeed it is no small sacrifice that the town is going to make.

HOVSTAD: The town?

ASLAKSEN: But I don't understand. Is it the Baths—?

PETER STOCKMANN: At a provisional estimate, the alterations that the Medical Officer asserts to be desirable will cost somewhere about twenty thousand pounds.

ASLAKSEN: That is a lot of money, but—

PETER STOCKMANN: Of course it will be necessary to raise a municipal loan.

HOVSTAD [*getting up*]: Surely you never mean that the town must pay—?

ASLAKSEN: Do you mean that it must come out of the municipal funds?— out of the ill-filled pockets of the small tradesmen?

PETER STOCKMANN: Well, my dear Mr. Aslaksen, where else is the money to come from?

ASLAKSEN: The gentlemen who own the Baths ought to provide that.

PETER STOCKMANN: The proprietors of the Baths are not in a position to incur any further expense.

ASLAKSEN: Is that absolutely certain, Mr. Mayor.

PETER STOCKMANN: I have satisfied myself that it is so. If the town wants these very extensive alterations, it will have to pay for them.

ASLAKSEN: But, damn it all—I beg your pardon—this is quite another matter, Mr. Hovstad!

HOVSTAD: It is, indeed.

PETER STOCKMANN: The most fatal part of it is that we shall be obliged to shut the Baths for a couple of years.

HOVSTAD: Shut them? Shut them altogether?

ASLAKSEN: For two years?

PETER STOCKMANN: Yes, the work will take as long as that—at least.

ASLAKSEN: I'm damned if we will stand that, Mr. Mayor! What are we householders to live upon in the meantime?

PETER STOCKMANN: Unfortunately that is an extremely difficult question to answer, Mr. Aslaksen. But what would you have us do? Do you suppose we shall have a single visitor in the town, if we go about proclaiming that our water is polluted, that we are living over a plague spot, that the entire town—

ASLAKSEN: And the whole thing is merely imagination?

PETER STOCKMANN: With the best will in the world, I have not been able to come to any other conclusion.

ASLAKSEN: Well then I must say it is absolutely unjustifiable of Dr. Stockmann—I beg your pardon, Mr. Mayor—

PETER STOCKMANN: What you say is lamentably true, Mr. Aslaksen. My brother has unfortunately always been a headstrong man.

ASLAKSEN: After this, do you mean to give him your support, Mr. Hovstad?

HOVSTAD: Can you suppose for a moment that I—?

PETER STOCKMANN: I have drawn up a short *résumé* of the situation as it appears from a reasonable man's point of view. In it I have indicated how certain possible defects might suitably be remedied without outrunning the resources of the Baths Committee.

HOVSTAD: Have you got it with you, Mr. Mayor.

PETER STOCKMANN [*fumbling in his pocket*]: Yes, I brought it with me in case you should—

ASLAKSEN: Good Lord, there he is!

PETER STOCKMANN: Who? My brother?

HOVSTAD: Where? Where?

ASLAKSEN: He has just gone through the printing-room.

PETER STOCKMANN: How unlucky! I don't want to meet him here, and I had still several things to speak to you about.

HOVSTAD [*pointing to the door on the right*]: Go in there for the present.

PETER STOCKMANN: But—?

HOVSTAD: You will only find Billing in there.

ASLAKSEN: Quick, quick, Mr. Mayor—he is just coming.

PETER STOCKMANN: Yes, very well; but see that you get rid of him quickly. [*Goes out through the door on the right, which* ASLAKSEN *opens for him and shuts after him.*]

HOVSTAD: Pretend to be doing something, Aslaksen. [*Sits down and writes.* ASLAKSEN *begins foraging among a heap of newspapers that are lying on a chair.*]

DR. STOCKMANN [*coming in from the printing-room*]: Here I am again. [*Puts down his hat and stick.*]

HOVSTAD [*writing*]: Already, Doctor? Hurry up with what we were speaking about, Aslaksen. We are very pressed for time today.

DR. STOCKMANN [*to* ASLAKSEN]: No proof for me to see yet, I hear.

ASLAKSEN [*without turning round*]: You couldn't expect it yet, Doctor.

DR. STOCKMANN: No, no; but I am impatient, as you can understand. I shall not know a moment's peace of mind till I see it in print.

HOVSTAD: Hm!—It will take a good while yet, won't it, Aslaksen?

ASLAKSEN: Yes, I am almost afraid it will.

DR. STOCKMANN: All right, my dear friends; I will come back. I do not mind coming back twice if necessary. A matter of such great importance—the welfare of the town at stake—it is no time to shirk trouble. [*Is just going, but stops and comes back.*] Look here—there is one thing more I want to speak to you about.

HOVSTAD: Excuse me, but could it not wait till some other time?

DR. STOCKMANN: I can tell you in half a dozen words. It is only this. When my article is read tomorrow and it is realised that I have been quietly working the whole winter for the welfare of the town—

HOVSTAD: Yes but, Doctor—

DR. STOCKMANN: I know what you are going to say. You don't see how on earth it was any more than my duty—my obvious duty as a citizen. Of course it wasn't; I know that as well as you. But my fellow citizens, you know—! Good Lord, think of all the good souls who think so highly of me—!

ASLAKSEN: Yes, our townsfolk have had a very high opinion of you so far, Doctor.

DR. STOCKMANN: Yes, and that is just why I am afraid they—. Well, this is the point; when this reaches them, especially the poorer classes, and sounds in their ears like a summons to take the town's affairs into their own hands for the future—

HOVSTAD [*getting up*]: Ahem! Doctor, I won't conceal from you the fact—

DR. STOCKMANN: Ah!—I knew there was something in the wind! But I won't hear a word of it. If anything of that sort is being set on foot—

HOVSTAD: Of what sort?

DR. STOCKMANN: Well, whatever it is—whether it is a demonstration in my honour, or a banquet, or a subscription list for some presentation to me —whatever it is, you must promise me solemnly and faithfully to put a stop to it. You too, Mr. Aslaksen; do you understand?

HOVSTAD: You must forgive me, Doctor, but sooner or later we must tell you the plain truth—

[*He is interrupted by the entrance of* MRS. STOCKMANN, *who comes in from the street door.*]

MRS. STOCKMANN [*seeing her husband*]: Just as I thought!

HOVSTAD [*going towards her*]: You too, Mrs. Stockmann?

DR. STOCKMANN: What on earth do *you* want here, Katherine?

MRS. STOCKMANN: I should think you know very well what I want.

HOVSTAD: Won't you sit down? Or perhaps—

MRS. STOCKMANN: No, thank you; don't trouble. And you must not be offended at my coming to fetch my husband; I am the mother of three children, you know.

DR. STOCKMANN: Nonsense!—we know all about that.

MRS. STOCKMANN: Well, one would not give you credit for much thought for your wife and children today; if you had had that, you would not have gone and dragged us all into misfortune.

DR. STOCKMANN: Are you out of your senses, Katherine! Because a man has a wife and children, is he not to be allowed to proclaim the truth—is he not to be allowed to be an actively useful citizen—is he not to be allowed to do a service to his native town!

MRS. STOCKMANN: Yes, Thomas—in reason.

ASLAKSEN: Just what I say. Moderation in everything.

MRS. STOCKMANN: And that is why you wrong us, Mr. Hovstad, in enticing my husband away from his home and making a dupe of him in all this.

HOVSTAD: I certainly am making a dupe of no one—

DR. STOCKMANN: Making a dupe of me! Do you suppose *I* should allow myself to be duped!

MRS. STOCKMANN: It is just what you do. I know quite well you have more brains than anyone in the town, but you are extremely easily duped, Thomas. [*To* HOVSTAD.] Please to realise that he loses his post at the Baths if you print what he has written—

ASLAKSEN: What!

HOVSTAD: Look here, Doctor—

DR. STOCKMANN [*laughing*]: Ha—ha!—just let them try! No, no—they will take good care not to. I have got the compact majority behind me, let me tell you!

MRS. STOCKMANN: Yes, that is just the worst of it—your having any such horrid thing behind you.

DR. STOCKMANN: Rubbish, Katherine!—Go home and look after your house and leave me to look after the community. How can you be so afraid, when I am so confident and happy? [*Walks up and down, rubbing his hands.*] Truth and the People will win the fight, you may be certain! I see the whole of the broad-minded middle class marching like a victorious army—! [*Stops beside a chair.*] What the deuce is that lying there?

ASLAKSEN: Good Lord!

HOVSTAD: Ahem!

DR. STOCKMANN: Here we have the topmost pinnacle of authority! [*Takes the Mayor's official hat carefully between his finger-tips and holds it up in the air.*]

MRS. STOCKMANN: The Mayor's hat!

DR. STOCKMANN: And here is the staff of office too. How in the name of all that's wonderful—?

HOVSTAD: Well, you see—

DR. STOCKMANN: Oh, I understand. He has been here trying to talk you over. Ha—ha!—he made rather a mistake there! And as soon as he caught sight of me in the printing-room—. [*Bursts out laughing.*] Did he run away, Mr. Aslaksen?

ASLAKSEN [*hurriedly*]: Yes, he ran away, Doctor.

DR. STOCKMANN: Ran away without his stick or his—. Fiddlesticks! Peter doesn't run away and leave his belongings behind him. But what the deuce have you done with him? Ah!—in there, of course. Now you shall see, Katherine!

MRS. STOCKMANN: Thomas—please don't—!

ASLAKSEN: Don't be rash, Doctor.

[DR. STOCKMANN *has put on the Mayor's hat and taken his stick in his hand. He goes up to the door, opens it, and stands with his hand to his hat at the salute.* PETER STOCKMANN *comes in, red with anger.* BILLING *follows him.*]

PETER STOCKMANN: What does this tomfoolery mean?

DR. STOCKMANN: Be respectful, my good Peter. I am the chief authority in the town now. [*Walks up and down.*]

MRS. STOCKMANN [*almost in tears*]: Really, Thomas!

PETER STOCKMANN [*following him about*]: Give me my hat and stick.

DR. STOCKMANN [*in the same tone as before*]: If you are chief constable, let me tell you that I am the Mayor—I am the master of the whole town, please understand!

PETER STOCKMANN: Take off my hat, I tell you. Remember it is part of an official uniform.

DR. STOCKMANN: Pooh! Do you think the newly awakened lion-hearted people are going to be frightened by an official hat? There is going to be a revolution in the town tomorrow, let me tell you. You thought you could turn me out; but now I shall turn you out—turn you out of all your various offices. Do you think I cannot? Listen to me. I have triumphant social forces behind me. Hovstad and Billing will thunder in the "People's Messenger," and Aslaksen will take the field at the head of the whole Householders' Association—

ASLAKSEN: That I won't, Doctor.

DR. STOCKMANN: Of course you will—

PETER STOCKMANN: Ah!—may I ask then if Mr. Hovstad intends to join this agitation.

HOVSTAD: No, Mr. Mayor.

ASLAKSEN: No, Mr. Hovstad is not such a fool as to go and ruin his paper and himself for the sake of an imaginary grievance.

DR. STOCKMANN [*looking round him*]: What does this mean?

HOVSTAD: You have represented your case in a false light, Doctor, and therefore I am unable to give you my support.

BILLING: And after what the Mayor was so kind as to tell me just now, I—

DR. STOCKMANN: A false light! Leave that part of it to me. Only print my article; I am quite capable of defending it.

HOVSTAD: I am not going to print it. I cannot and will not and dare not print it.

DR. STOCKMANN: You dare not? What nonsense!—you are the editor; and an editor controls his paper, I suppose!

ASLAKSEN: No, it is the subscribers, Doctor.

PETER STOCKMANN: Fortunately, yes.

ASLAKSEN: It is public opinion—the enlightened public—householders and people of that kind; they control the newspapers.

DR. STOCKMANN [*composedly*]: And I have all these influences against me?

ASLAKSEN: Yes, you have. It would mean the absolute ruin of the community if your article were to appear.

DR. STOCKMANN: Indeed.

PETER STOCKMANN: My hat and stick, if you please. [DR. STOCKMANN *takes off the hat and lays it on the table with the stick.* PETER STOCKMANN *takes them up.*] Your authority as mayor has come to an untimely end.

DR. STOCKMANN: We have not got to the end yet. [*To* HOVSTAD.] Then it is quite impossible for you to print my article in the "People's Messenger"?

HOVSTAD: Quite impossible—out of regard for your family as well.

MRS. STOCKMANN: You need not concern yourself about his family, thank you, Mr. Hovstad.

PETER STOCKMANN [*taking a paper from his pocket*]: It will be sufficient, for the guidance of the public, if this appears. It is an official statement. May I trouble you?

HOVSTAD [*taking the paper*]: Certainly; I will see that it is printed.

DR. STOCKMANN: But not mine. Do you imagine that you can silence me and stifle the truth! You will not find it so easy as you suppose. Mr. Aslaksen, kindly take my manuscript at once and print it as a pamphlet —at my expense. I will have four hundred copies—no, five—six hundred.

ASLAKSEN: If you offered me its weight in gold, I could not lend my press for any such purpose, Doctor. It would be flying in the face of public opinion. You will not get it printed anywhere in the town.

DR. STOCKMANN: Then give it back to me.

HOVSTAD [*giving him the MS.*]: Here it is.

DR. STOCKMANN [*taking his hat and stick*]: It shall be made public all the same. I will read it out at a mass meeting of the townspeople. All my fellow-citizens shall hear the voice of truth!

PETER STOCKMANN: You will not find any public body in the town that will give you the use of their hall for such a purpose.

ASLAKSEN: Not a single one, I am certain.

BILLING: No, I'm damned if you will find one.

MRS. STOCKMANN: But this is too shameful! Why should every one turn against you like that?

DR. STOCKMANN [*angrily*]: I will tell you why. It is because all the men in this town are old women—like you; they all think of nothing but their families, and never of the community.

MRS. STOCKMANN [*putting her arm into his*]: Then I will show them that an —an old woman can be a man for once. I am going to stand by you, Thomas!

DR. STOCKMANN: Bravely said, Katherine! It shall be made public—as I am a living soul! If I can't hire a hall, I shall hire a drum, and parade the town with it and read it at every street-corner.

PETER STOCKMANN: You are surely not such an arrant fool as that!

DR. STOCKMANN: Yes, I am.

ASLAKSEN: You won't find a single man in the whole town to go with you.

BILLING: No, I'm damned if you will.

MRS. STOCKMANN: Don't give in, Thomas. I will tell the boys to go with you.

DR. STOCKMANN: That is a splendid idea!

MRS. STOCKMANN: Morten will be delighted; and Ejlif will do whatever he does.

DR. STOCKMANN: Yes, and Petra!—and you too, Katherine!

MRS. STOCKMANN: No, I won't do that; but I will stand at the window and watch you, that's what I will do.

DR. STOCKMANN [*puts his arm round her and kisses her*]: Thank you, my dear! Now you and I are going to try a fall, my fine gentlemen! I am going to see whether a pack of cowards can succeed in gagging a patriot who wants to purify society! [*He and his wife go out by the street door.*]

PETER STOCKMANN [*shaking his head seriously*]: Now he has sent *her* out of her senses, too.

ACT IV

[SCENE: *A big old-fashioned room in* CAPTAIN HORSTER'S *house. At the back folding-doors, which are standing open, lead to an ante-room. Three windows in the left-hand wall. In the middle of the opposite wall a platform has been erected. On this is a small table with two candles, a water-bottle and glass, and a bell. The room is lit by lamps placed between the windows. In the foreground on the left there is a table with candles and a chair. To the right is a door and some chairs standing near it. The room is nearly filled with a crowd of townspeople of all sorts, a few women and schoolboys being amongst them. People are still streaming in from the back, and the room is soon filled.*]

1ST CITIZEN [*meeting another*]: Hullo, Lamstad! You here too?

2ND CITIZEN: I go to every public meeting, I do.

3RD CITIZEN: Brought your whistle too, I expect!

2ND CITIZEN: I should think so. Haven't you?

3RD CITIZEN: Rather! And old Evensen said he was going to bring a cow-horn, he did.

2ND CITIZEN: Good old Evensen! [*Laughter among the crowd.*]

4TH CITIZEN [*coming up to them*]: I say, tell me what is going on here to-night.

2ND CITIZEN: Dr. Stockmann is going to deliver an address attacking the Mayor.

4TH CITIZEN: But the Mayor is his brother.

1ST CITIZEN: That doesn't matter; Dr. Stockmann's not the chap to be afraid.

3RD CITIZEN: But he is in the wrong; it said so in the "People's Messenger."

2ND CITIZEN: Yes, I expect he must be in the wrong this time, because neither the Householders' Association nor the Citizens' Club would lend him their hall for his meeting.

1ST CITIZEN: He couldn't even get the loan of the hall at the Baths.

2ND CITIZEN: No, I should think not.

A MAN IN ANOTHER PART OF THE CROWD: I say—who are we to back up in this?

ANOTHER MAN, BESIDE HIM: Watch Aslaksen, and do as he does.

BILLING [pushing his way through the crowd, with a writing-case under his arm]: Excuse me, gentlemen—do you mind letting me through? I am reporting for the "People's Messenger." Thank you very much! [He sits down at the table on the left.]

A WORKMAN: Who was that?

SECOND WORKMAN: Don't you know him? It's Billing, who writes for Aslaksen's paper.

[CAPTAIN HORSTER brings in MRS. STOCKMANN and PETRA through the door on the right. EJLIF and MORTEN follow them in.]

HORSTER: I thought you might all sit here; you can slip out easily from here, if things get too lively.

MRS. STOCKMANN: Do you think there will be a disturbance?

HORSTER: One can never tell—with such a crowd. But sit down, and don't be uneasy.

MRS. STOCKMANN [sitting down]: It was extremely kind of you to offer my husband the room.

HORSTER: Well, if nobody else would—

PETRA [who has sat down beside her mother]: And it was a plucky thing to do, Captain Horster.

HORSTER: Oh, it is not such a great matter as all that.

[HOVSTAD and ASLAKSEN make their way through the crowd.]

ASLAKSEN [going up to HORSTER]: Has the Doctor not come yet?

HORSTER: He is waiting in the next room. [Movement in the crowd by the door at the back.]

HOVSTAD: Look—here comes the Mayor!

BILLING: Yes, I'm damned if he hasn't come after all!

[PETER STOCKMANN *makes his way gradually through the crowd, bows courteously, and takes up a position by the wall on the left. Shortly afterwards* DR. STOCKMANN *comes in by the right-hand door. He is dressed in a black frock-coat, with a white tie. There is a little feeble applause, which is hushed down. Silence is obtained.*]

DR. STOCKMANN [*in an undertone*]: How do you feel, Katherine?

MRS. STOCKMANN: All right, thank you. [*Lowering her voice.*] Be sure not to lose your temper, Thomas.

DR. STOCKMANN: Oh, I know how to control myself. [*Looks at his watch, steps on to the platform, and bows.*] It is a quarter past—so I will begin. [*Takes his MS. out of his pocket.*]

ASLAKSEN: I think we ought to elect a chairman first.

DR. STOCKMANN: No, it is quite unnecessary.

SOME OF THE CROWD: Yes—yes!

PETER STOCKMANN: I certainly think too that we ought to have a chairman.

DR. STOCKMANN: But I have called this meeting to deliver a lecture, Peter.

PETER STOCKMANN: Dr. Stockmann's lecture may possibly lead to a considerable conflict of opinion.

VOICES IN THE CROWD: A chairman! A chairman!

HOVSTAD: The general wish of the meeting seems to be that a chairman should be elected.

DR. STOCKMANN [*restraining himself*]: Very well—let the meeting have its way.

ASLAKSEN: Will the Mayor be good enough to undertake the task?

THREE MEN [*clapping their hands*]: Bravo! Bravo!

PETER STOCKMANN: For various reasons, which you will easily understand, I must beg to be excused. But fortunately we have amongst us a man who I think will be acceptable to you all. I refer to the President of the Householders' Association, Mr. Aslaksen!

SEVERAL VOICES: Yes—Aslaksen! Bravo Aslaksen!

[DR. STOCKMANN *takes up his MS. and walks up and down the platform.*]

ASLAKSEN: Since my fellow-citizens choose to entrust me with this duty, I cannot refuse.

[*Loud applause.* ASLAKSEN *mounts the platform.*]

BILLING [*writing*]: "Mr. Aslaksen was elected with enthusiasm."

ASLAKSEN: And now, as I am in this position, I should like to say a few brief words. I am a quiet and peaceable man, who believes in discreet moderation, and—and—in moderate discretion. All my friends can bear witness to that.

SEVERAL VOICES: That's right! That's right, Aslaksen!

ASLAKSEN: I have learnt in the school of life and experience that moderation is the most valuable virtue a citizen can possess—

PETER STOCKMANN: Hear, hear!

ASLAKSEN: —And moreover that discretion and moderation are what enable a man to be of most service to the community. I would therefore suggest to our esteemed fellow-citizen, who has called this meeting, that he should strive to keep strictly within the bounds of moderation.

A MAN BY THE DOOR: Three cheers for the Moderation Society!

A VOICE: Shame!

SEVERAL VOICES: Sh!—Sh!

ASLAKSEN: No interruptions, gentlemen, please! Does anyone wish to make any remarks?

PETER STOCKMANN: Mr. Chairman.

ASLAKSEN: The Mayor will address the meeting.

PETER STOCKMANN: In consideration of the close relationship in which, as you all know, I stand to the present Medical Officer of the Baths, I should have preferred not to speak this evening. But my official position with regard to the Baths and my solicitude for the vital interests of the town compel me to bring forward a motion. I venture to presume that there is not a single one of our citizens present who considers it desirable that unreliable and exaggerated accounts of the sanitary condition of the Baths and the town should be spread abroad.

SEVERAL VOICES: No, no! Certainly not! We protest against it!

PETER STOCKMANN: Therefore I should like to propose that the meeting should not permit the Medical Officer either to read or to comment on his proposed lecture.

DR. STOCKMANN [*impatiently*]: Not permit—! What the devil—!

MRS. STOCKMANN [*coughing*]: Ahem!—ahem!

DR. STOCKMANN [*collecting himself*]: Very well. Go ahead!

PETER STOCKMANN: In my communication to the "People's Messenger," I have put the essential facts before the public in such a way that every fair-minded citizen can easily form his own opinion. From it you will see that the main result of the Medical Officer's proposals—apart from their constituting a vote of censure on the leading men of the town— would be to saddle the ratepayers with an unnecessary expenditure of at least some thousands of pounds.

[*Sounds of disapproval among the audience, and some cat-calls.*]

ASLAKSEN [*ringing his bell*]: Silence, please, gentlemen! I beg to support the Mayor's motion. I quite agree with him that there is something behind this agitation started by the Doctor. He talks about the Baths; but it is a revolution he is aiming at—he wants to get the administration of the town put into new hands. No one doubts the honesty of the Doctor's intentions—no one will suggest that there can be any two opinions as to that. I myself am a believer in self-government for the people, provided it does not fall too heavily on the ratepayers. But that would be the case here; and that is why I will see Dr. Stockmann damned—I beg your pardon—before I go with him in the matter. You can pay too dearly for a thing sometimes; that is my opinion.

[*Loud applause on all sides.*]

HOVSTAD: I, too, feel called upon to explain my position. Dr. Stockmann's agitation appeared to be gaining a certain amount of sympathy at first, so I supported it as impartially as I could. But presently we had reason to suspect that we had allowed ourselves to be misled by misrepresentation of the state of affairs—

DR. STOCKMANN: Misrepresentation—!

HOVSTAD: Well, let us say a not entirely trustworthy representation. The Mayor's statement has proved that. I hope no one here has any doubt as to my liberal principles; the attitude of the "People's Messenger" towards important political questions is well known to every one. But the advice of experienced and thoughtful men has convinced me that in purely local matters a newspaper ought to proceed with a certain caution.

ASLAKSEN: I entirely agree with the speaker.

HOVSTAD: And, in the matter before us, it is now an undoubted fact that Dr. Stockmann has public opinion against him. Now, what is an editor's first and most obvious duty, gentlemen? Is it not to work in harmony with his readers? Has he not received a sort of tacit mandate to work persistently and assiduously for the welfare of those whose opinions he represents? Or is it possible I am mistaken in that?

VOICES FROM THE CROWD: No, no! You are quite right!

HOVSTAD: It has cost me a severe struggle to break with a man in whose house I have been lately a frequent guest—a man who till today has been able to pride himself on the undivided goodwill of his fellow-citizens—a man whose only, or at all events whose essential failing, is that he is swayed by his heart rather than his head.

A FEW SCATTERED VOICES: That is true! Bravo, Stockmann!

HOVSTAD: But my duty to the community obliged me to break with him. And there is another consideration that impels me to oppose him, and, as far as possible, to arrest him on the perilous course he has adopted; that is, consideration for his family—

DR. STOCKMANN: Please stick to the water-supply and drainage!

HOVSTAD:—consideration, I repeat, for his wife and his children for whom he has made no provision.

MORTEN: Is that us, mother?

MRS. STOCKMANN: Hush!

ASLAKSEN: I will now put the Mayor's proposition to the vote.

DR. STOCKMANN: There is no necessity! Tonight I have no intention of dealing with all that filth down at the Baths. No; I have something quite different to say to you.

PETER STOCKMANN [*aside*]: What is coming now?

A DRUNKEN MAN [*by the entrance door*]: I am a rate-payer! And therefore I have a right to speak too! And my entire—firm—inconceivable opinion is—

A NUMBER OF VOICES: Be quiet, at the back there!

OTHERS: He is drunk! Turn him out! [*They turn him out.*]

DR. STOCKMANN: Am I allowed to speak?

ASLAKSEN [*ringing his bell*]: Dr. Stockmann will address the meeting.

DR. STOCKMANN: I should like to have seen anyone, a few days ago, dare to attempt to silence me as has been done tonight! I would have defended my sacred rights as a man, like a lion! But now it is all one to me; I have something of even weightier importance to say to you. [*The crowd presses nearer to him,* MORTEN KIIL *conspicuous among them.*]

DR. STOCKMANN [*continuing*]: I have thought and pondered a great deal, these last few days—pondered over such a variety of things that in the end my head seemed too full to hold them—

PETER STOCKMANN [*with a cough*]: Ahem!

DR. STOCKMANN: —but I got them clear in my mind at last, and then I saw the whole situation lucidly. And that is why I am standing here to-night. I have a great revelation to make to you, my fellow-citizens! I will impart to you a discovery of a far wider scope than the trifling matter that our water-supply is poisoned and our medicinal Baths are standing on pestiferous soil.

A NUMBER OF VOICES [*shouting*]: Don't talk about the Baths! We won't hear you! None of that!

DR. STOCKMANN: I have already told you that what I want to speak about is the great discovery I have made lately—the discovery that all the sources of our *moral* life are poisoned and that the whole fabric of our civic community is founded on the pestiferous soil of falsehood.

VOICES OF DISCONCERTED CITIZENS: What is that he says?

PETER STOCKMANN: Such an insinuation—!

ASLAKSEN [*with his hand on his bell*]: I call upon the speaker to moderate his language.

DR. STOCKMANN: I have always loved my native town as a man only can love the home of his youthful days. I was not old when I went away from here; and exile, longing and memories cast as it were an additional halo over both the town and its inhabitants. [*Some clapping and applause.*] And there I stayed, for many years, in a horrible hole far away up north. When I came into contact with some of the people that lived scattered about among the rocks, I often thought it would of been more service to the poor half-starved creatures if a veterinary doctor had been sent up there, instead of a man like me. [*Murmurs among the crowd.*]

BILLING [*laying down his pen*]: I'm damned if I have ever heard—!

HOVSTAD: It is an insult to a respectable population!

DR. STOCKMANN: Wait a bit! I do not think anyone will charge me with having forgotten my native town up there. I was like one of the eider-ducks brooding on its nest, and what I hatched was—the plans for these Baths. [*Applause and protests.*] And then when fate at last decreed for me the great happiness of coming home again—I assure you, gentlemen, I thought I had nothing more in the world to wish for. Or rather, there was one thing I wished for—eagerly, untiringly, ardently—and that was to be able to be of service to my native town and the good of the community.

PETER STOCKMANN [*looking at the ceiling*]: You chose a strange way of doing it—ahem!

DR. STOCKMANN: And so, with my eyes blinded to the real facts, I revelled in happiness. But yesterday morning—no, to be precise, it was yester-day afternoon—the eyes of my mind were opened wide, and the first thing I realised was the colossal stupidity of the authorities—.[*Uproar, shouts and laughter.* MRS. STOCKMANN *coughs persistently.*]

PETER STOCKMANN: Mr. Chairman!

ASLAKSEN [*ringing his bell*]: By virtue of my authority—!

DR. STOCKMANN: It is a pretty thing to catch me up on a word, Mr. As-laksen. What I mean is only that I got scent of the unbelievable piggish-ness our leading men had been responsible for down at the Baths. I can't stand leading men at any price!—I have had enough of such people in my time. They are like billy-goats in a young plantation; they do mis-chief everywhere. They stand in a free man's way, whichever way he turns, and what I should like best would be to see them exterminated like any other vermin—. [*Uproar.*]

PETER STOCKMANN: Mr. Chairman, can we allow such expressions to pass?

ASLAKSEN [*with his hand on his bell*]: Doctor—!

DR. STOCKMANN: I cannot understand how it is that I have only now ac-quired a clear conception of what these gentry are, when I had almost daily before my eyes in this town such an excellent specimen of them —my brother Peter—slow-witted and hide-bound in prejudice—. [*Laughter, uproar and hisses.* MRS. STOCKMANN *sits coughing assiduously.* AS-LAKSEN *rings his bell violently.*]

THE DRUNKEN MAN [*who has got in again*]: Is it me he is talking about? My name's Petersen, all right—but devil take me if I—

ANGRY VOICES: Turn out that drunken man! Turn him out. [*He is turned out again.*]

PETER STOCKMANN: Who was that person?

1st CITIZEN: I don't know who he is, Mr. Mayor.

2nd CITIZEN: He doesn't belong here.

3rd CITIZEN: I expect he is a navvy from over at—[*the rest is inaudible*].

ASLAKSEN: He had obviously had too much beer.—Proceed, Doctor; but please strive to be moderate in your language.

DR. STOCKMANN: Very well, gentlemen, I will say no more about our leading men. And if anyone imagines, from what I have just said, that my object is to attack these people this evening, he is wrong—absolutely wide of the mark. For I cherish the comforting conviction that these parasites —all these venerable relics of a dying school of thought—are most admirably paving the way for their own extinction; they need no doctor's help to hasten their own extinction; they need no doctor's help to hasten their end. Nor is it folk of that kind who constitute the most pressing danger to the community. It is not they who are most instrumental in poisoning the sources of our moral life and infecting the ground on which we stand. It is not they who are the most dangerous enemies of truth and freedom amongst us.

SHOUTS FROM ALL SIDES: Who then? Who is it? Name! Name!

DR. STOCKMANN: You may depend upon it I shall name them! That is precisely the great discovery I made yesterday. [*Raises his voice.*] The most dangerous enemy of truth and freedom amongst us is the compact majority—yes, the damned compact Liberal majority—that is it! Now you know! [*Tremendous uproar. Most of the crowd are shouting, stamping and hissing. Some of the older men among them exchange stolen glances and seem to be enjoying themselves.* MRS. STOCKMANN *gets up, looking anxious.* EJLIF *and* MORTEN *advance threateningly upon some schoolboys who are playing pranks.* ASLAKSEN *rings his bell and begs for silence.* HOVSTAD *and* BILLING *both talk at once, but are inaudible. At last quiet is restored.*]

ASLAKSEN: As chairman, I call upon the speaker to withdraw the ill-considered expressions he has just used.

DR. STOCKMANN: Never, Mr. Aslaksen! It is the majority in our community that denies me my freedom and seeks to prevent my speaking the truth.

HOVSTAD: The majority always has right on its side.

BILLING: And truth too, by God!

DR. STOCKMANN: The majority *never* has right on its side. Never, I say! That is one of these social lies against which an independent, intelligent man must wage war. Who is it that constitute the majority of the population in a country? Is it the clever folk or the stupid? I don't imagine you will dispute the fact that at present the stupid people are in an absolutely overwhelming majority all the world over. But, good Lord!—you can never pretend that it is right that the stupid folk should govern the clever ones! [*Uproar and cries.*] Oh, yes—you can shout me down, I know! but you cannot answer me. The majority has *might* on its side —unfortunately; but *right* it has *not.* I am in the right—I and a few other scattered individuals. The minority is always in the right. [*Renewed uproar.*]

HOVSTAD: Aha!—so Dr. Stockmann has become an aristocrat since the day before yesterday!

DR. STOCKMANN: I have already said that I don't intend to waste a word on the puny, narrow-chested, short-winded crew whom we are leaving astern. Pulsating life no longer concerns itself with them. I am thinking of the few, the scattered few amongst us, who have absorbed new and vigorous truths. Such men stand, as it were, at the outposts, so far ahead that the compact majority has not yet been able to come up with them; and there they are fighting for truths that are too newly-born into the world of consciousness to have any considerable number of people on their side as yet.

HOVSTAD: So the Doctor is a revolutionary now!

DR. STOCKMANN: Good heavens—of course I am, Mr. Hovstad! I propose to raise a revolution against the lie that the majority has the monopoly on the truth. What sort of truths are they that the majority usually supports? They are truths that are of such advanced age that they are beginning to break up. And if a truth is as old as that, it is also in a fair way to become a lie, gentlemen. [*Laughter and mocking cries.*] Yes, believe me or not, as you like; but truths are by no means as long-lived as Methuselah—as some folks imagine. A normally constituted truth lives, let us say, as a rule seventeen or eighteen, or at most twenty years; seldom longer. But truths as aged as that are always worn frightfully thin, and nevertheless it is only then that the majority recognises them and recommends them to the community as wholesome moral nourishment. There is no great nutritive value in that sort of fare, I can assure you; and, as a doctor, I ought to know. These "majority truths" are like last year's cured meat—like rancid, tainted ham; and they are the origin of the moral scurvy that is rampant in our communities.

ASLAKSEN: It appears to me that the speaker is wandering a long way from his subject.

PETER STOCKMANN: I quite agree with the Chairman.

DR. STOCKMANN: Have you gone clean out of your senses, Peter? I am sticking as closely to my subject as I can; for my subject is precisely this, that it is the masses, the majority—this infernal compact majority—that poisons the sources of our moral life and infects the ground we stand on.

HOVSTAD: And all this because the great, broad-minded majority of the people is prudent enough to show deference only to well-ascertained and well-approved truths?

DR. STOCKMANN: Ah, my good Mr. Hovstad, don't talk nonsense about well-ascertained truths! The truths of which the masses now approve are the very truths that the fighters at the outposts held to in the days of our grandfathers. We fighters at the outposts nowadays no longer approve of them; and I do not believe there is any other well-ascertained truth except this, that no community can live a healthy life if it is nourished only on such old marrowless truths.

HOVSTAD: But instead of standing there using vague generalities, it would be interesting if you would tell us what these old marrowless truths are, that we are nourished on.

[*Applause from many quarters.*]

DR. STOCKMANN: Oh, I could give you a whole string of such abominations; but to begin with I will confine myself to one well-approved truth, which at bottom is a foul lie, but upon which nevertheless Mr. Hovstad and the "People's Messenger" and all the "Messenger's" supporters are nourished.

HOVSTAD: And that is—?

DR. STOCKMANN: That is, the doctrine you have inherited from your forefathers and proclaim thoughtlessly far and wide—the doctrine that the public, the crowd, the masses, are the essential part of the population —that they constitute the People—that the common folk, the ignorant and incomplete element in the community, have the same right to pronounce judgment and to approve, to direct and to govern, as the isolated, intellectually superior personalities in it.

BILLING: Well, damn me if ever I—

HOVSTAD [*at the same time, shouting out*]: Fellow-citizens, take good note of that!

A NUMBER OF VOICES [*angrily*]: Oho!—we are not the People! Only the superior folk are to govern, are they!

A WORKMAN: Turn the fellow out, for talking such rubbish!

ANOTHER: Out with him!

ANOTHER [*calling out*]: Blow your horn, Evensen!

[*A horn is blown loudly, amidst hisses and an angry uproar.*]

DR. STOCKMANN [*when the noise has somewhat abated*]: Be reasonable! Can't you stand hearing the voice of truth for once? I don't in the least expect you to agree with me all at once; but I must say I did expect Mr. Hovstad to admit I was right, when he had recovered his composure a little. He claims to be a freethinker—

VOICES [*in murmurs of astonishment*]: Freethinker, did he say? Is Hovstad a freethinker?

HOVSTAD [*shouting*]: Prove it, Dr. Stockmann! When have I said so in print?

DR. STOCKMANN [*reflecting*]: No, confound it, you are right!—you have never had the courage to. Well, I won't put you in a hole, Mr. Hovstad. Let us say it is I that am the freethinker, then. I am going to prove to you, scientifically, that the "People's Messenger" leads you by the nose in a shameful manner when it tells you that you—that the common people, the crowd, the masses, are the real essence of the People. That is only a newspaper lie, I tell you! The common people are nothing more than the raw material of which a People is made. [*Groans, laughter and uproar.*] Well, isn't that the case. Isn't there an enormous difference between a well-bred and an ill-bred strain of animals? Take, for instance, a common barn-door hen. What sort of eating do you get from a shrivelled up old scrag of a fowl like that? Not much, do you! And what sort of eggs does it lay? A fairly good crow or a raven can lay pretty nearly as good an egg. But take a well-bred Spanish or Japanese hen, or a good pheasant or a turkey—then you will see the difference. Or take the case of dogs, with whom we humans are on such intimate terms. Think first of an ordinary common cur—I mean one of the horrible, coarse-haired, low-bred curs that do nothing but run about the streets and befoul the walls of the houses. Compare one of these curs with a poodle whose sires for many generations have been bred in a gentleman's house, where they have had the best of food and had the opportunity of hearing soft voices and music. Do you not think that the poodle's brain is developed to quite a different degree from that of the cur? Of course it is. It is puppies of well-bred poodles like that, that showmen train to do incredibly clever tricks—things that a common cur could never learn to do even if it stood on its head. [*Uproar and mocking cries.*]

A CITIZEN [*calls out*]: Are you going to make out we are dogs, now?

ANOTHER CITIZEN: We are not animals, Doctor!

DR. STOCKMANN: Yes but, bless my soul, we *are*, my friend! It is true we are the finest animals anyone could wish for; but, even amongst us, exceptionally fine animals are rare. There is a tremendous difference between poodle-men and cur-men. And the amusing part of it is, that Mr. Hovstad quite agrees with me as long as it is a question of four-footed animals—

HOVSTAD: Yes, it is true enough as far as they are concerned.

DR. STOCKMANN: Very well. But as soon as I extend the principle and apply it to two-legged animals, Mr. Hovstad stops short. He no longer dares to think independently, or to pursue his ideas to their logical conclusion; so he turns the whole theory upside down and proclaims in the "People's Messenger" that it is the barn-door hens and street curs that are the finest specimens in the menagerie. But that is always the way, as long as a man retains the traces of common origin and has not worked his way up to intellectual distinction.

HOVSTAD: I lay no claim to any sort of distinction. I am the son of humble countryfolk, and I am proud that the stock I come from is rooted deep among the common people he insults.

VOICES: Bravo, Hovstad! Bravo! Bravo!

DR. STOCKMANN: The kind of common people I mean are not only to be found low down in the social scale; they crawl and swarm all around us—even in the highest social positions. You have only to look at your own fine, distinguished Mayor! My brother Peter is every bit as plebian as anyone that walks in two shoes—[*laughter and hisses.*]

PETER STOCKMANN: I protest against personal allusions of this kind.

DR. STOCKMANN [*imperturbably*]: —and that, not because he is, like myself, descended from some old rascal of a pirate from Pomerania or thereabouts—because that is who we are descended from—

PETER STOCKMANN: An absurd legend. I deny it!

DR. STOCKMANN:—but because he thinks what his superiors think and holds the same opinions as they. People who do that are, intellectually speaking, common people; and that is why my magnificent brother Peter is in reality so very far from any distinction—and consequently also so far from being liberal-minded.

PETER STOCKMANN: Mr. Chairman—!

HOVSTAD: So it is only the distinguished men that are liberal-minded in this country? We are learning something quite new! [*Laughter.*]

DR. STOCKMANN: Yes, that is part of my new discovery too. And another part of it is that broad-mindedness is almost precisely the same thing as morality. That is why I maintain that it is absolutely inexcusable in the "People's Messenger" to proclaim, day in and day out, the false doctrine that it is the masses, the crowd, the compact majority, that have the monopoly of broad-mindedness and morality—and that vice and corruption and every kind of intellectual depravity are the result of culture, just as all the filth that is draining into our Baths is the result of the tanneries up at Mölledal! [*Uproar and interruptions.* DR. STOCKMANN *is undisturbed, and goes on, carried away by his ardour, with a smile.*] And yet this same "People's Messenger" can go on preaching that the masses ought to be elevated to higher conditions of life! But, bless my soul, if the "Messenger's" teaching is to be depended upon, this very raising up the masses would mean nothing more or less than setting them straightway upon the paths of depravity! Happily the theory that culture demoralises is only an old falsehood that our forefathers believed in and we have inherited. No, it is ignorance, poverty, ugly conditions of life, that do the devil's work! In a house which does not get aired and swept every day—my wife Katherine maintains that the floor ought to be scrubbed as well, but that is a debatable question—in such a house, let me tell you, people will lose within two or three years the power of thinking or acting in a moral manner. Lack of oxygen weakens the conscience. And there must be a plentiful lack of oxygen in very many houses in this town, I should think, judging from the fact that the whole compact majority can be unconscientious enough to wish to build the town's prosperity on a quagmire of falsehood and deceit.

ASLAKSEN: We cannot allow such a grave accusation to be flung at a citizen community.

A CITIZEN: I move that the Chairman direct the speaker to sit down.

VOICES [*angrily*]: Hear, hear! Quite right! Make him sit down!

DR. STOCKMAN [*losing his self-control*]: Then I will go and shout the truth at every street corner! I will write it in other towns' newspapers! The whole country shall know what is going on here!

HOVSTAD: It almost seems as if Dr. Stockmann's intention were to ruin the town.

DR. STOCKMANN: Yes, my native town is so dear to me that I would rather ruin it than see it flourishing upon a lie.

ASLAKSEN: This is really serious. [*Uproar and cat-calls.* MRS. STOCKMANN *coughs, but to no purpose; her husband does not listen to her any longer.*]

HOVSTAD [*shouting above the din*]: A man must be a public enemy to wish to ruin a whole community!

DR. STOCKMANN [*with growing fervour*]: What does the destruction of a community matter, if it lives on lies! It ought to be razed to the ground, I tell you! All who live by lies ought to be exterminated like vermin! You will end by infecting the whole country; you will bring about such a state of things that the whole country will deserve to be ruined. And if things come to that pass, I shall say from the bottom of my heart: Let the whole country perish, let all these people be exterminated!

VOICES FROM THE CROWD: That is talking like an out-and-out enemy of the people!

BILLING: There sounded the voice of the people, by all that's holy!

THE WHOLE CROWD [*shouting*]: Yes, yes! He is an enemy of the people! He hates his country! He hates his own people!

ASLAKSEN: Both as a citizen and as an individual, I am profoundly disturbed by what we have had to listen to. Dr. Stockmann has shown himself in a light I should never have dreamed of. I am unhappily obliged to subscribe to the opinion which I have just heard my estimable fellow-citizens utter; and I propose that we should give expression to that opinion in a resolution. I propose a resolution as follows: "This meeting declares that it considers Dr. Thomas Stockmann, Medical Officer of the Baths, to be an enemy of the people." [*A storm of cheers and applause. A number of men surround the* DOCTOR *and hiss him.* MRS. STOCKMANN *and* PETRA *have got up from their seats.* MORTEN *and* EJLIF *are fighting the other schoolboys for hissing; some of their elders separate them.*]

DR. STOCKMANN [*to the men who are hissing him*]: Oh, you fools! I tell you that—

ASLAKSEN [*ringing his bell*]: We cannot hear you now, Doctor. A formal vote is about to be taken; but, out of regard for personal feelings, it shall be by ballot and not verbal. Have you any clean paper, Mr. Billing?

BILLING: I have both blue and white here.

ASLAKSEN [*going to him*]: That will do nicely; we shall get on more quickly that way. Cut it up into small strips—yes, that's it. [*To the meeting.*] Blue means no; white means yes. I will come round myself and collect votes. PETER STOCKMANN *leaves the hall.* ASLAKSEN *and one or two others go round the room with the slips of paper in their hats.*]

1ST CITIZEN [*to* HOVSTAD]: I say, what has come to the Doctor? What are we to think of it?

HOVSTAD: Oh, you know how headstrong he is.

2ND CITIZEN [*to* BILLING]: Billing, you go to their house—have you ever noticed if the fellow drinks?

BILLING: Well I'm hanged if I know what to say. There are always spirits on the table when you go.

3RD CITIZEN: I rather think he goes quite off his head sometimes.

1ST CITIZEN: I wonder if there is any madness in his family?

BILLING: I shouldn't wonder if there were.

4TH CITIZEN: No, it is nothing more than sheer malice; he wants to get even with somebody for something or other.

BILLING: Well certainly he suggested a rise in his salary on one occasion lately, and did not get it.

THE CITIZENS [*together*]: Ah!—then it is easy to understand how it is!

THE DRUNKEN MAN [*who has got amongst the audience again*]: I want a blue one, I do! And I want a white one too!

VOICES: It's that drunken chap again! Turn him out!

MORTEN KIIL [*going up to* DR. STOCKMANN]: Well, Stockmann, do you see what these monkey tricks of yours lead to?

DR. STOCKMANN: I have done my duty.

MORTEN KIIL: What was that you said about the tanneries at Mölledal?

DR. STOCKMANN: You heard well enough. I said they were the source of all the filth.

MORTEN KIIL: My tannery too?

DR. STOCKMANN: Unfortunately your tannery is by far the worst.

MORTEN KIIL: Are you going to put that in the papers?

DR. STOCKMANN: I shall conceal nothing.

MORTEN KIIL: That may cost you dear, Stockmann. [*Goes out.*]

A STOUT MAN [*going up to* CAPTAIN HORSTER, *without taking any notice of the ladies*]: Well, Captain, so you lend your house to enemies of the people?

HORSTER: I imagine I can do what I like with my own possessions, Mr. Vik.

THE STOUT MAN: Then you can have no objection to my doing the same with mine.

HORSTER: What do you mean, sir?

THE STOUT MAN: You shall hear from me in the morning. [*Turns his back on him and moves off.*]

PETRA: Was that not your owner, Captain Horster?

HORSTER: Yes, that was Mr. Vik the ship-owner.

ASLAKSEN [*with the voting-papers in his hands, gets up on to the platform and rings his bell*]: Gentlemen, allow me to announce the result. By the votes of every one here except one person—

A YOUNG MAN: That is the drunk chap!

ASLAKSEN: By the votes of every one here except a tipsy man, this meeting of citizens declares Dr. Thomas Stockmann to be an enemy of the people. [*Shouts and applause.*] Three cheers for our ancient and honourable citizen community! [*Renewed applause.*] Three cheers for our able and energetic Mayor, who has so loyally suppressed the promptings of family feeling! [*Cheers.*] The meeting is dissolved. [*Gets down.*]

BILLING: Three cheers for the Chairman!

THE WHOLE CROWD: Three cheers for Aslaksen! Hurrah!

DR. STOCKMANN: My hat and coat, Petra! Captain, have you room on your ship for passengers to the New World?

HORSTER: For you and yours we will make room, Doctor.

DR. STOCKMANN [*as* PETRA *helps him into his coat*]: Good. Come, Katherine! Come, boys!

MRS. STOCKMANN [*in an undertone*]: Thomas, dear, let us go out by the back way.

DR. STOCKMANN: No back ways for me, Katherine. [*Raising his voice.*] You will hear more of this enemy of the people, before he shakes the dust off his shoes upon you! I am not so forgiving as a certain Person; I do not say: "I forgive you, for ye know not what ye do."

ASLAKSEN [*shouting*]: That is a blasphemous comparison, Dr. Stockmann!

BILLING: It is, by God! It's dreadful for an earnest man to listen to.

A COARSE VOICE: Threatens us now, does he!

OTHER VOICES [*excitedly*]: Let's go and break his windows! Duck him in the fjord!

ANOTHER VOICE: Blow your horn, Evensen! Pip, pip!

[*Horn-blowing, hisses, and wild cries.* DR. STOCKMANN *goes out through the hall with his family,* HORSTER *elbowing a way for them.*]

THE WHOLE CROWD [*howling after them as they go*]: Enemy of the People! Enemy of the People!

BILLING [*as he puts his papers together*]: Well, I'm damned if I go and drink toddy with the Stockmanns tonight!

[*The crowd presses towards the exit. The uproar continues outside; shouts of "Enemy of the People!" are heard from without.*]

ACT V

[SCENE: DR. STOCKMANN'S *study. Bookcases, and cabinets containing specimens, line the walls. At the back is a door leading to the hall; in the foreground on the left, a door leading to the sitting-room. In the right-hand wall are two windows, of which all the panes are broken. The* DOCTOR'S *desk, littered with books and papers, stands in the middle of the room, which is in disorder. It is morning.* DR. STOCKMANN *in dressing-gown, slippers and a smoking-cap, is bending down and raking with an umbrella under one of the cabinets. After a little while he rakes out a stone.*]

DR. STOCKMANN [*calling through the open sitting-room door*]: Katherine, I have found another one.

MRS. STOCKMANN [*from the sitting-room*]: Oh, you will find a lot more yet, I expect.

DR. STOCKMANN [*adding the stone to a heap of others on the table*]: I shall treasure these stones as relics. Ejlif and Morten shall look at them every day, and when they are grown up they shall inherit them as heirlooms. [*Rakes about under a bookcase.*] Hasn't—what the deuce is her name?—the girl, you know—hasn't she been to fetch the glazier yet?

MRS. STOCKMANN [*coming in*]: Yes, but he said he didn't know if he would be able to come to-day.

DR. STOCKMANN: You will see he won't dare to come.

MRS. STOCKMANN: Well, that is just what Randine thought—that he didn't dare to, on account of the neighbours. [*Calls into the sitting-room.*] What is it you want, Randine? Give it to me. [*Goes in, and comes out again directly.*] Here is a letter for you, Thomas.

DR. STOCKMANN: Let me see it. [*Opens and reads it.*] Ah!—of course.

MRS. STOCKMANN: Who is it from?

DR. STOCKMANN: From the landlord. Notice to quit.

MRS. STOCKMANN: Is it possible? Such a nice man—

DR. STOCKMANN [*looking at the letter*]: Does not dare do otherwise, he says. Doesn't like doing it, but dare not do otherwise—on account of his fellow-citizens—out of regard for public opinion. Is in a dependent position—dare not offend certain influential men—

MRS. STOCKMANN: There, you see, Thomas!

DR. STOCKMANN: Yes, yes, I see well enough; the whole lot of them in the town are cowards; not a man among them dares do anything for fear of the others. [*Throws the letter on to the table.*] But it doesn't matter to us, Katherine. We are going to sail away to the New World, and—

MRS. STOCKMANN: But, Thomas, are you sure we are well advised to take this step?

DR. STOCKMANN: Are you suggesting that I should stay here, where they have pilloried me as an enemy of the people—branded me—broken my windows! And just look here, Katherine—they have torn a great rent in my black trousers too!

MRS. STOCKMANN: Oh, dear!—and they are the best pair you have got!

DR. STOCKMANN: You should never wear your best trousers when you go out to fight for freedom and truth. It is not that I care so much about the trousers, you know; you can always sew them up again for me. But that the common herd should dare to make this attack on me, as if they were my equals—that is what I cannot, for the life of me, swallow!

MRS. STOCKMANN: There is no doubt they have behaved very ill to you, Thomas; but is that sufficient reason for our leaving our native country for good and all?

DR. STOCKMANN: If we went to another town, do you suppose we should not find the common people just as insolent as they are here? Depend upon it, there is not much to choose between them. Oh, well, let the curs snap—that is not the worst part of it. The worst is that, from one end of this country to the other, every man is the slave of his Party. Although, as far as that goes, I daresay it is not much better in the free West either; the compact majority, and liberal public opinion, and all that infernal old bag of tricks are probably rampant there too. But there things are done on a larger scale, you see. They may kill you, but they won't put you to death by slow torture. They don't squeeze a free man's soul in a vice, as they do here. And, if need be, one can live in solitude. [*Walks up and down.*] If only I knew where there was a virgin forest or a small South Sea island for sale, cheap—

MRS. STOCKMANN: But think of the boys, Thomas!

DR. STOCKMANN [*standing still*]: What a strange woman you are, Katherine! Would you prefer to have the boys grow up in a society like this? You saw for yourself last night that half the population are out of their minds; and if the other half have not lost their senses, it is because they are mere brutes, with no sense to lose.

MRS. STOCKMANN: But, Thomas dear, the imprudent things you said had something to do with it, you know.

DR. STOCKMANN: Well, isn't what I said perfectly true? Don't they turn every idea topsy-turvy? Don't they make a regular hotch-potch of right and wrong? Don't they say that the things I know are true, are lies? The craziest part of it all is the fact of these "liberals," men of full age, going about in crowds imagining that they are the broad-minded party? Did you ever hear anything like it, Katherine!

MRS. STOCKMANN: Yes, yes, it's mad enough of them, certainly; but—[PETRA *comes in from the sitting-room.*] Back from school already?

PETRA: Yes. I have been given notice of dismissal.

MRS. STOCKMANN: Dismissal?

DR. STOCKMANN: You too?

PETRA: Mrs. Busk gave me my notice; so I thought it was best to go at once.

DR. STOCKMANN: You were perfectly right, too!

MRS. STOCKMANN: Who would have thought Mrs. Busk was a woman like that!

PETRA: Mrs. Busk isn't a bit like that, mother; I saw quite plainly how it hurt her to do it. But she didn't dare do otherwise, she said; and so I got my notice.

DR. STOCKMANN [*laughing and rubbing his hands*]: She didn't dare do otherwise, either! It's delicious!

MRS. STOCKMANN: Well, after the dreadful scenes last night—

PETRA: It was not only that. Just listen to this, father!

DR. STOCKMANN: Well?

PETRA: Mrs. Busk showed me no less than three letters she received this morning—

DR. STOCKMANN: Anonymous, I suppose?

PETRA: Yes.

DR. STOCKMANN: Yes, because they didn't dare to risk signing their names, Katherine!

PETRA: And two of them were to the effect that a man, who has been our guest here, was declaring last night at the Club that my views on various subjects are extremely emancipated—

DR. STOCKMANN: You did not deny that, I hope?

PETRA: No, you know I wouldn't. Mrs. Busk's own views are tolerably emancipated, when we are alone together; but now that this report about me is being spread, she dare not keep me on any longer.

MRS. STOCKMANN: And some one who had been a guest of ours! That shows you the return you get for your hospitality, Thomas!

DR. STOCKMANN: We won't live in such a disgusting hole any longer. Pack up as quickly as you can, Katherine; the sooner we can get away, the better.

MRS. STOCKMANN: Be quiet—I think I hear some one in the hall. See who it is, Petra.

PETRA [*opening the door*]: Oh, it's you, Captain Horster! Do come in.

HORSTER [*coming in*]: Good morning. I thought I would just come in and see how you were.

DR. STOCKMANN [*shaking his hand*]: Thanks—that is really kind of you.

MRS. STOCKMANN: And thank you, too, for helping us through the crowd, Captain Horster.

PETRA: How did you manage to get home again?

HORSTER: Oh, somehow or other. I am fairly strong, and there is more sound than fury about these folk.

DR. STOCKMANN: Yes, isn't their swinish cowardice astonishing? Look here, I will show you something! There are all the stones they have thrown through my windows. Just look at them! I'm hanged if there are more than two decently large bits of hardstone in the whole heap; the rest are nothing but gravel—wretched little things. And yet they stood out there bawling and swearing that they would do me some violence; but as for *doing* anything—you don't see much of that in this town.

HORSTER: Just as well for you this time, Doctor!

DR. STOCKMANN: True enough. But it makes one angry all the same; because if some day it should be a question of a national fight in real earnest, you will see that public opinion will be in favour of taking to one's heels, and the compact majority will turn tail like a flock of sheep, Captain Horster. That is what is so mournful to think of; it gives me so much concern, that—. No, devil take it, it is ridiculous to care about it! They have called me an enemy of the people, so an enemy of the people let me be!

MRS. STOCKMANN: You will never be that, Thomas.

DR. STOCKMANN: Don't swear to that, Katherine. To be called an ugly name may have the same effect as a pin-scratch in the lung. And that hateful name—I can't get quit of it. It is sticking here in the pit of my stomach, eating into me like a corrosive acid. And no magnesia will remove it.

PETRA: Bah!—you should only laugh at them, father.

HORSTER: They will change their minds some day, Doctor.

MRS. STOCKMANN: Yes, Thomas, as sure as you are standing here.

DR. STOCKMANN: Perhaps, when it is too late. Much good may it do them! They may wallow in their filth then and rue the day when they drove a patriot into exile. When do you sail, Captain Horster?

HORSTER: Hm!—that was just what I had come to speak about—

DR. STOCKMANN: Why, has anything gone wrong with the ship?

HORSTER: No; but what has happened is that I am not to sail in it.

PETRA: Do you mean that you have been dismissed from your command?

HORSTER [*smiling*]: Yes, that's just it.

PETRA: You too.

MRS. STOCKMANN: There, you see, Thomas!

DR. STOCKMANN: And that for the truth's sake! Oh, if I had thought such a thing possible—

HORSTER: You mustn't take it to heart; I shall be sure to find a job with some ship-owner or other, elsewhere.

DR. STOCKMANN: And that is this man Vik—a wealthy man, independent of every one and everything—! Shame on him!

HORSTER: He is quite an excellent fellow otherwise; he told me himself he would willingly have kept me on, if only he had dared—

DR. STOCKMANN: But he didn't dare? No, of course not.

HORSTER: It is not such an easy matter, he said, for a party man—

DR. STOCKMANN: The worthy man spoke the truth. A party is like a sausage machine; it mashes up all sorts of heads together into the same mince-meat—fatheads and blockheads, all in one mash!

MRS. STOCKMANN: Come, come, Thomas dear!

PETRA [*to* HORSTER]: If only you had not come home with us, things might not have come to this pass.

HORSTER: I do not regret it.

PETRA [*holding out her hand to him*]: Thank you for that!

HORSTER [*to* DR. STOCKMANN]: And so what I came to say was that if you are determined to go away, I have thought of another plan—

DR. STOCKMANN: That's splendid!—if only we can get away at once.

MRS. STOCKMANN: Hush!—wasn't that some one knocking?

PETRA: That is uncle, surely.

DR. STOCKMANN: Aha! [*Calls out.*] Come in!

MRS. STOCKMANN: Dear Thomas, promise me definitely—.

[PETER STOCKMANN *comes in from the hall.*]

PETER STOCKMANN: Oh, you are engaged. In that case, I will—

DR. STOCKMANN: No, no, come in.

PETER STOCKMANN: But I wanted to speak to you alone.

MRS. STOCKMANN: We will go into the sitting-room in the meanwhile.

HORSTER: And I will look in again later.

DR. STOCKMANN: No, go in there with them, Captain Horster; I want to hear more about—.

HORSTER: Very well, I will wait, then. [*He follows* MRS. STOCKMANN *and* PETRA *into the sitting-room.*]

DR. STOCKMANN: I daresay you find it rather draughty here to-day. Put your hat on.

PETER STOCKMANN: Thank you, if I may. [*Does so.*] I think I caught cold last night; I stood and shivered—

DR. STOCKMANN: Really? I found it warm enough.

PETER STOCKMANN: I regret that it was not in my power to prevent those excesses last night.

DR. STOCKMANN: Have you anything particular to say to me besides that?

PETER STOCKMANN [*taking a big letter from his pocket*]: I have this document for you, from the Baths Committee.

DR. STOCKMANN: My dismissal?

PETER STOCKMANN: Yes, dating from to-day. [*Lays the letter on the table.*] It gives us pain to do it; but, to speak frankly, we dared not do otherwise on account of public opinion.

DR. STOCKMANN [*smiling*]: Dared not? I seem to have heard that word before, to-day.

PETER STOCKMANN: I must beg you to understand your position clearly. For the future you must not count on any practice whatever in the town.

DR. STOCKMANN: Devil take the practice! But why are you so sure of that?

PETER STOCKMANN: The Householders' Association is circulating a list from house to house. All right-minded citizens are being called upon to give up employing you; and I can assure you that not a single head of a family will risk refusing his signature. They simply dare not.

DR. STOCKMANN: No, no; I don't doubt it. But what then?

PETER STOCKMANN: If I might advise you, it would be best to leave the place for a little while—

DR. STOCKMANN: Yes, the propriety of leaving the place *has* occurred to me.

PETER STOCKMANN: Good. And then, when you have had six months to think things over, if, after mature consideration, you can persuade your-self to write a few words of regret, acknowledging your error—

DR. STOCKMANN: I might have my appointment restored to me, do you mean?

PETER STOCKMANN: Perhaps. It is not at all impossible.

DR. STOCKMANN: But what about public opinion, then? Surely you would not dare to do it on account of public feeling.

PETER STOCKMANN: Public opinion is an extremely mutable thing. And, to be quite candid with you, it is a matter of great importance to us to have some admission of that sort from you in writing.

DR. STOCKMANN: Oh, that's what you are after, is it! I will just trouble you to remember what I said to you lately about foxy tricks of that sort!

PETER STOCKMANN: Your position was quite different then. At that time you had reason to suppose you had the whole town at your back—

DR. STOCKMANN: Yes, and now I feel I have the whole town *on* my back— [*flaring up*]. I would not do it if I had the devil and his dam on my back—! Never—never, I tell you!

PETER STOCKMANN: A man with a family has no right to behave as you do. You have no right to do it, Thomas.

DR. STOCKMANN: I have no right! There is only one single thing in the world a free man has no right to do. Do you know what that is?

PETER STOCKMANN: No.

DR. STOCKMANN: Of course you don't, but I will tell you. A free man has no right to soil himself with filth; he has no right to behave in a way that would justify his spitting in his own face.

PETER STOCKMANN: This sort of thing sounds extremely plausible, of course; and if there were no other explanation for your obstinacy—. But as it happens that there is.

DR. STOCKMANN: What do you mean?

PETER STOCKMANN: You understand very well what I mean. But, as your brother and as a man of discretion, I advise you not to build too much upon expectations and prospects that may so very easily fail you.

DR. STOCKMANN: What in the world is all this about?

PETER STOCKMANN: Do you really ask me to believe that you are ignorant of the terms of Mr. Kiil's will?

DR. STOCKMANN: I know that the small amount he possesses is to go to an institution for indigent old workpeople. How does that concern me?

PETER STOCKMANN: In the first place, it is by no means a small amount that is in question. Mr. Kiil is a fairly wealthy man.

DR. STOCKMANN: I had no notion of that!

PETER STOCKMANN: Hm!—hadn't you really? Then I suppose you had no notion, either, that a considerable portion of his wealth will come to your children, you and your wife having a life-rent of the capital. Has he never told you so?

DR. STOCKMANN: Never, on my honour! Quite the reverse; he has consistently done nothing but fume at being so unconscionably heavily taxed. But are you perfectly certain of this, Peter?

PETER STOCKMANN: I have it from an absolutely reliable source.

DR. STOCKMANN: Then, thank God, Katherine is provided for—and the children too! I must tell her this at once—[*calls out*] Katherine, Katherine!

PETER STOCKMANN [*restraining him*]: Hush, don't say a word yet!

MRS. STOCKMANN [*opening the door*]: What is the matter?

DR. STOCKMANN: Oh, nothing, nothing; you can go back.

[*She shuts the door.* DR. STOCKMANN *walks up and down in his excitement.*] Provided for!—Just think of it, we are all provided for! And for life! What a blessed feeling it is to know one is provided for!

PETER STOCKMANN: Yes, but that is just exactly what you are not. Mr. Kiil can alter his will any day he likes.

DR. STOCKMANN: But he won't do that, my dear Peter. The "Badger" is much too delighted at my attack on you and your wise friends.

PETER STOCKMANN [*starts and looks intently at him*]: Ah, that throws a light on various things.

DR. STOCKMANN: What things?

PETER STOCKMANN: I see that the whole thing was a combined manoeuvre on your part and his. These violent, reckless attacks that you have made against the leading men of the town, under the pretence that it was in the name of truth—

DR. STOCKMANN: What about them?

PETER STOCKMANN: I see that they were nothing else than the stipulated price for that vindictive old man's will.

DR. STOCKMANN [*almost speechless*]: Peter—you are the most disgusting plebeian I have ever met in all my life.

PETER STOCKMANN: All is over between us. Your dismissal is irrevocable— we have a weapon against you now. [*Goes out.*]

DR. STOCKMANN: For shame! For shame! [*Calls out.*] Katherine, you must have the floor scrubbed after him! Let—what's her name—devil take it, the girl who has always got soot on her nose—

MRS. STOCKMANN [*in the sitting-room*]: Hush, Thomas, be quiet!

PETRA [*coming to the door*]: Father, grandfather is here, asking if he may speak to you alone.

DR. STOCKMANN: Certainly he may. [*Going to the door.*] Come in, Mr. Kiil. [MORTEN KIIL *comes in.* DR. STOCKMANN *shuts the door after him.*] What can I do for you? Won't you sit down?

MORTEN KIIL: I won't sit. [*Looks around.*] You look very comfortable here to-day, Thomas.

DR. STOCKMANN: Yes, don't we!

MORTEN KIIL: Very comfortable—plenty of fresh air. I should think you have got enough today of that oxygen you were talking about yesterday. Your conscience must be in splendid order today, I should think.

DR. STOCKMANN: It is.

MORTEN KIIL: So I should think. [*Taps his chest.*] Do you know what I have got here?

DR. STOCKMANN: A good conscience, too, I hope.

MORTEN KIIL: Bah!—No, it is something better than that. [*He takes a thick pocket-book from his breast-pocket, opens it, and displays a packet of papers.*]

DR. STOCKMANN [*looking at him in astonishment*]: Shares in the Baths?

MORTEN KIIL: They were not difficult to get today.

DR. STOCKMANN: And you have been buying—?

MORTEN KIIL: As many as I could pay for.

DR. STOCKMANN: But, my dear Mr. Kiil—consider the state of the Baths' affairs!

MORTEN KIIL: If you behave like a reasonable man, you can soon set the Baths on their feet again.

DR. STOCKMANN: Well, you can see for yourself that I have done all I can, but—. They are all mad in this town!

MORTEN KIIL: You said yesterday that the worst of this pollution came from my tannery. If that is true, then my grandfather and my father before me, and I myself, for many years past, have been poisoning the town like three destroying angels. Do you think I am going to sit quiet under that reproach?

DR. STOCKMANN: Unfortunately I am afraid you will have to.

MORTEN KIIL: No, thank you. I am jealous of my name and reputation. They call me "the Badger," I am told. A badger is a kind of pig, I believe; but I am not going to give them the right to call me that. I mean to live and die a clean man.

DR. STOCKMANN: And how are you going to set about it?

MORTEN KIIL: You shall cleanse me, Thomas.

DR. STOCKMANN: I!

MORTEN KIIL: Do you know what money I have bought these shares with? No, of course you can't know—but I will tell you. It is the money that Katherine and Petra and the boys will have when I am gone. Because I have been able to save a little bit after all, you know.

DR. STOCKMANN [*flaring up*]: And you have gone and taken Katherine's money for *this!*

MORTEN KIIL: Yes, the whole of the money is invested in the Baths now. And now I just want to see whether you are quite stark, staring mad, Thomas! If you still make out that these animals and other nasty things of that sort come from my tannery, it will be exactly as if you were to flay broad strips of skin from Katherine's body, and Petra's, and the boys'; and no decent man would do that—unless he were mad.

DR. STOCKMANN [*walking up and down*]: Yes, but I *am* mad; I *am* mad!

MORTEN KIIL: You cannot be so absurdly mad as all that, when it is a question of your wife and children.

DR. STOCKMANN [*standing still in front of him*]: Why couldn't you consult me about it, before you went and bought all that trash?

MORTEN KIIL: What is done cannot be undone.

DR. STOCKMANN [*walks about uneasily*]: If only I were not so certain about it—! But I am absolutely convinced that I am right.

MORTEN KIIL [*weighing the pocket-book in his hand*]: If you stick to your mad idea, this won't be worth much, you know. [*Puts the pocket-book in his pocket.*]

DR. STOCKMANN: But, hang it all! it might be possible for science to discover some prophylactic, I should think—or some antidote of some kind—

MORTEN KIIL: To kill these animals, do you mean?

DR. STOCKMANN: Yes, or to make them innocuous.

MORTEN KIIL: Couldn't you try some rat's-bane?

DR. STOCKMANN: Don't talk nonsense! They all say it is only imagination, you know. Well, let it go at that! Let them have their own way about it! Haven't the ignorant, narrow-minded curs reviled me as an enemy of the people?—and haven't they been ready to tear the clothes off my back too?

MORTEN KIIL: And broken all your windows to pieces!

DR. STOCKMANN: And then there is my duty to my family. I must talk it over with Katherine; she is great on those things.

MORTEN KIIL: That is right; be guided by a reasonable woman's advice.

DR. STOCKMANN [*advancing towards him*]: To think you could do such a preposterous thing! Risking Katherine's money in this way, and putting me in such a horribly painful dilemma! When I look at you, I think I see the devil himself—.

MORTEN KIIL: Then I had better go. But I must have an answer from you before two o'clock—yes or no. If it is no, the shares go to a charity, and that this very day.

DR. STOCKMANN: And what does Katherine get?

MORTEN KIIL: Not a halfpenny. [*The door leading to the hall opens, and* HOVSTAD *and* ASLAKSEN *make their appearance.*] Look at those two!

DR. STOCKMANN [*staring at them*]: What the devil!—have *you* actually the face to come into my house?

HOVSTAD: Certainly.

ASLAKSEN: We have something to say to you, you see.

MORTEN KIIL [*in a whisper*]: Yes or no—before two o'clock.

ASLAKSEN [*glancing at* HOVSTAD]: Aha! [MORTEN KIIL *goes out.*]

DR. STOCKMANN: Well, what do you want with me? Be brief.

HOVSTAD: I can quite understand that you are annoyed with us for our attitude at the meeting yesterday—

DR. STOCKMANN: Attitude, do you call it? Yes, it was a charming attitude! I call it weak, womanish—damnably shameful!

HOVSTAD: Call it what you like, we could not do otherwise.

DR. STOCKMANN: You *dared* not do otherwise—isn't that it?

HOVSTAD: Well, if you like to put it that way.

ASLAKSEN: But why did you not let us have word of it beforehand?—just a hint to Mr. Hovstad or to me?

DR. STOCKMANN: A hint? Of what?

ASLAKSEN: Of what was behind it all.

DR. STOCKMANN: I don't understand you in the least.

ASLAKSEN [*with a confidential nod*]: Oh yes, you do, Dr. Stockmann.

HOVSTAD: It is no good making a mystery of it any longer.

DR. STOCKMANN [*looking first at one of them and then at the other*]: What the devil do you both mean?

ASLAKSEN: May I ask if your father-in-law is not going round the town buying up all the shares in the Baths?

DR. STOCKMANN: Yes, he has been buying Baths shares today; but—

ASLAKSEN: It would have been more prudent to get some one else to do it —some one less nearly related to you.

HOVSTAD: And you should not have let your name appear in the affair. There was no need for anyone to know that the attack on the Baths came from you. You ought to have consulted me, Dr. Stockmann.

DR. STOCKMANN [*looks in front of him; then a light seems to dawn on him and he says in amazement*]: Are such things conceivable? Are such things possible?

ASLAKSEN [*with a smile*]: Evidently they are. But it is better to use a little *finesse,* you know.

HOVSTAD: And it is much better to have several persons in a thing of that sort; because the responsibility of each individual is lessened, when there are others with him.

DR. STOCKMANN [*composedly*]: Come to the point, gentlemen. What do you want?

ASLAKSEN: Perhaps Mr. Hovstad had better—

HOVSTAD: No, you tell him, Aslaksen.

ASLAKSEN: Well, the fact is that, now we know the bearings the whole affair, we think we might venture to put the "People's Messenger" at your disposal.

DR. STOCKMANN: Do you dare do that now? What about public opinion? Are you not afraid of a storm breaking upon our heads?

HOVSTAD: We will try to weather it.

ASLAKSEN: And you must be ready to go off quickly on a new tack, Doctor. As soon as your invective has done its work—

DR. STOCKMANN: Do you mean, as soon as my father-in-law and I have got hold of the shares at a low figure?

HOVSTAD: Your reasons for wishing to get the control of the Baths are mainly scientific, I take it.

DR. STOCKMANN: Of course; it was for scientific reasons that I persuaded the old "Badger" to stand in with me in the matter. So we will tinker at the conduit-pipes a little, and dig up a little bit of the shore, and it shan't cost the town a sixpence. That will be all right—eh?

HOVSTAD: I think so—if you have the "People's Messenger" behind you.

ASLAKSEN: The Press is a power in a free community, Doctor.

DR. STOCKMANN: Quite so. And so is public opinion. And you, Mr. Aslaksen —I suppose you will be answerable for the Householders' Association?

ASLAKSEN: Yes, and for the Temperance Society. You may rely on that.

DR. STOCKMANN: But, gentlemen—I really am ashamed to ask the question —but, what return do you—?

HOVSTAD: We should prefer to help you without any return whatever, believe me. But the "People's Messenger" is in rather a shaky condition; it doesn't go really well; and I should be very unwilling to suspend the paper now, when there is so much work to do here in the political way.

DR. STOCKMANN: Quite so; that would be a great trial to such a friend of the people as you are. [*Flares up.*] But I am an enemy of the people, remember! [*Walks about the room.*] Where have I put my stick? Where the devil is my stick?

HOVSTAD: What's that?

ASLAKSEN: Surely you never mean—?

DR. STOCKMANN [*standing still*]: And suppose I don't give you a single penny of all I get out of it? Money is not very easy to get out of us rich folk, please to remember!

HOVSTAD: And you please to remember that this affair of the shares can be represented in two ways!

DR. STOCKMANN: Yes, and you are just the man to do it. If I don't come to the rescue of the "People's Messenger," you will certainly take an evil view of the affair; you will hunt me down, I can well imagine—pursue me—try to throttle me as a dog does a hare.

HOVSTAD: It is a natural law; every animal must fight for its own livelihood.

ASLAKSEN: And get its food where it can, you know.

DR. STOCKMANN [*walking about the room*]: Then you go and look for yours in the gutter; because I am going to show you which is the strongest animal of us three! [*Finds an umbrella and brandishes it above his head.*] Ah, now—!

HOVSTAD: You are surely not going to use violence!

ASLAKSEN: Take care what you are doing with that umbrella.

DR. STOCKMANN: Out of the window with you, Mr. Hovstad!

HOVSTAD [*edging to the door*]: Are you quite mad!

DR. STOCKMANN: Out of the window, Mr. Aslaksen! Jump, I tell you! You will have to do it, sooner or later.

ASLAKSEN [*running round the writing-table*]: Moderation, Doctor—I am a delicate man—I can stand so little—[*calls out*] help, help!

[MRS. STOCKMAN, PETRA *and* HORSTER *come in from the sitting-room.*]

MRS. STOCKMANN: Good gracious, Thomas! What is happening?

DR. STOCKMAN [*brandishing the umbrella*]: Jump out, I tell you! Out into the gutter!

HOVSTAD: An assault on an unoffending man! I call you to witness, Captain Horster. [*Hurries out through the hall.*]

ASLAKSEN [*irresolutely*]: If only I knew the way about here—. [*Steals out through the sitting-room.*]

MRS. STOCKMANN [*holding her husband back*]: Control yourself, Thomas!

DR. STOCKMANN [*throwing down the umbrella*]: Upon my soul, they have escaped after all.

MRS. STOCKMANN: What did they want you to do?

DR. STOCKMANN: I will tell you later on; I have something else to think about now. [*Goes to the table and writes something on a calling-card.*] Look there, Katherine; what is written there?

MRS. STOCKMANN: Three big *Noes;* what does that mean.

DR. STOCKMANN: I will tell you that too, later on. [*Holds out the card to* PETRA.] There, Petra; tell sooty-face to run over to the "Badger's" with that, as quick as she can. Hurry up! [PETRA *takes the card and goes out to the hall.*]

DR. STOCKMANN: Well, I think I have had a visit from every one of the devil's messengers today! But now I am going to sharpen my pen till they can feel its point; I shall dip it in venom and gall; I shall hurl my ink-pot at their heads!

MRS. STOCKMANN: Yes, but we are going away, you know, Thomas.

[PETRA *comes back.*]

DR. STOCKMANN: Well?

PETRA: She has gone with it.

DR. STOCKMANN: Good.—Going away, did you say? No, I'll be hanged if we are going away! We are going to stay where we are, Katherine!

PETRA: Stay here?

MRS. STOCKMANN: Here, in the town?

DR. STOCKMANN: Yes, here. This is the field of battle—this is where the fight will be. This is where I shall triumph! As soon as I have had my trousers sewn up I shall go out and look for another house. We must have a roof over our heads for the winter.

HORSTER: That you shall have in my house.

DR. STOCKMANN: Can I?

HORSTER: Yes, quite well. I have plenty of room, and I am almost never at home.

MRS. STOCKMANN: How good of you, Captain Horster!

PETRA: Thank you!

DR. STOCKMANN [*grasping his hand*]: Thank you, thank you! That is one trouble over! Now I can set to work in earnest at once. There is an endless amount of things to look through here, Katherine! Luckily I shall have all my time at my disposal; because I have been dismissed from the Baths, you know.

MRS. STOCKMANN [*with a sigh*]: Oh yes, I expected that.

DR. STOCKMANN: And they want to take my practice away from me too. Let them! I have got the poor people to fall back upon, anyway—those that don't pay anything! and, after all, they need me most, too. But, by Jove, they will have to listen to me; I shall preach to them in season and out of season, as it says somewhere.

MRS. STOCKMANN: But, dear Thomas, I should have thought events had showed you what use it is to preach.

DR. STOCKMANN: You are really ridiculous, Katherine. do you want me to let myself be beaten off the field by public opinion and the compact majority and all that deviltry? No, thank you! And what I want to do is so simple and clear and straightforward. I only want to drum into the heads of these curs the fact that the liberals are the most insidious enemies of freedom—that party programmes strangle every young and vigorous truth—that considerations of expediency turn morality and justice upside down—and that they will end by making life here unbearable. Don't you think, Captain Horster, that I ought to be able to make people understand that?

HORSTER: Very likely; I don't know much about such things myself.

DR. STOCKMANN: Well, look here—I will explain! It is the party leaders that must be exterminated. A party leader is like a wolf, you see—like a voracious wolf. He requires a certain number of smaller victims to prey upon every year, if he is to live. Just look at Hovstad and Aslaksen! How many smaller victims have they not put an end to—or at any rate maimed and mangled until they are fit for nothing except to be house holders or subscribers to the "People's Messenger"! [*Sits down on the edge of the table.*] Come here, Katherine—look how beautifully the sun shines to-day! And this lovely spring air I am drinking in!

MRS. STOCKMANN: Yes, if only we could live on sunshine and spring air, Thomas.

DR. STOCKMANN: Oh, you will have to pinch and save a bit—then we shall. get along. That gives me very little concern. What is much worse is, that I know of no one who is liberal-minded and high-minded enough to venture to take up my work after me.

PETRA: Don't think about that, father; you have plenty of time before you. —Hullo, here are the boys already!

[EJLIF *and* MORTEN *come in from the sitting-room.*]

MRS. STOCKMANN: Have you got a holiday?

MORTEN: No; but we were fighting with the other boys between lessons—

EJLIF: That isn't true; it was the other boys were fighting with us.

MORTEN: Well, and then Mr. Rörlund said we had better stay at home for a day or two.

DR. STOCKMANN [*snapping his fingers and getting up from the table*]: I have it! I have it, by Jove! You shall never set foot in the school again!

THE BOYS: No more school!

MRS. STOCKMANN: But, Thomas—

DR. STOCKMANN: Never, I say. I will educate you myself; that is to say, you shan't learn a blessed thing—

MORTEN: Hooray!

DR. STOCKMANN: —but I will make liberal-minded and high-minded men of you. You must help me with that, Petra.

PETRA: Yes, father, you may be sure I will.

DR. STOCKMANN: And my school shall be in the room where they insulted me and called me an enemy of the people. But we are too few as we are; I must have at least twelve boys to begin with.

MRS. STOCKMANN: You will certainly never get them in this town.

DR. STOCKMANN: We shall. [*To the boys.*] Don't you know any street urchins —regular ragamuffins—?

MORTEN: Yes, father, I know lots!

DR. STOCKMANN: That's capital! Bring me some specimens of them. I am going to experiment with curs, just for once; there may be some exceptional heads amongst them.

MORTEN: And what are we going to do, when you have made liberal-minded and high-minded men of us?

DR. STOCKMANN: Then you shall drive all the wolves out of the country, my boys!

[EJLIF *looks rather doubtful about it;* MORTEN *jumps about crying "Hurrah!"*]

MRS. STOCKMANN: Let us hope it won't be the wolves that will drive you out of the country, Thomas.

DR. STOCKMANN: Are you out of your mind, Katherine? Drive me out! Now —when I am the strongest man in the town!

MRS. STOCKMANN: The strongest—now?

DR. STOCKMANN: Yes, and I will go so far as to say that now I am the strongest man in the whole world.

MORTEN: I say!

DR. STOCKMANN [*lowering his voice*]: Hush! You mustn't say anything about it yet; but I have made a great discovery.

MRS. STOCKMANN: Another one?

DR. STOCKMANN: Yes [*Gathers them round him, and says confidentially*]: It is this, let me tell you—that the strongest man in the world is he who stands most alone.

MRS. STOCKMANN [*smiling and shaking her head*]: Oh, Thomas, Thomas!

PETRA [*encouragingly, as she grasps her father's hands*]: Father!

CAESAR AND CLEOPATRA

A HISTORY

Prologue

[*In the doorway of the temple of Ra in Memphis. Deep gloom. An august personage with a hawk's head is mysteriously visible by his own light in the darkness within the temple. He surveys the modern audience with great contempt; and finally speaks the following words to them.*]

Peace! Be silent and hearken unto me, ye quaint little islanders. Give ear, ye men with white paper on your breasts and nothing written thereon (to signify the innocency of your minds). Hear me, ye women who adorn yourselves alluringly and conceal your thoughts from your men, leading them to believe that ye deem them wondrous strong and masterful whilst in truth ye hold them in your hearts as children without judgment. Look upon my hawk's head; and know that I am Ra, who was once in Egypt a mighty god. Ye cannot kneel nor prostrate yourselves; for ye are packed in rows without freedom to move, obstructing one another's vision; neither do any of ye regard it as seemly to do aught until ye see all the rest do so too; wherefore it commonly happens that in great emergencies ye do nothing, though each telleth his fellow that something must be done. I ask you not for worship, but for silence. Let not your men speak nor your women cough; for I am come to draw you back two thousand years over the graves of sixty generations. Ye poor posterity, think not that ye are the first. Other fools before ye have seen the sun rise and set, and the moon change her shape and her hour. As they were so ye are; and yet not so great; for the pyramids my people built stand to this day; whilst the dustheaps on which ye slave, and which ye call empires, scatter in the wind even as ye pile your dead sons' bodies on them to make yet more dust.

Hearken to me then, oh ye compulsorily educated ones. Know that even as there is an old England and a new, and ye stand perplexed between the twain; so in the days when I was worshipped was there an old Rome and a new, and men

SOURCE: Reprinted with the permission of The Society of Authors, London.

standing perplexed between them. And the old Rome was poor and little, and greedy and fierce, and evil in many ways; but because its mind was little and its work was simple, it knew its own mind and did its own work; and the gods pitied it and helped it and strengthened it and shielded it; for the gods are patient with littleness. Then the old Rome, like the beggar on horseback, presumed on the favor of the gods, and said, "Lo! there is neither riches nor greatness in our littleness: the road to riches and greatness is through robbery of the poor and slaughter of the weak." So they robbed their own poor until they became great masters of that art, and knew by what laws it could be made to appear seemly and honest. And when they had squeezed their own poor dry, they robbed the poor of other lands, and added those lands to Rome until there came a new Rome, rich and huge. And I, Ra, laughed; for the minds of the Romans remained the same size whilst their dominion spread over the earth.

Now mark me, that ye may understand what ye are presently to see. Whilst the Romans still stood between the old Rome and the new, there arose among them a mighty soldier: Pompey the Great. And the way of the soldier is the way of death; but the way of the gods is the way of life; and so it comes that a god at the end of his way is wise and a soldier at the end of his way is a fool. So Pompey held by the old Rome, in which only soldiers could become great; but the gods turned to the new Rome, in which any man with wit enough could become what he would. And Pompey's friend Julius Caesar was on the side of the gods; for he saw that Rome had passed beyond the control of the little old Romans. This Caesar was a great talker and a politician: he bought men with words and with gold, even as ye are bought. And when they would not be satisfied with words and gold, and demanded also the glories of war, Caesar in his middle age turned his hand to that trade; and they that were against him when he sought their welfare, bowed down before him when he became a slayer and a conqueror; for such is the nature of you mortals. And as for Pompey, the gods grew tired of his triumphs and his airs of being himself a god; for he talked of law and duty and other matters that concerned not a mere human worm. And the gods smiled on Caesar; for he lived the life they had given him boldly, and was not forever rebuking us for our indecent ways of creation, and hiding our handiwork as a shameful thing. Ye know well what I mean; for this is one of your own sins.

And thus it fell out between the old Rome and the new, that Caesar said, "Unless I break the law of old Rome, I cannot take my share in ruling her; and the gift of ruling that the gods gave me will perish without fruit." But Pompey said, "The law is above all; and if thou break it thou shalt die." Then said Caesar, "I will break it: kill me who can." And he broke it. And Pompey went for him, as ye say, with a great army to slay him and uphold the old Rome. So Caesar fled across the Adriatic sea; for the high gods had a lesson to teach him, which lesson they shall also teach you in due time if ye continue to forget them and to worship that cad among gods, Mammon. Therefore before they raised Caesar to be master of the world, they were minded to throw him down into the dust, even beneath the feet of Pompey, and blacken his face before the nations. And Pompey they raised higher than ever, he and his laws and his high mind that aped the gods, so that his fall might be the more terrible. And Pompey followed Caesar, and overcame him with all the majesty of old Rome, and stood over him and over the whole world even as ye stand over it with your fleet that covers thirty miles of the sea. And when Caesar was brought down to utter nothingness, he made a last stand to die honorably, and did not despair; for he said, "Against me there is Pompey, and the old Rome, and the law and the legions: all all against me; but high above these are the gods; and Pompey is a fool." And the gods laughed and approved; and on the field of Pharsalia the impossible came to pass; the blood and iron ye pin your faith on fell before the spirit of man; for the spirit of man is the will of the gods; and Pompey's power crumbled in his hand, even as the power of imperial Spain crumbled when it was set against your fathers in the days when England was little, and knew her own mind, and had a mind to know instead of a circulation of newspapers. Wherefore look to it, lest some little people whom ye would enslave rise up and become in the hand of God the scourge of your boastings and your injustices and your lusts and stupidities.

And now, would ye know the end of Pompey, or will ye sleep while a god speaks? Heed my words well; for Pompey went where ye are gone, even to Egypt, where there was a Roman occupation even as there was but now a British one. And Caesar pursued Pompey to Egypt: a Roman fleeing, and a Roman pursuing: dog eating dog. And the Egyptians said, "Lo: these Romans which have lent money to our kings and levied a distraint upon us with their arms, call forever upon us to be loyal to them by betraying our own country to them. But now behold two Romes! Pompey's Rome and Caesar's Rome! To which of the twain shall we pretend to be loyal?" So they turned in their perplexity to a soldier that had once served Pompey, and that knew the way of Rome and was full of her lusts. And they said to him, "Lo: in thy country dog eats dog; and both dogs are coming to eat us: what counsel hast thou to give us?" And this soldier, whose name was Lucius Septimius, and whom ye shall presently see before ye, replied, "Ye shall diligently consider which is the bigger dog of the two; and ye shall kill the other dog for his sake and thereby earn his favor." And the Egyptians said, "Thy counsel is expedient; but if we kill a man outside the law we set ourselves in the place of the gods; and this we dare not do. But thou, being a Roman, art accustomed to this kind of killing; for thou hast imperial instincts. Wilt thou therefore kill the lesser dog for us?" And he said, "I will; for I have made my home in Egypt; and I desire consideration and influence among you." And they said, "We knew well thou wouldst not do it for nothing: thou shalt have thy reward." Now when Pompey came, he came alone in a little galley, putting his trust in the law and the constitution. And it was plain to the people of Egypt that Pompey was now but a very small dog. So when he set his foot on the shore he was greeted by his old comrade Lucius Septimius, who welcomed him with one hand and with the other smote off his head, and kept it as it were a pickled cabbage to make a present to Caesar. And mankind shuddered; but the gods laughed; for Septimius was but a knife that Pompey had sharpened; and when it turned against his own throat they said that Pompey had better have made Septimius a ploughman than so brave and readyhanded a slayer. Therefore again I bid you beware, ye who would all be Pompeys if ye dared; for war is a wolf that may come to your own door.

Are ye impatient with me? Do ye crave for a story of an unchaste woman? Hath the name of Cleopatra tempted ye hither? Ye foolish ones; Cleopatra is as yet but a child that is whipped by her nurse. And what I am about to shew you for the good of your souls is how Caesar, seeking Pompey in Egypt, found Cleopatra; and how he received that present of a pickled cabbage that was once the head of Pompey; and what things happened between the old Caesar and the child queen before he left Egypt and battled his way back to Rome to be slain there as Pompey was slain, by men in whom the spirit of Pompey still lived. All this ye shall see; and ye shall marvel, after your ignorant manner, that men twenty centuries ago were already just such as you, and spoke and lived as ye speak and live, no worse and no better, no wiser and no sillier. And the two thousand years that have past are to me, the god Ra, but a moment; nor is this day any other than the day in which Caesar set foot in the land of my people. And now I leave you; for ye are a dull folk, and instruction is wasted on you; and I had not spoken so much but that it is in the nature of a god to struggle forever with the dust and the darkness, and to drag from them, by the force of his longing for the divine, more life and more light. Settle ye therefore in your seats and keep silent; for ye are about to hear a man speak, and a great man he was, as ye count greatness. And fear not that I shall speak to you again: the rest of the story must ye learn from them that lived it. Farewell; and do not presume to applaud me. [*The temple vanishes in utter darkness.*]

[*1912*]

An Alternative to the Prologue

[*An October night on the Syrian border of Egypt towards the end of the XXXIII Dynasty, in the year 706 by Roman computation, afterwards reckoned by Christian computation as 48* B.C. *A great radiance of silver fire, the dawn of a moonlit night, is rising in the east. The stars and the cloudless sky are our own contemporaries, nineteen and a half centuries younger than we know them; but you would not guess that from their appearance. Below them are two notable drawbacks of civilization: a palace, and soldiers. The palace, an old, low, Syrian building of whitened mud, is not so ugly as Buckingham Palace; and the officers in the courtyard are more highly civilized than modern English officers: for example, they do not dig up the corpses of their dead enemies and mutilate them, as we dug up Cromwell and the Mahdi. They are in two groups: one intent on the gambling of their captain Belzanor, a warrior of fifty, who, with his spear on the ground beside his knee, is stooping to throw dice with a sly-looking young Persian recruit; the other gathered about a guardsman who has just finished telling a naughty story (still current in English barracks) at which they are laughing uproariously. They are about a dozen in number, all highly aristocratic young Egyptian guardsmen, handsomely equipped with weapons and armor, very unEnglish in point of not being ashamed of and uncomfortable in their professional dress; on the contrary, rather ostentatiously and arrogantly warlike, as valuing themselves on their military caste.*

Belzanor is a typical veteran, tough and wilful; prompt, capable and crafty where brute force will serve; helpless and boyish when it will not: an active sergeant, an incompetent general, a deplorable dictator. Would, if influentially connected, be employed in the two last capacities by a modern European State on the strength of his success in the first. Is rather to be pitied just now in view of the fact that Julius Caesar is invading his country. Not knowing this, is intent on his game with the Persian, whom, as a foreigner, he considers quite capable of cheating him.

His subalterns are mostly handsome young fellows whose interest in the game and the story symbolize with tolerable completeness the main interests in life of which they are conscious. Their spears are leaning against the walls, or lying on the ground ready to their hands. The corner of the courtyard forms a triangle of which one side is the front of the palace, with a doorway, the other a wall with a gateway. The storytellers are on the palace side: the gamblers, on the gateway side. Close to the gateway, against the wall, is a stone block high enough to enable a Nubian sentinel, standing on it, to look over the wall. The yard is lighted by a torch stuck in the wall. As the laughter from the group round the storyteller dies away, the kneeling Persian, winning the throw, snatches up the stake from the ground.]

BELZANOR: By Apis, Persian, thy gods are good to thee.

THE PERSIAN: Try yet again, O captain. Double or quits!

BELZANOR: No more. I am not in the vein.

THE SENTINEL [*poising his javelin as he peers over the wall*]: Stand. Who goes there?

[*They all start, listening. A strange voice replies from without.*]

VOICE: The bearer of evil tidings.

BELZANOR [*calling to the sentry*]: Pass him.

THE SENTINEL [*grounding his javelin*]: Draw near, O bearer of evil tidings.

BELZANOR [*pocketing the dice and picking up his spear*]: Let us receive this man with honor. He bears evil tidings.

[*The guardsmen seize their spears and gather about the gate, leaving a way through for the new comer.*]

PERSIAN [*rising from his knee*]: Are evil tidings, then, so honorable?

BELZANOR: O barbarous Persian, hear my instruction. In Egypt the bearer of good tidings is sacrificed to the gods as a thank offering; but no god will accept the blood of the messenger of evil. When we have good tidings, we are careful to send them in the mouth of the cheapest slave we can find. Evil tidings are borne by young noblemen who desire to bring themselves into notice. [*They join the rest at the gate.*]

THE SENTINEL: Pass, O young captain; and bow the head in the House of the Queen.

VOICE: Go anoint thy javelin with fat of swine, O Blackamoor: for before morning the Romans will make thee eat it to the very butt.

[*The owner of the voice, a fairhaired dandy, dressed in a different fashion from that affected by the guardsmen, but no less extravagantly, comes through the gateway laughing. He is somewhat battlestained; and his left forearm, bandaged, comes through a torn sleeve. In his right hand he carries a Roman sword in its sheath. He swaggers down the courtyard, the Persian on his right, Belzanor on his left, and the guardsmen crowding down behind him.*]

BELZANOR: Who are thou that laughest in the House of Cleopatra the Queen, and in the teeth of Belzanor, the captain of her guard?

THE NEW COMER: I am Bel Affris, descended from the gods.

BELZANOR [*ceremoniously*]: Hail, cousin!

ALL [*except the Persian*]: Hail, cousin!

PERSIAN: All the Queen's guards are descended from the gods, O stranger, save myself. I am Persian, and descended from many kings.

BEL AFFRIS [*to the guardsmen*]: Hail, cousins! [*To the Persian, condescendingly*] Hail, mortal!

BELZANOR: You have been in battle, Bel Affris; and you are a soldier among soldiers. You will not let the Queen's women have the first of your tidings.

BEL AFFRIS: I have no tidings, except that we shall have our throats cut presently, women, soldiers, and all.

PERSIAN [*to Belzanor*]: I told you so.

THE SENTINEL [*who has been listening*]: Woe, alas!

BEL AFFRIS [*calling to him*]: Peace, peace poor Ethiop: destiny is with the gods who painted thee black. [*To Belzanor*] What has this mortal [*indicating the Persian*] told you?

BELZANOR: He says that the Roman Julius Caesar, who has landed on our shores with a handful of followers, will make himself master of Egypt. He is afraid of the Roman soldiers. [*The guardsmen laugh with boisterous scorn*]. Peasants, brought up to scare crows and follow the plough! Sons of smiths and millers and tanners! And we nobles, consecrated to arms, descended from the gods!

PERSIAN: Belzanor: the gods are not always good to their poor relations.

BELZANOR [*hotly, to the Persian*]: Man to man, are we worse than the slaves of Caesar?

BEL AFFRIS [*stepping between them*]: Listen, cousin. Man to man, we Egyptians are as gods above the Romans.

THE GUARDSMEN [*exultantly*]: Aha!

BEL AFFRIS: But this Caesar does not pit man against man: he throws a legion at you where you are weakest as he throws a stone from a catapult; and that legion is as a man with one head, a thousand arms, and no religion. I have fought against them; and I know.

BELZANOR [*derisively*]: Were you frightened, cousin?

[*The guardsmen roar with laughter, their eyes sparkling at the wit of their captain.*]

BEL AFFRIS: No, cousin; but I was beaten. They were frightened (perhaps); but they scattered us like chaff.

[*The guardsmen, much damped, utter a growl of contemptuous disgust.*]

BELZANOR: Could you not die?

BEL AFFRIS: No: that was too easy to be worthy of a descendant of the gods. Besides, there was no time: all was over in a moment. The attack came just where we least expected it.

BELZANOR: That shews that the Romans are cowards.

BEL AFFRIS: They care nothing about cowardice, these Romans: they fight to win. The pride and honor of war are nothing to them.

PERSIAN: Tell us the tale of the battle. What befell?

THE GUARDSMEN [*gathering eagerly round Bel Affris*]: Ay: the tale of the battle.

BEL AFFRIS: Know then, that I am a novice in the guard of the temple of Ra in Memphis, serving neither Cleopatra nor her brother Ptolemy, but only the high gods. We went a journey to inquire of Ptolemy why he had driven Cleopatra into Syria, and how we of Egypt should deal with the Roman Pompey, newly come to our shores after his defeat by Caesar at Pharsalia. What, think ye, did we learn? Even that Caesar is coming also in hot pursuit of his foe, and that Ptolemy has slain Pompey, whose severed head he holds in readiness to present to the conqueror. [*Sensation among the guardsmen*]. Nay, more: we found that Caesar is already come; for we had not made half a day's journey on our way back when we came upon a city rabble flying from his legions, whose landing they had gone out to withstand.

BELZANOR: And ye, the temple guard! did ye not withstand these legions?

BEL AFFRIS: What man could, that we did. But there came the sound of a trumpet whose voice was as the cursing of a black mountain. Then saw we a moving wall of shields coming towards us. You know how the heart burns when you charge a fortified wall; but how if the fortified wall were to charge you?

THE PERSIAN [*exulting in having told them so*]: Did I not say it?

BEL AFFRIS: When the wall came nigh, it changed into a line of men—common fellows enough, with helmets, leather tunics, and breastplates. Every man of them flung his javelin: the one that came my way drove through my shield as through a papyrus—lo there! [*he points to the bandage on his left arm*] and would have gone through my neck had I not stooped. They were charging at the double then, and were upon us with short swords almost as soon as their javelins. When a man is close to you with such a sword, you can do nothing with our weapons: they are all too long.

THE PERSIAN: What did you do?

BEL AFFRIS: Doubled my fist and smote my Roman on the sharpness of his jaw. He was but mortal after all: he lay down in a stupor; and I took his sword and laid it on. [*Drawing the sword*] Lo! a Roman sword with Roman blood on it!

THE GUARDSMEN [*approvingly*]: Good! [*They take the sword and hand it round, examining it curiously*].

THE PERSIAN: And your men?

BEL AFFRIS: Fled. Scattered like sheep.

BELZANOR [*furiously*]: The cowardly slaves! Leaving the descendants of the gods to be butchered!

BEL AFFRIS [*with acid coolness*]: The descendants of the gods did not stay to be butchered, cousin. The battle was not to the strong; but the race was to the swift. The Romans who have no chariots, sent a cloud of horsemen in pursuit, and slew multitudes. Then our high priest's captain rallied a dozen descendants of the gods and exhorted us to die fighting. I said to myself: surely it is safer to stand than to lose my breath and be stabbed in the back; so I joined our captain and stood. Then the Romans treated us with respect; for no man attacks a lion when the field is full of sheep, except for the pride and honor of war, of which these Romans know nothing. So we escaped with our lives; and I am come to warn you that you must open your gates to Caesar; for his advance guard is scarce an hour behind me; and not an Egyptian warrior is left standing between you and his legions.

THE SENTINEL: Woe, alas! [*He throws down his javelin and flies into the palace*].

BELZANOR: Nail him to the door, quick! [*The guardsmen rush for him with their spears; but he is too quick for them*]. Now this news will run through the palace like fire through stubble.

BEL AFFRIS: What shall we do to save the women from the Romans?

BELZANOR: Why not kill them?

PERSIAN: Because we should have to pay blood money for some of them. Better let the Romans kill them: it is cheaper.

BELZANOR [*awestruck at his brain power*]: O subtle one! O serpent!

BEL AFFRIS: But your Queen?

BELZANOR: True: we must carry off Cleopatra.

BEL AFFRIS: Will ye not await her command?

BELZANOR: Command! a girl of sixteen! Not we. At Memphis ye deem her a Queen: here we know better. I will take her on the crupper of my horse. When we soldiers have carried her out of Caesar's reach, then the priests and the nurses and the rest of them can pretend she is a queen again, and put their commands into her mouth.

PERSIAN: Listen to me, Belzanor.

BELZANOR: Speak, O subtle beyond thy years.

THE PERSIAN: Cleopatra's brother Ptolemy is at war with her. Let us sell her to him.

THE GUARDSMEN: O subtle one! O serpent!

BELZANOR: We dare not. We are descended from the gods; but Cleopatra is descended from the river Nile; and the lands of our fathers will grow no grain if the Nile rises not to water them. Without our father's gifts we should live the lives of dogs.

PERSIAN: It is true: the Queen's guard cannot live on its pay. But hear me further, O ye kinsmen of Osiris.

THE GUARDSMEN: Speak, O subtle one. Hear the serpent begotten!

PERSIAN: Have I heretofore spoken truly to you of Caesar, when you thought I mocked you?

THE GUARDSMEN: Truly, truly.

BELZANOR [*reluctantly admitting it*]: So Bel Affris says.

PERSIAN: Hear more of him, then. This Caesar is a great lover of women: he makes them his friends and counsellors.

BELZANOR: Faugh! This rule of women will be the ruin of Egypt.

THE PERSIAN: Let it rather be the ruin of Rome! Caesar grows old now: he is past fifty and full of labors and battles. He is too old for the young women; and the old women are too wise to worship him.

BEL AFFRIS: Take heed, Persian. Caesar is by this time almost within earshot.

PERSIAN: Cleopatra is not yet a woman: neither is she wise. But she already troubles men's wisdom.

BELZANOR: Ay: that is because she is descended from the river Nile and a black kitten of the sacred White Cat. What then?

PERSIAN: Why, sell her secretly to Ptolemy, and then offer ourselves to Caesar as volunteers to fight for the overthrow of her brother and the rescue of our Queen, the Great Granddaughter of the Nile.

THE GUARDSMEN: O serpent!

PERSIAN: He will listen to us if we come with her picture in our mouths. He will conquer and kill her brother, and reign in Egypt with Cleopatra for his Queen. And we shall be her guard.

THE GUARDSMEN: O subtlest of all the serpents! O admiration! O wisdom!

BEL AFFRIS: He will also have arrived before you have done talking, O word spinner.

BELZANOR: That is true. [*An affrighted uproar in the palace interrupts him*]. Quick: the flight has begun: guard the door. [*They rush to the door and form a cordon before it with their spears. A mob of women-servants and nurses surges out. Those in front recoil from the spears, screaming to those behind to keep back. Belzanor's voice dominates the disturbance as he shouts*] Back there. In again, unprofitable cattle.

THE GUARDSMEN: Back, unprofitable cattle.

BELZANOR: Send us out Ftatateeta, the Queen's chief nurse.

THE WOMEN [*calling into the palace*]: Ftatateeta, Ftatateeta. Come, come. Speak to Belzanor.

A WOMAN: Oh, keep back. You are thrusting me on the spearheads.

[*A huge grim woman, her face covered with a network of tiny wrinkles, and her eyes old, large, and wise; sinewy handed, very tall, very strong; with the mouth of a bloodhound and the jaws of a bulldog, appears on the threshold. She is dressed like a person of consequence in the palace, and confronts the guardsmen insolently.*]

FTATATEETA: Make way for the Queen's chief nurse.

BELZANOR [*with solemn arrogance*]: Ftatateeta: I am Belzanor, the captain of the Queen's guard, descended from the gods.

FTATATEETA [*retorting his arrogance with interest*]: Belzanor: I am Ftatateeta, the Queen's chief nurse; and your divine ancestors were proud to be painted on the wall in the pyramids of the kings whom my fathers served.

[*The women laugh triumphantly.*]

BELZANOR [*with grim humor*]: Ftatateeta: daughter of a long-tongued, swivel-eyed chameleon, the Romans are at hand. [*A cry of terror from the women: they would fly but for the spears*] Not even the descendants of the gods can resist them; for they have each man seven arms, each carrying seven spears. The blood in their veins is boiling quicksilver; and their wives become mothers in three hours, and are slain and eaten the next day.

[*A shudder of horror from the women. Ftatateeta, despising them and scorning the soldiers, pushes her way through the crowd and confronts the spear points undismayed.*]

FTATATEETA: Then fly and save yourselves, O cowardly sons of the cheap clay gods that are sold to fish porters; and leave us to shift for ourselves.

BELZANOR: Not until you have first done our bidding, O terror of manhood. Bring out Cleopatra the Queen to us; and then go whither you will.

FTATATEETA [*with a derisive laugh*]: Now I know why the gods have taken her out of our hands. [*The guardsmen start and look at one another*]. Know, thou foolish soldier, that the Queen has been missing since an hour past sundown.

BELZANOR [*furiously*]: Hag: you have hidden her to sell to Caesar or her brother. [*He grasps her by the left wrist, and drags her, helped by a few of the guard, to the middle of the courtyard, where, as they fling her on her knees, he draws a murderous looking knife*]. Where is she? Where is she? or— [*he threatens to cut her throat*].

FTATATEETA [*savagely*]: Touch me, dog; and the Nile will not rise on your fields for seven times seven years of famine.

BELZANOR [*frightened, but desperate*]: I will sacrifice: I will pay. Or stay. [*To the Persian*] You, O subtle one: your father's lands lie far from the Nile. Slay her.

PERSIAN [*threatening her with the knife*]: Persia has but one god; yet he loves the blood of old women. Where is Cleopatra?

FTATATEETA: Persian: as Osiris lives, I do not know. I chid her for bringing evil days upon us by talking to the sacred cats of the priests, and carrying them in her arms. I told her she would be left alone here when the Romans came as a punishment for her disobedience. And now she is gone—run away—hidden. I speak the truth. I call Osiris to witness—

THE WOMEN [*protesting officiously*]: She speaks the truth, Belzanor.

BELZANOR: You have frightened the child: she is hiding. Search—quick— into the palace—search every corner.

[*The guards, led by Belzanor, shoulder their way into the palace through the flying crowd of women, who escape through the courtyard gate.*]

FTATATEETA [*screaming*]: Sacrilege! Men in the Queen's chambers! Sa—[*her voice dies away as the Persian puts his knife to her throat*].

BEL AFFRIS [*laying a hand on Ftatateeta's left shoulder*]: Forbear her yet a moment, Persian. [*To Ftatateeta, very significantly*] Mother: your gods are asleep or away hunting; and the sword is at your throat. Bring us to where the Queen is hid, and you shall live.

FTATATEETA [*contemptuously*]: Who shall stay the sword in the hand of a fool, if the high gods put it there? Listen to me, ye young men without understanding. Cleopatra fears me; but she fears the Romans more. There is but one power greater in her eyes than the wrath of the Queen's nurse and the cruelty of Caesar; and that is the power of the Sphinx that sits in the desert watching the way to the sea. What she would have it know, she tells into the ears of the sacred cats; and on her birthday she sacrifices to it and decks it with poppies. Go ye therefore into the desert and seek Cleopatra in the shadow of the Sphinx; and on your heads see to it that no harm comes to her.

BEL AFFRIS [*to the Persian*]: May we believe this, O subtle one?

PERSIAN: Which way come the Romans?

BEL AFFRIS: Over the desert, from the sea, by this very Sphinx.

PERSIAN [*to Ftatateeta*]: O mother of guile! O aspic's tongue! You have made up this tale so that we two may go into the desert and perish on the spears of the Romans. [*Lifting his knife*] Taste death.

FTATATEETA: Not from thee, baby.

[*She snatches his ankle from under him and flies stooping along the palace wall, vanishing in the darkness within its precinct. Bel Affris roars with laughter as the Persian tumbles. The guardsmen rush out of the palace with Belzanor and a mob of fugitives, mostly carrying bundles*].

PERSIAN: Have you found Cleopatra?

BELZANOR: She is gone. We have searched every corner.

THE NUBIAN SENTINEL [*appearing at the door of the palace*]: Woe! Alas! Fly, fly!

BELZANOR: What is the matter now?

THE NUBIAN SENTINEL: The sacred white cat has been stolen.

ALL: Woe! woe!

[*General panic. They all fly with cries of consternation. The torch is thrown down and extinguished in the rush. The noise of the fugitives dies away. Darkness and dead silence*].

Act I

[*The same darkness into which the temple of Ra and the Syrian palace vanished. The same silence. Suspense. Then the blackness and stillness break softly into silver mist and strange airs as the windswept harp of Memnon plays at the dawning of the moon. It rises full over the desert; and a vast horizon comes into relief, broken by a huge shape which soon reveals itself in the spreading radiance as a Sphinx pedestalled on the sands. The light still clears, until the upraised eyes of the image are distinguished looking straight forward and upward in infinite fearless vigil, and a mass of color between its great paws defines itself as a heap of red poppies on which a girl lies motionless, her silken vest heaving gently and regularly with the breathing of a dreamless sleeper, and her braided hair glittering in a shaft of moonlight like a bird's wing.*

Suddenly there comes from afar a vaguely fearful sound (it might be the bellow of a Minotaur softened by great distance) and Memnon's music stops. Silence: then a few faint high-ringing trumpet notes. Then silence again. Then a man comes from the south with stealing steps, ravished by the mystery of the night, all wonder, and halts, lost in contemplation, opposite the left flank of the Sphinx, whose bosom, with its burden, is hidden from him by its massive shoulder.]

THE MAN: Hail, Sphinx: salutation from Julius Caesar! I have wandered in many lands, seeking the lost regions from which my birth into this world exiled me, and the company of creatures such as I myself. I have found flocks and pastures, men and cities, but no other Caesar, no air native to me, no man kindred to me, none who can do my day's deed, and think my night's thought. In the little world yonder, Sphinx, my place is as high as yours in this great desert; only I wander, and you sit still; I conquer, and you endure; I work and wonder, you watch and wait; I look up and am dazzled, look down and am darkened, look round and am puzzled, whilst your eyes never turn from looking out—out of the world—to the lost region—the home from which we have strayed. Sphinx, you and I, strangers to the race of men, are no strangers to one another: have I not been conscious of you and of this place since I was born? Rome is a madman's dream: this is my Reality. These starry lamps of yours I have seen from afar in Gaul, in Britain, in Spain, in Thessaly, signaling great secrets to some eternal sentinel below, whose post I never could find. And here at last is their sentinel—an image of the constant and immortal part of my life, silent, full of thoughts, alone in the silver desert. Sphinx, Sphinx: I have climbed mountains at night to hear in the distance the stealthy footfall of the winds that chase your sands in forbidden play—our invisible children, O Sphinx, laughing in whispers. My way hither was the way of destiny; for I am he of whose genius you are the symbol: part brute, part woman, and part god— nothing of man in me at all. Have I read your riddle, Sphinx?

THE GIRL [*who has wakened, and peeped cautiously from her nest to see who is speaking*]: Old gentleman.

CAESAR [*starting violently, and clutching his sword*]: Immortal gods!

THE GIRL: Old gentleman: dont run away.

CAESAR [*stupefied*]: "Old gentleman: dont run away"!!! This! to Julius Caesar!

THE GIRL [*urgently*]: Old gentleman.

CAESAR: Sphinx: you presume on your centuries. I am younger than you, though your voice is but a girl's voice as yet.

THE GIRL: Climb up here, quickly; or the Romans will come and eat you.

CAESAR [*running forward past the Sphinx's shoulder, and seeing her*]: A child at its breast! a divine child!

THE GIRL: Come up quickly. You must get up at its side and creep round.

CAESAR [*amazed*]: Who are you?

THE GIRL: Cleopatra, Queen of Egypt.

CAESAR: Queen of the Gypsies, you mean.

CLEOPATRA: You must not be disrespectful to me, or the Sphinx will let the Romans eat you. Come up. It is quite cozy here.

CAESAR [*to himself*]: What a dream! What a magnificent dream! Only let me not wake, and I will conquer ten continents to pay for dreaming it out to the end.

[*He climbs to the Sphinx's flank, and presently reappears to her on the pedestal, stepping round to its right shoulder*].

CLEOPATRA: Take care. Thats right. Now sit down: you may have its other paw. [*She seats herself comfortably on its left paw*]. It is very powerful and will protect us; but [*shivering, and with plaintive loneliness*] it would not take any notice of me or keep me company. I am glad you have come: I was very lonely. Did you happen to see a white cat anywhere?

CAESAR [*sitting slowly down on the right paw in extreme wonderment*]: Have you lost one?

CLEOPATRA: Yes: the sacred white cat: is it not dreadful? I brought him here to sacrifice him to the Sphinx; but when we got a little way from the city a black cat called him, and he jumped out of my arms and ran away to it. Do you think that the black cat can have been my great-great-great-grandmother?

CAESAR [*staring at her*]: Your great-great-great-grandmother! Well, why not? Nothing would surprise me on this night of nights.

CLEOPATRA: I think it must have been. My great-grandmother's great-grandmother was a black kitten of the sacred white cat; and the river Nile made her his seventh wife. That is why my hair is so wavy. And I always want to be let do as I like, no matter whether it is the will of the gods or not: that is because my blood is made with Nile water.

CAESAR: What are you doing here at this time of night? Do you live here?

CLEOPATRA: Of course not: I am the Queen; and I shall live in the palace at Alexandria when I have killed my brother, who drove me out of it. When I am old enough I shall do just what I like. I shall be able to poison the slaves and see them wriggle, and pretend to Ftatateeta that she is going to be put into the fiery furnace.

CAESAR: Hm! Meanwhile why are you not at home and in bed?

CLEOPATRA: Because the Romans are coming to eat us all. You are not at home and in bed either.

CAESAR [*with conviction*]: Yes I am. I live in a tent; and I am now in that tent, fast asleep and dreaming. Do you suppose that I believe you are real, you impossible little dream witch?

CLEOPATRA [*giggling and leaning trustfully towards him*]: You are a funny old gentleman. I like you.

CAESAR: Ah, that spoils the dream. Why dont you dream that I am young?

CLEOPATRA: I wish you were; only I think I should be more afraid of you. I like men, especially young men with round strong arms; but I am afraid of them. You are old and rather thin and stringy; but you have a nice voice; and I like to have somebody to talk to, though I think you are a little mad. It is the moon that makes you talk to yourself in that silly way.

CAESAR: What! you heard that, did you? I was saying my prayers to the great Sphinx.

CLEOPATRA: But this isnt the great Sphinx.

CAESAR [*much disappointed, looking up at the statue*]: What!

CLEOPATRA: This is only a dear little kitten of a Sphinx. Why, the great Sphinx is so big that it has a temple between its paws. This is my pet Sphinx. Tell me: do you think the Romans have any sorcerers who could take us away from the Sphinx by magic?

CAESAR: Why? Are you afraid of the Romans?

CLEOPATRA [*very seriously*]: Oh, they would eat us if they caught us. They are barbarians. Their chief is called Julius Caesar. His father was a tiger and his mother a burning mountain; and his nose is like an elephant's trunk. [*Caesar involuntarily rubs his nose*]. They all have long noses, and ivory tusks, and little tails, and seven arms with a hundred arrows in each; and they live on human flesh.

CAESAR: Would you like me to shew you a real Roman?

CLEOPATRA [*terrified*]: No. You are frightening me.

CAESAR: No matter: this is only a dream—

CLEOPATRA [*excitedly*]: It is not a dream: it is not a dream. See, see. [*She plucks a pin from her hair and jabs it repeatedly into his arm*].

CAESAR: Ffff—Stop. [*Wrathfully*] How dare you?

CLEOPATRA [*abashed*]: You said you were dreaming. [*Whimpering*] I only wanted to shew you—

CAESAR [*gently*]: Come, come: dont cry. A queen mustnt cry. [*He rubs his arm, wondering at the reality of the smart*]. Am I awake? [*He strikes his hand against the Sphinx to test its solidity. It feels so real that he begins to be alarmed, and says perplexedly*] Yes. I— [*quite panicstricken*] no: impossible: madness, madness! [*Desperately*] Back to camp—to camp. [*He rises to spring down from the pedestal*].

CLEOPATRA [*flinging her arms in terror round him*]: No: you shant leave me. No, no, no: dont go. I'm afraid—afraid of the Romans.

CAESAR [*as the conviction that he is really awake forces itself on him*]: Cleopatra: can you see my face well?

CLEOPATRA: Yes. It is so white in the moonlight.

CAESAR: Are you sure it is the moonlight that makes me look whiter than an Egyptian? [*Grimly*] Do you notice that I have a rather long nose?

CLEOPATRA [*recoiling, paralysed by a terrible suspicion*]: Oh!

CAESAR: It is a Roman nose, Cleopatra.

CLEOPATRA: Ah! [*With a piercing scream she springs up; darts round the left shoulder of the Sphinx; scrambles down to the sand; and falls on her knees in frantic supplication, shrieking*] Bite him in two, Sphinx: bite him in two. I meant to sacrifice the white cat—I did indeed—I [*Caesar, who has slipped down from the pedestal, touches her on the shoulder*]—Ah! [*She buries her head in her arms*].

CAESAR: Cleopatra: shall I teach you a way to prevent Caesar from eating you?

CLEOPATRA [*clinging to him piteously*]: Oh do, do, do. I will steal Ftatateeta's jewels and give them to you. I will make the river Nile water your lands twice a year.

CAESAR: Peace, peace, my child. Your gods are afraid of the Romans: you see the Sphinx dare not bite me, nor prevent me carrying you off to Julius Caesar.

CLEOPATRA [*in pleading murmurings*]: You wont, you wont. You said you wouldnt.

CAESAR: Caesar never eats women.

CLEOPATRA [*springing up full of hope*]: What!

CAESAR [*impressively*]: But he eats girls [*she relapses*] and cats. Now you are a silly little girl; and you are descended from the black kitten. You are both a girl and a cat.

CLEOPATRA [*trembling*]: And will he eat me?

CAESAR: Yes; unless you make him believe that you are a woman.

CLEOPATRA: Oh, you must get a sorcerer to make a woman of me. Are you a sorcerer?

CAESAR: Perhaps. But it will take a long time; and this very night you must stand face to face with Caesar in the palace of your fathers.

CLEOPATRA: No, no. I darent.

CAESAR: Whatever dread may be in your soul—however terrible Caesar may be to you—you must confront him as a brave woman and a great queen; and you must feel no fear. If your hand shakes: if your voice quavers; then—night and death! [*She moans*]. But if he thinks you worthy to rule, he will set you on the throne by his side and make you the real ruler of Egypt.

CLEOPATRA [*despairingly*]: No: he will find me out: he will find me out.

CAESAR [*rather mournfully*]: He is easily deceived by women. Their eyes dazzle him; and he sees them not as they are, but as he wishes them to appear to him.

CLEOPATRA [*hopefully*]: Then we will cheat him. I will put on Ftatateeta's headdress; and he will think me quite an old woman.

CAESAR: If you do that he will eat you at one mouthful.

CLEOPATRA: But I will give him a cake with my magic opal and seven hairs of the white cat baked in it; and—

CAESAR [*abruptly*]: Pah! you are a little fool. He will eat your cake and you too. [*He turns contemptuously from her*].

CLEOPATRA [*running after him and clinging to him*]: Oh please, please! I will do whatever you tell me. I will be good. I will be your slave.

[*Again the terrible bellowing note sounds across the desert, now closer at hand. It is the bucina, the Roman war trumpet*].

CAESAR: Hark!

CLEOPATRA [*trembling*]: What was that?

CAESAR: Caesar's voice.

CLEOPATRA [*pulling at his hand*]: Let us run away. Come. Oh, come.

CAESAR: You are safe with me until you stand on your throne to receive Caesar. Now lead me thither.

CLEOPATRA [*only too glad to get away*]: I will, I will. [*Again the bucina*]. Oh come, come, come: the gods are angry. Do you feel the earth shaking?

CAESAR: It is the tread of Caesar's legions.

CLEOPATRA [*drawing him away*]: This way, quickly. And let us look for the white cat as we go. It is he that has turned you into a Roman.

CAESAR: Incorrigible, oh, incorrigible! Away!

[*He follows her, the bucina sounding louder as they steal across the desert. The moonlight wanes: the horizon again shews black against the sky, broken only by the fantastic silhouette of the Sphinx. The sky itself vanishes in darkness, from which there is no relief until the gleam of a distant torch falls on great Egyptian pillars supporting the roof of a majestic corridor. At the further end of this corridor a Nubian slave appears carrying the torch. Caesar, still led by Cleopatra, follows him. They come down the corridor, Caesar peering keenly about at the strange architecture, and at the pillar shadows between which, as the passing torch makes them hurry noiselessly backwards, figures of men with wings and hawk's heads, and vast black marble cats, seem to flit in and out of ambush. Further along, the wall turns a corner and makes a spacious transept in which Caesar sees, on his right, a throne, and behind the throne a door. On each side of the throne is a slender pillar with a lamp on it*].

CAESAR: What place is this?

CLEOPATRA: This is where I sit on the throne when I am allowed to wear my crown and robes. [*The slave holds his torch to shew the throne*].

CAESAR: Order the slave to light the lamps.

CLEOPATRA [*shyly*]: Do you think I may?

CAESAR: Of course. You are the Queen. [*She hesitates.*] Go on.

CLEOPATRA [*timidly, to the slave*]: Light all the lamps.

FTATATEETA [*suddenly coming from behind the throne*]: Stop. [*The slave stops. She turns sternly to Cleopatra, who quails like a naughty child*]. Who is this you have with you; and how dare you order the lamps to be lighted without my permission? [*Cleopatra is dumb with apprehension.*]

CAESAR: Who is she?

CLEOPATRA: Ftatateeta.

FTATATEETA [*arrogantly*]: Chief nurse to—

CAESAR [*cutting her short*]: I speak to the Queen. Be silent. [*To Cleopatra*] Is this how your servants know their places? Send her away; and do you [*to the slave*] do as the Queen has bidden. [*The slave lights the lamps. Meanwhile Cleopatra stands hesitating, afraid of Ftatateeta*]. You are the Queen: send her away.

CLEOPATRA [*cajoling*]: Ftatateeta, dear: you must go away—just for a little.

CAESAR: You are not commanding her to go away: you are begging her. You are no Queen. You will be eaten. Farewell. [*He turns to go*].
CLEOPATRA [*clutching him*]: No, no, no. Dont leave me.
CAESAR: A Roman does not stay with queens who are afraid of their slaves.
CLEOPATRA: I am not afraid. Indeed I am not afraid.
FTATATEETA: We shall see who is afraid here. [*Menacingly*] Cleopatra—
CAESAR: On your knees, woman: am I also a child that you dare trifle with me? [*He points to the floor at Cleopatra's feet. Ftatateeta, half cowed, half savage, hesitates. Caesar calls to the Nubian*] Slave. [*The Nubian comes to him*] Can you cut off a head? [*The Nubian nods and grins ecstatically, showing all his teeth. Caesar takes his sword by the scabbard, ready to offer the hilt to the Nubian, and turns again to Ftatateeta, repeating his gesture*]. Have you remembered yourself, mistress?

[*Ftatateeta, crushed, kneels before Cleopatra, who can hardly believe her eyes.*]

FTATATEETA [*hoarsely*]: O Queen, forget not thy servant in the days of thy greatness.
CLEOPATRA [*blazing with excitement*]: Go. Begone. Go away. [*Ftatateeta rises with stooped head, and moves backwards towards the door. Cleopatra watches her submission eagerly, almost clapping her hands, which are trembling. Suddenly she cries*] Give me something to beat her with.

[*She snatches a snake-skin from the throne and dashes after Ftatateeta, whirling it like a scourge in the air. Caesar makes a bound and manages to catch her and hold her while Ftatateeta escapes*].

CAESAR: You scratch, kitten, do you?
CLEOPATRA [*breaking from him*]: I will beat somebody. I will beat him. [*She attacks the slave.*] There, there, there! [*The slave flies for his life up the corridor and vanishes. She throws the snake-skin away and jumps on the step of the throne with her arms waving, crying*] I am a real Queen at last—a real, real Queen! Cleopatra the Queen! [*Caesar shakes his head dubiously, the advantage of the change seeming open to question from the point of view of the general welfare of Egypt. She turns and looks at him exultantly. Then she jumps down from the steps, runs to him, and flings her arms round him rapturously, crying*] Oh, I love you for making me a Queen.
CAESAR: But queens love only kings.
CLEOPATRA: I will make all the men I love kings. I will make you a king. I will have many young kings, with round, strong arms; and when I am tired of them I will whip them to death; but you shall always be my king: my nice, kind, wise, good old king.

CAESAR: Oh, my wrinkles, my wrinkles! And my child's heart! You will be the most dangerous of all Caesar's conquests.

CLEOPATRA [*appalled*]: Caesar! I forgot Caesar. [*Anxiously*] You will tell him that I am a Queen, will you not?—a real Queen. Listen! [*stealthily coaxing him*] let us run away and hide until Caesar is gone.

CAESAR: If you fear Caesar, you are no true queen; and though you were to hide beneath a pyramid, he would go straight to it and lift it with one hand. And then—! [*he chops his teeth together*].

CLEOPATRA [*trembling*]: Oh!

CAESAR: Be afraid if you dare. [*The note of the bucina resounds again in the distance. She moans with fear. Caesar exults in it, exclaiming*] Aha! Caesar approaches the throne of Cleopatra. Come: take your place. [*He takes her hand and leads her to the throne. She is too downcast to speak*]. Ho, there, Teetatota. How do you call your slaves?

CLEOPATRA [*spiritlessly, as she sinks on the throne and cowers there, shaking*]: Clap your hands.

[*He claps his hands. Ftatateeta returns.*]

CAESAR: Bring the Queen's robes, and her crown, and her women; and prepare her.

CLEOPATRA [*eagerly—recovering herself a little*]: Yes, the crown, Ftatateeta: I shall wear the crown.

FTATATEETA: For whom must the Queen put on her state?

CAESAR: For a citizen of Rome. A king of kings, Totateeta.

CLEOPATRA [*stamping at her*]: How dare you ask questions? Go and do as you are told. [*Ftatateeta goes out with a grim smile. Cleopatra goes on eagerly, to Caesar*] Caesar will know that I am a Queen when he sees my crown and robes, will he not?

CAESAR: No. How shall he know that you are not a slave dressed up in the Queen's ornaments?

CLEOPATRA: You must tell him.

CAESAR: He will not ask me. He will know Cleopatra by her pride, her courage, her majesty, and her beauty. [*She looks very doubtful*] Are you trembling?

CLEOPATRA [*shivering with dread*]: No, I—I—[*in a very sickly voice*] No.

[*Ftatateeta and three women come in with the regalia.*]

FTATATEETA: Of all the Queen's women, these three alone are left. The rest are fled. [*They begin to deck Cleopatra, who submits, pale and motionless*].

CAESAR: Good, good. Three are enough. Poor Caesar generally has to dress himself.

FTATATEETA [*contemptuously*]: The queen of Egypt is not a Roman barbarian. [*To Cleopatra*] Be brave, my nursling. Hold up your head before this stranger.

CAESAR [*admiring Cleopatra, and placing the crown on her head*]: Is it sweet or bitter to be a Queen, Cleopatra?

CLEOPATRA: Bitter.

CAESAR: Cast out fear; and you will conquer Caesar. Tota: are the Romans at hand?

FTATATEETA: They are at hand; and the guard has fled.

THE WOMEN [*wailing subduedly*]: Woe to us!

[*The Nubian comes running down the hall.*]

NUBIAN: The Romans are in the courtyard.

[*He bolts through the door. With a shriek, the women fly after him. Ftatateeta's jaw expresses savage resolution: she does not budge. Cleopatra can hardly restrain herself from following them. Caesar grips her wrist, and looks steadfastly at her. She stands like a martyr*].

CAESAR: The Queen must face Caesar alone. Answer "So be it."

CLEOPATRA [*white*]: So be it.

CAESAR [*releasing her*]: Good.

[*A tramp and tumult of armed men is heard. Cleopatra's terror increases. The bucina sounds close at hand, followed by a formidable clangor of trumpets. This is too much for Cleopatra: she utters a cry and darts towards the door. Ftatateeta stops her ruthlessly.*]

FTATATEETA: You are my nursling. You have said "So be it"; and if you die for it, you must make the Queen's word good.

[*She hands Cleopatra to Caesar, who takes her back, almost beside herself with apprehension, to the throne*].

CAESAR: Now, if you quail—! [*He seats himself on the throne*].

[*She stands on the step, all but unconscious, waiting for death. The Roman soldiers troop in tumultuously through the corridor, headed by their ensign with his eagle, and their bucinator, a burly fellow with his instrument coiled round his body, its brazen bell shaped like the head of a howling wolf. When they reach the transept, they stare in amazement at the throne; dress into ordered rank opposite; draw their swords and lift them in the air with a shout of Hail, Caesar. Cleopatra turns and stares wildly at Caesar; grasps the situation; and, with a great sob of relief, falls into his arms.*]

Act II

[*Alexandria. A hall on the first floor of the Palace, ending in a loggia approached by two steps. Through the arches of the loggia the Mediterranean can be seen, bright in the morning sun. The clean lofty walls, painted with a procession of the Egyptian theocracy, presented in profile as flat ornament, and the absence of mirrors, sham perspectives, stuffy upholstery and textiles, make the place handsome, wholesome, simple and cool, or, as a rich English manufacturer would express it, poor, bare, ridiculous and unhomely. For Tottenham Court Road civilization is to this Egyptian civilization as glass bead and tattoo civilization is to Tottenham Court Road.*

The young king Ptolemy Dionysus (aged ten) is at the top of the steps, on his way in through the loggia, led by his guardian Pothinus, who has him by the hand. The court is assembled to receive him. It is made up of men and women (some of the women being officials) of various complexions and races, mostly Egyptian; some of them, comparatively fair, from lower Egypt, some, much darker, from upper Egypt; with a few Greeks and Jews. Prominent in a group on Ptolemy's right hand is Theodotus, Ptolemy's tutor. Another group, on Ptolemy's left, is headed by Achillas, the general of Ptolemy's troops. Theodotus is a little old man, whose features are as cramped and wizened as his limbs, except his tall straight forehead, which occupies more space than all the rest of his face. He maintains an air of magpie keenness and profundity, listening to what the others say with the sarcastic vigilance of a philosopher listening to the exercises of his disciples. Achillas is a tall handsome man of thirty-five, with a fine black beard curled like the coat of a poodle. Apparently not a clever man, but distinguished and dignified. Pothinus is a vigorous man of fifty, a eunuch, passionate, energetic and quick witted, but of common mind and character; impatient and unable to control his temper. He has fine tawny hair, like fur. Ptolemy, the King, looks much older than an English boy of ten; but he has the childish air, the habit of being in leading strings, the mixture of impotence and petulance, the appearance of being excessively washed, combed and dressed by other hands, which is exhibited by court-bred princes of all ages.

All receive the King with reverences. He comes down the steps to a chair of state which stands a little to his right, the only seat in the hall. Taking his place before it, he looks nervously for instructions to Pothinus, who places himself at his left hand.]

POTHINUS: The king of Egypt has a word to speak.

THEODOTUS [*in a squeak which he makes impressive by sheer self-opinionativeness*]: Peace for the King's word!

PTOLEMY [*without any vocal inflexions: he is evidently repeating a lesson*]: Take notice of this all of you. I am the first-born son of Auletes the Flute Blower who was your King. My sister Berenice drove him from his throne and reigned in his stead but—but—[*he hesitates*]—

POTHINUS [*stealthily prompting*]:—but the gods would not suffer—

PTOLEMY: Yes—the gods would not suffer—not suffer—[*He stops; then, crest-fallen*] I forgot what the gods would not suffer.

THEODOTUS: Let Pothinus, the King's guardian, speak for the King.

POTHINUS [*suppressing his impatience with difficulty*]: The King wished to say that the gods would not suffer the impiety of his sister to go unpunished.

PTOLEMY [*hastily*]: Yes: I remember the rest of it. [*He resumes his monotone*]. Therefore the gods sent a stranger one Mark Antony a Roman captain of horsemen across the sands of the desert and he set my father again upon the throne. And my father took Berenice my sister and struck her head off. And now that my father is dead yet another of his daughters my sister Cleopatra would snatch the kingdom from me and reign in my place. But the gods would not suffer—[*Pothinus coughs admonitorily*]—the gods—the gods would not suffer—

POTHINUS [*prompting*]:—will not maintain—

PTOLEMY: Oh yes—will not maintain such iniquity they will give her head to the axe even as her sister's. But with the help of the witch Ftatateeta she hath cast a spell on the Roman Julius Caesar to make him uphold her false pretense to rule in Egypt. Take notice then that I will not suffer —that I will not suffer—[*pettishly, to Pothinus*] What is it that I will not suffer?

POTHINUS [*suddenly exploding with all the force and emphasis of political passion*]: The King will not suffer a foreigner to take from him the throne of our Egypt. [*A shout of applause.*] Tell the King, Achillas, how many soldiers and horsemen follow the Roman?

THEODOTUS: Let the King's general speak!

ACHILLAS: But two Roman legions, O King. Three thousand soldiers and scarce a thousand horsemen.

[*The court breaks into derisive laughter; and a great chattering begins, amid which Rufio, a Roman officer, appears in the loggia. He is a burly, black-bearded man of middle age, very blunt, prompt and rough, with small clear eyes, and plump nose and cheeks, which, however, like the rest of his flesh, are in ironhard condition.*]

RUFIO [*from the steps*]: Peace, ho! [*The laughter and chatter cease abruptly*]. Caesar approaches.

THEODOTUS [*with much presence of mind*]: The King permits the Roman commander to enter!

[*Caesar, plainly dressed, but wearing an oak wreath to conceal his baldness, enters from the loggia, attended by Britannus, his secretary, a Briton, about forty, tall, solemn, and already slightly bald, with a heavy, drooping, hazel-colored moustache trained so as to lose its ends in a pair of trim whiskers. He is carefully dressed in blue, with portfolio, inkhorn, and reed pen at his girdle.*]

His serious air and sense of the importance of the business in hand is in marked contrast to the kindly interest of Caesar, who looks at the scene, which is new to him, with the frank curiosity of a child, and then turns to the king's chair: Britannus and Rufio posting themselves near the steps at the other side.]

CAESAR [*looking at Pothinus and Ptolemy*]: Which is the King? the man or the boy?

POTHINUS: I am Pothinus, the guardian of my lord the King.

CAESAR [*patting Ptolemy kindly on the shoulder*]: So you are the King. Dull work at your age, eh? [*To Pothinus*] Your servant, Pothinus. [*He turns away unconcernedly and comes slowly along the middle of the hall, looking from side to side at the courtiers until he reaches Achillas*]. And this gentleman?

THEODOTUS: Achillas, the King's general.

CAESAR [*to Achillas, very friendly*]: A general, eh? I am a general myself. But I began too old, too old. Health and many victories, Achillas!

ACHILLAS: As the gods will, Caesar.

CAESAR [*turning to Theodotus*]: And you, sir, are—?

THEODOTUS: Theodotus, the King's tutor.

CAESAR: You teach men how to be kings, Theodotus. That is very clever of you. [*Looking at the gods on the walls as he turns away from Theodotus and goes up again to Pothinus*] And this place?

POTHINUS: The council chamber of the chancellors of the King's treasury, Caesar.

CAESAR: Ah! that reminds me. I want some money.

POTHINUS: The King's treasury is poor, Caesar.

CAESAR: Yes: I notice that there is but one chair in it.

RUFIO [*shouting gruffly*]: Bring a chair there, some of you, for Caesar.

PTOLEMY [*rising shyly to offer his chair*]: Caesar—

CAESAR [*kindly*]: No, no, my boy: that is your chair of state. Sit down.

[*He makes Ptolemy sit down again. Meanwhile Rufio, looking about him, sees in the nearest corner an image of the god Ra, represented as a seated man with the head of a hawk. Before the image is a bronze tripod, about as large as a three-legged stool, with a stick of incense burning on it. Rufio, with Roman resourcefulness and indifference to foreign superstitions, promptly seizes the tripod; shakes off the incense; blows away the ash; and dumps it down behind Caesar, nearly in the middle of the hall.*]

RUFIO: Sit on that, Caesar.

[*A shiver runs through the court, followed by a hissing whisper of* Sacrilege!]

CAESAR [*seating himself*]: Now, Pothinus, to business. I am badly in want of money.

BRITANNUS [*disapproving of these informal expressions*]: My master would say that there is a lawful debt due to Rome by Egypt, contracted by the King's deceased father to the Triumvirate; and that it is Caesar's duty to his country to require immediate payment.

CAESAR [*blandly*]: Ah, I forgot. I have not made my companions known here. Pothinus: this is Britannus, my secretary. He is an islander from the western end of the world, a day's voyage from Gaul. [*Britannus bows stiffly*]. This gentleman is Rufio, my comrade in arms. [*Rufio nods*]. Pothinus: I want 1,600 talents.

[*The courtiers, appalled, murmur loudly, and Theodotus and Achillas appeal mutely to one another against so monstrous a demand.*]

POTHINUS [*aghast*]: Forty million sesterces! Impossible. There is not so much money in the King's treasury.

CAESAR [*encouragingly*]: Only sixteen hundred talents, Pothinus. Why count it in sesterces? A sestertius is only worth a loaf of bread.

POTHINUS: And a talent is worth a racehorse. I say it is impossible. We have been at strife here, because the King's sister Cleopatra falsely claims his throne. The King's taxes have not been collected for a whole year.

CAESAR: Yes they have, Pothinus. My officers have been collecting them all morning. [*Renewed whisper and sensation, not without some stifled laughter, among the courtiers*].

RUFIO [*bluntly*]: You must pay, Pothinus. Why waste words? You are getting off cheaply enough.

POTHINUS [*bitterly*]: Is it possible that Caesar, the conqueror of the world, has time to occupy himself with such a trifle as our taxes?

CAESAR: My friend: taxes are the chief business of a conqueror of the world.

POTHINUS: Then take warning, Caesar. This day, the treasures of the temple and the gold of the King's treasury shall be sent to the mint to be melted down for our ransom in the sight of the people. They shall see us sitting under bare walls and drinking from wooden cups. And their wrath be on your head, Caesar, if you force us to this sacrilege!

CAESAR: Do not fear, Pothinus: the people know how well wine tastes in wooden cups. In return for your bounty, I will settle this dispute about the throne for you, if you will. What say you?

POTHINUS: If I say no, will that hinder you?

RUFIO [*defiantly*]: No.

CAESAR: You say the matter has been at issue for a year, Pothinus. May I have ten minutes at it?

POTHINUS: You will do your pleasure, doubtless.

CAESAR: Good! But first, let us have Cleopatra here.

THEODOTUS: She is not in Alexandria: she is fled into Syria.

CAESAR: I think not. [*To Rufio*] Call Totateeta.

RUFIO [*calling*]: Ho there, Teetatota.

[*Ftatateeta enters the loggia, and stands arrogantly at the top of the steps.*]

FTATATEETA: Who pronounces the name of Ftatateeta, the Queen's chief nurse?

CAESAR: Nobody can pronounce it, Tota, except yourself. Where is your mistress?

[*Cleopatra, who is hiding behind Ftatateeta, peeps out at them, laughing. Caesar rises.*]

CAESAR: Will the Queen favor us with her presence for a moment?

CLEOPATRA [*pushing Ftatateeta aside and standing haughtily on the brink of the steps*]: Am I to behave like a Queen?

CAESAR: Yes.

[*Cleopatra immediately comes down to the chair of state; seizes Ptolemy; drags him out of his seat; then takes his place in the chair. Ftatateeta seats herself on the step of the loggia, and sits there, watching the scene with sibylline intensity.*]

PTOLEMY [*mortified, and struggling with his tears*]: Caesar: this is how she treats me always. If I am king why is she allowed to take everything from me?

CLEOPATRA: You are not to be King, you little cry-baby. You are to be eaten by the Romans.

CAESAR [*touched by Ptolemy's distress*]: Come here, my boy, and stand by me.

[*Ptolemy goes over to Caesar, who, resuming his seat on the tripod, takes the boy's hand to encourage him. Cleopatra, furiously jealous, rises and glares at them.*]

CLEOPATRA [*with flaming cheeks*]: Take your throne: I dont want it. [*She flings away from the chair, and approaches Ptolemy, who shrinks from her*]. Go this instant and sit down in your place.

CAESAR: Go, Ptolemy. Always take a throne when it is offered to you.

RUFIO: I hope you will have the good sense to follow your own advice when we return to Rome, Caesar.

[*Ptolemy slowly goes back to the throne, giving Cleopatra a wide berth, in evident fear of her hands. She takes his place beside Caesar.*]

CAESAR: Pothinus—

CLEOPATRA [*interrupting him*]: Are you not going to speak to me?

CAESAR: Be quiet. Open your mouth again before I give you leave; and you shall be eaten.

CLEOPATRA: I am not afraid. A queen must not be afraid. Eat my husband there, if you like: he is afraid.

CAESAR [*starting*]: Your husband! What do you mean?

CLEOPATRA [*pointing to Ptolemy*]: That little thing.

[*The two Romans and the Briton stare at one another in amazement.*]

THEODOTUS: Caesar: you are a stranger here, and not conversant with our laws. The kings and queens of Egypt may not marry except with their own royal blood. Ptolemy and Cleopatra are born king and consort just as they are born brother and sister.

BRITANNUS [*shocked*]: Caesar: this is not proper.

THEODOTUS [*outraged*]: How!

CAESAR [*recovering his self-possession*]: Pardon him, Theodotus: he is a barbarian, and thinks that the customs of his tribe and island are the laws of nature.

BRITANNUS: On the contrary, Caesar, it is these Egyptians who are barbarians; and you do wrong to encourage them. I say it is a scandal.

CAESAR: Scandal or not, my friend, it opens the gate of peace. [*He addresses Pothinus seriously*]. Pothinus: hear what I propose.

RUFIO: Hear Caesar there.

CAESAR: Ptolemy and Cleopatra shall reign jointly in Egypt.

ACHILLAS: What of the King's younger brother and Cleopatra's younger sister?

RUFIO [*explaining*]: There is another little Ptolemy, Caesar: so they tell me.

CAESAR: Well, the little Ptolemy can marry the other sister; and we will make them both a present of Cyprus.

POTHINUS [*impatiently*]: Cyprus is of no use to anybody.

CAESAR: No matter: you shall have it for the sake of peace.

BRITANNUS [*unconsciously anticipating a later statesman*]: Peace with honor, Pothinus.

POTHINUS [*mutinously*]: Caesar: be honest. The money you demand is the price of our freedom. Take it; and leave us to settle our own affairs.

THE BOLDER COURTIERS [*encouraged by Pothinus's tone and Caesar's quietness*]: Yes, yes. Egypt for the Egyptians!

[*The conference now becomes an altercation, the Egyptians becoming more and more heated. Caesar remains unruffled; but Rufio grows fiercer and doggeder, and Britannus haughtily indignant.*]

RUFIO [*contemptuously*]: Egypt for the Egyptians! Do you forget that there is a Roman army of occupation here, left by Aulus Gabinius when he set up your toy king for you?

ACHILLAS [*suddenly asserting himself*]: And now under my command. *I* am the Roman general here, Caesar.

CAESAR [*tickled by the humor of the situation*]: And also the Egyptian general, eh?

POTHINUS [*triumphantly*]: That is so, Caesar.

CAESAR [*to Achillas*]: So you can make war on the Egyptians in the name of Rome, and on the Romans—on me, if necessary—in the name of Egypt?

ACHILLAS: That is so, Caesar.

CAESAR: And which side are you on at present, if I may presume to ask, general?

ACHILLAS: On the side of the right and of the gods.

CAESAR: Hm! How many men have you?

ACHILLAS: That will appear when I take the field.

RUFIO [*truculently*]: Are your men Romans? If not, it matters not how many there are, provided you are no stronger than 500 to ten.

POTHINUS: It is useless to try to bluff us, Rufio. Caesar has been defeated before and may be defeated again. A few weeks ago Caesar was flying for his life before Pompey: a few months hence he may be flying for his life before Cato and Juba of Numidia, the African King.

ACHILLAS [*following up Pothinus's speech menacingly*]: What can you do with 4,000 men?

THEODOTUS [*following up Achillas's speech with a raucous squeak*]: And without money? Away with you.

ALL THE COURTIERS [*shouting fiercely and crowding towards Caesar*]: Away with you. Egypt for the Egyptians! Begone.

[*Rufio bites his beard, too angry to speak. Caesar sits as comfortably as if he were at breakfast, and the cat were clamoring for a piece of Finnan-haddie.*]

CLEOPATRA: Why do you let them talk to you like that, Caesar? Are you afraid?

CAESAR: Why, my dear, what they say is quite true.

CLEOPATRA: But if you go away, I shall not be Queen.

CAESAR: I shall not go away until you are Queen.

POTHINUS: Achillas: if you are not a fool, you will take that girl whilst she is under your hand.

RUFIO [*daring them*]: Why not take Caesar as well, Achillas?

POTHINUS [*retorting the defiance with interest*]: Well said, Rufio. Why not?

RUFIO: Try, Achillas. [*Calling*] Guard there.

[*The loggia immediately fills with Caesar's soldiers, who stand, sword in hand, at the top of the steps, waiting the word to charge from their centurion, who carries a cudgel. For a moment the Egyptians face them proudly: then they retire sullenly to their former places.*]

BRITANNUS: You are Caesar's prisoners, all of you.

CAESAR [*benevolently*]: Oh no, no, no. By no means. Caesar's guests, gentlemen.

CLEOPATRA: Wont you cut their heads off?

CAESAR: What! Cut off your brother's head?

CLEOPATRA: Why not? He would cut off mine, if he got the chance. Wouldnt
you, Ptolemy?

PTOLEMY [*pale and obstinate*]: I would. I will, too, when I grow up.

[*Cleopatra is rent by a struggle between her newly-acquired dignity as a queen,
and a strong impulse to put out her tongue at him. She takes no part in the scene
which follows, but watches it with curiosity and wonder, fidgeting with the
restlessness of a child, and sitting down on Caesar's tripod when he rises.*]

POTHINUS: Caesar: if you attempt to detain us—

RUFIO: He will succeed, Egyptian: make up your mind to that. We hold the
palace, the beach, and the eastern harbor. The road to Rome is open; and
you shall travel it if Caesar chooses.

CAESAR [*courteously*]: I could do no less, Pothinus, to secure the retreat of my
own soldiers. I am accountable for every life among them. But you are
free to go. So are all here, and in the palace.

RUFIO [*aghast at this clemency*]: What! Renegades and all?

CAESAR [*softening the expression*]: Roman army of occupation and all, Rufio.

POTHINUS [*bewildered*]: But—but—but—

CAESAR: Well, my friend?

POTHINUS: You are turning us out of our own palace into the streets; and
you tell us with a grand air that we are free to go! It is for you to go.

CAESAR: Your friends are in the street, Pothinus. You will be safer there.

POTHINUS: This is a trick. I am the king's guardian: I refuse to stir. I stand
on my right here. Where is your right?

CAESAR: It is in Rufio's scabbard, Pothinus. I may not be able to keep it there
if you wait too long.

[*Sensation.*]

POTHINUS [*bitterly*]: And this is Roman justice!

THEODOTUS: But not Roman gratitude, I hope.

CAESAR: Gratitude! Am I in your debt for any service, gentlemen?

THEODOTUS: Is Caesar's life of so little account to him that he forgets that
we have saved it?

CAESAR: My life! Is that all?

THEODOTUS: Your life. Your laurels. Your future.

POTHINUS: It is true. I can call a witness to prove that but for us, the Roman
army of occupation, led by the greatest soldier in the world, would now

have Caesar at its mercy. [*Calling through the loggia*] Ho, there, Lucius Septimius [*Caesar starts, deeply moved*]: if my voice can reach you, come forth and testify before Caesar.

CAESAR [*shrinking*]: No, no.

THEODOTUS: Yes, I say. Let the military tribune bear witness.

[*Lucius Septimius, a clean shaven, trim athlete of about 40, with symmetrical features, resolute mouth, and handsome, thin Roman nose, in the dress of a Roman officer, comes in through the loggia and confronts Caesar, who hides his face with his robe for a moment; then, mastering himself, drops it, and confronts the tribune with dignity.*]

POTHINUS: Bear witness, Lucius Septimius. Caesar came hither in pursuit of his foe. Did we shelter his foe?

LUCIUS: As Pompey's foot touched the Egyptian shore, his head fell by the stroke of my sword.

THEODOTUS [*with viperish relish*]: Under the eyes of his wife and child! Remember that, Caesar! They saw it from the ship he had just left. We have given you a full and sweet measure of vengeance.

CAESAR [*with horror*]: Vengeance!

POTHINUS: Our first gift to you, as your galley came into the roadstead, was the head of your rival for the empire of the world. Bear witness, Lucius Septimius: is it not so?

LUCIUS: It is so. With this hand, that slew Pompey, I placed his head at the feet of Caesar.

CAESAR: Murderer! So would you have slain Caesar, had Pompey been victorious at Pharsalia.

LUCIUS: Woe to the vanquished, Caesar! When I served Pompey, I slew as good men as he, only because he conquered them. His turn came at last.

THEODOTUS [*flatteringly*]: The deed was not yours, Caesar, but ours—nay, mine; for it was done by my counsel. Thanks to us, you keep your reputation for clemency, and have your vengeance too.

CAESAR: Vengeance! Vengeance!! Oh, if I could stoop to vengeance, what would I not exact from you as the price of this murdered man's blood? [*They shrink back, appalled and disconcerted*]. Was he not my son-in-law, my ancient friend, for 20 years the master of great Rome, for 30 years the compeller of victory? Did not I, as a Roman, share his glory? Was the Fate that forced us to fight for the mastery of the world, of our making? Am I Julius Caesar, or am I a wolf, that you fling to me the grey head of the old soldier, the laurelled conqueror, the mighty Roman, treacherously struck down by this callous ruffian, and then claim my gratitude for it! [*To Lucius Septimius*] Begone: you fill me with horror.

LUCIUS [*cold and undaunted*]: Pshaw! You have seen severed heads before,

Caesar, and severed right hands too, I think; some thousands of them, in Gaul, after you vanquished Vercingetorix. Did you spare him, with all your clemency? Was that vengeance?

CAESAR: No, by the gods! would that it had been! Vengeance at least is human. No, I say: those severed right hands, and the brave Vercingetorix basely strangled in a vault beneath the Capitol were [*with shuddering satire*] a wise severity, a necessary protection to the commonwealth, a duty of statesmanship—follies and fictions ten times bloodier than honest vengeance! What a fool was I then! To think that men's lives should be at the mercy of such fools! [*Humbly*] Lucius Septimius, pardon me: why should the slayer of Vercingetorix rebuke the slayer of Pompey? You are free to go with the rest. Or stay if you will: I will find a place for you in my service.

LUCIUS: The odds are against you, Caesar. I go. [*He turns to go out through the loggia*].

RUFIO [*full of wrath at seeing his prey escaping*]: That means that he is a Republican.

LUCIUS [*turning defiantly on the loggia steps*]: And what are you?

RUFIO: A Caesarian, like all Caesar's soldiers.

CAESAR [*courteously*]: Lucius: believe me, Caesar is no Caesarian. Were Rome a true republic, then were Caesar the first of Republicans. But you have made your choice. Farewell.

LUCIUS: Farewell. Come, Achillas, whilst there is yet time.

[*Caesar, seeing that Rufio's temper threatens to get the worse of him, puts his hand on his shoulder and brings him down the hall out of harm's way, Britannus accompanying them and posting himself on Caesar's right hand. This movement brings the three in a little group to the place occupied by Achillas, who moves haughtily away and joins Theodotus on the other side. Lucius Septimius goes out through the soldiers in the loggia. Pothinus, Theodotus and Achillas follow him with the courtiers, very mistrustful of the soldiers, who close up in their rear and go out after them, keeping them moving without much ceremony. The King is left in his chair, piteous, obstinate, with twitching face and fingers. During these movements Rufio maintains an energetic grumbling, as follows:—*]*

RUFIO [*as Lucius departs*]: Do you suppose he would let us go if he had our heads in his hands?

CAESAR: I have no right to suppose that his ways are any baser than mine.

RUFIO: Psha!

CAESAR: Rufio: if I take Lucius Septimius for my model, and become exactly like him, ceasing to be Caesar, will you serve me still?

BRITANNUS: Caesar: this is not good sense. Your duty to Rome demands that her enemies should be prevented from doing further mischief. [*Caesar,*

whose delight in the moral eye-to-business of his British secretary is inexhaust-
ible, smiles indulgently].

RUFIO: It is no use talking to him, Britannus: you may save your breath to
cool your porridge. But mark this, Caesar. Clemency is very well for
you; but what is it for your soldiers, who have to fight tomorrow the
men you spared yesterday? You may give what orders you please; but
I tell you that your next victory will be a massacre, thanks to your
clemency. *I,* for one, will take no prisoners. I will kill my enemies in the
field; and then you can preach as much clemency as you please: I shall
never have to fight them again. And now, with your leave, I will see
these gentry off the premises. [*He turns to go*].

CAESAR [*turning also and seeing Ptolemy*]: What! have they left the boy alone!
Oh shame, shame!

RUFIO [*taking Ptolemy's hand and making him rise*]: Come, your majesty!

PTOLEMY [*to Caesar, drawing away his hand from Rufio*]: Is he turning me out
of my palace?

RUFIO [*grimly*]: You are welcome to stay if you wish.

CAESAR [*kindly*]: Go, my boy. I will not harm you; but you will be safer
away, among your friends. Here you are in the lion's mouth.

PTOLEMY [*turning to go*]: It is not the lion I fear, but [*looking at Rufio*] the
jackal. [*He goes out through the loggia*].

CAESAR [*laughing approvingly*]: Brave boy!

CLEOPATRA [*jealous of Caesar's approbation, calling after Ptolemy*]: Little silly.
You think that very clever.

CAESAR: Britannus: attend the King. Give him in charge to that Pothinus
fellow. [*Britannus goes out after Ptolemy*].

RUFIO [*pointing to Cleopatra*]: And this piece of goods? What is to be done
with her? However, I suppose I may leave that to you. [*He goes out
through the loggia*].

CLEOPATRA [*flushing suddenly and turning on Caesar*]: Did you mean me to go
with the rest?

CAESAR [*a little preoccupied, goes with a sigh to Ptolemy's chair, whilst she waits
for his answer with red cheeks and clenched fists*]: You are free to do just as
you please, Cleopatra.

CLEOPATRA: Then you do not care whether I stay or not?

CAESAR [*smiling*]: Of course I had rather you stayed.

CLEOPATRA: Much, much rather?

CAESAR [*nodding*]: Much, much rather.

CLEOPATRA: Then I consent to stay, because I am asked. But I do not want
to, mind.

CAESAR: That is quite understood. [*Calling*] Totateeta.

[*Ftatateeta, still seated, turns her eyes on him with a sinister expression, but
does not move.*]

CLEOPATRA [*with a splutter of laughter*]: Her name is not Totateeta: it is Ftatateeta. [*Calling*] Ftatateeta. [*Ftatateeta instantly rises and comes to Cleopatra*].

CAESAR [*stumbling over the name*]: Tfatafeeta will forgive the erring tongue of a Roman. Tota: the Queen will hold her state here in Alexandria. Engage women to attend upon her; and do all that is needful.

FTATATEETA: Am I then the mistress of the Queen's household:

CLEOPATRA [*sharply*]: No: *I* am the mistress of the Queen's household. Go and do as you are told, or I will have you thrown into the Nile this very afternoon, to poison the poor crocodiles.

CAESAR [*shocked*]: Oh no, no.

CLEOPATRA: Oh yes, yes. You are very sentimental, Caesar; but you are clever; and if you do as I tell you, you will soon learn to govern.

[*Caesar, quite dumbfounded by this impertinence, turns in his chair and stares at her. Ftatateeta, smiling grimly, and shewing a splendid set of teeth, goes, leaving them alone together.*]

CAESAR: Cleopatra: I really think I must eat you, after all.

CLEOPATRA [*kneeling beside him and looking at him with eager interest, half real, half affected to shew how intelligent she is*]: You must not talk to me now as if I were a child.

CAESAR: You have been growing up since the sphinx introduced us the other night; and you think you know more than I do already.

CLEOPATRA [*taken down, and anxious to justify herself*]: No: that would be very silly of me: of course I know that. But—[*suddenly*] are you angry with me?

CAESAR: No.

CLEOPATRA [*only half believing him*]: Then why are you so thoughtful?

CAESAR [*rising*]: I have work to do, Cleopatra.

CLEOPATRA [*drawing back*]: Work! [*Offended*] You are tired of talking to me; and that is your excuse to get away from me.

CAESAR [*sitting down again to appease her*]: Well, well: another minute. But then—work!

CLEOPATRA: Work! what nonsense! You must remember that you are a king now: I have made you one. Kings dont work.

CAESAR: Oh! Who told you that, little kitten? Eh?

CLEOPATRA: My father was King of Egypt; and he never worked. But he was a great king, and cut off my sister's head because she rebelled against him and took the throne from him.

CAESAR: Well; and how did he get his throne back again?

CLEOPATRA [*eagerly, her eyes lighting up*]: I will tell you. A beautiful young man, with strong round arms, came over the desert with many horsemen, and slew my sister's husband and gave my father back his throne.

[*Wistfully*] I was only twelve then. Oh, I wish he would come again, now that I am queen. I would make him my husband.

CAESAR: It might be managed, perhaps; for it was I who sent that beautiful young man to help your father.

CLEOPATRA [*enraptured*]: You know him!

CAESAR [*nodding*]: I do.

CLEOPATRA: Has he come with you? [*Caesar shakes his head: she is cruelly disappointed*]. Oh, I wish he had, I wish he had. If only I were a little older; so that he might not think me a mere kitten, as you do! But perhaps that is because you are old. He is many many years younger than you, is he not?

CAESAR [*as if swallowing a pill*]: He is somewhat younger.

CLEOPATRA: Would he be my husband, do you think, if I asked him?

CAESAR: Very likely.

CLEOPATRA: But I should not like to ask him. Could you not persuade him to ask me—without knowing that I wanted him to?

CAESAR [*touched by her innocence of the beautiful young man's character*]: My poor child!

CLEOPATRA: Why do you say that as if you were sorry for me? Does he love anyone else?

CAESAR: I am afraid so.

CLEOPATRA [*tearfully*]: Then I shall not be his first love.

CAESAR: Not quite the first. He is greatly admired by women.

CLEOPATRA: I wish I could be the first. But if he loves me, I will make him kill all the rest. Tell me: is he still beautiful? Do his strong round arms shine in the sun like marble?

CAESAR: He is in excellent condition—considering how much he eats and drinks.

CLEOPATRA: Oh, you must not say common, earthly things about him; for I love him. He is a god.

CAESAR: He is a great captain of horsemen, and swifter of foot than any other Roman.

CLEOPATRA: What is his real name?

CAESAR [*puzzled*]: His real name?

CLEOPATRA: Yes, I always call him Horus, because Horus is the most beautiful of our gods. But I want to know his real name.

CAESAR: His name is Mark Antony.

CLEOPATRA [*musically*]: Mark Antony, Mark Antony, Mark Antony! What a beautiful name! What a beautiful name! [*She throws her arms round Caesar's neck*]. Oh, how I love you for sending him to help my father! Did you love my father very much?

CAESAR: No, my child; but your father, as you say, never worked. I always work. So when he lost his crown he had to promise me 16,000 talents to get it back for him.

CLEOPATRA: Did he ever pay you?

CAESAR: Not in full.

CLEOPATRA: He was quite right: it was too dear. The whole world is not worth 16,000 talents.

CAESAR: That is perhaps true, Cleopatra. Those Egyptians who work paid as much of it as he could drag from them. The rest is still due. But as I most likely shall not get it, I must go back to my work. So you must run away for a little and send my secretary to me.

CLEOPATRA [coaxing]: No: I want to stay and hear you talk about Mark Antony.

CAESAR: But if I do not get to work, Pothinus and the rest of them will cut us off from the harbor; and then the way from Rome will be blocked.

CLEOPATRA: No matter: I dont want you to go back to Rome.

CAESAR: But you want Mark Antony to come from it.

CLEOPATRA [springing up]: Oh yes, yes, yes: I forgot. Go quickly and work, Caesar; and keep the way over the sea open for my Mark Antony. [She runs out through the loggia, kissing her hand to Mark Antony across the sea].

CAESAR [going briskly up the middle of the hall to the loggia steps]: Ho, Britannus. [He is startled by the entry of a wounded Roman soldier, who confronts him from the upper step]. What now?

SOLDIER [pointing to his bandaged head]: This, Caesar; and two of my comrades killed in the market place.

CAESAR [quiet, but attending]: Ay. Why?

SOLDIER: There is an army come to Alexandria, calling itself the Roman army.

CAESAR: The Roman army of occupation. Ay?

SOLDIER: Commanded by one Achillas.

CAESAR: Well?

SOLDIER: The citizens rose against us when the army entered the gates. I was with two others in the market place when the news came. They set upon us. I cut my way out; and here I am.

CAESAR: Good. I am glad to see you alive. [Rufio enters the loggia hastily, passing behind the soldier to look out through one of the arches at the quay beneath]. Rufio: we are besieged.

RUFIO: What! Already?

CAESAR: Now or tomorrow: what does it matter? We shall be besieged.

[Britannus runs in.]

BRITANNUS: Caesar—

CAESAR [anticipating him]: Yes: I know. [Rufio and Britannus come down the hall *from the loggia at opposite sides, past Caesar, who waits for a moment near the step to say to the soldier*] Comrade: give the word to turn out on the beach and stand by the boats. Get your wound attended to. Go. [*The soldier hurries out. Caesar comes down the hall between Rufio and Britannus*] Rufio: we have some ships in the west harbor. Burn them.

RUFIO [*staring*]: Burn them!!

CAESAR: Take every boat we have in the east harbor, and seize the Pharos —that island with the lighthouse. Leave half our men behind to hold the beach and the quay outside this palace: that is the way home.

RUFIO [*disapproving strongly*]: Are we to give up the city?

CAESAR: We have not got it, Rufio. This palace we have; and—what is that building next door?

RUFIO: The theatre.

CAESAR: We will have that too: it commands the strand. For the rest, Egypt for the Egyptians!

RUFIO: Well, you know best, I suppose. Is that all?

CAESAR: That is all. Are those ships burnt yet?

RUFIO: Be easy: I shall waste no more time. [*He runs out*].

BRITANNUS: Caesar: Pothinus demands speech of you. In my opinion he needs a lesson. His manner is most insolent.

CEASAR: Where is he?

BRITANNUS: He waits without.

CEASAR: Ho there! admit Pothinus.

[*Pothinus appears in the loggia, and comes down the hall very haughtily to Caesar's left hand.*].

CAESAR: Well, Pothinus?

POTHINUS: I have brought you our ultimatum, Caesar.

CAESAR: Ultimatum! The door was open: you should have gone out through it before you declared war. You are my prisoner now. [*He goes to the chair and loosens his toga*].

POTHINUS [*scornfully*]: I your prisoner! Do you know that you are in Alexandria, and that King Ptolemy, with an army outnumbering your little troop a hundred to one, is in possession of Alexandria?

CAESAR [*unconcernedly taking off his toga and throwing it on the chair*]: Well, my friend, get out if you can. And tell your friends not to kill any more Romans in the market place. Otherwise my soldiers, who do not share my celebrated clemency, will probably kill you. Britannus: pass the word to the guard; and fetch my armor. [*Britannus runs out. Rufio returns*]. Well?

RUFIO [*pointing from the loggia to a cloud of smoke drifting over the harbor*]: See there! [*Pothinus runs eagerly up the steps to look out*].

CAESAR: What, ablaze already! Impossible!

RUFIO: Yes, five good ships, and a barge laden with oil grappled to each. But it is not my doing: the Egyptians have saved me the trouble. They have captured the west harbor.

CAESAR [*anxiously*]: And the east harbor? The lighthouse, Rufio?

RUFIO [*with a sudden splutter of raging ill usage, coming down to Caesar and scolding him*]: Can I embark a legion in five minutes? The first cohort is already on the beach. We can do no more. If you want faster work, come and do it yourself.

CAESAR [*soothing him*]: Good, good. Patience, Rufio, patience.

RUFIO: Patience! Who is impatient here, you or I? Would I be here, if I could not oversee them from the balcony?

CAESAR: Forgive me, Rufio; and [*anxiously*] hurry them as much as—

[*He is interrupted by an outcry as of an old man in the extremity of misfortune. It draws near rapidly; and Theodotus rushes in, tearing his hair. and squeaking the most lamentable exclamations. Rufio steps back to stare at him, amazed at his frantic condition. Pothinus turns to listen.*]

THEODOTUS [*on the steps, with uplifted arms*]: Horror unspeakable! Woe, alas! Help!

RUFIO: What now?

CAESAR [*frowning*]: Who is slain?

THEODOTUS: Slain! Oh, worse than the death of ten thousand men! Loss irreparable to mankind!

RUFIO: What has happened, man?

THEODOTUS [*rushing down the hall between them*]: The fire has spread from your ships. The first of the seven wonders of the world perishes. The library of Alexandria is in flames.

RUFIO: Psha! [*Quite relieved, he goes up to the loggia and watches the preparations of the troops on the beach*].

CAESAR: Is that all?

THEODOTUS [*unable to believe his senses*]: All! Caesar: will you go down to posterity as a barbarous soldier too ignorant to know the value of books?

CAESAR: Theodotus: I am an author myself; and I tell you it is better that the Egyptians should live their lives than dream them away with the help of books.

THEODOTUS [*kneeling, with genuine literary emotion: the passion of the pedant*]: Caesar: once in ten generations of men, the world gains an immortal book.

CAESAR [*inflexible*]: If it did not flatter mankind, the common executioner would burn it.

THEODOTUS: Without history, death will lay you beside your meanest soldier.

CAESAR: Death will do that in any case. I ask no better grave.

THEODOTUS: What is burning there is the memory of mankind.

CAESAR: A shameful memory. Let it burn.

THEODOTUS [*wildly*]: Will you destroy the past?

CAESAR: Ay, and build the future with its ruins. [*Theodotus, in despair, strikes himself on the temples with his fists*]. But harken, Theodotus, teacher of kings: you who valued Pompey's head no more than a shepherd values an onion, and who now kneel to me, with tears in your old eyes, to plead for a few sheepskins scrawled with errors. I cannot spare you a man or a bucket of water just now; but you shall pass freely out of the palace. Now, away with you to Achillas; and borrow his legions to put out the fire. [*He hurries him to the steps*].

POTHINUS [*significantly*]: You understand, Theodotus: I remain a prisoner.

THEODOTUS: A prisoner!

CAESAR: Will you stay to talk whilst the memory of mankind is burning? [*Calling through the loggia*] Ho there! Pass Theodotus out. [*To Theodotus*] Away with you.

THEODOTUS [*To Pothinus*]: I must go to save the library. [*He hurries out*].

CAESAR: Follow him to the gate, Pothinus. Bid him urge your people to kill no more of my soldiers, for your sake.

POTHINUS: My life will cost you dear if you take it, Caesar.

[*He goes out after Theodotus. Rufio, absorbed in watching the embarkation, does not notice the departure of the two Egyptians.*]

RUFIO [*shouting from the loggia to the beach*]: All ready, there?

A CENTURION [*from below*]: All ready. We wait for Caesar.

CAESAR: Tell them Caesar is coming—the rogues! [*Calling*] Britannicus. [*This magniloquent version of his secretary's name is one of Caesar's jokes. In later years it would have meant, quite seriously and officially, Conqueror of Britain*].

RUFIO [*calling down*]: Push off, all except the longboat. Stand by it to embark, Caesar's guard there. [*He leaves the balcony and comes down into the hall*]. Where are those Egyptians? Is this more clemency? Have you let them go?

CAESAR [*chuckling*]: I have let Theodotus go to save the library. We must respect literature, Rufio.

RUFIO [*raging*]: Folly on folly's head! I believe if you could bring back all the dead of Spain, Gaul, and Thessaly to life, you would do it that we might have the trouble of fighting them over again.

CAESAR: Might not the gods destroy the world if their only thought were to be at peace next year? [*Rufio, out of all patience, turns away in anger. Caesar suddenly grips his sleeve, and adds slyly in his ear*] Besides, my friend: every Egyptian we imprison means imprisoning two Roman soldiers to guard him. Eh?

RUFIO: Agh! I might have known there was some fox's trick behind your fine talking. [*He gets away from Caesar with an ill-humored shrug, and goes to the balcony for another look at the preparations; finally goes out*].

CAESAR: Is Britannus asleep? I sent him for my armor an hour ago. [*Calling*] Britannicus, thou British islander. Britannicus!

[*Cleopatra runs in through the loggia with Caesar's helmet and sword, snatched from Britannus, who follows her with a cuirass and greaves. They come down to Caesar, she to his left hand, Britannus to his right.*]

CLEOPATRA: I am going to dress you, Caesar. Sit down. [*He obeys*]. These Roman helmets are so becoming! [*She takes off his wreath*]. Oh! [*She bursts out laughing at him*].

CAESAR: What are you laughing at?

CLEOPATRA: Youre bald [*beginning with a big B, and ending with a splutter*].

CAESAR [*almost annoyed*]: Cleopatra! [*He rises, for the convenience of Britannus, who puts the cuirass on him*].

CLEOPATRA: So that is why you wear the wreath—to hide it.

BRITANNUS: Peace, Egyptian: they are the bays of the conqueror. [*He buckles the cuirass*].

CLEOPATRA: Peace, thou: islander! [*To Caesar*] You should rub your head with strong spirits of sugar, Caesar. That will make it grow.

CAESAR [*with a wry face*]: Cleopatra: do you like to be reminded that you are very young?

CLEOPATRA [*pouting*]: No.

CAESAR [*sitting down again, and setting out his leg for Britannus, who kneels to put on his greaves*]: Neither do I like to be reminded that I am—middle aged. Let me give you ten of my superfluous years. That will make you 26, and leave me only—no matter. Is it a bargain?

CLEOPATRA: Agreed. 26, mind. [*She puts the helmet on him*]. Oh! How nice! You look only about 50 in it!

BRITANNUS [*looking up severely at Cleopatra*]: You must not speak in this manner to Caesar.

CLEOPATRA: Is it true that when Caesar caught you on that island, you were painted all over blue?

BRITANNUS: Blue is the color worn by all Britons of good standing. In war we stain our bodies blue; so that though our enemies may strip us of our clothes and our lives, they cannot strip us of our respectability. [*He rises*].

CLEOPATRA [*with Caesar's sword*]: Let me hang this on. Now you look splendid. Have they made any statues of you in Rome?

CAESAR: Yes, many statues.

CLEOPATRA: You must send for one and give it to me.

RUFIO [*coming back into the loggia, more impatient than ever*]: Now Caesar: have you done talking? The moment your foot is aboard there will be no holding our men back: the boats will race one another for the light-house.

CAESAR [*drawing his sword and trying the edge*]: Is this well set today, Britannus? At Pharsalia it was as blunt as a barrel-hoop.

BRITANNUS: It will split one of the Egyptian's hairs today, Caesar. I have set it myself.

CLEOPATRA [*suddenly throwing her arms in terror round Caesar*]: Oh, you are not really going into battle to be killed?

CAESAR: No, Cleopatra. No man goes to battle to be killed.

CLEOPATRA: But they do get killed. My sister's husband was killed in battle. You must not go. Let him go [*pointing to Rufio. They all laugh at her*]. Oh please, please dont go. What will happen to me if you never come back?

CAESAR [*gravely*]: Are you afraid?

CLEOPATRA [*shrinking*]: No.

CAESAR [*with quiet authority*]: Go to the balcony; and you shall see us take the Pharos. You must learn to look on battles. Go. [*She goes, downcast, and looks out from the balcony*]. That is well. Now, Rufio. March.

CLEOPATRA [*suddenly clapping her hands*]: Oh, you will not be able to go!

CAESAR: Why? What now?

CLEOPATRA: They are drying up the harbor with buckets—a multitude of soldiers—over there [*pointing out across the sea to her left*]—they are dipping up the water.

RUFIO [*hastening to look*]: It is true. The Egyptian army! Crawling over the edge of the west harbor like locusts. [*With sudden anger he strides down to Caesar*]. This is your accursed clemency, Caesar. Theodotus has brought them.

CAESAR [*delighted at his own cleverness*]: I meant him to, Rufio. They have come to put out the fire. The library will keep them busy whilst we seize the lighthouse. Eh?

[*He rushes out buoyantly through the loggia, followed by Britannus*].

RUFIO [*disgustedly*]: More foxing! Agh! [*He rushes off. A shout from the soldiers announces the appearance of Caesar below*].

CENTURION [*below*]: All aboard. Give way there. [*Another shout*].

CLEOPATRA [*waving her scarf through the loggia arch*]: Goodbye, goodbye, dear Caesar. Come back safe. Goodbye!

Act III

[*The edge of the quay in front of the palace, looking out west over the east harbor of Alexandria to Pharos island, just to the end of which, and connected with it by a narrow mole, is the famous lighthouse, a gigantic square tower of white marble diminishing in size storey by storey to the top, on which stands a cresset beacon. The island is joined to the main land by the Heptastadium, a great mole or causeway five miles long bounding the harbor on the south.*]

In the middle of the quay a Roman sentinel stands on guard, pilum in hand, looking out to the lighthouse with strained attention, his left hand shading his eyes. The pilum is a stout wooden shaft 4-1/2 feet long, with an iron spit about three feet long fixed in it. The sentinel is so absorbed that he does not notice the approach from the north end of the quay of four Egyptian market porters carrying rolls of carpet, preceded by Ftatateeta and Apollodorus the Sicilian. Apollodorus is a dashing young man of about 24, handsome and debonair, dressed with deliberate aestheticism in the most delicate purples and dove greys, with ornaments of bronze, oxydized silver, and stones of jade and agate. His sword, designed as carefully as a medieval cross, has a blued blade shewing through an openwork scabbard of purple leather and filigree. The porters, conducted by Ftatateeta, pass along the quay behind the sentinel to the steps of the palace, where they put down their bales and squat on the ground. Apollodorus does not pass along with them: he halts, amused by the preoccupation of the sentinel.]

APOLLODORUS [*calling to the sentinel*]: Who goes there, eh?

SENTINEL [*starting violently and turning with his pilum at the charge, revealing himself as a small, wiry, sandy-haired, conscientious young man with an elderly face*]: Whats this? Stand. Who are you?

APOLLODORUS: I am Apollodorus the Sicilian. Why, man, what are you dreaming of? Since I came through the lines beyond the theatre there, I have brought my caravan past three sentinels, all so busy staring at the lighthouse that not one of them challenged me. Is this Roman discipline?

SENTINEL: We are not here to watch the land but the sea. Caesar has just landed on the Pharos. [*Looking at Ftatateeta*] What have you here? Who is this piece of Egyptian crockery?

FTATATEETA: Apollodorus: rebuke this Roman dog; and bid him bridle his tongue in the presence of Ftatateeta, the mistress of the Queen's household.

APOLLODORUS: My friend: this is a great lady, who stands high with Caesar.

SENTINEL [*not at all impressed, pointing to the carpets*]: And what is all this truck?

APOLLODORUS: Carpets for the furnishing of the Queen's apartments in the palace. I have picked them from the best carpets in the world; and the Queen shall choose the best of my choosing.

SENTINEL: So you are the carpet merchant?

APOLLODORUS [*hurt*]: My friend: I am a patrician.

SENTINEL: A patrician! A patrician keeping a shop instead of following arms!

APOLLODORUS: I do not keep a shop. Mine is a temple of the arts. I am a worshipper of beauty. My calling is to choose beautiful things for beautiful queens. My motto is Art for Art's sake.

SENTINEL: That is not the password.

APOLLODORUS: It is a universal password.

SENTINEL: I know nothing about universal passwords. Either give me the password for the day or get back to your shop.

[*Ftatateeta, roused by his hostile tone, steals towards the edge of the quay with the step of a panther, and gets behind him.*]

APOLLODORUS: How if I do neither?
SENTINEL: Then I will drive this pilum through you.
APOLLODORUS: At your service, my friend.

[*He draws his sword, and springs to his guard with unruffled grace*].

FTATATEETA [*suddenly seizing the sentinel's arms from behind*]: Thrust your knife into the dog's throat, Apollodorus.

[*The chivalrous Apollodorus laughingly shakes his head; breaks ground away from the sentinel towards the palace; and lowers his point*].

SENTINEL [*struggling vainly*]: Curse on you! Let me go. Help ho!
FTATATEETA [*lifting him from the ground*]: Stab the little Roman reptile. Spit him on your sword.

[*A couple of Roman soldiers, with a centurion, come running along the edge of the quay from the north end. They rescue their comrade, and throw off Ftatateeta, who is sent reeling away on the left hand of the sentinel.*]

CENTURION [*an unattractive man of fifty, short in his speech and manners, with a vinewood cudgel in his hand*]: How now? What is all this?
FTATATEETA [*to Apollodorus*]: Why did you not stab him? There was time!
APOLLODORUS: Centurion: I am here by order of the Queen to—
CENTURION [*interrupting him*]: The Queen! Yes, yes: [*to the sentinel*] pass him in. Pass all these bazaar people in to the Queen, with their goods. But mind you pass no one out that you have not passed in—not even the Queen herself.
SENTINEL: This old woman is dangerous: she is as strong as three men. She wanted the merchant to stab me.
APOLLODORUS: Centurion: I am not a merchant. I am a patrician and a votary of art.
CENTURION: Is the woman your wife?
APOLLODORUS [*horrified*]: No, no! [*Correcting himself politely*] Not that the lady is not a striking figure in her own way. But [*emphatically*] she is not my wife.
FTATATEETA [*to the centurion*]: Roman: I am Ftatateeta, the mistress of the Queen's household.

CENTURION: Keep your hands off our men, mistress; or I will have you pitched into the harbor, though you were as strong as ten men. [*To his men*] To your posts: march!

[*He returns with his men the way they came*].

FTATATEETA [*looking malignantly after him*]: We shall see whom Isis loves best: her servant Ftatateeta or a dog of a Roman.
SENTINEL [*to Apollodorus, with a wave of his pilum towards the palace*]: Pass in there; and keep your distance. [*Turning to Ftatateeta*] Come within a yard of me, you old crocodile; and I will give you this [*the pilum*] in your jaws.
CLEOPATRA [*calling from the palace*]: Ftatateeta, Ftatateeta.
FTATATEETA [*looking up, scandalized*]: Go from the window, go from the window. There are men here.
CLEOPATRA: I am coming down.
FTATATEETA [*distracted*]: No, no. What are you dreaming of? O ye gods, ye gods! Apollodorus: bid your men pick up your bales; and in with me quickly.
APOLLODORUS: Obey the mistress of the Queen's household.
FTATATEETA [*impatiently, as the porters stoop to lift the bales*]: Quick, quick: she will be out upon us. [*Cleopatra comes from the palace and runs across the quay to Ftatateeta*]. Oh that ever I was born!
CLEOPATRA [*eagerly*]: Ftatateeta: I have thought of something. I want a boat —at once.
FTATATEETA: A boat! No, no: you cannot, Apollodorus: speak to the Queen.
APOLLODORUS [*gallantly*]: Beautiful queen: I am Apollodorus the Sicilian, your servant, from the bazaar. I have brought you the three most beautiful Persian carpets in the world to choose from.
CLEOPATRA: I have no time for carpets today. Get me a boat.
FTATATEETA: What whim is this? You cannot go on the water except in the royal barge.
APOLLODORUS: Royalty, Ftatateeta, lies not in the barge but in the Queen. [*To Cleopatra*] The touch of your majesty's foot on the gunwale of the meanest boat in the harbor will make it royal. [*He turns to the harbor and calls seaward*] Ho there, boatman! Pull in to the steps.
CLEOPATRA: Apollodorus: you are my perfect knight; and I will always buy my carpets through you. [*Apollodorus bows joyously. An oar appears above the quay; and the boatman, a bullet-headed, vivacious, grinning fellow, burnt almost black by the sun, comes up a flight of steps from the water on the sentinel's right, oar in hand, and waits at the top*]. Can you row, Apollodorus?
APOLLODORUS: My oars shall be your majesty's wings. Whither shall I row my Queen?
CLEOPATRA: To the lighthouse. Come. [*She makes for the steps*].
SENTINEL [*opposing her with his pilum at the charge*]: Stand. You cannot pass.

CLEOPATRA [*flushing angrily*]: How dare you? Do you know that I am the Queen?

SENTINEL: I have my orders. You cannot pass.

CLEOPATRA: I will make Caesar have you killed if you do not obey me.

SENTINEL: He will do worse to me if I disobey my officer. Stand back.

CLEOPATRA: Ftatateeta: strangle him.

SENTINEL [*alarmed—looking apprehensively at Ftatateeta, and brandishing his pilum*]: Keep off, there.

CLEOPATRA [*running to Apollodorus*]: Apollodorus: make your slaves help us.

APOLLODORUS: I shall not need their help, lady. [*He draws his sword*]. Now, soldier: choose which weapon you will defend yourself with. Shall it be sword against pilum, or sword against sword?

SENTINEL: Roman against Sicilian, curse you. Take that. [*He hurls his pilum at Apollodorus, who drops expertly on one knee. The pilum passes whizzing over his head and falls harmless. Apollodorus, with a cry of triumph, springs up and attacks the sentinel, who draws his sword and defends himself, crying*] Ho there, guard. Help!

[*Cleopatra, half frightened, half delighted, takes refuge near the palace, where the porters are squatting among the bales. The boatman, alarmed, hurries down the steps out of harm's way, but stops, with his head just visible above the edge of the quay, to watch the fight. The sentinel is handicapped by his fear of an attack in the rear from Ftatateeta. His swordsmanship, which is of rough and ready sort, is heavily taxed, as he has occasionally to strike at her to keep her off between a blow and a guard with Apollodorus. The centurion returns with several soldiers. Apollodorus springs back towards Cleopatra as this reinforcement confronts him.*]

CENTURION [*coming to the sentinel's right hand*]: What is this? What now?

SENTINEL [*painting*]: I could do well enough by myself if it werent for the old woman. Keep her off me: that is all the help I need.

CENTURION: Make your report, soldier. What has happened?

FTATATEETA: Centurion: he would have slain the Queen.

SENTINEL [*bluntly*]: I would, sooner than let her pass. She wanted to take boat, and go—so she said—to the lighthouse. I stopped her, as I was ordered to; and she set this fellow on me.

[*He goes to pick up his pilum and returns to his place with it*].

CENTURION [*turning to Cleopatra*]: Cleopatra: I am loth to offend you; but without Caesar's express order we dare not let you pass beyond the Roman lines.

APOLLODORUS: Well, Centurion; and has not the lighthouse been within the Roman lines since Caesar landed there?

CLEOPATRA: Yes, yes. Answer that, if you can.

CENTURION [*to Apollodorus*]: As for you, Apollodorus, you may thank the gods that you are not nailed to the palace door with a pilum for your meddling.

APOLLODORUS [*urbanely*]: My military friend, I was not born to be slain by so ugly a weapon. When I fall, it will be [*holding up his sword*] by this white queen of arms, the only weapon fit for an artist. And now that you are convinced that we do not want to go beyond the lines, let me finish killing your sentinel and depart with the Queen.

CENTURION [*as the sentinel makes an angry demonstration*]: Peace there, Cleopatra: I must abide by my orders, and not by the subtleties of this Sicilian. You must withdraw into the palace and examine your carpets there.

CLEOPATRA [*pouting*]: I will not: I am the Queen. Caesar does not speak to me as you do. Have Caesar's centurions changed manners with his scullions?

CENTURION [*sulkily*]: I do my duty. That is enough for me.

APOLLODORUS: Majesty: when a stupid man is doing something he is ashamed of, he always declares that it is his duty.

CENTURION [*angry*]: Apollodorus—

APOLLODORUS [*interrupting him with defiant elegance*]. I will make amends for that insult with my sword at fitting time and place. Who says artist, says duellist. [*To Cleopatra*] Hear my counsel, star of the east. Until word comes to these soldiers from Caesar himself, you are a prisoner. Let me go to him with a message from you, and a present; and before the sun has stooped half way to the arms of the sea, I will bring you back Caesar's order of release.

CENTURION [*sneering at him*]: And you will sell the Queen the present, no doubt.

APOLLODORUS: Centurion: the Queen shall have from me, without payment, as the unforced tribute of Sicilian taste to Egyptian beauty, the richest of these carpets for her present to Caesar.

CLEOPATRA [*exultantly, to the centurion*]: Now you see what an ignorant common creature you are!

CENTURION [*curtly*]: Well, a fool and his wares are soon parted. [*He turns to his men*] Two more men to this post here; and see that no one leaves the palace but this man and his merchandize. If he draws his sword again inside the lines, kill him. To your posts. March.

[*He goes out, leaving two auxiliary sentinels with the other.*]

APOLLODORUS [*with polite goodfellowship*]: My friends: will you not enter the palace and bury our quarrel in a bowl of wine? [*He take out his purse, jingling the coins in it*]. The Queen has presents for you all.

SENTINEL [*very sulky*]: You heard our orders. Get about your business.

FIRST AUXILIARY: Yes: you ought to know better. Off with you.

SECOND AUXILIARY [*looking longingly at the purse—this sentinel is a hooknosed man, unlike his comrade, who is squab faced*]: Do not tantalize a poor man.

APOLLODORUS [*to Cleopatra*]: Pearl of Queens: the centurion is at hand; and the Roman soldier is incorruptible when his officer is looking. I must carry your word to Caesar.

CLEOPATRA [*who has been meditating among the carpets*]: Are these carpets very heavy?

APOLLODORUS: It matters not how heavy. There are plenty of porters.

CLEOPATRA: How do they put the carpets into boats? Do they throw them down?

APOLLODORUS: Not into small boats, majesty. It would sink them.

CLEOPATRA: Not into that man's boat, for instance? [*pointing to the boatman*].

APOLLODORUS: No. Too small.

CLEOPATRA: But you can take a carpet to Caesar in it if I send one?

APOLLODORUS: Assuredly.

CLEOPATRA: And you will have it carried gently down the steps and take great care of it?

APOLLODORUS: Depend on me.

CLEOPATRA: Great, great care?

APOLLODORUS: More than of my own body.

CLEOPATRA: You will promise me not to let the porters drop it or throw it about?

APOLLODORUS: Place the most delicate glass goblet in the palace in the heart of the roll, Queen; and if it be broken, my head shall pay for it.

CLEOPATRA: Good. Come, Ftatateeta. [*Ftatateeta comes to her. Apollodorus offers to squire them into the palace*]. No, Apollodorus, you must not come. I will choose a carpet for myself. You must wait here. [*She runs into the palace*].

APOLLODORUS [*to the porters*]: Follow this lady [*indicating Ftatateeta*] and obey her.

[*The porters rise and take up their bales.*]

FTATATEETA [*addressing the porters as if they were vermin*]: This way. And take your shoes off before you put your feet on those stairs.

[*She goes in, followed by the porters with the carpets. Meanwhile Apollodorus goes to the edge of the quay and looks out over the harbor. The sentinels keep their eyes on him malignantly.*]

APOLLODORUS [*addressing the sentinel*]: My friend—

SENTINEL [*rudely*]: Silence there.

FIRST AUXILIARY: Shut your muzzle, you.

SECOND AUXILIARY [*in a half whisper, glancing apprehensively towards the north end of the quay*]: Cant you wait a bit?

APOLLODORUS: Patience, worthy three-headed donkey. [*They mutter ferociously; but he is not at all intimidated*]. Listen: were you set here to watch me, or to watch the Egyptians?

SENTINEL: We know our duty.

APOLLODORUS: Then why dont you do it? There is something going on over there [*pointing southwestward to the mole*].

SENTINEL [*sulkily*]: I do not need to be told what to do by the like of you.

APOLLODORUS: Blockhead. [*He begins shouting*] Ho there, Centurion. Hoiho!

SENTINEL: Curse your meddling. [*Shouting*] Hoiho! Alarm! Alarm!

FIRST AND SECOND AUXILIARIES: Alarm! alarm! Hoiho!

[*The Centurion comes running in with his guard.*]

CENTURION: What now? Has the old woman attacked you again? [*Seeing Apollodorus*] Are you here still?

APOLLODORUS [*pointing as before*]: See there. The Egyptians are moving. They are going to recapture the Pharos. They will attack by sea and land: by land along the great mole; by sea from the west harbor. Stir yourselves, my military friends: the hunt is up. [*A clangor of trumpets from several points along the quay*]. Aha! I told you so.

CENTURION [*quickly*]: The two extra men pass the alarm to the south posts. One man keep guard here. The rest with me—quick.

[*The two auxiliary sentinels run off to the south. The centurion and his guard run off northward; and immediately afterwards the bucina sounds. The four porters come from the palace carrying a carpet, followed by Ftatateeta.*]

SENTINEL [*handling his pilum apprehensively*]: You again!

[*The porters stop*].

FTATATEETA: Peace, Roman fellow: you are now singlehanded. Apollodorus: this carpet is Cleopatra's present to Caesar. It has rolled up in it ten precious goblets of the thinnest Iberian crystal, and a hundred eggs of the sacred blue pigeon. On your honor, let not one of them be broken.

APOLLODORUS: On my head be it! [*To to porters*] Into the boat with them carefully.

[*The porters carry the carpet to the steps.*]

FIRST PORTER [*looking down at the boat*]: Beware what you do, sir. Those eggs of which the lady speaks must weigh more than a pound apiece. This boat is too small for such a load.

BOATMAN [*excitedly rushing up the steps*]: Oh thou injurious porter! Oh thou unnatural son of a she-camel! [*To Apollodorus*] My boat, sir, hath often carried five men. Shall it not carry your lordship and a bale of pigeon's eggs? [*To the porter*] Thou mangey dromedary, the gods shall punish thee for this envious wickedness.

FIRST PORTER [*stolidly*]: I cannot quit this bale now to beat thee; but another day I will lie in wait for thee.

APOLLODORUS [*going between them*]: Peace there. If the boat were but a single plank, I would get to Caesar on it.

FTATATEETA [*anxiously*]: In the name of the gods, Apollodorus, run no risks with the bale.

APOLLODORUS: Fear not, thou venerable grotesque: I guess its great worth. [*To the porters*] Down with it, I say; and gently; or ye shall eat nothing but stick for ten days.

[*The boatman goes down the steps, followed by the porters with the bale: Ftatateeta and Apollodorus watching from the edge.*]

APOLLODORUS: Gently, my sons, my children—[*with sudden alarm*] gently, ye dogs. Lay it level in the stern—so—tis well.

FTATATEETA [*screaming down at one of the porters*]: Do not step on it, do not step on it. Oh thou brute beast!

FIRST PORTER [*ascending*]: Be not excited, mistress: all is well.

FTATATEETA [*panting*]: All well! Oh, thou hast given my heart a turn! [*She clutches her side, gasping*].

[*The four porters have now come up and are waiting at the stairhead to be paid.*]

APOLLODORUS: Here, ye hungry ones. [*He gives money to the first porter, who holds it in his hand to shew to the others. They crowd greedily to see how much it is, quite prepared, after the Eastern fashion, to protest to heaven against their patron's stinginess. But his liberality overpowers them*].

FIRST PORTER: O bounteous prince!

SECOND PORTER: O lord of the bazaar!

THIRD PORTER: O favored of the gods!

FOURTH PORTER: O father to all the porters of the market.

SENTINEL [*enviously, threatening them fiercely with his pilum*]: Hence, dogs: off. Out of this. [*They fly before him northward along the quay*].

APOLLODORUS: Farewell, Ftatateeta. I shall be at the lighthouse before the Egyptians. [*He descends the steps.*]

FTATATEETA: The gods speed thee and protect my nursling!

[*The sentry returns from chasing the porters and looks down at the boat, standing near the stairhead lest Ftatateeta should attempt to escape.*]

APOLLODORUS [*from beneath, as the boat moves off*]: Farewell, valiant pilum
  pitcher.
SENTINEL: Farewell, shopkeeper.
APOLLODORUS: Ha, ha! Pull, thou brave boatman, pull. Soho-o-o-o-o! [*He
  begins to sing in barcarolle measure to the rhythm of the oars*]

> My heart, my heart, spread out thy wings:
> Shake off thy heavy load of love—

Give me the oars, O son of a snail.

SENTINEL [*threatening Ftatateeta*]: Now mistress: back to your henhouse. In
  with you.
FTATATEETA [*falling on her knees and stretching her hands over the waters*]: Gods
  of the seas, bear her safely to the shore!
SENTINEL: Bear who safely? What do you mean?
FTATATEETA [*looking darkly at him*]: Gods of Egypt and of Vengeance, let this
  Roman fool be beaten like a dog by his captain for suffering her to be
  taken over the waters.
SENTINEL: Accursed one: is she then in the boat? [*He calls over the sea*] Hoiho,
  there, boatman! Hoiho!
APOLLODORUS [*singing in the distance*]:

> My heart, my heart, be whole and free:
> Love is thine only enemy.

[*Meanwhile Rufio, the morning's fighting done, sits munching dates on a faggot
of brushwood outside the door of the lighthouse, which towers gigantic to the
clouds on his left. His helmet, full of dates, is between his knees; and a leathern
bottle of wine is by his side. Behind him the great stone pedestal of the lighthouse
is shut in from the open sea by a low stone parapet, with a couple of steps in
the middle to the broad coping. A huge chain with a hook hangs down from
the lighthouse crane above his head. Faggots like the one he sits on lie beneath
it ready to be drawn up to feed the beacon. Caesar is standing on the step at
the parapet looking out anxiously, evidently ill at ease. Britannus comes out of
the lighthouse door.*]

RUFIO: Well, my British islander. Have you been up to the top?
BRITANNUS: I have. I reckon it at 200 feet high.
RUFIO: Anybody up there?
BRITANNUS: One elderly Tyrian to work the crane; and his son, a well
  conducted youth of 14.
RUFIO [*looking at the chain*]: What! An old man and a boy work that! Twenty
  men, you mean.

BRITANNUS: Two only, I assure you. They have counterweights, and a machine with boiling water in it which I do not understand: it is not of British design. They use it to haul up barrels of oil and faggots to burn in the brazier on the roof.

RUFIO: But—

BRITANNUS: Excuse me: I came down because there are messengers coming along the mole to us from the island. I must see what their business is. [*He hurries out past the lighthouse*].

CAESAR [*coming away from the parapet, shivering and out of sorts*]: Rufio: this has been a mad expedition. We shall be beaten. I wish I knew how our men are getting on with that barricade across the great mole.

RUFIO [*angrily*]: Must I leave my food and go starving to bring you a report?

CAESAR [*soothing him nervously*]: No, Rufio, no. Eat, my son, eat. [*He takes another turn, Rufio chewing dates meanwhile*]. The Egyptians cannot be such fools as not to storm the barricade and swoop down on us here before it is finished. It is the first time I have ever run an avoidable risk. I should not have come to Egypt.

RUFIO: An hour ago you were all for victory.

CAESAR [*apologetically*]: Yes: I was a fool—rash, Rufio—boyish.

RUFIO: Boyish! Not a bit of it. Here [*offering him a handful of dates*].

CAESAR: What are these for?

RUFIO: To eat. Thats whats the matter with you. When a man comes to your age, he runs down before his midday meal. Eat and drink; and then have another look at our chances.

CAESAR [*taking the dates*]: My age! [*He shakes his head and bites a date*]. Yes, Rufio: I am an old man—worn out now—true, quite true. [*He gives way to melancholy contemplation, and eats another date*]. Achillas is still in his prime: Ptolemy is a boy. [*He eats another date, and plucks up a little*]. Well, every dog has his day; and I have had mine: I cannot complain. [*With sudden cheerfulness*] These dates are not bad, Rufio. [*Britannus returns, greatly excited, with a leathern bag. Caesar is himself again in a moment*]. What now?

BRITANNUS [*triumphantly*]: Our brave Rhodian mariners have captured a treasure. There! [*He throws the bag down at Caesar's feet*]. Our enemies are delivered into our hands.

CAESAR: In that bag?

BRITTANUS: Wait till you hear, Caesar. This bag contains all the letters which have passed between Pompey's party and the army of occupation here.

CAESAR: Well?

BRITTANUS [*impatient of Caesar's slowness to grasp the situation*]: Well, we shall now know who your foes are. The name of every man who has plotted against you since you crossed the Rubicon may be in these papers, for all we know.

CAESAR: Put them in the fire.

BRITANNUS: Put them—[*he gasps*]!!!

CAESAR: In the fire. Would you have me waste the next three years of my life of proscribing and condemning men who will be my friends when I have proved that my friendship is worth more than Pompey's was— than Cato's is. O incorrigible British islander: am I a bull dog, to seek quarrels merely to shew how stubborn my jaws are?

BRITANNUS: But your honor—the honor of Rome—

CAESAR: I do not make human sacrifices to my honor, as your Druids do. Since you will not burn these, at least I can drown them. [*He picks up the bag and throws it over the parapet into the sea*].

BRITANNUS: Caesar: this is mere eccentricity. Are traitors to be allowed to go free for the sake of a paradox?

RUFIO [*rising*]: Caesar: when the islander has finished preaching, call me again. I am going to have a look at the boiling water machine. [*He goes into the lighthouse.*]

BRITANNUS [*with genuine feeling*]: O Caesar, my great master, if I could but persuade you to regard life seriously, as men do in my country!

CAESAR: Do they truly do so, Britannus?

BRITANNUS: Have you not been there? Have you not seen them? What Briton speaks as you do in your moments of levity? What Briton neglects to attend the services at the sacred grove? What Briton wears clothes of many colors as you do, instead of plain blue, as all solid, well esteemed men should? These are moral questions with us.

CAESAR: Well, well, my friend: some day I shall settle down and have a blue toga, perhaps. Meanwhile, I must get on as best I can in my flippant Roman way. [*Apollodorus comes past the lighthouse*]. What now?

BRITANNUS [*turning quickly, and challenging the stranger with official haughtiness*]: What is this? Who are you? How did you come here?

APOLLODORUS: Calm yourself, my friend: I am not going to eat you. I have come by boat, from Alexandria, with precious gifts for Caesar.

CAESAR: From Alexandria!

BRITANNUS [*severely*]: This is Caesar, sir.

RUFIO [*appearing at the lighthouse door*]: Whats the matter now?

APOLLODORUS: Hail, great Caesar! I am Apollodorus the Sicilian, an artist.

BRITANNUS: An artist! Why have they admitted this vagabond?

CAESAR: Peace, man. Apollodorus is a famous patrician amateur.

BRITANNUS [*disconcerted*]: I crave the gentleman's pardon. [*To Caesar*] I understood him to say that he was a professional.

[*Somewhat out of countenance, he allows Apollodorus to approach Caesar, changing places with him. Rufio, after looking Apollodorus up and down with marked disparagement, goes to the other side of the platform*].

CAESAR: You are welcome, Apollodorus. What is your business?

APOLLODORUS: First, to deliver to you a present from the Queen of Queens.

CAESAR: Who is that?

APOLLODORUS: Cleopatra of Egypt.

CAESAR [*taking him into his confidence in his most winning manner*]: Apollodorus: this is no time for playing with presents. Pray you, go back to the Queen, and tell her that if all goes well I shall return to the palace this evening.

APOLLODORUS: Caesar: I cannot return. As I approached the lighthouse, some fool threw a great leathern bag into the sea. It broke the nose of my boat; and I had hardly time to get myself and my charge to the shore before the poor little cockleshell sank.

CAESAR: I am sorry, Apollodorus. The fool shall be rebuked. Well, well: what have you brought me? The Queen will be hurt if I do not look at it.

RUFIO: Have we time to waste on this trumpery? The Queen is only a child.

CAESAR: Just so: that is why we must not disappoint her. What is the present, Apollodorus?

APOLLODORUS: Caesar: it is a Persian carpet—a beauty! And in it are—so I am told—pigeons' eggs and crystal goblets and fragile precious things. I dare not for my head have it carried up that narrow ladder from the causeway.

RUFIO: Swing it up by the crane, then. We will send the eggs to the cook; drink our wine from the goblets; and the carpet will make a bed for Caesar.

APOLLODORUS: The crane! Caesar: I have sworn to tender this bale of carpet as I tender my own life.

CAESAR [*cheerfully*]: Then let them swing you up at the same time; and if the chain breaks, you and the pigeons' eggs will perish together.

[*He goes to the chain and looks up along it, examining it curiously.*].

APOLLODORUS [*to Britannus*]: Is Caesar serious?

BRITANNUS: His manner is frivolous because he is an Italian; but he means what he says.

APOLLODORUS: Serious or not, he spake well. Give me a squad of soldiers to work the crane.

BRITANNUS: Leave the crane to me. Go and await the descent of the chain.

APOLLODORUS: Good. You will presently see me there [*turning to them all and pointing with an eloquent gesture to the sky above the parapet*] rising like the sun with my treasure.

[*He goes back the way he came. Britannus goes into the lighthouse.*]

RUFIO [*ill-humoredly*]: Are you really going to wait here for this foolery, Caesar?

CAESAR [*backing away from the crane as it gives signs of working*]: Why not?

RUFIO: The Egyptians will let you know why not if they have the sense to make a rush from the shore end of the mole before our barricade is finished. And here we are waiting like children to see a carpet full of pigeons' eggs.

[*The chain rattles, and is drawn up high enough to clear the parapet. It then swings round out of sight behind the lighthouse.*]

CAESAR: Fear not, my son Rufio. When the first Egyptian takes his first step along the mole, the alarm will sound; and we two will reach the barricade from our end before the Egyptians reach it from their end—we two, Rufio: I, the old man, and you, his biggest boy. And the old man will be there first. So peace; and give me some more dates.

APOLLODORUS [*from the causeway below*]: Soho, haul away. So-ho-o-o-o!

[*The chain is drawn up and comes round again from behind the lighthouse. Apollodorus is swinging in the air with his bale of carpet at the end of it. He breaks into song as he soars above the parapet*]

> Aloft, aloft, behold the blue
> That never shone in woman's eyes

Easy there: stop her. [*He ceases to rise*]. Further round!

[*The chain comes forward above the platform*].

RUFIO [*calling up*]: Lower away there. [*The chain and its load begin to descend*].

APOLLODORUS [*calling up*]: Gently—slowly—mind the eggs.

RUFIO [*calling up*]: Easy there—slowly—slowly.

[*Apollodorus and the bale are deposited safely on the flags in the middle of the platform. Rufio and Caesar help Apollodorus to cast off the chain from the bale.*]

RUFIO: Haul up.

[*The chain rises clear of their heads with a rattle. Britannus comes from the lighthouse and helps them to uncord the carpet.*]

APOLLODORUS [*when the cords are loose*]: Stand off, my friends: let Caesar see.

[*He throws the carpet open*].

RUFIO: Nothing but a heap of shawls. Where are the pigeons' eggs?

APOLLODORUS: Approach, Caesar; and search for them among the shawls.

RUFIO [*drawing his sword*]: Ha, treachery! Keep back, Caesar: I saw the shawl move: there is something alive there.

BRITANNUS [*drawing his sword*]: It is a serpent.

APOLLODORUS: Dares Caesar thrust his hand into the sack where the serpent moves?

RUFIO [*turning on him*]: Treacherous dog—

CAESAR: Peace. Put up your swords. Apollodorus: your serpent seems to breathe very regularly. [*He thrusts his hand under the shawls and draws out a bare arm*]: This is a pretty little snake.

RUFIO [*drawing out the other arm*]: Let us have the rest of you.

[*They pull Cleopatra up by the wrists into a sitting position. Britannus, scandalized, sheathes his sword with a drive of protest.*]

CLEOPATRA [*gasping*]: Oh, I'm smothered. Oh, Caesar, a man stood on me in the boat; and a great sack of something fell upon me out of the sky; and then the boat sank; and then I was swung up into the air and bumped down.

CAESAR [*petting her as she rises and takes refuge on his breast*]: Well, never mind: here you are safe and sound at last.

RUFIO: Ay; and now that she is here, where are we to do with her?

BRITANNUS: She cannot stay here, Caesar, without the companionship of some matron.

CLEOPATRA [*jealously, to Caesar, who is obviously perplexed*]: Arent you glad to see me?

CAESAR: Yes, yes; *I* am very glad. But Rufio is very angry; and Britannus is shocked.

CLEOPATRA [*contemptuously*]: You can have their heads cut off, can you not?

CAESAR: They would not be so useful with their heads cut off as they are now, my sea bird.

RUFIO [*to Cleopatra*]: We shall have to go away presently and cut some of your Egyptians' heads off. How will you like being left here with the chance of being captured by that little brother of yours if we are beaten?

CLEOPATRA: But you mustnt leave me alone. Caesar: you will not leave me alone, will you?

RUFIO: What! not when the trumpet sounds and all our lives depend on Caesar's being at the barricade before the Egyptians reach it? Eh?

CLEOPATRA: Let them lose their lives: they are only soldiers.

CAESAR [*gravely*]: Cleopatra: when that trumpet sounds, we must take every man his life in his hand, and throw it in the face of Death. And of my soldiers who have trusted me there is not one whose hand I shall not hold more sacred than your head. [*Cleopatra is overwhelmed. Her eyes fill with tears*]. Apollodorus: you must take her back to the palace.

APOLLODORUS: Am I a dolphin, Caesar, to cross the seas with young ladies on my back? My boat is sunk: all yours are either at the barricade or have returned to the city. I will hail one if I can: that is all I can do. [*He goes back to the causeway*].

CLEOPATRA [*struggling with her tears*]: It does not matter. I will not go back. Nobody cares for me.

CAESAR: Cleopatra—

CLEOPATRA: You want me to be killed.

CAESAR [*still more gravely*]: My poor child: your life matters little here to anyone but yourself.

[*She gives way altogether at this, casting herself down on the faggots weeping. Suddenly a great tumult is heard in the distance, bucinas and trumpets sounding through a storm of shouting. Britannus rushes to the parapet and looks along the mole. Caesar and Rufio turn to one another with quick intelligence*].

CAESAR: Come, Rufio.

CLEOPATRA [*scrambling to her knees and clinging to him*]: No no. Do not leave me, Caesar. [*He snatches his skirt from her clutch*]. Oh!

BRITANNUS [*from the parapet*]: Caesar: we are cut off. The Egyptians have landed from the west harbor between us and the barricade!!!

RUFIO [*running to see*]: Curses! It is true. We are caught like rats in a trap.

CAESAR [*ruthfully*]: Rufio, Rufio: my men at the barricade are between the sea party and the shore party. I have murdered them.

RUFIO [*coming back from the parapet to Caesar's right hand*]: Ay: that comes of fooling with this girl here.

APOLLODORUS [*coming up quickly from the causeway*]: Look over the parapet, Caesar.

CAESAR: We have looked, my friend. We must defend ourselves here.

APOLLODORUS: I have thrown the ladder into the sea. They cannot get in without it.

RUFIO: Ay; and we cannot get out. Have you thought of that?

APOLLODORUS: Not get out! Why not? You have ships in the east harbor.

BRITANNUS [*hopefully, at the parapet*]: The Rhodian galleys are standing in towards us already. [*Caesar quickly joins Britannus at the parapet*].

RUFIO [*to Apollodorus, impatiently*]: And by what road are we to walk to the galleys, pray?

APOLLODORUS [*with gay, defiant rhetoric*]: By the road that leads everywhere —the diamond path of the sun and moon. Have you never seen the child's shadow play of The Broken Bridge? "Ducks and geese with ease get over"—eh? [*He throws away his cloak and cap, and binds his sword on his back*].

RUFIO: What are you talking about?

APOLLODORUS: I will shew you. [*Calling to Britannus*] How far off is the nearest galley?

BRITANNUS: Fifty fathom.

CAESAR: No, no: they are further off than they seem in this clear air to your British eyes. Nearly quarter of a mile, Apollodorus.

APOLLODORUS: Good. Defend yourselves here until I send you a boat from that galley.

RUFIO: Have you wings, perhaps?

APOLLODORUS: Water wings, soldier. Behold!

[*He runs up the steps between Caesar and Britannus to the coping of the parapet; springs into the air; and plunges head foremost into the sea.*]

CAESAR [*like a schoolboy—wildly excited*]: Bravo, bravo! [*Throwing off his cloak*] By Jupiter, I will do that too.

RUFIO [*seizing him*]: You are mad. You shall not.

CAESAR: Why not? Can I not swim as well as he?

RUFIO [*frantic*]: Can an old fool dive and swim like a young one? He is twenty-five and you are fifty.

CAESAR [*breaking loose from Rufio*]: Old!!!

BRITANNUS [*shocked*]: Rufio: you forget yourself.

CAESAR: I will race you to the galley for a week's pay, father Rufio.

CLEOPATRA: But me! me!! me!!! what is to become of me?

CAESAR: I will carry you on my back to the galley like a dolphin. Rufio: when you see me rise to the surface, throw her in: I will answer for her. And then in with you after her, both of you.

CLEOPATRA: No, no, NO. I shall be drowned.

BRITANNUS: Caesar: I am a man and a Briton, not a fish. I must have a boat. I cannot swim.

CLEOPATRA: Neither can I.

CAESAR [*to Britannus*]: Stay here, then, alone, until I recapture the light-house: I will not forget you. Now, Rufio.

RUFIO: You have made up your mind to this folly?

CAESAR: The Egyptians have made it up for me. What else is there to do? And mind where you jump: I do not want to get your fourteen stone in the small of my back as I come up. [*He runs up the steps and stands on the coping*].

BRITANNUS [*anxiously*]: One last word, Caesar. Do not let yourself be seen in the fashionable part of Alexandria until you have changed your clothes.

CAESAR [*calling over the sea*]: Ho, Apollodorus: [*he points skyward and quotes the barcarolle*]

The white upon the blue above—

APOLLODORUS [*swimming in the distance*]:

Is purple on the green below—

CAESAR [*exultantly*]: Aha! [*He plunges into the sea*].
CLEOPATRA [*running excitedly to the steps*]: Oh, let me see. He will be drowned

[*Rufio seizes her*]—Ah—ah—ah—ah! [*He pitches her screaming into the sea. Rufio and Britannus roar with laughter*].

RUFIO [*looking down after her*]: He has got her. [*To Britannus*] Hold the fort, Briton. Caesar will not forget you. [*He springs off*].
BRITANNUS [*running to the steps to watch them as they swim*]: All safe, Rufio?
RUFIO [*swimming*]: All safe.
CAESAR [*swimming further off*]: Take refuge up there by the beacon; and pile the fuel on the trap door, Britannus.
BRITANNUS [*calling in reply*]: I will first do so, and then commend myself to my country's gods. [*A sound of cheering from the sea. Britannus gives full vent to his excitement*]. The boat has reached him: Hip, hip, hip, hurrah!

Act IV

[*Cleopatra's sousing in the east harbor of Alexandria was in October 48 B.C. In March 47 she is passing the afternoon in her boudoir in the palace, among a bevy of her ladies, listening to a slave girl who is playing the harp in the middle of the room. The harpist's master, an old musician, with a lined face, prominent brows, white beard, moustache and eyebrows twisted and horned at the ends, and a consciously keen and pretentious expression, is squatting on the floor close to her on her right, watching her performance. Ftatateeta is in attendance near the door, in front of a group of female slaves. Except the harp player all are seated: Cleopatra in a chair opposite the door on the other side of the room; the rest on the ground. Cleopatra's ladies are all young, the most conspicuous being Charmian and Iras, her favorites. Charmian is a hatchet faced, terra cotta colored little goblin, swift in her movements, and neatly finished at the hands and feet. Iras is a plump, goodnatured creature, rather fatuous, with a profusion of red hair, and a tendency to giggle on the slightest provocation.*]

CLEOPATRA: Can I—
FTATATEETA [*insolently, to the player*]: Peace, thou! The Queen speaks. [*The player stops*].
CLEOPATRA [*to the old musician*]: I want to learn to play the harp with my own hands. Caesar loves music. Can you teach me?
MUSICIAN: Assuredly I and no one else can teach the Queen. Have I not discovered the lost method of the ancient Egyptians, who could make

a pyramid tremble by touching a bass string? All the other teachers are quacks: I have exposed them repeatedly.

CLEOPATRA: Good: you shall teach me. How long will it take?

MUSICIAN: Not very long: only four years. Your Majesty must first become proficient in the philosophy of Pythagoras.

CLEOPATRA: Has she [*indicating the slave*] become proficient in the philosophy of Pythagoras?

MUSICIAN: Oh, she is but a slave. She learns as a dog learns.

CLEOPATRA: Well, then, I will learn as a dog learns; for she plays better than you. You shall give me a lesson every day for a fortnight. [*The musician hastily scrambles to his feet and bows profoundly*]. After that, whenever I strike a false note you shall be flogged; and if I strike so many that there is not time to flog you, you shall be thrown into the Nile to feed the crocodiles. Give the girl a piece of gold; and send them away.

MUSICIAN [*much taken aback*]: But true art will not be thus forced.

FTATATEETA [*pushing him out*]: What is this? Answering the Queen, forsooth. Out with you.

[*He is pushed out by Ftatateeta, the girl following with her harp, amid the laughter of the ladies and slaves.*]

CLEOPATRA: Now, can any of you amuse me? Have you any stories or any news?

IRAS: Ftatateeta—

CLEOPATRA: Oh, Ftatateeta, Ftatateeta, always Ftatateeta. Some new tale to set me against her.

IRAS: No: this time Ftatateeta has been virtuous. [*All the ladies laugh—not the slaves*]. Pothinus has been trying to bribe her to let him speak with you.

CLEOPATRA [*wrathfully*]: Ha! you all sell audiences with me, as if I saw whom you please, and not whom I please. I should like to know how much of her gold piece that harp girl will have to give up before she leaves the palace.

IRAS: We can easily find out that for you.

[*The ladies laugh.*]

CLEOPATRA [*frowning*]: You laugh; but take care, take care. I will find out some day how to make myself served as Caesar is served.

CHARMIAN: Old hooknose! [*They laugh again*].

CLEOPATRA [*revolted*]: Silence. Charmian: do not you be a silly little Egyptian fool. Do you know why I allow you all to chatter impertinently just as you please, instead of treating you as Ftatateeta would treat you if she were Queen?

CHARMIAN: Because you try to imitate Caesar in everything; and he lets everybody say what they please to him.

CLEOPATRA: No; but because I asked him one day why he did so; and he said "Let your women talk; and you will learn something from them." What have I to learn from them? I said. "What they are," said he; and oh! you should have seen his eye as he said it. You would have curled up, you shallow things. [*They laugh. She turns fiercely on Iras*]: At whom are you laughing—at me or at Caesar?

IRAS: At Caesar.

CLEOPATRA: If you were not a fool, you would laugh at me; and if you were not a coward you would not be afraid to tell me so. [*Ftatateeta returns*]. Ftatateeta: they tell me that Pothinus has offered you a bribe to admit him to my presence.

FTATATEETA [*protesting*]: Now by my father's gods—

CLEOPATRA [*cutting her short despotically*]: Have I not told you not to deny things? You would spend the day calling your father's gods to witness to your virtues if I let you. Go take the bribe; and bring in Pothinus. [*Ftatateeta is about to reply*]. Dont answer me. Go.

[*Ftatateeta goes out; and Cleopatra rises and begins to prowl to and fro between her chair and the door, meditating. All rise and stand.*]

IRAS [*as she reluctantly rises*]: Heigho! I wish Caesar were back in Rome.

CLEOPATRA [*threateningly*]: It will be a bad day for you all when he goes. Oh, if I were not ashamed to let him see that I am as cruel at heart as my father, I would make you repent that speech! Why do you wish him away?

CHARMIAN: He makes you so terribly prosy and serious and learned and philosophical. It is worse than being religious, at our ages. [*The ladies laugh*].

CLEOPATRA: Cease that endless cackling, will you. Hold your tongues.

CHARMIAN [*with mock resignation*]: Well, well: we must try to live up to Caesar.

[*They laugh again. Cleopatra rages silently as she continues to prowl to and fro. Ftatateeta comes back with Pothinus, who halts on the threshold.*]

FTATATEETA [*at the door*]: Pothinus craves the ear of the—

CLEOPATRA: There, there: that will do: let him come in. [*She resumes her seat. All sit down except Pothinus, who advances to the middle of the room. Ftatateeta takes her former place*]. Well, Pothinus: what is the latest news from your rebel friends?

POTHINUS [*haughtily*]: I am no friend of rebellion. And a prisoner does not receive news.

CLEOPATRA: You are no more a prisoner than I am—than Caesar is. These six months we have been besieged in this palace by my subjects. You are allowed to walk on the beach among the soldiers. Can I go further myself, or can Caesar?

POTHINUS: You are but a child, Cleopatra, and do not understand these matters. [*The ladies laugh. Cleopatra looks inscrutably at him.*]

CHARMIAN: I see you do not know the latest news, Pothinus.

POTHINUS: What is that?

CHARMIAN: That Cleopatra is no longer a child. Shall I tell you how to grow much older, and much, much wiser in one day?

POTHINUS: I should prefer to grow wiser without growing older.

CHARMIAN: Well, go up to the top of the lighthouse; and get somebody to take you by the hair and throw you into the sea. [*The ladies laugh*].

CLEOPATRA: She is right, Pothinus: you will come to the shore with much conceit washed out of you. [*The ladies laugh. Cleopatra rises impatiently*]. Begone, all of you. I will speak with Pothinus alone. Drive them out, Ftatateeta. [*They run out laughing. Ftatateeta shuts the door on them*]. What are you waiting for?

FTATATEETA: It is not meet that the Queen remain alone with—

CLEOPATRA [*interrupting her*]: Ftatateeta: must I sacrifice you to your father's gods to teach you that *I* am Queen of Egypt, and not you?

FTATATEETA [*indignantly*]: You are like the rest of them. You want to be what these Romans call a New Woman.

[*She goes out, banging the door*].

CLEOPATRA [*sitting down again*]: Now, Pothinus: why did you bribe Ftatateeta to bring you hither?

POTHINUS [*studying her gravely*]: Cleopatra: what they tell me is true. You are changed.

CLEOPATRA: Do you speak with Caesar every day for six months: and you will be changed.

POTHINUS: It is the common talk that you are infatuated with this old man?

CLEOPATRA: Infatuated? What does that mean? Made foolish, is it not? Oh no: I wish I were.

POTHINUS: You wish you were made foolish! How so?

CLEOPATRA: When I was foolish, I did what I liked, except when Ftatateeta beat me; and even then I cheated her and did it by stealth. Now that Caesar has made me wise, it is no use my liking or disliking: I do what must be done, and have no time to attend to myself. That is not happiness; but it is greatness. If Caesar were gone, I think I could govern the Egyptians; for what Caesar is to me, I am to the fools around me.

POTHINUS [*looking hard at her*]: Cleopatra: this may be the vanity of youth.

CLEOPATRA: No, no: it is not that I am so clever, but that the others are so stupid.

POTHINUS [*musingly*]: Truly, that is the great secret.

CLEOPATRA: Well, now tell me what you came to say?

POTHINUS [*embarrassed*]: I! Nothing.

CLEOPATRA: Nothing!

POTHINUS: At least—to beg for my liberty: that is all.

CLEOPATRA: For that you would have knelt to Caesar. No, Pothinus: you came with some plan that depended on Cleopatra being a little nursery kitten. Now that Cleopatra is a Queen, the plan is upset.

POTHINUS [*bowing his head submissively*]: It is so.

CLEOPATRA [*exultant*]: Aha!

POTHINUS [*raising his eyes keenly to hers*]: Is Cleopatra then indeed a Queen, and no longer Caesar's prisoner and slave?

CLEOPATRA: Pothinus: we are all Caesar's slaves—all we in this land of Egypt —whether we will or no. And she who is wise enough to know this will reign when Caesar departs.

POTHINUS: You harp on Caesar's departure.

CLEOPATRA: What if I do?

POTHINUS: Does he not love you?

CLEOPATRA: Love me! Pothinus: Caesar loves no one. Who are those we love. Only those whom we do not hate: all people are strangers and enemies to us except those we love. But it is not so with Caesar. He has no hatred in him: he makes friends with everyone as he does with dogs and children. His kindness to me is a wonder: neither mother, father, nor nurse have ever taken so much care for me, or thrown open their thoughts to me so freely.

POTHINUS: Well: is not this love?

CLEOPATRA: What! when he will do as much for the first girl he meets on his way back to Rome? Ask his slave, Britannus: he has been just as good to him. Nay, ask his very horse! His kindness is not for anything in me: it is in his own nature.

POTHINUS: But how can you be sure that he does not love you as men love women?

CLEOPATRA: Because I cannot make him jealous. I have tried.

POTHINUS: Hm! Perhaps I should have asked, then, do you love him?

CLEOPATRA: Can one love a god? Besides, I love another Roman: one whom I saw long before Caesar—no god, but a man—one who can love and hate—one whom I can hurt and who would hurt me.

POTHINUS: Does Caesar know this?

CLEOPATRA: Yes.

POTHINUS: And he is not angry?

CLEOPATRA: He promises to send him to Egypt to please me!

POTHINUS: I do not understand this man.

CLEOPATRA [*with superb contempt*]: You understand Caesar! How could you? [*Proudly*] I do—by instinct.

POTHINUS [*deferentially, after a moment's thought*]: Your Majesty caused me to be admitted today. What message has the Queen for me?

CLEOPATRA: This. You think that by making my brother king, you will rule in Egypt because you are his guardian and he is a little silly.

POTHINUS: The Queen is pleased to say so.

CLEOPATRA: The Queen is pleased to say this also. That Caesar will eat up you, and Achillas, and my brother, as a cat eats up mice; and that he will put on this land of Egypt as a shepherd puts on his garment. And when he has done that, he will return to Rome, and leave Cleopatra here as his viceroy.

POTHINUS [*breaking out wrathfully*]: That he shall never do. We have a thousand men to his ten; and we will drive him and his beggarly legions into the sea.

CLEOPATRA [*with scorn, getting up to go*]: You rant like any common fellow. Go, then, and marshal your thousands; and make haste; for Mithridates of Pergamos is at hand with reinforcements for Caesar. Caesar has held you at bay with two legions: we shall see what he will do with twenty.

POTHINUS: Cleopatra—

CLEOPATRA: Enough, enough: Caesar has spoiled me for talking to weak things like you.

[*She goes out. Pothinus, with a gesture of rage, is following, when Ftatateeta enters and stops him.*]

POTHINUS: Let me go forth from this hateful place.

FTATATEETA: What angers you?

POTHINUS: The curse of all the gods of Egypt be upon her! She sold her country to the Roman, that she may buy it back from him with her kisses.

FTATATEETA: Fool: did she not tell you that she would have Caesar gone?

POTHINUS: You listened?

FTATATEETA: I took care that some honest woman should be at hand whilst you were with her.

POTHINUS: Now by the gods—

FTATATEETA: Enough of your gods! Caesar's gods are all powerful here. It is no use you coming to Cleopatra: you are only an Egyptian. She will not listen to any of her own race: she treats us all as children.

POTHINUS: May she perish for it!

FTATATEETA [*balefully*]: May your tongue wither for that wish! Go! send for Lucius Septimius, the slayer of Pompey. He is a Roman: maybe she will listen to him. Begone!

POTHINUS [*darkly*]: I know to whom I must go now.

FTATATEETA [*suspiciously*]: To whom, then?

POTHINUS: To a greater Roman than Lucius. And mark this, mistress. You thought, before Caesar came, that Egypt should presently be ruled by you and your crew in the name of Cleopatra. I set myself against it—

FTATATEETA [*interrupting him—wrangling*]: Ay; that it might be ruled by you and your crew in the name of Ptolemy.

POTHINUS: Better me, or even you, than a woman with a Roman heart; and that is what Cleopatra is now become. Whilst I live, she shall never rule. So guide yourself accordingly. [*He goes out*].

[*It is by this time drawing on to dinner time. The table is laid on the roof of the palace; and thither Rufio is now climbing, ushered by a majestic palace official, wand of office in hand, and followed by a slave carrying an inlaid stool. After many stairs they emerge at last into a massive colonnade on the roof. Light curtains are drawn between the columns on the north and east to soften the westering sun. The official leads Rufio to one of these shaded sections. A cord for pulling the curtains apart hangs down between the pillars.*]

THE OFFICIAL [*bowing*]: The Roman commander will await Caesar here.

[*The slave sets down the stool near the southernmost column, and slips out through the curtains.*]

RUFIO [*sitting down, a little blown*]: Pouf! That was a climb. How high have we come?

THE OFFICIAL: We are on the palace roof, O Beloved of Victory!

RUFIO: Good! the Beloved of Victory has no more stairs to get up.

[*A second official enters from the opposite end, walking backwards.*]

THE SECOND OFFICIAL: Caesar approaches.

[*Caesar, fresh from the bath, clad in a new tunic of purple silk, comes in, beaming and festive, followed by two slaves carrying a light couch, which is hardly more than an elaborately designed bench. They place it near the northmost of the two curtained columns. When this is done they slip out through the curtains; and the two officials, formally bowing, follow them. Rufio rises to receive Caesar.*]

CAESAR [*coming over to him*]: Why, Rufio! [*Surveying his dress with an air of admiring astonishment*] A new baldrick! A new golden pommel to your sword! And you have had your hair cut! But not your beard—? impossible! [*He sniffs at Rufio's beard*]. Yes, perfumed, by Jupiter Olympus!

RUFIO [*growling*]: Well: is it to please myself?

CAESAR [*affectionately*]: No, my son Rufio, but to please me—to celebrate my birthday.

RUFIO [*contemptuously*]: Your birthday! You always have a birthday when there is a pretty girl to be flattered or an ambassador to be conciliated. We had seven of them in ten months last year.

CAESAR [*contritely*]: It is true, Rufio! I shall never break myself of these petty deceits.

RUFIO: Who is to dine with us—besides Cleopatra?

CAESAR: Apollodorus the Sicilian.

RUFIO: That popinjay!

CAESAR: Come! the popinjay is an amusing dog—tells a story; sings a song; and saves us the trouble of flattering the Queen. What does she care for old politicans and camp-fed bears like us? No, Apollodorus is good company, Rufio, good company.

RUFIO: Well, he can swim a bit and fence a bit: he might be worse, if he only knew how to hold his tongue.

CAESAR: The gods forbid he should ever learn! Oh, this military life! this tedious, brutal life of action! That is the worst of us Romans: we are mere doers and drudgers: a swarm of bees turned into men. Give me a good talker—one with wit and imagination enough to live without continually doing something!

RUFIO: Ay! a nice time he would have of it with you when dinner was over! Have you noticed that I am before my time?

CAESAR: Aha! I thought that meant something. What is it?

RUFIO: Can we be overheard here?

CAESAR: Our privacy invites eavesdropping. I can remedy that. [*He claps his hands twice. The curtains are drawn, revealing the roof garden with a banqueting table set across in the middle for four persons, one at each end, and two side by side. The side next Caesar and Rufio is blocked with golden wine vessels and basins. A gorgeous major-domo is superintending the laying of the table by a staff of slaves. The colonnade goes round the garden at both sides to the further end, where a gap in it, like a great gateway, leaves the view open to the sky beyond the western edge of the roof, except in the middle, where a life size image of Ra, seated on a huge plinth, towers up, with hawk head and crown of asp and disk. His altar, which stands at his feet, is a single white stone.*] Now everybody can see us, nobody will think of listening to us. [*He sits down on the bench left by the two slaves*].

RUFIO [*sitting down on his stool*]: Pothinus wants to speak to you. I advise you to see him: there is some plotting going on here among the women.

CAESAR: Who is Pothinus?

RUFIO: The fellow with hair like squirrel's fur—the little King's bear leader, whom you kept prisoner.

CAESAR [*annoyed*]: And has he not escaped?

RUFIO: No.

CAESAR [*rising imperiously*]: Why not? You have been guarding this man instead of watching the enemy. Have I not told you always to let prisoners escape unless there are special orders to the contrary? Are there not enough mouths to be fed without him?

RUFIO: Yes; and if you would have a little sense and let me cut his throat, you would save his rations. Anyhow he wont escape. Three sentries have told him they would put a pilum through him if they saw him again. What more can they do? He prefers to stay and spy on us. So would I if I had to do with generals subject to fits of clemency.

CAESAR [*resuming his seat, argued down*]: Hm! And so he wants to see me.

RUFIO: Ay. I have brought him with me. He is waiting there [*jerking his thumb over his shoulder*] under guard.

CAESAR: And you want me to see him?

RUFIO [*obstinately*]: I dont want anything. I daresay you will do what you like. Dont put it on to me.

CEASAR [*with an air of doing it expressly to indulge Rufio*]: Well, well: let us have him.

RUFIO [*calling*]: Ho there, guard! Release your man and send him up. [*Beckoning*]. Come along!

[*Pothinus enters and stops mistrustfully between the two, looking from one to the other.*]

CAESAR [*graciously*]: Ah, Pothinus! You are welcome. And what is the news this afternoon?

POTHINUS: Ceasar: I come to warn you of a danger, and to make you an offer.

CAESAR: Never mind the danger. Make the offer.

RUFIO: Never mind the offer. Whats the danger?

POTHINUS: Ceasar: you think that Cleopatra is devoted to you.

CAESAR [*gravely*]: My friend: I already know what I think. Come to your offer.

POTHINUS: I will deal plainly. I know not by what strange gods you have been enabled to defend a palace and a few yards of beach against a city and an army. Since we cut you off from Lake Mareotis, and you dug wells in the salt sea sand and brought up buckets of fresh water from them, we have known that your gods are irresistible, and that you are a worker of miracles. I no longer threaten you—

RUFIO [*sarcastically*]: Very handsome of you, indeed.

POTHINUS: So be it: you are the master. Our gods sent the north west winds to keep you in our hands; but you have been too strong for them.

CAESAR [*gently urging him to come to the point*]: Yes, yes, my friend. But what then?

RUFIO: Spit it out, man. What have you to say?

POTHINUS: I have to say that you have a traitress in your camp. Cleopatra—

THE MAJOR-DOMO [*at the table, announcing*]: The Queen! [*Caesar and Rufio rise*].

RUFIO [*aside to Pothinus*]: You should have spat it out sooner, you fool. Now it is too late.

[*Cleopatra, in gorgeous raiment, enters in state through the gap in the colonnade, and comes down past the image of Ra and past the table to Caesar. Her retinue, headed by Ftatateeta, joins the staff at the table. Caesar gives Cleopatra his seat, which she takes.*]

CLEOPATRA [*quickly, seeing Pothinus*]: What is he doing here?

CAESAR [*seating himself beside her, in the most amiable of tempers*]: Just going to tell me something about you. You shall hear it. Proceed, Pothinus.

POTHINUS [*disconcerted*]: Caesar—[*he stammers*]

CAESAR: Well, out with it.

POTHINUS: What I have to say is for your ear, not for the Queen's.

CLEOPATRA [*with subdued ferocity*]: There are means of making you speak. Take care.

POTHINUS [*defiantly*]: Caesar does not employ those means.

CAESAR: My friend: when a man has anything to tell in this world, the difficulty is not to make him tell it, but to prevent him from telling it too often. Let me celebrate my birthday by setting you free. Farewell: we shall not meet again.

CLEOPATRA [*angrily*]: Caesar: this mercy is foolish.

POTHINUS [*to Caesar*]: Will you not give me a private audience? Your life may depend on it. [*Caesar rises loftily*].

RUFIO [*aside to Pothinus*]: Ass! Now we shall have some heroics.

CAESAR [*oratorically*]: Pothinus—

RUFIO [*interrupting him*]: Caesar: the dinner will spoil if you begin preaching your favorite sermon about life and death.

CLEOPATRA [*priggishly*]: Peace, Rufio. I desire to hear Caesar.

RUFIO [*bluntly*]: Your Majesty has heard it before. You repeated it to Apollodorus last week; and he thought it was all your own. [*Caesar's dignity collapses. Much tickled, he sits down again and looks roguishly at Cleopatra, who is furious. Rufio calls as before*] Ho there, guard! Pass the prisoner out. He is released. [*To Pothinus*] Now off with you. You have lost your chance.

POTHINUS [*his temper overcoming his prudence*]: I will speak.

CAESAR [*to Cleopatra*]: You see. Torture would not have wrung a word from him.

POTHINUS: Caesar: you have taught Cleopatra the arts by which the Romans govern the world.

CAESAR: Alas! They cannot even govern themselves. What then?

POTHINUS: What then? Are you so besotted with her beauty that you do not see that she is impatient to reign in Egypt alone, and that her heart is set on your departure?

CLEOPATRA [rising]: Liar!

CAESAR [shocked]: What! Protestations! Contradictions!

CLEOPATRA [ashamed, but trembling with suppressed rage]: No. I do not deign to contradict. Let him talk. [She sits down again].

POTHINUS: From her own lips I have heard it. You are to be her catspaw: you are to tear the crown from her brother's head and set it on her own, delivering us all into her hand—delivering yourself also. And then Caesar can return to Rome, or depart through the gate of death, which is nearer and surer.

CAESAR [calmly]: Well, my friend; and is not this very natural?

POTHINUS [astonished]: Natural! Then you do not resent treachery?

CAESAR: Resent! O thou foolish Egyptian, what have I to do with resentment? Do I resent the wind when it chills me, or the night when it makes me stumble in darkness? Shall I resent youth when it turns from age, and ambition when it turns from servitude? To tell me such a story as this is but to tell me that the sun will rise tomorrow.

CLEOPATRA [unable to contain herself]: But it is false—false. I swear it.

CAESAR: It is true, though you swore it a thousand times, and believed all you swore. [She is convulsed with emotion. To screen her, he rises and takes Pothinus to Rufio, saying] Come, Rufio: let us see Pothinus past the guard. I have a word to say to him. [Aside to them] We must give the Queen a moment to recover herself. [Aloud] Come. [He takes Pothinus and Rufio out with him, conversing with them meanwhile]. Tell your friends, Pothinus, that they must not think I am opposed to a reasonable settlement of the country's affairs—[They pass out of hearing].

CLEOPATRA [in a stifled whisper]: Ftatateeta, Ftatateeta.

FTATATEETA [hurrying to her from the table and petting her]: Peace, child: be comforted–

CLEOPATRA [interrupting her]: Can they hear us?

FTATATEETA: No, dear heart, no.

CLEOPATRA: Listen to me. If he leaves the Palace alive, never see my face again.

FTATATEETA: He? Poth—

CLEOPATRA [striking her on the mouth]: Strike his life out as I strike his name from your lips. Dash him down from the wall. Break him on the stones. Kill, kill, kill him.

FTATATEETA [shewing all her teeth]: The dog shall perish.

CLEOPATRA: Fail in this, and you go out from before me forever.

FTATATEETA [*resolutely*]: So be it. You shall not see my face until his eyes are darkened.

[*Caesar comes back, with Apollodorus, exquisitely dressed, and Rufio.*]

CLEOPATRA [*to Ftatateeta*]: Come soon—soon. [*Ftatateeta turns her meaning eyes for a moment on her mistress; then goes grimly away past Ra and out. Cleopatra runs like a gazelle to Caesar*] So you have come back to me, Caesar. [*Caressingly*] I thought you were angry. Welcome, Apollodorus. [*She gives him her hand to kiss, with her other arm about Caesar*].

APOLLODORUS: Cleopatra grows more womanly beautiful from week to week.

CLEOPATRA: Truth, Apollodorus?

APOLLODORUS: Far, far short of the truth! Friend Rufio threw a pearl into the sea: Caesar fished up a diamond.

CAESAR: Caesar fished up a touch of rheumatism, my friend. Come: to dinner! to dinner! [*They move towards the table*].

CLEOPATRA [*skipping like a young fawn*]: Yes, to dinner. I have ordered such a dinner for you, Caesar!

CAESAR: Ay? What are we to have?

CLEOPATRA: Peacocks' brains.

CAESAR [*as if his mouth watered*]: Peacocks' brains, Apollodorus!

APOLLODORUS: Not for me. I prefer nightingales' tongues.

[*He goes to one of the two covers set side by side*].

CLEOPATRA: Roast boar, Rufio!

RUFIO [*gluttonously*]: Good! [*He goes to the seat next Apollodorus, on his left*].

CAESAR [*looking at his seat, which is at the end of the table, to Ra's left hand*]: What has become of my leathern cushion?

CLEOPATRA [*at the opposite end*]: I have got new ones for you.

THE MAJOR-DOMO: These cushions, Caesar, are of Maltese gauze, stuffed with rose leaves.

CAESAR: Rose leaves! Am I a caterpillar? [*He throws the cushions away and seats himself on the leather mattress underneath*].

CLEOPATRA: What a shame! My new cushions!

THE MAJOR-DOMO [*at Caesar's elbow*]: What shall we serve to whet Caesar's appetite?

CAESAR: What have you got?

THE MAJOR-DOMO: Sea hedgehogs, black and white sea acorns, sea nettles, beccaficoes, purple shellfish—

CAESAR: Any oysters?

THE MAJOR-DOMO: Assuredly.

CAESAR: British oysters?

THE MAJOR-DOMO [*assenting*]: British oysters, Caesar.

CAESAR: Oysters, then. [*The Major-Domo signs to a slave at each order; and the slave goes out to execute it*]. I have been in Britain—that western land of romance—the last piece of earth on the edge of the ocean that surrounds the world. I went there in search of its famous pearls. The British pearl was a fable; but in searching for it I found the British oyster.

APOLLODORUS: All posterity will bless you for it. [*To the Major-Domo*] Sea hedgehogs for me.

RUFIO: Is there nothing solid to begin with?

THE MAJOR-DOMO: Fieldfares with asparagus—

CLEOPATRA [*interrupting*]: Fattened fowls! have some fattened fowls, Rufio.

RUFIO: Ay, that will do.

CLEOPATRA [*greedily*]: Fieldfares for me.

THE MAJOR-DOMO: Caesar will deign to choose his wine? Sicilian, Lesbian, Chian—

RUFIO [*contemptuously*]: All Greek.

APOLLODORUS: Who would drink Roman wine when he could get Greek. Try the Lesbian, Caesar.

CAESAR: Bring me my barley water.

RUFIO [*with intense disgust*]: Ugh! Bring me my Falernian.

[*The Falernian is presently brought to him*].

CLEOPATRA [*pouting*]: It is waste of time giving you dinners, Caesar. My scullions would not condescend to your diet.

CAESAR [*relenting*]: Well, well: let us try the Lesbian. [*The Major-Domo fills Caesar's goblet; then Cleopatra's and Apollodorus's*]. But when I return to Rome, I will make laws against these extravagances. I will even get the laws carried out.

CLEOPATRA [*coaxingly*]: Never mind. Today you are to be like other people: idle, luxurious, and kind.

[*She stretches her hand to him along the table*].

CAESAR: Well, for once I will sacrifice my comfort—[*kissing her hand*] there! [*He takes a draught of wine*]. Now are you satisifed?

CLEOPATRA: And you no longer believe that I long for your departure for Rome?

CAESAR: I no longer believe anything. My brains are asleep. Besides, who knows whether I shall return to Rome?

RUFIO [*alarmed*]: How? Eh? What?

CAESAR: What has Rome to shew me that I have not seen already? One year of Rome is like another, except that I grow older, whilst the crowd in the Appian Way is always the same age.

APOLLODORUS: It is no better here in Egypt. The old men, when they are tired of life, say "We have seen everything except the source of the Nile."

CAESAR [*his imagination catching fire*]: And why not see that? Cleopatra: will you come with me and track the flood to its cradle in the heart of the regions of mystery? Shall we leave Rome behind us—Rome, that has achieved greatness only to learn how greatness destroys nations of men who are not great! Shall I make you a new kingdom, and build you a holy city there in the great unknown?

CLEOPATRA [*rapturously*]: Yes, yes. You shall.

RUFIO: Ay: now he will conquer Africa with two legions before we come to the roast boar.

APOLLODORUS: Come: no scoffing. This is a noble scheme: in it Caesar is no longer merely the conquering soldier, but the creative poet-artist. Let us name the holy city, and consecrate it with Lesbian wine.

CAESAR: Cleopatra shall name it herself.

CLEOPATRA: It shall be called Caesar's Gift to his Beloved.

APOLLODORUS: No, no. Something vaster than that—something universal, like the starry firmament.

CAESAR [*prosaically*]: Why not simply The Cradle of the Nile?

CLEOPATRA: No: the Nile is my ancestor; and he is a god. Oh! I have thought of something. The Nile shall name it himself. Let us call upon him. [*To the Major-Domo*] Send for him. [*The three men stare at one another; but the Major-Domo goes out as if he had received the most matter-of-fact order*]. And [*to the retinue*] away with you all.

[*The retinue withdraws, making obeisance. A priest enters, carrying a minia-ture sphinx with a tiny tripod before it. A morsel of incense is smoking in the tripod. The priest comes to the table and places the image in the middle of it. The light begins to change to the magenta purple of the Egyptian sunset, as if the god had brought a strange colored shadow with him. The three men are determined not to be impressed; but they feel curious in spite of themselves.*]

CAESAR: What hocus-pocus is this?

CLEOPATRA: You shall see. And it is not hocus-pocus. To do it properly, we should kill something to please him; but perhaps he will answer Caesar without that if we spill some wine to him.

APOLLODORUS [*turning his head to look up over his shoulder at Ra*]: Why not appeal to our hawkheaded friend here?

CLEOPATRA [*nervously*]: Sh! He will hear you and be angry.

RUFIO [*phlegmatically*]: The source of the Nile is out of his district, I expect.

CLEOPATRA: No: I will have my city named by nobody but my dear little sphinx, because it was in its arms that Caesar found me asleep. [*She languishes at Caesar then turns curtly to the priest*]. Go. I am a priestess, and have power to take your charge from you. [*The priest makes a reverence and goes out*]. Now let us call on the Nile all together. Perhaps he will rap on the table.

CAESAR: What! table rapping! Are such superstitions still believed in this year 707 of the Republic?

CLEOPATRA: It is no superstition: our priests learn lots of things from the tables. Is it not so, Apollodorus?

APOLLODORUS: Yes: I profess myself a converted man. When Cleopatra is priestess, Apollodorus is a devotee. Propose the conjuration.

CLEOPATRA: You must say with me "Send us thy voice, Father Nile."

ALL FOUR [*holding their glasses together before the idol*]: Send us thy voice, Father Nile.

[*The death cry of a man in mortal terror and agony answers them. Appalled, the men set down their glasses, and listen. Silence. The purple deepens in the sky. Caesar, glancing at Cleopatra, catches her pouring out her wine before the god, with gleaming eyes, and mute assurances of gratitude and worship. Apollodorus springs up and runs to the edge of the roof to peer down and listen.*]

CAESAR [*looking piercingly at Cleopatra*]: What was that?

CLEOPATRA [*petulantly*]: Nothing. They are beating some slave.

CAESAR: Nothing.

RUFIO: A man with a knife in him, I'll swear.

CAESAR [*rising*]: A murder!

APOLLODORUS [*at the back, waving his hand for silence*]: S-sh! Silence. Did you hear that?

CAESAR: Another cry?

APOLLODORUS [*returning to the table*]: No, a thud. Something fell on the beach, I think.

RUFIO [*grimly, as he rises*]: Something with bones in it, eh?

CAESAR [*shuddering*]: Hush, hush, Rufio.

[*He leaves the table and returns to the colonnade: Rufio following at his left elbow, and Apollodorus at the other side*].

CLEOPATRA [*still in her place at the table*]: Will you leave me, Caesar? Apollodorus: are you going?

APOLLODORUS: Faith, dearest Queen, my appetite is gone.

CAESAR: Go down to the courtyard, Apollodorus; and find out what has happened.

[*Apollodorus nods and goes out, making for the staircase by which Rufio ascended.*]

CLEOPATRA: Your soldiers have killed somebody, perhaps. What does it matter?

[*The murmur of a crowd rises from the beach below. Caesar and Rufio look at one another.*]

CAESAR: This must be seen to.

[*He is about to follow Apollodorus when Rufio stops him with a hand on his arm as Ftatateeta comes back by the far end of the roof, with dragging steps, a drowsy satiety in her eyes and in the corners of the bloodhound lips. For a moment Caesar suspects that she is drunk with wine. Not so Rufio: he knows well the red vintage that has inebriated her*].

RUFIO [*in a low tone*]: There is some mischief between these two.
FTATATEETA: The Queen looks again on the face of her servant.

[*Cleopatra looks at her for a moment with an exultant reflection of her murderous expression. Then she flings her arms round her; kisses her repeatedly and savagely; and tears off her jewels and heaps them on her. The two men turn from the spectacle to look at one another. Ftatateeta drags herself sleepily to the altar; kneels before Ra; and remains there in prayer. Caesar goes to Cleopatra, leaving Rufio in the colonnade.*]

CAESAR [*with searching earnestness*]: Cleopatra: what has happened?
CLEOPATRA [*in mortal dread of him, but with her utmost cajolery*]: Nothing, dearest Caesar. [*With sickly sweetness, her voice almost failing*] Nothing. I am innocent. [*She approaches him affectionately*] Dear Caesar: are you angry with me? Why do you look at me so? I have been here with you all the time. How can I know what has happened?
CAESAR [*reflectively*]: That is true.
CLEOPATRA [*greatly relieved, trying to caress him*]: Of course it is true. [*He does not respond to the caress*] You know it is true, Rufio.

[*The murmur without suddenly swells to a roar and subsides.*]

RUFIO: I shall know presently. [*He makes for the altar in the burly trot that serves him for a stride, and touches Ftatateeta on the shoulder*]. Now, mistress: I shall want you. [*He orders her, with a gesture, to go before him*].
FTATATEETA [*rising and glowering at him*]: My place is with the Queen.
CLEOPATRA: She has done no harm, Rufio.
CAESAR [*to Rufio*]: Let her stay.
RUFIO [*sitting down on the altar*]: Very well. Then my place is here too; and you can see what is the matter for yourself. The city is in a pretty uproar, it seems.
CAESAR [*with grave displeasure*]: Rufio: there is a time for obedience.
RUFIO: And there is a time for obstinacy. [*He folds his arms doggedly*].
CAESAR [*to Cleopatra*]: Send her away.

CLEOPATRA [*whining in her eagerness to propitiate him*]: Yes, I will. I will do whatever you ask me, Caesar, always, because I love you. Ftatateeta: go away.

FTATATEETA: The Queen's word is my will. I shall be at hand for the Queen's call. [*She goes out past Ra, as she came*].

RUFIO [*following her*]: Remember, Caesar, your bodyguard is also within call.

[*He follows her out*].

[*Cleopatra, presuming upon Caesar's submission to Rufio, leaves the table and sits down on the bench in the colonnade.*]

CLEOPATRA: Why do you allow Rufio to treat you so? You should teach him his place.

CAESAR: Teach him to be my enemy, and to hide his thoughts from me as you are now hiding yours?

CLEOPATRA [*her fears returning*]: Why do you say that, Caesar? Indeed, indeed, I am not hiding anything. You are wrong to treat me like this. [*She stifles a sob*]. I am only a child; and you turn into stone because you think some one has been killed. I cannot bear it. [*She purposely breaks down and weeps. He looks at her with profound sadness and complete coldness. She looks up to see what effect she is producing. Seeing that he is unmoved, she sits up, pretending to struggle with her emotion and to put it bravely away*]. But there: I know you hate tears: you shall not be troubled with them. I know you are not angry, but only sad; only I am so silly, I cannot help being hurt when you speak coldly. Of course you are quite right: it is dreadful to think of anyone being killed or even hurt; and I hope nothing really serious has—[*her voice dies away under his contemptuous penetration*].

CAESAR: What has frightened you into this? What have you done? [*A trumpet sounds on the beach below*]. Aha! that sounds like the answer.

CLEOPATRA [*sinking back trembling on the bench and covering her face with her hands*]: I have not betrayed you, Caesar: I swear it.

CAESAR: I know that. I have not trusted you. [*He turns from her, and is about to go out when Apollodorus and Britannus drag in Lucius Septimius to him. Rufio follows. Caesar shudders*]. Again, Pompey's murderer!

RUFIO: The town has gone mad, I think. They are for tearing the palace down and driving us into the sea straight away. We laid hold of this renegade in clearing them out of the courtyard.

CAESAR: Release him. [*They let go his arms*]. What has offended the citizens, Lucius Septimius?

LUCIUS: What did you expect, Caesar? Pothinus was a favorite of theirs.

CAESAR: What has happened to Pothinus? I set him free, here, not half an hour ago. Did they not pass him out?

LUCIUS: Ay, through the gallery arch sixty feet above ground, with three inches of steel in his ribs. He is as dead as Pompey. We are quits now, as to killing—you and I.

CAESAR [*shocked*]: Assassinated!—our prisoner, our guest! [*He turns reproachfully on Rufio*] Rufio—

RUFIO [*emphatically—anticipating the question*]: Whoever did it was a wise man and a friend of yours [*Cleopatra is greatly emboldened*]; but none of us had a hand in it. So it is no use to frown at me. [*Caesar turns and looks at Cleopatra*].

CLEOPATRA [*violently—rising*]: He was slain by order of the Queen of Egypt. I am not Julius Caesar the dreamer, who allows every slave to insult him. Rufio has said I did well: now the others shall judge me too. [*She turns to the others*]. This Pothinus sought to make me conspire with him to betray Caesar to Achillas and Ptolemy. I refused; and he cursed me and came privily to Caesar to accuse me of his own treachery. I caught him in the act; and he insulted me—me, the Queen! to my face. Caesar would not avenge me: he spoke him fair and set him free. Was I right to avenge myself? Speak, Lucius.

LUCIUS: I do not gainsay it. But you will get little thanks from Caesar for it.

CLEOPATRA: Speak, Apollodorus. Was I wrong?

APOLLODORUS: I have only one word of blame, most beautiful. You should have called upon me, your knight; and in a fair duel I should have slain the slanderer.

CLEOPATRA [*passionately*]: I will be judged by your very slave, Caesar. Britannus: speak. Was I wrong?

BRITANNUS: Were treachery, falsehood, and disloyalty left unpunished, society must become like an arena full of wild beasts, tearing one another to pieces. Caesar is in the wrong.

CAESAR [*with quiet bitterness*]: And so the verdict is against me, it seems.

CLEOPATRA [*vehemently*]: Listen to me, Caesar. If one man in all Alexandria can be found to say that I did wrong, I swear to have myself crucified on the door of the palace by my own slaves.

CAESAR: If one man in all the world can be found, now or forever, to know that you did wrong, that man will have either to conquer the world as I have, or be crucified by it [*The uproar in the streets again reaches them*]. Do you hear? These knockers at your gate are also believers in vengeance and in stabbing. You have slain their leader: it is right that they shall slay you. If you doubt it, ask your four counsellors here. And then in the name of that right [*he emphasizes the word with great scorn*] shall I not slay them for murdering their Queen, and be slain in my turn by their countrymen as the invader of their fatherland? Can Rome do less then than slay these slayers, too, to shew the world how Rome avenges her sons and her honor. And so, to the end of history, murder shall breed murder, always in the name of right and honor and peace, until the gods are tired of blood and create a race that can understand. [*Fierce uproar. Cleopatra becomes white with terror*]. Hearken, you who must not be insulted. Go near enough to catch their words: you will find them bitterer than the tongue of Pothinus. [*Loftily, wrapping himself up in an impenetrable dignity*] Let the Queen of Egypt now give her orders for vengeance, and take her measures for defence; for she has renounced Caesar. [*He turns to go*].

CLEOPATRA [*terrified, running to him and falling on her knees*]: You will not desert me, Caesar. You will defend the palace.

CAESAR: You have taken the powers of life and death upon you. I am only a dreamer.

CLEOPATRA: But they will kill me.

CAESAR: And why not?

CLEOPATRA: In pity—

CAESAR: Pity! What! has it come to this so suddenly, that nothing can save you now but pity? Did it save Pothinus?

[*She rises, wringing her hands, and goes back to the bench in despair. Apollodorus shews his sympathy with her by quietly posting himself behind the bench. The sky has by this time become the most vivid purple, and soon begins to change to a glowing pale orange, against which the colonnade and the great image shew darklier and darklier.*]

RUFIO: Caesar: enough of preaching. The enemy is at the gate.

CAESAR [*turning on him and giving way to his wrath*]: Ay; and what has held him baffled at the gate all these months? Was it my folly, as you deem it, or your wisdom? In this Egyptian Red Sea of blood, whose hand has held all your heads above the waves? [*Turning on Cleopatra*] And yet, when Caesar says to such an one, "Friend, go free," you, clinging for your little life to my sword, dare steal out and stab him in the back? And you, soldiers and gentlemen, and honest servants as you forget that you are, applaud this assassination, and say "Caesar is in the wrong." By the gods, I am tempted to open my hand and let you all sink into the flood.

CLEOPATRA [*with a ray of cunning hope*]: But, Caesar, if you do, you will perish yourself.

[*Caesar's eyes blaze.*]

RUFIO [*greatly alarmed*]: Now, by great Jove, you filthy little Egyptian rat, that is the very word to make him walk out alone into the city and leave us here to be cut to pieces. [*Desperately, to Caesar*] Will you desert us because we are a parcel of fools? I mean no harm by killing: I do it as a cat, by instinct. We are all dogs at your heels; but we have served you faithfully.

CAESAR [*relenting*]: Alas, Rufio, my son, my son: as dogs we are like to perish now in the streets.

APOLLODORUS [*at his post behind Cleopatra's seat*]: Caesar: what you say has an Olympian ring in it: it must be right; for it is fine art. But I am still on the side of Cleopatra. If we must die, she shall not want the devotion of a man's heart nor the strength of a man's arm.

CLEOPATRA [*sobbing*]: But I dont want to die.

CAESAR [*sadly*]: Oh, ignoble, ignoble!

LUCIUS [*coming forward between Caesar and Cleopatra*]: Hearken to me, Caesar. It may be ignoble; but I also mean to live as long as I can.

CAESAR: Well, my friend, you are likely to outlive Caesar. Is it any magic of mine, think you, that has kept your army and this whole city at bay for so long? Yesterday, what quarrel had they with me that they should risk their lives against me? But today we have flung them down their hero, murdered; and now every man of them is set upon clearing out this nest of assassins—for such we are and no more. Take courage then; and sharpen your sword. Pompey's head has fallen; and Caesar's head is ripe.

APOLLODORUS: Does Caesar despair?

CAESAR [*with infinite pride*]: He who has never hoped can never despair. Caesar, in good or bad fortune, looks his fate in the face.

LUCIUS: Look it in the face, then; and it will smile as it always has on Caesar.

CAESAR [*with involuntary haughtiness*]: Do you presume to encourage me?

LUCIUS: I offer you my services. I will change sides if you will have me.

CAESAR [*suddenly coming down to earth again, and looking sharply at him, divining that there is something behind the offer*]: What! At this point?

LUCIUS [*firmly*]: At this point.

RUFIO: Do you suppose Caesar is mad, to trust you?

LUCIUS: I do not ask him to trust me until he is victorious. I ask for my life, and for a command in Caesar's army. And since Caesar is a fair dealer, I will pay in advance.

CAESAR: Pay! How?

LUCIUS: With a piece of good news for you.

[*Caesar divines the news in a flash.*]

RUFIO: What news?

CAESAR [*with an elate and buoyant energy which makes Cleopatra sit up and stare*]: What news! What news, did you say, my son Rufio? The relief has arrived: what other news remains for us? Is it not so, Lucius Septimius? Mithridates of Pergamos is on the march.

LUCIUS: He has taken Pelusium.

CAESAR [*delighted*]: Lucius Septimius: you are henceforth my officer. Rufio: the Egyptians must have sent every soldier from the city to prevent Mithridates crossing the Nile. There is nothing in the streets now but mob—mob!

LUCIUS: It is so. Mithridates is marching by the great road to Memphis to cross above the Delta. Achillas will fight him there.

CAESAR [*all audacity*]: Achillas shall fight Caesar there. See, Rufio. [*He runs to the table; snatches a napkin; and draws a plan on it with his finger dipped in wine, whilst Rufio and Lucius Septimius crowd about him to watch, all looking closely, for the light is now almost gone*]: Here is the palace [*pointing to his plan*]: Here is the theatre. You [*to Rufio*] take twenty men and pretend to go by that street [*pointing it out*]; and whilst they are stoning you, out go the cohorts by this and this. My streets are right, are they, Lucius?

LUCIUS: Ay, that is the fig market—

CAESAR [*too much excited to listen to him*]: I saw them the day we arrived. Good! [*He throws the napkin on the table, and comes down again into the colonnade*]. Away, Britannus: tell Petronius that within an hour half our forces must take ship for the western lake. See to my horse and armor. [*Britannus runs out*] With the rest, *I* shall march round the lake and up the Nile to meet Mithridates. Away, Lucius; and give the word. [*Lucius hurries out after Britannus*]. Apollodorus: lend me your sword and your right arm for this campaign.

APOLLODORUS: Ay, and my heart and life to boot.

CAESAR [*grasping his hand*]: I accept both. [*Mighty handshake*]. Are you ready for work?

APOLLODORUS: Ready for Art—the Art of War [*he rushes out after Lucius, totally forgetting Cleopatra*].

RUFIO: Come! this is something like business.

CAESAR [*buoyantly*]: Is it not, my only son? [*He claps his hands. The slaves hurry in to the table*]. No more of this mawkish revelling: away with all this stuff: shut it out of my sight and be off with you. [*The slaves begin to remove the table; and the curtains are drawn, shutting in the colonnade*]. You understand about the streets, Rufio?

RUFIO: Ay, I think I do. I will get through them, at all events.

[*The bucina sounds busily in the courtyard beneath.*]

CAESAR: Come, then: we must talk to the troops and hearten them. You down to the beach: I to the courtyard. [*He makes for the staircase*].

CLEOPATRA [*rising from her seat, where she has been quite neglected all this time, and stretching out her hands timidly to him*]: Caesar.

CAESAR [*turning*]: Eh?

CLEOPATRA: Have you forgotten me?

CAESAR [*indulgently*]: I am busy now, my child, busy. When I return your affairs shall be settled. Farewell; and be good and patient.

[*He goes, preoccupied and quite indifferent. She stands with clenched fists, in speechless rage and humiliation.*]

RUFIO: That game is played and lost, Cleopatra. The woman always gets the worst of it.

CLEOPATRA [*haughtily*]: Go. Follow your master.

RUFIO [*in her ear, with rough familiarity*]: A word first. Tell your executioner that if Pothinus had been properly killed—in the throat—he would not have called out. Your man bungled his work.

CLEOPATRA [*enigmatically*]: How do you know it was a man?

RUFIO [*startled, and puzzled*]: It was not you: you were with us when it happened. [*She turns her back scornfully on him. He shakes his head, and draws the curtains to go out. It is now a magnificent moonlit night. The table has been removed. Ftatateeta is seen in the light of the moon and stars, again in prayer before the white altar-stone of Ra. Rufio starts; closes the curtains again softly; and says in a low voice to Cleopatra*] Was it she? with her own hand?

CLEOPATRA [*threateningly*]: Whoever it was, let my enemies beware of her. Look to it, Rufio, you who dare make the Queen of Egypt a fool before Caesar.

RUFIO [*looking grimly at her*]: I will look to it, Cleopatra.

[*He nods in confirmation of the promise, and slips out through the curtains, loosening his sword in its sheath as he goes*].

ROMAN SOLDIERS [*in the courtyard below*]: Hail, Caesar! Hail, hail!

[*Cleopatra listens. The bucina sounds again, followed by several trumpets.*]

CLEOPATRA [*wringing her hands and calling*]: Ftatateeta. Ftatateeta. It is dark; and I am alone. Come to me. [*Silence*] Ftatateeta. [*Louder*] Ftatateeta.

[*Silence. In a panic she snatches the cord and pulls the curtains apart*].

[*Ftatateeta is lying dead on the altar of Ra, with her throat cut. Her blood deluges the white stone.*]

Act V

[*High noon. Festival and military pageant on the esplanade before the palace. In the east harbor Caesar's galley, so gorgeously decorated that it seems to be rigged with flowers, is alongside the quay, close to the steps Apollodorus descended when he embarked with the carpet. A Roman guard is posted there in*] *charge of a gangway, whence a red floorcloth is laid down the middle of the esplanade, turning off to the north opposite the central gate in the palace front, which shuts in the esplanade on the south side. The broad steps of the gate, crowded with Cleopatra's ladies, all in their gayest attire, are like a flower garden. The façade is lined by her guard, officered by the same gallants to whom Bel Affris announced the coming of Caesar six months before in the old palace on the Syrian border. The north side is lined by Roman soldiers, with the townsfolk on tiptoe behind them, peering over their heads at the cleared esplanade, in which the officers stroll about, chatting. Among these are Belzanor and the Persian; also the centurion, vinewood cudgel in hand, battle worn, thick-booted, and much outshone, both socially and decoratively, by the Egyptian officers.*]

[*Apollodorus makes his way through the townsfolk and calls to the officers from behind the Roman line.*]

APOLLODORUS: Hullo! May I pass?

CENTURION: Pass Apollodorus the Sicilian there!

[*The soldiers let him through*].

BELZANOR: Is Caesar at hand?

APOLLODORUS: Not yet. He is still in the market place. I could not stand any more of the roaring of the soldiers! After half an hour of the enthusiasm of an army, one feels the need of a little sea air.

PERSIAN: Tell us the news. Hath he slain the priests?

APOLLODORUS: Not he. They met him in the market place with ashes on their heads and their gods in their hands. They placed the gods at his feet. The only one that was worth looking at was Apis: a miracle of gold and ivory work. By my advice he offered the chief priest two talents for it.

BELZANOR [*appalled*]: Apis the all-knowing for two talents! What said the chief Priest?

APOLLODORUS: He invoked the mercy of Apis, and asked for five.

BELZANOR: There will be famine and tempest in the land for this.

PERSIAN: Pooh! Why did not Apis cause Caesar to be vanquished by Achillas? Any fresh news from the war, Apollodorus?

APOLLODORUS: The little King Ptolemy was drowned.

BELZANOR: Drowned! How?

APOLLODORUS: With the rest of them. Caesar attacked them from three sides at once and swept them into the Nile. Ptolemy's barge sank.

BELZANOR: A marvellous man, this Caesar! Will he come soon, think you?

APOLLODORUS: He was settling the Jewish question when I left.

[*A flourish of trumpets from the north, and commotion among the townsfolk, announces the approach of Caesar.*]

PERSIAN: He has made short work of them. Here he comes.

[*He hurries to his post in front of the Egyptian lines*].

BELZANOR [*following him*]: Ho there! Caesar comes.

[*The soldiers stand at attention, and dress their lines. Apollodorus goes to the Egyptian line.*]

CENTURION [*hurrying to the gangway guard*]: Attention there! Caesar comes.

[*Caesar arrives in state with Rufio: Britannus following. The soldiers receive him with enthusiastic shouting.*]

CAESAR: I see my ship awaits me. The hour of Caesar's farewell to Egypt has arrived. And now, Rufio, what remains to be done before I go?

RUFIO [*at his left hand*]: You have not yet appointed a Roman governor for this province.

CAESAR [*looking whimsically at him, but speaking with perfect gravity*]: What say you to Mithridates of Pergamos, my reliever and rescuer, the great son of Eupator?

RUFIO: Why, that you will want him elsewhere. Do you forget that you have some three or four armies to conquer on your way home?

CAESAR: Indeed! Well, what say you to yourself?

RUFIO [*incredulously*]: I! I a governor! What are you dreaming of? Do you not know that I am only the son of a freedman?

CAESAR [*affectionately*]: Has not Caesar called you his son? [*Calling to the whole assembly*] Peace awhile there; and hear me.

THE ROMAN SOLDIERS: Hear .Caesar.

CAESAR: Hear the service, quality, rank and name of the Roman governor. By service, Caesar's shield; by quality, Caesar's friend; by rank, a Roman soldier. [*The Roman soldiers give a triumphant shout*]. By name, Rufio. [*They shout again*].

RUFIO [*kissing Caesar's hand*]: Ay: I am Caesar's shield; but of what use shall I be when I am no longer on Caesar's arm? Well, no matter—[*He becomes husky, and turns away to recover himself*].

CAESAR: Where is that British Islander of mine?

BRITANNUS [*coming forward on Caesar's right hand*]: Here, Caesar.

CAESAR: Who bade you, pray, thrust yourself into the battle of the Delta, uttering the barbarous cries of your native land, and affirming yourself a match for any four of the Egyptians, to whom you applied unseemly epithets?

BRITANNUS: Caesar: I ask you to excuse the language that escaped me in the heat of the moment.

CAESAR: And how did you, who cannot swim, cross the canal with us when we stormed the camp?

BRITANNUS: Caesar: I clung to the tail of your horse.

CAESAR: These are not the deeds of a slave, Britannus, but of a free man.

BRITANNUS: Caesar: I was born free.

CAESAR: But they call you Caesar's slave.

BRITANNUS: Only as Caesar's slave have I found real freedom.

CAESAR [moved]: Well said. Ungrateful that I am, I was about to set you free; but now I will not part from you for a million talents.

[He claps him friendly on the shoulder. Britannus, gratified, but a trifle shamefaced, takes his hand and kisses it sheepishly].

BELZANOR [to the Persian]: This Roman knows how to make men serve him.

PERSIAN: Ay: men too humble to become dangerous rivals to him.

BELZANOR: O subtle one! O cynic!

CAESAR [seeing Apollodorus in the Egyptian corner, and calling to him]: Apollodorus: I leave the art of Egypt in your charge. Remember: Rome loves art and will encourage it ungrudgingly.

APOLLODORUS: I understand, Caesar. Rome will produce no art itself; but it will buy up and take away whatever the other nations produce.

CAESAR: What! Rome produce no art! Is peace not an art? is war not an art? is government not an art? is civilization not an art? All these we give you in exchange for a few ornaments. You will have the best of the bargain. [Turning to Rufio] And now, what else have I to do before I embark? [Trying to recollect] There is something I cannot remember: what can it be? Well, well: it must remain undone: we must not waste this favorable wind. Farewell, Rufio.

RUFIO: Caesar: I am loth to let you go to Rome without your shield. There are too many daggers there.

CAESAR: It matters not: I shall finish my life's work on my way back; and then I shall have lived long enough. Besides: I have always disliked the idea of dying: I had rather be killed. Farewell.

RUFIO [with a sigh, raising his hands and giving Caesar up as incorrigible]: Farewell. [They shake hands].

CAESAR [waving his hand to Apollodorus]: Farewell, Apollodorus, and my friends, all of you. Aboard!

[The gangway is run out from the quay to the ship. As Caesar moves towards it, Cleopatra, cold and tragic, cunningly dressed in black, without ornaments or decoration of any kind, and thus making a striking figure among the brilliantly dressed bevy of ladies as she passes through it, comes from the palace and stands on the steps. Caesar does not see her until she speaks.]

CLEOPATRA: Has Cleopatra no part in this leavetaking?

CAESAR [*enlightened*]: Ah, I knew there was something. [*To Rufio*] How could you let me forget her, Rufio? [*Hastening to her*] Had I gone without seeing you, I should never have forgiven myself. [*He takes her hands, and brings her into the middle of the esplanade. She submits stonily*]. Is this mourning for me?

CLEOPATRA: No.

CAESAR [*remorsefully*]: Ah, that was thoughtless of me! It is for your brother.

CLEOPATRA: No.

CAESAR: For whom, then?

CLEOPATRA: Ask the Roman governor whom you have left us.

CAESAR: Rufio?

CLEOPATRA: Yes: Rufio. [*She points at him with deadly scorn*]. He who is to rule here in Caesar's name, in Caesar's way, according to Caesar's boasted laws of life.

CAESAR [*dubiously*]: He is to rule as he can, Cleopatra. He has taken the work upon him, and will do it in his own way.

CLEOPATRA: Not in your way, then?

CAESAR [*puzzled*]: What do you mean by my way?

CLEOPATRA: Without punishment. Without revenge. Without judgment.

CAESAR [*approvingly*]: Ay: that is the right way, the great way, the only possible way in the end. [*To Rufio*] Believe it, Rufio, if you can.

RUFIO: Why, I believe it, Caesar. You have convinced me of it long ago. But look you. You are sailing for Numidia today. Now tell me: if you meet a hungry lion there, you will not punish it for wanting to eat you?

CAESAR [*wondering what he is driving at*]: No.

RUFIO: Nor revenge upon it the blood of those it has already eaten.

CAESAR: No.

RUFIO: Nor judge it for its guiltiness.

CAESAR: No.

RUFIO: What, then, will you do to save your life from it?

CAESAR [*promptly*]: Kill it, man, without malice, just as it would kill me. What does this parable of the lion mean?

RUFIO: Why, Cleopatra had a tigress that killed men at her bidding. I thought she might bid it kill you some day. Well, had I not been Caesar's pupil, what pious things might I not have done to that tigress! I might have punished it. I might have revenged Pothinus on it.

CAESAR [*interjects*]: Pothinus!

RUFIO [*continuing*]: I might have judged it. But I put all these follies behind me; and, without malice, only cut its throat. And that is why Cleopatra comes to you in mourning.

CLEOPATRA [*vehemently*]: He has shed the blood of my servant Ftatateeta. On your head be it as upon his, Caesar, if you hold him free of it.

CAESAR [*energetically*]: On my head be it, then; for it was well done. Rufio: had you set yourself in the seat of the judge, and with hateful ceremonies and appeals to the gods handed that woman over to some hired executioner to be slain before the people in the name of justice, never again would I have touched your hand without a shudder. But this was natural slaying: I feel no horror at it.

[*Rufio, satisfied, nods at Cleopatra, mutely inviting her to mark that.*]

CLEOPATRA [*pettish and childish in her impotence*]: No: not when a Roman slays an Egyptian. All the world will now see how unjust and corrupt Caesar is.

CAESAR [*taking her hands coaxingly*]: Come: do not be angry with me. I am sorry for that poor Totateeta. [*She laughs in spite of herself*]. Aha! you are laughing. Does that mean reconciliation?

CLEOPATRA [*angry with herself for laughing*]: No, no, NO!! But it is so ridiculous to hear you call her Totateeta.

CAESAR: What! As much a child as ever, Cleopatra! Have I not made a woman of you after all?

CLEOPATRA: Oh, it is you who are a great baby: you make me seem silly because you will not behave seriously. But you have treated me badly; and I do not forgive you.

CAESAR: Bid me farewell.

CLEOPATRA: I will not.

CAESAR [*coaxing*]: I will send you a beautiful present from Rome.

CLEOPATRA [*proudly*]: Beauty from Rome to Egypt indeed! What can Rome give me that Egypt cannot give me?

APOLLODORUS: That is true, Caesar. If the present is to be really beautiful, I shall have to buy it for you in Alexandria.

CAESAR: You are forgetting the treasures for which Rome is most famous, my friend. You cannot buy them in Alexandria.

APOLLODORUS: What are they, Caesar?

CAESAR: Her sons. Come, Cleopatra: forgive me and bid me farewell; and I will send you a man, Roman from head to heel and Roman of the noblest; not old and ripe for the knife; not lean in the arms and cold in the heart; not hiding a bald head under his conqueror's laurels; not stooped with the weight of the world on his shoulders; but brisk and fresh, strong and young, hoping in the morning, fighting in the day, and revelling in the evening. Will you take such a one in exchange for Caesar?

CLEOPATRA [*palpitating*]: His name, his name?

CAESAR: Shall it be Mark Antony? [*She throws herself into his arms*].

RUFIO: You are a bad hand at a bargain, mistress, if you will swop Caesar for Antony.

CAESAR: So now you are satisfied.

CLEOPATRA: You will not forget.

CAESAR: I will not forget. Farewell: I do not think we shall meet again. Farewell.

[*He kisses her on the forehead. She is much affected and begins to sniff. He embarks*].

THE ROMAN SOLDIERS [*as he sets his foot on the gangway*]: Hail, Caesar; and farewell!

[*He reaches the ship and returns Rufio's wave of the hand.*]

APOLLODORUS [*to Cleopatra*]: No tears, dearest Queen: they stab your servant to the heart. He will return some day.

CLEOPATRA: I hope not. But I cant help crying, all the same.

[*She waves her handkerchief to Caesar; and the ship begins to move*].

THE ROMAN SOLDIERS [*drawing their swords and raising them in the air*]: Hail, Caesar!

Notes to *CAESAR AND CLEOPATRA*

Cleopatra's Cure for Baldness

For the sake of conciseness in a hurried situation I have made Cleopatra recommend rum. This, I am afraid, is an anachronism: the only real one in the play. To balance it, I give a couple of the remedies she actually believed in. They are quoted by Galen from Cleopatra's book on Cosmetic.

"For bald patches, powder red sulphuret of arsenic and take it up with oak gum, as much as it will bear. Put on a rag and apply, having soaped the place well first. I have mixed the above with a foam of nitre, and it worked well."

Several other receipts follow, ending with: "The following is the best of all, acting for fallen hairs, when applied with oil or pomatum; acts for falling off of eyelashes or for people getting bald all over. It is wonderful. Of domestic mice burnt, one part; of vine rag burnt, one part; of horse's teeth burnt, one part; of bear's grease one; of deer's marrow one; of reed bark one. To be pounded when dry, and mixed with plenty of honey til it gets the consistency of honey; then the bear's grease and marrow to be mixed (when melted), the medicine to be put in a brass flask, and the bald part rubbed til it sprouts."

Concerning these ingredients, my fellow-dramatist Gilbert Murray, who, as a Professor of Greek, has applied to classical antiquity the methods of high scholarship (my own method is pure divination), writes to me as follows: "Some of this I dont understand, and possibly Galen did not, as he quotes your heroine's own language. Foam of nitre is, I think, something like soapsuds. Reed bark is an odd expression. It might mean the outside membrane of a reed: I do not know what it ought to be called. In the burnt mice receipt I take it that you first mixed the solid powders with honey, and then added the grease. I expect Cleopatra preferred it because in most of the others you have to lacerate the skin, prick it, or rub it till it bleeds. I do not know what vine rag is. I translate literally."

Apparent Anachronisms

The only way to write a play which shall convey to the general public an impression of antiquity is to make the characters speak blank verse and abstain from reference to steam, telegraphy, or any of the material conditions of their existence. The more ignorant men are, the more convinced are they that their little parish and their little chapel is an apex to which civilization and philosophy has painfully struggled up the pyramid of time from a desert of savagery. Savagery, they think, became barbarism; barbarism became ancient civilization; ancient civilization became Pauline Christianity; Pauline Christianity became Roman Catholicism; Roman Catholicism became the Dark Ages; and the Dark Ages were finally enlightened by the Protestant instincts of the English race. The whole process is summed up as Progress with a capital P. And any elderly gentleman of Progressive temperament will testify that the improvement since he was a boy is enormous.

Now if we count the generations of Progressive elderly gentlemen since, say, Plato, and add together the successive enormous improvements to which each of them has testified, it will strike us at once as an unaccountable fact that the world, instead of having been improved in 67 generations out of all recognition, presents, on the whole, a rather less dignified appearance in Ibsen's *Enemy of the People* than in Plato's *Republic*. And in truth, the period of time covered by history is far too short to allow of any perceptible progress in the popular sense of Evolution of the Human Species. The notion that there has been any such Progress since Caesar's time (less than 20 centuries) is too absurd for discussion. All the savagery, barbarism, dark ages and the rest of it of which we have any record as existing in the past, exists at the present moment. A British carpenter or stonemason may point out that he gets twice as much money for his labor as his father did in the same trade, and that his suburban house, with its bath, its cottage piano, its drawing room suite, and its album of photographs, would have shamed the plainness of his grandmother's. But the descendants of feudal barons, living in squalid lodgings on a salary of fifteen shillings a week instead of in castles on princely revenues, do not congratulate the world on the change. Such changes, in fact, are not to the point. It has been known, as far back as our records go, that man running wild in the woods is different from man kennelled in a city slum; that a dog seems to understand a shepherd better than a hewer of wood and drawer of water can understand an astronomer; and that breeding, gentle nurture, and luxurious food and shelter will produce a kind of man with whom the common laborer is socially incompatible. The same thing is true of horses and dogs. Now there is clearly room for great changes in the world by increasing the percentage of individuals who are carefully bred and gently nurtured, even to finally making the most of every man and woman born. But that possibility existed in the days of the Hittites as much as it does today. It does not give the slightest real support to the common assumption that the civilized contemporaries of the Hittites were unlike their civilized descendants today.

This would appear the tritest commonplace if it were not that the ordinary citizen's ignorance of the past combines with his idealization of the present to mislead and flatter him. Our latest book on the new railway across Asia describes the dulness of the Siberian farmer and the vulgar pursepride of the Siberian man of business without the least consciousness that the string of contemptuous instances given might have been saved by writing simply "Farmers and provincial plutocrats in Siberia are exactly what they are in England." The latest professor descanting on the civilization of the Western Empire in the fifth century feels bound to assume, in the teeth of his own researches, that the Christian was one sort of animal and the Pagan another. It might as well be assumed as indeed it generally is assumed by implication, that a murder committed with a poisoned arrow is different from a murder committed with a Mauser rifle. All such notions are illusions. Go back to the first syllable of recorded time, and there you will find your Christian and your Pagan, your yokel and your poet, helot and hero, Don Quixote and Sancho, Tamino and Papageno, Newton and bushman unable to count eleven, all alive and contemporaneous, and all convinced that they are the heirs of all the ages and the privileged recipients of THE truth (all others damnable heresies), just as you have them today, flourishing in countries each of which is the bravest and best that ever sprang at Heaven's command from out the azure main.

Again, there is the illusion of "increased command over Nature," meaning that cotton is cheap and that ten miles of country road on a bicycle have replaced four on foot. But even if man's increased command over Nature included any increased command over himself (the only sort of command relevant to his evolution into a higher being), the fact remains that it is only by running away from the increased command over Nature to country places where Nature is still in primitive command over Man that he can recover from the effects of the smoke, the stench, the foul air, the overcrowding, the racket, the ugliness, the dirt which the cheap cotton costs us. If manufacturing activity means Progress, the town must be more advanced than the country; and the field laborers and village artisans of today must be much less changed from servants of Job than the proletariat of modern London from the proletariat of Caesar's Rome. Yet the cockney proletarian is so inferior to the village laborer that it is only by steady recruiting from the country that London is kept alive. This does not seem as if the change since Job's time were Progress in the popular sense: quite the reverse. The common stock of discoveries in physics has accumulated a little: that is all.

One more illustration. Is the Englishman prepared to admit that the American is his superior as a human being? I ask this question because the scarcity of labor in America relatively to the demand for it has led to a development of machinery there, and a consequent "increase of command over Nature" which makes many of our English methods appear almost medieval to the up-to-date Chicagoan. This means that the American has an advantage over the Englishman of exactly the same nature that the Englishman has over the contemporaries of Cicero. Is the Englishman prepared to draw the same conclusion in both cases? I think not. The American, of course, will draw it cheerfully; but I must then ask him whether, since a modern negro has a greater "command over Nature" than Washington had, we are also to accept the conclusion, involved in his former one, that humanity has progressed from Washington to the *fin de siècle* negro.

Finally, I would point out that if life is crowned by its success and devotion in industrial organization and ingenuity, we had better worship the ant and the bee (as moralists urge us to do in our childhood), and humble ourselves before the arrogance of the birds of Aristophanes.

My reason then for ignoring the popular conception of Progress in Caesar and Cleopatra is that there is no reason to suppose that any Progress has taken place since their time. But even if I shared the popular delusion, I do not see that I could have made any essential difference in the play. I can only imitate humanity as I know it. Nobody knows whether Shakespeare thought that ancient Athenian joiners, weavers, or bellows menders were any different from Elizabethan ones; but it is quite certain that he could not have made them so, unless, indeed, he had played the literary man and made Quince say, not "Is all our company here?" but "Bottom: was not that Socrates that passed us at the Piraeus with Glaucon and Polemarchus on his way to the house of Kephalus?" And so on.

Cleopatra

Cleopatra was only sixteen when Caesar went to Egypt; but in Egypt sixteen is a riper age than it is in England. The childishness I have ascribed to her, as far as it is childishness of character and not lack of experience, is not a matter of years. It may be observed in our own climate at the present day in many women of fifty. It is a mistake to suppose that the difference between wisdom and folly has anything to do with the difference between physical age and physical youth. Some women are younger at seventy than most women at seventeen.

It must be borne in mind, too, that Cleopatra was a queen, and was therefore not the typical Greek-cultured, educated Egyptian lady of her time. To represent her by any such type would be as absurd as to represent George IV by a type founded on the attainments of Sir Isaac Newton. It is true that an ordinarily well educated Alexandrian girl of her time would no more have believed bogey stories about the Romans than the daughter of a modern Oxford professor would believe them about the Germans (though, by the way, it is possible to talk great nonsense at Oxford about foreigners when we are at war with them). But I do not feel bound to believe that Cleopatra was well educated. Her father, the illustrious Flute Blower, was not at all a parent of the Oxford professor type. And Cleopatra was chip of the old block.

Britannus

I find among those who have read this play in manuscript a strong conviction that an ancient Briton could not possibly have been like a modern one. I see no reason to adopt this curious view. It is true that the Roman and Norman conquests must have for a time disturbed the normal British type produced by the climate. But Britannus, born before these events, represents the unadulterated Briton who fought Caesar and impressed Roman observers much as we should expect the ancestors of Mr. Podsnap to impress the cultivated Italians of their time.

I am told that it is not scientific to treat national character as a product of climate. This only shews the wide difference between common knowledge and the intellectual game called science. We have men of exactly the same stock, and speaking the same language, growing in Great Britain, in Ireland, and in America. The result is three of the most distinctly marked nationalities under the sun. Racial characteristics are quite another matter. The difference between a Jew and a Gentile has nothing to do with the difference between an Englishman and a German. The characteristics of Britannus are local characteristics, not race characteristics. In an ancient Briton they would, I take it, be exaggerated, since modern Britain, disforested, drained, urbanified and consequently cosmopolized, is presumably less characteristically British than Caesar's Britain.

And again I ask does anyone who, in the light of a competent knowledge of his own age, has studied history from contemporary documents, believe that 67 generations of promiscuous marriage have made any appreciable difference in the human fauna of these isles? Certainly I do not.

Julius Caesar

As to Caesar himself, I have purposely avoided the usual anachronism of going to Caesar's books, and concluding that the style is the man. That is only true of authors who have the specific literary genius, and have practised long enough to attain complete self-expression in letters. It is not true even on these conditions in an age when literature is conceived as a game of style, and not as a vehicle of self-expression by the author. Now Caesar was an amateur stylist writing books of travel and campaign histories in a style so impersonal that the authenticity of the later volumes is disputed. They reveal some of his qualities just as the Voyage of a Naturalist Round the World reveals some of Darwin's, without expressing his private personality. An Englishman reading them would say that Caesar was a man of great common sense and good taste, meaning thereby a man without originality or moral courage.

In exhibiting Caesar as a much more various person than the historian of the Gallic wars, I hope I have not been too much imposed on by the dramatic illusion to which all great men owe part of their reputation and some of the whole of it. I admit that reputations gained in war are specially questionable. Able civilians taking up the profession of arms, like Caesar and Cromwell, in middle age, have snatched all its laurels from opponent commanders bred to it, apparently because capable persons engaged in military pursuits are so scarce that the existence of two of them at the same time in the same hemisphere is extremely rare. The capacity of any conqueror is therefore more likely than not to be an illusion produced by the incapacity of his adversary. At all events, Caesar might have won his battles without being wiser than Charles XII or Nelson or Joan of Arc, who were, like most modern "self-made" millionaires, half-witted geniuses, enjoying the worship accorded by all races to certain forms of insanity. But Caesar's victories were only advertisements for an eminence that would never have become popular without them. Caesar is greater off the battle field than on it. Nelson off his quarterdeck was so quaintly out of the question that when his head was injured at the battle of the Nile, and his conduct became for some years openly scandalous, the difference was not important enough to be noticed. It may, however, be said that peace hath her illusory reputations no less than war. And it is certainly true that in civil life mere capacity for work—the power of killing a dozen secretaries under you, so to speak, as a life-or-death courier kills horses—enables men with common ideas and superstitions to distance all competitors in the strife of political ambition. It was this power of work that astonished Cicero as the most prodigious of Caesar's gifts, as it astonished later observers in Napoleon before it wore him out. How if Caesar were nothing but a Nelson and a Gladstone combined! a prodigy of vitality without any special quality of mind! nay, with ideas that were worn out before he was born, as Nelson's and Gladstone's were! I have considered that possibility too, and rejected it. I cannot cite all the stories about Caesar which seem to me to shew that he was genuinely original; but let me at least point out that I have been careful to attribute nothing but originality to him. Originality gives a man an air of frankness, generosity, and magnanimity by enabling him to estimate the value of truth, money, or success in any particular instance quite independently of convention and moral generalization. He therefore will not, in the ordinary Treasury bench fashion, tell a lie which everybody knows to be a lie (and consequently expects him as a matter of good taste to tell.) His lies are not found out: they pass for candors. He understands the paradox of money, and gives it away when he can get most for it: in other words, when its value is least, which is just when a common man tries hardest to get it. He knows that the real moment of success is not the moment apparent to the crowd. Hence, in order to produce an impression of complete disinterestedness and magnanimity, he has only to act with entire selfishness; and this is perhaps the only sense in which a man can be said to be *naturally* great. It is in this sense that I have represented Caesar as great. Having virtue, he has no need of goodness. He is neither forgiving, frank, nor generous, because a man who is too great to resent has nothing to forgive; a man who says things that other people are afraid to say need be no more frank than Bismarck was; and there is no generosity in giving things you do not want to people of whom you intend to make use. This distinction between virtue and goodness is not understood in England: hence the poverty of our drama in heroes. Our stage attempts at them are mere goody-goodies. Goodness, in its popular British sense of self-denial, implies that man is vicious by nature, and that supreme goodness is supreme martyrdom. Not sharing that pious opinion, I have not given countenance to it in any of my plays. In this I follow the precedent of the ancient myths, which represent the hero as vanquishing his enemies, not in fair fight, but with enchanted sword, superequine horse and magical invulnerability, the possession of which, from the vulgar moralistic point of view, robs his exploits of any merit whatever.

As to Caesar's sense of humor, there is no more reason to assume that he lacked it than to assume that he was deaf or blind. It is said that on the occasion of his assassination by a conspiracy of moralists (it is always your moralist who makes assassination a duty, on the scaffold or off it), he defended himself until the good Brutus struck him, when he exclaimed "What! you too, Brutus!" and disdained further fight. If this be true, he must have been an incorrigible comedian. But even if we waive this story, or accept the traditional sentimental interpretation of it, there is still abundant evidence of his lightheartedness and adventurousness. Indeed it is clear from his whole history that what has been called his ambition was an instinct for exploration. He had much more of Columbus and Franklin in him than of Henry V.

However, nobody need deny Caesar a share, at least, of the qualities I have attributed to him. All men, much more Julius Caesars, possess all qualities in some degree. The really interesting question is whether I am right in assuming that the way to produce an impression of greatness is by exhibiting a man, not as mortifying his nature by doing his duty, in the manner which our system of putting little men into great positions (not having enough great men in our influential families to go round) forces us to inculcate, but as simply doing what he naturally wants to do. For this raises the question whether our world has not been wrong in its moral theory for the last 2,500 years or so. It must be a constant puzzle to many of us that the Christian era, so excellent in its intentions, should have been practically such a very discreditable episode in the history of the race. I doubt if this is altogether due to the vulgar and sanguinary sensationalism of our religious legends, with their substitution of gross physical torments and public executions for the passion of humanity. Islam, substituting voluptuousness for torment (a merely superficial difference, it is true) has done no better. It may have been the failure of Christianity to emancipate itself from expiatory theories of moral responsibility, guilt, innocence, reward, punishment, and the rest of it, that baffled its intention of changing the world. But these are bound up in all philosophies of creation as opposed to cosmism. They may therefore be regarded as the price we pay for popular religion.

Luigi Pirandello (1867–1936)

SIX CHARACTERS IN SEARCH
OF AN AUTHOR

translated by Edward Storer

THE CHARACTERS

SIX CHARACTERS

THE FATHER
THE MOTHER
THE STEPDAUGHTER
THE SON
MADAME PACE
THE BOY ⎫
THE CHILD ⎭   *These two do not speak.*

ACTORS

THE MANAGER
LEADING LADY
LEADING MAN
SECOND LADY
L'INGÉNUE
JUVENILE LEAD

OTHER ACTORS *and* ACTRESSES
PROMPTER
MANAGER'S SECRETARY
PROPERTY MAN
MACHINIST
DOORKEEPER
SCENE SHIFTERS

[*Daytime: the stage of a theater.*]

SOURCE: Reprinted from *Naked Masks: Five Plays* by Luigi Pirandello, edited by Eric Bentley, with the permission of E. P. Dutton & Co., Inc. Copyright 1922, 1952 by E. P. Dutton & Co., Inc. Renewal, 1950 in the names of Stefano, Fausto and Lietta Pirandello. Reprinted from the Dutton Paperback Edition.

773

Act 1

[*N.B. The Comedy is without acts or scenes. The performance is interrupted once, without the curtain being lowered, when* THE MANAGER *and the chief characters withdraw to arrange the scenario. A second interruption of the action takes place when, by mistake the stage hands let the curtain down.*

The spectators will find the curtain raised and the stage as it usually is during the daytime. It will be half dark, and empty, so that from the beginning the public may have the impression of an impromptu performance.

PROMPTER'S *box and a small table and chair for* THE MANAGER.

Two other small tables and several chairs scattered about as during rehearsals.

The ACTORS *and* ACTRESSES *of the company enter from the back of the stage: First one, then another, then two together: nine or ten in all. They are about to rehearse a Pirandello play:* Mixing It Up. *Some of the company move off towards their dressing rooms. The* PROMPTER, *who has the "book" under his arm, is waiting for* THE MANAGER *in order to begin the rehearsal.*

The ACTORS *and* ACTRESSES, *some standing, some sitting, chat and smoke. One perhaps reads a paper; another cons his part.*

Finally, THE MANAGER *enters and goes to the table prepared for him. His* SECRETARY *brings him his mail, through which he glances. The* PROMPTER *takes his seat, turns on a light, and opens the "book."*]

THE MANAGER [*throwing a letter down on the table*]: I can't see. [*to* PROPERTY MAN] Let's have a little light, please!

PROPERTY MAN: Yes sir, yes, at once. [*A light comes down on to the stage.*]

THE MANAGER [*clapping his hands*]: Come along! Come along! Second act of *Mixing it Up.* [*Sits down.*]

[*The* ACTORS *and* ACTRESSES *go from the front of the stage to the wings, all except the three who are to begin the rehearsal.*]

THE PROMPTER [*reading the "book"*]: "Leo Gala's house. A curious room serving as dining-room and study."

THE MANAGER [*to* PROPERTY MAN]: Fix up the old red room.

PROPERTY MAN [*noting it down*]: Red set. All right!

THE PROMPTER [*continuing to read from the "book"*]: "Table already laid and writing desk with books and papers. Bookshelves. Exit rear to Leo's bedroom. Exit left to kitchen. Principal exit to right."

THE MANAGER [*energetically*]: Well, you understand: The principal exit over there; here, the kitchen. [*turning to* ACTOR *who is to play the part of Socrates*] You make your entrances and exits here. [*to* PROPERTY MAN] The baize doors at the rear, and curtains.

PROPERTY MAN [*noting it down*]: Right-o!

PROMPTER [*reading as before*]: "When the curtain rises, Leo Gala, dressed in cook's cap and apron is busy beating an egg in a cup. Philip, also dressed as a cook, is beating another egg. Guido Venanzi is seated and listening."

LEADING MAN [*to* MANAGER]: Excuse me, but must I absolutely wear a cook's cap?

THE MANAGER [*annoyed*]: I imagine so. It says so there anyway. [*pointing to the "book"*]

LEADING MAN: But it's ridiculous!

THE MANAGER: Ridiculous? Ridiculous? Is it my fault if France won't send us any more good comedies, and we are reduced to putting on Pirandello's works where nobody understands anything, and where the author plays the fool with us all? [*The* ACTORS *grin.* THE MANAGER *goes to* LEADING MAN *and shouts.*] Yes sir, you put on the cook's cap and beat eggs. Do you suppose that with all this egg-beating business you are on an ordinary stage? Get that out of your head. You represent the shell of the eggs you are beating! [*laughter and comments among the* ACTORS] Silence! and listen to my explanations, please! [*to* LEADING MAN]: "The empty form of reason without the fullness of instinct, which is blind" —You stand for reason, your wife is instinct. It's a mixing up of the parts, according to which you who act your own part become the puppet of yourself. Do you understand?

LEADING MAN: I'm hanged if I do.

THE MANAGER: Neither do I. But let's get on with it. It's sure to be a glorious failure anyway. [*confidentially*]: But I say, please face three-quarters. Otherwise, what with the abstruseness of the dialogue, and the public that won't be able to hear you, the whole thing will go to hell. Come on! come on!

PROMPTER: Pardon sir, may I get into my box? There's a bit of a draught.

THE MANAGER: Yes, yes, of course!

[*At this point, the* DOORKEEPER *has entered from the stage door and advances towards* THE MANAGER'S *table, taking off his braided cap. During this manoeuver, the* SIX CHARACTERS *enter, and stop by the door at back of stage, so that when the* DOORKEEPER *is about to announce their coming to* THE MANAGER, *they are already on the stage. A tenuous light surrounds them, almost as if irradiated by them—the faint breath of their fantastic reality.*

This light will disappear when they come forward towards the ACTORS. *They preserve, however, something of the dream lightness in which they seem almost suspended; but this does not detract from the essential reality of their forms and expressions.*]

[*He who is known as* THE FATHER *is a man of about 50: hair, reddish in color, thin at the temples; he is not bald, however; thick moustaches, falling over his still fresh mouth, which often opens in an empty and uncertain smile. He is fattish, pale; with an especially wide forehead. He has blue, oval-shaped eyes, very clear and piercing. Wears light trousers and a dark jacket. He is alternatively mellifluous and violent in his manner.*]

[THE MOTHER *seems crushed and terrified as if by an intolerable weight of shame and abasement. She is dressed in modest black and wears a thick widow's veil of crêpe. When she lifts this, she reveals a wax-like face. She always keeps her eyes downcast.*]

[THE STEPDAUGHTER *is dashing, almost impudent, beautiful. She wears mourning too, but with great elegance. She shows contempt for the timid half-frightened manner of the wretched* BOY *(14 years old, and also dressed in black); on the other hand, she displays a lively tenderness for her little sister,* THE CHILD *(about four), who is dressed in white, with a black silk sash at the waist.*]

[THE SON *(22) tall, severe in his attitude of contempt for* THE FATHER, *supercilious and indifferent to* THE MOTHER. *He looks as if he had come on the stage against his will.*]

DOORKEEPER [*cap in hand*]: Excuse me, sir. . . .

THE MANAGER [*rudely*]: Eh? What is it?

DOORKEEPER [*timidly*]: These people are asking for you, sir.

THE MANAGER [*furious*]: I am rehearsing, and you know perfectly well no one's allowed to come in during rehearsals! [*turning to the* CHARACTERS]: Who are you, please? What do you want?

THE FATHER [*coming forward a little, followed by the others, who seem embarrassed*]: As a matter of fact . . . we have come here in search of an author. . . .

THE MANAGER [*half angry, half amazed*]: An author? What author?

THE FATHER: Any author, sir.

THE MANAGER: But there's no author here. We are not rehearsing a new piece.

THE STEPDAUGHTER [*vivaciously*]: So much the better, so much the better! We can be your new piece.

AN ACTOR [*coming forward from the others*]: Oh, do you hear that?

THE FATHER [*to* STEPDAUGHTER]: Yes, but if the author isn't here . . . [*to* MANAGER] . . . unless you would be willing. . . .

THE MANAGER: You are trying to be funny.

THE FATHER: No, for Heaven's sake, what are you saying? We bring you a drama, sir.

THE STEPDAUGHTER: We may be your fortune.

THE MANAGER: Will you oblige me by going away? We haven't time to waste with mad people.

THE FATHER [*mellifluously*]: Oh sir, you know well that life is full of infinite absurdities, which, strangely enough, do not even need to appear plausible, since they are true.

THE MANAGER: What the devil is he talking about?

THE FATHER: I say that to reverse the ordinary process may well be considered a madness: that is, to create credible situations, in order that they may appear true. But permit me to observe that if this be madness, it is the sole *raison d'être* of your profession, gentlemen. [*The* ACTORS *look hurt and perplexed*]

THE MANAGER [*getting up and looking at him*]: So our profession seems to you one worthy of madmen then?

THE FATHER: Well, to make seem true that which isn't true . . . without any need . . . for a joke as it were . . . Isn't that your mission, gentlemen: to give life to fantastic characters on the stage?

THE MANAGER [*interpreting the rising anger of the* COMPANY]: But I would beg you to believe, my dear sir, that the profession of the comedian is a noble one. If today, as things go, the playwrights give us stupid comedies to play and puppets to represent instead of men, remember we are proud to have given life to immortal works here on these very boards! [*The* ACTORS, *satisfied, applaud their* MANAGER.]

THE FATHER [*interrupting furiously*]: Exactly, perfectly, to living beings more alive than those who breathe and wear clothes: being less real perhaps, but truer! I agree with you entirely. [*The* ACTORS *look at one another in amazement.*]

THE MANAGER: But what do you mean? Before, you said . . .

THE FATHER: No, excuse me, I meant it for you, sir, who were crying out that you had no time to lose with madmen, while no one better than yourself knows that nature uses the instrument of human fantasy in order to pursue her high creative purpose.

THE MANAGER: Very well—but where does all this take us?

THE FATHER: Nowhere! It is merely to show you that one is born to life in many forms, in many shapes, as tree, or as stone, as water, as butterfly, or as woman. So one may also be born a character in a play.

THE MANAGER [*with feigned comic dismay*]: So you and these other friends of yours have been born characters?

THE FATHER: Exactly, and alive as you see! [MANAGER *and* ACTORS *burst out laughing*]

THE FATHER [*hurt*]: I am sorry you laugh, because we carry in us a drama, as you can guess from this woman here, veiled in black.

THE MANAGER [*losing patience at last and almost indignant*]: Oh, chuck it! Get away please! Clear out of here! [*to* PROPERTY MAN] For Heaven's sake, turn them out!

THE FATHER [*resisting*]: No, no, look here, we. . . .

THE MANAGER [*roaring*]: We come here to work, you know.

LEADING ACTOR: One cannot let oneself be made such a fool of.

THE FATHER [*determined, coming forward*]: I marvel at your incredulity, gentlemen. Are you not accustomed to seeing the characters created by an author spring to life in yourselves and face each other? Just because there is no "book" [*pointing to the* PROMPTER'S *box*] which contains us, you refuse to believe. . . .

THE STEPDAUGHTER [*advances towards* MANAGER, *smiling and coquettish*]: Believe me, we are really six most interesting characters, sir; side-tracked however.

THE FATHER: Yes, that is the word! [*to* MANAGER *all at once*] In the sense, that is, that the author who created us alive no longer wished, or was no longer able, materially to put us into a work of art. And this was a real crime, sir; because he who has had the luck to be born a character can laugh even at death. He cannot die. The man, the writer, the instrument of the creation will die, but his creation does not die. And to live for ever, it does not need to have extraordinary gifts or to be able to work wonders. Who was Sancho Panza? Who was Don Abbondio? Yet they live eternally because—live germs as they were—they had the fortune to find a fecundating matrix, a fantasy which could raise and nourish them: make them live forever!

THE MANAGER: That is quite all right. But what do you want here, all of you?

THE FATHER: We want to live.

THE MANAGER [*ironically*]: For Eternity?

THE FATHER: No, sir, only for a moment . . . in you.

AN ACTOR: Just listen to him!

LEADING LADY: They want to live, in us! . . .

JUVENILE LEAD [*pointing to the* STEPDAUGHTER]: I've no objection, as far as that one is concerned!

THE FATHER: Look here! Look here! The comedy has to be made. [*to the* MANAGER] But if you and your actors are willing, we can soon concert it among ourselves.

THE MANAGER [*annoyed*]: But what do you want to concert? We don't go in for concerts here. Here we play dramas and comedies!

THE FATHER: Exactly! That is just why we have come to you.

THE MANAGER: And where is the "book"?

THE FATHER: It is in us! [*The* ACTORS *laugh.*] The drama is in us, and we are the drama. We are impatient to play it. Our inner passion drives us on to this.

THE STEPDAUGHTER [*disdainful, alluring, treacherous, full of impudence*]: My passion, sir! Ah, if you only knew! My passion for him! [*Points to the* FATHER *and makes a pretence of embracing him. Then she breaks out into a loud laugh.*]

THE FATHER [*angrily*]: Behave yourself! And please don't laugh in that fashion.

THE STEPDAUGHTER: With your permission, gentlemen, I, who am a two months' orphan, will show you how I can dance and sing. [*Sings and then dances* Prenez garde à Tchou-Tchin-Tchou]

Les chinois sont un peuple malin,
De Shanghaî à Pékin,

Ils ont mis des écriteaux partout:
Prenez garde à Tchou-Tchin-Tchou.

ACTORS and ACTRESSES: Bravo! Well done! Tip-top!

THE MANAGER: Silence! This isn't a café concert, you know! [*turning to the* FATHER *in consternation*] Is she mad?

THE FATHER: Mad? No, she's worse than mad.

THE STEPDAUGHTER [*to* MANAGER]: Worse? Worse? Listen! Stage this drama for us at once! Then you will see that at a certain moment I . . . when this little darling here . . . [*takes the* CHILD *by the hand and leads her to the* MANAGER] Isn't she a dear? [*takes her up and kisses her*] Darling! Darling! [*puts her down again and adds feelingly*] Well, when God suddenly takes this dear little child away from that poor mother there; and this imbecile here [*seizing hold of the* BOY *roughly and pushing him forward*] does the stupidest things, like the fool he is, you will see me run away. Yes, gentlemen, I shall be off. But the moment hasn't arrived yet. After what has taken place between him and me [*indicates the* FATHER *with a horrible wink*] I can't remain any longer in this society, to have to witness the anguish of this mother here for that fool . . . [*Indicates the* SON] Look at him! Look at him! See how indifferent, how frigid he is, because he is the legitimate son. He despises me, despises him [*pointing to the* BOY], despises this baby here; because . . . we are bastards. [*goes to the* MOTHER *and embraces her*] And he doesn't want to recognize her as his mother —she who is the common mother of us all. He looks down upon her as if she were only the mother of us three bastards. Wretch! [*She says all this very rapidly, excitedly. At the word "bastards" she raises her voice, and almost spits out the final "Wretch!"*]

THE MOTHER [*to the* MANAGER, *in anguish*]: In the name of these two little children, I beg you . . . [*She grows faint and is about to fall.*] Oh God!

THE FATHER [*coming forward to support her as do some of the* ACTORS]: Quick, a chair, a chair for this poor widow!

THE ACTORS: Is it true? Has she really fainted?

THE MANAGER: Quick, a chair! Here!

[*One of the* ACTORS *brings a chair, the others proffer assistance. The* MOTHER *tries to prevent the* FATHER *from lifting the veil which covers her face.*]

THE FATHER: Look at her! Look at her!

THE MOTHER: No, stop; stop it please!

THE FATHER [*raising her veil*]: Let them see you!

THE MOTHER [*rising and covering her face with her hands, in desperation*]: I beg you, sir, to prevent this man from carrying out his plan which is loathsome to me.

THE MANAGER [*dumbfounded*]: I don't understand at all. What is the situation? Is this lady your wife? [*to the* FATHER]

THE FATHER: Yes, gentlemen: my wife!

THE MANAGER: But how can she be a widow if you are alive? [*The* ACTORS *find relief for their astonishment in a loud laugh.*]

THE FATHER: Don't laugh! Don't laugh like that, for Heaven's sake. Her drama lies just here in this: she has had a lover, a man who ought to be here.

THE MOTHER [*with a cry*]: No! No!

THE STEPDAUGHTER: Fortunately for her, he is dead. Two months ago as I said. We are mourning, as you see.

THE FATHER: He isn't here you see, not because he is dead. He isn't here— look at her a moment and you will understand—because her drama isn't a drama of the love of two men for whom she was incapable of feeling anything except possibly a little gratitude—gratitude not for me but for the other. She isn't a woman, she is a mother, and her drama—powerful, sir, I assure you—lies, as a matter of fact, all in these four children she has had by two men.

THE MOTHER: I had them? Have you got the courage to say that I wanted them? [*to the* COMPANY] It was his doing. It was he who gave me that other man, who forced me to go away with him.

THE STEPDAUGHTER: It isn't true.

THE MOTHER [*startled*]: Not true, isn't it?

THE STEPDAUGHTER: No, it isn't true, it just isn't true.

THE MOTHER: And what can you know about it?

THE STEPDAUGHTER: It isn't true. Don't believe it. [*to* MANAGER] Do you know why she says so? For that fellow there. [*indicates the* SON] She tortures herself, destroys herself on account of the neglect of that son there; and she wants him to believe that if she abandoned him when he was only two years old, it was because he [*indicates the* FATHER] made her do so.

THE MOTHER [*vigorously*]: He forced me to it, and I call God to witness it. [*to the* MANAGER] Ask him [*indicates the* FATHER] if it isn't true. Let him speak. You [*to* DAUGHTER] are not in a position to know anything about it.

THE STEPDAUGHTER: I know you lived in peace and happiness with my father while he lived. Can you deny it?

THE MOTHER: No, I don't deny it . . .

THE STEPDAUGHTER: He was always full of affection and kindness for you. [*to the* BOY, *angrily*] It's true, isn't it? Tell them! Why don't you speak, you little fool?

THE MOTHER: Leave the poor boy alone. Why do you want to make me appear ungrateful, daughter? I don't want to offend your father. I have answered him that I didn't abandon my house and my son through any fault of mine, nor from any wilful passion.

THE FATHER: It is true. It was my doing.

LEADING MAN [*to the* COMPANY]: What a spectacle!

LEADING LADY: We are the audience this time.

JUVENILE LEAD: For once, in a way.

THE MANAGER [*beginning to get really interested*]: Let's hear them out. Listen!

THE SON: Oh yes, you're going to hear a fine bit now. He will talk to you of the Demon of Experiment.

THE FATHER: You are a cynical imbecile. I've told you so already a hundred times. [*to the* MANAGER] He tries to make fun of me on account of this expression which I have found to excuse myself with.

THE SON [*with disgust*]: Yes, phrases! phrases!

THE FATHER: Phrases! Isn't everyone consoled when faced with a trouble or fact he doesn't understand, by a word, some simple word, which tells us nothing and yet calms us?

THE STEPDAUGHTER: Even in the case of remorse. In fact, especially then.

THE FATHER: Remorse? No, that isn't true. I've done more than use words to quieten the remorse in me.

THE STEPDAUGHTER: Yes, there was a bit of money too. Yes, yes, a bit of money. There were the hundred lire he was about to offer me in payment, gentlemen. . . . [*sensation of horror among the* ACTORS]

THE SON [*to the* STEPDAUGHTER]: This is vile.

THE STEPDAUGHTER: Vile? There they were in a pale blue envelope on a little mahogany table in the back of Madame Pace's shop. You know Madam Pace—one of those ladies who attract poor girls of good family into their ateliers, under the pretext of their selling *robes et manteaux.*

THE SON: And he thinks he has bought the right to tyrannize over us all with those hundred lire he was going to pay; but which, fortunately— note this, gentlemen—he had no chance of paying.

THE STEPDAUGHTER: It was a near thing, though, you know! [*laughs ironically*]

THE MOTHER [*protesting*]: Shame, my daughter, shame!

THE STEPDAUGHTER: Shame indeed! This is my revenge! I am dying to live that scene. . . . The room . . . I see it . . . Here is the window with the mantels exposed, there the divan, the lookingglass, a screen, there in front of the window the little mahogany table with the blue envelope containing one hundred lire. I see it. I see it. I could take hold of it. . . . But you, gentlemen, you ought to turn your backs now: I am almost nude, you know. But I don't blush: I leave that to him. [*indicating* FATHER]

THE MANAGER: I don't understand this at all.

THE FATHER: Naturally enough. I would ask you, sir, to exercise your authority a little here, and let me speak before you believe all she is trying to blame me with. Let me explain.

THE STEPDAUGHTER: Ah yes, explain it in your own way.

THE FATHER: But don't you see that the whole trouble lies here. In words, words. Each one of us has within him a whole world of things, each man of us his own special world. And how can we ever come to an understanding if I put in the words I utter the sense and value of things as I see them; while you who listen to me must inevitably translate them according to the conception of things each one of you has within himself. We think we understand each other, but we never really do. Look here! This woman [*indicating the* MOTHER] takes all my pity for her as a specially ferocious form of cruelty.

THE MOTHER: But you drove me away.

THE FATHER: Do you hear her? I drove her away! She believes I really sent her away.

THE MOTHER: You know how to talk, and I don't; but, believe me sir [*to* MANAGER], after he had married me . . . who knows why? . . . I was a poor insignificant woman. . . .

THE FATHER: But, good Heaven! it was just for your humility that I married you. I loved this simplicity in you. [*He stops when he sees she makes signs to contradict him, opens his arms wide in sign of desperation, seeing how hopeless it is to make himself understood.*] You see she denies it. Her mental deafness, believe me, is phenomenal, the limit [*touches his forehead*]: deaf, deaf, mentally deaf! She had plenty of feeling. Oh yes, a good heart for the children; but the brain—deaf, to the point of desperation—!

THE STEPDAUGHTER: Yes, but ask him how his intelligence has helped us.

THE FATHER: If we could see all the evil that may spring from good, what should we do? [*At this point the* LEADING LADY *who is biting her lips with rage at seeing the* LEADING MAN *flirting with the* STEPDAUGHTER, *comes forward and says to the* MANAGER:]

LEADING LADY: Excuse me, but are we going to rehearse today?

MANAGER: Of course, of course; but let's hear them out.

JUVENILE LEAD: This is something quite new.

L'INGÉNUE: Most interesting!

LEADING LADY: Yes, for the people who like that kind of thing. [*casts a glance at* LEADING MAN]

THE MANAGER [*to* FATHER]: You must please explain yourself quite clearly. [*Sits down*]

THE FATHER: Very well then: listen! I had in my service a poor man, a clerk, a secretary of mine, full of devotion, who became friends with her. [*Indicating the* MOTHER] They understood one another, were kindred souls in fact, without, however, the least suspicion of any evil existing. They were incapable even of thinking of it.

THE STEPDAUGHTER: So he thought of it—for them!

THE FATHER: That's not true. I meant to do good to them—and to myself, I confess, at the same time. Things had come to the point that I could not say a word to either of them without their making a mute appeal, one to the other, with their eyes. I could see them silently asking each other how I was to be kept in countenance, how I was to be kept quiet. And this, believe me, was just about enough of itself to keep me in a constant rage, to exasperate me beyond measure.

THE MANAGER: And why didn't you send him away then—this secretary of yours?

THE FATHER: Precisely what I did, sir. And then I had to watch this poor woman drifting forlornly about the house like an animal without a master, like an animal one has taken in out of pity.

THE MOTHER: Ah yes! . . .

THE FATHER [*suddenly turning to the* MOTHER]: It's true about the son anyway, isn't it?

THE MOTHER: He took my son away from me first of all.

THE FATHER: But not from cruelty. I did it so that he should grow up healthy and strong by living in the country.

THE STEPDAUGHTER [*pointing to him ironically*]: As one can see.

THE FATHER [*quickly*]: Is it my fault if he has grown up like this? I sent him to a wet nurse in the country, a peasant, as *she* did not seem to me strong enough, though she is of humble origin. That was, anyway, the reason I married her. Unpleasant all this may be, but how can it be helped? My mistake possibly, but there we are! All my life I have had these confounded aspirations towards a certain moral sanity. [*At this point the* STEPDAUGHTER bursts out into a noisy laugh.] Oh, stop it! Stop it! I can't stand it.

THE MANAGER: Yes, please stop it, for Heaven's sake.

THE STEPDAUGHTER: But imagine moral sanity from him, if you please—the client of certain ateliers like that of Madame Pace!

THE FATHER: Fool! That is the proof that I am a man! This seeming contradiction, gentlemen, is the strongest proof that I stand here a live man before you. Why, it is just for this very incongruity in my nature that I have had to suffer what I have. I could not live by the side of that woman [*indicating the* MOTHER] any longer; but not so much for the boredom she inspired me with as for the pity I felt for her.

THE MOTHER: And so he turned me out—.

THE FATHER: —well provided for! Yes, I sent her to that man, gentlemen . . . to let her go free of me.

THE MOTHER: And to free himself.

THE FATHER: Yes, I admit it. It was also a liberation for me. But great evil has come of it. I meant well when I did it; and I did it more for her sake than mine. I swear it. [*Crosses his arms on his chest; then turns suddenly to the* MOTHER] Did I ever lose sight of you until that other man carried you off to another town, like the angry fool he was? And on account of my pure interest in you . . . my pure interest, I repeat, that had no base motive in it . . . I watched with the tenderest concern the new family that grew up around her. She can bear witness to this. [*points to the* STEPDAUGHTER]

THE STEPDAUGHTER: Oh yes, that's true enough. When I was a kiddie, so so high, you know, with plaits over my shoulders and knickers longer than my skirts, I used to see him waiting outside the school for me to come out. He came to see how I was growing up.

THE FATHER: This is infamous, shameful!

THE STEPDAUGHTER: No. Why?

THE FATHER: Infamous! Infamous! [*Then excitedly to* MANAGER, *explaining*] After she [*indicating* MOTHER] went away, my house seemed suddenly empty. She was my incubus, but she filled my house. I was like a dazed fly alone in the empty rooms. This boy here [*indicating the* SON] was educated away from home, and when he came back, he seemed to me to be no more mine. With no mother to stand between him and me, he grew up entirely for himself, on his own, apart, with no tie of intellect or affection binding him to me. And then—strange but true—I was driven, by curiosity at first and then by some tender sentiment, towards her family, which had come into being through my will. The thought of her began gradually to fill up the emptiness I felt all around me. I wanted to know if she were happy in living out the simple daily duties of life. I wanted to think of her as fortunate and happy because far away from the complicated torments of my spirit. And so, to have proof of this, I used to watch that child coming out of school.

THE STEPDAUGHTER: Yes, yes. True. He used to follow me in the street and smiled at me, waved his hand, like this. I would look at him with interest, wondering who he might be. I told my mother, who guessed at once. [*The* MOTHER *agrees with a nod.*] Then she didn't want to send me to school for some days; and when I finally went back, there he was again—looking so ridiculous—with a paper parcel in his hands. He came close to me, caressed me, and drew out a fine straw hat from the parcel, with a bouquet of flowers—all for me!

THE MANAGER: A bit discursive this, you know!

THE SON [*contemptuously*]: Literature! Literature!

THE FATHER: Literature indeed! This is life, this is passion!

THE MANAGER: It may be, but it won't act.

THE FATHER: I agree. This is only the part leading up. I don't suggest this should be staged. She [*pointing to the* STEPDAUGHTER], as you see, is no longer the flapper with plaits down her back—.

THE STEPDAUGHTER: —and the knickers showing below the skirt!

THE FATHER: The drama is coming now, sir; something new, complex, most interesting.

THE STEPDAUGHTER: As soon as my father died. . . .

THE FATHER: —there was absolute misery for them. They came back here, unknown to me. Through her stupidity! [*pointing to the* MOTHER] It is true she can barely write her own name; but she could anyhow have got her daughter to write to me that they were in need. . . .

THE MOTHER: And how was I to divine all this sentiment in him?

THE FATHER: That is exactly your mistake, never to have guessed any of my sentiments.

THE MOTHER: After so many years apart, and all that had happened. . . .

THE FATHER: Was it my fault if that fellow carried you away? It happened quite suddenly; for after he had obtained some job or other, I could find no trace of them; and so, not unnaturally, my interest in them dwindled. But the drama culminated unforeseen and violent on their return, when I was impelled by my miserable flesh that still lives. . . . Ah! what misery, what wretchedness is that of the man who is alone and disdains debasing *liaisons!* Not old enough to do without women, and not young enough to go and look for one without shame. Misery? It's worse than misery; it's a horror; for no woman can any longer give him love; and when a man feels this. . . . One ought to do without, you say? Yes, yes, I know. Each of us when he appears before his fellows is clothed in a certain dignity. But every man knows what unconfessable things pass within the secrecy of his own heart. One gives way to the temptation, only to rise from it again, afterwards, with a great eagerness to reestablish one's dignity, as if it were a tombstone to place on the grave of one's shame, and a monument to hide and sign the memory of our weaknesses. Everybody's in the same case. Some folks haven't the courage to say certain things, that's all!

THE STEPDAUGHTER: All appear to have the courage to do them though.

THE FATHER: Yes, but in secret. Therefore, you want more courage to say these things. Let a man but speak these things out, and folks at once label him a cynic. But it isn't true. He is like all the others, better indeed, because he isn't afraid to reveal with the light of the intelligence the red shame of human bestiality on which most men close their eyes so as not to see it. Woman—for example, look at her case! She turns tantalizing inviting glances on you. You seize her. No sooner does she feel herself in your grasp than she closes her eyes. It is the sign of her mission, the sign by which she says to man:. "Blind yourself, for I am blind."

THE STEPDAUGHTER: Sometimes she can close them no more: when she no longer feels the need of hiding her shame to herself, but dry-eyed and dispassionately, sees only that of the man who has blinded himself without love. Oh, all these intellectual complications make me sick, disgust me—all this philosophy that uncovers the beast in man, and then seeks to save him, excuse him . . . I can't stand it, sir. When a man seeks to "simplify" life bestially, throwing aside every relic of humanity, every chaste aspiration, every pure feeling, all sense of ideality, duty, modesty, shame . . . then nothing is more revolting and nauseous than a certain kind of remorse—crocodiles' tears, that's what it is.

THE MANAGER: Let's come to the point. This is only discussion.

THE FATHER: Very good, sir! But a fact is like a sack which won't stand up when it is empty. In order that it may stand up, one has to put into it the reason and sentiment which have caused it to exist. I couldn't possibly know that after the death of that man, they had decided to return here, that they were in misery, and that she [*pointing to the* MOTHER] had gone to work as a modiste, and at a shop of the type of that of Madame Pace.

THE STEPDAUGHTER: A real high-class modiste, you must know, gentlemen. In appearance, she works for the leaders of the best society; but she arranges matters so that these elegant ladies serve her purpose . . . without prejudice to other ladies who are . . . well . . . only so so.

THE MOTHER: You will believe me, gentlemen, that it never entered my mind that the old hag offered me work because she had her eye on my daughter.

THE STEPDAUGHTER: Poor mamma! Do you know, sir, what that woman did when I brought her back the work my mother had finished? She would point out to me that I had torn one of my frocks, and she would give it back to my mother to mend. It was I who paid for it, always I; while this poor creature here believed she was sacrificing herself for me and these two children here, sitting up at night sewing Madame Pace's robes.

THE MANAGER: And one day you met there. . . .

THE STEPDAUGHTER: Him, him. Yes, sir, an old client. There's a scene for you to play! Superb!

THE FATHER: She, the Mother arrived just then. . . .

THE STEPDAUGHTER [*treacherously*]: Almost in time!

THE FATHER [*crying out*]: No, in time! in time! Fortunately I recognized her . . . in time. And I took them back home with me to my house. You can imagine now her position and mine: she, as you see her; and I who cannot look her in the face.

THE STEPDAUGHTER: Absurd! How can I possibly be expected—after that—to be a modest young miss, a fit person to go with his confounded aspirations for "a solid moral sanity"?

THE FATHER: For the drama lies all in this—in the conscience that I have, that each one of us has. We believe this conscience to be a single thing, but it is many-sided. There is one for this person, and another for that. Diverse consciences. So we have this illusion of being one person for all, of having a personality that is unique in all our acts. But it isn't true. We perceive this when, tragically perhaps, in something we do, we are, as it were, suspended, caught up in the air on a kind of hook. Then we perceive that all of us was not in that act, and that it would be an atrocious injustice to judge us by that action alone, as if all our existence were summed up in that one deed. Now do you understand the perfidy of this girl? She surprised me in a place where she ought not to have known me, just as I could not exist for her; and she now seeks to attach to me a reality such as I could never suppose I should have to assume for her in a shameful and fleeting moment of my life. I feel this above all else. And the drama, you will see, acquires a tremendous value from this point. Then there is the position of the others . . . his . . . [*indicating the* SON]

THE SON [*shrugging his shoulders scornfully*]: Leave me alone! I don't come into this.

THE FATHER: What? You don't come into this?

THE SON: I've got nothing to do with it, and don't want to have; because you know well enough I wasn't made to be mixed up in all this with the rest of you.

THE STEPDAUGHTER: We are only vulgar folk! He is the fine gentleman. You may have noticed, Mr. Manager, that I fix him now and again with a look of scorn while he lowers his eyes—for he knows the evil he has done me.

THE SON [*scarcely looking at her*]: I?

THE STEPDAUGHTER: You! you! I owe my life on the streets to you. Did you or did you not deny us, with your behavior, I won't say the intimacy of home, but even that mere hospitality which makes guests feel at their ease? We were intruders who had come to disturb the kingdom of your legitimacy. I should like to have you witness, Mr. Manager, certain scenes between him and me. He says I have tyrannized over everyone. But it was just his behavior which made me insist on the reason for which I had come into the house—this reason he calls "vile"—into his house, with my mother, who is his mother too. And I came as mistress of the house.

THE SON: It's easy for them to put me always in the wrong. But imagine, gentlemen, the position of a son, whose fate it is to see arrive one day at his home a young woman of impudent bearing, a young woman who inquires for his father, with whom who knows what business she has. This young man has then to witness her return bolder than ever, accompanied by that child there. He is obliged to watch her treat his father in an equivocal and confidential manner. She asks money of him in a way that lets one suppose he must give it her, *must*, do you understand, because he has every obligation to do so.

THE FATHER: But I have, as a matter of fact, this obligation. I owe it to your mother.

THE SON: How should I know? When had I ever seen or heard of her? One day there arrive with her [*indicating* STEPDAUGHTER] that lad and this baby here. I am told: "This is *your* mother too, you know." I divine from her manner [*indicating* STEPDAUGHTER *again*] why it is they have come home. I had rather not say what I feel and think about it. I shouldn't even care to confess to myself. No action can therefore be hoped for from me in this affair. Believe me, Mr. Manager, I am an "unrealized" character, dramatically speaking; and I find myself not at all at ease in your company. Leave me out of it, I beg you.

THE FATHER: What? It is just because you are so that . . .

THE SON: How do you know what I am like? When did you ever bother your head about me?

THE FATHER: I admit it. I admit it. But isn't that a situation in itself? This aloofness of yours which is so cruel to me and to your mother, who returns home and sees you almost for the first time grown up, who doesn't recognize you but knows you are her son . . . [*pointing out the* MOTHER *to the* MANAGER] See, she's crying!

THE STEPDAUGHTER [*angrily, stamping her foot*]: Like a fool!

THE FATHER [*indicating* STEPDAUGHTER]: She can't stand him, you know. [*then referring again to the* SON]: He says he doesn't come into the affair, whereas he is really the hinge of the whole action. Look at that lad who is always clinging to his mother, frightened and humiliated. It is on account of this fellow here. Possibly his situation is the most painful of all. He feels himself a stranger more than the others. The poor little chap feels mortified, humiliated at being brought into a home out of charity as it were. [*in confidence*]—: He is the image of his father. Hardly talks at all. Humble and quiet.

THE MANAGER: Oh, we'll cut him out. You've no notion what a nuisance boys are on the stage . . .

THE FATHER: He disappears soon, you know. And the baby too. She is the first to vanish from the scene. The drama consists finally in this: when that mother re-enters my house, her family born outside of it, and shall we say superimposed on the original, ends with the death of the little girl, the tragedy of the boy and the flight of the elder daughter. It cannot go on, because it is foreign to its surroundings. So after much torment, we three remain: I, the mother, that son. Then, owing to the disappearance of that extraneous family, we too find ourselves strange to one another. We find we are living in an atmosphere of mortal desolation which is the revenge, as he [*indicating* SON] scornfully said of the Demon of Experiment, that unfortunately hides in me. Thus, sir, you see when faith is lacking, it becomes impossible to create certain states of happiness, for we lack the necessary humility. Vaingloriously, we try to substitute ourselves for this faith, creating thus for the rest of the world a reality which we believe after their fashion, while, actually, it doesn't exist. For each one of us has his own reality to be respected before God, even when it is harmful to one's very self.

THE MANAGER: There is something in what you say. I assure you all this interests me very much. I begin to think there's the stuff for a drama in all this, and not a bad drama either.

THE STEPDAUGHTER [*coming forward*]: When you've got a character like me.

THE FATHER [*shutting her up, all excited to learn the decision of the* MANAGER]: You be quiet!

THE MANAGER [*reflecting, heedless of interruption*]: It's new . . . hem . . . yes . . .

THE FATHER: Absolutely new!

THE MANAGER: You've got a nerve though, I must say, to come here and fling it at me like this . . .

THE FATHER: You will understand, sir, born as we are for the stage . . .

THE MANAGER: Are you amateur actors then?

THE FATHER: No, I say born for the stage, because . . .

THE MANAGER: Oh, nonsense. You're an old hand, you know.

THE FATHER: No sir, no. We act that rôle for which we have been cast, that rôle which we are given in life. And in my own case, passion itself, as usually happens, becomes a trifle theatrical when it is exalted.

THE MANAGER: Well, well, that will do. But you see, without an author . . . I could give you the address of an author if you like . . .

THE FATHER: No, no. Look here! You must be the author.

THE MANAGER: I? What are you talking about?

THE FATHER: Yes, you, you! Why not?

THE MANAGER: Because I have never been an author: that's why.

THE FATHER: Then why not turn author now? Everybody does it. You don't want any special qualities. Your task is made much easier by the fact that we are all here alive before you . . .

THE MANAGER: It won't do.

THE FATHER: What? When you see us live our drama . . .

THE MANAGER: Yes, that's all right. But you want someone to write it.

THE FATHER: No, no. Someone to take it down, possibly, while we play it, scene by scene! It will be enough to sketch it out at first, and then try it over.

THE MANAGER: Well . . . I am almost tempted. It's a bit of an idea. One might have a shot at it.

THE FATHER: Of course. You'll see what scenes will come out of it. I can give you one, at once . . .

THE MANAGER: By Jove, it tempts me. I'd like to have a go at it. Let's try it out. Come with me to my office. [*turning to the* ACTORS] You are at liberty for a bit, but don't stop out of the theater for long. In a quarter of an hour, twenty minutes, all back here again! [*to the* FATHER] We'll see what can be done. Who knows if we don't get something really extraordinary out of it?

THE FATHER: There's no doubt about it. They [*indicating the* CHARACTERS] had better come with us too, hadn't they?

THE MANAGER: Yes, yes. Come on! come on! [*moves away and then turning to the* ACTORS] Be punctual, please! [MANAGER *and the* SIX CHARACTERS *cross the stage and go off. The other* ACTORS *remain, looking at one another in astonishment.*]

LEADING MAN: Is he serious? What the devil does he want to do?

JUVENILE LEAD: This is rank madness.

THIRD ACTOR: Does he expect to knock up a drama in five minutes?

JUVENILE LEAD: Like the improvisers!

LEADING LADY: If he thinks I'm going to take part in a joke like this . . .

JUVENILE LEAD: I'm out of it anyway.

FOURTH ACTOR: I should like to know who they are. [*alludes to* CHARACTERS]

THIRD ACTOR: What do you suppose? Madmen or rascals!

JUVENILE LEAD: And he takes them seriously!

L'INGENUE: Vanity! He fancies himself as an author now.

LEADING MAN: It's absolutely unheard of. If the stage has come to this . . . well I'm . . .

FIFTH ACTOR: It's rather a joke.

THIRD ACTOR: Well, we'll see what's going to happen next.

[*Thus talking, the* ACTORS *leave the stage; some going out by the little door at the back; others retiring to their dressing-rooms. The curtain remains up. The action of the play is suspended for twenty minutes*]

Act II

[*The stage call-bells ring to warn the company that the play is about to begin again.*]

THE STEPDAUGHTER [*comes out of the* MANAGER'S *office along with the* CHILD *and the* BOY. *As she comes out of the office, she cries*]: Nonsense! Nonsense! Do it yourselves! I'm not going to mix myself up in this mess. [*turning to the* CHILD *and coming quickly with her on to the stage*] Come on, Rosetta, let's run!

[THE BOY *follows them slowly, remaining a little behind and seeming perplexed*]

THE STEPDAUGHTER [*stops, bends over the* CHILD *and takes the latter's face between her hands*]: My little darling! You're frightened, aren't you? You don't know where we are, do you?[*pretending to reply to a question of the* CHILD] What is the stage? It's a place, baby, you know, where people play at being serious, a place where they act comedies. We've got to act a comedy now, dead serious, you know; and you're in it also, little one. [*embraces her, pressing the little head to her breast, and rocking the* CHILD *for a moment*] Oh darling, darling, what a horrid comedy you've got to play! What a wretched part they've found for you! A garden . . . a fountain . . . look . . . just suppose, kiddie, it's here. Where, you say? Why, right here in the middle. It's all pretence you know. That's the trouble, my pet: it's all make-believe here. It's better to imagine it though, because if they fix it up for you, it'll only be painted cardboard, painted cardboard for the rockery, the water, the plants . . . Ah, but I think a baby like this one would sooner have a make-believe fountain than a real one, so she could play with it. What a joke it'll be for the others! But for you, alas! not quite such a joke: you who are real, baby dear, and really play by a real fountain that is big and green and beautiful, with ever so many bamboos around it that are reflected in the water, and a whole lot of little ducks swimming about . . . No, Rosetta, no, your mother doesn't bother about you on account of that wretch of a son there. I'm in the devil of a temper, and as for that lad . . . [*seizes* BOY *by the arm to force him to take one of his hands out of his pockets*] What have you got there? What are you hiding? [*pulls his hand out of his pocket, looks into it and catches the glint of a revolver*] Ah, where did you get this? [THE BOY, *very pale in the face, looks at her, but does not answer.*] Idiot! If I'd been in your place, instead of killing myself, I'd have shot one of those two, or both of them: father and son.

[THE FATHER *enters from the office, all excited from his work.* THE MANAGER *follows him.*]

THE FATHER: Come on, come on, dear! Come here for a minute! We've arranged everything. It's all fixed up.
THE MANAGER [*also excited*]: If you please, young lady, there are one or two points to settle still. Will you come along?
THE STEPDAUGHTER [*following him towards the office*]: Ouff! what's the good, if you've arranged everything.

[THE FATHER, MANAGER *and* STEPDAUGHTER *go back into the office again (off) for a moment. At the same time,* THE SON, *followed by* THE MOTHER, *comes out.*]

THE SON [*looking at the three entering office*]: Oh this is fine, fine! And to think I can't even get away!

[THE MOTHER *attempts to look at him, but lowers her eyes immediately when he turns away from her. She then sits down.* THE BOY *and* THE CHILD *approach her. She casts a glance again at the* SON, *and speaks with humble tones, trying to draw him into conversation.*]

THE MOTHER: And isn't my punishment the worst of all? [*Then seeing from the* SON'S *manner that he will not bother himself about her*] My God! Why are you so cruel? Isn't it enough for one person to support all this torment? Must you then insist on others seeing it also?
THE SON [*half to himself, meaning the* MOTHER *to hear, however*]: And they want to put it on the stage! If there was at least a reason for it! He thinks he has got at the meaning of it all. Just as if each one of us in every circumstance of life couldn't find his own explanation of it! [*pauses*] He

complains he was discovered in a place where he ought not to have been seen, in a moment of his life which ought to have remained hidden and kept out of the reach of that convention which he has to maintain for other people. And what about my case? Haven't I had to reveal what no son ought ever to reveal: how father and mother live and are man and wife for themselves quite apart from that idea of father and mother which we give them? When this idea is revealed, our life is then linked at one point only to that man and that woman; and as such it should shame them, shouldn't it?

[THE MOTHER *hides her face in her hands. From the dressing-rooms and the little door at the back of the stage the* ACTORS *and* STAGE MANAGER *return, followed by the* PROPERTY MAN, *and the* PROMPTER. *At the same moment,* THE MANAGER *comes out of his office, accompanied by the* FATHER *and the* STEP-DAUGHTER.]

THE MANAGER: Come on, come on, ladies and gentlemen! Heh! you there, machinist!

MACHINIST: Yes, sir?

THE MANAGER: Fix up the white parlor with the floral decorations. Two wings and a drop with a door will do. Hurry up!

[THE MACHINIST *runs off at once to prepare the scene, and arranges it while* THE MANAGER *talks with the* STAGE MANAGER, *the* PROPERTY MAN, *and the* PROMPTER *on matters of detail*].

THE MANAGER [*to* PROPERTY MAN]: Just have a look, and see if there isn't a sofa or divan in the wardrobe . . .

PROPERTY MAN: There's the green one.

THE STEPDAUGHTER: No, no! Green won't do. It was yellow, ornamented with flowers—very large! and most comfortable!

PROPERTY MAN: There isn't one like that.

THE MANAGER: It doesn't matter. Use the one we've got.

THE STEPDAUGHTER: Doesn't matter? It's most important!

THE MANAGER: We're only trying it now. Please don't interfere. [*to* PROPERTY MAN] See if we've got a shop window—long and narrowish.

THE STEPDAUGHTER: And the little table! The little mahogany table for the pale blue envelope!

PROPERTY MAN [*to* MANAGER]: There's that little gilt one.

THE MANAGER: That'll do fine.

THE FATHER: A mirror.

THE STEPDAUGHTER: And the screen! We must have a screen. Otherwise how can I manage?

PROPERTY MAN: That's all right, Miss. We've got any amount of them.

THE MANAGER [*to the* STEPDAUGHTER]: We want some clothes pegs too, don't we?

THE STEPDAUGHTER: Yes, several, several!

THE MANAGER: See how many we've got and bring them all.

PROPERTY MAN: All right!

[*The* PROPERTY MAN *hurries off to obey his orders. While he is putting the things in their places, the* MANAGER *talks to the* PROMPTER *and then with the* CHARACTERS *and the* ACTORS.]

THE MANAGER [*to* PROMPTER]: Take your seat. Look here: this is the outline of the scenes, act by act. [*hands him some sheets of paper*] And now I'm going to ask you to do something out of the ordinary.

PROMPTER: Take it down in shorthand?

THE MANAGER [*pleasantly surprised*]: Exactly! Can you do shorthand?

PROMPTER: Yes, a little.

MANAGER: Good! [*turning to a stage hand*] Go and get some paper from my office, plenty, as much as you can find.

[*The* STAGE HAND *goes off, and soon returns with a handful of paper which he gives to the* PROMPTER.]

THE MANAGER [*to* PROMPTER]: You follow the scenes as we play them, and try and get the points down, at any rate the most important ones. [*then addressing the* ACTORS] Clear the stage, ladies and gentlemen! Come over here [*pointing to the Left*] and listen attentively.

LEADING LADY: But, excuse me, we . . .

THE MANAGER [*guessing her thought*]: Don't worry! You won't have to improvise.

LEADING MAN: What have we to do then?

THE MANAGER: Nothing. For the moment you just watch and listen. Everybody will get his part written out afterwards. At present we're going to try the thing as best we can. They're going to act now.

THE FATHER [*as if fallen from the clouds into the confusion of the stage*]: We? What do you mean, if you please, by a rehearsal?

THE MANAGER: A rehearsal for them. [*points to the* ACTORS]

THE FATHER: But since we are the characters . . .

THE MANAGER: All right: "characters" then, if you insist on calling yourselves such. But here, my dear sir, the characters don't act. Here the actors do the acting. The characters are there, in the "book"—[*pointing towards* PROMPTER'S *box*] when there is a "book"!

THE FATHER: I won't contradict you; but excuse me, the actors aren't the characters. They want to be, they pretend to be, don't they? Now if these gentlemen here are fortunate enough to have us alive before them . . .

THE MANAGER: Oh this is grand! You want to come before the public yourselves then?

THE FATHER: As we are . . .

THE MANAGER: I can assure you it would be a magnificent spectacle!

LEADING MAN: What's the use of us here anyway then?

THE MANAGER: You're not going to pretend that you can act? It makes me laugh! [*The* ACTORS *laugh.*] There, you see, they are laughing at the notion. But, by the way, I must cast the parts. That won't be difficult. They cast themselves. [*To the* SECOND LADY LEAD] You play the Mother. [*To the* FATHER] We must find her a name.

THE FATHER: Amalia, sir.

THE MANAGER: But that is the real name of your wife. We don't want to call her by her real name.

THE FATHER: Why ever not, if it is her name? . . . Still, perhaps, if that lady must . . . [*makes a slight motion of the hand to indicate the* SECOND LADY LEAD] I see this woman here [*means the* MOTHER] as Amalia. But do as you like. [*gets more and more confused*] I don't know what to say to you. Already, I begin to hear my own words ring false, as if they had another sound . . .

THE MANAGER: Don't you worry about it. It'll be our job to find the right tones. And as for her name, if you want her Amalia, Amalia it shall be; and if you don't like it, we'll find another! For the moment though, we'll call the characters in this way: [*to* JUVENILE LEAD] You are the Son; [*to the* LEADING LADY] You naturally are the Stepdaughter . . .

THE STEPDAUGHTER [*excitedly*]: What? what? I, that woman there? [*bursts out laughing*]

THE MANAGER [*angry*]: What is there to laugh at?

LEADING LADY [*indignant*]: Nobody has ever dared to laugh at me. I insist on being treated with respect; otherwise I go away.

THE STEPDAUGHTER: No, no, excuse me . . . I am not laughing at you . . .

THE MANAGER [*to* STEPDAUGHTER]: You ought to feel honored to be played by . . .

LEADING LADY [*at once, contemptuously*]: "That woman there" . . .

THE STEPDAUGHTER: But I wasn't speaking of you, you know. I was speaking of myself—whom I can't see at all in you! That is all. I don't know . . . but . . . you . . . aren't in the least like me . . .

THE FATHER: True. Here's the point. Look here, sir, our temperaments, our souls . . .

THE MANAGER: Temperament, soul, be hanged. Do you suppose the spirit of the piece is in you? Nothing of the kind!

THE FATHER: What, haven't we our own temperaments, our own souls?

THE MANAGER: Not at all. Your soul or whatever you like to call it takes shape here. The actors give body and form to it, voice and gesture. And my actors—I may tell you—have given expression to much more lofty material than this little drama of yours, which may or may not hold up on the stage. But if it does, the merit of it, believe me, will be due to my actors.

THE FATHER: I don't dare contradict you, sir; but, believe me, it is a terrible suffering for us who are as we are, with these bodies of ours, these features to see . . .

THE MANAGER [*cutting him short and out of patience*]: Good heavens! The make-up will remedy all that, man, the make-up . . .

THE FATHER: Maybe. But the voice, the gestures . . .

THE MANAGER: Now, look here! On the stage, you as yourself, cannot exist. The actor here acts you, and that's an end to it!

THE FATHER: I understand. And now I think I see why our author who conceived us as we are, all alive, didn't want to put us on the stage after all. I haven't the least desire to offend your actors. Far from it! But when I think that I am to be acted by . . . I don't know by whom . . .

LEADING MAN [*on his dignity*]: By me, if you've no objection!

THE FATHER [*humbly, mellifluously*]: Honored, I assure you, sir. [*bows*] Still, I must say that try as this gentleman may, with all his good will and wonderful art, to absorb me into himself . . .

LEADING MAN: Oh chuck it! "Wonderful art!" Withdraw that, please!

THE FATHER: The performance he will give, even doing his best with make-up to look like me . . .

LEADING MAN: It will certainly be a bit difficult! [*The* ACTORS *laugh.*]

THE FATHER: Exactly! It will be difficult to act me as I really am. The effect will be rather—apart from the make-up—according as to how he supposes I am, as he senses me—if he does sense me—and not as I inside of myself feel myself to be. It seems to me then that account should be taken of this by everyone whose duty it may become to criticize us . . .

THE MANAGER: Heavens! The man's starting to think about the critics now! Let them say what they like. It's up to us to put on the play if we can. [*looking around*] Come on! come on! Is the stage set? [*to the* ACTORS *and* CHARACTERS] Stand back—stand back! Let me see, and don't let's lose any more time! [*to the* STEPDAUGHTER] Is it all right as it is now?

THE STEPDAUGHTER: Well, to tell the truth, I don't recognize the scene.

THE MANAGER: My dear lady, you can't possibly suppose that we can construct that shop of Madame Pace piece by piece here? [*to the* FATHER] You said a white room with flowered wall paper, didn't you?

THE FATHER: Yes.

THE MANAGER: Well then. We've got the furniture right, more or less. Bring that little table a bit further forward. [*The* STAGE HANDS *obey the order. To*

PROPERTY MAN] You go and find an envelope, if possible, a pale blue one; and give it to that gentleman. [*indicates* FATHER]

PROPERTY MAN: An ordinary envelope?

MANAGER *and* FATHER: Yes, yes, an ordinary envelope.

PROPERTY MAN: At once, sir. [*Exit*]

THE MANAGER: Ready, everyone! First scene—the Young Lady. [*The* LEADING LADY *comes forward.*] No, no, you must wait. I meant her. [*indicating the* STEPDAUGHTER] You must watch—

THE STEPDAUGHTER [*adding at once*]: How I shall play it, how I shall live it! . . .

LEADING LADY [*offended*]: I shall live it also, you may be sure, as soon as I begin!

THE MANAGER [*with his hands to his head*]: Ladies and gentlemen, if you please! No more useless discussions! Scene I: the young lady with Madame Pace: Oh! [*looks around as if lost*] And this Madame Pace, where is she?

THE FATHER: She isn't with us, sir.

THE MANAGER: Then what the devil's to be done?

THE FATHER: But she is alive too.

THE MANAGER: Yes, but where is she?

THE FATHER: One minute. Let me speak! [*turning to the* ACTRESSES] If these ladies would be so good as to give me their hats for a moment . . .

THE ACTRESSES [*half surprised, half laughing, in chorus*]: What?
Why?
Our hats?
What does he say?

THE MANAGER: What are you going to do with the ladies' hats? [*The* ACTORS *laugh.*]

THE FATHER: Oh nothing. I just want to put them on these pegs for a moment. And one of the ladies will be so kind as to take off her mantle . . .

THE ACTORS: Oh, what d'you think of that? Only the mantle?
He must be mad.

SOME ACTRESSES: But why? Mantles as well?

THE FATHER: To hang them up here for a moment. Please be so kind, will you?

THE ACTRESSES [*taking off their hats, one or two also their cloaks, and going to hang them on the racks*]: After all, why not?
There you are?
This is really funny.
We've got to put them on show.

THE FATHER: Exactly; just like that, on show.

THE MANAGER: May we know why?

THE FATHER: I'll tell you. Who knows if, by arranging the stage for her, she does not come here herself, attracted by the very articles of her trade? [*inviting the* ACTORS *to look towards the exit at back of stage*] Look! Look!

[*The door at the back of stage opens and* MADAME PACE *enters and takes a few steps forward. She is a fat, oldish woman with puffy oxygenated hair. She is rouged and powdered, dressed with a comical elegance in black silk. Round her waist is a long silver chain from which hangs a pair of scissors. The* STEPDAUGH-TER *runs over to her at once amid the stupor of the* ACTORS.]

THE STEPDAUGHTER [*turning towards her*]: There she is! There she is!
THE FATHER [*radiant*]: It's she! I said so, didn't I? There she is!
THE MANAGER [*conquering his surprise, and then becoming indignant*]: What sort of a trick is this?
LEADING MAN [*almost at the same time*]: What's going to happen next?
JUVENILE LEAD: Where does *she* come from?
L'INGÉNUE: They've been holding her in reserve, I guess.
LEADING LADY: A vulgar trick!
THE FATHER [*dominating the protests*]: Excuse me, all of you! Why are you so anxious to destroy in the name of a vulgar, commonplace sense of truth, this reality which comes to birth attracted and formed by the magic of the stage itself, which has indeed more right to live here than you, since it is much truer than you—if you don't mind my saying so? Which is the actress among you who is to play Madame Pace? Well, here is Madame Pace herself. And you will allow, I fancy, that the actress who acts her will be less true than this woman here, who is herself in person. You see my daughter recognized her and went over to her at once. Now you're going to witness the scene!

[*But the scene between the* STEPDAUGHTER *and* MADAME PACE *has already begun despite the protest of the* ACTORS *and the reply of* THE FATHER. *It has begun quietly, naturally, in a manner impossible for the stage. So when the* ACTORS, *called to attention by* THE FATHER, *turn round and see* MADAME PACE, *who has placed one hand under the* STEPDAUGHTER'S *chin to raise her head, they observe her at first with great attention, but hearing her speak in an unintelligible manner their interest begins to wane.*]

THE MANAGER: Well? well?
LEADING MAN: What does she say?
LEADING LADY: One can't hear a word.
JUVENILE LEAD: Louder! Louder please!
THE STEPDAUGHTER [*leaving* MADAME PACE, *who smiles a Sphinx-like smile, and advancing towards the* ACTORS]: Louder? Louder? What are you talking

about? These aren't matters which can be shouted at the top of one's voice. If I have spoken them out loud, it was to shame him and have my revenge. [*indicates* FATHER] But for Madame it's quite a different matter.

THE MANAGER: Indeed? indeed? But here, you know, people have got to make themselves heard, my dear. Even we who are on the stage can't hear you. What will it be when the public's in the theater? And anyway, you can very well speak up now among yourselves, since we shan't be present to listen to you as we are now. You've got to pretend to be alone in a room at the back of a shop where no one can hear you.

[THE STEPDAUGHTER *coquettishly and with a touch of malice makes a sign of disagreement two or three times with her finger.*]

THE MANAGER: What do you mean by no?

THE STEPDAUGHTER [*sotto voce, mysteriously*]: There's someone who will hear us if she [*indicating* MADAME PACE] speaks out loud.

THE MANAGER [*in consternation*]: What? Have you got someone else to spring on us now? [*The* ACTORS *burst out laughing.*]

THE FATHER: No, no sir. She is alluding to me. I've got to be here—there behind that door, in waiting; and Madame Pace knows it. In fact, if you will allow me, I'll go there at once, so I can be quite ready. [*moves away*]

THE MANAGER [*stopping him*]: No! wait! wait! We must observe the conventions of the theater. Before you are ready . . .

THE STEPDAUGHTER [*interrupting him*]: No, get on with it at once! I'm just dying, I tell you, to act this scene. If he's ready, I'm more than ready.

THE MANAGER [*shouting*]: But, my dear young lady, first of all, we must have the scene between you and this lady . . . [*indicates* MADAME PACE] Do you understand? . . .

THE STEPDAUGHTER: Good Heavens! She's been telling me what you know already: that Mamma's work is badly done again, that the material's ruined; and that if I want her to continue to help us in our misery I must be patient . . .

MADAME PACE [*coming forward with an air of great importance*]: Yes indeed, sir, I no wanta take advantage of her, I no wanta be hard . . .

[*Note:* MADAME PACE *is supposed to talk in a jargon half Italian, half English*]

THE MANAGER [*alarmed*]: What? What? She talks like that? [*The* ACTORS *burst out laughing again.*]

THE STEPDAUGHTER [*also laughing*]: Yes, yes, that's the way she talks, half English, half Italian! Most comical it is!

MADAME PACE: Itta seem not verra polite gentlemen laugha atta me eef I traya best speaka English.

THE MANAGER: *Diamine!* Of course! Of course! Let her talk like that! Just what we want. Talk just like that, Madame, if you please! The effect will be certain. Exactly what was wanted to put a little comic relief into the crudity of the situation. Of course she talks like that! Magnificent!

THE STEPDAUGHTER: Magnificent? Certainly! When certain suggestions are made to one in language of that kind, the effect is certain, since it seems almost a joke. One feels inclined to laugh when one hears her talk about an "old signore" "who wanta talka nicely with you." Nice old signore, eh, Madame?

MADAME PACE: Not so old, my dear, not so old! And even if you no lika him, he won't make any scandal!

THE MOTHER [*Jumping up amid the amazement and consternation of the* ACTORS *who had not been noticing her. They move to restrain her.*]: You old devil! You murderess!

THE STEPDAUGHTER [*running over to calm her* MOTHER]: Calm yourself, mother, calm yourself! Please don't . . .

THE FATHER [*going to her also at the same time*]: Calm yourself! Don't get excited! Sit down now!

THE MOTHER: Well then, take that woman away out of my sight!

THE STEPDAUGHTER [*to* MANAGER]: It is impossible for my mother to remain here.

THE FATHER [*to* MANAGER]: They can't be here together. And for this reason, you see: that woman there was not with us when we came . . . If they are on together, the whole thing is given away inevitably, as you see.

THE MANAGER: It doesn't matter. This is only a first rough sketch—just to get an idea of the various points of the scene, even confusedly . . . [*turning to the* MOTHER *and leading her to her chair*] Come along, my dear lady, sit down now, and let's get on with the scene . . .

[*Meanwhile, the* STEPDAUGHTER, *coming forward again, turns to* MADAME PACE.]

THE STEPDAUGHTER: Come on, Madame, come on!

MADAME PACE [*offended*]: No, no, *grazie.* I not do anything witha your mother present.

THE STEPDAUGHTER: Nonsense! Introduce this "old signore" who wants to talk nicely to me. [*addressing the company imperiously*] We've got to do this scene one way or another, haven't we? Come on! [*to* MADAME PACE] You can go!

MADAME PACE: Ah yes! I go'way! I go'way! Certainly! [*Exits furious*]

THE STEPDAUGHTER [*to the* FATHER]: Now you make your entry. No, you needn't go over there. Come here. Let's suppose you've already come in. Like that, yes! I'm here with bowed head, modest-like. Come on! Out with your voice! Say "Good morning, Miss" in that peculiar tone, that special tone . . .   ·

THE MANAGER: Excuse me, but are you the Manager, or am I? [*to the* FATHER, *who looks undecided and perplexed*] Get on with it, man! Go down there to the back of the stage. You needn't go off. Then come right forward here.

[THE FATHER *does as he is told, looking troubled and perplexed at first. But as soon as he begins to move, the reality of the action affects him, and he begins to smile and to be more natural. The* ACTORS *watch intently.*]

THE MANAGER [*sotto voce, quickly to the* PROMPTER *in his box*]: Ready! ready? Get ready to write now.

THE FATHER [*coming forward and speaking in a different tone*]: Good afternoon, Miss!

THE STEPDAUGHTER [*head bowed down slightly, with restrained disgust*]: Good afternoon!

THE FATHER [*Looks under her hat which partly covers her face. Perceiving she is very young, he makes an exclamation, partly of surprise, partly of fear lest he compromise himself in a risky adventure*]: Ah . . . but . . . ah . . . I say . . . this is not the first time that you have come here, is it?

THE STEPDAUGHTER [*modestly*]: No sir.

THE FATHER: You've been here before, eh? [*then seeing her nod agreement*] More than once? [*waits for her to answer, looks under her hat, smiles, and then says*] Well then, there's no need to be so shy, is there? May I take off your hat?

THE STEPDAUGHTER [*anticipating him and with veiled disgust*]: No sir . . . I'll do it myself. [*takes it off quickly*]

[THE MOTHER, *who watches the progress of the scene with* THE SON *and the other two* CHILDREN *who cling to her, is on thorns; and follows with varying expressions of sorrow, indignation, anxiety, and horror the words and actions of the other two. From time to time she hides her face in her hands and sobs.*]

THE MOTHER: Oh, my God, my God!

THE FATHER [*playing his part with a touch of gallantry*]: Give it to me! I'll put it down. [*takes hat from her hands*] But a dear little head like yours ought to have a smarter hat. Come and help me choose one from the stock, won't you?

L'INGÉNUE [*interrupting*]: I say . . . those are our hats, you know.

THE MANAGER [*furious*]: Silence! silence! Don't try and be funny, if you please . . . We're playing the scene now, I'd have you notice. [*to the* STEPDAUGHTER] Begin again, please!

THE STEPDAUGHTER [*continuing*]: No thank you, sir.

THE FATHER: Oh, come now. Don't talk like that. You must take it. I shall be upset if you don't. There are some lovely little hats here; and then —Madame will be pleased. She expects it, anyway, you know.

THE STEPDAUGHTER: No, no! I couldn't wear it!

THE FATHER: Oh, you're thinking about what they'd say at home if they saw you come in with a new hat? My dear girl, there's always a way round these little matters, you know.

THE STEPDAUGHTER [*all keyed up*]: No, it's not that. I couldn't wear it because I am . . . as you see . . . you might have noticed . . . [*showing her black dress*]

THE FATHER: . . . in mourning! Of course: I beg your pardon: I'm frightfully sorry . . .

THE STEPDAUGHTER [*forcing herself to conquer her indignation and nausea*]: Stop! Stop! It's I who must thank you. There's no need for you to feel mortified or specially sorry. Don't think any more of what I've said. [*tries to smile*] I must forget that I am dressed so . . .

THE MANAGER [*interrupting and turning to the* PROMPTER]: Stop a minute! Stop! Don't write that down. Cut out that last bit. [*then to the* FATHER *and* STEPDAUGHTER] Fine! it's going fine! [*to the* FATHER *only*] And now you can go on as we arranged. [*to the* ACTORS] Pretty good that scene, where he offers her the hat, eh?

THE STEPDAUGHTER: The best's coming now. Why can't we go on?

THE MANAGER: Have a little patience! [*to the* actors] Of course, it must be treated rather lightly.

LEADING MAN: Still, with a bit of go in it!

LEADING LADY: Of course! It's easy enough! [*to* LEADING MAN] Shall you and I try it now?

LEADING MAN: Why, yes! I'll prepare my entrance. [*Exit in order to make his entrance*]

THE MANAGER [*to* LEADING LADY]: See here! The scene between you and Madame Pace is finished. I'll have it written out properly after. You remain here . . . oh, where are you going?

LEADING LADY: One minute. I want to put my hat on again. [*goes over to hatrack and puts her hat on her head*]

THE MANAGER: Good! You stay here with your head bowed down a bit.

THE STEPDAUGHTER: But she isn't dressed in black.

LEADING LADY: But I shall be, and much more effectively than you.

THE MANAGER [*to* STEPDAUGHTER]: Be quiet please, and watch! You'll be able to learn something. [*clapping his hands*] Come on! come on! Entrance, please!

[*The door at rear of stage opens, and the* LEADING MAN *enters with the lively manner of an old gallant. The rendering of the scene by the* ACTORS *from the very first words is seen to be quite a different thing, though it has not in any way the air of a parody. Naturally, the* STEPDAUGHTER *and the* FATHER, *not being able to recognize themselves in the* LEADING LADY *and the* LEADING MAN, *who deliver their words in different tones and with a different psychology, express, sometimes with smiles, sometimes with gestures, the impression they receive.*]

LEADING MAN: Good afternoon, Miss . . .

THE FATHER [*at once unable to contain himself*]: No! no!

[THE STEPDAUGHTER, *noticing the way the* LEADING MAN *enters, bursts out laughing.*]

THE MANAGER [*furious*]: Silence! And you, please, just stop that laughing. If we go on like this, we shall never finish.

THE STEPDAUGHTER: Forgive me, sir, but it's natural enough. This lady [*indicating* LEADING LADY] stands there still; but if she is supposed to be me, I can assure you that if I heard anyone say "Good afternoon" in that manner and in that tone, I should burst out laughing as I did.

THE FATHER: Yes, yes, the manner, the tone . . .

THE MANAGER: Nonsense! Rubbish! Stand aside and let me see the action.

LEADING MAN: If I've got to represent an old fellow who's coming into a house of an equivocal character . . .

THE MANAGER: Don't listen to them, for Heaven's sake! Do it again! It goes fine. [*waiting for the* ACTORS *to begin again*] Well?

LEADING MAN: Good afternoon, Miss.

LEADING LADY: Good afternoon.

LEADING MAN [*imitating the gesture of the* FATHER *when he looked under the hat, and then expressing quite clearly first satisfaction and then fear*]: Ah, but . . . I say . . . this is not the first time that you have come here, is it?

THE MANAGER: Good, but not quite so heavily. Like this. [*acts himself*] "This isn't the first time that you have come here" . . . [*to* LEADING LADY] And you say: "No, sir."

LEADING LADY: No, sir.

LEADING MAN: You've been here before, more than once.

THE MANAGER: No, no, stop! Let her nod "yes" first. "You've been here before, eh?" [*the* LEADING LADY *lifts up her head slightly and closes her eyes as though in disgust. Then she inclines her head twice.*]

THE STEPDAUGHTER [*unable to contain herself*]: Oh my God! [*Puts a hand to her mouth to prevent herself from laughing*]

THE MANAGER [*turning round*]: What's the matter?

THE STEPDAUGHTER: Nothing, nothing!

THE MANAGER [*to* LEADING MAN]: Go on!

LEADING MAN: You've been here before, eh? Well then, there's no need to be so shy, is there? May I take off your hat?

[*The* LEADING MAN *says this last speech in such a tone and with such gestures that the* STEPDAUGHTER, *though she has her hand to her mouth, cannot keep from laughing.*]

LEADING LADY [*indignant*]: I'm not going to stop here to be made a fool of by that woman there.

LEADING MAN: Neither am I! I'm through with it!

THE MANAGER [*shouting to* STEPDAUGHTER]: Silence! for once and all, I tell you!

THE STEPDAUGHTER: Forgive me! forgive me!

THE MANAGER: You haven't any manners: that's what it is! You go too far.

THE FATHER [*endeavoring to intervene*]: Yes, it's true, but excuse her . . .

THE MANAGER: Excuse what? It's absolutely disgusting.

THE FATHER: Yes, sir, but believe me, it has such a strange effect when . . .

THE MANAGER: Strange? Why strange? Where is it strange?

THE FATHER: No, sir; I admire your actors—this gentleman here, this lady; but they are certainly not us!

THE MANAGER: I should hope not. Evidently they cannot be you, if they are actors.

THE FATHER: Just so: actors! Both of them act our parts exceedingly well. But, believe me, it produces quite a different effect on us. They want to be us, but they aren't, all the same.

THE MANAGER: What is it then anyway?

THE FATHER: Something that is . . . that is theirs—and no longer ours . . .

THE MANAGER: But naturally, inevitably. I've told you so already.

THE FATHER: Yes, I understand . . . I understand . . .

THE MANAGER: Well then, let's have no more of it! [*turning to the* ACTORS] We'll have the rehearsals by ourselves, afterwards, in the ordinary way. I never could stand rehearsing with the author present. He's never satisfied! [*turning to* FATHER *and* STEPDAUGHTER] Come on! Let's get on with it again; and try and see if you can't keep from laughing.

THE STEPDAUGHTER: Oh, I shan't laugh any more. There's a nice little bit coming from me now: you'll see.

THE MANAGER: Well then: when she says "Don't think any more of what I've said. I must forget, etc.," you [*addressing the* FATHER] come in sharp with "I understand, I understand"; and then you ask her . . .

THE STEPDAUGHTER [*interrupting*]: What?

THE MANAGER: Why she is in mourning.

THE STEPDAUGHTER: Not at all! See here: when I told him that it was useless for me to be thinking about my wearing mourning, do you know how he answered me? "Ah well," he said, "then let's take off this little frock."

THE MANAGER: Great! Just what we want, to make a riot in the theater!

THE STEPDAUGHTER: But it's the truth!

THE MANAGER: What does that matter? Acting is our business here. Truth up to a certain point, but no further.

THE STEPDAUGHTER: What do you want to do then?

THE MANAGER: You'll see, you'll see! Leave it to me.

THE STEPDAUGHTER: No sir! What you want to do is to piece together a little romantic sentimental scene out of my disgust, out of all the reasons, each more cruel and viler than the other, why I am what I am. He is to ask me why I'm in mourning; and I'm to answer with tears in my eyes, that it is just two months since papa died. No sir, no! He's got to say to me; as he did say: "Well, let's take off this little dress at once." And I; with my two months' mourning in my heart, went there behind that screen, and with these fingers tingling with shame . . .

THE MANAGER [*running his hands through his hair*]: For Heaven's sake! What are you saying?

THE STEPDAUGHTER [*crying out excitedly*]: The truth! The truth!

THE MANAGER: It may be. I don't deny it, and I can understand all your horror; but you must surely see that you can't have this kind of thing on the stage. It won't go.

THE STEPDAUGHTER: Not possible, eh? Very well! I'm much obliged to you— but I'm off!

THE MANAGER: Now be reasonable! Don't lose your temper!

THE STEPDAUGHTER: I won't stop here! I won't! I can see you've fixed it all up with him in your office. All this talk about what is possible for the stage . . . I understand! He wants to get at his complicated "cerebral drama," to have his famous remorses and torments acted; but I want to act my part, *my part!*

THE MANAGER [*annoyed, shaking his shoulders*]: Ah! Just *your* part! But, if you will pardon me, there are other parts than yours: his [*indicating the* FATHER] and hers! [*indicating the* MOTHER] On the stage you can't have a character becoming too prominent and overshadowing all the others. The thing is to pack them all into a neat little framework and then act what is actable. I am aware of the fact that everyone has his own interior life which he wants very much to put forward. But the difficulty lies in this fact: to set out just so much as is necessary for the stage, taking the other characters into consideration, and at the same time hint at the unrevealed interior life of each. I am willing to admit, my dear young lady, that from your point of view it would be a fine idea if each character could tell the public all his troubles in a nice monologue or a regular one-hour lecture. [*good-humoredly*] You must restrain yourself, my dear, and in your own interest, too; because this fury of yours, this exaggerated disgust you show, may make a bad impression, you know. After you have confessed to me that there were others before him at Madame Pace's and more than once . . .

THE STEPDAUGHTER [*bowing her head, impressed*]: It's true. But remember those others mean him for me all the same.

THE MANAGER [*not understanding*]: What? The others? What do you mean?

THE STEPDAUGHTER: For one who has gone wrong, sir, he who was responsible for the first fault is responsible for all that follow. He is responsible for my faults, was, even before I was born. Look at him, and see if it isn't true!

THE MANAGER: Well, well! And does the weight of so much responsibility seem nothing to you? Give him a chance to act it, to get it over!

THE STEPDAUGHTER: How? How can he act all his "noble remorses," all his "moral torments," if you want to spare him the horror of being discovered one day—after he had asked her what he did ask her—in the arms of her, that already fallen woman, that child, sir, that child he used to watch come out of school? [*She is moved*]

[THE MOTHER *at this point is overcome with emotion, and breaks out into a fit of crying. All are touched. A long pause*]

THE STEPDAUGHTER [*as soon as the* MOTHER *becomes a little quieter, adds resolutely and gravely*]: At present, we are unknown to the public. Tomorrow, you will act us as you wish, treating us in your own manner. But do you really want to see drama, do you want to see it flash out as it really did?

THE MANAGER: Of course! That's just what I do want, so I can use as much of it as is possible.

THE STEPDAUGHTER: Well then, ask that Mother there to leave us.

THE MOTHER [*changing her low plaint into a sharp cry*]: No! No! Don't permit it, sir, don't permit it!

THE MANAGER: But it's only to try it.

THE MOTHER: I can't bear it. I can't.

THE MANAGER: But since it has happened already . . . I don't understand!

THE MOTHER: It's taking place now. It happens all the time. My torment isn't a pretended one. I live and feel every minute of my torture. Those two children there—have you heard them speak? They can't speak any more. They cling to me to keep my torment actual and vivid for me. But for themselves, they do not exist, they aren't any more. And she [*indicating* STEPDAUGHTER] has run away, she has left me, and is lost. If I now see her here before me, it is only to renew for me the tortures I have suffered for her too.

THE FATHER: The eternal moment! She [*indicating the* STEPDAUGHTER] is here to catch me, fix me, and hold me eternally in the stocks for that one fleeting and shameful moment of my life. She can't give it up! And you sir, cannot either fairly spare me it.

THE MANAGER: I never said I didn't want to act it. It will form, as a matter of fact, the nucleus of the whole first act right up to her surprise. [*indicating the* MOTHER]

THE FATHER: Just so! This is my punishment: the passion in all of us that must culminate in her final cry.

THE STEPDAUGHTER: I can hear it still in my ears. It's driven me mad, that cry —You can put me on as you like; it doesn't matter. Fully dressed, if you like—provided I have at least the arm bare; because, standing like this [*she goes close to the* FATHER *and leans her head on his breast*] with my head so, and my arms round his neck, I saw a vein pulsing in my arm here; and then, as if that live vein had awakened disgust in me, I closed my eyes like this, and let my head sink on his breast. [*turning to the* MOTHER] Cry out, mother! Cry out! [*buries head in* FATHER'S *breast, and with her shoulders raised as if to prevent her hearing the cry, adds in tones of intense emotion*] Cry out as you did then!

THE MOTHER [*coming forward to separate them*]: No! My daughter, my daughter! [*and after having pulled her away from him*] You brute! you brute! She is my daughter! Don't you see she's my daughter?

THE MANAGER [*walking backwards towards footlights*]: Fine! fine! Damned good! And then, of course—curtain!

THE FATHER [*going towards him excitedly*]: Yes, of course, because that's the way it really happened.

THE MANAGER [*convinced and pleased*]: Oh, yes, no doubt about it. Curtain here, curtain!

[*At the reiterated cry of* THE MANAGER, THE MACHINIST *lets the curtain down, leaving* THE MANAGER *and* THE FATHER *in front of it before the footlights.*]

THE MANAGER: The darned idiot! I said "curtain" to show the act should end there, and he goes and lets it down in earnest. [*To the* FATHER, *while he pulls the curtain back to go onto the stage again*] Yes, yes, it's all right. Effect certain! That's the right ending. I'll guarantee the first act, at any rate.

Act III

[*When the curtain goes up again, it is seen that the stage hands have shifted the bit of scenery used in the last part, and have rigged up instead at the back of the stage a drop, with some trees, and one or two wings. A portion of a fountain basin is visible.* THE MOTHER *is sitting on the* Right *with the two children by her side.* THE SON *is on the same side, but away from the others. He seems bored, angry, and full of shame.* THE FATHER *and* THE STEPDAUGHTER *are also seated towards the* Right *front. On the other side* (Left) *are the* ACTORS, *much in the positions they occupied before the curtain was lowered. Only* THE MANAGER *is standing up in the middle of the stage, with his hand closed over his mouth, in the act of meditating.*]

THE MANAGER [*shaking his shoulders after a brief pause*]: Ah yes: the second act! Leave it to me, leave it all to me as we arranged, and you'll see! It'll go fine!

THE STEPDAUGHTER: Our entry into his house [*indicates* FATHER] in spite of him . . . [*indicates the* SON]

THE MANAGER [*out of patience*]: Leave it to me, I tell you!

THE STEPDAUGHTER: Do let it be clear, at any rate, that it is in spite of my wishes.

THE MOTHER [*from her corner, shaking her head*]: For all the good that's come of it . . .

THE STEPDAUGHTER [*turning towards her quickly*]: It doesn't matter. The more harm done us, the more remorse for him.

THE MANAGER [*impatiently*]: I understand! Good Heavens! I understand! I'm taking it into account.

THE MOTHER [*supplicatingly*]: I beg you, sir, to let it appear quite plain that for conscience' sake I did try in every way . . .

THE STEPDAUGHTER [*interrupting indignantly and continuing for the* MOTHER]: . . . to pacify me, to dissuade me from spiting him. [*to* MANAGER] Do as she wants: satisfy her, because it is true! I enjoy it immensely. Anyhow, as you can see, the meeker she is, the more she tries to get at his heart, the more distant and aloof does he become.

THE MANAGER: Are we going to begin this second act or not?

THE STEPDAUGHTER: I'm not going to talk any more now. But I must tell you this: you can't have the whole action take place in the garden, as you suggest. It isn't possible!

THE MANAGER: Why not?

THE STEPDAUGHTER: Because he [*indicates the* SON *again*] is always shut up alone in his room. And then there's all the part of that poor dazed looking boy there which takes place indoors.

THE MANAGER: Maybe! On the other hand, you will understand—we can't change scenes three or four times in one act.

THE LEADING MAN: They used to once.

THE MANAGER: Yes, when the public was up to the level of that child there.

THE LEADING LADY: It makes the illusion easier.

THE FATHER [*irritated*]: The illusion! For Heaven's sake, don't say illusion. Please don't use that word, which is particularly painful for us.

THE MANAGER [*astounded*]: And why, if you please?

THE FATHER: It's painful, cruel, really cruel; and you ought to understand that.

THE MANAGER: But why? What ought we to say then? The illusion, I tell you, sir, which we've got to create for the audience . . .

THE LEADING MAN: With our acting.

THE MANAGER: The illusion of a reality.

THE FATHER: I understand; but you, perhaps, do not understand us. Forgive me! You see . . . here for you and your actors, the thing is only—and rightly so . . . a kind of game . . .

THE LEADING LADY [*interrupting indignantly*]: A game! We're not children here, if you please! We are serious actors.

THE FATHER: I don't deny it. What I mean is the game, or play, of your art, which has to give, as the gentleman says, a perfect illusion of reality.

THE MANAGER: Precisely——!

THE FATHER: Now, if you consider the fact that we [*indicates himself and the other five* CHARACTERS], as we are, have no other reality outside of this illusion . . .

THE MANAGER [*astonished, looking at his* ACTORS, *who are also amazed*]: And what does that mean?

THE FATHER [*after watching them for a moment with a wan smile*]: As I say, sir, that which is a game of art for you is our sole reality. [*Brief pause. He goes a step or two nearer the* MANAGER *and adds*] But not only for us, you know, by the way. Just you think it over well. [*looks him in the eyes*] Can you tell me who you are?

THE MANAGER [*perplexed, half smiling*]: What? Who am I? I am myself.

THE FATHER: And if I were to tell you that that isn't true, because you are I? . . .

THE MANAGER: I should say you were mad——! [*The* ACTORS *laugh.*]

THE FATHER: You're quite right to laugh: because we are all making believe here. [*to* MANAGER] And you can therefore object that it's only for a joke that that gentleman there [*indicates the* LEADING MAN], who naturally is himself, has to be me, who am on the contrary myself—this thing you see here. You see I've caught you in a trap! [*The* ACTORS *laugh.*]

THE MANAGER [*annoyed*]: But we've had all this over once before. Do you want to begin again?

THE FATHER: No, no! that wasn't my meaning! In fact, I should like to re-quest you to abandon this game of art [*looking at the* LEADING LADY *as if anticipating her*] which you are accustomed to play here with your actors, and to ask you seriously once again: who are you?

THE MANAGER [*astonished and irritated, turning to his* ACTORS]: If this fellow here hasn't got a nerve! A man who calls himself a character comes and asks me who I am!

THE FATHER [*with dignity, but not offended*]: A character, sir, may always ask a man who he is. Because a character has really a life of his own, marked with his especial characteristics; for which reason he is always "some-body." But a man—I'm not speaking of you now—may very well be "nobody."

THE MANAGER: Yes, but you are asking these questions of me, the boss, the manager! Do you understand?

THE FATHER: But only in order to know if you, as you really are now, see yourself as you once were with all the illusions that were yours then, with all the things both inside and outside of you as they seemed to you —as they were then indeed for you. Well, sir, if you think of all those illusions that mean nothing to you now, of all those things which don't even *seem* to you to exist any more, while once they *were* for you, don't you feel that that—I won't say these boards—but the very earth under your feet is sinking away from you when you reflect that in the same way this *you* as you feel it today—all this present reality of yours—is fated to seem a mere illusion to you tomorrow?

THE MANAGER [*without having understood much, but astonished by the specious argument*]: Well, well! And where does all this take us anyway?

THE FATHER: Oh, nowhere! It's only to show you that if we [*indicating the* CHARACTERS] have no other reality beyond illusion, you too must not count overmuch on your reality as you feel it today, since, like that of yesterday, it may prove an illusion for you tomorrow.

THE MANAGER [*determining to make fun of him*]: Ah, excellent! Then you'll be saying next that you, with this comedy of yours that you brought here to act, are truer and more real than I am.

THE FATHER [*with the greatest seriousness*]: But of course; without doubt!

THE MANAGER: Ah, really?

THE FATHER: Why, I thought you'd understand that from the beginning.

THE MANAGER: More real than I?

THE FATHER: If your reality can change from one day to another . . .

THE MANAGER: But everyone knows it can change. It is always changing, the same as anyone else's.

THE FATHER [*with a cry*]: No, sir, not ours! Look here! That is the very difference! Our reality doesn't change: it can't change! It can't be other than what it is, because it is already fixed forever. It's terrible. Ours is an immutable reality which should make you shudder when you approach us if you are really conscious of the fact that your reality is a mere transitory and fleeting illusion, taking this form today and that tomorrow, according to the conditions, according to your will, your sentiments, which in turn are controlled by an intellect that shows them to you today in one manner and tomorrow . . . who knows how? . . . Illusions of reality represented in this fatuous comedy of life that never ends, nor can ever end! Because if tomorrow it were to end . . . then why, all would be finished.

THE MANAGER: Oh for God's sake, will you *at least* finish with this philosophizing and let us try and shape this comedy which you yourself have brought me here? You argue and philosophize a bit too much, my dear sir. You know you seem to me almost, almost . . . [*stops and looks him over from head to foot*] Ah, by the way, I think you introduced yourself to me as a—what shall . . . we say—a "character," created by an author who did not afterwards care to make a drama of his own creations.

THE FATHER: It is the simple truth, sir.

THE MANAGER: Nonsense! Cut that out, please! None of us believes it, because it isn't a thing, as you must recognize yourself, which one can believe seriously. If you want to know, it seems to me you are trying to imitate the manner of a certain author whom I heartily detest—I warn you—although I have unfortunately bound myself to put on one of his works. As a matter of fact, I was just starting to rehearse it, when you arrived. [*turning to the* ACTORS] And this is what we've gained—out of the frying-pan into the fire!

THE FATHER: I don't know to what author you may be alluding, but believe me I feel what I think; and I seem to be philosophizing only for those who do not think what they feel, because they blind themselves with their own sentiment. I know that for many people this self-blinding seems much more "human"; but the contrary is really true. For man never reasons so much and becomes so introspective as when he suffers; since he is anxious to get at the cause of his sufferings, to learn who has produced them, and whether it is just or unjust that he should have to bear them. On the other hand, when he is happy, he takes his happiness as it comes and doesn't analyze it, just as if happiness were his right. The animals suffer without reasoning about their sufferings. But take the case of a man who suffers and begins to reason about it. Oh no! it can't be allowed! Let him suffer like an animal, and then—ah yes, he is "human!"

THE MANAGER: Look here! Look here! You're off again, philosophizing worse than ever.

THE FATHER: Because I suffer, sir! I'm not philosophizing: I'm crying aloud the reason of my sufferings.

THE MANAGER [*makes brusque movement as he is taken with a new idea*]: I should like to know if anyone has ever heard of a character who gets right out of his part and perorates and speechifies as you do. Have you ever heard of a case? I haven't.

THE FATHER: You have never met such a case, sir, because authors, as a rule, hide the labor of their creations. When the characters are really alive before their author, the latter does nothing but follow them in their action, in their words, in the situations which they suggest to him; and he has to will them the way they will themselves—for there's trouble if he doesn't. When a character is born, he acquires at once such an independence, even of his own author, that he can be imagined by everybody even in many other situations where the author never dreamed of placing him; and so he acquires for himself a meaning which the author never thought of giving him.

THE MANAGER: Yes, yes, I know this.

THE FATHER: What is there then to marvel at in us? Imagine such a misfortune for characters as I have described to you: to be born of an author's fantasy, and be denied life by him; and then answer me if these characters left alive, and yet without life, weren't right in doing what they did do and are doing now, after they have attempted everything in their power to persuade him to give them their stage life. We've all tried him in turn, I, she [*indicating the* STEPDAUGHTER] and she. [*indicating the* MOTHER]

THE STEPDAUGHTER: It's true. I too have sought to tempt him, many, many

times, when he had been sitting at his writing table, feeling a bit melancholy, at the twilight hour. He would sit in his armchair too lazy to
switch on the light, and all the shadows that crept into his room were
full of our presence coming to tempt him. [*as if she saw herself still there
by the writing table, and was annoyed by the presence of the* ACTORS] Oh, if
you would only go away, go away and leave us alone—mother here
with that son of hers—I with that Child—that Boy there always alone
—and then I with him—[*just hints at the* FATHER]—and then I alone, alone
. . . in those shadows! [*makes a sudden movement as if in the vision she has
of herself illuminating those shadows she wanted to seize hold of herself*] Ah!
my life! my life! Oh, what scenes we proposed to him—and I tempted
him more than any of the others!

THE FATHER: Maybe. But perhaps it was your fault that he refused to give
us life: because you were too insistent, too troublesome.

THE STEPDAUGHTER: Nonsense! Didn't he make me so himself? [*goes close to
the* MANAGER *to tell him as if in confidence*] In my opinion he abandoned
us in a fit of depression, of disgust for the ordinary theater as the public
knows it and likes it.

THE SON: Exactly what it was, sir; exactly that!

THE FATHER: Not at all! Don't believe it for a minute. Listen to me! You'll
be doing quite right to modify, as you suggest, the excesses both of this
girl here, who wants to do too much, and of this young man, who won't
do anything at all.

THE SON: No, nothing!

THE MANAGER: You too get over the mark occasionally, my dear sir, if I may
say so.

THE FATHER: I? When? Where?

THE MANAGER: Always! Continuously! Then there's this insistence of yours
in trying to make us believe you are a character. And then too, you must
really argue and philosophize less, you know, much less.

THE FATHER: Well, if you want to take away from me the possibility of
representing the torment of my spirit which never gives me peace, you
will be suppressing me: that's all. Every true man, sir, who is a little
above the level of the beasts and plants does not live for the sake of
living, without knowing how to live; but he lives so as to give a meaning
and a value of his own to life. For me this is *everything*. I cannot give
up this, just to represent a mere fact as she [*indicating the* STEPDAUGH-
TER] wants. It's all very well for her, since her "vendetta" lies in the
"fact." I'm not going to do it. It destroys my *raison d'être*.

THE MANAGER: Your *raison d'être*! Oh, we're going ahead fine! First she starts
off, and then you jump in. At this rate, we'll never finish.

THE FATHER: Now, don't be offended! Have it your own way—provided,
however, that within the limits of the parts you assign us each one's
sacrifice isn't too great.

THE MANAGER: You've got to understand that you can't go on arguing at your own pleasure. Drama is action, sir, action and not confounded philosophy.

THE FATHER: All right. I'll do just as much arguing and philosophizing as everybody does when he is considering his own torments.

THE MANAGER: If the drama permits! But for Heaven's sake, man, let's get along and come to the scene.

THE STEPDAUGHTER: It seems to me we've got too much action with our coming into his house. [*indicating* FATHER] You said, before, you couldn't change the scene every five minutes.

THE MANAGER: Of course not. What we've got to do is to combine and group up all the facts in one simultaneous, close-knit action. We can't have it as you want, with your little brother wandering like a ghost from room to room, hiding behind doors and meditating a project which— what did you say it did to him?

THE STEPDAUGHTER: Consumes him, sir, wastes him away!

THE MANAGER: Well, it may be. And then at the same time, you want the little girl there to be playing in the garden . . . one in the house, and the other in the garden: isn't that it?

THE STEPDAUGHTER: Yes, in the sun, in the sun! That is my only pleasure: to see her happy and careless in the garden after the misery and squalor of the horrible room where we all four slept together. And I had to sleep with her—I, do you understand?—with my vile contaminated body next to hers; with her folding me fast in her loving little arms. In the garden, whenever she spied me, she would run to take me by the hand. She didn't care for the big flowers, only the little ones; and she loved to show me them and pet me.

THE MANAGER: Well then, we'll have it in the garden. Everything shall happen in the garden; and we'll group the other scenes there. [*calls a* STAGE HAND] Here, a back-cloth with trees and something to do as a fountain basin. [*turning round to look at the back of the stage*] Ah, you've fixed it up. Good! [*to* STEPDAUGHTER] This is just to give an idea, of course. The Boy, instead of hiding behind the doors, will wander about here in the garden, hiding behind the trees. But it's going to be rather difficult to find a child to do that scene with you where she shows you the flowers. [*turning to the* YOUTH] Come forward a little, will you please? Let's try it now! Come along! come along! [*Then seeing him come shyly forward, full of fear and looking lost*] It's a nice business, this lad here. What's the matter with him? We'll have to give him a word or two to say. [*goes close to him, puts a hand on his shoulders, and leads him behind one of the trees*] Come on! come on! Let me see you a little! Hide here . . . yes, like that. Try and show your head just a little as if you were looking for someone . . . [*goes back to observe the effect, when the* BOY *at once goes through the action*] Excellent! fine! [*turning to* STEPDAUGHTER] Suppose the little girl there were to surprise him as he looks round, and run over to him, so we could give him a word or two to say?

THE STEPDAUGHTER: It's useless to hope he will speak, as long as that fellow there is here . . . [*indicates the* SON] You must send him away first.

THE SON [*jumping up*]: Delighted! delighted! I don't ask for anything better. [*begins to move away*]

THE MANAGER [*at once stopping him*]: No! No! Where are you going? Wait a bit!

[*The* MOTHER *gets up, alarmed and terrified at the thought that he is really about to go away. Instinctively she lifts her arms to prevent him, without, however, leaving her seat.*]

THE SON [*to* MANAGER, *who stops him*]: I've got nothing to do with this affair. Let me go please! Let me go!

THE MANAGER: What do you mean by saying you've got nothing to do with this?

THE STEPDAUGHTER [*calmly, with irony*]: Don't bother to stop him: he won't go away.

THE FATHER: He has to act the terrible scene in the garden with his mother.

THE SON [*suddenly resolute and with dignity*]: I shall act nothing at all. I've said so from the very beginning. [*to the* MANAGER] Let me go!

THE STEPDAUGHTER [*going over to the* MANAGER]: Allow me? [*puts down the* MANAGER'S *arm which is restraining the* SON] Well, go away then, if you want to! [*The* SON *looks at her with contempt and hatred. She laughs and says*] You see, he can't, he can't go away! He is obliged to stay here, indissolubly bound to the chain. If I, who fly off when that happens which has to happen, because I can't bear him—if I am still here and support that face and expression of his, you can well imagine that he is unable to move. He has to remain here, has to stop with that nice father of his, and that mother whose only son he is. [*turning to the* MOTHER] Come on, mother, come along! [*turning to* MANAGER *to indicate her*] You see, she was getting up to keep him back. [*to the* MOTHER, *beckoning her with her hand*] Come on! come on! [*then to* MANAGER] You can imagine how little she wants to show these actors of yours what she really feels; but so eager is she to get near him that . . . There, you see? She is willing to act her part. [*And in fact, the* MOTHER *approaches him; and as soon as the* STEPDAUGHTER *has finished speaking, opens her arms to signify that she consents*]

THE SON [*suddenly*]: No! No! If I can't go away, then I'll stop here; but I repeat: I act nothing!

THE FATHER [*to* MANAGER *excitedly*]: You can force him, sir.

THE SON: Nobody can force me.

THE FATHER: I can.

THE STEPDAUGHTER: Wait a minute, wait . . . First of all, the baby has to go to the fountain . . . [*runs to take the* CHILD *and leads her to the fountain*]

THE MANAGER: Yes, yes of course; that's it. Both at the same time.

[*The second* LADY LEAD *and the* JUVENILE LEAD *at this point separate themselves from the group of* ACTORS. *One watches the* MOTHER *attentively; the other moves about studying the movements and manner of the* SON *whom he will have to act.*]

THE SON [*to* MANAGER]: What do you mean by both at the same time? It isn't right. There was no scene between me and her. [*indicates the* MOTHER] Ask her how it was!

THE MOTHER: Yes, it's true. I had come into his room . . .

THE SON: Into my room, do you understand? Nothing to do with the garden.

THE MANAGER: It doesn't matter. Haven't I told you we've got to group the action?

THE SON [*observing the* JUVENILE LEAD *studying him*]: What do you want?

THE JUVENILE LEAD: Nothing! I was just looking at you.

THE SON [*turning towards the* SECOND LADY LEAD]: Ah! she's at it too: to re-act her part! [*indicating the* MOTHER]

THE MANAGER: Exactly! And it seems to me that you ought to be grateful to them for their interest.

THE SON: Yes, but haven't you yet perceived that it isn't possible to live in front of a mirror which not only freezes us with the image of ourselves, but throws our likeness back at us with a horrible grimace?

THE FATHER: That is true, absolutely true. You must see that.

THE MANAGER [*to* SECOND LADY LEAD *and* JUVENILE LEAD]: He's right! Move away from them!

THE SON: Do as you like. I'm out of this!

THE MANAGER: Be quiet, you, will you? And let me hear your mother! [*to* MOTHER] You were saying you had entered . . .

THE MOTHER: Yes, into his room, because I couldn't stand it any longer. I went to empty my heart to him of all the anguish that tortures me . . . But as soon as he saw me come in . . .

THE SON: Nothing happened! There was no scene. I went away, that's all! I don't care for scenes!

THE MOTHER: It's true, true. That's how it was.

THE MANAGER: Well now, we've got to do this bit between you and him. It's indispensable.

THE MOTHER: I'm ready . . . when you are ready. If you could only find a chance for me to tell him what I feel here in my heart.

THE FATHER [*going to* SON *in a great rage*]: You'll do this for your mother, for your mother, do you understand?

THE SON [*quite determined*]: I do nothing!

THE FATHER [*taking hold of him and shaking him*]: For God's sake, do as I tell you! Don't you hear your mother asking you for a favor? Haven't you even got the guts to be a son?

THE SON [*taking hold of the* FATHER]: No! No! And for God's sake stop it, or else . . . [*General agitation. The* MOTHER, *frightened, tries to separate them*]

THE MOTHER [*pleading*]: Please! please!

THE FATHER [*not leaving hold of the* SON]: You've got to obey, do you hear?

THE SON [*almost crying from rage*]: What does it mean, this madness you've got? [*They separate.*] Have you no decency, that you insist on showing everyone our shame? I won't do it! I won't! And I stand for the will of our author in this. He didn't want to put us on the stage, after all!

THE MANAGER: Man alive! You came here . . .

THE SON [*indicating* FATHER]: *He* did! I didn't!

THE MANAGER: Aren't you here now?

THE SON: It was his wish, and he dragged us along with him. He's told you not only the things that did happen, but also things that have never happened at all.

THE MANAGER: Well, tell me then what did happen. You went out of your room without saying a word?

THE SON: Without a word, so as to avoid a scene!

THE MANAGER: And then what did you do?

THE SON: Nothing . . . walking in the garden . . . [*hesitates for a moment with expression of gloom*]

THE MANAGER [*coming closer to him, interested by his extraordinary reserve*]: Well, well . . . walking in the garden . . .

THE SON [*exasperated*]: Why on earth do you insist? It's horrible! [*The* MOTHER *trembles, sobs, and looks towards the fountain.*]

THE MANAGER [*slowly observing the glance and turning towards the* SON *with increasing apprehension*]: The baby?

THE SON: There in the fountain . . .

THE FATHER [*pointing with tender pity to the* MOTHER]: She was following him at the moment . . .

THE MANAGER [*to the* SON, *anxiously*]: And then you . . .

THE SON: I ran over to her; I was jumping in to drag her out when I saw something that froze my blood . . . the boy there, standing stock still, with eyes like a madman's, watching his little drowned sister, in the fountain! [*The* STEPDAUGHTER *bends over the fountain to hide the* CHILD. *She sobs.*] Then . . . [*A revolver shot rings out behind the trees where the* BOY *is hidden.*]

THE MOTHER [*With a cry of terror runs over in that direction together with several of the* ACTORS *amid general confusion*]: My son! My son! [*Then amid the cries and exclamations one hears her voice*] Help! Help!

THE MANAGER [*pushing the* ACTORS *aside while they lift up the* BOY *and carry him off*]: Is he really wounded?

SOME ACTORS: He's dead! dead!

OTHER ACTORS: No, no, it's only make believe, it's only pretence!

THE FATHER [*with a terrible cry*]: Pretence? Reality, sir, reality!

THE MANAGER: Pretence? Reality? To hell with it all! Never in my life has such a thing happened to me. I've lost a whole day over these people, a whole day!

Lorraine Hansberry (1930–1965)

A RAISIN IN THE SUN

To Mama: in gratitude for the dream

What happens to a dream deferred?
Does it dry up
Like a raisin in the sun?
Or fester like a sore—
And then run?
Does it stink like rotten meat:
Or crust and sugar over—
Like a syrupy sweet?

Maybe it just sags
Like a heavy load.

Or does it explode?

—Langston Hughes*

RUTH YOUNGER
TRAVIS YOUNGER
WALTER LEE YOUNGER [BROTHER]
BENEATHA YOUNGER
LENA YOUNGER [MAMA]

JOSEPH ASAGAI
GEORGE MURCHISON
KARL LINDNER
BOBO
MOVING MEN

The action of the play is set in Chicago's Southside, sometime between World War II and the present.

ACT ONE

SCENE 1: *Friday morning.*
SCENE 2: *The following morning.*

SOURCE: Reprinted with the permission of Random House, Inc. Copyright © 1958, 1959 by Lorraine Hansberry.

*Copyright 1951 by Langston Hughes. Reprinted from *The Panther and the Lash* by Langston Hughes, with the permission of Alfred A. Knopf, Inc.

ACT TWO

SCENE 1: *Later, the same day.*
SCENE 2: *Friday night, a few weeks later.*
SCENE 3: *Moving day, one week later.*

ACT THREE

An hour later.

ACT 1
Scene One

[*The* YOUNGER *living room would be a comfortable and well-ordered room if it were not for a number of indestructible contradictions to this state of being. Its furnishings are typical and undistinguished and their primary feature now is that they have clearly had to accommodate the living of too many people for too many years and—they are tired. Still, we can see that at some time, a time probably no longer remembered by the family (except perhaps for* MAMA) *the furnishings of this room were actually selected with care and love and even hope —and brought to this apartment and arranged with taste and pride. That was a long time ago. Now the once loved pattern of the couch upholstery has to fight to show itself from under acres of crocheted doilies and couch covers which have themselves finally come to be more important than the upholstery. And here a table or a chair has been moved to disguise the worn places in the carpet; but the carpet has fought back by showing its weariness, with depressing uniformity, elsewhere on its surface. Weariness has, in fact, won in this room. Everything has been polished, washed, sat on, used, scrubbed too often. All pretenses but living itself have long since vanished from the very atmosphere of this room.*

Moreover, a section of this room, for it is not really a room unto itself, though the landlord's lease would make it seem so, slopes backward to provide a small kitchen area, where the family prepares the meals that are eaten in the living room proper, which must also serve as dining room. The single window that has been provided for these "two" rooms is located in this kitchen area. The sole natural light the family may enjoy in the course of a day is only that which fights its way through this little window.

At left, a door leads to a bedroom which is shared by MAMA *and her daughter,* BENEATHA. *At right, opposite, is a second room (which in the beginning of the life of this apartment was probably a breakfast room) which serves as a bedroom for* WALTER *and his wife,* RUTH.

Time: Sometime between World War II and the present.
Place: Chicago's Southside.
At Rise: It is morning dark in the living room. TRAVIS *is asleep on the make-down bed at center. An alarm clock sounds from within the bedroom at right, and presently* RUTH *enters from that room and closes the door behind her. She crosses sleepily toward the window. As she passes her sleeping son she reaches*

down and shakes him a little. At the window she raises the shade and a dusky Southside morning light comes in feebly. She fills a pot with water and puts it on to boil. She calls to the boy, between yawns, in a slightly muffled voice. RUTH *is about thirty. We can see that she was a pretty girl, even exceptionally so, but now it is apparent that life has been little that she expected, and disappointment has already begun to hang in her face. In a few years, before thirty-five even, she will be known among her people as a "settled woman."] She crosses to her son and gives him a good, final, rousing shake.*

RUTH: Come on now, boy, it's seven thirty! [*Her son sits up at last, in a stupor of sleepiness*] I say hurry up, Travis! You ain't the only person in the world got to use a bathroom! [*The child, a sturdy, handsome little boy of ten or eleven, drags himself out of the bed and almost blindly takes his towels and "today's clothes" from drawers and a closet and goes out to the bathroom, which is in an outside hall and which is shared by another family or families on the same floor.* RUTH *crosses to the bedroom door at right and opens it and calls in to her husband*] Walter Lee! . . . It's after seven thirty! Lemme see you do some waking up in there now! [*She waits*] You better get up from there, man! It's after seven thirty I tell you. [*She waits again*] All right, you just go ahead and lay there and next thing you know Travis be finished and Mr. Johnson'll be in there and you'll be fussing and cussing round here like a mad man! And be late too! [*She waits, at the end of patience*] Walter Lee—it's time for you to get up!
[*She waits another second and then starts to go into the bedroom, but is apparently satisfied that her husband has begun to get up. She stops, pulls the door to, and returns to the kitchen area. She wipes her face with a moist cloth and runs her fingers through her sleep-disheveled hair in a vain effort and ties an apron around her housecoat. The bedroom door at right opens and her husband stands in the doorway in his pajamas, which are rumpled and mismated. He is a lean, intense young man in his middle thirties, inclined to quick nervous movements and erratic speech habits—and always in his voice there is a quality of indictment*]
WALTER: Is he out yet?
RUTH: What you mean *out?* He ain't hardly got in there good yet.
WALTER [*Wandering in, still more oriented to sleep than to a new day*]: Well, what was you doing all that yelling for if I can't even get in there yet? [*Stopping and thinking*] Check coming today?
RUTH: They *said* Saturday and this is just Friday and I hopes to God you ain't going to get up here first thing this morning and start talking to me 'bout no money—'cause I 'bout don't want to hear it.
WALTER: Something the matter with you this morning?
RUTH: No—I'm just sleepy as the devil. What kind of eggs you want?
WALTER: Not scrambled. [RUTH *starts to scramble eggs*] Paper come? [RUTH *points impatiently to the rolled up* Tribune *on the table, and he gets it and*

spreads it out and vaguely reads the front page] Set off another bomb yesterday.

RUTH [*Maximum indifference*]: Did they?

WALTER [*Looking up*]: What's the matter with you?

RUTH: Ain't nothing the matter with me. And don't keep asking me that this
morning.

WALTER: Ain't nobody bothering you. [*Reading the news of the day absently
again*] Say Colonel McCormick is sick.

RUTH [*Affecting tea-party interest*]: Is he now? Poor thing.

WALTER [*Sighing and looking at his watch*]: Oh, me. [*He waits*] Now what is
that boy doing in that bathroom all this time? He just going to have to
start getting up earlier. I can't be being late to work on account of him
fooling around in there.

RUTH [*Turning on him*]: Oh, no he ain't going to be getting up no earlier no
such thing! It ain't his fault that he can't get to bed no earlier nights
'cause he got a bunch of crazy good-for-nothing clowns sitting up
running their mouths in what is supposed to be his bedroom after ten
o'clock at night . . .

WALTER: That's what you mad about, ain't it? The things I want to talk
about with my friends just couldn't be important in your mind could
they?

[*He rises and finds a cigarette in her handbag on the table and crosses to the
little window and looks out, smoking and deeply enjoying this first one*]

RUTH [*Almost matter of factly, a complaint too automatic to deserve emphasis*]:
Why you always got to smoke before you eat in the morning?

WALTER [*At the window*]: Just look at 'em down there . . . Running and
racing to work . . . [*He turns and faces his wife and watches her a moment
at the stove, and then, suddenly*] You look young this morning, baby.

RUTH [*Indifferently*]: Yeah?

WALTER: Just for a second—stirring them eggs. It's gone now—just for a
second it was—you looked real young again. [*Then, drily*] It's gone now
—you look like yourself again.

RUTH: Man, if you don't shut up and leave me alone.

WALTER [*Looking out to the street again*]: First thing a man ought to learn in
life is not to make love to no colored woman first thing in the morning.
You all some evil people at eight o'clock in the morning.

[TRAVIS *appears in the hall doorway, almost fully dressed and quite wide awake
now, his towels and pajamas across his shoulders. He opens the door and signals
for his father to make the bathroom in a hurry*]

TRAVIS [*Watching the bathroom*]: Daddy, come on!

[WALTER *gets his bathroom utensils and flies out to the bathroom*]

RUTH: Sit down and have your breakfast, Travis.

TRAVIS: Mama, this is Friday. [*Gleefully*] Check coming tomorrow, huh?

RUTH: You get your mind off money and eat your breakfast.

TRAVIS [*Eating*]: This is the morning we supposed to bring the fifty cents to school.

RUTH: Well, I ain't got no fifty cents this morning.

TRAVIS: Teacher say we have to.

RUTH: I don't care what teacher say. I ain't got it. Eat your breakfast, Travis.

TRAVIS: I *am* eating.

RUTH: Hush up now and just eat!

[*The boy gives her an exasperated look for her lack of understanding, and eats grudgingly*]

TRAVIS: You think Grandmama would have it?

RUTH: No! And I want you to stop asking your grandmother for money, you hear me?

TRAVIS [*Outraged*]: Gaaaleee! I don't ask her, she just gimme it sometimes!

RUTH: Travis Willard Younger—I got too much on me this morning to be—

TRAVIS: Maybe Daddy—

RUTH: *Travis!*

[*The boy hushes abruptly. They are both quiet and tense for several seconds*]

TRAVIS [*Presently*]: Could I maybe go carry some groceries in front of the supermarket for a little while after school then?

RUTH: Just hush, I said. [*Travis jabs his spoon into his cereal bowl viciously, and rests his head in anger upon his fists*] If you through eating, you can get over there and make up your bed.

[*The boy obeys stiffly and crosses the room, almost mechanically, to the bed and more or less carefully folds the covering. He carries the bedding into his mother's room and returns with his books and cap*]

TRAVIS [*Sulking and standing apart from her unnaturally*]: I'm gone.

RUTH [*Looking up from the stove to inspect him automatically*]: Come here. [*He crosses to her and she studies his head*] If you don't take this comb and fix this here head, you better! [TRAVIS *puts down his books with a great sigh of oppression, and crosses to the mirror. His mother mutters under her breath about his 'slubbornness'*] 'Bout to march out of here with that head looking just like chickens slept in it! I just don't know where you get your slubborn ways . . . And get your jacket, too. Looks chilly out this morning.

TRAVIS [*With conspicuously brushed hair and jacket*]: I'm gone.

RUTH: Get carfare and milk money—[*Waving one finger*]—and not a single penny for no caps, you hear me?

TRAVIS [*With sullen politeness*]: Yes'm.

[*He turns in outrage to leave. His mother watches after him as in his frustration he approaches the door almost comically. When she speaks to him, her voice has become a very gentle tease*]

RUTH [*Mocking; as she thinks he would say it*]: Oh, Mama makes me so mad sometimes, I don't know what to do! [*She waits and continues to his back as he stands stock-still in front of the door*] I wouldn't kiss that woman good-bye for nothing in this world this morning! [*The boy finally turns around and rolls his eyes at her, knowing the mood has changed and he is vindicated; he does not, however, move toward her yet*] Not for nothing in this world! [*She finally laughs aloud at him and holds out her arms to him and we see that it is a way between them, very old and practiced. He crosses to her and allows her to embrace him warmly but keeps his face fixed with masculine rigidity. She holds him back from her presently and looks at him and runs her fingers over the features of his face. With utter gentleness—*] Now—whose little old angry man are you?

TRAVIS [*The masculinity and gruffness start to fade at last*]: Aw gaalee— Mama . . .

RUTH [*Mimicking*]: Aw—gaaaaalleeeee, Mama! [*She pushes him, with rough playfulness and finality, toward the door*] Get on out of here or you going to be late.

TRAVIS [*In the face of love, new aggressiveness*]: Mama, could I *please* go carry groceries?

RUTH: Honey, it's starting to get so cold evenings.

WALTER [*Coming in from the bathroom and drawing a make-believe gun from a make-believe holster and shooting at his son*]: What is it he wants to do?

RUTH: Go carry groceries after school at the supermarket.

WALTER: Well, let him go . . .

TRAVIS [*Quickly, to the ally*]: I *have* to—she won't gimme the fifty cents . . .

WALTER [*To his wife only*]: Why not?

RUTH [*Simply, and with flavor*]: 'Cause we don't have it.

WALTER [*To RUTH only*]: What you tell the boy things like that for? [*Reaching down into his pants with a rather important gesture*] Here, son—

[*He hands the boy the coin, but his eyes are directed to his wife's. TRAVIS takes the money happily*]

TRAVIS: Thanks, Daddy.

[*He starts out.* RUTH *watches both of them with murder in her eyes.* WALTER *stands and stares back at her with defiance, and suddenly reaches into his pocket again on an afterthought*]

WALTER [*Without even looking at his son, still staring hard at his wife*]: In fact, here's another fifty cents . . . Buy yourself some fruit today—or take a taxicab to school or something!
TRAVIS: Whoopee—

[*He leaps up and clasps his father around the middle with his legs, and they face each other in mutual appreciation; slowly* WALTER LEE *peeks around the boy to catch the violent rays from his wife's eyes and draws his head back as if shot*]

WALTER: You better get down now—and get to school, man.
TRAVIS [*At the door*]: O.K. Good-bye.

[*He exits*]

WALTER: [*After him, pointing with pride*] That's *my* boy. [*She looks at him in disgust and turns back to her work*] You know what I was thinking 'bout in the bathroom this morning?
RUTH: No.
WALTER: How come you always try to be so pleasant!
RUTH: What is there to be pleasant 'bout!
WALTER: You want to know what I was thinking 'bout in the bathroom or not!
RUTH: I know what you thinking 'bout.
WALTER [*Ignoring her*]: 'Bout what me and Willy Harris was talking about last night.
RUTH [*Immediately—a refrain*]: Willy Harris is a good-for-nothing loud mouth.
WALTER: Anybody who talks to me has got to be a good-for-nothing loud mouth, ain't he? And what you know about who is just a good-for-nothing loud mouth? Charlie Atkins was just a "good-for-nothing loud mouth" too, wasn't he! When he wanted me to go in the dry-cleaning business with him. And now—he's grossing a hundred thousand a year. A hundred thousand dollars a year! You still call *him* a loud mouth!
RUTH [*Bitterly*]: Oh, Walter Lee . . .

[*She folds her head on her arms over the table*]

WALTER [*Rising and coming to her and standing over her*]: You tired, ain't you? Tired of everything. Me, the boy, the way we live—this beat-up hole —everything. Ain't you? [*She doesn't look up, doesn't answer*] So tired— moaning and groaning all the time, but you wouldn't do nothing to help, would you? You couldn't be on my side that long for nothing, could you?

RUTH: Walter, please leave me alone.

WALTER: A man needs for a woman to back him up . . .

RUTH: Walter—

WALTER: Mama would listen to you. You know she listen to you more than she do me and Bennie. She think more of you. All you have to do is just sit down with her when you drinking your coffee one morning and talking 'bout things like you do and—[*He sits down beside her and demonstrates graphically what he thinks her methods and tone should be*]—you just sip your coffee, see, and say easy like that you been thinking 'bout that deal Walter Lee is so interested in, 'bout the store and all, and sip some more coffee, like what you saying ain't really that important to you— And the next thing you know, she be listening good and asking you questions and when I come home—I can tell her the details. This ain't no fly-by-night proposition, baby. I mean we figured it out, me and Willy and Bobo.

RUTH [*With a frown*]: Bobo?

WALTER: Yeah. You see, this little liquor store we got in mind cost seventy-five thousand and we figured the initial investment on the place be 'bout thirty thousand, see. That be ten thousand each. Course, there's a couple of hundred you got to pay so's you don't spend your life just waiting for them clowns to let your license get approved—

RUTH: You mean graft?

WALTER [*Frowning impatiently*]: Don't call it that. See there, that just goes to show you what women understand about the world. Baby, don't *nothing* happen for you in this world 'less you pay *somebody* off!

RUTH: Walter, leave me alone! [*She raises her head and stares at him vigorously —then says, more quietly*] Eat your eggs, they gonna be cold.

WALTER [*Straightening up from her and looking off*]: That's it. There you are. Man say to his woman: I got me a dream. His woman say: Eat your eggs. [*Sadly, but gaining in power*] Man say: I got to take hold of this here world, baby! And a woman will say: Eat your eggs and go to work. [*Passionately now*] Man say: I got to change my life, I'm choking to death, baby! And his woman say—[*In utter anguish as he brings his fists down on his thighs*]—Your eggs is getting cold!

RUTH [*Softly*]: Walter, that ain't none of our money.

WALTER [*Not listening at all or even looking at her*]: This morning, I was lookin' in the mirror and thinking about it . . . I'm thirty-five years old; I been married eleven years and I got a boy who sleeps in the living room—

[*Very, very quietly*]—and all I got to give him is stories about how rich white people live . . .

RUTH: Eat your eggs, Walter.

WALTER: *Damn my eggs . . . damn all the eggs that ever was!*

RUTH: Then go to work.

WALTER [*Looking up at her*]: See—I'm trying to talk to you 'bout myself— [*Shaking his head with the repetition*]—and all you can say is eat them eggs and go to work.

RUTH [*Wearily*]: Honey, you never say nothing new. I listen to you every day, every night and every morning, and you never say nothing new. [*Shrugging*] So you would rather *be* Mr. Arnold than be his chauffeur. So—I would *rather* be living in Buckingham Palace.

WALTER: That is just what is wrong with the colored woman in this world . . . Don't understand about building their men up and making 'em feel like they somebody. Like they can do something.

RUTH [*Drily, but to hurt*]: There *are* colored men who do things.

WALTER: No thanks to the colored woman.

RUTH: Well, being a colored woman, I guess I can't help myself none.

[*She rises and gets the ironing board and sets it up and attacks a huge pile of rough-dried clothes, sprinkling them in preparation for the ironing and then rolling them into tight fat balls*]

WALTER [*Mumbling*]: We one group of men tied to a race of women with small minds.

[*His sister* BENEATHA *enters. She is about twenty, as slim and intense as her brother. She is not as pretty as her sister-in-law, but her lean, almost intellectual face has a handsomeness of its own. She wears a bright-red flannel nightie, and her thick hair stands wildly about her head. Her speech is a mixture of many things; it is different from the rest of the family's insofar as education has permeated her sense of English—and perhaps the Midwest rather than the South has finally—at last—won out in her inflection; but not altogether, because over all of it is a soft slurring and transformed use of vowels which is the decided influence of the Southside. She passes through the room without looking at either* RUTH *or* WALTER *and goes to the outside door and looks, a little blindly, out to the bathroom. She sees that it has been lost to the Johnsons. She closes the door with a sleepy vengeance and crosses to the table and sits down a little defeated*]

BENEATHA: I am going to start timing those people.

WALTER: You should get up earlier.

BENEATHA [*Her face in her hands. She is still fighting the urge to go back to bed*]: Really—would you suggest dawn? Where's the paper?

WALTER [*Pushing the paper across the table to her as he studies her almost clinically, as though he has never seen her before*]: You a horrible-looking chick at this hour.

BENEATHA [*Drily*]: Good morning, everybody.

WALTER [*Senselessly*]: How is school coming?

BENEATHA [*In the same spirit*]: Lovely. Lovely. And you know, biology is the greatest. [*Looking up at him*] I dissected something that looked just like you yesterday.

WALTER: I just wondered if you've made up your mind and everything.

BENEATHA [*Gaining in sharpness and impatience*]: And what did I answer yesterday morning—and the day before that?

RUTH [*From the ironing board, like someone disinterested and old*]: Don't be so nasty, Bennie.

BENEATHA [*Still to her brother*]: And the day before that and the day before that!

WALTER [*Defensively*]: I'm interested in you. Something wrong with that? Ain't many girls who decide—

WALTER *and* BENEATHA [*In unison*]:—"to be a doctor."

[*Silence*]

WALTER: Have we figured out yet just exactly how much medical school is going to cost?

RUTH: Walter Lee, why don't you leave that girl alone and get out of here to work?

BENEATHA [*Exits to the bathroom and bangs on the door*]: Come on out of there, please!

[*She comes back into the room*]

WALTER [*Looking at his sister intently*]: You know the check is coming tomorrow.

BENEATHA [*Turning on him with a sharpness all her own*]: That money belongs to Mama, Walter, and it's for her to decide how she wants to use it. I don't care if she wants to buy a house or a rocket ship or just nail it up somewhere and look at it. It's hers. Not ours—*hers.*

WALTER [*Bitterly*]: Now ain't that fine! You just got your mother's interest at heart, ain't you, girl? You such a nice girl—but if Mama got that money she can always take a few thousand and help you through school too—can't she?

BENEATHA: I have never asked anyone around here to do anything for me!

WALTER: No! And the line between asking and just accepting when the time comes is big and wide—ain't it!

BENEATHA [*With fury*]: What do you want from me, Brother—that I quit school or just drop dead, which!

WALTER: I don't want nothing but for you to stop acting holy 'round here. Me and Ruth done made some sacrifices for you—why can't you do something for the family?

RUTH: Walter, don't be dragging me in it.

WALTER: You are in it—Don't you get up and go work in somebody's kitchen for the last three years to help put clothes on her back?

RUTH: Oh, Walter—that's not fair . . .

WALTER: It ain't that nobody expects you to get on your knees and say thank you, Brother; thank you, Ruth; thank you, Mama—and thank you, Travis, for wearing the same pair of shoes for two semesters—

BENEATHA [*Dropping to her knees*]: Well—I *do*—all right?—thank everybody . . . and forgive me for ever wanting to be anything at all . . . forgive me, forgive me!

RUTH: Please stop it! Your mama'll hear you.

WALTER: Who the hell told you you had to be a doctor? If you so crazy 'bout messing 'round with sick people—then go be a nurse like other women —or just get married and be quiet . . .

BENEATHA: Well— you finally got it said . . . It took you three years but you finally got it said. Walter, give up; leave me alone—it's Mama's money.

WALTER: *He was my father, too!*

BENEATHA: So what? He was mine, too—and Travis' grandfather—but the insurance money belongs to Mama. Picking on me is not going to make her give it to you to invest in any liquor stores—[*Underbreath, dropping into a chair*]—and I for one say, God bless Mama for that!

WALTER [*To* RUTH]: See—did you hear? Did you hear!

RUTH: Honey, please go to work.

WALTER: Nobody in this house is ever going to understand me.

BENEATHA: Because you're a nut.

WALTER: Who's a nut?

BENEATHA: You—you are a nut. Thee is mad, boy.

WALTER [*Looking at his wife and his sister from the door, very sadly*]: The world's most backward race of people, and that's a fact.

BENEATHA [*Turning slowly in her chair*]: And then there are all those prophets who would lead us out of the wildernesss—[WALTER *slams out of the house*]—into the swamps!

RUTH: Bennie, why you always gotta be pickin' on your brother? Can't you be a little sweeter sometimes? [*Door opens.* WALTER *walks in*]

WALTER [*To Ruth*]: I need some money for carfare.

RUTH [*Looks at him, then warms; teasing, but tenderly*]: Fifty cents? [*She goes to her bag and gets money*] Here, take a taxi.

[WALTER *exits.* MAMA *enters. She is a woman in her early sixties, full-bodied and strong. She is one of those women of a certain grace and beauty who wear it so unobtrusively that it takes a while to notice. Her dark-brown face is surrounded by the total whiteness of her hair, and, being a woman who has adjusted to many things in life and overcome many more, her face is full of strength. She has, we can see, wit and faith of a kind that keep her eyes lit and full of interest and expectancy. She is, in a word, a beautiful woman. Her bearing is perhaps most like the noble bearing of the women of the Hereros of Southwest Africa—rather as if she imagines that as she walks she still bears a basket or a vessel upon her head. Her speech, on the other hand, is as careless as her carriage is precise—she is inclined to slur everything—but her voice is perhaps not so much quiet as simply soft]*

MAMA: Who that 'round here slamming doors at this hour?

[She crosses through the room, goes to the window, opens it, and brings in a feeble little plant growing doggedly in a small pot on the window sill. She feels the dirt and puts it back out]

RUTH: That was Walter Lee. He and Bennie was at it again.
MAMA: My children and they tempers. Lord, if this little old plant don't get more sun than it's been getting it ain't never going to see spring again. *[She turns from the window]* What's the matter with you this morning, Ruth? You looks right peaked. You aiming to iron all them things? Leave some for me. I'll get to 'em this afternoon. Bennie honey, it's too drafty for you to be sitting 'round half dressed. Where's your robe?
BENEATHA: In the cleaners.
MAMA: Well, go get mine and put it on.
BENEATHA: I'm not cold, Mama, honest.
MAMA: I know—but you so thin . . .
BENEATHA *[Irritably]*: Mama, I'm not cold.
MAMA *[Seeing the make-down bed as TRAVIS has left it]*: Lord have mercy, look at that poor bed. Bless his heart—he tries, don't he?

[She moves to the bed TRAVIS has sloppily made up]

RUTH: No—he don't half try at all 'cause he knows you going to come along behind him and fix everything. That's just how come he don't know how to do nothing right now—you done spoiled that boy so.
MAMA: Well—he's a little boy. Ain't supposed to know 'bout housekeeping. My baby, that's what he is. What you fix for his breakfast this morning?
RUTH *[Angrily]*: I feed my son, Lena!
MAMA: I ain't meddling—*[Underbreath; busy-bodyish]* I just noticed all last week he had cold cereal, and when it starts getting this chilly in the fall a child ought to have some hot grits or something when he goes out in the cold—
RUTH *[Furious]*: I gave him hot oats—is that all right!
MAMA: I ain't meddling. *[Pause]* Put a lot of nice butter on it? *[RUTH shoots her an angry look and does not reply]* He likes lots of butter.

RUTH [*Exasperated*]: Lena—

MAMA [*To* BENEATHA. MAMA *is inclined to wander conversationally sometimes*]: What was you and your brother fussing 'bout this morning?

BENEATHA: It's not important, Mama.

[*She gets up and goes to look out at the bathroom, which is apparently free, and she picks up her towels and rushes out*]

MAMA: What was they fighting about?

RUTH: Now you know as well as I do.

MAMA [*Shaking her head*]: Brother still worrying hisself sick about that money?

RUTH: You know he is.

MAMA: You had breakfast?

RUTH: Some coffee.

MAMA: Girl, you better start eating and looking after yourself better. You almost thin as Travis.

RUTH: Lena—

MAMA: Un-hunh?

RUTH: What are you going to do with it?

MAMA: Now don't you start, child. It's too early in the morning to be talking about money. It ain't Christian.

RUTH: It's just that he got his heart set on that store—

MAMA: You mean that liquor store that Willy Harris want him to invest in?

RUTH: Yes—

MAMA: We ain't no business people, Ruth. We just plain working folks.

RUTH: Ain't nobody business people till they go into business. Walter Lee say colored people ain't never going to start getting ahead till they start gambling on some different kinds of things in the world—investments and things.

MAMA: What done got into you, girl? Walter Lee done finally sold you on investing.

RUTH: No. Mama, something is happening between Walter and me. I don't know what it is—but he needs something—something I can't give him any more. He needs this chance, Lena.

MAMA [*Frowning deeply*]: But liquor, honey—

RUTH: Well—like Walter say—I spec people going to always be drinking themselves some liquor.

MAMA: Well—whether they drinks it or not ain't none of my business. But whether I go into business selling it to 'em *is*, and I don't want that on my ledger this late in life. [*Stopping suddenly and studying her daughter-in-law*] Ruth Younger, what's the matter with you today? You look like you could fall over right there.

RUTH: I'm tired.

MAMA: Then you better stay home from work today.

RUTH: I can't stay home. She'd be calling up the agency and screaming at them, "My girl didn't come in today—send me somebody! My girl didn't come in!" Oh, she just have a fit . . .

MAMA: Well, let her have it. I'll just call her up and say you got the flu—

RUTH [*Laughing*]: Why the flu?

MAMA: 'Cause it sounds respectable to 'em. Something white people get, too. They know 'bout the flu. Otherwise they think you been cut up or something when you tell 'em you sick.

RUTH: I got to go in. We need the money.

MAMA: Somebody would of thought my children done all but starved to death the way they talk about money here late. Child, we got a great big old check coming tomorrow.

RUTH [*Sincerely, but also self-righteously*]: Now that's your money. It ain't got nothing to do with me. We all feel like that—Walter and Bennie and me—even Travis.

MAMA [*Thoughtfully, and suddenly very far away*]: Ten thousand dollars—

RUTH: Sure is wonderful.

MAMA: Ten thousand dollars.

RUTH: You know what you should do, Miss Lena? You should take yourself a trip somewhere. To Europe or South America or someplace—

MAMA [*Throwing up her hands at the thought*]: Oh, child!

RUTH: I'm serious. Just pack up and leave! Go on away and enjoy yourself some. Forget about the family and have yourself a ball for once in your life—

MAMA [*Drily*]: You sound like I'm just about ready to die. Who'd go with me? What I look like wandering 'round Europe by myself?

RUTH: Shoot—these here rich white women do it all the time. They don't think nothing of packing up they suitcases and piling on one of them big steamships and—swoosh!—they gone, child.

MAMA: Something always told me I wasn't no rich white woman.

RUTH: Well—what are you going to do with it then?

MAMA: I ain't rightly decided. [*Thinking. She speaks now with emphasis*] Some of it got to be put away for Beneatha and her schoolin'—and ain't nothing going to touch that part of it. Nothing. [*She waits several seconds, trying to make up her mind about something, and looks at* RUTH *a little tentatively before going on*] Been thinking that we maybe could meet the notes on a little old two-story somewhere, with a yard where Travis could play in the summertime, if we use part of the insurance for a down payment and everybody kind of pitch in. I could maybe take on a little day work again, few days a week—

RUTH [*Studying her mother-in-law furtively and concentrating on her ironing, anxious to encourage without seeming to*]: Well, Lord knows, we've put enough rent into this here rat trap to pay for four houses by now . . .

MAMA [*Looking up at the words "rat trap" and then looking around and leaning back and sighing—in a suddenly reflective mood—*]: "Rat trap"—yes, that's all it is. [*Smiling*] I remember just as well the day me and Big Walter moved in here. Hadn't been married but two weeks and wasn't planning on living here no more than a year. [*She shakes her head at the dissolved dream*] We was going to set away, little by little, don't you know, and buy a little place out in Morgan Park. We had even picked out the house. [*Chuckling a little*] Looks right dumpy today. But Lord, child, you should know all the dreams I had 'bout buying that house and fixing it up and making me a little garden in the back—[*She waits and stops smiling*] And didn't none of it happen.

[*Dropping her hands in a futile gesture*]

RUTH [*Keeps her head down, ironing*]: Yes, life can be a barrel of disappointments, sometimes.

MAMA: Honey, Big Walter would come in here some nights back then and slump down on that couch there and just look at the rug, and look at me and look at the rug and then back at me—and I'd know he was down then . . . really down. [*After a second very long and thoughtful pause; she is seeing back to times that only she can see*] And then, Lord, when I lost that baby—little Claude—I almost thought I was going to lose Big Walter too. Oh, that man grieved hisself! He was one man to love his children.

RUTH: Ain't nothin' can tear at you like losin' your baby.

MAMA: I guess that's how come that man finally worked hisself to death like he done. Like he was fighting his own war with this here world that took his baby from him.

RUTH: He sure was a fine man, all right. I always liked Mr. Younger.

MAMA: Crazy 'bout his children! God knows there was plenty wrong with Walter Younger—hard-headed, mean, kind of wild with women—plenty wrong with him. But he sure loved his children. Always wanted them to have something—be something. That's where Brother gets all these notions, I reckon. Big Walter used to say, he'd get right wet in the eyes sometimes, lean his head back with the water standing in his eyes and say, "Seem like God didn't see fit to give the black man nothing but dreams—but He did give us children to make them dreams seem worth while." [*She smiles*] He could talk like that, don't you know.

RUTH: Yes, he sure could. He was a good man, Mr. Younger.

MAMA: Yes, a fine man—just couldn't never catch up with his dreams, that's all.

[BENEATHA *comes in, brushing her hair and looking up to the ceiling, where the sound of a vacuum cleaner has started up*]

BENEATHA: What could be so dirty on that woman's rugs that she has to vacuum them every single day?

RUTH: I wish certain young women 'round here who I could name would take inspiration about certain rugs in a certain apartment I could also mention.

BENEATHA [*Shrugging*]: How much cleaning can a house need, for Christ's sakes.

MAMA [*Not liking the Lord's name used thus*]: Bennie!

RUTH: Just listen to her—just listen!

BENEATHA: Oh, God!

MAMA: If you use the Lord's name just one more time—

BENEATHA [*A bit of a whine*]: Oh, Mama—

RUTH: Fresh—just fresh as salt, this girl!

BENEATHA [*Drily*]: Well—if the salt loses its savor—

MAMA: Now that will do. I just ain't going to have you 'round here reciting the scriptures in vain—you hear me?

BENEATHA: How did I manage to get on everybody's wrong side by just walking into a room?

RUTH: If you weren't so fresh—

BENEATHA: Ruth, I'm twenty years old.

MAMA: What time you be home from school today?

BENEATHA: Kind of late. [*With enthusiasm*] Madeline is going to start my guitar lessons today.

[MAMA *and* RUTH *look up with the same expression*]

MAMA: Your *what* kind of lessons?

BENEATHA: Guitar.

RUTH: Oh, Father!

MAMA: How come you done taken it in your mind to learn to play the guitar?

BENEATHA: I just want to, that's all.

MAMA [*Smiling*]: Lord, child, don't you know what to do with yourself? How long it going to be before you get tired of this now—like you got tired of that little play-acting group you joined last year? [*Looking at* RUTH] And what was it the year before that?

RUTH: The horseback-riding club for which she bought that fifty-five-dollar riding habit that's been hanging in the closet ever since!

MAMA [*To* BENEATHA]: Why you got to flit so from one thing to another, baby?

BENEATHA [*Sharply*]: I just want to learn to play the guitar. Is there anything wrong with that?

MAMA: Ain't nobody trying to stop you. I just wonders sometimes why you has to flit so from one thing to another all the time. You ain't never done nothing with all that camera equipment you brought home—

BENEATHA: I don't flit! I—I experiment with different forms of expression—

RUTH: Like riding a horse?

BENEATHA: —People have to express themselves one way or another.

MAMA: What is it you want to express?

BENEATHA [*Angrily*]: Me! [MAMA *and* RUTH *look at each other and burst into raucous laughter*] Don't worry—I don't expect you to understand.

MAMA [*To change the subject*]: Who you going out with tomorrow night?

BENEATHA [*With displeasure*]: George Murchison again.

MAMA [*Pleased*]: Oh—you getting a little sweet on him?

RUTH: You ask me, this child ain't sweet on nobody but herself—[*Under-breath*] Express herself!

[*They laugh*]

BENEATHA: Oh—I like George all right, Mama. I mean I like him enough to go out with him and stuff, but—

RUTH [*For devilment*]: What does *and stuff* mean?

BENEATHA: Mind your own business.

MAMA: Stop picking at her now, Ruth. [*A thoughtful pause, and then a suspicious sudden look at her daughter as she turns in her chair for emphasis*] What *does* it mean?

BENEATHA [*Wearily*]: Oh, I just mean I couldn't ever really be serious about George. He's—he's so shallow.

RUTH: Shallow—what do you mean he's shallow? He's *Rich!*

MAMA: Hush, Ruth.

BENEATHA: I know he's rich. He knows he's rich, too.

RUTH: Well—what other qualities a man got to have to satisfy you, little girl?

BENEATHA: You wouldn't even begin to understand. Anybody who married Walter could not possibly understand.

MAMA [*Outraged*]: What kind of way is that to talk about your brother?

BENEATHA: Brother is a flip—let's face it.

MAMA [*To* RUTH, *helplessly*]: What's a flip?

RUTH [*Glad to add kindling*]: She's saying he's crazy.

BENEATHA: Not crazy. Brother isn't really crazy yet—he—he's an elaborate neurotic.

MAMA: Hush your mouth!

BENEATHA: As for George. Well. George looks good—he's got a beautiful car and he takes me to nice places and, as my sister-in-law says, he is probably the richest boy I will ever get to know and I even like him sometimes—but if the Youngers are sitting around waiting to see if their little Bennie is going to tie up the family with the Murchisons, they are wasting their time.

RUTH: You mean you wouldn't marry George Murchison if he asked you someday? That pretty, rich thing? Honey, I knew you was odd—

BENEATHA: No I would not marry him if all I felt for him was what I feel now. Besides, George's family wouldn't really like it.

MAMA: Why not?

BENEATHA: Oh, Mama—The Murchisons are honest-to-God-real-*live*-rich colored people, and the only people in the world who are more snobbish than rich white people are rich colored people. I thought everybody knew that. I've met Mrs. Murchison. She's a scene!

MAMA: You must not dislike people 'cause they well off, honey.

BENEATHA: Why not? It makes just as much sense as disliking people 'cause they are poor, and lots of people do that.

RUTH [*A wisdom-of-the-ages manner. To* MAMA]: Well, she'll get over some of this—

BENEATHA: Get over it? What are you talking about, Ruth? Listen, I'm going to be a doctor. I'm not worried about who I'm going to marry yet—if I ever get married.

MAMA *and* RUTH: *If!*

MAMA: Now, Bennie—

BENEATHA: Oh, I probably will . . . but first I'm going to be a doctor, and George, for one, still thinks that's pretty funny. I couldn't be bothered with that. I am going to be a doctor and everybody around here better understand that!

MAMA [*Kindly*]: 'Course you going to be a doctor, honey, God willing.

BENEATHA [*Drily*]: God hasn't got a thing to do with it.

MAMA: Beneatha—that just wasn't necessary.

BENEATHA: Well—neither is God. I get sick of hearing about God.

MAMA: Beneatha!

BENEATHA: I mean it! I'm just tired of hearing about God all the time. What has He got to do with anything? Does he pay tuition?

MAMA: You 'bout to get your fresh little jaw slapped!

RUTH: That's just what she needs, all right!

BENEATHA: Why? Why can't I say what I want to around here, like everybody else?

MAMA: It don't sound nice for a young girl to say things like that—you wasn't brought up that way. Me and your father went to trouble to get you and Brother to church every Sunday.

BENEATHA: Mama, you don't understand. It's all a matter of ideas, and God is just one idea I don't accept. It's not important. I am not going out and be immoral or commit crimes because I don't believe in God. I don't even think about it. It's just that I get tired of Him getting credit for all

the things the human race achieves through its own stubborn effort.
There simply is no blasted God—there is only man and it is he who
makes miracles!

[MAMA *absorbs this speech, studies her daughter and rises slowly and crosses
to* BENEATHA *and slaps her powerfully across the face. After, there is only silence
and the daughter drops her eyes from her mother's face, and* MAMA *is very tall
before her*]

MAMA: Now—you say after me, in my mother's house there is still God.
[*There is a long pause and* BENEATHA *stares at the floor wordlessly.* MAMA
repeats the phrase with precision and cool emotion] In my mother's house
there is still God.
BENEATHA: In my mother's house there is still God.

[*A long pause*]

MAMA [*Walking away from* BENEATHA, *too disturbed for triumphant posture.
Stopping and turning back to her daughter*]: There are some ideas we ain't
going to have in this house. Not long as I am at the head of this family.
BENEATHA: Yes, ma'am.

[MAMA *walks out of the room*]

RUTH [*Almost gently, with profound understanding*]: You think you a woman,
Bennie—but you still a little girl. What you did was childish—so you
got treated like a child.
BENEATHA: I see. [*Quietly*] I also see that everybody thinks it's all right for
Mama to be a tyrant. But all the tyranny in the world will never put
a God in the heavens!

[*She picks up her books and goes out*]

RUTH [*Goes to* MAMA'S *door*]: She said she was sorry.
MAMA [*Coming out, going to her plant*]: They frightens me, Ruth. My children.
RUTH: You got good children, Lena. They just a little off sometimes—but
they're good.
MAMA: No—there's something come down between me and them that don't
let us understand each other and I don't know what it is. One done
almost lost his mind thinking 'bout money all the time and the other
done commence to talk about things I can't seem to understand in no
form or fashion. What is it that's changing, Ruth?

RUTH [*Soothingly, older than her years*]: Now . . . you taking it all too seriously. You just got strong-willed children and it takes a strong woman like you to keep 'em in hand.

MAMA [*Looking at her plant and sprinkling a little water on it*]: They spirited all right, my children. Got to admit they got spirit—Bennie and Walter. Like this little old plant that ain't never had enough sunshine or nothing —and look at it . . .

[*She has her back to* RUTH, *who has had to stop ironing and lean against something and put the back of her hand to her forehead*]

RUTH [*Trying to keep* MAMA *from noticing*]: You . . . sure . . . loves that little old thing, don't you? . . .

MAMA: Well, I always wanted me a garden like I used to see sometimes at the back of the houses down home. This plant is close as I ever got to having one. [*She looks out of the window as she replaces the plant*] Lord, ain't nothing as dreary as the view from this window on a dreary day, is there? Why ain't you singing this morning, Ruth? Sing that "No Ways Tired." That song always lifts me up so—[*She turns at last to see that* RUTH *has slipped quietly into a chair, in a state of semiconsciousness*] Ruth! Ruth honey—what's the matter with you . . . Ruth!

CURTAIN

Scene Two

[*It is the following morning; a Saturday morning, and house cleaning is in progress at the* YOUNGERS: *Furniture has been shoved hither and yon and* MAMA *is giving the kitchen-area walls a washing down.* BENEATHA, *in dungarees, with a handkerchief tied around her face, is spraying insecticide into the cracks in the walls. As they work, the radio is on and a Southside disk-jockey program is inappropriately filling the house with a rather exotic saxophone blues.* TRAVIS, *the sole idle one, is leaning on his arms, looking out of the window.*]

TRAVIS: Grandmama, that stuff Bennie is using smells awful. Can I go downstairs, please?

MAMA: Did you get all them chores done already? I ain't seen you doing much.

TRAVIS: Yes'm—finished early. Where did Mama go this morning?

MAMA [*Looking at* BENEATHA]: She had to go on a little errand.

TRAVIS: Where?

MAMA: To tend to her business.

TRAVIS: Can I go outside then?

MAMA: Oh, I guess so. You better stay right in front of the house, though . . . and keep a good lookout for the postman.

TRAVIS: Yes'm. [*He starts out and decides to give his* AUNT BENEATHA *a good swat on the legs as he passes her*] Leave them poor little old cockroaches alone, they ain't bothering you none.

[*He runs as she swings the spray gun at him both viciously and playfully.* WALTER *enters from the bedroom and goes to the phone*]

MAMA: Look out there, girl, before you be spilling some of that stuff on that child!

TRAVIS [*Teasing*]: That's right—look out now!

[*He exits*]

BENEATHA [*Drily*]: I can't imagine that it would hurt him—it has never hurt the roaches.

MAMA: Well, little boys' hides ain't as tough as Southside roaches.

WALTER [*Into phone*]: Hello—Let me talk to Willy Harris.

MAMA: You better get over there behind the bureau. I seen one marching out of there like Napoleon yesterday.

WALTER: Hello, Willy? It ain't come yet. It'll be here in a few minutes. Did the lawyer give you the papers?

BENEATHA: There's really only one way to get rid of them, Mama—

MAMA: How?

BENEATHA: Set fire to this building.

WALTER: Good. Good. I'll be right over.

BENEATHA: Where did Ruth go, Walter?

WALTER: I don't know.

[*He exits abruptly*]

BENEATHA: Mama, where did Ruth go?

MAMA [*Looking at her with meaning*]: To the doctor, I think.

BENEATHA: The doctor? What's the matter? [*They exchange glances*] You don't think—

MAMA [*With her sense of drama*]: Now I ain't saying what I think. But I ain't never been wrong 'bout a woman neither.

[*The phone rings*]

BENEATHA [*At the phone*]: Hay-lo . . . [*Pause, and a moment of recognition*] Well—when did you get back! . . . And how was it? . . . Of course I've missed you—in my way . . . This morning? No . . . house cleaning and all that and Mama hates it if I let people come over when the house is like this . . . You *have?* Well, that's different . . . What is it—Oh, what the hell, come on over . . . Right, see you then.

[*She hangs up*]

MAMA [*Who has listened vigorously, as is her habit*]: Who is that you inviting over here with this house looking like this? You ain't got the pride you was born with!

BENEATHA: Asagai doesn't care how houses look, Mama—he's an intellectual.

MAMA: *Who?*

BENEATHA: Asagai—Joseph Asagai. He's an African boy I met on campus. He's been studying in Canada all summer.

MAMA: What's his name?

BENEATHA: Asagai, Joseph. Ah-sah-guy . . . He's from Nigeria.

MAMA: Oh, that's the little country that was founded by slaves way back . . .

BENEATHA: No, Mama—that's Liberia.

MAMA: I don't think I never met no African before.

BENEATHA: Well, do me a favor and don't ask him a whole lot of ignorant questions about Africans. I mean, do they wear clothes and all that—

MAMA: Well, now, I guess if you think we so ignorant 'round here maybe you shouldn't bring your friends here—

BENEATHA: It's just that people ask such crazy things. All anyone seems to know about when it comes to Africa is Tarzan—

MAMA [*Indignantly*]: Why should I know anything about Africa?

BENEATHA: Why do you give money at church for the missionary work?

MAMA: Well, that's to help save people.

BENEATHA: You mean save them from *heathenism*—

MAMA [*Innocently*]: Yes.

BENEATHA: I'm afraid they need more salvation from the British and the French.

[RUTH *comes in forlornly and pulls off her coat with dejection. They both turn to look at her*]

RUTH [*Dispiritedly*]: Well, I guess from all the happy faces—everybody knows.

BENEATHA: You pregnant?

MAMA: Lord have mercy, I sure hope it's a little old girl. Travis ought to have a sister.

[BENEATHA *and* RUTH *give her a hopeless look for this grandmotherly enthusiasm*]

BENEATHA: How far along are you?

RUTH: Two months.

BENEATHA: Did you mean to? I mean did you plan it or was it an accident?

MAMA: What do you know about planning or not planning?

BENEATHA: Oh, Mama.

RUTH [*Wearily*]: She's twenty years old, Lena.

BENEATHA: Did you plan it, Ruth?

RUTH: Mind your own business.

BENEATHA: It is my business—where is he going to live, on the *roof*? [*There is silence following the remark as the three women react to the sense of it*] Gee —I didn't mean that, Ruth, honest. Gee, I don't feel like that at all. I— I think it is wonderful.

RUTH [*Dully*]: Wonderful.

BENEATHA: Yes—really.

MAMA [*Looking at* RUTH, *worried*]: Doctor say everything going to be all right?

RUTH [*Far away*]: Yes—she says everything is going to be fine . . .

MAMA [*Immediately suspicious*]: "She"—What doctor you went to?

[RUTH *folds over, near hysteria*]

MAMA [*Worriedly hovering over* RUTH]: Ruth honey—what's the matter with you—you sick?

[RUTH *has her fists clenched on her thighs and is fighting hard to suppress a scream that seems to be rising in her*]

BENEATHA: What's the matter with her, Mama?

MAMA [*Working her fingers in* RUTH'S *shoulder to relax her*]: She be all right. Women gets right depressed sometimes when they get her way. [*Speaking softly, expertly, rapidly*] Now you just relax. That's right . . . just lean back, don't think 'bout nothing at all . . . nothing at all—

RUTH: I'm all right . . .

[*The glassy-eyed look melts and then she collapses into a fit of heavy sobbing. The bell rings*]

BENEATHA: Oh, my God—that must be Asagai.

MAMA [*To* RUTH]: Come on now, honey. You need to lie down and rest awhile . . . then have some nice hot food.

[*They exit,* RUTH'S *weight on her mother-in-law.* BENEATHA, *herself profoundly disturbed, opens the door to admit a rather dramatic-looking young man with a large package*]

ASAGAI: Hello, Alaiyo—

BENEATHA [*Holding the door open and regarding him with pleasure*]: Hello
. . . [*Long pause*] Well—come in. And please excuse everything. My
mother was very upset about my letting anyone come here with the
place like this.

ASAGAI [*Coming into the room*]: You look disturbed too . . . Is something
wrong?

BENEATHA [*Still at the door, absently*]: Yes . . . we've all got acute ghetto-itus.
[*She smiles and comes toward him, finding a cigarette and sitting*] So—sit
down! How was Canada?

ASAGAI [*A sophisticate*]: Canadian.

BENEATHA [*Looking at him*]: I'm very glad you are back.

ASAGAI [*Looking back at her in turn*]: Are you really?

BENEATHA: Yes—very.

ASAGAI: Why—you were quite glad when I went away. What happened?

BENEATHA: You went away.

ASAGAI: Ahhhhhhhh.

BENEATHA: Before—you wanted to be so serious before there was time.

ASAGAI: How much time must there be before one knows what one feels?

BENEATHA [*Stalling this particular conversation. Her hands pressed together, in a
deliberately childish gesture*]: What did you bring me?

ASAGAI [*Handing her the package*]: Open it and see.

BENEATHA [*Eagerly opening the package and drawing out some records and the
colorful robes of a Nigerian woman*]: Oh, Asagai! . . . You got them for me!
. . . How beautiful . . . and the records too! [*She lifts out the robes and
runs to the mirror with them and holds the drapery up in front of herself*]

ASAGAI [*Coming to her at the mirror*]: I shall have to teach you how to drape
it properly. [*He flings the material about her for the moment and stands back
to look at her*] Ah—*Oh-pay-gay-day, oh-gbah-mu-shay.* [*A Yoruba exclamation for admiration*] You wear it well . . . very well . . . mutilated hair
and all.

BENEATHA [*Turning suddenly*]: My hair—what's wrong with my hair?

ASAGAI [*Shrugging*]: Were you born with it like that?

BENEATHA [*Reaching up to touch it*]: No . . . of course not.

[*She looks back to the mirror, disturbed*]

ASAGAI [*Smiling*]: How then?

BENEATHA: You know perfectly well how . . . as crinkly as yours . . . that's
how.

ASAGAI: And it is ugly to you that way?

BENEATHA [*Quickly*]: Oh, no—not ugly . . . [*More slowly, apologetically*] But
it's so hard to manage when it's, well—raw.

ASAGAI: And so to accommodate that—you mutilate it every week?

BENEATHA: It's not mutilation!

ASAGAI [*Laughing aloud at her seriousness*]: Oh . . . please! I am only teasing you because you are so very serious about these things. [*He stands back from her and folds his arms across his chest as he watches her pulling at her hair and frowning in the mirror*] Do you remember the first time you met me at school? . . . [*He laughs*] You came up to me and you said—and I thought you were the most serious little thing I had ever seen—you said: [*He imitates her*] "Mr. Asagai—I want very much to talk with you. About Africa. You see, Mr. Asagai, I am looking for my *identity*.

[*He laughs*]

BENEATHA [*Turning to him, not laughing*]: Yes—

[*Her face is quizzical, profoundly disturbed*]

ASAGAI [*Still teasing and reaching out and taking her face in his hands and turning her profile to him*]: Well . . . it is true that this is not so much a profile of a Hollywood queen as perhaps a queen of the Nile—[*A mock dismissal of the importance of the question*] But what does it matter? Assimilationism is so popular in your country.

BENEATHA [*Wheeling, passionately, sharply*]: I am not an assimilationist!

ASAGAI [*The protest hangs in the room for a moment and* ASAGAI *studies her, his laughter fading*]: Such a serious one. [*There is a pause*] So—you like the robes? You must take excellent care of them—they are from my sister's personal wardrobe.

BENEATHA [*With incredulity*]: You—you sent all the way home—for me?

ASAGAI [*With charm*]: For you—I would do much more . . . Well, that is what I came for. I must go.

BENEATHA: Will you call me Monday?

ASAGAI: Yes . . . We have a great deal to talk about. I mean about identity and time and all that.

BENEATHA: Time?

ASAGAI: Yes. About how much time one needs to know what one feels.

BENEATHA: You never understood that there is more than one kind of feeling which can exist between a man and a woman—or, at least, there should be.

ASAGAI [*Shaking his head negatively but gently*]: No. Between a man and a woman there need be only one kind of feeling. I have that for you . . . Now even . . . right this moment . . .

BENEATHA: I know—and by itself—it won't do. I can find that anywhere.

ASAGAI: For a woman it should be enough.

BENEATHA: I know—because that's what it says in all the novels that men write. But it isn't. Go ahead and laugh—but I'm not interested in being someone's little episode in America or—[*With feminine vengeance*]—one of them! [ASAGAI *has burst into laughter again*] That's funny as hell, huh!

ASAGAI: It's just that every American girl I have known has said that to me. White—black—in this you are all the same. And the same speech, too!

BENEATHA [*Angrily*]: Yuk, yuk, yuk!

ASAGAI: It's how you can be sure that the world's most liberated women are not liberated at all. You all talk about it too much!

[MAMA *enters and is immediately all social charm because of the presence of a guest*]

BENEATHA: Oh—Mama—this is Mr. Asagai.

MAMA: How do you do?

ASAGAI [*Total politeness to an elder*]: How do you do, Mrs. Younger. Please forgive me for coming at such an outrageous hour on a Saturday.

MAMA: Well, you are quite welcome. I just hope you understand that our house don't always look like this. [*Chatterish*] You must come again. I would love to hear all about—[*Not sure of the name*]—your country. I think it's so sad the way our American Negroes don't know nothing about Africa 'cept Tarzan and all that. And all that money they pour into these churches when they ought to be helping you people over there drive out them French and Englishmen done taken away your land.

[*The mother flashes a slightly superior look at her daughter upon completion of the recitation*]

ASAGAI [*Taken aback by this sudden and acutely unrelated expression of sympathy*]: Yes . . . yes . . .

MAMA [*Smiling at him suddenly and relaxing and looking him over*]: How many miles is it from here to where you come from?

ASAGAI: Many thousands.

MAMA [*Looking at him as she would* WALTER]: I bet you don't half look after yourself, being away from your mama either. I spec you better come 'round here from time to time and get yourself some decent home-cooked meals . . .

ASAGAI [*Moved*]: Thank you. Thank you very much. [*They are all quiet, then—*] Well . . . I must go. I will call you Monday, Alaiyo.

MAMA: What's that he call you?

ASAGAI: Oh—"Alaiyo." I hope you don't mind. It is what you would call a nickname, I think. It is a Yoruba word. I am a Yoruba.

MAMA [*Looking at* BENEATHA]: I—I thought he was from—

ASAGAI [*Understanding*]: Nigeria is my country. Yoruba is my tribal origin—

BENEATHA: You didn't tell us what Alaiyo means . . . for all I know, you might be calling me Little Idiot or something . . .

ASAGAI: Well . . . let me see . . . I do not know how just to explain it . . . The sense of a thing can be so different when it changes languages.

BENEATHA: You're evading.

ASAGAI: No—really it is difficult . . . [*Thinking*] It means . . . it means One for Whom Bread—Food—Is Not Enough. [*He looks at her*] Is that all right?

BENEATHA [*Understanding, softly*]: Thank you.

MAMA [*Looking from one to the other and not understanding any of it*]: Well . . . that's nice . . . You must come see us again—Mr.—

ASAGAI: Ah-sah-guy . . .

MAMA: Yes . . . Do come again.

ASAGAI: Good-bye.

[*He exits*]

MAMA [*After him*]: Lord, that's a pretty thing just went out here! [*Insinuatingly, to her daughter*] Yes, I guess I see why we done commence to get so interested in Africa 'round here. Missionaries my aunt Jenny!

[*She exits*]

BENEATHA: Oh, Mama! . . .

[*She picks up the Nigerian dress and holds it up to her in front of the mirror again. She sets the headdress on haphazardly and then notices her hair again and clutches at it and then replaces the headdress and frowns at herself. Then she starts to wriggle in front of the mirror as she thinks a Nigerian woman might.* TRAVIS *enters and regards her*]

TRAVIS: You cracking up?

BENEATHA: Shut up.

[*She pulls the headdress off and looks at herself in the mirror and clutches at her hair again and squinches her eyes as if trying to imagine something. Then, suddenly, she gets her raincoat and kerchief and hurriedly prepares for going out*]

MAMA [*Coming back into the room*]: She's resting now. Travis, baby, run next door and ask Miss Johnson to please let me have a little kitchen cleanser. This here can is empty as Jacob's kettle.

TRAVIS: I just came in.

MAMA: Do as you told. [*He exits and she looks at her daughter*] Where you going?

BENEATHA [*Halting at the door*]: To become a queen of the Nile!

[*She exits in a breathless blaze of glory.* RUTH *appears in the bedroom door-way*]

MAMA: Who told you to get up?

RUTH: Ain't nothing wrong with me to be lying in no bed for. Where did Bennie go?

MAMA [*Drumming her fingers*]: Far as I could make out—to Egypt. [RUTH *just looks at her*] What time is it getting to?

RUTH: Ten twenty. And the mailman going to ring that bell this morning just like he done every morning for the last umpteen years.

[TRAVIS *comes in with the cleanser can*]

TRAVIS: She say to tell you that she don't have much.

MAMA [*Angrily*]: Lord, some people I could name sure is tight-fisted! [*Directing her grandson*] Mark two cans of cleanser down on the list there. If she that hard up for kitchen cleanser, I sure don't want to forget to get her none!

RUTH: Lena—maybe the woman is just short on cleanser—

MAMA [*Not listening*]: —Much baking powder as she done borrowed from me all these years, she could of done gone into the baking business!

[*The bell sounds suddenly and sharply and all three are stunned—serious and silent—mid-speech. In spite of all the other conversations and distractions of the morning, this is what they have been waiting for, even* TRAVIS, *who looks helplessly from his mother to his grandmother.* RUTH *is the first to come to life again*]

RUTH [*To* TRAVIS]: *Get down them steps, boy!*

[TRAVIS *snaps to life and flies out to get the mail*]

MAMA [*Her eyes wide, her hand to her breast*]: You mean it done really come?

RUTH [*Excited*]: Oh, Miss Lena!

MAMA [*Collecting herself*]: Well . . . I don't know what we all so excited about 'round here for. We known it was coming for months.

RUTH: That's a whole lot different from having it come and being able to hold it in your hands . . . a piece of paper worth ten thousand dollars . . . [TRAVIS *bursts back into the room. He holds the envelope high above his head, like a little dancer, his face is radiant and he is breathless. He moves to his grandmother with sudden slow ceremony and puts the envelope into her hands. She accepts it, and then merely holds it and looks at it*] Come on! Open it . . . Lord have mercy, I wish Walter Lee was here!

TRAVIS: Open it, Grandmama!

MAMA [*Staring at it*]: Now you all be quiet. It's just a check.

RUTH: Open it . . .

MAMA [*Still staring at it*]: Now don't act silly . . . We ain't never been no people to act silly 'bout no money—

RUTH [*Swiftly*]: We ain't never had none before—*open it!*

[MAMA *finally makes a good strong tear and pulls out the thin blue slice of paper and inspects it closely. The boy and his mother study it raptly over* MAMA'S *shoulders*]

MAMA: *Travis!* [*She is counting off with doubt*] Is that the right number of zeros.

TRAVIS: Yes'm . . . ten thousand dollars. Gaalee, Grandmama, you rich.

MAMA [*She holds the check away from her, still looking at it. Slowly her face sobers into a mask of unhappiness*]: Ten thousand dollars. [*She hands it to* RUTH] Put it away somewhere, Ruth. [*She does not look at* RUTH: *her eyes seem to be seeing something somewhere very far off*] Ten thousand dollars they give you. Ten thousand dollars.

TRAVIS [*To his mother, sincerely*]: What's the matter with Grandmama—don't she want to be rich?

RUTH [*Distractedly*]: You go on out and play now, baby. [TRAVIS *exits.* MAMA *starts wiping dishes absently, humming intently to herself.* RUTH *turns to her, with kind exasperation*] You've gone and got yourself upset.

MAMA [*Not looking at her*]: I spec if it wasn't for you all . . . I would just put that money away or give it to the church or something.

RUTH: Now what kind of talk is that. Mr. Younger would just be plain mad if he could hear you talking foolish like that.

MAMA [*Stopping and staring off*]: Yes . . . he sure would. [*Sighing*] We got enough to do with that money, all right. [*She halts then, and turns and looks at her daughter-in-law hard;* RUTH *avoids her eyes and* MAMA *wipes her hands with finality and starts to speak firmly to* RUTH] Where did you go today, girl?

RUTH: To the doctor.

MAMA [*Impatiently*]: Now, Ruth . . . you know better than that. Old Doctor Jones is strange enough in his way but there ain't nothing 'bout him make somebody slip and call him "she"—like you done this morning.

RUTH: Well, that's what happened—my tongue slipped.

MAMA: You went to see that woman, didn't you?

RUTH [*Defensively, giving herself away*]: What woman you talking about?

MAMA [*Angrily*]: That woman who—

[WALTER *enters in great excitement*]

WALTER: Did it come?

MAMA [*Quietly*]: Can't you give people a Christian greeting before you start asking about money?

WALTER [*To* RUTH]: Did it come? [RUTH *unfolds the check and lays it quietly before him, watching him intently with thoughts of her own.* WALTER *sits down and grasps it close and counts off the zeros*] Ten thousand dollars— [*He turns suddenly, frantically to his mother and draws some papers out of his breast pocket*] Mama—look. Old Willy Harris put everything on paper—

MAMA: Son—I think you ought to talk to your wife . . . I'll go on out and leave you alone if you want—

WALTER: I can talk to her later—Mama, look—

MAMA: Son—

WALTER: WILL SOMEBODY PLEASE LISTEN TO ME TODAY!

MAMA [*Quietly*]: I don't 'low no yellin' in this house, Walter Lee, and you know it— [WALTER *stares at them in frustration and starts to speak several times*] And there ain't going to be no investing in no liquor stores. I don't aim to have to speak on that again.

[*A long pause*]

WALTER: Oh—so you don't aim to have to speak on that again? So *you* have decided . . . [*Crumpling his papers*] Well, *you* tell that to my boy tonight when you put him to sleep on the living-room couch . . . [*Turning to* MAMA *and speaking directly to her*] Yeah—and tell it to my wife, Mama, tomorrow when she has to go out of here to look after somebody elses' kids. And tell it to *me*, Mama, every time we need a new pair of curtains and I have to watch *you* go out and work in somebody's kitchen. Yeah, you tell me then!

[WALTER *starts out*]

RUTH: Where you going?

WALTER: I'm going out!

RUTH: Where?

WALTER: Just out of this house somewhere—

RUTH [*Getting her coat*]: I'll come too.

WALTER: I don't want you to come!

RUTH: I got something to talk to you about, Walter.

WALTER: That's too bad.

MAMA [*Still quietly*]: Walter Lee—[*She waits and he finally turns and looks at her*] Sit down.

WALTER: I'm a grown man, Mama.

MAMA: Ain't nobody said you wasn't grown. But you still in my house and my presence. And as long as you are—you'll talk to your wife civil. Now sit down.

RUTH [*Suddenly*]: Oh, let him go on out and drink himself to death! He makes me sick to my stomach! [*She flings her coat against him*]

WALTER [*Violently*]: And you turn mine too, baby! [RUTH *goes into their bedroom and slams the door behind her*] That was my greatest mistake—

MAMA [*Still quietly*]: Walter, what is the matter with you?

WALTER: Matter with me? Ain't nothing the matter with *me!*

MAMA: Yes there is. Something eating you up like a crazy man. Something more than me not giving you this money. The past few years I been watching it happen to you. You get all nervous acting and kind of wild in the eyes—[WALTER *jumps up impatiently at her words*] I said sit there now, I'm talking to you!

WALTER: Mama—I don't need no nagging at me today.

MAMA: Seem like you getting to a place where you always tied up in some kind of knot about something. But if anybody ask you 'bout it you just yell at 'em and bust out the house and go out and drink somewheres. Walter Lee, people can't live with that. Ruth's a good, patient girl in her way—but you getting to be too much. Boy, don't make the mistake of driving that girl away from you.

WALTER: Why—what she do for me?

MAMA: She loves you.

WALTER: Mama—I'm going out. I want to go off somewhere and be by myself for a while.

MAMA: I'm sorry 'bout your liquor store, son. It just wasn't the thing for us to do. That's what I want to tell you about—

WALTER: I got to go out, Mama—

[*He rises*]

MAMA: It's dangerous, son.

WALTER: What's dangerous?

MAMA: When a man goes outside his home to look for peace.

WALTER [*Beseechingly*]: Then why can't there never be no peace in this house then?

MAMA: You done found it in some other house?

WALTER: No—there ain't no woman! Why do women always think there's a woman somewhere when a man gets restless. [*Coming to her*] Mama —Mama—I want so many things . . .

MAMA: Yes, son—

WALTER: I want so many things that they are driving me kind of crazy . . . Mama—look at me.

MAMA: I'm looking at you. You a good-looking boy. You got a job, a nice wife, a fine boy and—

WALTER: A job. [*Looks at her*] Mama, a job? I open and close car doors all day long. I drive a man around in his limousine and I say, "Yes, sir; no, sir; very good, sir; shall I take the Drive, sir?" Mama, that ain't no kind of job . . . that ain't nothing at all. [*Very quietly*] Mama, I don't know if I can make you understand.

MAMA: Understand what, baby?

WALTER [*Quietly*]: Sometimes it's like I can see the future stretched out in front of me—just plain as day. The future, Mama. Hanging over there at the edge of my days. Just waiting for me—a big, looming blank space —full of *nothing*. Just waiting for *me*. [*Pause*] Mama—sometimes when I'm downtown and I pass them cool, quiet-looking restaurants where them white boys are sitting back and talking 'bout things . . . sitting there turning deals worth millions of dollars . . . sometimes I see guys don't look much older than me—

MAMA: Son—how come you talk so much 'bout money?

WALTER [*With immense passion*]: Because it is life, Mama!

MAMA [*Quietly*]: Oh—[*Very quietly*] So now it's life. Money is life. Once upon a time freedom used to be life—now it's money. I guess the world really do change . . .

WALTER: No—it was always money, Mama. We just didn't know about it.

MAMA: No . . . something has changed. [*She looks at him*] You something new, boy. In my time we was worried about not being lynched and getting to the North if we could and how to stay alive and still have a pinch of dignity too . . . Now here come you and Beneatha—talking 'bout things we ain't never even thought about hardly, me and your daddy. You ain't satisfied or proud of nothing we done. I mean that you had a home; that we kept you out of trouble till you was grown; that you don't have to ride to work on the back of nobody's streetcar—You my children—but how different we done become.

WALTER: You just don't understand, Mama, you just don't understand.

MAMA: Son—do you know your wife is expecting another baby?] WALTER *stands, stunned, and absorbs what his mother has said*] That's what she wanted to talk to you about. [WALTER *sinks down into a chair*] This ain't for me to be telling—but you ought to know. [*She waits*] I think Ruth is thinking 'bout getting rid of that child.

WALTER [*Slowly understanding*]: No—no—Ruth wouldn't do that.

MAMA: When the world gets ugly enough—a woman will do anything for her family. *The part that's already living.*

WALTER: You don't know Ruth, Mama, if you think she would do that.

[RUTH *opens the bedroom door and stands there a little limp*]

RUTH [*Beaten*]: Yes I would too, Walter. [*Pause*] I gave her a five-dollar down payment.

[*There is total silence as the man stares at his wife and the mother stares at her son*]

MAMA [*Presently*]: Well—[*Tightly*] Well—son, I'm waiting to hear you say something . . . I'm waiting to hear how you be your father's son. Be the man he was . . . [*Pause*] Your wife say she going to destroy your child. And I'm waiting to hear you talk like him and say we a people who give children life, not who destroys them—[*She rises*] I'm waiting to see you stand up and look like your daddy and say we done give up one baby to poverty and that we ain't going to give up nary another one . . . I'm waiting.

WALTER: Ruth—

MAMA: If you a son of mine, tell her! [WALTER *turns, looks at her and can say nothing. She continues, bitterly*] You . . . you are a disgrace to your father's memory. Somebody get me my hat.

CURTAIN

ACT II
Scene One

[*Time: Later the same day.*
At rise: RUTH *is ironing again. She has the radio going. Presently* BENEATHA'S *bedroom door opens and* RUTH'S *mouth falls and she puts down the iron in fascination.*]

RUTH: What have we got on tonight!

BENEATHA [*Emerging grandly from the doorway so that we can see her thoroughly robed in the costume Asagai brought*]: You are looking at what a well-dressed Nigerian woman wears—[*She parades for* RUTH, *her hair completely hidden by the headdress; she is coquettishly fanning herself with an ornate oriental fan, mistakenly more like Butterfly than any Nigerian that ever was*] Isn't it beautiful? [*She promenades to the radio and, with an arrogant flourish, turns off the good loud blues that is playing*] Enough of this assimilationist junk! [RUTH *follows her with her eyes as she goes to the phonograph and puts on a record and turns and waits ceremoniously for the music to come up. Then, with a shout—*] OCOMOGOSIAY!

[RUTH *jumps. The music comes up, a lovely Nigerian melody.* BENEATHA *listens, enraptured, her eyes far away—"back to the past." She begins to dance.* RUTH *is dumfounded*]

RUTH: What kind of dance is that?

BENEATHA: A folk dance.

RUTH [*Pearl Bailey*]: What kind of folks do that, honey?

BENEATHA: It's from Nigeria. It's a dance of welcome.

RUTH: Who you welcoming?

BENEATHA: The men back to the village.

RUTH: Where they been?

BENEATHA: How should I know—out hunting or something. Anyway, they are coming back now . . .

RUTH: Well, that's good.

BENEATHA [*With the record*]:

Alundi, alundi
Alundi alunya
Jop pu a jeepua
Ang gu soooooooooo

Ai yai yae . . .
Ayehaye—alundi . . .

[WALTER *comes in during this performance; he has obviously been drinking. He leans against the door heavily and watches his sister, at first with distaste. Then his eyes look off—"back to the past"—as he lifts both his fists to the roof, screaming*]

WALTER: YEAH . . . AND ETHIOPIA STRETCH FORTH HER HANDS AGAIN! . . .

RUTH [*Drily, looking at him*]: Yes—and Africa sure is claiming her own tonight. [*She gives them both up and starts ironing again*]

WALTER [*All in a drunken, dramatic shout*]: Shut up! . . . I'm digging them drums . . . them drums move me! . . . [*He makes his weaving way to his wife's face and leans in close to her*] In my *heart of hearts*—[*He thumps his chest*]—I am much warrior!

RUTH [*Without even looking up*]: In your heart of hearts you are much drunkard.

WALTER [*Coming away from her and starting to wander around the room, shouting*]: Me and Jomo . . . [*Intently, in his sister's face. She has stopped dancing to watch him in this unknown mood*] That's my man, Kenyatta. [*Shouting and thumping his chest*] FLAMING SPEAR! HOT DAMN! [*He is suddenly in possession of an imaginary spear and actively spearing enemies all over the room*] OCOMOGOSIAY . . . THE LION IS WAKING . . . OWIMOWEH! [*He pulls his shirt open and leaps up on a table and gestures with his spear. The bell rings.* RUTH *goes to answer*]

BENEATHA [*To encourage* WALTER, *thoroughly caught up with this side of him*]: OCOMOGOSIAY, FLAMING SPEAR!

WALTER [*On the table, very far gone, his eyes pure glass sheets. He sees what we cannot, that he is a leader of his people, a great chief, a descendant of Chaka, and that the hour to march has come*]: Listen, my black brothers—

BENEATHA: OCOMOGOSIAY!

WALTER: —Do you hear the waters rushing against the shores of the coast-lands—

BENEATHA: OCOMOGOSIAY!

WALTER: —Do you hear the screeching of the cocks in yonder hills beyond where the chiefs meet in council for the coming of the mighty war—

BENEATHA: OCOMOGOSIAY!

WALTER: —Do you hear the beating of the wings of the birds flying low over the mountains and the low places of our land—

[RUTH *opens the door.* GEORGE MURCHISON *enters*]

BENEATHA: OCOMOGOSIAY!

WALTER: —Do you hear the singing of the women, singing the war songs of our fathers to the babies in the great houses . . . singing the sweet war songs? OH, DO YOU HEAR, MY BLACK BROTHERS!

BENEATHA [*Completely gone*]: We hear you, Flaming Spear—

WALTER: Telling us to prepare for the greatness of the time—[*To* GEORGE] Black Brother!

[*He extends his hand for the fraternal clasp*]

GEORGE: Black Brother, hell!

RUTH [*Having had enough, and embarrassed for the family*]: Beneatha, you got company—what's the matter with you? Walter Lee Younger, get down off that table and stop acting like a fool . . .

[WALTER *comes down off the table suddenly and makes a quick exit to the bathroom*]

RUTH: He's had a little to drink . . . I don't know what her excuse is.

GEORGE [*To* BENEATHA]: Look honey, we're going *to* the theatre—we're not going to be *in* it . . . so go change, huh?

RUTH: You expect this boy to go out with you looking like that?

BENEATHA [*Looking at* GEORGE]: That's up to George. If he's ashamed of his heritage—

GEORGE: Oh, don't be so proud of yourself, Bennie—just because you look eccentric.

BENEATHA: How can something that's natural be eccentric?

GEORGE: That's what being eccentric means—being natural. Get dressed.

BENEATHA: I don't like that, George.

RUTH: Why must you and your brother make an argument out of everything people say?

BENEATHA: Because I hate assimilationist Negroes!

RUTH: Will somebody please tell me what assimila-who-ever means!

GEORGE: Oh, it's just a college girl's way of calling people Uncle Toms—but that isn't what it means at all.

RUTH: Well, what does it mean?

BENEATHA [*Cutting* GEORGE *off and staring at him as she replies to* RUTH]: It means someone who is willing to give up his own culture and submerge himself completely in the dominant, and in this case, *oppressive* culture!

GEORGE: Oh, dear, dear, dear! Here we go! A lecture on the African past! On our Great West African Heritage! In one second we will hear all about the great Ashanti empires; the great Songhay civilizations; and the great sculpture of Bénin—and then some poetry in the Bantu—and the whole monologue will end with the word *heritage!* [*Nastily*] Let's face it, baby, your heritage is nothing but a bunch of raggedy-assed spirituals and some grass huts!

BENEATHA: *Grass huts!* [RUTH *crosses to her and forcibly pushes her toward the bedroom*] See there . . . you are standing there in your splendid ignorance talking about people who were the first to smelt iron on the face of the earth! [RUTH *is pushing her through the door*] The Ashanti were performing surgical operations when the English—[RUTH *pulls the door to, with* BENEATHA *on the other side, and smiles graciously at* GEORGE. BENEATHA *opens the door and shouts the end of the sentence defiantly at* GEORGE]—were still tattooing themselves with blue dragons . . . [*She goes back inside*]

RUTH: Have a seat, George. [*They both sit.* RUTH *folds her hands rather primly on her lap, determined to demonstrate the civilization of the family*] Warm, ain't it? I mean for September. [*Pause*] Just like they always say about Chicago weather: If it's too hot or cold for you, just wait a minute and it'll change. [*She smiles happily at this cliché of clichés*] Everybody say it's got to do with them bombs and things they keep setting off. [*Pause*] Would you like a nice cold beer?

GEORGE: No, thank you. I don't care for beer. [*He looks at his watch*] I hope she hurries up.

RUTH: What time is the show?

GEORGE: It's an eight-thirty curtain. That's just Chicago, though. In New York standard curtain time is eight forty.

[*He is rather proud of this knowledge*]

RUTH [*Properly appreciating it*]: You get to New York a lot?

GEORGE [*Offhand*]: Few times a year.

RUTH: Oh—that's nice. I've never been to New York.

[WALTER *enters. We feel he has relieved himself, but the edge of unreality is still with him*]

WALTER: New York ain't got nothing Chicago ain't. Just a bunch of hustling people all squeezed up together—being "Eastern."

[*He turns his face into a screw of displeasure*]

GEORGE: Oh—you've been?

WALTER: *Plenty* of times.

RUTH [*Shocked at the lie*]: Walter Lee Younger!

WALTER [*Staring her down*]: Plenty! [*Pause*] What we got to drink in this house? Why don't you offer this man some refreshment. [*To* GEORGE] They don't know how to entertain people in this house, man.

GEORGE: Thank you—I don't really care for anything.

WALTER [*Feeling his head; sobriety coming*]: Where's Mama?

RUTH: She ain't come back yet.

WALTER [*Looking* MURCHISON *over from head to toe, scrutinizing his carefully casual tweed sports jacket over cashmere V-neck sweater over soft eyelet shirt and tie, and soft slacks, finished off with white buckskin shoes*]: Why all you college boys wear them fairyish-looking white shoes?

RUTH: Walter Lee!

[GEORGE MURCHISON *ignores the remark*]

WALTER [*To* RUTH]: Well, they look crazy as hell—white shoes, cold as it is.

RUTH [*Crushed*]: You have to excuse him—

WALTER: No he don't! Excuse me for what? What you always excusing me for! I'll excuse myself when I needs to be excused! [*A pause*] They look as funny as them black knee socks Beneatha wears out of here all the time.

RUTH: It's the college *style*, Walter.

WALTER: Style, hell. She looks like she got burnt legs or something!

RUTH: Oh, Walter—

WALTER [*An irritable mimic*]: Oh, Walter! Oh, Walter! [*To* MURCHISON] How's your old man making out? I understand you all going to buy that big hotel on the Drive? [*He finds a beer in the refrigerator, wanders over to* MURCHISON, *sipping and wiping his lips with the back of his hand, and straddling a chair backwards to talk to the other man*] Shrewd move. Your old man is all right, man. [*Tapping his head and half winking for emphasis*] I mean he knows how to operate. I mean he thinks *big*, you know what I mean, I mean for a *home*, you know? But I think he's kind of running out of ideas now. I'd like to talk to him. Listen, man, I got some plans that could turn this city upside down. I mean I think like he does. *Big*. Invest big, gamble big, hell, lose *big* if you have to, you know what I mean. It's hard to find a man on this whole Southside who understands my kind of thinking—you dig? [*He scrutinizes* MURCHISON *again, drinks his beer, squints his eyes and leans in close, confidential, man to man*] Me and you ought to sit down and talk sometimes, man. Man, I got me some ideas . . .

MURCHISON [*With boredom*]: Yeah—sometimes we'll have to do that, Walter.

WALTER [*Understanding the indifference, and offended*]: Yeah—well, when you get the time, man. I know you a busy little boy.

RUTH: Walter, please—

WALTER [*Bitterly, hurt*]: I know ain't nothing in this world as busy as you colored college boys with your fraternity pins and white shoes . . .

RUTH [*Covering her face with humiliation*]: Oh, Walter Lee—

WALTER: I see you all all the time—with the books tucked under your arms —going to your [*British A—a mimic*] "clahsses." And for what! What the hell you learning over there? Filling up your heads—[*Counting off on his fingers*]—with the sociology and the psychology—but they teaching you how to be a man? How to take over and run the world? They teaching you how to run a rubber plantation or a steel mill? Naw—just to talk proper and read books and wear white shoes . . .

GEORGE [*Looking at him with distaste, a little above it all*]: You're all wacked up with bitterness, man.

WALTER [*Intently, almost quietly, between the teeth, glaring at the boy*]: And you —ain't you bitter, man? Ain't you just about had it yet? Don't you see no stars gleaming that you can't reach out and grab? You happy?—You contented son-of-a-bitch—you happy? You got it made? Bitter? Man, I'm a volcano. Bitter? Here I am a giant—surrounded by ants! Ants who can't even understand what it is the giant is talking about.

RUTH [*Passionately and suddenly*]: Oh, Walter—ain't you with nobody!

WALTER [*Violently*]: No! 'Cause ain't nobody with me! Not even my own mother!

RUTH: Walter, that's a terrible thing to say!

[BENEATHA *enters, dressed for the evening in a cocktail dress and earrings*]

GEORGE: Well—hey, you look great.

BENEATHA: Let's go, George. See you all later.

RUTH: Have a nice time.

GEORGE: Thanks. Good night. [*To* WALTER, *sarcastically*] Good night, *Prometheus.*

[BENEATHA *and* GEORGE *exit*]

WALTER [*To* RUTH]: Who is Prometheus?

RUTH: I don't know. Don't worry about it.

WALTER [*In fury, pointing after* GEORGE]: See there—they get to a point where they can't insult you man to man—they got to go talk about something ain't nobody never heard of!

RUTH: How do you know it was an insult? [*To humor him*] Maybe Prometheus is a nice fellow.

WALTER: Prometheus! I bet there ain't even no such thing! I bet that simple-minded clown—

RUTH: Walter—

[*She stops what she is doing and looks at him*]

WALTER [*Yelling*]: Don't start!

RUTH: Start what?

WALTER: Your nagging! Where was I? Who was I with? How much money did I spend?

RUTH [*Plaintively*]: Walter Lee—why don't we just try to talk about it. . .

WALTER [*Not listening*]: I been out talking with people who understand me. People who care about the things I got on my mind.

RUTH [*Wearily*]: I guess that means people like Willy Harris.

WALTER: Yes, people like Willy Harris.

RUTH [*With a sudden flash of impatience*]: Why don't you all just hurry up and go into the banking business and stop talking about it!

WALTER: Why? You want to know why? 'Cause we all tied up in a race of people that don't know how to do nothing but moan, pray and have babies!

[*The line is too bitter even for him and he looks at her and sits down*]

RUTH: Oh, Walter . . . [*Softly*] Honey, why can't you stop fighting me?

WALTER [*Without thinking*]: Who's fighting you? Who even cares about you?

[*This line begins the retardation of his mood*]

RUTH: Well—[*She waits a long time, and then with resignation starts to put away her things*] I guess I might as well go on to bed . . . [*More or less to herself*] I don't know where we lost it . . . but we have . . . [*Then, to him*] I–I'm sorry about this new baby, Walter. I guess maybe I better go on and do what I started . . . I guess I just didn't realize how bad things was with us . . . I guess I just didn't really realize—[*She starts out to the bedroom and stops*] You want some hot milk?

WALTER: Hot milk?

RUTH: Yes—hot milk.

WALTER: Why hot milk?

RUTH: 'Cause after all that liquor you come home with you ought to have something hot in your stomach.

WALTER: I don't want no milk.

RUTH: You want some coffee then?

WALTER: No, I don't want no coffee. I don't want nothing hot to drink. [*Almost plaintively*] Why you always trying to give me something to eat?

RUTH [*Standing and looking at him helplessly*]: What else can I give you, Walter Lee Younger?

[*She stands and looks at him and presently turns to go out again. He lifts his head and watches her going away from him in a new mood which began to emerge when he asked her "Who cares about you?"*]

WALTER: It's been rough, ain't it, baby? [*She hears and stops but does not turn around and he continues to her back*] I guess between two people there ain't never as much understood as folks generally thinks there is. I mean like between me and you—[*She turns to face him*] How we gets to the place where we scared to talk softness to each other. [*He waits, thinking hard himself*] Why you think it got to be like that? [*He is thoughtful, almost as a child would be*] Ruth, what is it gets into people ought to be close?

RUTH: I don't know, honey. I think about it a lot.

WALTER: On account of you and me, you mean? The way things are with us. The way something done come down between us.

RUTH: There ain't so much between us, Walter . . . Not when you come to me and try to talk to me. Try to be with me . . . a little even.

WALTER [*Total honesty*]: Sometimes . . . sometimes . . . I don't even know how to try.

RUTH: Walter—

WALTER: Yes?

RUTH [*Coming to him, gently and with misgiving, but coming to him*]: Honey . . . life don't have to be like this. I mean sometimes people can do things so that things are better . . . You remember how we used to talk when Travis was born . . . about the way we were going to live . . . the kind of house . . . [*She is stroking his head*] Well, it's all starting to slip away from us . . .

[MAMA *enters, and* WALTER *jumps up and shouts at her*]

WALTER: Mama, where have you been?

MAMA: My—them steps is longer than they used to be. Whew! [*She sits down and ignores him*] How you feeling this evening, Ruth?

[RUTH *shrugs, disturbed some at having been prematurely interrupted and watching her husband knowingly*]

WALTER: Mama, where have you been all day?

MAMA [*Still ignoring him and leaning on the table and changing to more comfortable shoes*]: Where's Travis?

RUTH: I let him go out earlier and he ain't come back yet. Boy, is he going to get it!

WALTER: Mama!

MAMA [*As if she has heard him for the first time*]: Yes, son?

WALTER: Where did you go this afternoon?

MAMA: I went downtown to tend to some business that I had to tend to.

WALTER: What kind of business?

MAMA: You know better than to question me like a child, Brother.

WALTER [*Rising and bending over the table*]: Where were you, Mama? [*Bringing his fists down and shouting*] Mama, you didn't go do something with that insurance money, something crazy?

[*The front door opens slowly, interrupting him, and* TRAVIS *peeks his head in, less than hopefully*]

TRAVIS [*To his mother*]: Mama, I—

RUTH: "Mama I" nothing! You're going to get it, boy! Get on in that bedroom and get yourself ready!

TRAVIS: But I—

MAMA: Why don't you all never let the child explain hisself.

RUTH: Keep out of it now, Lena.

[MAMA *clamps her lips together, and* RUTH *advances toward her son menacingly*]

RUTH: A thousand times I have told you not to go off like that—

MAMA [*Holding out her arms to her grandson*]: Well—at least let me tell him something. I want him to be the first one to hear . . . Come here, Travis. [*The boy obeys, gladly*] Travis–[*She takes him by the shoulder and looks into his face*]–you know that money we got in the mail this morning?

TRAVIS: Yes'm—

MAMA: Well—what you think your grandmama gone and done with that money?

TRAVIS: I don't know, Grandmama.

MAMA [*Putting her finger on his nose for emphasis*]: She went out and she bought you a house! [*The explosion comes from* WALTER *at the end of the revelation and he jumps up and turns away from all of them in a fury.* MAMA *continues, to* TRAVIS] You glad about the house? It's going to be yours when you get to be a man.

TRAVIS: Yeah—I always wanted to live in a house.

MAMA: All right, gimme some sugar then—[TRAVIS *puts his arms around her neck as she watches her son over the boy's shoulder. Then, to* TRAVIS, *after the embrace*] Now when you say your prayers tonight, you thank God and your grandfather—'cause it was him who give you the house—in his way.

RUTH [*Taking the boy from* MAMA *and pushing him toward the bedroom*]: Now you get out of here and get ready for your beating.

TRAVIS: Aw, Mama—

RUTH: Get on in there—[*Closing the door behind him and turning radiantly to her mother-in-law*] So you went and did it!

MAMA [*Quietly, looking at her son with pain*]: Yes, I did.

RUTH [*Raising both arms classically*]: Praise God! [*Looks at* WALTER *a moment, who says nothing. She crosses rapidly to her husband*] Please, honey—let me be glad . . . you be glad too. [*She has laid her hands on his shoulders, but he shakes himself free of her roughly, without turning to face her*] Oh, Walter . . . a home . . . a home. [*She comes back to* MAMA] Well—where is it? How big is it? How much it going to cost?

MAMA: Well—

RUTH: When we moving?

MAMA [*Smiling at her*]: First of the month.

RUTH [*Throwing back her head with jubilance*]: Praise God!

MAMA [*Tentatively, still looking at her son's back turned against her and* RUTH]: It's—it's a nice house too . . . [*She cannot help speaking directly to him. An imploring quality in her voice, her manner, makes her almost like a girl now*] Three bedrooms—nice big one for you and Ruth. . . . Me and Beneatha still have to share our room, but Travis have one of his own —and [*With difficulty*] I figure if the—new baby—is a boy, we could get one of them double-decker outfits . . . And there's a yard with a little patch of dirt where I could maybe get to grow me a few flowers . . . and a nice big basement . . .

RUTH: Walter honey, be glad—

MAMA [*Still to his back, fingering things on the table*]: 'Course I don't want to make it sound fancier than it is . . . It's just a plain little old house— but it's made good and solid—and it will be *ours*. Walter Lee—it makes a difference in a man when he can walk on floors that belong to him . . .

RUTH: Where is it?

MAMA [*Frightened at this telling*]: Well—well—it's out there in Clybourne Park—

[RUTH'S *radiance fades abruptly, and* WALTER *finally turns slowly to face his mother with incredulity and hostility*]

RUTH: Where?

MAMA [*Matter-of-factly*]: Four o six Clybourne Street, Clybourne Park.

RUTH: Clybourne Park? Mama, there ain't no colored people living in Clybourne Park.

MAMA [*Almost idiotically*]: Well, I guess there's going to be some now.

WALTER [*Bitterly*]: So that's the peace and comfort you went out and bought for us today!

MAMA [*Raising her eyes to meet his finally*]: Son—I just tried to find the nicest place for the least amount of money for my family.

RUTH [*Trying to recover from the shock*]: Well—well—'course I ain't one never been 'fraid of no crackers, mind you—but—well, wasn't there no other houses nowhere?

MAMA: Them houses they put up for colored in them areas way out all seem to cost twice as much as other houses. I did the best I could.

RUTH [*Struck senseless with the news, in its various degrees of goodness and trouble, she sits a moment, her fists propping her chin in thought, and then she starts to rise, bringing her fists down with vigor, the radiance spreading from cheek to cheek again*]: Well—well!—All I can say is—if this is my time in life —*my time*—to say good-bye—[*And she builds with momentum as she starts to circle the room with an exuberant, almost tearfully happy release*]—to these Goddamned cracking walls!—[*She pounds the walls*]—and these marching roaches!—[*She wipes at an imaginary army of marching roaches*]— and this cramped little closet which ain't now or never was no kitchen! . . . then I say it loud and good, *Hallelujah! and good-bye misery . . . I don't never want to see your ugly face again!* [*She laughs joyously, having practically destroyed the apartment, and flings her arms up and lets them come down happily, slowly, reflectively, over her abdomen, aware for the first time perhaps that the life therein pulses with happiness and not despair*] Lena?

MAMA [*Moved, watching her happiness*]: Yes, honey?

RUTH [*Looking off*]: Is there—is there a whole lot of sunlight?

MAMA [*Understanding*]: Yes, child, there's a whole lot of sunlight.

[*Long Pause*]

RUTH [*Collecting herself and going to the door of the room* TRAVIS *is in*]: Well— I guess I better see 'bout Travis. [*To* MAMA] Lord, I sure don't feel like whipping nobody today!

[*She exits*]

MAMA [*The mother and son are left alone now and the mother waits a long time, considering deeply, before she speaks*]: Son—you—you understand what I done, don't you? [WALTER *is silent and sullen*] I—I just seen my family falling apart today . . . just falling to pieces in front of my eyes . . . We couldn't of gone on like we was today. We was going backwards 'stead of forwards—talking 'bout killing babies and wishing each other was dead . . . When it gets like that in life—you just got to do something different, push on out and do something bigger . . . [*She waits*] I wish you say something, son . . . I wish you'd say how deep inside you you think I done the right thing—

WALTER [*Crossing slowly to his bedroom door and finally turning there and speaking measuredly*]: What you need me to say you done right for? *You* the head of this family. You run our lives like you want to. It was your money and you did what you wanted with it. So what you need for me to say it was all right for? [*Bitterly, to hurt her as deeply as he knows is possible*] So you butchered up a dream of mine—you—who always talking 'bout your children's dreams . . .

MAMA: Walter Lee—

[*He just closes the door behind him. MAMA sits alone, thinking heavily*]

CURTAIN

Scene Two

[*Time: Friday night. A few weeks later.*
At rise: Packing crates mark the intention of the family to move. BENEATHA and GEORGE come in, presumably from an evening out again.]

GEORGE: O.K. . . . O.K., whatever you say . . . [*They both sit on the couch. He tries to kiss her. She moves away*] Look, we've had a nice evening; let's not spoil it, huh? . . .

[*He again turns her head and tries to nuzzle in and she turns away from him, not with distaste but with momentary lack of interest; in a mood to pursue what they were talking about*]

BENEATHA: I'm *trying* to talk to you.
GEORGE: We always talk.
BENEATHA: Yes—and I love to talk.
GEORGE [*Exasperated; rising*]: I know it and I don't mind it sometimes . . . I want you to cut it out, see—The moody stuff, I mean. I don't like it. You're a nice-looking girl . . . all over. That's all you need, honey, forget the atmosphere. Guys aren't going to go for the atmosphere— they're going to go for what they see. Be glad for that. Drop the Garbo routine. It doesn't go with you. As for myself, I want a nice—[*Groping*]—simple [*Thoughtfully*]—sophisticated girl . . . not a poet—O.K.?

[*She rebuffs him again and he starts to leave*]

BENEATHA: Why are you angry?

GEORGE: Because this is stupid! I don't go out with you to discuss the nature of "quiet desperation" or to hear all about your thoughts—because the world will go on thinking what it thinks regardless—

BENEATHA: Then why read books? Why go to school?

GEORGE [*With artificial patience, counting on his fingers*]: It's simple. You read books—to learn facts—to get grades—to pass the course—to get a degree. That's all—it has nothing to do with thoughts.

[*A long pause*]

BENEATHA: I see. [*A longer pause as she looks at him*] Good night, George.

[GEORGE *looks at her a little oddly, and starts to exit. He meets* MAMA *coming in*]

GEORGE: Oh—hello, Mrs. Younger.

MAMA: Hello, George, how you feeling?

GEORGE: Fine—fine, how are you?

MAMA: Oh, a little tired. You know them steps can get you after a day's work. You all have a nice time tonight?

GEORGE: Yes—a fine time. Well, good night.

MAMA: Good night. [*He exits.* MAMA *closes the door behind her*] Hello, honey. What you sitting like that for?

BENEATHA: I'm just sitting.

MAMA: Didn't you have a nice time?

BENEATHA: No.

MAMA: No? What's the matter?

BENEATHA: Mama, George is a fool—honest. [*She rises*]

MAMA [*Hustling around unloading the packages she has entered with. She stops*]: Is he, baby?

BENEATHA: Yes.

[BENEATHA *makes up* TRAVIS' *bed as she talks*]

MAMA: You sure?

BENEATHA: Yes.

MAMA: Well—I guess you better not waste your time with no fools.

[BENEATHA *looks up at her mother, watching her put groceries in the refrigerator. Finally she gathers up her things and starts into the bedroom. At the door she stops and looks back at her mother*]

BENEATHA: Mama—

MAMA: Yes, baby—
BENEATHA: Thank you.
MAMA: For what?
BENEATHA: For understanding me this time.

[*She exits quickly and the mother stands, smiling a little, looking at the place where* BENEATHA *just stood.* RUTH *enters*]

RUTH: Now don't you fool with any of this stuff, Lena—
MAMA: Oh, I just thought I'd sort a few things out.

[*The phone rings.* RUTH *answers*]

RUTH [*At the phone*]: Hello—Just a minute. [*Goes to door*] Walter, it's Mrs. Arnold. [*Waits. Goes back to the phone. Tense*] Hello. Yes, this is his wife speaking . . . He's lying down now. Yes . . . well, he'll be in tomorrow. He's been very sick. Yes—I know we should have called, but we were so sure he'd be able to come in today. Yes—yes, I'm very sorry. Yes . . . Thank you very much. [*She hangs up.* WALTER *is standing in the doorway of the bedroom behind her*] That was Mrs. Arnold.
WALTER [*Indifferently*]: Was it?
RUTH: She said if you don't come in tomorrow that they are getting a new man . . .
WALTER: Ain't that sad—ain't that crying sad.
RUTH: She said Mr. Arnold has had to take a cab for three days . . . Walter, you ain't been to work for three days! [*This is a revelation to her*] Where you been, Walter Lee Younger? [WALTER *looks at her and starts to laugh*] You're going to lose your job.
WALTER: That's right . . .
RUTH: Oh, Walter, and with your mother working like a dog every day—
WALTER: That's sad too—Everything is sad.
MAMA: What you been doing for these three days, son?
WALTER: Mama—you don't know all the things a man what got leisure can find to do in this city . . . What's this—Friday night? Well—Wednesday I borrowed Willy Harris' car and I went for a drive . . . just me and myself and I drove and drove . . . Way out . . . way past South Chicago, and I parked the car and I sat and looked at the steel mills all day long. I just sat in the car and looked at them big black chimneys for hours. Then I drove back and I went to the Green Hat. [*Pause*] And Thursday—Thursday I borrowed the car again and I got in it and I pointed it the other way and I drove the other way—for hours—way, way up to Wisconsin, and I looked at the farms. I just drove and looked at the farms. Then I drove back and I went to the Green Hat. [*Pause*] And today—today I didn't get the car. Today I just walked. All over the

Southside. And I looked at the Negroes and they looked at me and finally I just sat down on the curb at Thirty-ninth and South Parkway and I just sat there and watched the Negroes go by. And then I went to the Green Hat. You all sad? You all depressed? And you know where I am going right now—

[RUTH *goes out quietly*]

MAMA: Oh, Big Walter, is this the harvest of our days?

WALTER: You know what I like about the Green Hat? [*He turns the radio on and a steamy, deep blues pours into the room*] I like this little cat they got there who blows a sax . . . He blows. He talks to me. He ain't but 'bout five feet tall and he's got a conked head and his eyes is always closed and he's all music—

MAMA [*Rising and getting some papers out of her handbag*]: Walter—

WALTER: And there's this other guy who plays the piano . . . and they got a sound. I mean they can work on some music . . . They got the best little combo in the world in the Green Hat . . . You can just sit there and drink and listen to them three men play and you realize that don't nothing matter worth a damn, but just being there—

MAMA: I've helped do it to you, haven't I, son? Walter, I been wrong.

WALTER: Naw—you ain't never been wrong about nothing, Mama.

MAMA: Listen to me, now. I say I been wrong, son. That I been doing to you what the rest of the world been doing to you. [*She stops and he looks up slowly at her and she meets his eyes pleadingly*] Walter—what you ain't never understood is that I ain't got nothing, don't own nothing, ain't never really wanted nothing that wasn't for you. There ain't nothing as precious to me . . . There ain't nothing worth holding on to, money, dreams, nothing else—if it means—if it means it's going to destroy my boy. [*She puts her papers in front of him and he watches her without speaking or moving*] I paid the man thirty-five hundred dollars down on the house. That leaves sixty-five hundred dollars. Monday morning I want you to take this money and take three thousand dollars and put it in a savings account for Beneatha's medical schooling. The rest you put in a checking account—with your name on it. And from now on any penny that come out of it or that go in it is for you to look after. For you to decide. [*She drops her hands a little helplessly*] It ain't much, but it's all I got in the world and I'm putting it in your hands. I'm telling you to be the head of this family from now on like you supposed to be.

WALTER [*Stares at the money*]: You trust me like that, Mama?

MAMA: I ain't never stop trusting you. Like I ain't never stop loving you.

[*She goes out, and* WALTER *sits looking at the money on the table as the music continues in its idiom, pulsing in the room. Finally, in a decisive gesture, he gets up, and, in mingled joy and desperation, picks up the money. At the same moment,* TRAVIS *enters for bed*]

TRAVIS: What's the matter, Daddy? You drunk?

WALTER [*Sweetly, more sweetly than we have ever known him*]: No, Daddy ain't drunk. Daddy ain't going to never be drunk again. . . .

TRAVIS: Well, Good night, Daddy.

[*The* FATHER *has come from behind the couch and leans over, embracing his son*]

WALTER: Son, I feel like talking to you tonight.

TRAVIS: About what?

WALTER: Oh, about a lot of things. About you and what kind of man you going to be when you grow up. . . . Son—son, what do you want to be when you grow up?

TRAVIS: A bus driver.

WALTER [*Laughing a little*]: A what? Man, that ain't nothing to want to be!

TRAVIS: Why not?

WALTER: 'Cause, man—it ain't big enough—you know what I mean.

TRAVIS: I don't know then. I can't make up my mind. Sometimes Mama asks me that too. And sometimes when I tell you I just want to be like you —she says she don't want me to be like that and sometimes she says she does. . . .

WALTER [*Gathering him up in his arms*]: You know what, Travis? In seven years you going to be seventeen years old. And things is going to be very different with us in seven years, Travis. . . . One day when you are seventeen I'll come home—home from my office downtown somewhere—

TRAVIS: You don't work in no office, Daddy.

WALTER: No—but after tonight. After what your daddy gonna do tonight, there's going to be offices—a whole lot of offices. . . .

TRAVIS: What you gonna do tonight, Daddy?

WALTER: You wouldn't understand yet, son, but your daddy's gonna make a transaction . . . a business transaction that's going to change our lives. . . . That's how come one day when you 'bout seventeen years old I'll come home and I'll be pretty tired, you know what I mean, after a day of conferences and secretaries getting things wrong the way they do . . . 'cause an executive's life is hell, man—[*The more he talks the farther away he gets*] And I'll pull the car up on the driveway . . . just a plain black Chrysler, I think, with white walls—no—black tires. More elegant. Rich people don't have to be flashy . . . though I'll have to get something a little sportier for Ruth—maybe a Cadillac convertible to do her shopping in. . . . And I'll come up the steps to the house and the gardener will be clipping away at the hedges and he'll say, "Good evening, Mr. Younger." And I'll say, "Hello, Jefferson, how are you this evening?" And I'll go inside and Ruth will come downstairs and meet me at the door and we'll kiss each other and she'll take my arm and we'll go up to your room to see you sitting on the floor with the catalogues of all the great schools in America around you. . . . All the great schools in the world! And—and I'll say, all right son—it's your seventeenth birthday, what is it you've decided? . . . Just tell me where you want to go to school and you'll *go*. Just tell me, what it is you want to be— and you'll *be* it. . . . Whatever you want to be—Yessir! [*He holds his arms open for* TRAVIS] You just name it, son . . . [TRAVIS *leaps into them*] and I hand you the world!

[WALTER'S *voice has risen in pitch and hysterical promise and on the last line he lifts* TRAVIS *high*]

[*BLACKOUT*]

Scene Three

[*Time: Saturday, moving day, one week later.*
Before the curtain rises, RUTH'S *voice, a strident, dramatic church alto, cuts through the silence.*
It is, in the darkness, a triumphant surge, a penetrating statement of expectation: "*Oh, Lord, I don't feel no ways tired! Children, oh, glory hallelujah!*"
As the curtain rises we see that RUTH *is alone in the living room, finishing up the family's packing. It is moving day. She is nailing crates and tying cartons.* BENEATHA *enters, carrying a guitar case, and watches her exuberant sister-in-law.*]

RUTH: Hey!
BENEATHA [*Putting away the case*]: Hi.
RUTH [*Pointing at a package*]: Honey—look in that package there and see what I found on sale this morning at the South Center. [RUTH *gets up and moves to the package and draws out some curtains*] Lookahere—handturned hems!
BENEATHA: How do you know the window size out there?
RUTH [*Who hadn't thought of that*]: Oh—Well, they bound to fit something in the whole house. Anyhow, they was too good a bargain to pass up. [RUTH *slaps her head, suddenly remembering something*] Oh, Bennie—I meant to put a special note on that carton over there. That's your mama's good china and she wants 'em to be very careful with it.
BENEATHA: I'll do it.

[BENEATHA *finds a piece of paper and starts to draw large letters on it*]

RUTH: You know what I'm going to do soon as I get in that new house?

BENEATHA: What?

RUTH: Honey—I'm going to run me a tub of water up to here . . . [*With her fingers practically up to her nostrils*] And I'm going to get in it—and I am going to sit . . . and sit . . . and sit in that hot water and the first person who knocks to tell *me* to hurry up and come out—

BENEATHA: Gets shot at sunrise.

RUTH [*Laughing happily*]: You said it, sister! [*Noticing how large* BENEATHA *is absent-mindedly making the note*] Honey, they ain't going to read that from no airplane.

BENEATHA [*Laughing herself*]: I guess I always think things have more emphasis if they are big, somehow.

RUTH [*Looking up at her and smiling*]: You and your brother seem to have that as a philosophy of life. Lord, that man—done changed so 'round here. You know—you know what we did last night? Me and Walter Lee?

BENEATHA: What?

RUTH [*Smiling to herself*]: We went to the movies. [*Looking at* BENEATHA *to see if she understands*] We went to the movies. You know the last time me and Walter went to the movies together?

BENEATHA: No.

RUTH: Me neither. That's how long it been. [*Smiling again*] But we went last night. The picture wasn't much good, but that didn't seem to matter. We went—and we held hands.

BENEATHA: Oh, Lord!

RUTH: We held hands—and you know what?

BENEATHA: What?

RUTH: When we come out of the show it was late and dark and all the stores and things was closed up . . . and it was kind of chilly and there wasn't many people on the streets . . . and we was still holding hands, me and Walter.

BENEATHA: You're killing me.

[WALTER *enters with a large package. His happiness is deep in him; he cannot keep still with his new-found exuberance. He is singing and wiggling and snapping his fingers. He puts his package in a corner and puts a phonograph record, which he has brought in with him, on the record player. As the music comes up he dances over to* RUTH *and tries to get her to dance with him. She gives in at last to his raunchiness and in a fit of giggling allows herself to be drawn into his mood and together they deliberately burlesque an old social dance of their youth*]

BENEATHA [*Regarding them a long time as they dance, then drawing in her breath for a deeply exaggerated comment which she does not particularly mean*]: Talk about—olddddddddddd-fashionedddddddd—Negroes!

WALTER [*Stopping momentarily*]: What kind of Negroes?

[*He says this in fun. He is not angry with her today, nor with anyone. He starts to dance with his wife again*]

BENEATHA: Old-fashioned.

WALTER [*As he dances with* RUTH]: You know, when these *New Negroes* have their convention—[*Pointing at his sister*]—that is going to be the chairman of the Committee on Unending Agitation. [*He goes on dancing, then stops*] Race, race, race! . . . Girl, I do believe you are the first person in the history of the entire human race to successfully brainwash yourself. [BENEATHA *breaks up and he goes on dancing. He stops again, enjoying his tease*] Damn, even the N double A C P takes a holiday sometimes! [BENEATHA *and* RUTH *laugh. He dances with* RUTH *some more and starts to laugh and stops and pantomimes someone over an operating table*] I can just see that chick someday looking down at some poor cat on an operating table before she starts to slice him, saying . . . [*Pulling his sleeves back maliciously*] "By the way, what are your views on civil rights down there? . . ."

[*He laughs at her again and starts to dance happily. The bell sounds*]

BENEATHA: Sticks and stones may break my bones but . . . words will never hurt me!

[BENEATHA *goes to the door and opens it as* WALTER *and* RUTH *go on with the clowning.* BENEATHA *is somewhat surprised to see a quiet-looking middle-aged white man in a business suit holding his hat and a briefcase in his hand and consulting a small piece of paper*]

MAN: Uh—how do you do, miss. I am looking for a Mrs.—[*He looks at the slip of paper*] Mrs. Lena Younger?

BENEATHA [*Smoothing her hair with slight embarrassment*]: Oh—yes, that's my mother. Excuse me [*She closes the door and turns to quiet the other two*] Ruth! Brother! Somebody's here. [*Then she opens the door. The man casts a curious quick glance at all of them*] Uh—come in please.

MAN [*Coming in*]: Thank you.

BENEATHA: My mother isn't here just now. Is it business?

MAN: Yes . . . well, of a sort.

WALTER [*Freely, the Man of the House*]: Have a seat. I'm Mrs. Younger's son. I look after most of her business matters.

[RUTH *and* BENEATHA *exchange amused glances*]

MAN [*Regarding* WALTER, *and sitting*]: Well—My name is Karl
Lindner . . .

WALTER [*Stretching out his hand*]: Walter Younger. This is my wife—[RUTH
nods politely]—and my sister.

LINDNER: How do you do.

WALTER [*Amiably, as he sits himself easily on a chair, leaning with interest
forward on his knees and looking expectantly into the newcomer's face*]: What
can we do for you, Mr. Lindner!

LINDNER [*Some minor shuffling of the hat and briefcase on his knees*]: Well—I am
a representative of the Clybourne Park Improvement Association—

WALTER [*Pointing*]: Why don't you sit your things on the floor?

LINDNER: Oh—yes. Thank you. [*He slides the briefcase and hat under the
chair*] And as I was saying—I am from the Clybourne Park Improvement
Association and we have had it brought to our attention at the last
meeting that you people—or at least your mother—has bought a piece
of residential property at—[*He digs for the slip of paper again*]—four o six
Clybourne Street. . . .

WALTER: That's right. Care for something to drink? Ruth, get Mr. Lindner
a beer.

LINDNER [*Upset for some reason*]: Oh—no, really. I mean thank you very
much, but no thank you.

RUTH [*Innocently*]: Some coffee?

LINDNER: Thank you, nothing at all.

[BENEATHA *is watching the man carefully*]

LINDNER: Well, I don't know how much you folks know about our organization. [*He is a gentle man; thoughtful and somewhat labored in his manner*]
It is one of these community organizations set up to look after—oh, you
know, things like block upkeep and special projects and we also have
what we call our New Neighbors Orientation Committee . . .

BENEATHA [*Drily*]: Yes—and what do they do?

LINDNER [*Turning a little to her and then returning the main force to* WALTER]:
Well—it's what you might call a sort of welcoming committee, I guess.
I mean they, we, I'm the chairman of the committee—go around and see
the new people who move into the neighborhood and sort of give them
the lowdown on the way we do things out in Clybourne Park.

BENEATHA [*With appreciation of the two meanings, which escape* RUTH *and* WAL-
TER]: Un-huh.

LINDNER: And we also have the category of what the association calls—[*He
looks elsewhere*]—uh—special community problems . . .

BENEATHA: Yes—and what are some of those?

WALTER: Girl, let the man talk.

LINDNER [*With understated relief*]: Thank you. I would sort of like to explain this thing in my own way. I mean I want to explain to you in a certain way.

WALTER: Go ahead.

LINDNER: Yes. Well. I'm going to try to get right to the point. I'm sure we'll all appreciate that in the long run.

BENEATHA: Yes.

WALTER: Be still now!

LINDNER: Well—

RUTH [*Still innocently*]: Would you like another chair—you don't look comfortable.

LINDNER [*More frustrated than annoyed*]: No, thank you very much. Please. Well—to get right to the point I—[*A great breath, and he is off at last*] I am sure you people must be aware of some of the incidents which have happened in various parts of the city when colored people have moved into certain areas—[BENEATHA *exhales heavily and starts tossing a piece of fruit up and down in the air*] Well—because we have what I think is going to be a unique type of organization in American community life—not only do we deplore that kind of thing—but we are trying to do something about it. [BENEATHA *stops tossing and turns with a new and quizzical interest to the man*] We feel—[*gaining confidence in his mission because of the interest in the faces of the people he is talking to*]—we feel that most of the trouble in this world, when you come right down to it—[*He hits his knee for emphasis*]—most of the trouble exists because people just don't sit down and talk to each other.

RUTH [*Nodding as she might in church, pleased with the remark*]: You can say that again, mister.

LINDNER [*More encouraged by such affirmation*]: That we don't try hard enough in this world to understand the other fellow's problem. The other guy's point of view.

RUTH: Now that's right.

[BENEATHA *and* WALTER *merely watch and listen with genuine interest*]

LINDNER: Yes—that's the way we feel out in Clybourne Park. And that's why I was elected to come here this afternoon and talk to you people. Friendly like, you know, the way people should talk to each other and see if we couldn't find some way to work this thing out. As I say, the whole business is a matter of *caring* about the other fellow. Anybody can see that you are a nice family of folks, hard working and honest I'm sure. [BENEATHA *frowns slightly, quizzically, her head tilted regarding him*] Today everybody knows what it means to be on the outside of *something*. And of course, there is always somebody who is out to take the advantage of people who don't always understand.

WALTER: What do you mean?

LINDNER: Well—you see our community is made up of people who've worked hard as the dickens for years to build up that little community. They're not rich and fancy people; just hard-working, honest people who don't really have much but those little homes and a dream of the kind of community they want to raise their children in. Now, I don't say we are perfect and there is a lot wrong in some of the things they want. But you've got to admit that a man, right or wrong, has the right to want to have the neighborhood he lives in a certain kind of way. And at the moment the overwhelming majority of our people out there feel that people get along better, take more of a common interest in the life of the community, when they share a common background. I want you to believe me when I tell you that race prejudice simply doesn't enter into it. It is a matter of the people of Clybourne Park believing, rightly or wrongly, as I say, that for the happiness of all concerned that our Negro families are happier when they live in their *own* communities.

BENEATHA [*With a grand and bitter gesture*]: This, friends, is the Welcoming Committee!

WALTER [*Dumfounded, looking at* LINDNER]: Is this what you came marching all the way over here to tell us?

LINDNER: Well, now we've been having a fine conversation. I hope you'll hear me all the way through.

WALTER [*Tightly*]: Go ahead, man.

LINDNER: You see—in the face of all things I have said, we are prepared to make your family a very generous offer . . .

BENEATHA: Thirty pieces and not a coin less!

WALTER: Yeah?

LINDNER [*Putting on his glasses and drawing a form out of the briefcase*]: Our association is prepared, through the collective effort of our people, to buy the house from you at a financial gain to your family.

RUTH: Lord have mercy, ain't this the living gall!

WALTER: All right, you through?

LINDNER: Well, I want to give you the exact terms of the financial arrangement—

WALTER: We don't want to hear no exact terms of no arrangements. I want to know if you got any more to tell us 'bout getting together?

LINDNER [*Taking off his glasses*]: Well—I don't suppose that you feel . . .

WALTER: Never mind how I feel—you got any more to say 'bout how people ought to sit down and talk to each other? . . . Get out of my house, man.

[*He turns his back and walks to the door*]

LINDNER [*Looking around at the hostile faces and reaching and assembling his hat and briefcase*]: Well—I don't understand why you people are reacting this way. What do you think you are going to gain by moving into a neighborhood where you just aren't wanted and where some elements —well—people can get awful worked up when they feel that their whole way of life and everything they've ever worked for is threatened.

WALTER: Get out.

LINDNER [*At the door, holding a small card*]: Well—I'm sorry it went like this.

WALTER: Get out.

LINDNER [*Almost sadly regarding* WALTER]: You just can't force people to change their hearts, son.

[*He turns and puts his card on a table and exits.* WALTER *pushes the door to with stinging hatred, and stands looking at it.* RUTH *just sits and* BENEATHA *just stands. They say nothing.* MAMA *and* TRAVIS *enter*]

MAMA: Well—this all the packing got done since I left out of here this morning. I testify before God that my children got all the energy of the dead. What time the moving men due?

BENEATHA: Four o'clock. You had a caller, Mama.

[*She is smiling, teasingly*]

MAMA: Sure enough—who?

BENEATHA [*Her arms folded saucily*]: The Welcoming Committee.

[WALTER *and* RUTH *giggle*]

MAMA [*Innocently*]: Who?

BENEATHA: The Welcoming Committee. They said they're sure going to be glad to see you when you get there.

WALTER [*Devilishly*]: Yeah, they said they can't hardly wait to see your face.

[*Laughter*]

MAMA [*Sensing their facetiousness*]: What's the matter with you all?

WALTER: Ain't nothing the matter with us. We just telling you 'bout the gentleman who came to see you this afternoon. From the Clybourne Park Improvement Association.

MAMA: What he want?

RUTH [*In the same mood as* BENEATHA *and* WALTER]: To welcome you, honey.

WALTER: He said they can't hardly wait. He said the one thing they don't have, that they just *dying* to have out there is a fine family of colored people! [*To* RUTH *and* BENEATHA] Ain't that right!

RUTH *and* BENEATHA [*Mockingly*]: Yeah! He left his card in case—

[*They indicate the card, and* MAMA *picks it up and throws it on the floor—*

understanding and looking off as she draws her chair up to the table on which she has put her plant and some sticks and some cord]

MAMA: Father, give us strength. [*Knowingly—and without fun*] Did he threaten us?

BENEATHA: Oh—Mama—they don't do it like that any more. He talked Brotherhood. He said everybody ought to learn how to sit down and hate each other with good Christian fellowship.

[*She and* WALTER *shake hands to ridicule the remark*]

MAMA [*Sadly*]: Lord, protect us . . .

RUTH: You should hear the money those folks raised to buy the house from us. All we paid and then some.

BENEATHA: What they think we going to do—eat 'em?

RUTH: No, honey, marry 'em.

MAMA [*Shaking her head*]: Lord, Lord, Lord . . .

RUTH: Well—that's the way the crackers crumble. Joke.

BENEATHA [*Laughingly noticing what her mother is doing*]: Mama, what are you doing?

MAMA: Fixing my plant so it won't get hurt none on the way . . .

BENEATHA: Mama, you going to take *that* to the new house?

MAMA: Un-huh—

BENEATHA: That raggedy-looking old thing?

MAMA [*Stopping and looking at her*]: It expresses *me*.

RUTH [*With delight, to* BENEATHA]: So there, Miss Thing!

[WALTER *comes to* MAMA *suddenly and bends down behind her and squeezes her in his arms with all his strength. She is overwhelmed by the suddenness of it and, though delighted, her manner is like that of* RUTH *with* TRAVIS]

MAMA: Look out now, boy! You make me mess up my thing here!

WALTER [*His face lit, he slips down on his knees beside her, his arms still about her*]: Mama . . . you know what it means to climb up in the chariot?

MAMA [*Gruffly, very happy*]: Get on away from me now . . .

RUTH [*Near the gift-wrapped package, trying to catch* WALTER'S *eye*]: Psst—

WALTER: What the old song say, Mama . . .

RUTH: Walter—Now?

[*She is pointing at the package*]

WALTER [*Speaking the lines, sweetly, playfully, in his mother's face*]:

> I got wings . . . you got wings . . .
> All God's Children got wings . . .

MAMA: Boy—get out of my face and do some work . . .
WALTER:

> When I get to heaven gonna put on my wings,
> Gonna fly all over God's heaven . . .

BENEATHA [*Teasingly, from across the room*]: Everybody talking 'bout heaven ain't going there!
WALTER [*To* RUTH, *who is carrying the box across to them*]: I don't know, you think we ought to give her that . . . Seems to me she ain't been very appreciative around here.
MAMA [*Eying the box, which is obviously a gift*]: What is that?
WALTER [*Taking it from* RUTH *and putting it on the table in front of* MAMA]: Well —what you all think? Should we give it to her?
RUTH: Oh—she was pretty good today.
MAMA: I'll good you—

[*She turns her eyes to the box again*]

BENEATHA: Open it, Mama.

[*She stands up, looks at it, turns and looks at all of them, and then presses her hands together and does not open the package*]

WALTER [*Sweetly*]: Open it, Mama. It's for you. [MAMA *looks in his eyes. It is the first present in her life without its being Christmas. Slowly she opens her package and lifts out, one by one, a brand-new sparkling set of gardening tools.* WALTER *continues, prodding*] Ruth made up the note—read it . . .
MAMA [*Picking up the card and adjusting her glasses*]: "To our own Mrs. Miniver—Love from Brother, Ruth and Beneatha." Ain't that lovely . . .
TRAVIS [*Tugging at his father's sleeve*]: Daddy, can I give her mine now?
WALTER: All right, son. [TRAVIS *flies to get his gift*] Travis didn't want to go in with the rest of us, Mama. He got his own. [*Somewhat amused*] We don't know what it is . . .
TRAVIS [*Racing back in the room with a large hatbox and putting it in front of his grandmother*]: Here!
MAMA: Lord have mercy, baby. You done gone and bought your grandmother a hat?
TRAVIS [*Very Proud*]: Open it!

[*She does and lifts out an elaborate, but very elaborate, wide gardening hat, and all the adults break up at the sight of it*]

RUTH: Travis, honey, what is that?

TRAVIS [*Who thinks it is beautiful and appropriate*]: It's a gardening hat! Like the ladies always have on in the magazines when they work in their gardens.

BENEATHA [*Giggling fiercely*]: Travis—we were trying to make Mama Mrs. Miniver—not Scarlett O'Hara!

MAMA [*Indignantly*]: What's the matter with you all! This here is a beautiful hat! [*Absurdly*] I always wanted me one just like it!

[*She pops it on her head to prove it to her grandson, and the hat is ludicrous and considerably oversized*]

RUTH: Hot dog! Go, Mama!

WALTER [*Doubled over with laughter*]: I'm sorry, Mama—but you look like you ready to go out and chop you some cotton sure enough!

[*They all laugh except* MAMA, *out of deference to* TRAVIS' *feelings*]

MAMA [*Gathering the boy up to her*]: Bless your heart—this is the prettiest hat I ever owned—[WALTER, RUTH *and* BENEATHA *chime in—noisily, festively and insincerely congratulating* TRAVIS *on his gift*] What are we all standing around here for? We ain't finished packin' yet. Bennie, you ain't packed one book.

[*The bell rings*]

BENEATHA: That couldn't be the movers . . . it's not hardly two good yet—

[BENEATHA *goes into her room.* MAMA *starts for door*]

WALTER [*Turning, stiffening*]: Wait—wait—I'll get it.

[*He stands and looks at the door*]

MAMA: You expecting company, son?

WALTER [*Just looking at the door*]: Yeah—yeah . . .

[MAMA *looks at* RUTH, *and they exchange innocent and unfrightened glances*]

MAMA [*Not understanding*]: Well, let them in, son.

BENEATHA [*From her room*]: We need some more string.

MAMA: Travis—you run to the hardware and get me some string cord.

[MAMA *goes out and* WALTER *turns and looks at* RUTH. TRAVIS *goes to a dish for money*]

RUTH: Why don't you answer the door, man?

WALTER [*Suddenly bounding across the floor to her*]: 'Cause sometimes it hard to let the future begin! [*Stooping down in her face*]

> *I got wings! You got wings!*
> *All Gods children got wings*

[*He crosses to the door and throws it open. Standing there is a very slight little man in a not too prosperous business suit and with haunted frightened eyes and a hat pulled down tightly, brim up, around his forehead.* TRAVIS *passes between the men and exits.* WALTER *leans deep in the man's face, still in his jubilance*]

> *When I get to heaven gonna put on my wings,*
> *Gonna fly all over God's heaven . . .*

[*The little man just stares at him*]

> *Heaven—*

[*Suddenly he stops and looks past the little man into the empty hallway*]

Where's Willy, man?

BOBO: He ain't with me.

WALTER [*Not disturbed*]: Oh—come on in. You know my wife.

BOBO [*Dumbly, taking off his hat*]: Yes—h'you, Miss Ruth.

RUTH [*Quietly, a mood apart from her husband already, seeing* BOBO]: Hello, Bobo.

WALTER: You right on time today . . . Right on time. That's the way! [*He slaps* BOBO *on his back*] Sit down . . . lemme hear.

[RUTH *stands stiffly and quietly in back of them, as though somehow she senses death, her eyes fixed on her husband*]

BOBO [*His frightened eyes on the floor, his hat in his hands*]: Could I please get a drink of water, before I tell you about it, Walter Lee?

[WALTER *does not take his eyes off the man.* RUTH *goes blindly to the tap and gets a glass of water and brings it to* BOBO]

WALTER: There ain't nothing wrong, is there?

BOBO: Lemme tell you—

WALTER: Man—didn't nothing go wrong?

BOBO: Lemme tell you—Walter Lee. [*Looking at* RUTH *and talking to her more than to* WALTER] You know how it was. I got to tell you how it was. I mean first I got to tell you how it was all the way . . . I mean about the money I put in, Walter Lee . . .

WALTER [*With taut agitation now*]: What about the money you put in?

BOBO: Well—it wasn't much as we told you—me and Willy—[*He stops*] I'm sorry, Walter. I got a bad feeling about it. I got a real bad feeling about it . . .

WALTER: Man, what you telling me about all this for? . . . Tell me what happened in Springfield . . .

BOBO: Springfield.

RUTH [*Like a dead woman*]: What was supposed to happen in Springfield?

BOBO [*To her*]: This deal that me and Walter went into with Willy—Me and Willy was going to go down to Springfield and spread some money 'round so's we wouldn't have to wait so long for the liquor license . . . That's what we were going to do. Everybody said that was the way you had to do, you understand, Miss Ruth?

WALTER: Man—what happened down there?

BOBO [*A pitiful man, near tears*]: I'm trying to tell you, Walter.

WALTER [*Screaming at him suddenly*]: THEN TELL ME, GODDAMMIT . . . WHAT'S THE MATTER WITH YOU?

BOBO: Man . . . I didn't go to no Springfield, yesterday.

WALTER [*Halted, life hanging in the moment*]: Why not?

BOBO [*The long way, the hard way to tell*]: 'Cause I didn't have no reasons to . . .

WALTER: Man, what are you talking about!

BOBO: I'm talking about the fact that when I got to the train station yesterday morning—eight o'clock like we planned . . . Man—*Willy didn't never show up.*

WALTER: Why . . . where was he . . . where is he?

BOBO: That's what I'm trying to tell you . . . I don't know . . . I waited six hours . . . I called his house . . . and I waited . . . six hours . . . I waited in that train station six hours . . . [*Breaking into tears*] That was all the extra money I had in the world . . . [*Looking up at* WALTER *with the tears running down his face*] Man, *Willy is gone.*

WALTER: Gone, what you mean Willy is gone? Gone where? You mean he went by himself. You mean he went off to Springfield by himself—to take care of getting the license—[*Turns and looks anxiously at* RUTH] You mean maybe he didn't want too many people in on the business down there? [*Looks to* RUTH *again, as before*] You know Willy got his own ways. [*Looks back to* BOBO] Maybe you was late yesterday and he just went on down there without you. Maybe—maybe—he's been callin' you at home trying' to tell you what happened or something. Maybe—maybe —he just got sick. He's somewhere—he's got to be somewhere. We just got to find him—me and you got to find him. [*Grabs* BOBO *senselessly by the collar and starts to shake him*] We got to!

BOBO [*In sudden angry, frightened agony*]: What's the matter with you, Walter! *When a cat take off with your money he don't leave you no maps!*

WALTER [*Turning madly, as though he is looking for* WILLY *in the very room*]: Willy! . . . Willy . . . don't do it . . . Please don't do it . . . Man, not with that money . . . Man, please, not with that money . . . Oh, God . . . Don't let it be true . . . [*He is wandering around, crying out for* WILLY *and looking for him or perhaps for help from God*] Man . . . I trusted you . . . Man, I put my life in your hands . . . [*He starts to crumple down on the floor as* RUTH *just covers her face in horror.* MAMA *opens the door and comes into the room, with* BENEATHA *behind her*] Man . . . [*He starts to pound the floor with his fists, sobbing wildly*] *That money is made out of my father's flesh* . . .

BOBO [*Standing over him helplessly*]: I'm sorry, Walter . . . [*Only* WALTER'S *sobs reply.* BOBO *puts on his hat*] I had my life staked on this deal, too . . .

[*He exits*]

MAMA [*To* WALTER]: Son—[*She goes to him, bends down to him, talks to his bent head*] Son . . . Is it gone? Son, I gave you sixty-five hundred dollars. Is it gone? All of it? Beneatha's money too?

WALTER [*Lifting his head slowly*]: Mama . . . I never . . . went to the bank at all . . .

MAMA [*Not wanting to believe him*]: You mean . . . your sister's school money . . . you used that too . . . Walter? . . .

WALTER: Yessss! . . . All of it . . . It's all gone . . .

[*There is total silence.* RUTH *stands with her face covered with her hands;* BENEATHA *leans forlornly against a wall, fingering a piece of red ribbon from the mother's gift.* MAMA *stops and looks at her son without recognition and then, quite without thinking about it, starts to beat him senselessly in the face.* BENEATHA *goes to them and stops it*]

BENEATHA: Mama!

[MAMA *stops and looks at both of her children and rises slowly and wanders vaguely, aimlessly away from them*]

MAMA: I seen . . . him . . . night after night . . . come in . . . and look at that rug . . . and then look at me . . . the red showing in his eyes . . . the veins moving in his head . . . I seen him grow thin and old before he was forty . . . working and working and working like

somebody's old horse . . . killing himself . . . and you—you give it all
away in a day . . .

BENEATHA: Mama—

MAMA: Oh, God . . . [*She looks up to Him*] Look down here—and show me
the strength.

BENEATHA: Mama—

MAMA [*Folding over*]: Strength . . .

BENEATHA [*Plaintively*]: Mama . . .

MAMA: Strength!

CURTAIN

Act III

[*An hour later.*
*At curtain, there is a sullen light of gloom in the living room, gray light not
unlike that which began the first scene of Act One.*
At left we can see WALTER *within his room, alone with himself. He is stretched
out on the bed, his shirt out and open, his arms under his head. He does not
smoke, he does not cry out, he merely lies there, looking up at the ceiling, much
as if he were alone in the world.*
In the living room BENEATHA *sits at the table, still surrounded by the now almost
ominous packing crates. She sits looking off. We feel that this is a mood struck
perhaps an hour before, and it lingers now, full of empty sound of profound
disappointment. We see on a line from her brother's bedroom the sameness of
their attitudes. Presently the bell rings and* BENEATHA *rises without ambition
or interest in answering. It is* ASAGAI, *smiling broadly, striding into the room
with energy and happy expectation and conversation.*]

ASAGAI: I came over . . . I had some free time. I thought I might help with
the packing. Ah, I like the look of packing crates! A household in
preparation for a journey! It depresses some people . . . but for
me . . . it is another feeling. Something full of the flow of life, do you
understand? Movement, progress . . . It makes me think of Africa.

BENEATHA: Africa!

ASAGAI: What kind of a mood is this? Have I told you how deeply you move
me?

BENEATHA: He gave away the money, Asagai . . .

ASAGAI: Who gave away what money?

BENEATHA: The insurance money. My brother gave it away.

ASAGAI: Gave it away?

BENEATHA: He made an investment! With a man even Travis wouldn't have
trusted.

ASAGAI: And it's gone?

BENEATHA: Gone!

ASAGAI: I'm very sorry . . . And you, now?

BENEATHA: Me? . . . Me? . . . Me I'm nothing . . . Me. When I was very small . . . we used to take our sleds out in the wintertime and the only hills we had were the ice-covered stone steps of some houses down the street. And we used to fill them in with snow and make them smooth and slide down them all day . . . and it was very dangerous you know . . . far too steep . . . and sure enough one day a kid named Rufus came down too fast and hit the sidewalk . . . and we saw his face just split open right there in front of us . . . And I remember standing there looking at his bloody open face thinking that was the end of Rufus. But the ambulance came and they took him to the hospital and they fixed the broken bones and they sewed it all up . . . and the next time I saw Rufus he just had a little line down the middle of his face . . . I never got over that . . .

[WALTER *sits up, listening on the bed. Throughout this scene it is important that we feel his reaction at all times, that he visibly respond to the words of his sister and* ASAGAI]

ASAGAI: What?

BENEATHA: That that was what one person could do for another, fix him up —sew up the problem, make him all right again. That was the most marvelous thing in the world . . . I wanted to do that. I always thought it was the one concrete thing in the world that a human being could do. Fix up the sick, you know—and make them whole again. This was truly being God . . .

ASAGAI: You wanted to be God?

BENEATHA: No—I wanted to cure. It used to be so important to me. I wanted to cure. It used to matter. I used to care. I mean about people and how their bodies hurt . . .

ASAGAI: And you've stopped caring?

BENEATHA: Yes—I think so.

ASAGAI: Why?

[WALTER *rises, goes to the door of his room and is about to open it, then stops and stands listening, leaning on the door jamb*]

BENEATHA: Because it doesn't seem deep enough, close enough to what ails mankind—I mean this thing of sewing up bodies or administering drugs. Don't you understand? It was a child's reaction to the world. I thought that doctors had the secret to all the hurts. . . . That's the way a child sees things—or an idealist.

ASAGAI: Children see things very well sometimes—and idealists even better.

BENEATHA: I know that's what you think. Because you are still where I left off—you still care. This is what you see for the world, for Africa. You with the dreams of the future will patch up all Africa—you are going to cure the Great Sore of colonialism with Independence—

ASAGAI: Yes!

BENEATHA: Yes—and you think that one word is the penicillin of the human spirit: "Independence!" But then what?

ASAGAI: That will be the problem for another time. First we must get there.

BENEATHA: And where does it end?

ASAGAI: End? Who even spoke of an end? To life? To living?

BENEATHA: An end to misery!

ASAGAI [*Smiling*]: You sound like a French intellectual.

BENEATHA: No! I sound like a human being who just had her future taken right out of her hands! While I was sleeping in my bed in there, things were happening in this world that directly concerned me—and nobody asked me, consulted me—they just went out and did things—and changed my life. Don't you see there isn't any real progress, Asagai, there is only one large circle that we march in, around and around, each of us with our own little picture—in front of us—our own little mirage that we think is the future.

ASAGAI: That is the mistake.

BENEATHA: What?

ASAGAI: What you just said—about the circle. It isn't a circle—it is simply a long line—as in geometry, you know, one that reaches into infinity. And because we cannot see the end—we also cannot see how it changes. And it is very odd but those who see the changes are called "idealists" —and those who cannot, or refuse to think, they are the "realists." It is very strange, and amusing too, I think.

BENEATHA: You—you are almost religious.

ASAGAI: Yes . . . I think I have the religion of doing what is necessary in the world—and of worshipping man—because he is so marvelous, you see.

BENEATHA: Man is foul! And the human race deserves its misery!

ASAGAI: You see: *you* have become the religious one in the old sense. Already, and after such a small defeat, you are worshipping despair.

BENEATHA: From now on, I worship the truth—and the truth is that people are puny, small and selfish. . . .

ASAGAI: Truth? Why is it that you despairing ones always think that only you have the truth? I never thought to see *you* like that. You! Your brother made a stupid, childish mistake—and you are grateful to him. So that now you can give up the ailing human race on account of it. You talk about what good is struggle; what good is anything? Where are we all going? And why are we bothering?

BENEATHA: *And you cannot answer it!* All your talk and dreams about Africa and Independence. Independence and then what? What about all the crooks and petty thieves and just plain idiots who will come into power to steal and plunder the same as before—only now they will be black and do it in the name of the new Independence—You cannot answer that.

ASAGAI [*Shouting over her*]: *I live the answer!* [*Pause*] In my village at home it is the exceptional man who can even read a newspaper . . . or who ever *sees* a book at all. I will go home and much of what I will have to say will seem strange to the people of my village . . . But I will teach and work and things will happen, slowly and swiftly. At times it will seem that nothing changes at all . . . and then again . . . the sudden dramatic events which make history leap into the future. And then quiet again. Retrogression even. Guns, murder, revolution. And I even will have moments when I wonder if the quiet was not better than all that death and hatred. But I will look about my village at the illiteracy and disease and ignorance and I will not wonder long. And perhaps . . . perhaps I will be a great man . . . I mean perhaps I will hold on to the substance of truth and find my way always with the right course . . . and perhaps for it I will be butchered in my bed some night by the servants of empire . . .

BENEATHA: *The martyr!*

ASAGAI: . . . or perhaps I shall live to be a very old man, respected and esteemed in my new nation . . . And perhaps I shall hold office and this is what I'm trying to tell you, Alaiyo; perhaps the things I believe now for my country will be wrong and outmoded, and I will not understand and do terrible things to have things my way or merely to keep my power. Don't you see that there will be young men and women, not British soldiers then, but my own black countrymen . . . to step out of the shadows some evening and slit my then useless throat? Don't you see they have always been there . . . that they always will be. And that such a thing as my own death will be an advance? They who might kill me even . . . actually replenish me!

BENEATHA: Oh, Asagai, I know all that.

ASAGAI: Good! Then stop moaning and groaning and tell me what you plan to do.

BENEATHA: Do?

ASAGAI: I have a bit of a suggestion.

BENEATHA: What?

ASAGAI [*Rather quietly for him*]: That when it is all over—that you come home with me—

BENEATHA [*Slapping herself on the forehead with exasperation born of misunderstanding*]: Oh—Asagai—at this moment you decide to be romantic!

ASAGAI [*Quickly understanding the misunderstanding*]: My dear, young creature of the New World—I do not mean across the city—I mean across the ocean; home—to Africa.

BENEATHA [*Slowly understanding and turning to him with murmured amazement*]: To—to Nigeria?

ASAGAI: Yes! . . . [*Smiling and lifting his arms playfully*] Three hundred years later the African Prince rose up out of the seas and swept the maiden back across the middle passage over which her ancestors had come—

BENEATHA [*Unable to play*]: Nigeria?

ASAGAI: Nigeria. Home. [*Coming to her with genuine romantic flippancy*] I will show you our mountains and our stars; and give you cool drinks from gourds and teach you the old songs and the ways of our people—and, in time, we will pretend that—[*very softly*]—you have only been away for a day—

[*She turns her back to him, thinking. He swings her around and takes her full in his arms in a long embrace which proceeds to passion*]

BENEATHA [*Pulling away*]: You're getting me all mixed up—

ASAGAI: Why?

BENEATHA: Too many things—too many things have happened today. I must sit down and think. I don't know what I feel about anything right this minute.

[*She promptly sits down and props her chin on her fist*]

ASAGAI [*Charmed*]: All right, I shall leave you. No—don't get up. [*Touching her, gently, sweetly*] Just sit awhile and think . . . Never be afraid to sit awhile and think. [*He goes to door and looks at her*] How often I have looked at you and said, "Ah—so this is what the New World hath finally wrought . . ."

[*He exits.* BENEATHA *sits on alone. Presently* WALTER *enters from his room and starts to rummage through things, feverishly looking for something. She looks up and turns in her seat*]

BENEATHA [*Hissingly*]: Yes—just look at what the New World hath wrought! . . . Just look! [*She gestures with bitter disgust*] There he is! *Monsieur le petit bourgeois noir*—himself! There he is—Symbol of a Rising Class! Entrepreneur! Titan of the system! [WALTER *ignores her completely and continues frantically and destructively looking for something and hurling things to floor and tearing things out of their place in his search.* BENEATHA *ignores the eccentricity of his actions and goes on with the monologue of insult*] Did you dream of yachts on Lake Michigan, Brother? Did you see yourself on that Great Day sitting down at the Conference Table, surrounded by all the mighty bald-headed men in America? All halted, waiting, breathless, waiting for your pronouncements on industry? Waiting for you—

Chairman of the Board? [WALTER *finds what he is looking for—a small piece of white paper—and pushes it in his pocket and puts on his coat and rushes out without ever having looked at her. She shouts after him*] I look at you and I see the final triumph of stupidity in the world!

[*The door slams and she returns to just sitting again.* RUTH *comes quickly out of* MAMA'S *room*]

RUTH: Who was that?

BENEATHA: Your husband.

RUTH: Where did he go?

BENEATHA: Who knows—maybe he has an appointment at U. S. Steel.

RUTH [*Anxiously, with frightened eyes*]: You didn't say nothing bad to him, did you?

BENEATHA: Bad? Say anything bad to him? No—I told him he was a sweet boy and full of dreams and everything is strictly peachy keen, as the ofay kids say!

[MAMA *enters from her bedroom. She is lost, vague, trying to catch hold, to make some sense of her former command of the world, but it still eludes her. A sense of waste overwhelms her gait; a measure of apology rides on her shoulders. She goes to her plant, which has remained on the table, looks at it, picks it up and takes it to the window sill and sits it outside, and she stands and looks at it a long moment. Then she closes the window, straightens her body with effort and turns around to her children*]

MAMA: Well—ain't it a mess in here, though? [*A false cheerfulness, a beginning of something*] I guess we all better stop moping around and get some work done. All this unpacking and everything we got to do. [RUTH *raises her head slowly in response to the sense of the line; and* BENEATHA *in similar manner turns very slowly to look at her mother*] One of you all better call the moving people and tell 'em not to come.

RUTH: Tell 'em not to come?

MAMA: Of course, baby. Ain't no need in 'em coming all the way here and having to go back. They charges for that too. [*She sits down, fingers to her brow, thinking*] Lord, ever since I was a little girl. I always remembers people saying, "Lena—Lena Eggleston, you aims too high all the time. You needs to slow down and see life a little more like it is. Just slow down some." That's what they always used to say down home— "Lord, that Lena Eggleston is a high-minded thing. She'll get her due one day!"

RUTH: No, Lena . . .

MAMA: Me and Big Walter just didn't never learn right.

RUTH: Lena, no! We gotta go. Bennie—tell her . . . [*She rises and crosses to* BENEATHA *with her arms outstretched.* BENEATHA *doesn't respond*] Tell her we can still move . . . the notes ain't but a hundred and twenty-five a month. We got four grown people in this house—we can work . . .

MAMA [*To herself*]: Just aimed too high all the time—

RUTH [*Turning and going to* MAMA *fast—the words pouring out with urgency and desperation*]: Lena—I'll work . . . I'll work twenty hours a day in all the kitchens in Chicago . . . I'll strap my baby on my back if I have to and scrub all the floors in America and wash all the sheets in America if I have to—but we got to move . . . We got to get out of here . . .

[MAMA *reaches out absently and pats* RUTH'S *hand*]

MAMA: No—I sees things differently now. Been thinking 'bout some of the things we could do to fix this place up some. I seen a second-hand bureau over on Maxwell Street just the other day that could fit right there. [*She points to where the new furniture might go.* RUTH *wanders away from her*] Would need some new handles on it and then a little varnish and then it look like something brand-new. And—we can put up them new curtains in the kitchen . . . Why this place be looking fine. Cheer us all up so that we forget trouble ever came . . . [*To* RUTH] And you could get some nice screens to put up in your room round the baby's bassinet . . . [*She looks at both of them, pleadingly*] Sometimes you just got to know when to give up some things . . . and hold on to what you got.

[WALTER *enters from the outside, looking spent and leaning against the door, his coat hanging from him*]

MAMA: Where you been, son?

WALTER [*Breathing hard*]: Made a call.

MAMA: To who, son?

WALTER: To The Man.

MAMA: What man, baby?

WALTER: The Man, Mama. Don't you know who The Man is?

RUTH: Walter Lee?

WALTER: *The Man.* Like the guys in the streets say—The Man. Captain Boss—Mistuh Charley . . . Old Captain Please Mr. Bossman . . .

BENEATHA [*Suddenly*]: Lindner!

WALTER: That's right! That's good. I told him to come right over.

BENEATHA [*Fiercely, understanding*]: For what? What do you want to see him for!

WALTER [*Looking at his sister*]: We going to do business with him.

MAMA: What you talking 'bout son?

WALTER: Talking 'bout life, Mama. You all always telling me to see life like it is. Well—I laid in there on my back today . . . and I figured it out. Life just like it is. Who gets and who don't get. [*He sits down with his coat on and laughs*] Mama, you know it's all divided up. Life is. Sure enough. Between the takers and the "tooken." [*He laughs*] I've figured it out finally. [*He looks around at them*] Yeah. Some of us always getting "tooken." [*He laughs*] People like Willy Harris, they don't never get "tooken." And you know why the rest of us do? 'Cause we all mixed up. Mixed up bad. We get to looking 'round for the right and the wrong; and we worry about it and cry about it and stay up nights trying to figure out 'bout the wrong and the right of things all the time . . . And all the time, man, them takers is out there operating, just taking and taking. Willy Harris? Shoot—Willy Harris don't even count. He don't even count in the big scheme of things. But I'll say one thing for old Willy Harris . . . he's taught me something. He's taught me to keep my eye on what counts in this world. Yeah—[*Shouting out a little*] Thanks, Willy!

RUTH: What did you call that man for, Walter Lee?

WALTER: Called him to tell him to come on over to the show. Gonna put on a show for the man. Just what he wants to see. You see, Mama, the man came here today and he told us that them people out there where you want us to move—well they so upset they willing to pay us not to move out there. [*He laughs again*] And—and oh, Mama—you would of been proud of the way me and Ruth and Bennie acted. We told him to get out . . . Lord have mercy! We told the man to get out. Oh, we was some proud folks this afternoon, yeah. [*He lights a cigarette*] We were still full of that old-time stuff . . .

RUTH [*Coming toward him slowly*]: You talking 'bout taking them people's money to keep us from moving in that house?

WALTER: I ain't just talking 'bout it, baby—I'm telling you that's what's going to happen.

BENEATHA: Oh, God! Where is the bottom! Where is the real honest-to-God bottom so he can't go any farther!

WALTER: See—that's the old stuff. You and that boy that was here today. You all want everybody to carry a flag and a spear and sing some marching songs, huh? You wanna spend your life looking into things and trying to find the right and the wrong part, huh? Yeah. You know what's going to happen to that boy someday—he'll find himself sitting in a dungeon, locked in forever—and the takers will have the key! Forget it, baby! There ain't no causes—there ain't nothing but taking in this world, and he who takes most is smartest—and it don't make a damn bit of difference *how*.

MAMA: You making something inside me cry, son. Some awful pain inside me.

WALTER: Don't cry, Mama. Understand. That white man is going to walk in that door able to write checks for more money than we ever had. It's important to him and I'm going to help him . . . I'm going to put on the show, Mama.

MAMA: Son—I come from five generations of people who was slaves and sharecroppers—but ain't nobody in my family never let nobody pay 'em no money that was a way of telling us we wasn't fit to walk the earth. We ain't never been that poor. [*Raising her eyes and looking at him*] We ain't never been that dead inside.

BENEATHA: Well—we are dead now. All the talk about dreams and sunlight that goes on in this house. All dead.

WALTER: What's the matter with you all! I didn't make this world! It was give to me this way! Hell, yes, I want me some yachts someday! Yes, I want to hang some real pearls 'round my wife's neck. Ain't she supposed to wear no pearls? Somebody tell me—tell me, who decides which women is suppose to wear some pearls in this world. I tell you I am a *man*—and I think my wife should wear pearls in this world!

[*This last line hangs a good while and* WALTER *begins to move about the room. The word "Man" has penetrated his consciousness; he mumbles it to himself repeatedly between strange agitated pauses as he moves about*]

MAMA: Baby, how you going to feel on the inside?

WALTER: Fine! . . . Going to feel fine . . . a man . . .

MAMA: You won't have nothing left then, Walter Lee.

WALTER [*Coming to her*]: I'm going to feel fine, Mama. I'm going to look that son-of-a-bitch in the eyes and say—[*He falters*]—and say, "All right, Mr. Lindner—[*He falters even more*]—that's your neighborhood out there. You got the right to keep it like you want. You got the right to have it like you want. Just write the check and—the house is yours." And, and I am going to say—[*His voice almost breaks*] And you—you people just put the money in my hand and you won't have to live next to this bunch of stinking niggers! . . . [*He straightens up and moves away from his mother, walking around the room*] Maybe—maybe I'll just get down on my black knees . . . [*He does so;* RUTH *and* BENNIE *and* MAMA *watch him in frozen horror*] Captain, Mistuh, Bossman. [*He starts crying*] A-hee-hee-hee! [*Wringing his hand in profoundly anguished imitation*] Yasssssuh! Great White Father, just gi' ussen de money, fo' God's sake, and we's ain't gwine come out deh and dirty up yo' white folks neighborhood . . .

[*He breaks down completely, then gets up and goes into the bedroom*]

BENEATHA: That is not a man. That is nothing but a toothless rat.

MAMA: Yes—death done come in this here house. [*She is nodding, slowly, reflectively*] Done come walking in my house. On the lips of my children. You what supposed to be my beginning again. You—what supposed to be my harvest. [*To* BENEATHA] You—you mourning your brother?

BENEATHA: He's no brother of mine.

MAMA: What you say?

BENEATHA: I said that that individual in that room is no brother of mine.

MAMA: That's what I thought you said. You feeling like you better than he is today? [BENEATHA *does not answer*] Yes? What you tell him a minute ago? That he wasn't a man? Yes? You give him up for me? You done wrote his epitaph too—like the rest of the world? Well, who give you the privilege?

BENEATHA: Be on my side for once! You saw what he just did, Mama! You saw him—down on his knees. Wasn't it you who taught me—to despise any man who would do that. Do what he's going to do.

MAMA: Yes—I taught you that. Me and your daddy. But I thought I taught you something else too . . . I thought I taught you to love him.

BENEATHA: Love him? There is nothing left to love.

MAMA: There is always something left to love. And if you ain't learned that, you ain't learned nothing. [*Looking at her*] Have you cried for that boy today? I don't mean for yourself and for the family 'cause we lost the money. I mean for him; what he been through and what it done to him. Child, when do you think is the time to love somebody the most; when they done good and made things easy for everybody? Well then, you ain't through learning—because that ain't the time at all. It's when he's at his lowest and can't believe in hisself 'cause the world done whipped him so. When you starts measuring somebody, measure him right, child, measure him right. Make sure you done taken into account what hills and valleys he come through before he got to wherever he is.

[TRAVIS *bursts into the room at the end of the speech, leaving the door open*]

TRAVIS: Grandmama—the moving men are downstairs! The truck just pulled up.

MAMA [*Turning and looking at him*]: Are they, baby? They downstairs?

[*She sighs and sits.* LINDNER *appears in the doorway. He peers in and knocks lightly, to gain attention, and comes in. All turn to look at him*]

LINDNER [*Hat and briefcase in hand*]: Uh—hello . . . [RUTH *crosses mechanically to the bedroom door and opens it and lets it swing open freely and slowly as the light comes up on* WALTER *within, still in his coat, sitting at the far corner of the room. He looks up and out through the room to* LINDNER]

RUTH: He's here.

[*A long minute passes and* WALTER *slowly gets up*]

LINDNER [*Coming to the table with efficiency, putting his briefcase on the table and starting to unfold papers and unscrew fountain pens*]: Well, I certainly was glad to hear from you people. [WALTER *has begun the trek out of the room, slowly and awkwardly, rather like a small boy, passing the back of his sleeve across his mouth from time to time*] Life can really be so much simpler than people let it be most of the time. Well—with whom do I negotiate? You, Mrs. Younger, or your son here? [MAMA *sits with her hands folded on her lap and her eyes closed as* WALTER *advances.* TRAVIS *goes closer to* LINDNER *and looks at the papers curiously*] Just some official papers, sonny.

RUTH: Travis, you go downstairs.

MAMA [*Opening her eyes and looking into* WALTER'S]: No. Travis, you stay right here. And you make him understand what you doing, Walter Lee. You teach him good. Like Willy Harris taught you. You show where our five generations come to. Go ahead, son—

WALTER [*Looks down into his boy's eyes.* TRAVIS *grins at him merrily and* WALTER *draws him beside him with his arm lightly around his shoulders*]: Well, Mr. Lindner. [BENEATHA *turns away*] We called you—[*There is a profound, simple groping quality in his speech*]—because, well, me and my family [*He looks around and shifts from one foot to the other*] Well—we are very plain people . . .

LINDNER: Yes—

WALTER: I mean—I have worked as a chauffeur most of my life—and my wife here, she does domestic work in people's kitchens. So does my mother. I mean—we are plain people . . .

LINDNER: Yes, Mr. Younger—

WALTER [*Really like a small boy, looking down at his shoes and then up at the man*]: And—uh—well, my father, well, he was a laborer most of his life.

LINDNER [*Absolutely confused*]: Uh, yes—

WALTER [*Looking down at his toes once again*]: My father almost beat a man to death once because this man called him a bad name or something, you know what I mean?

LINDNER: No, I'm afraid I don't.

WALTER [*Finally straightening up*]: Well, what I mean is that we come from people who had a lot of pride. I mean—we are very proud people. And that's my sister over there and she's going to be a doctor—and we are very proud—

LINDNER: Well—I am sure that is very nice, but—

WALTER [*Starting to cry and facing the man eye to eye*]: What I am telling you is that we called you over here to tell you that we are very proud and that this is—this is my son, who makes the sixth generation of our family in this country, and that we have all thought about your offer and we have decided to move into our house because my father—my father—he earned it. [MAMA *has her eyes closed and is rocking back and forth as though she were in church, with her head nodding the amen yes*] We don't want to make no trouble for nobody or fight no causes—but we will try to be good neighbors. That's all we got to say. [*He looks the man absolutely in the eyes*] We don't want your money.

[*He turns and walks away from the man*]

LINDNER [*Looking around at all of them*]: I take it then that you have decided to occupy.

BENEATHA: That's what the man said.

LINDNER [*To* MAMA *in her reverie*]: Then I would like to appeal to you, Mrs. Younger. You are older and wiser and understand things better I am sure . . .

MAMA [*Rising*]: I am afraid you don't understand. My son said we was going to move and there ain't nothing left for me to say. [*Shaking her head with double meaning*] You know how these young folks is nowadays, mister. Can't do a thing with 'em. Good-bye.

LINDNER [*Folding up his materials*]: Well—if you are that final about it . . . There is nothing left for me to say. [*He finishes. He is almost ignored by the family, who are concentrating on* WALTER LEE. *At the door* LINDNER *halts and looks around*] I sure hope you people know what you're doing. [*He shakes his head and exits*]

RUTH [*Looking around and coming to life*]: Well, for God's sake—if the moving men are here—LET'S GET THE HELL OUT OF HERE!

MAMA [*Into action*]: Ain't it the truth. Look at all this here mess. Ruth, put Travis' good jacket on him . . . Walter Lee, fix your tie and tuck your shirt in, you look just like somebody's hoodlum. Lord have mercy, where is my plant? [*She flies to get it amid the general bustling of the family, who are deliberately trying to ignore the nobility of the past moment*] You all start on down . . . Travis child, don't go empty-handed . . . Ruth, where did I put that box with my skillets in it? I want to be in charge of it myself . . . I'm going to make us the biggest dinner we ever ate tonight . . . Beneatha, what's the matter with them stockings? Pull them things up, girl . . .

[*The family starts to file out as two moving men appear and begin to carry out the heavier pieces of furniture, bumping into the family as they move about*]

BENEATHA: Mama, Asagai—asked me to marry him today and go to Africa—

MAMA [*In the middle of her getting-ready activity*]: He did? You ain't old enough to marry nobody—[*Seeing the moving men lifting one of her chairs precariously*] Darling, that ain't no bale of cotton, please handle it so we can sit in it again. I had that chair twenty-five years . . .

[*The movers sigh with exasperation and go on with their work*]

BENEATHA [*Girlishly and unreasonably trying to pursue the conversation*]: To go to Africa, Mama—be a doctor in Africa . . .

MAMA [*Distracted*]: Yes, baby—

WALTER: Africa! What he want you to go to Africa for?

BENEATHA: To practice there . . .

WALTER: Girl, if you don't get all them silly ideas out your head! You better marry yourself a man with some loot . . .

BENEATHA [*Angrily, precisely as in the first scene of the play*]: What have you got to do with who I marry!

WALTER: Plenty. Now I think George Murchison—

[*He and* BENEATHA *go out yelling at each other vigorously;* BENEATHA *is heard saying that she would not marry* GEORGE MURCHISON *if he were Adam and she were Eve, etc. The anger is loud and real till their voices diminish.* RUTH *stands at the door and turns to* MAMA *and smiles knowingly*]

MAMA [*Fixing her hat at last*]: Yeah—they something all right, my children . . .

RUTH: Yeah—they're something. Let's go, Lena.

MAMA [*Stalling, starting to look around at the house*]: Yes—I'm coming. Ruth—

RUTH: Yes?

MAMA [*Quietly, woman to woman*]: He finally come into his manhood today, didn't he? Kind of like a rainbow after the rain . . .

RUTH [*Biting her lip lest her own pride explode in front of* MAMA]: Yes, Lena.

[WALTER'S *voice calls for them raucously*]

MAMA [*Waving* RUTH *out vaguely*]: All right, honey—go on down. I be down directly.

[RUTH *hesitates, then exits.* MAMA *stands, at last alone in the living room, her plant on the table before her as the lights start to come down. She looks around at all the walls and ceilings and suddenly, despite herself, while the children call below, a great heaving thing rises in her and she puts her fist to her mouth, takes a final desperate look, pulls her coat about her, pats her hat and goes out. The lights dim down. The door opens and she comes back in, grabs her plant, and goes out for the last time*]

CURTAIN

Eugène Ionesco (b.1912)

THE PICTURE

Translated by Donald Watson

CHARACTERS

THE LARGE GENTLEMAN
THE PAINTER
ALICE
THE NEIGHBOUR

The Set

[*A big room with one very big desk as the only piece of furniture. A leather armchair in front of the desk, in which the* LARGE GENTLEMAN *is sitting.*

A door on the right, another on the left; a window in the right-hand corner.

The LARGE GENTLEMAN *is expensively but tastelessly dressed. He is in his shirt-sleeves; his jacket is hanging over the armchair. The* PAINTER *is very poorly dressed and ill-shaven; he might almost be taken for a tramp. He is wearing a loosely-tied cravat and carrying his canvas rolled up under his arm.*

ALICE *is a very old woman, with a dirty apron, and clumsy shoes or dirty slippers. She has untidy hair, wears glasses, walks with a white stick and has only one arm; she sniffs a great deal.*

The PAINTER *is excessively shy and looks rather simple.*

When the Curtain rises the LARGE GENTLEMAN *is sitting at his desk. He is constantly looking at his wrist-watch and fingering his many-coloured tie.*

Facing him, near the right-hand door, the PAINTER *is standing at a respectful distance.*]

SOURCE: Reprinted from *Hunger and Thirst and Other Plays* by Eugène Ionesco, with the permission of Grove Press, Inc. Copyright 1968 by Calder & Boyars, Ltd.

LARGE GENTLEMAN: Come closer, step right up . . . [*The Painter does not move.*] You see, it took me a long time to get under way. No, it wasn't easy. The problems that faced me were insoluble, but I managed to solve them; and yet that wasn't the end of my troubles. Believe me, there are no such things as miracles: I'm sure you realize that.

PAINTER: Yes sir, I realize that.

LARGE G: I'm a bulldog, so I stuck to it, never let go. You see, all that really matters is to hang on like grim death.

PAINTER: Like grim death, yes, sir.

LARGE G: Nothing falls from Heaven all prepared and ready to eat, like manna in the wilderness. [*With a sweeping movement of the arm to take in the room, the desk and himself.*] Glance around and you'll see the result of my labours, all this is mine. What do you think of it, eh? Tell me what you think of it.

PAINTER: Why yes, indeed, I . . .

LARGE G. [*mopping his brow*]: The fruit of my toil, the sweat of my brow. I'm proud of it.

PAINTER: Oh . . . you've every right to be.

LARGE G: Come closer. [*The Painter takes half a step forward.*] Yes, I've every right to be proud. I think I can say, without boasting, that others can learn from my example, and so can you. I'm not selfish about it, unlike most people who have reached the top as I have, through will-power, tenacity, energy and work. I just said there were no such things as miracles. Well, I was wrong. There is *one* miracle.

PAINTER: One miracle?

LARGE G: Yes. Don't misunderstand me. The one and only miracle, the supreme miracle—is work.

PAINTER: Yes, of course: the miracle of work.

LARGE G: There you are, you've said it yourself. I know I'm right. [*Once more indicating the walls and the desk.*] And the proof is all around me: my efforts materialized in *this house.*

PAINTER: No doubt about that. [*He shifts his canvas from one arm to the other.*]

LARGE G: *I* am a self-made man. Life for me has been one long struggle. Life is a pitiless battlefield, and you advance over the bodies of the fallen! I wonder if you agree.

PAINTER: Oh yes, sir! I do.

LARGE G: A pitiless battlefield . . . but a fair fight: the survival of the fittest.

PAINTER: Survival of the fittest, yes, sir.

LARGE G: And in the end it almost gives you a feeling of pleasure, a kind of deep and bitter satisfaction, the joy of a job well done . . . And you can sleep at night, with a quiet mind.

PAINTER: Quiet. Yes, sir.

LARGE G: But what sort of quiet is it? I'll tell you: it's the calm after the storm.

PAINTER: Oh yes, after . . . after the storm.

LARGE G: Come closer, closer. Since my early childhood I've had a very hard life. My father . . . but we won't speak of him; perhaps it wasn't entirely his fault, he's dead. So are my grandparents. As for my mother, she married again, married a drunkard. My father drank a lot too, but he was my father. While the other, how can I put it, was only my stepfather, and hardly *that!* Anyhow, my mother died too. [*Emotionally.*] You can't imagine what it is for a young chap, hurled into the jungle of life . . . but I came through.

PAINTER [*getting emotional too*]: Yes, sir, I know.

LARGE G: No, no, my lad, you can't possibly imagine.

PAINTER: It was like that for me too . . . My mother . . .

LARGE G: No, my dear boy, no, it's not the same. We're all so different from one another.

PAINTER: Oh yes, that's true!

LARGE G: You see that window over the street. [*He motions the Painter to go to it.*] Go and look out, go on.

PAINTER [*still with his rolled-up canvas, goes to the window*]: Here?

LARGE G: What can you see?

PAINTER: People passing.

LARGE G: What are they doing?

PAINTER: Just passing.

LARGE G: You're not very observant. Have another look. There aren't two of them alike.

PAINTER: No, I suppose there aren't.

LARGE G: I know. It's not the first time I've looked at them. I'm always watching them, when I'm not seeing people, in my moments of meditation.

PAINTER [*coming back quietly to his first position, his canvas still under his arm*]: Yes, sir.

LARGE G: I can see them from the inside . . . do put your picture down! And yet they're all alike: that's the whole mystery of life . . . [*The Painter again shifts his picture from one arm to the other, there being nowhere for him to put it down.*] Must you keep on shifting that picture from side to side? It's not a rifle.

PAINTER: Very sorry, sir.

LARGE G: Sit down, my boy.

PAINTER [*once more looking in vain for a seat*]: Yes, sir.

LARGE G: You see, my lad. I've twenty years of the Stock Exchange behind me. I gambled and I won. [*With a wave of the hand.*] Now I have the telephone.

[*The telephone rings.*]

And it works. That should convince you.

PAINTER: Yes, sir.

LARGE G: *I* don't want to convince you. You must feel convinced in your-self. The Stock Exchange toughens a man. The Stock Exchange is like life—you have to make up your mind and stick to it.

PAINTER: Yes, sir.

LARGE G. [*almost sobbing*]: Many a night, old chap, I've spent on a bed of straw, in the workhouse, any old place; I educated myself, with no-one to help me; I've never felt really young.

PAINTER: Please don't cry, sir.

LARGE G: I live in this house, and it's my house, with my sister . . . She's a lot older than I am . . . And yet I've always had—believe me, I don't want to brag, you'll think I'm joking . . .

PAINTER: Oh no, sir! No!

LARGE G. [*motioning him to keep quiet*]: I've always had a taste for the arts; good music, good books, good painting, films . . . Unfortunately I've never had much time for reading, for going to museums, concerts or theatres . . . We can never do what we want in life. [*Loudly.*] I tell you, when people say they do what they want in life, they don't know what they're talking about.

PAINTER: No, sir. Indeed they don't.

LARGE G: I was too tired in the evenings, after the Stock Exchange, as you'll easily understand; but I've the soul of an artist. Just to show you, old chap, that I don't in any way look down on creative artists, as perhaps you might be tempted to think, because I know what you're . . .

PAINTER: I . . . I wouldn't dream of such a thing!

LARGE G: Good for you, but why don't you pull up a chair?

[*The* PAINTER *reacts as before.*]

LARGE G: I don't in any way look down on creative artists; on the contrary I admire them, the good ones I mean, the real artists, the sincere ones . . . because you see [*With a broad smile:*] in art . . . and especially in painting . . . as you're a painter . . .

PAINTER [*embarrassed*]: Oh, sir, I'm not a well-known . . .

LARGE G: . . . just as in business, you must have a professional conscience; otherwise it's no good. If you take my advice, *you* can turn your *art* into a way to get on in life. In its own fashion, art is as good a battlefield as anything else. Question of temperament. After all, it's happiness we're each of us looking for; we're team mates sharing the same ideal; that's why, when all's said and done, men *can* get along together: any form of society must be founded on the common aims of its members. That is the principle of all humanism.

PAINTER: Ah! Humanism's a great thing.

[*For a few moments both are lost in reflection.*]

LARGE G: Why don't you pull up a chair and put your picture down?

[*The* PAINTER *reacts as before.*]

As you've let me talk to you so confidentially, I'm going to tell you everything. You don't mind, do you? I like confiding in people.

PAINTER: Oh no, of course not! It's an honour I was hardly expecting.

LARGE G: Very kind of you, thank you. I like confiding in people, but not just anybody, only those I can trust. I believe you are almost the first person . . .

PAINTER: I shall try, sir, to be worthy of the confidence you . . .

LARGE G: But you are. I know. I feel when I can trust someone. Now you've only just arrived, come to sell your picture.

PAINTER [*shyly*]: Yes . . . if I could . . . I should like . . . very much . . .

LARGE G: And yet, you're not the first. You are—you know, old chap, I've got intuition, and that's what's brought me success—you are one of those noble creatures, so rare nowadays, who absorb things, who enjoy listening to others and sharing their troubles; I'm sure you are, how shall I say, I'm not mistaken, am I? . . .

PAINTER: I hope not, sir.

LARGE G: You are one of those people for whom others really exist; you're not a selfish man: selfish—that's the word.

PAINTER: Yes, that's the word.

LARGE G: Don't deny it . . . no false modesty . . . I'm not flattering you. I know it's the truth . . . I never tell a lie, my boy!

PAINTER: I never said that . . .

LARGE G: And so, at the end of this victorious struggle, which has made me what I am . . . which has helped me to achieve . . . [*Impressive gesture.*] I needn't repeat myself . . . all this, when the battle had ended in triumph, old chap, the battle that gave me everything . . . there was always something missing. Perhaps the one thing needful. [*He stands up*] I am not a happy man. [*He sits down again.*]

PAINTER [*sorry for him*]: Not happy, sir?

LARGE G: I'm afraid you'd never think that, would you? The human heart is so complicated! I'm hungry for beauty. It's missing from my life. I've never managed to satisfy my taste, I might almost say my passion, for the arts. In other fields I succeeded in everything, but I failed, for instance, to find a wife who could understand me, though of course, as you know, it's not easy.

PAINTER: No, indeed it isn't.

LARGE G: But is it really impossible?

PAINTER: Perhaps not really impossible.

LARGE G: Frankly, it *is* impossible.

PAINTER: You're right. It's impossible.

LARGE G: No, not *impossible.*

PAINTER: Well, perhaps not, after all.

LARGE G: No, no, I still can't believe it's really impossible. Anyway, we'll see. Just imagine, all the finest qualities of body and soul combined in *one* woman . . . who's intelligent, that's the word . . .

PAINTER: Yes, that's the word.

LARGE G: And lovely to look at . . . lovely. A beautiful woman who understands everything. But beautiful, old chap, above all she must be beautiful . . . Unfortunately such a woman has never crossed my path.

PAINTER [*dreamily*]: The path of life . . .

LARGE G: At least I could have beauty reflected in the house. [*Sweeping gesture.*] These bare walls, believe me . . .

PAINTER: Oh, I do, sir.

LARGE G: These bare walls weigh me down.

PAINTER [*indicating the canvas rolled up under his arm*]: Perhaps, perhaps you might like this picture . . . perhaps, in a way . . . it might . . .

LARGE G: I ask myself one question: can art take the place of the woman of my dreams, that good and beautiful woman, above all beautiful, I miss so much?

PAINTER: Try. Look and see. [*He shows the picture.*]

LARGE G: Of course, there's my sister. She's much older than I am, lives in this house, hasn't made much of her life, no harm in her, what would she do without me? I've given her a home, I look after all her needs, give her bed and board, she's in the kitchen now, takes care of me as best she can, does all the housework, I don't say she's not fond of me, but . . . well . . . I see you understand, sisterly affection, that's not what I'm after, it's not *that* . . .

PAINTER: No, it wouldn't be that . . .

LARGE G: Mind you, I'm not blaming her, not blaming her at all. And yet if she'd been beautiful, I'd have enjoyed looking at her. When I come home in the evening, tired of the ugliness of life, I'd like to be able to gaze at a beautiful face, a graceful figure . . . She's all I have, old chap, in life. And she's ugly.

PAINTER: What a shame!

LARGE G: Yes, my boy, it's unfortunate! But it wouldn't do any good to hide the truth.

PAINTER: Quite right, sir. Of course that wouldn't do any good.

LARGE G: And yet, you know, even my sister hasn't destroyed the deep desire for beauty inside me, no, she's made it more vital, more intense, [*Sigh.*] more poignant than ever . . . You can't imagine how poignant it is.

PAINTER [*very sorry for him*]: I *do* understand, sir.

LARGE G: What I admire in you is your sympathy and understanding. You must be a genuine artist. From now on you have a place in my heart and in my home. We are friends.

PAINTER: Oh, I'm very flattered, very happy to . . .

LARGE G: You understand everything, straightaway. And yet there are so many people who don't understand my life at all and never even take the trouble to come and see me.

PAINTER: They *ought* to . . .

LARGE G: My sister's not by any means to be despised, she's not a bad sort, not entirely without a sense of beauty. But with her it's as if beauty were buried in the murky depths of the soul; her artistic impulse has been swallowed up in the dark waters of oblivion. It has to be fished out of her subconscious. My sister only lives, dear boy, in the world of necessity, she has no sense of humour, she forges her own chains, no freedom. I ask you, my boy, what are we without beauty and music and poetry . . . what would we be like, eh?

PAINTER: Er, we'd be, er . . .

LARGE G: Yes, I'm asking you, what would we be like?

PAINTER: Er . . . I . . . I don't know, sir.

LARGE G: Then I'll tell you . . .

[*Banging his fist hard on the table.*]

. . . brutes, sir.

PAINTER [*slightly alarmed*]: Oh . . . perhaps not . . .

LARGE G: Yes, we would. Brutes! No doubt about it. Without beauty, no charity; without charity, no truth. It's all one and indivisible!

PAINTER: And yet, and yet . . .

LARGE G: And yet what? There's no 'and yet' about it, no contradiction possible; didn't you say just now that you understood me?

PAINTER: Yes, I understand you, sir.

LARGE G: Well then?

[*The* PAINTER *is rather embarrassed; he puts his picture under the arm.*]

Sit down, dear boy, sit down.

[*The* PAINTER *reacts as before.*]

She's dependent on me, I earn my living, of course, I'm in a position to feed another mouth.

PAINTER: [*weakly*]: Your sister's mouth, sir?

LARGE G: That's who we're talking about, isn't it? What's the matter with you?

PAINTER: I'm sorry, sir. I *was* listening.

LARGE G: Well, briefly, I've only one thing against her, and even *that*—you see, I think it's only fair to admit it—even *that* is not her fault. What I have against her is that she's no ornament in a house that's too plain, anyway, too bare, too grim . . . Otherwise, I wouldn't be buying pictures . . . I have to buy pictures because my sister's ugly, and that costs money.

PAINTER: Not really, sir, you know, a man like you . . .

LARGE G: Right, cards on the table, how much do you want?

PAINTER [*taken by surprise, embarrassed*]: I . . . I . . . I don't know, sir . . .

LARGE G: What's your price? Give me a figure, but don't exceed the normal price for a masterpiece.

PAINTER [*embarrassed*]: I only came here, sir, just to ask quite simply . . . if you'd mind glancing at this picture . . . and if you'd mind . . .

LARGE G: Talk, talk, talk! You came here to sell your goods, didn't you? No more beating about the bush. As for me, I've just told you, for the reasons I've just indicated I am, or to be precise may eventually become, a buyer, providing your work satisfies certain aesthetic as well as financial considerations, which are merely the expression of my sincere and noble ideals in art and economics.

PAINTER [*more and more embarrassed*]: Yes, sir, of course . . . Naturally.

LARGE G: As far as finance is concerned, your figure will have to be modest, and it's up to you to let me know the price; as for the artistic quality of the work, which should be of the highest order, I trust my own judgment.

PAINTER: To start with, just have a look at it, and you can tell me afterwards if it interests you or not . . . The first thing is to know if you like it.

LARGE G. [*gets up and goes to the Painter, then sits down again*]: It can only interest me if the price falls within certain financial limits; it's a principle of mine, dear boy, believe me, just a matter of principle.

PAINTER: Yes, sir, of course, I understand . . .

LARGE G: Glad you do.

PAINTER: And yet . . .

LARGE G: Yet what?

PAINTER [*stammering*]: You must, I mean . . . Perhaps you should . . . look first . . .

LARGE G: First, the price, my dear chap, aesthetics later.

PAINTER: It's all rather embarrassing. Just glance at it.

LARGE G: No. You can't teach me anything about embarrassing situations; I won't look until I've heard your practical requirements. I've told you, it's a principle. You did say you understood me, didn't you?

PAINTER: Oh yes, oh yes!

LARGE G: Well then. Your price?

PAINTER: Hm! Er . . . do you know . . .

LARGE G: What should I be knowing? What do you think I don't know yet?

PAINTER: Well, you must be aware . . . [*Making an effort.*] A painter of my type, a contemporary painter, for example Rembrandt or Rubens . . .

LARGE G: I don't know the gentlemen, though I'm not lacking in culture . . .

PAINTER: I'm quite sure you're not . . . Rembrandt or Rubens . . .

LARGE G: I hope it's not non-representational painting?

PAINTER: Oh no, sir. I have done some, but I'm past that stage now, I'm back to realistic subjects.

LARGE G: Glad to hear you've turned over a new leaf. Congratulations.

PAINTER: So, if you'll allow me . . . Rembrandt or Rubens would sell a picture like this . . . for 500,000 francs . . . I can let you have mine for 400,000.

LARGE G. [*stupefied*]: 400,000 francs! You don't know the value of money! Poor fellow! Don't you realize that's a *fortune*? It's giving money away for the least effort. It's not every day that I earn a sum like that on the Stock Exchange! And I hope you now understand that the Stock Exchange is a desperate battle that wears a man out; a race won by the strongest runner . . . Whereas *you*, you just sit there quietly in front of your easel. No, my lad, no, 400,000 times no!

PAINTER: My work's not easy either, not everyone can do it.

LARGE G: Back to business.

PAINTER: I can offer it to you for 300,000 francs.

LARGE G: 3 or 400,000 it's almost the same.

PAINTER: For 250,000 . . . 200,000 . . .

LARGE G: 3 or 200,000, it's still the same.

PAINTER: 100,000.

LARGE G. [*throwing up his arms*]: 100,000! 1 or 200,000 what's the difference?

PAINTER: 80,000 . . . [*The Large Gentleman shakes his head.*] 70,000 . . . [*Shakes his head.*] 60,000 . . .

LARGE G: Between 70 and 60, you know . . . [*Shakes his head.*]

PAINTER: 50,000 . . .

LARGE G: From 60,000 to 50,000's not much of a jump. Take a big one, my lad, take several.

PAINTER: But you must admit I've lowered my price considerably.

LARGE G: I admit nothing of the sort.

PAINTER [*taking his courage in both hands*]: In that case, sir, I'm very sorry . . . I'd only be undervaluing my own work . . . [*With an effort.*] For I too have my principles . . .

LARGE G: Good for you. If you do have principles, keep them to yourself. And your picture too.

PAINTER: It's a pity, sir. Goodbye, sir! [*He makes for the door.*]

LARGE G. [*almost begging*]: One moment! Look here, my dear chap, you're not going to leave me with these bare dirty walls, these ugly walls that torture me with their lack of beauty! Think again, think of others for once!

PAINTER [*near the door, with a forced smile*]: Beauty, you know, has to be paid for, too . . .

LARGE G: Rubbish! An artist like you, the kind I hope you are, is not just a tradesman; he should be a priest who serves beauty, like the vestal virgins.

PAINTER: I have to live, sir.

LARGE G: What about me, don't I have to look after my sister? Please show a little human feeling . . .

PAINTER [*coming back*]: Perhaps you're right.

LARGE G: I'm not asking you to offer it to me . . . for nothing. That'd make me angry. I don't want to be in anyone's debt.

PAINTER: I'll let you have it for 40,000 . . .

LARGE G: 14,000 francs? What an idea, that's far too much!

PAINTER: I said . . . I said . . . 40, not 14. 40,000 francs.

LARGE G: I'm neither deaf nor dumb. You said 14,000 francs!

PAINTER: Oh no, sir, I didn't: 40!

LARGE G: I see you're going back on your last word, which I couldn't accept anyway. You're not a man of honour: a man of honour is a man of his word.

PAINTER: 40, sir.

LARGE G: 14 . . .

PAINTER: I'm sorry: 40. I really did say: 40.

LARGE G: 40 what?

PAINTER: 40,000.

LARGE G. [*dumbfounded*]: 40,000. [*Sarcastically.*] And you think I'm going to believe you? You won't catch me.

PAINTER: But . . .

LARGE G. [*his arms folded*]: No "buts". We'll say no more about it. Goodbye, dear boy . . .

PAINTER: Very well! Goodbye, sir! [*He moves to the door again.*] Goodbye, sir. [*He goes out.*]

[LARGE G. *runs after him.*]

LARGE G: I say, old chap, I say. [*He goes out for a moment and comes back pulling the Painter by the sleeve.*] . . . Wait . . . after all, I'd like to do something to help you. I'll give you 400 . . .

PAINTER: 400,000 francs? Ooh!

LARGE G: Ha ha! [*Loud laughter.*] You're joking.

PAINTER [*laughing too*]: You never know!

LARGE G: I'll give you 400 francs, and that's my final offer, 400 francs, take it or leave it.

PAINTER: All right, sir. Agreed. That's fine.

LARGE G: I was sure we'd come to an understanding. I know you artists, and you should get to know me too!

PAINTER [*sincerely*]: Yes indeed!

LARGE G: I respect you, my friend.

PAINTER: Thank you, sir. You know, I should have been most upset if we'd not come to an agreement.

LARGE G: And so should I! A friendly settlement without costs is better than a long-drawn-out law-suit, however expensive.

PAINTER: I agree with you entirely.

LARGE G: You're very kind.

PAINTER: I'll unroll the picture.

LARGE G: Oh, I could have done that by myself; it's not absolutely essential. A picture is a picture. So long as it's a work of art, that's all I ask; it'll decorate the wall, liven up this gloomy room a bit, so that it won't be so unpleasant to live in . . .

PAINTER: Of course.

LARGE G: Of course.

PAINTER: Of course.

LARGE G: Using the same expression proves we're in perfect agreement.

PAINTER: Yes, the agreement is perfect.

[*They both laugh.*]

LARGE G. [*back to business again*]: But perhaps we could look at the picture all the same . . . just . . . as a matter of form . . .

PAINTER: Ah?

LARGE G: It's not troubling you, I hope?

PAINTER: Oh . . . not at all . . . perhaps I am in rather a hurry . . . but then . . . for your sake . . .

LARGE G: My dear fellow, I want to know what I'm buying; I've a right to! I don't buy anything with my eyes shut! Not even painting!

PAINTER: Fair enough; you're quite within your rights.

LARGE G: Come on then, quickly, as you say you're in a hurry.

PAINTER: Straightaway, sir. [*He unrolls his huge picture.*]

LARGE G. [*as the Painter unrolls the picture which trails on the floor*]: Well . . . well . . . well I never . . .

PAINTER [*timidly, the picture still not quite unrolled*]: What do you think of it, sir?

LARGE G: Nothing at all just yet, dear boy. After all, I must *see* it . . . Roll it right out . . . Come along, faster, faster . . .

PAINTER: Yes sir, yes.

[*He spreads it out over the floor and gets caught up in it.*]

LARGE G. [*watching him, without helping*]: You're so clumsy! Look out, don't spoil my picture!

PAINTER: I'm so sorry.

LARGE G: Oh dear oh dear oh dear . . .

PAINTER: There you are, sir, that's it . . .

LARGE G: At last!

PAINTER: What do you think of it?

LARGE G. [*like a real connoisseur*]: Hmm! Well, well . . .

PAINTER: There it is.

LARGE G: It's a portrait . . . the portrait of a woman . . . Yes, that's right, it's not non-representational.

PAINTER: No.

LARGE G: Don't walk all over it then. How careless you are. I told you to look out.

PAINTER: Sorry, sir.

LARGE G. [*dissatisfied*]: It's representational.

PAINTER: That's what you wanted. I told you it was.

LARGE G: We never agreed on a definition of the term. I have good taste, you know. You can trust my judgement. Naturally I should have preferred . . . a non-representational picture, or if not, really . . . representational . . .

PAINTER: I thought you would.

LARGE G: Still, it's . . . what it is.

PAINTER: Yes, of course, it is what it is; but still, being what it is . . . what is it really? You, who have such good taste?

LARGE G: I can hardly give you a definite opinion yet, when I can't see it properly, spread out like that over the floor . . . a play is made to be acted, and a picture to be hung on the wall. On the ground it might be an ordnance survey map. You can just pick out a few details here, a few more there, a maze of lines and squiggles, the border, a few colours . . . the total effect escapes you.

PAINTER: Escapes, yes, escapes.

LARGE G: And you must realize that there's an essential difference between a mat and a Matisse, even if they do share a syllable.

PAINTER: Yes, but Matisse has got two.

LARGE G. [*without moving*]: Hang it up for me; now you're here you can give me a hand.

PAINTER: Of course I will.

[*He begins to roll the picture up.*]

LARGE G: You're not going to walk off with it, are you?

PAINTER: No, sir, no. I'm re-rolling it so I can re-unroll it again on the wall. [*He makes for the back wall with the half rolled picture.*]

LARGE G: It's just as you like, of course. You're free to do what you want.

PAINTER: Oh no, sir, I'm entirely at your service.

LARGE G: Anyway, you don't roll it up before you hang it up . . . [*Profoundly.*] I should say you'd do just the opposite.

PAINTER: [*right close to the wall*]: It'll have to be hung very high.

LARGE G: Of course it will, otherwise it'll drag on the floor. I have to tell you everything.

PAINTER: If it's to be hung very high on the wall, we'll need a ladder.

LARGE G. [*calling out to the kitchen*]: Alice! Alice!

ALICE'S CRACKED VOICE: Yes.

[*She rushes in. She is indeed very old: her shoulders are hunched and you can see her white hair straggling over her shawl; she wears thick-rimmed dark glasses, mittens, an apron and has only one arm. She is carrying a white stick.*]

Here I am . . .

LARGE G: Well, hurry up and bring a ladder . . .

ALICE: What for?

LARGE G: Mind your own business.

ALICE: All right.

[*She goes out.*]

LARGE G: That's my sister.

PAINTER: Yes sir, I was afraid it was.

LARGE G: Hurry up, hurry up, Alice, come along . . .

[*Tapping his foot.*]

Quickly now.

ALICE: I'm coming.

[*She comes back. The first you see is the end of the ladder.*]

PAINTER: I could . . . give her a hand.

LARGE G: She needs one; then she'll have two. Why don't you help her?

ALICE [*to the Painter who helps her as she struggles to carry the ladder with her one good hand and her stump*]: Thank you, sir, it's heavy and I'm tired; an old woman like me, sir, with only one arm, just think of it.

LARGE G: Always the same self-pity. The gentleman isn't interested.

[*They both carry the ladder and place it against the back wall.*]

ALICE: Here?

LARGE G: No, there! Mind! Go on! Be careful, don't spoil anything, don't scratch the wall. Ah! . . . Not like that . . . [*To Alice.*] Pass him the picture, pass it to him.

[*The* PAINTER *climbs the ladder and* ALICE *hands him the rolled-up picture.*]

PAINTER [*trying to hang it up*]: Here, sir?
LARGE G: Wait. [*He goes to the middle of the stage, thinks for a moment, and then:*] Too high.

[*The* PAINTER *moves it from place to place, following the* LARGE GENTLEMAN'S *directions, while* ALICE *flurries about in a disorganized fashion, without saying a word.*]

Too low! To the right! To the left. More to the left! No, no! . . . To the right! To the left! To the right! Too low! Too high! Too low! No! . . . It's to the right of the left, not to the left of the right. I hope it's not upside down. Hang it symmetrically. I said "symmetrically", it's very important. There, there, be careful, there! Don't move now. Fix it there and let it unroll.

[*The fixed canvas unrolls: a large picture, a kind of tapestry appears, representing a very beautiful woman, evidently royal; the back of a throne is seen; she is holding a sceptre and dressed in a crimson robe; her eyes are black.*]

Well, well . . .
ALICE: Who is it?
LARGE G: Be quiet!
PAINTER [*timidly, from the top of the ladder*]: What do you think, sir?
LARGE G: I know quite well what I think, but I can't tell you a thing while you're stuck in the way, come down from the ladder, quickly, quickly.
PAINTER: Yes, sir.

[*He comes down very fast.*]

LARGE G: Now then, Alice, stand to one side, don't block the view, and stop putting your tongue out.
ALICE: All right, yes, all right.
LARGE G: Well, get rid of the ladder, then! You're not going to leave it there till Christmas!
PAINTER: Straightaway, sir.
LARGE G: Alice, don't waste time. Can't you help the artist move the ladder? Where's your head?
ALICE: I'm doing my best. [*She sobs.*] All the time he's scolding me, sir, if you only knew . . .

PAINTER: Oh, don't scold her, sir.

LARGE G. [*to the Painter*]: It's no business of yours. [*To Alice:*] This isn't the time for tears and recriminations; it's the time for making a bargain. *Push* the ladder, then, both of you.

PAINTER: Yes, sir.

[*The* PAINTER, *and* ALICE *weeping, push the ladder aside.*]

LARGE G: That'll do!

[*Trembling, the other two stop.*]

Now let me look and decide.

[*He steps up to it, back from it and then up to it again, like a true connoisseur.*]

PAINTER: Your honest opinion . . .

LARGE G. [*to Alice*]: Alice, don't stand there glued to the wall, so close to the picture. How can I see it properly? And a comparison is hardly in your favour. Turn your face to the wall.

ALICE [*to the Painter*]: You see, sir, you see, I annoy him just by being here. [*She turns her back to the audience.*]

PAINTER [*to Alice*]: You're making me quite upset. [*Timidly:*] You're making her quite upset, sir . . .

[ALICE *turns to face the audience, tears streaming down her face.*]

LARGE G: Alice, you're a fool!

[ALICE *weeps more loudly.*]

PAINTER: Don't cry, Madame.

LARGE G: Stick to your own affairs. You're a painter, not a comforter.

PAINTER: I beg your pardon.

LARGE G. [*to Alice*]: How can I concentrate on the picture with all your tears and your nonsense? [*To the Painter*]: All day long she's crying, all day long. She spends her whole life preventing me from enjoying beauty. I've had enough of her. She's a disgrace.

PAINTER: She has no artistic impulse.

LARGE G: She's utterly devoid of any.

PAINTER: Not entirely.

ALICE [*sobbing*]: What's an artistic impulse?

LARGE G: A feeling for words.

ALICE [*weeping*]: A feeling for what?

LARGE G. [*to the Painter*]: You see, what did I say . . .

PAINTER: Oh sir! She's more to be pitied than blamed! It's just like any other disability . . .

LARGE G: Oh dear, disabilities . . . she's got too many of them already! She's not hungry for art, that's the greatest calamity for me. That's the real reason why we don't get on together. [*To Alice*:] Get back to your pots and pans!

ALICE [*wiping her eyes on her apron*]: All right, all right, all right . . .

[*She goes to the door leading to the kitchen and leaves it half open; every now and then she listens to what is being said and watches the action, sometimes coming on stage again.*]

LARGE G. [*to the Painter*]: Brothers and sisters have I one . . 🌼

PAINTER [*timidly*]: Now's the time to exercise your judgment, sir.

LARGE G. [*looking for a few moments in silence at the picture, while the Painter appears deeply moved*]: That's just what I am exercising, dear boy . . . Hmmm . . . and not perhaps to your advantage.

PAINTER [*with a forced smile*]: Never mind, sir, never mind, it can't be helped.

LARGE G: Well then . . . look here, the more I think about this piece of work of yours, the less I know what to think of it; I want to tell you exactly how it strikes me.

PAINTER: Yes, yes . . .

LARGE G: It has faults, of course, I quite see what you were trying to do, it's a portrait. The portrait of a woman, if I'm not mistaken . . .

PAINTER: No sir, indeed you're not.

LARGE G: Well . . . so it represents a woman, a seated woman . . . I'm just trying to work it out . . . sitting in a chair and holding a sceptre. It's like a big photograph: a portrait. So it must be non-representational painting. Right?

PAINTER: Exactly.

LARGE G: The chair this woman is sitting on looks very like a throne. It may even be a throne. But you can't see the lower part of it, though you can imagine how it is . . .

PAINTER: You can imagine how it is, yes, sir, at least I hope you can.

ALICE [*her head appearing*]: That's the main thing, if you can imagine it.

LARGE G. [*to Alice*]: Be quiet! [*To the Painter:*] She has a sceptre but no crown, so she must be a queen. The lower part you can only imagine must be the legs of this chair or throne. It's only in so far as they can be imagined, without actually being seen, that your picture can be called non-representational.

PAINTER: In that respect, yes, sir.

LARGE G: This princess, this woman, is also treated in a semi-representational, semi-non-representational, style, because, although you can imagine them, you can't really see the woman's feet or legs or thighs or pelvis either.

PAINTER: Oh yes, sir, that's perfectly correct.

LARGE G: How you realized this woman *is* a woman is just one of the mysteries of the painter's art, and there I must congratulate you.

ALICE: It's by suggestion.

PAINTER: Thank you, sir.

LARGE G: Wait! The mystery must be solved. How *can* you realize it's a woman when you can only just see the top half of her bosom, the nipples being carefully, I might almost say modestly, concealed by a lace bodice. You can't see the woman's breasts, and yet you're quite sure they're there . . . The way they're suggested is very striking, unmistakable. As for her legs, you can only imagine they exist by a simple logical deduction. But they're not in any way suggested. [*Decisively.*] That's one of the faults.

PAINTER: I apologise, sir, I'm really very sorry.

LARGE G: For you see, my dear chap, art and logic are two different things, and if you have to call on logic to understand art, art in other words life, vanishes; only logic, in other words death, remains.

PAINTER: Death?

LARGE G: Yes. I mean: the death of art.

PAINTER: I follow you, sir.

LARGE G: Good.

ALICE [*showing herself*]: I knew it, oh dear oh dear!

LARGE G. [*to Alice*]: Mind your own business! Go away, go away!

[ALICE *disappears, only to appear again a moment later.*]

In the same way—to take another example—if to understand logic, you have to call on art, logic vanishes, and nothing's left but dead art. You understand that this is only a manner of speaking, for art will live eternally. And so of course will logic. You really do understand?

PAINTER: Yes, sir. I understand you perfectly.

LARGE G: Good. This then is your weak point, the principal objection I have to make; in your work one has to imagine, and even that is not always possible, what one cannot see. There's a glaring contradiction there and consequently a confusion of styles as well: an uneasy mixture of the representational with the non-representational.

PAINTER: Yes, sir, unfortunately I see that. Your criticism is justified, but what can be done about it?

LARGE G: It's too late now . . . Perhaps you didn't allow sufficiently for this basic principle: logic works by demonstration, and art by suggestion.

PAINTER: I didn't know the principle.

LARGE G: From now on, you can think about it. After that, it's simple enough: this woman of yours, real or imaginary, representational or non-representational, is very well painted: she has brown hair, green eyes, a pale complexion, lips, nose, mouth, etc . . . What's more, now I can see she's really meant to be a queen.

ALICE: Every woman's a queen for him. He sees them everywhere, at the corner of every street, street-walking queens.

[ALICE *pops her head back.*]

PAINTER: Yes, sir. She is a queen.

LARGE G: Be quiet! Don't interrupt! I want to interpret it for myself. I think I've shown myself quite capable.

PAINTER: I shan't say a word, sir.

LARGE G: Your queen is holding a sceptre, which is the perfect symbol of royalty . . . but unfortunately I notice she has no crown . . . Real or imaginary, your portrait, dear boy, is incomplete . . .

PAINTER: Yes indeed. Oh, I'm really terribly sorry . . . terribly, terribly sorry . . . What can I do? [*He wrings his hands.*]

LARGE G: You should have been sorry before! There are some good qualities in your picture too, but I shall pass them over in respectful silence. In your own interest.

PAINTER: Very well.

LARGE G: To sum up, then: you need to make several essential alterations to this picture of yours. I can't take it from you in its present state.

PAINTER: Oh!

LARGE G: You can bring it back to me later. We'll discuss it another time, not now. Take it away.

PAINTER: Oh, sir . . . sir! . . . it's so awkward and heavy to carry. If you like, I'll let you have it for 300 francs.

LARGE G: Out of the question.

ALICE [*snivelling in the doorway*]: Oh please, please . . . don't be so heartless, you're not being kind to him . . . he's not a kind man, sir, he's hard, he's always been hard.

LARGE G: Alice, what business is it of yours, eh? Pots and pans!

ALICE: All right, all right, I'm going, don't be cross with me. [*She disappears for a moment, then pokes her head round the door again.*]

LARGE G: [*to the Painter*]: Just as a favour, my friend, I'm willing to keep it . . . for a while . . . on loan. In a month or two I'll have made up my mind whether I want to keep it for good or not. Of course I shan't be able to pay you anything.

PAINTER [*falling over himself in thanks*]: Thank you, sir, thank you with all my heart. Thank you for offering to keep it here.

LARGE G: It's just as a favour.

PAINTER: I know, sir, and I'm most grateful.

LARGE G: That way, it's off your hands. Not off mine, but there . . .

PAINTER: I'm afraid not!

LARGE G: If I have the time, if I find it's worth while and your picture's capable of improvement, I'll make the necessary changes myself.

PAINTER: I'd be so grateful. How can I thank you?

LARGE G: For the loan of it, I shall ask you . . . to pay me a small sum, we'll arrange all that, dear boy, don't worry about it. I'm only doing this, because of my feeling for art and my interest in you.

PAINTER: Very generous of you, sir.

LARGE G: Unless . . . but we'll see later. If I think we could . . . make anything out of it, I'll give you a fair percentage. You're not on the telephone?

PAINTER: No, sir.

LARGE G: Oh, these artists! They're all alike!

PAINTER: I'm afraid so . . .

LARGE G: Doesn't matter . . . I've got your address. I'll write, send you a telegram. Well then . . . [*In a jocular way:*] Now I'm turning you out, you see I've work to do. Our business is settled.

PAINTER: Thank you. Goodbye, sir.

LARGE G: Our business is settled.

[*As the* PAINTER *prepares to leave,* ALICE *comes forward.*]

ALICE [*to the Painter*]: Goodbye, sir, goodbye . . . look after yourself and best of luck!

[*The* LARGE GENTLEMAN *gazes at the picture; from now on he becomes more and more submissive, while* ALICE *changes her character and becomes astonishingly aggressive; as soon as the* PAINTER *leaves, the* LARGE GENTLEMAN *starts slumping and looks round-shouldered.*]

LARGE G. [*timidly*]: It's not bad, is it? Not bad at all, eh?

ALICE: Another of your ideas! Why do you want to buy a nasty picture like that? Funny thing to want. What came over you? You must be mad! At your age too!

LARGE G. [*already weakening, but still with some trace of his former authority*]: That's my affair, I'm within my rights. After all we've got to have something on the walls, you don't understand . . . to make the place beautiful.

ALICE: Sheer snobbery . . . and we can do without *that.* Just look at it! All your haggling's a waste of time. We'll have nothing to eat, not a rag to our backs. You'll ruin us, with your stupid ideas. Better for you if you'd thought about the contract; and the paper-work; how's all that getting on, eh? Time is money.

LARGE G: Don't worry, Alice, we'll make some.

ALICE: You'd better start by seeing about the certificate.

LARGE G. [*stealing a glance at the picture*]: Certificate?

ALICE: Yes. I suppose it's the first you've heard of it. I've got to go to the Town Hall about the certificate.

LARGE G: The Town Hall?

ALICE: The Town Hall. But as I've already been to the Town Hall about the certificate, it can't be about the certificate. So it must be something else. But as I've already been about something else, it can't be about that either. I wonder what it can be . . . [*The Large Gentleman is silent; Alice raises her stick.*] Eh? What's it all about? You've never given it a thought, I suppose? What do you do with your time? Waste it all gazing at her, do you? Dirty little tyke! Get on with your work!

LARGE G. [*goes fearfully back to his desk, still casting furtive glances at the picture as he moves reluctantly away*]: I *am* getting on with it!

ALICE [*pursuing the Large Gentleman, who takes refuge behind his desk*]: Snake in the grass! Boozer! You'd spend your life gazing at her! . . . Oh! My breath . . . I can't get my breath . . .

LARGE G: For goodness' sake, don't get in such a state, Alice. I promise you I'm getting on with my work!

ALICE: You always *say* that! Liar! Reptile! Good thing I'm here to keep you up to scratch!

LARGE G: I'm doing my best.

ALICE: You don't put your heart into it! *That's* all *you* think about! [*She points to the picture and raises her stick as if she were going to strike it.*]

LARGE G: Now then, Alice, my dear . . . Alice . . . it cost money, and it's going to make us some too.

ALICE [*hesitating*]: Oh. I don't know what's holding me back . . . I really don't know . . . It's all *your* fault, blockhead, not the fault of that misbegotten, revolting creature over there . . .

LARGE G: Don't hit me . . . don't hit me!

ALICE: The fine gentleman wants some pictures, does he! Pictures of beautiful women . . . nude women! What do you think of that!

LARGE G. [*sheltering behind the desk*]: She isn't nude, on the contrary it seems to me she's very respectably dressed.

ALICE: The way you look at her, with those piercing eyes of yours, it's just as though she hadn't a stich on.

LARGE G: It's a useful acquisition, you don't understand.

ALICE: That's what you think, he didn't even say how much he'd pay you, for the loan.

LARGE G: He'll pay through the nose, don't you worry, it'll all be arranged . . . Meanwhile we'll both benefit from his masterpiece, yes, *you'll* benefit from it too.

ALICE: Me? Benefit from that slut! Who do you take me for?

LARGE G: I did the painter a favour, I took it off his hands, he was very pleased, it's good business, he's very grateful, he'll pay us a lot of money.

ALICE: He'll give you nothing, or hardly anything; I know artists and poets, they're not worth twopence, their sort . . . they and their tarts!

LARGE G: That's not fair.

ALICE: He was only too glad to get rid of it, no-one wants it. You'll never see him again, no flies on him, he had you on all right. You're the only one wants any of his trash . . . I'll throw it away, I will, throw it in the dustbin, into the dustbin!

LARGE G: You may think it's unwise of me to sell the golden egg before I've caught the goose . . . but I've great hopes, by Jove, yes I've great hopes . . .

ALICE: Founded on what? Meanwhile you'll spend day after day, week after week, month after month, a whole lifetime, just looking at her, wasting your time, making eyes at her, like a filthy toad . . . [*Snivelling.*] Selfish brute! Instead of looking after me, when I'm so ill, you cram the house with pictures until there's no room for more.

LARGE G: There's only one.

ALICE: A thousand too many! The house is stuffed with them! Instead of looking after me . . .

LARGE G: But I give you everything you need.

ALICE: I don't go without anything, I suppose.

LARGE G: Not as far as I can help it.

ALICE: What about my rheumatism?

LARGE G: You've got that already!

ALICE: And my broken spectacles!

LARGE G: I bought you some more. You're wearing them.

ALICE: They're not the same.

LARGE G: They're just as good.

ALICE [*shouting, her stick raised*]: It's not true, you liar, you rat!

LARGE G. [*lifting his eyes to Heaven*]: Will she never understand that I'm a man of high ideals!

ALICE: I'll see you don't budge from this desk! You'll stay here . . . here . . .

[*The* LARGE GENTLEMAN *sits down at his desk at the place indicated by* ALICE *with her stick.*]

Where are those contracts? Where are they?

LARGE G. [*pointing to the drawer*]: They're here!

ALICE: And you leave them lying there in a drawer! Are they ready?

LARGE G: They won't take long.

ALICE: Lazy good-for-nothing! Take them out at once. What are your clients going to say? They'll all leave you everyone of them.

[*The* LARGE GENTLEMAN *takes some papers out of his drawer and sets them in front of him.*]

Get to work! You haven't even started them!

LARGE G: I have . . . just.

ALICE: There you sit, gossiping with I don't know who . . .

LARGE G: *I* didn't ask him to come!

ALICE: . . . boasting and bragging. That's all you're good for. And the painter's an idiot, an imbecile without talent, anyone could do as well, a four-year-old child would be better than that . . .

LARGE G: Children do it without thinking.

ALICE: Leaving their pictures in anyone's house, with any old snob, any old simpleton who knows nothing about it, who just pretends . . .

LARGE G: I don't pretend.

ALICE: That's worse still!

LARGE G. [*timidly*]: . . . not true . . .

ALICE: Be quiet! Get on with those contracts! If they're not finished this evening, no soup, no pudding, no supper. People who don't work, don't eat . . .

LARGE G. [*timidly*]: It'll be finished by this evening.

ALICE: Promises! I know what *they're* worth! You'll show them to *me* when they're finished, can't trust *you*, I have to check everything, as if I'd nothing else to do . . .

LARGE G. [*still timid*]: I shan't finish them if you don't leave me alone . . .

ALICE: If they're not ready, look out for yourself . . . Look out for the stick! And no supper, mind.

LARGE G. [*as before*]: All right, Alice.

ALICE: I'll go and wash up your dirty dishes . . . I'll leave the kitchen door open . . . And watch yourself, that's all . . .

LARGE: Oh, I won't . . .

ALICE: I'll have my eye on you . . . [*She points to the picture.*] And if I catch you ogling her, if I catch you . . .

LARGE G. [*as before*]: I promise!

ALICE: Don't let me catch you, that's all! [*Looks at the picture and spits at it.*] I'll pay her out. You'll see what I'll do to her! [*She goes hobbling out left to the kitchen, muttering angrily; before leaving she has time to say:*] I'm watching you!

[*The* LARGE GENTLEMAN *looks at his papers and utters a sigh of relief; after a moment he wipes his brow, turns his head cautiously to take a brief glance at the picture and then bends over his papers again.*]

ALICE'S VOICE [*off*]: No playing about! I'm here! Got my eye on you.
LARGE G. [*startled*]: No, no, Alice.

[*He goes back to work. Then another anxious glance at the kitchen door, followed by yet another; he seems reassured; he half gets up, then a little move; just at that moment the noise of breaking crockery is heard from the kitchen and* ALICE'S *voice: "Damn". The* LARGE GENTLEMAN *sits down again quickly, frightened out of his wits, as though the pile of dishes had been dropped on his head, and then he sets feverishly to work.*]

LARGE G: Seven and eight, fifteen; fifteen times three, forty-five; forty-five divided by three, fifteen; fifteen minus eight, seven; seven and one, eight . . . That makes eight million . . . eight million multiplied by ten, that makes eighty million . . . yes . . . eighty million, eighty million . . . eighty million . . . ten times eighty million is eight hundred million . . . a profit of eight hundred million, income tax paid . . . tax paid . . . a profit of eight hundred million . . . in two weeks that's not bad . . . it could be better . . . much better, much better!

[ALICE *can be heard snoring.*]

Is she asleep? Or is she pretending? [*Very loud.*] Eight hundred million! Eight hundred!

[ALICE *goes on snoring.*]

[*He yells out to the kitchen.*] Eight hundred million! Eight hundred mil-l-ion! [*He stops; the snoring continues.*] She's asleep . . . I've made eight hundred million, so I think I might be allowed a little amusement! [*He looks at the picture.*] An amusement that costs nothing! [*He stands up and tip-toes to the picture, then changes his mind. Cautiously he goes to the kitchen door, puts his head round and then withdraws it; meanwhile the snoring continues; he closes the kitchen door quietly so that the noise of the snoring fades and then dies away: the Large Gentleman peers through the keyhole, clamps his ear to the door and then stands erect, reassured; he goes to the middle of the stage, humming but still on tip-toe, and very cautiously as he approaches the picture; he stands in front of it, back to the public, at first with his hands folded behind him.*] A good bargain that! . . . Isn't she beautiful? I've not wasted my money! I've even made some . . . Alice can say what she likes! . . . [*He strokes the arms of the woman in the picture.*] A still queen is better than a dead life! I believe I'm turning into a poet . . . turning into a poet . . . That's what I needed for inspiration . . . I'm going to be a poet, a poet . . . Hail to thee, blithe skylark. Her skin is so smooth . . . Supposing I tried, supposing I tried . . . painting can appeal to the palate too . . .

[*Smacking kisses over the portrait.*]

Darling! [*He sniffs.*] She smells nice . . . oil paint . . . [*He flattens himself against the picture.*] You're so beautiful . . . [*He steps away.*] Must keep at a distance . . . to appreciate it better . . . Good, good, good . . . it really is tremendously inspiring! To me, if not to Alice . . . And to think we have the same mother and father . . . it must have been a mistake . . . [*To the picture.*] Oh wonderful woman, so eloquent in your silence!

[*He takes a step to the left and to the right.*]

If I step to the left or the right everything changes. You look even lovelier, you're radiant from every side . . . it's all a question of perspective! It's so easy! Just change my position slightly, ever so little, as though I were dancing . . . Oh I'll learn to dance, for your sake! One step's enough, for perfect proportion. It's because one always looks at the world from the same angle that it seems so ugly, so inflexible. I'm not inflexible any more.

[*Another step to the right, then to the left; in a ridiculously pompous declamatory style.*]

They muddy waste becomes a meadow, the sky is an ocean with islands of delight . . . oases in the desert . . . rivers flowing through dry sand . . . You are a path of violets . . . You remind me of great cities engulfed by the waves . . . you remind me . . . you remind me . . . What was it, what was it? I am young again, bursting into leaf and turning green . . . well, well, well . . . I'm even blossoming . . . [*He goes up to the picture and strokes the painted arms.*] I'm in flower. [*Standing sideways to the audience, he shows his rosette of the Legion of Honour, so that all can see.*] I'm in flower . . . Ah! I'm turning into a poet, I'm really becoming a poet . . .

[ALICE *pops her head in; the* LARGE GENTLEMAN *is too preoccupied to notice.*]

What do you want of me? What do you want?
ALICE: Pervert! You ought to be ashamed!

LARGE G. [*completely flattened against the picture*]: Your eyes are so soft and warm they're melting me . . . [*He climbs up one or two rungs of the ladder to kiss the painted woman more easily.*]

ALICE [*coming forward on to the stage; the Large Gentleman still does not see her*]: Nothing can replace the warmth of a sister's affection!

LARGE G. [*as before*]: Alas, life is short and art is long!

ALICE [*hobbling round in circles*]: Art is the opium of the people. So is life.

LARGE G. [*coming down from the ladder*]: I shall stand back to come closer to you . . .

ALICE [*as before*]: You'd better stand a long way back! [*She snivels.*] At his age too! At his age! And then she's so plain, so plain . . . she might at least be beautiful, but he's chosen the plainest!

[*The* LARGE GENTLEMAN *is blowing kisses to the picture; at the same time* ALICE *is spitting at it and threatening it with her stick.*]

What does he find so wonderful about her?

LARGE G. [*esctatically*]: What do you want of me?

ALICE [*as before*]: What has she got that I haven't got? I admit she's two arms, and I've only one and a half, but I *have* got legs, and she hasn't . . . And if I've lost a hand, it's only an accident of old age!

LARGE G. [*as before*]: My young sovereign!

ALICE [*as before*]: It's a trick! That picture's at least thirty years old . . .

LARGE G. [*as before*]: She must be about twenty, twenty for ever and ever.

ALICE [*as before*]: Add that to the woman's age and it makes sixty, it makes her eighty years old, as old as I am.

LARGE G. [*as before*]: And yet she lacks something . . . not much . . .

ALICE [*as before*]: And if she's only twenty, he's old enough to be her father . . .

LARGE G. [*as before*]: She's not quite real enough, or quite unreal . . .

ALICE [*as before*]: How his imagination runs away with him! She's got nothing others haven't got, nothing at all . . . [*Snivelling to the Large Gentleman :*] You haven't even paid for her, you thief . . .

LARGE G. [*to Alice*]: Don't interrupt my aesthetic ecstacy with your moaning and groaning!

ALICE [*to Large Gentleman*]: But she's just a make-believe queen . . . make-believe! . . . Oh dear oh dear . . . what's to become of us, he'll ruin himself because of her . . .

LARGE G. [*to the picture*]: I can see what you need . . .

ALICE [*snivelling*]: I've a pain in my nose . . . a pain in my eyes . . .

LARGE G. [*happy to have made the discovery*]: I've got it . . . I'll make a few changes . . .

ALICE [*snivelling*]: He doesn't think about my rheumatism . . .

LARGE G. [*he goes to the drawer, opens it and takes out a crown; then he climbs the ladder again and tries in vain to put the crown on the painted woman's head.*] I'm going to crown her . . .

ALICE [*as before*]: Unnecessary expense! [*To the picture.*] All because of you! Because of you! [*to the Large Gentleman.*] Selfish scoundrel!

LARGE G: The crown was there, in the special drawer for crowns . . . It didn't cost me anything . . . But it's expensive all the same!

ALICE: It's expensive all the same!

LARGE G. [*climbing the ladder*]: That's it, just the thing . . .

ALICE: What a silly idea! Oh dear oh dear . . . old devil, he only thinks of his own amusement, never of other people's . . .

[*The* LARGE GENTLEMAN *tries in vain to fix the crown on the painted woman's head.*]

LARGE G: Oh dear, it won't stick, it won't fix on!

ALICE: I told you you couldn't, you're too old for that now . . .

LARGE G. [*persisting*]: It won't fix . . .

ALICE: Cranky ideas! It's terrible!

LARGE G. [*in despair*]: I didn't start painting soon enough . . . And now it's too late.

ALICE: What a way to spend his time! And all for that idiot!

LARGE G. [*on the ladder*]: Let's try something else . . .

ALICE [*weeping*]: Oh dear oh dear!

LARGE G. [*at the picture*]: Try and hold it in your arms, then . . . [*He tries to put the crown in the woman's arms, but of course does not succeed.*] I can't do it! She doesn't want it! [*He starts snivelling too*].

ALICE [*as before*]: Serve you right!

LARGE G. [*as before*]: It's such a shame!

ALICE [*as before*]: That'll teach you!

LARGE G. [*as before, to Alice*]: Well why don't you help me?

ALICE: You expect *me* to help! What sauce!

[*While the* LARGE GENTLEMAN *still tries in vain to fit the crown on the picture,* ALICE *, in tears, goes into the kitchen, or to the corner of the room, to fetch a pail of water. Coming back with the pail she throws the contents over the* LARGE GENTLEMAN'S *shoulders.*]

Take that! Casanova!

LARGE G. [*caught by surprise, drops the crown on the floor*]: You're going too far, Alice! [*He comes down from the ladder.*] Alice, what did you do that for? [*After shaking himself like a poodle, he glares threateningly at her.*]

ALICE: I feel ill! Oh, I'm going to faint! I've a pain in my head, I want to be sick! I can't stand up, I'm going to fall! . . . going to fall! go and fetch a chair, what are you doing! You'd be better off buying chairs, they're more useful than pictures.

LARGE G: All right . . . all right . . .

ALICE: Take the pail with you!

LARGE G: Yes . . . yes . . .

[*He picks up the pail and casts a glance at the picture.*]

She's so beautiful, even without a crown!

ALICE [*snivelling*]: I'm going to fall . . . Hurry up.

LARGE G: Oh . . . I shall never have any peace . . . never be myself! [*He makes reluctantly for the kitchen, carrying the pail, and as he disappears he is heard saying:*] Never be myself!

ALICE [*straightening herself up, while the* LARGE GENTLEMAN *is off stage, and facing the picture.*] Loathsome creature! [*She threatens it.*]

LARGE G. [*coming back with an armchair that has a fairly high back.*]: Here! Sit down! [*He sets the chair down to the right of the picture.*]

ALICE: No next to her! Not next to her! [*She sits down all the same.*]

LARGE G: It's only because the comparison's not in your favour! [*In the hand he is holding behind his back, it can now be seen he is carrying a pistol.*]

ALICE: What impertinence! You've never used your eyes properly, never looked at me! You don't know how to! It's a bad picture, a baby could do better!

[*She gets up and hobbles about, striking the floor with her stick.*]

LARGE G. [*sweetly*]: You've a blind man's stick and you use it as though you were deaf!

ALICE [*as before*]: All right, I can hear you, hear you quite clearly, thank you!

LARGE G. [*still more sweetly*]: Sit down . . . you're tired . . . rest a bit! Here's the chair!

ALICE [*as before*]: What are you fussing about the chair for? Leave things where they are. You turn everything upside down.

LARGE G. [*as before*]: You were about to faint . . . sit down and you'll feel better.

ALICE [*as before*]: I haven't the time. And I've things to do. I'll work till I drop, like a horse . . .

LARGE G. [*suddenly very harsh*]: Don't move.

ALICE [*as before*]: You needn't think you can stop me.

[*The* LARGE GENTLEMAN *points the pistol at her.*]

Ah! Murderer! Murderer! [*Sits down, terrified.*] He's got a pistol! Murderer!

LARGE G: Didn't the doctor say you must have rest?

ALICE [*trembling in front of the pistol*]: Why don't you send me away to the mountains?

LARGE G: I haven't any mountains to hand. I've nothing but a pistol.

ALICE: Your finger might slip on the trigger.

LARGE G: You can slip in the mountains too! Keep quite still . . . And it's my finger, not yours.

ALICE: What's wrong with you . . . Tell me . . . Say something . . . you're my brother . . . it's only words that are important, all the rest is nonsense.

LARGE G: For me it's the opposite! Keep quiet . . . Don't move . . . I don't want you to speak or move again, without my permission! [*Pointing the pistol at her.*] Careful now!

ALICE [*snivelling*]: Oh . . . accidents happen so quickly . . .

LARGE G: Exactly. Stop crying. Not allowed!

ALICE: Why are you frightening your sister like this? Why do you want to kill her?

LARGE G: That's my affair!

ALICE: I'm sorry . . . I'm sorry . . . [*At a sudden movement of her head, her shawl falls back revealing her grey, dirty, unkempt hair.*] Now my shawl's fallen on the floor . . . Look what you've done! Let me pick it up!

LARGE G: Not my fault. Leave it alone or I warn you, this'll go off . . .

ALICE: I haven't got another one . . . I'm cold . . . It'll get dirty! [*She starts to pick it up.*]

LARGE G: No! No cheating!

ALICE: Stop playing with that pistol!

LARGE G: Not allowed to move or cry, be careful, it's loaded.

ALICE: I shan't move or speak again, don't fire, brother dear . . . I'm not cheating . . .

LARGE G: Sit up straight . . . lean against the back of the chair.

ALICE: It hurts me, I can't!

LARGE G: There's no such word as can't . . . Bend your knees . . . go on . . . go on..

[ALICE, *terrified, obeys painfully.*]

ALICE: My rheumatism . . .

LARGE G. [*playing dangerously with the pistol*]: I don't want to hear . . . go on, go on!

ALICE: With that pistol, if you're not careful, you might kill the neighbour's birds!

LARGE G: A lot I care! [*He sticks the pistol under Alice's nose.*] Lay your arm along the arm of the chair. [*She hesitates and pulls a face.*] Look sharp, get a move on! Keep still and not a word!

ALICE: An old woman like me, your sister who's always spoilt you and now you want to kill me . . . if you've no pity for me, remember my age!

LARGE G: For the last time, be quiet! You're too old to talk! Look out! [*He brandishes the pistol.*] Lose your temper and it'll go off! Come on, your arm along the arm of the chair, one on top of the other . . . Do you hear? [*She obeys, trembling.*] An excellent target!

ALICE: Ooh!

LARGE G: Remember the pistol, it's loaded! Head up, head on high . . .

[ALICE *tries to speak.*]

Ssh! Dear oh dear!

[*Tapping with his foot.*]

Not one movement . . . Smile! Smile, can't you!

[*He holds the pistol against her cheek.* ALICE *smiles and keeps this fixed smile to the end. He moves away a little, after having roughly snatched off* ALICE'S *second shawl, which he throws over her knees.*]

Ready now! I'm going to fire! [*A shot.*]

ALICE: Ah!

[ALICE *has a low-cut dress and we can now see that her bosom is the same as that of the woman in the picture. As she moves in her fright, her white wig and her spectacles fall off; we can see she has brown hair, and her face and her eyes are exactly like those of the painted woman.*]

LARGE G: Well! Well! Well!

[*At this moment an arm grows on* ALICE'S *stump.*]

And there's her arm too!

[*According to the production, it could be only at this moment that* ALICE *takes off her spectacles with her new-found hand. Spectacles, wig, etc. lie on the floor, all that remains of the dead.*]

Hurrah! Hurrah!

[*He fires the pistol into the air.*]

My idea was an inspiration, a wonderful inspiration! [*He jumps for joy, then stops.*] And the sceptre!

[*And now* ALICE'S *white stick becomes luminous; if this effect is difficult to realize, the* LARGE GENTLEMAN *can throw* ALICE'S *stick aside and place in her hand a sceptre he has taken from the drawer; to make the stick luminous it only needs an electric light bulb at the end—*ALICE *is radiant.*]

And there's the sceptre! Bravo! Bravo! Master painter, I congratulate you! [*He shakes himself by the hand.*] Now she needs the crown! [*He sets the crown on* ALICE'S *head. It is luminous too*] It's a masterpiece! I've created a masterpiece! [*He sobs for joy as he gazes at her.*] I could weep for joy. She outshines the model! I've improved on the painter. Don't need him any more! Want no more of his pictures! I can make them myself . . . and better ones! I shall found an Academy of Beauty! [*He bows grotesquely to the picture and to the lovely motionless Alice.*] Your Majesty! Your Majesty! Without a crown! And crowned! Your Majesty! Your Majesty! [*Then, to the audience.*] I am perfect! I was right!

[*The door on the right opens and the neighbour appears, she is exactly like* ALICE *before her transformation.*]

NEIGHBOUR [*coming in with a chair*]: Oh, I beg your pardon! [*The* LARGE GENTLEMAN, *slightly embarrassed, breaks off.*]
Am I disturbing you?
LARGE G: Oh no! . . . well in fact, no . . . I was jumping about like that, because I was happy . . .
NEIGHBOUR: I brought my knitting along, and my chair too, because I know you haven't any to spare in your place . . . it's cold at home . . . and it's not much warmer here . . . I don't want to be a nuisance.
LARGE G: Why don't you come in, then?

[*This conversation has taken place by the door; the* NEIGHBOUR *now comes into the room.*]

NEIGHBOUR [*seeing Alice*]: So you've been buying statues of queens! Beautifying the home!
LARGE G: As you see!
NEIGHBOUR: And a picture too? It looks as if it was copied from the statue . . . without the crown . . .
LARGE G. [*with a burst of gratified laughter.*]: Just the opposite . . . it's the statue that's a copy of the picture, or rather an improvement on it, with the crown added . . .
NEIGHBOUR: Oh yes . . . it's better than the model . . . it's magnificent!
LARGE G: I'm an artist!
NEIGHBOUR: . . . there's more weight about it, more flesh . . . I never knew you were such a genius! My congratulations!

LARGE G: Never judge by appearances again . . .
NEIGHBOUR: You'd think she was alive. She's beautiful.
LARGE G: Ha! Ha! Ha! It's Alice!
NEIGHBOUR: It can't be . . . Oh please do the same for me . . .
LARGE G: It's hard work. It costs money.
NEIGHBOUR: I'd give you my last farthing.
LARGE G: Very well. When you appeal to me like that, I give way. [*Aside.*] I'll get hundreds of thousands, when I sell her! [*To the Neighbour.*] Put your chair there, sit down and do as I say, like this.

[ALICE *and the* NEIGHBOUR *are on either side of the picture.*]

We'll start!

[*He takes out his pistol.*]

NEIGHBOUR: Oh . . . a paint gun, I love *them* . . .
LARGE G: Now you must sit quite still . . .

[*The* NEIGHBOUR *sits motionless on the chair.*]

We start . . .

[*The door on the right opens and the* PAINTER *appears.*]

PAINTER: Good morning, sir!
LARGE G: What do you want?
PAINTER [*still shy*]: I'm sorry sir. You told me to come back in three weeks' time, to know if you're taking my picture . . . if you decide . . .
LARGE G: Why don't you look and see what I've done!
PAINTER: Ooh! . . . it's marvellous . . .
LARGE G: My sister . . .
PAINTER: It can't be . . . she looks wise and beautiful, like a goddess!
LARGE G: I undertook to re-educate her! Sometimes by fear, sometimes by persuasion . . .
PAINTER: By fear!
LARGE G. [*showing the pistol*]: With this. [*He puts the pistol to his temple.*]
PAINTER: Oh . . . please . . . don't do that . . . you'll do something dreadful . . .
LARGE G: No I won't . . .

[*He fires a shot.*]

PAINTER: Aah! Sir!

LARGE G. [*laughing*]: I told you it wasn't dangerous . . . it's just to frighten you . . . you see, I've done better than you . . .

PAINTER: Oh much better, sir . . . it's true you told me you had talent, but I never believed you had as much as this . . . such an achievement, you know, reveals the touch of a master, rather than beginners' luck! . . . But what am I going to do?

LARGE G: *I've* become an artist. *You* must be a business man!

PAINTER [*in despair*]: The only thing left for me to do is to take my picture down!

LARGE G: First, you must give me forty million for the loan.

PAINTER: I haven't such a large sum on me!

LARGE G: You can pay it in instalments . . . In forty days, a million a day . . . and ten million interest!

PAINTER: Yes, sir, that's reasonable! Meanwhile I'll leave it with you . . .

LARGE G: That'll be eighty million! . . . Agreed. You may go.

PAINTER [*about to go*]: Goodbye, sir. I really do admire you. [*He stops on his way to the door. Very foolishly:*] You had one twin sister before, now you've two twin sisters; with this lady you'll have three twin sisters.

[*During this time the* LARGE GENTLEMAN *has taken two other crowns from the desk drawer.*]

LARGE G. [*putting one crown on the Neighbour's head, and the other on his own*]: And I'll make the fourth!

PAINTER: Well really!

LARGE G: Let me get on with my work!

[*Pistol shots into the air, fire crackers and flashing lights.*]

CURTAIN

Edward Albee (b. 1928)

THE ZOO STORY

For William Flanagan

A Play in One Scene

THE PLAYERS:

PETER:	*A man in his early forties, neither fat nor gaunt, neither handsome nor homely. He wears tweeds, smokes a pipe, carries horn-rimmed glasses. Although he is moving into middle age, his dress and his manner would suggest a man younger.*
JERRY:	*A man in his late thirties, not poorly dressed, but carelessly. What was once a trim and lightly muscled body has begun to go to fat; and while he is no longer handsome, it is evident that he once was. His fall from physical grace should not suggest debauchery; he has, to come closest to it, a great weariness.*

[THE SCENE: *It is Central Park; a Sunday afternoon in summer; the present. There are two park benches, one toward either side of the stage; they both face the audience. Behind them: foilage, trees, sky. At the beginning,* PETER *is seated on one of the benches.*]

STAGE DIRECTIONS:

[*As the curtain rises,* PETER *is seated on the bench stage-right. He is reading a book. He stops reading, cleans his glasses, goes back to reading.* JERRY *enters.*]

JERRY: I've been to the zoo. [PETER *doesn't notice*] I said, I've been to the zoo. MISTER, I'VE BEEN TO THE ZOO!

PETER: Hm? . . . What? . . . I'm sorry, were you talking to me?

JERRY: I went to the zoo, and then I walked until I came here. Have I been walking north?

PETER [*Puzzled*]: North? Why . . . I . . . I think so. Let me see.

JERRY [*Pointing past the audience*]: Is that Fifth Avenue?

PETER: Why yes; yes, it is.

JERRY: And what is that cross street there; that one, to the right?

PETER: That? Oh, that's Seventy-fourth Street.

JERRY: And the zoo is around Sixty-fifth Street; so, I've been walking north.

PETER [*Anxious to get back to his reading*]: Yes; it would seem so.

JERRY: Good old north.

PETER [*Lightly, by reflex*]: Ha, ha.

JERRY [*After a slight pause*]: But not due north.

PETER: I . . . well, no, not due north; but, we . . . call it north. It's northerly.

JERRY [*Watches as* PETER, *anxious to dismiss him, prepares his pipe*]: Well, boy; you're not going to get lung cancer, are you?

PETER [*Looks up, a little annoyed, then smiles*]: No, sir. Not from this.

JERRY: No, sir. What you'll probably get is cancer of the mouth, and then you'll have to wear one of those things Freud wore after they took one whole side of his jaw away. What do they call those things?

PETER [*Uncomfortable*]: A prosthesis?

JERRY: The very thing! A prosthesis. You're an educated man, aren't you? Are you a doctor?

PETER: Oh, no; no. I read about it somewhere; *Time* magazine, I think. [*He turns to his book*]

JERRY: Well, *Time* magazine isn't for blockheads.

PETER: No, I suppose not.

JERRY [*After a pause*]: Boy, I'm glad that's Fifth Avenue there.

PETER [*Vaguely*]: Yes.

JERRY: I don't like the west side of the park much.

PETER: Oh? [*Then, slightly wary, but interested*] Why?

JERRY [*Offhand*]: I don't know.

PETER: Oh. [*He returns to his book*]

JERRY [*He stands for a few seconds, looking at* PETER, *who finally looks up again, puzzled*]: Do you mind if we talk?

PETER [*Obviously minding*]: Why . . . no, no.

JERRY: Yes you do; you do.

PETER [*Puts his book down, his pipe out and away, smiling*]: No, really; I don't mind.

JERRY: Yes you do.

PETER [*Finally decided*]: No; I don't mind at all, really.

JERRY: It's . . . it's a nice day.

PETER [*Stares unnecessarily at the sky*]: Yes. Yes, it is; lovely.

JERRY: I've been to the zoo.

PETER: Yes, I think you said so . . . didn't you?

JERRY: You'll read about it in the papers tomorrow, if you don't see it on your TV tonight. You have TV, haven't you?

PETER: Why yes, we have two; one for the children.

JERRY: You're married!

PETER [*With pleased emphasis*]: Why, certainly.

JERRY: It isn't a law, for God's sake.

PETER: No . . . no, of course not.

JERRY: And you have a wife.

PETER [*Bewildered by the seeming lack of communication*]: Yes!

JERRY: And you have children.

PETER: Yes; two.

JERRY: Boys?

PETER: No, girls . . . both girls.

JERRY: But you wanted boys.

PETER: Well . . . naturally, every man wants a son, but . . .

JERRY [*Lightly mocking*]: But that's the way the cookie crumbles?

PETER [*Annoyed*]: I wasn't going to say that.

JERRY: And you're not going to have any more kids, are you?

PETER [*A bit distantly*]: No. No more. [*Then back, and irksome*] Why did you say that? How would you know about that?

JERRY: The way you cross your legs, perhaps; something in the voice. Or maybe I'm just guessing. Is it your wife?

PETER [*Furious*]: That's none of your business! [*A silence*] Do you understand? [JERRY *nods.* PETER *is quiet now*] Well, you're right. We'll have no more children.

JERRY [*Softly*]: That *is* the way the cookie crumbles.

PETER [*Forgiving*]: Yes . . . I guess so.

JERRY: Well, now; what else?

PETER: What were you saying about the zoo . . . that I'd read about it, or see . . . ?

JERRY: I'll tell you about it, soon. Do you mind if I ask you questions?

PETER: Oh, not really.

JERRY: I'll tell you why I do it; I don't talk to many people—except to say like: give me a beer, or where's the john, or what time does the feature go on, or keep your hands to yourself, buddy. You know—things like that.

PETER: I must say I don't . . .

JERRY: But every once in a while I like to talk to somebody, really *talk;* like to get to know somebody, know all about him.

PETER [*Lightly laughing, still a little uncomfortable*]: And am I the guinea pig for today?

JERRY: On a sun-drenched Sunday afternoon like this? Who better than a nice married man with two daughters and . . . uh . . . a dog? [PETER *shakes his head*] No? Two dogs. [PETER *shakes his head again*] Hm. No dogs? [PETER *shakes his head, sadly*] Oh, that's a shame. But you look like an animal man. CATS? [PETER *nods his head, ruefully*] Cats! But, that can't be your idea. No, sir. Your wife and daughters? [PETER *nods his head*] Is there anything else I should know?

PETER [*He has to clear his throat*]: There are . . . there are two parakeets. One . . . uh . . . one for each of my daughters.

JERRY: Birds.

PETER: My daughters keep them in a cage in their bedroom.

JERRY: Do they carry disease? The birds.

PETER: I don't believe so.

JERRY: That's too bad. If they did you could set them loose in the house and the cats could eat them and die, maybe. [PETER *looks blank for a moment, then laughs*]. And what else? What do you do to support your enormous household?

PETER: I . . . uh . . . I have an executive position with a . . . a small publishing house. We . . . uh . . . we publish textbooks.

JERRY: That sounds nice; very nice. What do you make?

PETER [*Still cheerful*]: Now look here!

JERRY: Oh, come on.

PETER: Well, I make around eighteen thousand a year, but I don't carry more than forty dollars at any one time . . . in case you're a . . . a holdup man . . . ha, ha, ha.

JERRY [*Ignoring the above*]: Where do you live? [PETER *is reluctant*] Oh, look; I'm not going to rob you, and I'm not going to kidnap your parakeets, your cats, or your daughters.

PETER [*Too loud*]: I live between Lexington and Third Avenue, on Seventy-fourth Street.

JERRY: That wasn't so hard, was it?

PETER: I didn't mean to seem . . . ah . . . it's that you don't really carry on a conversation; you just ask questions. and I'm . . . I'm normally . . . uh . . . reticent. Why do you just stand there?

JERRY: I'll start walking around in a little while, and eventually I'll sit down. [*Recalling*] Wait until you see the expression on his face.

PETER: What? Whose face? Look here; is this something about the zoo?

JERRY [*Distantly*]: The what?

PETER: The zoo; the zoo. Something about the zoo.

JERRY: The zoo?

PETER: You've mentioned it several times.

JERRY [*Still distant, but returning abruptly*]: The zoo? Oh, yes; the zoo. I was there before I came here. I told you that. Say, what's the dividing line between upper-middle-middle-class and lower-upper-middle-class?

PETER: My dear fellow, I . . .

JERRY: Don't my dear fellow me.

PETER [*Unhappily*]: Was I patronizing? I believe I was; I'm sorry. But, you see, your question about the classes bewildered me.

JERRY: And when you're bewildered you become patronizing?

PETER: I . . . I don't express myself too well, sometimes. [*He attempts a joke on himself*] I'm in publishing, not writing.

JERRY [*Amused, but not at the humor*]: So be it. The truth *is: I* was being patronizing.

PETER: Oh, now; you needn't say that.

[*It is at this point that Jerry may begin to move about the stage with slowly increasing determination and authority, but pacing himself, so that the long speech about the dog comes at the high point of the arc*]

JERRY: All right. Who are your favorite writers? Baudelaire and J. P. Marquand?

PETER [*Wary*]: Well, I like a great many writers; I have a considerable . . . catholicity of taste, if I may say so. Those two men are fine, each in his way. [*Warming up*] Baudelaire, of course . . . uh . . . is by far the finer of the two, but Marquand has a place . . . in our . . . uh . . . national . . .

JERRY: Skip it.

PETER: I . . . sorry.

JERRY: Do you know what I did before I went to the zoo today? I walked all the way up Fifth Avenue from Washington Square; all the way.

PETER: Oh; you live in the Village! [*This seems to enlighten* PETER]

JERRY: No, I don't. I took the subway down to the Village so I could walk all the way up Fifth Avenue to the zoo. It's one of those things a person has to do; sometimes a person has to go a very long distance out of his way to come back a short distance correctly.

PETER [*Almost pouting*]: Oh, I thought you lived in the Village.

JERRY: What were you trying to do? Make sense out of things? Bring order? The old pigeonhole bit? Well, that's easy; I'll tell you. I live in a four-story brownstone roominghouse on the upper West Side between Columbus Avenue and Central Park West. I live on the top floor; rear; west. It's a laughably small room, and one of my walls is made of beaverboard; this beaverboard separates my room from another laughably small room, so I assume that the two rooms were once one room, a small room, but not necessarily laughable. The room beyond my beaverboard wall is occupied by a colored queen who always keeps his door open; well, not always, but *always* when he's plucking his eyebrows, which he does with Buddhist concentration. This colored queen has rotten teeth, which is rare, and he has a Japanese kimono, which is also pretty rare; and he wears this kimono to and from the john in the hall, which is pretty frequent. I mean, he goes to the john a lot. He never bothers me, and he never brings anyone up to his room. All he does is pluck his eyebrows, wear his kimono and go to the john. Now, the two front rooms on my floor are a little larger, I guess; but they're pretty small, too. There's a Puerto Rican family in one of them, a husband, a wife, and some kids; I don't know how many. These people entertain a lot. And in the other front room, there's somebody living there, but I don't know who it is. I've never seen who it is. Never. Never ever.

PETER [*Embarrassed*]: Why . . . why do you live there?

JERRY [*From a distance again*]: I don't know.

PETER: It doesn't sound like a very nice place . . . where you live.

JERRY: Well, no; it isn't an apartment in the East Seventies. But, then again, I don't have one wife, two daughters, two cats and two parakeets. What I do have, I have toilet articles, a few clothes, a hot plate that I'm not supposed to have, a can opener, one that works with a key, you know; a knife, two forks, and two spoons, one small, one large; three plates, a cup, a saucer, a drinking glass, two picture frames, both empty, eight or nine books, a pack of pornographic playing cards, regular deck, an old Western Union typewriter that prints nothing but capital letters, and a small strongbox without a lock which has in it . . . what? Rocks! Some rocks . . . sea-rounded rocks I picked up on the beach when I was a kid. Under which . . . weighed down . . . are some letters . . . please letters . . . please why don't you do this, and please when will you do that letters. And when letters, too. When will you write? When will you come? When? These letters are from more recent years.

PETER [*Stares glumly at his shoes, then*]: About those two empty picture frames . . . ?

JERRY: I don't see why they need any explanation at all. Isn't it clear? I don't have pictures of anyone to put in them.

PETER: Your parents . . . perhaps . . . a girl friend . . .

JERRY: You're a very sweet man, and you're possessed of a truly enviable innocence. But good old Mom and good old Pop are dead . . . you know? . . . I'm broken up about it, too . . . I mean really. BUT. That particular vaudeville act is playing the cloud circuit now, so I don't see how I can look at them, all neat and framed. Besides, or, rather, to be pointed about it, good old Mom walked out on good old Pop when I was ten and a half years old; she embarked on an adulterous turn of our southern states . . . a journey of a year's duration . . . and her most constant companion . . . among others, among many others . . . was a Mr. Barleycorn. At least, that's what good old Pop told me after he went down . . . came back . . . brought her body north. We'd received the news between Christmas and New Year's, you see, that good old Mom had parted with the ghost in some dump in Alabama. And, with-

out the ghost . . . she was less welcome. I mean, what was she? A stiff
. . . a northern stiff. At any rate, good old Pop celebrated the New Year
for an even two weeks and then slapped into the front of a somewhat
moving city omnibus, which sort of cleaned things out family-wise.
Well no; then there was Mom's sister, who was given neither to sin nor
the consolations of the bottle. I moved in on her, and my memory of
her is slight excepting I remember still that she did all things dourly:
sleeping, eating, working, praying. She dropped dead on the stairs to her
apartment, my apartment then, too, on the afternoon of my high school
graduation. A terribly middle-European joke, if you ask me.

PETER: Oh, my; oh, my.

JERRY: Oh, your what? But that was a long time ago, and I have no feeling
about any of it that I care to admit to myself. Perhaps you can see,
though, why good old Mom and good old Pop are frameless. What's
your name? Your first name?

PETER: I'm Peter.

JERRY: I'd forgotten to ask you. I'm Jerry.

PETER [*With a slight, nervous laugh*]: Hello, Jerry.

JERRY [*Nods his hello*]: And let's see now; what's the point of having a girl's
picture, especially in two frames? I have two picture frames, you
remember. I never see the pretty little ladies more than once, and most
of them wouldn't be caught in the same room with a camera. It's odd,
and I wonder if it's sad.

PETER: The girls?

JERRY: No. I wonder if it's sad that I never see the little ladies more than
once. I've never been able to have sex with, or, how is it put? . . . make
love to anybody more than once. Once; that's it. . . . Oh, wait; for a
week and a half, when I was fifteen . . . and I hang my head in shame
that puberty was late . . . I was a h-o-m-o-s-e-x-u-a-l. I mean, I was
queer . . . [*Very fast*] . . . queer, queer, queer . . . with bells ringing,
banners snapping in the wind. And for those eleven days, I met at least
twice a day with the park superintendent's son . . . a Greek boy, whose
birthday was the same as mine, except he was a year older. I think I was
very much in love . . . maybe just with sex. But that was the jazz of
a very special hotel, wasn't it? And now; oh, do I love the little ladies;
really, I love them. For about an hour.

PETER: Well, it seems perfectly simple to me. . . .

JERRY [*Angry*]: Look! Are you going to tell me to get married and have
parakeets?

PETER [*Angry himself*]: Forget the parakeets! And stay single if you want to.
It's no business of mine. I didn't start this conversation in the . . .

JERRY: All right, all right. I'm sorry. All right? You're not angry?

PETER [*Laughing*]: No, I'm not angry.

JERRY [*Relieved*]: Good. [*Now back to his previous tone*]. Interesting that you asked me about the picture frames. I would have thought that you would have asked me about the pornographic playing cards.

PETER [*With a knowing smile*]: Oh, I've seen those cards.

JERRY: That's not the point. [*Laughs*] I suppose when you were a kid you and your pals passed them around, or you had a pack of your own.

PETER: Well, I guess a lot of us did.

JERRY: And you threw them away just before you got married.

PETER: Oh, now; look here. I didn't *need* anything like that when I got older.

JERRY: No?

PETER [*Embarrassed*]: I'd rather not talk about these things.

JERRY: So? Don't. Besides, I wasn't trying to plumb your post-adolescent sexual life and hard times; what I wanted to get at is the value difference between pornographic playing cards when you're a kid, and pornographic playing cards when you're older. It's that when you're a kid you use the cards as a substitute for a real experience, and when you're older you use real experience as a substitute for the fantasy. But I imagine you'd rather hear about what happened at the zoo.

PETER [*Enthusiastic*]: Oh, yes; the zoo. [*Then, awkward*] That is . . . if you. . . .

JERRY: Let me tell you about why I went . . . well, let me tell you some things. I've told you about the fourth floor of the roominghouse where I live. I think the rooms are better as you go down, floor by floor. I guess they are; I don't know. I don't know any of the people on the third and second floors. Oh, wait! I do know that there's a lady living on the third floor, in the front. I know because she cries all the time. Whenever I go out or come back in, whenever I pass her door, I always hear her crying, muffled, but . . . very determined. Very determined indeed. But the one I'm getting to, and all about the dog, is the landlady. I don't like to use words that are too harsh in describing people. I don't like to. But the landlady is a fat, ugly, mean, stupid, unwashed, misanthropic, cheap, drunken bag of garbage. And you may have noticed that I very seldom use profanity, so I can't describe her as well as I might.

PETER: You describe her . . . vividly.

JERRY: Well, thanks. Anyway, she has a dog, and I will tell you about the dog, and she and her dog are the gatekeepers of my dwelling. The woman is bad enough; she leans around in the entrance hall, spying to see that I don't bring in things or people, and when she's had her mid-afternoon pint of lemon-flavored gin she always stops me in the hall, and grabs ahold of my coat or my arm, and she presses her disgusting body up against me to keep me in a corner so she can talk to me. The smell of her body and her breath . . . you can't imagine it . . . and somewhere, somewhere in the back of that pea-sized brain of hers, an organ developed just enough to let her eat, drink, and emit, she has some foul parody of sexual desire. And I, Peter, I am the object of her sweaty lust.

PETER: That's disgusting. That's . . . horrible.

JERRY: But I have found a way to keep her off. When she talks to me, when she presses herself to my body and mumbles about her room and how I should come there, I merely say: but, Love; wasn't yesterday enough for you, and the day before? Then she puzzles, she makes slits of her tiny eyes, she sways a little, and then, Peter . . . and it is at this moment that I think I might be doing some good in that tormented house . . . a simple-minded smile begins to form on her unthinkable face, and she giggles and groans as she thinks about yesterday and the day before; as she believes and relives what never happened. Then, she motions to that black monster of a dog she has, and she goes back to her room. And I am safe until our next meeting.

PETER: It's so . . . unthinkable. I find it hard to believe that people such as that really *are.*

JERRY [*Lightly mocking*]: It's for reading about, isn't it?

PETER [*Seriously*]: Yes.

JERRY: And fact is better left to fiction. You're right, Peter. Well, what I have been meaning to tell you about is the dog; I shall, now.

PETER [*Nervously*]: Oh, yes; the dog.

JERRY: Don't go. You're not thinking of going, are you?

PETER: Well . . . no, I don't think so.

JERRY [*As if to a child*]: Because after I tell you about the dog, do you know what then? Then . . . then I'll tell you about what happened at the zoo.

PETER [*Laughing faintly*]: You're . . . you're full of stories, aren't you?

JERRY: You don't *have* to listen. Nobody is holding you here; remember that. Keep that in your mind.

PETER *Irritably*]: I know that.

JERRY: You do? Good.

[*The following long speech, it seems to me, should be done with a great deal of action, to achieve a hypnotic effect on Peter, and on the audience, too. Some specific actions have been suggested, but the director and the actor playing Jerry might best work it out for themselves*]

ALL RIGHT. [*As if reading from a huge billboard*] THE STORY OF JERRY AND THE DOG! [*Natural again*] What I am going to tell you has something to do with how sometimes it's necessary to go a long distance out of the way in order to come back a short distance correctly; or, maybe I only think that it has something to do with that. But, it's why I went to the zoo today, and why I walked north . . . northerly, rather . . . until I came here. All right. The dog, I think I told you, is a black monster of a beast: an oversized head, tiny, tiny ears, and eyes . . . bloodshot, infected, maybe; and a body you can see the ribs through the skin. The dog is black, all black; all black except for the bloodshot eyes, and . . . yes . . . and an open sore on its . . . *right* forepaw; that is red, too. And, oh yes; the poor monster, and I do believe it's an old dog . . . it's certainly a misused one . . . almost always has an erection . . . of sorts. That's red, too. And . . . what else? . . . oh, yes; there's a gray-yellow-white color, too, when he bares his fangs. Like this: Grrrrrr! Which is what he did when he saw me for the first time . . . the day I moved in. I worried about that animal the very first minute I met him. Now, animals don't take to me like Saint Francis had birds hanging off him all the time. What I mean is: animals are indifferent to me . . . like people [*He smiles slightly*] . . . most of the time. But this dog wasn't indifferent. From the very beginning he'd snarl and then go for me, to get one of my legs. Not like he was rabid, you know; he was sort of a stumbly dog, but he wasn't half-assed, either. It was a good, stumbly run; but I always got away. He got a piece of my trouser leg, look, you can see right here, where it's mended; he got that the second day I lived there; but, I kicked free and got upstairs fast, so that was that. [*Puzzles*] I still don't know to this day how the other roomers manage it, but you know what I *think:* I think it had to do only with me. Cozy. So. Anyway, this went on for over a week, whenever I came in; but never when I went out. That's funny. Or, it *was* funny. I could pack up and live in the street for all the dog cared. Well, I thought about it up in my room one day, one of the times after I'd bolted upstairs, and I made up my mind. I decided: First, I'll kill the dog with kindness, and if that doesn't work . . . I'll just kill him. [PETER *winces*] Don't react, Peter; just listen. So, the next day I went out and bought a bag of hamburgers, medium rare, no catsup, no onion; and on the way home I threw away all the rolls and kept just the meat.

[*Action for the following, perhaps*]

When I got back to the roominghouse the dog was waiting for me. I half opened the door that led into the entrance hall, and there he was; waiting for me. It figured. I went in, very cautiously, and I had the hamburgers, you remember; I opened the bag, and I set the meat down about twelve feet from where the dog was snarling at me. Like so! He snarled; stopped snarling; sniffed; moved slowly; then faster; then faster toward the meat; Well, when he got to it he stopped, and he looked at me. I smiled; but tentatively, you understand. He turned his face back to the hamburgers, smelled, sniffed some more, and then . . . RRRAAAAGGGGGHHHH, like that . . . he tore into them. It was as if he had never eaten anything in his life before, except like garbage. Which might very well have been the truth. I don't think the landlady ever eats anything but garbage. But. He ate all the hamburgers, almost all at once, making sounds in his throat like a woman. *Then,* when he'd finished the meat, the hamburger, and tried to eat the paper, too, he sat down and smiled. I think he smiled; I know cats do. It was a very gratifying few moments. Then, BAM, he snarled and made for me again. He didn't get me this time, either. So, I got upstairs, and I lay down on my bed and started to think about the dog again. To be truthful, I was offended, and I was damn mad, too. It was six perfectly good hamburgers with not enough pork in them to make it disgusting. I was offended. But, after a while, I decided to try it for a few more days. If you think about it, this dog had what amounted to an antipathy toward me; really. And, I wondered if I mightn't overcome this antipathy. So, I tried it for five more days, but it was always the same: snarl, sniff; move; faster; stare; gobble; RAAGGGHHH; smile; snarl; BAM. Well, now; by this time Columbus Avenue was strewn with hamburger rolls and I was less offended than disgusted. So, I decided to kill the dog.

[PETER *raises a hand in protest*]

Oh, don't be so alarmed, Peter; I didn't succeed. The day I tried to kill the dog I bought only one hamburger and what I thought was a murderous portion of rat poison. When I bought the hamburger I asked the man not to bother with the roll, all I wanted was the meat. I expected some reaction from him, like: we don't sell no hamburgers without rolls; or, wha' d'ya wanna do, eat it out'a ya han's? But no; he smiled benignly, wrapped up the hamburger in waxed paper and said: A bite for ya pussy-cat? I wanted to say: No, not really; it's part of a plan to poison a dog I know. But, you can't say "a dog I know" without sounding funny; so I said, a little too loud, I'm afraid, and too formally: YES, A BITE FOR MY PUSSY-CAT. People looked up. It always happens when I try to simplify things; people look up. But that's neither hither nor thither. So. On my way back to the roominghouse, I kneaded the hamburger and the rat poison together between my hands, at that point feeling as much sadness as disgust. I opened the door to the entrance hall, and there the monster was, waiting to take the offering and then jump me. Poor bastard; he never learned that the moment he took to smile before he went for me gave me time enough to get out of range. BUT, there he was; malevolence with an erection, waiting. I put the poison patty down, moved toward the stairs and watched. The poor animal gobbled the food down as usual, smiled, which made me almost sick, and then, BAM. But, I sprinted up the stairs, as usual, and the dog didn't get me, as usual. AND IT CAME TO PASS THAT THE BEAST WAS DEATHLY ILL. I knew this because he no longer attended me, and because the landlady sobered up. She stopped me in the hall the same evening of the attempted murder and confided the information that God had struck her puppy-dog a surely fatal blow. She had forgotten her bewildered lust, and her eyes were wide open for the first time. They looked like the dog's eyes. She sniveled and implored me to pray for the animal. I wanted to say to her: Madam, I have myself to pray for, the colored queen, the Puerto Rican family, the person in the front room whom I've never seen, the woman who cries deliberately behind her closed door, and the rest of the people in all roominghouses, everywhere; besides, Madam, I don't understand how to pray. But . . . to simplify things . . . I told her I would pray. She looked up. She said that I was a liar, and that I probably wanted the dog to die. I told her, and there was so much truth here, that I didn't want the dog to die. I didn't, and not just because I'd poisoned him. I'm afraid that I must tell you I wanted the dog to live so that I could see what our new relationship might come to.

[PETER *indicates his increasing displeasure and slowly growing antagonism*]

Please understand, Peter; that sort of thing is important. You must believe me; it *is* important. We have to know the effect of our actions. [*Another deep sigh*] Well, anyway; the dog recovered. I have no idea why, unless he was a descendant of the puppy that guarded the gates of hell or some such resort. I'm not up on my mythology. [*He pronounces the word myth-o-logy*] Are you?

[PETER *sets to thinking, but* JERRY *goes on*]

At any rate, and you've missed the eight-thousand-dollar question, Peter; at any rate, the dog recovered his health and the landlady recovered her thirst, in no way altered by the bow-wow's deliverance. When I came home from a movie that was playing on Forty-second Street, a movie I'd seen, or one that was very much like one or several I'd seen, after the landlady told me puppykins was better, I was so hoping for the dog to be waiting for me. I was . . . well, how would you put it . . . enticed? . . . fascinated? . . . no, I don't think so . . . heart-shatteringly anxious, that's it; I was heart-shatteringly anxious to confront my friend again.

[PETER *reacts scoffingly*]

Yes, Peter; friend. That's the only word for it. I was heart-shatteringly et cetera to confront my doggy friend again. I came in the door and advanced, unafraid, to the center of the entrance hall. The beast was there . . . looking at me. And, you know, he looked better for his scrape with the nevermind. I stopped; I looked at him; he looked at me. I think . . . I think we stayed a long time that way . . . still, stone-statue . . . just looking at one another. I looked more into his face than he looked into mine. I mean, I can concentrate longer at looking into a dog's face than a dog can concentrate at looking into mine, or into anybody else's face, for that matter. But during that twenty seconds or two hours that we looked into each other's face, we made contact. Now, here is what I had wanted to happen: I loved the dog now, and I wanted him to love me. I had tried to love, and I had tried to kill, and both had been unsuccessful by themselves. I hoped . . . and I don't really know why I expected the dog to understand anything, much less my motivations . . . I hoped that the dog would understand.

[PETER *seems to be hypnotized*]

It's just . . . it's just that . . . [JERRY *is abnormally tense, now*] . . . it's just that if you can't deal with people, you have to make a start somewhere. WITH ANIMALS! [*Much faster now, and like a conspirator*] Don't you see? A person has to have some way of dealing with SOME-THING. If not with people . . . if not with people . . . SOMETHING. With a bed, with a cockroach, with a mirror . . . no, that's too hard, that's one of the last steps. With a cockroach, with a . . . with a . . . with a carpet, a roll of toilet paper . . . no, not that, either . . . that's a mirror, too; always check bleeding. You see how hard it is to find things? With a street corner, and too many lights, all colors reflecting on the oily-wet streets . . . with a wisp of smoke, a wisp . . . of smoke . . . with . . . with pornographic playing cards, with a strong-box . . . WITHOUT A LOCK . . . with love, with vomiting, with crying, with fury because the pretty little ladies aren't pretty little ladies, with making money with your body which is an act of love and I could prove it, with howling because you're alive; with God. How about that? WITH GOD WHO IS A COLORED QUEEN WHO WEARS A KIMONO AND PLUCKS HIS EYEBROWS, WHO IS A WOMAN WHO CRIES WITH DETERMINATION BEHIND HER CLOSED DOOR . . . with God who, I'm told, turned his back on the whole thing some time ago . . . with . . . some day, with people. [JERRY *sighs the next word heavily*] People. With an idea; a concept. And where better, where ever better in this humiliating excuse for a jail, where better to communicate one single, simpleminded idea than in an en-trance hall? Where? It would be A START! Where better to make a beginning . . . to understand and just possibly be understood . . . a beginning of an understanding, than with . . .

[*Here* JERRY *seems to fall into almost grotesque fatigue*]

. . . than with A DOG. Just that; a dog.

[*Here there is a silence that might be prolonged for a moment or so; then* JERRY *wearily finishes his story*]

A dog. It seemed like a perfectly sensible idea. Man is a dog's best friend, remember. So: the dog and I looked at each other. I longer than the dog. And what I saw then has been the same ever since. Whenever the dog and I see each other we both stop where we are. We regard each other with a mixture of sadness and suspicion, and then we feign indifference. We walk past each other safely; we have an understanding. It's very sad, but you'll have to admit that it is an understanding. We had made many attempts at contact, and we had failed. The dog has returned to garbage, and I to solitary but free passage. I have not returned. I mean to say, I have *gained* solitary free passage, if that much further loss can be said to be gain. I have learned that neither kindness nor cruelty by themselves, independent of each other, creates any effect beyond themselves; and I have learned that the two combined, together, at the same time, are the teaching emotion. And what is gained is loss. And what has been the result: the dog and I have attained a compromise; more of a bargain, really. We neither love nor hurt because we do not try to reach each other. And, *was* trying to feed the dog an act of love? And, perhaps, was the dog's attempt to bite me *not* an act of love? If we can so misunderstand, well then, why have we invented the word love in the first place?

[*There is silence.* JERRY *moves to* PETER'S *bench and sits down beside him. This is the first time* JERRY *has sat down during the play*]

The Story of Jerry and the Dog: the end.

[PETER *is silent*]

Well, Peter? [JERRY *is suddenly cheerful*] Well, Peter? Do you think I could sell that story to the *Reader's Digest* and make a couple of hundred bucks for *The Most Unforgettable Character I've Ever Met?* Huh?

[JERRY *is animated, but* PETER *is disturbed*]

Oh, come on now, Peter; tell me what you think.

PETER [*Numb*]: I . . . I don't understand what . . . I don't think I . . . [*Now, almost tearfully*] Why did you tell me all of this?
JERRY: Why not?
PETER: I DON'T UNDERSTAND!
JERRY [*Furious, but whispering*]: That's a lie.
PETER: No. No, it's not.
JERRY [*Quietly*]: I tried to explain it to you as I went along. I went slowly; it all has to do with . . .
PETER: I DON'T WANT TO HEAR ANY MORE. I don't understand you, or your landlady, or her dog. . . .

JERRY: *Her* dog! I thought it was my . . . No. No, you're right. It *is* her dog. [*Looks at* PETER *intently, shaking his head*] I don't know what I was thinking about; of course you don't understand. [*In a monotone, wearily*] I don't live in your block; I'm not married to two parakeets, or whatever your setup is. I am a *permanent transient,* and my home is the sickening roominghouses on the West Side of New York City, which is the greatest city in the world. Amen.

PETER: I'm . . . I'm sorry; I didn't mean to . . .

JERRY: Forget it. I suppose you don't quite know what to make of me, eh?

PETER [*A joke*]: We get all kinds in publishing. [*Chuckles*]

JERRY: You're a funny man. [*He forces a laugh*] You know that? You're a very . . . a richly comic person.

PETER [*Modestly, but amused*]: Oh, now, not really. [*Still chuckling*]

JERRY: Peter, do I annoy you, or confuse you?

PETER [*Lightly*]: Well, I must confess that this wasn't the kind of afternoon I'd anticipated.

JERRY: You mean, I'm not the gentleman you were expecting.

PETER: I wasn't expecting anybody.

JERRY: No, I don't imagine you were. But I'm here, and I'm not leaving.

PETER [*Consulting his watch*]: Well, you may not be, but I must be getting home soon.

JERRY: Oh, come on; stay a while longer.

PETER: I really should get home; you see . . .

JERRY [*Tickles* PETER'S *ribs with his fingers*]: Oh, come on.

PETER [*He is very ticklish; as* JERRY *continues to tickle him his voice becomes falsetto*]: No, I . . . OHHHHH! Don't do that. Stop, Stop. Ohhh, no, no.

JERRY: Oh, come on.

PETER [*As* JERRY *tickles*]: Oh, hee, hee, hee. I must go. I . . . hee, hee, hee. After all, stop, stop, hee, hee, hee, after all, the parakeets will be getting dinner ready soon. Hee, hee. And the cats are setting the table. Stop, stop, and, and . . . [PETER *is beside himself now*] . . . and we're having . . . hee, hee . . . uh . . . ho, ho, ho.

[JERRY *stops tickling* PETER, *but the combination of the tickling and his own mad whimsy has* PETER *laughing almost hysterically. As his laughter continues, then subsides,* JERRY *watches him, with a curious fixed smile*]

JERRY: Peter?

PETER: Oh, ha, ha, ha, ha, ha. What? What?

JERRY: Listen, now.

PETER: Oh, ho, ho. What . . . what is it, Jerry? Oh, my.

JERRY [*Mysteriously*]: Peter, do you want to know what happened at the zoo?

PETER: Ah, ha, ha. The what? Oh, yes; the zoo. Oh, ho, ho. Well, I had my own zoo there for a moment with . . . hee, hee, the parakeets getting dinner ready, and the . . . ha, ha, whatever it was, the . . .

JERRY [*Calmly*]: Yes, that was very funny, Peter. I wouldn't have expected it. But do you want to hear about what happened at the zoo, or not?

PETER: Yes. Yes, by all means; tell me what happened at the zoo. Oh, my. I don't know what happened to me.

JERRY: Now I'll let you in on what happened at the zoo; but first, I should tell you why I went to the zoo. I went to the zoo to find out more about the way people exist with animals, and the way animals exist with each other, and with people too. It probably wasn't a fair test, what with everyone separated by bars from everyone else, the animals for the most part from each other, and always the people from the animals. But, if it's a zoo, that's the way it is. [*He pokes* PETER *on the arm*] Move over.

PETER [*Friendly*]: I'm sorry, haven't you enough room? [*He shifts a little*]

JERRY [*Smiling slightly*]: Well, all the animals are there, and all the people are there, and it's Sunday and all the children are there. [*He pokes* PETER *again*] Move over.

PETER [*Patiently, still friendly*]: All right.

[*He moves some more, and* JERRY *has all the room he might need*]

JERRY: And it's a hot day, so all the stench is there, too, and all the balloon sellers, and all the ice cream sellers, and all the seals are barking, and all the birds are screaming. [*Pokes* PETER *harder*] Move over!

PETER [*Beginning to be annoyed*]: Look here, you have more than enough room! [*But he moves more, and is now fairly cramped at one end of the bench*]

JERRY: And I am there, and it's feeding time at the lions' house, and the lion keeper comes into the lion cage, one of the lion cages, to feed one of the lions. [*Punches* PETER *on the arm, hard*] MOVE OVER!

PETER [*Very annoyed*]: I can't move over any more, and stop hitting me. What's the matter with you?

JERRY: Do you want to hear the story? [*Punches* PETER'S *arm again*]

PETER [*Flabbergasted*]: I'm not so sure! I certainly don't want to be punched in the arm.

JERRY [*Punches* PETER'S *arm again*]: Like that?

PETER: Stop it! What's the matter with you?

JERRY: I'm crazy, you bastard.

PETER: That isn't funny.

JERRY: Listen to me, Peter. I want this bench. You go sit on the bench over there, and if you're good I'll tell you the rest of the story.

PETER [*Flustered*]: But . . . whatever for? What *is* the matter with you? Besides, I see no reason why I should give up this bench. I sit on this bench almost every Sunday afternoon, in good weather. It's secluded here; there's never anyone sitting here, so I have it all to myself.

JERRY [*Softly*]: Get off this bench, Peter; I want it.

PETER [*Almost whining*]: No.

JERRY: I said I want this bench, and I'm going to have it. Now get over there.

PETER: People can't have everything they want. You should know that; it's a rule; people can have some of the things they want, but they can't have everything.

JERRY [*Laughs*]: Imbecile! You're slow-witted!

PETER: Stop that!

JERRY: You're a vegetable! Go lie down on the ground.

PETER [*Intense*]: Now *you* listen to me. I've put up with you all afternoon.

JERRY: Not really.

PETER: LONG ENOUGH. I've put up with you long enough. I've listened to you because you seemed . . . well, because I thought you wanted to talk to somebody.

JERRY: You put things well; economically, and, yet . . . oh, what is the word I want to put justice to your . . . JESUS, you make me sick . . . get off here and give me my bench.

PETER: MY BENCH!

JERRY [*Pushes* PETER *almost, but not quite, off the bench*]: Get out of my sight.

PETER [*Regaining his position*]: God da . . . mn you. That's enough! I've had enough of you. I will not give up this bench; you can't have it, and that's that. Now, go away.

[JERRY *snorts but does not move*]

Go away, I said.

[JERRY *does not move*]

Get away from here. If you don't move on . . . you're a bum . . . that's what you are. . . . If you don't move on, I'll get a policeman here and make you go.

[JERRY *laughs, stays*]

I warn you, I'll call a policeman.

JERRY [*Softly*]: You won't find a policeman around here; they're all over on the west side of the park chasing fairies down from trees or out of the bushes. That's all they do. That's their function. So scream your head off; it won't do you any good.

PETER: POLICE! I warn you, I'll have you arrested. POLICE! [*Pause*] I said POLICE! [*Pause*] I feel ridiculous.

JERRY: You look ridiculous: a grown man screaming for the police on a bright Sunday afternoon in the park with nobody harming you. If a policeman *did* fill his quota and come sludging over this way he'd probably take you in as a nut.

PETER [*With disgust and impotence*]: Great God, I just came here to read, and now you want me to give up the bench. You're mad.

JERRY: Hey, I got news for you, as they say. I'm on your precious bench, and you're never going to have it for yourself again.

PETER [*Furious*]: Look, you; get off my bench. I don't care if it makes any sense or not. I want this bench to myself; I want you OFF IT!

JERRY [*Mocking*]: Aw . . . look who's mad.

PETER: GET OUT!

JERRY: No.

PETER: I WARN YOU!

JERRY: Do you know how ridiculous you look *now?*

PETER [*His fury and self-consciousness have possessed him*]: It doesn't matter. [*He is almost crying*] GET AWAY FROM MY BENCH!

JERRY: Why? You have everything in the world you want; you've told me about your home, and your family, and *your own* little zoo. You have everything, and now you want this bench. Are these the things men fight for? Tell me, Peter, is this bench, this iron and this wood, is this your honor? Is this the thing in the world you'd fight for? Can you think of anything more absurd?

PETER: Absurd? Look, I'm not going to talk to you about honor, or even try to explain it to you. Besides, it isn't a question of honor; but even if it were, you wouldn't understand.

JERRY [*Contemptuously*]: You don't even know what you're saying, do you? This is probably the first time in your life you've had anything more trying to face than changing your cats' toilet box. Stupid! Don't you have any idea, not even the slightest, what other people *need?*

PETER: Oh, boy, listen to you; well, you don't need this bench. That's for sure.

JERRY: Yes; yes, I do.

PETER [*Quivering*]: I've come here for years; I have hours of great pleasure, great satisfaction, right here. And that's important to a man. I'm a responsible person, and I'm a GROWNUP. This is my bench, and you have no right to take it away from me.

JERRY: Fight for it, then. Defend yourself; defend your bench.

PETER: You've *pushed* me to it. Get up and fight.

JERRY: Like a man?

PETER [*Still angry*]: Yes, like a man, if you insist on mocking me even further.

JERRY: I'll have to give you credit for one thing: you *are* a vegetable, and a slightly nearsighted one, I think . . .

PETER: THAT'S ENOUGH. . . .

JERRY: . . . but, you know, as they say on TV all the time—you know— and I mean this, Peter, you have a certain dignity; it surprises me. . . .

PETER: STOP!

JERRY [*Rises lazily*]: Very well, Peter, we'll battle for the bench, but we're not evenly matched.

[*He takes out and clicks open an ugly-looking knife*]

PETER [*Suddenly awakening to the reality of the situation*]: You *are* mad! You're stark raving mad! YOU'RE GOING TO KILL ME!

[*But before* PETER *has time to think what do do,* JERRY *tosses the knife at* PETER'S *feet*]

JERRY: There you go. Pick it up. You have the knife and we'll be more evenly matched.

PETER [*Horrified*]: No!

JERRY [*Rushes over to* PETER, *grabs him by the collar;* PETER *rises; their faces almost touch*]: Now you pick up that knife and you fight with me. You fight for your self-respect; you fight for that goddamned bench.

PETER [*Struggling*]: No! Let . . . let go of me! He . . . Help!

JERRY [*Slaps* PETER *on each "fight"*]: You fight, you miserable bastard; fight for that bench; fight for your parakeets; fight for your cats, fight for your two daughters; fight for your wife; fight for your manhood, you pathetic little vegetable. [*Spits in* PETER'S *face*] You couldn't even get your wife with a male child.

PETER [*Breaks away, enraged*]: It's a matter of genetics, not manhood, you . . . you monster.

[*He darts down, picks up the knife and backs off a little; he is breathing heavily*]

I'll give you one last chance; get out of here and leave me alone!

[*He holds the knife with a firm arm, but far in front of him, not to attack, but to defend*]

JERRY [*Sighs heavily*]: So be it!

[*With a rush he charges* PETER *and impales himself on the knife. Tableau: For just a moment, complete silence,* JERRY *impaled on the knife at the end of* PETER'S *still firm arm. Then* PETER *screams, pulls away, leaving the knife in* JERRY. JERRY *is motionless, on point. Then he, too, screams, and it must be the sound of an infuriated and fatally wounded animal. With the knife in him, he stumbles back to the bench that* PETER *had vacated. He crumbles there, sitting, facing* PETER, *his eyes wide in agony, his mouth open*]

PETER [*Whispering*]: Oh my God, oh my God, oh my God. . . .

[*He repeats these words many times, very rapidly*]

JERRY [JERRY *is dying; but now his expression seems to change. His features relax, and while his voice varies, sometimes wrenched with pain, for the most part he seems removed from his dying. He smiles*]: Thank you, Peter. I mean that, now; thank you very much.

[PETER'S *mouth drops open. He cannot move; he is transfixed*]

Oh, Peter, I was so afraid I'd drive you away. [*He laughs as best he can*] You don't know how afraid I was you'd go away and leave me. And now I'll tell you what happened at the zoo. I think . . . I think this is what happened at the zoo . . . I think. I think that while I was at the zoo I decided that I would walk north . . . northerly, rather . . . until I found you . . . or somebody . . . and I decided that I would talk to you . . . I would tell you things . . . and things that I would tell you would . . . Well, here we are. You see? Here we *are*. But . . . I don't know . . . could I have planned all this? No . . . no, I couldn't have. But I think I did. And now I've told you what you wanted to know, haven't I? And now you know all about what happened at the zoo. And now you know what you'll see in your TV, and the face I told you about . . . you remember . . . the face I told you about . . . my face, the face you see right now. Peter . . . Peter? . . . Peter . . . thank you. I came unto you [*He laughs, so faintly*] and you have comforted me. Dear Peter.

PETER [*Almost fainting*]: Oh my God!
JERRY: You'd better go now. Somebody might come by, and you don't want to be here when anyone comes.
PETER [*Does not move, but begins to weep*]: Oh my God, oh my God.
JERRY [*Most faintly, now; he is very near death*]: You won't be coming back here any more, Peter; you've been dispossessed. You've lost your bench, but you've defended your honor. And Peter, I'll tell you something now; you're not really a vegetable; it's all right, you're an animal. You're an animal, too. But you'd better hurry now, Peter. Hurry, you'd better go . . . see?

[JERRY *takes a handkerchief and with great effort and pain wipes the knife handle clean of fingerprints*]

Hurry away, Peter.

[PETER *begins to stagger away*]

Wait . . . wait, Peter. Take your book . . . book. Right here . . . beside me . . . on your bench . . . my bench, rather. Come . . . take your book.

[PETER *starts for the book, but retreats*]

Hurry . . . Peter.

[PETER *rushes to the bench, grabs the book, retreats*]

Very good, Peter . . . very good. Now . . . hurry away.

[PETER *hesitates for a moment, then flees, stage-left*]

Hurry away. . . . [*His eyes are closed now*] Hurry away, your parakeets are making the dinner . . . the cats . . . are setting the table . . .

PETER [*Off stage*]:

[*A pitiful howl*]

OH MY GOD!

JERRY:

[*His eyes still closed, he shakes his head and speaks; a combination of scornful mimicry and supplication*]

Oh . . . my . . . God.

[*He is dead*]

CURTAIN

Rhetorical Index

A B C D E F G H I J   9 8 7 6 5 4 3 2 1